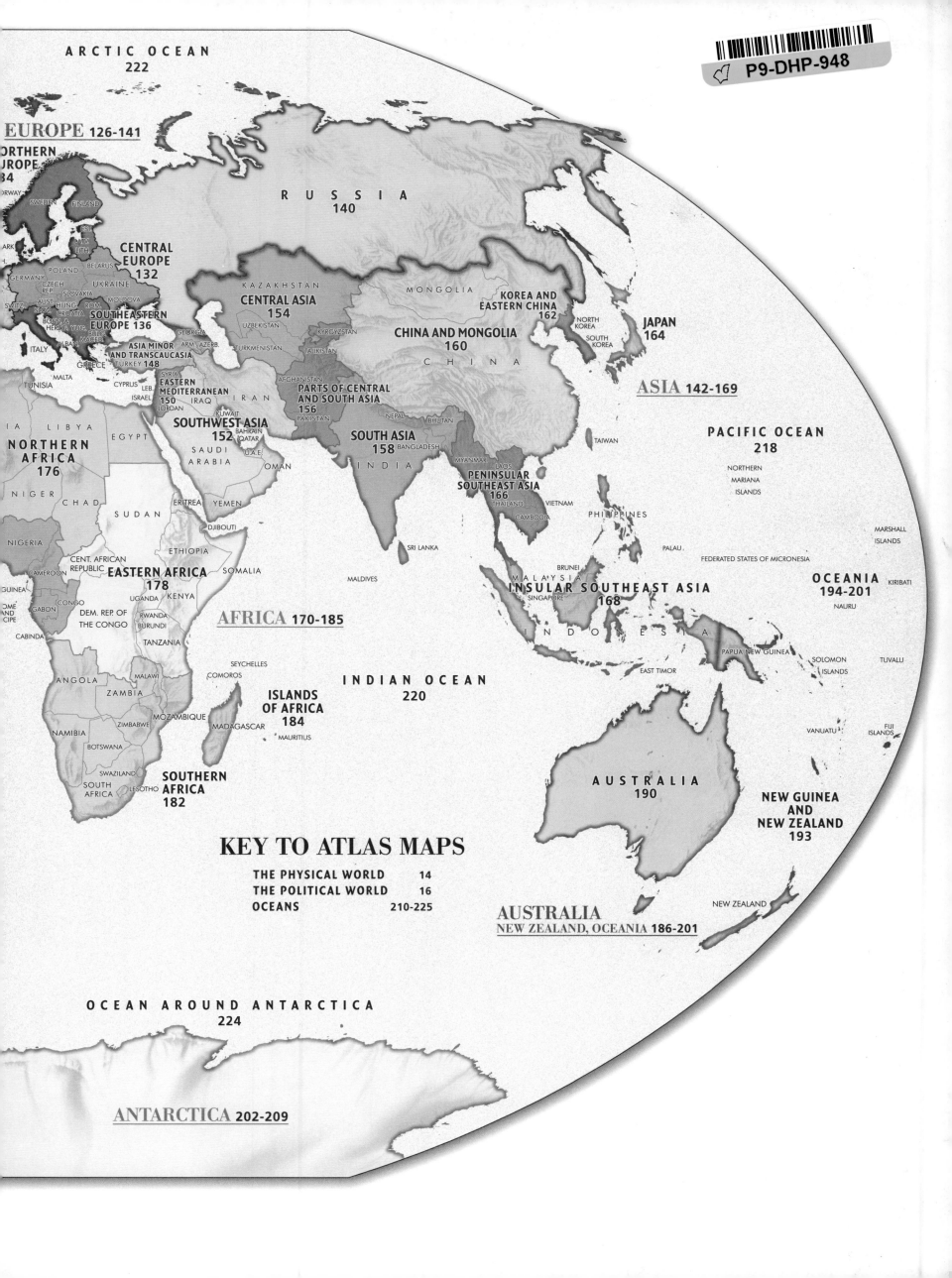

ARCTIC OCEAN 222

EUROPE 126-141

NORTHERN EUROPE 134

CENTRAL EUROPE 132

SOUTHEASTERN EUROPE 136

ASIA MINOR AND TRANSCAUCASIA 148

EASTERN MEDITERRANEAN 150

SOUTHWEST ASIA 152

CENTRAL ASIA 154

PARTS OF CENTRAL AND SOUTH ASIA 156

SOUTH ASIA 158

CHINA AND MONGOLIA 160

KOREA AND EASTERN CHINA 162

JAPAN 164

ASIA 142-169

PACIFIC OCEAN 218

PENINSULAR SOUTHEAST ASIA 166

INSULAR SOUTHEAST ASIA 168

OCEANIA 194-201

NORTHERN AFRICA 176

EASTERN AFRICA 178

AFRICA 170-185

ISLANDS OF AFRICA 184

INDIAN OCEAN 220

SOUTHERN AFRICA 182

AUSTRALIA 190

NEW GUINEA AND NEW ZEALAND 193

AUSTRALIA NEW ZEALAND, OCEANIA 186-201

OCEAN AROUND ANTARCTICA 224

ANTARCTICA 202-209

KEY TO ATLAS MAPS

THE PHYSICAL WORLD   14
THE POLITICAL WORLD   16
OCEANS   210-225

NATIONAL
GEOGRAPHIC

FAMILY
REFERENCE
ATLAS *of the World*

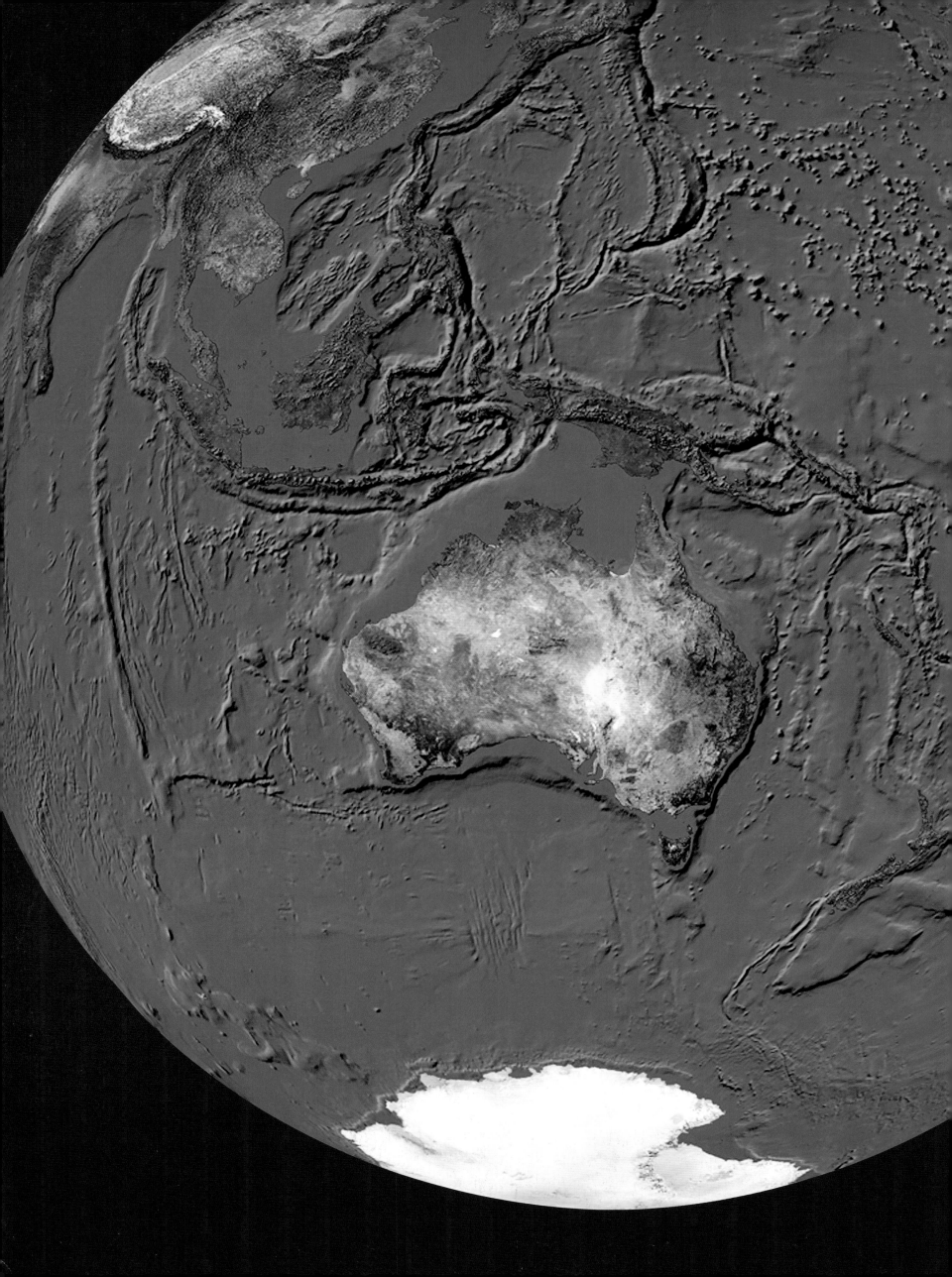

NATIONAL GEOGRAPHIC

FAMILY REFERENCE ATLAS *of the World*

NATIONAL GEOGRAPHIC, WASHINGTON, D.C.

NATIONAL GEOGRAPHIC

Family Reference Atlas of the World

One of the world's largest nonprofit scientific and educational organizations, the National Geographic Society was founded in 1888 "for the increase and diffusion of geographic knowledge." Fulfilling this mission, the Society educates and inspires millions every day through its magazines, books, television programs, videos, maps and atlases, research grants, the National Geographic Bee, teacher workshops, and innovative classroom materials. The Society is supported through membership dues, charitable gifts, and income from the sale of its educational products. This support is vital to National Geographic's mission to increase global understanding and promote conservation of our planet through exploration, research, and education.

For more information, please call 1-800-NGS LINE (647-5463) or write to the following address:

National Geographic Society
1145 17th Street N.W.
Washington, D.C. 20036-4688 U.S.A.

Visit the Society's Web site at www.nationalgeographic.com.

Library of Congress Cataloging in Publication data is available upon request.

This atlas was made possible by the contributions of numerous experts and organizations around the world, including the following:

Center for International Earth Science Information Network (CIESIN), Columbia University

Central Intelligence Agency (CIA)

Conservation International

Cooperative Association for Internet Data Analysis (CAIDA)

Earth Science System Education Program, Michigan State University

Global Land Cover Group, University of Maryland

Lunar and Planetary Institute

National Aeronautics and Space Administration (NASA) and the NASA Ames Research Center, NASA Goddard Space Flight Center, NASA Jet Propulsion Laboratory (JPL), NASA Marshall Space Flight Center

National Imagery and Mapping Agency (NIMA)

National Oceanic and Atmospheric Administration (NOAA) and the National Climatic Data Center, National Environmental Satellite, Data, and Information Service; National Geophysical Data Center; National Ocean Service

National Science Foundation

Population Reference Bureau

Scripps Institution of Oceanography

Smithsonian Institution

United Nations (UN) and the UN Conference on Trade and Development, UN Development Programme, UN Educational, Scientific, and Cultural Organization (UNESCO), UN Environment Programme (UNEP), UN Population Division, Food and Agriculture Organization (FAO), International Telecommunication Union (ITU), World Conservation Monitoring Centre (WCMC)

U.S. Board on Geographic Names

U.S. Department of Agriculture

U.S. Department of Commerce: Bureau of the Census, National Oceanic and Atmospheric Administration

U.S. Department of Energy

U.S. Department of the Interior: Bureau of Land Management, National Park Service, U.S. Geological Survey

U.S. Department of State: Office of the Geographer

World Bank

World Health Organization/Pan American Health Organization (WHO/PAHO)

World Resources Institute (WRI)

World Trade Organization (WTO)

Worldwatch Institute

World Wildlife Fund (WWF)

For a complete listing of contributors, see page 348.

INTRODUCTION

Dear Readers,

Geography is not always a gentle pursuit. Those who first discerned the shapes of continents, the paths of rivers, and the heights of mountains were resolute individuals with a passion for discovery. Only through their accounts could we begin to construct our sense of place and eventually to control our future. Today satellites rain down data, and electronic communications bind people together, but our world grows less gentle, and our destiny remains unclear. No one had anticipated that an ozone hole over Antarctica could threaten populations with ultraviolet radiation. No one had pieced together, until too late, how nationless men in Afghanistan could launch global terror.

National Geographic's *Family Reference Atlas of the World* comes to you at a time when physical geography—the study of landforms, climate, vegetation, soils, and water—is critical to the health of the planet, and when human geography—the study of people's relationships to their locations, and ultimately each other—is increasingly urgent. Think of it as survival data for a global culture in which no country exists in a vacuum, where a shift in ocean currents off Peru can affect crop growth in Africa and where foreign ships can introduce exotic species that disrupt entire ecosystems.

This book presents the findings of geographers who now have access to powerful information-gathering tools. High above the Earth, satellites and specially equipped aircraft collect critical information about the planet and beam it into digital databases called Geographic Information Systems (GIS). From the perspective provided by these modern technologies, scientists can layer data and recombine it to understand the myriad factors affecting everything from a small corner of the globe to the ocean that spans it.

Throughout the *Atlas,* maps, diagrams, and other illustrations help readers understand the basic physical realities of the Earth and how the human hand has divided those realities into political entities. Using spatial data collected by the most renowned research institutions, we have developed thematic maps that explain such vital issues as environmental stresses, energy extraction, population growth, plate tectonics, and biospheric cycles. Cultural maps of the world trace the spread of languages and religions, and a geologic time line outlines the unfathomably long history of Earth itself.

Since the first explorers dared to look beyond a faraway ridge, human curiosity has boldly pursued these questions: Who are we? Where are we? What is our proper place in this creation? The *Family Reference Atlas* will help give you that sense of place and lead to a better understanding of our astonishing—and fragile—world. In these uneasy times, it will provide an easily accessible reference book, essential for you, your family, and all informed and responsible citizens.

PRESIDENT AND CHIEF EXECUTIVE OFFICER

TABLE OF CONTENTS

HOW TO USE THIS ATLAS   8
Map Policies / Physical Maps / Political Maps / World Thematic
Maps / Regional Maps / Map Symbols

WORLD ■

INTRODUCTION   12
PHYSICAL WORLD   14
POLITICAL WORLD   16
PHYSICAL HEMISPHERES AND POLITICAL POLES   18
STRUCTURE OF THE EARTH   20
Continents Adrift in Time / Geologic Time / Geologic Forces
Change the Face of the Planet / Plate Tectonics
EARTH'S ROCKY EXTERIOR   22
Rock Classes / The Rock Cycle / Rock Class Distribution / Reading
Earth History from Rocks
WORLD LANDFORMS   24
Major Landform Types / Endogenic Landforms / Exogenic Landforms /
Other Landforms / Landforms Created by Wind / Landforms
Created by Water / Landforms Created by Ice
SURFACE OF THE EARTH   28
Surface by the Numbers / Distribution of Earth's Elevations and
Depths (Hypsometry)/ A Slice of Earth / Earth Surface Elevations
and Depths
WORLD LAND COVER   30
Global Land Cover Composition
WORLD CLIMATE   32
January and July Solar Energy, Average Temperature, Cloud Cover,
Precipitation / Major Factors that Influence Climate / Temperature
Change over Time / Climate Zones / Climographs
WORLD WEATHER   36
Major Factors that Influence Weather / Cloud Types / Hurricanes /
Lightning / El Niño and La Niña
WORLD BIOSPHERE   38
The Biosphere from Space / Biosphere Dynamics / Earth System
Dynamics / Size of the Biosphere / The Biosphere over Time
WORLD BIODIVERSITY   40
The Natural World / Species Diversity / Threatened Ecoregions /
Threatened Species / Projected Biodiversity Status
WORLD POPULATION   42
Lights of the World / Population Pyramids / Population Growth /
Population Density / Regional Population Growth Disparities /
Fertility / Urban Population Densities / Urban Population Growth /
Life Expectancy / Migration / Most Populous Nations / Most
Crowded Nations / Demographic Extremes
WORLD LANGUAGES   46
Voices of the World / Vanishing Languages / Evolution of Languages /
How Many Speak What? / Major Language Families Today
WORLD RELIGIONS   48
Major Religions / Sacred Places / Adherents Worldwide / Adherents
by Continent / Adherents by Country
WORLD ECONOMY   50
Predominant Economy / Labor Migration / Top GDP Growth
Rates / The World's Richest and Poorest Countries / World
Employment / Gross Domestic Product / Major Manufacturers
WORLD TRADE   52
Investment Flows / Growth of World Trade / Merchandise Exports /
Main Trading Nations / World Debt / Trade Blocs / Trade Flow:
Fuels / Trade Flow: Agricultural Products / Top Merchandise
Exporters and Importers / Top Commercial Services Exporters
and Importers
WORLD FOOD   54
Land Use and Commercial Agriculture / Fishing and Aquaculture /
World Agricultural Production / Undernourishment in the
Developing World / Diet / World Grain Production
WORLD ENERGY   56
Annual Energy Consumption / Energy Production / Fossil Fuel
Extraction / Biomass, Hydroelectric, and Nuclear Energy /
Renewable Energy
WORLD MINERALS   58
World Mineral Production / World Minerals by Economic Value
WORLD HEALTH AND EDUCATION   60
Expenditures on Health / Income Levels: Indicators of Health and
Literacy / Access to Safe Drinking Water / Access to Sanitation
Services / Number of Physicians per 100,000 Population / Infant
Mortality / AIDS / Malaria / Tuberculosis / Life Expectancy /
Causes of Death / Literacy / Expenditures on Education

ENVIRONMENTAL STRESSES   62
Global Climate Change / Depletion of the Ozone Layer / Pollution /
Water Scarcity / Soil Degradation and Desertification / Deforestation
WORLD PROTECTED LANDS   64
World Heritage Sites / Protected Areas / The World Heritage Site
System / Endemism
TECHNOLOGY AND GLOBALIZATION   66
Centers of Technological Innovation / Milestones in Technology /
Teledensity, Fiber-Optic Cables, and Satellites / Nuclear Powers
THE INTERNET   68
Mapping the Spread of a Computer Virus / Worldwide Distribution
of Internet Resources

NORTH AMERICA ■

INTRODUCTION   70
NORTH AMERICA, PHYSICAL AND POLITICAL   74
CANADA   76
Canada, Greenland, St.-Pierre and Miquelon
UNITED STATES, PHYSICAL   78
UNITED STATES, POLITICAL   80
UNITED STATES   82
Temperature and Precipitation / Land Use, Agriculture, and
Fishing / Population / Industry and Mining
UNITED STATES, MAJOR HIGHWAYS   84
UNITED STATES, FEDERAL LANDS   86
  NORTHEAST   88
  Connecticut, Maine, Massachusetts, New Hampshire, New Jersey,
  New York, Pennsylvania, Rhode Island, Vermont
  SOUTH ATLANTIC   90
  Delaware, District of Columbia, Florida, Georgia, Maryland, North
  Carolina, South Carolina, Virginia, West Virginia
  GREAT LAKES   92
  Illinois, Indiana, Michigan, Ohio, Wisconsin
  MIDDLE SOUTH   94
  Alabama, Arkansas, Kentucky, Louisiana, Mississippi, Tennessee
  TEXAS AND OKLAHOMA   96
  Oklahoma, Texas
  NORTHERN PLAINS   98
  Iowa, Kansas, Minnesota, Missouri, Nebraska, North Dakota,
  South Dakota
  ROCKY MOUNTAINS   100
  Arizona, Colorado, Idaho, Montana, New Mexico, Utah, Wyoming
  WEST COAST   102
  California, Nevada, Oregon, Washington
  ALASKA   104
  HAWAII   106
MEXICO AND CENTRAL AMERICA   108
Belize, Costa Rica, El Salvador, Guatemala, Honduras, Mexico,
Nicaragua, Panama
BAHAMAS AND GREATER ANTILLES   110
Bahamas, Bermuda, Cayman Islands, Cuba, Dominican Republic,
Haiti, Jamaica, Puerto Rico, Turks and Caicos Islands
LESSER ANTILLES   112
Anguilla, Antigua and Barbuda, Aruba, Barbados, British Virgin
Islands, Dominica, Guadeloupe, Grenada, Martinique, Montserrat,
Netherlands Antilles, St. Kitts and Nevis, St. Lucia, St. Vincent and
the Grenadines, Trinidad and Tobago, U.S. Virgin Islands

SOUTH AMERICA ■

INTRODUCTION   114
SOUTH AMERICA, PHYSICAL AND POLITICAL   118
NORTHERN SOUTH AMERICA   120
Colombia, Ecuador, French Guiana, Guyana, Suriname, Venezuela
CENTRAL SOUTH AMERICA   122
Bolivia, Brazil, Paraguay, Peru
SOUTHERN SOUTH AMERICA   124
Argentina, Chile, Falkland Islands, Uruguay

EUROPE

INTRODUCTION	126
EUROPE, PHYSICAL AND POLITICAL	130
CENTRAL EUROPE	132
Austria, Belarus, Czech Republic, Germany, Hungary, Liechtenstein, Moldova, Poland, Slovakia, Switzerland, Ukraine	
NORTHERN EUROPE	134
Denmark, Estonia, Faroe Islands, Finland, Iceland, Latvia, Lithuania, Norway, Sweden	
SOUTHEASTERN EUROPE	136
Albania, Bosnia and Herzegovina, Bulgaria, Croatia, Greece, Italy, Macedonia, Malta, Romania, San Marino, Slovenia, Vatican City, Yugoslavia	
WESTERN EUROPE	138
Andorra, Belgium, France, Gibraltar, Ireland, Luxembourg, Monaco, Netherlands, Portugal, Spain, United Kingdom	
RUSSIA: EUROPE/ASIA	140

ASIA

INTRODUCTION	142
ASIA, PHYSICAL AND POLITICAL	146
ASIA MINOR AND TRANSCAUCASIA	148
Armenia, Azerbaijan, Cyprus, Georgia, Turkey	
EASTERN MEDITERRANEAN	150
Israel, Jordan, Lebanon, Syria	
SOUTHWEST ASIA	152
Bahrain, Iran, Iraq, Kuwait, Oman, Qatar, Saudi Arabia, United Arab Emirates, Yemen	
CENTRAL ASIA	154
Kazakhstan, Turkmenistan, Uzbekistan	
PARTS OF CENTRAL AND SOUTH ASIA	156
Afghanistan, Kyrgyzstan, Pakistan, Tajikistan	
SOUTH ASIA	158
Bangladesh, Bhutan, India, Maldives, Nepal, Sri Lanka	
CHINA AND MONGOLIA	160
China, Mongolia	
KOREA AND EASTERN CHINA	162
Eastern China, North Korea, South Korea	
JAPAN	164
PENINSULAR SOUTHEAST ASIA	166
Cambodia, Laos, Myanmar, Thailand, Vietnam	
INSULAR SOUTHEAST ASIA	168
Brunei, East Timor, Indonesia, Malaysia, Philippines, Singapore	

AFRICA

INTRODUCTION	170
AFRICA, PHYSICAL AND POLITICAL	174
NORTHERN AFRICA	176
Algeria, Chad, Egypt, Gambia, Libya, Mali, Mauritania, Morocco, Niger, Senegal, Tunisia, Western Sahara	
EASTERN AFRICA	178
Burundi, Central African Republic, Democratic Republic of the Congo, Djibouti, Eritrea, Ethiopia, Kenya, Rwanda, Somalia, Sudan, Tanzania, Uganda	
WEST-CENTRAL AFRICA	180
Benin, Burkina Faso, Cameroon, Congo, Côte d'Ivoire, Equatorial Guinea, Gabon, Ghana, Guinea, Guinea-Bissau, Liberia, Nigeria, Sao Tome & Principe, Sierra Leone, Togo	
SOUTHERN AFRICA	182
Angola, Botswana, Cabinda, Comoros, Lesotho, Madagascar, Malawi, Mozambique, Namibia, Seychelles, South Africa, Swaziland, Zambia, Zimbabwe	
ISLANDS OF AFRICA	184
Cape Verde, Comoros, Mauritius, Réunion, Sao Tome and Principe, Seychelles, Mayotte, St. Helena	

AUSTRALIA
NEW ZEALAND, OCEANIA

INTRODUCTION	186
AUSTRALIA, PHYSICAL AND POLITICAL	190
AUSTRALIA	192
Temperature and Precipitation / Land Use, Agriculture, and Fishing / Population / Industry and Mining	
NEW GUINEA AND NEW ZEALAND	193
New Zealand, Papua New Guinea	
ISLANDS OF OCEANIA	194
OCEANIA	196
Inset Maps / Flags and Facts	

ANTARCTICA

INTRODUCTION	202
ANTARCTICA, PHYSICAL AND POLITICAL	206
ANTARCTICA	208
Elevation of the Ice Sheet / Measurements of a Paradox / Ice on the Move / Ultimate Winds / Antarctic Treaty / Antarctic Convergence	

OCEANS

WORLD BATHYMETRY	210
OCEANOGRAPHY	212
The Ocean Floor / Major Surface Currents / Ocean Conveyor Belt	
LIMITS OF THE OCEANS & SEAS	214
ATLANTIC OCEAN	216
PACIFIC OCEAN	218
INDIAN OCEAN	220
ARCTIC OCEAN	222
OCEAN AROUND ANTARCTICA	224

SPACE

INTRODUCTION	226
MOON: NEAR SIDE	228
MOON: FAR SIDE	230
THE SOLAR SYSTEM	232
THE PLANETS	234
Sun, Mercury, Venus, Earth, Mars, Jupiter, Saturn, Uranus, Neptune, Pluto	
THE UNIVERSE	236
SPACE EXPLORATION TIME LINE	238

APPENDIX

AIRLINE DISTANCES IN KILOMETERS, ABBREVIATIONS, METRIC CONVERSIONS	240
GEOGRAPHIC COMPARISONS	242
POLITICAL ENTITIES AND STATUS	244
Independent States of the World / Dependencies of the World / Areas of Special Status / Areas Geographically Separated from Mainland Countries	
SPECIAL FLAGS	248
Development of the Stars and Stripes / International Flags / Regional Flags / Religious Flags / Specialized Flags	
FOREIGN TERMS	250
WORLD TIME ZONES	252
MAJOR CITIES OF THE WORLD	254
WORLD TEMPERATURE AND RAINFALL	256
GLOSSARY OF GEOGRAPHIC TERMS	260

INDEX

PLACE-NAME INDEX	262
MOON INDEX	346
ACKNOWLEDGMENTS	348
Consultants / Art and Illustrations / Satellite Images / Photography / Principal Reference Sources / Principal Online Sources / Key to Flags and Facts	

HOW TO USE THIS ATLAS

Map Policies

Maps are a rich, useful, and—to the extent humanly possible—accurate means of depicting the world. Yet maps inevitably make the world seem a little simpler than it really is. A neatly drawn boundary may in reality be a hotly contested war zone. The government-sanctioned, "official" name of a provincial city in an ethnically diverse region may bear little resemblance to the name its citizens routinely use. These cartographic issues often seem obscure and academic. But maps arouse passions. Despite our carefully reasoned map policies, users of National Geographic maps write us strongly worded letters when our maps are at odds with their worldviews.

How do National Geographic cartographers deal with these realities? With constant scrutiny,

considerable discussion, and help from many outside experts.

Examples:

Nations: Issues of national sovereignty and contested borders often boil down to "de facto versus de jure" discussions. Governments and international agencies frequently make official rulings about contested regions. These de jure decisions, no matter how legitimate, are often at odds with the wishes of individuals and groups, and they often stand in stark contrast to real-world situations. The inevitable conclusion: It is simplest and best to show the world as it is—de facto—rather than as we or others wish it to be.

Africa's Western Sahara, for example, was divided by Morocco and Mauritania after

the Spanish government withdrew in 1976. Although Morocco now controls the entire territory, the United Nations does not recognize Morocco's sovereignty over this still disputed area. This atlas shows the de facto Moroccan rule but includes an explanatory note.

Place-names: Ride a barge down the Danube, and you'll hear the river called Donau, Duna, Dunaj, Dunărea, Dunav, Dunay. These are local names. This atlas uses the conventional name, "Danube," on physical maps. On political maps, local names are used, with the conventional name in parentheses where space permits. Usage conventions for both foreign and domestic place-names are established by the U.S. Board on Geographic Names, a group with representatives from several federal agencies.

Physical Maps

Physical maps of the world, the continents, and the ocean floor reveal landforms and vegetation in stunning detail. Painted by relief artists John Bonner and Tibor Tóth, the maps have been edited for accuracy. Although painted maps are human interpretations, these depictions can emphasize subtle features that are sometimes invisible in satellite imagery.

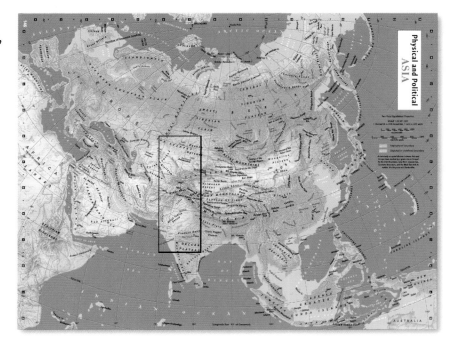

Physical features: Colors and shading illustrate variations in elevation, landforms and vegetation. Patterns indicate specific landscape features, such as sand, glaciers, and swamps.

Water features: Blue lines indicate rivers; other water bodies are shown as areas of blue. Lighter shading reflects the limits of the Continental Shelf.

Boundaries and political divisions are shown in red. Dotted lines indicate disputed or uncertain boundaries.

Political Maps

Political maps portray features such as international boundaries, the locations of cities, road networks, and other important elements of the world's human geography. Most index entries are keyed to the political maps, listing the page numbers and then the specific locations on the pages. (See page 262 for details on how to use the index.)

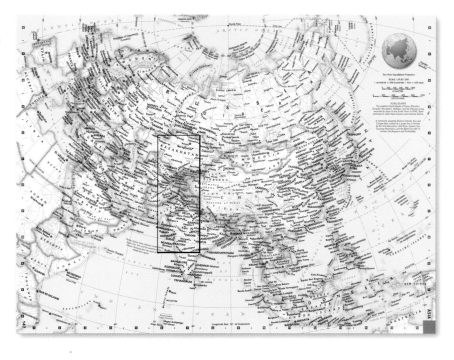

Physical features: Gray relief shading depicts surface features such as mountains, hills, and valleys.

Water features are shown in blue. Solid lines and filled-in areas indicate perennial water features; dashed lines and patterns indicate intermittent features.

Boundaries and political divisions are defined with both lines and colored bands; they vary according to whether a boundary is internal or international (for details, see map symbols key at right).

Cities: The regional political maps that form the bulk of this atlas depict four categories of cities or towns. The largest cities are shown in all capital letters (e.g., LONDON).

World Thematic Maps

Thematic maps reveal the rich patch-work and infinite interrelationships of our changing planet. The thematic section at the beginning of the atlas focuses on physical and biological topics such as geology, landforms, land cover, and biodiversity. It also charts human patterns, with information on population, languages, religions, and the world economy. Two-page spreads on energy and minerals illustrate how people have learned to use Earth's resources, while spreads devoted to environmental stresses and protected lands focus on the far-reaching effects of human activities and the need for resource conservation. Throughout this section of the atlas, maps are coupled with satellite imagery, charts, diagrams, photographs, and tabular information; together, they create a very useful framework for studying geographic patterns.

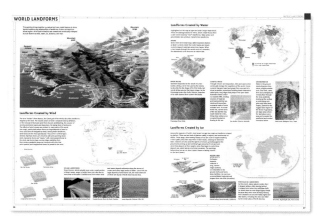

World Landforms

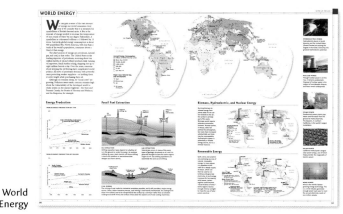

World Energy

Regional Maps

This atlas divides the continents into several subregions, each displayed on a two-page spread. Large-scale maps capture the political divisions and major surface features, while accompanying regional thematic maps lend insight into natural and human factors that give character to a region. Fact boxes, which include flag designs and information on populations, languages, religions, and economies, appear alongside the maps as practical reference tools.

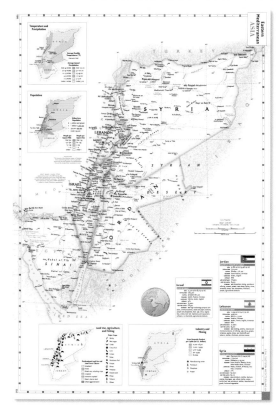

For more details on the regional map spreads, see pages 10–11.

Map Symbols

BOUNDARIES

	Defined
	Undefined or disputed
	Offshore line of separation
	International boundary (Physical Plates)
	Disputed or undefined boundary (Physical Plates)

CITIES

⊛ ★ ◉	Capitals
● ● ● ●	Towns

TRANSPORTATION

	Superhighway
	Road
	Auto ferry
	Highway tunnel
INTERSTATE **35** STATE **376** FEDERAL **50**	Highway numbers

WATER FEATURES

	Drainage
	Intermittent drainage
	Intermittent lake
	Dry salt lake
	Swamp
	Bank or shoal
	Coral reef
200	Depth curves in meters
51	Water surface elevation in meters
	Falls or rapids
	Aqueduct

PHYSICAL FEATURES

	Relief
⊙	Crater
	Lava and volcanic debris
+8850 (29035 ft)	Elevation in meters (feet in United States)
-86	Elevation in meters below sea level
⤬	Pass
	Sand
	Salt desert
	Below sea level
	Ice shelf
	Glacier

CULTURAL FEATURES

⚑	Oil field
	Canal
	Dam
	Wall
	U.S. national park
⬚	Site
∴	Ruin

INDEX AND GRID:
Beginning on page 262 is a full index of place-names found in this atlas. The edge of each map is marked with letters (in rows) and numbers (in columns), to which the index entries are referenced. As an example, "Pauini, river, *Braz.* **122** F6" (see inset below) refers to the grid section on page 122 where row F and column 6 meet. More examples and additional details about the index are included on page 262.

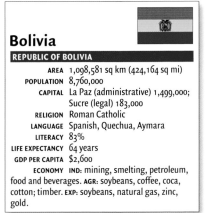

Patuca, river, *Hond.* **109** KI8
Patuxent Range, *Antarctica* **206** HII
Pátzcuaro, *Mex.* **108** JIO
Pau, *Fr.* **139** N9
Pauini, river, *Braz.* **122** F6
Pauini, *Braz.* **122** F6
Pauktaw, *Myanmar* **166** H4
Paulatuk, *N.W.T., Can.* **76** EII
Paulding, *Ohio, U.S.* **93** PII
Paulistana, *Braz.* **123** FI6
Paulo Afonso, *Braz.* **123** GI7
Pauls Valley, *Okla., U.S.* **96** HII

Bolivia

REPUBLIC OF BOLIVIA

AREA	1,098,581 sq km (424,164 sq mi)
POPULATION	8,760,000
CAPITAL	La Paz (administrative) 1,499,000; Sucre (legal) 183,000
RELIGION	Roman Catholic
LANGUAGE	Spanish, Quechua, Aymara
LITERACY	83%
LIFE EXPECTANCY	64 years
GDP PER CAPITA	$2,600
ECONOMY	**IND:** mining, smelting, petroleum, food and beverages. **AGR:** soybeans, coffee, coca, cotton; timber. **EXP:** soybeans, natural gas, zinc, gold.

FLAGS AND FACTS:
This atlas recognizes 192 independent nations. All of these countries, along with dependencies and U.S. states, are profiled in the continental sections of the atlas. Accompanying each entry are highlights of geographic, demographic, and economic data. These details provide a brief overview of each country, state, or territory; they are not intended to be comprehensive. A detailed description of the sources and policies used in compiling the listings is included in the Key to Flags and Facts on page 351.

Central
SOUTH AMERICA

122

Bolivia

REPUBLIC OF BOLIVIA

AREA	1,098,581 sq km (424,164 sq mi)
POPULATION	8,760,000
CAPITAL	La Paz (administrative) 1,499,000; Sucre (legal) 183,000
RELIGION	Roman Catholic
LANGUAGE	Spanish, Quechua, Aymara
LITERACY	83%
LIFE EXPECTANCY	64 years
GDP PER CAPITA	$2,600
ECONOMY	**IND:** mining, smelting, petroleum, food and beverages. **AGR:** soybeans, coffee, coca, cotton; timber. **EXP:** soybeans, natural gas, zinc, gold.

Temperature and Precipitation

Average Annual Precipitation

Over 80 inches	Over 200 cm
60–80 inches	150–200 cm
40–59 inches	100–149 cm
20–39 inches	50–99 cm
10–19 inches	25–49 cm
Under 10 inches	Under 25 cm

Average Monthly Temperatures (°F)

(January/July)

Brazil

FEDERATIVE REPUBLIC OF BRAZIL

AREA	8,511,965 sq km (3,286,488 sq mi)
POPULATION	173,816,000
CAPITAL	Brasília 2,073,000
RELIGION	Roman Catholic
LANGUAGE	Portuguese, Spanish, English, French
LITERACY	83%
LIFE EXPECTANCY	63 years
GDP PER CAPITA	$6,500
ECONOMY	**IND:** textiles, shoes, chemicals, cement. **AGR:** coffee, soybeans, wheat, rice; beef. **EXP:** manufactures, iron ore, soybeans, footwear.

TEMPERATURE AND PRECIPITATION MAPS:
These maps show climatic averages over time. Colors represent precipitation information; point symbols show average January and July temperatures for selected cities and towns.

LOCATORS: Each regional spread contains a locator map showing where the featured region lies within a continent. The region of interest is highlighted in color. Surrounding areas on the same continent appear in gray; other land areas are brown.

POPULATION MAPS: Colors indicate relative population density, with the most crowded areas shown in the darkest red-orange color. Geometric point symbols indicate the sizes of selected major cities and national capitals and their urban areas.

THEMATIC MAPS:
In combination, the four thematic maps on each regional spread—Temperature and Precipitation; Population; Land Use, Agriculture and Fishing; and Industry and Mining—provide a fascinating overview of the area's physical and cultural geography. Temperature and Precipitation maps show which areas receive the most rain, and what the average temperatures are at different times during the year. Population maps allow one to see, at a glance, which areas are the least and most crowded, and where the major urban centers are located. Land Use, Agriculture, and Fishing maps paint a general picture of the ways humans use land resources. And Industry and Mining maps indicate the relative economic well-being of countries (expressed in GDP per capita) and show major centers of mining, mineral processing, and manufacturing. Interesting relationships can be observed: For example, although mines can be located anywhere that mineral deposits occur, processing centers are only feasible in areas with inexpensive electricity and adequate access to transportation.

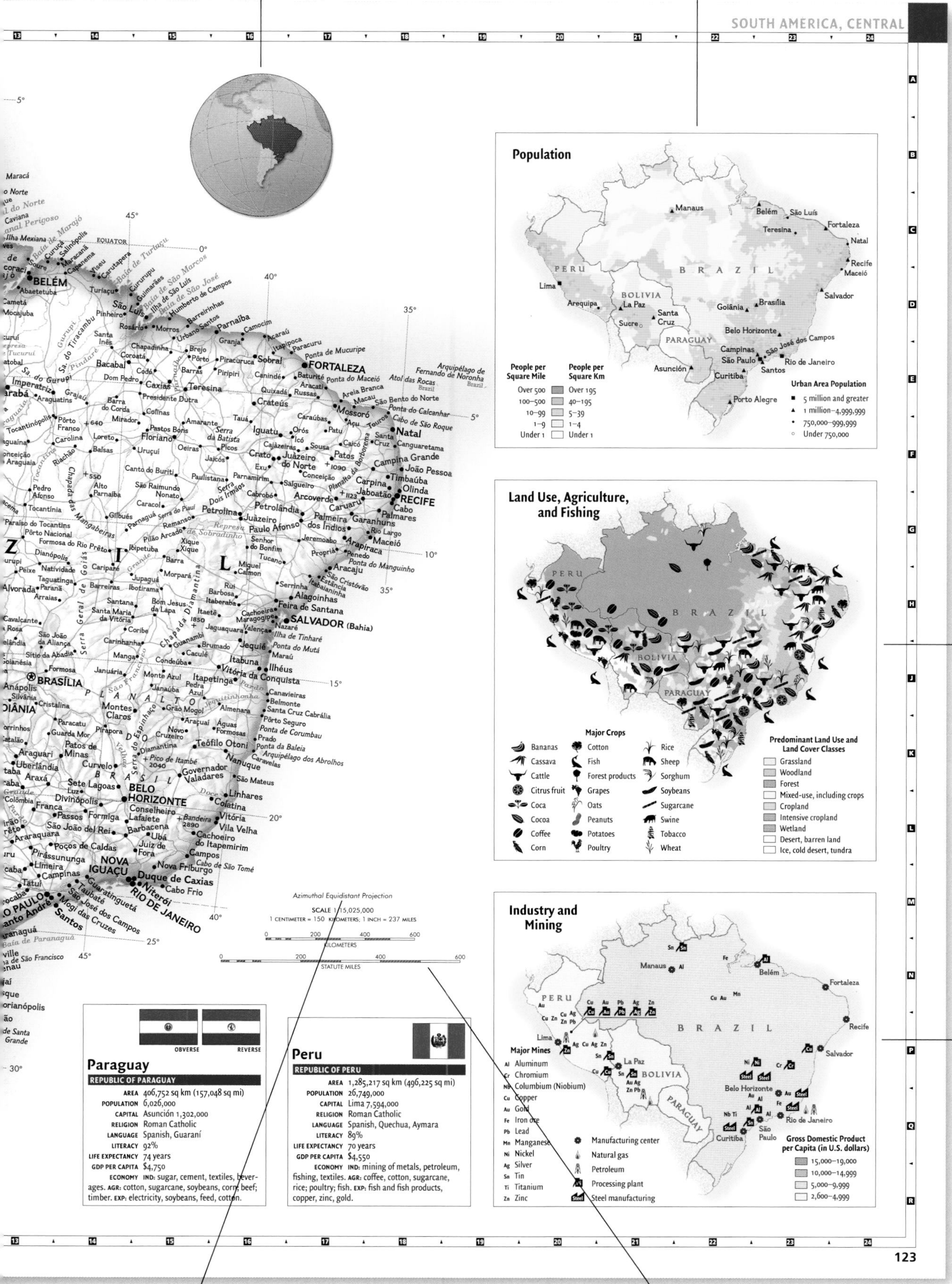

LAND USE, AGRICULTURE, AND FISHING MAPS:
The colors on these maps indicate predominant land use and land cover types—showing, for example, whether an area comprises mainly cropland or forest. Symbols for major crops give a general picture of each region's agricultural activity.

INDUSTRY AND MINING MAPS:
On these maps, major manufacturing centers, mines, and processing plants are shown with symbols; countries are colored according to gross domestic product (GDP) per capita. The GDP per-capita key breakdowns are consistent among all regions of a continent (e.g., the key categories for northern and southern South America match this key for central South America).

MAP PROJECTIONS: Map projections determine how land shapes are distorted when transferred from a sphere (the Earth) to a flat piece of paper. Many different projections are used in this atlas—each carefully chosen for a map's particular coverage area and purpose.

MAP SCALES: Scale information indicates the distance on Earth represented by a given length on the map.

SOUTH AMERICA, CENTRAL

Population

Land Use, Agriculture, and Fishing

Industry and Mining

Paraguay
REPUBLIC OF PARAGUAY
AREA 406,752 sq km (157,048 sq mi)
POPULATION 6,026,000
CAPITAL Asunción 1,302,000
RELIGION Roman Catholic
LANGUAGE Spanish, Guaraní
LITERACY 92%
LIFE EXPECTANCY 74 years
GDP PER CAPITA $4,750
ECONOMY IND: sugar, cement, textiles, beverages. AGR: cotton, sugarcane, soybeans, corn; beef; timber. EXP: electricity, soybeans, feed, cotton.

Peru
REPUBLIC OF PERU
AREA 1,285,217 sq km (496,225 sq mi)
POPULATION 26,749,000
CAPITAL Lima 7,594,000
RELIGION Roman Catholic
LANGUAGE Spanish, Quechua, Aymara
LITERACY 89%
LIFE EXPECTANCY 70 years
GDP PER CAPITA $4,550
ECONOMY IND: mining of metals, petroleum, fishing, textiles. AGR: coffee, cotton, sugarcane, rice; poultry; fish. EXP: fish and fish products, copper, zinc, gold.

123

THE WORLD

Some 93 million miles from the sun, Earth whirls in space, its exact origins shrouded in time. According to scientists, our planet and every other object in the solar system descend from a great cloud of interstellar gas and dust that condensed to form the sun about 4.6 billion years ago. Life is known to have found a foothold only on Earth—more than 3.5 billion years ago— but in recent years researchers have made intriguing discoveries about potential habitats for life on other planets or their moons.

Scientists continue to study habitats here at home as well. Using the very latest technologies, they are gaining a much better understanding of the natural processes that support life, shape landscapes, and keep the currents of the air and sea always in motion. They are learning, too, how we humans, relative newcomers among life-forms, are affecting our world, for better or worse.

Data collected by satellites help us to see our world in new ways and monitor changes as they unfold. Acting as eyes in the sky, satellites peer down from the heavens and beam back images as informative as they are beautiful. The images on these pages, for example, reveal global sea surface temperatures, replacing the blue of the oceans with colors approximating gradations of heat. Scientists monitor ocean temperatures for many purposes, not the least of which is to make climate forecasts and detect the possible onset of major climate shifts, such as those associated with El Niño and La Niña.

In the following pages are more images like these, as well as maps, charts, graphs, and text based on data from many sources— from high-flying to low-lying instruments, from the Internet to international organizations, and from futurists to historians. Together, they reveal the state of our world, this complex, dynamic realm we call Earth.

Reflecting the unprecedented accuracy and depth of detail provided by the MODIS instrument on NASA's Terra satellite, these images show sea surface temperatures measured over an eight-day period: Cold waters are black and dark green. Blue, purple, red, yellow, and white represent progressively warmer waters.

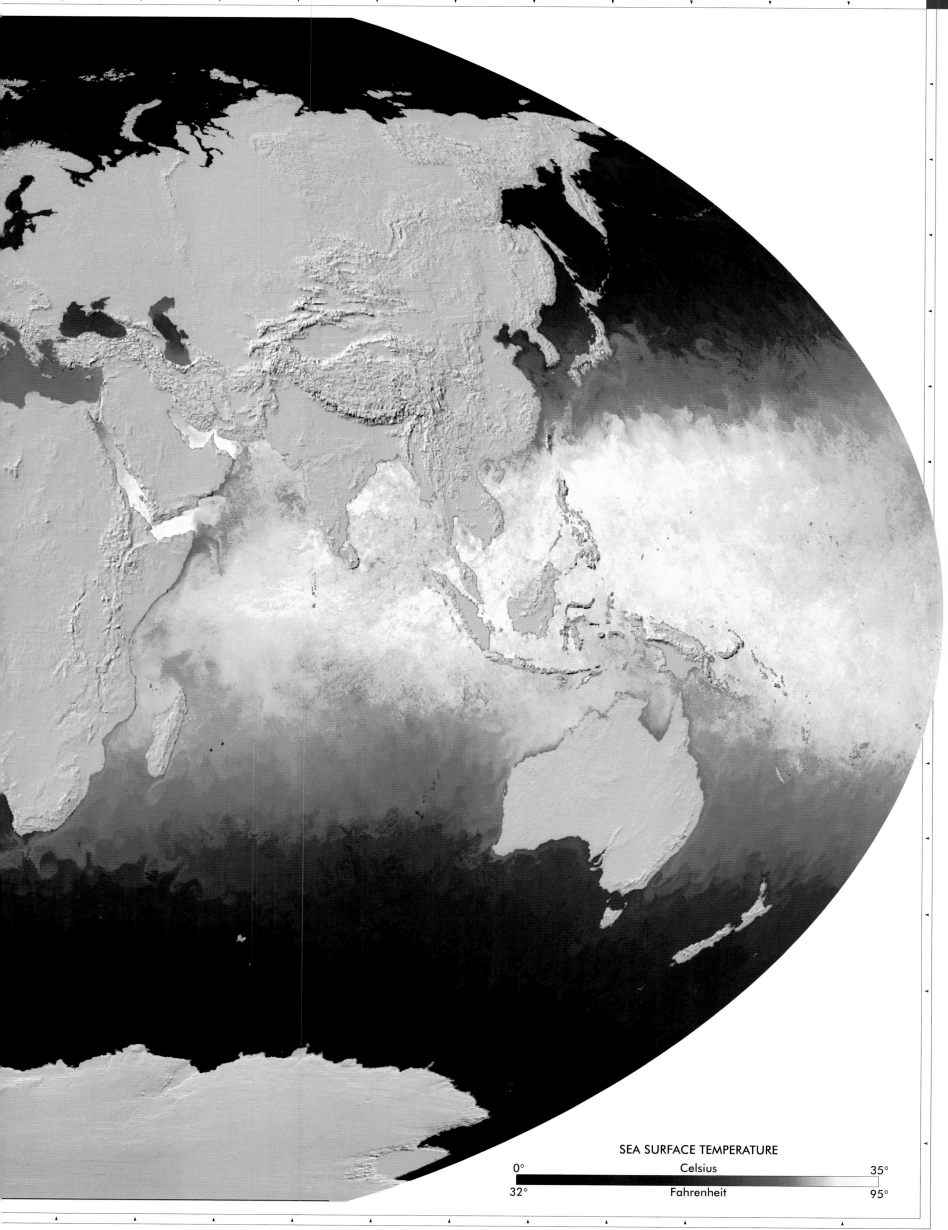

SEA SURFACE TEMPERATURE

| 0° | Celsius | 35° |
| 32° | Fahrenheit | 95° |

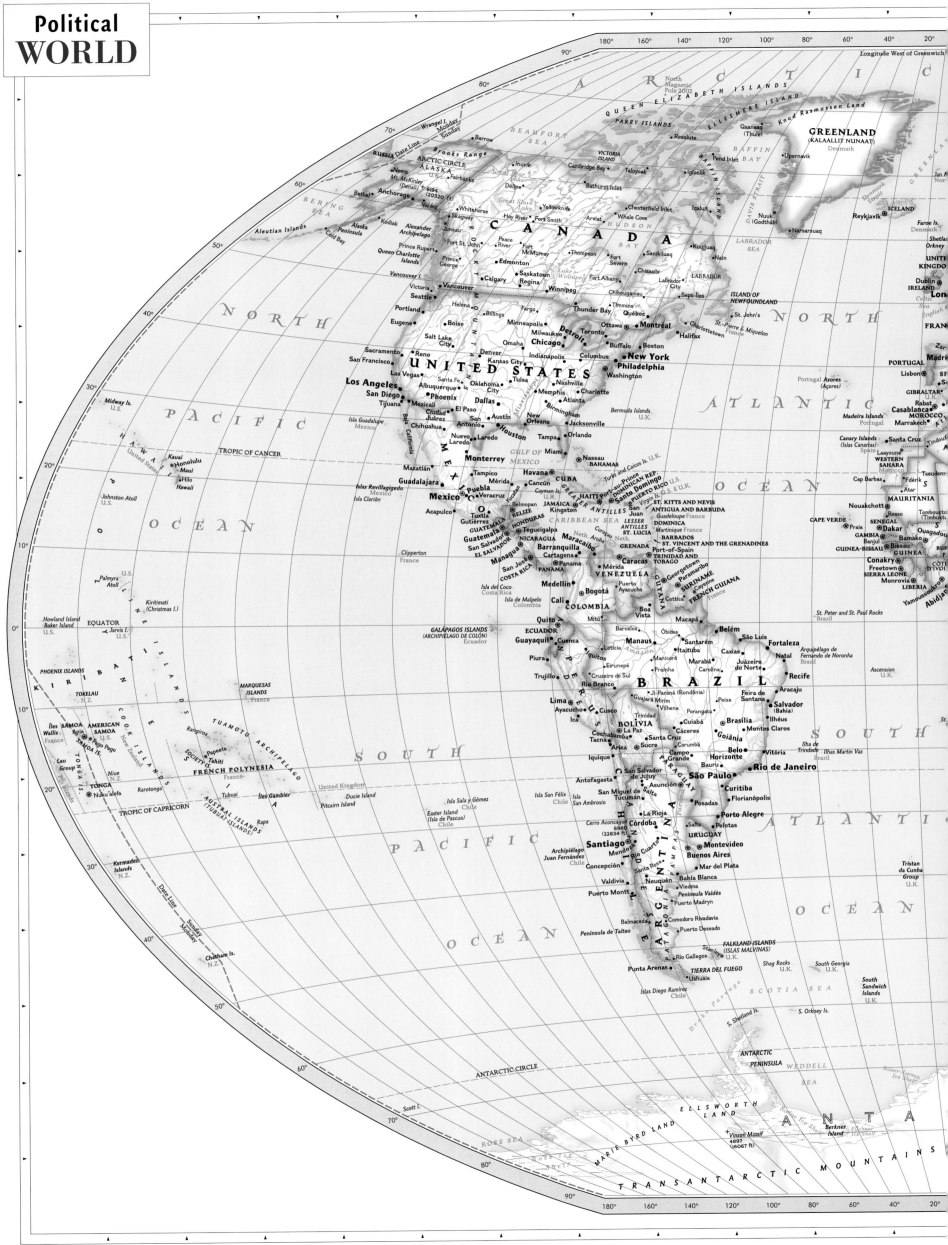

Winkel Tripel Projection, Central Meridian 0°

SCALE 1:80,470,600

1 CENTIMETER = 805 KILOMETERS; 1 INCH = 1270 MILES AT THE EQUATOR

0   500   1000   1500   2000   2500
KILOMETERS

0   500   1000   1500   2000   2500
STATUTE MILES

International boundaries and disputed territories, where scale
permits, reflect de facto status at the time of publication.

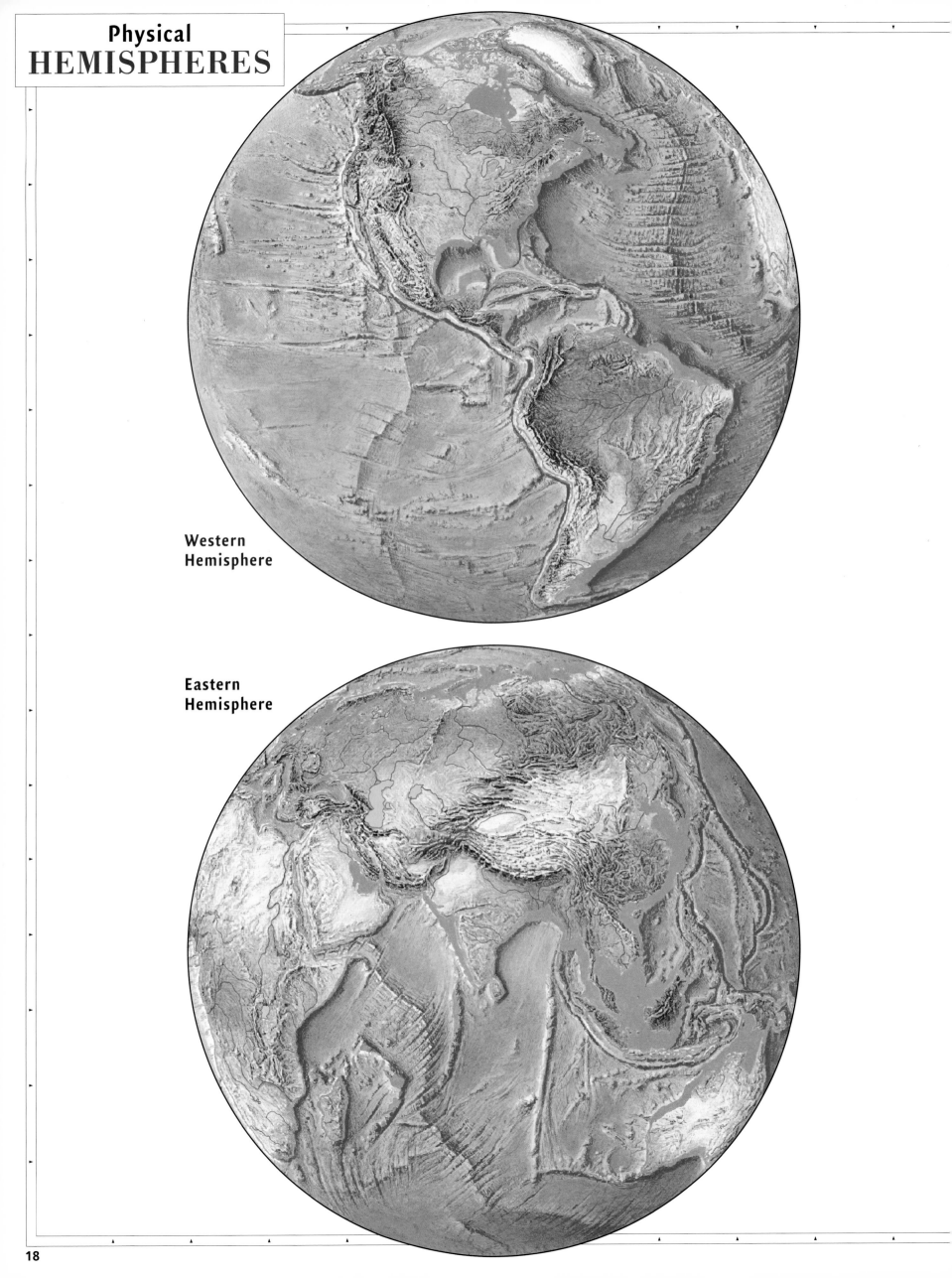

Western
Hemisphere

Eastern
Hemisphere

North Pole

Anchorage
Nome
Anadyr'
Bering Sea
180°
165°
150°
Kolyma

ALASKA
United States
Fairbanks
ARCTIC CIRCLE
Indigirka
135°

150°
135°
Yukon
Chukchi Sea
East Siberian Sea
Yakutsk

Barrow
Wrangel Island

Mackenzie
Beaufort Sea
120°

Great Slave L.
Great Bear Lake
New Siberian Islands
Tiksi
Lena
Laptev Sea
75°
105°

Yellowknife

CANADA
Banks Island
ARCTIC OCEAN

Victoria Island
North Magnetic Pole 2002
North Land
RUSSIA

150°
Queen Elizabeth Islands
North Pole ★
Limit of Multiyear Ice
Noril'sk
Yenisey
90°

Ellesmere Island
Kara Sea

Baffin Island
Baffin Bay
Franz Josef Land
Russia
Novaya Zemlya
Vorkuta
Ob'
60°

75°
Davis Strait

Svalbard
Norway
Barents Sea
75°

GREENLAND
Denmark
75°
Longyearbyen
Spitsbergen
Murmansk

Nuuk
(Godthåb)
Arkhangel'sk
45°

0 mi   600
0 km   600
Azimuthal Equidistant Projection
Greenland Sea
Winter Extent of Sea Ice

Reykjavík
ICELAND
ARCTIC CIRCLE
FINLAND

SWEDEN
Helsinki
30°
Norwegian Sea
30°

ATLANTIC OCEAN
NORWAY
15°
15°
0°

North Pole

South Pole

0°
15°
15°
ANTARCTIC CIRCLE
30°

30°
ATLANTIC OCEAN
Fimbul Ice Shelf
45°

South Orkney Is.
Cape Norvegia
Neumayer
Germany
Maitri
India

South Shetland Is.
Riiser-Larsen Ice Shelf
Queen Maud Land
Syowa
Japan
Molodezhnaya
Russia
60°

Joinville I.
Weddell Sea
Enderby Land
INDIAN OCEAN

60°
Larsen Ice Shelf
Halley
U.K.
Mawson
Australia

Antarctic Peninsula
Belgrano II
Argentina
Cape Darnley
75°

Alexander I.
Berkner Island
Amery Ice Shelf

75°
Ronne Ice Shelf
Zhongshan
China
Davis
Australia

Bellingshausen Sea
Vinson Massif
4897
ANTARCTICA
Polar Plateau
★ South Pole
Amundsen-Scott
U.S.
West Ice Shelf
90°

Ellsworth Land
Ellsworth Mts.
EAST
Mirnyy
Russia

Thurston I.
WEST
ANTARCTICA
ANTARCTICA
Shackleton Ice Shelf

90°
Amundsen Sea
Marie Byrd Land
Ross Ice Shelf
Casey
Australia
105°

105°
Getz Ice Shelf
Roosevelt I.
McMurdo
U.S.
Scott N.Z.
Wilkes Land

PACIFIC OCEAN
Mt. Erebus
3794
Victoria Land
Dumont d'Urville
France

0 mi   600
0 km   600
Azimuthal Equidistant Projection
⊙ Research station
Ross Sea
Cape Adare
South Magnetic Pole 2002

120°
135°
Balleny Islands
120°
ANTARCTIC CIRCLE
150°
165°
180°
165°

South Pole

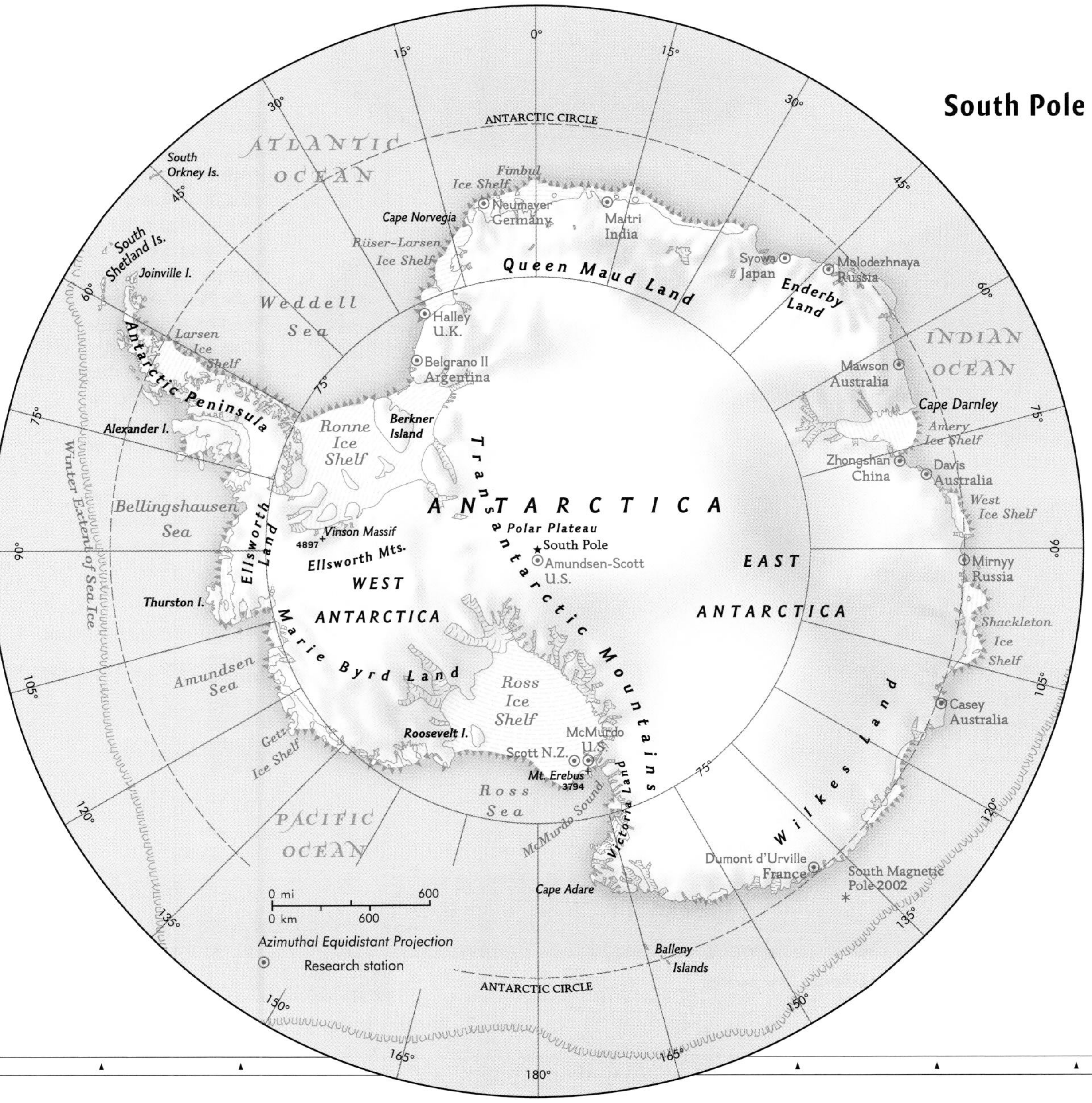

Like ice on a great lake, the Earth's crust, or the lithosphere, floats over the planet's molten innards, is cracked in many places, and is in slow but constant movement. Earth's surface is broken into 16 enormous slabs of rock, called plates, averaging thousands of miles wide and having a thickness of several miles. As they move and grind against each other, they push up mountains, spawn volcanoes, and generate earthquakes.

Although these often cataclysmic events capture our attention, the movements that cause them are imperceptible, a slow waltz of rafted rock that continues over eons.

How slow? The Mid-Atlantic Ridge (see "spreading" diagram, opposite) is being built by magma oozing between two plates, separating North America and Africa at the speed of a growing human fingernail.

The dividing lines between plates often mark areas of high volcanic and earthquake activity as plates strain against each other or one dives beneath another. In the Ring of Fire around the Pacific Basin, disastrous earthquakes have occurred in Kobe, Japan, and in Los Angeles and San Francisco, California. Volcanic eruptions have taken place at Pinatubo in the Philippines and Mount St. Helens in Washington State.

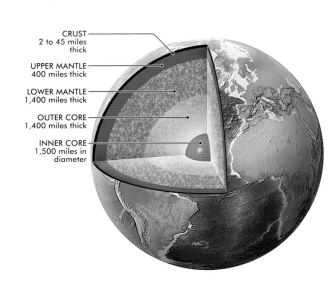

CRUST
2 to 45 miles thick

UPPER MANTLE
400 miles thick

LOWER MANTLE
1,400 miles thick

OUTER CORE
1,400 miles thick

INNER CORE
1,500 miles in diameter

Continents Adrift in Time

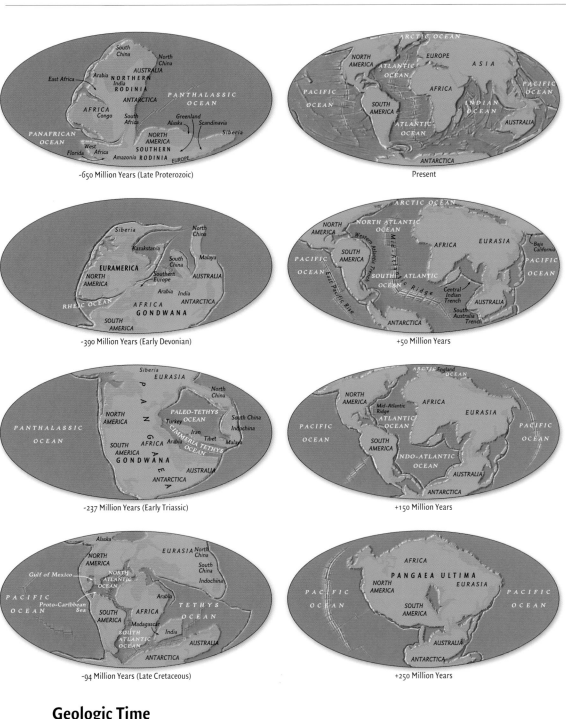

-650 Million Years (Late Proterozoic)

Present

-390 Million Years (Early Devonian)

+50 Million Years

-237 Million Years (Early Triassic)

+150 Million Years

-94 Million Years (Late Cretaceous)

+250 Million Years

As crustal plates drift, continents join and pull apart. Three times during the last billion years Earth's lands have merged, forming supercontinents. Rodinia, the huge landmass of the late Precambrian, began breaking apart 750 million years ago; in time, its pieces came together as Pannotia. This supercontinent rifted, too, splitting into the Paleozoic continents of Baltica (Europe) and Laurentia (North America)— which merged and became Euramerica— and Gondwana (Africa, (Antarctica, Arabia, India, and Australia). More than 250 years ago, these continents combined into Pangaea; in the Mesozoic era, Pangaea split and the Atlantic and Indian Oceans began forming. Though the Atlantic is widening, scientists predict it will close as seafloor recycles back into Earth's mantle. A new supercontinent— Pangaea Ultima—will eventually form.

KEY TO PALEO-GEOGRAPHIC MAPS

Seafloor spreading ridge

Subduction zone

Ancient landmass

Geologic Time

	4,500 MILLIONS OF YEARS AGO		3,500	3,000		2,500	2000	1500	1000
EON	A R C H E A N						P R O T E R O Z O I C		
ERA	EOARCHEAN		PALEOARCHEAN	MESOARCHEAN	NEOARCHEAN	PALEOPROTEROZOIC		MESOPROTEROZOIC	
PERIOD	No subdivision into periods					SIDERIAN / RHYACIAN / OROSIRIAN / STATHERIAN / CALYMMIAN		ECTASIAN / STENIAN / TONIAN	

Geologic Forces Change the Face of the Planet

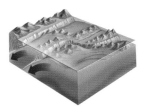  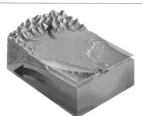   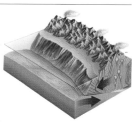

ACCRETION
As ocean plates move toward the edges of continents or island arcs and slide under them, seamounts are skimmed off and piled up in submarine trenches. The buildup can cause continents to grow.

FAULTING
Enormous crustal plates do not slide smoothly. Strain built up along their edges may release in a series of small jumps, felt as minor tremors on land. Extended buildup can cause a sudden jump, producing an earthquake.

COLLISION
When two continental plates converge, the result can be the greatest mountain-building process on Earth. The Himalaya rose when the Indian subcontinent collided with Eurasia, driving the land upward.

HOT SPOTS
In the cauldron of inner Earth, some areas burn hotter than others and periodically blast through their crustal covering as volcanoes. Such a "hot spot" built the Hawaiian Islands, leaving a string of oceanic protuberances.

SPREADING
At the divergent boundary known as the Mid-Atlantic Ridge, oozing magma forces two plates apart by as much as eight inches a year. If that rate had been constant, the ocean could have reached its current width in 30 million years.

SUBDUCTION
When an oceanic plate and a continental plate converge, the older and heavier sea plate takes a dive. Plunging back into the interior of the Earth, it is transformed into molten material, only to rise again as magma.

Plate Tectonics

Tectonic boundaries mark areas of geologic change in ocean floors, on the margins of continents, and even within continents, as seen in the Great Rift Valley of East Africa. Clusters of volcanoes and frequent earthquakes indicate unstable areas.

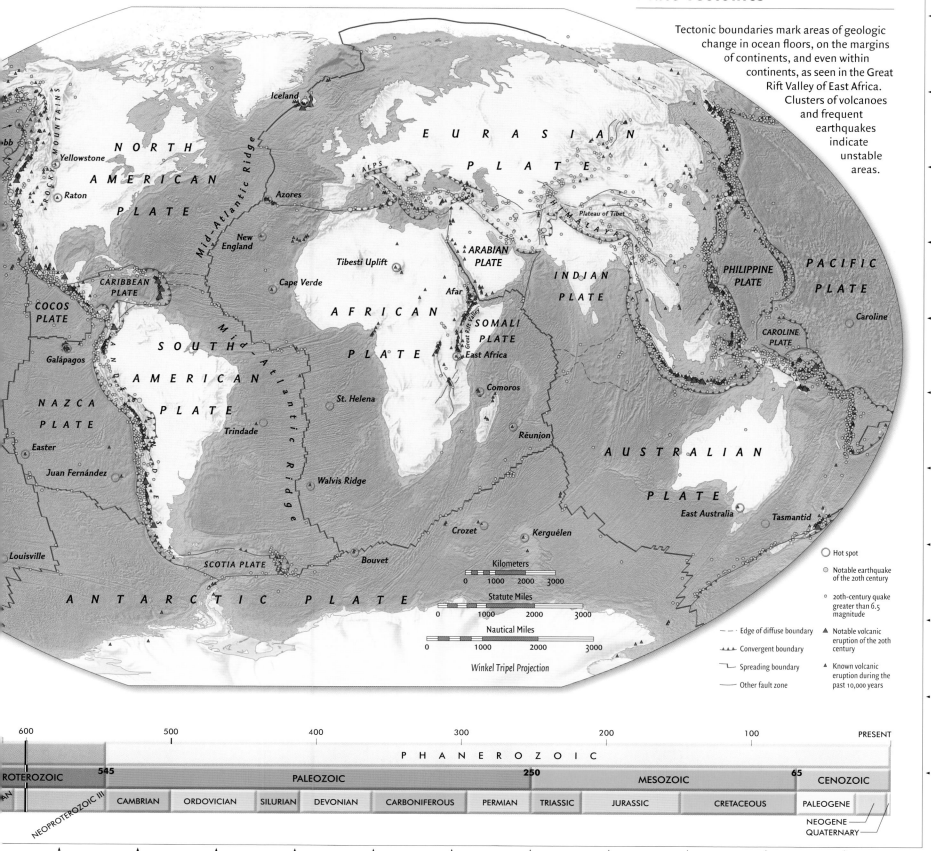

Winkel Tripel Projection

○ Hot spot
◉ Notable earthquake of the 20th century
○ 20th-century quake greater than 6.5 magnitude
- - - Edge of diffuse boundary
▲▲▲ Convergent boundary
⌐ Spreading boundary
— Other fault zone
▲ Notable volcanic eruption of the 20th century
▲ Known volcanic eruption during the past 10,000 years

Kilometers
0 1000 2000 3000
Statute Miles
0 1000 2000 3000
Nautical Miles
0 1000 2000 3000

| 600 | 500 | 400 | 300 | 200 | 100 | PRESENT |

P H A N E R O Z O I C

| ROTEROZOIC | 545 | PALEOZOIC | | | | | 250 | | MESOZOIC | | 65 | CENOZOIC |

| AN | NEOPROTEROZOIC III | CAMBRIAN | ORDOVICIAN | SILURIAN | DEVONIAN | CARBONIFEROUS | PERMIAN | TRIASSIC | JURASSIC | CRETACEOUS | PALEOGENE |

NEOGENE
QUATERNARY

Earth's outermost layer, the crust, is from two to forty-five miles (3 to 70 km) thick and comprises a large variety of rocks that are aggregates of one or more types of minerals.

Scientists recognize three main classes of rock. The igneous type forms when molten material cools and solidifies, either rapidly at the Earth's surface—as perhaps a lava flow—or more slowly underground, as an intrusion. Sedimentary rocks form from mineral or rock fragments, or from organic material that is eroded or dissolved, then deposited at Earth's surface. Metamorphic rocks form when rocks of any origin (igneous, sedimentary, or metamorphic) are subjected to very high temperature or pressure; this type also forms as rocks react with fluids deep within the crust. Igneous and metamorphic rocks make up 95 percent of the crust's volume. Sedimentary rocks make up only about 5 percent; even so, they cover a large percentage of Earth's surface.

As a result of plate tectonics, the crust is in constant slow motion; thus, rocks change positions over time. Their compositions also change as they are gradually modified by metamorphism and melting. Rocks form and re-form in a sequence known as the rock cycle (see below). Understanding their nature and origin is important because rocks contain materials that sustain modern civilization. For example, steel requires the processing of iron—mainly from ancient sedimentary rocks; copper is mined principally from slowly cooled igneous rocks called plutons; and petroleum derives from organic material trapped ages ago in relatively young sedimentary rocks.

Rock Classes

IGNEOUS Igneous rocks form when molten rock (magma) originating from deep within the Earth solidifies. The chemical composition of the magma and its cooling rate determine the final rock type.	**Intrusive (Plutonic)**	Intrusive igneous rocks are formed from magma that cools and solidifies deep beneath the Earth's surface. The insulating effect of the surrounding rock allows the magma to solidify very slowly. Slow cooling means the individual mineral grains have a long time to grow, so they grow to a relatively large size. Intrusive rocks have a characteristically coarse grain size.	Examples: gabbro, diorite, granite
	Extrusive (Volcanic)	Extrusive igneous rocks are formed from magma that cools and solidifies at or near the Earth's surface. Exposure to the relatively cool temperature of the atmosphere or water makes the erupted magma solidify very quickly. Rapid cooling means the individual mineral grains have only a short time to grow, so their final size is very tiny, or fine-grained. Sometimes the magma is quenched so rapidly that individual minerals have no time to grow. This is how volcanic glass forms.	Examples: basalt, andesite, and rhyolite

SEDIMENTARY Sedimentary rocks are formed from preexisting rocks or pieces of once living organisms. They form deposits that accumulate on the Earth's surface, often with distinctive layering or bedding.	**Clastic**	Clastic sedimentary rocks are made up of pieces (clasts) of preexisting rocks. Pieces of rock are loosened by weathering, then transported to a basin or depression where sediment is trapped. If the sediment is buried deeply, it becomes compacted and cemented, forming sedimentary rock. Clastic sedimentary rocks may have particles ranging in size from microscopic clay to huge boulders. Their names are based on their grain size.	Examples: sandstone, mudstone, conglomerate
	Chemical	Chemical sedimentary rocks are formed by chemical precipitation. This process begins when water traveling through rock dissolves some of the minerals, carrying them away from their source. Eventually these minerals are redeposited when the water evaporates.	Examples: evaporite, dolomite
	Biologic	Biologic sedimentary rocks form from once living organisms. They may comprise accumulated carbon-rich plant material or deposits of animal shells.	Examples: coal, chalk, limestone, chert

METAMORPHIC Metamorphic rocks are rocks that have been substantially changed from their original igneous, sedimentary, or earlier metamorphic form. Metamorphic rocks form when rocks are subjected to high heat; high pressure; hot, mineral-rich fluids; or, more commonly, some combination of these factors.	**Foliated**	Foliated rocks form when pressure squeezes the flat or elongated minerals within a rock so they become aligned. These rocks develop a platy or sheetlike structure that reflects the direction from which pressure was applied.	Examples: schist, gneiss, slate
	Nonfoliated	Nonfoliated metamorphic rocks do not have a platy or sheetlike structure. There are several ways that nonfoliated rocks can be produced. Some rocks, such as limestone, are made of minerals that are not flat or elongated; no matter how much pressure is applied, the grains will not align. Contact metamorphism occurs when hot igneous rock intrudes into preexisting rock. The preexisting rock is essentially baked by the heat, which changes the mineral structure without the addition of pressure.	Examples: marble, quartzite, hornfels

The Rock Cycle

To learn the origin and history of rocks, geologists study their mineralogy, texture, and fabric—characteristics that result from dynamic Earth-shaping processes driven by internal and external energy.

Internal energy is heat contained within the Earth. This intense heat creates convection currents in the mantle, which in turn cause tectonic plate movements and volcanism. External energy comes from the sun, which drives atmospheric processes that produce rain, snow, ice, and wind—powerful agents of weathering and erosion.

As internal energy builds and rebuilds Earth's rocky exterior, the forces of weathering and erosion break down surface materials and wear them away. Ultimately, soil particles and rock fragments, called sediments, are carried by rivers into the oceans, where they may lithify, or harden into solid rock. In time, these sedimentary rocks may be subjected to heat and pressure at great depth. Mineral and structural changes occur as the rocks break and fold; they are transformed into metamorphic rocks.

Rocks near a magma source may begin to melt. Eventually this hot material may erupt as lava from a volcano; as it cools on the surface, it recrystallizes into igneous rock. Hot rock may also solidify underground and later be carried upward by tectonic uplift. At the surface, the cycle continues as weathering and erosion break it down and wear it away.

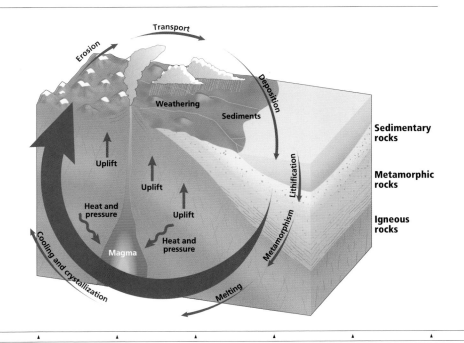

Rock Class Distribution

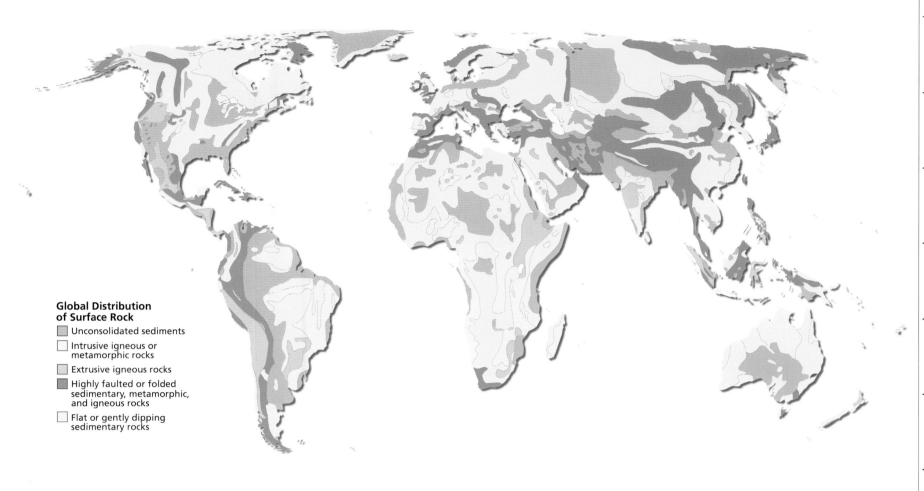

Global Distribution of Surface Rock
- ▢ Unconsolidated sediments
- ▢ Intrusive igneous or metamorphic rocks
- ▢ Extrusive igneous rocks
- ▢ Highly faulted or folded sedimentary, metamorphic, and igneous rocks
- ▢ Flat or gently dipping sedimentary rocks

Reading Earth History from Rocks

The Earth is 4.6 billion years old, with a long, complex history written in layers of rock. By reading sequences of rock, we can discover information about past environments and processes. The principle of superposition states that, provided rocks are not turned upside down by deformation, the oldest rocks are at the bottom of a sequence and younger rocks are found near the top. Unconformities tell us that uplift and erosion occurred before the deposition of younger sediments resumed. As an example, the rock sequence exposed in the Grand Canyon of Arizona indicates from oldest to youngest, the following major events:

During Precambrian time:
1. Deposition of Vishnu sediment (about 2 billion years ago)
2. Mountain building, metamorphism of Vishnu sediment into Vishnu schist, and intrusion of Zoroaster granite (1.8 to 1.4 billion years ago)
3. Uplift and erosion resulting in an unconformity (1.4 to 1.2 billion years ago)
4. Deposition of Unkar Group sediments (1.2 to 1.0 billion years ago)
5. Tilting (1 billion years ago)
6. Erosion resulting in angular unconformity (1 billion to 543 million years ago)

During the Phanerozoic (Cambrian-Recent) eon:
7. Deposition of Cambrian to Permian (and younger rocks not shown) sediments (543-520 million years ago), with disconformities indicating erosion and "missing" time where noted
8. Uplift and erosion of the Grand Canyon (20 million years ago to present)

The ages for these events are broadly defined by the radioisotopic dating of minerals in the metamorphic and igneous rocks, and by fossils and correlation to other rocks for the sedimentary rocks that are younger than the Precambrian-Cambrian boundary (543 million years ago).

Yavapai Point, Grand Canyon

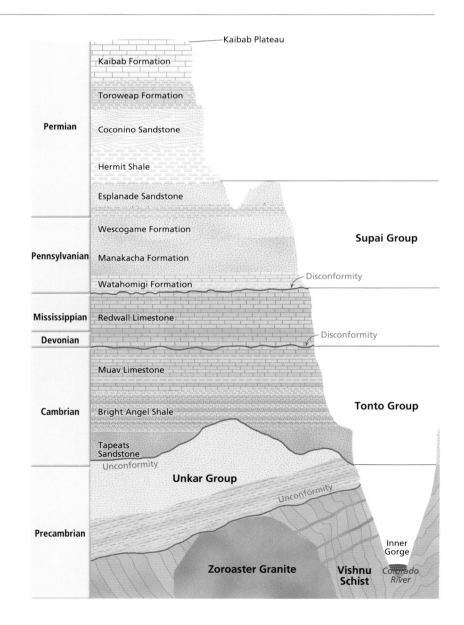

Kaibab Plateau

Permian	Kaibab Formation
	Toroweap Formation
	Coconino Sandstone
	Hermit Shale
	Esplanade Sandstone

Wescogame Formation

Supai Group

| Pennsylvanian | Manakacha Formation |
| | Watahomigi Formation |

Disconformity

| Mississippian | Redwall Limestone |

Disconformity

| Devonian | |
| | Muav Limestone |

| Cambrian | Bright Angel Shale |

Tonto Group

Tapeats Sandstone

Unconformity

Unkar Group

Unconformity

| Precambrian | |

Inner Gorge

Zoroaster Granite   **Vishnu Schist**   Colorado River

WORLD LANDFORMS

Seven major landform types are found on Earth's surface (see map); except for **ice caps,** all result from tectonic movements and denudational forces.

The loftiest landforms, **mountains,** often define the edges of tectonic plates. In places where continental plates converge, Earth's crust crumples into high ranges such as the Himalaya. Where oceanic plates dive beneath continental ones, volcanic mountains can rise. Volcanoes are common along the west coast of South America, which is part of the so-called Pacific Rim of Fire, the world's most active mountain-building zone.

Widely spaced mountains are another type, and examples of this landform are seen in the Basin and Range province of the western United States. These features are actually the tops of heavily eroded, faulted mountains. The eroded material filled adjacent valleys, giving these old summits the look of widely spaced mountains.

Extensive, relatively flat lands that are higher than surrounding areas are known as **plateaus.** Formed by uplift, they include the Guiana Highlands of South America.

Hills and low plateaus are rounded natural elevations of land with some local relief. The Canadian Shield and Ozarks of North America provide good examples.

Depressions, large basins delimited by higher lands, are found on the Mongolian Plateau and in other parts of the world.

Plains are extensive areas of level or rolling treeless country. Examples include the steppes of Russia, the Ganges River plains, and the outback of Australia.

Major Landform Types
- Mountains
- Widely spaced mountains
- High plateaus
- Hills and low plateaus
- Depressions
- Plains
- Ice caps

Endogenic Landforms

LANDFORMS THAT RESULT FROM "INTERNAL" PROCESSES

Forces deep within the Earth give rise to mountains and other endogenic landforms. Some mountains (e.g., the Himalaya) were born when continental plates collided. Others rose in the form of volcanoes (the Cascades of North America, Mount Fuji of Japan) as sea plates subducted beneath continental plates or as plates moved over hot spots in Earth's mantle (Hawaii). Still others were thrust up by tectonic uplift (parts of the western United States). Rifting and faulting, which occur along plate boundaries and sometimes within the plates themselves, also generate vertical tectonic landforms; these can be seen in Africa's Rift Valley and along the San Andreas Fault of California.

Clockwise from above: The Wasatch Range in Utah, uplifted by tectonic forces; the San Andreas Fault in California, a fracture in Earth's crust marking a plate boundary; Mount Fuji in Japan, a volcanic peak; Crater Lake in Oregon, a deep lake inside the caldera of Mount Mazama.

Exogenic Landforms

LANDFORMS THAT RESULT FROM "EXTERNAL" PROCESSES

External agents create exogenic landforms. Weathering by rain, groundwater, and other natural elements slowly breaks down rocks, such as the limestone in karst landscapes or the granite in an exfoliation dome (Yosemite's Half Dome). Erosion removes weathered material and transports it from place to place. In the American Southwest, erosion continues to shape the spires of Bryce Canyon and the walls of slot canyons.

Clockwise from above: tower karst in China, weathered limestone in humid climate; Bryce Canyon in Utah, eroded sedimentary rocks in arid climate; slot canyon in the American Southwest, sedimentary rock eroded by water; Half Dome in Yosemite, California, weathered granite batholith.

Other Landforms

Some landforms are the impact sites (or craters) of asteroids, comets, and meteorites. The most readily observable are Meteor Crater in Arizona and New Quebec Crater in eastern Canada. Other landforms include man-made dams and open-pit mines, as well as biogenic features such as coral reefs made by coral polyps and giant mounds built by termites.

Meteor Crater, Arizona

Termite mound, Cape York Peninsula, Australia

WORLD LANDFORMS

All of Earth's features are created and continually reshaped by such factors as wind, water, ice, tectonics, and humans. This painting brings together 34 natural and man-made features to show typical locations and relationships of landforms; it does not depict an actual region.

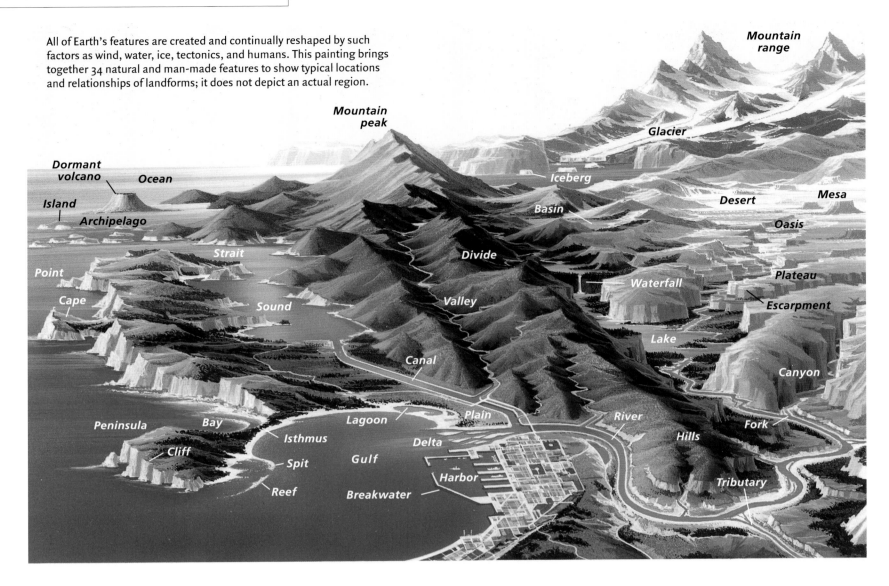

Labels in illustration: Mountain range, Mountain peak, Glacier, Iceberg, Dormant volcano, Ocean, Basin, Desert, Mesa, Island, Archipelago, Oasis, Strait, Divide, Plateau, Point, Waterfall, Escarpment, Cape, Sound, Valley, Lake, Canal, Canyon, Peninsula, Bay, Lagoon, Plain, River, Fork, Hills, Cliff, Isthmus, Delta, Spit, Gulf, Harbor, Tributary, Reef, Breakwater

Landforms Created by Wind

The term "eolian" (from Aeolus, the Greek god of the winds) describes landforms shaped by the wind. The erosive action of wind is characterized by deflation, or the removal of dust and sand from dry soil; sandblasting, the erosion of rock by wind-borne sand; and deposition, the laying down of sediments. The effects of wind erosion are evident in many parts of the world (see map), particularly where there are large deposits of sand or loess (dust and silt dropped by wind). Among desert landforms, sand dunes may be the most spectacular. They come in several types (below): **Barchan dunes** are crescents with arms pointing downwind; **transverse dunes** are "waves," with crests perpendicular to the wind; **star dunes** have curving ridges radiating from their centers; **parabolic dunes** are crescents with arms that point upwind; and **longitudinal dunes** lie parallel to the wind.

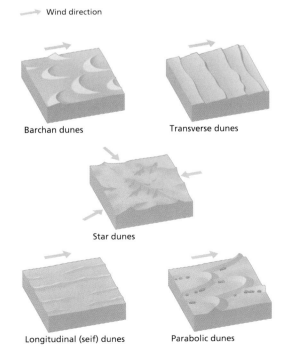

→ Wind direction

Barchan dunes

Transverse dunes

Star dunes

Longitudinal (seif) dunes

Parabolic dunes

SIBERIA
EUROPE
ASIA
NORTH AMERICA
GOBI
SAHARA
AFRICA
SOUTH AMERICA
KALAHARI DESERT
AUSTRALIA
ANTARCTICA

☐ Desert
☐ Loess deposit

EOLIAN LANDFORMS

Desert dunes, which actually cover only a small portion of desert areas, range in height from just a few feet to more than a thousand. Coastal dunes form when wind and waves deposit sediments along the shores of oceans and other large bodies of water. Loess hills are large deposits of wind-borne silt, the most extensive of which are found in North America and Asia.

Desert dunes: Death Valley National Park

Coastal dunes: Dune du Nord, Quebec

Loess deposits: Palouse Hills, Washington

Landforms Created by Water

Highlighted on the map at right are Earth's major watersheds. These are drainage basins for rivers, which create fluvial (from a Latin word meaning "river") landforms. Wave action and groundwater also produce characteristic landforms.

RIVERS

Some rivers form broad loops called meanders (below) as faster currents erode their outer banks and slower currents deposit materials along inner banks. When a river breaks through the narrow neck of a meander, the abandoned curve becomes an oxbow lake.

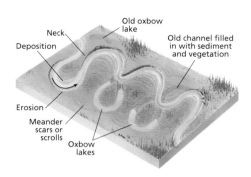

The world's ten largest watersheds
Other major watersheds

RIVER DELTAS

Sediment deposited at a river's mouth builds a delta, a term first used by the ancient Greeks to describe the Nile Delta; its triangular shape resembles the fourth letter of the Greek alphabet. Not all deltas have that classic shape: The Mississippi River forms a bird's-foot delta.

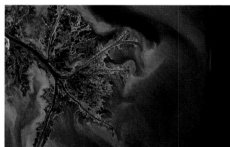

Mississippi River Delta

COASTAL AREAS

Through erosion and deposition, tides and wave action continually reshape the coastlines of the world. Ocean currents transport sand and gravel from one part of a shore to another, sometimes building beach extensions called spits, long ridges that project into open water.

Relentless waves undercut coastal cliffs, eroding volumes of material and leaving behind sea stacks and sea arches, remnants made of more resistant rock. As ocean levels rise, narrow arms of the sea (fjords) may reach inland for miles, filling deep valleys once occupied by glaciers flowing to the sea.

Sea stacks: Victoria, Australia

GROUNDWATER

Water in the ground slowly dissolves limestone, a highly soluble rock. Over time, caves form and underground streams flow through the rock; sinkholes develop at the surface as underlying rock gives way. Karst landscapes, named for the rugged Karst region of the former Yugoslavia, are large areas of unusual landforms created by weathered and eroded limestone.

Karst cave: Kickapoo Cave, Texas

Landforms Created by Ice

Among the legacies of Earth's most recent ice age (see map) are landforms shaped by glaciers. There are two kinds of glaciers: valley, or alpine, and continental ice sheets. These large, slow-moving masses of ice can crush or topple anything in their paths; they even stop rivers in their tracks, creating ice-dammed lakes. Glaciers are also powerful agents of erosion, grinding against the ground and picking up and carrying huge amounts of rock and soil, which they deposit at their margins when they begin to melt; these deposits are called lateral and terminal moraines. The paintings below show how an ice sheet (upper) leaves a lasting imprint on the land (lower).

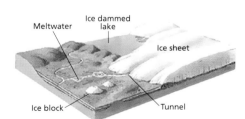

Greatest extent of ice during last ice age

BEFORE AND AFTER (LEFT)

Meltwater deposits material in long, narrow ridges (eskers). Ice embedded in the ground melts and forms lakes (kettles). Ice overruns unconsolidated materials and shapes them into hills (drumlins).

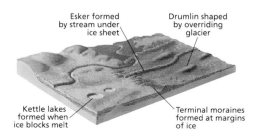

Glacial valley: Sierra Nevada, California

POSTGLACIAL LANDFORMS

As they move, alpine glaciers widen their V-shaped valleys, often leaving behind U-shaped ones when they withdraw (left). Ice sheets leave an even larger legacy simply because they cover more territory. Among their creations are drumlin fields (right) and lake basins, including the ones now filled by the Great Lakes of North America.

Drumlins: Kejimkujik Lake, Nova Scotia

SURFACE OF THE EARTH

Earth's largest features—oceans and continents—can be seen from thousands of miles out in space. So can some of its relatively smaller ones: vast plains and long mountain chains, huge lakes and great ice sheets. The sizes, shapes, locations, and interrelationships of these and innumerable other features, large and small, give Earth its unique appearance.

Mountains, plateaus, and plains give texture to the land. In North and South America, the Rockies and Andes rise above great basins and plains, while in Asia the Himalaya and Plateau of Tibet form the rugged core of Earth's largest continent. All are the result of powerful forces within the planet pushing up the land. Other features, such as valleys and canyons, were created when weathering and erosion wore down parts of the surface. Landmasses are not the only places with dramatic features: Lying beneath the oceans are enormous mountains and towering volcanoes, high plateaus and seemingly bottomless trenches.

Around most continents are shallow seas concealing gently sloping continental shelves. From the margins of these shelves, steeper continental slopes lead ever deeper into the abyss. Although scientists use different terms to describe their studies of the ocean depths (bathymetry) and the lay of the land (topography), Earth's surface is a continuum, with similar features giving texture to lands both above and below the sea level.

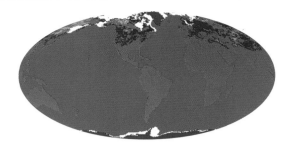

SNOW AND ICE
Just over 2 percent of Earth's water is locked in ice, snow, and glaciers. Ice and snow reflect solar energy back into space, thus regulating the temperature. Ocean levels can also be affected, rising or falling as polar ice sheets shrink or grow.

Surface by the Numbers

AREA
Total surface area: 196,938,000 square miles (510,066,000 sq km)
Land area: 57,393,000 square miles (148,647,000 sq km), 29.1 percent of total surface area
Water area: 139,545,000 square miles (361,419,000 sq km), 70.9 percent of total surface area

SURFACE FEATURES
Highest land: Mount Everest, 29,035 feet (8,850 m) above sea level
Lowest land: shore of Dead Sea, 1,349 feet (411 m) below sea level

OCEAN DEPTHS
Deepest part of ocean: Challenger Deep, in the Pacific Ocean southwest of Guam, 35,827 feet (10,920 m) below the surface
Average ocean depth: 12,205 feet (3,720 m)

CHEMICAL MAKEUP OF EARTH'S CRUST
As a percentage of the crust's weight: oxygen 46.6, silicon 27.7, aluminum 8.1, iron 5.0, calcium 3.6, sodium 2.8, potassium 2.6, magnesium 2.1, and other elements totaling 1.5.

Frozen fresh water / Liquid fresh water / Salt water

Other elements / Magnesium / Potassium / Sodium / Calcium / Iron / Aluminum / Oxygen / Silicon

Earth Surface Elevations and Depths

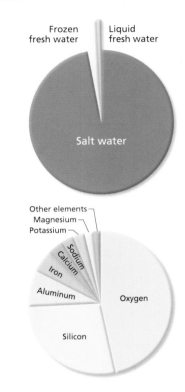

Rocky Mountains

NORTH AMERICA

PACIFIC OCEAN

Peru-Chile Trench

East Pacific Rise

A

Distribution of Earth's Elevations and Depths (Hypsometry)

Hypsometry measures the distribution of elevation and depth as a function of the area covered. At right, the "Raw %" curve shows two concentrations of average elevation: about 4,000 m (13,000 feet) below sea level and about 800 m (2,600 feet) above sea level. The "peaks" in the curve reflect the large, nearly flat areas of ocean floor, and vast land areas of Asia, Greenland, and Antarctica. The "Cumulative %" curve shows that about 72 percent of Earth's surface is below sea level, based on a worldwide 2-minute (latitude-longitude) grid and a 200-meter (650-foot) grouping of vertical data.

Cumulative %
Sea level
Raw %
100 90 80 70 60 50 40 30 20 10
9 8 7 6 5 4 3 2 1
-11,200 -4,000 0 4,000 9,000
Depth/elevation (in meters)

A Slice of Earth

Combining bathymetric and topographic data, this profile shows details of the Earth's crust—from the western Pacific Basin (A) to the Atlantic Basin; across Africa, the Himalaya, and the Japan Trench; then back to the western Pacific margin (B).

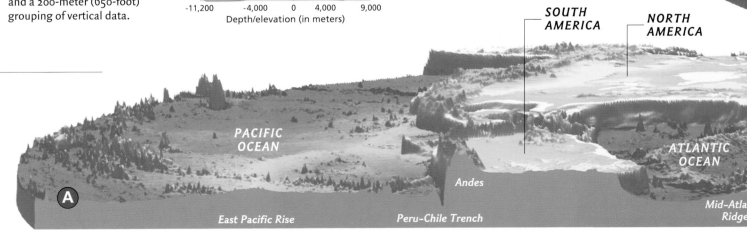

SOUTH AMERICA
NORTH AMERICA
PACIFIC OCEAN
ATLANTIC OCEAN
A
Andes
East Pacific Rise
Peru-Chile Trench
Mid-Atlantic Ridge

VEGETATIVE COVER
Forests and woodlands cover 28 percent of Earth's land areas, helping those regions retain heat and thus playing a major role in the shaping of climate. Vast grasslands hold grains that are an important element in the world food supply.

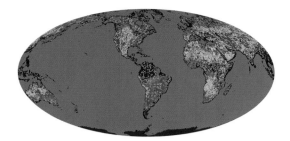

DAY AND NIGHT TEMPERATURE DIFFERENCES
Vegetative cover influences variations between day and night temperatures in an area. Rain forests and other heavily vegetated regions retain heat well and experience relatively small changes, while deserts (in red) are subject to extreme variations.

CLOUD COVER
This composite image shows the regions with the heaviest cloud cover (red) on a typical June day. The gradation to blue signifies decreasing cover. Clouds contain moisture, affect temperatures, and on any given day cover 50 to 70 percent of Earth's surface.

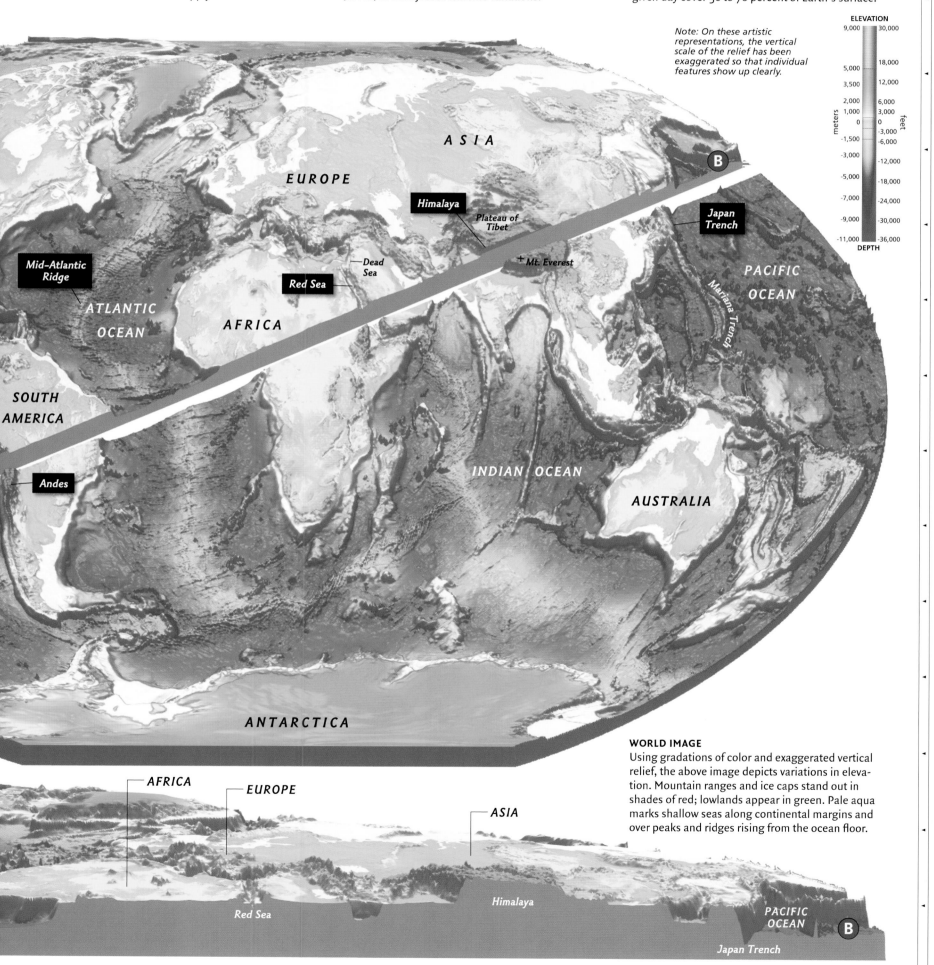

Note: On these artistic representations, the vertical scale of the relief has been exaggerated so that individual features show up clearly.

ELEVATION

meters	feet
9,000	30,000
5,000	18,000
3,500	12,000
2,000	6,000
1,000	3,000
0	0
-1,500	-3,000
-3,000	-6,000
-5,000	-12,000
-7,000	-18,000
	-24,000
-9,000	-30,000
-11,000	-36,000

DEPTH

ASIA

EUROPE

Himalaya

Plateau of Tibet

Japan Trench

Mid-Atlantic Ridge

Dead Sea

Red Sea

+ Mt. Everest

PACIFIC OCEAN

Mariana Trench

ATLANTIC OCEAN

AFRICA

SOUTH AMERICA

Andes

INDIAN OCEAN

AUSTRALIA

B

ANTARCTICA

WORLD IMAGE
Using gradations of color and exaggerated vertical relief, the above image depicts variations in elevation. Mountain ranges and ice caps stand out in shades of red; lowlands appear in green. Pale aqua marks shallow seas along continental margins and over peaks and ridges rising from the ocean floor.

AFRICA

EUROPE

ASIA

Red Sea

Himalaya

PACIFIC OCEAN

B

Japan Trench

WORLD LAND COVER

Reliable information on global vegetative cover is an important requirement for many Earth-system studies, and the best source for an overall view of the planet is satellite data. Such data allow for the creation of internally consistent, reproducible, and accurate land cover maps like the one at right, which is based on a year of global satellite imagery from the Advanced Very High Resolution Radiometer (AVHRR) at a spatial resolution of one kilometer.

The change of vegetation through time, or its phenology, is captured in the satellite record and used to differentiate classes of vegetative cover. By recording the data at different wavelengths of the electromagnetic spectrum, scientists can derive land cover types through spectral variation. Maps made from this information help identify places undergoing changes. Descriptions of the various land cover types are provided below.

EVERGREEN NEEDLELEAF FOREST
More than 60 percent of the land is covered by a forest canopy; tree height exceeds 5 meters. This land cover is typical of the boreal (northern) region. In many areas, trees are grown on plantations and logged for the making of paper and building products.

EVERGREEN BROADLEAF FOREST
More than 60 percent of the land is covered by a forest canopy; tree height exceeds 5 meters. Such forests dominate in the tropics and contain the greatest concentrations of biodiversity. In many areas, mechanized farms, ranches, and tree plantations are replacing this land cover.

Legend:
- Evergreen Needleleaf Forest
- Evergreen Broadleaf Forest
- Deciduous Needleleaf Forest
- Deciduous Broadleaf Forest
- Mixed Forest
- Woodland
- Wooded Grassland
- Closed Shrubland
- Open Shrubland
- Grassland
- Cropland
- Barren and Desert
- Urban and Built-Up
- Snow and Ice

DECIDUOUS NEEDLELEAF FOREST
More than 60 percent of the land is covered by a forest canopy; tree height exceeds 5 meters. Trees respond to cold seasons by shedding their leaves simultaneously. This class is dominant only in Siberia, taking the form of larch forests with a short June to August growing season.

DECIDUOUS BROADLEAF FOREST
More than 60 percent of the land is covered by a forest canopy; tree height exceeds 5 meters. In dry or cold seasons, trees shed their leaves simultaneously. Much of this forest has been converted to cropland in temperate regions, with large remnants found only on steep slopes.

MIXED FOREST
More than 60 percent of the land is covered by a forest canopy; tree height exceeds 5 meters. Both needleleaf and deciduous types appear, with neither having coverage of less than 25 percent or more than 75 percent. This type is largely found between temperate deciduous and boreal evergreen forests.

WOODLAND
Land has herbaceous or woody understories and tree canopy cover of 40 to 60 percent; trees exceed 5 meters and may be evergreen or deciduous. This type is common in the tropics and is most highly degraded in areas with long histories of human habitation, such as West Africa.

WOODED GRASSLAND
Land has herbaceous or woody understories and tree canopy cover of 10 to 40 percent; trees exceed 5 meters and may be evergreen or deciduous. This type includes classic African savanna, as well as open boreal woodlands that demarcate tree lines and the beginning of tundra ecosystems.

CLOSED SHRUBLAND
Bushes or shrubs dominate, with a canopy coverage of more than 40 percent. Bushes do not exceed 5 meters in height; shrubs or bushes can be evergreen or deciduous. Tree canopy is less than 10 percent. This land cover can be found where prolonged cold or dry seasons limit plant growth.

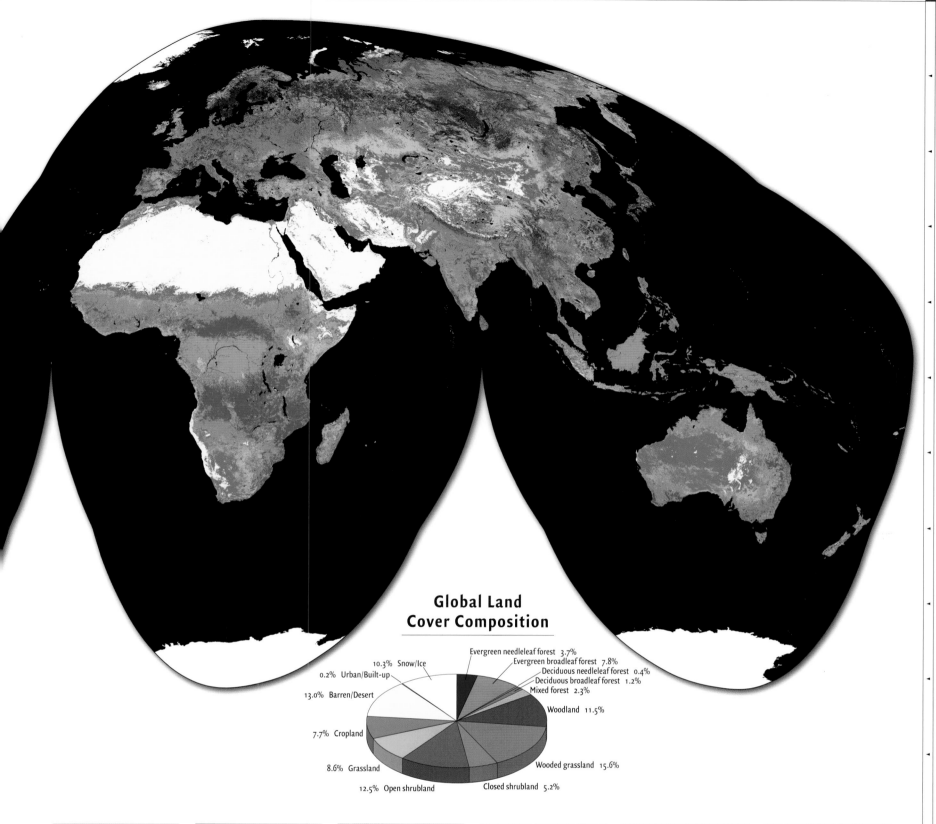

Global Land Cover Composition

- 10.3% Snow/Ice
- 0.2% Urban/Built-up
- 13.0% Barren/Desert
- 7.7% Cropland
- 8.6% Grassland
- 12.5% Open shrubland
- Closed shrubland 5.2%
- Wooded grassland 15.6%
- Woodland 11.5%
- Mixed forest 2.3%
- Deciduous broadleaf forest 1.2%
- Deciduous needleleaf forest 0.4%
- Evergreen broadleaf forest 7.8%
- Evergreen needleleaf forest 3.7%

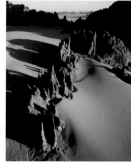

OPEN SHRUBLAND
Shrubs are dominant, with a canopy cover between 10 and 40 percent; they do not exceed 2 meters in height and can be evergreen or deciduous. The remaining land is either barren or characterized by annual herbaceous cover. This type occurs in semiarid or severely cold areas.

GRASSLAND
Land has continuous herbaceous cover and less than 10 percent tree or shrub canopy cover. This type occurs in a wide range of habitats. Perennial grasslands in the central United States and Russia, for example, are the most extensive and mark a line of decreased precipitation that limits agriculture.

CROPLAND
Crop-producing fields make up more than 80 percent of the landscape. Areas of high-intensity agriculture, including mechanized farming, stretch across temperate regions. Much agriculture in the developing world is fragmented, however, and occurs on small plots of land.

BARREN AND DESERT
Exposed soil, sand, or rocks are typical; the land never has more than 10 percent vegetated cover during any time of year. This class includes true deserts, such as the Sahara in Africa. Desertification, the expansion of deserts due to land degradation or climate change, is a problem in some areas.

URBAN AND BUILT-UP
Land cover includes buildings and other man-made structures. This class was mapped using the populated places layer that is part of the "Digital Chart of the World" (Danko, 1992). Urban and built-up cover represents the most densely developed areas of human habitation.

SNOW AND ICE
Land has permanent snow and ice; it never has more than 10 percent vegetated cover at any time of year. The greatest expanses of this class can be seen in Greenland, on other Arctic islands, and in Antarctica. Glaciers at high elevations form significant examples in Alaska, the Himalaya, and Iceland.

It has been said that "climate is what you expect; weather is what you get" (Robert A. Heinlein, science fiction writer). In other words, you can expect snow in Alaska in January, but you may or may not get it on a particular day. Weather describes the condition of the atmosphere over a short period of time, while climate describes average conditions over a longer period of time.

By definition, climate can be viewed as the slowly varying aspects of the air-water-land system. This variability can be seen in the long-term daily, monthly, and yearly averages for different weather conditions. Scientists present this data in many ways. They may use climographs (see page 34), which show information about specific places, or they may create maps, which can show regional and worldwide data. The maps at right, for example, focus on seasonal variations in solar energy, temperature, cloud cover, and precipitation.

The effects of climate can be seen in the distribution of Earth's life-forms. Temperature ranges and the amount of sunlight and precipitation determine what plants can grow in a region. They also affect which animal species can live there. People are more adaptable; even so, climate can be a limiting factor on the size of a population.

Knowing what to expect is important for planning purposes: The climate of a region affects whether a person needs to lay in supplies of heating oil, stock up on mosquito repellent, or do both. Tables with climatological data can be useful to individuals and community leaders alike. Knowing the coldest temperature ever recorded at a city on a particular day can help that city plan for its energy needs; knowing how average annual low temperatures have changed since 1850 in a particular state can provide clues to changes in insect migration. And if you know the average wind conditions at a place—as the Wright Brothers did when they chose to take flight from the Outer Banks of North Carolina—you might decide to meet your energy needs with wind power or even buy a sailplane and take flight yourself.

JANUARY SOLAR ENERGY

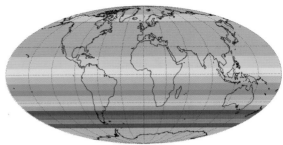

Watts per square yard

| 0 | 115.0 | 230.0 | 344.9 | 459.9 |

| 0 | 137.5 | 275 | 412.5 | 550 |

Watts per square meter

JULY SOLAR ENERGY

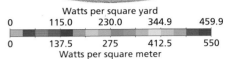

Watts per square yard

| 0 | 115.0 | 230.0 | 344.9 | 459.9 |

| 0 | 137.5 | 275 | 412.5 | 550 |

Watts per square meter

JANUARY AVERAGE TEMPERATURE

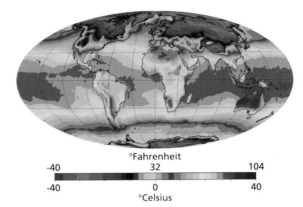

°Fahrenheit

| -40 | 32 | 104 |

| -40 | 0 | 40 |

°Celsius

JULY AVERAGE TEMPERATURE

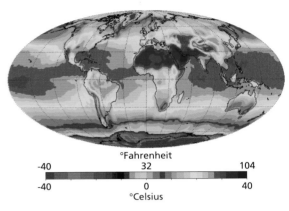

°Fahrenheit

| -40 | 32 | 104 |

| -40 | 0 | 40 |

°Celsius

JANUARY CLOUD COVER

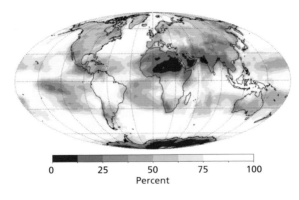

| 0 | 25 | 50 | 75 | 100 |

Percent

JULY CLOUD COVER

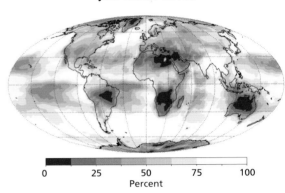

| 0 | 25 | 50 | 75 | 100 |

Percent

JANUARY PRECIPITATION

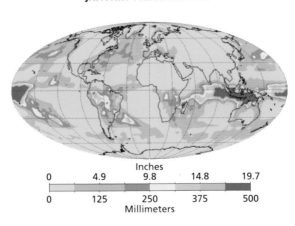

Inches

| 0 | 4.9 | 9.8 | 14.8 | 19.7 |

| 0 | 125 | 250 | 375 | 500 |

Millimeters

JULY PRECIPITATION

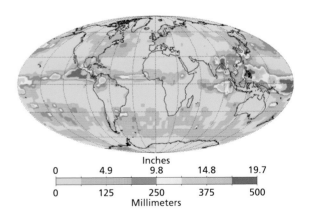

Inches

| 0 | 4.9 | 9.8 | 14.8 | 19.7 |

| 0 | 125 | 250 | 375 | 500 |

Millimeters

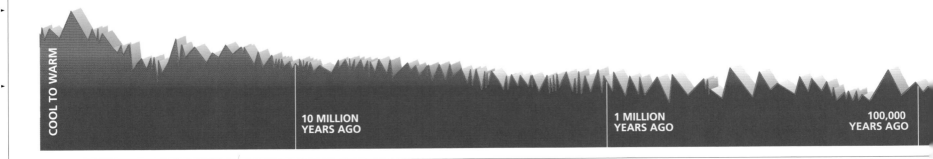

COOL TO WARM

10 MILLION YEARS AGO

1 MILLION YEARS AGO

100,000 YEARS AGO

Major Factors that Influence Climate

LATITUDE AND ANGLE OF THE SUN'S RAYS

As the Earth circles the sun, the tilt of its axis causes changes in the angle of the sun's rays and in the periods of daylight at different latitudes. Polar regions experience the greatest variation, with long periods of limited or no sunlight in winter and sometimes 24 hours of daylight in the summer.

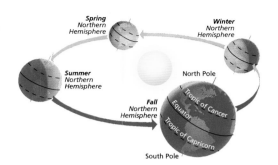

ELEVATION (ALTITUDE)

In general, climatic conditions become colder as elevation increases, just as they do when latitude increases. "Life zones" on a high mountain reflect the changes: Plants at the base are the same as those in surrounding countryside, but no trees at all can grow above the timberline. Snow crowns the highest elevations.

Mount Shasta, California

TOPOGRAPHY

Mountain ranges are natural barriers to air movement. In California (see diagram), winds off the Pacific carry moisture-laden air toward the coast. The Coastal Range allows for some condensation and light precipitation. Inland, the taller Sierra Nevada range wrings more significant precipitation from the air. On the leeward slopes of the Sierra Nevada, sinking air warms from compression, clouds evaporate, and dry conditions prevail.

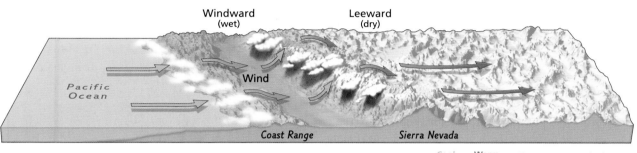

Temperature variations as air moves over mountains

EFFECTS OF GEOGRAPHY

The location of a place and its distance from mountains and bodies of water help determine its prevailing wind patterns and what types of air masses affect it. Coastal areas may enjoy refreshing breezes in summer, when cooler ocean air moves ashore. Places south and east of the Great Lakes can expect "lake effect" snow in winter, when cold air travels over relatively warmer waters. In spring and summer, people in the central United States watch for thunderstorms.

They live in "Tornado Alley," where three types of air masses often converge: cold and dry from the north, warm and dry from the southwest, and warm and moist from the Gulf of Mexico. The colliding air masses often spawn tornadic storms.

Cold winds over warm water
Cool onshore ocean winds
Desert winds
Warm onshore ocean winds

PREVAILING GLOBAL WIND PATTERNS

As shown at right, three large-scale wind patterns are found in the Northern Hemisphere and three are found in the Southern Hemisphere. These are average conditions and do not necessarily reflect conditions on a particular day. As seasons change, the wind patterns shift north or south. So does the intertropical convergence zone, which moves back and forth across the Equator. Sailors called this zone the doldrums because its winds are typically weak.

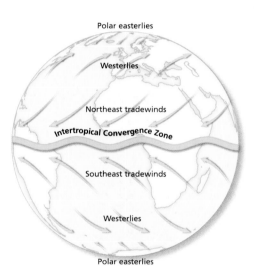

SURFACE OF THE EARTH

Just look at any globe or a world map showing land cover, and you will see another important influence on climate: the surface of the Earth. The amount of sunlight that is absorbed or reflected by the surface determines how much atmospheric heating occurs. Darker areas, such as heavily vegetated regions, tend to be good absorbers; lighter areas, such as snow- and ice-covered regions, tend to be good reflectors. The ocean absorbs and loses heat more slowly than land. Its waters gradually release heat into the atmosphere, which then distributes heat around the globe.

Temperature Change over Time

Cold and warm periods punctuate Earth's long history. Some were fairly short (perhaps hundreds of years); others spanned hundreds of thousands of years. In some cold periods, glaciers grew and spread over large regions. In subsequent warm periods, the ice retreated. Each period profoundly affected plant and animal life. The most recent cool period, often called the "Little Ice Age," ended in western Europe around 1850.

Since the turn of the 20th century, temperatures have been rising steadily throughout the world. But it is not yet clear how much of this warming is due to natural causes and how much derives from human activities, such as the burning of fossil fuels and the clearing of forests.

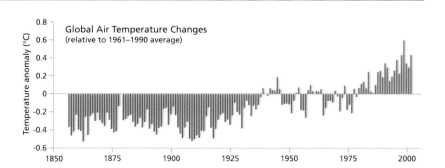

Climate Zones

Climate zones are primarily controlled by latitude—which governs the prevailing winds, the angle of the sun's rays, and the length of day throughout the year—and by geographical location with respect to mountains and oceans. Elevation, surface attributes, and other variables modify the primary controlling factors. Latitudinal banding of climate zones is most pronounced over Africa and Asia, where fewer north-south mountain ranges mean less disruption of prevailing winds. In the Western Hemisphere, the very tall, almost continuous mountain range that extends from western Canada to southern South America helps to create dry regions on its leeward slopes. Over the United States, where westerly winds prevail, areas to the east of the range lie in a "rain shadow" and are therefore drier. In northern parts of South America, where easterly trade winds prevail, the rain shadow lies west of the mountains. Ocean effects dominate much of western Europe and southern parts of Australia.

Climographs

The map at right shows the global distribution of climate zones, while the following 12 climographs (graphs of monthly temperature and precipitation) provide snapshots of the climate at specific places. Each place has a different climate type, which is described in general terms. Rainfall is shown in a bar graph format (scale on right side of the graph); temperature is expressed with a line graph (scale on left side). Places with highland and upland climates were not included because local changes in elevation can produce significant variations in local conditions.

Climatic Zones
(based on modified Köppen system)

Tropical
- Tropical wet
- Tropical wet & dry

Dry
- Semiarid
- Arid

Mild
- Marine west coast
- Mediterranean
- Humid subtropical

Continental
- Warm summer
- Cool summer
- Subarctic

Polar
- Tundra
- Ice sheet

High elevations
- Highlands
- Uplands

— Warm ocean current
— Cool ocean current

TROPICAL WET

This climate type has the most predictable conditions. Warm and rainy year-round, regions with a tropical wet climate experience little variation from month to month. This type is mainly found within a zone extending about 10 degrees on either side of the Equator. With as much as 60 inches (152 cm) of rain each year, the tropical wet climate supports lush vegetation.

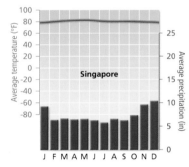

TROPICAL WET AND DRY

Because of seasonal reversals in wind direction (monsoons), this climate type is characterized by a slightly cooler dry season and a warmer, very moist wet season. The highest temperatures usually occur just before the wet season. Although average annual conditions may be similar to a tropical wet climate, the rainy season brings much more rain.

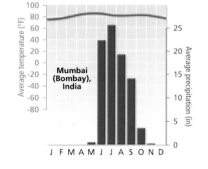

ARID

Centered between 20 and 30 degrees north and south latitude, this climate type is the result of a persistent high-pressure area and, along the western margins of continents, a cold ocean current. Rainfall amounts in regions with this climate type are negligible, and there is some seasonal variation in temperature. Desert vegetation is typically sparse.

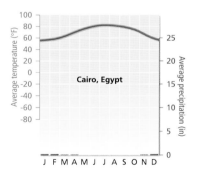

SEMIARID

Regions with a semiarid climate lie poleward of areas with a desert (arid) climate; they have a much greater range in monthly temperatures and receive significantly more rainfall than deserts. This climate type is often found in inland regions, in the rain shadow of mountain ranges. Annual rainfall amounts support mainly grasses and small shrubs.

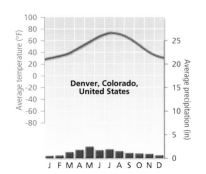

MARINE WEST COAST

This climate type is primarily found between 40 and 60 degrees latitude; it occurs on the west coasts of continents and across much of Europe. Prevailing westerly winds bring milder ocean air ashore, but sunny days are limited and precipitation is frequent. Except in the highest elevations, most precipitation falls as rain. This climate supports extensive forests.

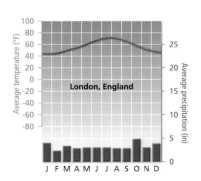

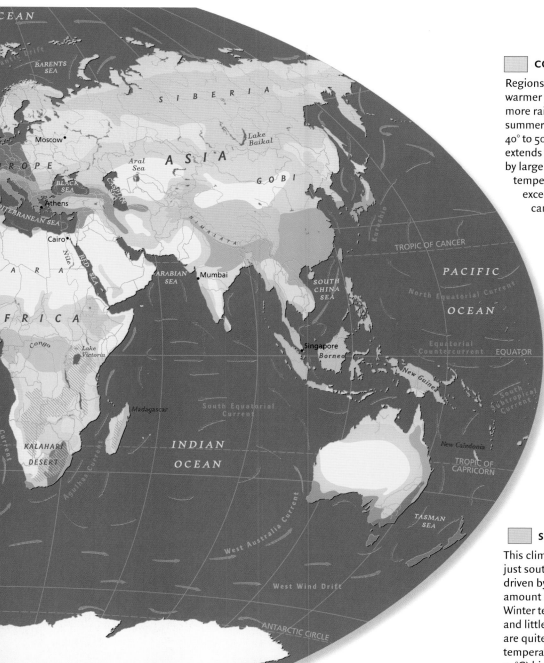

CONTINENTAL WARM SUMMER

Regions with this climate type have warmer year-round temperatures and more rainfall than regions with cool summers. This type is found from about 40° to 50° N (except in Europe, where it extends to about 60° N) and is marked by large variations in average monthly temperature. Summer averages can exceed 70°F (21°C); winter averages can be in the 20s (-7°C).

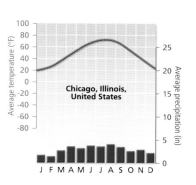

CONTINENTAL COOL SUMMER

Found only from about 40° to 60° N, this type is marked by temperature extremes. Summers are cool (around 60°F/15°C as a monthly average); winter months may have below-freezing average temperatures. Rainfall is moderate to abundant.

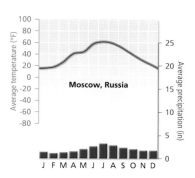

SUBARCTIC

This climate type is found along and just south of the Arctic Circle; it is driven by large seasonal swings in the amount of daylight a region receives. Winter tends to be cold with light snow and little melting. Summer months are quite warm for the latitude, with temperatures 70 or 80 degrees (21°–27°C) higher than monthly averages in winter; summer has significant rainfall.

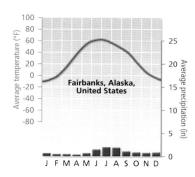

MEDITERRANEAN

This term describes the climate of much of the Mediterranean region. Such a climate is also found in narrow bands along the west coasts of continents that lie around 30 to 35 degrees poleward from the Equator. Summer months are typically warm to hot with dry conditions, while winter months are cool (but not cold) and provide modest precipitation.

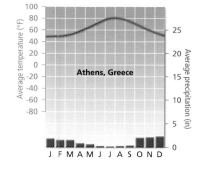

TUNDRA

Along the southern boundary of this climatic zone, ground-hugging plants meet the northernmost trees (the tree line). Here, the warmest average monthly temperature is below 50°F (10°C), with only one to four months having an average monthly temperature that is above freezing. Precipitation amounts are low, typically about ten inches (25 cm) or less annually.

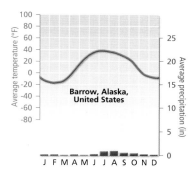

HUMID SUBTROPICAL

This climate type dominates eastern regions of continents at 30 to 35 degrees latitude. Here, warm ocean waters lead to warm and humid summers. Rainfall is greatest near the coast, supporting forest growth; precipitation is less farther west, supporting grasslands. Winter can bring cold waves and snowy periods, except in areas right on the coast.

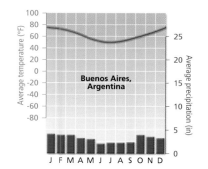

ICE SHEET

This climate type is found at high latitudes in interior Greenland and across most of Antarctica; average monthly temperatures are around zero degrees Fahrenheit (-18°C) and below. Snow defines the landscape, but precipitation is only about five inches (13 cm) or less annually. The combined effects of cold and dryness produce desert-like conditions.

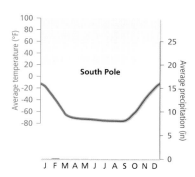

Step outside and you experience many facets of weather. Humidity, air temperature and pressure, wind speed and direction, cloud cover and type, and the amount and form of precipitation are all atmospheric characteristics of the momentary conditions we call weather.

The sun is ultimately responsible for the weather. Its rays are absorbed differently by land and water surfaces (equal amounts of solar radiation heat the ground more quickly than they do water). Differential warming, in turn, causes variations in the temperature and pressure of overlying air masses.

As an air mass warms, it becomes lighter and rises higher into the atmosphere. As an air mass cools, it becomes heavier and sinks. Pressure differences between masses of air generate winds, which tend to blow from high-pressure areas to areas of low pressure. Fast-moving, upper atmosphere winds known as jet streams help move weather systems around the world.

Large weather systems called cyclones rotate counterclockwise in the Northern Hemisphere (clockwise in the Southern

Hemisphere); they are also called "lows," because their centers are low-pressure areas. Clouds and precipitation are usually associated with these systems. Anticyclones, or "highs," rotate in the opposite direction and are high-pressure areas. They usually bring clearer skies and more settled weather.

The boundary between two air masses is called a front. Here, wind, temperature, and humidity change abruptly, producing atmospheric instability. When things get "out of balance" in the atmosphere, storms may develop, bringing rain or snow and sometimes thunder and lightning as well. Storms are among nature's great equalizers.

The weather you experience is influenced by many factors, including your location's latitude, elevation, and proximity to water bodies. Even the degree of urban development, which creates "heat islands," and the amount of snow cover, which chills an overlying air mass, play important roles.

The next time you watch a weather report on television, think about the many factors, some thousands of miles away, that help make the weather what it is.

The swirling cloud pattern and well-formed eye of Hurricane Floyd stand out in this NOAA satellite image from September 15, 1999. Floyd made landfall in North Carolina and caused major flooding in parts of the eastern United States. Hurricanes—tropical low-pressure systems with winds of at least 74 miles an hour—can be prolific rainmakers: In 1972 Agnes, like Floyd, dropped torrents on the eastern U.S.; in 2001 Allison inundated parts of Texas. Even so, non-tropical, or extratropical, low-pressure systems are primarily responsible for the precipitation that falls in the middle latitudes (30 to 60 degrees latitude).

Major Factors that Influence Weather

THE WATER CYCLE

As the sun warms the surface of the Earth, water rises in the form of water vapor from lakes, rivers, oceans, plants, the ground, and other sources. This process is called evaporation. Water vapor provides the moisture that forms clouds; it eventually returns to Earth in the form of precipitation, and the cycle continues.

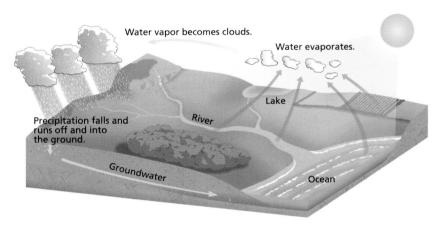

Water vapor becomes clouds.

Water evaporates.

Lake

Precipitation falls and runs off and into the ground.

River

Groundwater

Ocean

AIR MASSES

When air hovers for a while over a surface area with uniform humidity and temperature, it takes on the characteristics of the area below. For example, an air mass over the tropical Atlantic Ocean would become warm and humid; an air mass over the winter snow and ice of northern Canada would become cold and dry. These massive volumes of air often cover thousands of miles and reach to the stratosphere. Over time, mid-latitude cyclonic storms and global wind patterns move them to locations far from their source regions.

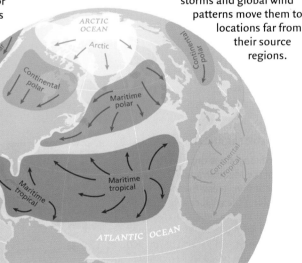

JET STREAM

A meandering current of high-speed wind, a jet stream is usually found around five to ten miles above Earth's surface. It generally flows west to east, often in a non-continuous wavy fashion, with cold, Equatorward dips (called troughs) and warm, Poleward bulges (called ridges). The polar jet separates cold and warm masses of air; the subtropical jet is less likely to be related to temperature differences. Fronts and low-pressure areas are typically located near a jet stream.

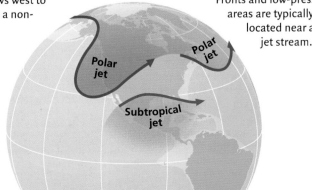

WEATHER FRONTS

The transition zone between two air masses of different humidity and temperature is called a front. Along a cold front, cold air displaces warm air; along a warm front, warm air displaces cold air. When neither air mass displaces the other, a stationary front develops. Towering clouds and intense storms may form along cold fronts, while widespread clouds and rain, snow, sleet, or drizzle may accompany warm fronts.

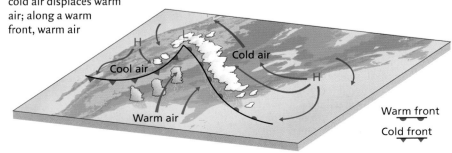

Warm front

Cold front

Cloud Types

Clouds are the visible collections of water droplets or ice particles in the atmosphere. Meteorologists classify them according to shape and altitude.

Fog is a ground-level cloud. Stratus clouds, which are flat or layered, are much longer and wider than they are tall. Altostratus (*alto* means "high") is a stratus cloud about 2 miles above the Earth. When these clouds rain or snow, they are called nimbostratus. Cirrostratus clouds lie at an altitude of about 4 miles.

The cumulus type is puffy. True cumulus clouds form about a mile above the surface of the Earth; they often develop as sunlight heats the ground and the ground, in turn, heats the air. This cloud type literally bubbles upward. If it becomes very tall, it can form a cumulonimbus (thunderstorm) cloud, with its top reaching an altitude of 7 miles or more.

Cumulus clouds can also develop in layers. Stratocumulus is a layered cumulus cloud about a mile above the ground. Altocumulus is a similar cloud at an altitude of 2 miles. Its greater distance from the ground makes the cumulus puffs appear smaller than those of stratocumulus clouds. The cirrocumulus type (with smaller puffs still) is found about 4 to 5 miles up.

Cirrus clouds occur at an altitude of 4 miles or more, where the temperature is always below freezing; hence, these clouds are always filled with ice crystals.

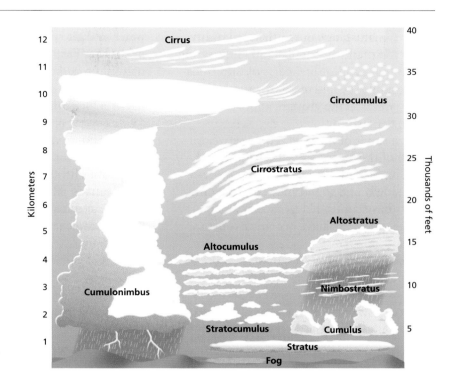

Hurricanes

Hurricanes and their counterparts in other places (typhoons near Japan and cyclones off India and Australia) are moderately large low-pressure systems that form most often during the warmer months of the year.

They occur mainly near the Equator, in regions with prevailing easterly winds. These systems develop winds between 75 and 150 miles an hour and, on some rare occasions, winds even stronger. As the storms move toward the middle latitudes, where the prevailing winds are mainly westerly, they can "recurve" (move toward the east). Some hurricanes have stayed nearly stationary at times, while others have made loops and spirals along their paths.

Lightning

To estimate the mean annual distribution of lightning (more than 1.2 billion intracloud and cloud-to-ground flashes), NASA scientists used five years of data from a satellite orbiting 460 miles above the Earth. Lightning distribution is linked to climate, with maximal occurrence in areas that see frequent thunderstorms (the red areas on the map below).

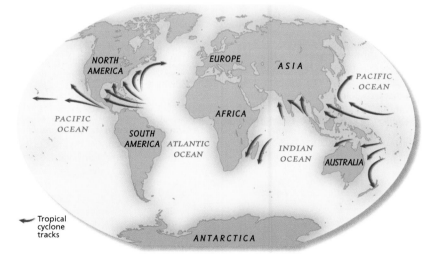

Tropical cyclone tracks

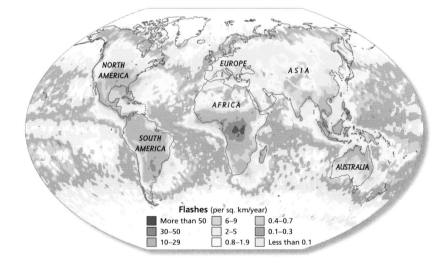

Flashes (per sq. km/year)
More than 50 | 6–9 | 0.4–0.7
30–50 | 2–5 | 0.1–0.3
10–29 | 0.8–1.9 | Less than 0.1

El Niño and La Niña

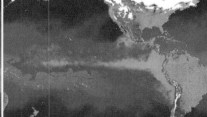

Periodic shifts in wind speed and direction in the tropical eastern Pacific can lead to changes in sea surface temperatures. In what scientists call El Niño events, prevailing easterly winds weaken or give way to westerly winds, and the normal upwelling process, which brings cool, nutrient-rich waters up from lower levels of the ocean, stops. This causes sea surface temperatures to rise, providing an unfavorable habitat for many fish. The warmer ocean conditions can also lead to more rainfall and floods along the west coast of the Americas. A stronger easterly wind flow, on the other hand, can increase upwelling and make the sea surface temperatures even colder, producing La Niña. Both phenomena can have far-reaching weather effects. For example, strong El Niño events often result in a weak Atlantic Ocean hurricane season; La Niña events can spell drought, even for normally dry California.

From left to right, the above image sequence shows how temperatures in the Pacific Ocean changed as the 1997-98 El Niño event evolved. The first image, from March 10, 1997, shows a mostly cool ocean (blue shades). By mid-June, sea surface temperatures (red shades) were above average from South America across much of the tropical Pacific. By mid-September, the warmth had extended from California southward to Chile and westward across most of the tropical Pacific. The final image, from late December 1997, shows an impressive El Niño, with surface temperatures about 15 degrees above average on the Fahrenheit scale.

To learn about weather extremes, see Geographic Comparisons on page 242.

Home to all living things, the biosphere is an intricate system made up of constantly interacting realms that support life: parts of the atmosphere (air), lithosphere (land), and hydrosphere (water in the ground, at the surface, and in the air).

As a result of the interaction between realms of the biosphere, Earth's flora and fauna have changed over the eons, sometimes slowly and sometimes rapidly. Some species have continued to evolve; others, like the dinosaurs, have become extinct.

Life, of course, interacts with the land, water, and air, playing a significant role in shaping Earth's face and influencing its natural processes. Billions of years ago one of the smallest life-forms, photosynthetic bacteria (organisms that produce oxygen as a by-product of their metabolism), helped provide the oxygen in the air we breathe.

Humans are currently Earth's dominant life-form. Through the ages, we have evolved the means to affect the planet in ways both positive and negative. At present, we are introducing changes to the biosphere at greater rates than natural processes may be able to accommodate, with industrialized societies increasing demands on Earth's resources at the expense of other organisms.

It is now clear that humans are able to greatly influence the fate of the biosphere. It is also clear that developing a better understanding of how the biosphere functions, and how its realms interact, is fundamental to sustaining it. This requires a multi- and interdisciplinary perspective that brings together different worldviews from each of the physical, biological, and social sciences.

The Biosphere from Space

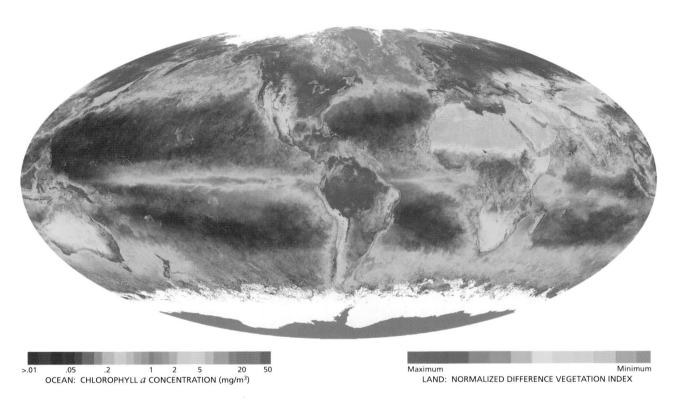

>.01   .05   .2   1   2   5   20   50
OCEAN: CHLOROPHYLL *a* CONCENTRATION (mg/m³)

Maximum   Minimum
LAND: NORMALIZED DIFFERENCE VEGETATION INDEX

Satellite technology enables us to monitor life on Earth. For example, satellite sensors help us measure the amount of chlorophyll—the green pigment used by plants during photosynthesis—on land and in masses of water. Satellite measurements can also provide an estimate of the distribution and abundance of both terrestrial vegetation and aquatic phytoplankton. By color-coding data (see the color scales for the world map), we can actually quantify changes in vegetation on land and in the oceans from season to season and from year to year. The map reveals an unequal distribution of life for the June-to-August period. Most of the Northern Hemisphere has become green, except in areas of low rainfall or poor soil. Spectacular phytoplankton blooms are evident in the equatorial Pacific. Vegetation has lightened in the southern winter, as the direct rays of the sun have moved northward.

Biosphere Dynamics

A fundamental characteristic of the biosphere is the interconnectivity among all of its components. Known as holoceonosis, this interrelationship means that when one part of the biosphere changes, so will others. The biosphere is a dynamic system where interactions are occurring all the time between and within living and nonliving components.

The main fuel that keeps the biosphere dynamic is the sun's energy, which is captured by the surface of the Earth and later harvested by plants and other photosynthetic organisms. The energy flows from these organisms through a living web that includes herbivores (plant feeders), carnivores (flesh feeders), and decomposers (detritus feeders). Energy from the sun also drives the recycling of water and all chemical elements necessary for life. The flow of energy and the continuous recycling of matter are two key processes of the biosphere.

Humans are part of this web of life. We have evolved, we interact with other living organisms, and we may become extinct. We have also developed large-scale organizations (societies, for example) that constitute the "sociosphere." Human interactions within this sphere occur through a diverse array of technologies and cultural frameworks and include activities such as fishing, agriculture, forestry, mining, and urban development. All are resource-utilization processes that can affect the biosphere on a global scale.

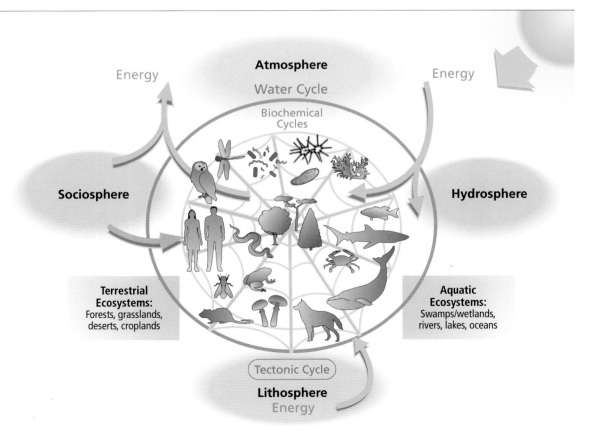

Earth System Dynamics

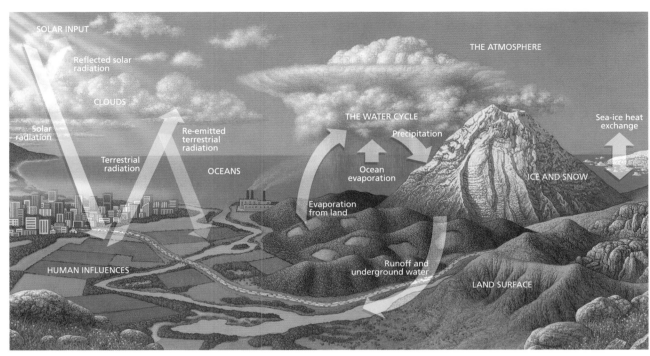

The Earth is a dynamic system driven by energy flow from the sun and the planet's interior. Electromagnetic energy from the sun is converted to heat energy in the atmosphere (the greenhouse effect). Energy imbalances cause atmospheric and oceanic currents and drive the water cycle—a result of which is the wearing down of landscapes. Energy flow from Earth's interior drives the tectonic cycle, which builds landscapes. The cycles vary because they derive from independent forces that operate on different time scales and with changing intensities. Variations in these cycles keep the complex interactions among the biosphere, lithosphere, hydrosphere, and atmosphere from reaching a balance; the tendency of Earth processes to reach a balance causes natural global change. People can influence these interactions: By modifying the chemical composition of the atmosphere, for example, humans can cause changes in the greenhouse effect.

Size of the Biosphere

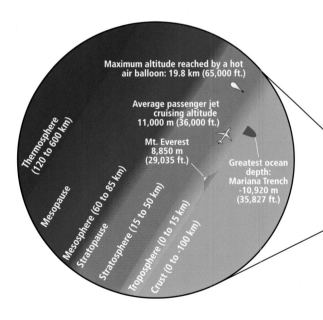

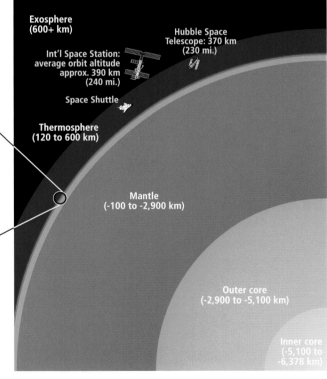

The biosphere reaches from the ocean floor to more than 10,000 meters (33,000 ft) above sea level. Most life, however, occurs in a zone extending from about 200 meters (650 ft) below the surface of the ocean to 6,000 meters (20,000 ft) above sea level. Humans can occupy much of the biosphere and exert influence on all of the regions within it.

Organisms that make up the biosphere vary greatly in size and number. Small life-forms generally reach very high numbers, while large ones may be relatively rare. Mycoplasmas, which are very small parasitic bacteria, can measure 0.2 to 0.3 micrometers (one micrometer is one-millionth of a meter, or three-millionths of a foot). Other organisms can be very large: Blue whales weigh about 110,000 kilograms (240,000 lbs) and reach a length of more than 25 meters (80 ft); they are the largest animals on Earth. Dinosaurs weighed as much as 80,000 kilograms (175,000 lbs) and measured up to 33 meters (108 ft) long.

The Biosphere over Time

Ever since life arose on Earth more than three billion years ago, the biosphere has gone through many changes (see time line at right). These have been driven, in part, by drifting continents, shifting sea levels, and the consequences of activities in the biosphere itself. Over millions of years, the addition of oxygen to the atmosphere allowed for the development of terrestrial ecosystems. But in fairly rapid fashion, humans have had a significant effect on the world's ecosystems; our ability to modify species through gene manipulation will further increase our impact.

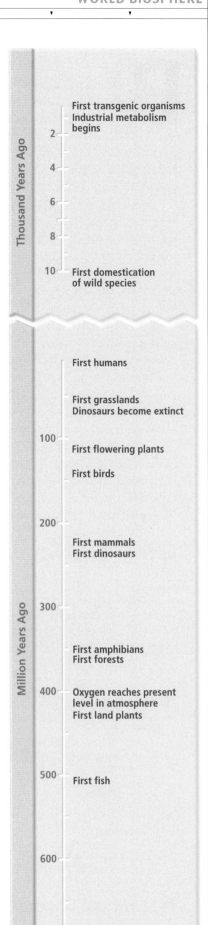

WORLD BIODIVERSITY

Biodiversity refers to three measures of Earth's intricate web of life: the number of different species, the genetic diversity within a species, and the variety of ecosystems in which species live. Greatest in the wet tropics, biodiversity is important for many reasons, including helping to provide food and medicine, breathable air, drinkable water, livable climates, protection from pests and diseases, and ecosystem stability.

Humankind is only one species in a vast array of life-forms. It is, however, an especially influential and increasingly disruptive actor in the huge cast of characters on the stage of planet Earth. Estimates of the total number of plant and animal species range from ten million to a hundred million; of these, fewer than two million have been described. Yet a substantial number of those species may be gone before we even have a chance to understand their value.

For most of human history, people have often looked at plants and animals simply as resources for meeting their own basic needs. Scientists today count more than a quarter million plant species, of which just nine provide three-quarters of all our food; in that respect, biodiversity has been an unimaginable luxury. It is ironic that as humankind's power to destroy other species grows, so does our ingenuity in finding new and beneficial uses for them.

Sometimes the benefits of preserving a species may have nothing to do with food or medicine. Before a worldwide ban on exports of elephant ivory, the estimated value of such exports was 40 million dollars a year for all of Africa. Now, in Kenya alone, the viewing value of elephants by tourists is thought to be 25 million dollars a year.

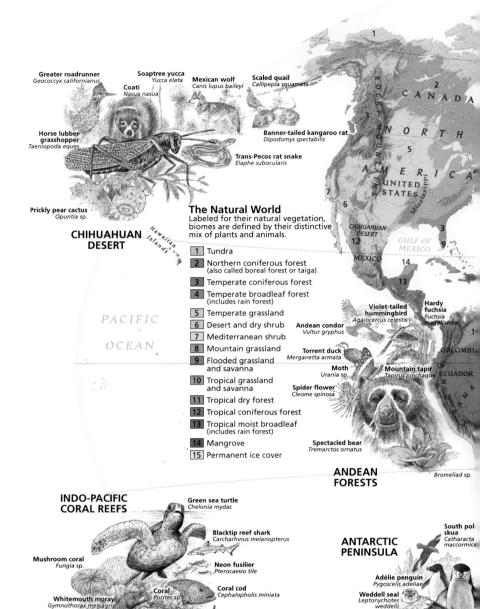

The Natural World
Labeled for their natural vegetation, biomes are defined by their distinctive mix of plants and animals.

1	Tundra
2	Northern coniferous forest (also called boreal forest or taiga)
3	Temperate coniferous forest
4	Temperate broadleaf forest (includes rain forest)
5	Temperate grassland
6	Desert and dry shrub
7	Mediterranean shrub
8	Mountain grassland
9	Flooded grassland and savanna
10	Tropical grassland and savanna
11	Tropical dry forest
12	Tropical coniferous forest
13	Tropical moist broadleaf (includes rain forest)
14	Mangrove
15	Permanent ice cover

Species Diversity

Among fauna and flora, insects make up the largest classification in terms of sheer number of species, with fungi ranked a distant second. At the other extreme, the categories with the smallest numbers—mammals, birds, and mollusks—also happen to be the classes with the greatest percentage of threatened species (see middle graph, below). This is not just a matter of proportion: These groups include the most at-risk species in terms of absolute numbers as well.

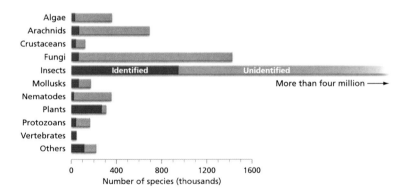

Algae
Arachnids
Crustaceans
Fungi
Insects — Identified / Unidentified — More than four million ⟶
Mollusks
Nematodes
Plants
Protozoans
Vertebrates
Others

0   400   800   1200   1600
Number of species (thousands)

Threatened Ecoregions

Earth is experiencing a great wave of extinctions, a process being driven by the reckless destruction of habitats by humans. Within this century, scientists say, half of all living species may be gone. In view of the situation, conservationists have now identified 25 biodiversity "hotspots," habitats for species that are found nowhere else in the wild and that are especially threatened. These hotspots contain the sole remaining habitats for 44 percent of all plant species and 35 percent of all the invertebrate species.

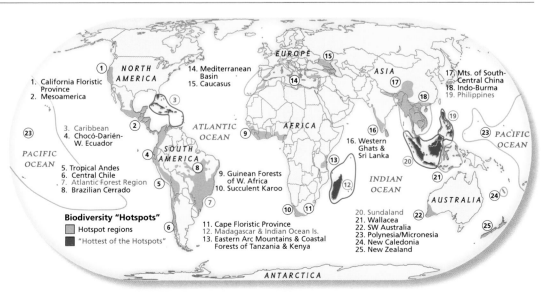

1. California Floristic Province
2. Mesoamerica
3. Caribbean
4. Chocó-Darién-W. Ecuador
5. Tropical Andes
6. Central Chile
7. Atlantic Forest Region
8. Brazilian Cerrado
9. Guinean Forests of W. Africa
10. Succulent Karoo
11. Cape Floristic Province
12. Madagascar & Indian Ocean Is.
13. Eastern Arc Mountains & Coastal Forests of Tanzania & Kenya
14. Mediterranean Basin
15. Caucasus
16. Western Ghats & Sri Lanka
17. Mts. of South-Central China
18. Indo-Burma
19. Philippines
20. Sundaland
21. Wallacea
22. SW Australia
23. Polynesia/Micronesia
24. New Caledonia
25. New Zealand

Biodiversity "Hotspots"
☐ Hotspot regions
■ "Hottest of the Hotspots"

Threatened Species

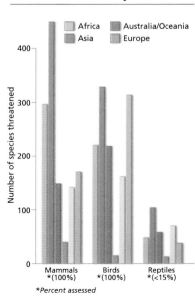

☐ Africa ■ Australia/Oceania
☐ Asia ☐ Europe

400
300
200
100
0

Number of species threatened

Mammals *(100%)   Birds *(100%)   Reptiles *(<15%)

*Percent assessed

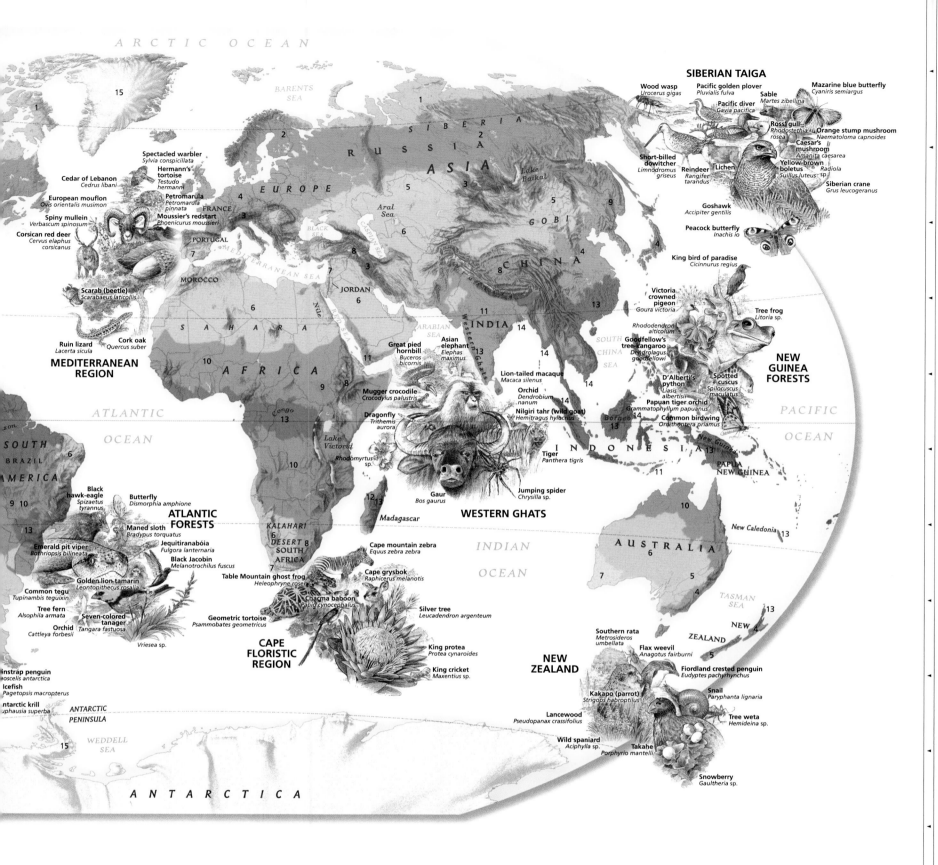

ARCTIC OCEAN

BARENTS SEA

SIBERIAN TAIGA

Wood wasp
Urocerus gigas

Pacific golden plover
Pluvialis fulva

Sable
Martes zibellina

Mazarine blue butterfly
Cyaniris semiargus

Pacific diver
Gavia pacifica

Ross' gull
Rhodostethia rosea

Orange stump mushroom
Naematoloma capnoides

Short-billed dowitcher
Limnodromus griseus

Reindeer
Rangifer tarandus

Lichen

Caesar's mushroom
Amanita caesarea

Yellow-brown boletus
Suillus luteus

Radiola sp.

Goshawk
Accipiter gentilis

Siberian crane
Grus leucogeranus

Peacock butterfly
Inachis io

King bird of paradise
Cicinnurus regius

SIBERIA

RUSSIA

ASIA

Lake Baikal

GOBI

CHINA

EUROPE

Aral Sea

FRANCE

PORTUGAL

BLACK SEA

Caspian Sea

MEDITERRANEAN SEA

MOROCCO

JORDAN

Nile

SAHARA

AFRICA

ARABIAN SEA

INDIA

Western Ghats

SOUTH CHINA SEA

Spectacled warbler
Sylvia conspicillata

Cedar of Lebanon
Cedrus libani

Hermann's tortoise
Testudo hermanni

Petromarula
Petromarula pinnata

European mouflon
Ovis orientalis musimon

Moussier's redstart
Phoenicurus moussieri

Spiny mullein
Verbascum spinosum

Corsican red deer
Cervus elaphus corsicanus

Scarab (beetle)
Scarabaeus laticollis

Ruin lizard
Lacerta sicula

Cork oak
Quercus suber

MEDITERRANEAN REGION

Great pied hornbill
Buceros bicornis

Asian elephant
Elephas maximus

Mugger crocodile
Crocodylus palustris

Dragonfly
Trithemis aurora

Lion-tailed macaque
Macaca silenus

Orchid
Dendrobium nanum

Nilgiri tahr (wild goat)
Hemitragus hylocrius

Gaur
Bos gaurus

Tiger
Panthera tigris

Jumping spider
Chrysilla sp.

Victoria crowned pigeon
Goura victoria

Rhododendron
Rhododendron alticolum

Goodfellow's tree-kangaroo
Dendrolagus goodfellowi

D'Alberti's python
Liasis albertisii

Papuan tiger orchid
Grammatophyllum papuanum

Spotted cuscus
Spilocuscus maculatus

Common birdwing
Ornithoptera priamus

Tree frog
Litoria sp.

NEW GUINEA FORESTS

Rhodomyrtus sp.

Madagascar

WESTERN GHATS

KALAHARI DESERT

SOUTH AFRICA

INDONESIA

Borneo

New Guinea

PAPUA NEW GUINEA

AUSTRALIA

New Caledonia

TASMAN SEA

SOUTH AMERICA

BRAZIL

ATLANTIC OCEAN

Black hawk-eagle
Spizaetus tyrannus

Butterfly
Dismorphia amphione

Maned sloth
Bradypus torquatus

Jequitiranabóia
Fulgora laternaria

Black Jacobin
Melanotrochilus fuscus

Emerald pit viper
Bothriopsis bilineata

Golden lion-tamarin
Leontopithecus rosalia

Common tegu
Tupinambis teguixin

Tree fern
Alsophila armata

Seven-colored tanager
Tangara fastuosa

Orchid
Cattleya forbesii

ATLANTIC FORESTS

Vriesea sp.

Lake Victoria

Congo

Table Mountain ghost frog
Heleophryne rosei

Chacma baboon
Papio cynocephalus

Geometric tortoise
Psammobates geometricus

CAPE FLORISTIC REGION

Cape mountain zebra
Equus zebra zebra

Cape grysbok
Raphicerus melanotis

Silver tree
Leucadendron argenteum

King protea
Protea cynaroides

King cricket
Maxentius sp.

INDIAN OCEAN

PACIFIC OCEAN

Southern rata
Metrosideros umbellata

Flax weevil
Anagotus fairburni

Fiordland crested penguin
Eudyptes pachyrhynchus

Snail
Paryphanta lignaria

Kakapo (parrot)
Strigops habroptilus

Tree weta
Hemideina sp.

NEW ZEALAND

NEW ZEALAND

Lancewood
Pseudopanax crassifolius

Wild spaniard
Aciphylla sp.

Takahe
Porphyrio mantelli

Snowberry
Gaultheria sp.

Chinstrap penguin
[Pygos]celis antarctica

Icefish
Pagetopsis macropterus

[A]ntarctic krill
[E]uphausia superba

ANTARCTIC PENINSULA

WEDDELL SEA

ANTARCTICA

Projected Biodiversity Status

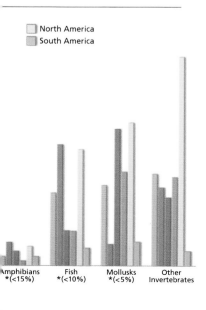

Amphibians *(<15%)*

Fish *(<10%)*

Mollusks *(<5%)*

Other Invertebrates

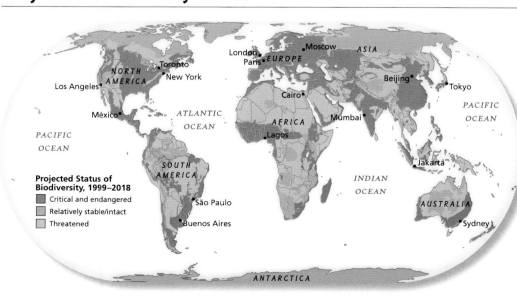

NORTH AMERICA

Toronto

London

Paris

Moscow

ASIA

EUROPE

Los Angeles

New York

Cairo

Beijing

Tokyo

México

ATLANTIC OCEAN

AFRICA

Mumbai

PACIFIC OCEAN

PACIFIC OCEAN

SOUTH AMERICA

Lagos

INDIAN OCEAN

Jakarta

Projected Status of Biodiversity, 1999–2018

Critical and endangered

Relatively stable/intact

Threatened

São Paulo

Buenos Aires

AUSTRALIA

Sydney

ANTARCTICA

Biodiversity is decreasing at a rapidly increasing rate. According to scientists, current extinction rates are from 50 to a hundred times greater than the historical average; some experts fear that as many as a quarter of the world's species could be lost just in the next quarter century. Species are not being killed off directly: The two leading causes of extinction are loss of habitats and the introduction of non-native plants and animals into habitats. Both causes tend to correspond to high human population levels.

While populations in many parts of the world are expanding, those of Europe, Australia, New Zealand, Japan, and other rich industrial areas show little to no growth, or may actually be shrinking. Many such countries must bring in immigrant workers to keep their economies thriving. A clear correlation exists between wealth and low fertility: the higher the incomes and educational levels, the lower the rates of reproduction.

Many governments keep vital statistics, recording births and deaths, and count their populations regularly to try to plan ahead.

The United States has taken a census every ten years since 1790, recording the ages, the occupations, and other important facts about its people. The United Nations helps less developed countries carry out censuses and improve their demographic information.

Governments of poor countries, with an average per capita income of $380 a year, may find that half their populations are under the age of 20. They are faced with the overwhelming tasks of providing adequate education and jobs while encouraging better family planning programs. Governments of nations with low birthrates find themselves with growing numbers of elderly people but

fewer workers able to provide tax money for health care and pensions.

In a mere 150 years, world population has grown fivefold, at an ever increasing pace. The industrial revolution helped bring about improvements in food supplies and advances in both medicine and public health, which allowed people to live longer and to have more healthy babies. Today, 15,000 people are born into the world every hour, and nearly all of them are in poor African, Asian, and South American nations. This situation concerns planners, who look to demographers (professionals who study all aspects of population) for important data.

Lights of the World

Satellite imagery offers a surprising view of the world at night. Bright lights in Europe, Asia, and the United States give a clear picture of densely populated areas with ample electricity. Reading this map requires great care, however. Some totally dark areas, like most of Australia, do in fact have very small populations, but other light-free areas—in China and Africa, for example—may simply hide dense populations with not enough electricity to be seen by a satellite. Wealthy areas with fewer people, such as Florida, may be using their energy wastefully. Ever since the 1970s, demographers have supplemented census data with information from satellite imagery.

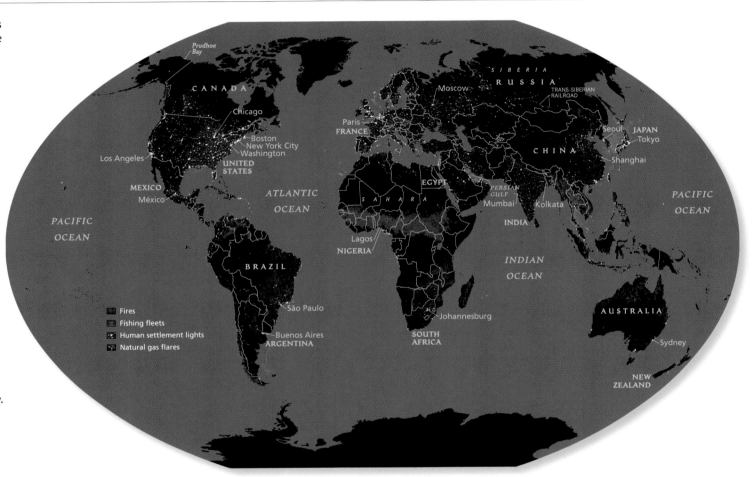

Fires
Fishing fleets
Human settlement lights
Natural gas flares

Population Pyramids

A population pyramid shows the number of males and females in every age group of a population. A pyramid for Ethiopia reveals that people younger than 20 far outnumber older people; one for Spain shows that most people are between 25 and 40.

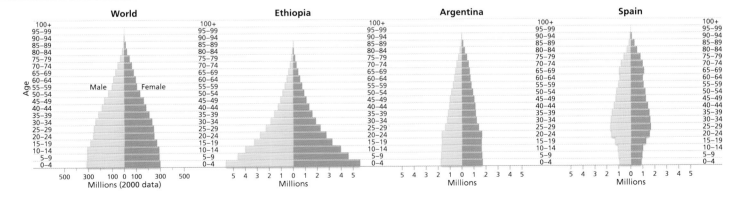

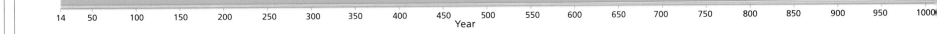

Population Growth

The population of the world is not distributed evenly. In this cartogram Canada is almost invisible, while China looks enormous because its population is 41 times greater than Canada's. In reality, both countries are similar in size. The shape of almost every country looks distorted when populations are compared in this way. Population sizes are constantly changing, however. In countries that are experiencing many more births than deaths, population totals are ballooning. In others, too few babies are born to replace the number of people who die, and populations are shrinking. A cartogram devoted solely to growth rates around the world would look quite different from this one.

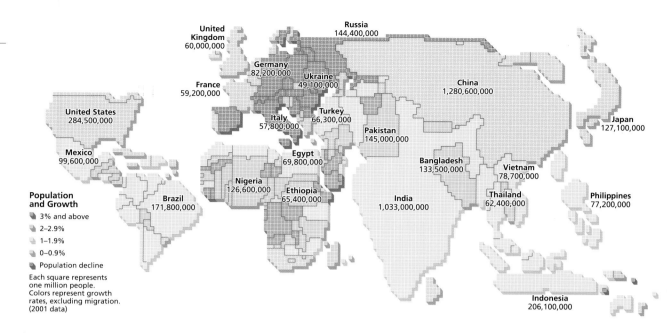

Population and Growth
- 3% and above
- 2–2.9%
- 1–1.9%
- 0–0.9%
- Population decline

Each square represents one million people. Colors represent growth rates, excluding migration. (2001 data)

United Kingdom 60,000,000
Russia 144,400,000
Germany 82,200,000
France 59,200,000
Ukraine 49,100,000
China 1,280,600,000
United States 284,500,000
Italy 57,800,000
Turkey 66,300,000
Japan 127,100,000
Mexico 99,600,000
Pakistan 145,000,000
Egypt 69,800,000
Bangladesh 133,500,000
Vietnam 78,700,000
Nigeria 126,600,000
Ethiopia 65,400,000
India 1,033,000,000
Thailand 62,400,000
Philippines 77,200,000
Brazil 171,800,000
Indonesia 206,100,000

Population Density

A country's population density is estimated by figuring out how many people would occupy one square mile if they were all spread out evenly. In reality, people live together most closely in cities, on seacoasts, and in river valleys. Singapore, a tiny country largely composed of a single city, has a high population density—more than 17,000 people per square mile. Greenland, by comparison, has less than one person per square mile because it is mostly covered by ice. Its people mainly fish for a living and dwell in small groups near the shore.

People per Square Mile / People per Square Km
- More than 500 / More than 195
- 150–500 / 60–195
- 25–149 / 10–59
- 1–24 / 1–9
- 0–1 / Less than 1
- No data / No data

Urban Area Population (in millions)
- ■ More than 20
- ▲ 15–20
- ● 10–14.9
- ○ 5–9.9

PACIFIC OCEAN
ATLANTIC OCEAN
PACIFIC OCEAN
INDIAN OCEAN

Chicago, New York, Los Angeles, México, Bogotá, Lima, Santiago, Buenos Aires, Rio de Janeiro, São Paulo, London, Paris, Moscow, Istanbul, Cairo, Tehran, Lahore, Delhi, Karachi, Mumbai, Bangalore, Hyderabad, Kolkata, Dhaka, Beijing, Tianjin, Wuhan, Seoul, Tokyo, Osaka, Shanghai, Hong Kong, Bangkok, Manila, Lagos, Kinshasa, Jakarta

Regional Population Growth Disparities

Two centuries ago, the population of the world began a phenomenal expansion. Even so, North America and Australia still have a long way to go before their population numbers equal those of Asia and Africa. China and India now have more than a billion people each, making Asia the most populous continent. Africa, which has the second greatest growth, does not yet approach Asia in numbers.

According to some experts, the world's population, now totaling more than six billion, will not start to level off until about the year 2200, when it could reach eleven billion. Nearly all the new growth will take place in Asia, Africa, and Latin America; however, Africa's share will be almost double that of its present level and China's share will decline.

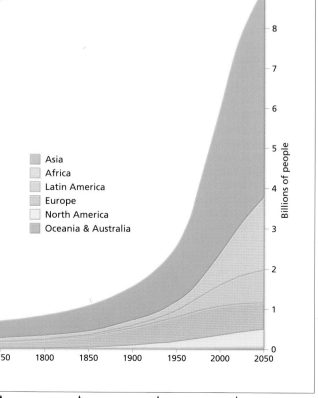

- Asia
- Africa
- Latin America
- Europe
- North America
- Oceania & Australia

Billions of people

Year: 1100 1150 1200 1250 1300 1350 1400 1450 1500 1550 1600 1650 1700 1750 1800 1850 1900 1950 2000 2050

WORLD POPULATION

Fertility

Fertility, or birthrate, measures the average number of children born to women in a given population. It can also be expressed as the number of live births per thousand people in a population per year. In low-income countries, with limited educational opportunities for girls and women, birthrates reach their highest levels.

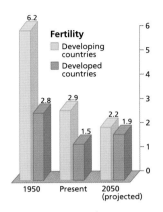

Fertility
- Developing countries
- Developed countries

6.2 / 2.8 — 1950
2.9 / 1.5 — Present
2.2 / 1.9 — 2050 (projected)

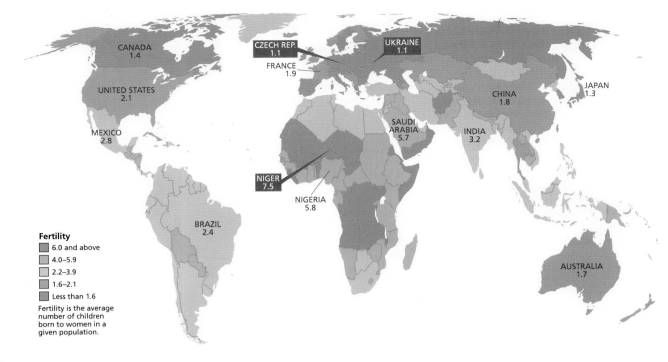

CANADA 1.4
CZECH REP. 1.1
UKRAINE 1.1
FRANCE 1.9
UNITED STATES 2.1
CHINA 1.8
JAPAN 1.3
MEXICO 2.8
SAUDI ARABIA 5.7
INDIA 3.2
NIGER 7.5
NIGERIA 5.8
BRAZIL 2.4
AUSTRALIA 1.7

Fertility
- 6.0 and above
- 4.0–5.9
- 2.2–3.9
- 1.6–2.1
- Less than 1.6

Fertility is the average number of children born to women in a given population.

Urban Population Densities

People around the world are leaving farms and moving to cities, where jobs and opportunities are better. In 2000 almost half the world's people lived in cities. The shift of population from the countryside to urban centers will probably continue in less developed countries for many years to come.

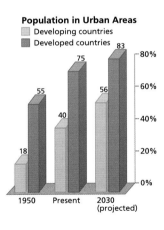

Population in Urban Areas
- Developing countries
- Developed countries

18 / 55 — 1950
40 / 75 — Present
56 / 83 — 2030 (projected)

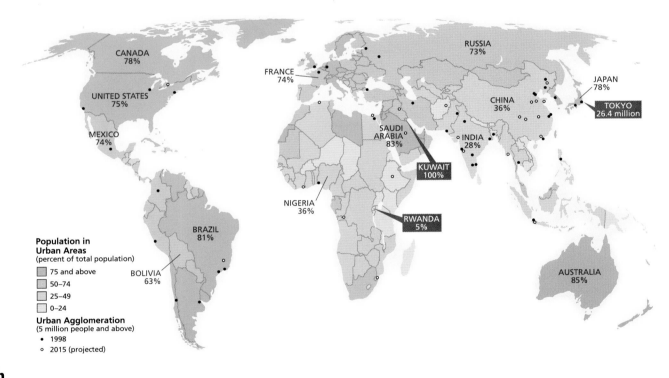

CANADA 78%
RUSSIA 73%
FRANCE 74%
JAPAN 78%
UNITED STATES 75%
CHINA 36%
TOKYO 26.4 million
MEXICO 74%
SAUDI ARABIA 83%
INDIA 28%
KUWAIT 100%
NIGERIA 36%
RWANDA 5%
BRAZIL 81%
BOLIVIA 63%
AUSTRALIA 85%

Population in Urban Areas (percent of total population)
- 75 and above
- 50–74
- 25–49
- 0–24

Urban Agglomeration (5 million people and above)
- 1998
- 2015 (projected)

Urban Population Growth

Urban populations are growing more than twice as fast as populations as a whole. Soon, the world's city dwellers will outnumber its rural inhabitants as towns become cities and cities merge into megacities with more than ten million people. Globalization speeds the process. Although cities generate wealth and provide better health care along with electricity, clean water, sewage treatment, and other benefits, they can also cause great ecological damage. Squatter settlements and slums may develop if cities cannot keep up with millions of new arrivals. Smog, congestion, pollution, and crime are other dangers. Good city management is a key to future prosperity.

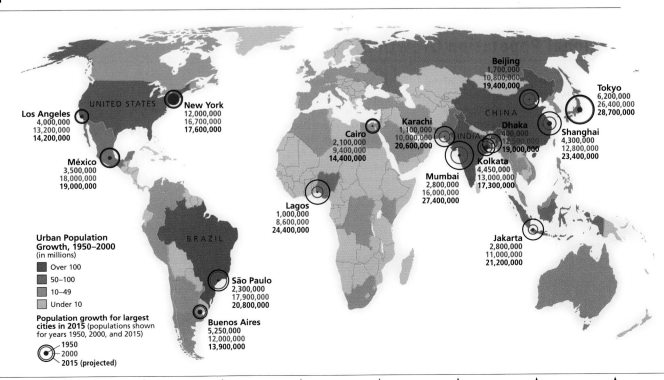

Los Angeles 4,000,000 / 13,200,000 / 14,200,000
New York 12,000,000 / 16,700,000 / 17,600,000
México 3,500,000 / 18,000,000 / 19,000,000
Beijing 1,700,000 / 10,800,000 / 19,400,000
Tokyo 6,200,000 / 26,400,000 / 28,700,000
Karachi 1,100,000 / 10,000,000 / 20,600,000
Dhaka 400,000 / 12,500,000 / 19,000,000
Shanghai 4,300,000 / 12,800,000 / 23,400,000
Cairo 2,100,000 / 9,400,000 / 14,400,000
Kolkata 4,450,000 / 13,000,000 / 17,300,000
Mumbai 2,800,000 / 16,000,000 / 27,400,000
Lagos 1,000,000 / 8,600,000 / 24,400,000
Jakarta 2,800,000 / 11,000,000 / 21,200,000
São Paulo 2,300,000 / 17,900,000 / 20,800,000
Buenos Aires 5,250,000 / 12,000,000 / 13,900,000

Urban Population Growth, 1950–2000 (in millions)
- Over 100
- 50–100
- 10–49
- Under 10

Population growth for largest cities in 2015 (populations shown for years 1950, 2000, and 2015)
- 1950
- 2000
- 2015 (projected)

Life Expectancy

Life expectancy for population groups does not mean that all people die by a certain age. It is an average of death statistics. High infant mortality equals low life expectancy: People who live to adulthood will probably reach old age; there are just fewer of them.

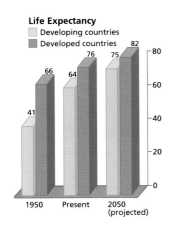

Life Expectancy
- Developing countries
- Developed countries

1950: 41, 66
Present: 64, 76
2050 (projected): 75, 82

CANADA 79
UNITED STATES 77
MEXICO 75
BRAZIL 68
ARGENTINA 73
FRANCE 79
RUSSIA 66
CHINA 71
JAPAN 81 years
SAUDI ARABIA 67
INDIA 61
NIGERIA 52
ZAMBIA 37 years
AUSTRALIA 79

Life Expectancy
(years)
- 70 and above
- 60–69
- 50–59
- 40–49
- Less than 40

Migration

International migration has reached its highest level, with foreign workers now providing the labor in several Middle Eastern nations and immigrant workers proving essential to rich countries with low birthrates. Refugees continue to escape grim political and environmental conditions, while businesspeople and tourists keep many economies spinning.

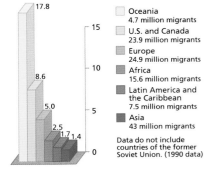

Migrant Population
(percent of regional population)

17.8 Oceania 4.7 million migrants
8.6 U.S. and Canada 23.9 million migrants
5.0 Europe 24.9 million migrants
2.5 Africa 15.6 million migrants
1.7 Latin America and the Caribbean 7.5 million migrants
1.4 Asia 43 million migrants

Data do not include countries of the former Soviet Union. (1990 data)

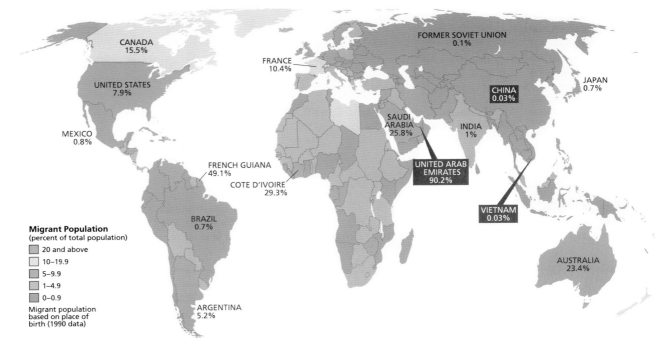

CANADA 15.5%
UNITED STATES 7.9%
MEXICO 0.8%
FRENCH GUIANA 49.1%
BRAZIL 0.7%
ARGENTINA 5.2%
FRANCE 10.4%
FORMER SOVIET UNION 0.1%
COTE D'IVOIRE 29.3%
SAUDI ARABIA 25.8%
UNITED ARAB EMIRATES 90.2%
INDIA 1%
CHINA 0.03%
JAPAN 0.7%
VIETNAM 0.03%
AUSTRALIA 23.4%

Migrant Population
(percent of total population)
- 20 and above
- 10–19.9
- 5–9.9
- 1–4.9
- 0–0.9

Migrant population based on place of birth (1990 data)

Most Populous Nations

(mid-2002 data)

1. China 1,280,712,000
2. India 1,049,464,000
3. United States 287,494,000
4. Indonesia 216,983,000
5. Brazil 173,816,000
6. Russia 143,524,000
7. Pakistan 143,481,000
8. Bangladesh 133,603,000
9. Nigeria 129,935,000
10. Japan 127,378,000
11. Mexico 101,743,000
12. Germany 82,406,000
13. Philippines 80,025,000
14. Vietnam 79,707,000
15. Egypt 71,244,000
16. Ethiopia 67,673,000
17. Turkey 67,264,000
18. Iran 65,554,000
19. Thailand 62,626,000
20. United Kingdom 60,224,000

Most Crowded Nations

Population Density (pop/sq. mi.)

1. Monaco 45,333
2. Singapore 17,320
3. Malta 3,157
4. Bahrain 2,688
5. Maldives 2,495
6. Bangladesh 2,401
7. Barbados 1,620
8. Taiwan 1,608
9. Mauritius 1,520
10. Nauru 1,412
11. South Korea 1,274
12. San Marino 1,166
13. Mayotte (Fr.) 1,139
14. Puerto Rico (U.S.) 1,139
15. Tuvalu 1,100
16. Lebanon 1,061
17. Netherlands 1,018
18. Marshall Islands 1,007
19. Martinique (Fr.) 897
20. Belgium and Japan 872

Demographic Extremes

Life Expectancy at Birth

Lowest (female):
38 Zambia
39 Angola, Zimbabwe, Mozambique
40 Malawi, Rwanda
41 Niger, Swaziland

Lowest (male):
37 Angola, Zambia, Mozambique
39 Malawi, Rwanda
40 Swaziland
41 Botswana, Niger, Zimbabwe

Highest (female):
84 Japan
83 France, San Marino, Switzerland
82 Australia, Italy, Martinque, Spain, Sweden

Highest (male):
78 Iceland
77 Japan, Sweden, Switzerland
76 Australia, Canada, Greece, Israel, Italy, Martinique, Norway, San Marino, Singapore

Population Age Structure

Highest % Population under Age 15
51% Uganda
50% Niger
49% Marshall Islands
48% Angola, Benin, Burkina Faso, Burundi, Chad, Dem. Rep. of Congo, Sao Tome and Principe, Yemen

Highest % Population over Age 65
23% Monaco
18% Italy
17% Belgium, Greece, Japan, Spain
16% Bulgaria, France, Germany, San Marino, United Kingdom

Until recently, a person's nationality and language were usually the same: A German spoke German, for example. The ability to use a specific language has often been viewed as a defining characteristic of a citizen. But there are only about 200 countries, while there are some 6,000 living languages. In one-fourth of all nations, no single language is spoken by a majority of the inhabitants. Canada is legally bilingual; India has 14 official languages; and French, Spanish, English, Portuguese, and German are each the official language of at least two nations.

Most languages are spoken by only a few hundred or a few thousand people. Over 200 languages are spoken by more than a million people; 23 languages have 50 million or more speakers.

How we define language makes it difficult to determine the exact number of languages. A dialect, for instance, is a variety of language used by a specific group of persons, with its own rules of grammar or pronunciation. Other linguistic systems that fail to attain the full status of languages are pidgins (contact languages used by groups with different native languages to communicate) and creoles (what pidgins are called when they are adopted as native languages).

Vanishing Languages

Some 10,000 languages—or more—are thought to have once existed (graph, right). This is an estimate; unlike extinct animals, dead languages rarely left traces, as most lacked a written form. About 6,000 still exist, but linguists fear that the rate of loss is quickening.

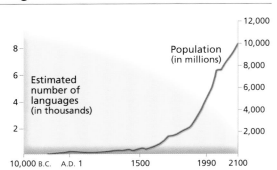

Evolution of Languages

Even as many languages have disappeared, a few dominant linguistic groups have spawned numerous related tongues. Thus, the Germanic language, which derived from Proto-Indo-European and was spoken by tribes that settled in northern and western Europe, has diversified into several major languages today.

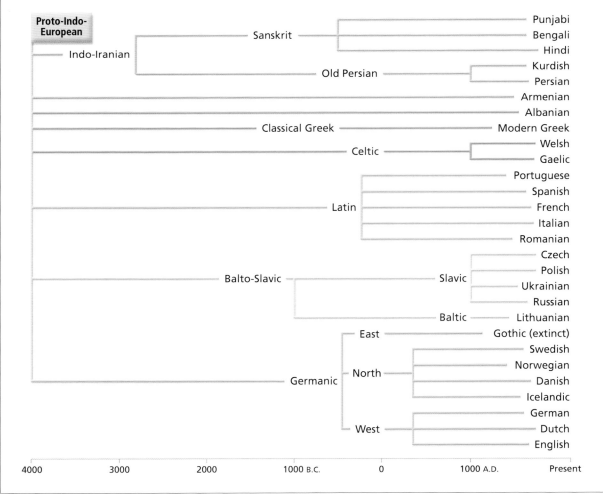

Voices of the World

AMERICAN INDIAN (NORTH)
More than 300 native languages were once spoken in the United States and Canada. Two-thirds survive, but the few speakers left are aging. Even as native languages fade, their sounds echo in place-names such as Chicago and Massachusetts.

1 Algonquian-Ritwan
2 Caddoan
3 Hokan
4 Iroquoian
5 Kiowa-Tanoan
6 Muskogean
7 Nadene
8 Penutian
9 Salishan
10 Siouan
11 Uto-Aztecan
12 Wakashan
13 Undetermined

AMERICAN INDIAN (MESO-)
Quiché and Yucatec, Mayan languages, are the region's strongest indigenous tongues. Most languages faded after European contact, but a few were documented by missionaries. Alonso de Molina recorded Nahuatl, the Aztec language, in the mid-1500s.

1 Macro-Chibchan
2 Mayan
3 Mixe-Zoquean
4 Oto-Manguean
5 Totonacan
6 Uto-Aztecan

AFRO-ASIATIC
The languages of ancient Babylon, Assyria, Egypt, and Palestine belonged to this family. Still thriving, the largest living Afro-Asiatic language, Arabic, spreads in tandem with Islam.

1 Berber
2 Chadic
3 Cushitic
4 Omotic
5 Semitic

ISOLATES
Dozens of rare languages—such as Basque in Spain and France, Burushaski in Pakistan—persist as linguistic islands. Despite decades of research, links to known language groups have yet to be verified. Chukchi, spoken in Siberia, is an example of a member of an isolated small language family.

Isolates and isolated small families

AMERICAN INDIAN (SOUTH)
Perhaps a thousand Indian languages that once had a voice here have disappeared. Two modest success stories: Quechua, the language of the Inca, has six million speakers; Guarani is the major language of Paraguay.

1 Arawakan
2 Kariban
3 Macro-Chibchan
4 Macro-Ge
5 Pano-Takanan
6 Quechumaran
7 Tukánoan
8 Tupian
9 Other
10 Undetermined

How Many Speak What?

Languages can paint vivid historical pictures of migration and colonization. English, Spanish, and Portuguese, for example, originated in parts of Europe with only a tenth of China's population and area; yet they rival Mandarin Chinese in total number of speakers. They spread because England, Spain, and Portugal built large overseas empires. India, which has been part of several empires, currently has 14 official languages and a population of 900 million; only a fifth of its people speak Hindi.

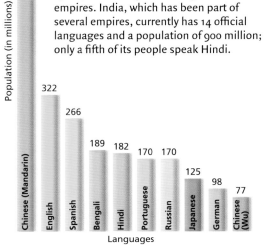

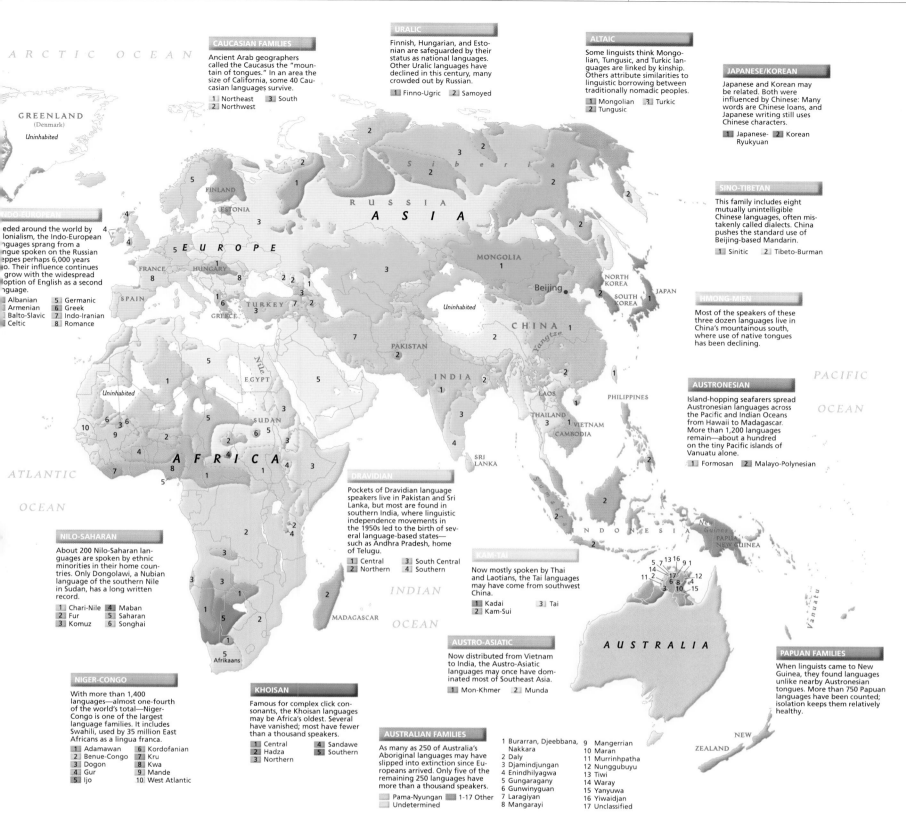

CAUCASIAN FAMILIES

Ancient Arab geographers called the Caucasus the "mountain of tongues." In an area the size of California, some 40 Caucasian languages survive.

1 Northeast   3 South
2 Northwest

URALIC

Finnish, Hungarian, and Estonian are safeguarded by their status as national languages. Other Uralic languages have declined in this century, many crowded out by Russian.

1 Finno-Ugric   2 Samoyed

ALTAIC

Some linguists think Mongolian, Tungusic, and Turkic languages are linked by kinship. Others attribute similarities to linguistic borrowing between traditionally nomadic peoples.

1 Mongolian   3 Turkic
2 Tungusic

JAPANESE/KOREAN

Japanese and Korean may be related. Both were influenced by Chinese: Many words are Chinese loans, and Japanese writing still uses Chinese characters.

1 Japanese-   2 Korean
Ryukyuan

SINO-TIBETAN

This family includes eight mutually unintelligible Chinese languages, often mistakenly called dialects. China pushes the standard use of Beijing-based Mandarin.

1 Sinitic   2 Tibeto-Burman

INDO-EUROPEAN

...eded around the world by ...lonialism, the Indo-European ...nguages sprang from a ...ngue spoken on the Russian ...eppes perhaps 6,000 years ...o. Their influence continues ...grow with the widespread ...option of English as a second ...nguage.

1 Albanian   5 Germanic
2 Armenian   6 Greek
3 Balto-Slavic 7 Indo-Iranian
4 Celtic   8 Romance

HMONG-MIEN

Most of the speakers of these three dozen languages live in China's mountainous south, where use of native tongues has been declining.

AUSTRONESIAN

Island-hopping seafarers spread Austronesian languages across the Pacific and Indian Oceans from Hawaii to Madagascar. More than 1,200 languages remain—about a hundred on the tiny Pacific islands of Vanuatu alone.

1 Formosan   2 Malayo-Polynesian

DRAVIDIAN

Pockets of Dravidian language speakers live in Pakistan and Sri Lanka, but most are found in southern India, where linguistic independence movements in the 1950s led to the birth of several language-based states—such as Andhra Pradesh, home of Telugu.

1 Central   3 South Central
2 Northern   4 Southern

NILO-SAHARAN

About 200 Nilo-Saharan languages are spoken by ethnic minorities in their home countries. Only Dongolawi, a Nubian language of the southern Nile in Sudan, has a long written record.

1 Chari-Nile   4 Maban
2 Fur   5 Saharan
3 Komuz   6 Songhai

KAM-TAI

Now mostly spoken by Thai and Laotians, the Tai languages may have come from southwest China.

1 Kadai   3 Tai
2 Kam-Sui

NIGER-CONGO

With more than 1,400 languages—almost one-fourth of the world's total—Niger-Congo is one of the largest language families. It includes Swahili, used by 35 million East Africans as a lingua franca.

1 Adamawan   6 Kordofanian
2 Benue-Congo 7 Kru
3 Dogon   8 Kwa
4 Gur   9 Mande
5 Ijo   10 West Atlantic

KHOISAN

Famous for complex click consonants, the Khoisan languages may be Africa's oldest. Several have vanished; most have fewer than a thousand speakers.

1 Central   4 Sandawe
2 Hadza   5 Southern
3 Northern

AUSTRO-ASIATIC

Now distributed from Vietnam to India, the Austro-Asiatic languages may once have dominated most of Southeast Asia.

1 Mon-Khmer   2 Munda

AUSTRALIAN FAMILIES

As many as 250 of Australia's Aboriginal languages may have slipped into extinction since Europeans arrived. Only five of the remaining 250 languages have more than a thousand speakers.

Pama-Nyungan   1-17 Other
Undetermined

1 Burarran, Djeebbana, Nakkara
2 Daly
3 Djamindjungan
4 Enindhilyagwa
5 Gungaragany
6 Gunwinyguan
7 Laragiyan
8 Mangarayi
9 Mangerrian
10 Maran
11 Murrinhpatha
12 Nunggubuyu
13 Tiwi
14 Waray
15 Yanyuwa
16 Yiwaidjan
17 Unclassified

PAPUAN FAMILIES

When linguists came to New Guinea, they found languages unlike nearby Austronesian tongues. More than 750 Papuan languages have been counted; isolation keeps them relatively healthy.

Major Language Families Today

Many of the world's languages belong to the Indo-European language group, which is thought to have ancient roots in the Russian steppes. The map at right illustrates how far members of this group—and others—have spread over the millennia. The map locates languages by territory; it does not indicate the number of speakers. For example, the Altaic group covers a vast area, but it has only about 135 million speakers. Austronesian, on the other hand, is shown only in the Philippines and Indonesia, but it has a quarter of a billion speakers.

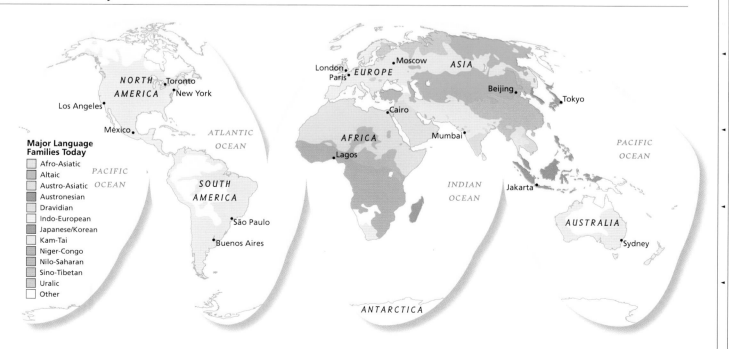

Major Language Families Today

Afro-Asiatic
Altaic
Austro-Asiatic
Austronesian
Dravidian
Indo-European
Japanese/Korean
Kam-Tai
Niger-Congo
Nilo-Saharan
Sino-Tibetan
Uralic
Other

WORLD RELIGIONS

The great power of religion comes from its ability to speak to the heart of individuals and societies. Since earliest human times, the urge to honor nature spirits or the belief in a supreme being has brought comfort and security in the face of fundamental questions of life and death.

Billions of people are now adherents of Hinduism, Buddhism, Judaism, Christianity, and Islam, all of which began in Asia. Universal elements of these faiths include ritual and prayer, sacred sites and pilgrimage, saints and martyrs, ritual clothing and implements, dietary laws and fasting, festivals and holy days, and special ceremonies for life's major moments. Sometimes otherworldly, most religions have moral and ethical guidelines that attempt to make life better on Earth as well. Their tenets and goals are taught not only at the church, synagogue, mosque, or temple but also through schools, storytelling, parables, painting, sculpture, even dance and drama.

The world's major religions blossomed from the teachings and revelations of individuals who heeded and transmitted the voice of God or discovered a way to salvation that could be understood by others. Abraham and Moses for Jews, the Buddha for Buddhists, Jesus Christ for Christians, and Muhammad for Muslims fulfilled the roles of divine teachers who experienced essential truths of existence.

Throughout history, priests, rabbis, clergymen, and imams have recited, interpreted, and preached the holy words of sacred texts and writings to the faithful. Today the world's religions, with their guidance here on Earth and hopes and promises for the afterlife, continue to exert an extraordinary force on billions of people.

Major Religions
- Eastern Orthodox
- Protestant
- Roman Catholic
- Other Christian
- Jewish
- Shia Muslim
- Sunni Muslim
- Hindu
- Lamaistic Buddhist
- Theravada Buddhist
- Buddhist and Shintoist
- Mahayana Buddhist, Confucianist, Taoist
- Sikh
- Indigenous

BUDDHISM
Founded about 2,500 years ago by Siddhartha Gautama—an Indian prince who became the Buddha, or Enlightened One—Buddhism accepts "four noble truths": Life is suffering; suffering has a cause (desire); the cause can be overcome; the way to overcome the cause is through ethical conduct, meditation, and wisdom.

CHRISTIANITY
Christian belief in eternal life is based on the example of Jesus Christ, a Jew born 2,000 years ago. The New Testament tells of his teaching, persecution, crucifixion, and resurrection. Today Christianity is found around the world in three main forms: Roman Catholicism, Eastern Orthodox, and Protestantism.

HINDUISM
Hinduism began in India more than 4,000 years ago and is still flourishing. Sacred texts known as the *Vedas* form the basis of Hindu faith and

Adherents Worldwide

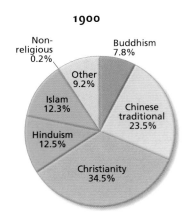

1900
- Non-religious 0.2%
- Buddhism 7.8%
- Other 9.2%
- Islam 12.3%
- Chinese traditional 23.5%
- Hinduism 12.5%
- Christianity 34.5%

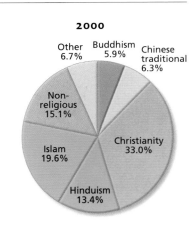

2000
- Other 6.7%
- Buddhism 5.9%
- Chinese traditional 6.3%
- Non-religious 15.1%
- Christianity 33.0%
- Islam 19.6%
- Hinduism 13.4%

The growth of Islam and the decline of Chinese traditional religion stand out as significant changes over the past one hundred years. Christianity, largest of the world's main faiths, has remained largely stable in number of adherents. Today more than one out of six people claim to be atheistic or nonreligious.

Adherents by Continent

In terms of religious adherents, Asia ranks first. This is not only because half the world's people live on that continent but also because three of the five major faiths are practiced there: Hinduism in South Asia; Buddhism in East and Southeast Asia; and Islam from Indonesia to the Central Asian republics to Turkey. Australia, Europe, North America, and South America are overwhelmingly Christian. Africa, with many millions of Muslims and Christians, retains large numbers of animists.

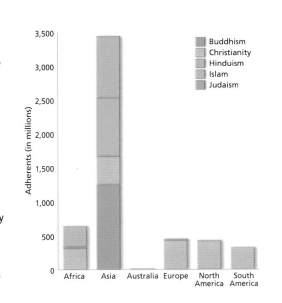

Legend:
- Buddhism
- Christianity
- Hinduism
- Islam
- Judaism

Adherents (in millions): Africa, Asia, Australia, Europe, North America, South America

Sacred Places

BUDDHISM
1. Bodhgaya: Where Buddha reached enlightenment
2. Kusinagara: Place of Buddha's death
3. Lumbini: Buddha's birthplace
4. Sarnath: Place where Buddha delivered his first sermon
5. Sanchi: Location of stupa that contains relics of Buddha

CHRISTIANITY
1. Jerusalem: Church of the Holy Sepulchre, Jesus's crucifixion
2. Bethlehem: Jesus's birthplace
3. Nazareth: Where Jesus grew up
4. Shore of the Sea of Galilee: Where Jesus gave the Sermon on the Mount
5. Rome and the Vatican: Tombs of St. Peter and St. Paul

HINDUISM
1. Varanasi (Benares): Most holy Hindu site, home of Shiva
2. Vrindavan: Krishna's birthplace
3. Allahabad: At confluence of Ganges and Yamuna rivers, purest place to bathe
4. Madurai: Temple of Minakshi, great goddess of the south
5. Badrinath: Vishnu's shrine

ISLAM
1. Mecca: Muhammad's birthplace
2. Medina: City of Muhammad's flight, or hegira
3. Jerusalem: Dome of the Rock, Muhammad's stepping-stone to heaven
4. Najaf (Shi'ite): Tomb of Imam Ali
5. Kerbala (Shi'ite): Tomb of Imam Hoseyn

JUDAISM
1. Jerusalem: Location of the Western Wall and first and second temples
2. Hebron: Tomb of the patriarchs and their wives
3. Safed: Where Kabbalah (Jewish mysticism) flourished
4. Tiberias: Where Talmud (source of Jewish law) first composed
5. Auschwitz: Symbol of six million Jews who perished in the Holocaust

ritual. The main trinity of gods comprises Brahma the creator, Vishnu the preserver, and Shiva the destroyer. Hindus believe in reincarnation.

ISLAM
Muslims believe that the Koran, Islam's sacred book, accurately records the spoken word of God (Allah) as revealed to the Prophet Muhammad, born in Mecca around A.D. 570. Strict adherents pray five times a day, fast during the holy month of Ramadan, and make at least one pilgrimage to Mecca, Islam's holiest city.

JUDAISM
The 4,000-year-old religion of the Jews stands as the oldest of the major faiths that believe in a single god. Judaism's traditions, customs, laws, and beliefs date back to Abraham, the founder, and to the Torah—the first five books of the Old Testament, believed to have been handed down to Moses on Mount Sinai.

Adherents by Country

COUNTRIES WITH THE MOST BUDDHISTS		COUNTRIES WITH THE MOST CHRISTIANS		COUNTRIES WITH THE MOST HINDUS		COUNTRIES WITH THE MOST MUSLIMS		COUNTRIES WITH THE MOST JEWS	
Country	Buddhists	Country	Christians	Country	Hindus	Country	Muslims	Country	Jews
1. China	105,829,000	1. United States	235,742,000	1. India	755,135,000	1. Indonesia	181,368,000	1. United States	5,621,000
2. Japan	69,931,000	2. Brazil	155,545,000	2. Nepal	18,354,000	2. Pakistan	141,650,000	2. Israel	3,951,000
3. Thailand	52,383,000	3. Mexico	95,169,000	3. Bangladesh	15,995,000	3. India	123,960,000	3. Russia	951,000
4. Vietnam	39,534,000	4. China	89,056,000	4. Indonesia	7,259,000	4. Bangladesh	110,805,000	4. France	591,000
5. Myanmar	33,145,000	5. Russia	84,308,000	5. Sri Lanka	2,124,000	5. Turkey	65,637,000	5. Argentina	490,000
6. Sri Lanka	12,879,000	6. Philippines	68,151,000	6. Pakistan	1,868,000	6. Egypt	65,612,000	6. Canada	403,000
7. Cambodia	9,462,000	7. India	62,341,000	7. Malaysia	1,630,000	7. Iran	65,439,000	7. Brazil	357,000
8. India	7,249,000	8. Germany	62,326,000	8. United States	1,032,000	8. Nigeria	63,300,000	8. Britain	302,000
9. South Korea	7,174,000	9. Nigeria	51,123,000	9. South Africa	959,000	9. China	38,208,000	9. Palestine*	273,000
10. Taiwan	4,686,000	10. Congo, Dem. Rep.	49,256,000	10. Myanmar	893,000	10. Algeria	30,690,000	10. Ukraine	220,000

*Non-sovereign nation

All figures are estimates based on data for the year 2000.
Countries with the highest reported nonreligious populations include China, Russia, United States, Germany, North Korea, Japan, India, Vietnam, France, and Italy.

WORLD ECONOMY

A global economic activity map (right) reveals striking differences between the Northern and Southern Hemispheres, particularly in the case of manufacturing. In the north are large clusters of manufacturing centers, but south of the Equator such centers make only scattered appearances on the map. The most notable concentrations of economic activity are seen in North America and Western Europe; these are followed by parts of eastern and southern Asia and a few areas of South America, southern Africa, and Australia.

There are different ways of looking at this activity. When examined by country, the United States leads in many areas, but united Western European countries have also become a major economic force. Indeed, in terms of manufacturing, Western Europe outpaces the U.S. in cars, chemicals, and food.

The world's second largest economy is found in China. Even so, Chinese workers take home only a fraction of the cash pocketed each week by their economic rivals in the West; they also have very few telephones and cars—two basic consumer products of the modern age. (When it comes to vehicles, Italy has more passenger cars per thousand people than any other country.)

The Middle East produces more fuel than any other region, but it has virtually no other economic output besides that commodity.

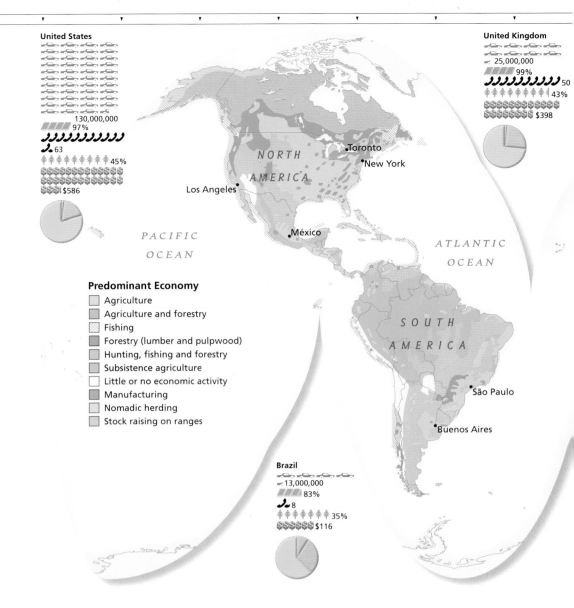

Predominant Economy
- Agriculture
- Agriculture and forestry
- Fishing
- Forestry (lumber and pulpwood)
- Hunting, fishing and forestry
- Subsistence agriculture
- Little or no economic activity
- Manufacturing
- Nomadic herding
- Stock raising on ranges

Labor Migration

People in search of jobs gravitate toward the strongest economies, unless immigration policies prevent them from doing so. Japan, for instance, has one of the world's most vigorous economies and a population that is more than 99 percent Japanese. Some nations are "labor importers," while some are "labor exporters." In the mid-1990s, Malaysia was the largest Asian importer (close to a million) and the Philippines was the largest Asian exporter (4.2 million). Europe, once a major labor exporter to North and South America, is now a major importer, especially from Africa.

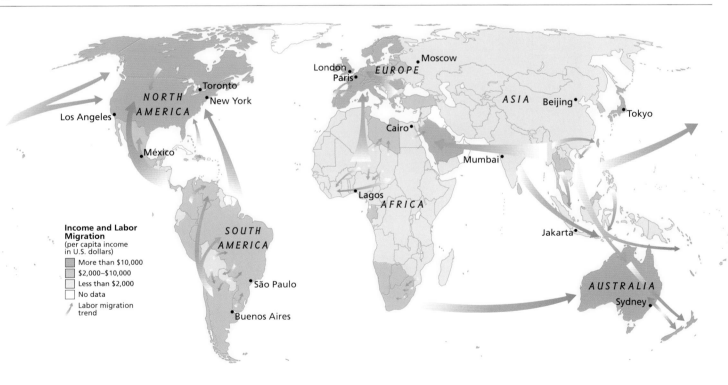

Income and Labor Migration
(per capita income in U.S. dollars)
- More than $10,000
- $2,000–$10,000
- Less than $2,000
- No data
- Labor migration trend

Top GDP Growth Rates

1995–2000 AVERAGE

1. Bosnia and Herzegovina	31%
2. Equatorial Guinea	29%
3. Rwanda	14%
4. Ireland	10%
5. China	9%
6. Maldives	8%
7. Mozambique	8%
8. Vietnam	7%
9. Dominican Republic	7%
10. Sudan	7%

The World's Richest and Poorest Countries

RICHEST	GDP PER CAPITA (2000)	POOREST	GDP PER CAPITA (2000)
1. Luxembourg	36,400 (figures in U.S. dollars)	1. Sierra Leone	510
2. United States	36,200	2. Congo, Dem. Rep. of the	600
3. Bermuda	33,000	3. Ethiopia	600
4. San Marino	32,000	4. Somalia	600
5. Switzerland	28,600	5. Eritrea	710
6. Norway	27,700	6. Tanzania	710
7. Monaco	27,000	7. Burundi	720
8. Singapore	26,500	8. Comoros	720
9. Denmark	25,500	9. Afghanistan	800
10. Belgium	25,300	10. Madagascar	800

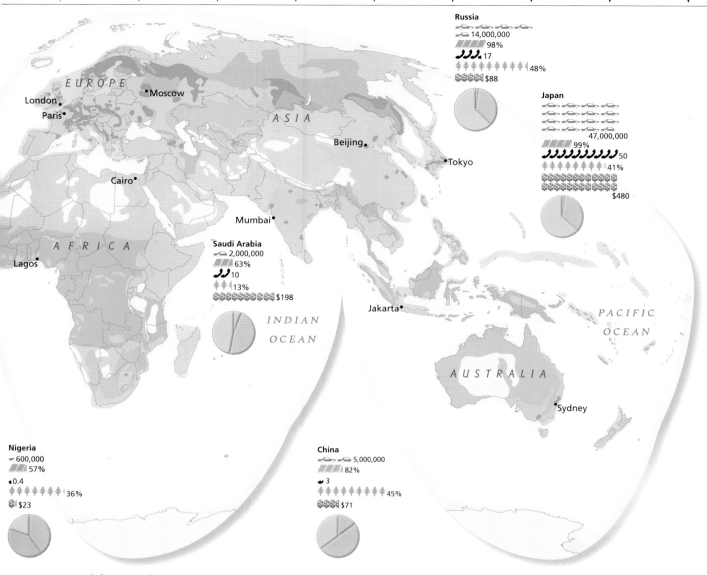

Russia
14,000,000
98%
17
48%
$88

Japan
47,000,000
99%
50
41%
$480

Saudi Arabia
2,000,000
63%
10
13% $198

Nigeria
600,000
57%
0.4
36%
$23

China
5,000,000
82%
3
45%
$71

Number of cars (symbol equals 3 million cars)

Women in adult work-force (symbol equals 5%)

Literacy rate (symbol equals 25%)

Average weekly income (symbol equals $20 U.S. equivalent)

Number of telephones per 100 people (symbol equals 5 telephones)

GDP by sector

Services   Agriculture

Industry

Major Manufacturers

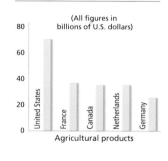

(All figures in billions of U.S. dollars)

Agricultural products

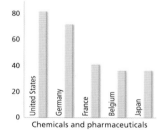

Automotive products

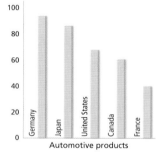

Chemicals and pharmaceuticals

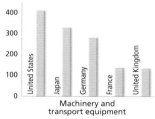

Machinery and transport equipment

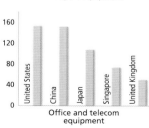

Office and telecom equipment

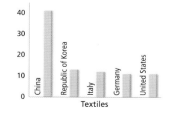

Textiles

World Employment

In the most developed nations, a majority of people work in industry or services: 80 percent of the workforce in the United Kingdom, for example, is in services; that figure is 72 percent in the United States. In those countries, only a tiny percentage works to raise food (just 3 percent in the U.S.). There are many places where that proportion is inverted: 67 percent of India's labor force works in agriculture.

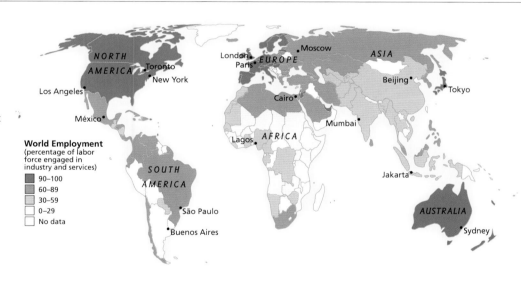

World Employment
(percentage of labor force engaged in industry and services)

- 90–100
- 60–89
- 30–59
- 0–29
- No data

Gross Domestic Product

The gross domestic product, or GDP, is the total market value of goods and services produced by a nation's economy in a given year. It is a convenient way of calculating the level of a nation's economic activity; it does not show average wealth of individuals. Thus, China may have close to half the GDP of the U.S., but its citizens' earnings, on average, are less than a tenth of what Americans make.

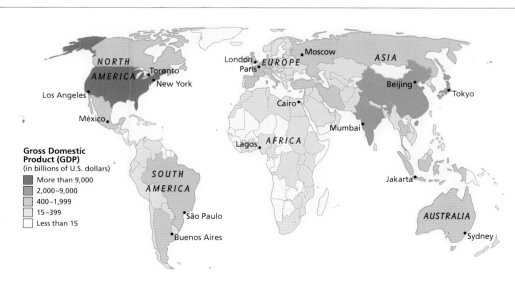

Gross Domestic Product (GDP)
(in billions of U.S. dollars)

- More than 9,000
- 2,000–9,000
- 400–1,999
- 15–399
- Less than 15

World trade has expanded at a dizzying pace in the decades since World War II ended. Moreover, it has been diversifying: The less developed nations continue to export raw materials (lumber, minerals, and fuel oils), the more developed nations export finished and manufactured products, and the most developed nations are the source of international investment.

The world seems to be divided into a more developed north and a less developed south. On the map below, economies that rely on single commodities for more than 40 percent of all exports are marked with black symbols, which are clearly more prevalent south of the Caribbean and Mediterranean Seas.

The capital flows among Europe, the United States, and Japan (see colored arrows) are investments in company stock and other financial instruments, such as commodity futures and derivatives. In the time it takes a shipment of timber from Cambodia to reach its home market, the market value of the stock in a technology company may have skyrocketed or plummeted.

The great ports of stocks and other financial instruments are stock exchanges. North America has ten exchanges and Europe has sixteen, while Asia has eight and the entire African continent has just one.

This disparity in the value of trade is also reflected in the other charts, maps, and graphs on these two pages. Among the top ten trading nations, for instance, are countries ranging in population from China's 1.2 billion down to Canada's 30 million, the Netherlands' 15 million, and Belgium's 10 million.

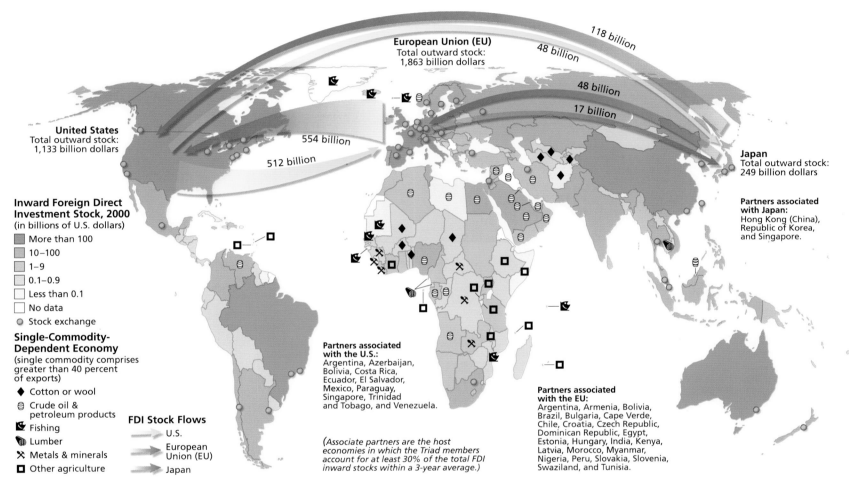

European Union (EU)
Total outward stock:
1,863 billion dollars

118 billion
48 billion
48 billion
17 billion

United States
Total outward stock:
1,133 billion dollars

554 billion
512 billion

Japan
Total outward stock:
249 billion dollars

Partners associated with Japan:
Hong Kong (China), Republic of Korea, and Singapore.

Inward Foreign Direct Investment Stock, 2000
(in billions of U.S. dollars)
- More than 100
- 10–100
- 1–9
- 0.1–0.9
- Less than 0.1
- No data
- Stock exchange

Single-Commodity-Dependent Economy
(single commodity comprises greater than 40 percent of exports)
- ◆ Cotton or wool
- Crude oil & petroleum products
- Fishing
- Lumber
- ✕ Metals & minerals
- ◻ Other agriculture

FDI Stock Flows
- → U.S.
- → European Union (EU)
- → Japan

Partners associated with the U.S.:
Argentina, Azerbaijan, Bolivia, Costa Rica, Ecuador, El Salvador, Mexico, Paraguay, Singapore, Trinidad and Tobago, and Venezuela.

Partners associated with the EU:
Argentina, Armenia, Bolivia, Brazil, Bulgaria, Cape Verde, Chile, Croatia, Czech Republic, Dominican Republic, Egypt, Estonia, Hungary, India, Kenya, Latvia, Morocco, Myanmar, Nigeria, Peru, Slovakia, Slovenia, Swaziland, and Tunisia.

(Associate partners are the host economies in which the Triad members account for at least 30% of the total FDI inward stocks within a 3-year average.)

Growth of World Trade

After World War II the export growth of manufactured goods greatly outstripped other exports. This graph shows the volume growth on a semi-log scale (a straight line represents constant growth) rather than a standard scale (a straight line indicates a constant increase in the absolute values in each year).

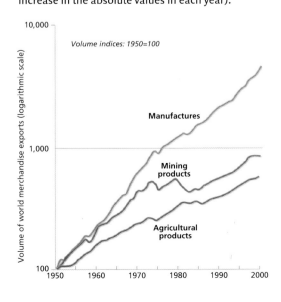

Volume indices: 1950=100

Volume of world merchandise exports (logarithmic scale)

10,000

Manufactures

1,000

Mining products

Agricultural products

100
1950 1960 1970 1980 1990 2000

Merchandise Exports

Manufactured goods account for three-quarters of world merchandise exports. Export values of two sub-types—machinery and office/telecom equipment—exceed the total export value of mining products; world exports in chemicals and automotive products exceed the export value of all agricultural products.

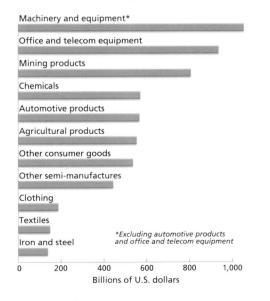

Machinery and equipment*
Office and telecom equipment
Mining products
Chemicals
Automotive products
Agricultural products
Other consumer goods
Other semi-manufactures
Clothing
Textiles
Iron and steel

*Excluding automotive products and office and telecom equipment

0   200   400   600   800   1,000
Billions of U.S. dollars

Main Trading Nations

The U.S., Germany, and Japan account for nearly 30 percent of total world merchandise trade. Ongoing negotiations among the 144 member nations of the World Trade Organization are tackling market-access barriers in agriculture, textiles, and clothing—areas where many developing countries hope to compete.

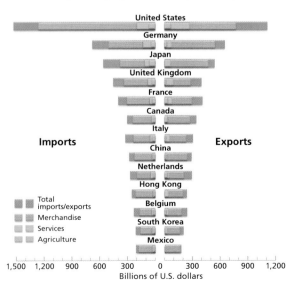

United States
Germany
Japan
United Kingdom
France
Canada
Italy
China
Netherlands
Hong Kong
Belgium
South Korea
Mexico

Imports   **Exports**

- Total imports/exports
- Merchandise
- Services
- Agriculture

1,500 1,200 900 600 300 0 300 600 900 1,200
Billions of U.S. dollars

World Debt

Measuring a nation's outstanding foreign debt in relation to its GDP indicates the size of future income needed to pay back the debt; it also shows how much a nation has relied in the past on foreign savings to finance investment and consumption expenditures. A high external debt ratio can pose a financial risk if debt service payments are not assured.

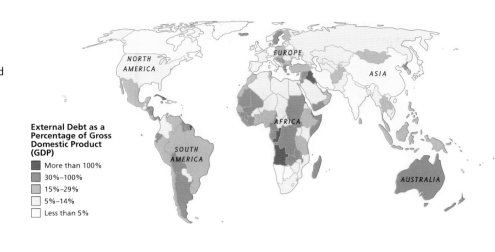

External Debt as a Percentage of Gross Domestic Product (GDP)
- More than 100%
- 30%–100%
- 15%–29%
- 5%–14%
- Less than 5%

Trade Blocs

Regional trade is on the rise. Agreements between neighboring countries to offer each other trade benefits can create larger markets and improve the economy of the region as a whole. But they can also lead to discrimination, especially when more efficient suppliers outside the regional agreements are prevented from supplying their goods and services.

Major Regional Trade Agreements
- **APEC** - Asia-Pacific Economic Cooperation
- **ASEAN** - Association of Southeast Asian Nations
- **COMESA** - Common Market for Eastern and Southern Africa
- **ECOWAS** - Economic Community of West African States
- **EU** - European Union
- **MERCOSUR** - Southern Common Market
- **APEC & NAFTA** (North American Free Trade Agreement)
- **APEC & ASEAN**

Trade Flow: Fuels

The leading exporters of fuel products are countries in the Middle East, Africa, Eastern Europe, and western Asia; all export more fuel than they consume. But intra-regional energy trade is growing, with some of the key producers—Canada, Indonesia, Norway, and the United Kingdom, for example—located in regions that are net energy importers.

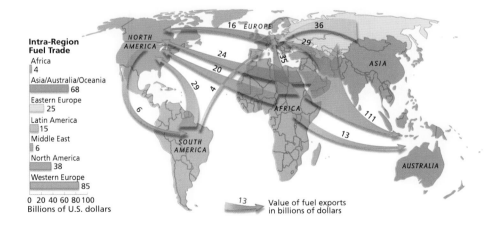

Intra-Region Fuel Trade
- Africa: 4
- Asia/Australia/Oceania: 68
- Eastern Europe: 25
- Latin America: 15
- Middle East: 6
- North America: 38
- Western Europe: 85

0 20 40 60 80 100
Billions of U.S. dollars

13 → Value of fuel exports in billions of dollars

Trade Flow: Agricultural Products

The world trade in agricultural products is less concentrated than trade in fuels, with processed goods making up the majority. Agricultural products encounter high export barriers, which limit the opportunities for some exporters to expand into foreign markets. Reducing such barriers is a major challenge for governments that are engaged in agricultural trade negotiations.

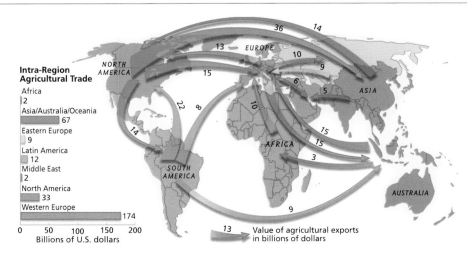

Intra-Region Agricultural Trade
- Africa: 2
- Asia/Australia/Oceania: 67
- Eastern Europe: 9
- Latin America: 12
- Middle East: 2
- North America: 33
- Western Europe: 174

0 50 100 150 200
Billions of U.S. dollars

13 → Value of agricultural exports in billions of dollars

Top Merchandise Exporters and Importers

	PERCENTAGE OF WORLD TOTAL	VALUE (BILLIONS)
TOP EXPORTERS		
United States	12.3	$781
Germany	8.7	$552
Japan	7.5	$479
France	4.7	$298
United Kingdom	4.5	$284
Canada	4.3	$277
China	3.9	$249
Italy	3.9	$238
Netherlands	3.3	$213
Hong Kong (China)	3.3	$202
Belgium	2.9	$186
South Korea	2.7	$172
Mexico	2.6	$166
Taiwan (China)	2.3	$148
Singapore	2.2	$138
TOP IMPORTERS		
United States	18.9	$1,258
Germany	7.5	$503
Japan	5.7	$380
United Kingdom	5.1	$337
France	4.6	$305
Canada	3.7	$245
Italy	3.5	$236
China	3.4	$225
Hong Kong (China)	3.2	$214
Netherlands	3.0	$198
Mexico	2.7	$183
Belgium	2.6	$173
South Korea	2.4	$160
Spain	2.3	$154
Taiwan (China)	2.1	$140

Top Commercial Services Exporters and Importers

	PERCENTAGE OF WORLD TOTAL	VALUE (BILLIONS)
TOP EXPORTERS		
United States	19.1	$275
United Kingdom	7.0	$100
France	5.7	$81
Germany	5.6	$80
Japan	4.8	$68
Italy	4.0	$57
Spain	3.7	$53
Netherlands	3.6	$52
Hong Kong (China)	2.9	$42
Belgium-Luxembourg	2.9	$42
Canada	2.6	$37
China	2.1	$30
Austria	2.1	$30
South Korea	2.0	$29
Singapore	1.9	$27
TOP IMPORTERS		
United States	13.8	$199
Germany	9.2	$132
Japan	8.1	$116
United Kingdom	5.7	$82
France	4.3	$62
Italy	3.9	$56
Netherlands	3.6	$51
Canada	2.9	$42
Belgium-Luxembourg	2.7	$38
China	2.5	$36
South Korea	2.3	$33
Spain	2.1	$31
Austria	2.0	$29
Ireland	2.0	$29
Hong Kong (China)	1.8	$26

The population of the planet, which already tops six billion, continues to increase by 230,000 new mouths a day. What will they eat? Where will the additional food come from?

Worldwide, agricultural production also continues to grow, but the food-producing regions are unevenly distributed around the globe. And though efforts to raise the levels of production even more (while relying less on chemical applications that damage the environment) are vitally important, they can go only so far in solving a great dilemma: How can we get more food to the millions of people who do not have enough to eat? Invariably, it is the economic situation of nations—which ones have food surpluses to sell; which ones need food and have or don't have enough money to buy it—that determines who goes hungry.

For people in the world's poorest regions, the situation is grim. The United Nations Food and Agriculture Organization reports that every night 815 million people in the developing world go to bed hungry and that malnourishment contributes to at least one-third of all child deaths. It also says that 13 million people in southern Africa face famine. Most cases of malnutrition are found in the developing countries of the tropics, where rapid population growth and other factors are depleting agricultural and financial resources.

Land Use and Commercial Agriculture

At various times and in various places, people began to till the land. The beginning of agriculture—cultivating soil, producing crops, and raising livestock—created a generally reliable food supply. Many historians believe that the planting and tending of crops also led to the first fixed settlements. Over thousands of years, the human population has grown in number, occupying more land and producing more food. Today most of the world's potential cropland is being cultivated. The challenge now is to balance population and land use.

Human occupation, commercial agriculture, and Earth's ecosystems (including woodlands, forests, and deserts, which feed far fewer people per acre than croplands) all have to be sustained. People must eat, but they also need viable ecosystems in which to live.

Predominant Land Use
- Grassland
- Forest
- Woodland
- Cropland
- Intensive cropland
- Mixed-use, including crops
- Wetland
- Desert, barren land
- Ice, cold desert, tundra

Major Crops
- Barley
- Beet sugar
- Cassava
- Cattle
- Citrus fruit
- Coffee
- Corn
- Forest products
- Grapes
- Millet
- Oats
- Potatoes
- Poultry
- Rice
- Sheep
- Soybeans
- Sugarcane
- Swine
- Tea
- Tobacco
- Wheat

Fishing and Aquaculture

Fish, a low-cost source of protein, is assuming a more central role in the human diet. Since 1950, the world's yearly catch of ocean fish has more than quadrupled. And an increase in fish-farming ponds and commercial production of seaweed, collectively called aquaculture, has spawned one of the fastest-growing areas of food production; it now accounts for one-quarter of the fish people eat. About 85 percent of aquaculture occurs in developing countries, with China (where the technique began some 4,000 years ago) accounting for two-thirds of total output. Experts project that by 2010, fish farming may overtake cattle ranching as a world food source.

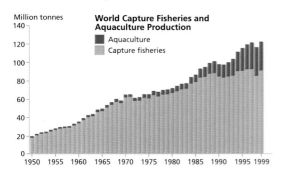

Million tonnes
World Capture Fisheries and Aquaculture Production
- Aquaculture
- Capture fisheries

1950 1955 1960 1965 1970 1975 1980 1985 1990 1995 1999

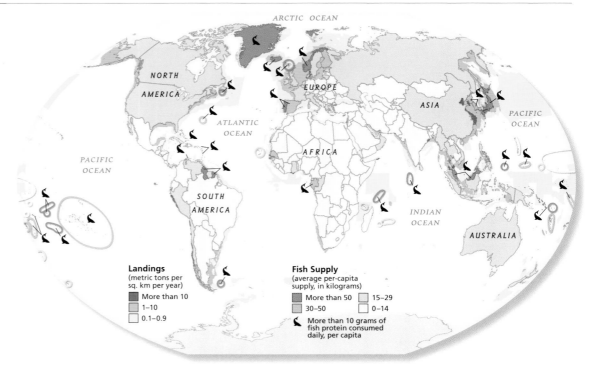

Landings
(metric tons per sq. km per year)
- More than 10
- 1–10
- 0.1–0.9

Fish Supply
(average per-capita supply, in kilograms)
- More than 50
- 30–50
- 15–29
- 0–14

More than 10 grams of fish protein consumed daily, per capita

World Agricultural Production

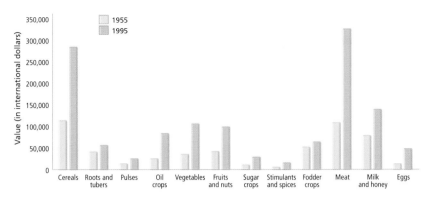

In the past few decades, world food production has more than kept pace with the burgeoning global population. Meat and cereals account for the most dramatic increases. New high-yield crops, additional irrigated land, and fertilizers have contributed to the rise in production. But there are related problems: Scientists warn that overuse of fertilizers causes nitrogen overload in Earth's waters and insufficient use, in particular in Africa, has long-term adverse consequences for food security.

Undernourishment in the Developing World

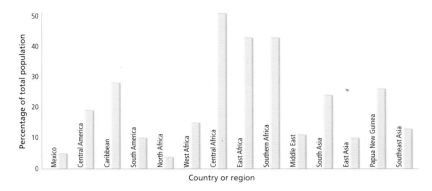

More food than ever is produced, but its distribution is uneven. Africa, in particular, is a continent of contrasts: Almost half the people in central, eastern, and southern Africa are undernourished, while a much lower percentage of people in the north and west are undernourished. The United Nations estimates that more than three-quarters of a billion people suffer from persistent malnourishment. Without access to adequate food, these populations cannot lead healthy, productive lives.

Diet

As shown at right, plants (primarily cereals) dominate the diets of people in Brazil, China, Nigeria, the Russian Federation, and Saudi Arabia, while fats, oils, and nonvegetable proteins (meat and fish) dominate diets in the United Kingdom and the United States.

World Grain Production

Humans rely on plant sources for carbohydrates, with grains (the edible parts of cereal plants) providing 80 percent of the food energy (calorie) supply. This means that the major grains—corn, wheat, and rice—are the foods that fuel humanity. Most cereal grains are grown in the Northern Hemisphere (see map), with the United States and France producing enough to be the largest exporters. Many parts of the world cannot grow cereal grains because they do not have productive farmland or the needed technology. Again and again throughout history, the actions of nations have been shaped by disparities in the supply and demand of grains, and by the knowledge that grains equal survival. Waverley Root, a food historian, once wrote: "[p]ossession of wheat or lack of it sways the destinies of nations; nor is it rare to find wheat being used as a political weapon.... [I]t is difficult to foresee any future in which it will not still exert a powerful influence on human history."

Type of Grain
- Corn
- Wheat
- Rice

Major Grain
Imports and Exports
(in thousands of
metric tons, 1999)

Exporters
United States 83,088
France 26,669
Argentina 17,346
Australia 17,209
Canada 17,047
China 7,124

Importers
Japan 23,243
Egypt 9,547
South Korea 8,115
Brazil 7,879
Iran 7,008

CORN
A staple in prehistoric Mexico and Peru, corn (or maize) is native to the New World. By the time Columbus's crew first tasted it, corn already was a hardy crop in much of North and South America.

WHEAT
Among the two oldest foods (barley is the other), wheat was important in ancient Mediterranean civilizations; today it is the most widely cultivated grain. Wheat grows best in temperate climates.

RICE
Originating in Asia many millennia ago, rice is the staple grain for about half the world's people. It is a labor-intensive plant that grows primarily in paddies (wet land) and thrives in the hot, humid tropics.

WORLD ENERGY

W e can gain a sense of the vast amount of energy our world consumes every year if we consider that it is measured in quadrillions of British thermal units. A Btu is the amount of energy needed to increase the temperature of one pound of water by one degree Fahrenheit. A quadrillion is a thousand trillions: a 1 followed by 15 zeros. Currently, global energy consumption is about 400 quadrillion Btu. North America, with less than a tenth of the world's population, consumes about a third of that energy.

The chief sources of energy are petroleum, natural gas, and coal, in that order. The United States is the leading importer of petroleum, receiving about ten million barrels of oil and refined products daily. Among oil exporters, Saudi Arabia is king, shipping up to eight million barrels a day. Over the years, concerns about keeping the oil flowing have complicated world politics. All sorts of paradoxes abound, with powerful users protecting weaker suppliers—or holding them at arm's length while purchasing their oil.

Although oil remains cheap, its "social costs" are growing. Pollution issues aside, concern remains high about the vulnerability of the developed world to choke points on the marine highway—the Suez and Panama Canals, the Straits of Hormuz and Malacca, and the Bosporus, for example.

Annual Energy Consumption
(in trillions of British thermal units)
- More than 20,000
- 10,000–20,000
- 1,000–9,999
- 100–999
- 10–99
- Less than 10

Major Coal, Natural Gas, and Oil Deposits
- Coal
- Natural gas
- Oil

- Oil transit chokepoint

Energy Production

WORLD ENERGY PRODUCTION BY TYPE

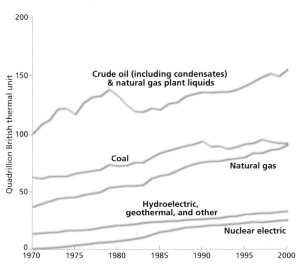

Crude oil (including condensates) & natural gas plant liquids

Coal

Natural gas

Hydroelectric, geothermal, and other

Nuclear electric

WORLD ENERGY PRODUCTION BY REGION

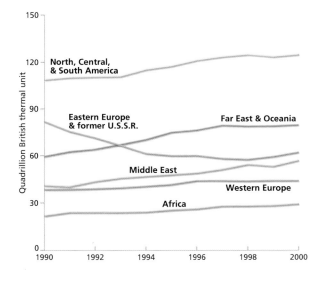

North, Central, & South America

Eastern Europe & former U.S.S.R.

Far East & Oceania

Middle East

Western Europe

Africa

Fossil Fuel Extraction

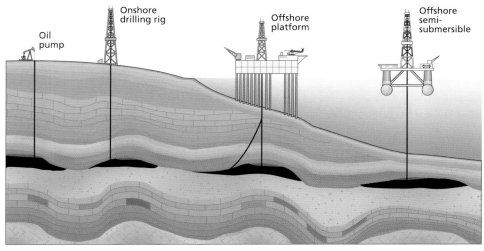

Oil pump

Onshore drilling rig

Offshore platform

Offshore semi-submersible

OIL EXTRACTION
Drilling-operation types depend on whether oil is in the ground or under the ocean. An onshore drilling rig uses a basic derrick; off-shore drilling is done with platform or semisubmersible designs (as shown above).

GAS EXTRACTION
Natural gas occurs in many of the same types of geologic structures as oil, and it is generally thought to have the same organic origins as oil. Gas-drilling operations are essentially the same as oil drilling.

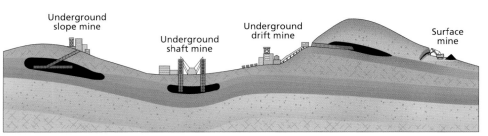

Underground slope mine

Underground shaft mine

Underground drift mine

Surface mine

COAL MINING
The mining of coal made the industrial revolution possible, and it still provides a major energy source. Once a labor-intensive process, coal mining is now heavily mechanized. An underground slope mine allows coal to be transported to the surface by a conveyor rather than an elevator. Underground drift mines and surface mines allow the easiest use of coal-cutting machinery.

Oil to Europe from Russia

Oil to Europe from Nigeria

London
Paris

Moscow

Beijing

Tokyo

Oil to Japan and South Korea from Middle East and Indonesia

Oil to Europe from Middle East

Cairo

Mumbai

Oil to India from Middle East

Oil from Middle East to Europe, North America, and Asia

Oil to Thailand from Middle East

PACIFIC OCEAN

Lagos

AFRICA

Oil to North America and Europe from Nigeria

INDIAN OCEAN

Jakarta

Oil to Australia from Middle East and Indonesia

AUSTRALIA

Sydney

ANTARCTICA

HYDROELECTRIC POWER
Hydroelectric plants in South America and the United States (Grand Coulee) are among the largest in the world. China has the greatest hydroelectric potential.

NUCLEAR POWER
Though nuclear power is on the rise, it remains problematic. Disposal of nuclear waste is the subject of considerable dispute, and fears remain widespread.

STEAM POWER
Geothermal power plants pipe steam and hot water from the ground to make electricity. The world's largest installation—The Geysers—is in California.

SOLAR POWER
California holds Earth's largest solar power arrays, one of which helps provide 160 megawatts of electric power.

WIND POWER
Harnessing the wind is the goal of the fastest growing energy technology. In the U.S., the wind industry generates enough power each year to meet the electricity needs of one million people.

Biomass, Hydroelectric, and Nuclear Energy

Burning biomass to release energy from plants does not cause a net increase in carbon dioxide; the carbon is already part of the cycle. Biomass would require extensive conversion, however. Nuclear power, in theory, does not pollute the atmosphere, but costs have increased substantially and risks may be unacceptable. Hydroelectric power is potentially a reliable energy source, but it is a limited resource.

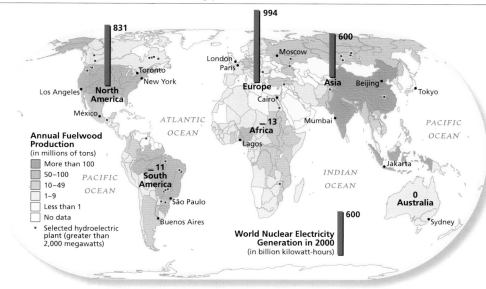

831
994
600

London
Paris
Moscow
Toronto
New York

Los Angeles
North America

México

Europe
Cairo

Asia
Beijing
Tokyo

13
Africa
Lagos

Mumbai

ATLANTIC OCEAN

PACIFIC OCEAN

11
South America

São Paulo

Buenos Aires

PACIFIC OCEAN

INDIAN OCEAN

Jakarta

0
Australia

Sydney

Annual Fuelwood Production
(in millions of tons)
- More than 100
- 50–100
- 10–49
- 1–9
- Less than 1
- No data
- Selected hydroelectric plant (greater than 2,000 megawatts)

600

World Nuclear Electricity Generation in 2000
(in billion kilowatt-hours)

Renewable Energy

Earth, wind, and sunshine are promising sources of natural, renewable energy. In many places it is possible to drill wells for a steady supply of steam, which can then be used to run turbines and generate electricity. As technology improves for harnessing wind power, certain regions of the world could become "Saudi Arabias of wind." Some areas receive enough intense sunlight to make reliance on solar power practical.

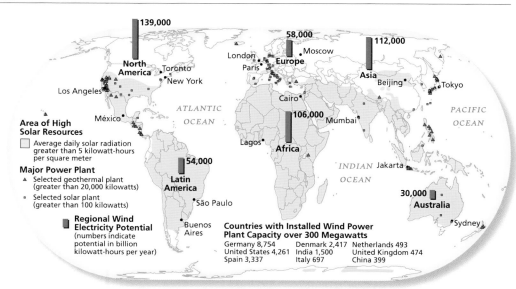

139,000
58,000
112,000

London
Paris
Moscow

North America
Toronto
New York

Los Angeles

Europe

Asia
Beijing
Tokyo

Cairo

México

ATLANTIC OCEAN

PACIFIC OCEAN

Lagos
Africa
106,000

Mumbai

54,000
Latin America

São Paulo

Buenos Aires

INDIAN OCEAN
Jakarta

30,000
Australia

Sydney

Area of High Solar Resources
- Average daily solar radiation greater than 5 kilowatt-hours per square meter

Major Power Plant
- ▲ Selected geothermal plant (greater than 20,000 kilowatts)
- ■ Selected solar plant (greater than 100 kilowatts)

Regional Wind Electricity Potential
(numbers indicate potential in billion kilowatt-hours per year)

Countries with Installed Wind Power Plant Capacity over 300 Megawatts

Germany 8,754	Denmark 2,417	Netherlands 493
United States 4,261	India 1,500	United Kingdom 474
Spain 3,337	Italy 697	China 399

WORLD MINERALS

The spatial pattern of world mineral production is the result of several factors: geology, climate, economic systems, and social preferences. This pattern can be seen on the map at right, which locates major production and processing sites for various mineral commodities (see below for profiles on 18 important minerals).

Plate movements, volcanism, and sedimentation are geologic processes that form valuable concentrations of minerals. The same geologic forces that formed the Andes, for example, are responsible for the porphyry copper deposits along South America's Pacific coast. Other processes concentrate copper in sedimentary basins and in volcanic arcs. Climatic factors, such as the tropical conditions that contribute to bauxite formation, are also important.

Mineral consumption by industries is positively correlated with income and differs greatly among countries. Developed nations use larger volumes of materials and a wider variety of mineral commodities than less developed countries. In developed nations, annual copper use is typically 5 to 10 kilograms per person; for less developed ones, usage is only a few kilograms per person. Recent economic growth has led to greater demand for many mineral resources. Meeting that need without causing harm to the environment will be one of the major challenges for societies in the 21st century.

World Mineral Production

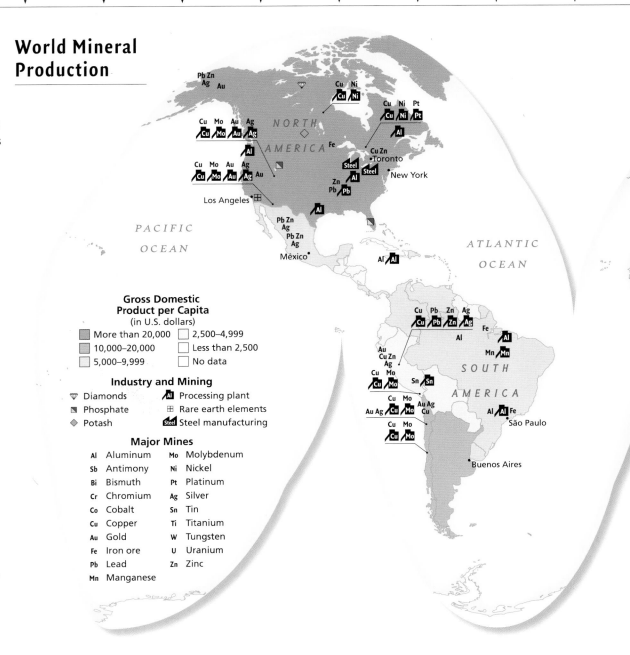

Gross Domestic Product per Capita
(in U.S. dollars)
- More than 20,000
- 10,000–20,000
- 5,000–9,999
- 2,500–4,999
- Less than 2,500
- No data

Industry and Mining
- ▽ Diamonds
- ◩ Phosphate
- ◇ Potash
- Ⓐl Processing plant
- ⊞ Rare earth elements
- Steel Steel manufacturing

Major Mines

Al	Aluminum	Mo	Molybdenum
Sb	Antimony	Ni	Nickel
Bi	Bismuth	Pt	Platinum
Cr	Chromium	Ag	Silver
Co	Cobalt	Sn	Tin
Cu	Copper	Ti	Titanium
Au	Gold	W	Tungsten
Fe	Iron ore	U	Uranium
Pb	Lead	Zn	Zinc
Mn	Manganese		

 Aluminum (Bauxite, Alumina, Aluminum)—Bauxite is the principal ore of aluminum. World production of this ore was 137 million tons in 2001. Australia was the largest bauxite producer (54 million tons) that year, followed by Guinea (15 million tons), Brazil (14 million tons), and Jamaica (13 million). Alumina, an intermediate product, is made by using the Bayer process to refine bauxite; it is then smelted, using the Hall-Heroult process, to make aluminum metal. The United States has the largest smelting capacity (4.3 million tons), followed by Russia (3.2 million tons), China (2.6 million tons), and Canada (2.6 million tons). Australia and Brazil also have significant aluminum smelting capacities. In 2001, the world production of aluminum was estimated at 23.4 million tons.

 Chromium—Chromite ($FeCr_2O_4$) is the principal ore mineral of chromium. In 2001, world chromium production was estimated at more than 12 million tons. South Africa has long been the largest producer on the planet; in 2001, it mined 5.4 million tons of contained chromium. Kazakhstan produced an additional 2.3 million tons that year. The main use of chromium is in the manufacture of stainless and heat-resistant steels. This substance is also used in the production of chromium chemicals and in acid-resistant refractories.

Copper—Chalcopyrite (Cu,FeS_2) is the principal ore of copper. In 2001, world mine production of copper was estimated at 13.2 million tons. Chile was the leading producer (4.7 million tons) that year, followed by the U.S. (1.3 million tons) and Indonesia (1.1 million tons). Other major producers include Australia, Canada, China, Peru, Kazakhstan, Russia, and Poland. Copper is prized, in particular, for its ability to conduct electrical current.

 Diamond (gem and industrial)—Diamonds are used both as gems and as materials to increase the hardness of cutting tools. The map locates the major producers of natural gems and industrial diamonds. Diamonds can also be produced synthetically, and about 90 percent of industrial diamonds are made this way. The world production of gem diamonds was estimated at 60.4 million carats in 2001. Botswana (16 million carats) was the largest producer, followed by Australia (13 million carats), Russia (11.6 million carats), South Africa (4.8 million carats), Angola (4.4 million carats), and the Congo (3.5 million carats).

 Gold—Native gold or electrum, an alloy with silver, are the common forms. Historically, gold was used as money or as a backup for paper money. Today, no major country backs its paper currency with gold, but private investors may hold gold as a hedge against economic uncertainty. Gold is also used in jewelry, as a dental material, and in electronic equipment. South Africa was the largest producer of mined gold in 2001 (400 metric tons), followed by the U.S. (350 metric tons), Australia (290 metric tons), and China (185 metric tons). Total world production that year was estimated at 2,530 tons.

 Iron Ore and Steel—Iron occurs in a wide variety of oxide (magnetite), sulfide (pyrite), carbonate (siderite), and silicate minerals found in sedimentary rock. In 2001, world production was one billion tons. The largest producers were China (220 million tons), Brazil (200 million tons), and Australia (160 million tons). Steel is produced by melting pig iron, an intermediate product of iron, in a furnace in the presence of oxygen and any alloying metals. In 2001, world crude steel production was 828 million tons. The European Union countries (157 million tons), China (135 million tons), and Japan (104 million tons) were the main producers.

 Lead—Galena (PbS) is the principal ore mineral of lead. In 2001, world mine production of lead was 3 million tons. Australia was the largest producer (700,000 tons), followed by China (560,000 tons) and the U.S. (420,000 tons). Peru and Mexico were also significant producers. Because of lead's toxicity the number of lead-containing products has been reduced in recent years, and automobile batteries with lead are now recycled. This effort has reduced the consumption of primary, or new lead, which is also used in solder, in television glass, and in the radiation shields for X-ray equipment.

 Manganese—This mineral originally was used as an additive to remove impurities from steel. Later it was employed as an alloying element. Manganese is also used in dry-cell batteries, as an additive in fertilizers and animal feed, and as a colorant for brick. World production was 7.26 million tons in 2001. South Africa (1.45 million tons) was the largest producer. Ukraine, Gabon, Brazil, China, and Australia each produced more than 800,000 tons.

 Nickel—Two very different types of deposits are the sources for nickel. In sulfide deposits found in ultramafic rock complexes, nickel occurs primarily in the mineral pentlandite (($Fe, Ni)_9S_8$). It is also produced from oxide and silicate minerals in laterite deposits, thick soils that form over ultramafic rock in tropical environments. World mine production was 1.26 million tons in 2001. Russia, the leading producer (265,000 tons), and Canada, in third place (183,000 tons), produce nickel from sulfide deposits. Australia, the second largest producer (184,000 tons), mines both types. New Caledonia and Indonesia, which rank fourth and fifth, respectively, focus only on laterite deposits. Nickel is used to make stainless steel and in electroplating.

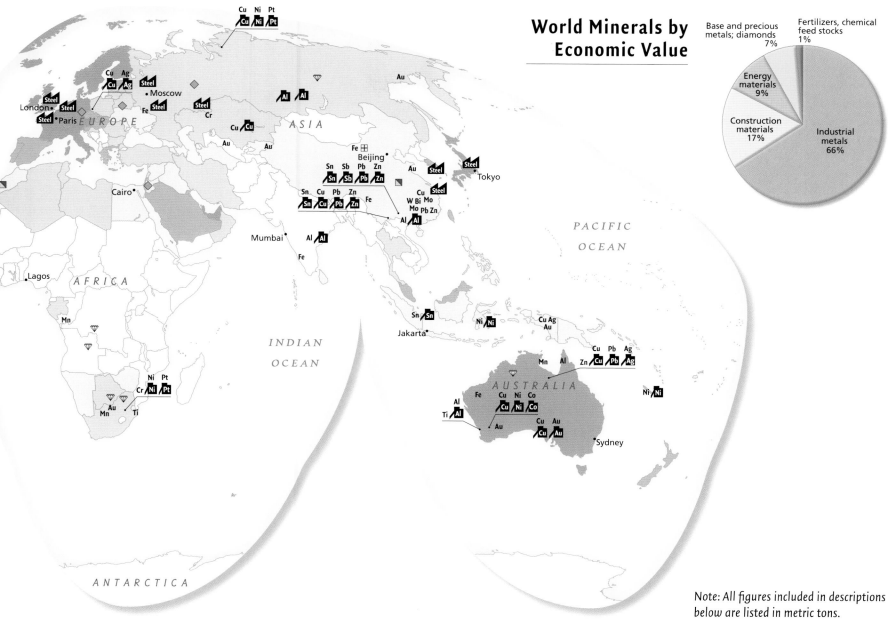

Cu Ni Pt

Cu Ag
Moscow
London Steel Steel
Steel Paris EUROPE
Fe Steel
Cairo

AFRICA

Lagos

Mn

INDIAN
OCEAN

ASIA
Al Al
Cr
Cu Cu
Au Au
Fe ⊞
Beijing
Sn Sb Pb Zn
Sn Cu Pb Zn Fe
W Bi Mo
Mo Pb Zn
Al Al
Mumbai Al Al
Fe
Au Steel
Steel Tokyo
Cu Steel

PACIFIC
OCEAN

Sn Sn
Jakarta
Ni Ni
Cu Ag
Au

Mn Al Cu Pb Ag
Zn Cu Pb Ag

AUSTRALIA
Fe Cu Ni Co
Cu Ni Co
Al
Ti Al
Au
Cu Au
Cu Au
Sydney

Ni Ni

Ni Pt
Cr Ni Pt
Au
Mn Ti

ANTARCTICA

World Minerals by Economic Value

Base and precious
metals; diamonds
7%

Fertilizers, chemical
feed stocks
1%

Energy
materials
9%

Construction
materials
17%

Industrial
metals
66%

Note: All figures included in descriptions
below are listed in metric tons.

Phosphate Rock—This substance is needed to make phosphoric acid and superphosphoric acid, which are used in the production of certain fertilizers. In 2001, the world production of phosphate rock was 128 million tons. The United States was the leading producer (34 million tons). Morocco and Western Sahara together accounted for 22 million tons; China (20 million tons) was the third largest producer in 2001. Russia and Tunisia also produce significant quantities of phosphate rock.

Platinum-Group Metals (Pt, Pd, Ru, Rh, Ir, Os)—These substances are used in jewelry; in catalytic converters, which clean the exhaust from cars; and in chemotherapy for cancer. World mine production of platinum and palladium was 163 tons and 177 tons, respectively, in 2001. South Africa was the leading producer of platinum (122 tons), followed by Russia (29 tons). Russia produced 90 tons of palladium, while South Africa mined 59 tons of this material. Other producers of platinum-group metals are the United States and Canada.

Potash—This term is the industrial name for a group of water-soluble salts that contain potassium. The main sources are certain evaporite deposits that include mixtures of the minerals halite ($NaCl$), sylvite (KCl), and carnallite ($KMg Cl_3 \cdot 6H_2O$); other potassium-, magnesium-, and bromine-bearing minerals; and saline brines. Most potash is used in fertilizer, while the remainder is employed in the production of potassium chemicals. Canada, which produced 8.8 million tons of potash in 2001, is the largest producer in the world, followed by Russia (4.4 million tons), Belarus (3.5 million tons), and Germany (3.34 million tons). Israel and Jordan continue to produce significant amounts of potash from the Dead Sea.

Rare Earths—This group of metals ranges from lanthanum to lutetium in the periodic table of elements. Rare earth metals are used in the making of a wide variety of products, including chemical catalysts for petroleum refining, rechargeable batteries, phosphors for TV and computer screens, and superalloys. World mine production of rare earth oxides was 85,500 tons in 2001. China, which mined 75,000 tons of rare earth oxides, was the largest producer that year. The United States was second, with 5,000 tons.

Silver—This substance has the highest electrical conductivity of all elements. It occurs in pure form; mixed with native gold in electrum; as a sulfide (argentite, Ag_2S); in a group of complex copper- lead- antimony- and arsenic-bearing minerals, such as tetrahedrite (($Cu,Fe, Zn, Ag)_{12}Sb_4S_{13}$); and as a trace constituent in galena. Silver is used in photographic materials, electronic products, jewelry, tableware, and coinage. In 2001, world mine production was 18,300 tons. Mexico, which mined 2,600 tons of silver, was the largest producer; it was followed by Peru (2,500 tons) and Australia (2,100 tons).

Tin—The most common use of tin is as a coating to prevent oxidation of a covered metal, such as steel in "tin cans." When alloyed with other metals, tin makes solder, pewter, and bronze. Window glass is manufactured by floating molten glass on molten tin. Organo-tin chemicals are used as pesticides, fungicides, and wood preservatives. The major ore mineral of tin is cassiterite (SnO_2). China, which mined 95,000 tons in 2001, was the world's largest producer that year. Indonesia (50,000 tons) and Peru (38,000 tons) were the second and third largest producers, respectively. World production in 2001 was 242,000 tons.

Titanium—About 95 percent of titanium is consumed as titanium oxide; the rest is processed to make titanium metal or sponge. Because titanium metal is light and has high strength, it is used in aircraft bodies and submarine hulls. The titanium-bearing minerals ilmenite ($FeTiO_3$) and rutile (TiO_2), which are common components in beach and dune sands, are processed into TiO_2 pigment used in paints. Japan, Russia, and the U.S. were among the largest makers of titanium sponge in 2001. Australia (1.2 million tons) and South Africa (1.1 million tons) were the largest producers of titanium-bearing mineral concentrates that year.

Tungsten—The main use of tungsten is in tungsten-carbide cutting tools. Because of its high melting point, this substance is added to certain steels to give them strength at high temperatures. It is also used in lightbulb filaments. Tungsten mainly occurs in two types of deposits—skarns that form in limestone adjacent to certain granites, and veins that form within and above certain granites. Scheelite ($CaWO_4$), or calcium tungstate, is the main ore mineral in skarn deposits, and wolframite (($Fe,Mn)WO_4$), an iron- and manganese-bearing tungstate, is the main ore mineral in vein deposits. In 2001, China produced 37,000 tons of tungsten, followed by Russia, with 3,600 tons. World production was 44,600 tons.

Zinc—The largest use of zinc is as a coating for steel; galvanized steel resists corrosion. Zinc is also used to make brass, solder, and batteries, and it is added to soil, rubber, and cosmetics. Sphalerite (ZnS), or zinc sulfide, is the principal ore mineral. In 2001, world mine production was 8.9 million tons. The largest producers were China (1.7 million tons), Australia (1.5 million tons), and Peru (1.1 million tons). Canada (950,000 tons) and the U.S. (830,000 tons) were also significant producers.

WORLD HEALTH AND EDUCATION

As the global economy began to recover in the 1990s, health and literacy rates began to improve as well, not only in the more industrialized nations but also in many developing nations. This is because health and literacy are intricately tied to economic conditions. Better economies and higher incomes mean that more people have access to at least basic health care, clean water, and sanitation facilities; more food is produced, and more people can buy it; and educational resources are more widely available.

On the health care front, new drugs and vaccines have given the world new tools for the control and prevention of communicable diseases. More children are vaccinated for diseases that have been among the most common causes of early death: measles, polio, tuberculosis, diptheria, pertussis, and neonatal tetanus, to name several.

In contrast to these gains, however, disparities between the wealthy and poor have continued to grow, with extreme poverty still a fact of life—or death. People in poverty suffer more often from disease, malnutrition, substance abuse, and family disintegration. They are less likely to avail themselves of educational opportunities, even if such opportunities are available. They endure more cases of mental illness (worldwide, one in four families has at least one member with a behavioral or mental health disorder). And they are more likely to die relatively young. Some of the poorest nations have actually seen declines in life expectancy (worldwide, two-fifths of all deaths are still premature).

In most countries, life expectancies have increased. But longer life spans can mean more cases of heart disease, cancer, diabetes, and other age-related ailments. Lifestyle-related diseases arising from smoking, obesity, and alcohol abuse are also serious problems. The emergence of HIV/AIDS and the growth of antibiotic-resistant infections have brought more health worries and more challenges for health care recipients and providers. Other health threats—the highly fatal Ebola virus, the hantavirus, food- and waterborne cryptosporidium, and various strains of *E. coli*—present additional challenges. Just in the past two decades, 29 new diseases have been identified.

Thanks to well-funded research programs and improved access to health care, many diseases have been conquered or held in check; still, serious threats exist and the poor remain the most vulnerable. Thanks to greater support for public schools in nearly every country, more children are learning to read and write; still, illiteracy remains a problem in many parts of the world. These are conditions with far-reaching consequences. Health and education are critical to a person's ability to find employment, to participate in government and society, and to enjoy life to the fullest.

Expenditures on Health

PUBLIC EXPENDITURE ON HEALTH AS A PERCENTAGE OF GROSS DOMESTIC PRODUCT

Countries with the **HIGHEST** spending:	Countries with the **LOWEST** spending:
1. United States	1. Myanmar
2. Lebanon	2. Afghanistan
3. Zimbabwe	3. Dem. Republic of the Congo
4. Andorra	4. Somalia
5. Switzerland	5. Nigeria
6. Fed. States of Micronesia	6. Burundi
7. Germany	7. Madagascar
8. Uruguay	8. Tajikistan
9. Marshall Islands	9. Central African Republic
10. Canada	10. Liberia

Income Levels: Indicators of Health and Literacy

Personal Income
- High income
- Upper middle income
- Lower middle income
- Low income

Access to Safe Drinking Water

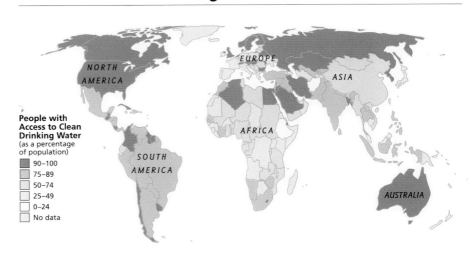

People with Access to Clean Drinking Water
(as a percentage of population)
- 90–100
- 75–89
- 50–74
- 25–49
- 0–24
- No data

Access to Sanitation Services

People with Access to Sanitation Services
(as a percentage of population)
- 90–100
- 75–89
- 50–74
- 25–49
- 0–24
- No data

Number of Physicians per 100,000 Population

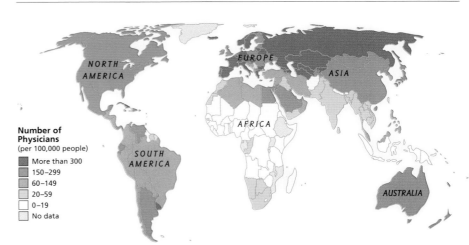

Number of Physicians
(per 100,000 people)
- More than 300
- 150–299
- 60–149
- 20–59
- 0–19
- No data

Infant Mortality

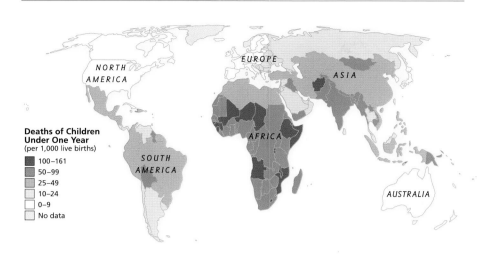

Deaths of Children Under One Year
(per 1,000 live births)
- 100–161
- 50–99
- 25–49
- 10–24
- 0–9
- No data

AIDS

AIDS
(percentage of adults, ages 15–45, living with AIDS)
- 20–36
- 10–19
- 5–9
- 2–4
- 0–1
- No data

Malaria

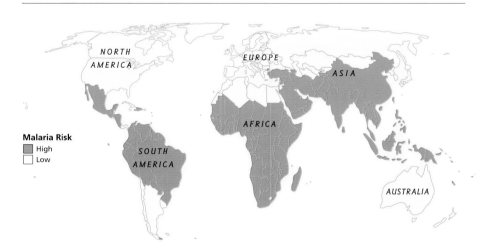

Malaria Risk
- High
- Low

Tuberculosis

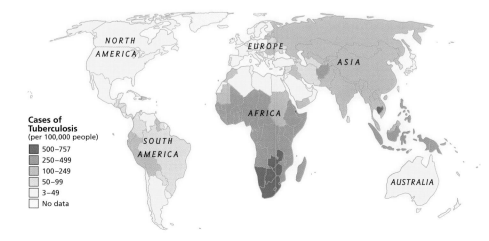

Cases of Tuberculosis
(per 100,000 people)
- 500–757
- 250–499
- 100–249
- 50–99
- 3–49
- No data

Life Expectancy

Worldwide, average life expectancy has gained four months every year since 1970. In the last part of the 20th century, however, it declined in some areas, especially in sub-Saharan Africa, where AIDS has overcome health gains, and in the former U.S.S.R., where economic depression has brought hardship.

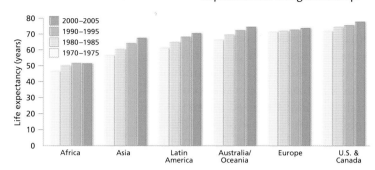

Causes of Death

Deaths due to infectious and parasitic diseases claim larger proportions of populations in the developing world than in the more industrialized nations. Chronic, non-communicable ailments such as heart disease, cancer, and diabetes are expected to increase in developing countries as a result of lifestyle changes related to economic growth. These changes include increased levels of smoking and obesity.

Causes of Death, Worldwide

- Other
- Diabetes mellitus
- Neuropsychiatric disorders
- Intentional injuries
- Digestive diseases
- Perinatal conditions
- Unintentional injuries
- Noncommunicable respiratory diseases
- Respiratory infections
- Cancers
- Infectious & parasitic diseases
- Cardiovascular diseases

Literacy

LITERACY RATES

Countries with the **HIGHEST** literacy rates:

1.	Andorra	100%
2.	Australia	100%
3.	Denmark	100%
4.	Estonia	100%
5.	Finland	100%
6.	Latvia	100%
7.	Liechtenstein	100%
8.	Luxembourg	100%
9.	Norway	100%
10.	Czech Republic	100%

Countries with the **LOWEST** literacy rates:

1.	Niger	14%
2.	Burkina Faso	19%
3.	Somalia	24%
4.	Eritrea	25%
5.	Nepal	28%
6.	Mali	31%
7.	Sierra Leone	31%
8.	Afghanistan	32%
9.	Senegal	33%
10.	Cambodia	35%

Expenditures on Education

PUBLIC EXPENDITURE ON EDUCATION AS A PERCENTAGE OF GDP PER CAPITA

Countries with the **HIGHEST** spending:

1.	Bhutan	30%
2.	Sweden	29%
3.	Ukraine	27%
4.	Ethiopia	25%
5.	Canada	24%
6.	Denmark	24%
7.	Finland	24%
8.	Moldova	24%
9.	Norway	23%
10.	Switzerland	23%

Countries with the **LOWEST** spending:

1.	Tajikistan	3%
2.	Myanmar	3%
3.	Kyrgyzstan	3%
4.	Armenia	3%
5.	Kazakhstan	4%
6.	Azerbaijan	4%
7.	Dominican Rep.	4%
8.	Madagascar	4%
9.	Bangladesh	5%
10.	Peru	5%

Most environmental damage is due to human activity. Some harmful actions are inadvertent—the release, for example, of chlorofluorocarbons (CFCs), once thought to be inert gases, into the atmosphere. Others are deliberate and include such acts as the disposal of sewage into rivers.

Among the root causes of human-induced damage are excessive consumption (mainly in industrialized countries) and rapid population growth (primarily in the developing nations). So, even though scientists may develop products and technologies that have no adverse effects on the environment, their efforts will be muted if both population and consumption continue to increase worldwide.

Socioeconomic and environmental indicators can reveal much about long-term trends; unfortunately, such data are not collected routinely in many countries. With respect to urban environmental quality, suitable indicators would include electricity consumption, numbers of automobiles, and rates of land conversion from rural to urban. The rapid conversion of countryside to built-up areas during the last 25 to 50 years is a strong indicator that change is occurring at an ever quickening pace.

Many types of environmental stress are interrelated and may have far-reaching consequences. Global warming, for one, will likely increase water scarcity, desertification, deforestation, and coastal flooding (due to rising sea level)—all of which can have a significant impact on human populations.

Legend:
- Areas most affected by acid rain
- Current tropical forest
- Cleared tropical forest
- Current temperate forest
- Cleared temperate forest
- Areas at highest risk of desertification
- Frequent pollution from shipping
- ✳ Major industrial accident
- ➡ Major oil spill
- ✳ Major oil rig explosion

Global Climate Change

The world's climate is constantly changing—over decades, centuries, and millennia. Currently, several lines of reasoning support the idea that humans are likely to live in a much warmer world before the end of this century. Atmospheric concentrations of carbon dioxide and other "greenhouse gases" are now well above historical levels, and simulation models predict that these gases will result in warming of the lower atmosphere (particularly in polar regions) but cooling of the stratosphere. Experimental evidence supports these predictions. Indeed, throughout the last decade the globally averaged annual surface temperature was higher than the hundred-year mean. Model simulations of the impacts of this warming are so alarming that most scientists and many policy people believe that immediate action must be taken to slow the changes.

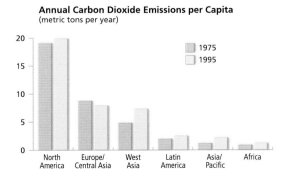

Annual Carbon Dioxide Emissions per Capita
(metric tons per year)

■ 1975
□ 1995

North America / Europe/Central Asia / West Asia / Latin America / Asia/Pacific / Africa

Depletion of the Ozone Layer

The ozone layer in the stratosphere has long shielded the biosphere from harmful solar ultraviolet radiation. Since the 1970s, however, the layer has been thinning over Antarctica—and more recently elsewhere. If the process continues, there will be significant effects on human health, including more cases of skin cancer and eye cataracts, and on biological systems. Fortunately, scientific understanding of the phenomenon came rather quickly.

Beginning in the 1950s, increasing amounts of CFCs (and other gases with similar properties) were released into the atmosphere. CFCs are chemically inert in the lower atmosphere but decompose in the stratosphere, subsequently destroying ozone. This understanding provided the basis for successful United Nations actions (Vienna Convention, 1985; Montreal Protocol, 1987) to phase out these gases.

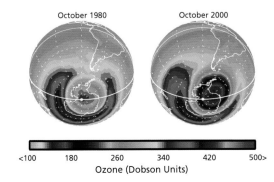

October 1980   October 2000

<100   180   260   340   420   500>
Ozone (Dobson Units)

Pollution

People know that water is not always pure and that beaches may be closed to bathers due to raw sewage. A worst-case example is the Minamata, Japan, disaster of the 1950s. More than a hundred people died and thousands were paralyzed after they ate fish containing mercury discharged from a local factory. Examples of water and soil pollution also include the contamination of groundwater, salinization of irrigated lands in semiarid regions, and the so-called chemical time bomb issue, where accumulated toxins are suddenly mobilized following a change in external conditions. Preventing and mitigating such problems requires the modernization of industrial plants, additional staff training, a better understanding of the problems, the development of more effective policies, and greater public support.

Urban air quality remains a serious problem, particularly in developing countries. In some developed countries, successful control measures have improved air quality over the past 50 years; in others, trends have actually reversed, with brown haze often hanging over metropolitan areas.

Solid and hazardous waste disposal is a universal urban problem, and the issue is on many political agendas. In the world's poorest countries, "garbage pickers" (usually women and children) are symbols of abject poverty. In North America, toxic wastes are frequently transported long distances. But transport introduces the risk of highway and rail accidents, causing serious local contamination.

Water Scarcity

Shortages of drinking water are increasing in many parts of the world, and studies indicate that by the year 2025, one billion people in northern China, Afghanistan, Pakistan, Iraq, Egypt, Tunisia, and other areas will face "absolute drinking water scarcity." But water is also needed by industry and agriculture, in hydroelectric-power production, and for transport. With increasing population, industrialization, and global warming, the situation can only worsen.

Water scarcity has already become a major brake on development in many countries, including Poland, Singapore, and parts of North America. In countries where artesian wells are pumping groundwater more rapidly than it can be replaced, water is actually being mined. In river basins where water is shared by several jurisdictions, social tensions will increase. This is particularly so in the Middle East, North Africa, and East Africa, where the availability of fresh water is less than 1,300 cubic yards (1,000 cu m) per capita per annum; water-rich countries such as Iceland, New Zealand, and Canada enjoy more than a hundred times as much.

Irrigation can be a particularly wasteful use of water. Some citrus-growing nations, for example, are exporting not only fruit but also so-called virtual water, which includes the water inside the fruit as well as the wasted irrigation water that drains away from the orchards. Many individuals and organizations believe that water scarcity is the major environmental issue of the 21st century.

Soil Degradation and Desertification

Deserts exist where rainfall is too little and too erratic to support life except in a few favored localities. Even in these "oases," occasional sandstorms may inhibit agricultural activity. In semiarid zones, lands can easily become degraded or desert-like if they are overused or subject to long or frequent drought. The Sahel of North Africa faced this situation in the 1970s and early 1980s, but rainfall subsequently returned to normal, and some of the land recovered.

Often, an extended drought over a wide area can trigger desertification if the land has already been degraded by human actions. Causes of degradation include overgrazing, overcultivation, deforestation, soil erosion, overconsumption of groundwater, and the salinization/waterlogging of irrigated lands.

An emerging issue is the effect of climate warming on desertification. Warming will probably lead to more drought in more parts of the world. Glaciers would begin to disappear, and the meltwater flowing through semiarid downstream areas would diminish.

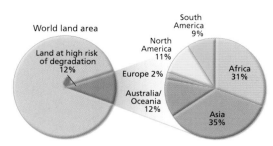

Deforestation

Widespread deforestation in the wet tropics is largely the result of short-term and unsustainable uses. In Mexico, Brazil, and Peru, only 30, 42, and 45 percent (respectively) of the total land still has a closed forest cover. But the situation is improving thanks to efforts by the FAO, UNEP, UNESCO, WWF/IUCN, and other international bodies. Venezuela enjoys a very high level of forest protection (63 percent). By comparison, Russia protects just 2 percent of its forests.

The loss of forests has contributed to atmospheric build-up of carbon dioxide (a greenhouse gas), changes in rainfall patterns (in Brazil at least), soil erosion, and soil nutrient losses. Deforestation in the wet tropics, where more than half of the world's species live, is the main cause of biodiversity loss.

In contrast to the tropics, the forest cover in the temperate zones has increased slightly in the last 50 years because of the adoption of conservation practices and because abandoned farmland has been replaced by forest.

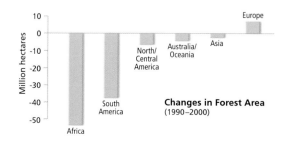

In recent years, environmental groups and world organizations have identified certain sites and land areas whose value is so great, and status is so critical, that they require special protection.

This protection takes various forms. UNESCO's World Heritage Committee has identified more than 700 sites that are of great cultural or natural value. Some are very famous: Stonehenge, the Great Wall of China, the Taj Mahal, the Great Barrier Reef, and the Grand Canyon, for example. Others are monuments to important and sometimes tragic chapters in history: Auschwitz in Poland and the Senegalese island of Gorée, which was for 400 years the largest slaving station on the African coast. Some sites are threatened natural features of great value: the Danube Delta in Romania, for instance, and Lake Baikal in Russia.

Conservationists have identified 25 world "hotspots" (see World Biodiversity, pp. 40-41) that make up less than 2 percent of Earth's lands but are the only remaining habitats for 44 percent of all plant species and 35 percent of all nonfish vertebrates. About half these sites are now designated protected areas.

Though "protected areas" vary greatly in their objectives, the extent to which they are integrated into the wider landscape, and the effectiveness with which they are managed, they provide powerful evidence of a nation's commitment to conservation.

World Heritage Sites
- Cultural
- Natural
- Mixed site (site with both cultural and natural value)

Protected Areas

An array of overlapping conventions designed to preserve everything from wetlands, seas, and wilderness to birds and biogenetic reserves protects approximately 9 percent of Earth's land area. In contrast, less than one percent of the total ocean area is protected.

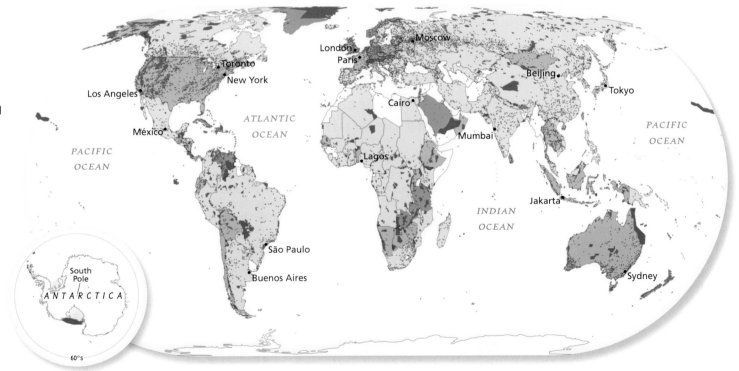

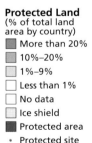

Protected Land
(% of total land area by country)
- More than 20%
- 10%–20%
- 1%–9%
- Less than 1%
- No data
- Ice shield
- Protected area
- Protected site

COUNTRIES WITH HIGHEST % PROTECTED AREA

Country (with total area >11,000 sq. mi.)	Percentage of land protected	GDP per capita (U.S. $)	Pop. density (sq. mi.)
Venezuela	60.8	6,200	70
Denmark	44.4	25,500	322
Saudi Arabia	42.1	10,500	25
Dominican Republic	31.7	5,700	456
Zambia	29.8	880	34
Switzerland	24.5	28,600	453
Tanzania	23.1	710	99
New Zealand	23.1	17,700	37
Bhutan	22.4	1,100	50
Norway	22.3	27,700	36

COUNTRIES WITH LOWEST % PROTECTED AREA

Country (with total area >11,000 sq. mi.)	Percentage of land protected	GDP per capita (U.S. $)	Pop. density (sq. mi.)
Iraq	0.0	2,500	139
United Arab Emirates	0.0	22,800	103
Yemen	0.0	820	88
Syria	0.1	3,100	231
Libya	0.1	8,900	8
Lesotho	0.2	2,400	186
Uruguay	0.3	9,300	49
Tunisia	0.3	6,500	154
Guyana	0.3	4,800	8
Afghanistan	0.3	800	106

PROTECTED AREAS BY REGION

Continent or region	Square miles protected	As percentage of total land area
North America	1,223,184	14.0
South America	642,373	9.3
Europe	1,100,461	11.2
Africa	805,420	6.8
Asia	969,127	7.8
Australia/Oceania	449,253	14.4
Antarctica	1,149	0.02
World	**5,190,969**	**8.9**

Endemism

Regional Share of Plant Endemism

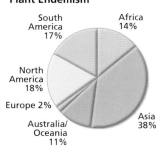

- South America 17%
- Africa 14%
- North America 18%
- Europe 2%
- Australia/Oceania 11%
- Asia 38%

Endemism—the presence of species found nowhere else—is a key criterion for determining conservation priorities, as areas with high levels of endemism are the most vulnerable to biodiversity loss. The highest levels of endemism occur on oceanic islands and in montane regions.

Ouratea dependens is one of thousands of plants unique to Madagascar.

The World Heritage Site System

NATURAL HERITAGE SITE
Canada's Tatshenshini-Alsek Provincial Wilderness holds the largest nonpolar ice cap and hundreds of valley glaciers; it is the last major stronghold for North America's grizzly bears. The park designation averted what would have been an enormous open-pit mine.

CULTURAL HERITAGE SITE
Site of some of the most important monuments of ancient Greece, the Acropolis illustrates the civilizations, myths, and religions that flourished there for a period of over 1,000 years. Europe claims about half of the world's cultural heritage sites, with over 300.

MIXED HERITAGE SITE
The town of Ohrid, on the shores of Lake Ohrid in the former Yugoslav Republic of Macedonia, exemplifies a mixed heritage site. The ten-million-year-old lake may be the oldest in Europe, and the town is one of the continent's oldest continuously inhabited sites.

The World Heritage List was established under the terms of the 1972 UNESCO "Convention Concerning the Protection of the World Cultural and Natural Heritage." The first 12 World Heritage Sites were named in 1978; among them were L'Anse aux Meadows in Canada, the site of the first Viking settlement in North America; the Galápagos Islands; the cathedral of Aachen, Germany; the historic city center of Cracow, Poland; the island of Gorée off Senegal; and Mesa Verde and Yellowstone National Parks in the United States.

New sites are added annually. In December 2001, the list comprised 721 sites, with 554 cultural, 144 natural, and 23 mixed sites, located in 124 countries, all party to the Convention. On average, 30 newly designated sites are added to the list each year, but 2000 must have been considered an auspicious time for listings: 61 sites were added that year, the largest number ever.

MOST VISITED NATURAL HERITAGE SITES

Name	Size of site (sq. mi.)	Country	Visitors per year
Canadian Rocky Mountain Parks	8,907	Canada	9,549,798
Great Smoky Mountains National Park	805	United States	9,457,323
Grand Canyon National Park	1,880	United States	4,219,726
Yosemite National Park	1,176	United States	3,453,345
Olympic National Park	1,425	United States	3,401,245
Yellowstone National Park	3,428	United States	2,841,290
Wet Tropics of Queensland	3,453	Australia	2,840,000
Great Barrier Reef	134,633	Australia	2,162,896
Glacier/Waterton National Park	1,767	U.S./Canada	2,135,172

TECHNOLOGY AND GLOBALIZATION

For better or worse, everyone on Earth is now your neighbor to a certain degree. This new reality is the culmination of a globalization process that began in the 19th century with the telegraph, which in recent years has been dubbed the "Victorian Internet." Just over 30 years after the invention of this device, Samuel F. B. Morse transmitted a special greeting to every telegraphic station in the United States. A few years later, *Scientific American* speculated that the telegraph would unite the world in peace.

Communication may not always lead to peace, but it does promote globalization. Information is traveling faster than ever before: In 2001, more data was sent over a cable in one second than was carried over the entire Internet in one month in 1997. A trillion bits of information can now be sent cross-country for 12 cents; in 1970 the cost would have been 150,000 dollars.

The flow of information is almost impossible to restrict. Work is under way to make the Internet available by wireless connection. For villages without phone lines or electric power, solar power could be the key to communication; for illiterate peoples, text-to-speech software could be used. Enormous technological strides have been made, but much remains to be done: Even now, hundreds of millions of people have never even made a phone call.

Centers of Technological Innovation

Recent studies have attempted to measure technological achievement and innovation in geographic terms.

The Technological Achievement Index focuses on (1) creation of technology (patents per capita and receipt of royalty and licensing fees), (2) spread of new innovations (the number of Internet hosts and technology exports), (3) spread of older innovations (use of telephones and electricity per capita), and (4) human skills (schooling).

The Technological Innovation score, on the other hand, singles out the most important locations in the new digital geography. Each hub of innovation is rated from 1 to 4 in these four areas: (1) local universities and research centers that can train workers and develop technologies, (2) companies that provide expertise and economic stability, (3) widespread entrepreneurial drive, and (4) availability of venture capital.

Technological Achievement Index
(from UNDP Human Development Report, 2001)
- Above 0.5
- .35–0.5
- 0.2–.34
- Below 0.2
- No data

Technological Innovation Score
(from *Wired* magazine, 2000)
- 16 (maximum)
- 4 (minimum)

16 Silicon Valley, U.S.	12 Albuquerque, U.S.
15 Boston, U.S.	12 Montréal, Canada
15 Stockholm-Kista, Sweden	12 Seattle, U.S.
15 Israel	12 Cambridge, U.K.
14 Raleigh-Durham-Chapel Hill, U.S.	12 Dublin, Ireland
14 London, U.K.	11 Los Angeles, U.S.
14 Helsinki, Finland	11 Malmö, Sweden & Copenhagen, Denmark
13 Austin, U.S.	11 Bavaria, Germany
13 San Francisco, U.S.	11 Flanders, Belgium
13 Taipei, Taiwan	11 Tokyo, Japan
13 Bangalore, India	11 Kyoto, Japan
12 New York City, U.S.	

11 Hsinchu, Taiwan	8 Santa Fe, U.S.
10 Virginia, U.S.	8 Glasgow-Edinburgh, U.K.
10 Thames Valley, U.K.	8 Saxony, Germany
10 Paris, France	8 Sophia Antipolis, France
10 Baden-Württemberg, Germany	8 Inchon, Rep. of Korea
10 Oulu, Finland	8 Kuala Lumpur, Malaysia
10 Melbourne, Australia	8 Campinas, Brazil
9 Chicago, U.S.	7 Singapore
9 Hong Kong, China	6 Trondheim, Norway
9 Queensland, Australia	4 El Ghazala, Tunisia
9 São Paulo, Brazil	4 Gauteng, South Africa
8 Salt Lake City, U.S.	

Milestones in Technology

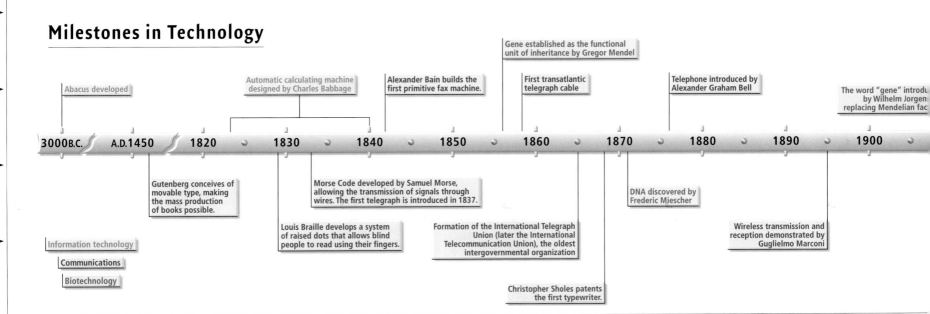

Abacus developed

Gutenberg conceives of movable type, making the mass production of books possible.

Automatic calculating machine designed by Charles Babbage

Louis Braille develops a system of raised dots that allows blind people to read using their fingers.

Morse Code developed by Samuel Morse, allowing the transmission of signals through wires. The first telegraph is introduced in 1837.

Alexander Bain builds the first primitive fax machine.

Formation of the International Telegraph Union (later the International Telecommunication Union), the oldest intergovernmental organization

Gene established as the functional unit of inheritance by Gregor Mendel

First transatlantic telegraph cable

Christopher Sholes patents the first typewriter.

DNA discovered by Frederic Miescher

Telephone introduced by Alexander Graham Bell

Wireless transmission and reception demonstrated by Guglielmo Marconi

The word "gene" introdu[ced] by Wilhelm Jorgen[son?] replacing Mendelian fac[tor]

3000 B.C. A.D. 1450 1820 1830 1840 1850 1860 1870 1880 1890 1900

Information technology
Communications
Biotechnology

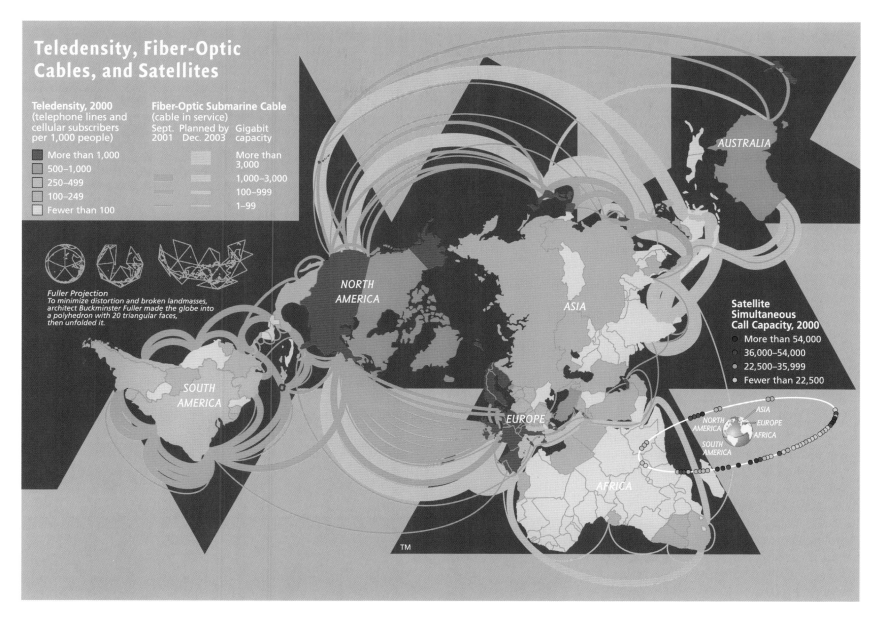

Teledensity, Fiber-Optic Cables, and Satellites

Teledensity, 2000
(telephone lines and cellular subscribers per 1,000 people)

- More than 1,000
- 500–1,000
- 250–499
- 100–249
- Fewer than 100

Fiber-Optic Submarine Cable
(cable in service)
Sept. 2001 / Planned by Dec. 2003 / Gigabit capacity

- More than 3,000
- 1,000–3,000
- 100–999
- 1–99

Fuller Projection
To minimize distortion and broken landmasses, architect Buckminster Fuller made the globe into a polyhedron with 20 triangular faces, then unfolded it.

AUSTRALIA

NORTH AMERICA

ASIA

SOUTH AMERICA

EUROPE

AFRICA

Satellite Simultaneous Call Capacity, 2000
- More than 54,000
- 36,000–54,000
- 22,500–35,999
- Fewer than 22,500

ASIA / NORTH AMERICA / EUROPE / SOUTH AMERICA / AFRICA

Nuclear Powers

Seven countries officially possess nuclear weapons: the United States, Russia, China, India, Pakistan, Great Britain, and France. Six other countries have given up whatever nuclear capability they might have achieved: Argentina, Brazil, South Africa, and three former Soviet republics (Ukraine, Belarus, and Kazakhstan). Five more countries are suspected nuclear powers: Iraq, Iran, North Korea, Algeria, and Libya. Lastly, Israel will not confirm or deny that it has the bomb, but it is thought to have over a hundred atomic weapons.

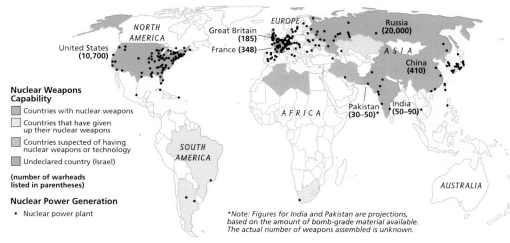

NORTH AMERICA — United States (10,700)
EUROPE — Great Britain (185), France (348)
Russia (20,000)
ASIA — China (410)
Pakistan (30–50)* / India (50–90)*
AFRICA
SOUTH AMERICA
AUSTRALIA

Nuclear Weapons Capability
- Countries with nuclear weapons
- Countries that have given up their nuclear weapons
- Countries suspected of having nuclear weapons or technology
- Undeclared country (Israel)

(number of warheads listed in parentheses)

Nuclear Power Generation
- Nuclear power plant

*Note: Figures for India and Pakistan are projections, based on the amount of bomb-grade material available. The actual number of weapons assembled is unknown.

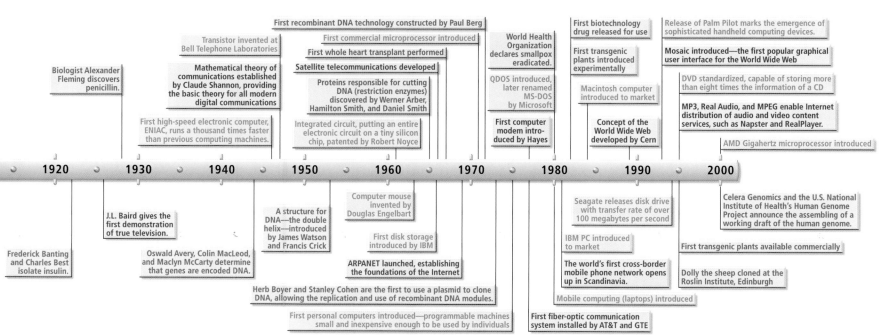

First recombinant DNA technology constructed by Paul Berg

Transistor invented at Bell Telephone Laboratories

First commercial microprocessor introduced

First biotechnology drug released for use

Release of Palm Pilot marks the emergence of sophisticated handheld computing devices.

Biologist Alexander Fleming discovers penicillin.

Mathematical theory of communications established by Claude Shannon, providing the basic theory for all modern digital communications

First whole heart transplant performed

Satellite telecommunications developed

World Health Organization declares smallpox eradicated.

First transgenic plants introduced experimentally

Mosaic introduced—the first popular graphical user interface for the World Wide Web

Proteins responsible for cutting DNA (restriction enzymes) discovered by Werner Arber, Hamilton Smith, and Daniel Smith

QDOS introduced, later renamed MS-DOS by Microsoft

Macintosh computer introduced to market

DVD standardized, capable of storing more than eight times the information of a CD

First high-speed electronic computer, ENIAC, runs a thousand times faster than previous computing machines.

Integrated circuit, putting an entire electronic circuit on a tiny silicon chip, patented by Robert Noyce

First computer modem introduced by Hayes

Concept of the World Wide Web developed by Cern

MP3, Real Audio, and MPEG enable Internet distribution of audio and video content services, such as Napster and RealPlayer.

AMD Gigahertz microprocessor introduced

| 1920 | 1930 | 1940 | 1950 | 1960 | 1970 | 1980 | 1990 | 2000 |

J.L. Baird gives the first demonstration of true television.

A structure for DNA—the double helix—introduced by James Watson and Francis Crick

Computer mouse invented by Douglas Engelbart

Seagate releases disk drive with transfer rate of over 100 megabytes per second

Celera Genomics and the U.S. National Institute of Health's Human Genome Project announce the assembling of a working draft of the human genome.

Frederick Banting and Charles Best isolate insulin.

Oswald Avery, Colin MacLeod, and Maclyn McCarty determine that genes are encoded DNA.

First disk storage introduced by IBM

IBM PC introduced to market

First transgenic plants available commercially

ARPANET launched, establishing the foundations of the Internet

The world's first cross-border mobile phone network opens up in Scandinavia.

Dolly the sheep cloned at the Roslin Institute, Edinburgh

Herb Boyer and Stanley Cohen are the first to use a plasmid to clone DNA, allowing the replication and use of recombinant DNA modules.

Mobile computing (laptops) introduced

First personal computers introduced—programmable machines small and inexpensive enough to be used by individuals

First fiber-optic communication system installed by AT&T and GTE

The "cooperative anarchy" of the global Internet, a vast collection of interconnected computer networks communicating through specific protocols (information exchange rules), defies easy characterization or measurement of its behavior. Still, a lack of understanding has not stalled development of technologies that enable and support Internet growth.

Old behavior models for telephone networks no longer apply to packet delivery (data sent over a network) and to application support over multiple links, routers, and Internet Service Providers (ISPs). The sheer volume of traffic and the high capacity of electronic pathways have made Internet monitoring and analysis a more challenging endeavor. Users and providers both benefit from measurements that detect and isolate problems, but watching every link is not practical or particularly effective.

Each ISP monitors its own infrastructure and quality of service; however, business and policy concerns often keep ISPs from sharing such information. Common sense supports creation of a measurement infrastructure that would yield maximal Internet coverage for a reasonable price. But dynamically changing network configurations, as well as complex business and geopolitical concerns, make it difficult to acquire a worldwide view of the Internet.

A BRIEF HISTORY

1960s: ARPANET, a system designed to promote the sharing of supercomputers by researchers in the United States, is commissioned by the Department of Defense.

1970s: People begin to use ARPANET to collaborate on research projects and discuss common interests. In 1974, a commercial version goes online for the first time.

1980s: Corporations begin to use the Internet for e-mail. As the Internet grows in importance, viruses start to create concerns about online privacy and security. New terms such as "hacker" come into use.

1990s: After the introduction of browsers for navigating the World Wide Web, Internet use expands rapidly (see graph below). By the late 1990s, 200 million people are connected, with online consumer spending totaling in the tens of billions of dollars. During this time, Internet-related companies attract enormous amounts of money from investors.

Early 2000s: Internet stock values take a deep plunge following the "dotcom" crash of April 2000. But rapid Internet growth continues, with more than 100 million new users each year. Satellite communications technology allows people to easily access the Internet with handheld devices.

Mapping the Spread of a Computer Virus

The graphics below illustrate two different ways of viewing Internet data. The world map shows the early (yellow), middle (orange), and late (red) stages in the spread of the CodeRed worm on July 19, 2001. Below the map, a computer-generated fish-eye view depicts the number of network hosts infected by the virus over the course of 24 hours. Each node represents a routable address prefix announced by Internet Service Providers (ISPs). Prefixes with no infected hosts appear gray, while prefixes with infected hosts are green to red, according to increasing numbers of infections. Although the entire set of announced prefixes is shown, details visible in the center of the fish-eye view focus on one branch of the address prefix tree. The 24.0.0.0/8 subtree clearly shows a large number of infections, which is not surprising because it contains prefixes belonging to @Home, RoadRunner, and AT&T broadband services, as well as other ISPs with large bases of residential and small business customers. As a class, home users and small businesses were among the most commonly infected by the CodeRed worm.

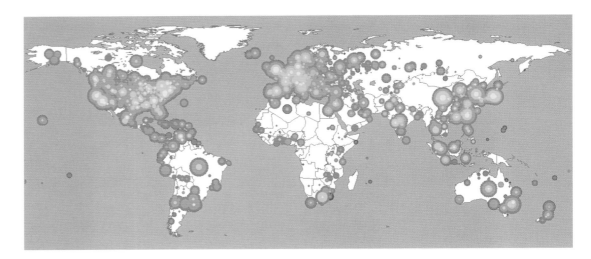

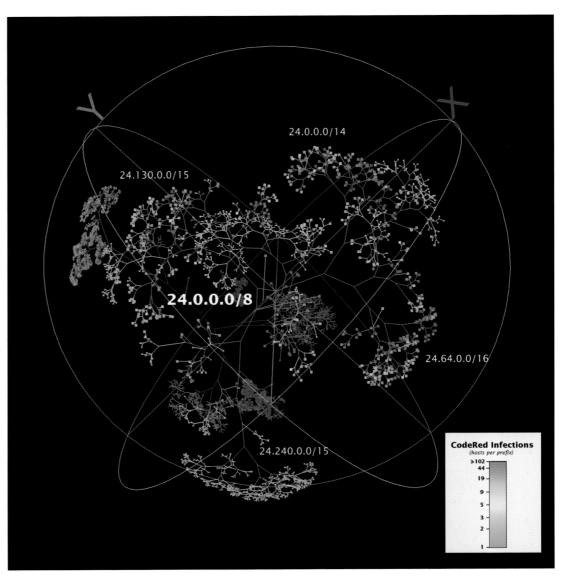

24.0.0.0/14

24.130.0.0/15

24.0.0.0/8

24.64.0.0/16

24.240.0.0/15

CodeRed Infections
(hosts per prefix)
>102
44
19
9
5
3
2
1

INTERNET USERS WORLDWIDE (estimated), 1995–2001

December 1995: 16 million

December 1998: 160 million

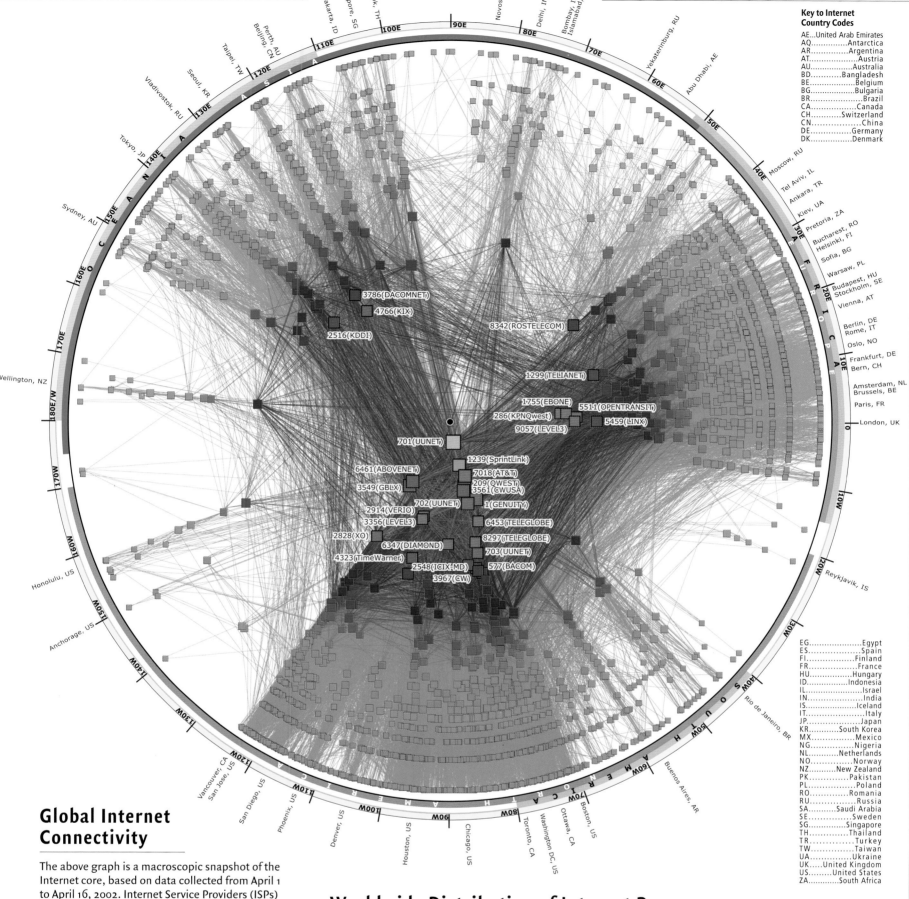

Key to Internet Country Codes

AE...United Arab Emirates
AQ..............Antarctica
AR..............Argentina
AT..................Austria
AU..............Australia
BD............Bangladesh
BE..................Belgium
BG................Bulgaria
BR....................Brazil
CA..................Canada
CH............Switzerland
CN....................China
DK................Denmark

Jakarta, ID
Perth, AU
Beijing, CN
Taipei, TW
Singapore, SG
Bangkok, TH
Novosibirsk, RU
Delhi, IN
Bombay, IN
Islamabad, PK
Yekaterinburg, RU
Abu Dhabi, AE
Moscow, RU
Tel Aviv, IL
Ankara, TR
Kiev, UA
Pretoria, ZA
Bucharest, RO
Helsinki, FI
Sofia, BG
Warsaw, PL
Budapest, HU
Stockholm, SE
Vienna, AT
Berlin, DE
Rome, IT
Oslo, NO
Frankfurt, DE
Bern, CH
Amsterdam, NL
Brussels, BE
Paris, FR
London, UK
Reykjavik, IS
Rio de Janeiro, BR
Buenos Aires, AR
Ottawa, CA
Boston, US
Washington DC, US
Toronto, CA
Chicago, US
Houston, US
Denver, US
Phoenix, US
San Diego, US
San Jose, US
Vancouver, CA
Anchorage, US
Honolulu, US
Wellington, NZ
Sydney, AU
Tokyo, JP
Vladivostok, RU
Seoul, KR

Node labels:
3786 (DACOMNET)
4766 (KIX)
2516 (KDDI)
8342 (ROSTELECOM)
1299 (TELIANET)
1755 (EBONE)
5511 (OPENTRANSIT)
286 (KPNQwest)
5459 (LINX)
9057 (LEVEL3)
701 (UUNET)
1239 (SprintLink)
6461 (ABOVENET)
7018 (AT&T)
209 (QWEST)
3561 (CWUSA)
3549 (GBLX)
702 (UUNET)
1 (GENUITY)
2914 (VERIO)
3356 (LEVEL3)
6453 (TELEGLOBE)
2828 (XO)
8297 (TELEGLOBE)
6347 (DIAMOND)
703 (UUNET)
4323 (TimeWarner)
2548 (ICIX-MD)
577 (BACOM)
3967 (CW)

EG..................Egypt
ES....................Spain
FI....................Finland
FR....................France
HU................Hungary
ID................Indonesia
IL......................Israel
IN......................India
IS....................Iceland
IT........................Italy
JP......................Japan
KR............South Korea
MX..................Mexico
NG..................Nigeria
NL............Netherlands
NO..................Norway
NZ..........New Zealand
PK................Pakistan
PL......................Poland
RO................Romania
RU....................Russia
SA..........Saudi Arabia
SE..................Sweden
SG..............Singapore
TH................Thailand
TR....................Turkey
TW..................Taiwan
UA................Ukraine
UK.....United Kingdom
US.........United States
ZA..............South Africa

Global Internet Connectivity

The above graph is a macroscopic snapshot of the Internet core, based on data collected from April 1 to April 16, 2002. Internet Service Providers (ISPs) are represented by squares, with better-connected ISPs found toward the center. The colors indicate "outdegree" (the number of "next-hop" systems that were observed accepting traffic from a link), from lowest (blue) to highest (yellow).

The top 13 network nodes are based in the United States, and one of the European ISPs in the top 15 is the European branch of an American company. While ISPs in Europe and Asia have many links with ISPs in the United States, there are few direct links between ISPs in Asia and Europe. Both technical (cabling and router placement and management) and policy factors (business and cost models, geopolitical considerations) contribute to the ISP associations represented in this graph.

Worldwide Distribution of Internet Resources

The worldwide distribution of Internet resources—ISPs, Autonomous System (AS) routers, address space—is highly nonuniform and is unrelated to a region's size or population. For this graph, Internet addresses of routable paths announced on June 11, 2001, were mapped to physical locations and compared with public demographic data.

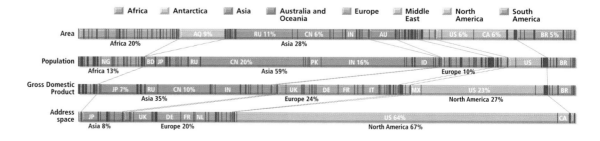

Legend: Africa | Antarctica | Asia | Australia and Oceania | Europe | Middle East | North America | South America

Area: Africa 20% | AQ 9% | RU 11% | CN 6% | IN | AU | US 6% | CA 6% | BR 5% | Asia 28%

Population: Africa 13% | NG | BD JP | RU | CN 20% | PK | IN 16% | ID | Europe 10% | US | BR | Asia 59%

Gross Domestic Product: JP 7% | RU | CN 10% | IN | UK | DE | FR | IT | MX | US 23% | BR | Asia 35% | Europe 24% | North America 27%

Address space: JP | UK | DE | FR | NL | US 64% | CA | Asia 8% | Europe 20% | North America 67%

December 2001: 528 million

NORTH AMERICA

Northern America is both incredibly old, geologically speaking, and relatively young, when viewed in terms of its human history.

About 200 million years ago, North America separated from Africa when the supercontinent Pangaea began to break apart. For a while, it was attached to Europe, but in time that connection was broken and the North American landmass began roughly assuming its current shape and size. Meanwhile, the other continents were still separating from one another and jockeying for position on the face of the planet.

Some of the oldest stones in the world are found in North America. Dating from nearly four billion years ago, they form the stout underbelly of Canada's frozen tundra. In the east, an ancient mountain system—the Appalachians—runs from the United States into Canada.

Millions of years of weathering and erosion, in the form of wind, rain, snow, heat, cold, and the Colorado River, have shaped the Grand Canyon into one of North America's geographic icons.

But not everything is so utterly ancient: North America's human history is only thousands of years old, while that of Africa, the birthplace of humankind, dates back millions of years. Just in the past couple of centuries, North America has experienced dramatic changes in its population, landscapes, and environment, an incredible transformation brought about by waves of immigration, booming economies, and relentless development.

PHYSICAL GEOGRAPHY

From the world's largest island (Greenland) and greatest concentration of fresh water (the Great Lakes) to such spectacular features as the Grand Canyon and Niagara Falls, North America holds a wealth of superlatives. It is also home to Earth's largest and tallest trees (the redwoods of California) and many of its biggest animals (grizzly bears, moose, and bison). The continent is known as well for dramatic extremes of climate—from the sauna-like 134°F (57°C) recorded in Death Valley to the brutally cold minus 87°F (-66°C) logged on Greenland's windswept ice cap.

Third largest of the continents, after Asia and Africa, North America encompasses 9.45 million square miles (24.5 million sq km); its northernmost tip is in Greenland (Kap Morris Jesup), and its southernmost point is in Panama (Península de Azuero).

Deeply indented with inlets and bays, North America claims the longest coastline when compared with other continents. Its land is surrounded by vast oceans and sizable seas—the Atlantic in the east, the Pacific in the west, the Arctic in the north, and the Gulf of Mexico and Caribbean Sea in the south. This geographic circumstance kept the continent isolated for millions of years, greatly influencing the development of its flora and fauna, as well as its human history. Into North America's coastal waters pour a number of mighty rivers, including the Saint Lawrence, Rio Grande, Yukon, Columbia, and Mississippi.

Three significant geologic features dominate the continental landmass: the Canadian (Laurentian) Shield; the great Western Cordillera, which includes the Rocky Mountains, Sierra Nevada, and Sierra Madre; and a colossal flatland that embraces the Great Plains, the Mississippi-Missouri River basin, and most of the Great Lakes region. Other major components include the ancient Appalachian Mountains and the predominantly volcanic islands of the Caribbean Sea. The continent peaks out at 20,320 feet (6,194 m) on the summit of Mount McKinley (Denali), in Alaska, and drops to 282 feet (86 m) below sea level in California's Death Valley.

The climates of North America range from the frigid conditions of the Arctic ice cap to the steamy tropics of Central America (considered part of North America) and the Caribbean; in between are variations of dry, mild, and continental climes.

The continent has an equally diverse biological heritage, ranging from seemingly endless tundra and coniferous forests in the north to vast deserts and dense rain forests in the south. North America once held huge herds of bison, antelope, elk, and other large wildlife, but such populations declined as the human population grew and spread across the continent.

HISTORY

Although the exact date will probably never be determined, North America's human history began sometime between 12,000 and 30,000 years ago, when Asiatic nomads crossed the Bering Strait into Alaska. The descendants of these people spread throughout the continent, evolving into distinct tribes with their own lifestyles and more than 550 different languages.

Most of these original Americans were still hunting and gathering when Europeans arrived in North America; however, several groups had already developed sophisticated cultures. By 1200 B.C., the Olmec of Mexico had created what is generally deemed the first "civilization" in the Western Hemisphere; theirs was a highly advanced society with a calendar, writing system, and stonework architecture. About a hundred years later, the Maya took root in Mexico and Central America, reaching an apex around A.D. 700 with the creation of an elaborate religion and sprawling temple cities. In central Mexico, the highly militaristic Toltec and Aztec forged sprawling empires that drew cultural inspiration from both the Olmec and Maya.

One of the most significant moments for North America—indeed, it was among the most influential events in world history—came in 1492, when a Spanish expedition under Christopher Columbus set foot on an island in the Bahamas. This initial landing ushered in an era of European exploration and settlement that would alter the social fabric of the entire continent. In the next few decades, Hernán Cortés vanquished the Aztec, and Spain claimed virtually the whole Caribbean region and Central America. Other Europeans soon followed—English, French, Dutch, Russians, and even Danes— the leading edge of a migration that would become one of the greatest in human history (more than 70 million people and still counting).

The Native American cultures were unable to compete: They were plagued by European diseases, against which they had little or no resistance; unable to counter the superior firepower of the invaders; and relentlessly driven from their lands. The continent's rich tribal mosaic gradually melted away, replaced by myriad European colonies. By the end of the 19th century, these colonies had been superseded by autonomous nation-states, such as Canada, Mexico, and the United States. Since 1960, many of the Caribbean isles have gained independence, yet quite a few remain colonial possessions under the British, French, Dutch, and U.S. flags.

During the last century, both the U.S. and Canada managed to propel themselves into the ranks of the world's richest nations. But the rest of the continent failed to keep pace, plagued by poverty, despotic governments, and social unrest. In the decades since World War II, many of the Spanish-speaking nations—Cuba, the Dominican Republic, Nicaragua, El Salvador, and Guatemala—have been racked by bloody revolution. The United States, on the other hand, ended the 20th century as the only true superpower, with a military presence and political, economic, and cultural influences that extend around the globe.

The ancient site of Palenque (A.D. 600–700), in Mexico's Yucatán region, was a Maya ceremonial center and royal enclave. Even in ruins, its massive stone palace remains an impressive structure.

CULTURE

North America's cultural landscape has changed profoundly over the past 500 years. Before the 16th century, the continent was fragmented into hundreds of different cultures developed along tribal lines. From the Inuit people of the Arctic to the Cuña Indians of the Panama jungle, a majority of North America's people had barely risen above Stone Age cultural levels. Noteworthy exceptions included the great civilizations of Mexico and Central America, the pueblo builders of the southwestern U.S., and the highly organized cultivators of the Great Lakes region and the Mississippi Valley. But for the most part, the average North American was migratory, had no concept of written language, and used stone or wooden tools.

The arrival of the Europeans brought permanent settlements, metal tools (and weapons), and written languages. The newcomers founded towns based on Old World models, some of which would evolve into world-class cities—New York, Los Angeles, Chicago, Toronto, and Mexico City among them. Native tongues gave way to a trio of European languages—English, Spanish, and French—now spoken by most of North America's 500 million people. And ancient beliefs yielded to new religions, like Roman Catholicism and Protestantism, which now dominate the continent's spiritual life. The Europeans brought ideas—concepts like democracy, capitalism, religious choice, and free speech—that continue to shape political, intellectual, and economic life.

Despite common historical threads, the coat that comprises today's North America is one of many colors. Mexico and Central America are dominated by Hispano-Indian culture and tend to have more in common with South America than with their neighbors north of the Rio Grande. Although Anglo-Saxon ways still hold sway in the U.S. and Canada, a surge of immigration from Latin America, Asia, and Pacific islands has introduced new cultural traditions. From the Rastafarians of Jamaica to the Creoles of Martinique, the Caribbean islands have fostered myriad microcultures that blend European, African, and Latin traditions.

ECONOMY

When it comes to business and industry, North America—and especially the United States—is the envy of the world. No other continent produces such an abundance of merchandise or profusion of crops, and no other major region comes close to North America's per capita resource and product consumption. From the high-tech citadels of Silicon Valley to the dream factories of Hollywood, the continent is a world leader in dozens of fields and industries, including computers, entertainment, aerospace, finance, medicine, defense, and agriculture.

The quest for monetary and material success can be traced all the way back to early European immigrants and the tireless work ethic they brought with them. These people, and their cultural descendants, sought to improve their standard of living by exploiting the natural wealth of the land. North America's forests, minerals, and farmlands stoked an industrial revolution that by the end of the 19th century had propelled the United States into the ranks of the richest and most powerful nations. Indeed, the continent has an abundance of natural resources: vast petroleum reserves in Alaska and around the Gulf of Mexico, huge coal deposits in the Appalachians and Rocky Mountains, swift-flowing rivers to produce hydropower, and fertile soils that lead to copious harvests.

But the most important product has always been ideas—the ability to imagine. Next is the ability to transform those ideas into reality through experimentation and hard work. Many of the innovations that revolutionized modern life—the telephone, electric light, motor vehicles, airplanes, computers, shopping malls, television, the Internet—were either invented or first mass-produced in the United States.

Globalization has spread U.S. goods—and by extension, American ideas and culture—around the planet. To a large extent the U.S. dollar has become the world currency, and the financial wizards of New York's Wall Street now control a lion's share of global investment funds. The creation of the North American Free Trade Association (NAFTA) in 1994 drew Canada and Mexico into the same economic web. But success has brought a host of concerns, not the least of which involves the continued exploitation of natural resources. North America is home to roughly 8 percent of the planet's people, yet its per capita consumption of energy is almost six times as great as the average for all other continents. Its appetite for timber, metals, and water resources is just as voracious.

Other parts of the continent continue to lag in terms of economic vitality. Most Caribbean nations—along with Costa Rica and Belize—now rely on the tourist industry to generate the bulk of their gross national product, while most Central American countries continue to bank on agricultural commodities such as bananas and coffee. Poverty has spurred millions of Mexicans, Central Americans, and Caribbean islanders to migrate northward (legally and illegally) in search of better lives. Finding ways to integrate these disenfranchised masses into the continent's economic miracle is one of the greatest challenges facing North America in the 21st century.

Physical and Political
NORTH AMERICA

Azimuthal Equidistant Projection

SCALE 1:28,768,000
1 CENTIMETER = 288 KILOMETERS, 1 INCH = 454 MILES

KILOMETERS

STATUTE MILES

International boundary

BERING SEA
AND THE
ALEUTIAN ISLANDS
Same Scale as Main Map

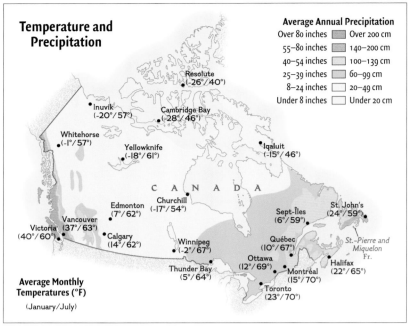

Temperature and Precipitation

Average Annual Precipitation

Over 80 inches		Over 200 cm
55–80 inches		140–200 cm
40–54 inches		100–139 cm
25–39 inches		60–99 cm
8–24 inches		20–49 cm
Under 8 inches		Under 20 cm

Resolute (-26°/40°)
Inuvik (-20°/57°)
Cambridge Bay (-28°/46°)
Whitehorse (-1°/57°)
Yellowknife (-18°/61°)
Iqaluit (-15°/46°)
C A N A D A
Edmonton (7°/62°)
Churchill (-17°/54°)
Sept-Îles (6°/59°)
St. John's (24°/59°)
Victoria (40°/60°)
Vancouver (37°/63°)
Calgary (14°/62°)
Winnipeg (-2°/67°)
Québec (10°/67°)
St.-Pierre and Miquelon Fr.
Thunder Bay (5°/64°)
Ottawa (12°/69°)
Montréal (15°/70°)
Halifax (22°/65°)
Toronto (23°/70°)

Average Monthly Temperatures (°F)
(January/July)

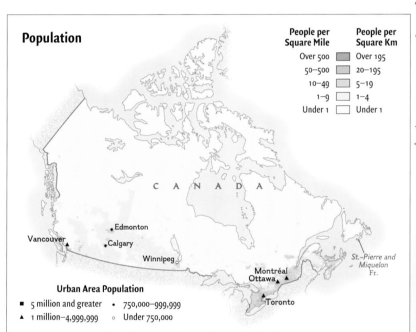

Population

People per Square Mile		People per Square Km
Over 500		Over 195
50–500		20–195
10–49		5–19
1–9		1–4
Under 1		Under 1

C A N A D A
Vancouver
Edmonton
Calgary
Winnipeg
Montréal
Ottawa
Toronto
St.-Pierre and Miquelon Fr.

Urban Area Population
- ■ 5 million and greater
- ▲ 1 million–4,999,999
- • 750,000–999,999
- ○ Under 750,000

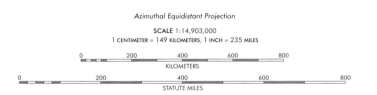

Azimuthal Equidistant Projection

SCALE 1:14,903,000
1 CENTIMETER = 149 KILOMETERS; 1 INCH = 235 MILES

0 200 400 600 800
KILOMETERS

0 200 400 600 800
STATUTE MILES

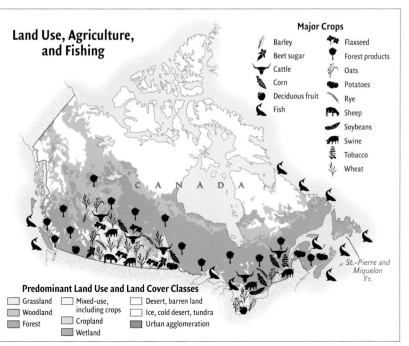

Land Use, Agriculture, and Fishing

Major Crops
- Barley
- Beet sugar
- Cattle
- Corn
- Deciduous fruit
- Fish
- Flaxseed
- Forest products
- Oats
- Potatoes
- Rye
- Sheep
- Soybeans
- Swine
- Tobacco
- Wheat

C A N A D A
St.-Pierre and Miquelon Fr.

Predominant Land Use and Land Cover Classes
- Grassland
- Woodland
- Forest
- Wetland
- Mixed-use, including crops
- Cropland
- Desert, barren land
- Ice, cold desert, tundra
- Urban agglomeration

Canada
CANADA

AREA	9,970,610 sq km (3,849,670 sq mi)
POPULATION	31,333,000
CAPITAL	Ottawa 1,094,000
RELIGION	Roman Catholic, Protestant
LANGUAGE	English, French
LITERACY	97%
LIFE EXPECTANCY	80 years
GDP PER CAPITA	$24,800

ECONOMY IND: processed and unprocessed minerals, food products, wood and paper products, transportation equipment. AGR: wheat, barley, oilseed, tobacco; dairy products; forest products; fish. EXP: motor vehicles and parts, newsprint, wood pulp, timber.

Greenland (Denmark)
GREENLAND

SOVEREIGN   LOCAL

AREA	2,175,600 sq km (840,004 sq mi)
POPULATION	56,000
CAPITAL	Godthåb (Nuuk) 14,000
LANGUAGES	Greenlandic (East Inuit), Danish, English
RELIGION	Evangelical Lutheran
LITERACY	NA
LIFE EXPECTANCY	68
GPD PER CAPITA	$20,000

ECONOMY IND: fish processing (shrimp and halibut), handicrafts, furs. AGR: forage crops, garden and greenhouse vegetables; sheep; fish. EXP: fish and fish products.

Industry and Mining

Major Mines

Al	Aluminum	Pb	Lead	U	Uranium
Co	Cobalt	Ni	Nickel	Zn	Zinc
Cu	Copper	Pt	Platinum		
Au	Gold	Ag	Silver		

Gross Domestic Product per Capita (in U.S. dollars)
- 30,000–36,200
- 20,000–29,999
- 10,000–19,999
- 1,700–9,999

CANADA

- Coal
- Diamonds
- Manufacturing center
- Petroleum
- Potash
- Processing plant

St.-Pierre and Miquelon Fr.

Montréal
Toronto

SOVEREIGN   LOCAL

St.-Pierre and Miquelon
(France)

TERRITORIAL COLLECTIVITY OF ST.-PIERRE AND MIQUELON

AREA	242 sq km (93 sq mi)
POPULATION	7,000
CAPITAL	Saint-Pierre 6,000
LANGUAGES	French
RELIGION	Roman Catholic
LITERACY	99%
LIFE EXPECTANCY	78
GDP PER CAPITA	$11,000

ECONOMY IND: fish processing and supply base for fishing fleets, tourism. AGR: vegetables; poultry; fish. EXP: fish and fish products, soybeans, animal feed, mollusks and crustaceans.

OCEAN

QUEEN ELIZABETH ISLANDS
SVERDRUP ISLANDS
PARRY ISLANDS
Melville Island
Bathurst Island
Cornwallis Island
Devon Island
Ellesmere Island
GREENLAND (KALAALLIT NUNAAT)

North Magnetic Pole 2002
Cape Columbia
Cape Sheridan
Cape Hecla
Ward Hunt I.
Alert
M'Clintock Inlet
Ayles Fjord
Yelverton Bay
Phillips Inlet
2604
Axel Heiberg Island
Eureka
Fosheim Pen.
Meighen I.
Ellef Ringnes I.
Amund Ringnes I.
Graham I.
Grinnell Pen.
Grise Fiord
Coburg Island
Jones Sound
Lady Ann Strait
1908
Philpots Island
Cape Byam Martin
Bylot Island
Pond Inlet
Brodeur Peninsula
Borden Peninsula
Arctic Bay
Borden Island
1615
C. Adair

BAFFIN BAY
Eglinton Fiord
Clyde River
Clyde Inlet
1905
Cape Raper
Henry Kater Pen.
Home Bay
Cape Hooper
Kangeeak Point
Qikiqtarjuaq
Padloping Island
Cape Dyer
Cumberland Peninsula
Pangnirtung
1067
Hoare Bay
Cape Mercy
Cumberland Sound
Cyrus Field Bay
Loks Land
Edgell Island
Qikiqtarjuaq

DAVIS STRAIT
ARCTIC CIRCLE

LABRADOR SEA
Cod Island
Okak Islands
South Aulatsivik I.
Nain
Davis Inlet
Hopedale
Makkovik
Cape Harrison
Indian Harbour
Hamilton Inlet
Rigolet
Cartwright
Sandwich Bay
Batteau
Port Hope Simpson
Battle Harbour
Belle Isle
L'Anse aux Meadows
St. Anthony
Grey Islands
Roddickton
La Scie
Fogo Island
Twillingate
Bonavista
Trinity Bay
Conception Bay
St. John's
Avalon Pen.
Trepassey B.
Cape Race
Grand Banks of Newfoundland

NUNAVUT
Baffin Island
Foxe Basin
Foxe Peninsula
Melville Peninsula
Prince Charles Island
Air Force I.
Iqaluit
Hall Pen.
Meta Incognita Pen.
Kimmirut
Big I.
Nottingham I.
Salisbury Island
Cape Dorset
Markham Bay
Frobisher Bay
Brevoort Island
Lemieux Islands

HUDSON STRAIT
Button Islands
Killiniq Island
Port Burwell
North Aulatsivik I.
Seven Islands Bay
Nachvak Fjord
Saglek Bay
Torngat Mts.
1652
Ungava Bay
Akpatok Island

NEWFOUNDLAND AND LABRADOR
LABRADOR
NOUVEAU-QUÉBEC
QUÉBEC

Kangirsuk
Kangiqsualujjuaq
Kuujjuaq
George
1169
North West River
Happy Valley-Goose Bay
Churchill Falls
Esker
Schefferville
Labrador City
Fermont
Pitaga

Ottawa Islands
Baie de Povungnituk
Inukjuak
Hopewell Islands
Sleeper Is.
King George Is.
North Belcher Is.
Belcher Islands
Long Island
Pte. Louis-XIV
Kuujjuarapik
Lac à l'Eau Claire
Lac Bienville
Lac Guillaume-Delisle
Lac Minto
Lac Payne
Lac Tassiuaq
Lac Wakuach
Sakami
Keyano
Chisasibi
Radisson
Eastmain
R. de Rupert
Nemiscau
Waskaganish
Mistassini
Lac Mistassini
Chibougamau
Lac Plétipi
Rés. Manicouagan
Rés. aux Feuilles

HUDSON BAY
JAMES BAY
Charlton Island
Akimiski Island
Attawapiskat
Fort Albany
Moosonee
C. Henrietta Maria
Long Island

MANITOBA
Churchill
Cape Churchill
Brochet
Reindeer L.
Southern Indian L.
Lynn Lake
Split Lake
Gillam
Nelson House
Thompson
Sipiwesk
Wabowden
Sherridon
The Pas
Grand Rapids
Norway House
Island Lake
Gods Lake
Swan River
Winnipegosis
Dauphin
Portage la Prairie
Neepawa
Gimli
Riverton
Berens River
Cat Lake
Red Lake
Winnipeg
Brandon
Steinbach

ONTARIO
Big Trout Lake
Kingfisher Lake
Sandy Lake
Lansdowne House
Fort Hope
Pickle Lake
Ogoki
Armstrong
Geraldton
Nakina
Hearst
Kapuskasing
Cochrane
Kenora
Sioux Lookout
Dryden
Graham
Nipigon
Atikokan
Fort Frances
Thunder Bay
Wawa
Franz
Chapleau
Timmins
Kirkland Lake
New Liskeard
Cobalt
Sault Ste. Marie
Thessalon
Elliot Lake
Capreol
Sudbury
Blind River
Espanola
North Bay
Pembroke
Barrie
Orillia
Peterborough
Oshawa
Kingston
TORONTO
Kitchener
Hamilton
London
Windsor

Lake Superior
Lake Michigan
Lake Huron
Georgian Bay
L. Nipissing
L. Simcoe
L. Ontario
Lake Erie

NOUVEAU-QUÉBEC
Matagami
Amos
La Sarre
Senneterre
Val-d'Or
Rouyn-Noranda
Chibougamau
Dolbeau
Chicoutimi
La Malbaie
La Tuque
Shawinigan
Trois-Rivières
Québec
Lévis
St-Hyacinthe
Granby
Sherbrooke
MONTRÉAL
Ottawa
Cornwall
Joliette

NEW BRUNSWICK
Edmundston
Moncton
Fredericton
Saint John
Bathurst
Chatham

PRINCE EDWARD ISLAND
Charlottetown
Summerside

NOVA SCOTIA
Halifax
Dartmouth
Truro
New Glasgow
Antigonish
Sydney
Glace Bay
Port Hawkesbury
Baddeck
Cape Breton Island
Amherst
Yarmouth
Shelburne
Liverpool
Bridgewater
Sable Island

GULF OF ST. LAWRENCE
Gaspé
Gaspé Peninsula
Mont-Joli
Matane
Rimouski
Rivière-du-Loup
Tadoussac
Forestville
Baie-Comeau
Sept-Îles
Havre-St-Pierre
Mingan
Port-Cartier
Natashquan
Blanc-Sablon
Pointe-aux-Anglais
Port-Menier
Île d'Anticosti
Îles de la Madeleine
Cape Ray
Channel-Port aux Basques
St. Pierre & Miquelon
Corner Brook
Stephenville
ISLAND OF NEWFOUNDLAND
Grand Falls
Botwood
Gander
Windsor

ATLANTIC OCEAN

MINNESOTA
WISCONSIN
MICHIGAN
NEW YORK
PENNSYLVANIA
OHIO
MAINE
VT
N.H.
NORTH DAKOTA

TRANS-CANADA HIGHWAYS

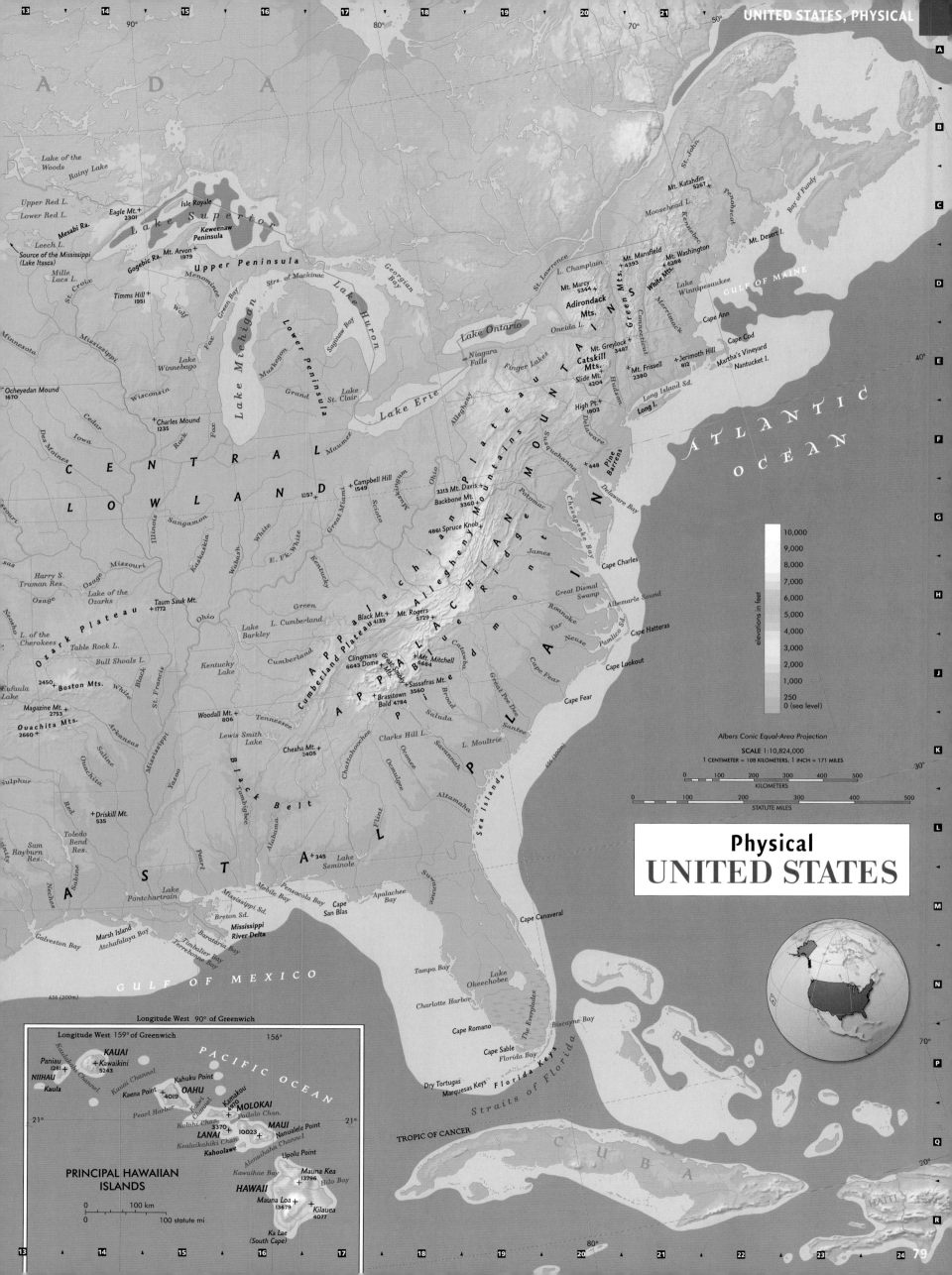

United States of America

UNITED STATES OF AMERICA

AREA	9,629,091 sq km (3,717,796 sq mi)
POPULATION	287,494,000
CAPITAL	Washington, D.C.
CAPITAL POP.	metro area: 4,396,000
	city proper: 572,000
RELIGION	Protestant, Roman Catholic, Jewish
LANGUAGE	English, Spanish
LITERACY	97%
LIFE EXPECTANCY	77 years
GDP PER CAPITA	$36,200
ECONOMY	IND: petroleum, steel, motor vehicles, aerospace. AGR: wheat, other grains, corn, fruits; beef; forest products; fish. EXP: capital goods, automobiles, industrial supplies and raw materials, consumer goods.

Albers Conic Equal-Area Projection

SCALE 1:10,824,000

1 CENTIMETER = 108 KILOMETERS; 1 INCH = 171 MILES

0   100   200   300   400   500
KILOMETERS

0   100   200   300   400   500
STATUTE MILES

Political
UNITED STATES

PRINCIPAL HAWAIIAN ISLANDS

Longitude West 90° of Greenwich

Longitude West 159° of Greenwich

0   100 km

0   100 statute mi

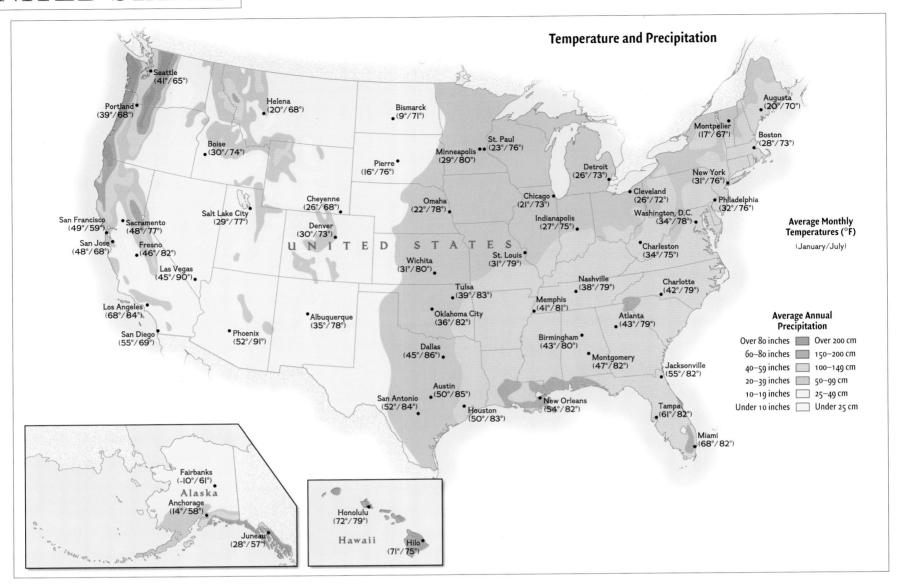

Temperature and Precipitation

Seattle
(41°/65°)

Portland
(39°/68°)

Helena
(20°/68°)

Bismarck
(9°/71°)

Augusta
(20°/70°)

Boise
(30°/74°)

St. Paul
(23°/76°)

Montpelier
(17°/67°)

Boston
(28°/73°)

Minneapolis
(29°/80°)

Pierre
(16°/76°)

Detroit
(26°/73°)

New York
(31°/76°)

San Francisco
(49°/59°)

Sacramento
(48°/77°)

Salt Lake City
(29°/77°)

Cheyenne
(26°/68°)

Omaha
(22°/78°)

Chicago
(21°/73°)

Cleveland
(26°/72°)

Philadelphia
(32°/76°)

San Jose
(48°/68°)

Fresno
(46°/82°)

Denver
(30°/73°)

UNITED STATES

Indianapolis
(27°/75°)

Washington, D.C.
(34°/78°)

Las Vegas
(45°/90°)

Wichita
(31°/80°)

St. Louis
(31°/79°)

Charleston
(34°/75°)

Los Angeles
(68°/84°)

Albuquerque
(35°/78°)

Tulsa
(39°/83°)

Nashville
(38°/79°)

Charlotte
(42°/79°)

San Diego
(55°/69°)

Phoenix
(52°/91°)

Oklahoma City
(36°/82°)

Memphis
(41°/81°)

Atlanta
(43°/79°)

Dallas
(45°/86°)

Birmingham
(43°/80°)

Montgomery
(47°/82°)

Jacksonville
(55°/82°)

San Antonio
(52°/84°)

Austin
(50°/85°)

New Orleans
(54°/82°)

Houston
(50°/83°)

Tampa
(61°/82°)

Miami
(68°/82°)

**Average Monthly
Temperatures (°F)**

(January/July)

**Average Annual
Precipitation**

Over 80 inches	Over 200 cm
60–80 inches	150–200 cm
40–59 inches	100–149 cm
20–39 inches	50–99 cm
10–19 inches	25–49 cm
Under 10 inches	Under 25 cm

Fairbanks
(-10°/61°)

Alaska

Anchorage
(14°/58°)

Juneau
(28°/57°)

Honolulu
(72°/79°)

Hawaii

Hilo
(71°/75°)

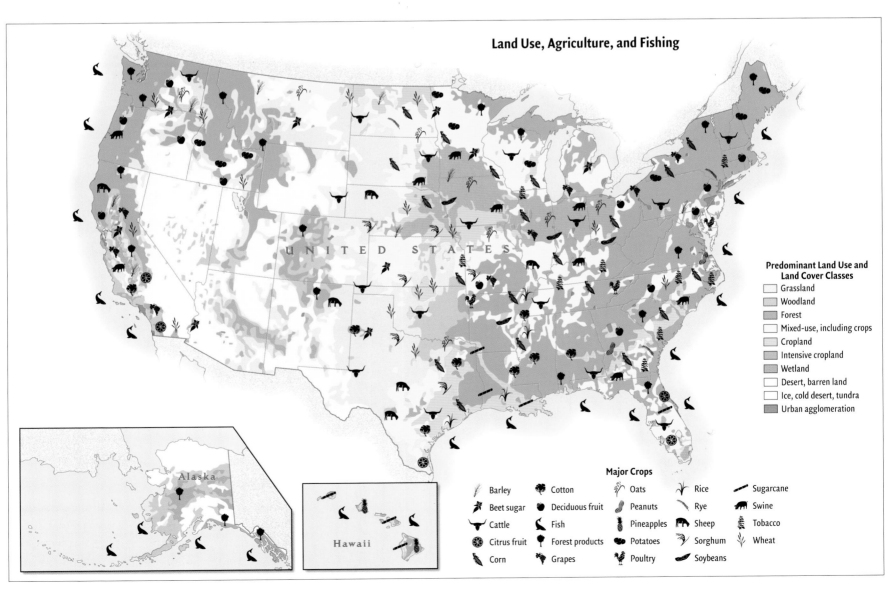

Land Use, Agriculture, and Fishing

UNITED STATES

**Predominant Land Use and
Land Cover Classes**

	Grassland
	Woodland
	Forest
	Mixed-use, including crops
	Cropland
	Intensive cropland
	Wetland
	Desert, barren land
	Ice, cold desert, tundra
	Urban agglomeration

Alaska

Hawaii

Major Crops

Barley	Cotton	Oats	Rice	Sugarcane
Beet sugar	Deciduous fruit	Peanuts	Rye	Swine
Cattle	Fish	Pineapples	Sheep	Tobacco
Citrus fruit	Forest products	Potatoes	Sorghum	Wheat
Corn	Grapes	Poultry	Soybeans	

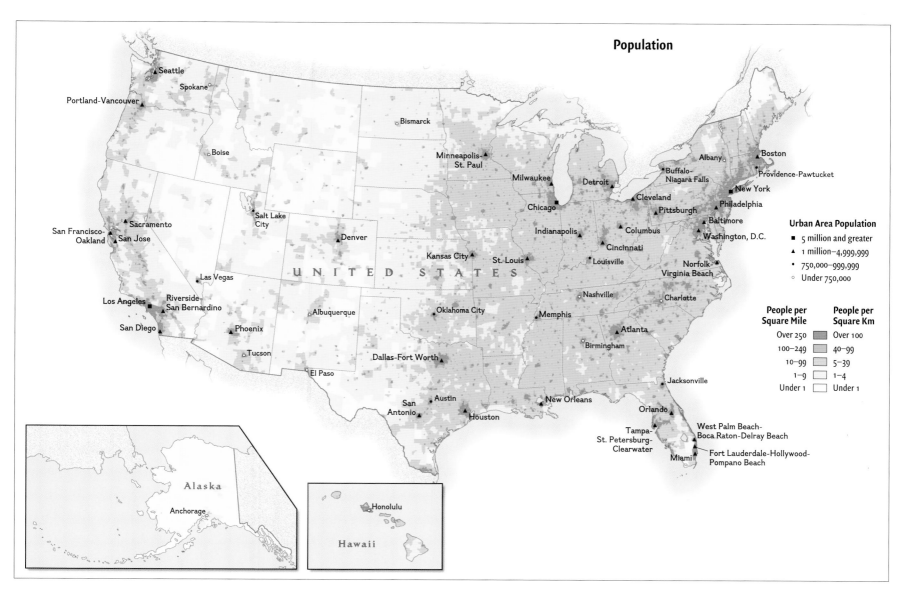

Population

Urban Area Population

- ■ 5 million and greater
- ▲ 1 million–4,999,999
- ▴ 750,000–999,999
- ○ Under 750,000

People per Square Mile		People per Square Km
Over 250		Over 100
100–249		40–99
10–99		5–39
1–9		1–4
Under 1		Under 1

Seattle
Spokane
Portland-Vancouver
Bismarck
Boise
Minneapolis-St. Paul
Milwaukee
Detroit
Albany
Buffalo-Niagara Falls
Boston
Providence-Pawtucket
Cleveland
New York
Chicago
Pittsburgh
Philadelphia
Salt Lake City
Sacramento
Denver
Indianapolis
Columbus
Baltimore
Washington, D.C.
San Francisco-Oakland
San Jose
Cincinnati
Kansas City
St. Louis
Louisville
Norfolk-Virginia Beach
Las Vegas
Los Angeles
Riverside-San Bernardino
Nashville
Charlotte
San Diego
Albuquerque
Oklahoma City
Memphis
Atlanta
Phoenix
Birmingham
Tucson
Dallas-Fort Worth
El Paso
Jacksonville
San Antonio
Austin
New Orleans
Houston
Orlando
Tampa-St. Petersburg-Clearwater
West Palm Beach-Boca Raton-Delray Beach
Miami
Fort Lauderdale-Hollywood-Pompano Beach

UNITED STATES

Alaska
Anchorage

Hawaii
Honolulu

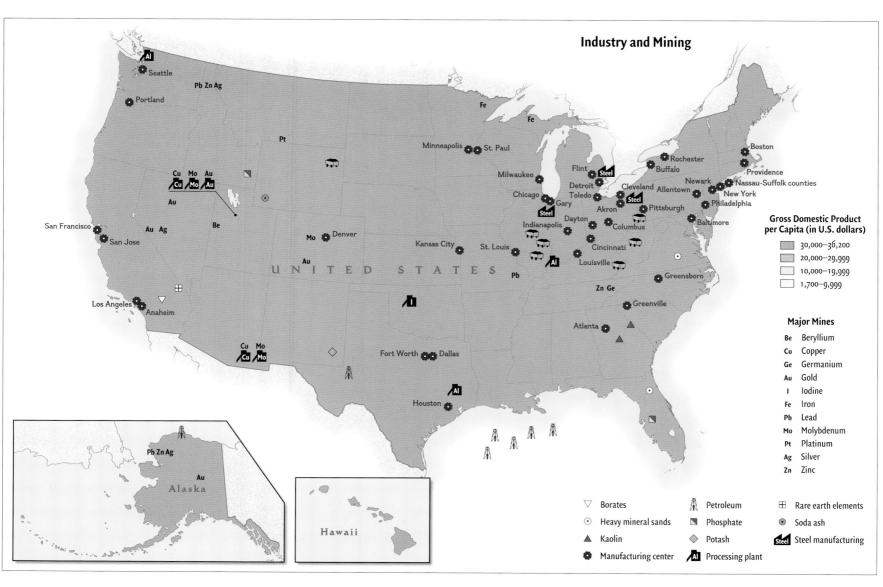

Industry and Mining

Gross Domestic Product per Capita (in U.S. dollars)

- 30,000–36,200
- 20,000–29,999
- 10,000–19,999
- 1,700–9,999

Major Mines

- Be Beryllium
- Cu Copper
- Ge Germanium
- Au Gold
- I Iodine
- Fe Iron
- Pb Lead
- Mo Molybdenum
- Pt Platinum
- Ag Silver
- Zn Zinc

Seattle
Portland
Pb Zn Ag
Fe
Fe
Pt
Minneapolis St. Paul
Rochester
Boston
Milwaukee
Flint
Buffalo
Providence
Detroit
Cleveland
Newark
Nassau-Suffolk counties
Cu Mo Au
Chicago
Toledo
Allentown
New York
Au
Gary
Akron
Pittsburgh
Philadelphia
Indianapolis
Dayton
Columbus
Baltimore
San Francisco
Au Ag
Be
Dayton
Cincinnati
San Jose
Mo
Denver
Kansas City
St. Louis
Au
Louisville
Pb
Greensboro
UNITED STATES
Zn Ge
Greenville
Cu Mo
Atlanta
Los Angeles
Anaheim
Fort Worth Dallas
Houston

Alaska
Pb Zn Ag
Au

Hawaii

- ▽ Borates
- ⊙ Heavy mineral sands
- ▲ Kaolin
- ✲ Manufacturing center
- Petroleum
- Phosphate
- ◇ Potash
- **Al** Processing plant
- ⊞ Rare earth elements
- Soda ash
- **Steel** Steel manufacturing

Major Highways
UNITED STATES

Albers Conic Equal-Area Projection

SCALE 1:10,824,000

1 Centimeter = 108 Kilometers; 1 Inch = 171 Miles

KILOMETERS

0 100 200 300 400 500

STATUTE MILES

0 100 200 300 400 500

PRINCIPAL HAWAIIAN ISLANDS

Longitude West 159° of Greenwich

Longitude West 90° of Greenwich

0 100 km
0 100 statute mi

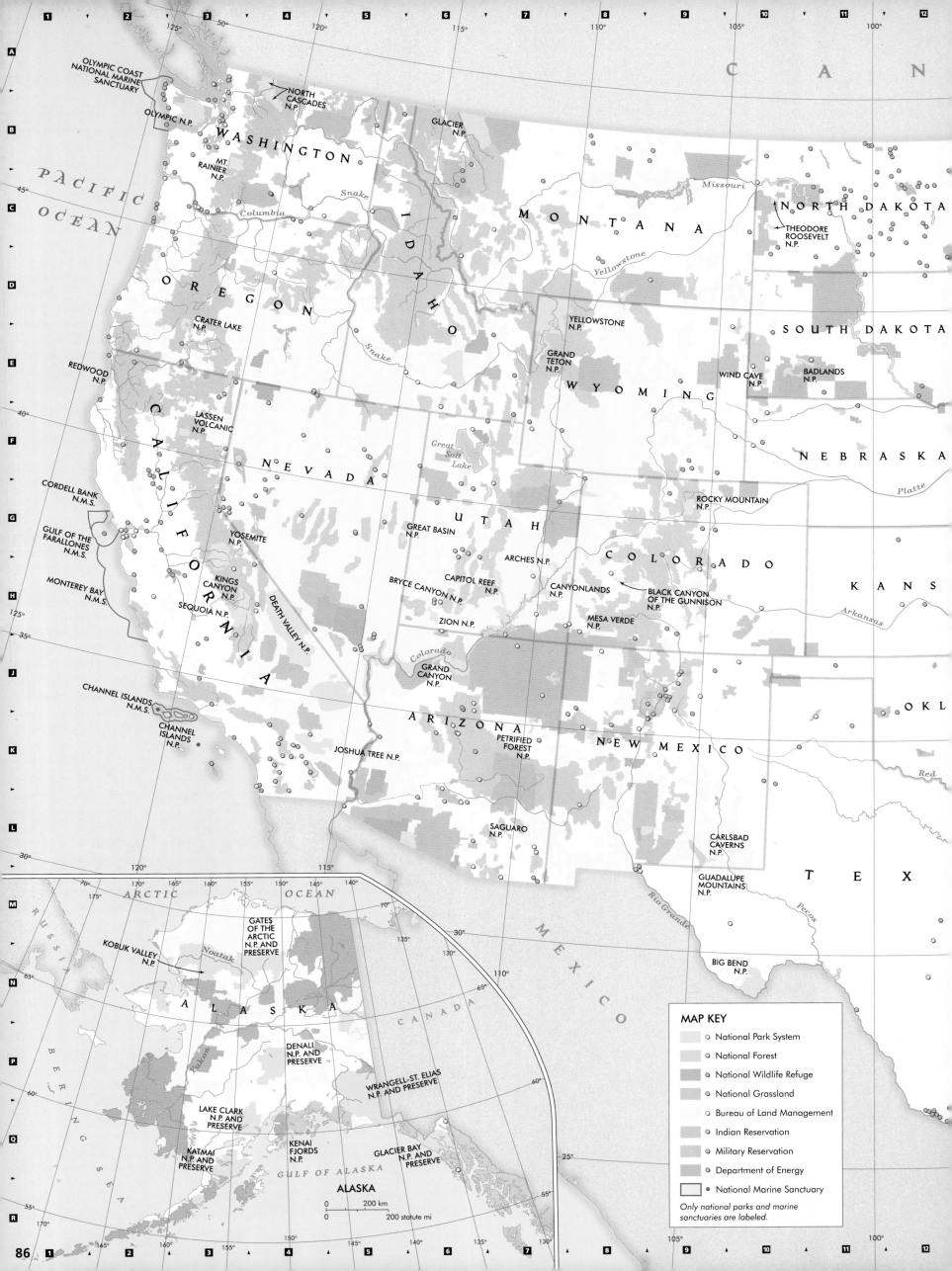

MAP KEY

- National Park System
- National Forest
- National Wildlife Refuge
- National Grassland
- Bureau of Land Management
- Indian Reservation
- Military Reservation
- Department of Energy
- National Marine Sanctuary

Only national parks and marine sanctuaries are labeled.

ALASKA

| 0 | 200 km |
| 0 | 200 statute mi |

CANADA

95° 90° 85° 80° 75° 70°

Lake of
the Woods

VOYAGEURS N.P.

ISLE ROYALE
N.P.

Lake Superior

*Georgian
Bay*

St. Lawrence

ACADIA
N.P.

MAINE

MINNESOTA

WISCONSIN

MICHIGAN

Lake Michigan

Lake Huron

Lake Ontario

Lake Erie

*Lake
Champlain*

VERMONT

NEW HAMPSHIRE

STELLWAGEN
BANK N.M.S.

MASSACHUSETTS

CONN.

RHODE ISLAND

IOWA

ILLINOIS

INDIANA

OHIO

CUYAHOGA
VALLEY N.P.

NEW YORK

PENNSYLVANIA

Hudson

NEW JERSEY

DELAWARE

MARYLAND

Mississippi

Missouri

MISSOURI

KENTUCKY

Ohio

WASHINGTON, D.C.

WEST
VIRGINIA

SHENANDOAH
N.P.

VIRGINIA

ATLANTIC

OCEAN

MAMMOTH
CAVE N.P

NORTH CAROLINA

MONITOR
N.M.S.

ARKANSAS

TENNESSEE

GREAT SMOKY
MOUNTAINS
N.P.

SOUTH
CAROLINA

Savannah

HOT
SPRINGS
N.P.

ALABAMA

GEORGIA

Mississippi

MISSISSIPPI

LOUISIANA

Brazos

GRAY'S
REEF
N.M.S.

FLORIDA

Federal Lands
UNITED STATES

GULF OF MEXICO

FLOWER GARDEN
BANKS N.M.S.

*Lake
Okeechobee*

BAHAMAS

Longitude West 90° of Greenwich

Longitude West 159° of Greenwich 156°

PACIFIC OCEAN

KAUAI

OAHU

MOLOKAI

21°

HAWAIIAN ISLANDS
HUMPBACK WHALE
NATIONAL MARINE
SANCTUARY

LANAI

MAUI

HALEAKALA N.P

21°

PRINCIPAL HAWAIIAN
ISLANDS

HAWAII

0 100 km

0 100 statute mi

HAWAII
VOLCANOES
NATIONAL PARK

EVERGLADES
N.P.

BISCAYNE N.P.

DRY TORTUGAS
N.P.

FLORIDA KEYS
N.M.S.

CUBA

Lambert Conformal Conic Projection, Standard Parallels 33° And 45°

SCALE 1:3,102,000
1 CENTIMETER = 31 KILOMETERS; 1 INCH = 49 MILES

0   50   100   150
KILOMETERS

0   50   100   150
STATUTE MILES

Elevations in feet

LAKE ONTARIO

LAKE ERIE

ONTARIO

NEW YORK

PENNSYLVANIA

OHIO

WEST VIRGINIA

MARYLAND

DELAWARE

NEW JERSEY

ADIRONDACK MOUNTAINS

CATSKILL MTS.

ALLEGHENY MTS.

Niagara R.

Finger Lakes

Oneida L.

Cayuga L.

Pymatuning Res.

Allegheny Res.

Saranac Lakes

Lake Champlain

Lake George

Delaware Bay

Cranberry Lake

Raquette L.

Black R.

Genesee R.

Susquehanna R.

Juniata R.

Delaware R.

Hudson R.

Mohawk R.

Chemung R.

Ohio R.

Monongahela R.

Great Sacandaga Lake

CONN

Massena, Malone, Norwood, Potsdam, Ogdensburg, Canton, Morristown, Gouverneur, Plattsburgh, Dannemora, Rouses Point, St. Alb., Swant., Mt. Mansfield 4393, Winooski, Burlington, Vergennes, Middlebu., VER., Tupper Lake, Saranac Lake, Lake Placid, Mt. Marcy 5344, Port Henry, Ticonderoga

Alexandria Bay, Clayton, Cape Vincent, Sackets Harbor, Carthage, Watertown, Ellisburg, Lowville, Boonville, 3899, FT. STANWIX N.M., Camden, Rome, Utica, Little Falls, Herkimer, Ilion, Gloversville, Johnstown, Amsterdam, Saratoga Springs, Rutland, Whitehall, Fair Haven, Granville, Glens Falls, Corinth, Schenectady, Cohoes, Troy, Albany, Mt. Greylock 3491, Benningt., MA., Pittsfield

Port Ontario, Pulaski, Lycoming, Oswego, Fulton, Hamilton, Cooperstown, Stamford, Ravena, Chatham, Catskill, Hudson, Westfie., Bristol

Kendall, Brockport, Greece, Irondequoit, Albion, Medina, Lockport, Niagara Falls, N. Tonawanda, Rochester, Fairport, Palmyra, Newark, Baldwinsville, Solvay, Canastota, Oneida, Syracuse, Batavia, Le Roy, Lyons, Geneva, Auburn, Seneca Falls, Canandaigua, Geneseo, Penn Yan, Homer, Cortland, Norwich, Oneonta, Sidney, Delhi, 2817, Saugerties, Kingston, 2380 Mt. Frissel, Hyde Park, Poughkeepsie, 2289, Torrington, New Brit.

Buffalo, Lackawanna, Amherst, Cheektowaga, E. Aurora, Hamburg, Farnham, Dunkirk, Gowanda, Springville, Dansville, Watkins Glen, Ithaca, Fredonia, Franklinville, Westfield 2115, North East, Erie, Wesleyville, Falconer, Salamanca, Jamestown, Hornell, Bath, Canisteo, Corning, Horseheads, Elmira, Waverly, Sayre, Johnson City, Endicott, Oswego, Binghamton, Deposit, Susquehanna, Liberty, Monticello, Newburgh, West Point, Danbury, Waterbury, Meride., Hamden, New Hav., Peekskill, Bridgeport

N. Springfield, Girard, Corry, Warren, Bradford, Smethport, Port Allegany, Coudersport, Galeton, Elkland, Mansfield, Wellsboro, Towanda, Canton, 2580, 2548, Olean, Cambridge Springs, Union City, Meadville, Titusville, Kane, Mt. Jewett, Austin, 2693, Carbondale, Honesdale, Middletown, West Point, New City, White Plains, Stroudsburg, Paterson, Yonkers, New Rochelle, Mount Vernon, Brentw.

Greenville, Oil City, Franklin, Johnsonburg, Ridgway, Emporium, St. Marys, Renovo, Eagles Mere, Williamsport, Montoursville, Muncy, Milton, Scranton, Archbald, Dickson City, Dunmore, Old Forge, Pittston, Kingston, Plymouth, Wilkes-Barre, Nanticoke, DELAWARE WATER GAP N.R.A., High Point 1803, 23, Morristown, E. Orange, Newark, NEW YORK, Jersey City, Hempstead, Levittown, Freeport, Patchog., Sharon, Farrell, Grove City, Polk, Clarion, Brookville, Brockway, Du Bois, Clearfield, Lock Haven, Jersey Shore, Bloomsburg, Hazleton, Shenandoah, Easton, Bethlehem, Allentown, Emmaus, Plainfield, New Brunswick, Edison, Elizabeth

New Castle, Butler, Beaver Falls, Kittanning, Indiana, Punxsutawney, Philipsburg, Bellefonte, State College, Sunbury, Shamokin, Mt. Carmel, Pottsville, Reading, Pottstown, Lansdale, Princeton, Freehold, Long Branch, Asbury Park

Aliquippa, McKees Rocks, Pittsburgh, Bethel Park, Duquesne, Penn Hills, Clairton, Monessen, McKeesport, Greensburg, Johnstown, Windber, 3136, Tyrone, Altoona, Hollidaysburg, Huntingdon, Lewistown, Mechanicsburg, Carlisle, Lebanon, Norristown, Bristol, Trenton, Levittown, Lakewood, Point Pleasant, PHILADELPHIA, W. Chester, Upper Darby, Chester, Camden, NEW JERSEY, Seaside Park

Washington, Monessen, Connellsville, Somerset, Bedford, Breezewood, Shippensburg, Chambersburg, Harrisburg, Steelton, Lancaster, Columbia, York, Woodbury, Glassboro, Barnegat, Barnegat Light, Waynesburg, Uniontown, Masontown, Mt. Davis 3213, Greencastle, Waynesboro, Hanover, Gettysburg, Woodstown, Hammonton, Tuckerton, Beach Haven

Vineland, Bridgeton, Pleasantville, Atlantic City, Ventnor City, Ocean City, Millville, Wildwood, Cape May

ST. LAWRENCE ISLANDS N.P.

75° 45° 42° 78° 39°

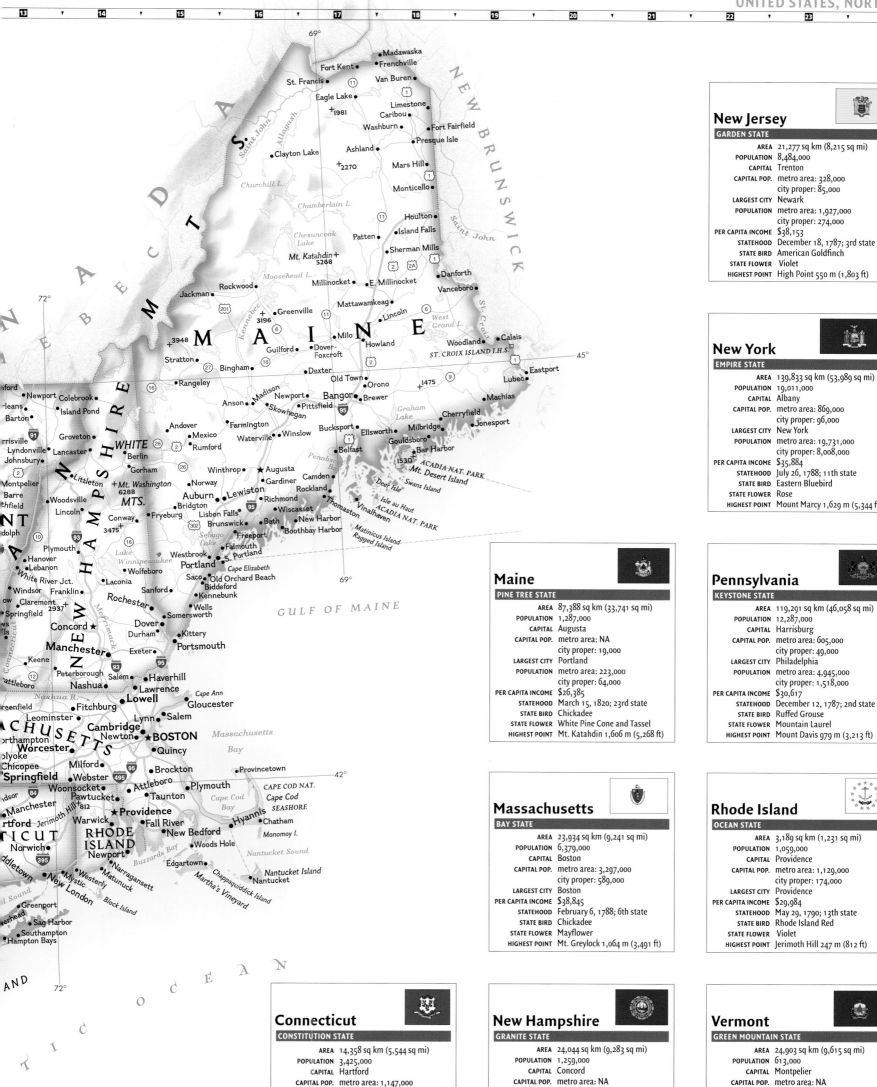

New Jersey
GARDEN STATE

AREA	21,277 sq km (8,215 sq mi)
POPULATION	8,484,000
CAPITAL	Trenton
CAPITAL POP.	metro area: 328,000
	city proper: 85,000
LARGEST CITY	Newark
POPULATION	metro area: 1,927,000
	city proper: 274,000
PER CAPITA INCOME	$38,153
STATEHOOD	December 18, 1787; 3rd state
STATE BIRD	American Goldfinch
STATE FLOWER	Violet
HIGHEST POINT	High Point 550 m (1,803 ft)

New York
EMPIRE STATE

AREA	139,833 sq km (53,989 sq mi)
POPULATION	19,011,000
CAPITAL	Albany
CAPITAL POP.	metro area: 869,000
	city proper: 96,000
LARGEST CITY	New York
POPULATION	metro area: 19,731,000
	city proper: 8,008,000
PER CAPITA INCOME	$35,884
STATEHOOD	July 26, 1788; 11th state
STATE BIRD	Eastern Bluebird
STATE FLOWER	Rose
HIGHEST POINT	Mount Marcy 1,629 m (5,344 ft)

Maine
PINE TREE STATE

AREA	87,388 sq km (33,741 sq mi)
POPULATION	1,287,000
CAPITAL	Augusta
CAPITAL POP.	metro area: NA
	city proper: 19,000
LARGEST CITY	Portland
POPULATION	metro area: 223,000
	city proper: 64,000
PER CAPITA INCOME	$26,385
STATEHOOD	March 15, 1820; 23rd state
STATE BIRD	Chickadee
STATE FLOWER	White Pine Cone and Tassel
HIGHEST POINT	Mt. Katahdin 1,606 m (5,268 ft)

Pennsylvania
KEYSTONE STATE

AREA	119,291 sq km (46,058 sq mi)
POPULATION	12,287,000
CAPITAL	Harrisburg
CAPITAL POP.	metro area: 605,000
	city proper: 49,000
LARGEST CITY	Philadelphia
POPULATION	metro area: 4,945,000
	city proper: 1,518,000
PER CAPITA INCOME	$30,617
STATEHOOD	December 12, 1787; 2nd state
STATE BIRD	Ruffed Grouse
STATE FLOWER	Mountain Laurel
HIGHEST POINT	Mount Davis 979 m (3,213 ft)

Massachusetts
BAY STATE

AREA	23,934 sq km (9,241 sq mi)
POPULATION	6,379,000
CAPITAL	Boston
CAPITAL POP.	metro area: 3,297,000
	city proper: 589,000
LARGEST CITY	Boston
PER CAPITA INCOME	$38,845
STATEHOOD	February 6, 1788; 6th state
STATE BIRD	Chickadee
STATE FLOWER	Mayflower
HIGHEST POINT	Mt. Greylock 1,064 m (3,491 ft)

Rhode Island
OCEAN STATE

AREA	3,189 sq km (1,231 sq mi)
POPULATION	1,059,000
CAPITAL	Providence
CAPITAL POP.	metro area: 1,129,000
	city proper: 174,000
LARGEST CITY	Providence
PER CAPITA INCOME	$29,984
STATEHOOD	May 29, 1790; 13th state
STATE BIRD	Rhode Island Red
STATE FLOWER	Violet
HIGHEST POINT	Jerimoth Hill 247 m (812 ft)

Connecticut
CONSTITUTION STATE

AREA	14,358 sq km (5,544 sq mi)
POPULATION	3,425,000
CAPITAL	Hartford
CAPITAL POP.	metro area: 1,147,000
	city proper: 122,000
LARGEST CITY	Bridgeport
POPULATION	metro area: 446,000
	city proper: 140,000
PER CAPITA INCOME	$41,930
STATEHOOD	January 9, 1788; 5th state
STATE BIRD	Robin
STATE FLOWER	Mountain Laurel
HIGHEST POINT	Mt. Frissel, South slope 725 m (2,380 ft)

New Hampshire
GRANITE STATE

AREA	24,044 sq km (9,283 sq mi)
POPULATION	1,259,000
CAPITAL	Concord
CAPITAL POP.	metro area: NA
	city proper: 41,000
LARGEST CITY	Manchester
POPULATION	metro area: 190,000
	city proper: 107,000
PER CAPITA INCOME	$33,928
STATEHOOD	June 21, 1788; 9th state
STATE BIRD	Purple Finch
STATE FLOWER	Purple Lilac
HIGHEST POINT	Mount Washington 1,917 m (6,288 ft)

Vermont
GREEN MOUNTAIN STATE

AREA	24,903 sq km (9,615 sq mi)
POPULATION	613,000
CAPITAL	Montpelier
CAPITAL POP.	metro area: NA
	city proper: 8,000
LARGEST CITY	Burlington
POPULATION	metro area: 156,000
	city proper: 39,000
PER CAPITA INCOME	$27,992
STATEHOOD	March 4, 1791; 14th state
STATE BIRD	Hermit Thrush
STATE FLOWER	Red Clover
HIGHEST POINT	Mount Mansfield 1,339 m (4,393 ft)

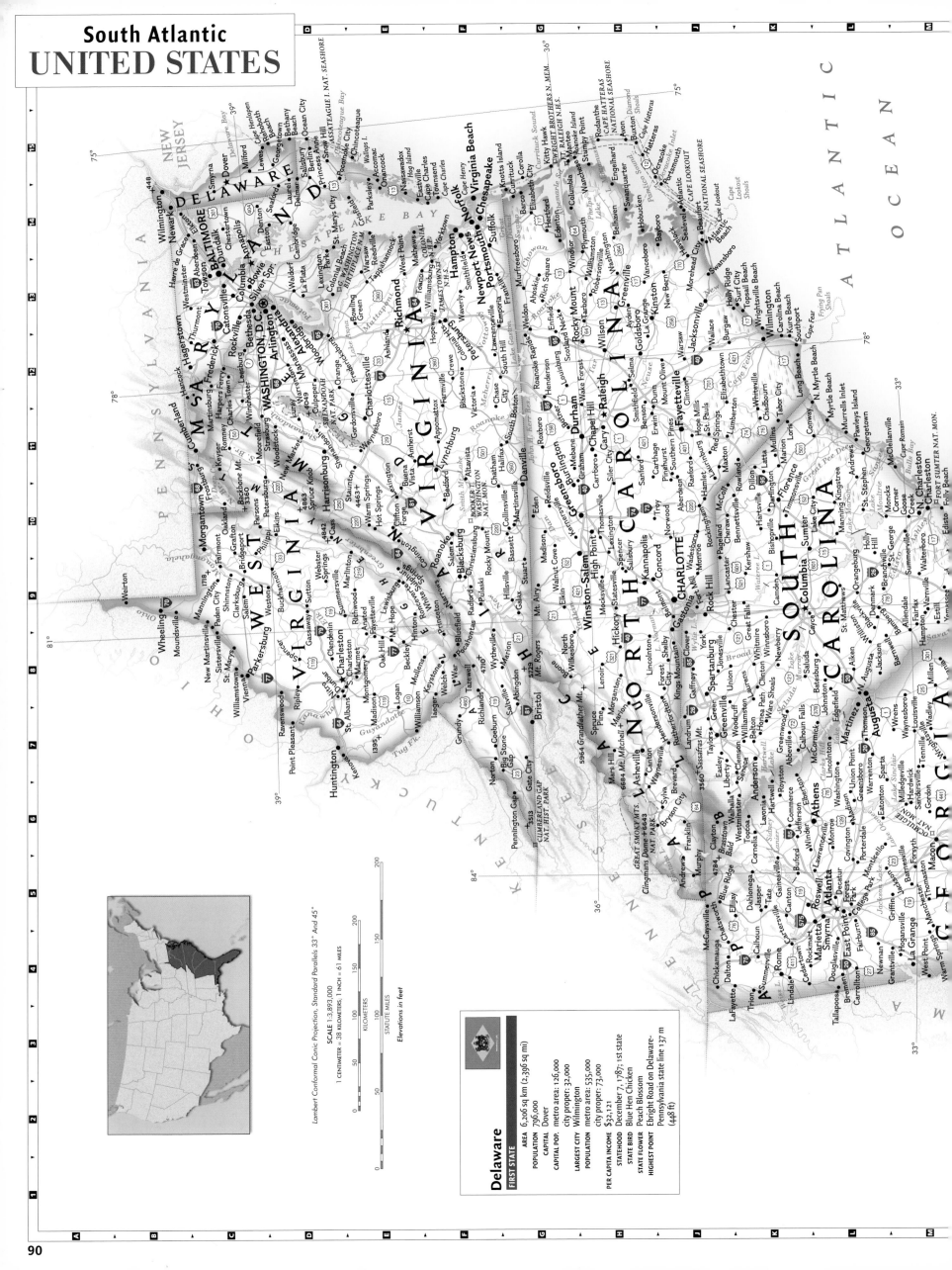

North Carolina
TAR HEEL STATE

AREA	136,421 sq km (52,672 sq mi)
POPULATION	8,186,000
CAPITAL	Raleigh
CAPITAL POP.	metro area: 936,000
	city proper: 276,000
LARGEST CITY	Charlotte
POPULATION	metro area: 1,417,000
	city proper: 541,000
PER CAPITA INCOME	$27,418
STATEHOOD	November 21, 1789; 12th state
STATE BIRD	Cardinal
STATE FLOWER	Flowering Dogwood
HIGHEST POINT	Mount Mitchell 2,037 m (6,684 ft)

South Carolina
PALMETTO STATE

AREA	80,779 sq km (31,189 sq mi)
POPULATION	4,063,000
CAPITAL	Columbia
CAPITAL POP.	metro area: 516,000
	city proper: 116,000
LARGEST CITY	Columbia
PER CAPITA INCOME	$24,594
STATEHOOD	May 23, 1788; 8th state
STATE BIRD	Carolina Wren
STATE FLOWER	Yellow Jessamine
HIGHEST POINT	Sassafras Mountain 1,085 m (3,560 ft)

Virginia
OLD DOMINION

AREA	109,625 sq km (42,326 sq mi)
POPULATION	7,188,000
CAPITAL	Richmond
CAPITAL POP.	metro area: 904,000
	city proper: 198,000
LARGEST CITY	Virginia Beach
POPULATION	metro area: 1,517,000
	city proper: 425,000
PER CAPITA INCOME	$32,295
STATEHOOD	June 25, 1788; 10th state
STATE BIRD	Cardinal
STATE FLOWER	Flowering Dogwood
HIGHEST POINT	Mount Rogers 1,746 m (5,729 ft)

West Virginia
MOUNTAIN STATE

AREA	62,759 sq km (24,231 sq mi)
POPULATION	1,802,000
CAPITAL	Charleston
CAPITAL POP.	metro area: 251,000
	city proper: 53,000
LARGEST CITY	Charleston
PER CAPITA INCOME	$22,725
STATEHOOD	June 20, 1863; 35th state
STATE BIRD	Cardinal
STATE FLOWER	Rhododendron
HIGHEST POINT	Spruce Knob 1,482 m (4,863 ft)

Maryland
OLD LINE STATE

AREA	31,849 sq km (12,297 sq mi)
POPULATION	5,375,000
CAPITAL	Annapolis
CAPITAL POP.	metro area: 78,590
	city proper: 36,000
LARGEST CITY	Baltimore
POPULATION	metro area: 2,440,000
	city proper: 651,000
PER CAPITA INCOME	$34,950
STATEHOOD	April 28, 1788; 7th state
STATE BIRD	Northern (Baltimore) Oriole
STATE FLOWER	Black-eyed Susan
HIGHEST POINT	Backbone Mountain 1,024 m (3,360 ft)

Georgia
EMPIRE STATE OF THE SOUTH

AREA	152,750 sq km (58,977 sq mi)
POPULATION	8,384,000
CAPITAL	Atlanta
CAPITAL POP.	metro area: 3,857,000
	city proper: 416,000
LARGEST CITY	Atlanta
PER CAPITA INCOME	$28,438
STATEHOOD	January 2, 1788; 4th state
STATE BIRD	Brown Thrasher
STATE FLOWER	Cherokee Rose
HIGHEST POINT	Brasstown Bald 1,458 m (4,784 ft)

District of Columbia
THE NATION'S CAPITAL

AREA	177 sq km (68 sq mi)
POPULATION	572,000
CAPITAL	
CAPITAL POP.	metro area: 4,396,000
	city proper: 572,000
PER CAPITA INCOME	$40,498
ESTABLISHMENT	1790–1791 (Site of capital chosen by George Washington, Maryland and Virginia then ceded a ten mile by ten mile area that included land from both states)
OFFICIAL BIRD	Wood Thrush
OFFICIAL FLOWER	American Beauty Rose
HIGHEST POINT	Tenleytown at Reno Reservoir 125 m (410 ft)

Florida
SUNSHINE STATE

AREA	155,214 sq km (59,928 sq mi)
POPULATION	16,397,000
CAPITAL	Tallahassee
CAPITAL POP.	metro area: 248,000
	city proper: 151,000
LARGEST CITY	Jacksonville
POPULATION	metro area: 959,000
	city proper: 736,000
PER CAPITA INCOME	$28,493
STATEHOOD	March 3, 1845; 27th state
STATE BIRD	Mockingbird
STATE FLOWER	Orange Blossom
HIGHEST POINT	Britton Hill 105 m (345 ft)

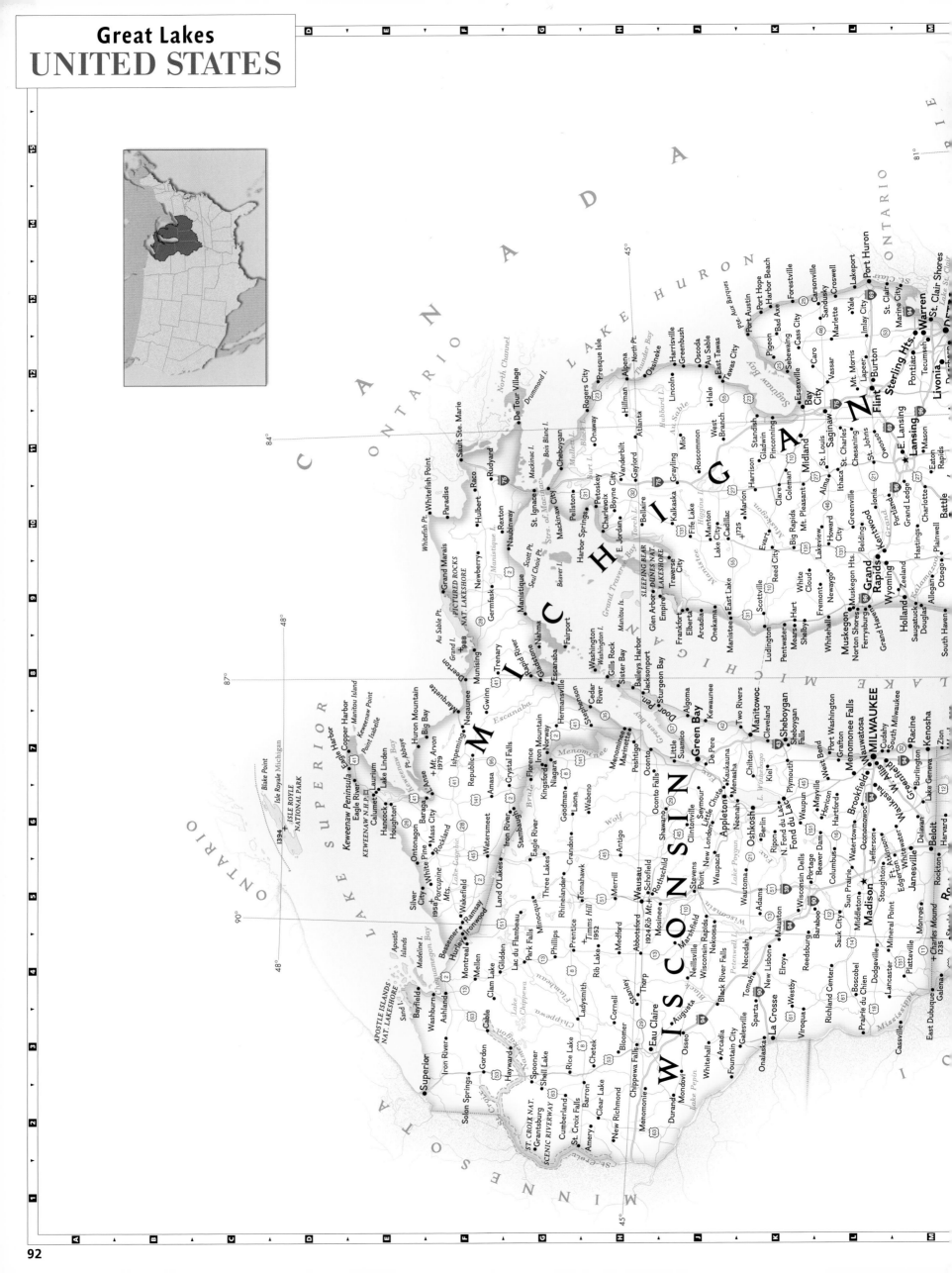

CANADA

ONTARIO

ONTARIO

LAKE HURON

St. Clair

Lake St. Clair

LAKE ERIE

81°

45°

LAKE SUPERIOR

ONTARIO

84°

48°

87°

90°

48°

45°

MICHIGAN

WISCONSIN

MINNESOTA

ISLE ROYALE NATIONAL PARK

APOSTLE ISLANDS NAT. LAKESHORE

ST. CROIX NAT. SCENIC RIVERWAY

PICTURED ROCKS NAT. LAKESHORE

SLEEPING BEAR DUNES NAT. LAKESHORE

Sault Ste. Marie

Whitefish Pt.
Whitefish Point
Paradise
Hulbert
Raco
Rudyard
De Tour Village
Drummond I.
Bois Blanc I.
Mackinac I.
St. Ignace
Mackinaw City
Cheboygan
Pellston
Harbor Springs
Petoskey
Boyne City
Charlevoix
E. Jordan
Bellaire
Kalkaska
Fife Lake
Manton
Cadillac
Lake City
McBain
Evart
Marion
Clare
Harrison
Gladwin
Standish
Sterling
West Branch
Roscommon
Grayling
Mio
Vanderbilt
Gaylord
Atlanta
Onaway
Rogers City
Presque Isle
Alpena
Hillman
Lincoln
Harrisville
Greenbush
Oscoda
Au Sable
East Tawas
Tawas City
Pte. Aux Barques
Port Austin
Port Hope
Harbor Beach
Bad Axe
Caseville
Pigeon
Sebewaing
Caro
Vassar
Essexville
Bay City
Saginaw
Midland
St. Louis
Alma
Ithaca
St. Charles
Chesaning
Owosso
St. Johns
E. Lansing
Lansing
Mason
Eaton Rapids
Charlotte
Grand Ledge
Portland
Ionia
Belding
Greenville
Howard City
Big Rapids
Reed City
White Cloud
Newaygo
Fremont
Hart
Shelby
Mears
Pentwater
Ludington
Scottville
Frankfort
Elberta
Arcadia
Onekama
Manistee
Empire
Glen Arbor
Traverse City
Torch L.
Beulah
Forestville
Carsonville
Sandusky
Croswell
Lexington
Yale
Imlay City
Marlette
Marine City
St. Clair
Port Huron
Lapeer
Mt. Morris
Burton
Flint
Pontiac
Tecumseh
Livonia
Warren
Sterling Hts.
St. Clair Shores

Manitou Island
Copper Harbor
Eagle Harbor
Point Isabelle
Keweenaw Peninsula
Eagle River
Laurium
Calumet
Hancock
Houghton
Keweenaw Bay
Baraga
L'Anse
Pt. Abbaye
Huron Mountain
Big Bay
Mt. Arvon
1979
Ishpeming
Negaunee
Marquette
Munising
Au Sable Pt.
Grand Marais
Grand I.
Deerton
Trenary
Rapid River
Gwinn
Republic
Amasa
Crystal Falls
Iron Mountain
Norway
Kingsford
Niagara
Florence
Goodman
Wabeno
Laona
Crandon
Three Lakes
Tomahawk
Rhinelander
Minocqua
Eagle River
Land O'Lakes
Watersmeet
Iron River
Stambaugh
Brule
Newberry
Germfask
Manistique
Thompson
Nahma
Gladstone
Escanaba
Gills Rock
Washington
Washington I.
Ellison Bay
Sister Bay
Baileys Harbor
Jacksonport
Sturgeon Bay
Kewaunee
Algoma
Two Rivers
Manitowoc
Cleveland
Sheboygan
Sheboygan Falls
Plymouth
Kiel
Chilton
Kaukauna
Appleton
Menasha
Neenah
Little Chute
Kimberly
Seymour
Clintonville
New London
Shawano
Oconto Falls
Oconto
Little Suamico
Green Bay
De Pere
Marinette
Menominee
Peshtigo
Coleman
Cedar River
Hermansville
Stephenson

Superior
Iron River
Gordon
Solon Springs
Bayfield
Washburn
Ashland
Mellen
Hayward
Spooner
Shell Lake
Clam Lake
Glidden
Cable
Madeline I.
Apostle Islands
Sand I.
Blake Point
1394
Silver City
Porcupine Mts.
1958
White Pine
Ontonagon
Rockland
Mass City
Greenland
Bruce Crossing
Bergland
Wakefield
Bessemer
Hurley
Ironwood
Montreal
Ramsay
Saxon
Mellen
Lac du Flambeau
Park Falls
Phillips
Prentice
Medford
Abbotsford
Marshfield
Neillsville
Black River Falls
Merrillan
Tomah
Sparta
La Crosse
Onalaska
Holmen
West Salem
Bangor
Viroqua
Westby
Coon Valley
Galesville
Arcadia
Independence
Whitehall
Blair
Osseo
Augusta
Eau Claire
Altoona
Chippewa Falls
Cornell
Ladysmith
Bruce
Rice Lake
Cumberland
Barron
Chetek
Bloomer
Stanley
Thorp
Cadott
Mondovi
Durand
Menomonie
Colfax
Boyceville
Baldwin
New Richmond
Amery
Clear Lake
Osceola
St. Croix Falls
Grantsburg
Solon Springs
Lake Pepin
Sand Lake
Rib Lake
Rothschild
Mosinee
Wausau
Schofield
Antigo
Wittenberg
Marion
Clintonville
Waupaca
Iola
Stevens Point
Wisconsin Rapids
Nekoosa
Adams
Friendship
Westfield
Wautoma
Berlin
Ripon
Green Lake
Princeton
Montello
Portage
Wisconsin Dells
Baraboo
Sauk City
Reedsburg
Richland Center
New Lisbon
Necedah
Mauston
Elroy
Hillsboro
Kendall
Wonewoc
Boscobel
Fennimore
Lancaster
Platteville
Dodgeville
Mineral Point
Prairie du Chien
Cassville
Boscobel
East Dubuque
Galena
Monroe
Brodhead
Darlington
Belmont
Mt. Horeb
Middleton
Madison
Stoughton
Edgerton
Milton
Janesville
Beloit
Delavan
Elkhorn
Lake Geneva
Harvard
Rockton
Sun Prairie
Columbus
Waterloo
Beaver Dam
Fond du Lac
N. Fond du Lac
Waupun
Mayville
Horicon
Hartford
West Bend
Grafton
Port Washington
Cedarburg
Menomonee Falls
Germantown
Jackson
Slinger
Hartland
Oconomowoc
Watertown
Jefferson
Ft. Atkinson
Whitewater
Palmyra
Waukesha
Brookfield
Wauwatosa
Milwaukee
W. Allis
Greenfield
Cudahy
South Milwaukee
Oak Creek
Franklin
Muskego
Burlington
Racine
Kenosha
Zion
Oshkosh
Omro
Winneconne
Neenah

CANADA
MINNESOTA

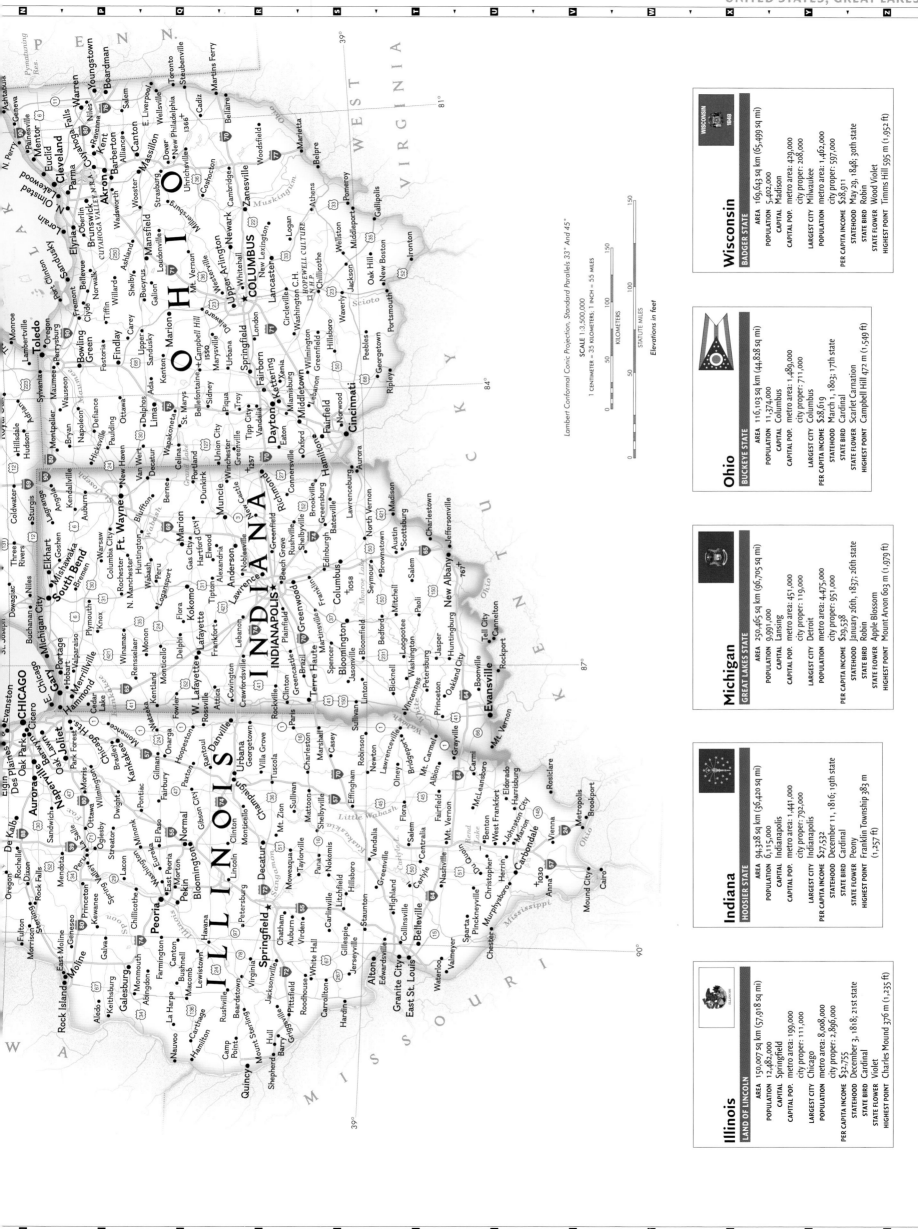

Alabama
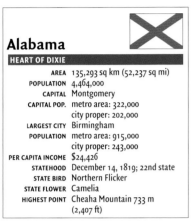

HEART OF DIXIE

AREA	135,293 sq km (52,237 sq mi)
POPULATION	4,464,000
CAPITAL	Montgomery
CAPITAL POP.	metro area: 322,000
	city proper: 202,000
LARGEST CITY	Birmingham
POPULATION	metro area: 915,000
	city proper: 243,000
PER CAPITA INCOME	$24,426
STATEHOOD	December 14, 1819; 22nd state
STATE BIRD	Northern Flicker
STATE FLOWER	Camelia
HIGHEST POINT	Cheaha Mountain 733 m (2,407 ft)

Arkansas

NATURAL STATE

AREA	137,742 sq km (53,182 sq mi)
POPULATION	2,692,000
CAPITAL	Little Rock
CAPITAL POP.	metro area: 559,000
	city proper: 183,000
LARGEST CITY	Little Rock
PER CAPITA INCOME	$22,912
STATEHOOD	June 15, 1836; 25th state
STATE BIRD	Mockingbird
STATE FLOWER	Apple Blossom
HIGHEST POINT	Magazine Mt. 839 m (2,753 ft)

Kentucky

BLUEGRASS STATE

AREA	104,665 sq km (40,411 sq mi)
POPULATION	4,066,000
CAPITAL	Frankfort
CAPITAL POP.	metro area: NA
	city proper: 28,000
LARGEST CITY	Lexington
POPULATION	metro area: 456,000
	city proper: 261,000
PER CAPITA INCOME	$25,057
STATEHOOD	June 1, 1792; 15th state
STATE BIRD	Cardinal
STATE FLOWER	Goldenrod
HIGHEST POINT	Black Mountain 1,263 m (4,145 ft)

Louisiana

PELICAN STATE

AREA	128,595 sq km (49,651 sq mi)
POPULATION	4,465,000
CAPITAL	Baton Rouge
CAPITAL POP.	metro area: 579,000
	city proper: 228,000
LARGEST CITY	New Orleans
POPULATION	metro area: 1,305,000
	city proper: 485,000
PER CAPITA INCOME	$24,084
STATEHOOD	April 30, 1812; 18th state
STATE BIRD	Brown Pelican
STATE FLOWER	Magnolia
HIGHEST POINT	Driskill Mountain 163 m (535 ft)

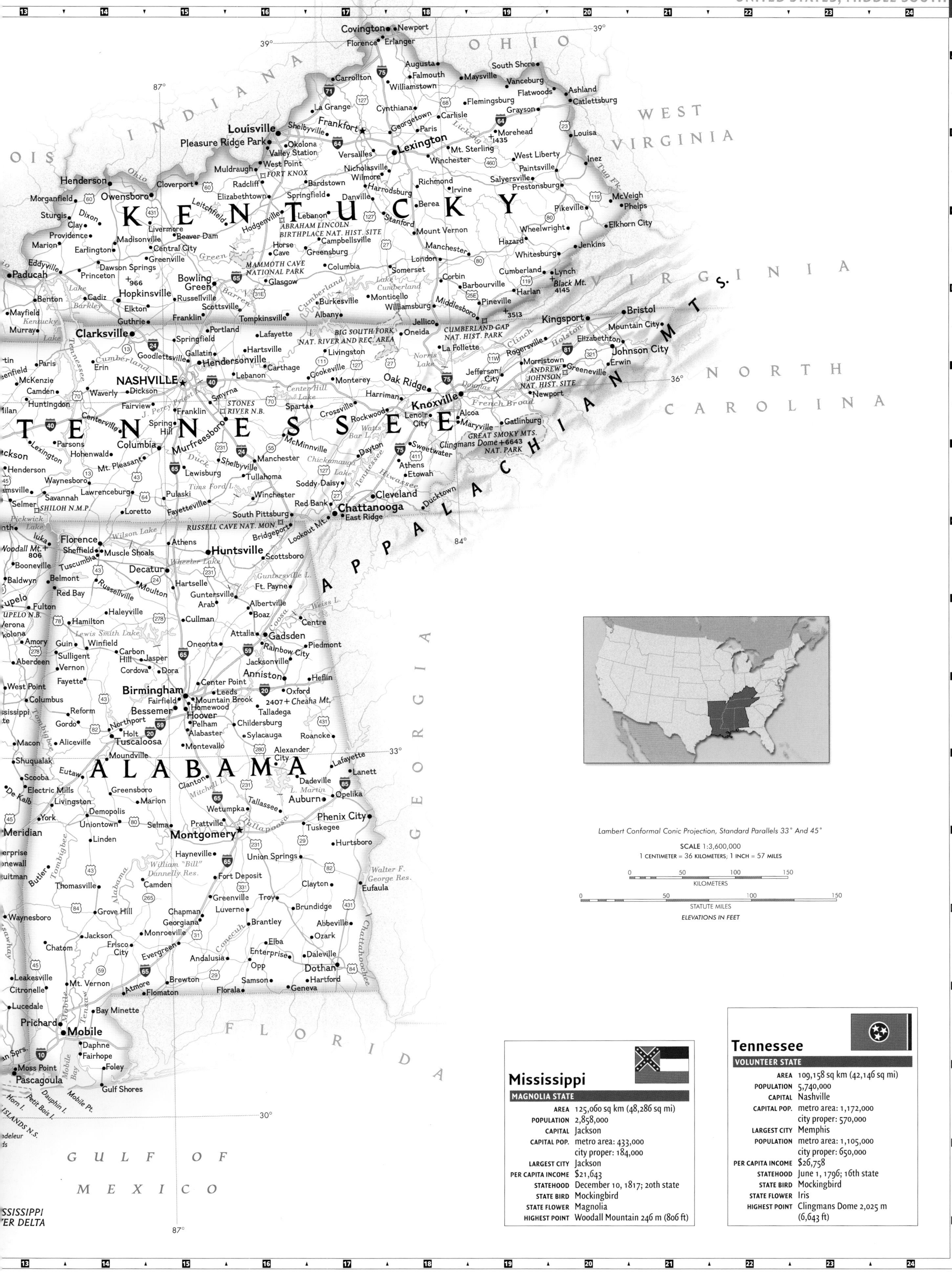

Lambert Conformal Conic Projection, Standard Parallels 33° And 45°

SCALE 1:3,600,000
1 CENTIMETER = 36 KILOMETERS; 1 INCH = 57 MILES

```
0        50        100        150
KILOMETERS

0        50        100        150
STATUTE MILES
```

ELEVATIONS IN FEET

Mississippi
MAGNOLIA STATE

AREA	125,060 sq km (48,286 sq mi)
POPULATION	2,858,000
CAPITAL	Jackson
CAPITAL POP.	metro area: 433,000 city proper: 184,000
LARGEST CITY	Jackson
PER CAPITA INCOME	$21,643
STATEHOOD	December 10, 1817; 20th state
STATE BIRD	Mockingbird
STATE FLOWER	Magnolia
HIGHEST POINT	Woodall Mountain 246 m (806 ft)

Tennessee
VOLUNTEER STATE

AREA	109,158 sq km (42,146 sq mi)
POPULATION	5,740,000
CAPITAL	Nashville
CAPITAL POP.	metro area: 1,172,000 city proper: 570,000
LARGEST CITY	Memphis
POPULATION	metro area: 1,105,000 city proper: 650,000
PER CAPITA INCOME	$26,758
STATEHOOD	June 1, 1796; 16th state
STATE BIRD	Mockingbird
STATE FLOWER	Iris
HIGHEST POINT	Clingmans Dome 2,025 m (6,643 ft)

95

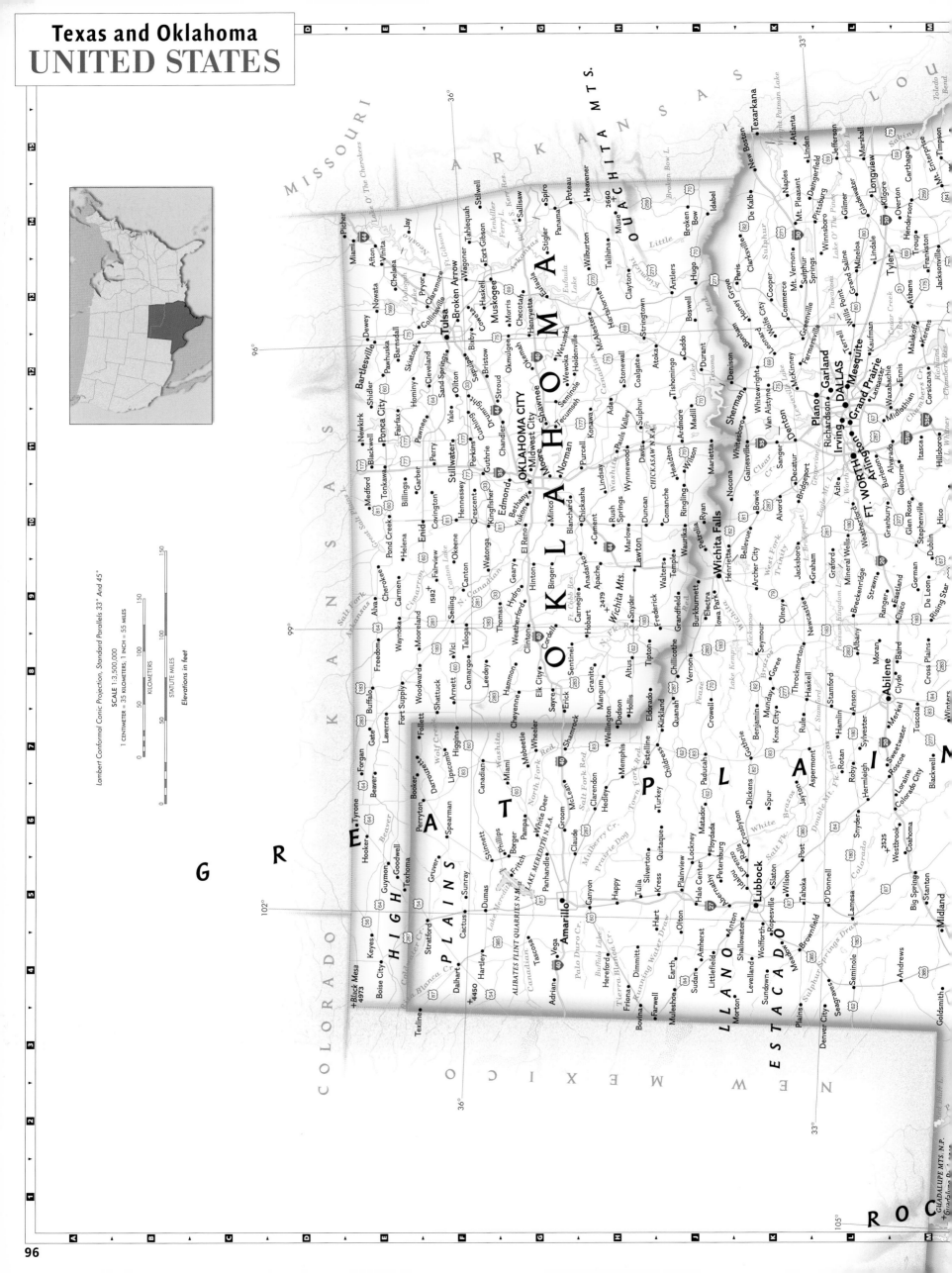

Lambert Conformal Conic Projection, Standard Parallels 33° And 45°

SCALE 1:3,500,000

1 CENTIMETER = 35 KILOMETERS, 1 INCH = 55 MILES

KILOMETERS

STATUTE MILES

Elevations in feet

MISSOURI

ARKANSAS

OUACHITA MTS.

LOU

K A N S A S

O K L A H O M A

COLORADO

NEW MEXICO

G R E A T   P L A I N S

HIGH PLAINS

LLANO ESTACADO

R O C

Texarkana

Tulsa

OKLAHOMA CITY

Wichita Falls

FT. WORTH

DALLAS

Garland

Mesquite

Grand Prairie

Plano

Richardson

Irving

Arlington

Abilene

Lubbock

Amarillo

Midland

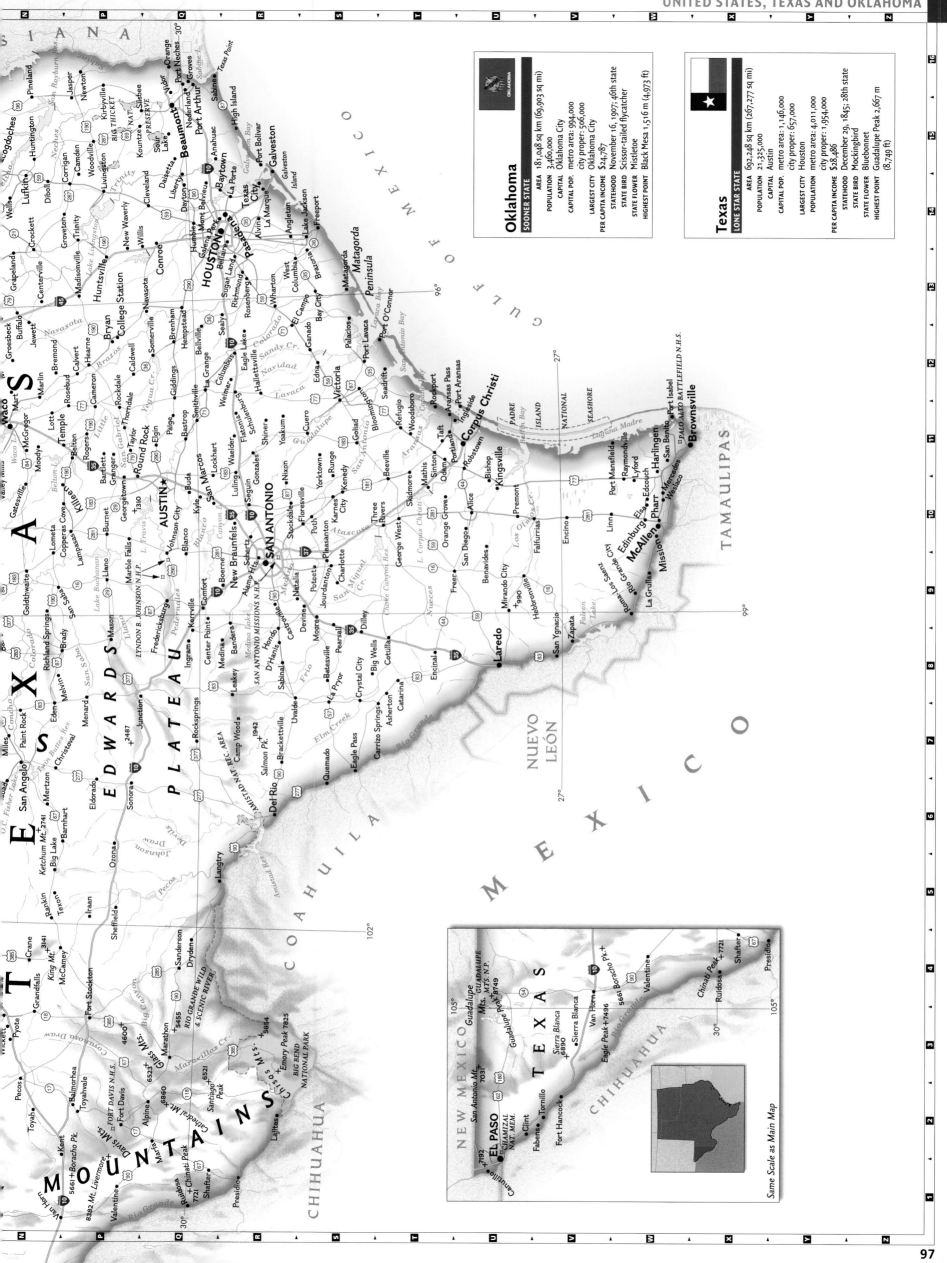

Northern Plains
UNITED STATES

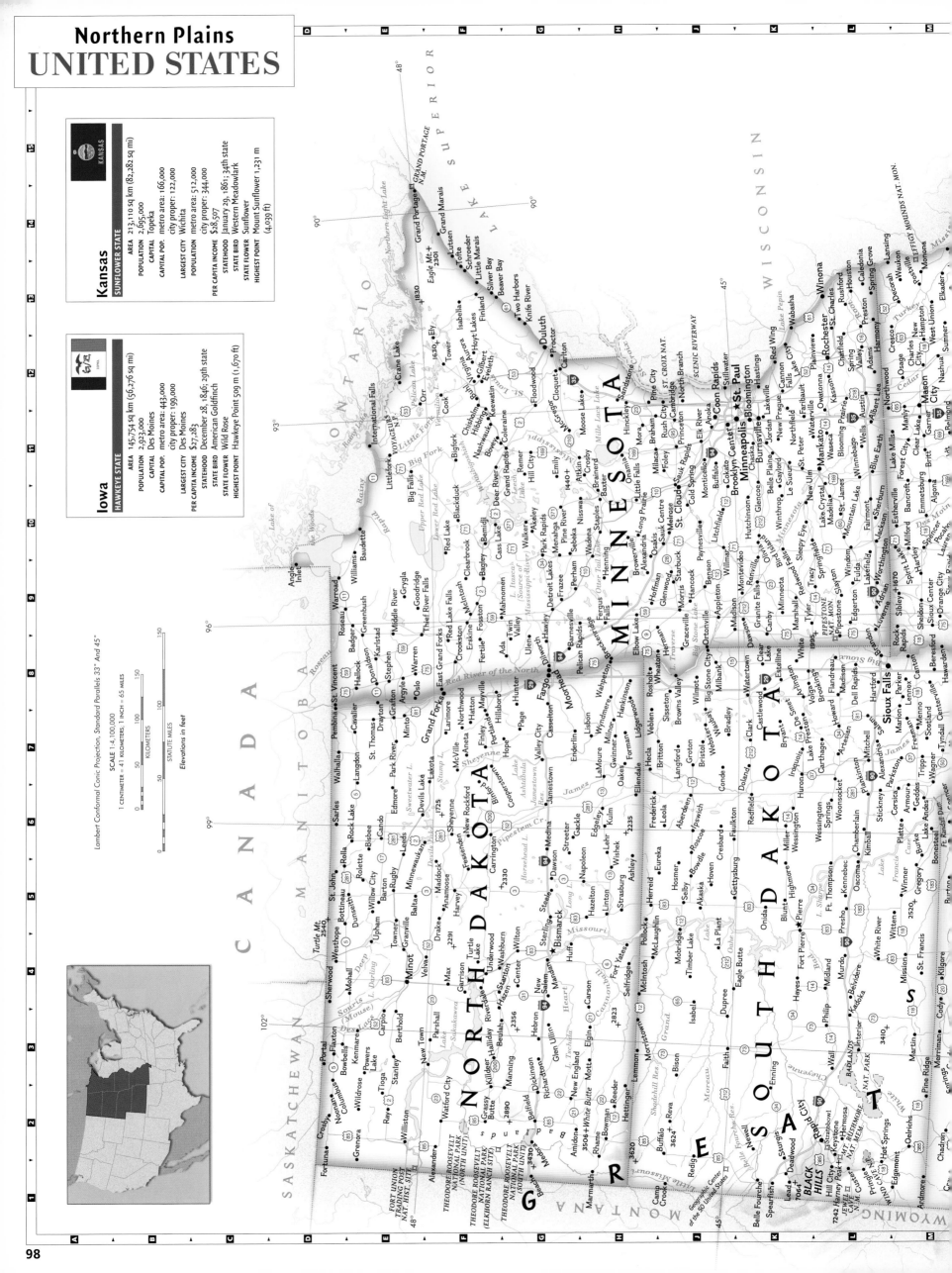
Lambert Conformal Conic Projection, Standard Parallels 33° And 45°

SCALE 1:4,100,000

1 CENTIMETER = 41 KILOMETERS; 1 INCH = 65 MILES

KILOMETERS

STATUTE MILES

Elevations in feet

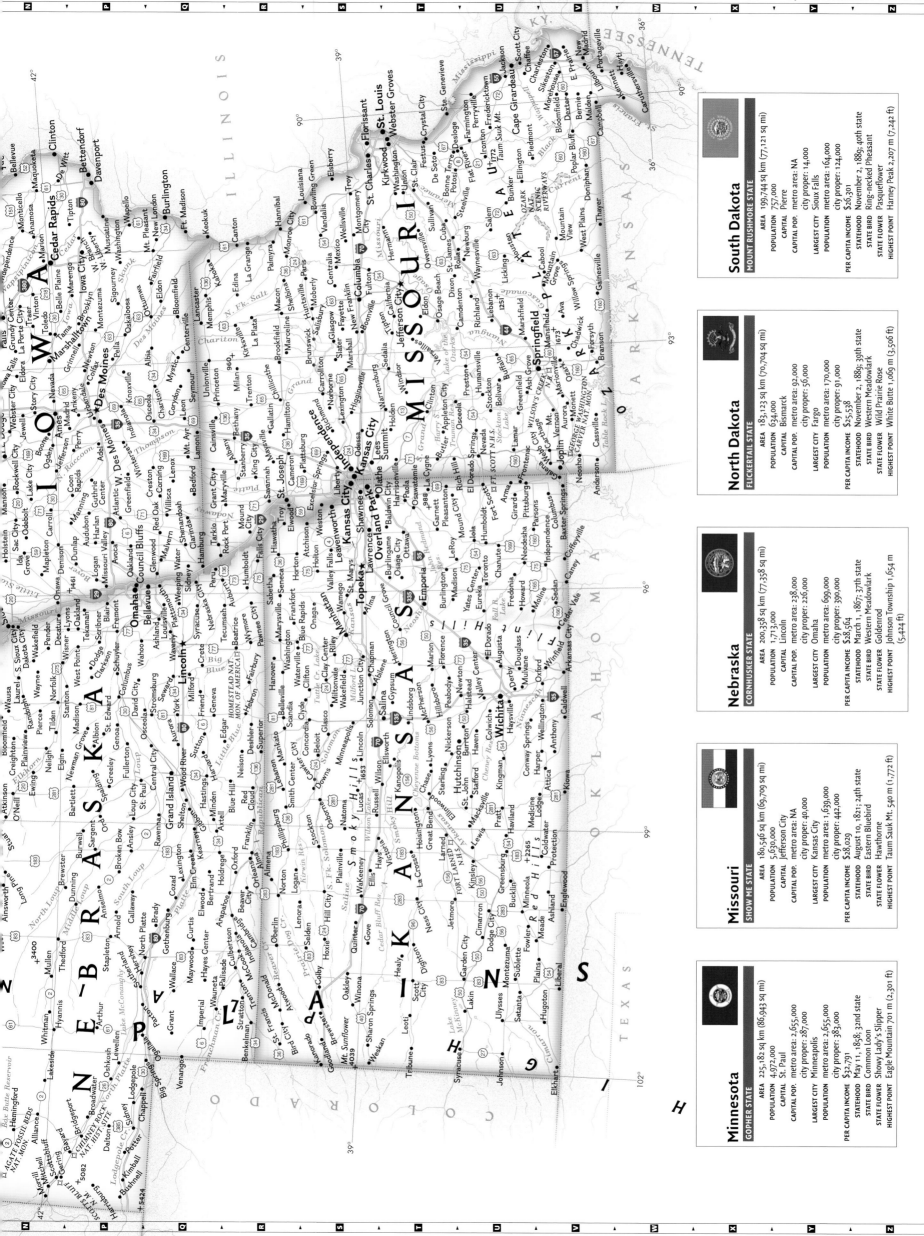

South Dakota
MOUNT RUSHMORE STATE

AREA	199,744 sq km (77,121 sq mi)
POPULATION	757,000
CAPITAL	Pierre
CAPITAL POP.	metro area: NA
	city proper: 14,000
LARGEST CITY	Sioux Falls
POPULATION	metro area: 164,000
	city proper: 124,000
PER CAPITA INCOME	$26,301
STATEHOOD	November 2, 1889; 40th state
STATE BIRD	Ring-necked Pheasant
STATE FLOWER	Pasqueflower
HIGHEST POINT	Harney Peak 2,207 m (7,242 ft)

North Dakota
FLICKERTAIL STATE

AREA	183,123 sq km (70,704 sq mi)
POPULATION	634,000
CAPITAL	Bismarck
CAPITAL POP.	metro area: 92,000
	city proper: 56,000
LARGEST CITY	Fargo
POPULATION	metro area: 170,000
	city proper: 91,000
PER CAPITA INCOME	$25,538
STATEHOOD	November 2, 1889; 39th state
STATE BIRD	Western Meadowlark
STATE FLOWER	Wild Prairie Rose
HIGHEST POINT	White Butte 1,069 m (3,506 ft)

Nebraska
CORNHUSKER STATE

AREA	200,358 sq km (77,358 sq mi)
POPULATION	1,713,000
CAPITAL	Lincoln
CAPITAL POP.	metro area: 238,000
	city proper: 226,000
LARGEST CITY	Omaha
POPULATION	metro area: 699,000
	city proper: 390,000
PER CAPITA INCOME	$28,564
STATEHOOD	March 1, 1867; 37th state
STATE BIRD	Western Meadowlark
STATE FLOWER	Goldenrod
HIGHEST POINT	Johnson Township 1,654 m (5,424 ft)

Missouri
SHOW ME STATE

AREA	180,546 sq km (69,709 sq mi)
POPULATION	5,630,000
CAPITAL	Jefferson City
CAPITAL POP.	metro area: NA
	city proper: 40,000
LARGEST CITY	Kansas City
POPULATION	metro area: 1,639,000
	city proper: 442,000
PER CAPITA INCOME	$28,029
STATEHOOD	August 10, 1821; 24th state
STATE BIRD	Eastern Bluebird
STATE FLOWER	Hawthorne
HIGHEST POINT	Taum Sauk Mt. 540 m (1,772 ft)

Minnesota
GOPHER STATE

AREA	225,182 sq km (86,943 sq mi)
POPULATION	4,972,000
CAPITAL	St. Paul
CAPITAL POP.	metro area: 2,655,000
	city proper: 287,000
LARGEST CITY	Minneapolis
POPULATION	metro area: 2,655,000
	city proper: 383,000
PER CAPITA INCOME	$32,791
STATEHOOD	May 11, 1858; 32nd state
STATE BIRD	Common Loon
STATE FLOWER	Showy Lady's Slipper
HIGHEST POINT	Eagle Mountain 701 m (2,301 ft)

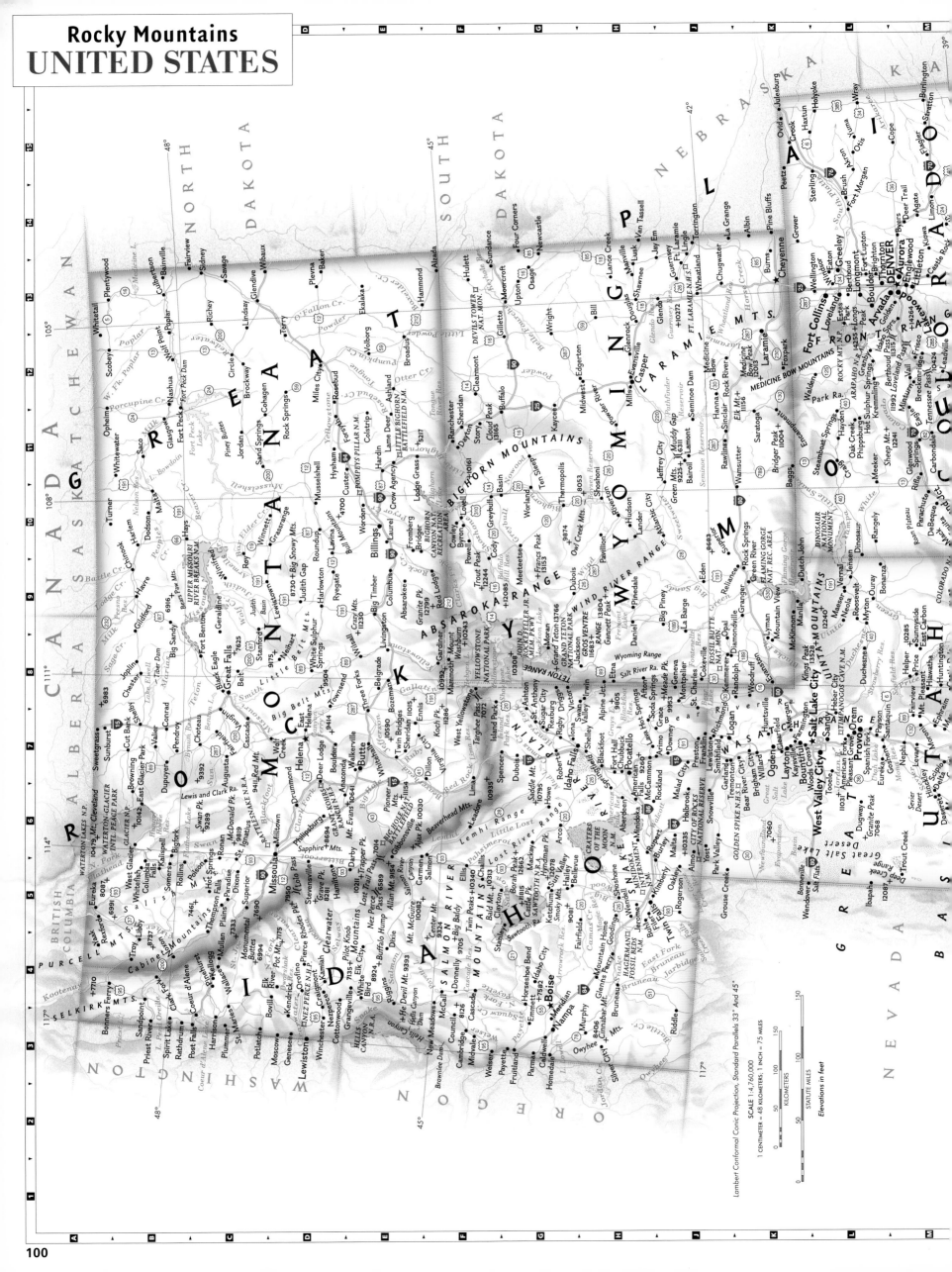

SCALE 1:4,760,000
Lambert Conformal Conic Projection, Standard Parallels 33° And 45°

1 CENTIMETER = 48 KILOMETERS; 1 INCH = 75 MILES

STATUTE MILES

KILOMETERS

Elevations in feet

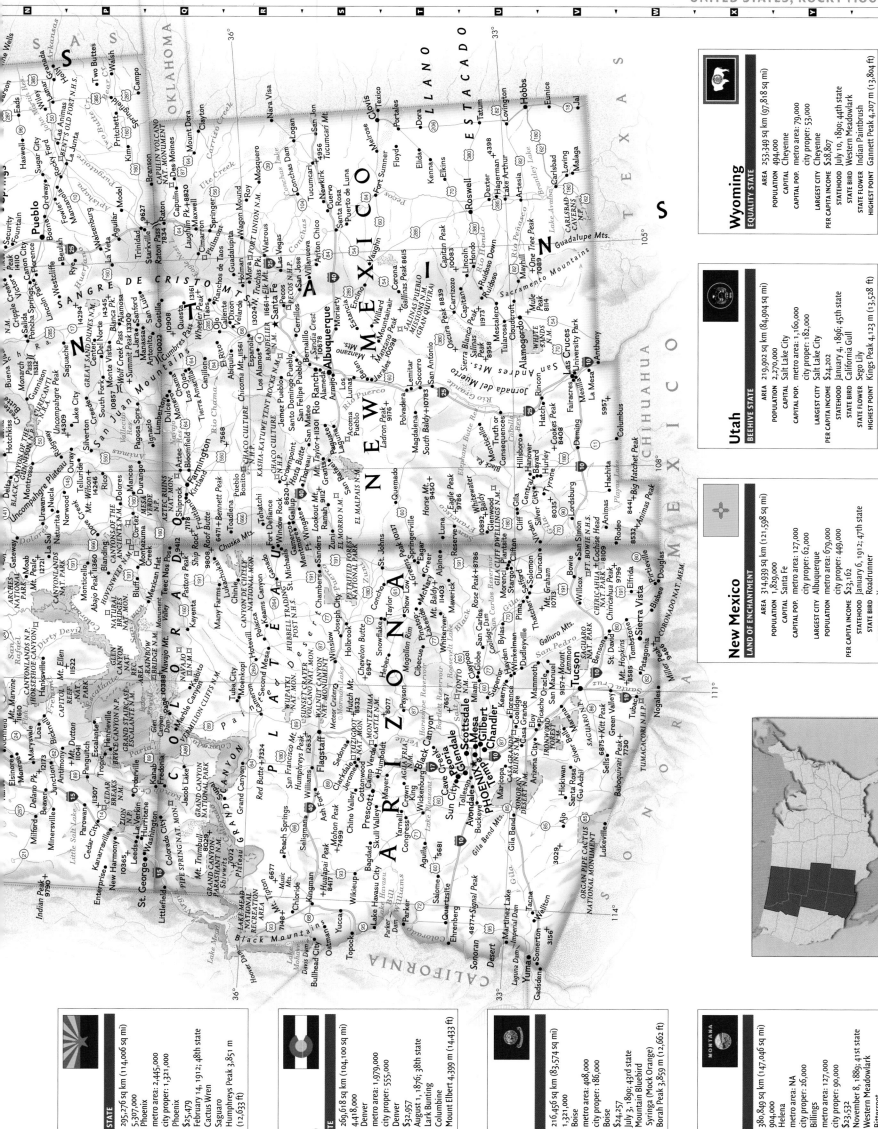

Wyoming
EQUALITY STATE

AREA	253,349 sq km (97,818 sq mi)
POPULATION	494,000
CAPITAL	Cheyenne
CAPITAL POP.	metro area: 79,000
	city proper: 53,000
LARGEST CITY	Cheyenne
PER CAPITA INCOME	$28,867
STATEHOOD	July 10, 1890; 44th state
STATE BIRD	Western Meadowlark
STATE FLOWER	Indian Paintbrush
HIGHEST POINT	Gannett Peak 4,207 m (13,804 ft)

Utah
BEEHIVE STATE

AREA	219,902 sq km (84,904 sq mi)
POPULATION	2,270,000
CAPITAL	Salt Lake City
CAPITAL POP.	metro area: 1,160,000
	city proper: 182,000
LARGEST CITY	Salt Lake City
PER CAPITA INCOME	$24,202
STATEHOOD	January 4, 1896; 45th state
STATE BIRD	California Gull
STATE FLOWER	Sego Lily
HIGHEST POINT	Kings Peak 4,123 m (13,528 ft)

New Mexico
LAND OF ENCHANTMENT

AREA	314,939 sq km (121,598 sq mi)
POPULATION	1,829,000
CAPITAL	Santa Fe
CAPITAL POP.	metro area: 127,000
	city proper: 62,000
LARGEST CITY	Albuquerque
POPULATION	metro area: 679,000
	city proper: 449,000
PER CAPITA INCOME	$23,102
STATEHOOD	January 6, 1912; 47th state
STATE BIRD	Roadrunner
STATE FLOWER	Yucca
HIGHEST POINT	Wheeler Peak 4,011 m (13,161 ft)

Arizona
GRAND CANYON STATE

AREA	295,276 sq km (114,006 sq mi)
POPULATION	5,207,000
CAPITAL	Phoenix
CAPITAL POP.	metro area: 2,445,000
	city proper: 1,321,000
LARGEST CITY	Phoenix
PER CAPITA INCOME	$25,479
STATEHOOD	February 14, 1912; 48th state
STATE BIRD	Cactus Wren
STATE FLOWER	Saguaro
HIGHEST POINT	Humphreys Peak 3,851 m (12,633 ft)

Colorado
CENTENNIAL STATE

AREA	269,618 sq km (104,100 sq mi)
POPULATION	4,418,000
CAPITAL	Denver
CAPITAL POP.	metro area: 1,979,000
	city proper: 555,000
LARGEST CITY	Denver
PER CAPITA INCOME	$32,957
STATEHOOD	August 1, 1876; 38th state
STATE BIRD	Lark Bunting
STATE FLOWER	Columbine
HIGHEST POINT	Mount Elbert 4,399 m (14,433 ft)

Idaho
GEM STATE

AREA	216,456 sq km (83,574 sq mi)
POPULATION	1,321,000
CAPITAL	Boise
CAPITAL POP.	metro area: 408,000
	city proper: 186,000
LARGEST CITY	Boise
PER CAPITA INCOME	$24,257
STATEHOOD	July 3, 1890; 43rd state
STATE BIRD	Mountain Bluebird
STATE FLOWER	Syringa (Mock Orange)
HIGHEST POINT	Borah Peak 3,859 m (12,662 ft)

Montana
TREASURE STATE

AREA	380,849 sq km (147,046 sq mi)
POPULATION	904,000
CAPITAL	Helena
CAPITAL POP.	metro area: NA
	city proper: 26,000
LARGEST CITY	Billings
POPULATION	metro area: 127,000
	city proper: 90,000
PER CAPITA INCOME	$23,532
STATEHOOD	November 8, 1889; 41st state
STATE BIRD	Western Meadowlark
STATE FLOWER	Bitterroot
HIGHEST POINT	Granite Peak 3,901 m (12,799 ft)

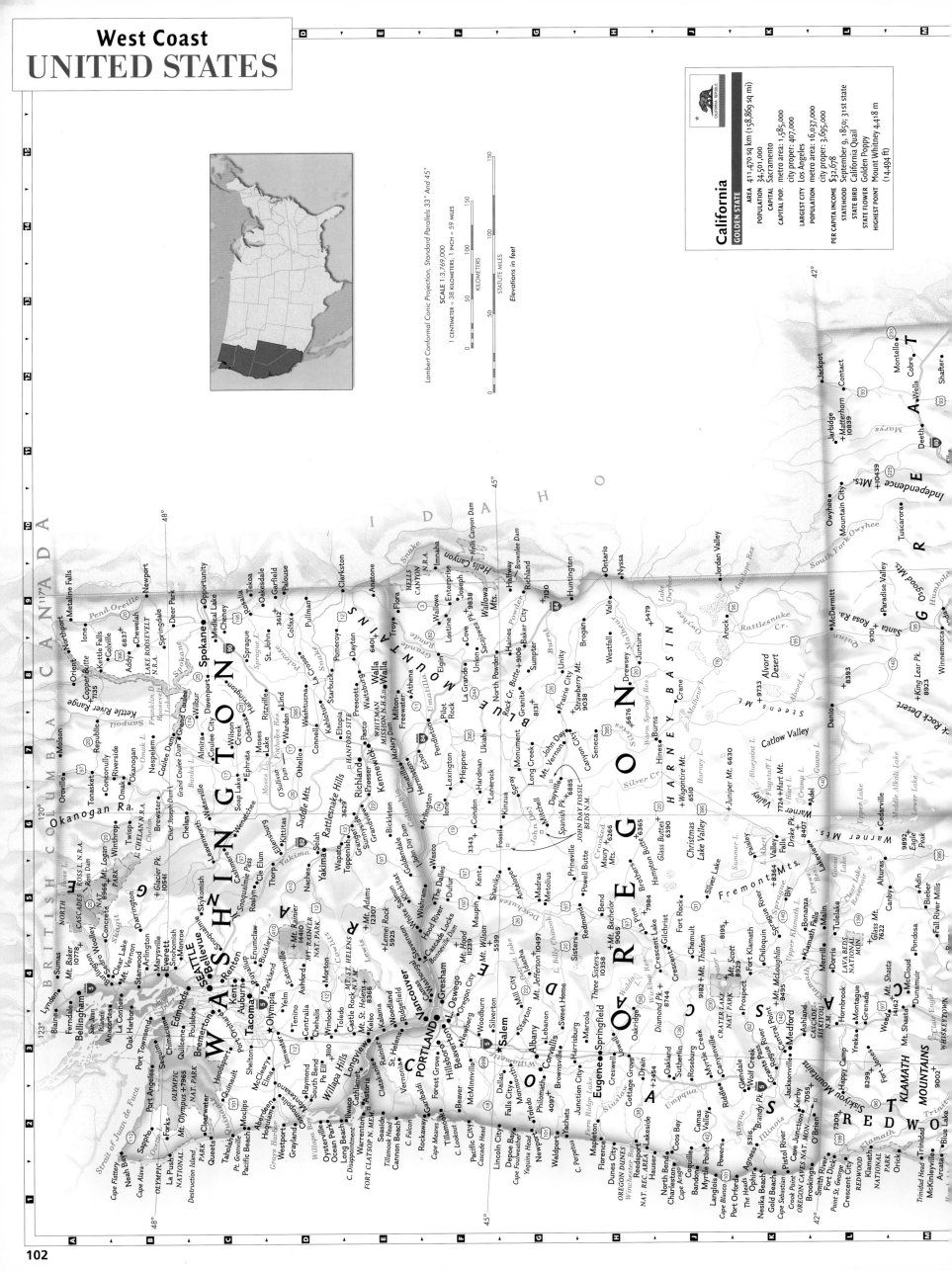

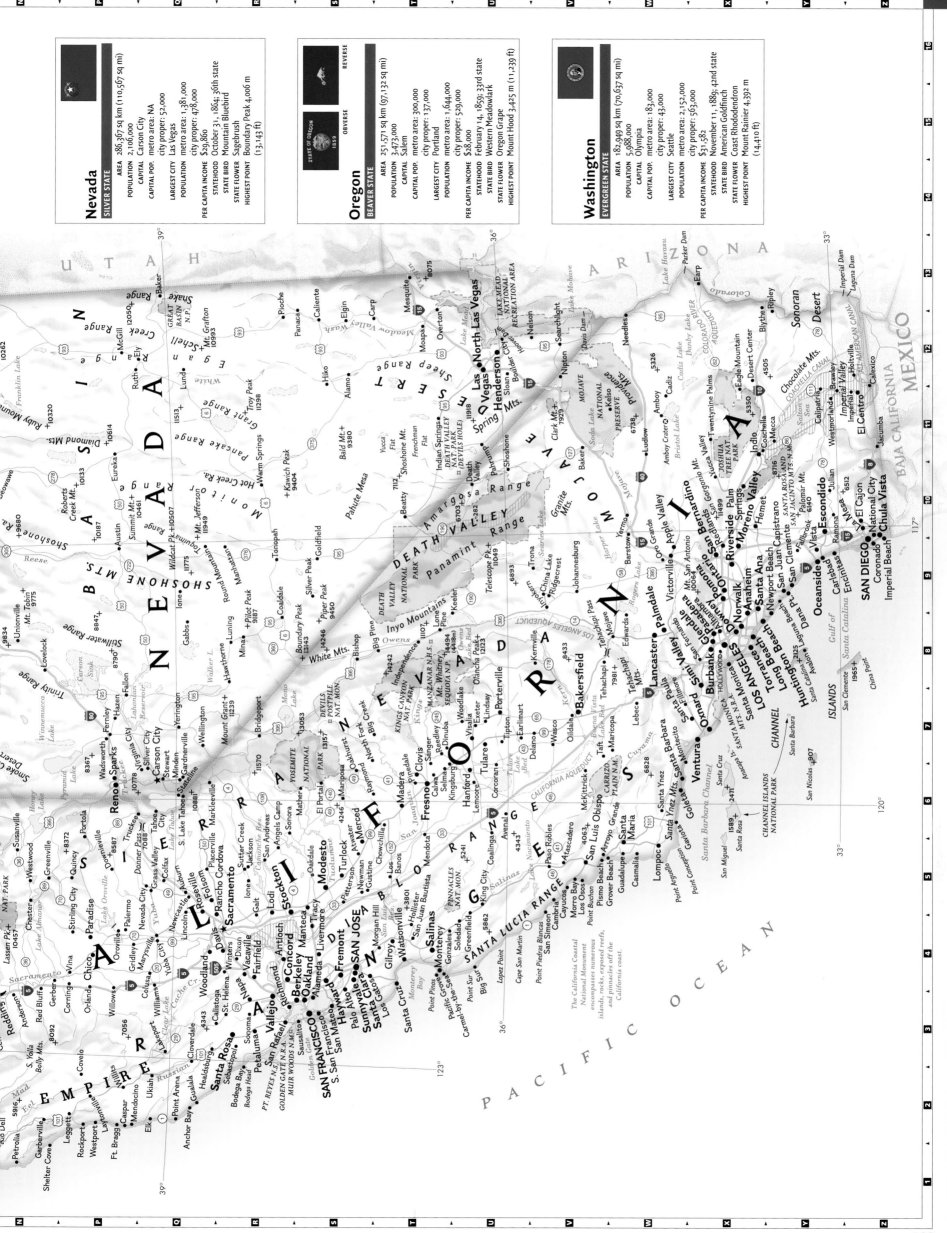

Nevada
SILVER STATE

AREA	286,367 sq km (110,567 sq mi)
POPULATION	2,106,000
CAPITAL	Carson City
CAPITAL POP.	metro area: NA
	city proper: 52,000
LARGEST CITY	Las Vegas
POPULATION	metro area: 1,381,000
	city proper: 478,000
PER CAPITA INCOME	$29,860
STATEHOOD	October 31, 1864; 36th state
STATE BIRD	Mountain Bluebird
STATE FLOWER	Sagebrush
HIGHEST POINT	Boundary Peak 4,006 m (13,143 ft)

Oregon
BEAVER STATE

REVERSE
STATE OF OREGON 1859 OBVERSE

AREA	251,571 sq km (97,132 sq mi)
POPULATION	3,473,000
CAPITAL	Salem
CAPITAL POP.	metro area: 300,000
	city proper: 137,000
LARGEST CITY	Portland
POPULATION	metro area: 1,644,000
	city proper: 529,000
PER CAPITA INCOME	$28,000
STATEHOOD	February 14, 1859; 33rd state
STATE BIRD	Western Meadowlark
STATE FLOWER	Oregon Grape
HIGHEST POINT	Mount Hood 3,425 m (11,239 ft)

Washington
EVERGREEN STATE

AREA	182,949 sq km (70,637 sq mi)
POPULATION	5,988,000
CAPITAL	Olympia
CAPITAL POP.	metro area: 183,000
	city proper: 43,000
LARGEST CITY	Seattle
POPULATION	metro area: 2,152,000
	city proper: 563,000
PER CAPITA INCOME	$31,582
STATEHOOD	November 11, 1889; 42nd state
STATE BIRD	American Goldfinch
STATE FLOWER	Coast Rhododendron
HIGHEST POINT	Mount Rainier 4,392 m (14,410 ft)

The California Coastal National Monument encompasses numerous islands, rocks, exposed reefs, and pinnacles off the California coast.

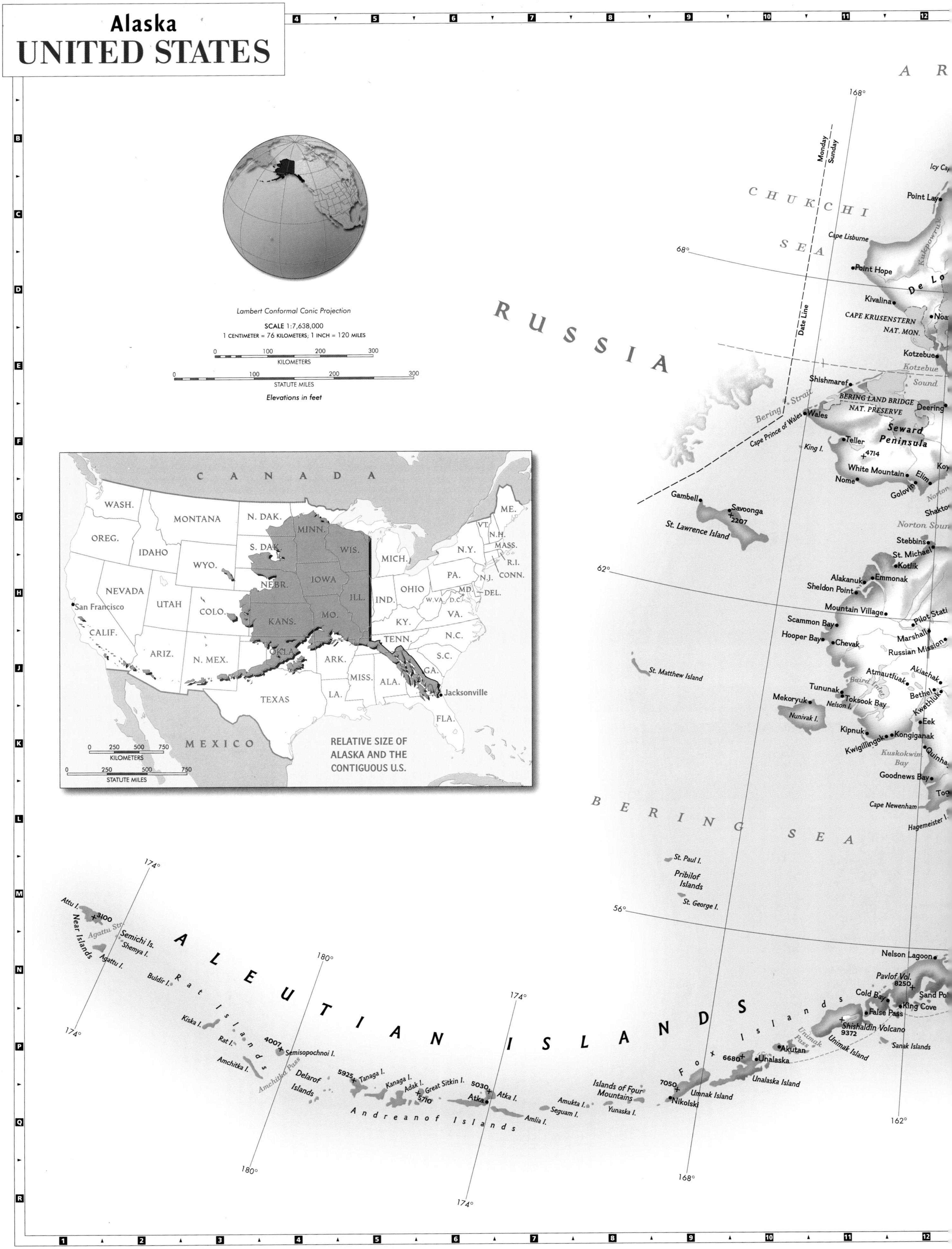

Alaska
UNITED STATES

Lambert Conformal Conic Projection

SCALE 1:7,638,000
1 CENTIMETER = 76 KILOMETERS; 1 INCH = 120 MILES

0 100 200 300
KILOMETERS

0 100 200 300
STATUTE MILES

Elevations in feet

CANADA

WASH.
OREG.
IDAHO
MONTANA
N. DAK.
MINN.
S. DAK.
WIS.
WYO.
NEBR.
IOWA
MICH.
N.Y.
VT.
N.H.
MASS.
R.I.
CONN.
N.J.
PA.
OHIO
IND.
ILL.
MO.
KANS.
COLO.
UTAH
NEVADA
CALIF.
San Francisco
ARIZ.
N. MEX.
OKLA.
TEXAS
ARK.
LA.
MISS.
ALA.
TENN.
KY.
VA.
W. VA.
D.C.
MD.
DEL.
N.C.
S.C.
GA.
FLA.
Jacksonville
ME.

MEXICO

RELATIVE SIZE OF
ALASKA AND THE
CONTIGUOUS U.S.

0 250 500 750
KILOMETERS

0 250 500 750
STATUTE MILES

RUSSIA

CHUKCHI SEA

A R
168°
68°
62°
56°

Icy Cap
Point Lay
Cape Lisburne
Point Hope
De Lo
Kivalina
Noa
CAPE KRUSENSTERN NAT. MON.
Kotzebue
Kotzebue Sound
Shishmaref
BERING LAND BRIDGE NAT. PRESERVE
Deering
Seward Peninsula
Wales
Cape Prince of Wales
King I.
Teller
+4714
White Mountain
Nome
Elim
Golovin
Koy
Norton
Gambell
Savoonga
2207
St. Lawrence Island
Shakto
Norton Sound
Stebbins
St. Michael
Kotlik
Alakanuk
Emmonak
Sheldon Point
Mountain Village
Scammon Bay
Pilot Stati
Hooper Bay
Chevak
Marshall
Russian Mission
St. Matthew Island
Atmautluak
Akiacha
Tununak
Baird Inle
Bethel
Mekoryuk
Toksook Bay
Kwethlik
Nelson I.
Nunivak I.
Eek
Kipnuk
Kongiganak
Kwigillingok
Quinha
Kuskokwim Bay
Goodnews Bay
Tog
Date Line
Monday Sunday
Bering Strait

BERING SEA

St. Paul I.
Pribilof Islands
St. George I.
Cape Newenham
Hagemeister I.
Nelson Lagoon
Pavlof Vol. 8250
Cold Bay
Sand Po
King Cove
False Pass
Shishaldin Volcano 9372
Sanak Islands

A L E U T I A N   I S L A N D S

174°
180°
174°
168°
162°

Attu I. +3100
Near Islands
Agattu Str.
Semichi Is.
Shenya I.
Agattu I.
Buldir I.
Rat Islands
Kiska I.
Rat I.
Amchitka I.
Semisopochnoi I. 4007
Amchitka Pass
Delarof Islands
5925 Tanaga I.
Kanaga I.
Adak I.
Great Sitkin I. 5030
Atka I. Atka
Andreanof Islands
3710
Amlia I.
Seguam I.
Amukta I.
Yunaska I.
Islands of Four Mountains
7050 Umnak Island
Nikolski
Umnak Island
6680 Unalaska
Akutan
Unalaska Island
Fox Islands
Unimak Pass
Unimak Island

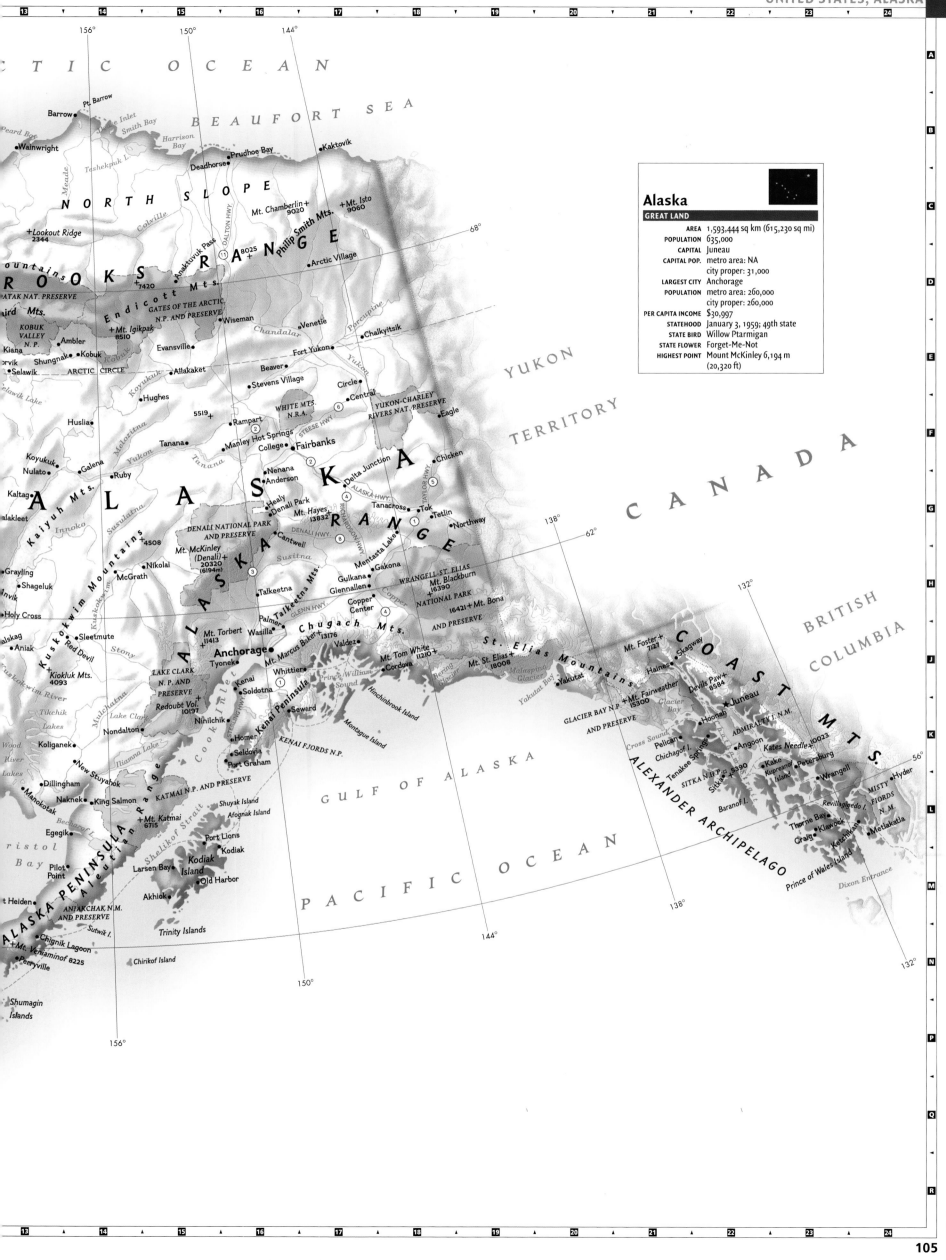

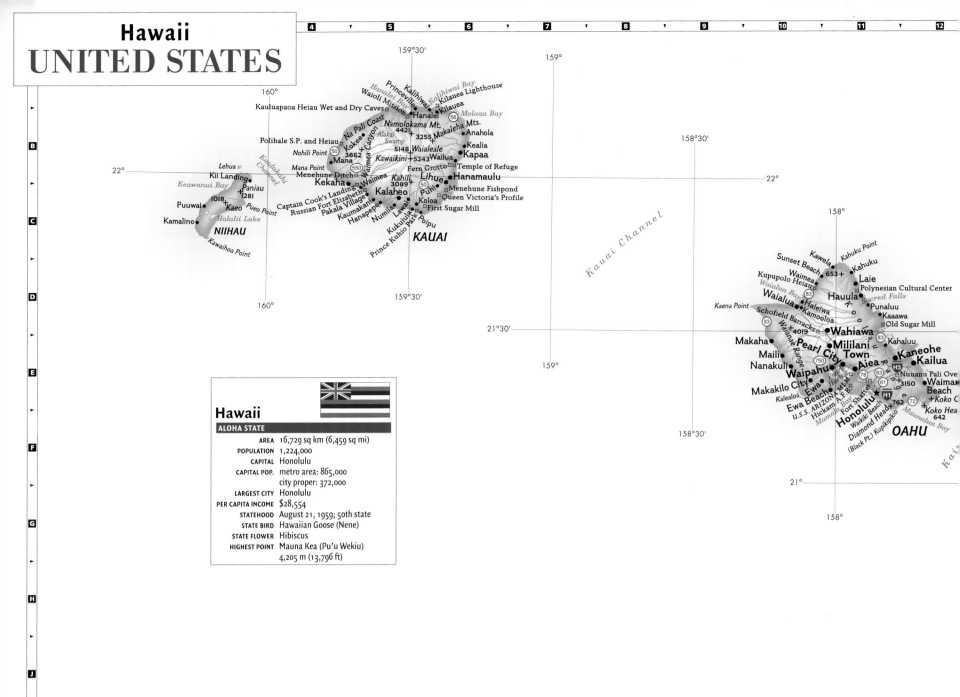

Hawaii

ALOHA STATE

AREA	16,729 sq km (6,459 sq mi)
POPULATION	1,224,000
CAPITAL	Honolulu
CAPITAL POP.	metro area: 865,000
	city proper: 372,000
LARGEST CITY	Honolulu
PER CAPITA INCOME	$28,554
STATEHOOD	August 21, 1959; 50th state
STATE BIRD	Hawaiian Goose (Nene)
STATE FLOWER	Hibiscus
HIGHEST POINT	Mauna Kea (Pu'u Wekiu)
	4,205 m (13,796 ft)

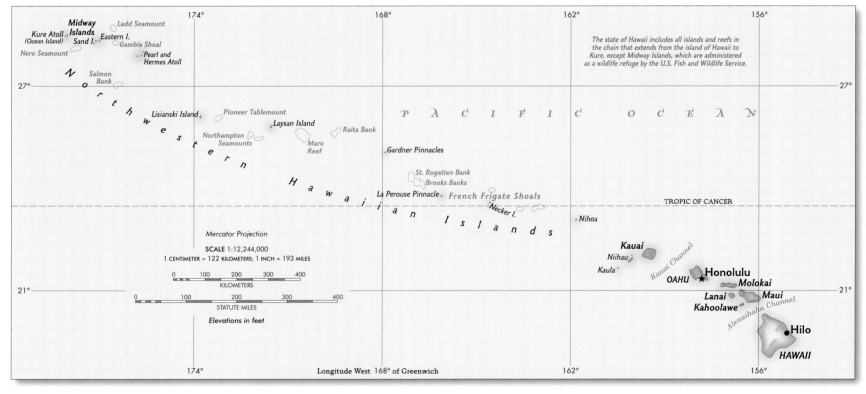

The state of Hawaii includes all islands and reefs in the chain that extends from the island of Hawaii to Kure, except Midway Islands, which are administered as a wildlife refuge by the U.S. Fish and Wildlife Service.

Mercator Projection

SCALE 1:12,244,000
1 CENTIMETER = 122 kilometers; 1 INCH = 193 miles

KILOMETERS

STATUTE MILES

Elevations in feet

Longitude West 168° of Greenwich

Oblique Mercator Projection

SCALE 1:1,370,000
1 CENTIMETER = 14 KILOMETERS; 1 INCH = 22 MILES

0   20   40   60
KILOMETERS

0   20   40   60
STATUTE MILES

Elevations in feet

21°30'
157°
156°30'
156°
21°
20°30'
157°
156°30'
20°30'

MOLOKAI
Kalaupapa
KALAUPAPA N.H.P.
Kauhako Crater 405
Kalawao
Papa Heiau
Ilio Point
658
Hoolehua
Kamakou 4970
Papohaku Beach
Maunaloa
(460)
1381
Kualapuu
Kaunakakai
Kamakou
Iliiliopae Heiau
Cape Halawa
Halawa Bay
Laau Point
(450)
Kapuaiwa Coconut Grove
Kamilola
Kawela
Kalaeloa Harbor
Kaunakakai Harbor
Kaloho Channel
Channel
Garden of the Gods
Keanapapa Point
Lanaihale
Shipwreck Beach
Kahana
Honokowai
Kaanapali
Honokahua
Waihee
(340)
4480
Kahakuloa
Lipoa Point
Nakalele Point
Haleki-Pihana Heiaus
Opana Point
Lower Paia
Pauwela
Haiku
Kaupakulua
Keanae
Wailua
Honomanu Bay
MAUI
LANAI
Lanai City
Lahaina
5788
Wailuku
Kahului
Paia
Puunene
Makawao
Luahiwa Petroglyphs
(30)
3370
Olowalu
Waikapu
(37)
Pukalani
(360)
HANA HWY.
Kaumalapau
Kahea Heiau
Kihei
(Kula) Waiohuli
Puu Nianiau
Piilanihale Heiau
Halulu Heiau
Kaunolu
Petroglyphs
(31)
Keokea
6849
Nanualele Point
Palaoa Point
Kealaikahiki Channel
Maalaea Bay
Red Hill
Haleakala Crater
Haou
Hana
Waiohonu Pictographs
Kaiwaloa Heiau & Olowalu Petroglyphs
Wailea
10023
HALEAKALA N.P.
Kipahulu
Kuikui Point
Makena
Haleakala Observatories
Loaloa Heiau
Kaupo
Puu Moaulanui
Puu Mahoe 2660
KAHOOLAWE
1477
Kealaikahiki Point
Kiakeana Point
Pohakueaea Point
Mamalu Bay
Kaka Point
20°30'
Waikahalulu Bay
Kamohio Bay
Alenuihaha Channel

Mookini Heiau
Kamehameha I Birthplace
Upolu Point
Kapaau (Kohala)
Halaula (Kohala Mill)
Makapala
Akoakoa Point
Hawi
Halawa
Kahei Homesteads
Lapakahi S.H.P.
Awini Plateau
1200
(270)
(250)
5505
Kaumu o Kaleihoohie
Kawaihae
Waipio Valley
Kukuihaele
Kapulena
Honokaa
HAWAII
Kaalaula
Waimea (Kamuela)
Paauhau
Paauilo
Ookala
(19)
Laupahoehoe
PUUKOHOLA HEIAU N.H.S.
Parker Ranch Headquarters
Kaula Gulch
Ninole
Kawaihae Bay
Puako
3249
Nohonaohae
Honokaa
(19)
Hakalau
Honomu
Pepeekeo
Papaikou
Waikoloa Village
Petroglyphs
Mauna Kea Observatory
Puu Makanaka
12414
Dr. D.
Douglas H.M.
(Kaluakauka)
Kolekole Stream
Akaka Falls
Anaehoomalu Bay
Kiholo Bay
Mauna Kea 13796
Mauna Kea Adz Quarry
Kapue Stream
Hilo Bay
Hilo
Leleiwi Point
Kaupulehu
Makolea Point
Keahole Point
Puuanahulu
Ahumoa 7024
Na Puu Kulua 5986
Humuula Saddle 6632
Kaumana Cave
Rainbow Falls
Haena
Keaau Ranch
KALOKO-HONOKOHAU N.H.P.
Huehue Ranch
Kalaoa
Keaau
Kaloli Point
Honokohau Settlement
8271
Hualalai
Kailua
Ahu a Umi Heiau
Kokoolau 8049
Puu Makaala
Kukui
(11)
Kurtistown
Kauakaiakaola Heiau
Holualoa
Puu Lehua 5200
Mountain View
Keauhou
Kahaluu
Mauna Loa
9307
Puu Kulua
9014
3707
(130)
446 Kapoho Crater
Keauhou Holua Slide
Kealakekua
Kulani 5518
Pahoa
Captain Cook
Mahinaakaka Heiau
19°30'
Captain Cook's Monument
Hikiau Heiau
13679
HAWAII VOLCANOES
Volcano
Kalalua 2181
Opihikao
Keei
4077
Chain of Craters
PUUHONUA O HONAUNAU N.H.P. (CITY OF REFUGE N.H.P.)
Honaunau
Keokea
Kealia
Hookena
Sulphur Cone 11329
Mauna Iki 3032
Mauna Ulu
Wahaula Heiau
Kauluoa Point
NAT. PARK
Hilina Pali 1050
Holei Pali
Petroglyphs
7843
Alika Cone
Puu o Keokeo 6875
Apua Point
Keauhou Landing
Papa Bay
Kuee Ruins
Hanamalo Point
Milolii
(11)
Pahala
Kaiholena 3800
Punaluu
Ninole
Kauna Point
Naalehu
2992
Waiohinu
Honuapo Bay
19°
Pohue Bay
Kahuku
Petroglyphs
Waikapuna Bay
Heiau o Molilele
Kaalualu Bay
Mahana Bay
Heiau o Kalalea
Ka Lae (South Cape)
155°30'
155°
20°
19°30'
19°
155°
155°30'

Belize
BELIZE
AREA 22,965 sq km (8,867 sq mi)
POPULATION 255,000
CAPITAL Belmopan 9,000
RELIGION Roman Catholic, Protestant
LANGUAGE English, Spanish, Mayan, Garifuna, Creole
LITERACY 70%
LIFE EXPECTANCY 71 years
GDP PER CAPITA $3,200
ECONOMY IND: garment production, food processing, tourism, construction. **AGR:** bananas, coca, citrus, sugarcane; lumber. **EXP:** sugar, bananas, citrus, clothing.

Costa Rica
REPUBLIC OF COSTA RICA
AREA 51,100 sq km (19,730 sq mi)
POPULATION 3,944,000
CAPITAL San José 983,000
RELIGION Roman Catholic, Evangelical
LANGUAGE Spanish, English
LITERACY 95%
LIFE EXPECTANCY 76 years
GDP PER CAPITA $6,700
ECONOMY IND: microprocessors, food processing, textiles and clothing, construction materials. **AGR:** coffee, pineapples, bananas, sugar; beef; timber. **EXP:** coffee, bananas, sugar, pineapples.

El Salvador
REPUBLIC OF EL SALVADOR
AREA 21,041 sq km (8,124 sq mi)
POPULATION 6,551,000
CAPITAL San Salvador 1,381,000
RELIGION Roman Catholic, Evangelical
LANGUAGE Spanish, Nahua
LITERACY 72%
LIFE EXPECTANCY 70 years
GDP PER CAPITA $4,000
ECONOMY IND: food processing, beverages, textiles, chemicals. **AGR:** coffee, sugar, corn, rice; shrimp, beef. **EXP:** raw materials, consumer goods, capital goods, fuels.

Guatemala
REPUBLIC OF GUATEMALA
AREA 108,889 sq km (42,042 sq mi)
POPULATION 12,063,000
CAPITAL Guatemala 3,366,000
RELIGION Roman Catholic, Protestant, indigenous Mayan beliefs
LANGUAGE Spanish, Amerindian languages
LITERACY 64%
LIFE EXPECTANCY 67 years
GDP PER CAPITA $3,700
ECONOMY IND: sugar, textiles and clothing, furniture, chemicals. **AGR:** sugarcane, corn, bananas, coffee; cattle. **EXP:** coffee, sugar, bananas, fruits and vegetables.

Honduras
REPUBLIC OF HONDURAS
AREA 112,088 sq km (43,277 sq mi)
POPULATION 6,732,000
CAPITAL Tegucigalpa 980,000
RELIGION Roman Catholic, Protestant
LANGUAGE Spanish, Amerindian dialects
LITERACY 73%
LIFE EXPECTANCY 69 years
GDP PER CAPITA $2,700
ECONOMY IND: sugar, coffee, textiles, clothing. **AGR:** bananas, coffee, citrus; beef; timber; shrimp. **EXP:** coffee, bananas, shrimp, lobster.

Mexico
UNITED MEXICAN STATES
AREA 1,958,201 sq km (756,066 sq mi)
POPULATION 101,743,000
CAPITAL Mexico City 18,268,000
RELIGION Roman Catholic, Protestant
LANGUAGE Spanish, various Mayan, Nahuatl, other indigenous languages
LITERACY 90%
LIFE EXPECTANCY 72 years
GDP PER CAPITA $9,100
ECONOMY IND: food and beverages, tobacco, chemicals, iron and steel. **AGR:** corn, wheat, soybeans, rice; beef; wood products. **EXP:** manufactured goods, oil and oil products, silver, fruits.

Nicaragua
REPUBLIC OF NICARAGUA
AREA 129,999 sq km (50,193 sq mi)
POPULATION 5,354,000
CAPITAL Managua 1,039,000
RELIGION Roman Catholic, Protestant
LANGUAGE Spanish, English, indigenous languages
LITERACY 66%
LIFE EXPECTANCY 69 years
GDP PER CAPITA $2,700
ECONOMY IND: food processing, chemicals, machinery and metal products, textiles. **AGR:** coffee, bananas, sugarcane, cotton; beef. **EXP:** coffee, shrimp and lobster, cotton, tobacco.

Panama
REPUBLIC OF PANAMA
AREA 77,082 sq km (29,762 sq mi)
POPULATION 2,939,000
CAPITAL Panama City 1,202,000
RELIGION Roman Catholic, Protestant
LANGUAGE Spanish, English
LITERACY 91%
LIFE EXPECTANCY 76 years
GDP PER CAPITA $6,000
ECONOMY IND: construction, petroleum refining, brewing, cement and other construction materials. **AGR:** bananas, rice, corn, coffee; livestock; shrimp. **EXP:** bananas, shrimp, sugar, coffee.

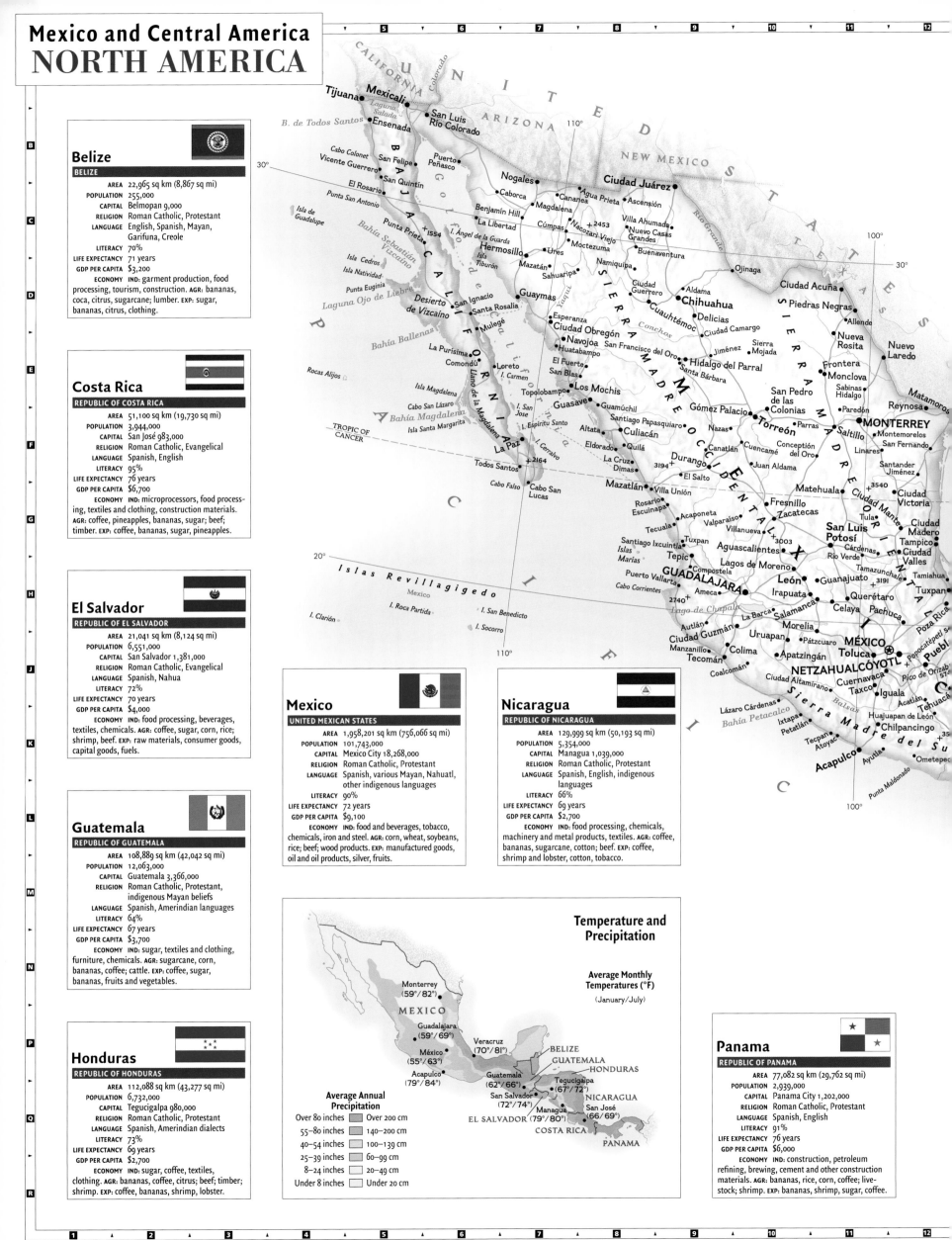

Temperature and Precipitation

Average Monthly Temperatures (°F)

(January/July)

Monterrey (59°/82°)
Guadalajara (59°/69°)
México (55°/63°)
Veracruz (70°/81°)
Acapulco (79°/84°)
Guatemala (62°/66°)
San Salvador (72°/74°)
Tegucigalpa (67°/72°)
Managua (79°/80°)
San José (66°/69°)

Average Annual Precipitation

Precipitation		Precipitation	
Over 80 inches		Over 200 cm	
55–80 inches		140–200 cm	
40–54 inches		100–139 cm	
25–39 inches		60–99 cm	
8–24 inches		20–49 cm	
Under 8 inches		Under 20 cm	

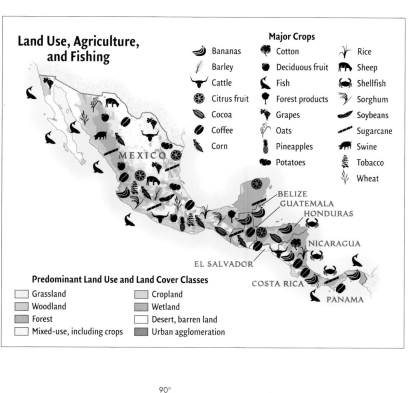

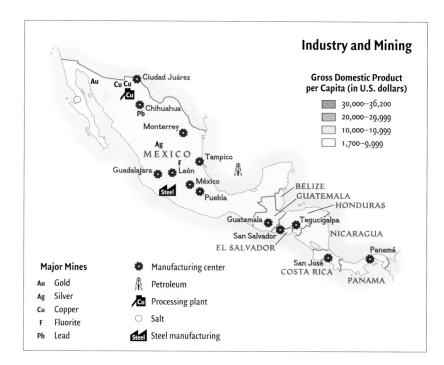

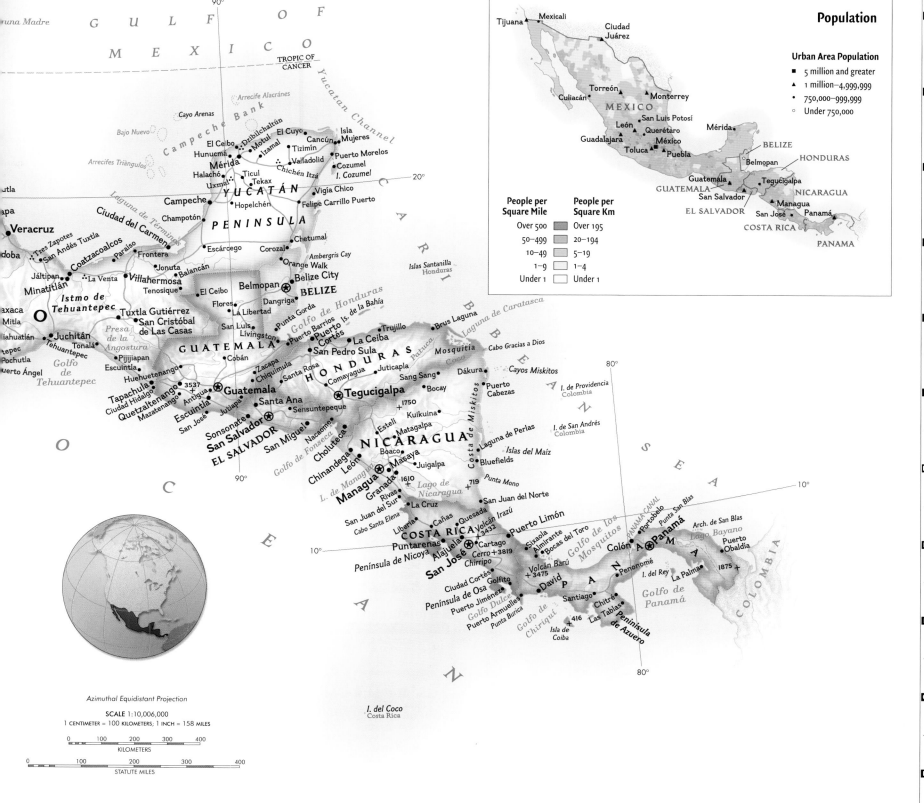

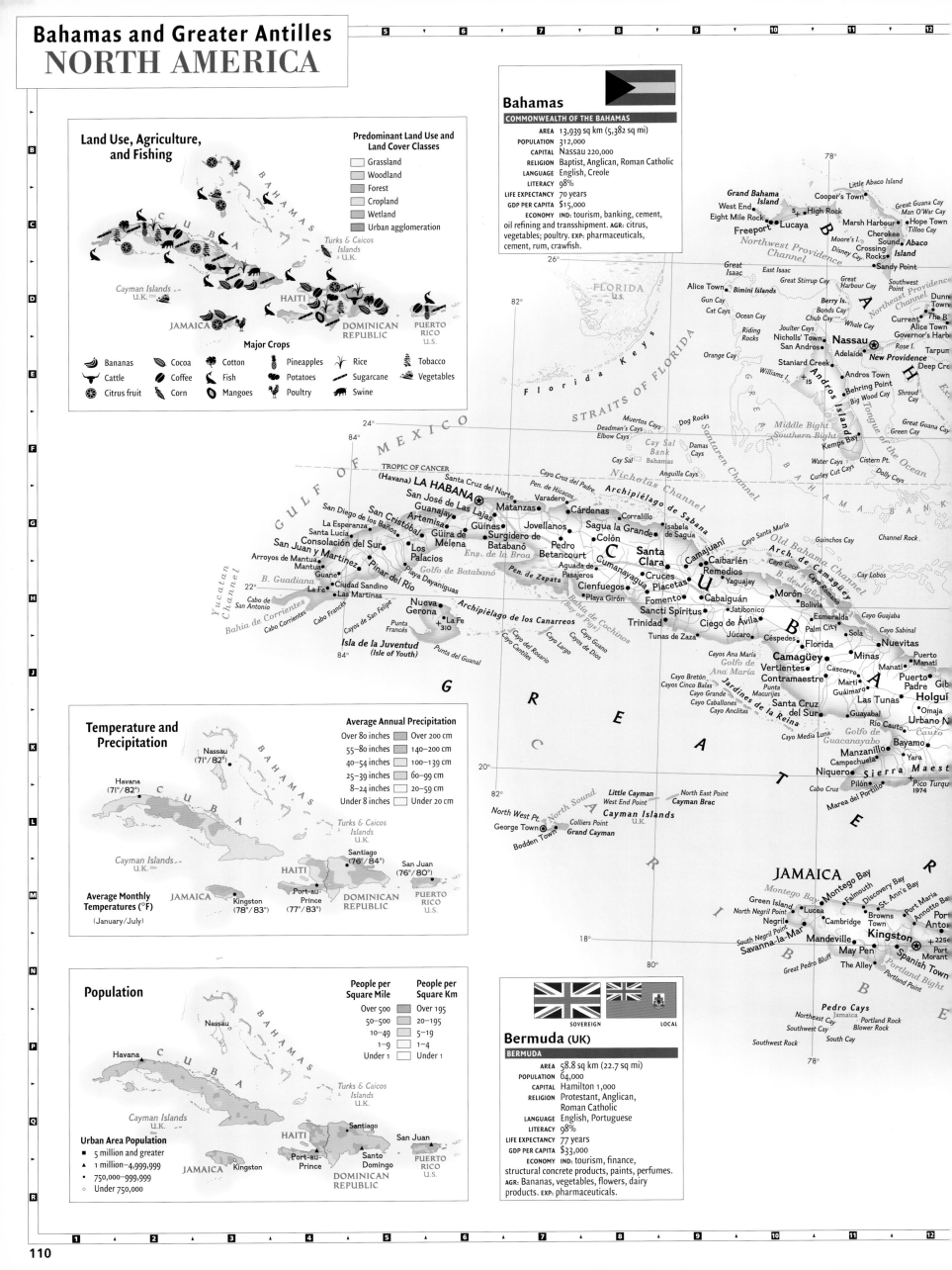

Land Use, Agriculture, and Fishing

Predominant Land Use and Land Cover Classes
- Grassland
- Woodland
- Forest
- Cropland
- Wetland
- Urban agglomeration

Major Crops
- Bananas
- Cattle
- Citrus fruit
- Cocoa
- Coffee
- Corn
- Cotton
- Fish
- Mangoes
- Pineapples
- Potatoes
- Poultry
- Rice
- Sugarcane
- Swine
- Tobacco
- Vegetables

Bahamas
COMMONWEALTH OF THE BAHAMAS
- **AREA** 13,939 sq km (5,382 sq mi)
- **POPULATION** 312,000
- **CAPITAL** Nassau 220,000
- **RELIGION** Baptist, Anglican, Roman Catholic
- **LANGUAGE** English, Creole
- **LITERACY** 98%
- **LIFE EXPECTANCY** 70 years
- **GDP PER CAPITA** $15,000
- **ECONOMY IND:** tourism, banking, cement, oil refining and transshipment. **AGR:** citrus, vegetables; poultry. **EXP:** pharmaceuticals, cement, rum, crawfish.

Temperature and Precipitation

Average Annual Precipitation
- Over 80 inches / Over 200 cm
- 55–80 inches / 140–200 cm
- 40–54 inches / 100–139 cm
- 25–39 inches / 60–99 cm
- 8–24 inches / 20–59 cm
- Under 8 inches / Under 20 cm

Average Monthly Temperatures (°F) (January/July)

- Nassau (71°/82°)
- Havana (71°/82°)
- Kingston (78°/83°)
- Port-au-Prince (77°/83°)
- Santiago (76°/84°)
- San Juan (76°/80°)

Population

People per Square Mile / People per Square Km
- Over 500 / Over 195
- 50–500 / 20–195
- 10–49 / 5–19
- 1–9 / 1–4
- Under 1 / Under 1

Urban Area Population
- ■ 5 million and greater
- ▲ 1 million–4,999,999
- ● 750,000–999,999
- ○ Under 750,000

Bermuda (UK)
BERMUDA
SOVEREIGN · LOCAL
- **AREA** 58.8 sq km (22.7 sq mi)
- **POPULATION** 64,000
- **CAPITAL** Hamilton 1,000
- **RELIGION** Protestant, Anglican, Roman Catholic
- **LANGUAGE** English, Portuguese
- **LITERACY** 98%
- **LIFE EXPECTANCY** 77 years
- **GDP PER CAPITA** $33,000
- **ECONOMY IND:** tourism, finance, structural concrete products, paints, perfumes. **AGR:** Bananas, vegetables, flowers, dairy products. **EXP:** pharmaceuticals.

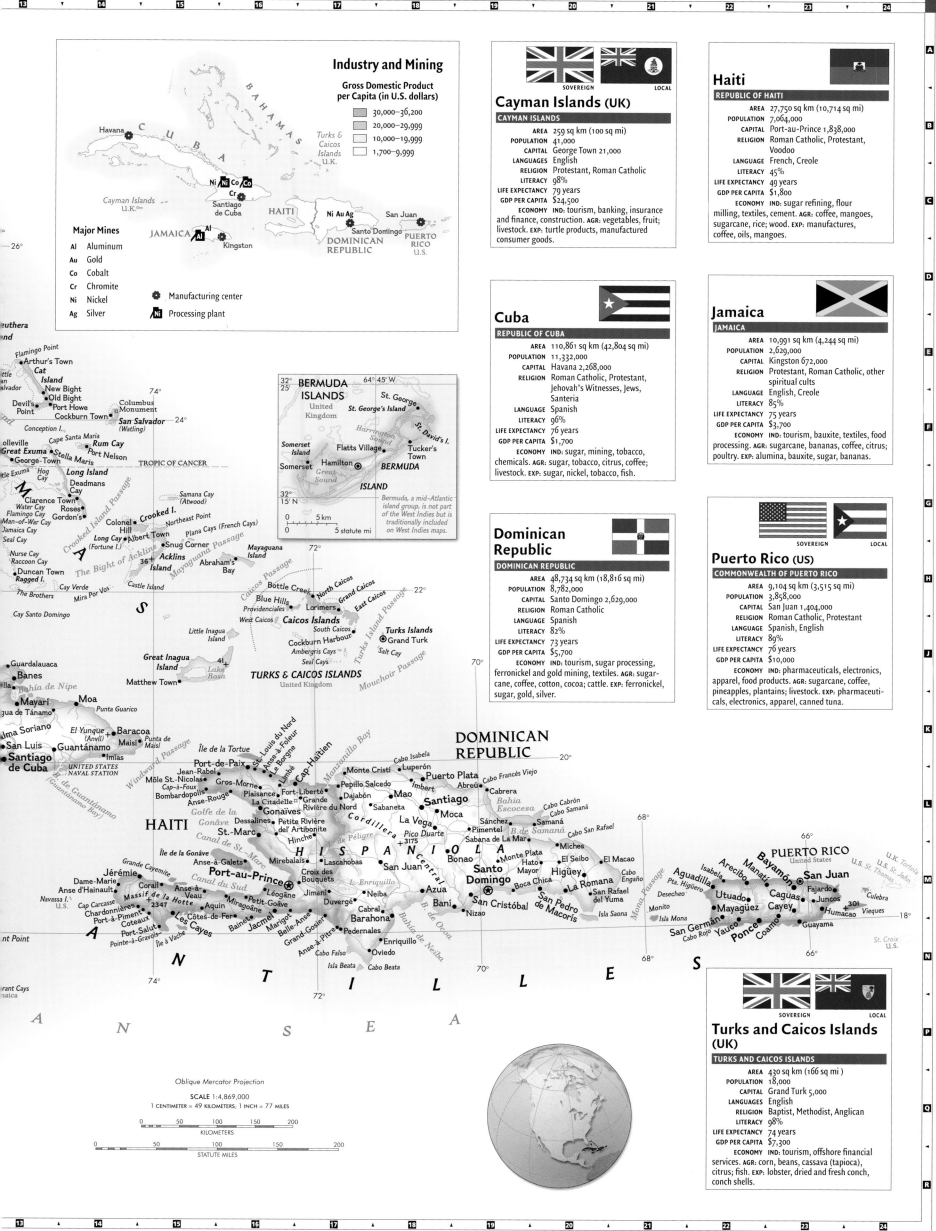

Industry and Mining

Gross Domestic Product per Capita (in U.S. dollars)

- 30,000–36,200
- 20,000–29,999
- 10,000–19,999
- 1,700–9,999

Major Mines

- Al — Aluminum
- Au — Gold
- Co — Cobalt
- Cr — Chromite
- Ni — Nickel
- Ag — Silver

- ✿ Manufacturing center
- Ni Processing plant

Cayman Islands (UK)

SOVEREIGN · LOCAL

CAYMAN ISLANDS

AREA 259 sq km (100 sq mi)
POPULATION 41,000
CAPITAL George Town 21,000
LANGUAGES English
RELIGION Protestant, Roman Catholic
LITERACY 98%
LIFE EXPECTANCY 79 years
GDP PER CAPITA $24,500
ECONOMY IND: tourism, banking, insurance and finance, construction. AGR: vegetables, fruit; livestock. EXP: turtle products, manufactured consumer goods.

Haiti

REPUBLIC OF HAITI

AREA 27,750 sq km (10,714 sq mi)
POPULATION 7,064,000
CAPITAL Port-au-Prince 1,838,000
RELIGION Roman Catholic, Protestant, Voodoo
LANGUAGE French, Creole
LITERACY 45%
LIFE EXPECTANCY 49 years
GDP PER CAPITA $1,800
ECONOMY IND: sugar refining, flour milling, textiles, cement. AGR: coffee, mangoes, sugarcane, rice; wood. EXP: manufactures, coffee, oils, mangoes.

Cuba

REPUBLIC OF CUBA

AREA 110,861 sq km (42,804 sq mi)
POPULATION 11,332,000
CAPITAL Havana 2,268,000
RELIGION Roman Catholic, Protestant, Jehovah's Witnesses, Jews, Santeria
LANGUAGE Spanish
LITERACY 96%
LIFE EXPECTANCY 76 years
GDP PER CAPITA $1,700
ECONOMY IND: sugar, mining, tobacco, chemicals. AGR: sugar, tobacco, citrus, coffee; livestock. EXP: sugar, nickel, tobacco, fish.

Jamaica

JAMAICA

AREA 10,991 sq km (4,244 sq mi)
POPULATION 2,629,000
CAPITAL Kingston 672,000
RELIGION Protestant, Roman Catholic, other spiritual cults
LANGUAGE English, Creole
LITERACY 85%
LIFE EXPECTANCY 75 years
GDP PER CAPITA $3,700
ECONOMY IND: tourism, bauxite, textiles, food processing. AGR: sugarcane, bananas, coffee, citrus; poultry. EXP: alumina, bauxite, sugar, bananas.

Dominican Republic

DOMINICAN REPUBLIC

AREA 48,734 sq km (18,816 sq mi)
POPULATION 8,782,000
CAPITAL Santo Domingo 2,629,000
RELIGION Roman Catholic
LANGUAGE Spanish
LITERACY 82%
LIFE EXPECTANCY 73 years
GDP PER CAPITA $5,700
ECONOMY IND: tourism, sugar processing, ferronickel and gold mining, textiles. AGR: sugarcane, coffee, cotton, cocoa; cattle. EXP: ferronickel, sugar, gold, silver.

Puerto Rico (US)

SOVEREIGN · LOCAL

COMMONWEALTH OF PUERTO RICO

AREA 9,104 sq km (3,515 sq mi)
POPULATION 3,858,000
CAPITAL San Juan 1,404,000
RELIGION Roman Catholic, Protestant
LANGUAGE Spanish, English
LITERACY 89%
LIFE EXPECTANCY 76 years
GDP PER CAPITA $10,000
ECONOMY IND: pharmaceuticals, electronics, apparel, food products. AGR: sugarcane, coffee, pineapples, plantains; livestock. EXP: pharmaceuticals, electronics, apparel, canned tuna.

Turks and Caicos Islands (UK)

SOVEREIGN · LOCAL

TURKS AND CAICOS ISLANDS

AREA 430 sq km (166 sq mi)
POPULATION 18,000
CAPITAL Grand Turk 5,000
LANGUAGES English
RELIGION Baptist, Methodist, Anglican
LITERACY 98%
LIFE EXPECTANCY 74 years
GDP PER CAPITA $7,300
ECONOMY IND: tourism, offshore financial services. AGR: corn, beans, cassava (tapioca), citrus; fish. EXP: lobster, dried and fresh conch, conch shells.

BERMUDA ISLANDS

United Kingdom

Bermuda, a mid-Atlantic island group, is not part of the West Indies but is traditionally included on West Indies maps.

0 — 5 km
0 — 5 statute mi

Oblique Mercator Projection

SCALE 1:4,869,000

1 CENTIMETER = 49 KILOMETERS; 1 INCH = 77 MILES

0 50 100 150 200
KILOMETERS

0 50 100 150 200
STATUTE MILES

Anguilla (UK)

ANGUILLA

AREA	91 sq km (35 sq mi)
POPULATION	13,000
CAPITAL	The Valley 1,000
RELIGION	Anglican, Methodist, Seventh-day Adventist, Baptist, Roman Catholic
LANGUAGE	English
LITERACY	95%
LIFE EXPECTANCY	76 years
GDP PER CAPITA	$8,200

ECONOMY IND: tourism, boat building, off-shore financial services. AGR: small quantities of tobacco, vegetables; cattle raising. EXP: lobster, fish, livestock, salt.

Antigua and Barbuda

ANTIGUA AND BARBUDA

AREA	440 sq km (170 sq mi)
POPULATION	67,000
CAPITAL	St. John's 24,000
RELIGION	Anglican, other Protestant, Roman Catholic
LANGUAGE	English, local dialects
LITERACY	89%
LIFE EXPECTANCY	71 years
GDP PER CAPITA	$8,200

ECONOMY IND: tourism, construction, light manufacturing (clothing, alcohol). AGR: cotton, fruits, vegetables, bananas; livestock. EXP: petroleum products, manufactures, machinery and transport equipment, food and live animals.

Aruba (Netherlands)

ARUBA

AREA	193 sq km (75 sq mi)
POPULATION	96,000
CAPITAL	Oranjestad 23,000
RELIGION	Roman Catholic, Protestant
LANGUAGE	Dutch, Papiamento, English, Spanish
LITERACY	97%
LIFE EXPECTANCY	79 years
GDP PER CAPITA	$28,000

ECONOMY IND: tourism, transshipment facilities, oil refining. AGR: aloes; livestock; fish. EXP: live animals and animal products, art and collectibles, machinery and electrical equipment, transport equipment.

Barbados

BARBADOS

AREA	430 sq km (166 sq mi)
POPULATION	269,000
CAPITAL	Bridgetown 136,000
RELIGION	Protestant, Roman Catholic
LANGUAGE	English
LITERACY	97%
LIFE EXPECTANCY	73 years
GDP PER CAPITA	$14,500

ECONOMY IND: tourism, sugar, light manufacturing, component assembly. AGR: sugarcane, vegetables, cotton. EXP: sugar and molasses, rum, other foods and beverages, chemicals.

British Virgin Islands (UK)

BRITISH VIRGIN ISLANDS

AREA	150 sq km (58 sq mi)
POPULATION	21,000
CAPITAL	Road Town 11,000
RELIGION	Methodist, Anglican, other Protestant dominations, Roman Catholic
LANGUAGE	English
LITERACY	98%
LIFE EXPECTANCY	76 years
GDP PER CAPITA	$16,000

ECONOMY IND: tourism, light industry, construction, rum. AGR: fruits, vegetables; livestock; fish. EXP: rum, fresh fish, fruits, animals.

Dominica

COMMONWEALTH OF DOMINICA

AREA	751 sq km (290 sq mi)
POPULATION	76,000
CAPITAL	Roseau 26,000
RELIGION	Roman Catholic, Protestant
LANGUAGE	English, French patois
LITERACY	94%
LIFE EXPECTANCY	74 years
GDP PER CAPITA	$4,000

ECONOMY IND: soap, coconut oil, tourism, copra. AGR: bananas, citrus, mangoes, root crops. EXP: bananas, soap, bay oil, vegetables.

Guadeloupe (France)

OVERSEAS DEPARTMENT OF FRANCE

AREA	1,780 sq km (687 sq mi)
POPULATION	461,000
CAPITAL	Basse-Terre 12,000
RELIGION	Roman Catholic, Hindu, pagan African
LANGUAGE	French
LITERACY	90%
LIFE EXPECTANCY	77 years
GDP PER CAPITA	$9,000

ECONOMY IND: construction, cement, rum, sugar. AGR: bananas, sugarcane, tropical fruits and vegetables; cattle. EXP: bananas, sugar, rum.

Grenada

GRENADA

AREA	344 sq km (133 sq mi)
POPULATION	104,000
CAPITAL	St. George's 36,000
RELIGION	Roman Catholic, Anglican, other Protestant
LANGUAGE	English, French patois
LITERACY	98%
LIFE EXPECTANCY	65 years
GDP PER CAPITA	$4,400

ECONOMY IND: food and beverages, textiles, light assembly operations, tourism. AGR: bananas, cocoa, nutmeg, mace. EXP: bananas, cocoa, nutmeg, fruit and vegetables.

Martinique (France)

OVERSEAS DEPARTMENT OF FRANCE

AREA	1,100 sq km (425 sq mi)
POPULATION	384,000
CAPITAL	Fort-de-France 93,000
RELIGION	Roman Catholic, Hindu, pagan African
LANGUAGE	French, Creole patois
LITERACY	93%
LIFE EXPECTANCY	78 years
GDP PER CAPITA	$11,000

ECONOMY IND: construction, rum, cement, oil refining. AGR: pineapples, avocados, bananas, flowers. EXP: refined petroleum products, bananas, rum, pineapples.

Montserrat (UK)

MONTSERRAT

AREA	100 sq km (39 sq mi)
POPULATION	4,000
CAPITAL	Plymouth (abandoned)
RELIGION	Anglican, Methodist, Roman Catholic, Pentecostal, Seventh-Day Adventist, other Christian denominations
LANGUAGE	English
LITERACY	97%
LIFE EXPECTANCY	78 years
GDP PER CAPITA	$5,000

ECONOMY IND: tourism, textiles, electronic appliances. AGR: cabbages, carrots, cucumbers, tomatoes; livestock products. EXP: Electronic components, plastic bags, apparel, hot peppers.

Netherlands Antilles (Netherlands)

NETHERLANDS ANTILLES

AREA	960 sq km (371 sq mi)
POPULATION	225,000
CAPITAL	Willemstad 125,000
RELIGION	Roman Catholic, Protestant, Jewish, Seventh-Day Adventist
LANGUAGE	Dutch, Papiamento, English, Spanish
LITERACY	98%
LIFE EXPECTANCY	75 years
GDP PER CAPITA	$11,400

ECONOMY IND: tourism, petroleum refining, petroleum transshipment facilities, light manufacturing. EXP: petroleum products.

St. Kitts and Nevis

FEDERATION OF SAINT KITTS AND NEVIS

AREA	261 sq km (101 sq mi)
POPULATION	39,000
CAPITAL	Basseterre 12,000
RELIGION	Anglican, other Protestant, Roman Catholic
LANGUAGE	English
LITERACY	97%
LIFE EXPECTANCY	71 years
GDP PER CAPITA	$7,000

ECONOMY IND: sugar processing, tourism, cotton, salt. AGR: sugarcane, rice, yams, vegetables; fish. EXP: machinery, food, electronics, beverages.

St. Lucia

SAINT LUCIA

AREA	617 sq km (238 sq mi)
POPULATION	166,000
CAPITAL	Castries 57,000
RELIGION	Roman Catholic, Protestant
LANGUAGE	English, French patois
LITERACY	67%
LIFE EXPECTANCY	73 years
GDP PER CAPITA	$4,500

ECONOMY IND: clothing, assembly of electronic components, beverages, corrugated cardboard boxes. AGR: bananas, coconuts, vegetables, citrus. EXP: bananas, clothing, cocoa, vegetables.

St. Vincent and the Grenadines

SAINT VINCENT AND THE GRENADINES

AREA	388 sq km (150 sq mi)
POPULATION	116,000
CAPITAL	Kingstown 28,000
RELIGION	Anglican, Methodist, Roman Catholic, other Protestant
LANGUAGE	English, French patois
LITERACY	96%
LIFE EXPECTANCY	73 years
GDP PER CAPITA	$2,800

ECONOMY IND: food processing, cement, furniture, clothing. AGR: bananas, coconuts, sweet potatoes, spices; cattle; fish. EXP: bananas, eddoes and dasheen (taro), arrowroot starch, tennis racquets.

Trinidad and Tobago

REPUBLIC OF TRINIDAD AND TOBAGO

AREA	5,131 sq km (1,981 sq mi)
POPULATION	1,306,000
CAPITAL	Port-of-Spain 54,000
RELIGION	Roman Catholic, Hindu, Anglican, Muslim, Presbyterian
LANGUAGE	English, Hindi, French, Spanish, Chinese
LITERACY	98%
LIFE EXPECTANCY	68 years
GDP PER CAPITA	$9,500

ECONOMY IND: petroleum, chemicals, tourism, food processing. AGR: cocoa, sugarcane, rice, citrus; poultry. EXP: petroleum and petroleum products, chemicals, steel products, fertilizer.

Virgin Islands (US)

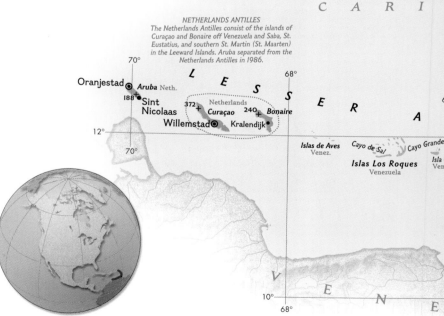

UNITED STATES VIRGIN ISLANDS

AREA	352 sq km (136 sq mi)
POPULATION	110,000
CAPITAL	Charlotte Amalie 11,000
RELIGION	Baptist, Roman Catholic, Episcopalian
LANGUAGE	English, Spanish, Creole
LITERACY	NA
LIFE EXPECTANCY	78 years
GDP PER CAPITA	$15,000

ECONOMY IND: tourism, petroleum refining, watch assembly, rum distilling. AGR: fruit, vegetables, sorghum; senepol cattle. EXP: refined petroleum products.

NETHERLANDS ANTILLES
The Netherlands Antilles consist of the islands of Curaçao and Bonaire off Venezuela and Saba, St. Eustatius, and southern St. Martin (St. Maarten) in the Leeward Islands. Aruba separated from the Netherlands Antilles in 1986.

Oblique Mercator Projection

SCALE 1:5,237,000
1 CENTIMETER = 52 KILOMETERS; 1 INCH = 83 MILES

KILOMETERS

STATUTE MILES

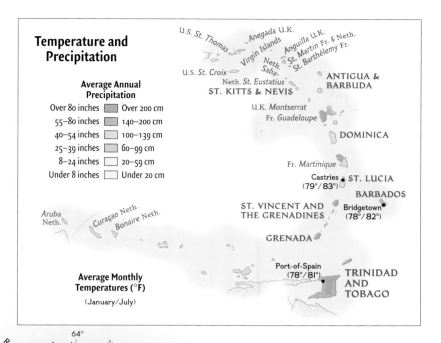

Temperature and Precipitation

Average Annual Precipitation

Over 80 inches	Over 200 cm
55–80 inches	140–200 cm
40–54 inches	100–139 cm
25–39 inches	60–99 cm
8–24 inches	20–59 cm
Under 8 inches	Under 20 cm

Average Monthly Temperatures (°F)
(January/July)

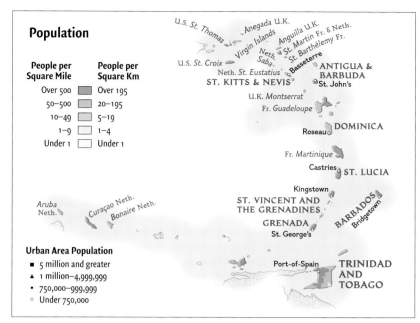

Population

People per Square Mile	People per Square Km
Over 500	Over 195
50–500	20–195
10–49	5–19
1–9	1–4
Under 1	Under 1

Urban Area Population
- ■ 5 million and greater
- ▲ 1 million–4,999,999
- • 750,000–999,999
- ○ Under 750,000

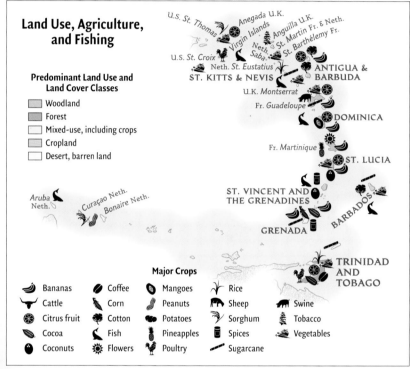

Land Use, Agriculture, and Fishing

Predominant Land Use and Land Cover Classes
- Woodland
- Forest
- Mixed-use, including crops
- Cropland
- Desert, barren land

Major Crops
- Bananas
- Cattle
- Citrus fruit
- Cocoa
- Coconuts
- Coffee
- Corn
- Cotton
- Fish
- Flowers
- Mangoes
- Peanuts
- Potatoes
- Pineapples
- Poultry
- Rice
- Sheep
- Sorghum
- Spices
- Sugarcane
- Swine
- Tobacco
- Vegetables

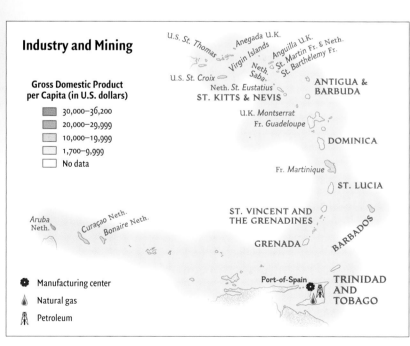

Industry and Mining

Gross Domestic Product per Capita (in U.S. dollars)
- 30,000–36,200
- 20,000–29,999
- 10,000–19,999
- 1,700–9,999
- No data

- ✿ Manufacturing center
- ▲ Natural gas
- ⛏ Petroleum

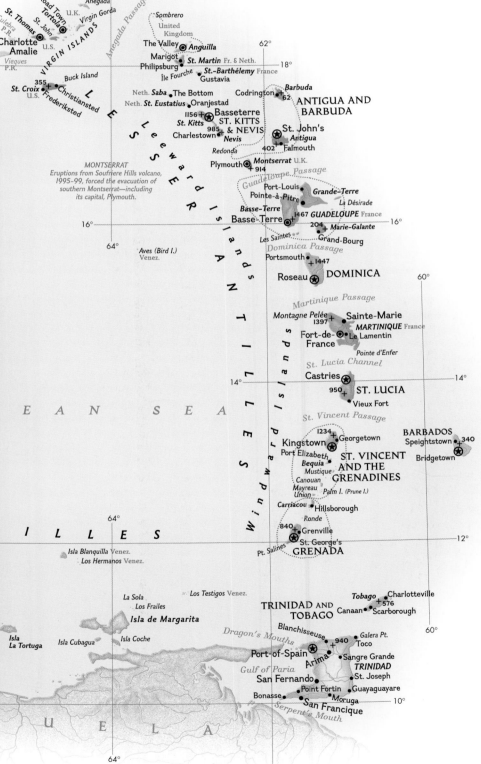

MONTSERRAT
Eruptions from Soufrière Hills volcano, 1995–99, forced the evacuation of southern Montserrat—including its capital, Plymouth.

SOUTH AMERICA

S outh America is a place of remarkable extremes— sweltering jungle heat and face-numbing cold, endless mountains and tropical forests that seem to stretch forever, the world's mightiest river and the planet's driest spot. While the region's coastal areas are highly developed, the heart of the continent remains largely vacant, a rugged expanse of mountains, desert, grassland, and forest that constitutes one of the world's last great wilderness treasures.

Although much of the continent remains wild and untamed, South America has its refined side. It provided a cradle for several ancient civilizations and in modern times has given birth to some of the world's biggest cities. South America has also

The Jamari River snakes its way through the Rondonia region of the Brazilian Amazon. The world's largest rain forest, the Amazon Basin sprawls across more than a third of the South American continent.

Among the most dramatic ruins in South America, the Inca citadel of Machu Picchu hovers 2,000 feet (610 meters) above the Urubamba River in the Peruvian Andes.

afforded us some of the great cultural highlights of the last hundred years—the astonishing discovery of the lost city of Machu Picchu in the Peruvian Andes, Evita Peron rousing crowds in Argentina, the alluring "Girl from Ipanema" on the beach in Brazil, and Pele's magic with a soccer ball.

PHYSICAL GEOGRAPHY

With a base along the Caribbean coast and an apex at Cape Horn, South America is shaped rather like an elongated triangle. Embracing a total area of nearly 6.9 million square miles (17.8 sq km), it's the fourth largest continent, bounded by the Atlantic Ocean in the east, the Pacific Ocean in the west, and the Caribbean Sea in the north. Its only connection to another land mass (North America) is the narrow Isthmus of Panama between Colombia and Panama. In the deep south, only the stormy Drake Passage separates South America from the Antarctic continent.

Despite its hefty size, South America has a relatively short coastline and few islands. However its offshore elements are distinctive: frigid Tierra del Fuego, the battle-torn Falklands (Malvinas), the biologically wondrous Galápagos, the spectacular fjord country of southern Chile, and untamed Marajó Island in the Amazon delta.

Three huge physical features dominate the South American mainland: the Andes mountains, the Amazon Basin, and a wide southern plain that encompasses the Pampas, the Gran Chaco, and much of Patagonia. The Andes cordillera, which runs all the way from northern Colombia to southern Chile and Argentina, is the world's longest mountain range. It's also one of the highest—more than 50 peaks over 20,000 feet (6,100 meters)—and one of the most active in terms of volcanism and earthquakes.

South America's hydrology is perhaps the most astounding of any continent. Rainwater spilling off the Andes creates the mighty Amazon River and its thousand plus tributaries, which in turn sustain the world's largest rain forest and greatest diversity of flora and fauna. Although the Amazon itself is not the planet's longest watercourse, it carries more liquid than the next ten biggest rivers combined. Spilling off a tabletop mountain in the northern Amazon is Angel Falls, the world's highest cascade at 3,212 feet (979 meters), and tumbling off an ancient lava cliff between Brazil and Argentina is thunderous Iguazu Falls.

Among the continent's other geographic oddities are wind-swept Patagonia and the super-dry Atacama Desert, which often goes without rain for hundreds of years. The endless Pampas prairie of Argentina and Uruguay was the birthplace of gaucho culture, while the Pantanal region of southern Brazil is among the Earth's great wetlands.

HISTORY

Like its continental cousin to the north, South America was first inhabited by nomads whose Asiatic ancestors crossed the Bering Strait during the last great ice age, sometime between 12,000 and 30,000 years ago. After crossing the Isthmus of Panama, they diffused throughout the continent and evolved into hundreds of different tribal groups with their own languages, customs, and traditions.

Starting around 3000 B.C., Amerindians living in the Andes region began to cultivate beans, squash, cotton, and potatoes. By 1000 B.C., villages along Peru's northern coastal plain had evolved into the Chavin culture, the continent's first true civilization. With a religion based on worship of the jaguar god, the Chavin built great ceremonial centers with mud-brick temples and pyramids. They also developed polychrome pottery,

intricate weaving, and South America's first metallurgy. By the 6th century A.D., the Chavin had been eclipsed by other sophisticated Peruvian cultures such as the Moche, Nasca, and Tiwanaku. The last of the region's great Amerindian cultures was the Inca, master stonemasons and soldiers who forged an empire that stretched from present-day southern Colombia to northern Chile and Argentina.

Christopher Columbus "discovered" South America in 1498 on his third voyage to the New World, but the landmass (and adjacent North America) didn't receive its current name until Italian mariner Amerigo Vespucci explored its coast (1499–1502) and first postulated that it was a continent unto itself rather than part of Asia. In their quest for riches, the Spanish conquistadors came into violent contact with local Amerindian groups, climaxing in Pizarro's invasion of the Andes and bloody triumph over the Inca Empire in the 1530s. While the Spaniards were busy conquering the west coast, the Portuguese were claiming the continent's eastern shore, an area they called Brazil after a local dyewood tree. Driven off their land, decimated by disease, and pressed into slavery, South America's native population quickly declined in all but the most remote regions. Within half a century of first contact, European hegemony over the entire continent was assured.

Three distinct groups—the military, wealthy families, and the Roman Catholic Church—came to dominate South America's new Iberian colonies by the end of the 16th century. Using Indian labor and millions of slaves imported from Africa, they developed a society based on sprawling ranches and European-style cities such as Lima and Bogota. Missions under the direction of the Jesuits and Franciscans were used to convert and control Indians in frontier areas. By the dawn of the 19th century—inspired by popular uprisings in the United States and France—South America's colonies had hatched their own revolutions. Between 1810 and 1824, Simón Bolívar and Jose de San Martín liberated all of the region's Spanish-speaking lands. Brazil declared its independence from Portugal in 1822.

Despite impressive economic gains in some countries—most notably Argentina—most of South America's independent states were stagnant by the early 20th century, struggling beneath a twin yoke of brutal military rule and neo-colonial economic exploitation. This status quo endured until the late 1990s, when democracy flowered across the continent.

CULTURE

A rich blend of Iberian, African, and Amerindian traditions, South America has one of the world's most lively and distinctive cultures. It's also one of the most urban. Despite romantic images of the Amazon and Machu Picchu, the vast majority of South Americans live in cities rather than the rain forest or mountains. A massive rural exodus since the 1950s has transformed South America into the most urbanized continent after Australia, a region that now boasts three of the world's 15 largest cities—Sao Paulo (18 million), Buenos Aires (12 million), and Rio de Janeiro (11 million). Ninety percent of these people live within 200 miles (320 km) of the coast, leaving huge expanses of the interior virtually unpopulated.

Several common threads bind the continent's 350 million people. Iberian languages dominate, with about half speaking Spanish and the other half Portuguese. There are several linguistic anomalies—French, Dutch, and English in the Guianas, and Amerindian dialects in the remote Amazon and Andes—but most South Americans don't need a translator when talking to one another. And despite recent inroads by Protestant missionaries—especially among remote Indian tribes and the urban poor—nearly 90 percent of South Americans adhere to the Roman Catholic faith.

Yet the continent also flaunts an amazing ethnic diversity. Although the majority of people can still trace their ancestors back to Spain or Portugal, waves of immigration have transformed South America into an ethnic smorgasbord. Amerindians and mixed-blood mestizos make up more than 80 percent of the population in Bolivia, Ecuador, and Peru. More than one-third of Argentines can boast Italian roots. Blond-haired, blue-eyed Germans populate many parts of Chile, Uruguay, and southern Brazil. Almost 40 percent of Brazilians and a high percentage of the residents of coastal Colombia and Venezuela are the descendants of African slaves. Asian Indians comprise the largest ethnic groups in both Surinam and Guyana.

This blend has produced a vibrant modern culture with influence far beyond the bounds of its South American cradle. Argentina's beloved tango—music, lyrics and dance steps born of the Buenos Aires ghettos—is now an icon of romance all around the world. Brazil's steamy port cities hatched sensual Afro-Latino rhythms such as samba and bossa nova, Peruvian pipe music has become synonymous with the Andes, while Colombia has produced a rousing Latino rock. South America's rich literary map includes everything from the magical realism of Gabriel Garcia Marquez and Mario Vargas Llosa to the sensual poems of Pablo Neruda and the poignant prose of Jose Luis Borges. A similar passion flows through soccer, the region's favorite game, where the likes of Pele and Maradona have led their respective national teams (Brazil and Argentina) to multiple World Cup titles.

ECONOMICS

Even though South America's colonies gained their independence at a relatively early stage, they were not able to achieve economic autonomy to any large extent. By the early 20th century, nearly all of them were dependent on commodity exports to Europe or the United States—bananas, rubber, sugar, coffee, timber, emeralds, copper, oil, and beef. In the short term some countries did very well with exports, especially Argentina, which counted

itself among the world's richest nations until the 1950s. But failure to make a full transition from resource extraction into modern business and industry spelled economic doom for the entire continent.

By the 1960s, most of South America was mired in negative or neutral economic growth, increasingly dependent on overseas aid, and plagued by unemployment and poverty. Corruption, military rule, and mismanagement augmented an already dire situation. Hyperinflation of several hundred percent per annum battered Brazil and Argentina in the 1980s, nearly crippling the continent's two largest economies. During the same era, narcotics became one of South America's most important money spinners—cocaine exported in great quantities from Colombia, Bolivia, and Peru. Yet by the 1990s, most countries saw light at the end of their dim economic tunnels. Although fundamental problems remain—like huge foreign debt—the region's nouvelle democracy spurred an era of relative prosperity.

South America still relies, to a large extent, on commodity exports—oil from Venezuela, coffee from Colombia, and copper from Chile. But recent decades have seen a dramatic shift toward manufacturing and niche agriculture. Brazil now earns more money from making automobiles and aircraft than from shipping rubber overseas. Chile has earned a worldwide market for its wine, fruit, and salmon.

Despite protests from indigenous tribes and environmental groups, South American governments have tried to spur even more growth by opening up the Amazon region to economic exploitation—the extraction of oil and timber and the transformation of rain forest into cattle ranches. But this practice is already wreaking widespread ecological havoc. The Amazon could very well be the key to the region's economic future—not by the decimation of the world's richest forest, but by the sustainable management and commercial development of its largely untapped biodiversity into medical, chemical, and nutritional products. Many researchers believe that potential treatments for cancer and other ailments may lie hidden in South America's shadowy rain forest.

Physical and Political
SOUTH AMERICA

Longitude West 55° of Greenwich

Azimuthal Equidistant Projection

SCALE 1:22,838,000
1 CENTIMETER = 228 KILOMETERS; 1 INCH = 360 MILES

0 200 400 600 800
KILOMETERS

0 200 400 600 800
STATUTE MILES

International boundary

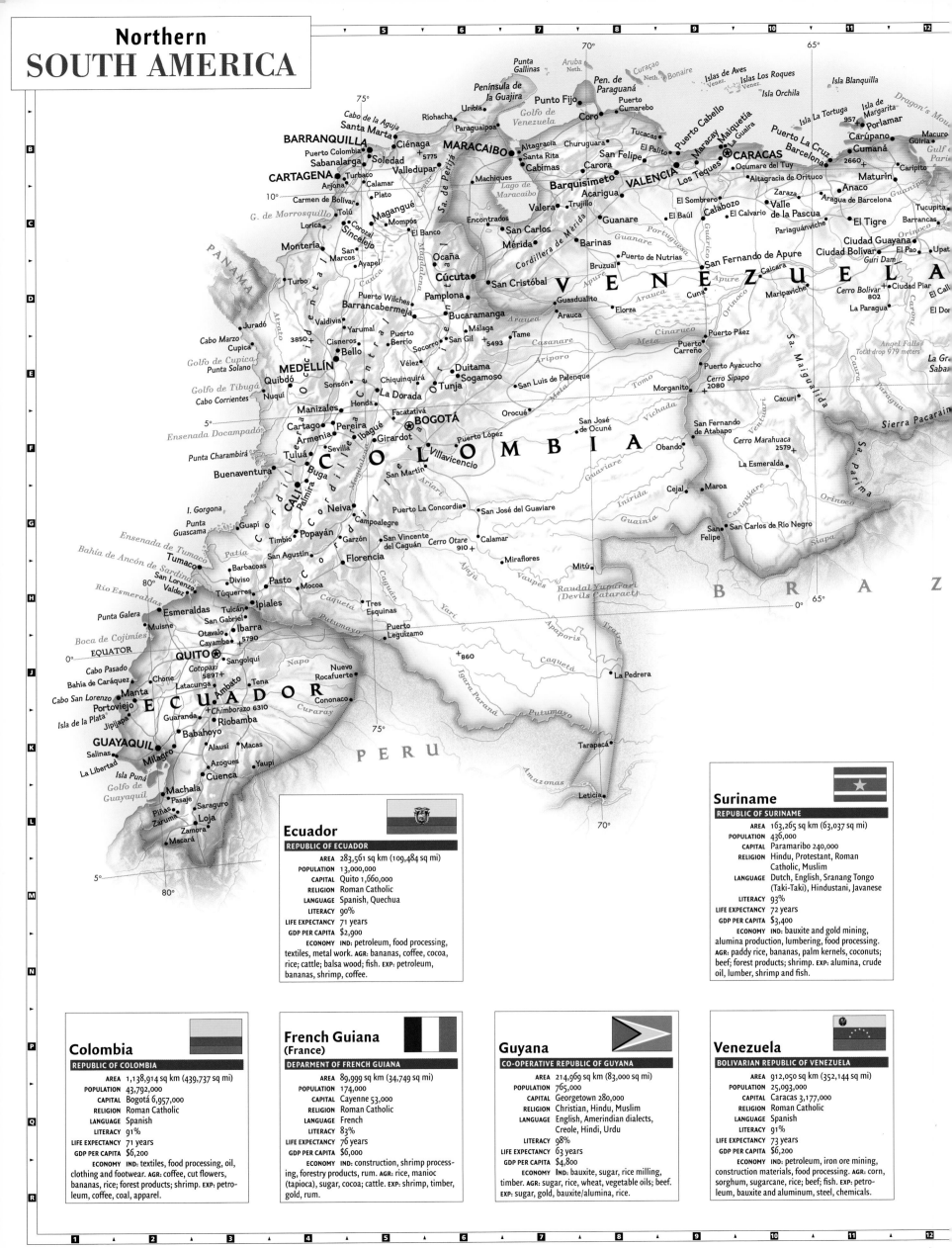

Ecuador
REPUBLIC OF ECUADOR
AREA 283,561 sq km (109,484 sq mi)
POPULATION 13,000,000
CAPITAL Quito 1,660,000
RELIGION Roman Catholic
LANGUAGE Spanish, Quechua
LITERACY 90%
LIFE EXPECTANCY 71 years
GDP PER CAPITA $2,900
ECONOMY IND: petroleum, food processing, textiles, metal work. AGR: bananas, coffee, cocoa, rice; cattle; balsa wood; fish. EXP: petroleum, bananas, shrimp, coffee.

Suriname
REPUBLIC OF SURINAME
AREA 163,265 sq km (63,037 sq mi)
POPULATION 436,000
CAPITAL Paramaribo 240,000
RELIGION Hindu, Protestant, Roman Catholic, Muslim
LANGUAGE Dutch, English, Sranang Tongo (Taki-Taki), Hindustani, Javanese
LITERACY 93%
LIFE EXPECTANCY 72 years
GDP PER CAPITA $3,400
ECONOMY IND: bauxite and gold mining, alumina production, lumbering, food processing. AGR: paddy rice, bananas, palm kernels, coconuts; beef; forest products; shrimp. EXP: alumina, crude oil, lumber, shrimp and fish.

Colombia
REPUBLIC OF COLOMBIA
AREA 1,138,914 sq km (439,737 sq mi)
POPULATION 43,792,000
CAPITAL Bogotá 6,957,000
RELIGION Roman Catholic
LANGUAGE Spanish
LITERACY 91%
LIFE EXPECTANCY 71 years
GDP PER CAPITA $6,200
ECONOMY IND: textiles, food processing, oil, clothing and footwear. AGR: coffee, cut flowers, bananas, rice; forest products; shrimp. EXP: petroleum, coffee, coal, apparel.

French Guiana
(France)
DEPARTMENT OF FRENCH GUIANA
AREA 89,999 sq km (34,749 sq mi)
POPULATION 174,000
CAPITAL Cayenne 53,000
RELIGION Roman Catholic
LANGUAGE French
LITERACY 83%
LIFE EXPECTANCY 76 years
GDP PER CAPITA $6,000
ECONOMY IND: construction, shrimp processing, forestry products, rum. AGR: rice, manioc (tapioca), sugar, cocoa; cattle. EXP: shrimp, timber, gold, rum.

Guyana
CO-OPERATIVE REPUBLIC OF GUYANA
AREA 214,969 sq km (83,000 sq mi)
POPULATION 765,000
CAPITAL Georgetown 280,000
RELIGION Christian, Hindu, Muslim
LANGUAGE English, Amerindian dialects, Creole, Hindi, Urdu
LITERACY 98%
LIFE EXPECTANCY 63 years
GDP PER CAPITA $4,800
ECONOMY IND: bauxite, sugar, rice milling, timber. AGR: sugar, rice, wheat, vegetable oils; beef. EXP: sugar, gold, bauxite/alumina, rice.

Venezuela
BOLIVARIAN REPUBLIC OF VENEZUELA
AREA 912,050 sq km (352,144 sq mi)
POPULATION 25,093,000
CAPITAL Caracas 3,177,000
RELIGION Roman Catholic
LANGUAGE Spanish
LITERACY 91%
LIFE EXPECTANCY 73 years
GDP PER CAPITA $6,200
ECONOMY IND: petroleum, iron ore mining, construction materials, food processing. AGR: corn, sorghum, sugarcane; rice; beef; fish. EXP: petroleum, bauxite and aluminum, steel, chemicals.

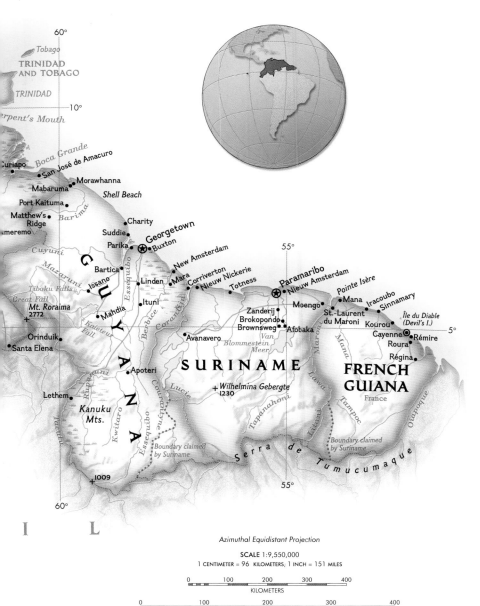

Tobago

TRINIDAD AND TOBAGO

TRINIDAD

60°

10°

'rpent's Mouth

Curiapo

Boca Grande

San José de Amacuro

Mabaruma

Morawhanna

Shell Beach

Matthew's Ridge

Port Kaituma

Barima

meremo

Charity

Suddie

Georgetown

Parika

Buxton

New Amsterdam

Bartica

Linden

Mara

Corriverton

Nieuw Nickerie

Nieuw Amsterdam

Totness

Paramaribo

Pointe Isère

Issano

Ituni

Moengo

Mana

Iracoubo

Sinnamary

Zanderij

Brokopondo

Brownsweg

St.-Laurent du Maroni

Île du Diable (Devil's I.)

Afobaka

Kourou

Cayenne

Rémire

Avanavero

Roura

Mt. Roraima 2772

Cuyuni

Mazaruni

Tiboku Falls

Essequibo

Great Fall

Berbice

Corantijn

Van Blommestein Meer

Régina

Mahdia

Orinduik

Santa Elena

Apoteri

SURINAME

FRENCH GUIANA

Wilhelmina Gebergte 1230

France

Lethem

Kanuku Mts.

Kwitaro

Rupununi

Lucie

Coppename

Saramacca

Suriname

Tapanahoni

Litani

Tampoc

Oiapoque

GUYANA

Boundary claimed by Suriname

Boundary claimed by Suriname

Serra de Tumucumaque

1009

55°

55°

5°

60°

I L

Azimuthal Equidistant Projection

SCALE 1:9,550,000
1 CENTIMETER = 96 KILOMETERS; 1 INCH = 151 MILES

0   100   200   300   400
KILOMETERS

0   100   200   300   400
STATUTE MILES

Temperature and Precipitation

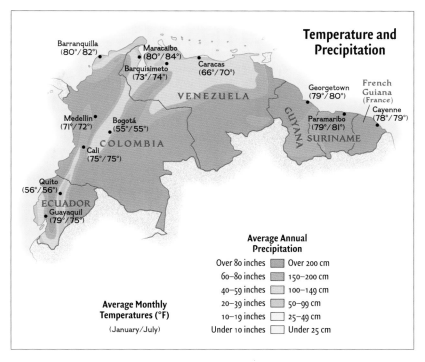

Barranquilla (80°/82°)

Maracaibo (80°/84°)

Barquisimeto (73°/74°)

Caracas (66°/70°)

VENEZUELA

Georgetown (79°/80°)

French Guiana (France)

Cayenne (78°/79°)

Medellín (71°/72°)

Bogotá (55°/55°)

GUYANA

Paramaribo (79°/81°)

SURINAME

COLOMBIA

Cali (75°/75°)

Quito (56°/56°)

ECUADOR

Guayaquil (79°/75°)

Average Annual Precipitation

	Over 80 inches	Over 200 cm
	60–80 inches	150–200 cm
	40–59 inches	100–149 cm
	20–39 inches	50–99 cm
	10–19 inches	25–49 cm
	Under 10 inches	Under 25 cm

Average Monthly Temperatures (°F)

(January/July)

Population

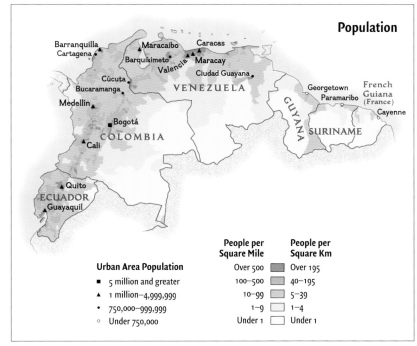

Barranquilla

Cartagena

Maracaibo

Caracas

Barquisimeto

Valencia

Maracay

Ciudad Guayana

Cúcuta

VENEZUELA

Georgetown

French Guiana (France)

Bucaramanga

Paramaribo

Cayenne

Medellín

GUYANA

SURINAME

Bogotá

COLOMBIA

Cali

Quito

ECUADOR

Guayaquil

Urban Area Population

■ 5 million and greater
▲ 1 million–4,999,999
● 750,000–999,999
○ Under 750,000

	People per Square Mile	People per Square Km
	Over 500	Over 195
	100–500	40–195
	10–99	5–39
	1–9	1–4
	Under 1	Under 1

Land Use, Agriculture, and Fishing

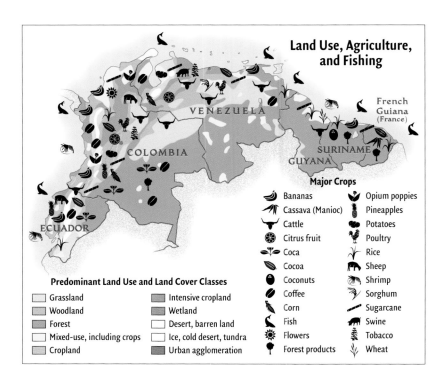

VENEZUELA

French Guiana (France)

SURINAME

COLOMBIA

GUYANA

ECUADOR

Major Crops

Bananas
Cassava (Manioc)
Cattle
Citrus fruit
Coca
Cocoa
Coconuts
Coffee
Corn
Fish
Flowers
Forest products

Opium poppies
Pineapples
Potatoes
Poultry
Rice
Sheep
Shrimp
Sorghum
Sugarcane
Swine
Tobacco
Wheat

Predominant Land Use and Land Cover Classes

Grassland		Intensive cropland
Woodland		Wetland
Forest		Desert, barren land
Mixed-use, including crops		Ice, cold desert, tundra
Cropland		Urban agglomeration

Industry and Mining

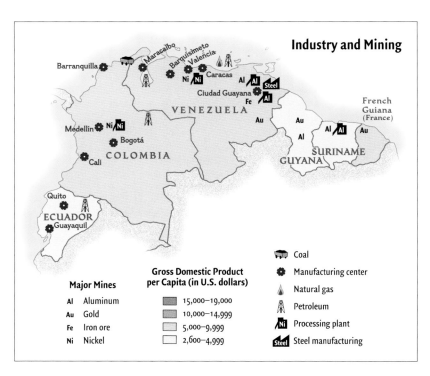

Barranquilla

Maracaibo

Barquisimeto

Valencia

Caracas

Ni Ni

Al Al Steel

Ciudad Guayana

Fe Al

Au

French Guiana (France)

VENEZUELA

Medellín Ni / Ni

Au

Al

Au

Bogotá

Al

COLOMBIA

Al Al

Cali

GUYANA

SURINAME

Quito

ECUADOR

Guayaquil

Major Mines

Al Aluminum
Au Gold
Fe Iron ore
Ni Nickel

Gross Domestic Product per Capita (in U.S. dollars)

	15,000–19,000
	10,000–14,999
	5,000–9,999
	2,600–4,999

🚃 Coal
⚙ Manufacturing center
△ Natural gas
⛽ Petroleum
Ni Processing plant
Steel Steel manufacturing

Bolivia

REPUBLIC OF BOLIVIA

AREA	1,098,581 sq km (424,164 sq mi)
POPULATION	8,760,000
CAPITAL	La Paz (administrative) 1,499,000; Sucre (legal) 183,000
RELIGION	Roman Catholic
LANGUAGE	Spanish, Quechua, Aymara
LITERACY	83%
LIFE EXPECTANCY	64 years
GDP PER CAPITA	$2,600
ECONOMY	IND: mining, smelting, petroleum, food and beverages. AGR: soybeans, coffee, coca, cotton; timber. EXP: soybeans, natural gas, zinc, gold.

Temperature and Precipitation

Manaus (79°/80°)
Belém (78°/79°)
Fortaleza (81°/79°)
Recife (80°/75°)
Lima (72°/61°)
La Paz (50°/44°)
Sucre (61°/57°)
Santa Cruz (80°/69°)
Brasília (70°/65°)
Salvador (Bahia) (79°/74°)
Belo Horizonte (73°/65°)
São Paulo (70°/59°)
Rio de Janeiro (79°/69°)
Asunción (82°/64°)
Curitiba (68°/54°)
Porto Alegre (76°/58°)

Average Annual Precipitation

Over 80 inches		Over 200 cm
60–80 inches		150–200 cm
40–59 inches		100–149 cm
20–39 inches		50–99 cm
10–19 inches		25–49 cm
Under 10 inches		Under 25 cm

Average Monthly Temperatures (°F)

(January/July)

Brazil

FEDERATIVE REPUBLIC OF BRAZIL

AREA	8,511,965 sq km (3,286,488 sq mi)
POPULATION	173,816,000
CAPITAL	Brasília 2,073,000
RELIGION	Roman Catholic
LANGUAGE	Portuguese, Spanish, English, French
LITERACY	83%
LIFE EXPECTANCY	63 years
GDP PER CAPITA	$6,500
ECONOMY	IND: textiles, shoes, chemicals, cement. AGR: coffee, soybeans, wheat, rice; beef. EXP: manufactures, iron ore, soybeans, footwear.

Azimuthal Equidistant Projection

SCALE 1:15,025,000
1 CENTIMETER = 150 KILOMETERS; 1 INCH = 237 MILES

0 200 400 600
KILOMETERS

0 200 400 600
STATUTE MILES

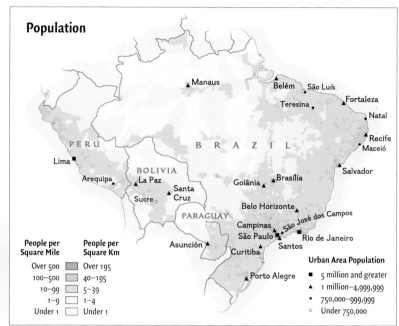

Population

PERU
BRAZIL
BOLIVIA
PARAGUAY

Lima
Arequipa
La Paz
Sucre
Santa Cruz
Asunción
Manaus
Belém
São Luís
Teresina
Fortaleza
Natal
Recife
Maceió
Salvador
Goiânia
Brasília
Belo Horizonte
Campinas
São José dos Campos
São Paulo
Rio de Janeiro
Santos
Curitiba
Porto Alegre

People per Square Mile	People per Square Km
Over 500	Over 195
100–500	40–195
10–99	5–39
1–9	1–4
Under 1	Under 1

Urban Area Population
■ 5 million and greater
▲ 1 million–4,999,999
● 750,000–999,999
○ Under 750,000

Land Use, Agriculture, and Fishing

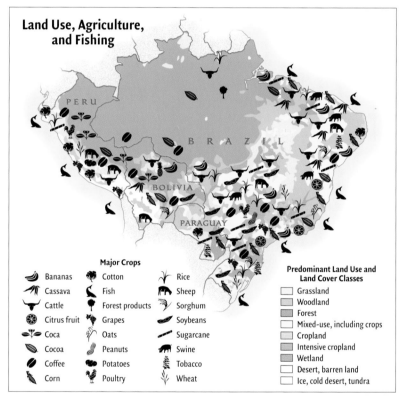

PERU
BRAZIL
BOLIVIA
PARAGUAY

Major Crops
🍌 Bananas
Cassava
Cattle
Citrus fruit
Coca
Cocoa
Coffee
Corn
Cotton
Fish
Forest products
Grapes
Oats
Peanuts
Potatoes
Poultry
Rice
Sheep
Sorghum
Soybeans
Sugarcane
Swine
Tobacco
Wheat

Predominant Land Use and Land Cover Classes
Grassland
Woodland
Forest
Mixed-use, including crops
Cropland
Intensive cropland
Wetland
Desert, barren land
Ice, cold desert, tundra

Industry and Mining

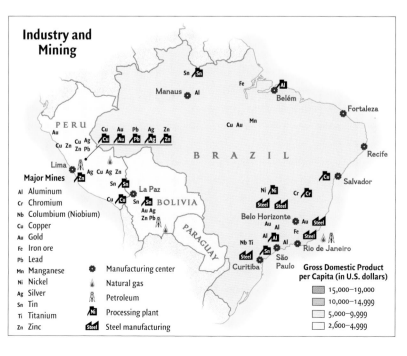

PERU
BRAZIL
BOLIVIA
PARAGUAY

Manaus
Belém
Fortaleza
Recife
Salvador
Lima
La Paz
Belo Horizonte
Rio de Janeiro
São Paulo
Curitiba

Major Mines
Al Aluminum
Cr Chromium
Nb Columbium (Niobium)
Cu Copper
Au Gold
Fe Iron ore
Pb Lead
Mn Manganese
Ni Nickel
Ag Silver
Sn Tin
Ti Titanium
Zn Zinc

✿ Manufacturing center
△ Natural gas
Petroleum
Ni Processing plant
Steel Steel manufacturing

Gross Domestic Product per Capita (in U.S. dollars)
15,000–19,000
10,000–14,999
5,000–9,999
2,600–4,999

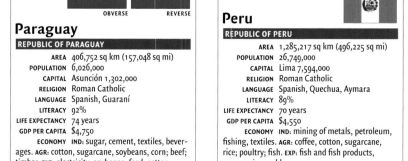

OBVERSE   REVERSE

Paraguay
REPUBLIC OF PARAGUAY
AREA 406,752 sq km (157,048 sq mi)
POPULATION 6,026,000
CAPITAL Asunción 1,302,000
RELIGION Roman Catholic
LANGUAGE Spanish, Guaraní
LITERACY 92%
LIFE EXPECTANCY 74 years
GDP PER CAPITA $4,750
ECONOMY IND: sugar, cement, textiles, beverages. AGR: cotton, sugarcane, soybeans, corn; beef; timber. EXP: electricity, soybeans, feed, cotton.

Peru
REPUBLIC OF PERU
AREA 1,285,217 sq km (496,225 sq mi)
POPULATION 26,749,000
CAPITAL Lima 7,594,000
RELIGION Roman Catholic
LANGUAGE Spanish, Quechua, Aymara
LITERACY 89%
LIFE EXPECTANCY 70 years
GDP PER CAPITA $4,550
ECONOMY IND: mining of metals, petroleum, fishing, textiles. AGR: coffee, cotton, sugarcane, rice; poultry; fish. EXP: fish and fish products, copper, zinc, gold.

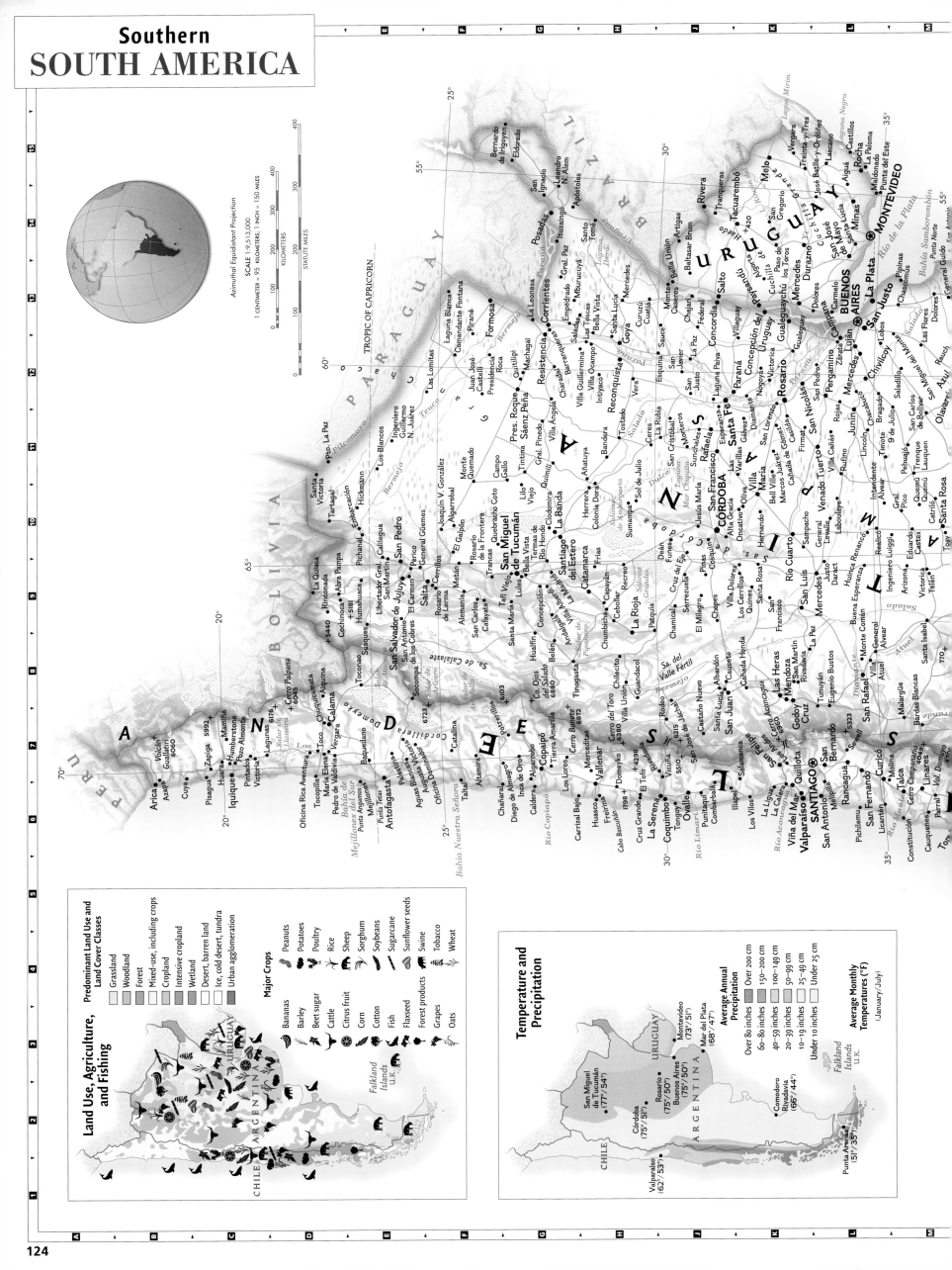

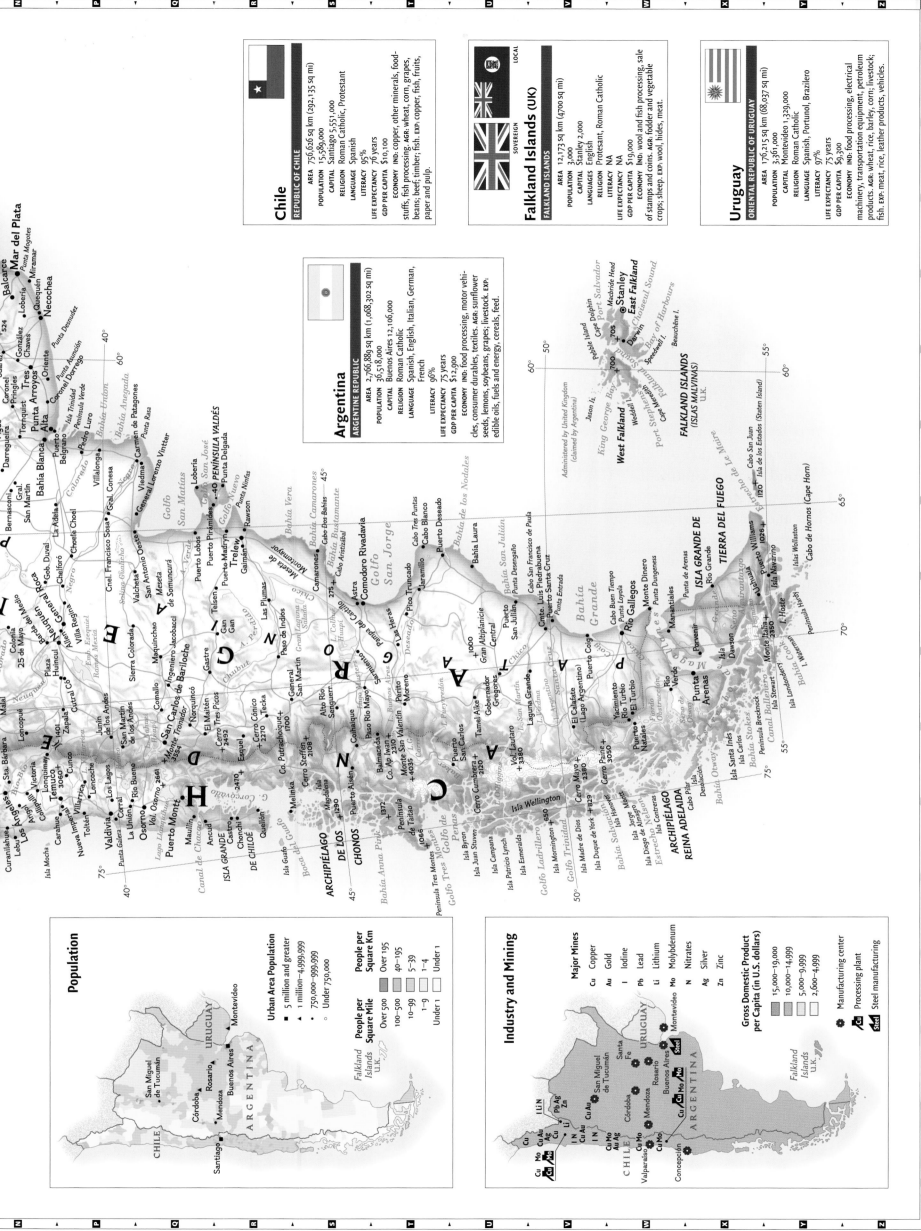

Chile
REPUBLIC OF CHILE
AREA 756,626 sq km (292,135 sq mi)
POPULATION 15,589,000
CAPITAL Santiago 5,551,000
RELIGION Roman Catholic, Protestant
LANGUAGE Spanish
LITERACY 95%
LIFE EXPECTANCY 76 years
GDP PER CAPITA $10,100
ECONOMY IND: copper, other minerals, foodstuffs, fish processing. AGR: wheat, corn, grapes, beans; beef; timber; fish. EXP: copper, fish, fruits, paper and pulp.

SOVEREIGN / LOCAL

Falkland Islands (UK)
FALKLAND ISLANDS
AREA 12,173 sq km (4700 sq mi)
POPULATION 3,000
CAPITAL Stanley 2,000
LANGUAGES English
RELIGION Protestant, Roman Catholic
LITERACY NA
LIFE EXPECTANCY NA
GDP PER CAPITA $19,000
ECONOMY IND: wool and fish processing, sale of stamps and coins. AGR: fodder and vegetable crops; sheep. EXP: wool, hides, meat.

Uruguay
ORIENTAL REPUBLIC OF URUGUAY
AREA 176,215 sq km (68,037 sq mi)
POPULATION 3,361,000
CAPITAL Montevideo 1,329,000
RELIGION Roman Catholic
LANGUAGE Spanish, Portuñol, Brazilero
LITERACY 97%
LIFE EXPECTANCY 75 years
GDP PER CAPITA $9,300
ECONOMY IND: food processing, electrical machinery, transportation equipment, petroleum products. AGR: wheat, rice, barley, corn; livestock; fish. EXP: meat, rice, leather products, vehicles.

Argentina
ARGENTINE REPUBLIC
AREA 2,766,889 sq km (1,068,302 sq mi)
POPULATION 36,518,000
CAPITAL Buenos Aires 12,106,000
RELIGION Roman Catholic
LANGUAGE Spanish, English, Italian, German, French
LITERACY 96%
LIFE EXPECTANCY 75 years
GDP PER CAPITA $12,900
ECONOMY IND: food processing, motor vehicles, consumer durables, textiles. AGR: sunflower seeds, lemons, soybeans, grapes; livestock. EXP: edible oils, fuels and energy, cereals, feed.

Population

Urban Area Population
■ 5 million and greater
▲ 1 million–4,999,999
● 750,000–999,999
○ Under 750,000

People per Square Mile / People per Square Km
Over 500 / Over 195
100–500 / 40–195
10–99 / 5–39
1–9 / 1–4
Under 1 / Under 1

Industry and Mining

Major Mines
Cu Copper
Au Gold
I Iodine
Pb Lead
Li Lithium
Mo Molybdenum
N Nitrates
Ag Silver
Zn Zinc

Gross Domestic Product per Capita (in U.S. dollars)
15,000–19,000
10,000–14,999
5,000–9,999
2,600–4,999

✹ Manufacturing center
⚙ Processing plant
Steel Steel manufacturing

EUROPE

Europe is the world's second smallest continent, after Australia. A cluster of peninsulas and islands extending from northwestern Asia, Europe encompasses more than 40 countries. Despite its northern location, most of its population enjoys a mild climate tempered by warm ocean currents such as the Gulf Stream.

Europe has been inhabited for some 40,000 years. During the last millennium Europeans explored the planet and established far-flung empires. Europe led the world in science and invention, and launched the industrial revolution. By the end of the 19th century, it dominated world commerce, spreading European ideas, languages, legal systems, and political patterns around the globe.

The 20th century brought unprecedented changes. Germany and its neighbors ignited two world wars. The Russian Revolution introduced communism. And Europe, weakened by war, lost its dominant position in the world along with its empires. New superpowers, the

White cliffs, 400 feet (122 m) high, guard England's south coast along the Strait of Dover. Here many historic naval battles were waged against France, only 18 miles (29 km) away. Composed of soft chalk, the cliffs are eroding.

United States and the Soviet Union, entered into a Cold War in 1947, pitting capitalism and democracy against communism and state control, thus dividing Europe in two. Western Europe, backed by the U.S., prospered with market economies, democracy, and free speech, while Eastern and Central European countries were separated from the West by a metaphoric "Iron Curtain." Their centrally planned economies, linked closely to the Soviet Union's, lagged behind the West and, despite full employment and social benefits, people suffered from a severe lack of personal freedom.

In Western Europe, age-old enemies started cooperating. In 1952 six countries founded a common market for coal and steel; it soon included more countries and more commodities until, in 1991, the European Union was formed. Border controls were eliminated between 15 member countries (in 1999, 12 members introduced a common European currency). Also in 1991, the Soviet Union collapsed. Germany, which had been split by the Cold War, was reunified. Eastern and Central Europe started the difficult transition toward Western-style democracy and privatization.

When chaos overtook the Balkans, Yugoslavia shattered into five countries. But other forces are working toward a cohesive Europe. People move freely throughout the continent; they share the same pop culture, pursue similar urban lifestyles, and rely heavily on cell phones and the Internet.

Environmental problems are often international. Acid rain from England kills life in Swedish lakes. A nuclear accident in Ukraine damages dozens of countries. The Danube and Rhine Rivers spread industrial pollution downstream. Wherever possible, regional solutions hold the most promise, like the projected cleanup of the Baltic Sea involving nine surrounding countries.

Although the European Union enforces strict environmental laws, Eastern Europe understood little about the environment until the 1990s. Some countries still contain toxic waste dumps, untreated sewage, and other hazards, but they have insufficient funds to meet the high costs of cleanup.

A political United States of Europe will probably never happen, but the economic advantages of the European Union have drawn applications from more than a dozen would-be members hoping to enter a new era of history.

PHYSICAL GEOGRAPHY

Europe is bounded by the Arctic Ocean in the north, the Atlantic Ocean in the west, the Mediterranean and Black Seas in the south, and the Caspian Sea in the southeast. The traditional landward boundary is a line following the Ural Mountains south across Russia from the Arctic Ocean, via the Ural River to the Caspian Sea. The line then continues west along the crest of the Caucasus Mountains between the Caspian and Black Seas, making Mount El'brus (18,510 ft; 5,642 m), on the northern side, the highest mountain in Europe. Waterways linking the Black Sea to the Mediterranean place a small part of Turkey in Europe.

Two mountain systems lie between icy tundra and boreal forest in the far north and the warm, dry, hilly Mediterranean coast in the south. Ancient, rugged highlands, worn down by successive Ice Age glaciers, arc southwestward from Scandinavia, through the British Isles, to the Iberian Peninsula, while an active Alpine system spreads east to west across southern Europe. Still rising from a collision of tectonic plates, these mountains include the Carpathians, the Alps, the Pyrenees, and their many spurs. The high point is Mont Blanc (15,771 ft; 4,807 m), shared by France and Italy. Three major navigable rivers—the Danube, the Rhine, and the Rhône—rise in the Alps. Europe's longest river, however, is the Volga, flowing southeast across Russia to the Caspian Sea. Movements in the Earth's crust cause earthquakes and volcanic eruptions in southern Europe and in Iceland. The best known volcanoes are Vesuvius, Etna, and Stromboli, in Italy.

Between Europe's two mountain systems, a rolling, fertile plain stretches across the continent from the Pyrenees to the Urals, well drained by several rivers. Some of the world's greatest cities are located here, including Paris, Berlin, and Moscow. Huge industrial areas on this plain are home to much of Europe's dense population.

HISTORY

Named for King Minos, the first civilization in Europe appeared in Crete about 2000 B.C. Minoans traded with Egypt and western Asia, produced impressive art and architecture, and developed a unique form of writing. Around 1450 B.C., their culture disappeared, probably after a major volcanic eruption or an invasion by warlike Mycenaeans. Homer's *Iliad* and *Odyssey* describe the Mycenaean era that followed.

Classical Greek civilization began in the eighth century B.C. The great achievements of the Greeks in philosophy, mathematics, natural sciences, political thought, and the arts have influenced European civilization ever since. Greece bequeathed its legacy to Rome, known for its builders, engineers, military strategists, and lawmakers. The Roman Empire eventually reached from Britain to Persia and lasted roughly 500 years, until invasions by Germanic tribes from the north destroyed it.

During Roman times a new religion, Christianity, entered Europe from western Asia. As Rome declined, the Christian church became the common thread binding Europeans together. It maintained schools and learning in its monasteries through the Middle Ages. In the 11th century, theological differences split Christianity into Orthodoxy in the east, led by patriarchs, and Roman Catholicism in the west, under popes.

Ottoman Turks introduced Islam to the Balkans through conquest during the 14th and 15th centuries. A hundred years later, the Protestant Reformation in northern Europe broke the unity of the Roman Catholic church and provoked a century of wars.

In the 15th and 16th centuries, the Renaissance, a rebirth of the arts, science, and culture, spread northward throughout the continent. Political power shifted to Western Europe, where strong nations emerged, notably England, France, Spain, and Portugal. Under powerful kings, worldwide explorations created mercantile empires, even as ideas of democracy and equality started circulating.

In the 18th century Britain's American colonies became independent and, in the wake of the French Revolution that toppled

Rome's greatest landmark, the Colosseum, was completed in A.D. 80; it held 50,000 spectators during gladiator fights and other events. Four stories high, this structure combines Greek esthetics with Roman building techniques.

the monarchy, Napoleon tried, but failed, to seize all of Europe. In 1815, a balance of power was reestablished among European countries until the forces of nationalism, socialism, and democracy exploded into two world wars a century later.

Following World War II, the Cold War between the U.S. and the Soviet Union replaced the old balance of power with a deadly balance of nuclear armaments, reducing Europe to lesser status. But by the time the Cold War came to an end in the 1990s, Western Europe had coalesced into the European Union. A large number of countries were also allied with the North Atlantic Treaty Organization (NATO), and Europe was embarking on a new era of economic and military cooperation.

CULTURE

Next to Asia, Europe has the world's densest population. Scores of distinct ethnic groups, speaking some 40 languages, inhabit more than 40 countries, which vary in size from European Russia to tiny Luxembourg, each with its own history and traditions. Yet Europe has a more uniform culture than any other continent. Its population is overwhelmingly of one race, Caucasian, despite the recent arrival of immigrants from Africa and Asia. Most of its languages fall into three groups with Indo-European roots: Germanic, Romance, or Slavic. One religion, Christianity, predominates in various forms, and social structures nearly everywhere are based on economic classes.

Great periods of creativity in the arts have occurred at various times all over the continent and shape its collective culture. Classical Greek sculpture and architecture are widely seen as paradigms of beauty. Gothic cathedrals of medieval France still

inspire awe. Renaissance works of art, from paintings by Leonardo da Vinci in Florence to plays by Shakespeare in England, are famous worldwide. Music composed by Mozart of Austria, Beethoven of Germany, and Tchaikovsky of Russia has passed far beyond Europe. Spanish artist Pablo Picasso transformed the Western world's concept of art. By the 20th century, European culture had penetrated everywhere.

The success of America's multibillion-dollar entertainment industry makes some Europeans feel culturally threatened. American movies flood the continent; American products and lifestyles are aggressively marketed. English is becoming the preferred second language for students all over Europe. Others see the blending of cultures as an inevitable aspect of globalization and a chance to export their own pop music, plays, architecture, fashions, and gourmet foods to other countries. A more imminent worry focuses on immigrant groups established as legitimate and illegal workers, refugees, and asylum seekers, who cling to their own habits, religions, and languages. Every European society is becoming multicultural, with political as well as cultural consequences.

ECONOMY

Europe is fortunate in having fertile soil, a temperate climate, ample natural resources, and a long, irregular coastline that gives most countries access to the sea and foreign trade. Navigable rivers often help the 13 landlocked countries.

Europe is currently undertaking two of the most far-reaching economic experiments in its history. Some 20 countries in Eastern and Central Europe are converting centrally planned, communist-style economies to the

democratic market system, while 12 highly developed countries in Western Europe have created a powerful "eurozone" by replacing their national money with the euro, a new currency shared by all of them.

The progress of many ex-Soviet bloc countries has been slower than anticipated due, in part, to a need for laws preventing corruption and abuse of the new system, and for institutions to assure sound financial management. Poland and Slovenia have been among the most successful. Russia and Belarus, on the other hand, have slipped into worsening poverty, causing some people to clamor for a return to the safety nets of communism.

The eurozone countries have not had a totally smooth transition to the single currency. The new European Central Bank could not keep the euro from losing a quarter of its value against the U.S. dollar in its first three years. But there are many advantages. Banking has become faster and easier, and the newly enlarged bond market has led to many corporate reforms and important mergers. A majority of voters in Britain, Sweden, and Denmark, called "euroskeptics," refused to adopt the euro in 1999 like other European Union members. But they will probably vote to do so as the eurozone grows in strength and influence.

Meanwhile, the advantages offered by the European Union encourage outside countries to practice the tough economic and fiscal policies that are prerequisites for membership. Thirteen more countries are currently candidates for admission, and ten that qualify will probably be admitted in 2004: Estonia, Latvia, Lithuania, Cyprus, Malta, the Czech Republic, Hungary, Poland, Slovakia, and Slovenia. With a population of 300 million, the European Union is now one of the largest economies in the world. Europeans speculate that in time the euro may rival the U.S. dollar as the principal global currency.

Physical and Political
EUROPE

A commonly accepted division between Asia and Europe—here marked by a green line—is formed by the Ural Mountains, Ural River, Caspian Sea, Caucasus Mountains, and the Black Sea with its outlets, the Bosporus and Dardanelles.

Azimuthal Equidistant Projection

SCALE 1:18,036,000

1 CENTIMETER = 180 KILOMETERS; 1 INCH = 284 MILES

International boundary

Austria
REPUBLIC OF AUSTRIA
AREA	83,856 sq km (32,377 sq mi)
POPULATION	8,149,000
CAPITAL	Vienna 2,066,000
RELIGION	Roman Catholic, Protestant
LANGUAGE	German
LITERACY	98%
LIFE EXPECTANCY	78 years
GDP PER CAPITA	$25,000

ECONOMY IND: construction, machinery, vehicles and parts, food. AGR: grains, potatoes, sugar beets, wine; dairy products; lumber. EXP: machinery and equipment, paper and paperboard, metal goods, chemicals.

Belarus
REPUBLIC OF BELARUS
AREA	207,598 sq km (80,154 sq mi)
POPULATION	9,936,000
CAPITAL	Minsk 1,664,000
RELIGION	Eastern Orthodox, Roman Catholic, Protestant, Jewish, Muslim
LANGUAGE	Byelorussian, Russian
LITERACY	98%
LIFE EXPECTANCY	68 years
GDP PER CAPITA	$7,500

ECONOMY IND: metal-cutting machine tools, tractors, trucks, earth movers. AGR: grain, potatoes, vegetables, sugar beets; beef. EXP: machinery and equipment, chemicals, metals, textiles.

Czech Republic
CZECH REPUBLIC
AREA	78,864 sq km (30,450 sq mi)
POPULATION	10,276,000
CAPITAL	Prague 1,202,000
RELIGION	Atheist, Roman Catholic, Protestant
LANGUAGE	Czech
LITERACY	100%
LIFE EXPECTANCY	75 years
GDP PER CAPITA	$12,900

ECONOMY IND: metallurgy, machinery and equipment, motor vehicles, glass. AGR: wheat, potatoes, sugar beets, hops; pigs. EXP: machinery and transport equipment, other manufactured goods, chemicals, raw materials and fuel.

Germany
FEDERAL REPUBLIC OF GERMANY
AREA	357,046 sq km (137,857 sq mi)
POPULATION	82,406,000
CAPITAL	Berlin 3,319,000
RELIGION	Protestant, Roman Catholic
LANGUAGE	German
LITERACY	99%
LIFE EXPECTANCY	78 years
GDP PER CAPITA	$23,400

ECONOMY IND: iron, steel, coal, cement. AGR: potatoes, wheat, sugar beets, fruit; cattle. EXP: machinery, vehicles, chemicals, metals and manufactures.

Liechtenstein
PRINCIPALITY OF LIECHTENSTEIN
AREA	160 sq km (62 sq mi)
POPULATION	34,000
CAPITAL	Vaduz 5,000
RELIGION	Roman Catholic, Protestant
LANGUAGE	German, Alemannic dialect
LITERACY	100%
LIFE EXPECTANCY	79 years
GDP PER CAPITA	$23,000

ECONOMY IND: electronics, metal manufacturing, textiles, ceramics. AGR: wheat, barley, corn, potatoes; livestock. EXP: small specialty machinery, dental products, stamps, hardware.

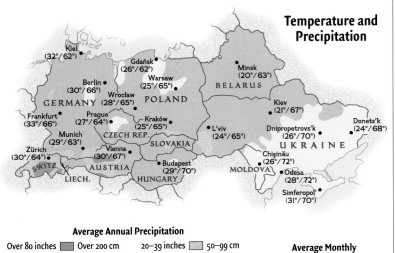

Temperature and Precipitation

Average Annual Precipitation
Over 80 inches	Over 200 cm
60–80 inches	150–200 cm
40–59 inches	100–149 cm
20–39 inches	50–99 cm
10–19 inches	25–49 cm
Under 10 inches	Under 25 cm

Average Monthly Temperatures (°F)
(January/July)

Hungary
REPUBLIC OF HUNGARY
AREA	93,030 sq km (35,919 sq mi)
POPULATION	10,146,000
CAPITAL	Budapest 1,812,000
RELIGION	Roman Catholic, Calvinist, Lutheran
LANGUAGE	Hungarian
LITERACY	99%
LIFE EXPECTANCY	72 years
GDP PER CAPITA	$11,200

ECONOMY IND: mining, metallurgy, construction materials, processed foods. AGR: wheat, corn, sunflower seed, potatoes; pigs. EXP: machinery and equipment, other manufactures, food products, raw materials.

Moldova
REPUBLIC OF MOLDOVA
AREA	33,999 sq km (13,217 sq mi)
POPULATION	4,258,000
CAPITAL	Chişinău 662,000
RELIGION	Eastern Orthodox
LANGUAGE	Moldovan, Russian, Gagauz
LITERACY	96%
LIFE EXPECTANCY	65 years
GDP PER CAPITA	$2,500

ECONOMY IND: food processing, agricultural machinery, foundry equipment, refrigerators and freezers. AGR: vegetables, fruits, wine, grain; beef. EXP: foodstuffs, wine, tobacco, textiles and footwear.

Poland

REPUBLIC OF POLAND

AREA 312,677 sq km (120,725 sq mi)
POPULATION 38,629,000
CAPITAL Warsaw 2,282,000
RELIGION Roman Catholic
LANGUAGE Polish
LITERACY 99%
LIFE EXPECTANCY 73 years
GDP PER CAPITA $8,500
ECONOMY IND: machine building, iron and steel, coal mining, chemicals. AGR: potatoes, fruits, vegetables, wheat; poultry. EXP: machinery and transport equipment, intermediate manufactured goods, miscellaneous manufactured goods, food and live animals.

Switzerland

SWISS CONFEDERATION

AREA 41,288 sq km (15,941 sq mi)
POPULATION 7,286,000
CAPITAL Bern 316,000
RELIGION Roman Catholic, Protestant
LANGUAGE German, French, Italian
LITERACY 99%
LIFE EXPECTANCY 80 years
GDP PER CAPITA $28,600
ECONOMY IND: machinery, chemicals, watches, textiles. AGR: grains, fruits, vegetables; meat. EXP: machinery, chemicals, metals, watches.

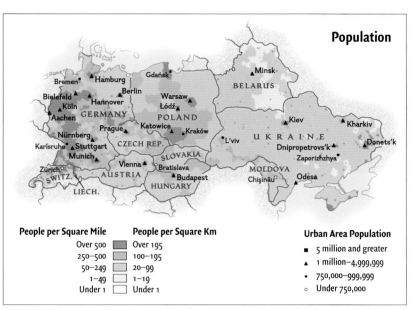

Population

People per Square Mile
Over 500
250–500
50–249
1–49
Under 1

People per Square Km
Over 195
100–195
20–99
1–19
Under 1

Urban Area Population
■ 5 million and greater
▲ 1 million–4,999,999
• 750,000–999,999
○ Under 750,000

Azimuthal Equidistant Projection

SCALE 1:8,024,000
1 CENTIMETER = 80 KILOMETERS; 1 INCH = 127 MILES

0 100 200 300
KILOMETERS

0 100 200 300
STATUTE MILES

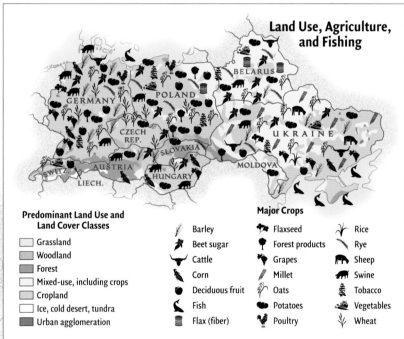

Land Use, Agriculture, and Fishing

Predominant Land Use and Land Cover Classes
Grassland
Woodland
Forest
Mixed-use, including crops
Cropland
Ice, cold desert, tundra
Urban agglomeration

Major Crops
Barley
Beet sugar
Cattle
Corn
Deciduous fruit
Fish
Flax (fiber)
Flaxseed
Forest products
Grapes
Millet
Oats
Potatoes
Poultry
Rice
Rye
Sheep
Swine
Tobacco
Vegetables
Wheat

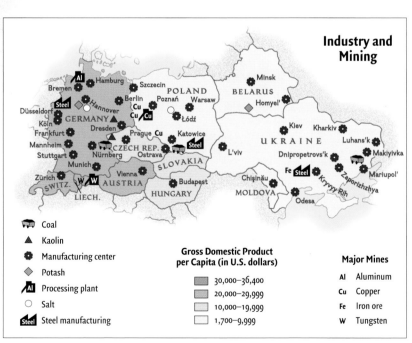

Industry and Mining

Coal
Kaolin
Manufacturing center
Potash
Processing plant
Salt
Steel manufacturing

Gross Domestic Product per Capita (in U.S. dollars)
30,000–36,400
20,000–29,999
10,000–19,999
1,700–9,999

Major Mines
Al Aluminum
Cu Copper
Fe Iron ore
W Tungsten

Slovakia

SLOVAK REPUBLIC

AREA 49,006 sq km (18,921 sq mi)
POPULATION 5,367,000
CAPITAL Bratislava 464,000
RELIGION Roman Catholic, atheist, Protestant
LANGUAGE Slovak, Hungarian
LITERACY NA
LIFE EXPECTANCY 74 years
GDP PER CAPITA $10,200
ECONOMY IND: metal and metal products, food and beverages, electricity, gas. AGR: grains, potatoes, sugar beets, hops; pigs; forest products. EXP: machinery and transport equipment, intermediate manufactured goods, miscellaneous manufactured goods, chemicals.

Ukraine

UKRAINE

AREA 604,001 sq km (233,206 sq mi)
POPULATION 48,225,000
CAPITAL Kiev 2,488,000
RELIGION Ukrainian Orthodox, Ukrainian Catholic (Uniate), Protestant, Jewish.
LANGUAGE Ukrainian, Russian, Romanian, Polish, Hungarian
LITERACY 98%
LIFE EXPECTANCY 66 years
GDP PER CAPITA $3,850
ECONOMY IND: coal, electric power, ferrous and nonferrous metals, machinery and transport equipment. AGR: grain, sugar beets, sunflower seeds, vegetables; beef. EXP: ferrous and nonferrous metals, fuel and petroleum products, machinery and transport equipment, food products.

Denmark
KINGDOM OF DENMARK

AREA	43,092 sq km (16,638 sq mi)
POPULATION	5,378,000
CAPITAL	Copenhagen 1,332,000
RELIGION	Evangelical Lutheran
LANGUAGE	Danish, Faroese, Greenlandic
LITERACY	100%
LIFE EXPECTANCY	77 years
GDP PER CAPITA	$25,500

ECONOMY IND: food processing, machinery and equipment, textiles and clothing, chemical products. AGR: Grain, potatoes, rape, sugar beets; pork and beef; fish. EXP: machinery and instruments, meat and meat products, dairy products, fish.

Latvia
REPUBLIC OF LATVIA

AREA	64,599 sq km (24,942 sq mi)
POPULATION	2,345,000
CAPITAL	Rīga 756,000
RELIGION	Lutheran, Roman Catholic, Russian Orthodox
LANGUAGE	Latvian, Lithuanian, Russian
LITERACY	100%
LIFE EXPECTANCY	69 years
GDP PER CAPITA	$7,200

ECONOMY IND: buses, vans, street and railroad cars, synthetic fibers. AGR: grain, sugar beets, potatoes, vegetables; beef; fish. EXP: wood and wood products, machinery and equipment, metals, textiles.

Norway
KINGDOM OF NORWAY

AREA	324,220 sq km (125,182 sq mi)
POPULATION	4,534,000
CAPITAL	Oslo 787,000
RELIGION	Evangelical Lutheran
LANGUAGE	Norwegian
LITERACY	100%
LIFE EXPECTANCY	79 years
GDP PER CAPITA	$27,700

ECONOMY IND: petroleum and gas, food processing, ship building, pulp and paper products. AGR: barley, other grains, potatoes; beef; fish. EXP: petroleum and petroleum products, machinery and equipment, metals, chemicals.

Sweden
KINGDOM OF SWEDEN

AREA	449,964 sq km (173,732 sq mi)
POPULATION	8,922,000
CAPITAL	Stockholm 1,626,000
RELIGION	Lutheran
LANGUAGE	Swedish
LITERACY	99%
LIFE EXPECTANCY	80 years
GDP PER CAPITA	$22,200

ECONOMY IND: iron and steel, precision equipment, wood pulp and paper products, processed foods. AGR: grains, sugar beets, potatoes; meat. EXP: machinery, motor vehicles, paper products, pulp and wood.

Estonia
REPUBLIC OF ESTONIA

AREA	45,099 sq km (17,413 sq mi)
POPULATION	1,358,000
CAPITAL	Tallinn 401,000
RELIGION	Evangelical Lutheran, Russian Orthodox, Eastern Orthodox
LANGUAGE	Estonian, Russian, Ukrainian
LITERACY	100%
LIFE EXPECTANCY	70 years
GDP PER CAPITA	$10,000

ECONOMY IND: oil shale, shipbuilding, electric motors, cement. AGR: potatoes, fruits, vegetables; livestock and dairy products; fish. EXP: machinery and equipment, wood products, textiles, food products.

Lithuania
REPUBLIC OF LITHUANIA

AREA	65,200 sq km (25,174 sq mi)
POPULATION	3,477,000
CAPITAL	Vilnius 579,000
RELIGION	Roman Catholic, Lutheran, Russian Orthodox, Protestant
LANGUAGE	Lithuanian, Polish, Russian
LITERACY	98%
LIFE EXPECTANCY	69 years
GDP PER CAPITA	$7,300

ECONOMY IND: metal-cutting machine tools, electric motors, television sets, refrigerators and freezers. AGR: grain, potatoes, sugar beets, flax; beef; fish. EXP: machinery and equipment, mineral products, chemicals, textiles and clothing.

Finland
REPUBLIC OF FINLAND

AREA	338,145 sq km (130,558 sq mi)
POPULATION	5,196,000
CAPITAL	Helsinki 936,000
RELIGION	Evangelical Lutheran
LANGUAGE	Finnish, Swedish
LITERACY	100%
LIFE EXPECTANCY	78 years
GDP PER CAPITA	$22,900

ECONOMY IND: metal products, shipbuilding, pulp and paper, copper refining. AGR: cereals, sugar beets, potatoes; dairy; fish. EXP: machinery and equipment, chemicals, metals, timber.

Iceland
REPUBLIC OF ICELAND

AREA	103,001 sq km (39,769 sq mi)
POPULATION	288,000
CAPITAL	Reykjavík 175,000
RELIGION	Evangelical Lutheran
LANGUAGE	Icelandic
LITERACY	100%
LIFE EXPECTANCY	80 years
GDP PER CAPITA	$24,800

ECONOMY IND: fish processing, aluminum smelting, ferrosilicon production, geothermal power. AGR: potatoes, turnips; cattle; fish. EXP: fish and fish products, animal products, aluminum, diatomite.

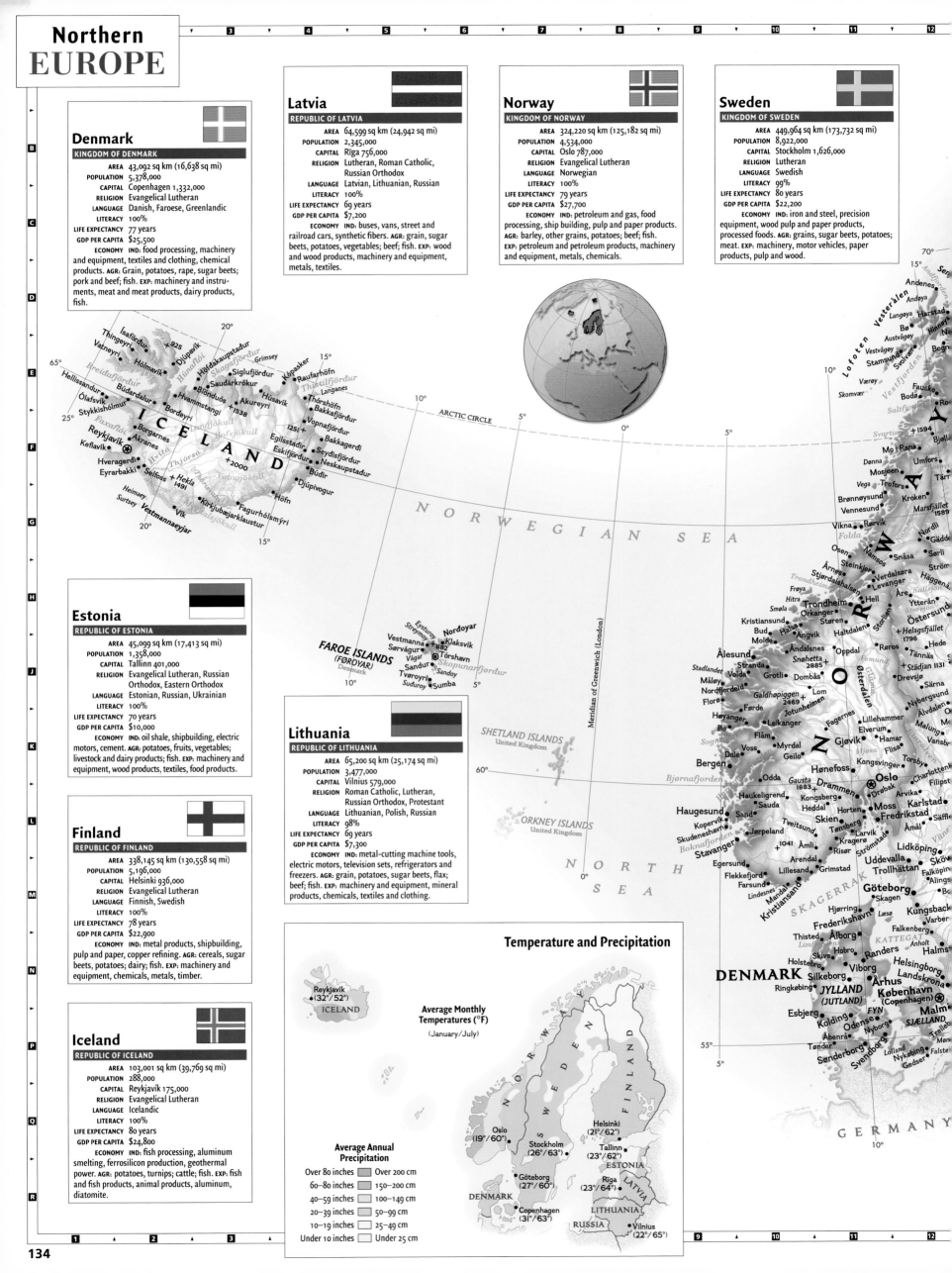

Temperature and Precipitation

Average Monthly Temperatures (°F)
(January/July)

Reykjavík (32°/52°) ICELAND

Oslo (19°/60°)
Stockholm (26°/63°)
Helsinki (21°/60°)
Tallinn (23°/62°)
Göteborg (27°/60°)
Rīga (23°/64°)
København (31°/63°)
Vilnius (22°/65°)

Average Annual Precipitation

Over 80 inches	Over 200 cm
60–80 inches	150–200 cm
40–59 inches	100–149 cm
20–39 inches	50–99 cm
10–19 inches	25–49 cm
Under 10 inches	Under 25 cm

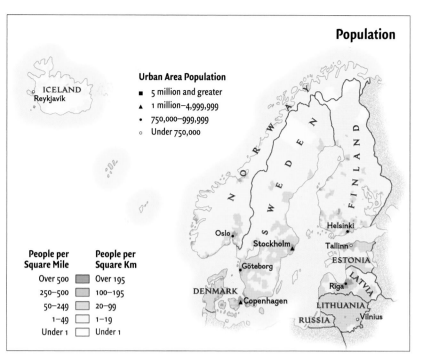

Faroe Islands (Denmark)

SOVEREIGN   LOCAL

FAROE ISLANDS

AREA 1,399 sq km (540 sq mi)
POPULATION 47,000
CAPITAL Torshavn 17,000
RELIGION Evangelical Lutheran
LANGUAGE Faroese (derived from old Norse),
Danish
LITERACY NA
LIFE EXPECTANCY 79 years
GDP PER CAPITA $20,000
ECONOMY IND: fishing, fish processing,
shipbuilding, construction. AGR: milk, potatoes,
vegetables; sheep; salmon. EXP: fish and fish
products, stamps, ships.

Population

Urban Area Population
■ 5 million and greater
▲ 1 million–4,999,999
● 750,000–999,999
○ Under 750,000

People per Square Mile	People per Square Km
Over 500	Over 195
250–500	100–195
50–249	20–99
1–49	1–19
Under 1	Under 1

Land Use, Agriculture, and Fishing

Predominant Land Use and Land Cover Classes
☐ Grassland
☐ Woodland
☐ Forest
☐ Mixed-use, including crops
☐ Cropland
☐ Ice, cold desert, tundra
☐ Urban agglomeration

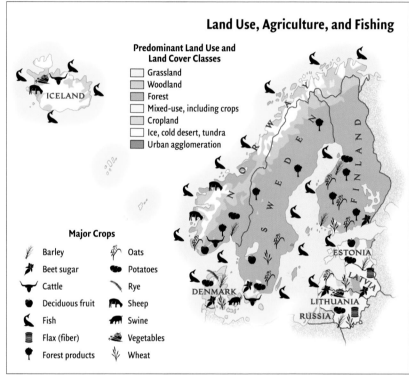

Major Crops

Barley	Oats
Beet sugar	Potatoes
Cattle	Rye
Deciduous fruit	Sheep
Fish	Swine
Flax (fiber)	Vegetables
Forest products	Wheat

Industry and Mining

Coal
Natural gas
Petroleum
Al Processing plant
Steel Steel manufacturing

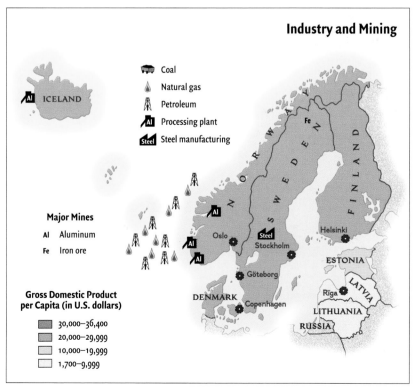

Major Mines

Al Aluminum
Fe Iron ore

Gross Domestic Product per Capita (in U.S. dollars)
☐ 30,000–36,400
☐ 20,000–29,999
☐ 10,000–19,999
☐ 1,700–9,999

Albania

REPUBLIC OF ALBANIA

- **AREA** 28,748 sq km (11,100 sq mi)
- **POPULATION** 3,134,000
- **CAPITAL** Tirana 299,000
- **RELIGION** Muslim, Albanian Orthodox, Roman Catholic
- **LANGUAGE** Albanian, Greek
- **LITERACY** 93%
- **LIFE EXPECTANCY** 72 years
- **GDP PER CAPITA** $3000
- **ECONOMY IND:** food processing, textiles and clothing, lumber, oil. **AGR:** wheat, corn, potatoes, vegetables; meat. **EXP:** textiles and footwear, asphalt, metals and metallic ores, crude oil.

Bosnia and Herzegovina

BOSNIA AND HERZEGOVINA

- **AREA** 51,129 sq km (19,741 sq mi)
- **POPULATION** 3,409,000
- **CAPITAL** Sarajevo 552,000
- **RELIGION** Muslim, Orthodox, Roman Catholic
- **LANGUAGE** Croatian, Serbian, Bosnian
- **LITERACY** NA
- **LIFE EXPECTANCY** 72 years
- **GDP PER CAPITA** $1,700
- **ECONOMY IND:** vehicle assembly, textiles, tobacco products, wooden furniture. **AGR:** wheat, corn, fruits, vegetables; livestock. **EXP:** NA.

Bulgaria

REPUBLIC OF BULGARIA

- **AREA** 110,912 sq km (42,823 sq mi)
- **POPULATION** 7,822,000
- **CAPITAL** Sofia 1,187,000
- **RELIGION** Bulgarian orthodox, Muslim
- **LANGUAGE** Bulgarian, Turkish
- **LITERACY** 98%
- **LIFE EXPECTANCY** 71 years
- **GDP PER CAPITA** $6,200
- **ECONOMY IND:** electricity, gas and water, food, beverages and tobacco. **AGR:** vegetables, fruits, tobacco; livestock. **EXP:** clothing, footwear, iron and steel, machinery and equipment.

Croatia

REPUBLIC OF CROATIA

- **AREA** 56,538 sq km (21,829 sq mi)
- **POPULATION** 4,320,000
- **CAPITAL** Zagreb 1,081,000
- **RELIGION** Roman Catholic, Orthodox
- **LANGUAGE** Croatian
- **LITERACY** 97%
- **LIFE EXPECTANCY** 74 years
- **GDP PER CAPITA** $5,800
- **ECONOMY IND:** chemicals and plastics, machine tools, fabricated metal, electronics. **AGR:** wheat, corn, sugar beets, sunflower seed; livestock. **EXP:** transport equipment, textiles, chemicals, foodstuffs.

Greece

HELLENIC REPUBLIC

- **AREA** 131,990 sq km (50,962 sq mi)
- **POPULATION** 10,968,000
- **CAPITAL** Athens 3,120,000
- **RELIGION** Greek Orthodox
- **LANGUAGE** Greek
- **LITERACY** 95%
- **LIFE EXPECTANCY** 79 years
- **GDP PER CAPITA** $17,200
- **ECONOMY IND:** tourism, food and tobacco processing, textiles, chemicals. **AGR:** wheat, corn, barley, sugar beets; beef. **EXP:** manufactured goods, food and beverages, petroleum products.

Italy

ITALIAN REPUBLIC

- **AREA** 301,277 sq km (116,324 sq mi)
- **POPULATION** 58,091,000
- **CAPITAL** Rome 2,651,000
- **RELIGION** Roman Catholic
- **LANGUAGE** Italian, German, French, Slovene
- **LITERACY** 98%
- **LIFE EXPECTANCY** 79 years
- **GDP PER CAPITA** $22,100
- **ECONOMY IND:** tourism, machinery, iron and steel, chemicals. **AGR:** fruits, vegetables, grapes, potatoes; beef; fish. **EXP:** engineering products, textiles and clothing, production machinery, motor vehicles.

Macedonia

FORMER YUGOSLAV REP. OF MACEDONIA

- **AREA** 25,713 sq km (9,928 sq mi)
- **POPULATION** 2,045,000
- **CAPITAL** Skopje 437,000
- **RELIGION** Macedonian Orthodox, Muslim
- **LANGUAGE** Macedonian, Albanian
- **LITERACY** NA
- **LIFE EXPECTANCY** 74 years
- **GDP PER CAPITA** $4,400
- **ECONOMY IND:** textiles, mining, metal fabrication & electrical equipment, chemicals. **AGR:** rice, tobacco, wheat, corn; beef. **EXP:** food, beverages, tobacco, miscellaneous manufactures.

Malta

REPUBLIC OF MALTA

- **AREA** 316 sq km (122 sq mi)
- **POPULATION** 380,000
- **CAPITAL** Valletta 82,000
- **RELIGION** Roman Catholic
- **LANGUAGE** Maltese, English
- **LITERACY** 89%
- **LIFE EXPECTANCY** 78 years
- **GDP PER CAPITA** $14,300
- **ECONOMY IND:** tourism, electronics, ship building and repair, construction. **AGR:** potatoes, cauliflower, grapes, wheat; pork. **EXP:** machinery and transport equipment, manufactures.

Romania

ROMANIA

- **AREA** 237,499 sq km (91,699 sq mi)
- **POPULATION** 22,382,000
- **CAPITAL** Bucharest 1,998,000
- **RELIGION** Romanian Orthodox, Protestant, Roman Catholic, Uniate Catholic
- **LANGUAGE** Romanian, Hungarian, German
- **LITERACY** 97%
- **LIFE EXPECTANCY** 70 years
- **GDP PER CAPITA** $5,900
- **ECONOMY IND:** textiles and footwear, light machinery and auto assembly, mining, timber. **AGR:** wheat, corn, sugar beets, sunflower seed; eggs. **EXP:** textiles and footwear, metals and metal products, machinery and equipment, minerals and fuels.

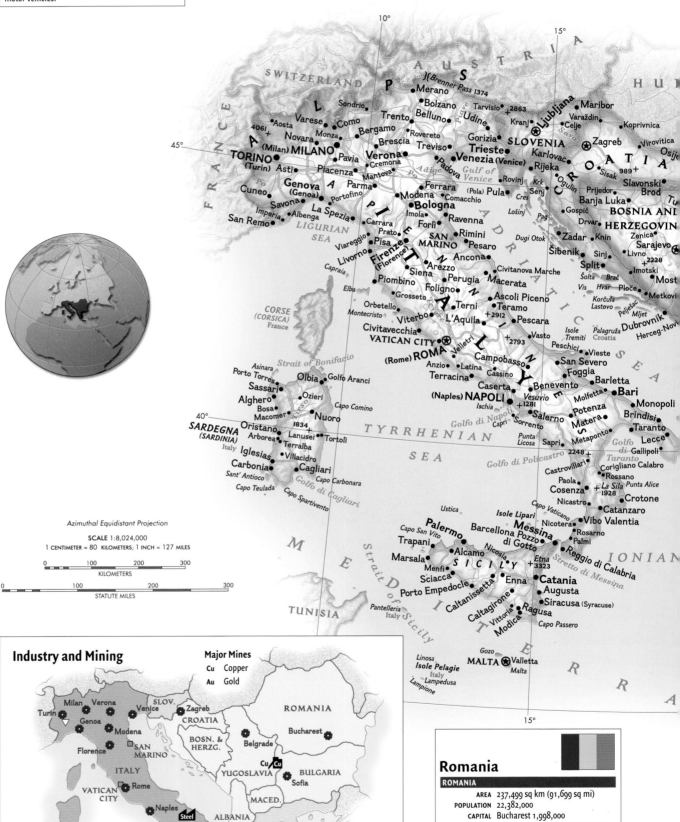

Azimuthal Equidistant Projection

SCALE 1:8,024,000
1 CENTIMETER = 80 KILOMETERS; 1 INCH = 127 MILES

KILOMETERS
0   100   200   300

STATUTE MILES
0   100   200   300

Industry and Mining

Major Mines
- Cu Copper
- Au Gold

Gross Domestic Product per Capita (in U.S. dollars)
- 30,000–36,400
- 20,000–29,999
- 10,000–19,999
- 1,700–9,999

- ✪ Manufacturing center
- Cu Processing plant
- Steel Steel manufacturing
- ▽ Talc

San Marino
REPUBLIC OF SAN MARINO
AREA 61 sq km (24 sq mi)
POPULATION 27,000
CAPITAL San Marino 5,000
RELIGION Roman Catholic
LANGUAGE Italian
LITERACY 96%
LIFE EXPECTANCY 71 years
GDP PER CAPITA $32,000
ECONOMY IND: tourism, banking, textiles, electronics. AGR: wheat, grapes, corn, olives; cattle. EXP: NA.

Vatican City
THE HOLY SEE (STATE OF THE VATICAN CITY)
AREA 0.4 sq km (0.2 sq mi)
POPULATION 1,000
RELIGION Roman Catholic
LANGUAGE Italian, Latin, French
LITERACY 100%
LIFE EXPECTANCY NA
GDP PER CAPITA NA
ECONOMY IND: printing and production of a small amount of mosaics and staff uniforms, worldwide banking and financial activities. AGR: NA. EXP: NA.

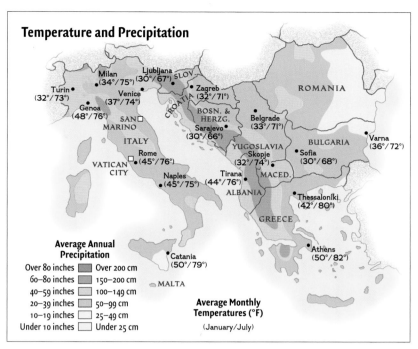

Temperature and Precipitation

Average Annual Precipitation

Over 80 inches	Over 200 cm
60–80 inches	150–200 cm
40–59 inches	100–149 cm
20–39 inches	50–99 cm
10–19 inches	25–49 cm
Under 10 inches	Under 25 cm

Average Monthly Temperatures (°F) (January/July)

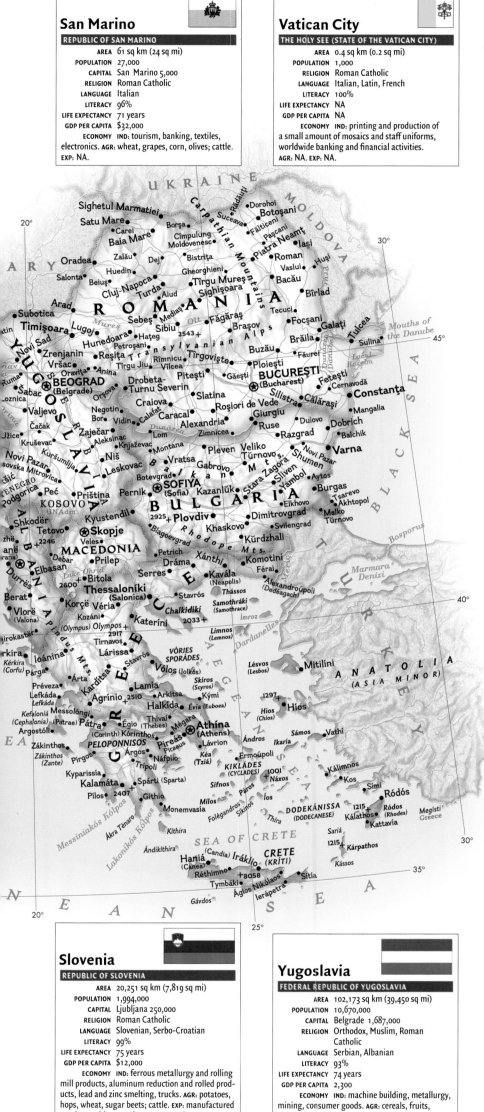

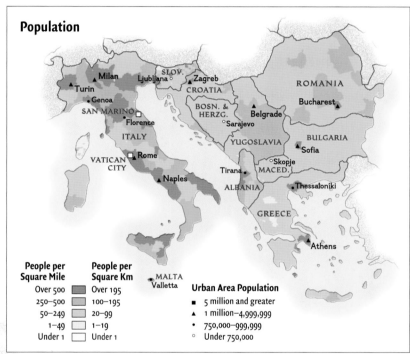

Population

People per Square Mile / People per Square Km

Over 500	Over 195
250–500	100–195
50–249	20–99
1–49	1–19
Under 1	Under 1

Urban Area Population
- ■ 5 million and greater
- ▲ 1 million–4,999,999
- • 750,000–999,999
- ○ Under 750,000

Slovenia
REPUBLIC OF SLOVENIA
AREA 20,251 sq km (7,819 sq mi)
POPULATION 1,994,000
CAPITAL Ljubljana 250,000
RELIGION Roman Catholic
LANGUAGE Slovenian, Serbo-Croatian
LITERACY 99%
LIFE EXPECTANCY 75 years
GDP PER CAPITA $12,000
ECONOMY IND: ferrous metallurgy and rolling mill products, aluminum reduction and rolled products, lead and zinc smelting, trucks. AGR: potatoes, hops, wheat, sugar beets; cattle. EXP: manufactured goods, machinery and transport equipment, chemicals, food.

Yugoslavia
FEDERAL REPUBLIC OF YUGOSLAVIA
AREA 102,173 sq km (39,450 sq mi)
POPULATION 10,670,000
CAPITAL Belgrade 1,687,000
RELIGION Orthodox, Muslim, Roman Catholic
LANGUAGE Serbian, Albanian
LITERACY 93%
LIFE EXPECTANCY 74 years
GDP PER CAPITA 2,300
ECONOMY IND: machine building, metallurgy, mining, consumer goods. AGR: cereals, fruits, vegetables, tobacco; cattle. EXP: manufactured goods, food and live animals, raw materials.

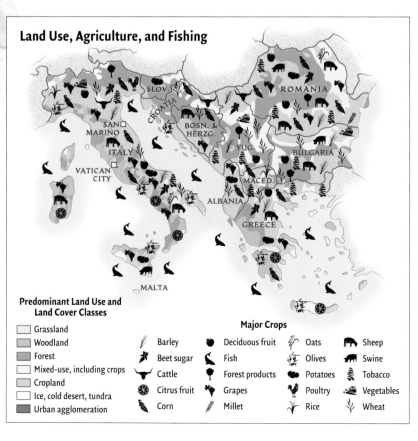

Land Use, Agriculture, and Fishing

Predominant Land Use and Land Cover Classes
- Grassland
- Woodland
- Forest
- Mixed-use, including crops
- Cropland
- Ice, cold desert, tundra
- Urban agglomeration

Major Crops
Barley, Beet sugar, Cattle, Citrus fruit, Corn, Deciduous fruit, Fish, Forest products, Grapes, Millet, Oats, Olives, Potatoes, Poultry, Rice, Sheep, Swine, Tobacco, Vegetables, Wheat

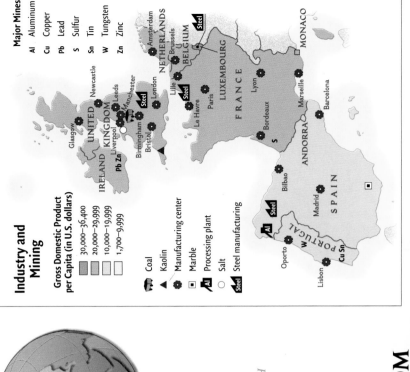

Industry and Mining

Major Mines

Al	Aluminum
Cu	Copper
Pb	Lead
S	Sulfur
Sn	Tin
W	Tungsten
Zn	Zinc

Gross Domestic Product per Capita (in U.S. dollars)

- 30,000–36,400
- 20,000–29,999
- 10,000–19,999
- 1,700–9,999

- Coal
- Kaolin
- ⚙ Manufacturing center
- ◼ Marble
- Processing plant
- ◻ Al Salt
- ○ Steel Steel manufacturing

Portugal
PORTUGUESE REPUBLIC

AREA 92,389 sq km (35,672 sq mi)
POPULATION 10,438,000
CAPITAL Lisbon 3,942,000
RELIGION Roman Catholic
LANGUAGE Portuguese
LITERACY 87%
LIFE EXPECTANCY 76 years
GDP PER CAPITA $15,800
ECONOMY IND: textiles and footwear, wood pulp, paper and cork, metalworking. **AGR:** grain, potatoes, olives, grapes; sheep. **EXP:** clothing and footwear, machinery, chemicals, cork and paper products.

Spain
KINGDOM OF SPAIN

AREA 504,782 sq km (194,897 sq mi)
POPULATION 41,298,000
CAPITAL Madrid 3,966,000
RELIGION Roman Catholic
LANGUAGE Spanish, Catalan, Galician, Basque
LITERACY 97%
LIFE EXPECTANCY 79 years
GDP PER CAPITA $18,000
ECONOMY IND: textiles and apparel, food and beverages, metals and metal manufactures, chemicals. **AGR:** grain, vegetables, olives, wine grapes; beef; fish. **EXP:** machinery, motor vehicles, foodstuffs, other consumer goods.

Monaco
PRINCIPALITY OF MONACO

AREA 1.9 sq km (0.7 sq mi)
POPULATION 34,000
CAPITAL Monaco 34,000
RELIGION Roman Catholic
LANGUAGE French, English, Italian, Monegasque
LITERACY 99%
LIFE EXPECTANCY 79 years
GDP PER CAPITA $27,000
ECONOMY IND: tourism, construction, small-scale industrial and consumer products. **AGR:** NA. **EXP:** Full customs integration with France.

Andorra
PRINCIPALITY OF ANDORRA

AREA 453 sq km (175 sq mi)
POPULATION 66,000
CAPITAL Andorra la Vella 21,000
RELIGION Roman Catholic
LANGUAGE Catalan, French, Castilian (Spanish)
LITERACY 100%
LIFE EXPECTANCY 83 years
GDP PER CAPITA $18,000
ECONOMY IND: tourism, cattle raising, timber, tobacco. **AGR:** tobacco, rye, wheat, barley, sheep. **EXP:** tobacco products, furniture.

Belgium
KINGDOM OF BELGIUM

AREA 30,518 sq km (11,783 sq mi)
POPULATION 10,299,000
CAPITAL Brussels 1,134,000
RELIGION Roman Catholic, Protestant
LANGUAGE Dutch, French, German
LITERACY 98%
LIFE EXPECTANCY 79 years
GDP PER CAPITA $25,300
ECONOMY IND: engineering and metal products, motor vehicle assembly, processed food and beverages, chemicals. **AGR:** sugar beets, fresh vegetables, fruits, grain; beef. **EXP:** machinery and equipment, chemicals, diamonds, metals and metal products.

France
FRENCH REPUBLIC

AREA 543,965 sq km (210,026 sq mi)
POPULATION 59,498,000
CAPITAL Paris 9,658,000
RELIGION Roman Catholic
LANGUAGE French
LITERACY 99%
LIFE EXPECTANCY 79 years
GDP PER CAPITA $24,400
ECONOMY IND: machinery, chemicals, automobiles, metallurgy. **AGR:** wheat, cereals, sugar beets, potatoes; beef; fish. **EXP:** machinery and transportation equipment, aircraft, plastics, chemicals.

Gibraltar (UK)
GIBRALTAR

AREA 6.5 sq km (2.5 sq mi)
POPULATION 27,000
CAPITAL Gibraltar 27,000
RELIGION Roman Catholic, Church of England, Muslim, Jewish
LANGUAGE English, Spanish, Italian, Portuguese, Russian
LITERACY NA
LIFE EXPECTANCY 79 years
GDP PER CAPITA $17,500
ECONOMY IND: tourism, banking and finance, ship building and repairing, support to large UK naval and air bases. **AGR:** NA. **EXP:** petroleum, manufactured goods.

Azimuthal Equidistant Projection

SCALE 1:8,425,000

1 CENTIMETER = 84 KILOMETERS; 1 INCH = 133 MILES

KILOMETERS
STATUTE MILES

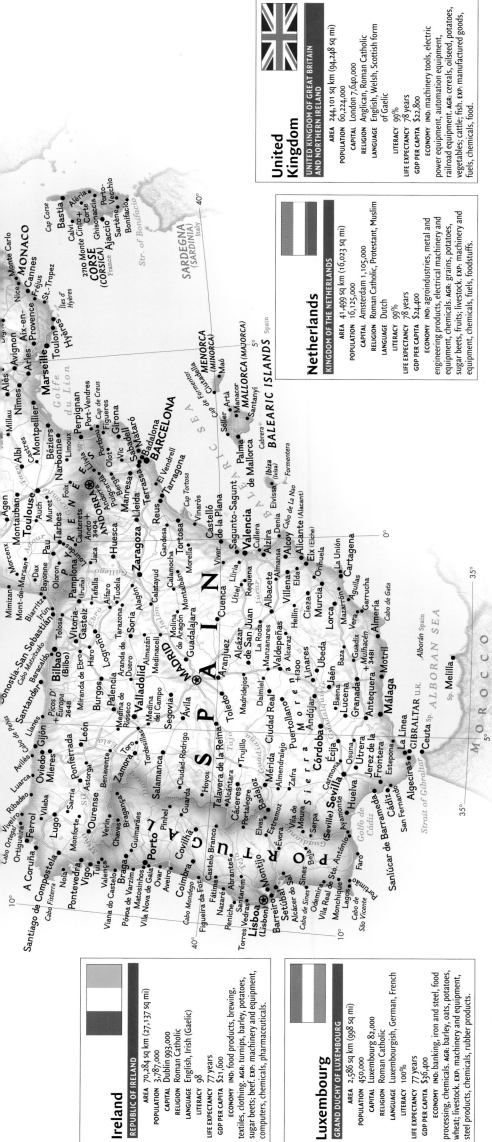

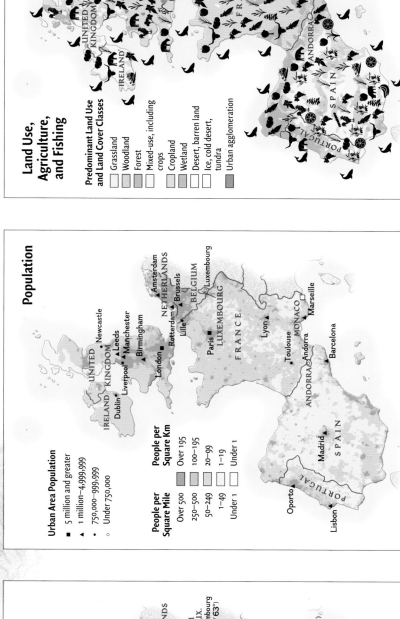

Ireland
REPUBLIC OF IRELAND

AREA 70,284 sq km (27,137 sq mi)
POPULATION 3,787,000
CAPITAL Dublin 993,000
RELIGION Roman Catholic
LANGUAGE English, Irish (Gaelic)
LITERACY 98
LIFE EXPECTANCY 77 years
GDP PER CAPITA $21,600
ECONOMY IND: food products, brewing, textiles, clothing. **AGR:** turnips, barley, potatoes, sugar beets; beef. **EXP:** machinery and equipment, computers, chemicals, pharmaceuticals.

Luxembourg
GRAND DUCHY OF LUXEMBOURG

AREA 2,586 sq km (998 sq mi)
POPULATION 450,000
CAPITAL Luxembourg 82,000
RELIGION Roman Catholic
LANGUAGE Luxembourgish, German, French
LITERACY 100%
LIFE EXPECTANCY 77 years
GDP PER CAPITA $36,400
ECONOMY IND: banking, iron and steel, food processing, chemicals. **AGR:** barley, oats, potatoes, wheat; livestock. **EXP:** machinery and equipment, steel products, chemicals, rubber products.

United Kingdom
UNITED KINGDOM OF GREAT BRITAIN AND NORTHERN IRELAND

AREA 244,101 sq km (94,248 sq mi)
POPULATION 60,224,000
CAPITAL London 7,640,000
RELIGION Anglican, Roman Catholic
LANGUAGE English, Welsh, Scottish form of Gaelic
LITERACY 99%
LIFE EXPECTANCY 78 years
GDP PER CAPITA $22,800
ECONOMY IND: machinery tools, electric power equipment, automation equipment, railroad equipment, automation systems, vegetables; cattle, fish. **EXP:** manufactured goods, fuels, chemicals, food.

Netherlands
KINGDOM OF THE NETHERLANDS

AREA 41,499 sq km (16,023 sq mi)
POPULATION 16,125,000
CAPITAL Amsterdam 1,105,000
RELIGION Roman Catholic, Protestant, Muslim
LANGUAGE Dutch
LITERACY 99%
LIFE EXPECTANCY 78 years
GDP PER CAPITA $24,400
ECONOMY IND: agroindustries, metal and engineering products, electrical machinery and equipment, chemicals. **AGR:** grains, potatoes, sugar beets; fruits; livestock. **EXP:** machinery and equipment, chemicals, fuels, foodstuffs.

Land Use, Agriculture, and Fishing

Major Crops
- Bananas
- Barley
- Beet sugar
- Cattle
- Citrus fruit
- Corn
- Deciduous fruit
- Fish
- Flaxseed
- Forest products
- Grapes
- Oats
- Olives
- Potatoes
- Poultry
- Rice
- Sheep
- Sugarcane
- Swine
- Tobacco
- Vegetables
- Wheat

Predominant Land Use and Land Cover Classes
- Grassland
- Woodland
- Forest
- Mixed-use, including crops
- Cropland
- Wetland
- Desert, barren land
- Ice, cold desert, tundra
- Urban agglomeration

Population

Urban Area Population
- 5 million and greater
- 1 million–4,999,999
- 750,000–999,999
- Under 750,000

People per Square Mile
- Over 500
- 250–500
- 50–249
- 1–49
- Under 1

People per Square Km
- Over 195
- 100–195
- 20–99
- 1–19
- Under 1

Temperature and Precipitation

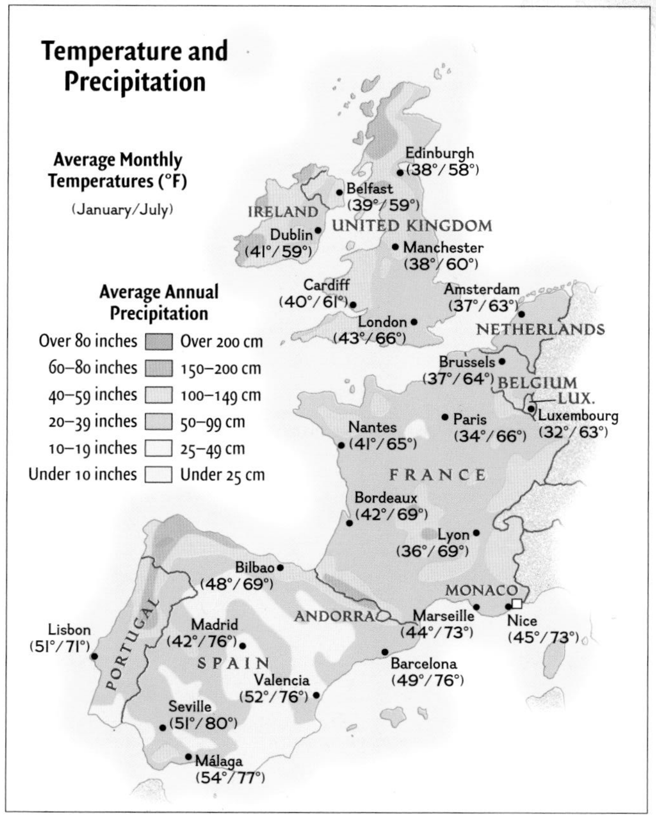

Average Monthly Temperatures (°F)
(January/July)

Average Annual Precipitation
- Over 80 inches — Over 200 cm
- 60–80 inches — 150–200 cm
- 40–59 inches — 100–149 cm
- 20–39 inches — 50–99 cm
- 10–19 inches — 25–49 cm
- Under 10 inches — Under 25 cm

Temperature labels:
- Edinburgh (38°/58°)
- Belfast (39°/59°)
- Dublin (41°/59°)
- Cardiff (40°/61°)
- London (43°/66°)
- Manchester (38°/60°)
- Amsterdam (37°/63°)
- Brussels (37°/64°)
- Paris (34°/66°)
- Luxembourg (32°/63°)
- Nantes (41°/65°)
- Bordeaux (42°/69°)
- Lyon (36°/69°)
- Nice (45°/73°)
- Marseille (44°/73°)
- Monaco
- Bilbao (48°/69°)
- Madrid (42°/76°)
- Valencia (52°/76°)
- Barcelona (49°/76°)
- Seville (51°/80°)
- Málaga (54°/77°)
- Lisbon (51°/71°)

Russia
EUROPE/ASIA

Europe - Asia Boundary

SVALBARD
Norway
BARENTS SEA
KARA SEA
GULF OF BOTHNIA
BALTIC SEA
BLACK SEA
CASPIAN SEA
SEA OF AZOV
ARCTIC CIRCLE
KALININGRAD OBLAST Russia
NOVAYA ZEMLYA
ZEMLYA FRANTSA IOSIFA (FRANZ JOSEF LAND) Russia
ST. PETERSBURG (Leningrad)
MOSKVA (Moscow)
NIZHNIY NOVGOROD
KAZAN'
SAMARA
PERM'
YEKATERINBURG
CHELYABINSK
OMSK
NOVOSIBIRSK
ROSTOV NA DONU
Volgograd (Stalingrad)
Arkhangel'sk (Archangel)
Murmansk
CAUCASUS MTS.
Caspian Depression
KAZAKHSTAN
FINLAND
SWEDEN
NORWAY
ESTONIA
LATVIA
LITHUANIA
BELARUS
UKRAINE
POLAND
GEORGIA
ARMENIA
AZERBAIJAN
CHINA
El'brus 5642
Gora Belukha 4506
A commonly accepted division between Asia and Europe–here marked by a green line–is formed by the Ural Mountains, Ural River, Caspian Sea, Caucasus Mountains, and the Black Sea with its outlets, the Bosporus and Dardanelles.

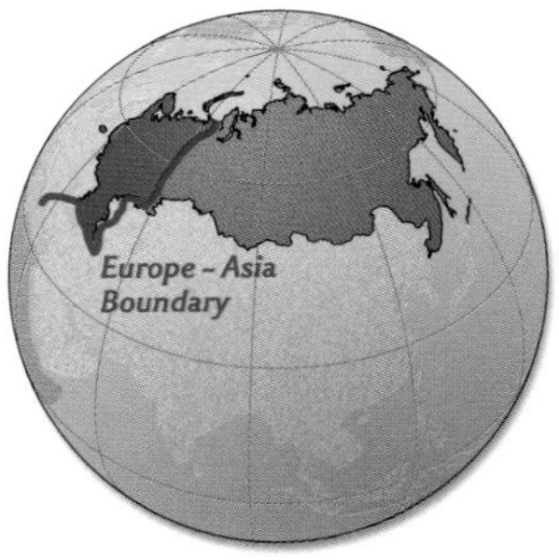

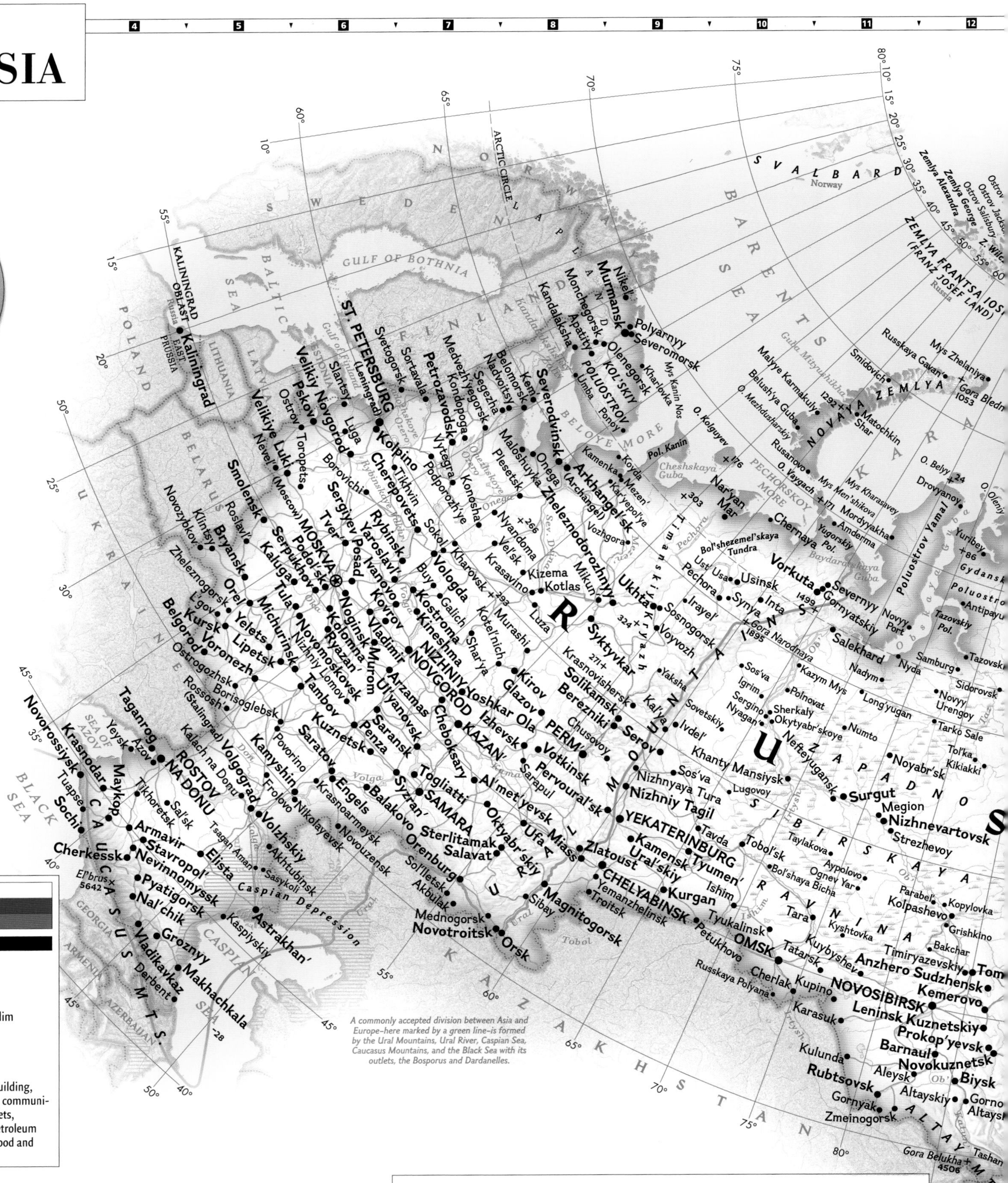

Russia

RUSSIAN FEDERATION

AREA	17,074,993 sq km (6,592,692 sq mi)
POPULATION	143,524,000
CAPITAL	Moscow 8,316,000
RELIGION	Russian Orthodox, Muslim
LANGUAGE	Russian
LITERACY	98%
LIFE EXPECTANCY	67 years
GDP PER CAPITA	$7,700

ECONOMY IND: mining, machine building, road and rail transportation equipment, communications equipment. AGR: grain, sugar beets, sunflower seed, vegetables; beef. EXP: petroleum and petroleum products, natural gas, wood and wood products, metals.

Industry and Mining

Gross Domestic Product Per Capita (in U.S. Dollars)
30,000–36,400
20,000–29,999
10,000–19,999
1,700–9,999
St. Petersburg
Moscow
Lipetsk
Rostov
Nizhniy Novgorod
Perm'
Ufa
Yekaterinburg
Chelyabinsk
Volgograd
Omsk
Barnaul
RUSSIA
Major Mines
Al Aluminum
Co Cobalt
Cu Copper
Au Gold
Fe Iron ore
Mo Molybdenum
Ni Nickel
Pt Platinum
Sn Tin
W Tungsten
Coal
Diamond mine
Manufacturing center
Natural gas
Petroleum
Phosphate
Potash
Processing plant
Steel manufacturing

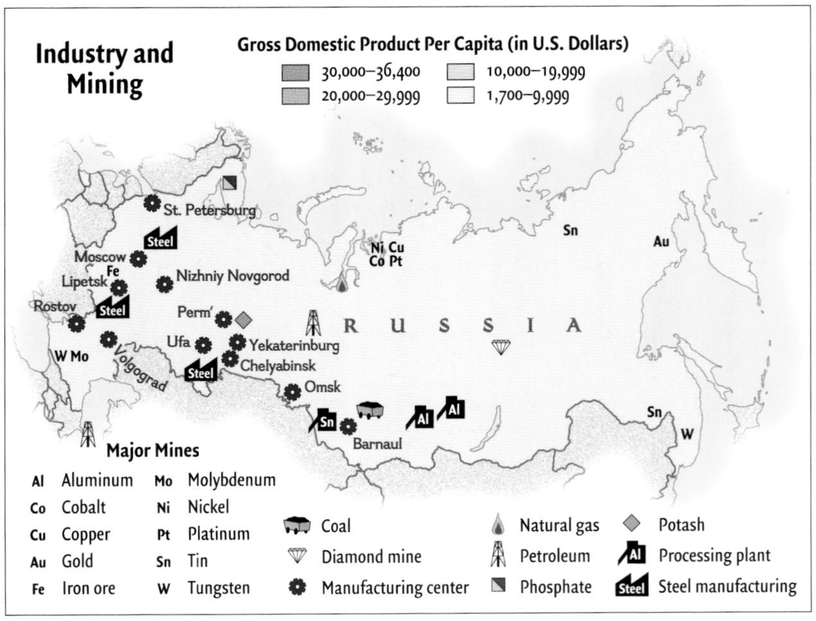

Land Use, Agriculture, and Fishing

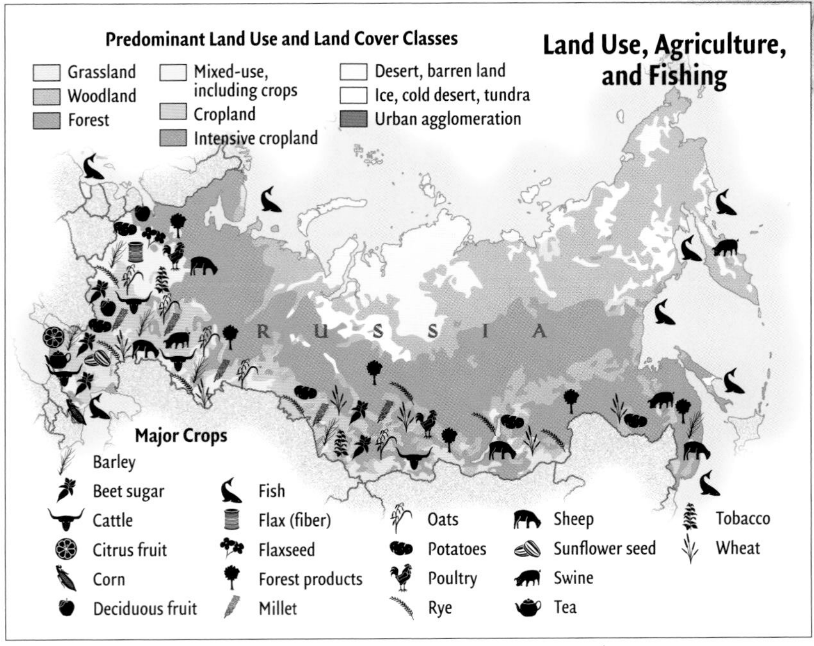

Predominant Land Use and Land Cover Classes
Grassland
Woodland
Forest
Mixed-use, including crops
Cropland
Intensive cropland
Desert, barren land
Ice, cold desert, tundra
Urban agglomeration
RUSSIA
Major Crops
Barley
Beet sugar
Cattle
Citrus fruit
Corn
Deciduous fruit
Fish
Flax (fiber)
Flaxseed
Forest products
Millet
Oats
Potatoes
Poultry
Rye
Sheep
Sunflower seed
Swine
Tea
Tobacco
Wheat

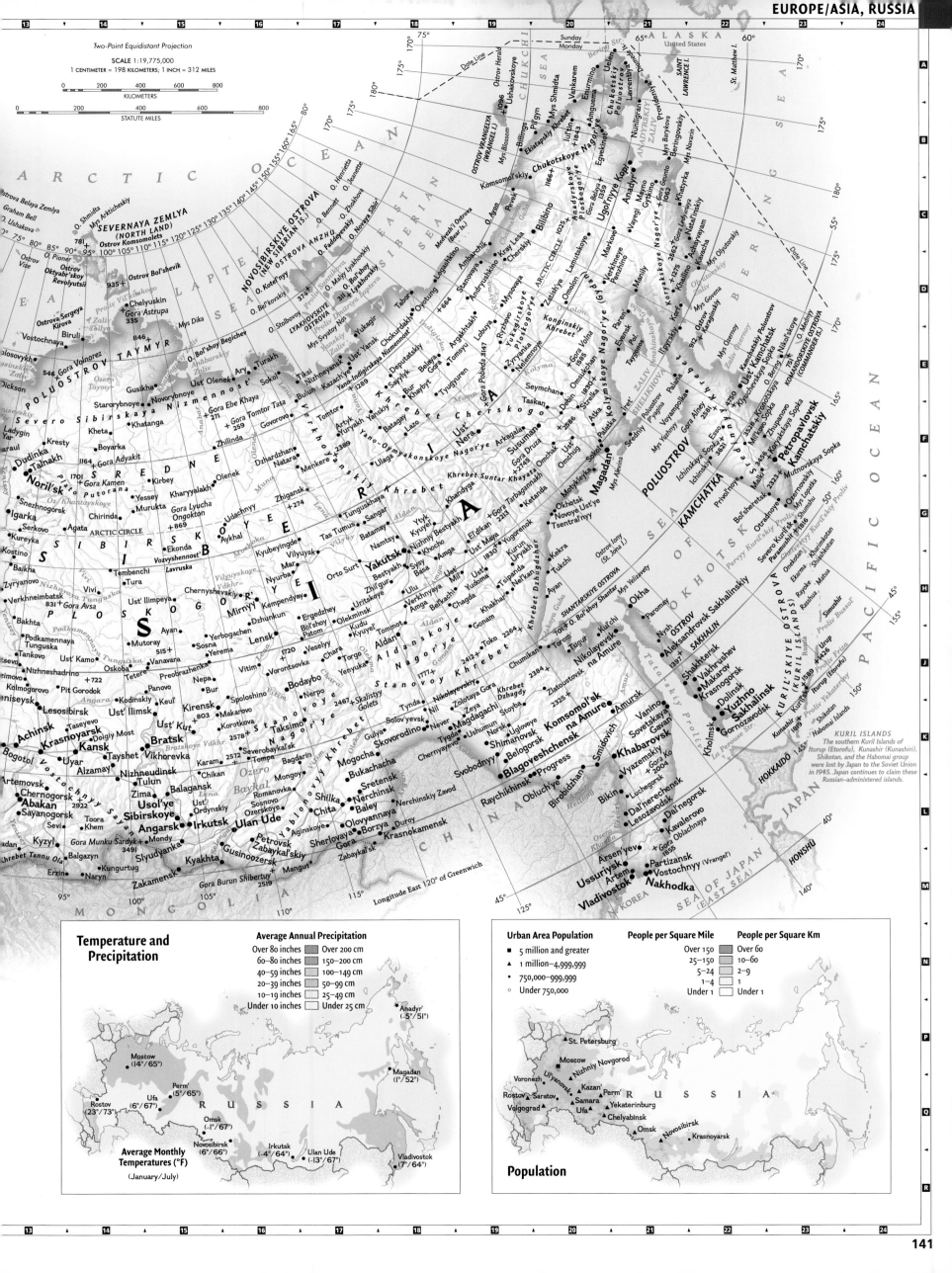

ASIA

The continent of Asia, occupying four-fifths of the giant Eurasian land mass, stretches across ten time zones from the Pacific Ocean in the east to the Ural Mountains and Black Sea in the west. It is the largest of continents, with dazzling geographic diversity and 30 percent of the Earth's land surface. Asia includes numerous island nations, such as Japan, the Philippines, Indonesia and Sri Lanka, as well as many of the world's major islands: Borneo, Sumatra, Honshu, Celebes, Java, and half of New Guinea.

Siberia, the huge Asian section of Russia, reaches deep inside the Arctic Circle and fills the continent's northern quarter. To its south lie the large countries of Kazakhstan, Mongolia, and China. In all, Asia contains 47 nations, accounting for 60 percent of the Earth's population—nearly 3.8 billion people—yet deserts, mountains, jungles, and inhospitable zones render much of Asia empty or underpopulated.

For millenia, people have lived near the seas and along great rivers.

Morning light illuminates 29,035-foot (8,850 m) Mount Everest, Earth's highest point, on the border of Nepal and Tibet. Local Tibetans honor the peak as "Goddess Mother of the World."

Monumental religious sculpture marks the vast complex of Angkor in northwest Cambodia. Heart of the Khmer empire from the 9th to the 15th centuries, Angkor's temples represented the cosmos.

Early civilizations arose in China along the Yellow River, in South Asia on the Indus, and in the Middle East along the Tigris and Euphrates. Today, Asia's large populations continue to thrive near inland water and coastal regions.

India and China, historically isolated from each other by the Himalaya Mountains and Myanmar's jungles, developed rich, vibrant cultures with art, literature, and philosophy of the highest order. China's 1.3 billion people and India's billion make up nearly two-thirds of Asia's population. These countries stand as rivals, each trying to modernize and assert itself while struggling with formidable problems of poverty, pollution, urbanization, and illiteracy.

Breakup of the Soviet Union in 1991 allowed for the creation of eight new Asian countries, five in Central Asia—Kazakhstan, Kyrgyzstan, Uzbekistan, Turkmenistan, and Tajikistan—and three in the Caucasus region—Georgia, Armenia, and Azerbaijan.

Asia's few democracies, including Israel, India, and Japan, contrast with much more authoritarian governments or military regimes, which are numerous and widespread. Monarchies in Bhutan, Nepal, Jordan, Saudi Arabia, and Brunei (a sultanate) pass rulership through family lines.

Events at the start of the 21st century have put new focus on the Middle East, the role of Islam, and control of religious extremism. More than half of Asia's countries are Muslim, yet they possess very different languages, climates, economies, and ethnic groups. But all share emotional links with their co-religionists and care deeply about the development of Islam in the decades ahead.

PHYSICAL GEOGRAPHY

Asia, the planet's youngest continent, displays continuing geologic activity. Volcanoes form a chain known as the "rim of fire" along the entire Pacific edge, from Siberia's Kamchatka Peninsula to the islands of the Philippines and Indonesia. The Indian subcontinent pushes into the heart of Asia, raising and contorting the towering Karakoram and Himalaya ranges. Earthquakes rattle China, Japan, and West Asia.

Geographic extremes allow Asia to claim many world records. Mount Everest, monarch of the Himalaya, is the planet's highest point at 29,035 feet (8,850 m). The super-salty Dead Sea lies 1,349 feet (411 m) below sea level—the lowest point. A site in Assam, India, receives an astonishing 39 feet (12 m) of rain each year, making it the wettest spot on Earth, and Siberia's ancient Lake Baikal, arcing 395 miles (636 km), plunges over a mile (5,371 ft; 1,637 m) as the world's deepest lake. It harbors many unique plant and animal species, including tens of thousands of freshwater seals.

The Caspian Sea, salty and isolated on the border of Europe and Asia, is the largest lake, measuring more than four times the area of Lake Superior. A 39,000-mile (62,800 km) coastline, longest of any continent's, allows all but 12 Asian nations direct access to the sea.

These landlocked countries, mostly in Central Asia (excepting Laos), form part of a great band across the middle latitudes comprised of deserts, mountains, and arid plateaus. The vast Tibetan Plateau, home to the yak, snow leopard, wild ass, and migrating antelope, gives rise to Asia's vital rivers: the Yellow, Yangzi, Indus, Ganges, Salween, and Mekong. At the heart of the continent exists a convergence of the world's mighty mountains: Himalaya, Karakoram, Hindu Kush, Pamir, and Kunlun.

Flowing sand dunes of the Arabian Peninsula contrast with steppes that extend for thousands of grassy miles from Europe to Mongolia. To the north, girdling Asia's northern latitudes, grow boreal forests made up of conifers—the taiga—largest unbroken woodlands in the world. Beyond the taiga lie frozen expanses of tundra.

Far to the south, monsoon winds bring annual rains to thickly populated regions of South and Southeast Asia. These wet, green domains support some of the world's last rain forests and amazing numbers of plants. Human impact through agriculture, animal grazing, and forestry has altered much of Asia's landscape and continues to threaten the natural realm.

HISTORY

Asia's great historical breadth encompasses thousands of years, vast distances, and a kaleidoscope of peoples. From China to Lebanon, from Siberia to Sri Lanka, Asia has more ethnic and national groups than any other continent. Their histories have evolved through peaceful growth and migration, but more often through military conquest.

The Fertile Crescent region of the Middle East saw the emergence of agriculture and early settlements some ten thousand years ago. Later, successful irrigation helped bring forth the first civilization in Sumer, today's southern Iraq; Sumerians invented the first wheeled vehicles, the potter's wheel, the first system of writing—cuneiform—and codes of law.

During the second millennium B.C., a pastoral people called Aryans, or Indo-Iranians, pushed into present-day Afghanistan and eastern Iran, then steadily occupied much of India, Western, and Central Asia.

Central Asia has always been a historic melting pot of flourishing cultures. More than two thousand years ago a braid of ancient caravan tracks—the Silk Road—carried precious goods between East Asia and the rest of the world: sleek horses, exotic foods, medicines, jewels, birds, and perfume. More practical were gunpowder, the magnetic compass, the printing press, mathematics, ceramics, and silk. Trade flourished especially during China's Han dynasty (206 B.C.–A.D. 220), Tang dynasty (A.D. 618-907), and the Mongol period (13th and 14th centuries). Mongols at their height came closer than any other people to conquering all of Asia, threatening Europe in the west and twice trying to invade Japan.

Another great expansion was the conquest and settlement of Siberia and Central Asia by Russians. The Trans-Siberian Railway, built between 1891 and 1905, opened up Siberia for settlement. During the 19th century, Russian armies and colonizers spread through Central Asia as well, claiming the khanates for an expanding Russian empire.

Today, colonial empires have ended and a seemingly stable community of nations with defined borders exists in Asia. Yet rivalries, threats, and war dominate many regions. Indochina is only now healing after decades of violence. The Korean Peninsula remains divided. Nuclear-armed India and Pakistan have fought three wars since independence in 1947. Religious and ethnic hostilities inflame many areas, nowhere more so than in the Middle East. Troubled Afghanistan, victim of almost continuous warfare since 1979, saw a U.S.-led invasion in 2001 to oust the Taliban government and destroy terrorist groups. Many claim peace will come to these areas only after economic stability, steps towards democracy, and recognition of human rights are achieved.

CULTURE

Numerous cultural forces, each linked to broad geographic areas, have formed and influenced Asia's rich civilizations and hundreds of ethnic groups. The two oldest are the cultural milieus of India and China.

India's culture still reverberates throughout countries as varied as Sri Lanka, Pakistan, Afghanistan, Nepal, Bangladesh, Burma, and across seas to Thailand, Cambodia, Singapore, and Indonesia. The world religions of Hinduism and Buddhism originated in India and spread as traders, scholars, and priests sought distant footholds. The island of Bali in predominantly Muslim Indonesia remains Hindu today. Many regions of Asia first encountered writing in the form of Sanskrit, the holy script of Hinduism.

China's civilization, more than four thousand years old, has profoundly influenced the development of all of East Asia, much of Southeast Asia, and parts of Central Asia. Chinese institutions such as government, warfare, architecture, the arts and sciences, and even chopsticks reached to the heart of other lands and peoples. Most important of all were the Chinese written language, a complex script with thousands of characters, and Confucianism, an ethical world view that affected philosophy, politics, and relations within society. Japan, Korea, and Vietnam especially absorbed these cultural gifts.

Today, most Chinese call themselves "Han," a term that embraces more than 90 percent of the population—a billion people—and thus makes them the world's largest ethnic group. In addition, China's government recognizes 55 other ethnic minorities within its borders.

Islam, a third great cultural influence in Asia, proved formidable in its energy and creative genius. Arabs from the 7th century onwards, spurred on by faith, moved rapidly into Southwest Asia. Their religion and culture, particularly Arabic writing, spread through Iran and Afghanistan to the Indian subcontinent. In time, shipping, commerce, and missionaries carried Islam on to the Malay Peninsula and Indonesian archipelago. Indonesia, the largest Muslim country with 175 million believers, and Pakistan and Bangladesh, each with over 100 million Muslims, attest to Islam's success.

Europeans, too, have affected Asia's cultures, from the conquests of Alexander the Great to today's multinational corporations. Colonial powers, especially Britain in India, France in Indochina, Holland in the Indonesian archipelago, and numerous countries in China, left a lasting mark even after nationalist movements forced them out in the late 1940s and early 1950s.

ECONOMY

Blessed with resources and teeming with energetic people, Asia still suffers from great disparities between rich and poor. The livelihood of most Asians rests on agriculture and age-old methods of production. Vietnamese women turn waterwheels by foot-power. Iranian farmers plow using buffaloes. Indian villagers, bent at the waist, plant rice seedlings by hand. Bangladeshi fishermen cast circular nets, hoping for a few small fish. Burmese lacquerwork, Chinese embroidery, Middle Eastern brassware, and Indonesian batik cloth represent local crafts.

Wet-rice cultivation from Japan southward has shaped life for hundreds of millions of Asians. To the west, across north China, Central Asia, and beyond to the Middle East, wheat growing has dominated. Plantation and cash crops, too, such as rubber, tea, palm oil, coconuts, sugar cane, and tobacco continue to sustain regional economies.

Across Asia, country dwellers have flocked in the millions to the cities, seeking jobs and a better life. From Jakarta to Baghdad, the growth of megacities represents a dramatic change over the past 50 years. In China, up to 80 million people form a floating population, seeking work wherever it can be found.

The emergence of post-war Japan as Asia's strongest economy set a model for newly industrialized countries such as South Korea, Hong Kong, Singapore, and Taiwan. Japan, with few natural resources, imports oil, foodstuffs, and textiles, but succeeds by exporting cars, chemicals, and electronics. Central Asian nations of the former Soviet Union have industrialized but require further diversification to rise above poverty. Lands in the Persian Gulf region have flourished from petroleum, and many countries now use light industry as a motor for growth. Tourism, too, plays its part and has helped Thailand, Nepal, parts of Indonesia and China, and Hong Kong.

India's liberalized economy has encouraged a large, growing middle class, and China—an economic dynamo with plentiful resources—may become the world's largest economy in 25 years.

Yet hunger for minerals, water, agricultural land, fuelwood, housing, and animal products poses great challenges for Asia as every nation tries to raise the standard of living of its people.

Physical and Political
ASIA

Two-Point Equidistant Projection
SCALE 1:39,821,000
1 CENTIMETER = 398 KILOMETERS; 1 INCH = 629 MILES

KILOMETERS
0 200 400 600 800 1000

STATUTE MILES
0 200 400 600 800

International boundary

Disputed or undefined boundary

A commonly accepted division between Asia and Europe—here marked by a green line—is formed by the Ural Mountains, Ural River, Caspian Sea, Caucasus Mountains, and the Black Sea with its outlets, the Bosporus and Dardanelles.

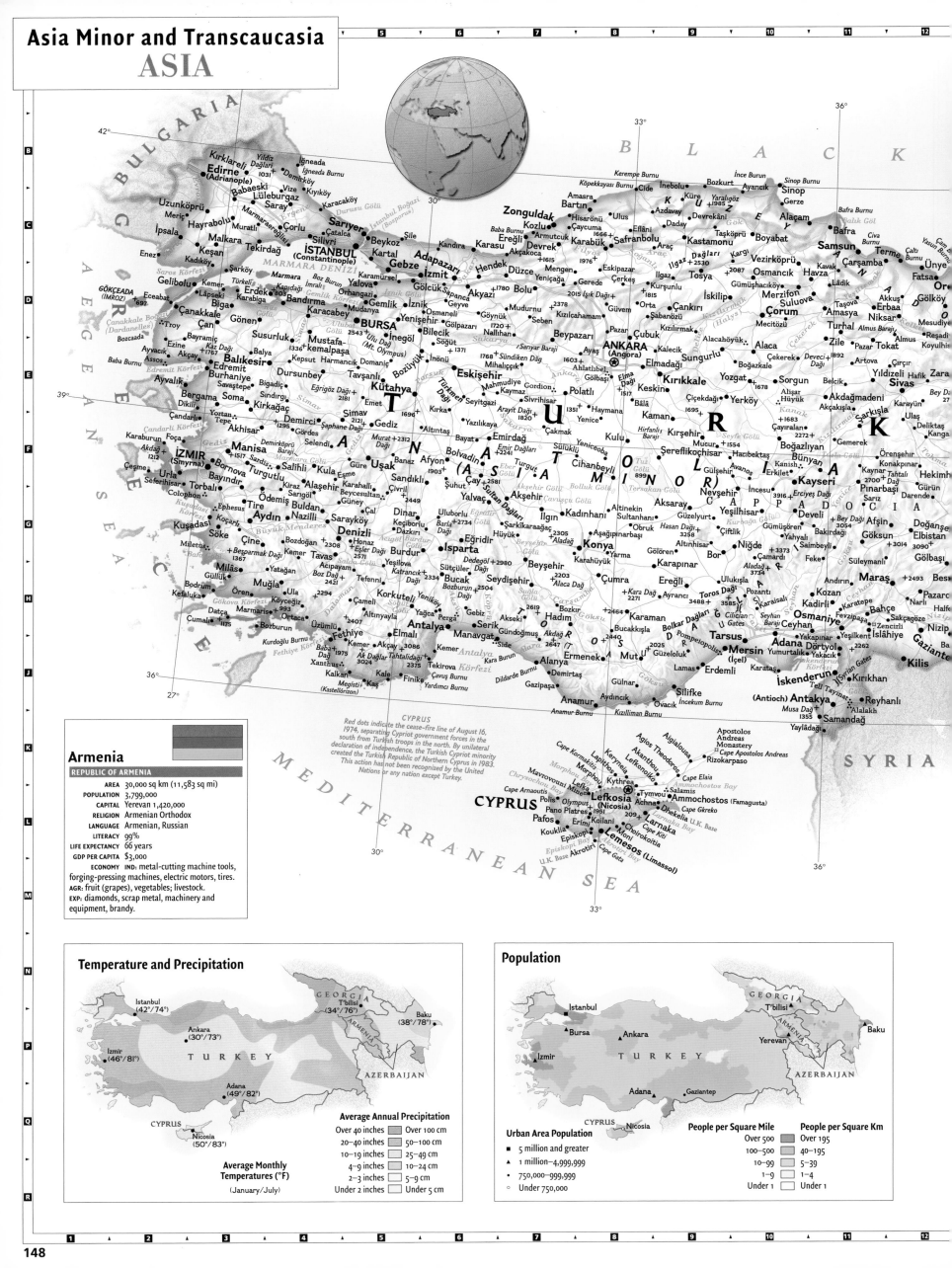

Asia Minor and Transcaucasia
ASIA

Armenia

REPUBLIC OF ARMENIA

AREA 30,000 sq km (11,583 sq mi)
POPULATION 3,799,000
CAPITAL Yerevan 1,420,000
RELIGION Armenian Orthodox
LANGUAGE Armenian, Russian
LITERACY 99%
LIFE EXPECTANCY 66 years
GDP PER CAPITA $3,000
ECONOMY IND: metal-cutting machine tools, forging-pressing machines, electric motors, tires. AGR: fruit (grapes), vegetables; livestock. EXP: diamonds, scrap metal, machinery and equipment, brandy.

Red dots indicate the cease-fire line of August 16, 1974, separating Cypriot government forces in the south from Turkish troops in the north. By unilateral declaration of independence, the Turkish Cypriot minority created the Turkish Republic of Northern Cyprus in 1983. This action has not been recognized by the United Nations or any nation except Turkey.

Temperature and Precipitation

Istanbul (42°/74°)
T'bilisi (34°/76°)
Baku (38°/78°)
Ankara (30°/73°)
Izmir (46°/81°)
Adana (49°/82°)
Nicosia (50°/83°)

Average Annual Precipitation

Over 40 inches / Over 100 cm
20–40 inches / 50–100 cm
10–19 inches / 25–49 cm
4–9 inches / 10–24 cm
2–3 inches / 5–9 cm
Under 2 inches / Under 5 cm

Average Monthly Temperatures (°F)

(January/July)

Population

Urban Area Population

■ 5 million and greater
▲ 1 million–4,999,999
• 750,000–999,999
○ Under 750,000

People per Square Mile

Over 500
100–500
10–99
1–9
Under 1

People per Square Km

Over 195
40–195
5–39
1–4
Under 1

Map Labels

RUSSIA · GEORGIA · ARMENIA · AZERBAIJAN · TURKEY · IRAN · IRAQ · CYPRUS

CAUCASUS MOUNTAINS · ABKHAZIA · SOUTH OSSETIA · AJARIA · NAGORNO-KARABAKH · NAXÇIVAN

BLACK SEA · CASPIAN SEA

T'BILISI (Tiflis) · Yerevan · BAKI (Baku) · Sumqayıt

Kazbek 5033 · Aragats 4090 · Ağrı Dağı (Mt. Ararat) 5137 · Bazar Dyuzi 4466 · Buzul Dağı 4168

Azerbaijan

REPUBLIC OF AZERBAIJAN

AREA	87,000 sq km (33,591 sq mi)
POPULATION	8,172,000
CAPITAL	Baku 1,964,000
RELIGION	Muslim, Russian Orthodox, Armenian Orthodox
LANGUAGE	Azerbaijani, Russian, Armenian
LITERACY	97%
LIFE EXPECTANCY	63 years
GDP PER CAPITA	$3,000

ECONOMY IND: petroleum, natural gas, chemicals and petrochemicals, textiles. AGR: cotton, grain, rice, grapes; cattle. EXP: oil and gas, machinery, cotton, foodstuffs.

Cyprus

REPUBLIC OF CYPRUS

AREA	5,897 sq km (2,277 sq mi)
POPULATION	893,000
CAPITAL	Nicosia 199,000
RELIGION	Greek Orthodox, Muslim
LANGUAGE	Greek, Turkish, English
LITERACY	94%
LIFE EXPECTANCY	77 years
GDP PER CAPITA	$13,430

ECONOMY IND: food, beverages, textiles, chemicals. AGR: potatoes, citrus, vegetables, barley. EXP: citrus, potatoes, grapes, textiles.

Georgia

GEORGIA

AREA	70,000 sq km (27,027 sq mi)
POPULATION	4,400,000
CAPITAL	T'bilisi 1,406,000
RELIGION	Georgian Orthodox, Muslim, Russian Orthodox, Armenian Apostolic
LANGUAGE	Georgian, Russian, Armenian, Azeri
LITERACY	99%
LIFE EXPECTANCY	65 years
GDP PER CAPITA	$4,600

ECONOMY IND: aircraft, food processing, machine tools, electric locomotives. AGR: citrus, grapes, tea, vegetables; livestock. EXP: citrus fruits, diverse types of machinery and metals, chemicals, fuel exports.

Turkey

REPUBLIC OF TURKEY

AREA	779,452 sq km (300,948 sq mi)
POPULATION	67,264,000
CAPITAL	Ankara 3,208,000
RELIGION	Muslim (mostly Sunni)
LANGUAGE	Turkish, Kurdish, Arabic, Armenian, Greek
LITERACY	85%
LIFE EXPECTANCY	71 years
GDP PER CAPITA	$6,800

ECONOMY IND: textiles, food processing, autos, mining. AGR: tobacco, cotton, grain, olives; livestock. EXP: apparel, foodstuffs, textiles, metal manufactures.

Industry and Mining

Istanbul · Ankara · İzmir · TURKEY · GEORGIA · ARMENIA · AZERBAIJAN · CYPRUS

Major Mines

B Boron

Manufacturing center

Petroleum

Gross Domestic Product per Capita (in U.S. dollars)

- 20,000–26,500
- 10,000–19,999
- 5,000–9,999
- 300–4,999

Land Use, Agriculture, and Fishing

TURKEY · GEORGIA · ARMENIA · AZERBAIJAN · CYPRUS

Major Crops

- Barley
- Beet sugar
- Cattle
- Citrus fruit
- Corn
- Cotton
- Dates
- Deciduous fruit
- Fish
- Forest products
- Grapes
- Millet
- Oats
- Olives
- Potatoes
- Poultry
- Rice
- Rye
- Sesame seed
- Sheep
- Swine
- Tea
- Tobacco
- Wheat

Predominant Land Use and Land Cover Classes

- Grassland
- Woodland
- Forest
- Mixed-use, including crops
- Cropland
- Intensive cropland
- Wetland
- Desert, barren land

Conic Projection

SCALE 1:4,628,000

1 CENTIMETER = 46.3 KILOMETERS; 1 INCH = 73.1 MILES

KILOMETERS 0 · 100 · 200

STATUTE MILES 0 · 100 · 200

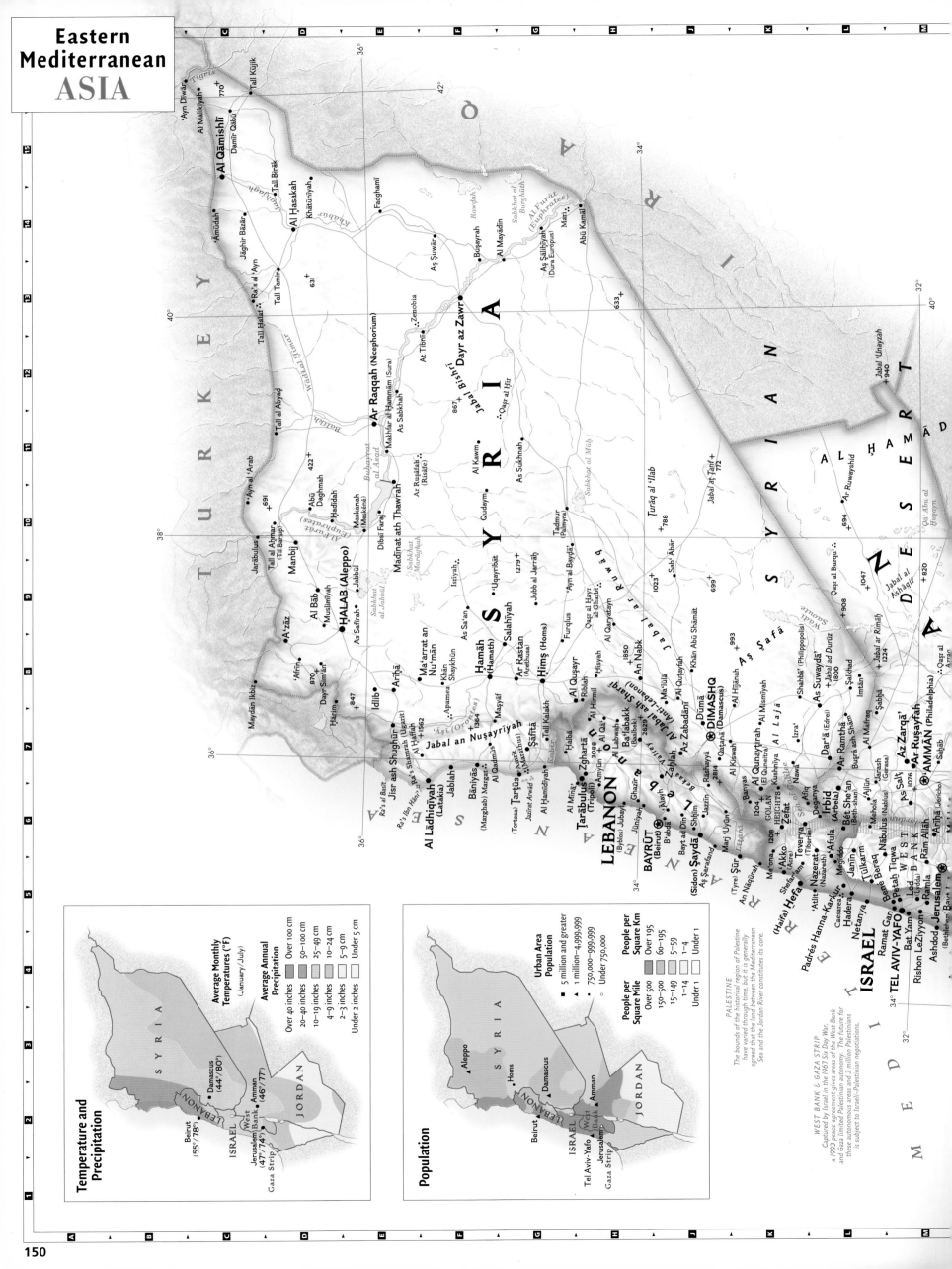

TURKEY

O

R

A

Q

SYRIAN

DESERT

Tigris

770+

'Ayn Diwār

Al Mālikīyah

Damīr Qābū

Tall Kūjik

Al Qāmishlī

Jāghir Bāzār

Tall al Birāk

'Āmūdah

Al Ḥasakah

Khātūnīyah

Ra's al 'Ayn

Tall Ḥalaf

Fadghamī

Khābūr

Tall al Abyaḍ

631+

Tall Tāmir

Buşayrah

Al Mayādīn

Aş Şuwār

Rawḍah

Sabkhat al Burghūth

Al Furāt (Euphrates)

Abū Kamāl

As Şālihīyah (Dura Europus)

Matt.

Jabal 'Unayzah +940

SYRIA

Jabal Bishrī

867+

Dayr az Zawr

At Tibnī

Zenobia

Makhfar al Hammām (Sura)

Ar Raqqah (Nicephorium)

As Sabkhah

Buḥayrat al Asad

Al Kawm

Qadaym

As Sukhnah

Qaşr al Ḥīr

Tadmur (Palmyra)

1023+

Sab' Ābār

633+

1047+

+694

+908

+820

Ar Ruwayshid

Qaşr al Burqu'

Jabal aṭ Ṭanf +772

Ţurāq al 'Ilab +788

699+

AL ḤAMĀD

Jabal al Ashqif

422+

Abū Daghmah

Ḥadīdah

Maskanah (Meskéné)

Dibsī Faraj

Madīnat ath Thawrah

Ar Ruṣāfah (Risafe)

Istiyah

'Uqayribāt

1279+

'Ayn al Bayḍā'

Jubb al Jarrāḥ

Al Qaryatayn

Qaşr al Ḥayr al Gharbī

Khān Abū Shāmāt

993+

Al Hījānah

As Şafā

Shahbā' (Philippopolis)

As Suwaydā'

Jabal ad Durūz 1800

Salkhad

Imtān

Şabḥā

Qaşr al 'Azraq

691+

'Ayn al 'Arab

Ayṇ

Dayr Sim'ān

870+

Hārim

847

Idlib

Arīḥā

Apamea

1562+

'Āfrīn

A'zāz

Al Bāb

Muslimīyah

HALAB (Aleppo)

Jabbūl

Sabkhat al Jabbūl

As Şafīrah

As Sa'an

Salahīyah

Ma'arrat an Nu'mān

Khān Shaykhūn

Al Ḥaffah

Maydān Ikbiz

TURKEY

Jarābulus

Tall al Aḥmar (Til Barsip)

Manbij

Jabal an Nuşayrīyah

1364+

Aşi (Orontes)

Maşyāf

Al Qadmūs

Ḥamāh (Hamath)

Ar Rastan (Arethusa)

Furqlus

'Ayn al Bayḍā'

1850+

An Nabk

Ma'lūlā

Al Quṭayfah

Dūmā

DIMASHQ (Damascus)

Qaṭanā

'Al Mismīyah

Al Lajā

Izra'

Nawā

Bā'labakk (Baalbek)

Al Qaryatayn

Al Mismīyah

Az Zabadānī

Shabbā'

Jabal ad Durūz

LEBANON

2629+

Jabal Lubnān (Mt. Lebanon)

Zaḥlah

Rāshayyā

2814

As Suwaydā'

A'ṣī

Ḥimṣ (Homs)

Hişyah

Riblah

Al Quşayr

Tall Kalakh

Şāfītā

Ḥabā

Tall Kalakh

Al Mīnā'

Al Ḥamīdīyah

Al Hirmil

Al Labwah

Ṭarābulus (Tripoli)

Zgharṭā

Amyūn

Al Qā'

Ghazīr

B'abdā

BAYRŪT (Beirut)

Jūnīyah

Jubayl

(Byblos)

Bayt ad Dīn

Shim

Şaydā (Sidon)

Bayt ad Dīn

Marj 'Uyūn

Al Litānī

Lītanī

Az Zabadānī

Dūmā

Al Kiswah

Banyas

Al Quyayṭirah (El Quneitra)

GOLAN HEIGHTS

Kushnīya

1208+

Nawā

Izra'

Dar'ā (Edrei)

Buşrā ash Shām

Al Mafraq

Jarash (Gerasa)

AMMĀN (Philadelphia)

Qaşr al 'Ammān

Buşrā ash Shām

Ar Ruṣayfah

Az Zarqā'

1076+

As Salṭ

'Ajlūn (Arbela)

Irbid

Jisr ash Shughūr

Lādhiqīyah (Latakia)

Jablah

Bāniyās

Tartūs (Tortosa)

(Marghab) Margat'

Jazīrat Arwād

Al Ladhiqīyah (Latakia)

Ra's al Basīt

Ra's Ibn Hāni'

Ra's Shamrah (Ugarit)

N U Ş A Y R Ī Y A H

Amrīt

(Tortosa)

Banyas

Sab' Bīyar

1224+ Jabal ar Rimāḥ

Şaydā

Şūr (Tyre)

An Nāqūrah

Zefat

Teverya (Tiberias)

Doganya

Degania

Sea of Galilee

Afīq

Bēt She'an (Beth-shan)

Meholá

'Ajlūn

Jarash (Gerasa)

Ma'ona

Akko (Acre)

Shefar'am

Nazerat (Nazareth)

'Afula

Megiddo

Janīn

Tūlkarm

Nābulus (Nablus)

WEST BANK

Ar Ramthā

Ḥefa (Haifa)

'Atlit

Karkur

Ḥadera

Netanya

Petaḥ Tiqwa

Ramat Gan

TEL AVIV-YAFO

Bat Yam

Rishon LeZiyyon

Ashdod

Lydda (Lod)

Ramla

Rām Allāh

Jerusalem

Bethlehem

ISRAEL

Caesarea

Padrés Hanna-Karkur

Bēte Bereq

Netanya

J O R D A N

M E D

32°

34°

36°

38°

40°

42°

34°

36°

Temperature and Precipitation

Average Monthly Temperatures (°F)
(January/July)

Average Annual Precipitation

Over 40 inches	Over 100 cm
20–40 inches	50–100 cm
10–19 inches	25–49 cm
4–9 inches	10–24 cm
2–3 inches	5–9 cm
Under 2 inches	Under 5 cm

SYRIA

LEBANON

ISRAEL

JORDAN

West Bank

Gaza Strip

Beirut (55°/78°)

Damascus (44°/80°)

Amman (46°/77°)

Jerusalem (47°/74°)

Population

Urban Area Population

■	5 million and greater
▲	1 million–4,999,999
■	750,000–999,999
○	Under 750,000

People per Square Mile	People per Square Km	
Over 500	Over 195
150–500	60–195
15–149	1–59
1–14	1–4
Under 1	Under 1

SYRIA

LEBANON

ISRAEL

JORDAN

West Bank

Gaza Strip

Aleppo

Homs

Damascus

Amman

Beirut

Tel Aviv-Yafo

Jerusalem

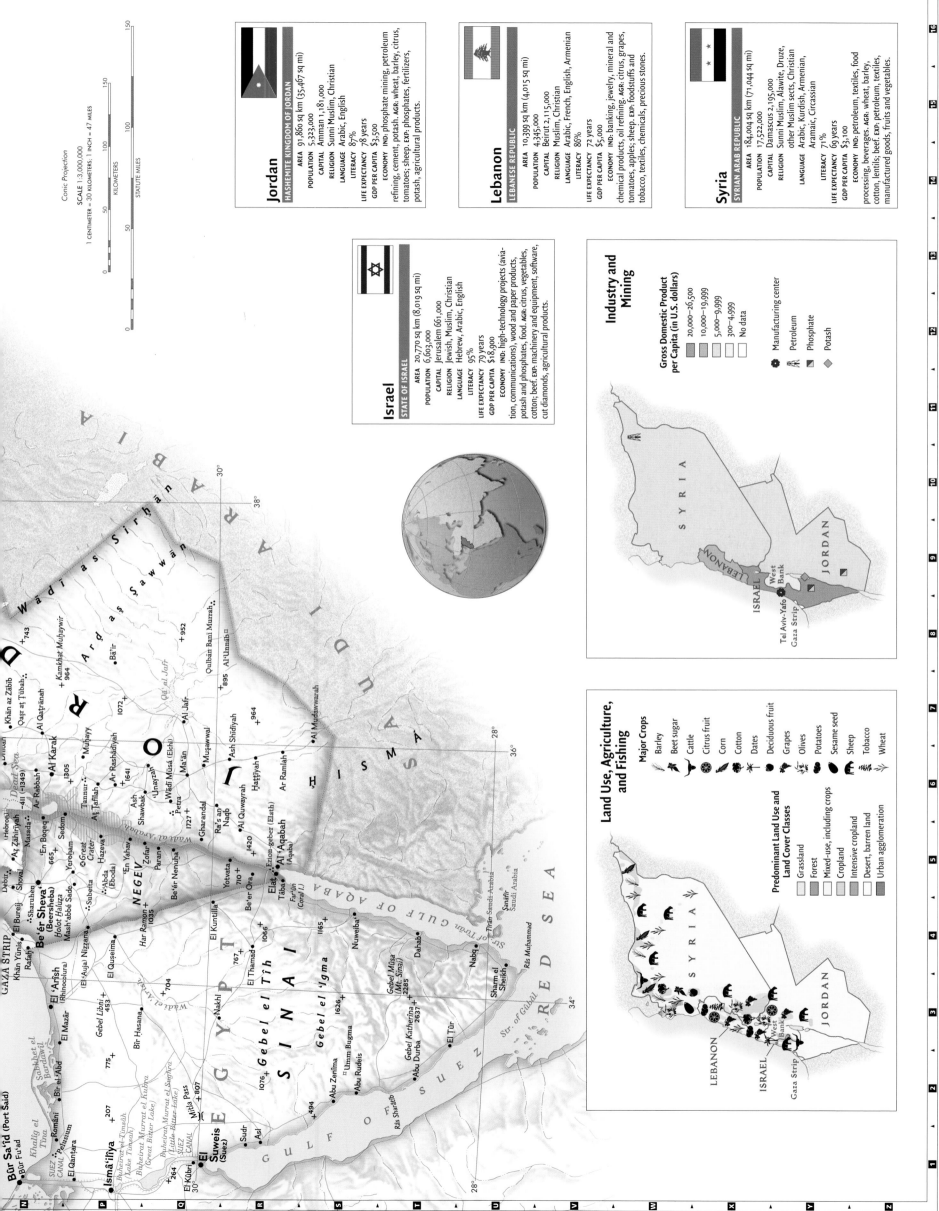

Jordan
HASHEMITE KINGDOM OF JORDAN
AREA 91,860 sq km (35,467 sq mi)
POPULATION 5,333,000
CAPITAL Amman 1,181,000
RELIGION Sunni Muslim, Christian
LANGUAGE Arabic, English
LITERACY 87%
LIFE EXPECTANCY 78 years
GDP PER CAPITA $3,500
ECONOMY IND: phosphate mining, petroleum refining, cement, potash. **AGR:** wheat, barley, citrus, tomatoes; sheep. **EXP:** phosphates, fertilizers, potash, agricultural products.

Lebanon
LEBANESE REPUBLIC
AREA 10,399 sq km (4,015 sq mi)
POPULATION 4,345,000
CAPITAL Beirut 2,115,000
RELIGION Muslim, Christian
LANGUAGE Arabic, French, English, Armenian
LITERACY 86%
LIFE EXPECTANCY 72 years
GDP PER CAPITA $5,000
ECONOMY IND: banking, jewelry, mineral and chemical products, oil refining. **AGR:** citrus, grapes, tomatoes, apples; sheep. **EXP:** foodstuffs and tobacco, textiles, chemicals, precious stones.

Syria
SYRIAN ARAB REPUBLIC
AREA 184,004 sq km (71,044 sq mi)
POPULATION 17,522,000
CAPITAL Damascus 2,195,000
RELIGION Sunni Muslim, Alawite, Druze, other Muslim sects, Christian
LANGUAGE Arabic, Kurdish, Armenian, Aramaic, Circassian
LITERACY 71%
LIFE EXPECTANCY 69 years
GDP PER CAPITA $3,100
ECONOMY IND: petroleum, textiles, food processing, beverages. **AGR:** wheat, barley, cotton, lentils; beef. **EXP:** petroleum, textiles, manufactured goods, fruits and vegetables.

Israel
STATE OF ISRAEL
AREA 20,770 sq km (8,019 sq mi)
POPULATION 6,603,000
CAPITAL Jerusalem 661,000
RELIGION Jewish, Muslim, Christian
LANGUAGE Hebrew, Arabic, English
LITERACY 95%
LIFE EXPECTANCY 79 years
GDP PER CAPITA $18,900
ECONOMY IND: high-technology projects (aviation, communications), wood and paper products, potash and phosphates, food. **AGR:** citrus, vegetables, cotton; beef. **EXP:** machinery and equipment, software, cut diamonds, agricultural products.

Conic Projection

SCALE 1:3,000,000
1 CENTIMETER = 30 KILOMETERS; 1 INCH = 47 MILES

Industry and Mining

Gross Domestic Product per Capita (in U.S. dollars)
- 20,000–26,500
- 10,000–19,999
- 5,000–9,999
- 300–4,999
- No data

- Manufacturing center
- Petroleum
- Phosphate
- Potash

Land Use, Agriculture, and Fishing

Major Crops
- Barley
- Beet sugar
- Cattle
- Citrus fruit
- Corn
- Cotton
- Dates
- Deciduous fruit
- Grapes
- Olives
- Potatoes
- Sesame seed
- Sheep
- Tobacco
- Wheat

Predominant Land Use and Land Cover Classes
- Grassland
- Forest
- Cropland
- Mixed-use, including crops
- Intensive cropland
- Desert, barren land
- Urban agglomeration

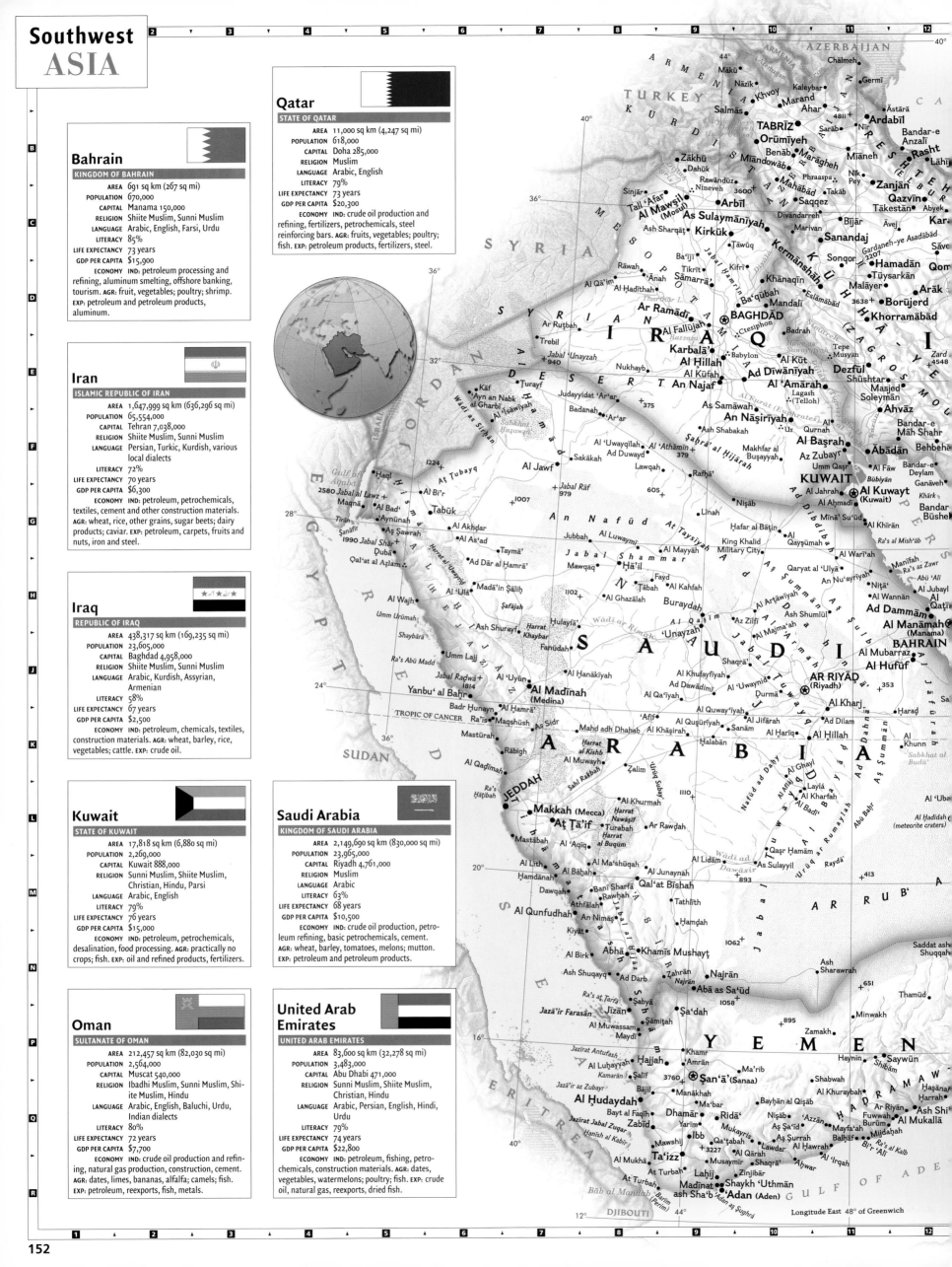

Bahrain
KINGDOM OF BAHRAIN
AREA 691 sq km (267 sq mi)
POPULATION 670,000
CAPITAL Manama 150,000
RELIGION Shiite Muslim, Sunni Muslim
LANGUAGE Arabic, English, Farsi, Urdu
LITERACY 85%
LIFE EXPECTANCY 73 years
GDP PER CAPITA $15,900
ECONOMY IND: petroleum processing and refining, aluminum smelting, offshore banking, tourism. AGR: fruit, vegetables; poultry; shrimp. EXP: petroleum and petroleum products, aluminum.

Iran
ISLAMIC REPUBLIC OF IRAN
AREA 1,647,999 sq km (636,296 sq mi)
POPULATION 65,554,000
CAPITAL Tehran 7,038,000
RELIGION Shiite Muslim, Sunni Muslim
LANGUAGE Persian, Turkic, Kurdish, various local dialects
LITERACY 72%
LIFE EXPECTANCY 70 years
GDP PER CAPITA $6,300
ECONOMY IND: petroleum, petrochemicals, textiles, cement and other construction materials. AGR: wheat, rice, other grains, sugar beets; dairy products; caviar. EXP: petroleum, carpets, fruits and nuts, iron and steel.

Iraq
REPUBLIC OF IRAQ
AREA 438,317 sq km (169,235 sq mi)
POPULATION 23,605,000
CAPITAL Baghdad 4,958,000
RELIGION Shiite Muslim, Sunni Muslim
LANGUAGE Arabic, Kurdish, Assyrian, Armenian
LITERACY 58%
LIFE EXPECTANCY 67 years
GDP PER CAPITA $2,500
ECONOMY IND: petroleum, chemicals, textiles, construction materials. AGR: wheat, barley, rice, vegetables; cattle. EXP: crude oil.

Kuwait
STATE OF KUWAIT
AREA 17,818 sq km (6,880 sq mi)
POPULATION 2,269,000
CAPITAL Kuwait 888,000
RELIGION Sunni Muslim, Shiite Muslim, Christian, Hindu, Parsi
LANGUAGE Arabic, English
LITERACY 79%
LIFE EXPECTANCY 76 years
GDP PER CAPITA $15,000
ECONOMY IND: petroleum, petrochemicals, desalination, food processing. AGR: practically no crops; fish. EXP: oil and refined products, fertilizers.

Oman
SULTANATE OF OMAN
AREA 212,457 sq km (82,030 sq mi)
POPULATION 2,564,000
CAPITAL Muscat 540,000
RELIGION Ibadhi Muslim, Sunni Muslim, Shiite Muslim, Hindu
LANGUAGE Arabic, English, Baluchi, Urdu, Indian dialects
LITERACY 80%
LIFE EXPECTANCY 72 years
GDP PER CAPITA $7,700
ECONOMY IND: crude oil production and refining, natural gas production, construction, cement. AGR: dates, limes, bananas, alfalfa; camels; fish. EXP: petroleum, reexports, fish, metals.

Qatar
STATE OF QATAR
AREA 11,000 sq km (4,247 sq mi)
POPULATION 618,000
CAPITAL Doha 285,000
RELIGION Muslim
LANGUAGE Arabic, English
LITERACY 79%
LIFE EXPECTANCY 73 years
GDP PER CAPITA $20,300
ECONOMY IND: crude oil production and refining, fertilizers, petrochemicals, steel reinforcing bars. AGR: fruits, vegetables; poultry; fish. EXP: petroleum products, fertilizers, steel.

Saudi Arabia
KINGDOM OF SAUDI ARABIA
AREA 2,149,690 sq km (830,000 sq mi)
POPULATION 23,065,000
CAPITAL Riyadh 4,761,000
RELIGION Muslim
LANGUAGE Arabic
LITERACY 63%
LIFE EXPECTANCY 68 years
GDP PER CAPITA $10,500
ECONOMY IND: crude oil production, petroleum refining, basic petrochemicals, cement. AGR: wheat, barley, tomatoes, melons; mutton. EXP: petroleum and petroleum products.

United Arab Emirates
UNITED ARAB EMIRATES
AREA 83,600 sq km (32,278 sq mi)
POPULATION 3,483,000
CAPITAL Abu Dhabi 471,000
RELIGION Sunni Muslim, Shiite Muslim, Christian, Hindu
LANGUAGE Arabic, Persian, English, Hindi, Urdu
LITERACY 79%
LIFE EXPECTANCY 74 years
GDP PER CAPITA $22,800
ECONOMY IND: petroleum, fishing, petrochemicals, construction materials. AGR: dates, vegetables, watermelons; poultry; fish. EXP: crude oil, natural gas, reexports, dried fish.

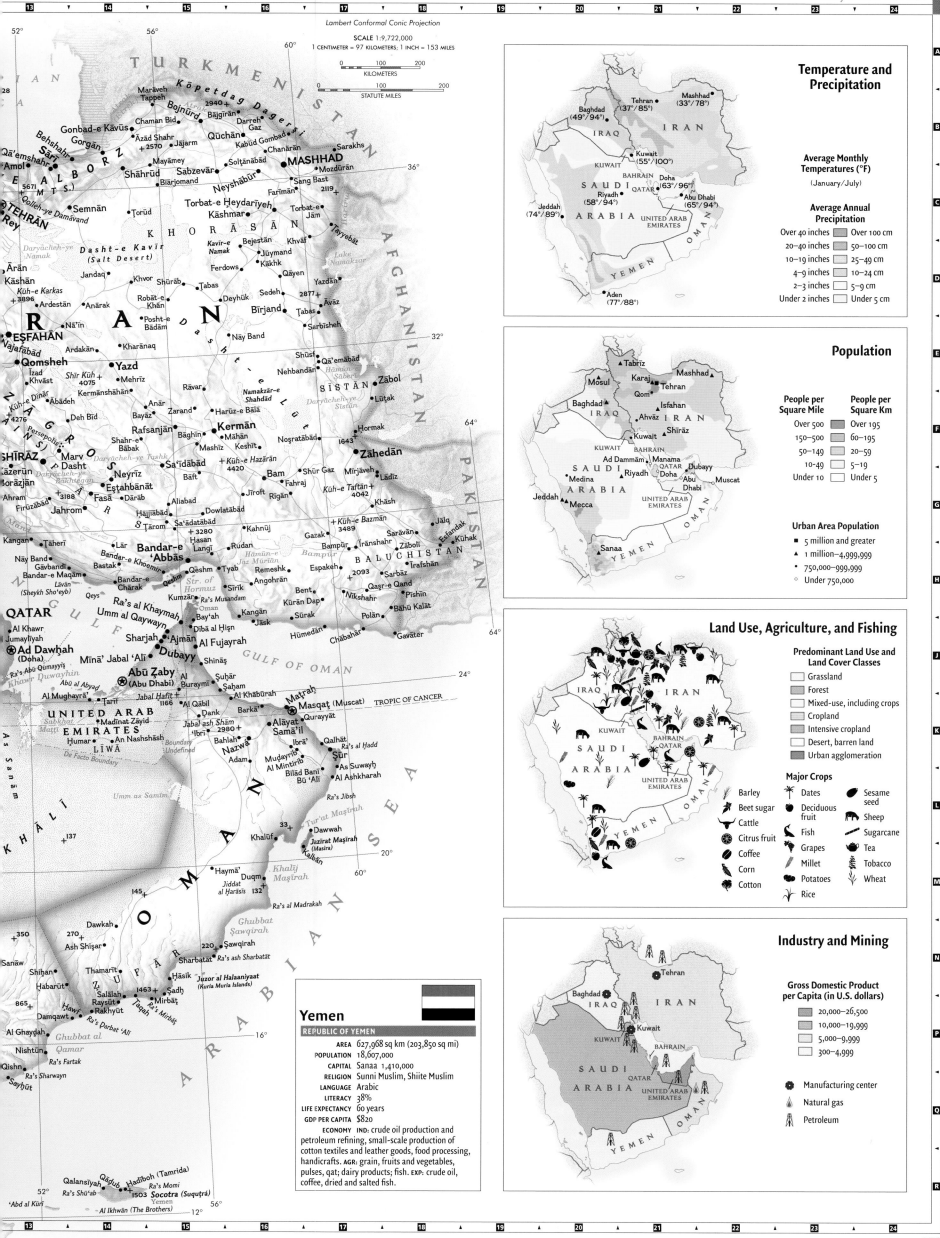

Central
ASIA

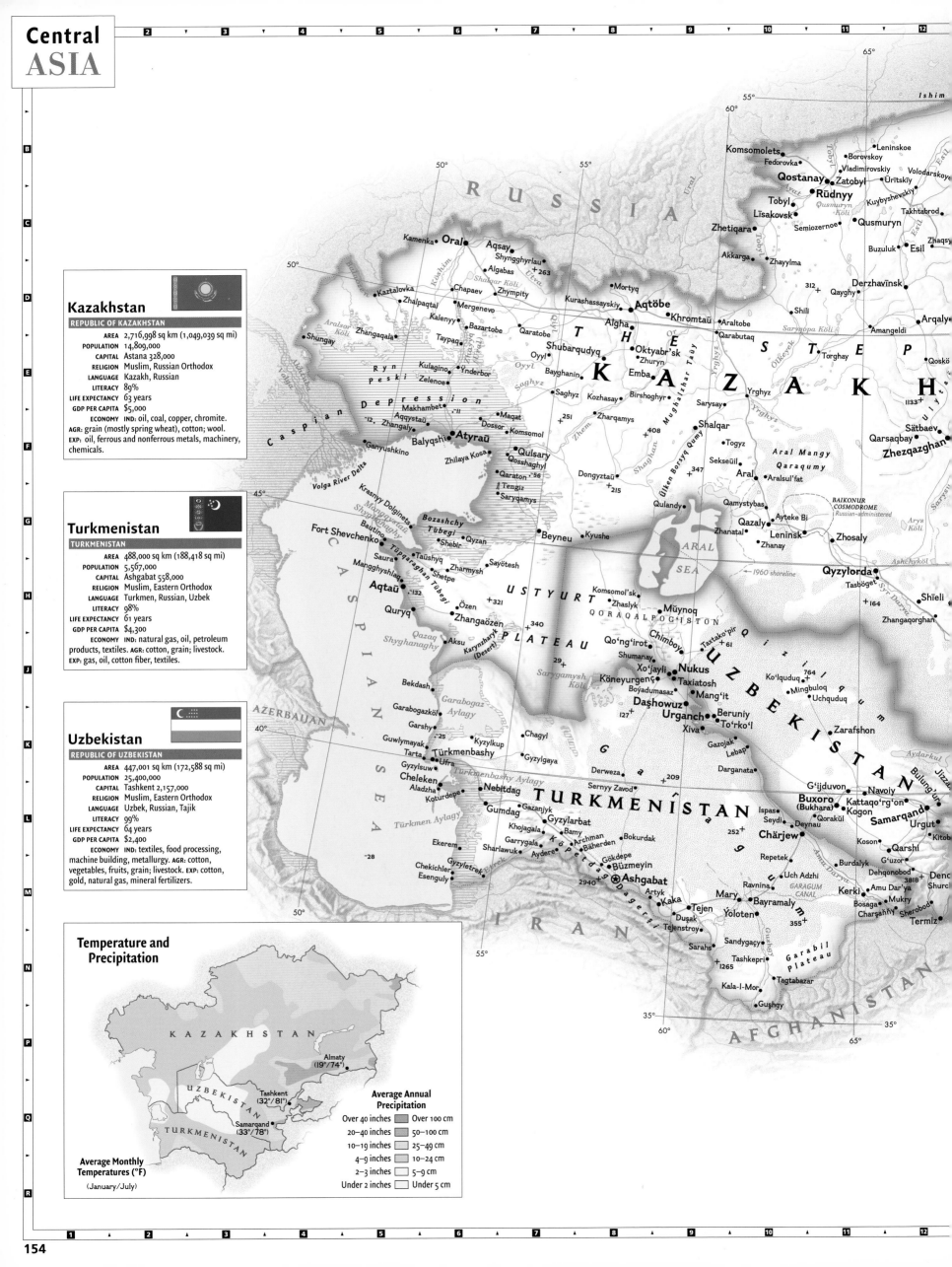

Kazakhstan
REPUBLIC OF KAZAKHSTAN
AREA 2,716,998 sq km (1,049,039 sq mi)
POPULATION 14,800,000
CAPITAL Astana 328,000
RELIGION Muslim, Russian Orthodox
LANGUAGE Kazakh, Russian
LITERACY 89%
LIFE EXPECTANCY 63 years
GDP PER CAPITA $5,000
ECONOMY IND: oil, coal, copper, chromite.
AGR: grain (mostly spring wheat), cotton; wool.
EXP: oil, ferrous and nonferrous metals, machinery,
chemicals.

Turkmenistan
TURKMENISTAN
AREA 488,000 sq km (188,418 sq mi)
POPULATION 5,567,000
CAPITAL Ashgabat 558,000
RELIGION Muslim, Eastern Orthodox
LANGUAGE Turkmen, Russian, Uzbek
LITERACY 98%
LIFE EXPECTANCY 61 years
GDP PER CAPITA $4,300
ECONOMY IND: natural gas, oil, petroleum
products, textiles. AGR: cotton, grain; livestock.
EXP: gas, oil, cotton fiber, textiles.

Uzbekistan
REPUBLIC OF UZBEKISTAN
AREA 447,001 sq km (172,588 sq mi)
POPULATION 25,400,000
CAPITAL Tashkent 2,157,000
RELIGION Muslim, Eastern Orthodox
LANGUAGE Uzbek, Russian, Tajik
LITERACY 99%
LIFE EXPECTANCY 64 years
GDP PER CAPITA $2,400
ECONOMY IND: textiles, food processing,
machine building, metallurgy. AGR: cotton,
vegetables, fruits, grain; livestock. EXP: cotton,
gold, natural gas, mineral fertilizers.

Temperature and Precipitation

Average Monthly Temperatures (°F)
(January/July)

Average Annual Precipitation

Over 40 inches	Over 100 cm
20–40 inches	50–100 cm
10–19 inches	25–49 cm
4–9 inches	10–24 cm
2–3 inches	5–9 cm
Under 2 inches	Under 5 cm

Almaty (19°/74°)
Tashkent (32°/81°)
Samarqand (33°/78°)

KAZAKHSTAN
UZBEKISTAN
TURKMENISTAN

RUSSIA

eppe
Petropavl
•Būlaevo
•Krasnoarmeysk
Zhelezinka
•Qyzyltū
Ertis
•Kachīry
•Kökshetaū
Golubovka
Shchūchīnsk
•Sharbaqty
Makinsk
•Aqsū
Bestobe
Pavlodar
•Aqköl
•Stepnogorsk
•Ereymentaū
Ekibastuz
•Lebyazh'e
Zhaltyr
Astana (Aqmola)
Capital since 1997
•Vishnevka
•Bayanauyl
adyzhenka
•Osakarovka
Znamenka
Kurchatov
Shemonaīkha
Lenīnogorsk
+Gora Belukha 4506
•Shaghan
Semey (Semipalatinsk)
Glūbokoe
•Belūsovka
Serebryansk
•Zyryanovsk
ALTAY MTS.
MONGOLIA
Tengiz Köli
KAZAKH
Temirtaū
•Tokarevka
SEMIPALATINSK NUCLEAR TEST RANGE (Closed in 1991)
Sarzhal
Öskemen (Ust' Kamenogorsk)
Shar
Georgīevka
•Rakhman Qaynary
•Samarskoye
+1608
Margaköl
+1366
Sorang
Qaraghandy
•Qarqaraly
•Qaynar
•Qaraūyl
Zharma
•Kökpekti
•Alekseyevka
Abay
•Qaraghayly
Boran
STAN
Atasu
•Aqadyr
+1305
•Ayaköz
Zaysan Köli
Tūghyl
Zaysan
C H I N A
Qarazhal
Aqshataū
U P L A N D S
Qongyrat
+1213
Barshatas
•Taskesken
+2992
Tarbaghatay Zhotasy
Urdzhar
Moyynty
Balqash
Aqtoghay
•Beskol'
Baqty
Sarysu
Saryesik-
Atyraū
Qumy
Kopbirlik
•Lepsi
Sasyqköl
Alaköl
Saryshagan
Balqash Köli
•Lepsinsk
Dzungarian Gate
Dostyq
Qaraqoyyn Köli
Ushtobe
Sarqan
Quyghan
Aqköl
Taldyqorghan
Tekeli
BETPAQDALA (DESERT)
Burylbaytal
Kirovskiy
Baqbaqty
•Saryözek
Panfilov
Ili (Ile)
1053
Shū
Qapshaghay Reservoir
Ili (Ile)
•Shonzhy
Moyynqum
Novotroitskoye
1537
Otar
Qapshaghay
Shelek
ALMATY *Capital until 1997*
•Kegen
Zhanatas
Čū
Lūgovoy
Georgīevka
•Kegen
Narynkol
Akkol'
Qarataū
Oytal
Khan Tängiri (Lord of the Sky) 6995
Taraz
Kyrgyz Range
Khan Tängiri
TIAN SHAN
Arys
Shymkent
Lenger
KYRGYZSTAN
irchiq
Iskandar
TOSHKENT (Tashkent)
Sirdaryo
Angren
Namangan
Qo'qon
Fergana Valley
Andijon
Guliston
Farg'ona
Bekobod
Sūkh
TAJIKISTAN

Lambert Conformal Conic Projection
SCALE 1:8,875,000
1 CENTIMETER = 89 KILOMETERS; 1 INCH = 140 MILES
0 100 200 300 KILOMETERS
0 100 200 300 STATUTE MILES

Land Use, Agriculture, and Fishing

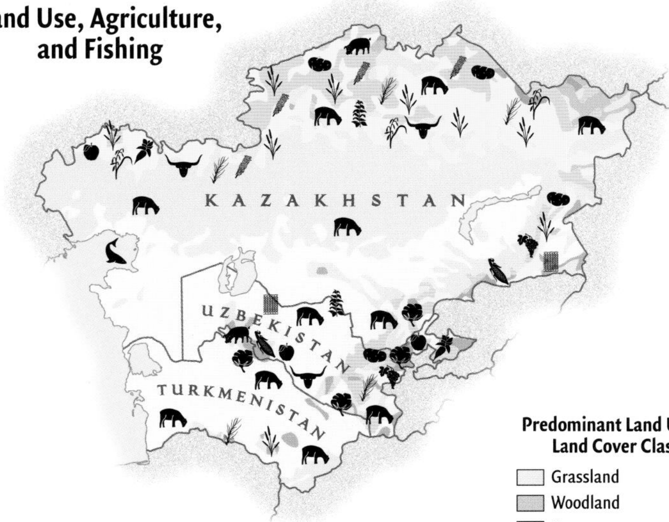

KAZAKHSTAN
UZBEKISTAN
TURKMENISTAN

Predominant Land Use and Land Cover Classes

- Grassland
- Woodland
- Forest
- Mixed-use, including crops
- Cropland
- Intensive cropland
- Desert, barren land
- Urban agglomeration

Major Crops

- Barley
- Beet sugar
- Cattle
- Corn
- Cotton
- Deciduous fruit
- Fish
- Grapes
- Jute
- Millet
- Oats
- Potatoes
- Sheep
- Swine
- Tobacco
- Wheat

Population

KAZAKHSTAN
Astana
Almaty
UZBEKISTAN
Tashkent
TURKMENISTAN
Ashgabat

Urban Area Population

- ■ 5 million and greater
- ▲ 1 million–4,999,999
- ● 750,000–999,999
- ○ Under 750,000

People per Square Mile	People per Square Km
Over 750	Over 290
250–750	100–290
25–249	10–99
5–24	2–9
Under 5	Under 2

Industry and Mining

KAZAKHSTAN
Öskemen
Cr
Cu Cu
UZBEKISTAN
Au Tashkent
TURKMENISTAN

- ■ Coal
- ✿ Manufacturing center
- ▲ Natural gas
- ⚒ Petroleum
- Cu Processing plant

Major Mines

- Au Gold
- Cr Chromite
- Cu Copper

Gross Domestic Product per Capita (in U.S. dollars)

- 20,000–26,500
- 10,000–19,999
- 5,000–9,999
- 300–4,999

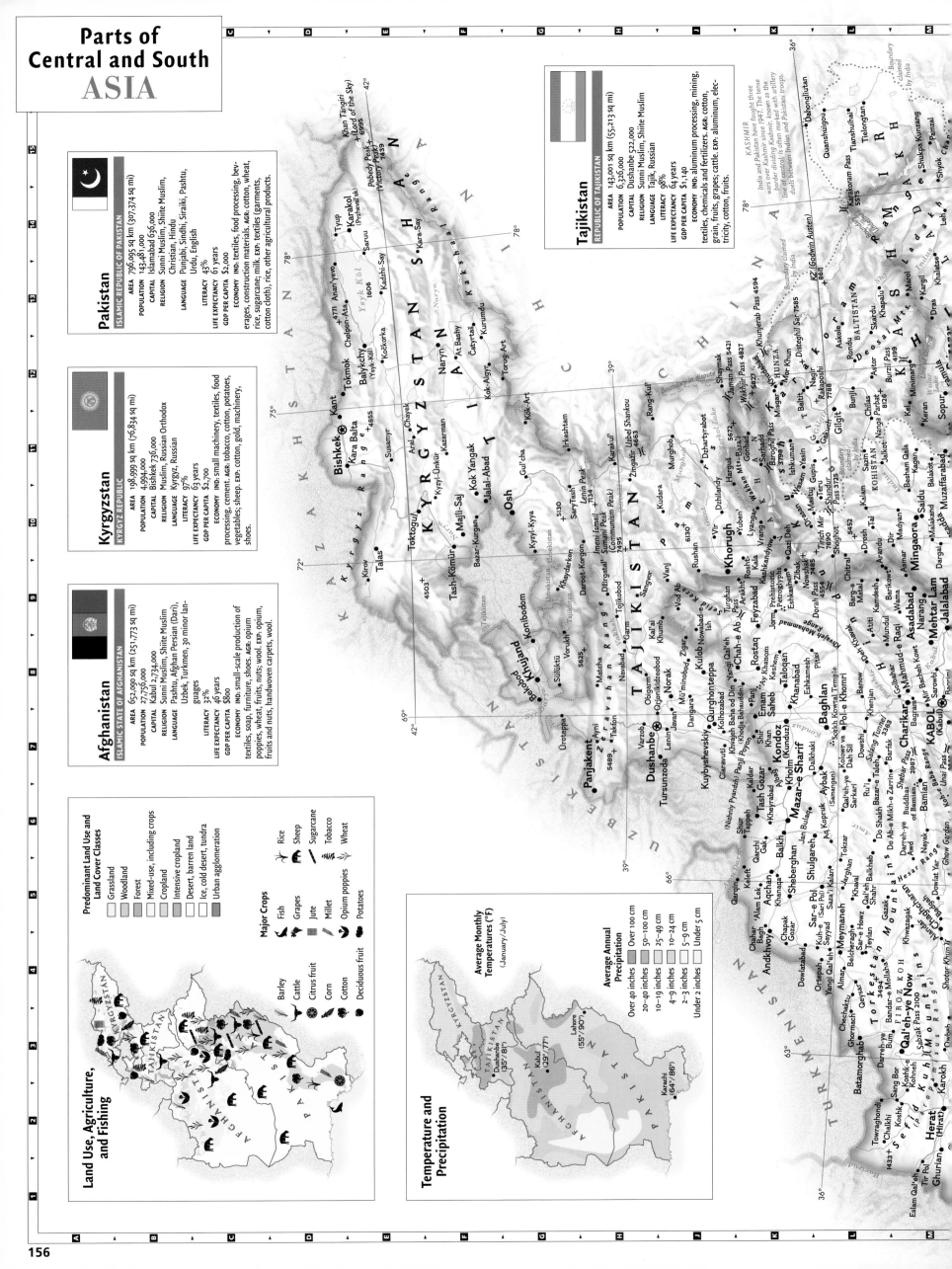

Parts of Central and South ASIA

Pakistan
ISLAMIC REPUBLIC OF PAKISTAN
AREA 796,095 sq km (307,374 sq mi)
POPULATION 143,481,000
CAPITAL Islamabad 636,000
RELIGION Sunni Muslim, Shiite Muslim, Christian, Hindu
LANGUAGE Punjabi, Sindhi, Siraiki, Pashtu, Urdu, English
LITERACY 43%
LIFE EXPECTANCY 61 years
GDP PER CAPITA $2,000
ECONOMY IND: textiles, food processing, beverages, construction materials. AGR: cotton, wheat, rice, sugarcane; milk. EXP: textiles (garments, cotton cloth), rice, other agricultural products.

Kyrgyzstan
KYRGYZ REPUBLIC
AREA 198,999 sq km (76,834 sq mi)
POPULATION 4,994,000
CAPITAL Bishkek 736,000
RELIGION Muslim, Russian Orthodox
LANGUAGE Kyrgyz, Russian
LITERACY 97%
LIFE EXPECTANCY 63 years
GDP PER CAPITA $2,700
ECONOMY IND: small machinery, textiles, food processing, cement. AGR: tobacco, cotton, potatoes, vegetables; sheep. EXP: cotton, gold, machinery, shoes.

Afghanistan
ISLAMIC STATE OF AFGHANISTAN
AREA 652,090 sq km (251,773 sq mi)
POPULATION 27,756,000
CAPITAL Kabul 2,734,000
RELIGION Sunni Muslim, Shiite Muslim
LANGUAGE Pashtu, Afghan Persian (Dari), Uzbek, Turkmen, 30 minor languages
LITERACY 32%
LIFE EXPECTANCY 46 years
GDP PER CAPITA $800
ECONOMY IND: small-scale production of textiles, soap, furniture, shoes. AGR: opium poppies, wheat, fruits, nuts; wool. EXP: opium, fruits and nuts, handwoven carpets, wool.

Tajikistan
REPUBLIC OF TAJIKISTAN
AREA 143,001 sq km (55,213 sq mi)
POPULATION 6,326,000
CAPITAL Dushanbe $22,000
RELIGION Sunni Muslim, Shiite Muslim
LANGUAGE Tajik, Russian
LITERACY 98%
LIFE EXPECTANCY 64 years
GDP PER CAPITA $1,140
ECONOMY IND: aluminum processing, mining, textiles, chemicals and fertilizers. AGR: cotton, grain, fruits, grapes; cattle. EXP: aluminum, electricity, cotton, fruits.

Land Use, Agriculture, and Fishing

Predominant Land Use and Land Cover Classes
- Grassland
- Woodland
- Forest
- Mixed-use, including crops
- Cropland
- Intensive cropland
- Desert, barren land
- Ice, cold desert, tundra
- Urban agglomeration

Major Crops
- Barley
- Cattle
- Citrus fruit
- Corn
- Cotton
- Deciduous fruit
- Fish
- Grapes
- Jute
- Millet
- Opium poppies
- Potatoes
- Rice
- Sheep
- Sugarcane
- Tobacco
- Wheat

Temperature and Precipitation

Average Monthly Temperatures (°F)
(January/July)

Average Annual Precipitation
- Over 100 cm — Over 40 inches
- 50–100 cm — 20–40 inches
- 25–49 cm — 10–19 inches
- 10–24 cm — 4–9 inches
- 5–9 cm — 2–3 inches
- Under 5 cm — Under 2 inches

Lahore (55°/90°)
Kabul (29°/77°)
Dushanbe (35°/81°)
Karachi (64°/86°)

KASHMIR
India and Pakistan have fought three wars over Kashmir since 1947. The tense area known as Kashmir is often divided by a border marked with artillery line of control. It is often the scene of duels between Indian and Pakistani troops.

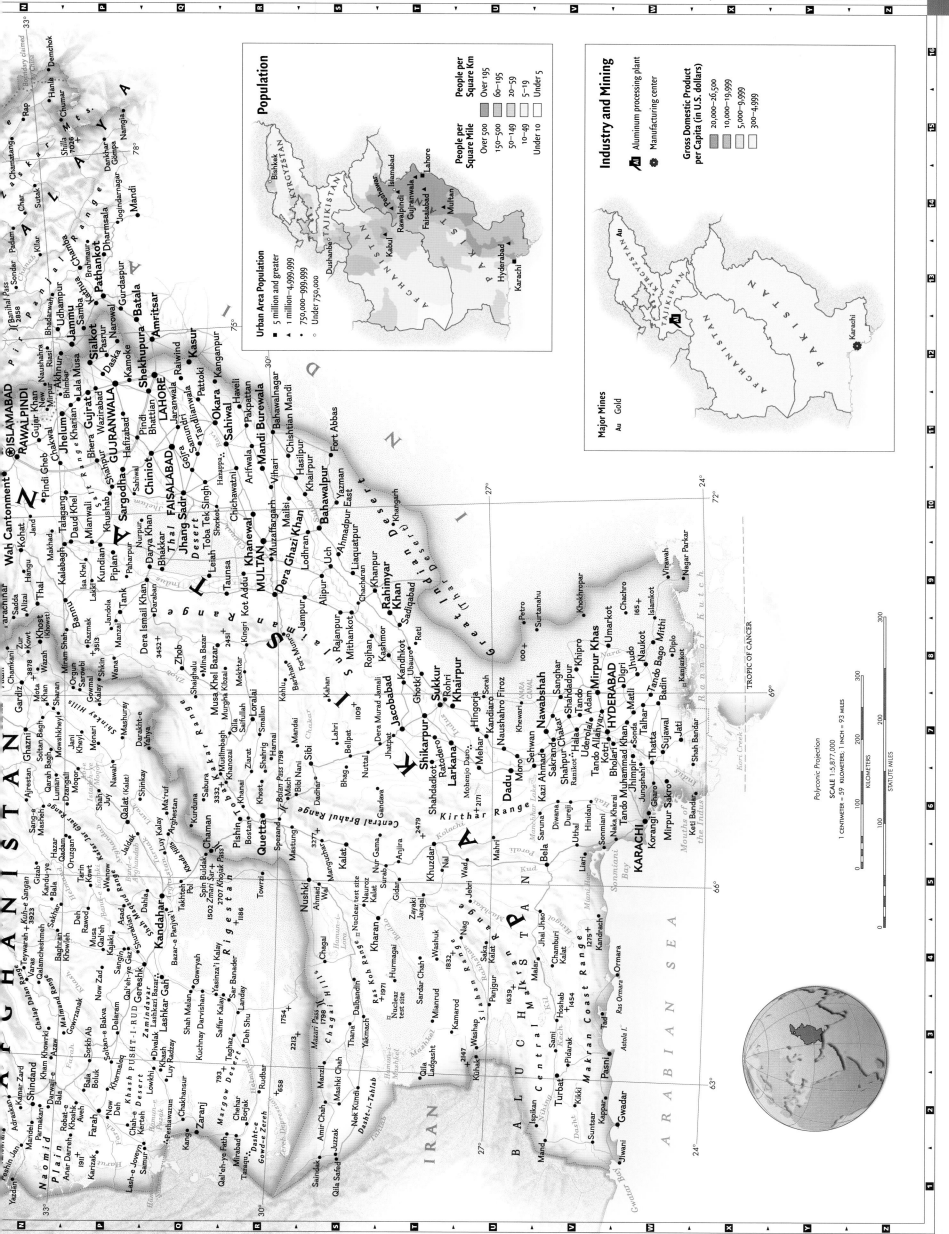

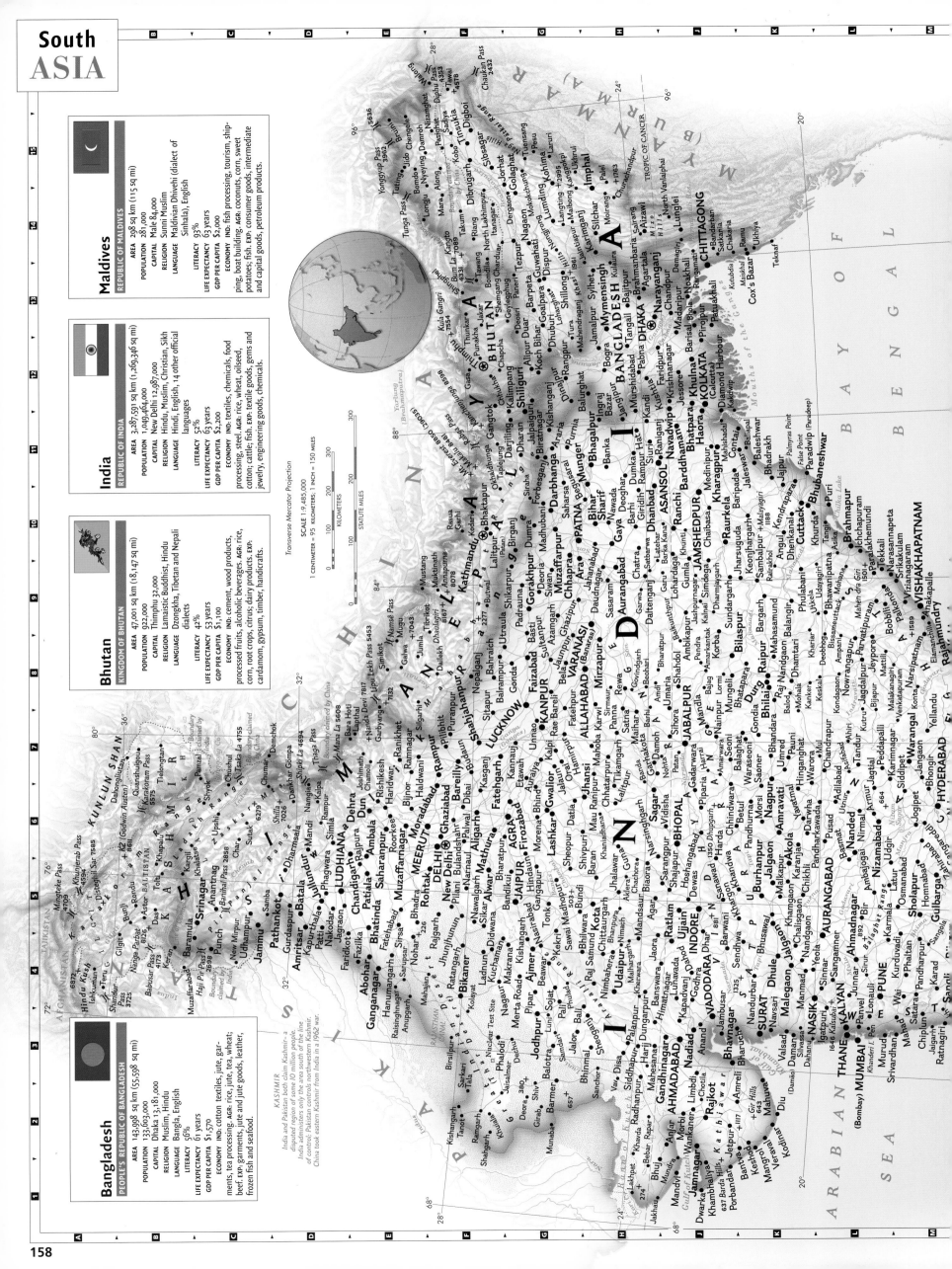

South ASIA

Maldives
REPUBLIC OF MALDIVES

AREA 298 sq km (115 sq mi)
POPULATION 281,000
CAPITAL Male 84,000
RELIGION Sunni Muslim
LANGUAGE Maldivian Dhivehi (dialect of Sinhala), English
LITERACY 93%
LIFE EXPECTANCY 63 years
GDP PER CAPITA $2,000
ECONOMY IND: fish processing, tourism, shipping, boat building. AGR: coconuts, corn, sweet potatoes; fish. EXP: consumer goods, intermediate and capital goods, petroleum products.

India
REPUBLIC OF INDIA

AREA 3,287,591 sq km (1,269,346 sq mi)
POPULATION 1,049,464,000
CAPITAL New Delhi 12,089,000
RELIGION Hindu, Muslim, Christian, Sikh
LANGUAGE Hindi, English, 14 other official languages
LITERACY 52%
LIFE EXPECTANCY 63 years
GDP PER CAPITA $2,200
ECONOMY IND: textiles, chemicals, food processing, steel, machinery. AGR: rice, wheat, oilseed, cotton; cattle; fish. EXP: textile goods, gems and jewelry, engineering goods, chemicals.

Bhutan
KINGDOM OF BHUTAN

AREA 47,001 sq km (18,147 sq mi)
POPULATION 922,000
CAPITAL Thimphu 32,000
RELIGION Lamaistic Buddhist, Hindu
LANGUAGE Dzongkha, Tibetan and Nepali dialects
LITERACY 42%
LIFE EXPECTANCY 53 years
GDP PER CAPITA $1,100
ECONOMY IND: cement, wood products, processed fruits, alcoholic beverages. AGR: rice, corn, root crops; citrus; dairy products. EXP: cardamom, gypsum, timber, handicrafts.

Bangladesh
PEOPLE'S REPUBLIC OF BANGLADESH

AREA 143,998 sq km (55,598 sq mi)
POPULATION 133,603,000
CAPITAL Dhaka 13,181,000
RELIGION Muslim, Hindu
LANGUAGE Bangla, English
LITERACY 56%
LIFE EXPECTANCY 61 years
GDP PER CAPITA $1,570
ECONOMY IND: cotton textiles, jute, garments; tea processing. AGR: rice, jute, tea, wheat; beef. EXP: garments, jute and jute goods, leather, frozen fish and seafood.

KASHMIR
India and Pakistan both claim Kashmir—a disputed region of some 10 million people. India administers only the area south of the line of control; Pakistan controls northwestern Kashmir. China took eastern Kashmir from India in a 1962 war.

Transverse Mercator Projection

SCALE 1:9,485,000
1 CENTIMETER = 95 KILOMETERS; 1 INCH = 150 MILES

KILOMETERS
STATUTE MILES

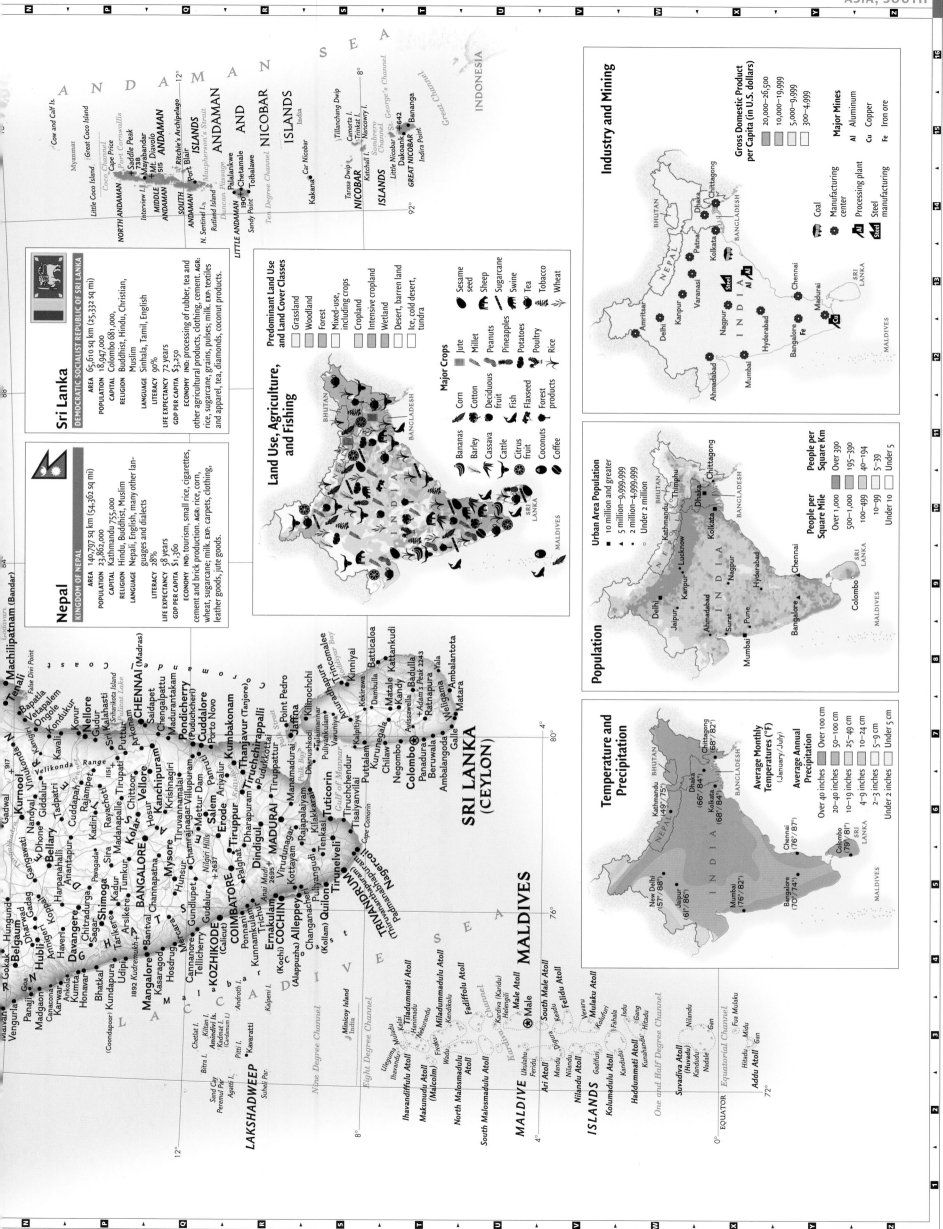

Sri Lanka
DEMOCRATIC SOCIALIST REPUBLIC OF SRI LANKA

AREA 65,610 sq km (25,332 sq mi)
POPULATION 18,947,000
CAPITAL Colombo 681,000
RELIGION Buddhist, Hindu, Christian, Muslim
LANGUAGE Sinhala, Tamil, English
LITERACY 90%
LIFE EXPECTANCY 72 years
GDP PER CAPITA $3,250
ECONOMY IND: processing of rubber, tea and other agricultural products, clothing, cement. AGR: rice, sugarcane, grains, pulses; milk. textiles and apparel, tea, diamonds, coconut products.

Nepal
KINGDOM OF NEPAL

AREA 140,797 sq km (54,362 sq mi)
POPULATION 23,862,000
CAPITAL Kathmandu 755,000
RELIGION Hindu, Buddhist, Muslim
LANGUAGE Nepali, English, many other languages and dialects
LITERACY 28%
LIFE EXPECTANCY 58 years
GDP PER CAPITA $1,360
ECONOMY IND: tourism, small rice, cigarettes, cement and brick production. AGR: rice, corn, wheat, sugarcane; milk. EXP: carpets, clothing, leather goods, jute goods.

Industry and Mining

Gross Domestic Product per Capita (in U.S. dollars)
20,000–26,500
10,000–19,999
5,000–9,999
300–4,999

Major Mines
Al Aluminum
Cu Copper
Fe Iron ore

Coal
Manufacturing center
Processing plant
Steel manufacturing

Land Use, Agriculture, and Fishing

Predominant Land Use and Land Cover Classes
Grassland
Woodland
Forest
Mixed-use, including crops
Cropland
Intensive cropland
Wetland
Desert, barren land
Ice, cold desert, tundra

Major Crops
Corn · Sesame seed
Cotton · Sheep
Deciduous fruit · Sugarcane
Fish · Swine
Flaxseed · Tea
Forest products · Tobacco
Bananas · Jute · Wheat
Barley · Millet
Cassava · Peanuts
Cattle · Pineapples
Citrus fruit · Potatoes
Coconuts · Poultry
Coffee · Rice

Population

Urban Area Population
10 million and greater
5 million–9,999,999
2 million–4,999,999
Under 2 million

People per Square Mile
Over 1,000
500–1,000
100–499
10–99
Under 10

People per Square Km
Over 390
195–390
40–194
5–39
Under 5

Temperature and Precipitation

Average Monthly Temperatures (°F) (January/July)
Over 40 inches
20–40 inches
10–19 inches
4–9 inches
2–3 inches
Under 2 inches

Average Annual Precipitation
Over 100 cm
50–100 cm
25–49 cm
10–24 cm
5–9 cm
Under 5 cm

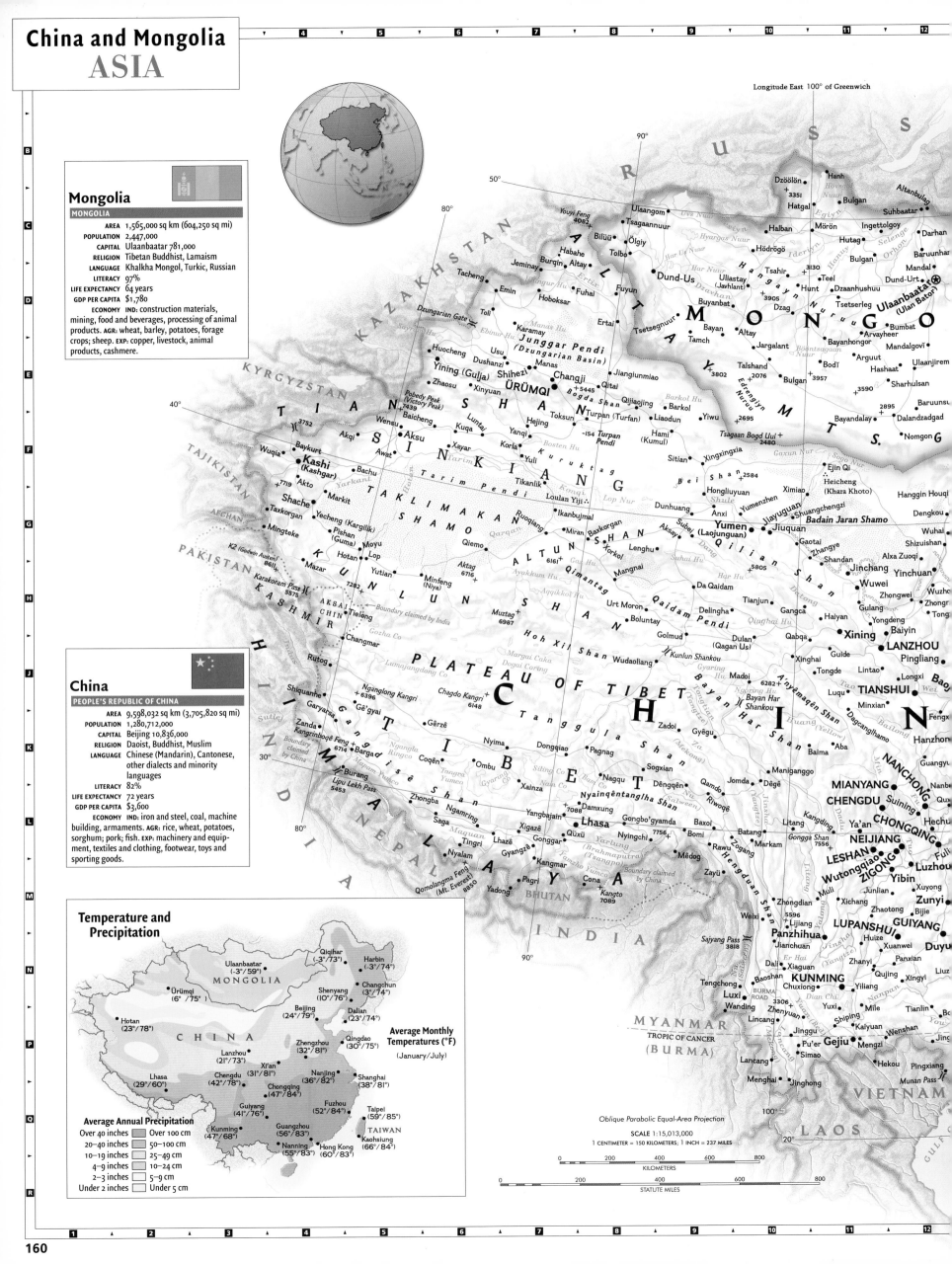

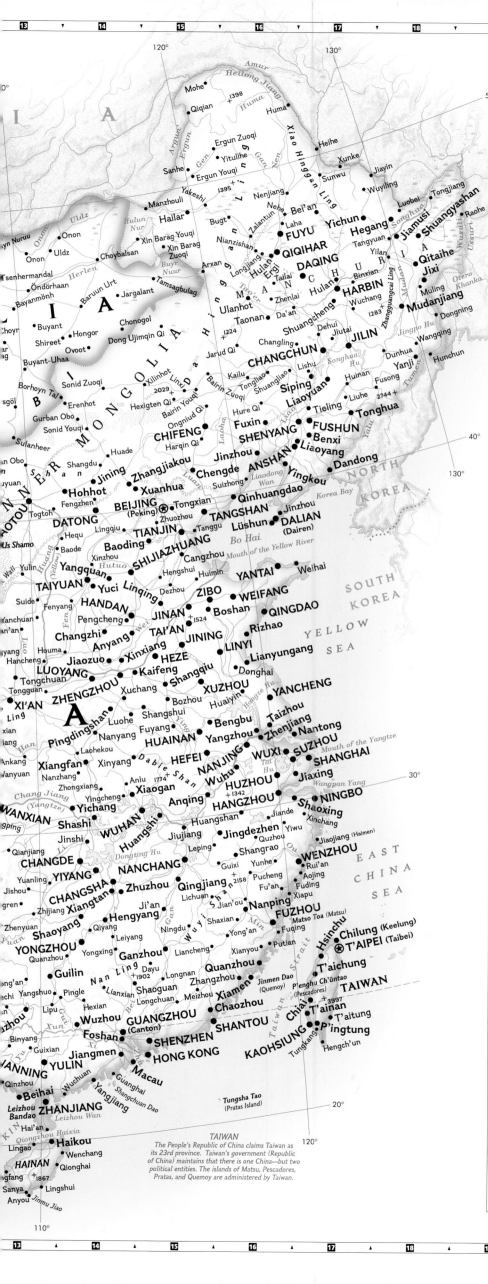

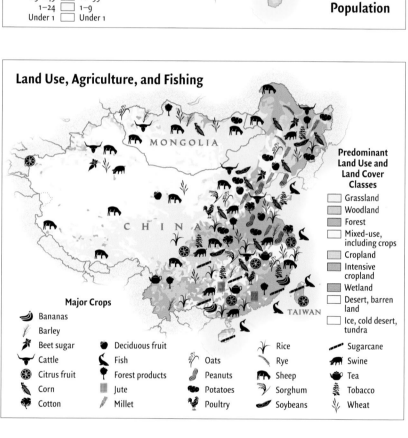

Population

Urban Area Population
- ■ 10 million and greater
- ▲ 4 million–9,999,999
- ▲ 2.5 million–3,999,999
- ○ 2 million–2,499,999

People per Square Mile	People per Square Km
Over 1000	Over 390
250–1000	100–390
25–249	10–99
1–24	1–9
Under 1	Under 1

Land Use, Agriculture, and Fishing

Predominant Land Use and Land Cover Classes
- Grassland
- Woodland
- Forest
- Mixed-use, including crops
- Cropland
- Intensive cropland
- Wetland
- Desert, barren land
- Ice, cold desert, tundra

Major Crops
- Bananas
- Barley
- Beet sugar
- Cattle
- Citrus fruit
- Corn
- Cotton
- Deciduous fruit
- Fish
- Forest products
- Jute
- Millet
- Oats
- Peanuts
- Potatoes
- Poultry
- Rice
- Rye
- Sheep
- Sorghum
- Soybeans
- Sugarcane
- Swine
- Tea
- Tobacco
- Wheat

Industry and Mining

Major Mines
Al	Aluminum
Sb	Antimony
Bi	Bismuth
Co	Cobalt
Cu	Copper
F	Fluorite
Au	Gold
Fe	Iron ore
Pb	Lead
Mo	Molybdenum
Ni	Nickel
Sn	Tin
Ti	Titanium
V	Vanadium
W	Tungsten
Zn	Zinc

Gross Domestic Product per Capita (in U.S. dollars)
- 20,000–26,500
- 10,000–19,999
- 5,000–9,999
- 300–4,999

- Coal
- Natural gas
- Petroleum
- Phosphate
- Processing plant
- Rare earth elements
- Steel manufacturing

TAIWAN
The People's Republic of China claims Taiwan as its 23rd province. Taiwan's government (Republic of China) maintains that there is one China—but two political entities. The islands of Matsu, Pescadores, Pratas, and Quemoy are administered by Taiwan.

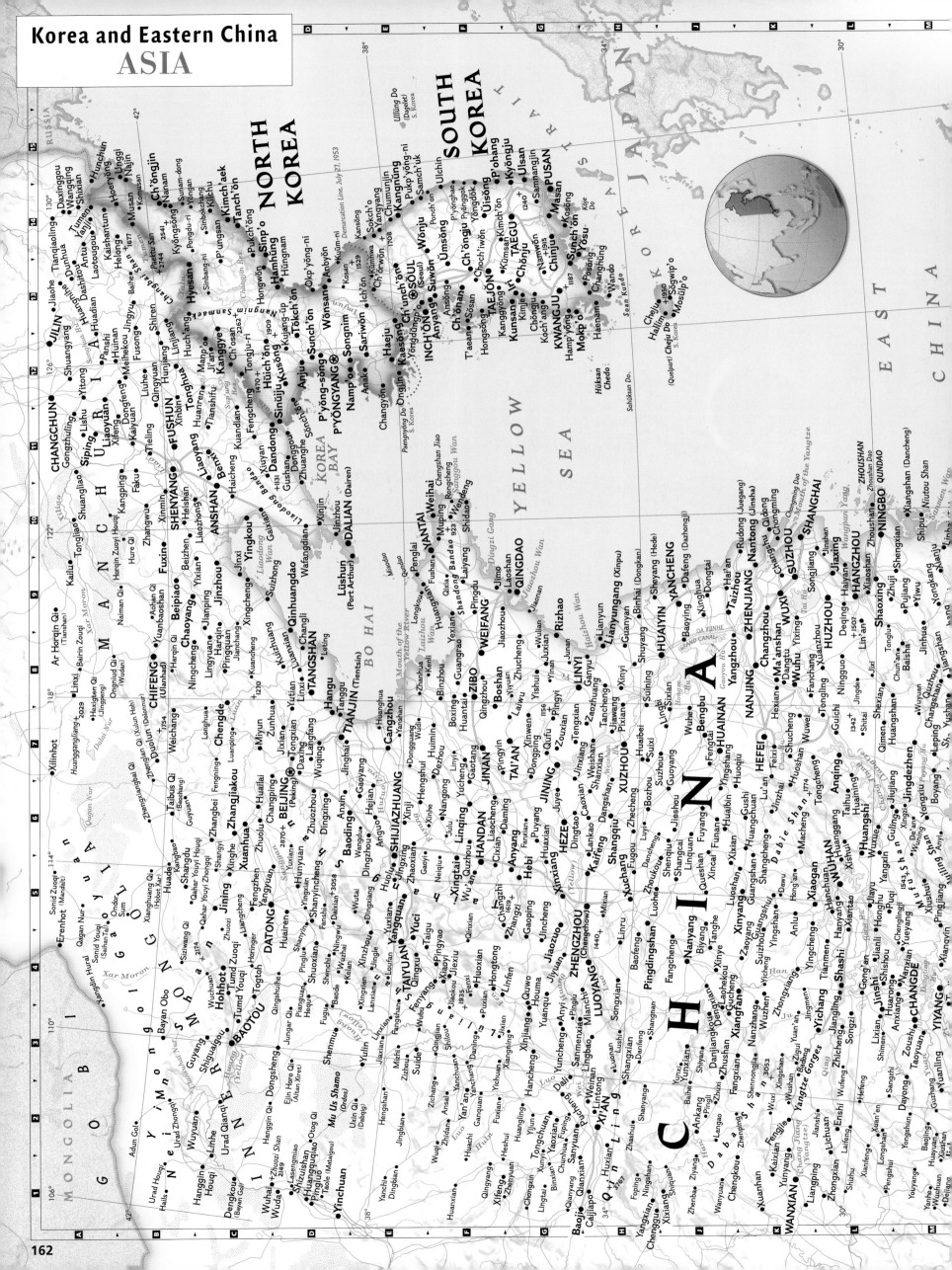

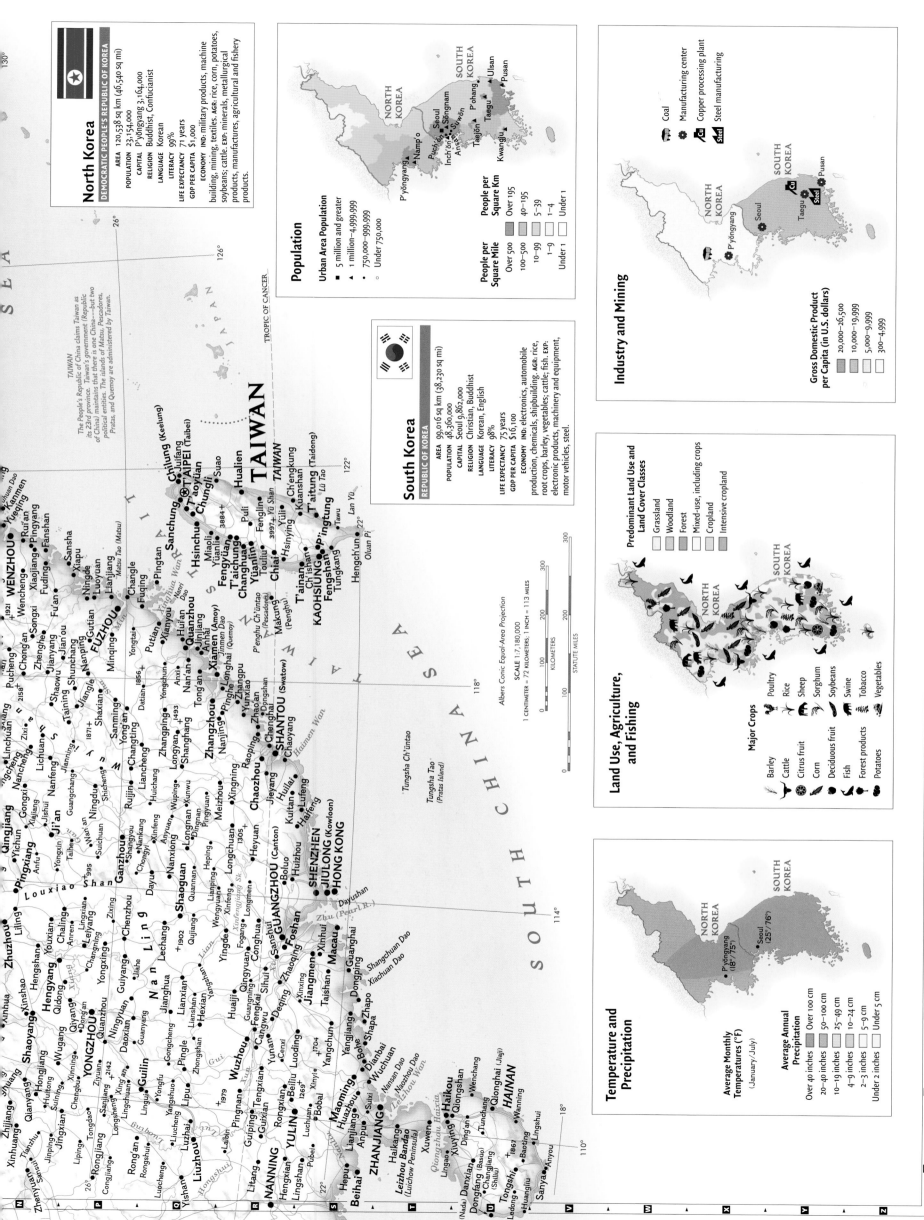

North Korea
DEMOCRATIC PEOPLE'S REPUBLIC OF KOREA

AREA 120,538 sq km (46,540 sq mi)
POPULATION 23,154,000
CAPITAL P'yŏngyang 3,164,000
RELIGION Buddhist, Confucianist
LANGUAGE Korean
LITERACY 99%
LIFE EXPECTANCY 71 years
GDP PER CAPITA $1,000
ECONOMY IND: military products, machine building, mining, textiles. **AGR:** rice, corn, potatoes, soybeans; cattle. **EXP:** minerals, metallurgical products, manufactures, agricultural and fishery products.

South Korea
REPUBLIC OF KOREA

AREA 99,016 sq km (38,230 sq mi)
POPULATION 48,360,000
CAPITAL Seoul 9,862,000
RELIGION Christian, Buddhist
LANGUAGE Korean, English
LITERACY 98%
LIFE EXPECTANCY 75 years
GDP PER CAPITA $16,100
ECONOMY IND: electronics, automobile production, chemicals, shipbuilding. **AGR:** rice, root crops, barley, vegetables; cattle; fish. **EXP:** electronic products, machinery and equipment, motor vehicles, steel.

TAIWAN
The People's Republic of China claims Taiwan as its 23rd province. Taiwan's government (Republic of China) maintains that there is one China—but two political entities. The islands of Matsu, Pescadores, Pratas, and Quemoy are administered by Taiwan.

Population

Urban Area Population
- ■ 5 million and greater
- ▲ 1 million–4,999,999
- ● 750,000–999,999
- ○ Under 750,000

People per Square Mile
- Over 500
- 100–500
- 10–99
- 1–9
- Under 1

People per Square Km
- Over 195
- 40–195
- 5–39
- 1–4
- Under 1

Industry and Mining

- Coal
- Manufacturing center
- Cu Copper processing plant
- Steel Steel manufacturing

Gross Domestic Product per Capita (in U.S. dollars)
- 20,000–26,500
- 10,000–19,999
- 5,000–9,999
- 300–4,999

Land Use, Agriculture, and Fishing

Predominant Land Use and Land Cover Classes
- Grassland
- Woodland
- Forest
- Mixed-use, including crops
- Cropland
- Intensive cropland

Major Crops
- Barley
- Cattle
- Citrus fruit
- Corn
- Deciduous fruit
- Fish
- Forest products
- Potatoes
- Poultry
- Rice
- Sheep
- Sorghum
- Soybeans
- Swine
- Tobacco
- Vegetables

Temperature and Precipitation

Average Monthly Temperatures (°F)
(January/July)

Average Annual Precipitation
- Over 100 cm — Over 40 inches
- 50–100 cm — 20–40 inches
- 25–49 cm — 10–19 inches
- 10–24 cm — 4–9 inches
- 5–9 cm — 2–3 inches
- Under 5 cm — Under 2 inches

Albers Conic Equal-Area Projection
SCALE 1:7,180,000
1 CENTIMETER = 72 KILOMETERS; 1 INCH = 113 MILES

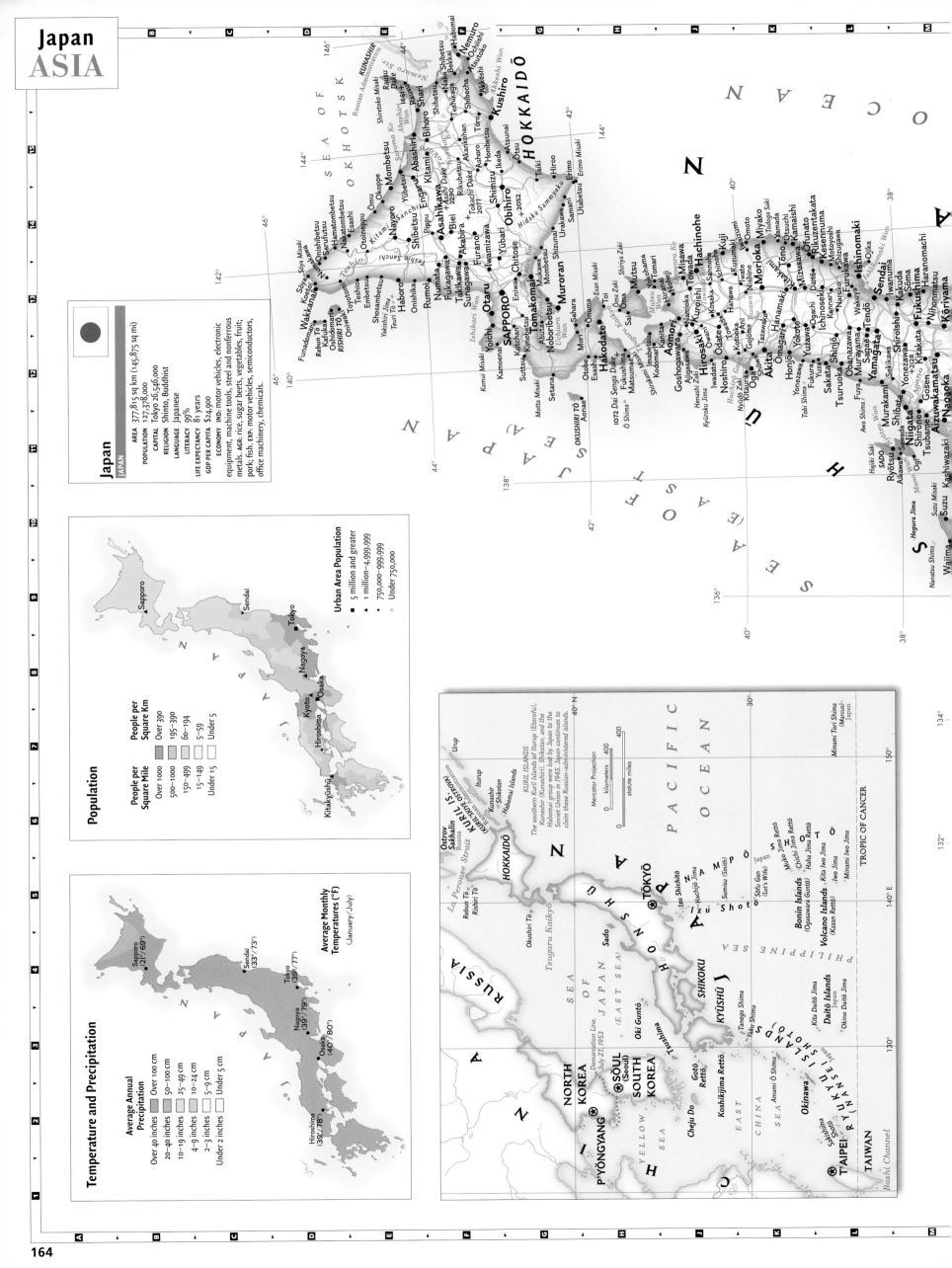

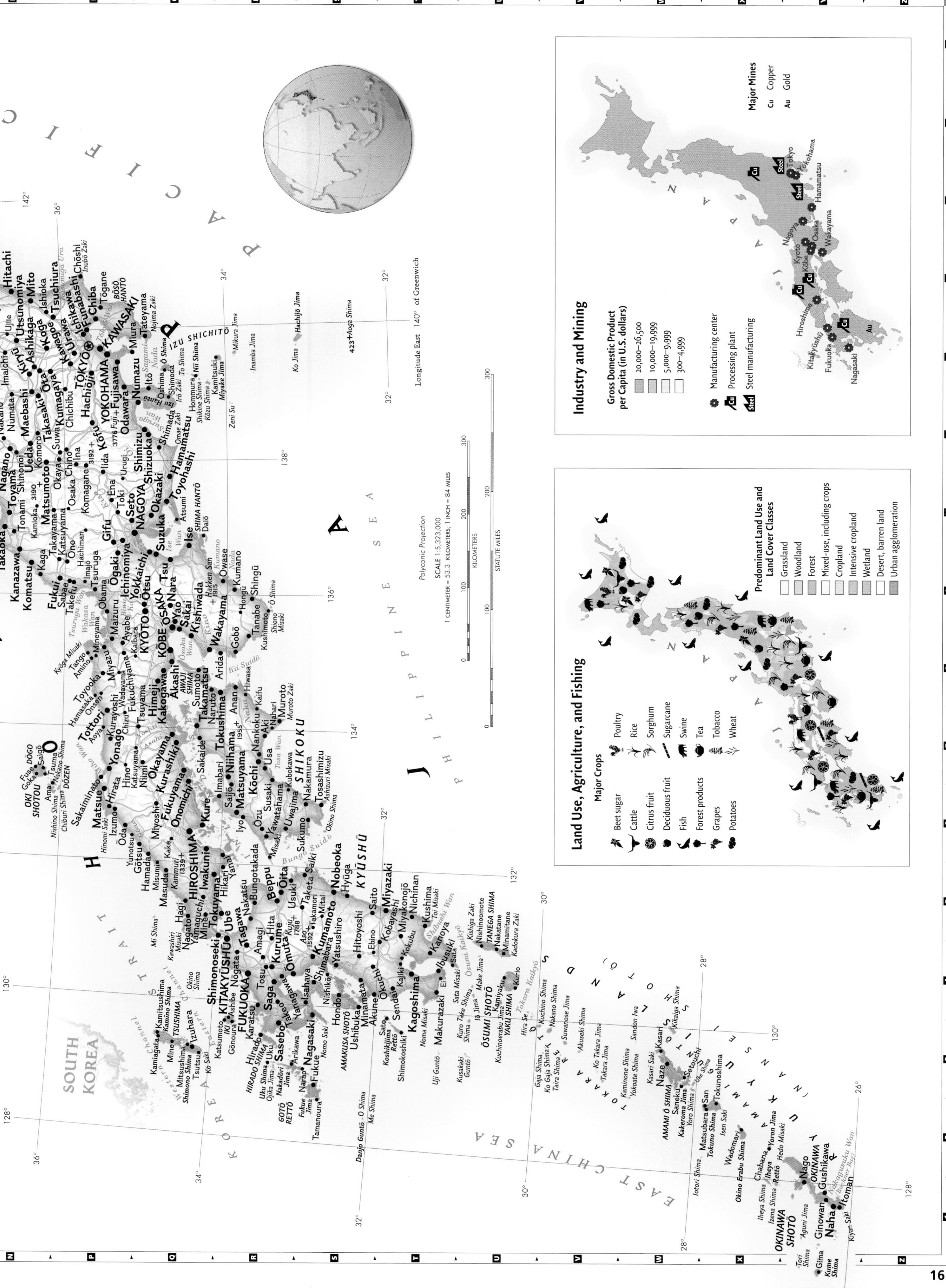

Industry and Mining

Gross Domestic Product per Capita (in U.S. dollars)
- 20,000–26,500
- 10,000–19,999
- 5,000–9,999
- 300–4,999

- ⚙ Manufacturing center
- Processing plant
- **Steel** Steel manufacturing

Major Mines
- Cu Copper
- Au Gold

Land Use, Agriculture, and Fishing

Major Crops
- Beet sugar
- Cattle
- Citrus fruit
- Deciduous fruit
- Fish
- Forest products
- Grapes
- Potatoes
- Poultry
- Rice
- Sorghum
- Sugarcane
- Swine
- Tea
- Tobacco
- Wheat

Predominant Land Use and Land Cover Classes
- Grassland
- Woodland
- Forest
- Mixed-use, including crops
- Cropland
- Intensive cropland
- Wetland
- Desert, barren land
- Urban agglomeration

Polyconic Projection

SCALE 1:5,323,000

1 CENTIMETER = 53.3 KILOMETERS, 1 INCH = 84 MILES

KILOMETERS

STATUTE MILES

0 100 200 300

Longitude East 140° of Greenwich

PACIFIC OCEAN

PHILIPPINE SEA

EAST CHINA SEA

KOREA STRAIT

SOUTH KOREA

TSUSHIMA

KYŪSHŪ

SHIKOKU

HONSHŪ

OKI SHOTŌ
DŌGO
DŌZEN

IZU SHICHITŌ

BŌSŌ HANTŌ

SHIMA HANTŌ

TOKYO
YOKOHAMA
KAWASAKI
CHIBA
NAGOYA
OSAKA
KOBE
KYOTO
HIROSHIMA
KITAKYŪSHŪ
FUKUOKA
NAGASAKI
KUMAMOTO
KAGOSHIMA
SAPPORO

Fuji 3776

ŌSUMI SHOTŌ
TANEGA SHIMA
YAKU SHIMA

AMAKUSA SHOTŌ
GOTŌ RETTŌ

TOKARA RETTŌ

AMAMI Ō SHIMA

OKINAWA SHOTŌ
OKINAWA
Naha
NANSEI SHOTŌ (RYUKYU ISLANDS)

Peninsular Southeast
ASIA

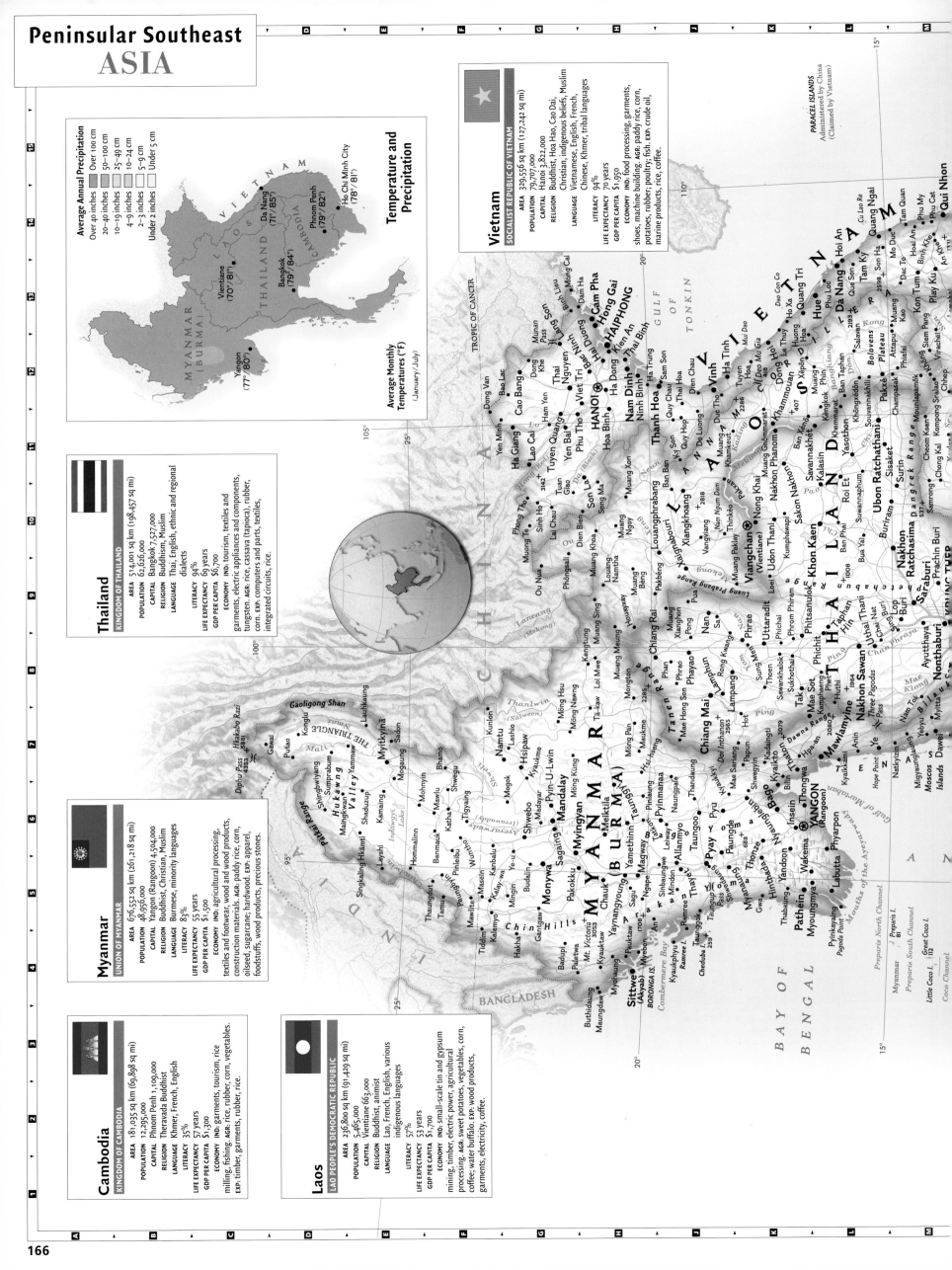

Average Annual Precipitation
- Over 100 cm — Over 40 inches
- 50–100 cm — 20–40 inches
- 25–49 cm — 10–19 inches
- 10–24 cm — 4–9 inches
- 5–9 cm — 2–3 inches
- Under 5 cm — Under 2 inches

Temperature and Precipitation

Da Nang (71°/85°)
Phnom Penh (79°/82°)
Ho Chi Minh City (78°/81°)
Vientiane (70°/81°)
Bangkok (79°/84°)
Yangon (77°/80°)

Average Monthly Temperatures (°F) (January/July)

Vietnam
SOCIALIST REPUBLIC OF VIETNAM
- AREA 329,556 sq km (127,242 sq mi)
- POPULATION 79,707,000
- CAPITAL Hanoi 3,822,000
- RELIGION Buddhist, Hoa Hao, Cao Dai, Christian, indigenous beliefs, Muslim
- LANGUAGE Vietnamese, English, French, Chinese, Khmer, tribal languages
- LITERACY 94%
- LIFE EXPECTANCY 70 years
- GDP PER CAPITA $1,950
- ECONOMY IND: food processing, garments, shoes, machine building. AGR: paddy rice, corn, potatoes, rubber; poultry, fish. EXP: crude oil, marine products, rice, coffee.

Thailand
KINGDOM OF THAILAND
- AREA 514,001 sq km (198,457 sq mi)
- POPULATION 62,626,000
- CAPITAL Bangkok 7,527,000
- RELIGION Buddhist, Muslim
- LANGUAGE Thai, English, ethnic and regional dialects
- LITERACY 94%
- LIFE EXPECTANCY 69 years
- GDP PER CAPITA $6,700
- ECONOMY IND: tourism, textiles and garments, electric appliances and components, tungsten. AGR: rice, cassava (tapioca), rubber, corn. EXP: computers and parts, textiles, integrated circuits, rice.

Myanmar
UNION OF MYANMAR
- AREA 676,552 sq km (261,218 sq mi)
- POPULATION 48,956,000
- CAPITAL Yangon (Rangoon) 4,504,000
- RELIGION Buddhist, Christian, Muslim
- LANGUAGE Burmese, minority languages
- LITERACY 83%
- LIFE EXPECTANCY 55 years
- GDP PER CAPITA $1,500
- ECONOMY IND: agricultural processing, textiles and footwear, wood and wood products, construction materials. AGR: paddy rice, corn, oilseed, sugarcane; hardwood. EXP: apparel, foodstuffs, wood products, precious stones.

Cambodia
KINGDOM OF CAMBODIA
- AREA 181,035 sq km (69,898 sq mi)
- POPULATION 12,295,000
- CAPITAL Phnom Penh 1,109,000
- RELIGION Theravada Buddhist
- LANGUAGE Khmer, French, English
- LITERACY 35%
- LIFE EXPECTANCY 57 years
- GDP PER CAPITA $1,300
- ECONOMY IND: garments, tourism, rice milling, fishing. AGR: rice, rubber, corn, vegetables. EXP: timber, garments, rubber, rice.

Laos
LAO PEOPLE'S DEMOCRATIC REPUBLIC
- AREA 236,800 sq km (91,429 sq mi)
- POPULATION 5,465,000
- CAPITAL Vientiane 665,000
- RELIGION Buddhist, animist
- LANGUAGE Lao, French, English, various indigenous languages
- LITERACY 57%
- LIFE EXPECTANCY 53 years
- GDP PER CAPITA $1,700
- ECONOMY IND: small-scale tin and gypsum mining, timber, electric power, agricultural processing. AGR: sweet potatoes, vegetables, corn, coffee; water buffalo. EXP: wood products, garments, electricity, coffee.

PARACEL ISLANDS
Administered by China
(Claimed by Vietnam)

GULF OF TONKIN

TROPIC OF CANCER

BAY OF BENGAL

BANGLADESH

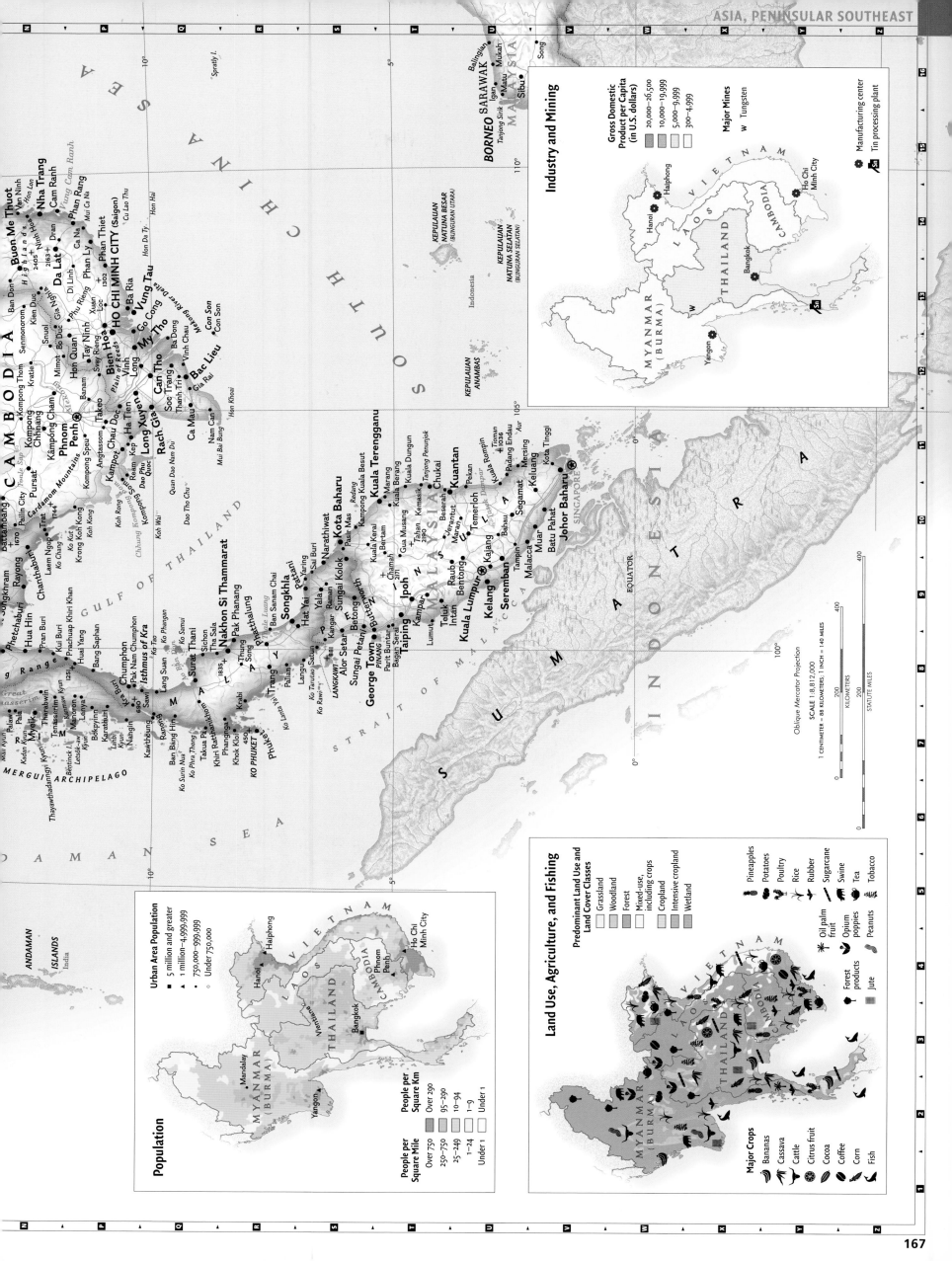

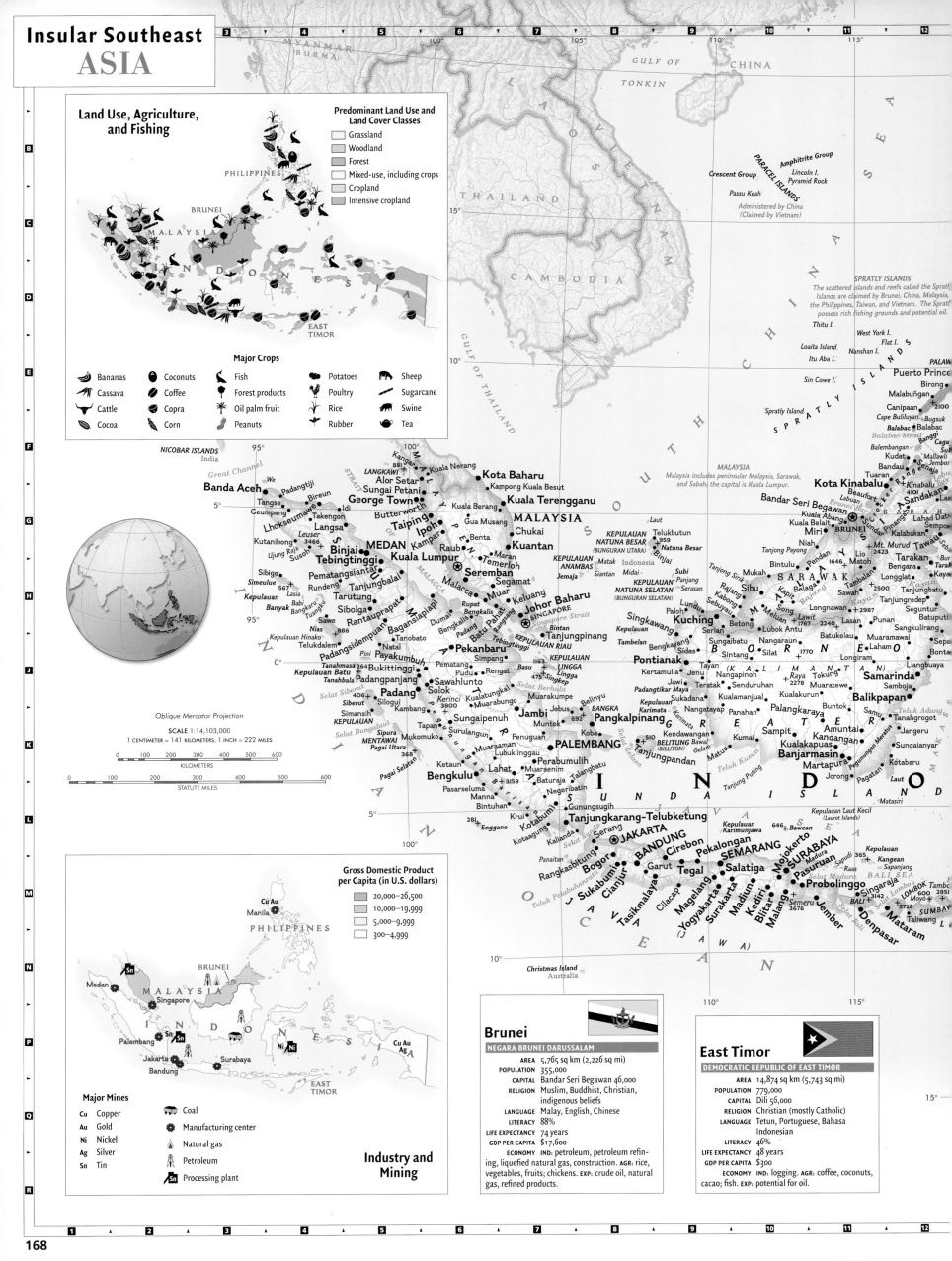

Insular Southeast ASIA

Land Use, Agriculture, and Fishing

Predominant Land Use and Land Cover Classes
- Grassland
- Woodland
- Forest
- Mixed-use, including crops
- Cropland
- Intensive cropland

Major Crops
- Bananas
- Cassava
- Cattle
- Cocoa
- Coconuts
- Coffee
- Copra
- Corn
- Fish
- Forest products
- Oil palm fruit
- Peanuts
- Potatoes
- Poultry
- Rice
- Rubber
- Sheep
- Sugarcane
- Swine
- Tea

Oblique Mercator Projection

SCALE 1:14,103,000
1 CENTIMETER = 141 KILOMETERS; 1 INCH = 222 MILES

KILOMETERS
0 100 200 300 400 500 600

STATUTE MILES
0 100 200 300 400 500 600

Gross Domestic Product per Capita (in U.S. dollars)
- 20,000–26,500
- 10,000–19,999
- 5,000–9,999
- 300–4,999

Major Mines
- Cu Copper
- Au Gold
- Ni Nickel
- Ag Silver
- Sn Tin
- Coal
- Manufacturing center
- Natural gas
- Petroleum
- Processing plant

Industry and Mining

Brunei
NEGARA BRUNEI DARUSSALAM
- AREA 5,765 sq km (2,226 sq mi)
- POPULATION 355,000
- CAPITAL Bandar Seri Begawan 46,000
- RELIGION Muslim, Buddhist, Christian, indigenous beliefs
- LANGUAGE Malay, English, Chinese
- LITERACY 88%
- LIFE EXPECTANCY 74 years
- GDP PER CAPITA $17,600
- ECONOMY IND: petroleum, petroleum refining, liquefied natural gas, construction. AGR: rice, vegetables, fruits; chickens. EXP: crude oil, natural gas, refined products.

East Timor
DEMOCRATIC REPUBLIC OF EAST TIMOR
- AREA 14,874 sq km (5,743 sq mi)
- POPULATION 779,000
- CAPITAL Dili 56,000
- RELIGION Christian (mostly Catholic)
- LANGUAGE Tetun, Portuguese, Bahasa Indonesian
- LITERACY 46%
- LIFE EXPECTANCY 48 years
- GDP PER CAPITA $300
- ECONOMY IND: logging. AGR: coffee, coconuts, cacao; fish. EXP: potential for oil.

Indonesia
REPUBLIC OF INDONESIA

AREA	1,904,569 sq km (735,358 sq mi)
POPULATION	216,983,000
CAPITAL	Jakarta 11,429,000
RELIGION	Muslim, Protestant, Roman Catholic, Hindu, Buddhist
LANGUAGE	Bahasa Indonesia, English, Dutch, Javanese and other local dialects
LITERACY	89%
LIFE EXPECTANCY	68 years
GDP PER CAPITA	$2,900
ECONOMY	IND: petroleum and natural gas, textiles, mining, rubber. AGR: rice, cassava (tapioca), peanuts, rubber; poultry. EXP: oil and gas, plywood, textiles, rubber.

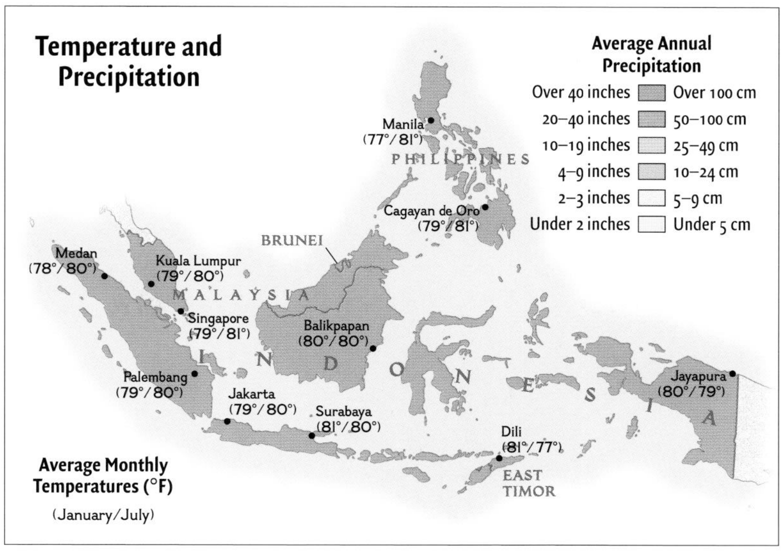

Temperature and Precipitation

Average Annual Precipitation

Over 40 inches	Over 100 cm
20–40 inches	50–100 cm
10–19 inches	25–49 cm
4–9 inches	10–24 cm
2–3 inches	5–9 cm
Under 2 inches	Under 5 cm

Average Monthly Temperatures (°F)

(January/July)

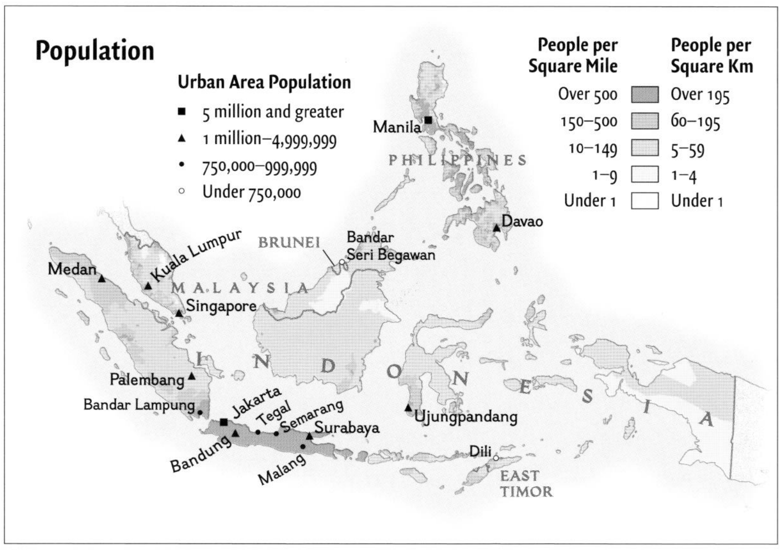

Population

Urban Area Population

- ■ 5 million and greater
- ▲ 1 million–4,999,999
- ● 750,000–999,999
- ○ Under 750,000

People per Square Mile	People per Square Km
Over 500	Over 195
150–500	60–195
10–149	5–59
1–9	1–4
Under 1	Under 1

Malaysia
MALAYSIA

East Timor gained independence on May 20, 2002 after being under United Nations administration since 1999. It was a Portuguese colony from the 16th century until 1975. Indonesia annexed East Timor in 1976 and held it until 1999.

AREA	329,749 sq km (127,317 sq mi)
POPULATION	24,370,000
CAPITAL	Kuala Lumpur 1,410,000
RELIGION	Muslim, Buddhist, Daoist, Hindu, Christian, Sikh, Shamanist
LANGUAGE	Bahasa Melayu, English, Chinese dialects, other regional dialects and indigenous languages
LITERACY	84%
LIFE EXPECTANCY	71 years
GDP PER CAPITA	$10,300
ECONOMY	IND: rubber and palm oil processing and manufacturing, light manufacturing industry, logging, agriculture processing. AGR: rubber, palm oil, subsistence crops, timber. EXP: electronic equipment, petroleum and liquefied natural gas, chemicals, palm oil.

Philippines
REPUBLIC OF THE PHILIPPINES

AREA	300,001 sq km (115,831 sq mi)
POPULATION	80,025,000
CAPITAL	Manila 10,069,000
RELIGION	Roman Catholic, Protestant, Muslim, Buddhist
LANGUAGE	Filipino (based on Tagalog), English, and eight major dialects
LITERACY	95%
LIFE EXPECTANCY	68 years
GDP PER CAPITA	$3,800
ECONOMY	IND: textiles, pharmaceuticals, chemicals, wood products. AGR: rice, coconuts, corn, sugarcane; pork; fish. EXP: electronic equipment, machinery and transport equipment, garments, coconut products.

Singapore
REPUBLIC OF SINGAPORE

AREA	618 sq km (239 sq mi)
POPULATION	4,248,000
CAPITAL	Singapore 4,108,000
RELIGION	Buddhist, Muslim, Christian, Hindu, Sikh, Taoist, Confucianist
LANGUAGE	Chinese, Malay, Tamil, English
LITERACY	94%
LIFE EXPECTANCY	80 years
GDP PER CAPITA	$26,500
ECONOMY	IND: electronics, chemicals, financial services, oil drilling equipment. AGR: rubber, copra, fruit, orchids; poultry. EXP: machinery and equipment (including electronics), chemicals, mineral fuels.

AFRICA

Africa is often called the continent of beginnings. Fossil and bone records of the earliest humans go back more than 4 million years, and perhaps 1.8 million years ago our early upright ancestor, *Homo erectus*, departed Africa on the long journey that eventually peopled the Earth. It now seems likely that every person today comes from a lineage that leads back to an ancient African. Innumerable cave paintings and petroglyphs, from the Sahara to South Africa, provide clues to the beliefs and way of life of these age-old hominids.

Second largest continent after Asia, Africa accounts for a fifth of the world's land surface. Its unforgettable form, bulging to the west, lies surrounded by oceans and seas and can be considered underpopulated because only slightly more than 10 percent of the world's population lives here. Yet Africa's 53 countries now contain more than 800 million people, two-thirds living in the countryside, mostly in coastal regions, near lakes, and along river courses.

Boundless stretches of sand are the highways of Saharan Niger. Fewer than 500 miles (805 km) of paved roads serve a nation three times as large as California. A caravan laden with salt heads toward markets at the desert's edge.

The mighty Sahara, largest desert in the world, covers more than a quarter of Africa's surface and divides the continent. Desert zones—Sahara, Kalahari, Namib—contrast with immense tropical rain forests. Watered regions of lakes and rivers lie beyond the Sahel, a vast semi-arid zone of short grasses that spans the continent south of the Sahara. Most of Africa is made up of savannah—high, rolling, grassy plains.

These savannahs have been home since earliest times to people often called Bantu, a reference to both social groupings and their languages. Other distinct physical types exist around the continent as well: BaMbuti (Pygmies), San (Bushmen), Nilo-Saharans, and Hamito-Semitics (Berbers and Cushites). Africa's astonishing 1,600 spoken languages—more than any other continent—reflect the great diversity of ethnic and social groups.

Near the Equator, perpetual ice and snow crown Mount Kilimanjaro, the continent's highest point at 19,340 feet (5,895 m). The Nile, longest river in the world at 4,241 miles (6,825 km), originates in mountains south of the Equator and flows north-northeast before finally delivering its life-giving waters into the Mediterranean Sea.

Africa, blessed with wondrous deserts, rivers, grasslands, forests, and multi-hued earth, and possessing huge reserves of mineral wealth and biodiversity, waits expectantly for a prosperous future.

Many obstacles, however, complicate the way forward. African countries experience great gaps in wealth between city and country, and many face growing slums around megacities such as Lagos and Cairo. Nearly 40 other African cities have populations over a million. Lack of clean water and the spread of diseases—malaria, tuberculosis, cholera, and AIDS—undermine people's health. In addition, war and huge concentrations of refugees displaced by fighting, persecution, and famine deter any chance of growth and stability. Africa today seems to stand between hope and hopelessness.

PHYSICAL

Africa stretches an astounding 5,000 miles (8,047 km) from north to south and 4,600 miles (7,403 km) from east to west. The continent rises from generally narrow coastal strips to form a gigantic plateau, with portions over 2,000 feet (610 m) in height. It has limited harbors and a coastline with few bays and inlets. Though formed by a series of expansive uplands, Africa has few true mountain chains. Main ranges in the north are the Atlas in Morocco and the Ahaggar in the Sahara. To the southeast, the Ethiopian highlands form a broad area of high topography. The massive volcanic peaks of Mount Kilimanjaro and Mount Kenya rise in dramatic isolation from surrounding plains. Between Uganda and the Congo, the Ruwenzori Range runs north to south and falls steeply in the west to the Rift Valley.

The East African Rift System is the continent's most dramatic geologic feature. This great rent actually begins in the Red Sea, then cuts southward to form the stunning landscape of lakes, volcanoes, and deep valleys that finally ends near the mouth of the Zambezi River. The Rift Valley, a region of active plate tectonics, marks the divide where East Africa is steadily being pulled away, eventually to become a mini-continent.

The Great Escarpment in southern Africa, a plateau edge that falls off to the coastal strip, is best represented by the stark, highly eroded Drakensberg Range, which reaches altitudes over 11,400 feet (3,475 m).

Madagascar, fourth largest island in the world, lies east of the main continent and is remarkable for its flora and fauna, including medicinal plants and lemur species.

Africa's great rivers include the Niger, Congo, and Zambezi, each regionally important for internal transport and fishing. The Nile drains 6 percent of the continent; its two main branches, the Blue Nile and the White Nile, meet at Khartoum in Sudan.

Wildlife still abounds in eastern and southern Africa and supports ecotourism, but hundreds of plant and animal species live precariously close to extinction.

HISTORY

After millions of years of human evolution there arose along the Nile River the brilliant civilization of Egypt. Mastery of agriculture and the river's annual flooding led to a series of dynasties that lasted for some 3,000 years, creating an astounding legacy of tombs, statuary, pyramids, temples, and hieroglyphic writing.

The long-standing power of Carthage ruled the western Mediterranean, but was conquered by the Roman Empire in 146 B.C. Rome and Byzantium henceforth controlled all of North Africa's coastal strip until the Arab influx from the 7th century onward. The Arabs quickly took all of North Africa and spread their language and religion. Arabic and Islam have been unifying forces ever since. Trans-Sahara trade and contact converted many sub-Saharan people, such as the Hausa of Nigeria, to Islam.

Indigenous kingdoms have punctuated Africa's history. Finds from Great Zimbabwe, a massive fortress-city and inland empire that flourished from the 11th to 15th centuries, show contacts with places as far away as India and China.

Along the Niger River, regional empires rose and fell between A.D. 800 and 1600. Slaves, ivory, gold, and kola nuts, used for flavoring and medicine, formed the basis of trade. In the Niger delta area, Yoruba, Ashanti, and Hausa states also had their periods of grandness. Longest lasting of all was Benin, a major African kingdom that survived from the 13th to 19th centuries.

The Swahili (literally, "coastal plain") culture arose from a mix of Arabs, local people, and others who from A.D. 900 onward spread to towns and cities of the east coast, along the Indian Ocean, from Somalia to Zanzibar. The Swahili language remains a major lingua franca in east, central, and southern Africa.

Colonialism's long period of domination, during which Portugal, Great Britain, France, Belgium, Germany, and Italy ruled the continent, spans from the mid-16th century to the mid-1900s. Portuguese arrived first in search of riches and the sea route to India. In time, commerce and Christianity pushed Europe into Africa.

The terrible slave trade shipped millions of Africans to North and South America and Arab regions. European presence encouraged exploration to find the sources of Africa's main rivers and to fill in blank spots on the map.

The Great Sphinx at Giza, four and a half thousand years old, portrays the face of King Khafre atop a lion's body. Giza's three colossal pyramids all stand near the Nile River, outside Cairo.

Europe's powers embarked on a "scramble for Africa," begun in the late 19th century, which led to partition of the entire continent by 1914. After the two world wars colonialism weakened. Independence for some countries began in the 1950s and came to most in the 1960s, in power transfers ranging from peaceful (Ghana, Senegal) to bloody (Kenya, Algeria). Freedom arrived in Rhodesia, with the new name Zimbabwe, in 1980, and in Namibia in 1990. The end of white rule in South Africa culminated with the election of Nelson Mandela in 1994.

CULTURE

Hunting, fishing, and gathering supported Africa's early humans. In time, agriculture led to permanent settlements and diversity in society, first along the Nile River and then in the south.

Village-based communities, resilient and lasting in their institutions, have formed the core of African life for thousands of years. With crop cultivation came domestication of animals—cattle, sheep, and goats. Iron-working reached sub-Saharan Africa from the north by about the 4th century B.C., allowing for new tools and weapons that accelerated change.

Kingdoms grew from the soil of village life. Kings and their courts resembled village elders in their roles as judges, mediators of disputes, and masters of trade. Early kingdoms in Mali, Ghana, and elsewhere conducted long-distance trade in gold, ivory, hides, jewels, feathers, and salt.

In some places, religious leaders became kings. Seen as divine, they assumed rights over land and cattle herds and in return took responsibility for the people's well-being.

Settled life allowed time and energy for arts, crafts, and other creative activities. In West Africa, artists, carvers, and bronze casters of Ife (12th–13th centuries) and Benin (16th–17th centuries) produced masterpieces in different mediums, culminating in terracotta heads and bronze statues and bas-reliefs of exquisite craftsmanship and naturalism. African art, especially sculpture, continues to hold a high place in world culture.

Rich traditions of oral narrative survive to preserve the history and collective memories of different tribes and groups. Bards known as *griots* tell tales and sing epic songs while accompanied by their instruments.

Traditional religion and ritual still have a powerful place in Africa, for health, wealth, good harvests, and to honor the forces of nature. The Dogon people retain a complex cosmology and perform a great ceremony every 60 years to mark the appearance of the star Sirius between two mountains.

Most major world religions are represented in Africa: Islam, Christianity, Judaism, even Hinduism. Islam predominates in the north, and south of the Sahara Christianity claims multitudes of followers—Islam and Christianity each claim about 300 million followers.

European languages and schooling, legacies of colonialism, have had lasting effects on modern Africa. Yet far from the cities one can still find blue-turbanned Tuareg wandering the Sahara, slender Masai on the savannahs of East Africa, Pygmies in the rain forests, and San (Bushmen) adapted to the Kalahari Desert's harsh conditions. Color, exuberance, and diversity manage to shine through the clouds of trouble that beset the nations of Africa.

ECONOMY

Africa ranks among the richest regions in the world in natural resources; it contains vast reserves of fossil fuels, precious metals, ores, and gems, including almost all of the world's chromium, much uranium, copper, tremendous underground gold reserves, and diamonds. West Africa exports major amounts of iron ore.

Yet Africa, the poorest continent, accounts for a mere 1 percent of world economic output. South Africa's economy alone nearly equals that of all other sub-Saharan countries.

With little history of refining and manufacturing (limited to parts of North and South Africa), small-scale agriculture dominates the activities of more than 60 percent of Africans: main crops are corn, wheat, rice, yams, potatoes, and cassava. Economic life revolves around farmsteads and village markets. Important cash crops include cacao, coffee, tea, fruit, and palm and vegetable oils.

Even though food production is increasing, agriculture takes place on only 6 percent of Africa's land and fails to keep pace with population growth—six children is the average for every woman, and in many countries nearly half the people are under 15. Most countries rely on imported food and loans. A cycle of crushing debt repayment, unemployment, and instability repels much-needed foreign investment.

Tourism, while offering hope to numerous countries, mostly in north, east, and southern Africa, highlights the need for conservation and interdependence between humans and the varied ecosystems that support Africa's plants and wildlife. Stresses today include poaching, overgrazing, and deforestation.

The Organization of African Unity (OAU) and numerous regional trading blocks try to encourage economic cooperation and political stability, essential for sustained growth. After decades of corruption, ruinous to many economies, Africans now realize that any hope for development lies with themselves and their leaders.

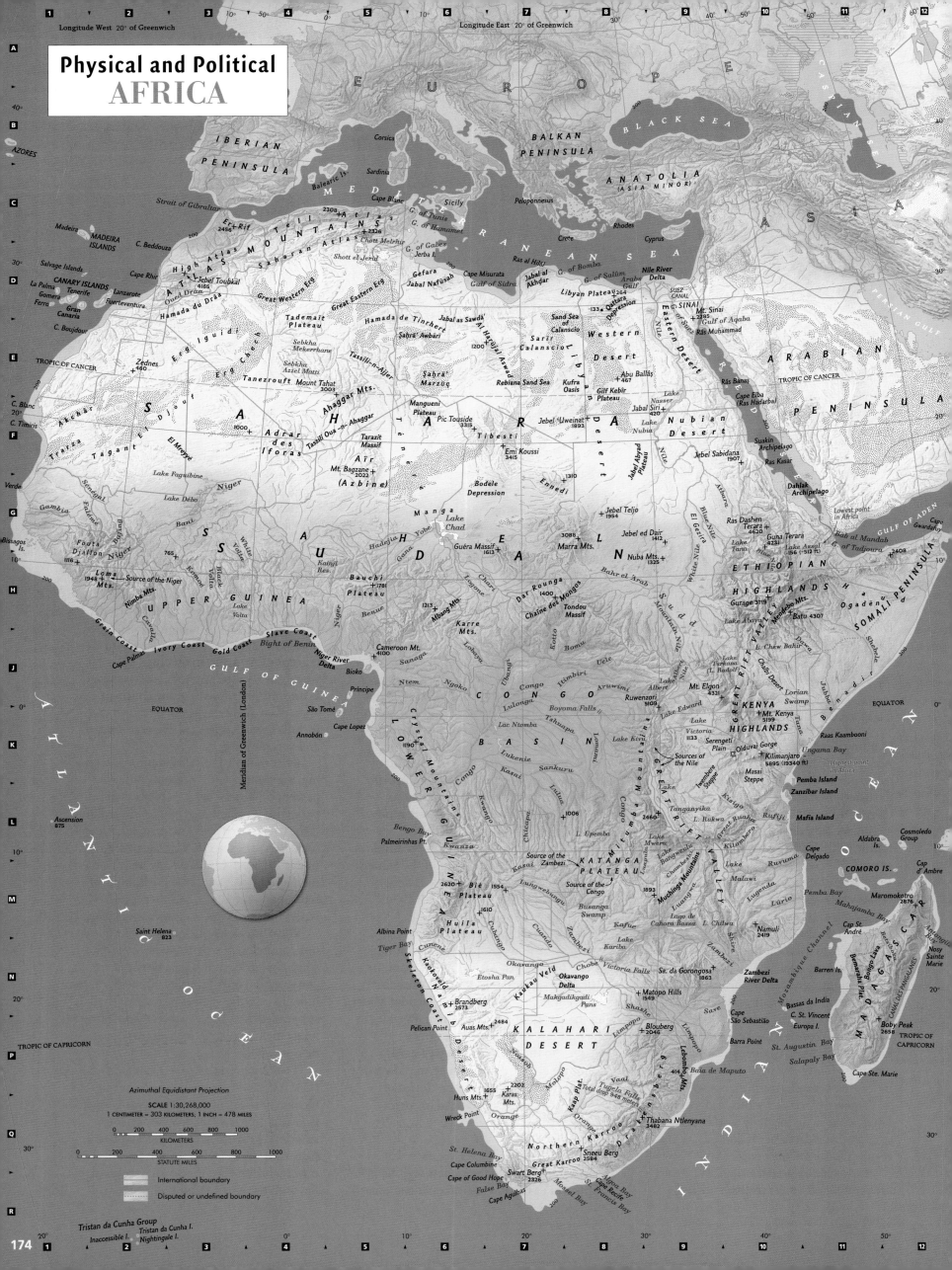

Physical and Political
AFRICA

EUROPE

AZORES

IBERIAN PENINSULA

Corsica

BALKAN PENINSULA

BLACK SEA

CASPIAN SEA

ANATOLIA (ASIA MINOR)

Cape Blanc

Sardinia

Balearic Is.

G. of Tunis

Sicily

Peloponnesus

Rhodes

Cyprus

Strait of Gibraltar

MEDITERRANEAN SEA

Crete

Madeira

MADEIRA ISLANDS

C. Beddouza

Er - Rif 2456

Tell Atlas 2308 +Atlas

Saharan Atlas + 2326

G. of Hammamet

Jerba I. G. of Gabes

Ras al Hilal

Cape Misurata

Gulf of Sidra

G. of Bomba

G. of Salûm

Arabs Gulf

Nile River Delta

SUEZ CANAL

SINAI Mt. Sinai 2285

Gulf of Aqaba

Ras Muhammad

Salvage Islands

CANARY ISLANDS

Cape Rhir

High Atlas

Jebel Toubkal 4165

ATLAS MOUNTAINS

Chott Melrhir

Shott el Jerid

Gefara

Jabal Nafûsah

Jabal al Akhdar

Libyan Plateau -133 +264

Qattara Depression

Eastern Desert

Gulf of Suez

Red

La Palma Gomera Ferro

Gran Canaria

Tenerife

Lanzarote Fuerteventura

C. Boujdour

Hamada du Drâa

Oued Drâa

Great Western Erg

Great Eastern Erg

Jabal as Sawdâ'

Al Haqûf al Aswad

Sand Sea of Calanscio

Western Desert

+ 467 Abu Ballâs

Lake Nasser

TROPIC OF CANCER

Zednes +460

Erg Iguidi

Tademaït Plateau

Hamada de Tinrhert

Sebkha Mekerrhane

Şahrâ' Awbârî

Sarir Calanscio

1200

Kufra Oasis

Gilf Kebir Plateau

Jabal Sîrî 420

Nubian Desert

Lake Nubia

ARABIAN PENINSULA

TROPIC OF CANCER

C. Blanc

C. Timiris

Akchâr

Erg Chech

Sebkha Azzel Matti

Tassili-n-Ajjer

Şahrâ' Marzûq

Rebiana Sand Sea

Ras Banas

Cape Elba (Ras Hadarba)

El Mreyé

Tanezrouft

Mount Tahat 3003

Ahaggar Mts.

Libyan Desert

Jebel 'Uweinat 1893

Suakin Archipelago

Ras Kasar

Trarza

Adrar des Iforas

1000

Mangueni Plateau

Pic Toussidé 3315

Tibesti

Jebel Sabidana 1907

Tagant

Tassili Oua-n-Ahaggar

Tarazit Massif

Dahlak Archipelago

Verde

Lake Faguibine

Aïr

Mt. Bagzane 2022

(Azbine)

Emi Koussi 3415

1310

Ennedi

Jabal Abyad Plateau

Lowest point in Africa

GULF OF ADEN

Cape Gwardafuy

Lake Débo

Niger

Bani

White Volta

Manga

Lake Chad

Bodèlè Depression

Jebel Teljo 1954

3088

Ras Dashen Terara 4620

Guna Terara 4231

Bab al Mandab

G. of Tadjoura 2408

Bissagos Is.

Gambia

Falémé

Senegal

Fouta Djallon

Niger

1116

765

Kainji Res.

Black Volta

Kémou

Hadjeia

Gana

Yobe

Guéra Massif 1613

Chari

Marra Mts.

Jebel ed Dair 1412

Nuba Mts. 1325

El Gezira

White Nile

Blue Nile

Lake Tana

Lake Assal -156 (-512 ft)

ETHIOPIAN

Loma Mts. 1948

Source of the Niger

SUDAN

Bauchi Plateau 1781

Benue

1213

Mbang Mts.

Dar Rounga 1400

Chaine des Mongos

Tondou Massif

Bahr el Arab

Bahr el Ghazal

S u d d

Mountain Nile

Gurage 3719

HIGHLANDS

Mendebo Mts.

Batu 4307

Ogadên

SOMALI PENINSULA

Nimba Mts.

UPPER GUINEA

Lake Volta

Karre Mts.

Togone

Kotto

Lake Abaya

L. Chew Bahir

Dawa

Shebele

Grain Coast

Cavalla

Ivory Coast

Cape Palmas

Gold Coast

Slave Coast

Bight of Benin

Niger River Delta

Cameroon Mt. 4100

Sanaga

Lobaye

Bomu

Uele

Lake Turkana (L. Rudolf)

Chalbi Desert

Lorian Swamp

Jubba

GULF OF GUINEA

Bioko

Principe

São Tomé

Cape Lopez

Annobón

Ntem

Ngoko

Ubangi

Congo

Itimbiri

Aruwimi

Congo

Lake Albert

Mt. Elgon 4321

Ruwenzori 5109

Lake Edward

KENYA HIGHLANDS

+Mt. Kenya 5199

GREAT RIFT VALLEY

Raas Kaambooni

Ungama Bay

EQUATOR

Meridian of Greenwich (London)

CONGO

Lulonga

Boyoma Falls

Lac Ntomba

Tshuapa

Lukenie

Lake Kivu

Lake Victoria 1133

Serengeti Plain

Olduvai Gorge

Highest point in Africa

EQUATOR

1190

LOWER GUINEA

Crystal Mountains

Congo

Kasai

Sankuru

Lomami

Lualaba

Iwembere Steppe

Kilimanjaro 5895 (19340 ft)

Masai Steppe

Pemba Island

Zanzibar Island

Ascension 875

ATLANTIC OCEAN

BASIN

Kasai

Kwango

Chicapa

Lukuga

L. Upemba

Sources of the Nile

Lake Tanganyika

2460

L. Rukwa Ruaha

Great

Kisigo

Rufiji

Mafia Island

Bengo Bay

Palmeirinhas Pt.

Kwanza

L. Mweru

Muchinga Mountains

Bangweulu

Chambeshi

Luangwa

Kilombero

Lake Malawi

Ruvuma

Cape Delgado

COMORO IS.

Cap d'Ambre

Source of the Zambezi

KATANGA PLATEAU

Mitumba Mountains

1893

Lugenda

Lúrio

Aldabra Is.

Cosmoledo Group

Saint Helena 823

2620 Biè 1554 Plateau

Source of the Congo

Busanga Swamp

Kafue

Lago de Cahora Bassa

L. Chilwa

Namuli 2419

Pemba Bay

Maromokotro 2876

1610

Huíla Plateau

Cubango

Cuanza

Zambezi

Lake Kariba

Shire

Mahajamba Bay

Albina Point

Cunene

Okavango

Cuando

Chobe

Victoria Falls

Sa. da Gorongosa 1863

Zambezi River Delta

Barren Is.

Cap St. André

Antongila Bay

Nosy Sainte Marie

Tiger Bay

Skeleton Coast

Etosha Pan

Kaukau Veld

Okavango Delta

Makgadikgadi Pans

Shashe

Save

Cape São Sebastião

Bemaraha Plat.

MADAGASCAR

TROPIC OF CAPRICORN

Brandberg 2573

Kalahari Namib Desert

Matopo Hills 1549

Limpopo

Bassas da India

C. St. Vincent

Europa I.

Barra Point

Boby Peak 2658

TROPIC OF CAPRICORN

Pelican Point

Auas Mts. 2484

KALAHARI DESERT

Blouberg 2046

Limpopo

St. Augustin Bay

Salapaly Bay

Cape Ste. Marie

1655 2202

Huns Mts.

Karas Mts.

Molopo

Vaal

Kaap Plat.

Tugela Falls Total drop 948 meters

414

Lebombo Mts.

Baia de Maputo

Wreck Point

Orange

Orange

Northern Karroo

Drakensberg

Thabana Ntlenyana 3482

MOZAMBIQUE CHANNEL

St. Helena Bay

Cape Columbine

Cape of Good Hope

False Bay

Great Karroo

Swart Berg 2326

Sneeu Berg 2584

St. Francis Bay

Algoa Bay

Cape Recife

Cape Agulhas

Mossel Bay

Azimuthal Equidistant Projection

SCALE 1:30,268,000

1 CENTIMETER = 303 KILOMETERS; 1 INCH = 478 MILES

0 200 400 600 800 1000
KILOMETERS

0 200 400 600 800 1000
STATUTE MILES

International boundary

Disputed or undefined boundary

Tristan da Cunha Group

Inaccessible I. Tristan da Cunha I.

Nightingale I.

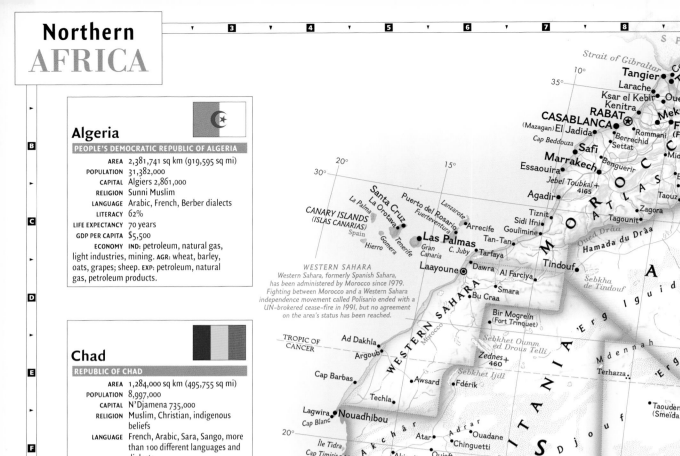

Algeria
PEOPLE'S DEMOCRATIC REPUBLIC OF ALGERIA
- **AREA** 2,381,741 sq km (919,595 sq mi)
- **POPULATION** 31,382,000
- **CAPITAL** Algiers 2,861,000
- **RELIGION** Sunni Muslim
- **LANGUAGE** Arabic, French, Berber dialects
- **LITERACY** 62%
- **LIFE EXPECTANCY** 70 years
- **GDP PER CAPITA** $5,500
- **ECONOMY IND:** petroleum, natural gas, light industries, mining. **AGR:** wheat, barley, oats, grapes; sheep. **EXP:** petroleum, natural gas, petroleum products.

Chad
REPUBLIC OF CHAD
- **AREA** 1,284,000 sq km (495,755 sq mi)
- **POPULATION** 8,997,000
- **CAPITAL** N'Djamena 735,000
- **RELIGION** Muslim, Christian, indigenous beliefs
- **LANGUAGE** French, Arabic, Sara, Sango, more than 100 different languages and dialects
- **LITERACY** 48%
- **LIFE EXPECTANCY** 51 years
- **GDP PER CAPITA** $1,000
- **ECONOMY IND:** cotton textiles, meat packing, beer brewing, natron (sodium carbonate). **AGR:** cotton, sorghum, millet, peanuts; cattle. **EXP:** cotton, cattle, textiles.

Egypt
ARAB REPUBLIC OF EGYPT
- **AREA** 1,001,449 sq km (386,662 sq mi)
- **POPULATION** 71,244,000
- **CAPITAL** Cairo 9,586,000
- **RELIGION** Sunni Muslim, Coptic Christian
- **LANGUAGE** Arabic, English, French
- **LITERACY** 51%
- **LIFE EXPECTANCY** 64 years
- **GDP PER CAPITA** $3,600
- **ECONOMY IND:** textiles, food processing, tourism, chemicals. **AGR:** cotton, rice, corn, wheat; cattle. **EXP:** crude oil and petroleum, cotton, textiles, metal products.

Gambia
REPUBLIC OF THE GAMBIA
- **AREA** 11,295 sq km (4,361 sq mi)
- **POPULATION** 1,456,000
- **CAPITAL** Banjul 418,000
- **RELIGION** Muslim, Christian
- **LANGUAGE** English, Mandinka, Wolof, Fula
- **LITERACY** 48%
- **LIFE EXPECTANCY** 54 years
- **GDP PER CAPITA** $1,100
- **ECONOMY IND:** processing peanuts, fish and hides, tourism, beverages. **AGR:** peanuts, millet, sorghum, rice; cattle. **EXP:** peanuts and peanut products, fish, cotton lint, palm kernels.

Libya
GREAT SOCIALIST PEOPLE'S LIBYAN ARAB JAMAHIRIYA
- **AREA** 1,759,540 sq km (679,362 sq mi)
- **POPULATION** 5,369,000
- **CAPITAL** Tripoli 1,776,000
- **RELIGION** Sunni Muslim
- **LANGUAGE** Arabic, Italian, English
- **LITERACY** 76%
- **LIFE EXPECTANCY** 76 years
- **GDP PER CAPITA** $8,900
- **ECONOMY IND:** petroleum, food processing, textiles, handicrafts. **AGR:** wheat, barley, olives, dates; sheep. **EXP:** crude oil, refined petroleum products.

Mali
REPUBLIC OF MALI
- **AREA** 1,240,192 sq km (478,841 sq mi)
- **POPULATION** 11,340,000
- **CAPITAL** Bamako 1,161,000
- **RELIGION** Muslim, indigenous beliefs
- **LANGUAGE** French, Bambara, numerous African languages
- **LITERACY** 31%
- **LIFE EXPECTANCY** 47 years
- **GDP PER CAPITA** $850
- **ECONOMY IND:** minor local consumer good production and food processing, construction, textiles, gold mining. **AGR:** cotton, millet, rice, corn; cattle. **EXP:** cotton, gold, livestock.

Mauritania
ISLAMIC REPUBLIC OF MAURITANIA
- **AREA** 1,030,700 sq km (397,955 sq mi)
- **POPULATION** 2,635,000
- **CAPITAL** Nouakchott 626,000
- **RELIGION** Muslim
- **LANGUAGE** Hasaniya Arabic, Wolof, Pular, Soninke, French
- **LITERACY** 47%
- **LIFE EXPECTANCY** 51 years
- **GDP PER CAPITA** $2,000
- **ECONOMY IND:** fish processing, mining of iron ore and gypsum. **AGR:** dates, millet, sorghum, rice; cattle. **EXP:** iron ore, fish and fish products, gold.

Morocco
KINGDOM OF MOROCCO
- **AREA** 712,550 sq km (275,117 sq mi)
- **POPULATION** 29,662,000
- **CAPITAL** Rabat 1,668,000
- **RELIGION** Muslim
- **LANGUAGE** Arabic, Berber dialects, French
- **LITERACY** 44%
- **LIFE EXPECTANCY** 69 years
- **GDP PER CAPITA** $3,500
- **ECONOMY IND:** phosphate rock mining and processing, food processing, leather goods, textiles. **AGR:** barley, wheat, citrus, wine; livestock. **EXP:** phosphates and fertilizers, food and beverages, minerals.

Niger
REPUBLIC OF NIGER
- **AREA** 1,267,000 sq km (489,191 sq mi)
- **POPULATION** 11,641,000
- **CAPITAL** Niamey 821,000
- **RELIGION** Muslim, indigenous beliefs, Christian
- **LANGUAGE** French, Hausa, Djerma
- **LITERACY** 14%
- **LIFE EXPECTANCY** 42 years
- **GDP PER CAPITA** $1,000
- **ECONOMY IND:** uranium mining, cement, brick, textiles. **AGR:** cowpeas, cotton, peanuts, millet; cattle. **EXP:** uranium ore, livestock products, cowpeas, onions.

Western Sahara, formerly Spanish Sahara, has been administered by Morocco since 1979. Fighting between Morocco and a Western Sahara independence movement called Polisario ended with a UN-brokered cease-fire in 1991, but no agreement on the area's status has been reached.

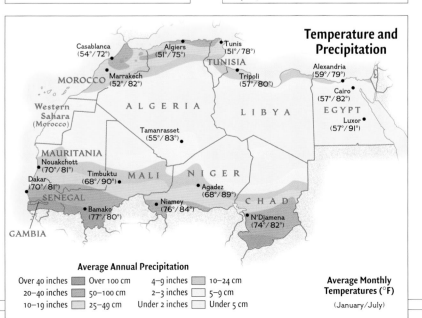

Temperature and Precipitation

Casablanca (54°/72°)
Algiers (51°/75°)
Tunis (51°/78°)
Alexandria (59°/79°)
Marrakech (52°/82°)
Tripoli (57°/80°)
Cairo (57°/82°)
Tamanrasset (55°/83°)
Luxor (57°/91°)
Nouakchott (70°/81°)
Timbuktu (68°/90°)
Dakar (70°/84°)
Niamey (76°/84°)
Agadez (68°/89°)
Bamako (77°/80°)
N'Djamena (74°/82°)

Average Annual Precipitation

Over 40 inches	Over 100 cm	4–9 inches	10–24 cm
20–40 inches	50–100 cm	2–3 inches	5–9 cm
10–19 inches	25–49 cm	Under 2 inches	Under 5 cm

Average Monthly Temperatures (°F)

(January/July)

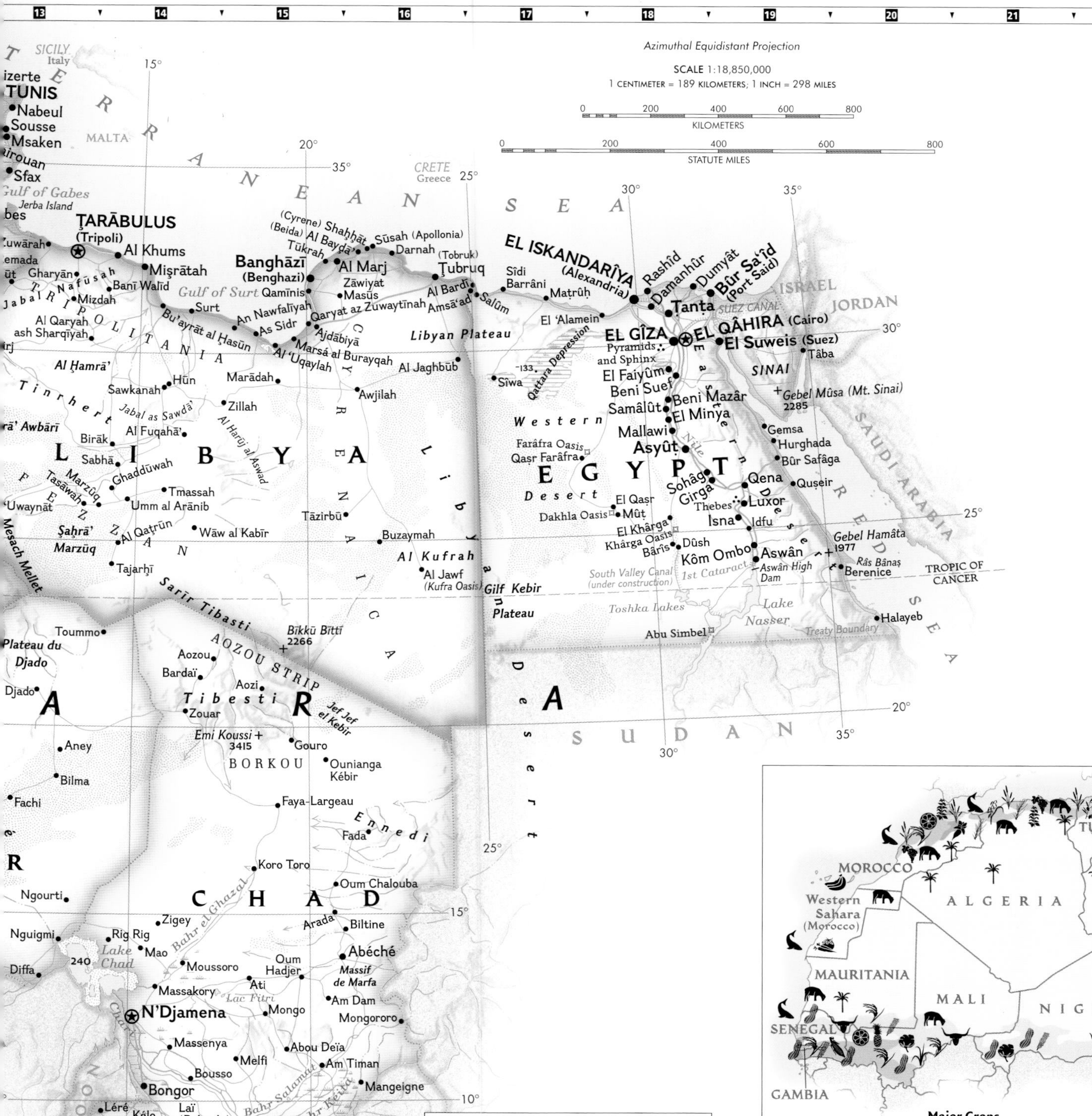

Azimuthal Equidistant Projection

SCALE 1:18,850,000
1 CENTIMETER = 189 KILOMETERS; 1 INCH = 298 MILES

0 200 400 600 800
KILOMETERS

0 200 400 600 800
STATUTE MILES

Map labels

SICILY
Italy
Bizerte
TUNIS
Nabeul
Sousse
Msaken
Kairouan
Sfax
Gulf of Gabes
Jerba Island
bes
MALTA

MEDITERRANEAN SEA

CRETE
Greece

TARĀBULUS
(Tripoli)
Al Khums
Mişrātah
Banghāzī
(Benghazi)
Al Marj
Zāwiyat
Qamīnis
Masūs
Bu'ayrāt al Ḥasūn
As Sidr
Ajdābiyā
Marsá al Burayqah
Al 'Uqaylah
An Nawfalīyah
Surt
Qaryat az Zūwaytīnah
Suwārah
'emada
Gharyān
Al Qaryah ash Sharqīyah
Banī Walīd
Mizdah
Al Hamrā'
Jabal Nafūsah
Tarhūnah

(Cyrene) Shaḥḥāt Sūsah (Apollonia)
(Beida) Al Bayḍā'
Tūkrah
Darnah (Tobruk)
Tubruq
Sīdi Barrāni
Salūm
Amsā'ad
Al Bardī
Matrūḥ
El 'Alamein

EL ISKANDARĪYA
(Alexandria)
Rashīd
Damanhūr
Dumyāṭ
Būr Sa'īd
(Port Said)
Tanta
Suez Canal
EL QÂHIRA (Cairo)
EL GÎZA
El Suweis (Suez)
Ṭâba

ISRAEL
JORDAN
SINAI
+ Gebel Mûsa (Mt. Sinai)
2285
SAUDI ARABIA
RED SEA

Libyan Plateau
Qattara Depression
-133
Sîwa
Pyramids and Sphinx
El Faiyûm
Beni Suef
Samâlût
Mallawi
Asyût
Sohâg
Girga
Thebes
Qena
Luxor
Isna
Idfu
El Qasr
Dakhla Oasis
Mût
El Khârga
Khârga Oasis
Bâris
Dûsh
Kôm Ombo
Aswân
Aswân High Dam
1st Cataract

Beni Mazâr
El Minya
Gemsa
Hurghada
Bûr Safâga
Qusêir
Gebel Ḥamâta
1977
Râs Bânas
Berenice

LIBYA
EGYPT
Western Desert
Farâfra Oasis
Qasr Farâfra

Al Jaghbūb
Awjilah
Marādah
Zillah
Ḥūn
Sawknah
Al Fuqahā'
Maradah
Buzaymah
Al Kufrah
Al Jawf (Kufra Oasis)

Jabal as Sawdā'
Al Harūj al Aswad
Waddān
Jālū
Tāzirbū

Gharyān
Ghaddūwah
Umm al Arānib
Tmassah
Al Qaṭrūn
Wāw al Kabīr
Murzuq
Tajarhī

Sabhā
Tasāwah
Birāk
Ghāt
'Awbārī

Sebha
Mizdah

TROPIC OF CANCER

South Valley Canal (under construction)
Gilf Kebir Plateau
Toshka Lakes
Abu Simbel
Lake Nasser
Halayeb
Treaty Boundary

SUDAN

Toummo
Plateau du Djado
Djado
AOZOU STRIP
Aozou
Bardaï
Aozi
Zouar
Tibesti
Jef Jef el Kebir
Emi Koussi + 3415
Gouro
Bïkkū Bïttï 2266
Ounianga Kébir
BORKOU
Faya-Largeau
Fada
Ennedi
Koro Toro
Oum Chalouba
Arada
Biltine
Abéché
Massif de Marfa
Am Dam
Mongororo

CHAD

Aney
Bilma
Fachi
Ngourti
Nguigmi
Rig Rig
Mao
Zigey
Lake Chad
240
Diffa
Moussoro
Massakory
Ati
Oum Hadjer
Mongo
Lac Fitri

N'Djamena
Massenya
Bousso
Melfi
Bongor
Abou Deïa
Am Timan
Mangeigne
Léré
Kélo
Laï (Behagle)
Palaï
Koumra
Sarh
Bahr Salamat
Moundou
Doba
Moïssala
Baïbokoum
Goré
CAMEROON
CENTRAL AFRICAN REPUBLIC
Bahr el Ghazal
Bahr Aouk
Bahr Keïta

Tunisia

REPUBLIC OF TUNISIA

AREA 163,610 sq km (63,170 sq mi)
POPULATION 9,782,000
CAPITAL Tunis 1,927,000
RELIGION Muslim
LANGUAGE Arabic, French
LITERACY 67%
LIFE EXPECTANCY 74 years
GDP PER CAPITA $6,500
ECONOMY IND: petroleum, mining, tourism, textiles, footwear. AGR: olives, olive oil, grain, dairy products. EXP: textiles, mechanical goods, phosphates and chemicals, agricultural products.

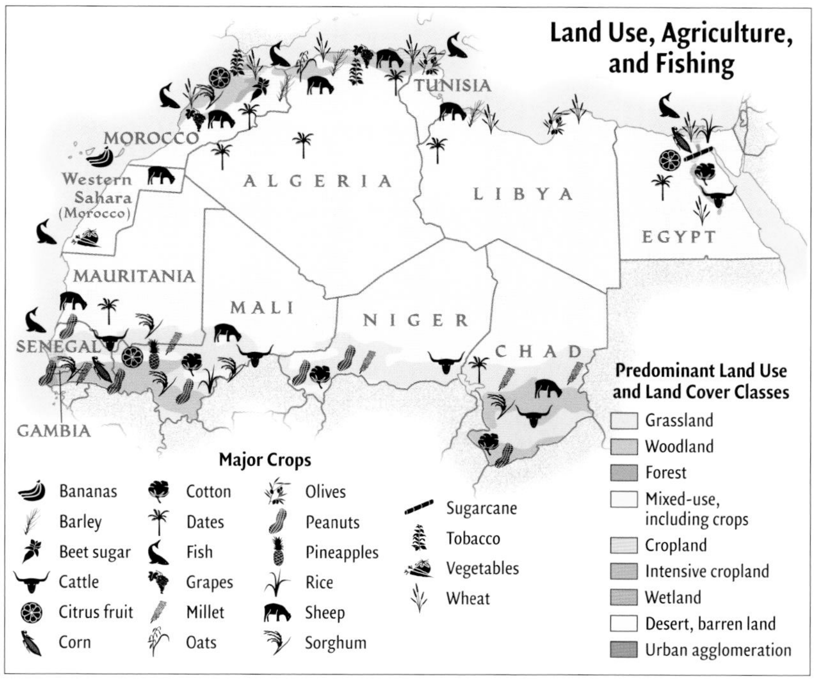

Senegal

REPUBLIC OF SENEGAL

AREA 196,722 sq km (75,955 sq mi)
POPULATION 9,908,000
CAPITAL Dakar 2,160,000
RELIGION Muslim, indigenous beliefs
LANGUAGE French, Wolof, Pulaar, Diola, Jola, Mandinka
LITERACY 33%
LIFE EXPECTANCY 63 years
GDP PER CAPITA $1,600
ECONOMY IND: agricultural and fish processing, phosphate mining, fertilizer production, petroleum refining. AGR: peanuts, millet, corn, sorghum; cattle; fish. EXP: fish, ground nuts, petroleum products, phosphates.

Land Use, Agriculture, and Fishing

TUNISIA
MOROCCO
Western Sahara (Morocco)
ALGERIA
LIBYA
EGYPT
MAURITANIA
MALI
NIGER
CHAD
SENEGAL
GAMBIA

Major Crops

Bananas
Barley
Beet sugar
Cattle
Citrus fruit
Corn
Cotton
Dates
Fish
Grapes
Millet
Oats
Olives
Peanuts
Pineapples
Rice
Sheep
Sorghum
Sugarcane
Tobacco
Vegetables
Wheat

Predominant Land Use and Land Cover Classes

Grassland
Woodland
Forest
Mixed-use, including crops
Cropland
Intensive cropland
Wetland
Desert, barren land
Urban agglomeration

Industry and Mining

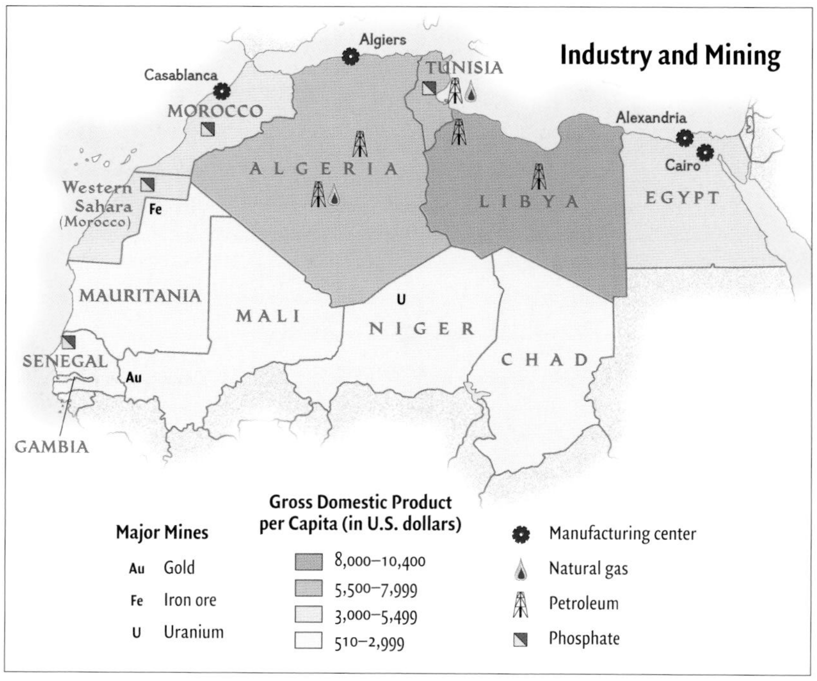

Algiers
Casablanca
TUNISIA
MOROCCO
Western Sahara (Morocco)
Fe
ALGERIA
LIBYA
Alexandria
Cairo
EGYPT
MAURITANIA
MALI
NIGER
CHAD
SENEGAL
GAMBIA
Au
U

Major Mines

Au Gold
Fe Iron ore
U Uranium

Gross Domestic Product per Capita (in U.S. dollars)

8,000–10,400
5,500–7,999
3,000–5,499
510–2,999

Manufacturing center
Natural gas
Petroleum
Phosphate

Population

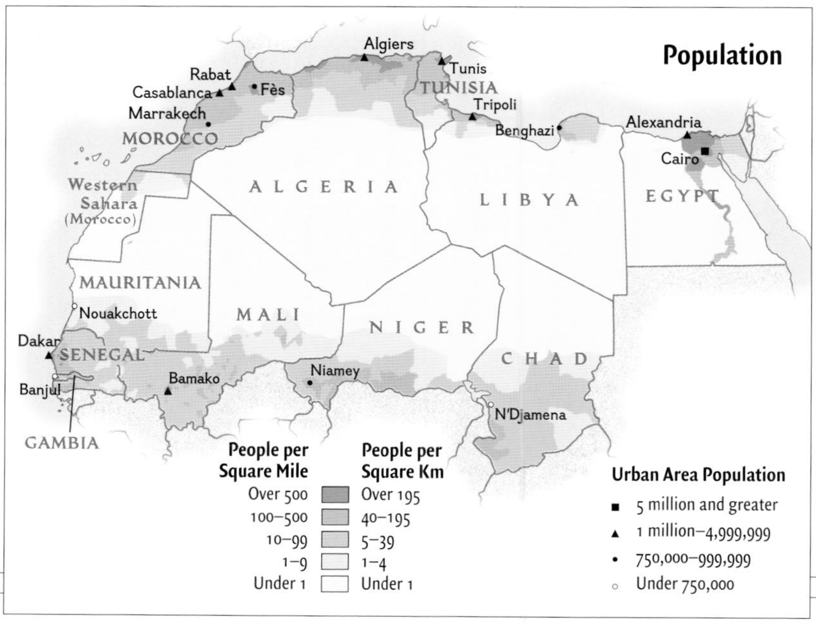

Algiers
Rabat
Casablanca
Fès
Tunis
Tripoli
Benghazi
Marrakech
MOROCCO
TUNISIA
Alexandria
Cairo
Western Sahara (Morocco)
ALGERIA
LIBYA
EGYPT
MAURITANIA
Nouakchott
MALI
NIGER
CHAD
Dakar
SENEGAL
Bamako
Niamey
Banjul
GAMBIA
N'Djamena

People per Square Mile

Over 500
100–500
10–99
1–9
Under 1

People per Square Km

Over 195
40–195
5–39
1–4
Under 1

Urban Area Population

5 million and greater
1 million–4,999,999
750,000–999,999
Under 750,000

Djibouti
REPUBLIC OF DJIBOUTI

AREA	23,200 sq km (8,958 sq mi)
POPULATION	652,000
CAPITAL	Djibouti 542,000
RELIGION	Muslim, Christian
LANGUAGE	French, Arabic, Somali, Afar
LITERACY	46%
LIFE EXPECTANCY	51 years
GDP PER CAPITA	$1,300
ECONOMY	IND: small-scale enterprises (dairy products, mineral-water bottling). AGR: fruits, vegetables; goats. EXP: reexports, hides and skins, coffee.

Burundi
REPUBLIC OF BURUNDI

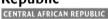

AREA	27,834 sq km (10,747 sq mi)
POPULATION	6,688,000
CAPITAL	Bujumbura 346,000
RELIGION	Roman Catholic, indigenous beliefs, Protestant, Muslim
LANGUAGE	Kirundi, French, Swahili
LITERACY	35%
LIFE EXPECTANCY	46 years
GDP PER CAPITA	$720
ECONOMY	IND: light consumer goods (blankets, shoes, soap), assembly of imported components. AGR: coffee, cotton, tea, corn; beef. EXP: coffee, tea, sugar, cotton.

Central African Republic
CENTRAL AFRICAN REPUBLIC

AREA	622,984 sq km (240,535 sq mi)
POPULATION	3,643,000
CAPITAL	Bangui 666,000
RELIGION	Protestant, Roman Catholic, indigenous beliefs, Muslim
LANGUAGE	French, Sango, Arabic, Hunsa, Swahili
LITERACY	60%
LIFE EXPECTANCY	44 years
GDP PER CAPITA	$1,700
ECONOMY	IND: diamond mining, sawmills, breweries, textiles. AGR: cotton, coffee, tobacco, manioc (tapioca); timber. EXP: food, textiles, petroleum products, machinery.

Congo,
Democratic Republic of the
DEMOCRATIC REPUBLIC OF THE CONGO

AREA	2,345,409 sq km (905,568 sq mi)
POPULATION	55,225,000
CAPITAL	Kinshasa 5,253,000
RELIGION	Roman Catholic, Protestant, Kimbanguist, Muslim, traditional
LANGUAGE	French, Lingala, Kingwana, Kikongo, Tshiluba
LITERACY	77%
LIFE EXPECTANCY	49 years
GDP PER CAPITA	$600
ECONOMY	IND: mining (diamonds, copper), mineral processing, consumer products. AGR: coffee, sugar, palm oil, rubber; wood products. EXP: diamonds, copper, coffee, cobalt.

Eritrea
STATE OF ERITREA

AREA	121,320 sq km (46,842 sq mi)
POPULATION	4,466,000
CAPITAL	Asmara 503,000
RELIGION	Muslim, Coptic Christian, Roman Catholic, Protestant
LANGUAGE	Afar, Arabic, Tigre, Kunama, Tigrinya
LITERACY	NA
LIFE EXPECTANCY	56 years
GDP PER CAPITA	$710
ECONOMY	IND: food processing, beverages, clothing and textiles. AGR: sorghum, lentils, vegetables, corn; livestock; fish. EXP: livestock, sorghum, textiles, food.

Ethiopia
FEDERAL DEMOCRATIC REPUBLIC OF ETHIOPIA

AREA	1,100,574 sq km (424,934 sq mi)
POPULATION	67,673,000
CAPITAL	Addis Ababa 2,753,000
RELIGION	Muslim, Ethiopian Orthodox, animist
LANGUAGE	Amharic, Tigrinya, Orominga, Guaraginga, Somali, Arabic
LITERACY	36%
LIFE EXPECTANCY	45 years
GDP PER CAPITA	$600
ECONOMY	IND: food processing, beverages, textiles, chemicals. AGR: cereals, pulses, coffee, oilseed; hides. EXP: coffee, gold, leather products, oilseeds.

Kenya
REPUBLIC OF KENYA

AREA	592,747 sq km (228,861 sq mi)
POPULATION	31,139,000
CAPITAL	Nairobi 2,343,000
RELIGION	Protestant, Roman Catholic, indigenous beliefs, Muslim
LANGUAGE	English, Kiswahili, indigenous languages
LITERACY	78%
LIFE EXPECTANCY	47 years
GDP PER CAPITA	$1,500
ECONOMY	IND: small scale consumer goods (plastic, furniture), agricultural products processing, oil refining. AGR: coffee, tea, corn, wheat; dairy products. EXP: tea, coffee, horticultural products, petroleum products.

Temperature and Precipitation

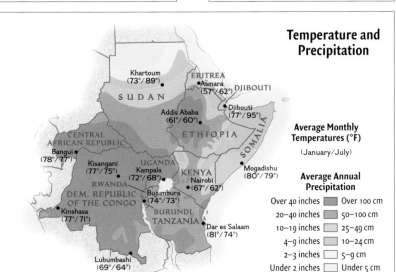

Khartoum	(73°/89°)	
Asmara	(57°/62°)	
Addis Ababa	(61°/60°)	
Djibouti	(77°/95°)	
Bangui	(78°/77°)	
Kisangani	(77°/75°)	
Kampala	(72°/68°)	
Nairobi	(67°/62°)	
Mogadishu	(80°/79°)	
Bujumbura	(74°/73°)	
Dar es Salaam	(81°/74°)	
Kinshasa	(77°/71°)	
Lubumbashi	(69°/64°)	

Average Monthly Temperatures (°F)
(January/July)

Average Annual Precipitation

Over 40 inches	Over 100 cm
20–40 inches	50–100 cm
10–19 inches	25–49 cm
4–9 inches	10–24 cm
2–3 inches	5–9 cm
Under 2 inches	Under 5 cm

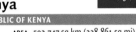

Azimuthal Equidistant Projection

SCALE 1:18,454,000
1 CENTIMETER = 185 KILOMETERS; 1 INCH = 291 MILES

KILOMETERS
STATUTE MILES

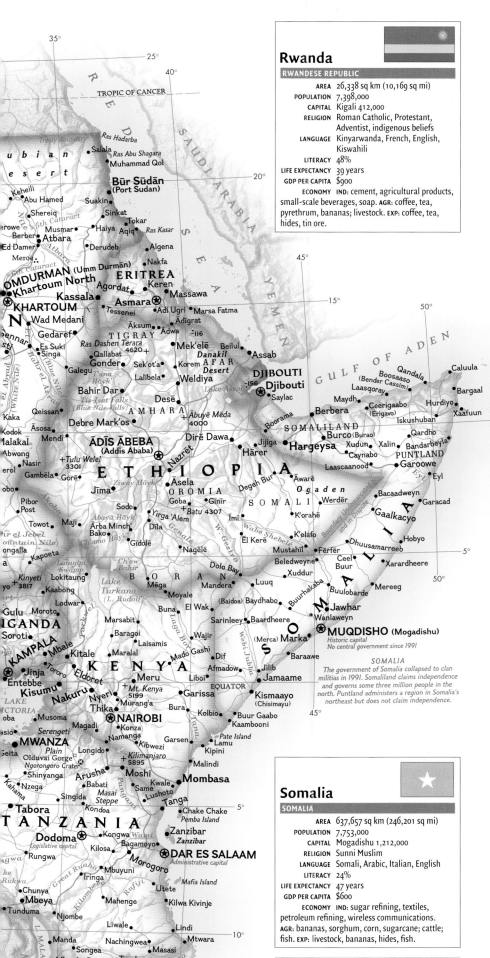

Rwanda
RWANDESE REPUBLIC
AREA	26,338 sq km (10,169 sq mi)
POPULATION	7,398,000
CAPITAL	Kigali 412,000
RELIGION	Roman Catholic, Protestant, Adventist, indigenous beliefs
LANGUAGE	Kinyarwanda, French, English, Kiswahili
LITERACY	48%
LIFE EXPECTANCY	39 years
GDP PER CAPITA	$900
ECONOMY	IND: cement, agricultural products, small-scale beverages, soap. AGR: coffee, tea, pyrethrum, bananas; livestock. EXP: coffee, tea, hides, tin ore.

Tanzania
UNITED REPUBLIC OF TANZANIA
AREA	945,087 sq km (364,900 sq mi)
POPULATION	37,188,000
CAPITAL	Dar Es Salaam (administrative) 2,115,000; Dodoma (legislative) 180,000
RELIGION	Christian, Muslim, indigenous beliefs
LANGUAGE	Swahili, English, Arabic, many local languages
LITERACY	68%
LIFE EXPECTANCY	52 years
GDP PER CAPITA	$710
ECONOMY	IND: agricultural processing (sugar, beer), diamond and gold mining, oil refining. AGR: coffee, sisal, tea, cotton; cattle. EXP: coffee, manufactured goods, cotton, cashew nuts.

Uganda
REPUBLIC OF UGANDA
AREA	236,036 sq km (91,134 sq mi)
POPULATION	24,699,000
CAPITAL	Kampala 1,274,000
RELIGION	Roman Catholic, Protestant, indigenous beliefs, Muslim
LANGUAGE	English, Ganda or Luganda, many local languages
LITERACY	62%
LIFE EXPECTANCY	43 years
GDP PER CAPITA	$1,100
ECONOMY	IND: sugar, brewing, tobacco, cotton textiles. AGR: coffee, tea, tobacco, cassava (tapioca); beef. EXP: coffee, fish and fish products, tea, electrical products.

Somalia
SOMALIA
AREA	637,657 sq km (246,201 sq mi)
POPULATION	7,753,000
CAPITAL	Mogadishu 1,212,000
RELIGION	Sunni Muslim
LANGUAGE	Somali, Arabic, Italian, English
LITERACY	24%
LIFE EXPECTANCY	47 years
GDP PER CAPITA	$600
ECONOMY	IND: sugar refining, textiles, petroleum refining, wireless communications. AGR: bananas, sorghum, corn, sugarcane; cattle; fish. EXP: livestock, bananas, hides, fish.

Sudan
REPUBLIC OF THE SUDAN
AREA	2,495,712 sq km (963,600 sq mi)
POPULATION	32,559,000
CAPITAL	Khartoum 2,853,000
RELIGION	Sunni Muslim, indigenous beliefs, Christian
LANGUAGE	Arabic, Nubian, Ta Bedawie, many local dialects
LITERACY	46%
LIFE EXPECTANCY	57 years
GDP PER CAPITA	$1,000
ECONOMY	IND: agricultural processing (sugar, beer), gold mining, oil refining, shoes. AGR: coffee, sisal, tea, cotton; cattle. EXP: coffee, manufactured goods, cotton, cashew nuts.

SOMALIA
The government of Somalia collapsed to clan militias in 1991. Somaliland claims independence and governs some three million people in the north. Puntland administers a region in Somalia's northeast but does not claim independence.

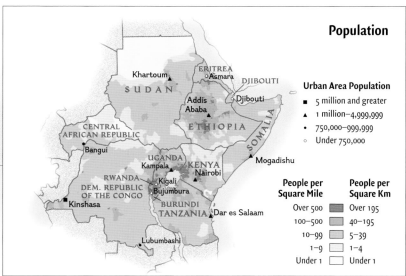

Population
Urban Area Population
- ■ 5 million and greater
- ▲ 1 million–4,999,999
- ● 750,000–999,999
- ○ Under 750,000

People per Square Mile	People per Square Km
Over 500	Over 195
100–500	40–195
10–99	5–39
1–9	1–4
Under 1	Under 1

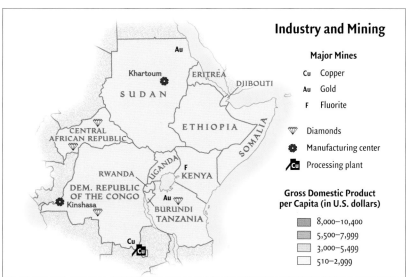

Industry and Mining
Major Mines
- Cu Copper
- Au Gold
- F Fluorite
- ▽ Diamonds
- ⚙ Manufacturing center
- Cu Processing plant

Gross Domestic Product per Capita (in U.S. dollars)
- 8,000–10,400
- 5,500–7,999
- 3,000–5,499
- 510–2,999

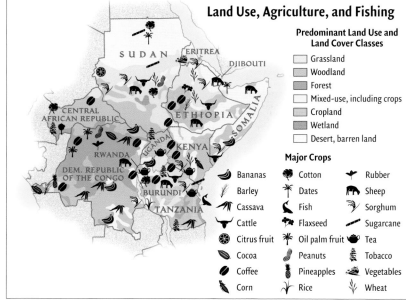
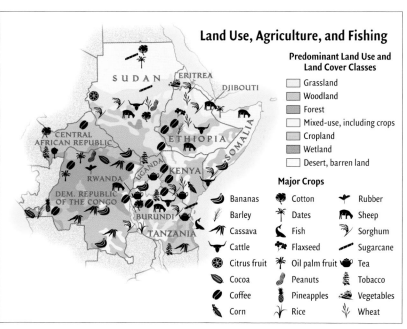

Land Use, Agriculture, and Fishing
Predominant Land Use and Land Cover Classes
- Grassland
- Woodland
- Forest
- Mixed-use, including crops
- Cropland
- Wetland
- Desert, barren land

Major Crops
Bananas	Cotton	Rubber
Barley	Dates	Sheep
Cassava	Fish	Sorghum
Cattle	Flaxseed	Sugarcane
Citrus fruit	Oil palm fruit	Tea
Cocoa	Peanuts	Tobacco
Coffee	Pineapples	Vegetables
Corn	Rice	Wheat

Azimuthal Equidistant Projection

SCALE 1:13,485,000
1 CENTIMETER = 135 KILOMETERS; 1 INCH = 213 MILES

KILOMETERS

STATUTE MILES

Benin
REPUBLIC OF BENIN
AREA	112,622 sq km (43,484 sq mi)
POPULATION	6,629,000
CAPITAL	Porto-Novo, 225,000,
RELIGION	Indigenous beliefs, Christian, Muslim
LANGUAGE	French, Fon, Yoruba, tribal languages
LITERACY	38%
LIFE EXPECTANCY	50 years
GDP PER CAPITA	$1,030

ECONOMY IND: textiles, cigarettes, beverages, food. AGR: corn, sorghum, cassava (tapioca), yams; poultry. EXP: cotton, crude oil, palm products, cocoa.

Burkina Faso
BURKINA FASO
AREA	274,200 sq km (105,869 sq mi)
POPULATION	12,603,000
CAPITAL	Ouagadougou 862,000
RELIGION	Muslim, indigenous beliefs, Roman Catholic
LANGUAGE	French, tribal languages
LITERACY	19%
LIFE EXPECTANCY	46 years
GDP PER CAPITA	$1,000

ECONOMY IND: cotton lint, beverages, agricultural processing, soap. AGR: peanuts, shea nuts, sesame, cotton; livestock. EXP: cotton, animal products, gold.

Cameroon
REPUBLIC OF CAMEROON
AREA	475,442 sq km (183,569 sq mi)
POPULATION	16,185,000
CAPITAL	Yaoundé 1,481,000
RELIGION	Indigenous beliefs, Christian, Muslim
LANGUAGE	French, English, 24 major African language groups
LITERACY	63%
LIFE EXPECTANCY	55 years
GDP PER CAPITA	$1,700

ECONOMY IND: petroleum production and refining, food processing, light consumer goods, textiles. AGR: coffee, cocoa, cotton, rubber; livestock. EXP: crude oil and petroleum products, lumber, cocoa beans, aluminum.

Côte d'Ivoire
REPUBLIC OF CÔTE D'IVOIRE
AREA	322,463 sq km (124,504 sq mi)
POPULATION	16,805,000
CAPITAL	Abidjan (administrative) 3,956,000; Yamoussoukro (legislative) 110,000
RELIGION	Christian, Muslim, indigenous beliefs
LANGUAGE	French, Dioula, 60 native languages
LITERACY	49%
LIFE EXPECTANCY	45 years
GDP PER CAPITA	$1,600

ECONOMY IND: mining, mineral processing, consumer products, cement. AGR: coffee, sugar, palm oil, rubber; wood products. EXP: diamonds, copper, coffee, cobalt.

Gabon
GABONESE REPUBLIC
AREA	267,667 sq km (103,347 sq mi)
POPULATION	1,233,000
CAPITAL	Libreville 573,000
RELIGION	Christian, indigenous beliefs
LANGUAGE	French, Fang, Myene, Bateke, Bapounou/Eschira, Bandjabi
LITERACY	63%
LIFE EXPECTANCY	50 years
GDP PER CAPITA	$6,300

ECONOMY IND: food and beverage, textile, lumbering and plywood, cement. AGR: cocoa, coffee, sugar, palm oil; cattle; okoume; fish. EXP: crude oil, timber, manganese, uranium.

Guinea
REPUBLIC OF GUINEA
AREA	245,857 sq km (94,926 sq mi)
POPULATION	8,381,000
CAPITAL	Conakry 1,272,000
RELIGION	Muslim, Christian, indigenous beliefs
LANGUAGE	French, tribal languages
LITERACY	36%
LIFE EXPECTANCY	46 years
GDP PER CAPITA	$1,300

ECONOMY IND: bauxite, gold, diamonds, light manufacturing. AGR: rice, coffee, pineapples, palm kernels; cattle; timber. EXP: bauxite, alumina, gold, diamonds.

Congo
REPUBLIC OF THE CONGO
AREA	342,000 sq km (132,047 sq mi)
POPULATION	3,206,000
CAPITAL	Brazzaville 1,360,000
RELIGION	Christian, animist, Muslim
LANGUAGE	French, Lingala, Monokutuba, many local languages, dialects
LITERACY	75%
LIFE EXPECTANCY	48 years
GDP PER CAPITA	$1,100

ECONOMY IND: petroleum extraction, cement kilning, lumbering, brewing. AGR: cassava (tapioca), sugar, rice, corn; forest products. EXP: petroleum products, capital equipment, construction materials, foodstuffs.

Equatorial Guinea
REPUBLIC OF EQUATORIAL GUINEA
AREA	28,051 sq km (10,831 sq mi)
POPULATION	483,000
CAPITAL	Malabo 33,000
RELIGION	Roman Catholic, pagan practices
LANGUAGE	Spanish, French, pidgin English, Fang, Bubi, Ibo
LITERACY	79%
LIFE EXPECTANCY	54 years
GDP PER CAPITA	$2,000

ECONOMY IND: petroleum, fishing, sawmiling, natural gas. AGR: coffee, cocoa, rice, yams; livestock; timber. EXP: petroleum, timber, cocoa.

Ghana
REPUBLIC OF GHANA
AREA	238,537 sq km (92,100 sq mi)
POPULATION	20,244,000
CAPITAL	Accra 1,925,000
RELIGION	Indigenous beliefs, Muslim, Christian
LANGUAGE	English, Akan, Moshi-Dagomba, Ewe, Ga
LITERACY	65%
LIFE EXPECTANCY	57 years
GDP PER CAPITA	$1,900

ECONOMY IND: mining, lumbering, light manufacturing, aluminum smelting. AGR: cocoa, rice, coffee, cassava (tapioca); timber. EXP: gold, cocoa, timber, tuna.

Guinea-Bissau
REPUBLIC OF GUINEA-BISSAU
AREA	36,125 sq km (13,948 sq mi)
POPULATION	1,257,000
CAPITAL	Bissau 292,000
RELIGION	Indigenous beliefs, Muslim, Christian
LANGUAGE	Portuguese, Crioulo, African languages
LITERACY	54%
LIFE EXPECTANCY	49 years
GDP PER CAPITA	$850

ECONOMY IND: agricultural products processing, beer, soft drinks. AGR: rice, corn, beans, cassava (tapioca); timber; fish. EXP: cashew nuts, shrimp, peanuts, palm kernels.

Liberia
REPUBLIC OF LIBERIA

AREA	111,369 sq km (43,000 sq mi)
POPULATION	3,288,000
CAPITAL	Monrovia 491,000
RELIGION	Indigenous beliefs, Muslim, Christian
LANGUAGE	English, tribal languages
LITERACY	38%
LIFE EXPECTANCY	51 years
GDP PER CAPITA	$1,100
ECONOMY	IND: rubber processing, palm oil processing, diamonds. AGR: rubber, coffee, cocoa, rice; sheep; timber. EXP: diamonds, iron ore, rubber, timber.

Sierra Leone
REPUBLIC OF SIERRA LEONE

AREA	71,740 sq km (27,699 sq mi)
POPULATION	5,615,000
CAPITAL	Freetown 837,000
RELIGION	Muslim, indigenous beliefs, Christian
LANGUAGE	English, Mende, Temne, Krio
LITERACY	31%
LIFE EXPECTANCY	46 years
GDP PER CAPITA	$510
ECONOMY	IND: diamond mining, small-scale manufacturing (beverages, textiles), petroleum refining. AGR: rice, coffee, cocoa, palm kernels; poultry; fish. EXP: diamonds, rutile, cocoa, coffee.

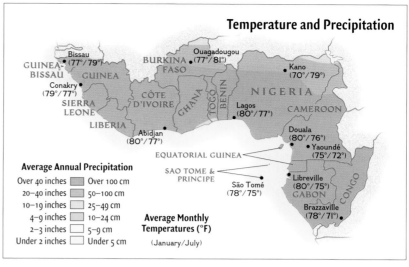

Temperature and Precipitation

Average Annual Precipitation

Over 40 inches	Over 100 cm
20–40 inches	50–100 cm
10–19 inches	25–49 cm
4–9 inches	10–24 cm
2–3 inches	5–9 cm
Under 2 inches	Under 5 cm

Average Monthly Temperatures (°F) (January/July)

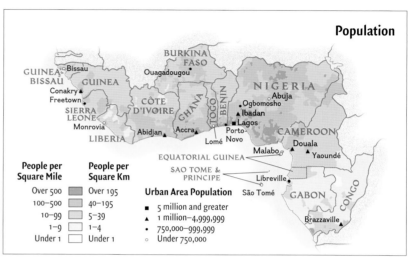

Population

People per Square Mile / People per Square Km

People per Square Mile	People per Square Km
Over 500	Over 195
100–500	40–195
10–99	5–39
1–9	1–4
Under 1	Under 1

Urban Area Population

- ■ 5 million and greater
- ▲ 1 million–4,999,999
- ● 750,000–999,999
- ○ Under 750,000

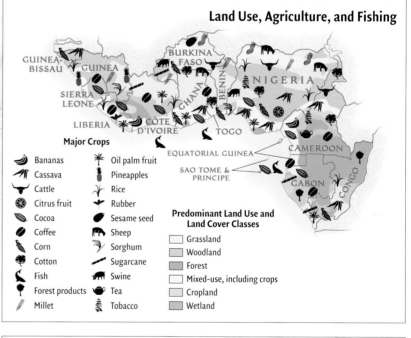

Land Use, Agriculture, and Fishing

Major Crops

- Bananas
- Cassava
- Cattle
- Citrus fruit
- Cocoa
- Coffee
- Corn
- Cotton
- Fish
- Forest products
- Millet
- Oil palm fruit
- Pineapples
- Rice
- Rubber
- Sesame seed
- Sheep
- Sorghum
- Sugarcane
- Swine
- Tea
- Tobacco

Predominant Land Use and Land Cover Classes

- Grassland
- Woodland
- Forest
- Mixed-use, including crops
- Cropland
- Wetland

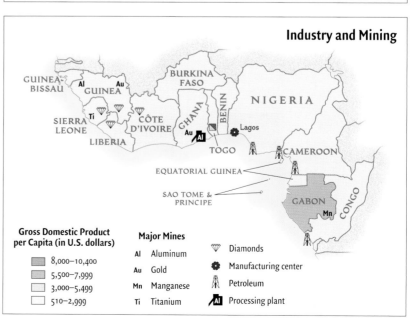

Industry and Mining

Gross Domestic Product per Capita (in U.S. dollars)

	8,000–10,400
	5,500–7,999
	3,000–5,499
	510–2,999

Major Mines

- Al Aluminum
- Au Gold
- Mn Manganese
- Ti Titanium
- ▽ Diamonds
- ⚙ Manufacturing center
- Petroleum
- Al Processing plant

Nigeria
FEDERAL REPUBLIC OF NIGERIA

AREA	923,768 sq km (356,669 sq mi)
POPULATION	129,935,000
CAPITAL	Abuja 420,000
RELIGION	Muslim, Christian, indigenous beliefs
LANGUAGE	English, Hausa, Yoruba, Ibo, Fulani
LITERACY	57%
LIFE EXPECTANCY	51 years
GDP PER CAPITA	$950
ECONOMY	IND: crude oil, mining, palm oil, cement. AGR: cocoa, peanuts, palm oil, corn; cattle; timber; fish. EXP: petroleum and petroleum products, cocoa, rubber.

Togo
TOGOLESE REPUBLIC

AREA	56,785 sq km (21,925 sq mi)
POPULATION	5,286,000
CAPITAL	Lomé 732,000
RELIGION	Indigenous beliefs, Christian, Muslim
LANGUAGE	French, Ewe, Mina, Kabye, Dagomba
LITERACY	52%
LIFE EXPECTANCY	54 years
GDP PER CAPITA	$1,500
ECONOMY	IND: phosphate mining, agricultural processing, cement, handicrafts. AGR: coffee, cocoa, cotton, yams; livestock; fish. EXP: cotton, phosphates, coffee, cocoa.

Angola
REPUBLIC OF ANGOLA
AREA	1,246,700 sq km (481,354 sq mi)
POPULATION	12,714,000
CAPITAL	Luanda 2,819,000
RELIGION	Indigenous beliefs, Roman Catholic, Protestant
LANGUAGE	Portuguese, Bantu
LITERACY	42%
LIFE EXPECTANCY	39 years
GDP PER CAPITA	$1,000

ECONOMY IND: petroleum, diamonds, cement, food. AGR: bananas, sugarcane, coffee, sisal; livestock; forest products; fish. EXP: crude oil, diamonds, refined petroleum products, gas.

Botswana
REPUBLIC OF BOTSWANA
AREA	600,372 sq km (231,805 sq mi)
POPULATION	1,591,000
CAPITAL	Gaborone 225,000
RELIGION	Indigenous beliefs, Christian
LANGUAGE	English, Setswana
LITERACY	70%
LIFE EXPECTANCY	37 years
GDP PER CAPITA	$6,600

ECONOMY IND: diamonds, copper, nickel, coal. AGR: sorghum, corn, millet, pulses; livestock. EXP: diamonds, vehicles, copper, nickel.

Lesotho
KINGDOM OF LESOTHO
AREA	30,355 sq km (11,720 sq mi)
POPULATION	2,208,000
CAPITAL	Maseru 271,000
RELIGION	Christian, indigenous beliefs
LANGUAGE	English, Sesotho, Zulu, Xhosa
LITERACY	83%
LIFE EXPECTANCY	49 years
GDP PER CAPITA	$2,400

ECONOMY IND: food, beverages, textiles, handicrafts. AGR: corn, wheat, pulses, sorghum; livestock. EXP: manufactures (clothing, footwear), wool and mohair, food and live animals.

Madagascar
REPUBLIC OF MADAGASCAR
AREA	587,041 sq km (226,658 sq mi)
POPULATION	16,913,000
CAPITAL	Antananarivo 1,689,000
RELIGION	Indigenous beliefs, Christian, Muslim
LANGUAGE	French, Malagasy
LITERACY	80%
LIFE EXPECTANCY	55 years
GDP PER CAPITA	$800

ECONOMY IND: meat processing, soap, breweries, tanneries. AGR: coffee, vanilla, sugarcane, cloves; livestock products. EXP: coffee, vanilla, shellfish, sugar.

Malawi
REPUBLIC OF MALAWI
AREA	118,484 sq km (45,747 sq mi)
POPULATION	10,917,000
CAPITAL	Lilongwe 523,000
RELIGION	Protestant, Roman Catholic, indigenous beliefs
LANGUAGE	English, Chichewa
LITERACY	58%
LIFE EXPECTANCY	37 years
GDP PER CAPITA	$900

ECONOMY IND: tobacco, tea, sugar, sawmill products. AGR: tobacco, sugarcane, cotton, tea; cattle. EXP: tobacco, tea, sugar, cotton.

Mozambique
REPUBLIC OF MOZAMBIQUE
AREA	799,380 sq km (308,642 sq mi)
POPULATION	19,608,000
CAPITAL	Maputo 1,134,000
RELIGION	Indigenous beliefs, Christian, Muslim
LANGUAGE	Portuguese, indigenous dialects
LITERACY	42%
LIFE EXPECTANCY	36 years
GDP PER CAPITA	$1,000

ECONOMY IND: food, beverages, chemicals (fertilizer, soap), petroleum products. AGR: cotton, cashew nuts, sugarcane, tea; beef. EXP: prawns, cashews, cotton, sugar.

Namibia
REPUBLIC OF NAMIBIA
AREA	824,292 sq km (318,261 sq mi)
POPULATION	1,821,000
CAPITAL	Windhoek 216,000
RELIGION	Christian, indigenous beliefs
LANGUAGE	English, Afrikaans, German, indigenous languages
LITERACY	38%
LIFE EXPECTANCY	41 years
GDP PER CAPITA	$4,300

ECONOMY IND: meatpacking, fish processing, dairy products, mining (diamonds, uranium). AGR: millet, sorghum, peanuts; livestock; fish. EXP: fish, diamonds, copper, gold.

South Africa
REPUBLIC OF SOUTH AFRICA
AREA	1,221,037 sq km (471,445 sq mi)
POPULATION	43,648,000
CAPITAL	Pretoria (administrative) 1,651,000; Cape Town (legislative) 2,993,000; Bloemfontein (judicial) 364,000
RELIGION	Christian, indigenous beliefs, Muslim, Hindu
LANGUAGE	Afrikaans, English, Ndebele, Pedi, Sotho, Swazi, Tsonga, Tswana, Venda, Xhosa, Zulu
LITERACY	82%
LIFE EXPECTANCY	48 years
GDP PER CAPITA	$8,500

ECONOMY IND: mining (platinum, gold), automobile assembly, metalworking, machinery. AGR: corn, wheat, sugarcane, fruits; beef. EXP: gold, diamonds, other metals and minerals, machinery and equipment.

S E Y C H E L L E S

Providence I.

Aldabra Is.
Assumption I.

Cosmoledo
Group

St. Pierre I.
Cerf I.

Astove I.

Farquhar Group

T A N Z A N I A

hilumba
ronga

LAKE MALAWI
(L. NYASA)
Ikhata Bay
Likoma I.
Cóbuè

Manjamba
Maniamba
Lichinga
Mecula
Maúa
Mandimba
Mangoche
Salima
Cuamba
Zomba
wonde
Blantyre
Chiromo
Mutarara
Cala
Quelimane
Marromeu
Chinde

Palma
Cabo Delgado
Negomane
Mocimboa da Praia
Mueda
Montepuez
Nantulo
Quissanga
Marrupa
Namapa
Ibo
Pemba
Mecúfi
Lúrio
Memba
Nacala
Lumbo
Moçambique
Angoche
Ilha Angoche
Mocuba
Mualama
Moma
Pebane

Moroni
COMOROS
Njazidja
(Grande Comore)
Nzwani (Anjouan)
(Mohéli) Mwali
Dzaoudzi
Mayotte
France

Îles Glorieuses
France

Cap d'Ambre
Antsiranana

Nosy Mitsio
Nosy Be
(Hell-Ville) Andoany
Ambilobe
Iharaña
(Vohemar)
Ambanja
Sambava
Antalaha
Maroantsetra
Presqu'île
de Masoala

Maromokotro
2876

Andapa

Baie de Sahamalaza

Baie de la
Mahajamba

Baie d'Antongila

Analalava

Mahajanga
Soalala
Marovoay

Besalampy

Île Juan de Nova
France

Nosy Vao
Nosy Barren

Maintirano

Belo-Tsiribihina

Morondava

Mandritsara

Maevatanana

Lac
Alaotra

Nosy
Ste. Marie
S.antierana-Ivongo

Ambatondrazaka

Miarinarivo
ANTANANARIVO
Andovoranto

Antsirabe
Mahanoro

CANAL DES
PANGALANES

Miandrivazo

Mahabo

Nosy-Varika

M A D A G A S C A R

Ambositra

Manja
Bekoropoka-Antongo
Morombe

Mangoky

Fianarantsoa

Beroroha

Ambohitra

Manakara

Boby 2658

Ihosy
Manakara

Mananjary

Ihosy
Manja

Farafangana
Vangaindrano

Betroka

Toliara

Onilahy

Ampanihy
Androka
Tsiombe

Bekily

Antanimora

Tôlañaro

Ambovombe

Cap Ste. Marie

M O Z A M B I Q U E

Dondo
Beira
Nova Sofala
Divinhe
Nova Mambone
Bartolomeu Dias
Macovane
Vilanculos
Ponta São Sebastião
Pomene
Massinga
Morrumbene
Ponta da Barra
Inhambane
Inharrime
Massinga
kixe
nhalouro

Zambeze
River Delta

TROPIC OF CAPRICORN

M O Z A M B I Q U E   C H A N N E L

40°
45°
50°
35°
40°
10°
15°
20°
25°
45°

Zambia
REPUBLIC OF ZAMBIA
AREA	752,614 sq km (290,586 sq mi)
POPULATION	9,959,000
CAPITAL	Lusaka 1,718,000
RELIGION	Christian, Muslim, Hindu
LANGUAGE	English, indigenous languages
LITERACY	78%
LIFE EXPECTANCY	37 years
GDP PER CAPITA	$880
ECONOMY	IND: copper mining and processing, construction, foodstuffs, beverages. AGR: corn, sorghum, rice, peanuts; cattle; coffee. EXP: copper, cobalt, electricity, tobacco.

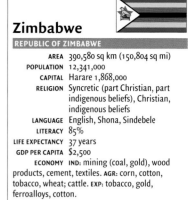

Zimbabwe
REPUBLIC OF ZIMBABWE
AREA	390,580 sq km (150,804 sq mi)
POPULATION	12,341,000
CAPITAL	Harare 1,868,000
RELIGION	Syncretic (part Christian, part indigenous beliefs), Christian, indigenous beliefs
LANGUAGE	English, Shona, Sindebele
LITERACY	85%
LIFE EXPECTANCY	37 years
GDP PER CAPITA	$2,500
ECONOMY	IND: mining (coal, gold), wood products, cement, textiles. AGR: corn, cotton, tobacco, wheat; cattle. EXP: tobacco, gold, ferroalloys, cotton.

Swaziland
KINGDOM OF SWAZILAND
AREA	17,364 sq km (6,704 sq mi)
POPULATION	1,124,000
CAPITAL	Mbabane 80,000
RELIGION	Protestant, indigenous beliefs, Muslim, Roman Catholic
LANGUAGE	English, Swazi
LITERACY	77%
LIFE EXPECTANCY	39 years
GDP PER CAPITA	$4,000
ECONOMY	IND: mining (coal and asbestos), wood pulp, sugar, soft drink concentrates. AGR: sugarcane, cotton, corn, tobacco; cattle. EXP: soft drink concentrates, sugar, wood pulp, cotton yarn.

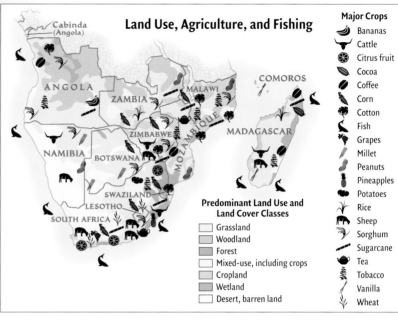

Land Use, Agriculture, and Fishing

Predominant Land Use and Land Cover Classes
- Grassland
- Woodland
- Forest
- Mixed-use, including crops
- Cropland
- Wetland
- Desert, barren land

Major Crops
- Bananas
- Cattle
- Citrus fruit
- Cocoa
- Coffee
- Corn
- Cotton
- Fish
- Grapes
- Millet
- Peanuts
- Pineapples
- Potatoes
- Rice
- Sheep
- Sorghum
- Sugarcane
- Tea
- Tobacco
- Vanilla
- Wheat

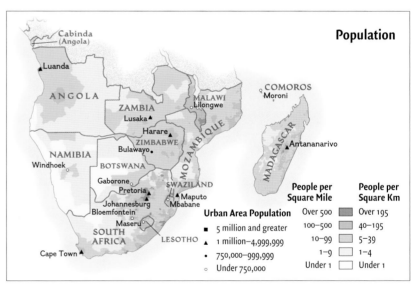

Population

Cabinda (Angola)
Luanda
ANGOLA
ZAMBIA
Lusaka
Harare
NAMIBIA
Windhoek
ZIMBABWE
Bulawayo
BOTSWANA
Gaborone
Pretoria
Johannesburg
Bloemfontein
Maseru
Maputo
Mbabane
SWAZILAND
LESOTHO
SOUTH AFRICA
Cape Town
MALAWI
Lilongwe
MOZAMBIQUE
COMOROS
Moroni
MADAGASCAR
Antananarivo

Urban Area Population
- ■ 5 million and greater
- ▲ 1 million–4,999,999
- ● 750,000–999,999
- ○ Under 750,000

People per Square Mile	People per Square Km
Over 500	Over 195
100–500	40–195
10–99	5–39
1–9	1–4
Under 1	Under 1

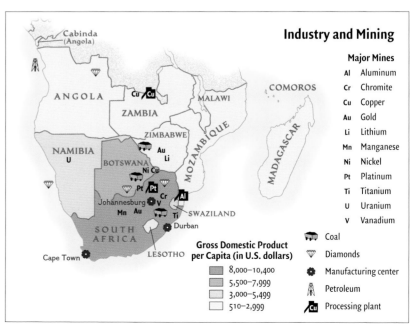

Industry and Mining

Cabinda (Angola)
ANGOLA
ZAMBIA
ZIMBABWE
NAMIBIA
BOTSWANA
SOUTH AFRICA
Cape Town
MALAWI
MOZAMBIQUE
COMOROS
MADAGASCAR
LESOTHO
SWAZILAND
Durban
Johannesburg

Major Mines
Al	Aluminum
Cr	Chromite
Cu	Copper
Au	Gold
Li	Lithium
Mn	Manganese
Ni	Nickel
Pt	Platinum
Ti	Titanium
U	Uranium
V	Vanadium

Gross Domestic Product per Capita (in U.S. dollars)
- 8,000–10,400
- 5,500–7,999
- 3,000–5,499
- 510–2,999

- Coal
- Diamonds
- Manufacturing center
- Petroleum
- Processing plant

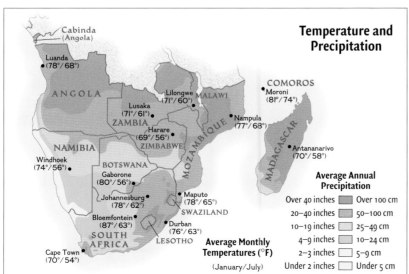

Temperature and Precipitation

Cabinda (Angola)
Luanda (78°/68°)
ANGOLA
Lusaka (71°/61°)
ZAMBIA
Lilongwe (71°/60°)
MALAWI
Moroni (81°/74°)
COMOROS
Harare (69°/56°)
ZIMBABWE
Nampula (77°/68°)
Antananarivo (70°/58°)
MADAGASCAR
NAMIBIA
Windhoek (74°/56°)
BOTSWANA
Gaborone (80°/56°)
Johannesburg (78°/62°)
Maputo (78°/65°)
SWAZILAND
Durban (76°/63°)
LESOTHO
Bloemfontein (87°/63°)
SOUTH AFRICA
Cape Town (70°/54°)
MOZAMBIQUE

Average Annual Precipitation
Over 40 inches	Over 100 cm
20–40 inches	50–100 cm
10–19 inches	25–49 cm
4–9 inches	10–24 cm
2–3 inches	5–9 cm
Under 2 inches	Under 5 cm

Average Monthly Temperatures (°F)
(January/July)

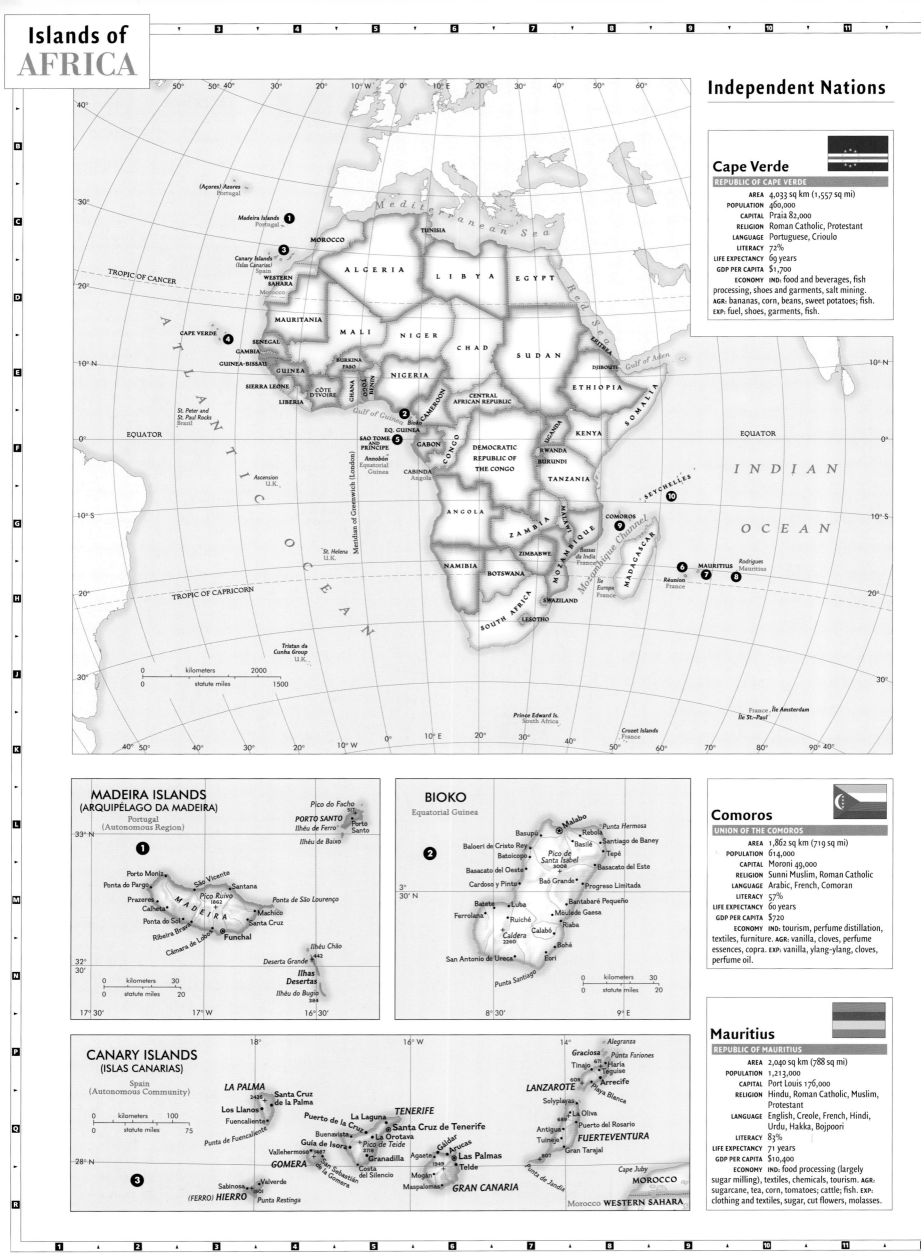

Islands of AFRICA

Independent Nations

Cape Verde
REPUBLIC OF CAPE VERDE

AREA	4,033 sq km (1,557 sq mi)
POPULATION	460,000
CAPITAL	Praia 82,000
RELIGION	Roman Catholic, Protestant
LANGUAGE	Portuguese, Crioulo
LITERACY	72%
LIFE EXPECTANCY	69 years
GDP PER CAPITA	$1,700

ECONOMY IND: food and beverages, fish processing, shoes and garments, salt mining. AGR: bananas, corn, beans, sweet potatoes; fish. EXP: fuel, shoes, garments, fish.

Comoros
UNION OF THE COMOROS

AREA	1,862 sq km (719 sq mi)
POPULATION	614,000
CAPITAL	Moroni 49,000
RELIGION	Sunni Muslim, Roman Catholic
LANGUAGE	Arabic, French, Comoran
LITERACY	57%
LIFE EXPECTANCY	60 years
GDP PER CAPITA	$720

ECONOMY IND: tourism, perfume distillation, textiles, furniture. AGR: vanilla, cloves, perfume essences, copra. EXP: vanilla, ylang-ylang, cloves, perfume oil.

Mauritius
REPUBLIC OF MAURITIUS

AREA	2,040 sq km (788 sq mi)
POPULATION	1,213,000
CAPITAL	Port Louis 176,000
RELIGION	Hindu, Roman Catholic, Muslim, Protestant
LANGUAGE	English, Creole, French, Hindi, Urdu, Hakka, Bojpoori
LITERACY	83%
LIFE EXPECTANCY	71 years
GDP PER CAPITA	$10,400

ECONOMY IND: food processing (largely sugar milling), textiles, chemicals, tourism. AGR: sugarcane, tea, corn, tomatoes; cattle; fish. EXP: clothing and textiles, sugar, cut flowers, molasses.

MADEIRA ISLANDS (ARQUIPÉLAGO DA MADEIRA)
Portugal (Autonomous Region)

BIOKO
Equatorial Guinea

CANARY ISLANDS (ISLAS CANARIAS)
Spain (Autonomous Community)

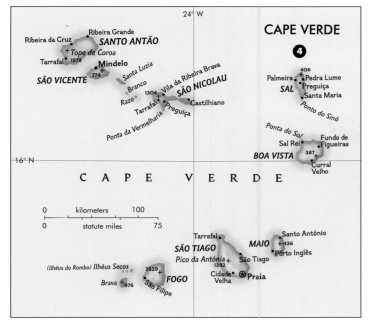

CAPE VERDE

4

Ribeira da Cruz · Ribeira Grande · *SANTO ANTÃO*
+Tope de Coroa 1979
Tarrafal · Mindelo 774 · Santa Luzia
SÃO VICENTE · Branco · Vila da Ribeira Brava
Razo 1304 · *SÃO NICOLAU* · Castilhiano
Tarrafal + · Preguiça
Ponta da Vermelharia

Palmeira · 406 · Pedra Lume
SAL · Preguiça · Santa Maria
Ponto do Sinó

Ponta do Sol · Fundo de Figueiras
Sal Rei · 387
BOA VISTA · Curral Velho

C A P E   V E R D E

0 kilometers 100
0 statute miles 75

16° N · 24° W

Tarrafal · Santo António
SÃO TIAGO · *MAIO* · +436
Pico da Antónia 1392 · São Tiago · Pôrto Inglês
(Ilhéus do Rombo) Ilhéus Secos · Cidade Velha · Praia
2829 · *FOGO*
Brava + 976 · São Filipe

SAO TOME AND PRINCIPE

5

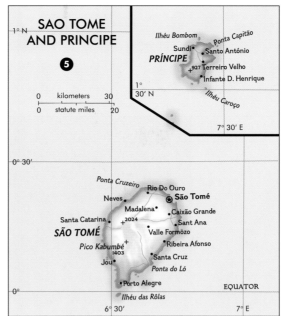

Ilhéu Bombom · Ponta Capitão
Sundi · Santo António
PRÍNCIPE
927 · Terreiro Velho
Infante D. Henrique
1° N
30' N · Ilhéu Caroço
7° 30' E

0 kilometers 30
0 statute miles 20

Ponta Cruzeiro · Rio Do Ouro
Neves · São Tomé
Santa Catarina · Madalena · Caixão Grande
SÃO TOMÉ · 2024 · Sant Ana
Valle Formózo
Pico Kabumbé 1403 · Ribeira Afonso
Jou · Santa Cruz
Ponta do Ló
Porto Alegre
0° · Ilhéu das Rôlas
6° 30' · EQUATOR · 7° E

RÉUNION

6

France · 55° 30' E

St.-Denis
Pointe des Galets · Ste.-Suzanna
Le Port · La Possession
St.-Paul · St.-André
21° S · Salazie
St.-Gilles-les-Bains · St.-Benoît
Piton des Neiges 3069
Trois-Bassins · 2896 + Cilaos
St.-Leu · La Plaine
Piton de la Fournaise 2631
Étang-Salé · Ste.-Rose
St.-Louis · Le Tampon
21° 30' · St.-Pierre · Pte. de la Table
St.-Philippe
St.-Joseph
43° E

0 kilometers 30
0 statute miles 20

MAURITIUS

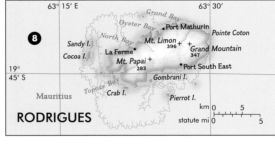

322 · Serpent I.
91 · Round Island
Flat Island
Canonniers Point · Gunners Quoin
20° S
Goodlands
Poudre d'Or
7 · Pamplemousses · Rivière du Rempart
Port Louis · 820 · Centre de Flacq
Beau Bassin · Trou d'Eau Douce
Quatre Bornes · Curepipe · Grande Rivière Sud Est
Tamarin · Rose Belle
Piton de la Rivière Noire 826 · Mahébourg
Chemin Grenier · River des Anguilles
Souillac
20° 30'
57° 30' E · 58°

0 kilometers 30
0 statute miles 20

63° 15' E · 63° 30'
Grand Bay
Oyster Bay · Port Mathurin
North Bay · Mt. Limon 396 · Pointe Coton
8 · Sandy I. · Grand Mountain
Cocoa I. · La Ferme · 347
Mt. Papai 283 · Port South East
19° 45' S · Gombrani I.
Topaze Bay · Crab I. · Pierrot I.
Mauritius
km 0 5
statute mi 0 5

RODRIGUES

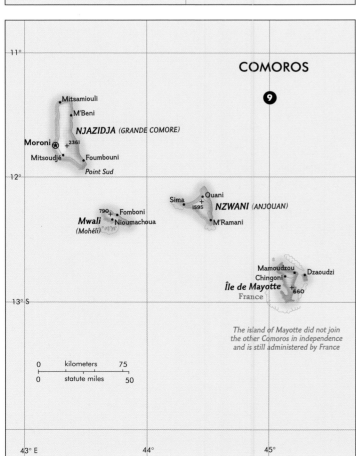

COMOROS

9

11°
Mitsamiouli
M'Beni
NJAZIDJA (GRANDE COMORE)
Moroni · 2361
Mitsoudjé · Foumbouni
Point Sud
12°
Ouani · Sima 1595 · *NZWANI (ANJOUAN)*
790 · Fomboni · M'Ramani
Mwali · Nioumachoua
(Mohéli)
Mamoudzou · Dzaoudzi
Chingoni
Île de Mayotte 660
France
13° S
43° E · 44° · 45°

The island of Mayotte did not join the other Comoros in independence and is still administered by France

0 kilometers 75
0 statute miles 50

SEYCHELLES

Bird
Denis
10
Aride
Curieuse · The Sisters
384 · Félicité
Praslin · 326 · Marie Anne
North Island · *La Digue*
Silhouette 716
North Point
Northwest Bay · Victoria
912 · Frigate
Cascade · *Mahé I.*
Anse Boileau · 378
Pointe du Sud
55° · 55° 30' E · 56°

0 kilometers 40
0 statute miles 30

Réunion (France)
OVERSEAS DEPARTMENT OF FRANCE

AREA	2510 sq km (969 sq mi)
POPULATION	742,000
CAPITAL	Saint-Denis 169,000
RELIGION	Roman Catholic, Hindu, Muslim, Buddhist
LANGUAGE	French, Creole
LITERACY	79%
LIFE EXPECTANCY	73 years
GDP PER CAPITA	$4,800
ECONOMY	IND: sugar, rum, cigarettes, handicraft items. AGR: sugarcane, vanilla, tobacco, tropical fruits. EXP: sugar, rum and molasses, perfume essences, lobster.

Sao Tome and Principe
DEM. REP. OF SAO TOME AND PRINCIPE

AREA	964 sq km (372 sq mi)
POPULATION	170,000
CAPITAL	São Tomé 67,000
RELIGION	Roman Catholic, Evangelical, Protestant, Seventh-Day Adventist
LANGUAGE	Portuguese
LITERACY	73%
LIFE EXPECTANCY	66 years
GDP PER CAPITA	$1,100
ECONOMY	IND: light construction, textiles, soap, beer; fish processing; timber. AGR: cocoa, coconuts, palm kernels, copra; poultry; fish. EXP: cocoa, copra, coffee, palm oil.

Seychelles
REPUBLIC OF SEYCHELLES

AREA	453 sq km (175 sq mi)
POPULATION	85,000
CAPITAL	Victoria 30,000
RELIGION	Roman Catholic, Anglican
LANGUAGE	English, French, Creole
LITERACY	58%
LIFE EXPECTANCY	71 years
GDP PER CAPITA	$7,700
ECONOMY	IND: fishing, tourism, processing of coconuts and vanilla, beverages. AGR: coconuts, cinnamon, vanilla, sweet potatoes; broiler chickens; tuna fish. EXP: fish, cinnamon bark, copra, petroleum products.

Dependencies

Mayotte (France)
TERRITORIAL COLLECTIVITY OF MAYOTTE

AREA	374 sq km (144 sq mi)
POPULATION	174,000
CAPITAL	Mamoudzou 43,000
RELIGION	Muslim, Christian
LANGUAGE	Mahorian, French
LITERACY	NA
LIFE EXPECTANCY	60 years
GDP PER CAPITA	$600
ECONOMY	IND: lobster and shrimp industry, construction. AGR: vanilla, ylang-ylang (perfume essence), coffee, copra. EXP: ylang-ylang, vanilla, copra, coconuts.

SOVEREIGN · LOCAL

St. Helena (U.K.)
ST. HELENA

AREA	308 sq km (119 sq mi)
POPULATION	7,000
CAPITAL	Jamestown 2,000
RELIGION	Anglican(majority), Baptist, Seventh-Day Adventist, Roman Catholic
LANGUAGE	English
LITERACY	97%
LIFE EXPECTANCY	77 years
GDP PER CAPITA	$2,500
ECONOMY	IND: construction, crafts, fishing. AGR: corn, potatoes, vegetables, timber, fish. EXP: fish, coffee, handicrafts.

AUSTRALIA
NEW ZEALAND, OCEANIA

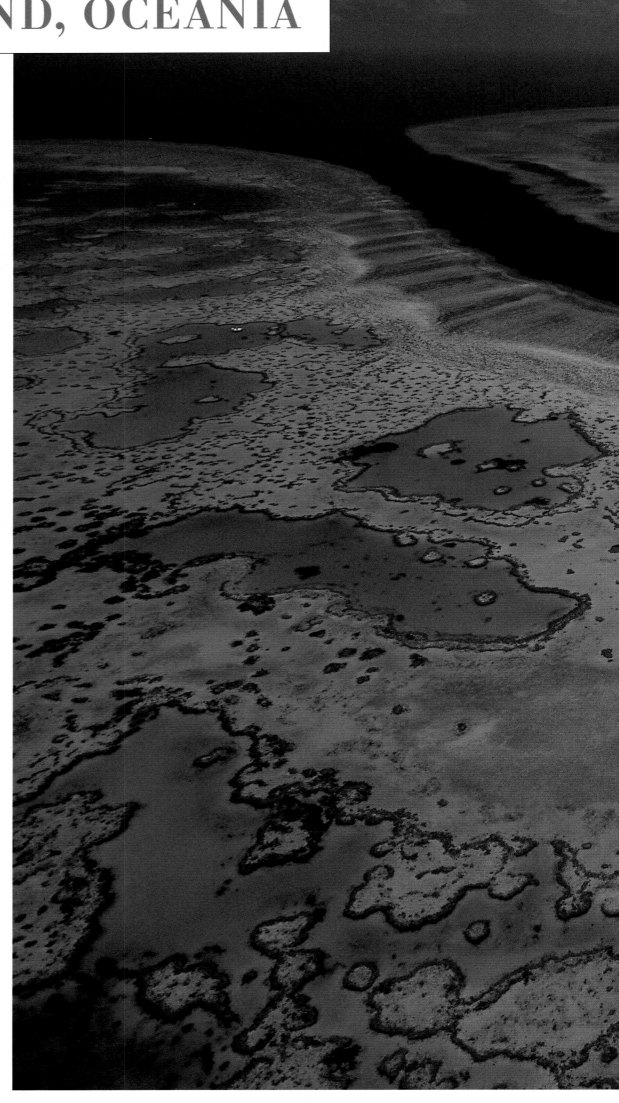

Smallest of continents and sixth largest country in the world, Australia is the lowest, flattest, and, apart from Antarctica, the driest continent.

Australia's land mass is relatively arid, but varied climatic zones give it surprising diversity and a rich ecology. Unlike Europe and North America, where much of the landscape dates back 20,000 years to when great ice sheets retreated, Australia's land is many millions of years old; it retains an ancient feeling and distinctive geography and endures extremes of droughts, floods, tropical cyclones, severe storms, and bushfires.

Off the coast of northeast Queensland lies the Great Barrier Reef, the world's largest coral reef, which extends about 1,250 miles (2,012 km). The Great Barrier Reef was formed and expanded over millions of years as tiny marine animals deposited their skeletons. Coral reefs, and the Great Barrier Reef especially, are considered the rain forests of the ocean for their complex

Largest structure ever built by living creatures, the Great Barrier Reef lies off Australia's northeast coast. Some 400 coral species and 1,500 species of fish inhabit its warm, shallow waters.

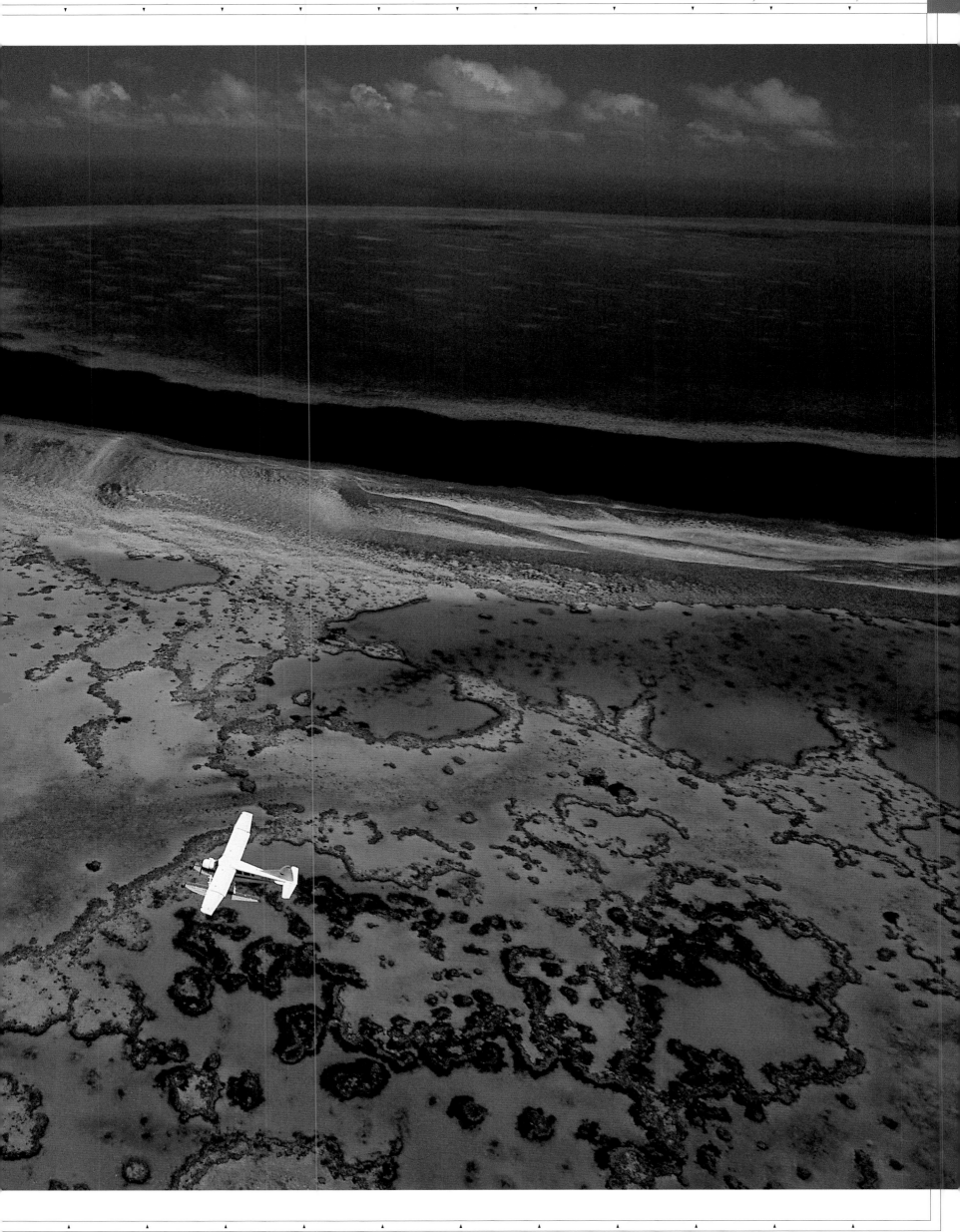

life forms and multilayered biodiversity.

The island of Tasmania lies off Australia's southeast coast. East from there, across the Tasman Sea, is the island nation of New Zealand, composed of South Island and North Island, respectively the 12th and 14th largest islands on Earth.

Extending into the massive Pacific Ocean north and east of Australia and New Zealand are the thousands of islands—which include 12 independent nations and more than 20 territories—that make up greater Oceania. The term Oceania normally designates all the islands of the Central and South Pacific, including Australia, New Zealand, and specifically the islands of Melanesia, Micronesia, and Polynesia, including Hawaii. Eons of isolation have allowed outstanding and bizarre life forms to evolve, such as the duck-billed platypus—a monotreme, or egg-laying mammal native to Australia and Tasmania—and New Zealand's kiwi, a timid, nocturnal, wingless bird.

Oceania has many ethnic groups and layers and types of society, from sophisticated cosmopolitan cities to near-Stone Age people in the New Guinea highlands. Many became Christian converts in the 19th century; as a result, Christianity is widespread and dominant in many countries today. Excluding Australia, some 12 million people live in Oceania, three-fourths of whom are found in Papua New Guinea and New Zealand.

Polynesia, which means "many islands," is the most extensive of the ocean realms. It can be seen as a huge triangle in the central-south Pacific, with the points being New Zealand in the southwest, Easter Island in the southeast, and Hawaii as the northern point. Other island groups include Tuvala, Tokelau, Wallis and Futuna, Samoa, Tonga, Cook Islands, and French Polynesia.

Micronesia, north and west of Polynesia, includes the islands and island groups of Nauru, Marshall Islands, Palau, Mariana Islands, Kiribati, and Guam.

Melanesia, one of the three main divisions of Oceania, includes the Solomon Islands, Vanuatu, New Caledonia, the Bismarck Archipelago, and Fiji, and sometimes takes in Papua New Guinea, where over 700 of the giant region's 1,200 languages are spoken.

PHYSICAL GEOGRAPHY

The continent of Australia can be divided into three parts, the Western Plateau, Central Lowlands, and Eastern Highlands. The Western Plateau consists of very old rocks, some over three billion years old. Much of the center of Australia is flat, but some ranges and the famous landmark Ayers Rock (Uluru) still rise up, everything around them having eroded away.

Much variety exists within the general context of a red, dusty, dry, flat continent, of which a third is desert and a third scrub and steppe. Sand dunes, mostly fixed and running north to south, and stony deserts mark the great tableland.

Many of Australia's rivers drain inland; though they erode their valleys near the highland sources, their lower courses are filling up with alluvium, and the rivers often end in salt lakes, dry for much of each year, when they become beds of salt and caked mud. Yet occasional spring rains in the outback can bring spectacular wildflowers.

Sparsely populated, Australia has nearly all its almost 20 million people along the east and southeast coasts, and of these about 40 percent live in the two cities of Sydney and Melbourne. Along the coasts are some fine harbors and long beaches and rocky headlands.

The Eastern Highlands rise gently from central Australia towards a series of high plateaus, the highest part around Mount Kosciuszko (7,310 ft; 2,228 m). The Great Escarpment runs from northern Queensland to the Victoria border in the south. Australia's highest waterfalls occur where rivers flow over the Great Escarpment.

The longest of all Australian river systems, the Murray River and its tributaries, including the long Darling River, drains part of Queensland, the major part of New South Wales and a large part of Victoria, finally flowing into the Indian Ocean just east of Adelaide.

Most of the Great Dividing Range that separates rivers flowing to Central Australia from those flowing to the Pacific runs across remarkably flat country dotted with lakes and airstrips. In ancient times volcanoes erupted in eastern Australia, and

lava plains covered large areas.

Australia is blessed with a fascinating mix of native flora and fauna. Its distinctive plants include the ubiquitous eucalyptus, sometimes called gum trees, and acacia, which Australians call wattles, each with several hundred species. Other common plants include bottlebrushes, paperbarks, and tea trees. Animals include the iconic kangaroo, koala, wallaby, wombat, and dog-like dingo, also the echidna, a spiny anteater, and numerous beloved birds, such as parrots, cockatoos, and kookaburras, and the emu, second largest of all birds after the ostrich.

Foreign animals have been introduced. The rabbit and fox have proven to be particular pests, overgrazing the land and killing and driving out native species. A fence built in 1907, still maintained, runs a thousand miles from the north coast to the south to prevent rabbits from invading Western Australia.

New Zealand is mountainous compared to Australia; it has peaks over 10,000 feet in the Southern Alps and considerably more rain, making the climate cooler and more temperate. Among New Zealand's oddities is a fossil lizard species, the tuatara; individuals can live up to 100 years.

The atolls, mountains, volcanoes, and sandy isles of greater Oceania, with limited land and small populations, have for most of history been isolated from the more settled parts of the world.

Peaks and promontories of the many islands of Polynesia form clouds and capture rain, making these islands very wet.

HISTORY

Australia's first inhabitants, the Aborigines, migrated there some 50 thousand or more years ago from Asia. Until the arrival of Europeans, the Aborigines had remained isolated from outside influences except for occasional trading in the north with Indonesian islanders.

In 1688 Englishman William Dampier landed on the northwest coast. Little interest was aroused, however, until Capt. James Cook noted the fertile east coast during his 1770 voyage, which stopped at Botany Bay, just south of today's Sydney. He claimed the entire continent for the British Empire

A member of the Arrernte people sits on Corroboree Rock at Atula Station in the Northern Territories. The rock shows ancient petroglyphs carved by her Aboriginal ancestors.

and named it New South Wales.

Australia's formative moment came when Britain began colonizing the east coast in 1788 as a penal colony, so as to relieve overcrowded prisons in England. Altogether, 161,000 English, Irish, and other convicts were forced to settle there. Prison transports ended in 1868, and by that time regular emigrants had already begun settling down under, as Australia was called for being so far south of the Equator. By the mid-1800s systematic, permanent colonization had completely replaced the old penal settlements.

Introduction of sheep proved vital, and the wool industry flourished. A gold strike in Victoria in 1851 attracted prospectors from all over the world. Other strikes followed, and with minerals, sheep, and grain forming the base of the economy, Australia developed rapidly, expanding across the whole continent.

By 1861, Australians had established the straight-line boundaries between the colonies, and the Commonwealth of Australia was born January 1, 1901, relying on British parliamentary and U.S. federal traditions. Australia and New Zealand share a common British heritage and many similar characteristics, and both are democracies that continue to honor the British monarch.

The great seafaring navigators of Polynesia and Micronesia took part in the last phase of mankind's settlement of the globe, into the widely dispersed islands of the great Pacific. Their particular genius and contribution was the development of seafaring and navigation skills and canoe technology, which let them sail back and forth among islands across great distances. The more diverse, land-based Melanesians fished along the coasts and practiced horticulture farther inland.

CULTURE

Australia's Aborigines were hunters and gatherers moving with the seasons, taking with them only those possessions necessary for hunting and preparing food. Perhaps 500 or more tribes lived in Australia at the time of Captain Cook in 1770.

Aboriginal society was based on a complex network of intricate kinship relationships. No formal government or authority existed, but social control was maintained by a system of beliefs called the Dreaming. These beliefs found expression in song, art, and dance. A rich oral tradition existed in which stories of the Dreamtime, the time of creation, or recent history were passed down. Aboriginal rock carvings and paintings date back at least 30,000 years.

Australia's Aborigines have faced two centuries and more of lost land, brutalization, and discrimination. In the 1960s an Aboriginal movement grew to press for full citizenship and improved education. Modern Aboriginal art has undergone a revival as Aboriginal artists have preserved their ancient values while learning from the contemporary world.

Most Australians are of British and Irish ancestry and the majority of the country lives in urban areas. The population has more than doubled since the end of World War II, spurred by an ambitious postwar immigration program, with many coming from Greece, Turkey, Italy, and Lebanon. In the 1970s Australia officially ended discriminatory immigration policies, and substantial Asian immigration followed. Today Asians make up some 7 percent of the population.

Largest church groups are the Anglican and Roman Catholic, though some say sport is the national religion; Australians are famous in cricket, rugby, and swimming.

The Maori—indigenous Polynesian people of New Zealand—arrived in different migrations starting around 1150, and a "great fleet" arrived in the 14th century, probably from Tahiti. Maori art boasts of beautiful wood carvings that adorn houses and fish hooks carved out of whale bone. In the 1840 Treaty of Waitangi, the Maori gave formal control of their land to the British, though they kept all other rights of livelihood.

ECONOMY

Australia dominates all of Oceania economically. Its connection to Asia grows more important as a supplier of raw material to other Pacific Rim countries and an importer of finished manufactured products. Japan is Australia's leading trade partner and thousands of children learn Japanese in Australian schools. The standard of living is high and people have considerable leisure time, a sign for Australians of a good life.

Most of the rich farmland and good ports are in the east, particularly the southeast, and the areas around Perth in Western Australia. Melbourne, Sydney, Brisbane, and Adelaide are the leading industrial and commercial cities.

Australia is highly industrialized. Its chief industries include mining, food processing, and the manufacture of industrial and transportation equipment, chemicals, iron and steel, textiles, machinery, and motor vehicles. Some lumbering is done in the east and southeast. Tropical and subtropical produce are also important, as are vineyards, dairy farms, and tobacco farms.

Chief export commodities are coal, gold, beef, and mutton, wool, minerals, cereals, and manufactured products. Australia's economic ties with Asia and the Pacific Rim have become increasingly important. Air transport and modern communications have shrunk the distances of Australia and Oceania, with landing strips on isolated atolls, in the desert outback, and in Papuan jungles.

Physical and Political
AUSTRALIA

Azimuthal Equidistant Projection

SCALE 1:13,170,000

1 CENTIMETER = 132 KILOMETERS, 1 INCH = 208 MILES

KILOMETERS

STATUTE MILES

— — — State boundary

Temperature and Precipitation

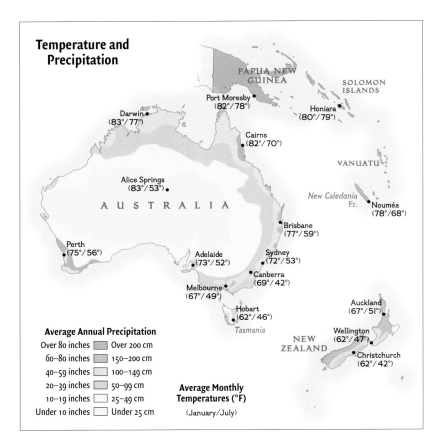

PAPUA NEW GUINEA
Port Moresby (82°/78°)
Darwin (83°/77°)
SOLOMON ISLANDS
Honiara (80°/79°)
Cairns (82°/70°)
VANUATU
Alice Springs (83°/53°)
AUSTRALIA
New Caledonia Fr.
Nouméa (78°/68°)
Brisbane (77°/59°)
Perth (75°/56°)
Adelaide (73°/52°)
Sydney (72°/53°)
Canberra (69°/42°)
Melbourne (67°/49°)
Hobart (62°/46°)
Tasmania
Auckland (67°/51°)
Wellington (62°/47°)
NEW ZEALAND
Christchurch (62°/42°)

Average Annual Precipitation

Over 80 inches		Over 200 cm	
60–80 inches		150–200 cm	
40–59 inches		100–149 cm	
20–39 inches		50–99 cm	
10–19 inches		25–49 cm	
Under 10 inches		Under 25 cm	

Average Monthly Temperatures (°F)

(January/July)

Population

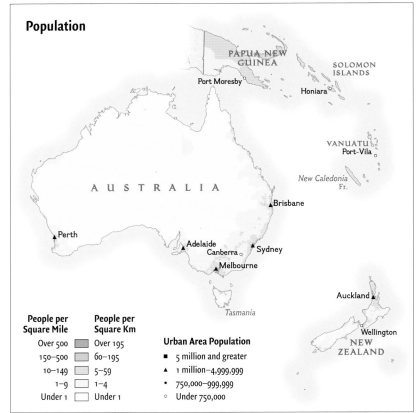

PAPUA NEW GUINEA
Port Moresby
SOLOMON ISLANDS
Honiara
VANUATU
Port-Vila
AUSTRALIA
New Caledonia Fr.
Brisbane
Perth
Adelaide
Canberra
Sydney
Melbourne
Tasmania
Auckland
Wellington
NEW ZEALAND

People per Square Mile	People per Square Km
Over 500	Over 195
150–500	60–195
10–149	5–59
1–9	1–4
Under 1	Under 1

Urban Area Population

- ■ 5 million and greater
- ▲ 1 million–4,999,999
- • 750,000–999,999
- ○ Under 750,000

Land Use, Agriculture, and Fishing

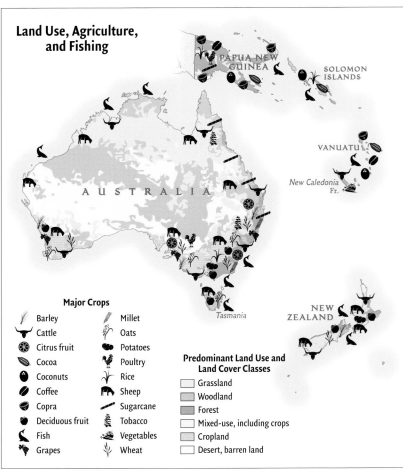

PAPUA NEW GUINEA
SOLOMON ISLANDS
VANUATU
AUSTRALIA
New Caledonia Fr.
Tasmania
NEW ZEALAND

Major Crops

Barley		Millet	
Cattle		Oats	
Citrus fruit		Potatoes	
Cocoa		Poultry	
Coconuts		Rice	
Coffee		Sheep	
Copra		Sugarcane	
Deciduous fruit		Tobacco	
Fish		Vegetables	
Grapes		Wheat	

Predominant Land Use and Land Cover Classes

- Grassland
- Woodland
- Forest
- Mixed-use, including crops
- Cropland
- Desert, barren land

Industry and Mining

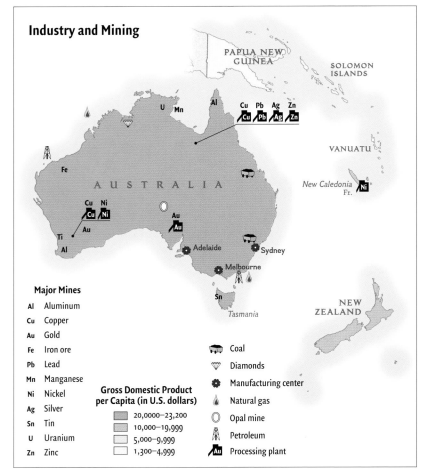

PAPUA NEW GUINEA
SOLOMON ISLANDS
U Mn Al
Cu Pb Ag Zn
VANUATU
Fe
AUSTRALIA
New Caledonia Fr.
Ni
Cu Ni
Au
Ti
Al
Au
Adelaide
Sydney
Melbourne
Sn
Tasmania
NEW ZEALAND

Major Mines

Al	Aluminum
Cu	Copper
Au	Gold
Fe	Iron ore
Pb	Lead
Mn	Manganese
Ni	Nickel
Ag	Silver
Sn	Tin
U	Uranium
Zn	Zinc

- Coal
- Diamonds
- Manufacturing center
- Natural gas
- Opal mine
- Petroleum
- Au Processing plant

Gross Domestic Product per Capita (in U.S. dollars)

- 20,0000–23,200
- 10,000–19,999
- 5,000–9,999
- 1,300–4,999

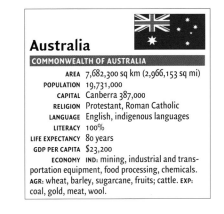

Australia

COMMONWEALTH OF AUSTRALIA

AREA	7,682,300 sq km (2,966,153 sq mi)
POPULATION	19,731,000
CAPITAL	Canberra 387,000
RELIGION	Protestant, Roman Catholic
LANGUAGE	English, indigenous languages
LITERACY	100%
LIFE EXPECTANCY	80 years
GDP PER CAPITA	$23,200
ECONOMY	IND: mining, industrial and transportation equipment, food processing, chemicals. AGR: wheat, barley, sugarcane, fruits; cattle. EXP: coal, gold, meat, wool.

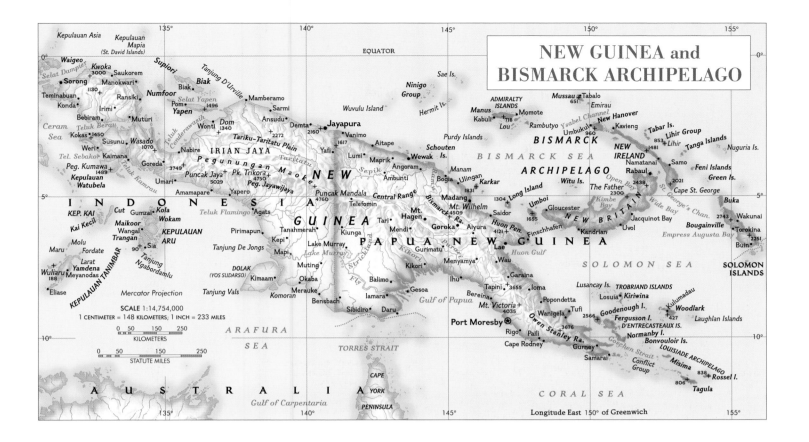

NEW GUINEA and BISMARCK ARCHIPELAGO

NEW ZEALAND

New Zealand

NEW ZEALAND

AREA	269,057 sq km (103,883 sq mi)
POPULATION	3,867,000
CAPITAL	Wellington 345,000
RELIGION	Protestant, Roman Catholic
LANGUAGE	English, Maori
LITERACY	99%
LIFE EXPECTANCY	78 years
GDP PER CAPITA	$17,700
ECONOMY	IND: food processing, wood and paper products, textiles, machinery. AGR: wheat, barley, potatoes, pulses; wool; fish. EXP: dairy products, meat, fish, wool.

Papua New Guinea

INDEPENDENT STATE OF PAPUA NEW GUINEA

AREA	461,691 sq km (178,260 sq mi)
POPULATION	5,016,000
CAPITAL	Port Moresby 259,000
RELIGION	Protestant, indigenous beliefs, Roman Catholic
LANGUAGE	715 indigenous languages
LITERACY	72%
LIFE EXPECTANCY	63 years
GDP PER CAPITA	$2,500
ECONOMY	IND: copra crushing, mining (gold, silver), crude oil production, construction. AGR: coffee, cocoa, coconuts, palm kernels; poultry. EXP: oil, gold, copper ore, logs.

Cape Mendocino

U N I T E D   S T A T E S

Washington ⊕

SAN FRANCISCO ●

Sierra Nevada

O C E A N

LOS ANGELES ●
SAN DIEGO ●
Tijuana ●

BAHAMAS

Golfo de California

M É X I C O

Baja California

Isla de Guadalupe
Mexico

Isla Cedros
Punta Eugenia

GULF
OF
MEXICO

CUBA

TROPIC OF CANCER

Rocas Alijos
Mexico

Cabo Falso   Mazatlán ●

HAITI

Islas Revillagigedo
Mexico

Isla San Benedicto

⊕ **MÉXICO**

DOMINICAN
REPUBLIC

JAMAICA

Isla Clarión   Isla Socorro

Belmopan ⊕   BELIZE

Isla Roca Partida

Acupulco ●

CARIBBEAN SEA

GUATEMALA   HONDURAS

Clipperton
France

Guatemala ⊛   ⊛ Tegucigalpa
San Salvador ⊛
EL SALVADOR   ● Managua

NICARAGUA

Managua

San José ●   PANAMA

COSTA RICA   ⊛ Panamá

CARACAS ⊛
VENEZUELA

Isla del Coco
Costa Rica

Golfo de Panamá

BOGOTÁ ⊛

EQUATOR

Isla de Malpelo
Colombia

COLOMBIA

Isla Darwin
Ecuador

Galápagos Islands
(Archipiélago de Colón)
Isla Fernandina
Isla Isabela

Isla Santiago
Isla Santa Cruz
Isla San Cristóbal

QUITO ⊛

ECUADOR

GUAYAQUIL ●

Isla Santa María

MARQUESAS ISLANDS
France

Eiao   Hatutu
Nuku Hiva   Ua Huka (51)
Ua Pu   Hiva Oa (50)
Tahuata   Mohotani (Motane)
Fatu Hiva

Caroline Island

TRUJILLO ●

BRAZIL

P E R U

Vostok Island

Flint Island

Mataiva   Napuka
Manihi   Pukapuka
Makatea   Takaroa   Tikei
Rangiroa
Moorea   Makemo   Tatakoto
● Papeete   Anaa
Tahiti (49)   Hikueru   Hao
IETY ISLANDS   FRENCH POLYNESIA
France

T U A M O T U   A R C H I P E L A G O (46)
(45)

LIMA ⊛

BOLIVIA
LA PAZ ⊛

Hereheretue
Îles Duc de Gloucester
Tematagi   Tureia
Moruroa   Marutea
Morane   Mangareva
Îles Gambier (52)   Temoe

United Kingdom

TROPIC OF CAPRICORN

Raivavae (Vavitu)
IS. (TUBUAI IS.)

Oeno Island
Henderson Island
Pitcairn Island (53)   Ducie Island

Rapa
Marotiri
(Îlots de Bass)

Sala-y-Gómez
Chile

Isla de Pascua
(Easter Island)
Chile

Isla San Félix   Isla San Ambrosio
Chile

Islas Juan Fernández
Chile

Valparaíso ●

Isla Róbinson Crusoe

Isla Santa
Clara

SANTIAGO ⊛

H   P A C I F I C   O C E A N

Isla Alejandro Selkirk

Concepción ●

Mercator Projection

SCALE 1:39,295,000 AT THE EQUATOR
1 CENTIMETER = 392 KILOMETERS; 1 INCH = 620 MILES

Isla Grande de Chiloé

0   500   1000   1500   2000
KILOMETERS

**Archipiélago de
los Chonos**

0   500   1000   1500   2000
STATUTE MILES

Golfo de Penas

(20) *Numbered islands correspond to larger-scale maps on the following pages.*

Isla Campana

Major Pacific Island Groups

● Mariana Islands
● Marshall Islands
● Caroline Islands
● Society Islands and
   Tuamotu Archipelago
● Other island

Isla Wellington

Isla Madre de Dios

**Archipiélago
Reina Adelaida**

Isla Santa Inés

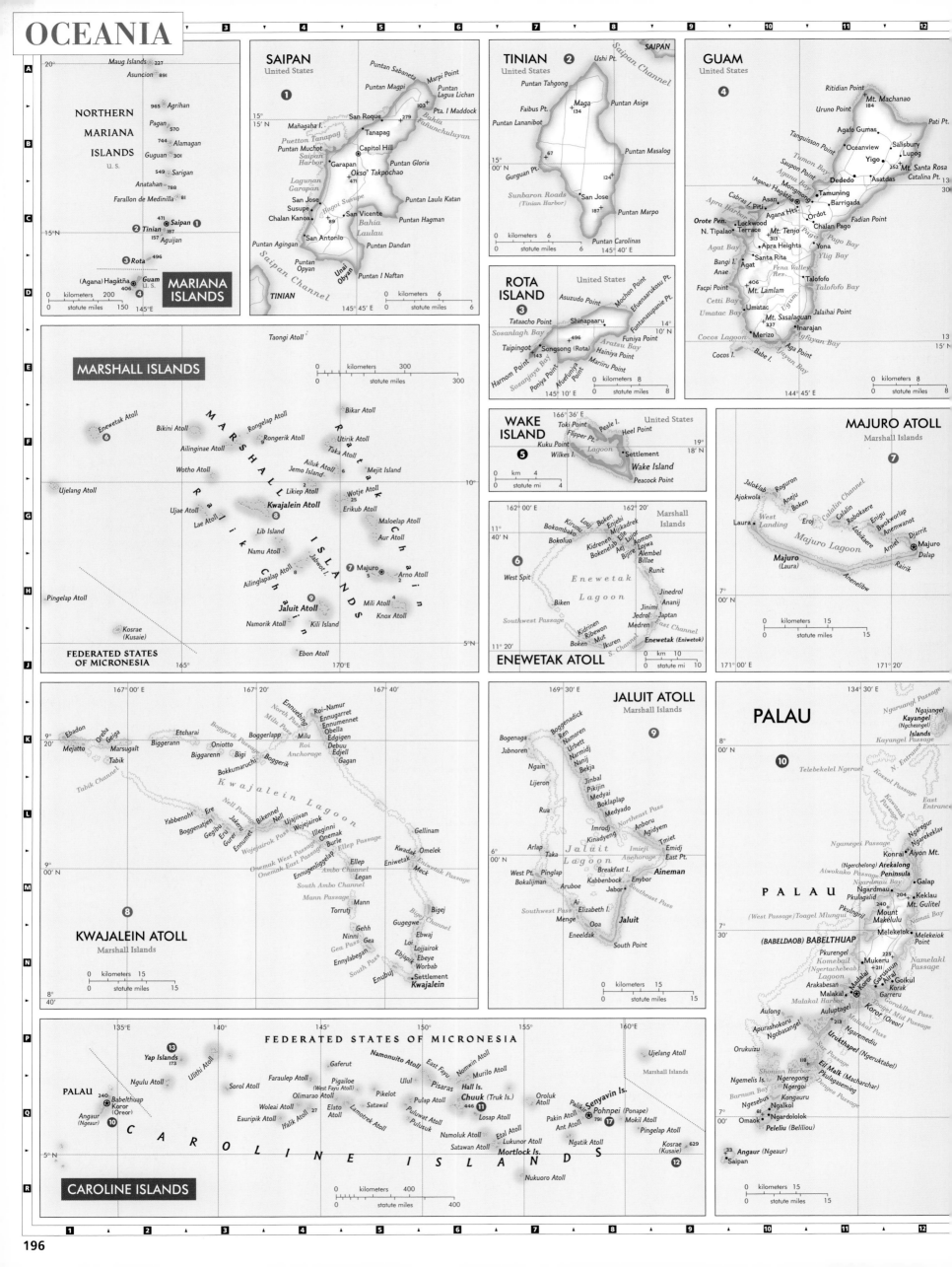

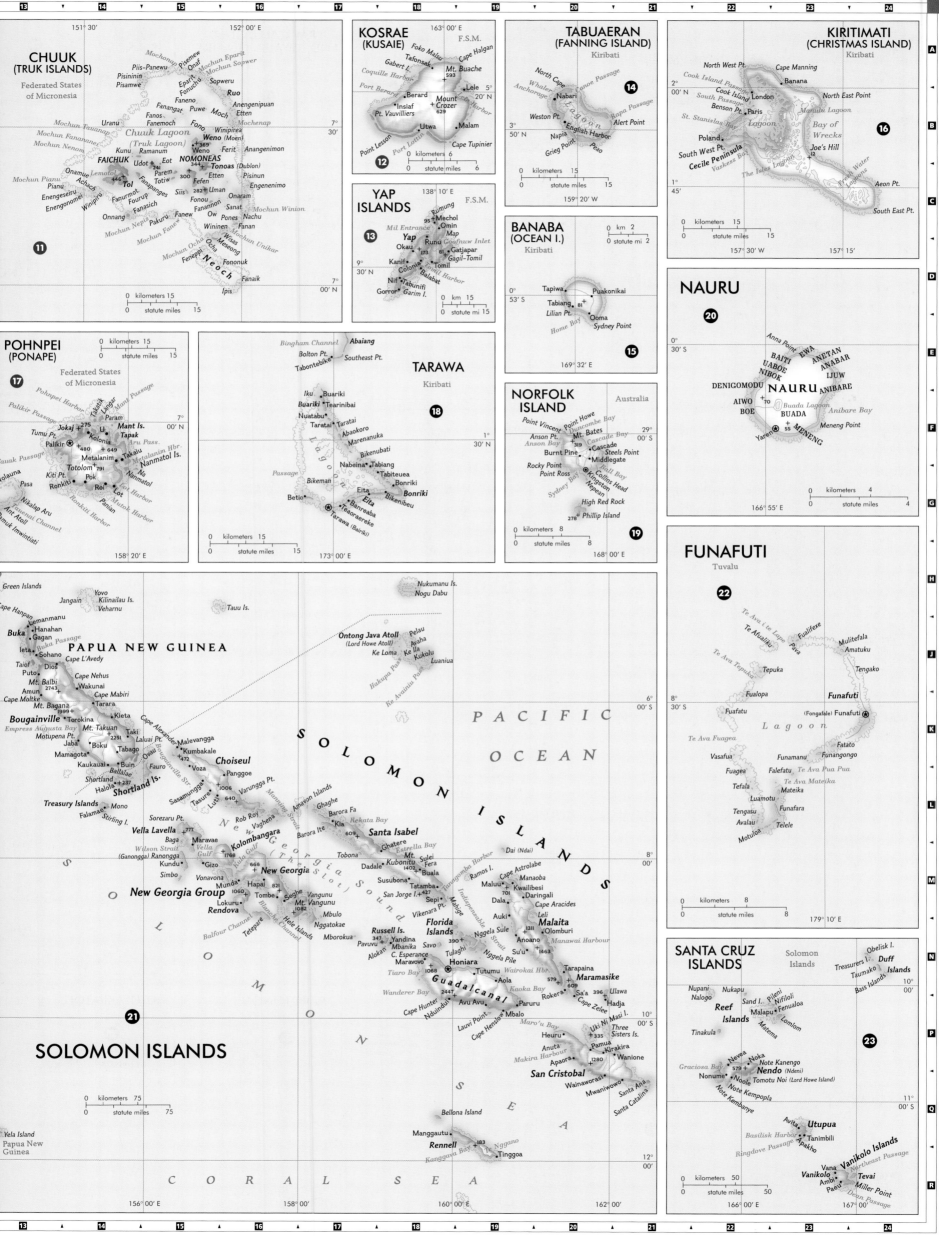

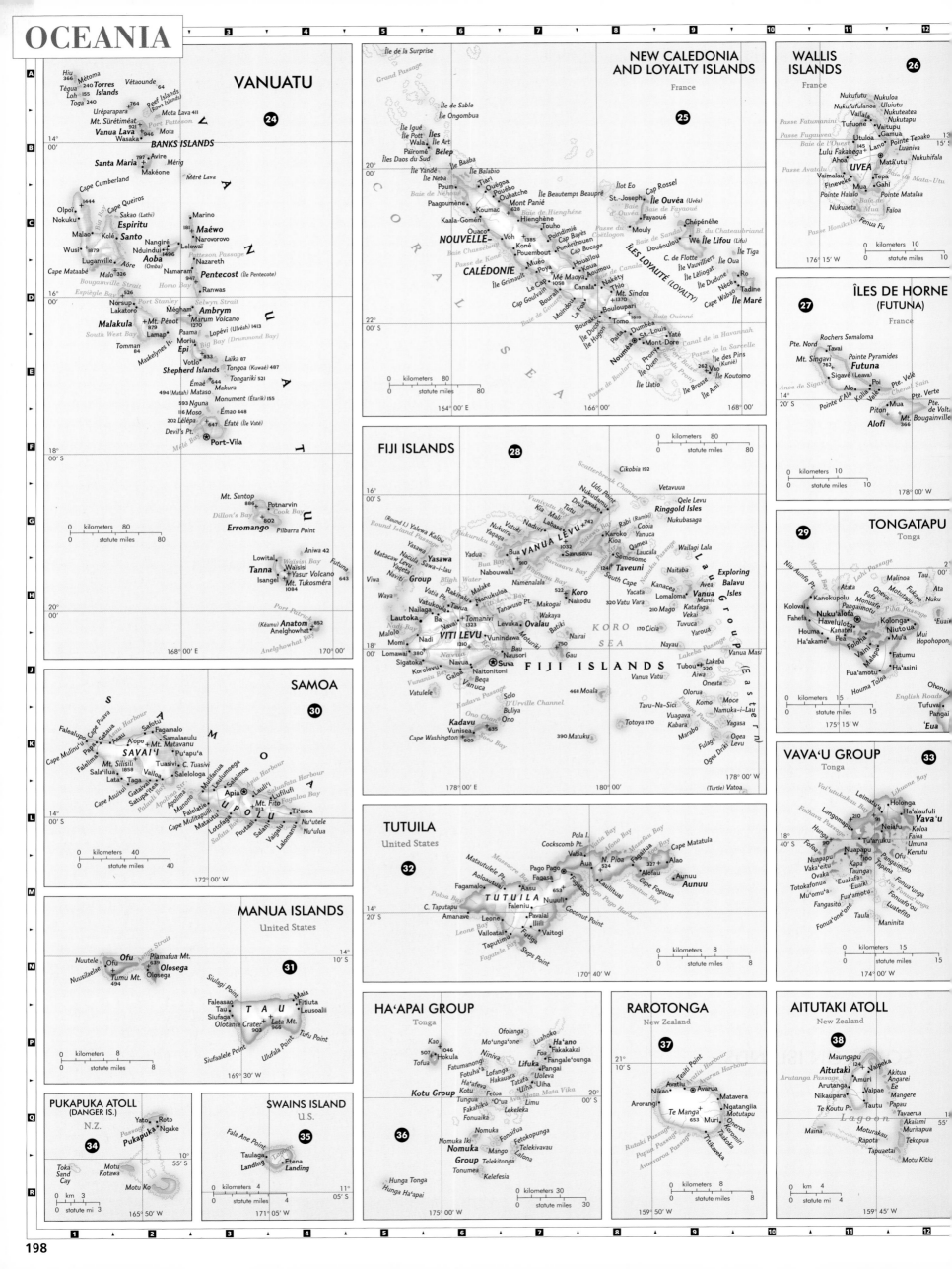

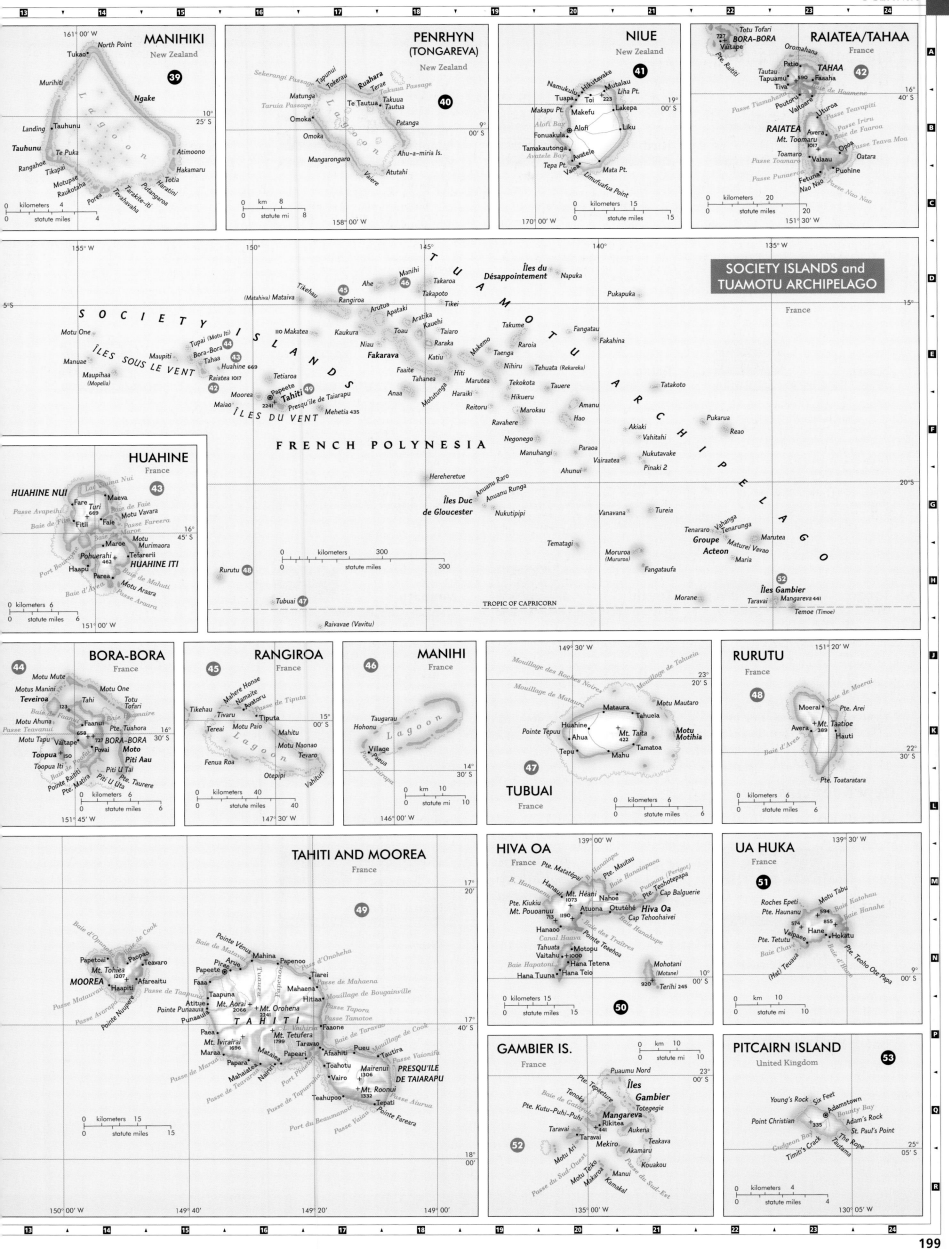

MANIHIKI
New Zealand

39

North Point
Tukao
Murihiti
Lagoon
Ngake
Landing • Tauhunu
Te Puka
Rangahoe
Tikapai
Motupae
Raukotaha
Porea Tevahavaha
Atimoono
Hakamaru
Haratini
Tarakite-iti
Putangaroa
Totia

kilometers 4
statute miles 4

161° 00' W
10° 25' S

PENRHYN
(TONGAREVA)
New Zealand

40

Sekerangi Passage
Tapunui
Tokerau
Ruahara
Terae
Te Tautua
Takuua Passage
Takuua
Tautua
Matunga
Taruia Passage
Omoka
Lagoon
Patanga
Omoka
Mangarongaro
Vaiere
Ahu-a-miria Is.
Atutahi

km 8
statute mi 8

158° 00' W
9° 00' S

NIUE
New Zealand

41

Namukulu
Tuapa
Hikutavake
Mutalau
Liha Pt.
Makapu Pt.
Makefu
Toi
223
Lakepa
Alofi Bay
Makefu
Fonuakula
Alofi
Liku
Tamakautonga
Avatele Bay
Avatele
Vaiea
Tepa Pt.
Limuftufua Point
Mata Pt.

kilometers 15
statute miles 15

170° 00' W
19° 00' S

RAIATEA/TAHAA
France

42

Totu Tofari
727 BORA-BORA
Vaitape
Pte. Raititi
Oromahana
Tautau
Patio
Tapuamu
TAHAA
Tiva
590
Faaaha
Poutoru
Baie de Haamene
Passe Tiamahana
Vaitoare
Uturoa
Passe Teavapiti
Passe Iriru
Avera
RAIATEA
Baie de Faaroa
Mt. Toomaru
1017
Opoa
Toamaro
Passe Toamaro
Vaiaau
Oatara
Passe Teava Moa
Puohine
Passe Punaeroa
Fetuna
Nao Nao
Passe Nao Nao

kilometers 20
statute miles 20

151° 30' W
16° 40' S

SOCIETY ISLANDS and TUAMOTU ARCHIPELAGO

155° W
150° W
145° W
140° W
135° W

T U A M O T U   A R C H I P E L A G O

5° S

S O C I E T Y   I S L A N D S

Manihi
Ahe
45
Takaroa
Îles du Désappointement
Napuka
Tikehau
Rangiroa
46
Takapoto
Tikei
Pukapuka
(Matahiva) Mataiva
Arutua
Apataki
France
15° S
Motu One
110 Makatea
Kaukura
Toau
Aratika
Kauehi
Taiaro
Takume
Fangatau
Tupai (Motu Iti)
Bora-Bora
44
Niau
Raraka
Makemo
Fakahina
Maupiti
ÎLES SOUS LE VENT
Tahaa
43
Fakarava
Katiu
Taenga
Raroia
Manuae
Huahine 669
Faaite
Hiti
Nihiru
Tehuata (Rekareka)
Maupihaa
Raiatea 1017
Tetiaroa
Tahanea
Marutea
Tekokota
(Mopelia)
42
Moorea
Papeete
49
Anaa
Motutunga
Haraiki
Tauere
Maiao
Tahiti
2241
Reitoru
Hikueru
Amanu
ÎLES DU VENT
Presqu'île de Taiarapu
Marokau
Takatoto
Mehetia 435
Ravahere
Hao
20° S
F R E N C H   P O L Y N E S I A
Negonego
Akiaki
Pukarua
Reao
Hereheretue
Anuanu Raro
Vahitake
Manuhangi
Paraoa
Nukutavake
Anuanu Runga
Vairaatea
Pinaki 2
Îles Duc de Gloucester
Nukutipipi
Ahunui
Vanavana
Tureia
Tenararo
Vahanga
Tenarunga
Tematagi
Moruroa (Mururoa)
Groupe Acteon
Marutea
Maria
Fangataufa
Matarei Vavao
52
Îles Gambier
Tubuai 47
Rurutu 48
Morane
Taravai
Mangareva 441
TROPIC OF CAPRICORN
Temoe (Timoe)
Raivavae (Vavitu)

kilometers 300
statute miles 300

151° 00' W

HUAHINE
France

43

HUAHINE NUI
Lac Fauna Nui
Passe Avapeihi
Fare
Turi 669
Maeva
Baie de Faie
Baie de Fitii
Fitii
Faie
Motu Vavara
Passe Fareera
16° 45' S
Maroe
Motu
Murimaora
Pohuerahi 462
Tefarerii
HUAHINE ITI
Haapu
Motu Araara
Parea
Baie de Mahuti
Port Bourayne
Baie d'Avea
Passe Araara

kilometers 6
statute miles 6

151° 00' W

BORA-BORA
France

44

Motu Mute
Motus Manini
Motu One
Teveiroa
Tahi
Totu Tofari
Baie de Faanui
123
Faanui
Pte. Tuahora
Motu Ahuna
658
727
BORA-BORA
16° 30' S
Passe Teavanui
Vaitape
Povai
Moto
Piti Aau
Motu Tapu
Toopua 150
Vaiotaha
Pte. Taurere
Toopua Iti
Piti U Tai
Baie de Povai
Pointe Raititi
Piti U Uta
Pte. Matira

kilometers 6
statute miles 6

151° 45' W

RANGIROA
France

45

Mahere Honae
Namaite
Avatoru
Passe de Tiputa
Tikehau
Tivaru
Tiputa
15° 00' S
Tereai
Motu Paio
Mahitu
Lagoon
Motu Naonao
Fenua Roa
Tevaro
Otepipi
Vahituri

kilometers 40
statute miles 40

147° 30' W

MANIHI
France

46

Taugarau
Hohonu
Lagoon
14° 30' S
Village
Paeua
Passe Tairapa

km 10
statute mi 10

146° 00' W

149° 30' W
Mouillage des Roches Noires
Mouillage de Tahueia
23° 20' S
Mouillage de Mataura
Mataura
Tahueia
Motu Mautaro
Huahine
Mt. Taita 422
Motu Motihia
Pointe Tepuu
Ahua
Tepu
Mahu
Tamatoa

TUBUAI
France

47

kilometers 6
statute miles 6

RURUTU
France

48

151° 20' W
Baie de Moerai
Moerai
Pte. Arei
Avera
Mt. Taatioe 389
Hauti
Baie d'Avea
22° 30' S
Pte. Toataratara

kilometers 6
statute miles 6

TAHITI AND MOOREA
France

49

17° 20' S

Papetoai
Paopao
Teavaro
Pointe Vénus
Mahina
Arue
Papenoo
Passe d'Onoheha
Mt. Tohiea 1207
Afareaitu
Papeete
Pirae
MOOREA
Faaa
Tiarei
Haapiti
Taapuna
Mahaena
Passe Taapuna
Atiue
Mahaena
Mouillage de Bougainville
Pointe Punaauia
Mt. Aorai 2066
Hitiaa
Passe Matauvau
Mt. Orohena 2241
Passe Tamotoe
Pointe Nuupere
Paea
TAHITI
Faaone
17° 40' S
Mt. Iviraira 1696
Faaone
Mouillage de Cook
Passe Avarapa
Mt. Tetufera 1799
Taravao
Pueu
Maraa
Taravao
Tautira
Papara
Matatea
Papeari
Toahotu
Port Phaeton
Passe Vaionifa
Passe de Maraa
Mahaiatea
Afaahiti
Mairenui 1306
Naihiti
Vairo
PRESQU'ÎLE DE TAIARAPU
Mt. Roonui 1332
Teahupoo
Tepati
Pointe Fareara
Passe de Toupaereu
Port du Beaumanoir
Passe Aturua
Passe Vaiau

kilometers 15
statute miles 15

150° 00' W
149° 40'
149° 20'
149° 00'

HIVA OA
France

50

139° 00' W
Pte. Matatépai
B. Hanaiapa
Pte. Mautau
B. Puamau (Perigot)
Hanauii
Mt. Héani 1073
Nahoe
Pte. Teohotepapa
Cap Balguerie
Pte. Kiukiu
Atuona
Hiva Oa
Mt. Pouoanuu 713
1190
Otutéhé
Cap Tehoohaivei
Hanaoo
Pointe Teaehoa
Tahuata
Motopu
Vaitahu +1000
Baie Hapatoni
Hana Tetena
Mohotani (Motane)
Hana Tuuna
Hana Teio
920
Terihi 245
10° 00' S
Canal Haava
Baie des Traîtres
Baie Hanahupe

kilometers 15
statute miles 15

UA HUKA
France

51

139° 30' W
Roches Epeti
Motu Tabu
Pte. Haunanu
Motu Katohau
574
594
855
Baie Hanahe
Pte. Tetutu
Vaipaee
Hane
Hokatu
Baie Chave
(Hat) Teuaua
Baie de Hane
Pte. Teoho Ote Papa
9° 00' S

km 10
statute mi 10

GAMBIER IS.
France

52

km 10
statute mi 10

23° 00' S
Puaumu Nord
Tenoka
Pte. Tepapure
Baie de Gatavake
Îles Gambier
Pte. Kutu-Puhi-Puhi
Totegegie
Taravai
Mangareva
Rikitea
441
Taravai
Aukena
Mekiro
Motu Ari
Taravai
Akamaru
Teakava
Motu Teko
Manui
Motu Makaroa
Kouakou
Kamaka
Passe du Sud-Ouest
Passe du Sud-Est

PITCAIRN ISLAND
United Kingdom

53

Young's Rock
Six Feet
Point Christian
Adamstown
Bounty Bay
Adam's Rock
St. Paul's Point
The Rope
Tautama
Gudgeon Bay
Timiti's Crack
25° 05' S

kilometers
statute miles

130° 05' W

Independent Nations

Fiji Islands

REPUBLIC OF THE FIJI ISLANDS

AREA 18,274 sq km (7,056 sq mi)
POPULATION 852,000
CAPITAL Suva 203,000
RELIGION Christian, Hindu, Muslim
LANGUAGE English, Fijian, Hindustani
LITERACY 92%
LIFE EXPECTANCY 68 years
GDP PER CAPITA $7,300
ECONOMY IND: tourism, sugar, clothing, copra. AGR: sugarcane, coconuts, cassava (tapioca), rice; cattle; fish. EXP: sugar, garments, gold, timber.

Kiribati
REPUBLIC OF KIRIBATI

AREA 717 sq km (277 sq mi)
POPULATION 95,000
CAPITAL Tarawa 32,000
RELIGION Roman Catholic, Protestant
LANGUAGE English, I-Kiribati
LITERACY NA
LIFE EXPECTANCY 60 years
GDP PER CAPITA $850
ECONOMY IND: fishing, handicrafts. AGR: copra, taro, breadfruit, sweet potatoes; fish. EXP: copra, coconuts, seaweed, fish.

Marshall Islands
REPUBLIC OF THE MARSHALL ISLANDS

AREA 181 sq km (70 sq mi)
POPULATION 54,000
CAPITAL Majuro, 25,000
RELIGION Christian (mostly Protestant)
LANGUAGE English, local dialects, Japanese
LITERACY 93%
LIFE EXPECTANCY 66 years
GDP PER CAPITA $1,670
ECONOMY IND: copra, fish, tourism, craft items from shell, wood, and pearls. AGR: coconuts, tomatoes, melons, cacao; pigs. EXP: fish, coconut oil, trochus shells.

Micronesia
FEDERATED STATES OF MICRONESIA

AREA 702 sq km (271 sq mi)
POPULATION 108,000
CAPITAL Palikir 11,000
RELIGION Roman Catholic, Protestant
LANGUAGE English, Trukese, Pohnpeian, Yapese, Kosrean
LITERACY 89%
LIFE EXPECTANCY NA
GDP PER CAPITA $2,000
ECONOMY IND: tourism, construction, fish processing, craft items from shell, wood, and pearls. AGR: black pepper, tropical fruits and vegetables, coconuts, cassava (tapioca); pigs. EXP: fish, garments, bananas, black pepper.

Nauru
REPUBLIC OF NAURU

AREA 21 sq km (8 sq mi)
POPULATION 12,000
CAPITAL Yaren 5,000
RELIGION Protestant, Roman Catholic
LANGUAGE Nauruan, English
LITERACY NA
LIFE EXPECTANCY 61 years
GDP PER CAPITA $5,000
ECONOMY IND: phosphate mining, financial services, coconut products. AGR: coconuts. EXP: phosphates.

Palau

REPUBLIC OF PALAU

AREA 487 sq km (188 sq mi)
POPULATION 20,000
CAPITAL Koror 14,000
RELIGION Christian, Modekngei (indigenous)
LANGUAGE English, Palauan, Japanese, three additional local languages
LITERACY 92%
LIFE EXPECTANCY 69 years
GDP PER CAPITA $7,100
ECONOMY IND: tourism, craft items, construction, garment making. AGR: coconuts, copra, cassava (tapioca), sweet potatoes. EXP: trochus (type of shellfish), tuna, copra, handicrafts.

Samoa

INDEPENDENT STATE OF SAMOA

AREA 2,831 sq km (1,093 sq mi)
POPULATION 171,000
CAPITAL Apia 35,000
RELIGION Protestant, Roman Catholic
LANGUAGE Samoan, English
LITERACY 97%
LIFE EXPECTANCY 70 years
GDP PER CAPITA $3,200
ECONOMY IND: food processing, building materials, auto parts. AGR: coconuts, bananas, taro, yams. EXP: coconut oil and cream, copra, fish, beer.

Solomon Islands
SOLOMON ISLANDS

AREA 28,450 sq km (10,985 sq mi)
POPULATION 479,000
CAPITAL Honiara 78,000
RELIGION Protestant, Roman Catholic, indigenous beliefs
LANGUAGE Melanesian pidgin, 120 indigenous languages, English
LITERACY NA
LIFE EXPECTANCY 72 years
GDP PER CAPITA $2,000
ECONOMY IND: fish (tuna), mining, timber. AGR: cocoa, beans, coconuts, palm kernels; cattle; timber; fish. EXP: timber, fish, palm oil, cocoa.

Tonga
KINGDOM OF TONGA

AREA 699 sq km (270 sq mi)
POPULATION 101,000
CAPITAL Nuku'alofa 33,000
RELIGION Christian
LANGUAGE Tongan, English
LITERACY 99%
LIFE EXPECTANCY 68 years
GDP PER CAPITA $2,200
ECONOMY IND: tourism, fishing. AGR: squash, coconuts, copra, bananas. EXP: squash, fish, vanilla beans.

Tuvalu
TUVALU

AREA 26 sq km (10 sq mi)
POPULATION 10,000
CAPITAL Funafuti 5,000
RELIGION Church of Tuvalu (Congregationalist), Seventh-Day Adventist, Baha'i
LANGUAGE Tuvaluan, English
LITERACY NA
LIFE EXPECTANCY 67 years
GDP PER CAPITA $1,100
ECONOMY IND: fishing, tourism, copra. AGR: coconuts; fish. EXP: copra.

Vanuatu
REPUBLIC OF VANUATU

AREA 14,760 sq km (5,700 sq mi)
POPULATION 212,000
CAPITAL Port-Vila 31,000
RELIGION Protestant, Roman Catholic, indigenous beliefs
LANGUAGE English, French, pidgin (Bislama)
LITERACY 53%
LIFE EXPECTANCY 61 years
GDP PER CAPITA $1,300
ECONOMY IND: food and fish freezing, wood processing, meat canning. AGR: copra, coconuts, cocoa, coffee; fish. EXP: copra, kava, beef, cocoa.

Dependencies

AUSTRALIA

SOVEREIGN   LOCAL

Norfolk Island
TERRITORY OF NORFOLK ISLAND

AREA 35 sq km (14 sq mi)
POPULATION 2,000
CAPITAL Kingston 1,000
RELIGION Protestant, Roman Catholic
LANGUAGE English, Norfolk
LITERACY NA
LIFE EXPECTANCY NA
GDP PER CAPITA $4,420
ECONOMY IND: tourism. AGR: pine seed, palm seed, cereals, vegetables; cattle. EXP: postage stamps, pine and palm seed, avocados.

Coral Sea Islands

CORAL SEA ISLANDS TERRITORY

AREA Less than 3 sq km (1 sq mi)
POPULATION none

UNITED KINGDOM

SOVEREIGN   LOCAL

Pitcairn Islands
PITCAIRN, HENDERSON, DUCIE, AND OENO ISLANDS

AREA 47 sq km (18 sq mi)
POPULATION 50
CAPITAL Adamstown 50
RELIGION Seventh-Day Adventist
LANGUAGE English, Pitcairnese
LITERACY NA
LIFE EXPECTANCY NA
GDP PER CAPITA NA
ECONOMY IND: postage stamps, handicrafts. AGR: fruits and vegetables; goats, chickens. EXP: fruits, vegetables, curios, stamps.

Dependencies

FRANCE

French Polynesia
TERRITORY OF FRENCH POLYNESIA
- AREA 4,167 sq km (1,609 sq mi)
- POPULATION 241,000
- CAPITAL Papeete 125,000
- RELIGION Protestant, Roman Catholic
- LANGUAGE French, Tahitian
- LITERACY 98%
- LIFE EXPECTANCY 75 years
- GDP PER CAPITA $10,800
- ECONOMY IND: tourism, pearls, agricultural processing, handicrafts. AGR: coconuts, vanilla, vegetables, fruits; poultry. EXP: cultured pearls, coconut products, mother-of-pearl, vanilla.

New Caledonia
TERRITORY OF NEW CALEDONIA AND DEPENDENCIES
- AREA 19,060 sq km (7,359 sq mi)
- POPULATION 220,000
- CAPITAL Nouméa 138,000
- RELIGION Roman Catholic, Protestant
- LANGUAGE French, 33 Melanesian-Polynesian dialects
- LITERACY 91%
- LIFE EXPECTANCY 73 years
- GDP PER CAPITA $15,000
- ECONOMY IND: nickel mining and smelting. AGR: vegetables; beef. EXP: ferronickels, nickel ore, fish.

Wallis and Futuna Islands
TERRITORY OF THE WALLIS AND FUTUNA ISLANDS
- AREA 274 sq km (106 sq mi)
- POPULATION 15,000
- CAPITAL Matâ'utu 1,000
- RELIGION Roman Catholic
- LANGUAGE French, Wallisian
- LITERACY 50%
- LIFE EXPECTANCY NA
- GDP PER CAPITA $2,000
- ECONOMY IND: copra, handicrafts, fishing, lumber. AGR: breadfruit, yams, taro, bananas; pigs. EXP: copra, chemicals, construction materials.

Clipperton Island
CLIPPERTON ISLAND
- AREA 7 sq km (3 sq mi)
- POPULATION none

NEW ZEALAND

Cook Islands
COOK ISLANDS
- AREA 240 sq km (93 sq mi)
- POPULATION 19,000
- CAPITAL Avarua 12,000
- RELIGION Christian
- LANGUAGE English, Maori
- LITERACY NA
- LIFE EXPECTANCY NA
- GDP PER CAPITA $5,000
- ECONOMY IND: fruit processing, tourism, fishing. AGR: copra, citrus, pineapples, tomatoes; pigs. EXP: copra, papayas, fresh and canned citrus fruit, coffee.

Niue
NIUE
- AREA 260 sq km (100 sq mi)
- POPULATION 2,000
- CAPITAL Alofi 1,000
- RELIGION Ekalesia Niue (a Protestant church), Latter-Day Saints, other Christian
- LANGUAGE Polynesian (related to Tongan and Samoan), English
- LITERACY 95%
- LIFE EXPECTANCY NA
- GDP PER CAPITA $2,800
- ECONOMY IND: tourism, handicrafts, food processing. AGR: coconuts, passion fruit, honey, limes; pigs. EXP: canned coconut cream, copra, honey, passion fruit products.

Tokelau
TOKELAU
- AREA 10 sq km (4 sq mi)
- POPULATION 2,000
- CAPITAL none
- RELIGION Congregational Christian Church, Roman Catholic
- LANGUAGE Tokelauan, English
- LITERACY NA
- LIFE EXPECTANCY NA
- GDP PER CAPITA $1,000
- ECONOMY IND: small-scale enterprises for copra production and woodworking, stamps, coins, fishing. AGR: coconuts, copra, breadfruit, papayas; pigs. EXP: stamps, copra, handicrafts.

UNITED STATES

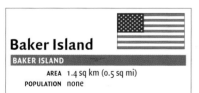

American Samoa
AMERICAN SAMOA
- AREA 199 sq km (77 sq mi)
- POPULATION 61,000
- CAPITAL Pago Pago 15,000
- RELIGION Christian Congregationalist, Roman Catholic, Protestant
- LANGUAGE Samoan, English
- LITERACY 97%
- LIFE EXPECTANCY 75 years
- GDP PER CAPITA $8,000
- ECONOMY IND: tuna canneries, handicrafts. AGR: bananas, coconuts, vegetables, taro; dairy products. EXP: canned tuna.

Guam
GUAM
- AREA 549 sq km (212 sq mi)
- POPULATION 158,000
- CAPITAL Hagåtña (Agana) 2,000
- RELIGION Roman Catholic
- LANGUAGE English, Chamorro, Japanese
- LITERACY 99%
- LIFE EXPECTANCY 78 years
- GDP PER CAPITA $21,000
- ECONOMY IND: US military, tourism, construction, transshipment services. AGR: fruits, copra, vegetables; eggs. EXP: mostly transshipments of refined petroleum products, construction materials, fish, food and beverage products.

Northern Mariana Islands
COMMONWEALTH OF THE NORTHERN MARIANA ISLANDS
- AREA 477 sq km (184 sq mi)
- POPULATION 78,000
- CAPITAL Saipan 7,000
- RELIGION Christian, traditional beliefs
- LANGUAGE English, Chamorro, Carolinian
- LITERACY 97%
- LIFE EXPECTANCY 76 years
- GDP PER CAPITA $12,500
- ECONOMY IND: tourism, construction, garments, handicrafts. AGR: coconuts, fruits, vegetables; cattle. EXP: garments.

Baker Island
BAKER ISLAND
- AREA 1.4 sq km (0.5 sq mi)
- POPULATION none

Howland Island
HOWLAND ISLAND
- AREA 1.6 sq km (0.6 sq mi)
- POPULATION None

Jarvis Island
JARVIS ISLAND
- AREA 4.5 sq km (1.7 sq mi)
- POPULATION none

Johnston Atoll
JOHNSTON ATOLL
- AREA 2.8 sq km (1.1 sq mi)
- POPULATION none

Kingman Reef
KINGMAN REEF
- AREA 1 sq km (0.4 sq mi)
- POPULATION none

Midway Islands
MIDWAY ISLANDS
- AREA 6.2 sq km (2.4 sq mi)
- POPULATION none

Palmyra Atoll
PALMYRA ATOLL
- AREA 11.9 sq km (4.6 sq mi)
- POPULATION none

Wake Island
WAKE ISLAND
- AREA 6.5 sq km (2.5 sq mi)
- POPULATION none

ANTARCTICA

O ften called the last wilderness on Earth, Antarctica's unspoiled expanses of austere frozen beauty remain largely untouched by humans. Driest, coldest, windiest, and least populated of Earth's seven continents, its 5.1 million square miles (13.2 million sq km) of ice-shrouded land sit at the bottom of the world, larger than Europe or Australia. An average elevation of 8,000 feet (2,438 m) makes it the highest continent as well.

Antarctica's ice cap, greatest body of ice in the world, holds some 70 percent of the Earth's fresh water. Yet despite all this ice and water, the Antarctic interior averages only two inches of precipitation per year, making it the largest desert in the world; the little snow that does fall, however, almost never melts.

The immensely heavy ice sheet, averaging over a mile (1.6 km) thick and in places reaching almost three miles (4.8 km) in thickness, compresses the land surface over much of the continent to below sea level. The weight actually deforms the South Pole, creating a slightly pear-shaped Earth.

A Ross Sea iceberg becomes a diving platform for hundreds of emperor penguin youngsters. Clumsy on land, they are marvelous swimmers and can live for 20 years or more.

Beneath the ice exists a continent of valleys, lakes, islands, and mountains, little dreamed of until the compilation of more than 2.5 million ice-thickness measurements revealed startling topography below. Less than 2 percent of Antarctica actually breaks through the ice cover to reveal stretches of coastline, islands, and features such as the outstanding Transantarctic Mountains, which extend for 1,800 miles (2, 897 km) and separate East and West Antarctica.

In spite of perpetual light during the Antarctic summer (December to March), little heat accumulates because the white, snowy landscape reflects more than 80 percent of the sun's incoming rays. During the half year of darkness, terrible cold and storms buffet the continent. The winter of 1983 saw the lowest temperature ever recorded on Earth—minus 128.6°F (-89.2°C).

Annual winter temperatures over the elevated central plateau average minus 80°F (-62.2°C), and this cold season causes the ice around Antarctica to grow quickly. Sea ice averaging six feet deep more than doubles the size of the continent, extending outward to create a belt ranging from 300 miles to more than 1,000 miles (483–1,609 km) wide.

In spring, melting ice coincides with calving of huge white and blue-green icebergs from the Antarctic glaciers. The largest iceberg ever spotted, in 1956, measured 208 miles (335 km) long by 60 miles (97 km) wide, slightly larger than Belgium.

Antarctica's Southern Ocean, which holds 10 percent of the world's sea water, swirls in rhythm with the Antarctic Circumpolar Current, largest, fastest current in the world, which sweeps clockwise around the globe unimpeded by any land. These high southern latitudes experience extremes of wind and weather. At around 60° south latitude, a remarkable interface of relatively warm waters from the southern Atlantic, Indian, and Pacific oceans and the cold Southern Ocean creates conditions for an eruption of rich nutrients, phytoplankton, and zooplankton. These form the base for a flourishing marine ecosystem. Though limited in numbers of species—for example, only about 120 kinds of the world's 20,000 fish swim here—Antarctica's animal life has adapted extremely well to so harsh a climate.

Seasonal feeding and energy storage in fats exemplify this specialization. Well-known animals of the far south include seals, whales, and distinctive birds such as flightless penguins, albatrosses, terns, and petrels.

PHYSICAL GEOGRAPHY

Every summer thousands of scientists travel to Antarctica to obtain vital information about the Earth's weather and ecology and the state of the southernmost continent. This interest attests to the region's role as a pristine laboratory, where measurements and rates of change in numerous scientific fields can point to larger issues of the world's environmental health.

Antarctica's oceanic and atmospheric system—indicator and element of climate change—is a main area of focus. Oceanographers attempt to understand more fully the global exchange of heat, sea-ice dynamics, salt and trace elements, and the entire marine biosphere. Other important research has included the 1985 discovery of a hole in the Earth's protective ozone layer by scientists at the British Halley research station. This find brought to prominence a major ecological threat.

Ice and sediment cores provide insight into the world's ancient climate and allow for comparison with conditions today. Studies of the Antarctic ice sheet help predict future sea levels, important news for the three billion people who live in coastal areas. If the Antarctic ice sheet were to melt, global seas would rise by an estimated 200 feet, inundating many oceanic islands and gravely altering the world's coastlines.

Three basic water masses comprise the Southern Ocean: Antarctic Surface Water, Circumpolar Deep Water, and Antarctic Bottom Water. Sharp boundaries separate the water masses, each with its own characteristics. These differences drive circulation around the continent and contribute to the global heat engine and overall transfer of energy around the world.

Prominent physical features include the Vinson Massif, Antarctica's highest mountain at 16,067 feet (4,897 m). Discovered only in 1958 by U.S. Navy aircraft, it was first climbed by an American team in 1966.

The Antarctic Peninsula, reaching like a long arm 800 miles (1,287 km) into the Southern Ocean toward the tip of South America, is made up of a mountain range and many islands linked together by ice. Seals, penguins, and other sea birds find it particularly suitable, and the peninsula's relative accessibility makes it the Antarctic area most visited by humans.

The continent's only sizable river, the Onyx, arises from a coastal glacier near McMurdo Sound. Every summer its waters flow inland for some 20 miles (32 km), replenishing and raising the surface level of Lake Vanda, one of several lakes in the Dry Valleys. These valleys, free of snow and ice unlike the rest of Antarctica, were created by ancient glaciers. They stretch to the coast from the Transantarctic Mountains, a range high enough here to prevent the great Polar Plateau ice sheet from flowing down to the sea through the Dry Valleys, perhaps the driest places on Earth.

Immense ice shelves, produced by the main plateau disgorging masses of ice, rim much of the continent's coast and extend far into the sea. Largest are the Ross Ice Shelf, the size of France, and the Ronne Ice Shelf.

Special names exist for the many different types of ice: frazil ice, an early stage of sea-ice growth in which crystals below the surface form an unstructured slush; nilas, a thin sheen of ice on the sea surface that bends but does not break with wave action; pancake ice, named for its flattened circular shape; pack ice, frozen sea water and floating ice driven together to form a continuous mass; and fast ice, that part of the sea-ice cover attached to land.

CULTURE, HISTORY, AND EXPLORATION

Heroism, hardship, and sacrifice marked the early decades of Antarctic exploration, and only in the early 20th century did men penetrate the continent to reveal its secrets and strange allure.

The search for Antarctica represented the last great adventure of global exploration. British Captain James Cook crossed three times into Antarctic waters between 1772 and 1775 and was probably the first to cross the Antarctic Circle. Though he never saw the continent, he believed in "a tract of land at

Scientists seeking to understand sea ice are suspended above the icescape. Pancake ice forms when a thin surface film of ice crystals breaks up and thickens into irregular disks.

the Pole that is the source of all the ice that is spread over this vast Southern Ocean."

His observations of marine mammals in great numbers lured whalers and sealers into the freezing southern waters in search of skins and oil. First sightings of the continent then followed in 1820.

Scientists seeking the south magnetic pole included British naval officer James Clark Ross, who between 1839–43 charted unknown territory, including a giant ice shelf later named after him, and located the approximate position of the south magnetic pole—the point toward which a compass needle points from any direction throughout surrounding areas.

In 1895, Norwegian whalers landed on the continent beyond the Antarctic Peninsula for the first time, and in 1898 a major Belgian scientific expedition overwintered in the Antarctic when their ship became stuck in pack ice for almost 13 months.

Douglas Mawson reached the south magnetic pole as part of Ernest Shackleton's 1907 Nimrod expedition. Later, Mawson led the Australasian Antarctic Expedition (1911–14), which produced observations in magnetism, geology, biology, and meteorology.

A race to reach the South Geographic Pole came to a climax in 1911–12. Norwegian Roald Amundsen's expedition reached the South Pole on December 14, 1911, after 97 days on the move, relying on husky dogs to pull their sleds. Simultaneously, the British team of Robert Falcon Scott and four companions set off unaware of Amundsen's swifter, better managed effort. Scott's use of ponies proved a mistake; his team reached the Pole 34 days later, only to find the Norwegian flag flying. The five men began the bitter return trip, but succumbed to cold, hunger, exhaustion, and bad weather, just 11 miles (18 km) from supplies. All died.

Another epic adventure involved Ernest Shackleton, whose British expedition aimed to traverse the entire continent. In 1915 Shackleton's main party of 28 men became stranded when sea ice trapped and crushed their ship. After more than a year on drifting ice, they sailed in lifeboats to Elephant Island at the tip of the Antarctic Peninsula. Shackleton and five others then embarked on an astonishing 800-mile (1,287 km) journey in a small boat to South Georgia, from where he eventually rescued his other men.

In 1935 Caroline Mikkelsen, wife of a Norwegian whaling captain, became the first woman to stand on Antarctica. Almost a dozen years later the United States Navy brought 4,700 men, 13 ships, and 23 aircraft to the continent, using icebreakers for the first time. The vast enterprise mapped large areas of the coastline and interior and took 70,000 aerial photographs.

The modern scientific era arrived with the 18-month-long International Geophysical Year (IGY, 1957–58), when many nations advanced knowledge of the continent. The Antarctic Treaty, signed in 1959 by 12 leading IGY participants, has done much to protect Antarctica.

Today some 60 research stations stand at many sites around Antarctica, and an ever-shifting population, including tourists, can reach as high as 20,000 people in the summer. Tourism brings its own troubles. Recently, species of non-native grasses, presumably carried on visitors' clothing, have been found on the continent. Further unintentional aliens, such as algae, crustaceans, and parasites arrive on floating plastic bottles and other man-made debris.

MINERALS AND ECONOMY

Many believe Antarctica has great resource wealth, but the harsh climate, short work season, and need to drill through thick ice make the recovery of these resources difficult.

Minerals under the ice include gold, uranium, cobalt, chromium, nickel, copper, iron, and platinum, as well as potentially large deposits of diamonds. Oil probably exists below the ocean floor, and coal deposits have been detected along the coast and throughout the Transantarctic Mountains.

A pressing reason to limit mineral exploration and drilling is Antarctica's extreme fragility. Sensitive plants, including rare moss beds on the Antarctic Peninsula, take three to four hundred years to grow, and a single human boot can cause tremendous damage.

In January 1998 an addition to the Antarctic Treaty, known as the Madrid Protocol, went into force, deeming Antarctica a natural reserve devoted to peace and science. It specifically banned mining and mineral exploitation of any kind until 2048.

But pressure builds yearly to find new mineral and petroleum deposits. Despite the ban, Russia and other countries appear to be actively exploring Antarctic oil, gas, and mineral resources. Also significant is the growing commercialization of Southern Ocean fisheries. Particularly vulnerable are the tiny shrimp-like krill that form a vital part of Antarctica's food chain. The collapse of fish and krill species might be analogous to the wholesale slaughter of fur seal populations in the late 1700s and early 1800s and the near destruction of the Southern Ocean's whales in the 20th century.

Antarctica already witnesses vehicle pollution; dumping of plastics, solid wastes, food, and batteries; burning of fossil fuels; and construction of roads and airstrips at the many scientific bases.

Even the most obvious resource of all—ice—may one day serve to relieve thirsty nations. Ships towing icebergs from Antarctica to all parts of the world could deliver this huge potential of fresh water, but at present such a project is simply too expensive.

Physical and Political
ANTARCTICA

Contributions from the following organizations are gratefully acknowledged: National Science Foundation, Washington, D.C.; Norwegian Polar Institute, Tromsø, Norway; British Antarctic Survey, Cambridge, United Kingdom; University of Cambridge, Scott Polar Institute, Cambridge, United Kingdom; U.S. Navy/NOAA Joint Ice Center, Washington, D.C.; U.S. Geological Survey; Lamont-Doherty Earth Observatory of Columbia University, Palisades, New York; National Aeronautics and Space Administration. Special thanks to Richard S. Williams, Jr., John Smellie, George E. Watson, and Guy Gutheridge.

ANTARCTIC PENINSULA AREA STATIONS

Argentina		**Korea, South**	
1 Esperanza	C4	10 King Sejong	C3
2 Jubany	C4	**Poland**	
3 Marambio	C4	11 Arctowski	C3
4 San Martín	E5	**Russia**	
Brazil		12 Bellingshausen	C3
5 Comandante Ferraz	C3	**Ukraine**	
Chile		13 Vernadsky	D4
6 Capitán Arturo Prat	C4	**United Kingdom**	
7 General Bernardo O'Higgins	C4	14 Rothera	E4
8 Presidente Eduardo Frei	C3	**United States**	
China		15 Palmer	D4
9 Great Wall	C3	**Uruguay**	
		16 Artigas	C3

DECEPTION ISLAND

Deception Island is the horseshoe-shaped summit of a largely submerged volcano with a flooded caldera. It was particularly active in the 19th century and late 18th centuries, and saw eruptions during two episodes in the 20th century (1906-12 and 1967-70), resulting in the destruction of scientific stations on the island. Now it is a popular destination for tourists, many of whom swim in the volcanically-heated waters.

Edward Bransfield charted this region in 1820, establishing the British claim to discovery of Antarctica. The following year members of a sealing expedition led by John Davis, an American, went ashore at Hughes Bay, the first known landing on the continent.

ANTARCTIC PENINSULA

A mountain range welded to clusters of islands by a relatively thin coat of ice, this 800-mile-long peninsula is popular with penguins and other seabirds, including gulls, skuas, and petrels and provides important habitat for several species of seals.

MINERALS

The mineral-resource potential of Antarctica is unknown. Geologists have located copper, lead, zinc, gold, and silver on the Antarctic Peninsula. Chromium and platinum may exist in the Pensacola Mountains, and low-grade coal lies in the Transantarctic Mountains. East Antarctica contains iron ore. Oil and natural gas are almost certainly present in sedimentary basins as deep as 14,000 m (46,000 ft) near Prydz Bay, the Ross Sea, and the Weddell Sea, but exploitation has been banned for at least 50 years. In 1991, Antarctic Treaty parties signed an agreement to prohibit "any activity relating to mineral resources other than scientific research." In 1998, Antarctic Treaty parties signed an agreement to establish the Committee for Environmental Protection (CEP). The CEP will help preserve the continent's immeasurable value as an archive of the world's climatic past and will enable it to continue to be a sensitive barometer of the planet's future.

CLIMATE

The southern polar region is substantially colder than its northern counterpart. The lofty ice sheet reflects as much as 90 percent of solar radiation back to space, whereas in the Arctic Ocean ice partly melts in summer and the dark waters absorb heat. The temperature difference between the equatorial and polar regions drives atmospheric circulation. Because the South Pole is colder than the North, winds are stronger in the Southern Hemisphere. The ice sheet contains a climate record that extends back at least 200,000 years at some locations. Ice cores preserve a record of past atmospheric composition, volcanic eruptions, and other environmental information.

KATABATIC WINDS

Upper-level air circulates toward Antarctica from the tropics. By the time it reaches the continent, most moisture has been lost. Intensely chilled, the air descends over the central polar plateau, where winds are typically light. Then, like cold air spilling out of an open refrigerator, the air pours downhill with increasing speed until it blasts the coast at as much as 300 km (180 mi) an hour.

METEORITES

More than 16,000 meteorite fragments have been recovered from blue-ice areas of the Antarctic ice sheet. Found in almost pristine condition and representing most classes of meteorites described previously from finds in Earth's other continents, they yield information about the origin and evolution of the solar system. Some meteorites found are thought to have their origin on Mars or the Earth's moon because of their unique geochemical composition.

LARSEN ICE SHELF

During the past few decades, the Larsen Ice Shelf has been disintegrating on the north and along its eastern margin to the south. In recent years, the break up appears to have accelerated.

PALMER LAND

U.S. sealer Nathaniel Brown Palmer sailed along the west coast of the peninsula in November 1820 in search of rookeries. The U.S. credited him with the discovery of Antarctica, a prize also claimed by Britain and Russia. The newest polar research ship operated by the U.S. National Science Foundation is named the R/V Nathaniel B. Palmer.

HIGHEST POINT

At 4,897 m (16,067 ft) Vinson Massif is the highest elevation on Antarctica. It was climbed first by a U.S. team in 1966.

ELEVATION OF THE ICE SHEET

Many mountaintops rise higher than Antarctica's highest point—Vinson Massif, 16,067 feet—but with an average elevation of 8,000 feet, the continent ranks as Earth's highest. Asia, its closest competitor, averages 3,000 feet. Roughly dome shaped, the ice sheet conceals much of the bedrock relief below. The 1,800-mile-long Transantarctic Mountains rival the Rockies in height, but only the peaks break through the ice.

This was the location of Shackleton Base, point of departure for the Commonwealth Trans-Antarctic Expedition, which crossed the continent by tractor in 1957-58. Led by Sir Vivian Fuchs, the expedition traveled 3,472 kilometers to Scott Base in 99 days. A major calving event in 1986 removed more than 11,500 sq km of ice from the Filchner Ice Shelf. The ice had been the location of several scientific and exploration bases for the past 50 years.

THE LONGEST WINTER

Over hundreds of thousands of square miles of high plateau, the sunless cold of winter lasts from April through September. From beginning to end of the season, temperatures average minus 80°F.

F. G. von Bellingshausen, a Russian, sighted what may have been the mainland during his circumnavigation in 1820.

In 1898, Adrien de Gerlache de Gomery, a Belgian, led the first expedition to endure the Antarctic winter, after his ship froze in pack ice.

ICE SHELVES

Large areas of floating glacier ice fringe the coast of Antarctica. The two largest ice shelves are the Ross Ice Shelf and the Ronne Ice Shelf, both separated by glacier ice that is grounded below sea level. Large tabular icebergs periodically calve from ice shelves.

VOLCANOES

Mt. Erebus, the Earth's southernmost volcano, and Deception Island have remained active throughout the past century. Because it contains areas of volcanically-heated ground, Mt. Melbourne is considered to be a dormant volcano. Several other volcanoes in Marie Byrd Land (Mt. Takahe, Mt. Waesche, and Mt. Berlin) are known to have erupted tephra, now preserved within Antarctic ice, within the last few thousand years.

Rear Adm. Richard E. Byrd, USN, established five scientific stations (named Little America I through V) on Ross Ice Shelf near the Bay of Whales, the first in 1928, the last in 1956. As the ice shelf flowed forward and calved off, the stations were carried out to sea.

In 1841 Sir James Clark Ross, U... penetrated the pack ice to disco... the ice shelf now named for hi...

In 1899, C. E. Borchgrevink led a British expedition that was the first to winter on the continent.

Azimuthal Equidistant Projection

SCALE 1:13,759,000

1 CENTIMETER = 137 KILOMETERS; 1 INCH = 217 MILES

KILOMETERS
0 100 200 300 400 500

STATUTE MILES
0 100 200 300 400 500

⊙ Year-round research station

Blue figures on the continent indicate thickness of the ice in meters.

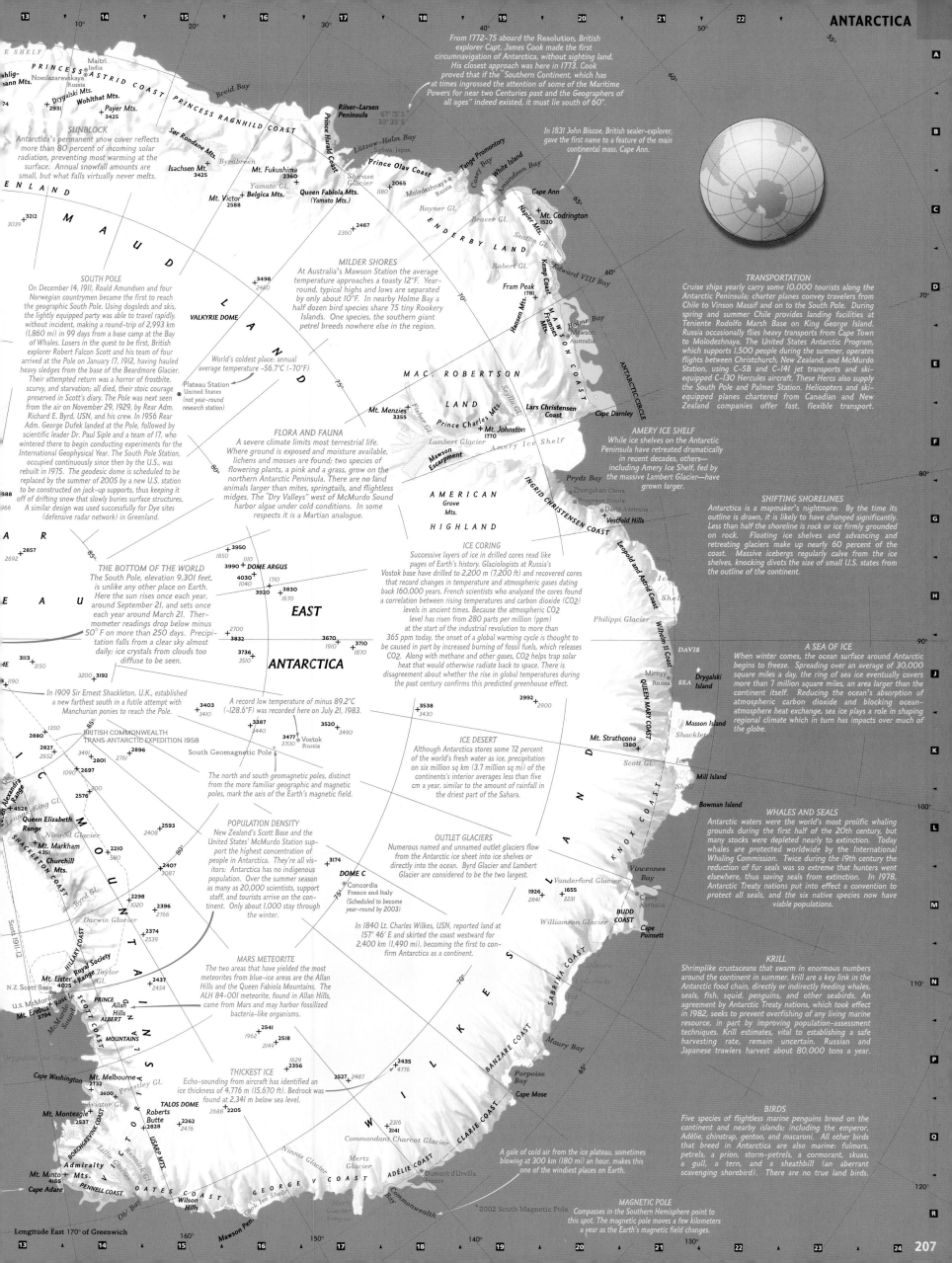

From 1772–75 aboard the Resolution, British explorer Capt. James Cook made the first circumnavigation of Antarctica, without sighting land. His closest approach was here in 1773. Cook proved that if the "Southern Continent, which has at times ingrossed the attention of some of the Maritime Powers for near two Centuries past and the Geographers of all ages" indeed existed, it must lie south of 60°.

In 1831 John Biscoe, British sealer-explorer, gave the first name to a feature of the main continental mass, Cape Ann.

SUNBLOCK
Antarctica's permanent snow cover reflects more than 80 percent of incoming solar radiation, preventing most warming at the surface. Annual snowfall amounts are small, but what falls virtually never melts.

MILDER SHORES
At Australia's Mawson Station the average temperature approaches a toasty 12°F. Year-round, typical highs and lows are separated by only about 10°F. In nearby Holme Bay a half dozen bird species share 75 tiny Rookery Islands. One species, the southern giant petrel breeds nowhere else in the region.

SOUTH POLE
On December 14, 1911, Roald Amundsen and four Norwegian countrymen became the first to reach the geographic South Pole. Using dogsleds and skis, the lightly equipped party was able to travel rapidly, without incident, making a round-trip of 2,993 km (1,860 mi) in 99 days from a base camp at the Bay of Whales. Losers in the quest to be first, British explorer Robert Falcon Scott and his team of four arrived at the Pole on January 17, 1912, having hauled heavy sledges from the base of the Beardmore Glacier. Their attempted return was a horror of frostbite, scurvy, and starvation; all died, their stoic courage preserved in Scott's diary. The Pole was next seen from the air on November 29, 1929, by Rear Adm. Richard E. Byrd, USN, and his crew. In 1956 Rear Adm. George Dufek landed at the Pole, followed by scientific leader Dr. Paul Siple and a team of 17, who wintered there to begin conducting experiments for the International Geophysical Year. The South Pole Station, occupied continuously since then by the U.S., was rebuilt in 1975. The geodesic dome is scheduled to be replaced by the summer of 2005 by a new U.S. station to be constructed on jack-up supports, thus keeping it off of drifting snow that slowly buries surface structures. A similar design was used successfully for Dye sites (defensive radar network) in Greenland.

World's coldest place: annual average temperature −56.7°C (−70°F)

FLORA AND FAUNA
A severe climate limits most terrestrial life. Where ground is exposed and moisture available, lichens and mosses are found; two species of flowering plants, a pink and a grass, grow on the northern Antarctic Peninsula. There are no land animals larger than mites, springtails, and flightless midges. The "Dry Valleys" west of McMurdo Sound harbor algae under cold conditions. In some respects it is a Martian analogue.

THE BOTTOM OF THE WORLD
The South Pole, elevation 9,301 feet, is unlike any other place on Earth. Here the sun rises once each year, around September 21, and sets once each year around March 21. Thermometer readings drop below minus 50°F on more than 250 days. Precipitation falls from a clear sky almost daily; ice crystals from clouds too diffuse to be seen.

In 1909 Sir Ernest Shackleton, U.K., established a new farthest south in a futile attempt with Manchurian ponies to reach the Pole.

A record low temperature of minus 89.2°C (−128.6°F) was recorded here on July 21, 1983.

BRITISH COMMONWEALTH TRANS-ANTARCTIC EXPEDITION 1958

South Geomagnetic Pole

The north and south geomagnetic poles, distinct from the more familiar geographic and magnetic poles, mark the axis of the Earth's magnetic field.

ICE CORING
Successive layers of ice in drilled cores read like pages of Earth's history. Glaciologists at Russia's Vostok base have drilled to 2,200 m (7,200 ft) and recovered cores that record changes in temperature and atmospheric gases dating back 160,000 years. French scientists who analyzed the cores found a correlation between rising temperatures and carbon dioxide (CO_2) levels in ancient times. Because the atmospheric CO_2 level has risen from 280 parts per million (ppm) at the start of the industrial revolution to more than 365 ppm today, the onset of a global warming cycle is thought to be caused in part by increased burning of fossil fuels, which releases CO_2. Along with methane and other gases, CO_2 helps trap solar heat that would otherwise radiate back to space. There is disagreement about whether the rise in global temperatures during the past century confirms this predicted greenhouse effect.

ICE DESERT
Although Antarctica stores some 72 percent of the world's fresh water as ice, precipitation on six million sq km (3.7 million sq mi) of the continent's interior averages less than five cm a year, similar to the amount of rainfall in the driest part of the Sahara.

POPULATION DENSITY
New Zealand's Scott Base and the United States' McMurdo Station support the highest concentration of people in Antarctica. They're all visitors: Antarctica has no indigenous population. Over the summer season as many as 20,000 scientists, support staff, and tourists arrive on the continent. Only about 1,000 stay through the winter.

OUTLET GLACIERS
Numerous named and unnamed outlet glaciers flow from the Antarctic ice sheet into ice shelves or directly into the ocean. Byrd Glacier and Lambert Glacier are considered to be the two largest.

In 1840 Lt. Charles Wilkes, USN, reported land at 157° 46' E and skirted the coast westward for 2,400 km (1,490 mi), becoming the first to confirm Antarctica as a continent.

MARS METEORITE
The two areas that have yielded the most meteorites from blue-ice areas are the Allan Hills and the Queen Fabiola Mountains. The ALH 84-001 meteorite, found in Allan Hills, came from Mars and may harbor fossilized bacteria-like organisms.

THICKEST ICE
Echo-sounding from aircraft has identified an ice thickness of 4,776 m (15,670 ft). Bedrock was found at 2,341 m below sea level.

A gale of cold air from the ice plateau, sometimes blowing at 300 km (180 mi) an hour, makes this one of the windiest places on Earth.

TRANSPORTATION
Cruise ships yearly carry some 10,000 tourists along the Antarctic Peninsula; charter planes convey travelers from Chile to Vinson Massif and on to the South Pole. During spring and summer Chile provides landing facilities at Teniente Rodolfo Marsh Base on King George Island. Russia occasionally flies heavy transports from Cape Town to Molodezhnaya. The United States Antarctic Program, which supports 1,500 people during the summer, operates flights between Christchurch, New Zealand, and McMurdo Station, using C-5B and C-141 jet transports and ski-equipped C-130 Hercules aircraft. These Hercs also supply the South Pole and Palmer Station. Helicopters and ski-equipped planes chartered from Canadian and New Zealand companies offer fast, flexible transport.

AMERY ICE SHELF
While ice shelves on the Antarctic Peninsula have retreated dramatically in recent decades, others—including the massive Lambert Glacier—have grown larger.

SHIFTING SHORELINES
Antarctica is a mapmaker's nightmare: By the time its outline is drawn, it is likely to have changed significantly. Less than half the shoreline is rock or ice firmly grounded on rock. Floating ice shelves and advancing and retreating glaciers make up nearly 60 percent of the coast. Massive icebergs regularly calve from the ice shelves, knocking divots the size of small U.S. states from the outline of the continent.

A SEA OF ICE
When winter comes, the ocean surface around Antarctic begins to freeze. Spreading over an average of 30,000 square miles a day, the ring of sea ice eventually covers more than 7 million square miles, an area larger than the continent itself. Reducing the ocean's absorption of atmospheric carbon dioxide and blocking ocean-atmosphere heat exchange, sea ice plays a role in shaping regional climate which in turn has impacts over much of the globe.

WHALES AND SEALS
Antarctic waters were the world's most prolific whaling grounds during the first half of the 20th century, but many stocks were depleted nearly to extinction. Today whales are protected worldwide by the International Whaling Commission. Twice during the 19th century the reduction of fur seals was so extreme that hunters went elsewhere, thus saving seals from extinction. In 1978, Antarctic Treaty nations put into effect a convention to protect all seals, and the six native species now have viable populations.

KRILL
Shrimplike crustaceans that swarm in enormous numbers around the continent in summer, krill are a key link in the Antarctic food chain, directly or indirectly feeding whales, seals, fish, squid, penguins, and other seabirds. An agreement by Antarctic Treaty nations, which took effect in 1982, seeks to prevent overfishing of any living marine resource, in part by improving population-assessment techniques. Krill estimates, vital to establishing a safe harvesting rate, remain uncertain. Russian and Japanese trawlers harvest about 80,000 tons a year.

BIRDS
Five species of flightless marine penguins breed on the continent and nearby islands; including the emperor, Adélie, chinstrap, gentoo, and macaroni. All other birds that breed in Antarctica are also marine: fulmars, petrels, a prion, storm-petrels, a cormorant, skuas, a gull, a tern, and a sheathbill (an aberrant scavenging shorebird). There are no true land birds.

MAGNETIC POLE
Compasses in the Southern Hemisphere point to this spot. The magnetic pole moves a few kilometers a year as the Earth's magnetic field changes.

Longitude East 170° of Greenwich

Elevation of the Ice Sheet

Antarctica is Earth's coldest, driest, and on average highest continent (about 8,000 ft; 2,438 m). The continent is covered by a vast ice sheet that blankets over 96 percent of the land mass. The highest point, located in East Antarctica, rises to 13,222 feet (4,030 m). The ice sheet is interrupted only by occasional mountain peaks that pierce the ice. One such peak is the Vinson Massif, Antarctica's highest point, which reaches an elevation of 16,067 feet (4,897 m) and is located in West Antarctica. Otherwise the icy surface is smooth (surface slopes rarely exceed more than 1 or 2 degrees). The shape of the ice sheet is determined in part by the weight of the ice itself, which causes the ice to flow outward. It is also determined in part by forces acting at the base of the ice sheet that tend to restrain it. The balance of these forces leads to a characteristically parabola-like shape. Depar-tures from this simple shape occur as the ice from the interior domes spreads slowly over hills and valleys in the rocky base and where coastal mountain ranges channel the flow into outlet glaciers. Ice shelves form where there is sufficient ice to spread over the ocean. Ice shelves are the lowest and flattest parts of the ice sheet and are the source of the huge tabular icebergs that intermittently calve into the coastal ocean.

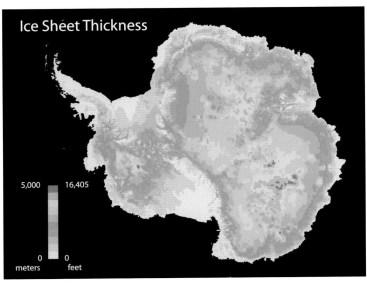

Surface Elevation

Vinson Massif
4897 m (16,067 ft)
Highest elevation
on Antarctica

5,000	16,405

| 0 | 0 |
| meters | feet |

Measurements of a Paradox

Ninety percent of the world's ice and 70 percent of the world's fresh water are found here, yet most of Antarctica is truly a desert. The snow equivalent of less than three inches of rain falls over the high interior of the continent each year. But snow and ice have been slowly accumulating on Antarctica for millions of years. More than 15,600 feet (4,755 m) deep at its thickest, the mean depth of the ice exceeds 6,600 feet (2,012 m). Ice is generally much thicker on the interior of the ice sheet than at edges. This is because ice flows from the interior to edges, where it eventually returns to the ocean either in the form of icebergs or by melting directly into the ocean. The few areas of thin ice on the interior lie over chains of subglacial mountains. Glaciologists measure ice thickness with either a downward-pointing radar or by seismic sounding, which records the echo from an explosive shot buried just beneath the surface of the ice sheet. The thickness measurements used for this map were collected by scientists from 15 nations over the last 50 years. Although in theory the amount of ice in the ice sheet is sufficient to raise global sea levels by approximately 187 feet (57 m), it is extremely unlikely that the entire ice sheet could be lost in the foreseeable future.

Ice Sheet Thickness

5,000	16,405

| 0 | 0 |
| meters | feet |

Ice on the Move

Glaciologists once thought that ice motion in Antarctica's interior was slow and relatively uniform, with just a few fast-moving outlet glaciers and some ice streams (in West Antarctica) drawing ice from the interior down to the ice shelves and the sea. A computer model of ice flow, based on new satellite elevation measurements, suggests a more intricate ice-movement pattern. Like rivers, coastal ice flows appear to be fed by complex systems of tributaries that penetrate hundreds of miles into major drainage basins, and the major streams identified in East Antarctica dwarf those of the West. New satellite-based radar images agree with this more dynamic view. Ice velocities in the streams can be ten times greater than the flow of the adjacent slow-moving ice, and the resulting stream boundaries are often heavily crevassed and detectable from space. The computer model combines measurements of surface elevation, ice sheet thickness, and snowfall to calculate the pattern of ice flow that would keep Antarctica in balance at its present shape. The resulting continent-wide baseline picture of this "balanced" flow generally resembles the actual situation, and detailed observations can be compared against it to uncover any changes occurring in the size and shape of the ice sheet.

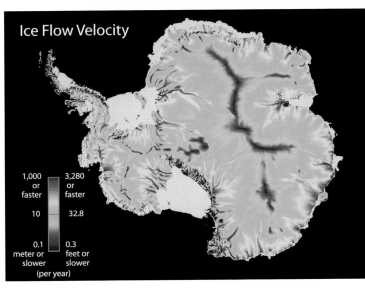

Ice Flow Velocity

1,000 or faster	3,280 or faster
10	32.8
0.1 meter or slower	0.3 feet or slower
(per year)	

Ultimate Winds

Katabatic winds—cold air pouring down glacial slopes—often blow at 80 miles (129 km) per hour and can exceed 180 miles (290 km) per hour. These winds, which drain cold air masses from central Antarctica under the influence of gravity, are funnelled down valleys outward towards the coast, as indicated by the streamline arrows (right) on the white background of the Antarctic continent. When katabatic winds reach the coastline they often turn westward to blow counterclockwise around the continent. Offshore, circumpolar winds and currents push against the sea ice that grows to surround Antarctica each winter, leading to drift distances of up to several miles per day. The resulting near-shore movement of the sea ice is known as the East Wind drift, due to the dominant winds from the east. In some locations, such as the Weddell Sea, the drift is forced northward along the Antarctic Peninsula. In this case, and in the Bellings-hausen, Amundsen, and Ross Seas, the combination of winds, currents, bathymetry, and topography leads to clockwise circulations known as gyres. In this image, the average sea-ice drift was determined from meteorological satellites. It illustrates the monthly average drift during the austral mid-winter, when sea-ice cover is at its maximum extent.

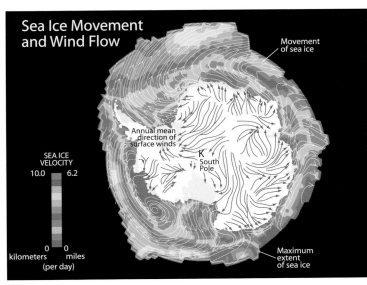

Sea Ice Movement and Wind Flow

Movement of sea ice

Annual mean direction of surface winds

K
South Pole

SEA ICE VELOCITY

10.0	6.2

0	0
kilometers	miles
(per day)	

Maximum extent of sea ice

Antarctic Treaty

On December 1, 1959, after a decade of secret meetings, 12 nations—Argentina, Australia, Belgium, Chile, France, Japan, New Zealand, Norway, South Africa, the Soviet Union (Russia), the United Kingdom, and the United States—signed the Antarctic Treaty to preserve the frozen continent for peaceful scientific use only, a major feat during the height of Cold War rivalries. Since then, 32 other nations have joined. The treaty includes all land, islands, and ice shelves south of 60° south latitude and enshrines the principles of peace, freedom of scientific research and exchange, and total banning of all military activity, nuclear testing, or disposal of radioactive waste. In addition, research stations are fully open to inspection, scientists may travel anywhere on the continent at any time, and countries can carry out aerial observations over any area.

A 1991 meeting prohibited mining in Antarctica. Other gatherings have asserted the importance of protecting wildlife, such as the Ross and fur seals, conserving unique biological habitats, and limiting human impact on sensitive ecological zones. The Antarctic Treaty made static all territorial claims held by 7 of the original 12 countries and prohibits any new claims. The treaty affirms that no country "rules the continent." For more than four decades it has proven to be an unprecedented example of international cooperation.

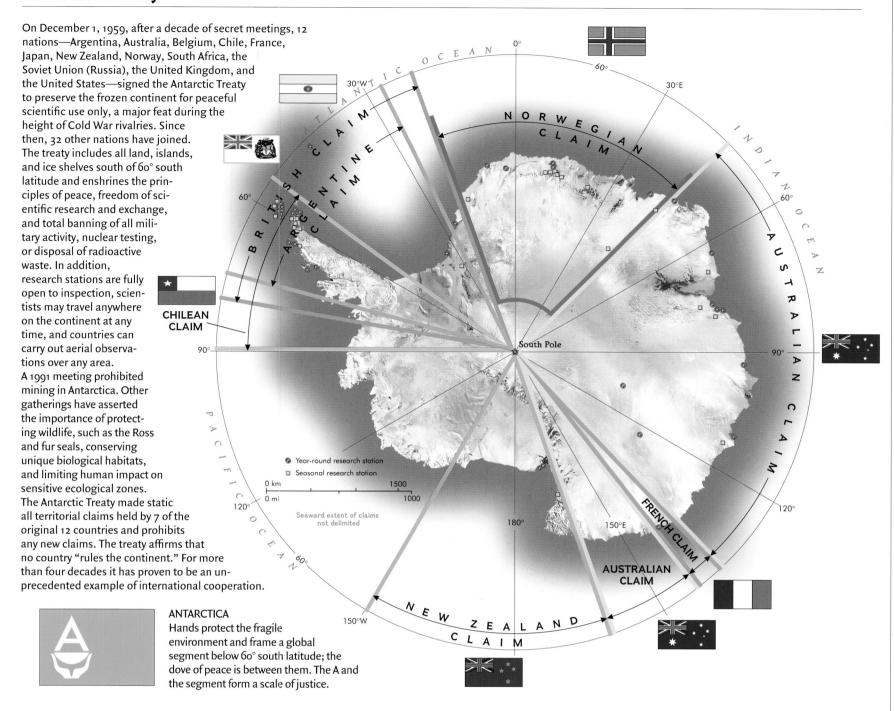

ANTARCTICA
Hands protect the fragile environment and frame a global segment below 60° south latitude; the dove of peace is between them. The A and the segment form a scale of justice.

Antarctic Convergence

The Antarctic Convergence refers to an undulating boundary in the seas that rings Antarctica roughly 950 miles (1,529 km) off the continental coast, between 50° and 60° south latitude. This narrow zone marks the meeting place of relatively warm waters from the southern Atlantic, Indian, and Pacific Oceans and the cold Antarctic Circumpolar Current. Because cold water sinks, it slips under the more buoyant warmer water and acts to power the great oceanic conveyor belt that affects life and weather around the world. The Antarctic Convergence also generates one of Earth's richest marine ecosystems. Mist and fog often rise at the interface of blended warm and cold waters. Immediately air becomes brisker

and marine life alters. Water temperatures can plummet a dozen degrees (Fahrenheit) or more upon entering the Southern Ocean. The Antarctic Convergence functions as a barrier and forms Antarctica's biological extent. It delimits the Southern Ocean, which holds 10 percent of the world's seawater, and thus creates a largely closed ecosystem and isolates the continent from warmer waters. Deep, cold waters permit the proliferation of diatoms—single-celled algae—that in turn support krill, shrimp-like organisms that exist in enormous numbers. Krill form a vital part of the food chain, directly or indirectly providing nutrition for Antarctica's amazing wildlife, particularly fish, seals, whales, and birds,

including five species of flightless penguins. Losses of this food source through over-harvesting by humans would seriously affect marine life. As one travels north into warmer regions beyond the Antarctic Convergence, krill—the basis of Antarctica's life—perish and disappear. The Southern Ocean's rich waters, full of plant and animal life, stand apart from the continent itself, frozen and incredibly harsh, where vegetation is limited to lichens, mosses, and a mere two species of flowering plants. A small insect known as the wingless midge represents the largest land animal. In contrast, large body size and slow growth mark many marine animals, all of which have adapted magnificently to the cold environment.

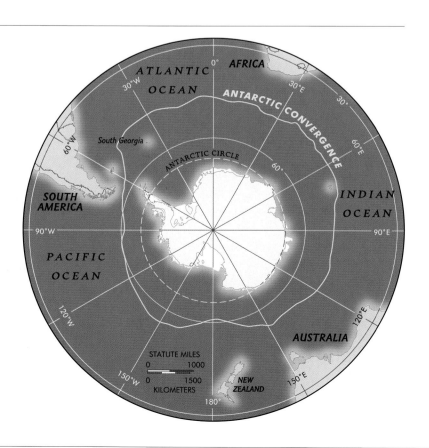

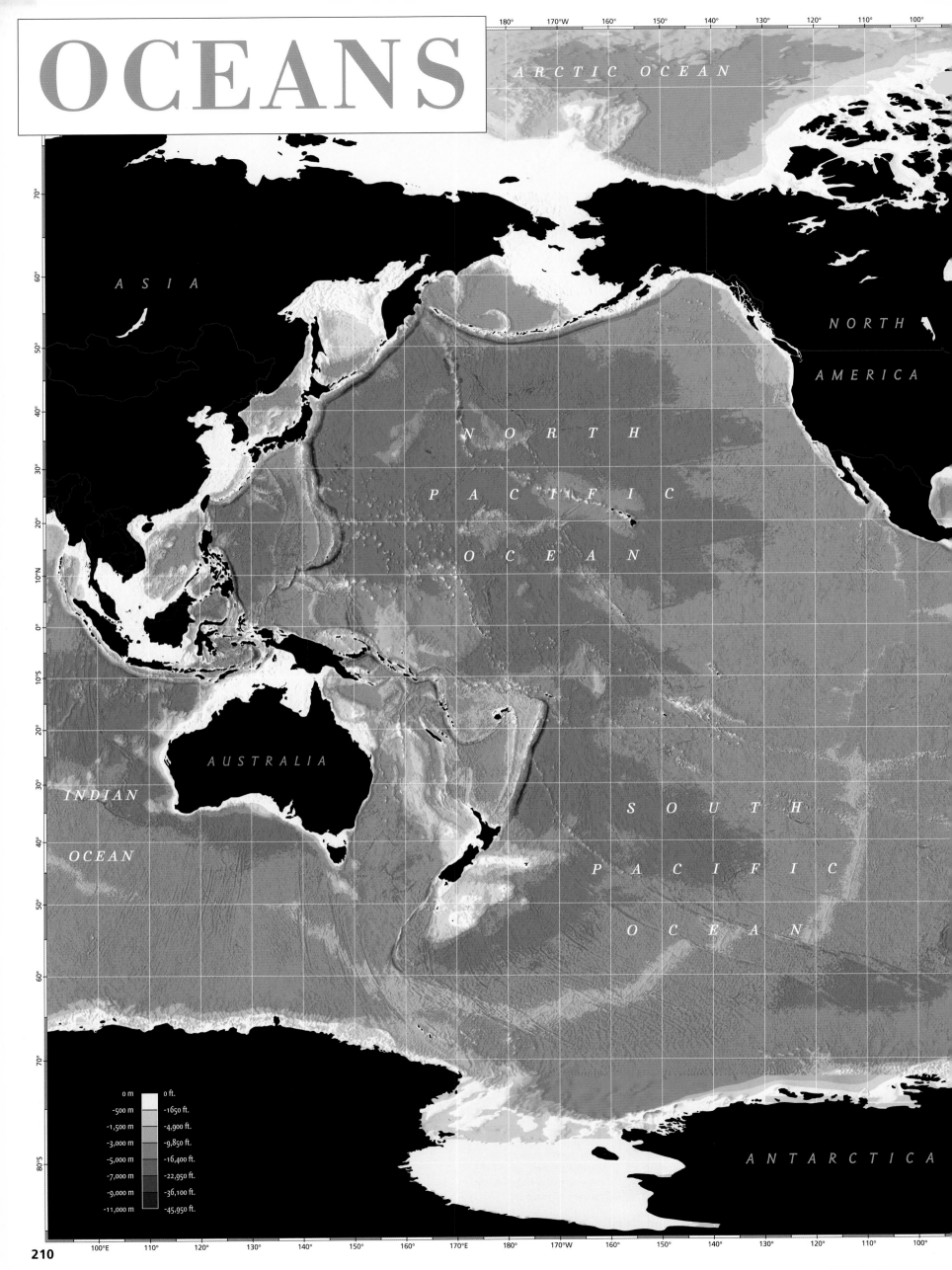

OCEANS

ARCTIC OCEAN

ASIA

NORTH

AMERICA

NORTH

PACIFIC

OCEAN

INDIAN

AUSTRALIA

OCEAN

SOUTH

PACIFIC

OCEAN

ANTARCTICA

0 m	0 ft.
-500 m	-1,650 ft.
-1,500 m	-4,900 ft.
-3,000 m	-9,850 ft.
-5,000 m	-16,400 ft.
-7,000 m	-22,950 ft.
-9,000 m	-36,100 ft.
-11,000 m	-45,950 ft.

100°E 110° 120° 130° 140° 150° 160° 170°E 180° 170°W 160° 150° 140° 130° 120° 110° 100°

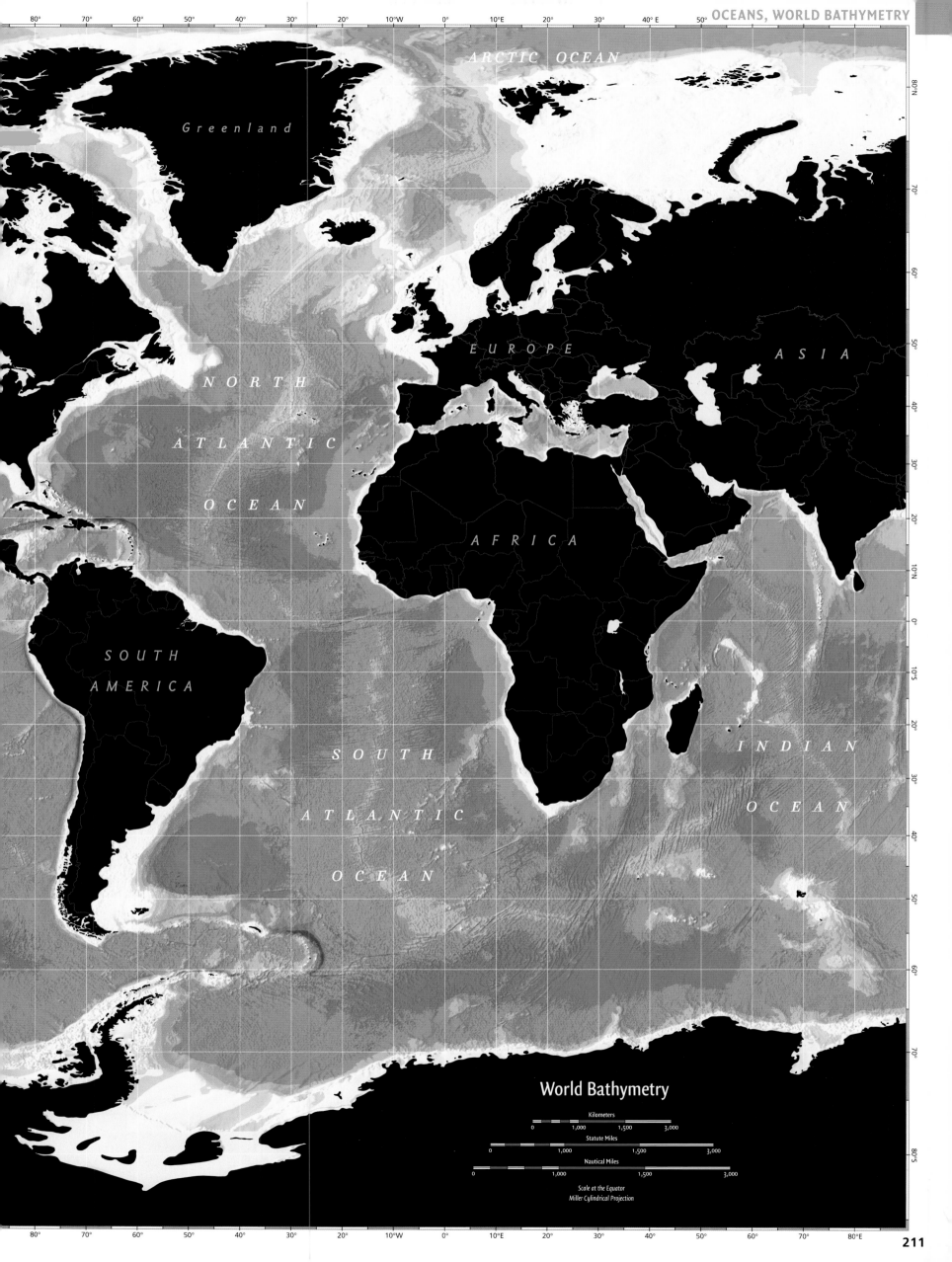

ARCTIC OCEAN

Greenland

EUROPE

ASIA

NORTH

ATLANTIC

OCEAN

AFRICA

SOUTH

AMERICA

SOUTH

ATLANTIC

INDIAN

OCEAN

OCEAN

World Bathymetry

Kilometers

0   1,000   1,500   3,000

Statute Miles

0   1,000   1,500   3,000

Nautical Miles

0   1,000   1,500   3,000

Scale at the Equator
Miller Cylindrical Projection

Earth is a watery planet: More than 70 percent of its surface is covered by interconnected bodies of salt water that together make up a continuous, global ocean. Over the centuries, people have created artificial boundaries that divide this great water body into smaller oceans with numerous seas, gulfs, bays, straits, and channels.

The global ocean is a dynamic participant in Earth's physical, chemical, and biological processes. Millions of years ago, life itself most likely evolved in its waters. These are restless waters, always in motion. Tidal movement—the regular rise and fall of the ocean surface—results from gravitational forces exerted by the sun and the moon. The spin of Earth on its axis, coupled with wind, generates surface currents that redistribute warm and cold water around the planet. Variations in the temperature and salinity of water keep the thermohaline circulation system moving; this enormous system of interconnected currents, at the surface and deep in the ocean, influences climate patterns and circulates nutrients.

Where marine and terrestrial realms meet, one may find reefs built by tiny coral polyps or see cliffs and sea stacks shaped by countless waves. Many coastal zones are threatened, however, by overdevelopment, pollution, and overfishing. Farther out, in the deep ocean, lie vast untouched plains, high mountains and ridges, and valleys with floors lying as much as seven miles (11 km) below the sea surface. Teeming with life, the ocean includes "rain forests of the sea" and a host of marine species—even creatures who dwell in superhot waters near hydrothermal vents.

New technology is helping scientists to explore ever deeper and farther and to create more accurate maps of the ocean. Some of this underwater world has been explored with diving vessels and satellite imagery, but so much more remains to be discovered.

The Ocean Floor

The ocean floor is dynamic and varied. From the edge of the continental shelf (the shelf break), the continental slope plunges to the continental rise, which reaches to the abyssal plain. Periodically, terrestrial rocks and sediment flow through submarine canyons and form alluvial fans. The Mid-Ocean Ridge builds new seafloor; erosion and subsidence create atolls and guyots; and subducting tectonic plates form deep trenches in the ocean floor.

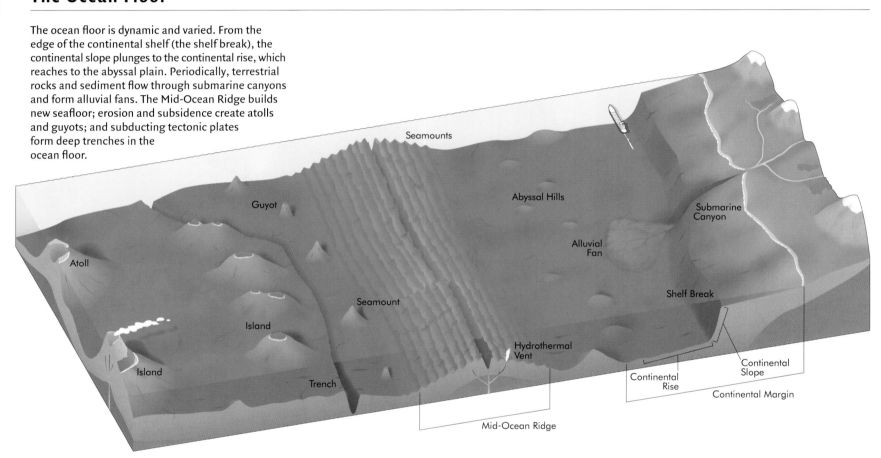

OCEAN WAVES
Waves may be born thousands of miles from shore, a result of large storms churning over the ocean. Wind pushing on the sea surface forms unorganized groups of waves that travel in all directions. In time, they organize into swell—groups of waves that can carry energy over thousands of miles of ocean. As the waves approach a surf zone, they steepen until their crests curl forward and break upon the beach.

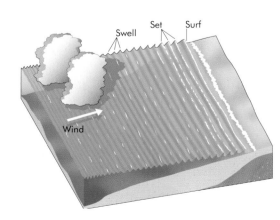

CORAL MORPHOLOGY
Coral reefs—Earth's largest structures with biological origins—form primarily in the tropics, where water is clear and warm. They begin as fringing reefs, colonies built along coastlines by tiny organisms known as coral polyps. As a coastal area subsides, a fringing reef becomes a barrier reef enclosing a protected lagoon. Corals on a reef's seaward side rely on spur and groove formations to withstand powerful waves.

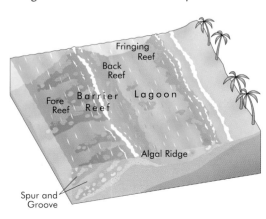

COASTAL MORPHOLOGY
The contours of a coast determine how approaching ocean waves release their energy. In bays, wave energy is dispersed; at headlands, it is concentrated. Waves approaching at an angle produce longshore currents, which flow parallel to shore and transport sediment. Rip currents, generated by wind and the return flow of water, move outward. Over time, waves and currents reshape the coastlines of the world.

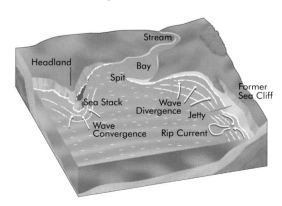

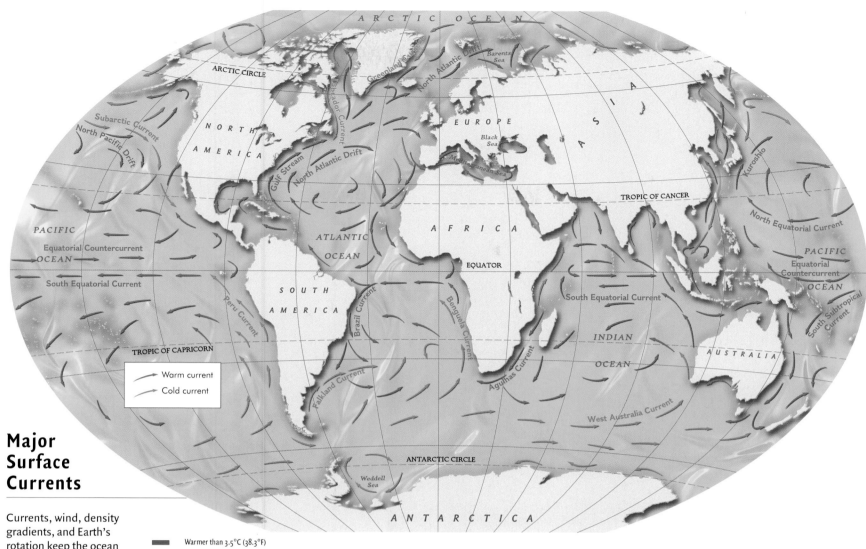

Major Surface Currents

Warm current

Cold current

Currents, wind, density gradients, and Earth's rotation keep the ocean in motion. As the Earth spins, wind and surface currents are deflected to the right in the Northern Hemisphere and to the left in the Southern Hemisphere. This effect creates enormous gyres that transport warm water from equatorial regions into the much colder polar regions. El Niño events in the Pacific, as well as the monsoon season in the Indian Ocean, alter surface currents.

Warmer than 3.5°C (38.3°F)

1°C – 3.5°C (33.8°F –38.3°F)

Cooler than 1°C (33.8°F)

S Sinking

U Upwelling

Ocean Conveyor Belt

The circulation of ocean water is often compared to a conveyor belt. Warm water flows into the North Atlantic, cools, becomes saltier (due to evaporation), and sinks because its density has increased. Then it flows south along the seafloor to Antarctica, chills further, and flows outward into the South Atlantic, Indian, and Pacific Oceans. In these warm waters, it rises and flows again toward the North Atlantic.

TIDES

Both the sun and moon exert gravitational force on the Earth's ocean, creating tides. But because the moon is closer, its tug is much greater. During spring tides, when the moon is new or full, the combined pull of the sun and moon causes very high and low tides. Neap tides occur during the first and third quarters of the moon; at those times, the difference between tides is much smaller.

MAPPING THE OCEAN

Mapping the ocean requires myriad devices. In space, some satellites carry microwave radars to record data on wind speed and sea height; others use visible and infrared radiometers to collect biological productivity data. Radar altimetry and scatterometry are also used to record wind speed and direction. Out in the ocean, profiling floats collect temperature and salinity data. Ships use acoustics to map the sea floor.

THERMOHALINE CIRCULATION SYSTEM

Differences in the relative densities of volumes of water—determined by temperature (thermo) and salinity (haline)—drive thermohaline circulation. In polar regions, density increases as water cools and as evaporation makes it saltier; the mass of water sinks and flows along the ocean floor. Near the Equator, water warms and rises to the surface. If this system shut down, significant climate effects could occur.

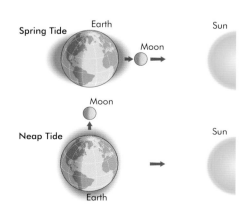

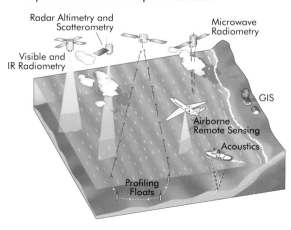

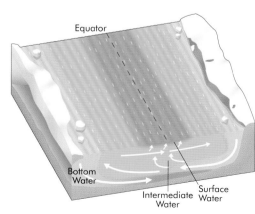

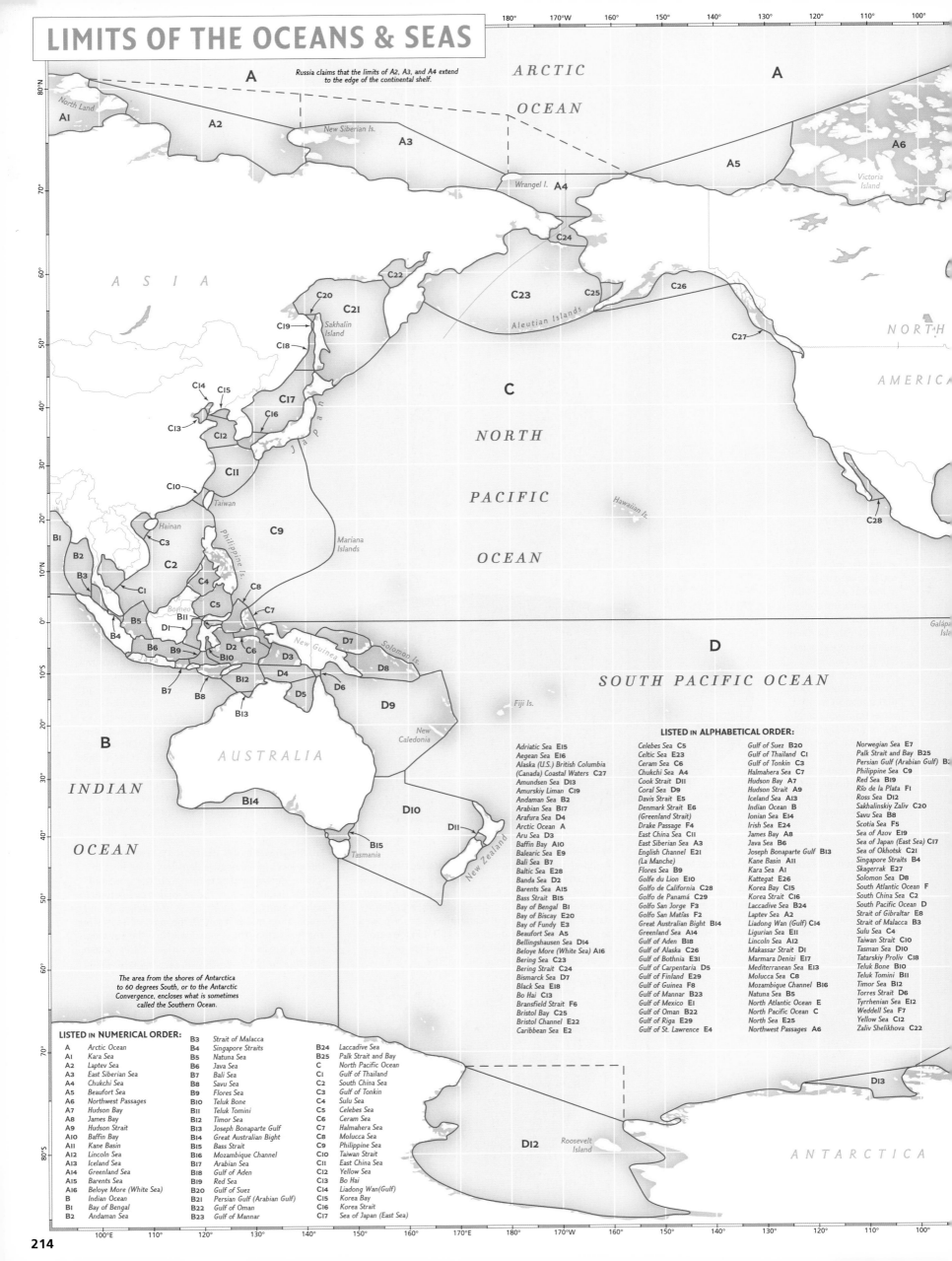

Russia claims that the limits of A2, A3, and A4 extend to the edge of the continental shelf.

The area from the shores of Antarctica to 60 degrees South, or to the Antarctic Convergence, encloses what is sometimes called the Southern Ocean.

LISTED IN ALPHABETICAL ORDER:

Adriatic Sea E15	Celebes Sea C5	Gulf of Suez B20	Norwegian Sea E7
Aegean Sea E16	Celtic Sea E23	Gulf of Thailand C1	Palk Strait and Bay B25
Alaska (U.S.) British Columbia	Ceram Sea C6	Gulf of Tonkin C3	Persian Gulf (Arabian Gulf) B21
(Canada) Coastal Waters C27	Chukchi Sea A4	Halmahera Sea C7	Philippine Sea C9
Amundsen Sea D13	Cook Strait D11	Hudson Bay A7	Red Sea B19
Amurskiy Liman C19	Coral Sea D9	Hudson Strait A9	Río de la Plata F1
Andaman Sea B2	Davis Strait E5	Iceland Sea A13	Ross Sea D12
Arabian Sea B17	Denmark Strait E6	Indian Ocean B	Sakhalinskiy Zaliv C20
Arafura Sea D4	(Greenland Strait)	Ionian Sea E14	Savu Sea B8
Arctic Ocean A	Drake Passage F4	Irish Sea E24	Scotia Sea F5
Aru Sea D3	East China Sea C11	James Bay A8	Sea of Azov E19
Baffin Bay A10	East Siberian Sea A3	Java Sea B6	Sea of Japan (East Sea) C17
Balearic Sea E9	English Channel E21	Joseph Bonaparte Gulf B13	Sea of Okhotsk C21
Bali Sea B7	(La Manche)	Kane Basin A11	Singapore Straits B4
Baltic Sea E28	Flores Sea B9	Kara Sea A1	Skagerrak E27
Banda Sea D2	Golfe du Lion E10	Kattegat E26	Solomon Sea D8
Barents Sea A15	Golfo de California C28	Korea Bay C15	South Atlantic Ocean F
Bass Strait B15	Golfo de Panamá C29	Korea Strait C16	South China Sea C2
Bay of Bengal B1	Golfo San Jorge F3	Laccadive Sea B24	South Pacific Ocean D
Bay of Biscay E20	Golfo San Matías F2	Laptev Sea A2	Strait of Gibraltar E8
Bay of Fundy E3	Great Australian Bight B14	Liadong Wan (Gulf) C14	Strait of Malacca B3
Beaufort Sea A5	Greenland Sea A14	Ligurian Sea E11	Sulu Sea C4
Bellingshausen Sea D14	Gulf of Aden B18	Lincoln Sea A12	Taiwan Strait C10
Beloye More (White Sea) A16	Gulf of Alaska C26	Makassar Strait D1	Tasman Sea D10
Bering Sea C23	Gulf of Bothnia E31	Marmara Denizi E17	Tatarskiy Proliv C18
Bering Strait C24	Gulf of Carpentaria D5	Mediterranean Sea E13	Teluk Bone B10
Bismarck Sea D7	Gulf of Finland E29	Molucca Sea C8	Teluk Tomini B11
Black Sea E18	Gulf of Guinea F8	Mozambique Channel B16	Timor Sea B12
Bo Hai C13	Gulf of Mannar B23	Natuna Sea B5	Torres Strait D6
Bransfield Strait F6	Gulf of Mexico E1	North Atlantic Ocean E	Tyrrhenian Sea E12
Bristol Bay C25	Gulf of Oman B22	North Pacific Ocean C	Weddell Sea F7
Bristol Channel E22	Gulf of Riga E29	North Sea E25	Yellow Sea C12
Caribbean Sea E2	Gulf of St. Lawrence E4	Northwest Passages A6	Zaliv Shelikhova C22

LISTED IN NUMERICAL ORDER:

A	Arctic Ocean	B3	Strait of Malacca	B24	Laccadive Sea
A1	Kara Sea	B4	Singapore Straits	B25	Palk Strait and Bay
A2	Laptev Sea	B5	Natuna Sea	C	North Pacific Ocean
A3	East Siberian Sea	B6	Java Sea	C1	Gulf of Thailand
A4	Chukchi Sea	B7	Bali Sea	C2	South China Sea
A5	Beaufort Sea	B8	Savu Sea	C3	Gulf of Tonkin
A6	Northwest Passages	B9	Flores Sea	C4	Sulu Sea
A7	Hudson Bay	B10	Teluk Bone	C5	Celebes Sea
A8	James Bay	B11	Teluk Tomini	C6	Ceram Sea
A9	Hudson Strait	B12	Timor Sea	C7	Halmahera Sea
A10	Baffin Bay	B13	Joseph Bonaparte Gulf	C8	Molucca Sea
A11	Kane Basin	B14	Great Australian Bight	C9	Philippine Sea
A12	Lincoln Sea	B15	Bass Strait	C10	Taiwan Strait
A13	Iceland Sea	B16	Mozambique Channel	C11	East China Sea
A14	Greenland Sea	B17	Arabian Sea	C12	Yellow Sea
A15	Barents Sea	B18	Gulf of Aden	C13	Bo Hai
A16	Beloye More (White Sea)	B19	Red Sea	C14	Liadong Wan(Gulf)
B	Indian Ocean	B20	Gulf of Suez	C15	Korea Bay
B1	Bay of Bengal	B21	Persian Gulf (Arabian Gulf)	C16	Korea Strait
B2	Andaman Sea	B22	Gulf of Oman	C17	Sea of Japan (East Sea)
		B23	Gulf of Mannar		

214

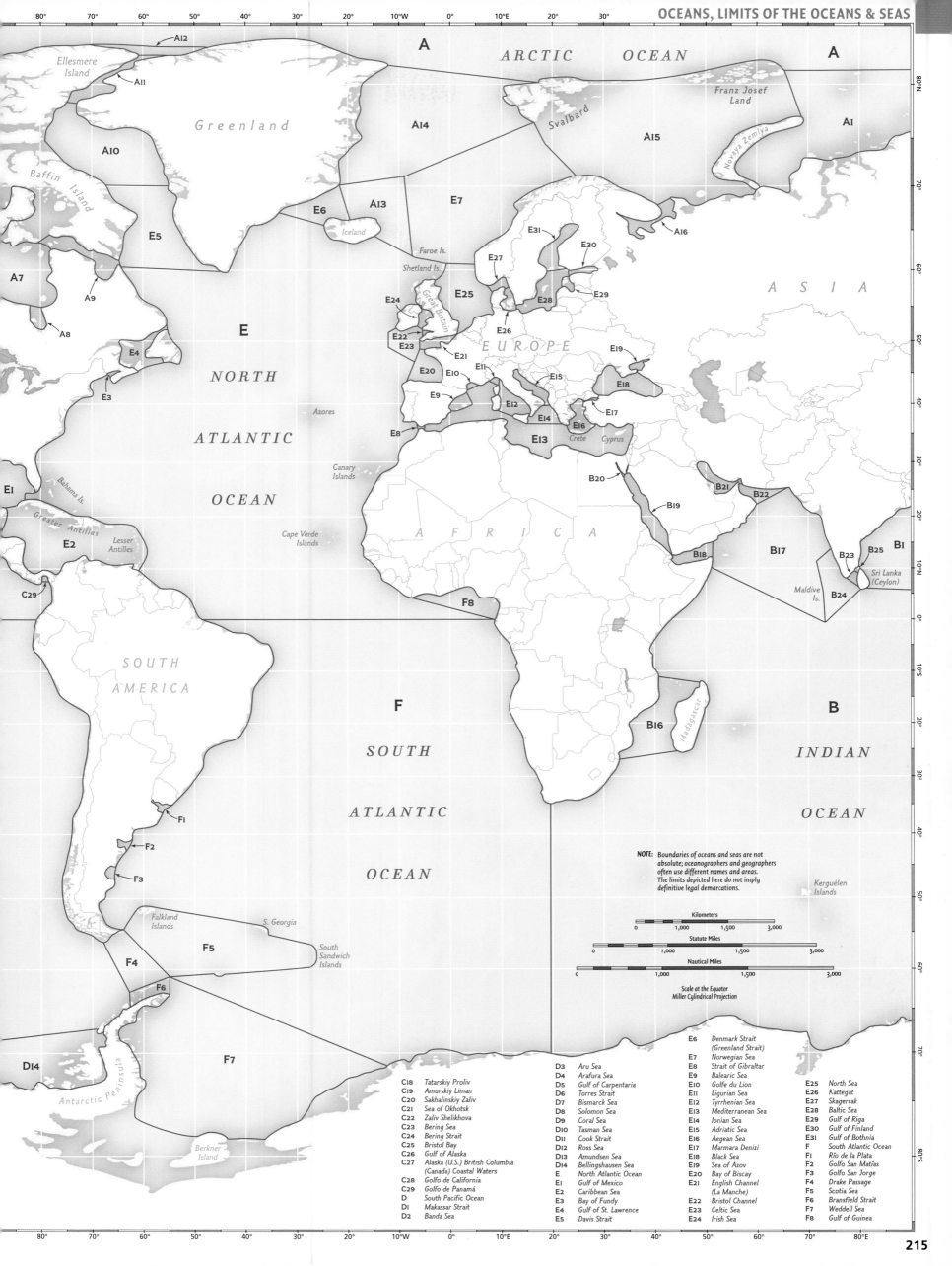

OCEANS, LIMITS OF THE OCEANS & SEAS

NOTE: Boundaries of oceans and seas are not absolute; oceanographers and geographers often use different names and areas. The limits depicted here do not imply definitive legal demarcations.

Kilometers
0   1,000   1,500   3,000

Statute Miles
0   1,000   1,500   3,000

Nautical Miles
0   1,000   1,500   3,000

Scale at the Equator
Miller Cylindrical Projection

C18	Tatarskiy Proliv	D3	Aru Sea
C19	Amurskiy Liman	D4	Arafura Sea
C20	Sakhalinskiy Zaliv	D5	Gulf of Carpentaria
C21	Sea of Okhotsk	D6	Torres Strait
C22	Zaliv Shelikhova	D7	Bismarck Sea
C23	Bering Sea	D8	Solomon Sea
C24	Bering Strait	D9	Coral Sea
C25	Bristol Bay	D10	Tasman Sea
C26	Gulf of Alaska	D11	Cook Strait
C27	Alaska (U.S.) British Columbia (Canada) Coastal Waters	D12	Ross Sea
C28	Golfo de California	D13	Amundsen Sea
C29	Golfo de Panamá	D14	Bellingshausen Sea
D	South Pacific Ocean	E	North Atlantic Ocean
D1	Makassar Strait	E1	Gulf of Mexico
D2	Banda Sea	E2	Caribbean Sea
		E3	Bay of Fundy
		E4	Gulf of St. Lawrence
		E5	Davis Strait

E6	Denmark Strait (Greenland Strait)	E25	North Sea
E7	Norwegian Sea	E26	Kattegat
E8	Strait of Gibraltar	E27	Skagerrak
E9	Balearic Sea	E28	Baltic Sea
E10	Golfe du Lion	E29	Gulf of Riga
E11	Ligurian Sea	E30	Gulf of Finland
E12	Tyrrhenian Sea	E31	Gulf of Bothnia
E13	Mediterranean Sea	F	South Atlantic Ocean
E14	Ionian Sea	F1	Río de la Plata
E15	Adriatic Sea	F2	Golfo San Matías
E16	Aegean Sea	F3	Golfo San Jorge
E17	Marmara Denizi	F4	Drake Passage
E18	Black Sea	F5	Scotia Sea
E19	Sea of Azov	F6	Bransfield Strait
E20	Bay of Biscay	F7	Weddell Sea
E21	English Channel (La Manche)	F8	Gulf of Guinea
E22	Bristol Channel		
E23	Celtic Sea		
E24	Irish Sea		

215

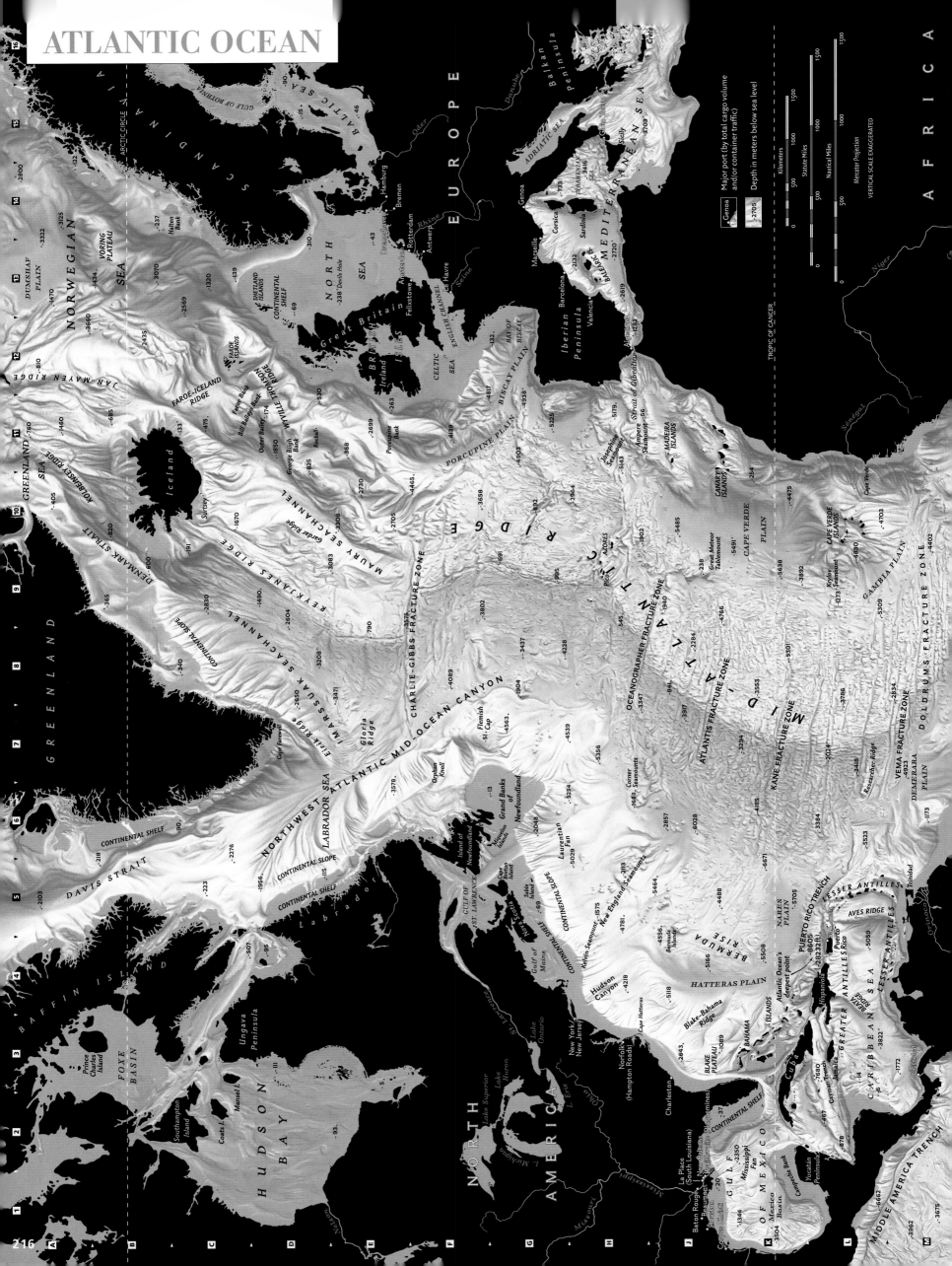

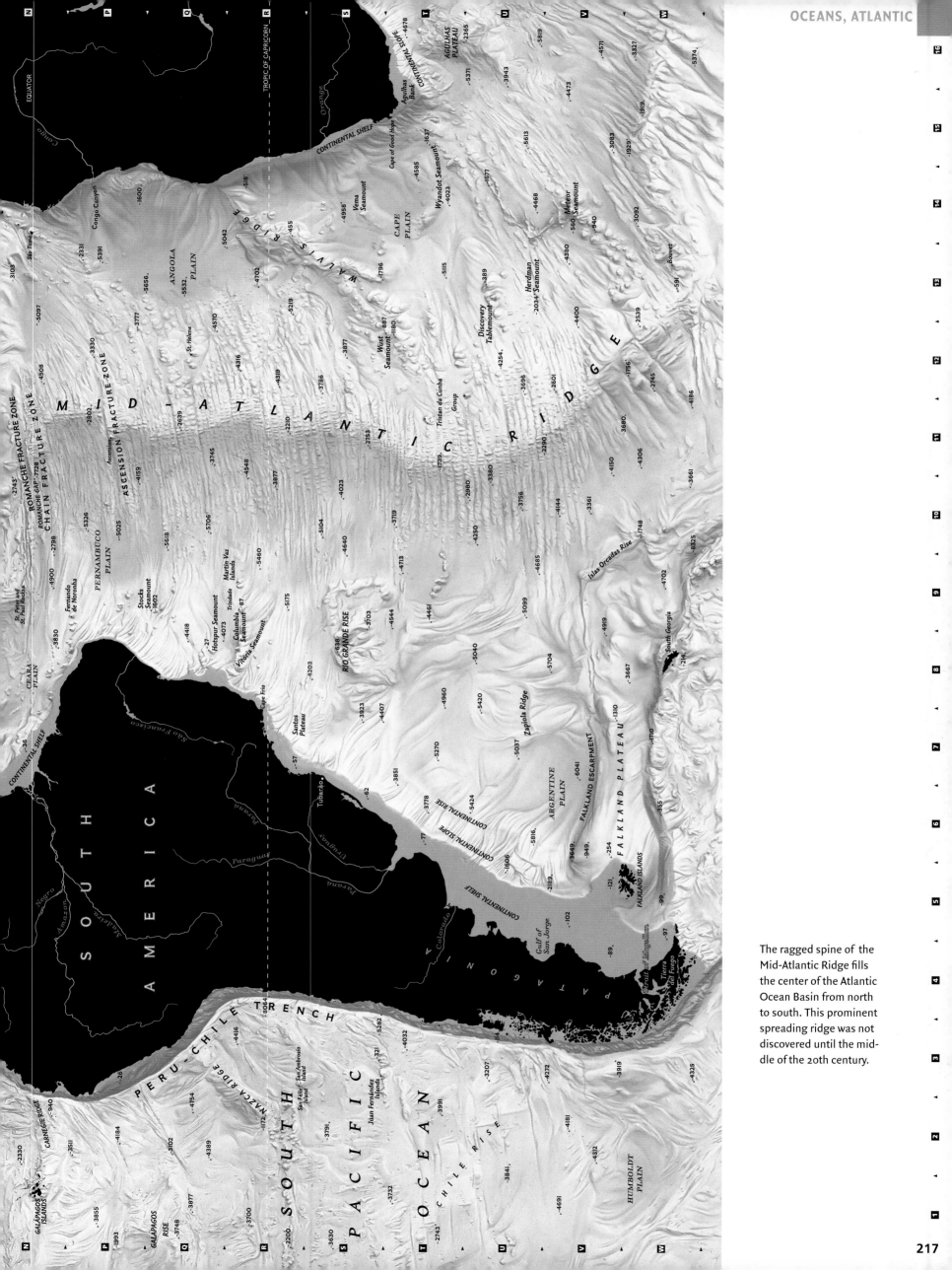

The ragged spine of the Mid-Atlantic Ridge fills the center of the Atlantic Ocean Basin from north to south. This prominent spreading ridge was not discovered until the middle of the 20th century.

NORTH AMERICA

GULF OF ALASKA

Kodiak Seamount -2289
Pratt Seamount -723
Welker Seamount -708
-44
Bowie Seamount
Gilbert Seamount

-3250

Eickelberg Seamount -2553
Vancouver
Seattle
Tacoma
JUAN DE FUCA RIDGE
CASCADIA BASIN
Columbia

TUFTS PLAIN
-5121
-3905
-2571
-1893

FRACTURE ZONE

PIONEER FRACTURE ZONE
-5413
-2933
Oakland

-5990
-2140
ZONE

FRACTURE

Fieberling Tablemount -426
Moonless Mountains
-4064
-2753
Isla de Guadalupe

-3502
Henderson Seamount -388
-3956
MOLOKAI FRACTURE ZONE
-1317
-4175
-1472
-2906

-3347
CLARION FRACTURE ZONE
-5351
Islas Revillagigedo

Los Angeles
Long Beach
PEDROS TRENCH
PATTON ESCARPMENT

TROPIC OF CANCER

-4700
-4137
-5157
-3182
-1594
Mathematicians Seamounts

-5029
-4609
-4688
-4299
-1954

-5121
-3877
PACIFIC BASIN
-2506
-3356
-3835

CLIPPERTON FRACTURE ZONE
-4170
-3928

MIDDLE AMERICA TRENCH
-6662
-2641
-3716 -3962 -3457
GUATEMALA BASIN
-2780 -3306
COLON RIDGE
GALÁPAGOS RIFT -2330
COCOS RIDGE
-3669
PANAMA BASIN
-3356
GALÁPAGOS IS.
CARNEGIE RIDGE
-1453

EQUATOR

SOUTH AMERICA

GALÁPAGOS FRACTURE ZONE
-1506
-2378
-4190
-3967
-2611
-3714

-4481
-4662
-26
-4718
-4526
MARQUESAS ISLANDS
-4440
MARQUESAS FRACTURE ZONE
-3840
-4078
-1690
-1993
-4303

-2710
-4022
-3804
GALÁPAGOS RISE
PERU BASIN

-3587
-1792
-4075
-3877
-4389
-4754

TUAMOTU ARCHIPELAGO
Pukapuka
-4138
PERU-CHILE TRENCH
NAZCA RIDGE

Tahiti
SOCIETY ISLANDS
-3844
-3839
EASTER FRACTURE ZONE
-3700
-5069
-328
-4416

AUSTRAL ISLANDS
-3839
Îles Gambier
-2969
-889
-8064
CHILE

President Thiers Bank
-4753
Morane
Pitcairn I.
Ducie I.
-769
Sala y Gómez
SALA Y GÓMEZ RIDGE
San Félix I.
San Ambrosio I.

Neilson Reef
Marotiri -3729
Easter I.
-3839
-3013
-3630
BASIN

-4716
-2819
-3694

CHALLENGER FRACTURE ZONE
-3732
Juan Fernández Islands -321
-5282

-3830
-3628
-2743
CHILE RISE
-3991

-4387
-4173
-2792
-4163
-3207
-14
-4032

PACIFIC BASIN
AGASSIZ FRACTURE ZONE
-4115
VALDIVIA FRACTURE ZONE
-3480
-3841

-3700
-4808
-4766
-4371

-5210
-4879
SOUTHEAST

EAST PACIFIC RISE

-4724
-4356
MENARD FRACTURE ZONE
-4118
-3324
-3379
-4691
PACIFIC
-4181
-4272

ELTANIN FRACTURE ZONE
-2923
-3323
-3387
BASIN
-4359
-3919
-5124
HUMBOLDT PLAIN
-4900
CONTINENTAL SHELF

-702

NORTH ATLANTIC OCEAN

Gulf of Maine
Hudson Canyon
Cape Hatteras -26
-5118
-2643
BLAKE PLATEAU
BAHAMA
ISLANDS
-5508
-8605 (-28232ft)
Atlantic Ocean's deepest point

GULF OF MEXICO
-1344
Mississippi Fan
MEXICO BASIN -3504
CONTINENTAL SHELF
Campeche Bank
Yucatan Peninsula
GREATER ANTILLES
-7680
CAYMAN TRENCH
-878
-6
CARIBBEAN SEA
-3822
BEATA RIDGE
LESSER ANTILLES
-1772

-183
-298
-318
-507
-95
-126
-878

Major port (by total cargo volume and/or container traffic)
-1218 Depth in meters below sea level

Kilometers
0 500 1000 1500 2000
Statute Miles
0 500 1000 1500 2000
Nautical Miles
0 500 1000 1500 2000
Mercator Projection
VERTICAL SCALE EXAGGERATED

The Pacific Ocean Basin is shrinking as it is subsumed under surrounding continents on all sides.

INDIAN OCEAN

A S I

Dead Sea
(-1349ft) -411
World's lowest point

Brahmaputra

Mt. Everest +
(29035ft) 8850
World's highest point

Tigris

Indus

PERSIAN GULF

-73

GULF OF OMAN

Dubai

TROPIC OF CANCER

ARABIAN PENINSULA

Nile

S A H A R A

-3372

Ra's al Hadd

-2643

-291

CONTINENTAL SHELF

Ganges

INDIA

-82

-59

Dubai — Major port (by total cargo volume and/or container traffic)

-2548 — Depth in meters below sea level

-3345

-22

-2577

-2821

BAY OF BENGAL

Kilometers
0 200 400 600 800 1000 1200

Statute Miles
0 200 400 600 800 1000 1200

Nautical Miles
0 200 400 600 800 1000 1200

Mercator Projection

VERTICAL SCALE EXAGGERATED

RED SEA

-2266

-5278

GULF OF ADEN

Socotra

-1706

Errér Tablemount

-368

-1906

A R A B I A N   S E A

-1940

ARABIAN BASIN

-2758

-2769

-2284

-4160

-4652

Ganges Fan

-3173

Andaman Islands

ANDAMAN BASIN

A F R I C A

-1534

-5106

CARLSBERG RIDGE

-2805

-1682

-3583

-3602

-4267

Lakshadweep

Maldive Islands

-2780

-4442

-4735

Colombo

Sri Lanka (Ceylon)

-1842

Indus Fan

OWEN FRACTURE ZONE

CHAGOS-LACCADIVE PLATEAU

EQUATOR

Lake Victoria

-3096

SOMALI BASIN

-3343

-1068

COCO-DE-MER SEAMOUNTS

-4738

-2919

-4025

-4179

-2302

-4547

-4962

Nikitin Seamount

-1549

-5166

-4993

Zanzibar I.

-3932

-4609

Seychelles

Amirante Isles

-5273

-13

-3511

MASCARENE PLATEAU

Chagos Archipelago

-5406

MID-INDIAN BASIN

MID-INDIAN RIDGE

-3619

Aldabra Is.

Farquhar Group

-3674

-13

AMIRANTE TRENCH

Agalega Islands

-6402

VEMA FRACTURE ZONE

Diego Garcia

-1906

CHAGOS TRENCH

-799

-5421

-5183

Comoro Islands

-10

Saya de Malha Bank

-7

-1240

Lake Malawi

-3621

MASCARENE BASIN

-1525

Nazareth Bank

-16

Cargados Carajos Bank

NINETYEAST RIDGE

Shire

-338

Tromelin

-38

RODRIGUES FRACTURE ZONE

-3996

OSBORN PLATEAU

-4983

Zambezi

Madagascar

-5194

MASCARENE PLAIN

Mauritius

-35

-4270

-1517

Rodrigues

EGERIA FRACTURE ZONE

-2619

MAURITIUS TRENCH

Réunion

-4521

-2599

-1584

Bassas da India

Limpopo

CONTINENTAL SHELF

-5967

-3919

-3429

-1922

-917

TROPIC OF CAPRICORN

-3292

Europa

-5340

-4634

MADAGASCAR BASIN

-6035

-2548

-2067

SOUTHWEST INDIAN RIDGE

BROKEN RIDGE

-1916

-4654

MADAGASCAR PLATEAU

-3974

-4305

-847

Richards Bay

-1555

NATAL BASIN

-4459

-5077

MOZAMBIQUE PLATEAU

Walters Shoal

-18

-5967

-3131

-3784

-2067

-4321

Cape of Hope

Cape Agulhas

Agulhas Bank

-1216

CONTINENTAL SLOPE

-516

-6110

ATLANTIS II FRACTURE ZONE

-4920

-3540

-3745

-4680

-4574

MOZAMBIQUE ESCARPMENT

-6291

-205

-1372

INDOMED FRACTURE ZONE

Amsterdam

St. Paul

-1423

-5536

-5371

-2590

-772

AGULHAS PLATEAU

-283

CROZET BASIN

-5195

-3261

-2315

PRINCE EDWARD FRACTURE ZONE

-2946

-2595

-4000

SOUTHEAST

-3943

AGULHAS BASIN

-5819

-638

CROZET PLATEAU

-2700

-4199

-4945

-451

-1976

-4080

-3330

-1244

Prince Edward Islands

Crozet Islands

-4590

-366

Kerguelen Islands

-2529

-4473

-2911

-4438

-430

-4181

ATLANTIC-INDIAN RIDGE

-3327

-247

Ob' Tablemount

-4270

-1710

KERGUELEN

-450

PLATEAU

-1124

-4571

-3049

-254

The Ninety East Ridge, the longest linear feature in the world, formed as ocean crust moved north over a hot spot deep in the Earth.

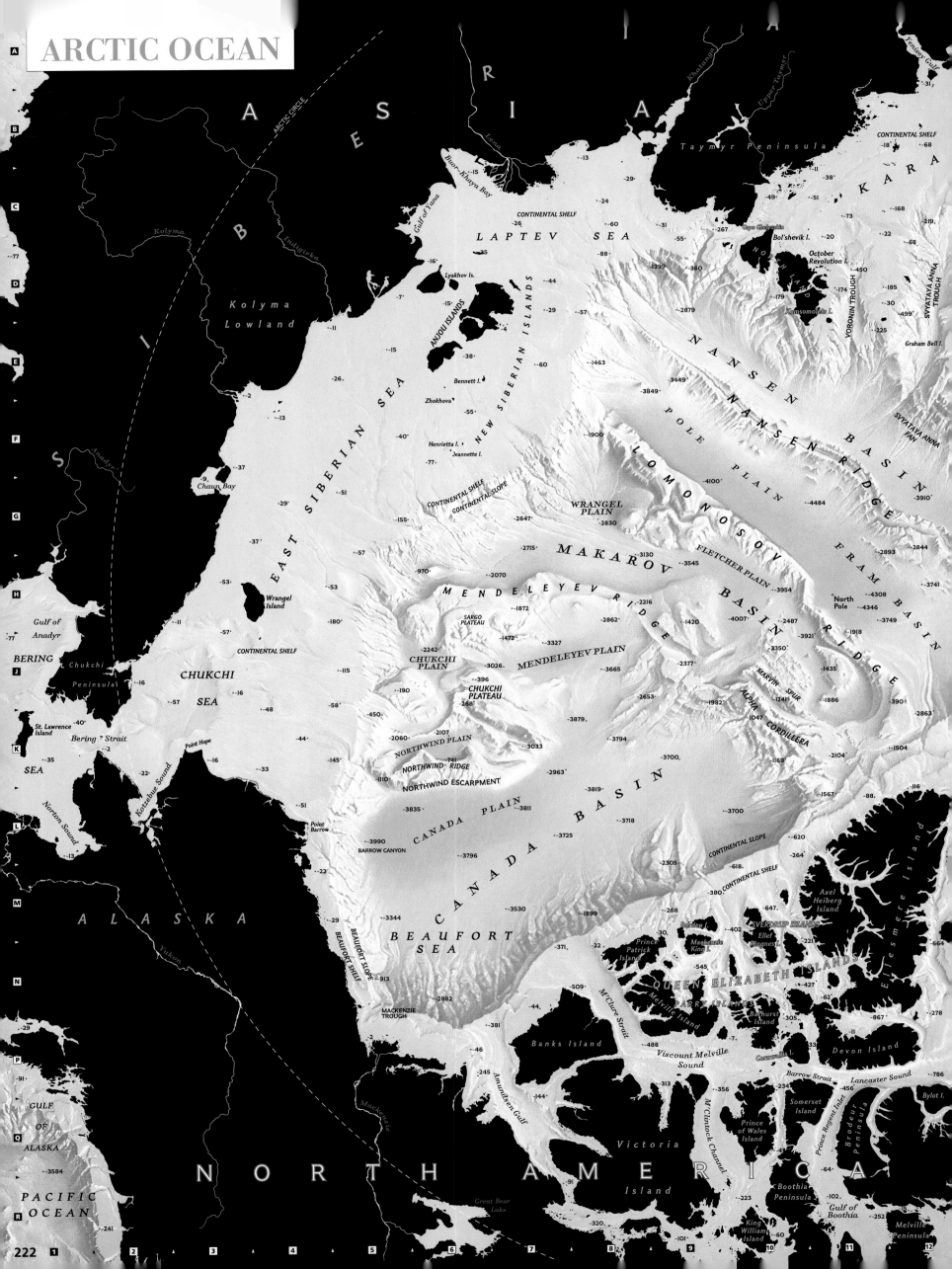

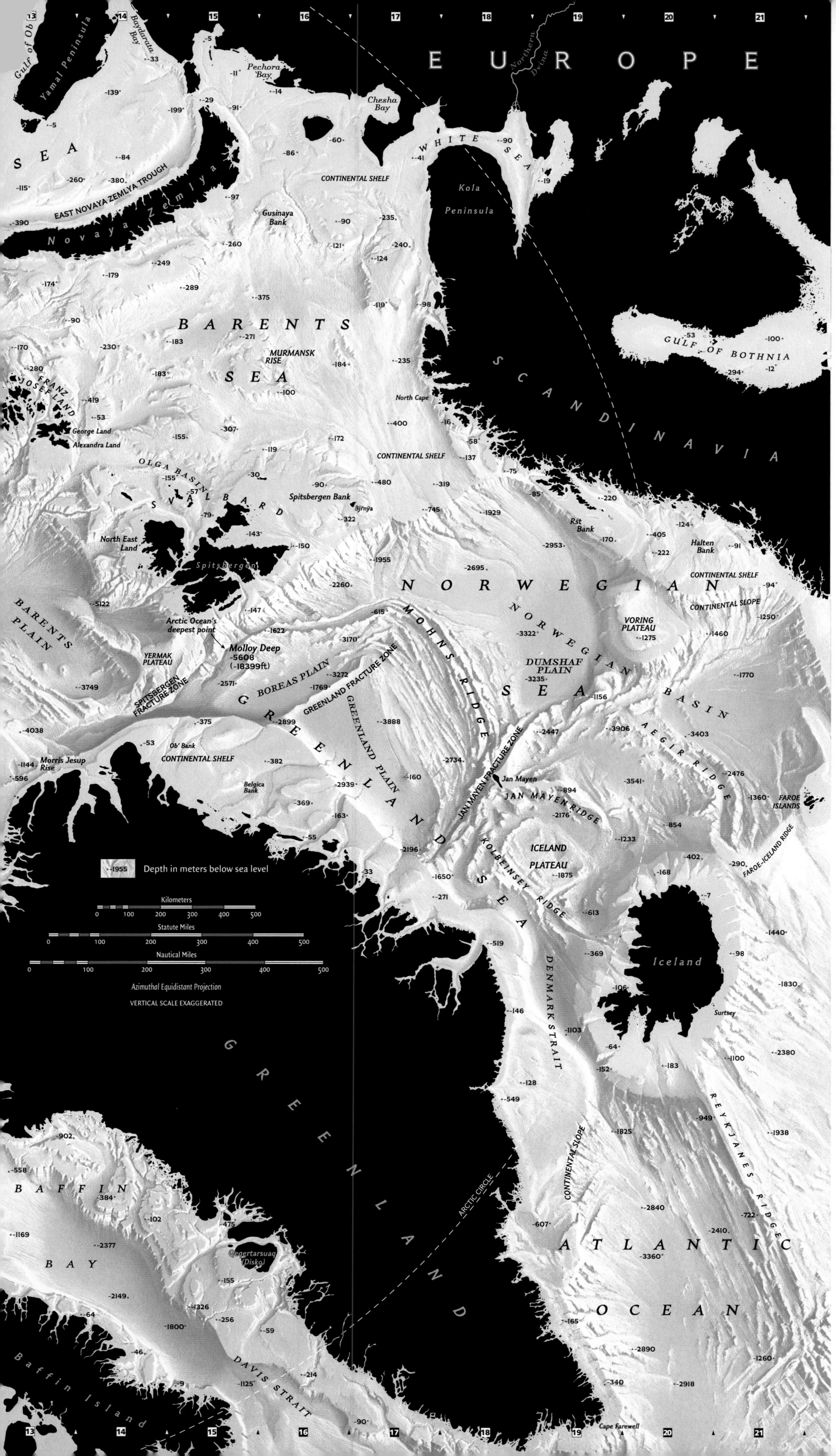

E U R O P E

Northern Dvina

SEA

Gulf of Ob
Yamal Peninsula
Baydaratskaya Bay
Pechora Bay
Chesha Bay
WHITE SEA
Kola Peninsula
SCANDINAVIA
GULF OF BOTHNIA

CONTINENTAL SHELF

EAST NOVAYA ZEMLYA TROUGH
Novaya Zemlya
Gusinaya Bank

North Cape

B A R E N T S
S E A
MURMANSK RISE

FRANZ JOSEF LAND
George Land
Alexandra Land
OLGA BASIN
S V A L B A R D
Spitsbergen Bank
Bjørnøya
Rst Bank
Halten Bank
CONTINENTAL SHELF
CONTINENTAL SHELF
CONTINENTAL SLOPE

North East Land
Spitsbergen

BARENTS PLAIN
YERMAK PLATEAU
Arctic Ocean's deepest point
Molloy Deep
-5608
(-18399ft)
SPITSBERGEN FRACTURE ZONE
BOREAS PLAIN
GREENLAND FRACTURE ZONE

N O R W E G I A N
S E A

VORING PLATEAU

DUMSHAF PLAIN

N O R W E G I A N   B A S I N

A E G I R   R I D G E

M O H N S   R I D G E

G R E E N L A N D   P L A I N

Ob' Bank
CONTINENTAL SHELF
Belgica Bank

Morris Jesup Rise

FAROE ISLANDS
FAROE-ICELAND RIDGE

JAN MAYEN FRACTURE ZONE
Jan Mayen
JAN MAYEN RIDGE

ICELAND PLATEAU

KOLBEINSEY RIDGE

G R E E N L A N D

-1955 Depth in meters below sea level

Kilometers
0 100 200 300 400 500
Statute Miles
0 100 200 300 400 500
Nautical Miles
0 100 200 300 400 500

Azimuthal Equidistant Projection
VERTICAL SCALE EXAGGERATED

Iceland
Surtsey

DENMARK STRAIT

R E Y K J A N E S   R I D G E

BAFFIN BAY

Qeqertarsuaq (Disko)

ARCTIC CIRCLE

CONTINENTAL SLOPE

A T L A N T I C

O C E A N

Baffin Island
DAVIS STRAIT

Cape Farewell

Water depths in the Arctic Ocean must often be measured from submarines under the ice. They discovered three almost parallel ridges crossing the Arctic Basin.

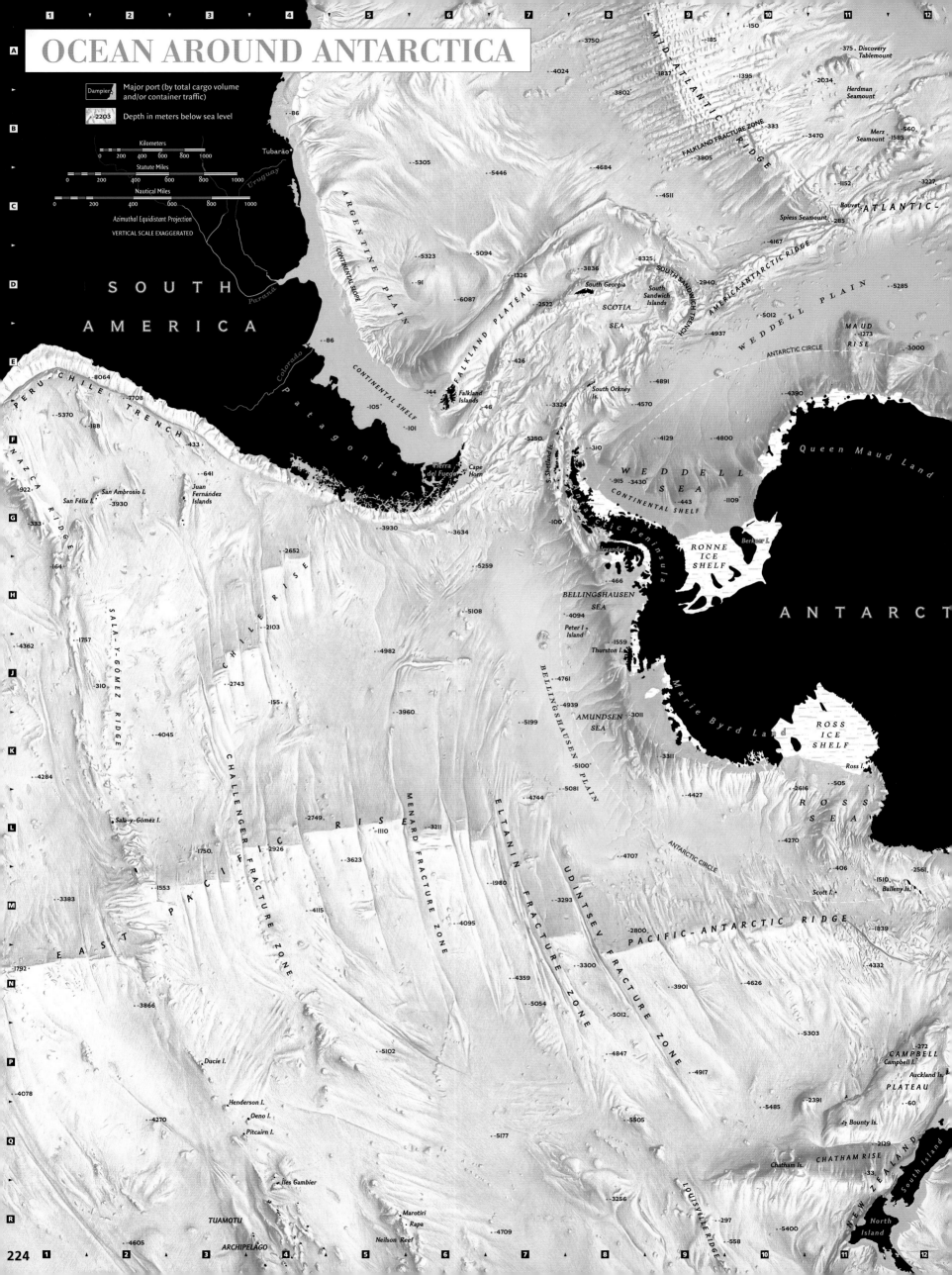

OCEAN AROUND ANTARCTICA

Dampier. Major port (by total cargo volume and/or container traffic)

-2203 Depth in meters below sea level

Kilometers
0 200 400 600 800 1000

Statute Miles
0 200 400 600 800 1000

Nautical Miles
0 200 400 600 800 1000

Azimuthal Equidistant Projection
VERTICAL SCALE EXAGGERATED

SOUTH

AMERICA

ATLANTIC-

MID-ATLANTIC RIDGE

FALKLAND FRACTURE ZONE

Discovery
Tablemount

Herdman
Seamount

Merz
Seamount

Bouvet

Spiess Seamount

AMERICA-ANTARCTIC RIDGE

SOUTH SANDWICH TRENCH

SOUTH SANDWICH RIDGE

WEDDELL PLAIN

MAUD
RISE

ANTARCTIC CIRCLE

ARGENTINE PLAIN

Continental Slope

FALKLAND PLATEAU

SCOTIA SEA

South Georgia

South Sandwich Islands

South Orkney Is.

Queen Maud Land

CONTINENTAL SHELF

Patagonia

Colorado

Parana

Uruguay

Falkland Islands

Tierra del Fuego

Cape Horn

S. Shetland Is.

WEDDELL SEA

CONTINENTAL SHELF

RONNE ICE SHELF

Berkner I.

ANTARCT

PERU-CHILE TRENCH

NAZCA RIDGE

San Félix I.

San Ambrosio I.

Juan Fernández Islands

CHILE RISE

Antarctic Peninsula

Alexander I.

BELLINGSHAUSEN SEA

Peter I Island

Thurston I.

SALA-Y-GÓMEZ RIDGE

BELLINGSHAUSEN PLAIN

AMUNDSEN SEA

Marie Byrd Land

ROSS ICE SHELF

Ross I.

Sala-y-Gómez I.

EAST PACIFIC RISE

CHALLENGER FRACTURE ZONE

MENARD FRACTURE ZONE

ELTANIN FRACTURE ZONE

UDINTSEV FRACTURE ZONE

ANTARCTIC CIRCLE

ROSS SEA

Scott I.

Balleny Is.

PACIFIC-ANTARCTIC RIDGE

CAMPBELL PLATEAU

Campbell I.

Auckland Is.

Bounty Is.

Ducie I.

Henderson I.

Oeno I.

Pitcairn I.

CHATHAM RISE

Chatham Is.

Iles Gambier

TUAMOTU

ARCHIPELAGO

Marotiri

Rapa

Neilson Reef

LOUISVILLE RIDGE

NEW ZEALAND

North Island

South Island

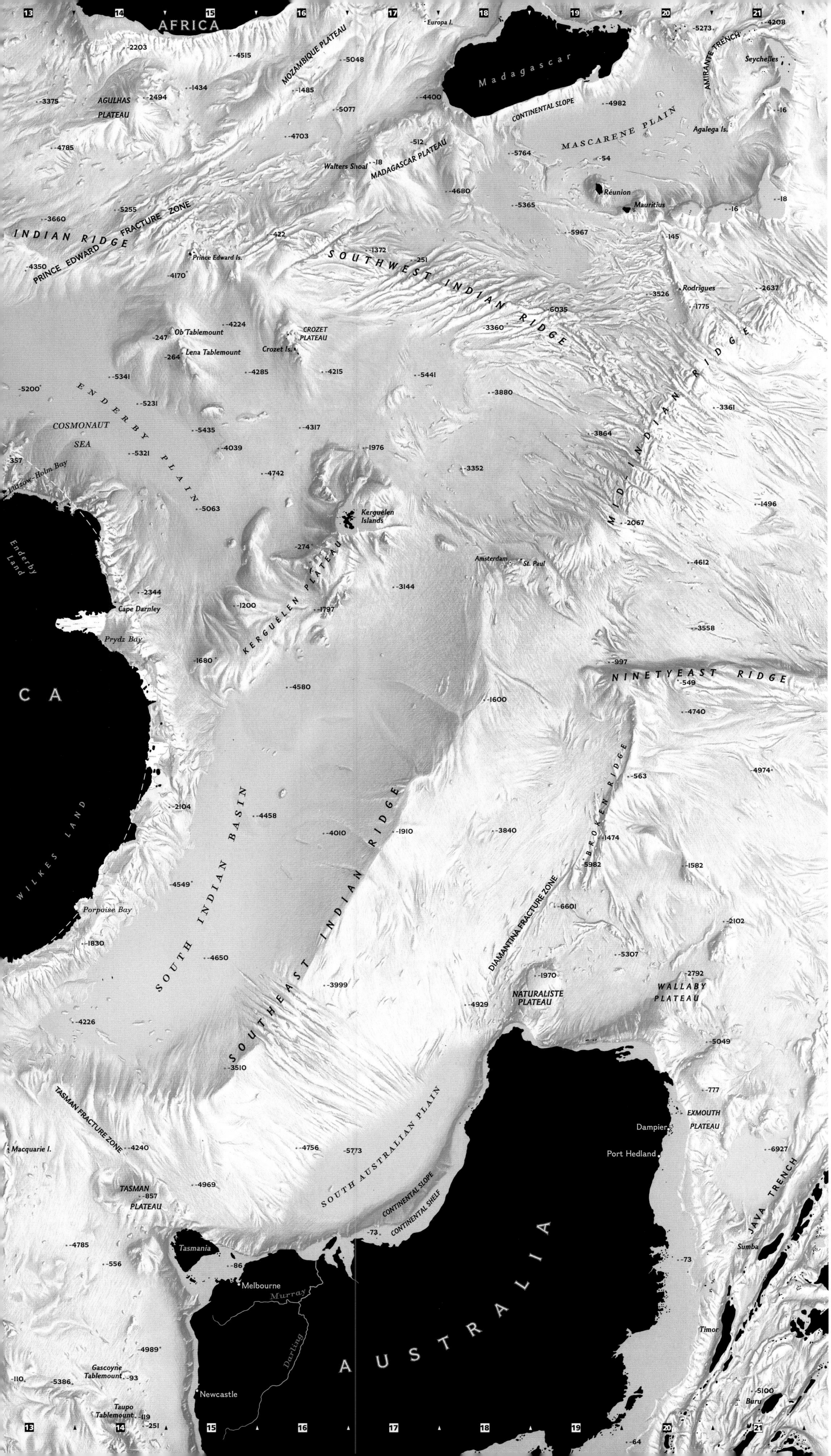

AFRICA

Madagascar

-2203
-4515
MOZAMBIQUE PLATEAU
-5048
-1485
Europa I.
-4400
Seychelles
-5273
-4208
AMIRANTE TRENCH
-16
-1434
AGULHAS PLATEAU
-2494
-3375
-5077
CONTINENTAL SLOPE
-4982
MASCARENE PLAIN
Agalega Is.
-4785
-4703
-512
-5764
-54
Walters Shoal
-18
MADAGASCAR PLATEAU
Réunion
Mauritius
-4680
-5365
-16
-18
-3660
-5255
PRINCE EDWARD FRACTURE ZONE
-422
-1372
-251
-5967
-145
INDIAN RIDGE
-4350
PRINCE EDWARD
Prince Edward Is.
-4170
SOUTHWEST INDIAN RIDGE
Rodrigues
-2637
-3526
-1775
-6035
Ob' Tablemount
-4224
CROZET PLATEAU
-3360
MID INDIAN RIDGE
-247
Lena Tablemount
Crozet Is.
-4285
-4215
-5441
-3880
-3361
-3864
-5200
-5341
ENDERBY PLAIN
-5231
-4317
-1976
-3352
-2067
-1496
COSMONAUT SEA
-5435
-4039
-357
-5321
-4742
Kerguelen Islands
Amsterdam
St. Paul
-4612
Lützow-Holm Bay
-5063
-274
-3144
-3558
Enderby Land
-2344
-1200
-997
NINETYEAST RIDGE
Cape Darnley
-1797
-549
Prydz Bay
-1680
-4580
-1600
-4740
CA
WILKES LAND
-2104
-4458
SOUTH INDIAN RIDGE
-4010
-1910
-3840
-563
BROKEN RIDGE
-4974
-1474
-4549
-5982
-1582
Porpoise Bay
-4650
SOUTH INDIAN BASIN
-2102
-1830
-6601
-5307
DIAMANTINA FRACTURE ZONE
-2792
WALLABY PLATEAU
-4226
-3999
-1970
NATURALISTE PLATEAU
-4929
-5049
SOUTHEAST INDIAN RIDGE
-3510
-777
EXMOUTH PLATEAU
Dampier
TASMAN FRACTURE ZONE
-4240
-4756
-5773
SOUTH AUSTRALIAN PLAIN
Port Hedland
-6927
JAVA TRENCH
Macquarie I.
TASMAN PLATEAU
-857
-4969
CONTINENTAL SLOPE
Sumba
-73
CONTINENTAL SHELF
-4785
Tasmania
-556
-86
-73
Timor
Melbourne
Murray
AUSTRALIA
-64
-4989
Darling
Gascoyne Tablemount
-93
-5100
-110
-5386
Buru
Newcastle
Taupo Tablemount
-119
-251

The ice-covered Antarctic continent is surrounded by deep, fairly flat underwater plains.

SPACE

In the first years of the new millennium, astronomers are conducting extensive surveys of space, registering millions of galaxies, each composed of billions of stars. Within the Milky Way galaxy, the Earth and eight other planets and their moons circle a single star, the sun. Instruments sensitive to stellar motions no faster than a brisk walk have revealed dozens of planets orbiting other nearby stars, but none of them resembles Earth. An instrumented probe scanning the surface of Mars has detected buried deposits of frozen water. There, future roving robots will seek evidence of past or present life.

Wherever we look, we see evidence of cataclysmic events, indicating that the status quo is but a fleeting condition in a universe evolving dramatically over time. The moon, pockmarked with impact craters, most likely was formed when a rogue planet struck the newborn Earth a glancing blow. Some suns, their atmospheres curiously enriched with telltale elements, may be "death stars" that swallowed whole planets long ago. The Milky Way is gradually devouring a small galaxy in the constellation Sagittarius, and elsewhere larger galaxies collide and distort each other.

At the limits of telescopic vision (and thus seen as they were more than 13 billion years ago), many galaxies seem small and roughly shaped; they are works in progress that may someday resemble the Milky Way. The entire universe is a work in progress. It began with the big bang and has been expanding ever since—accelerating, rather than slowing as long believed. A mysterious "dark energy" that exceeds all known forms of energy is thought to be the cause of this expansion; space is also pervaded by unseen "dark matter" that vastly exceeds the sum of all known substances.

In laboratories on Earth and on the drawing boards of spacecraft engineers, we are preparing to explore the next frontier of astronomical observation, looking for gravitational waves that may disturb the very fabric of space and time.

Greatly distended by a cosmic collision, the Tadpole galaxy stretches across the constellation Draco, about 420 million light-years from Earth. Countless other galaxies lie beyond.

The young Earth had no moon. At some point in Earth's early history, a rogue planet, larger than Mars, struck the Earth a great, glancing blow. Instantly, most of the rogue body and a sizable chunk of Earth were vaporized. The cloud rose to above 14,000 miles (22,500 km) altitude, where it condensed into innumerable solid particles that orbited the Earth as they aggregated into ever larger moonlets, which eventually combined to form the moon. This "giant impact" hypothesis of the moon's origin is based on computer simulations and on laboratory analyses of lunar rocks gathered by six teams of Apollo astronauts. It also fits with data on the lunar topography and environment from the United States' Clementine and Lunar Prospector spacecraft.

The airless lunar surface bakes in the sun at up to 243°F (117°C) for two weeks at a time. All the while, it is sprayed with the solar wind of subatomic particles. Then, for an equal period, the same spot is in the dark, cooling to about -272°F (-169°C) when the sun sets. Day and night, the moon is bombarded by micrometeoroids and larger space rocks. The moon's rotation is synchronized in a way that causes it to show the same face to the Earth at all times. One hemisphere always faces us, while the other always faces away. The lunar far side has been photographed only from spacecraft.

(Continued on page 230)

One square centimeter on this Lambert azimuthal equal-area projection equals 30,100 square kilometers on the moon; elevations of prominent features are stated in meters. Impact craters, including those (labeled in blue) commemorating the seven *Challenger* astronauts, predominate on the far side. Landing site labels are in red.

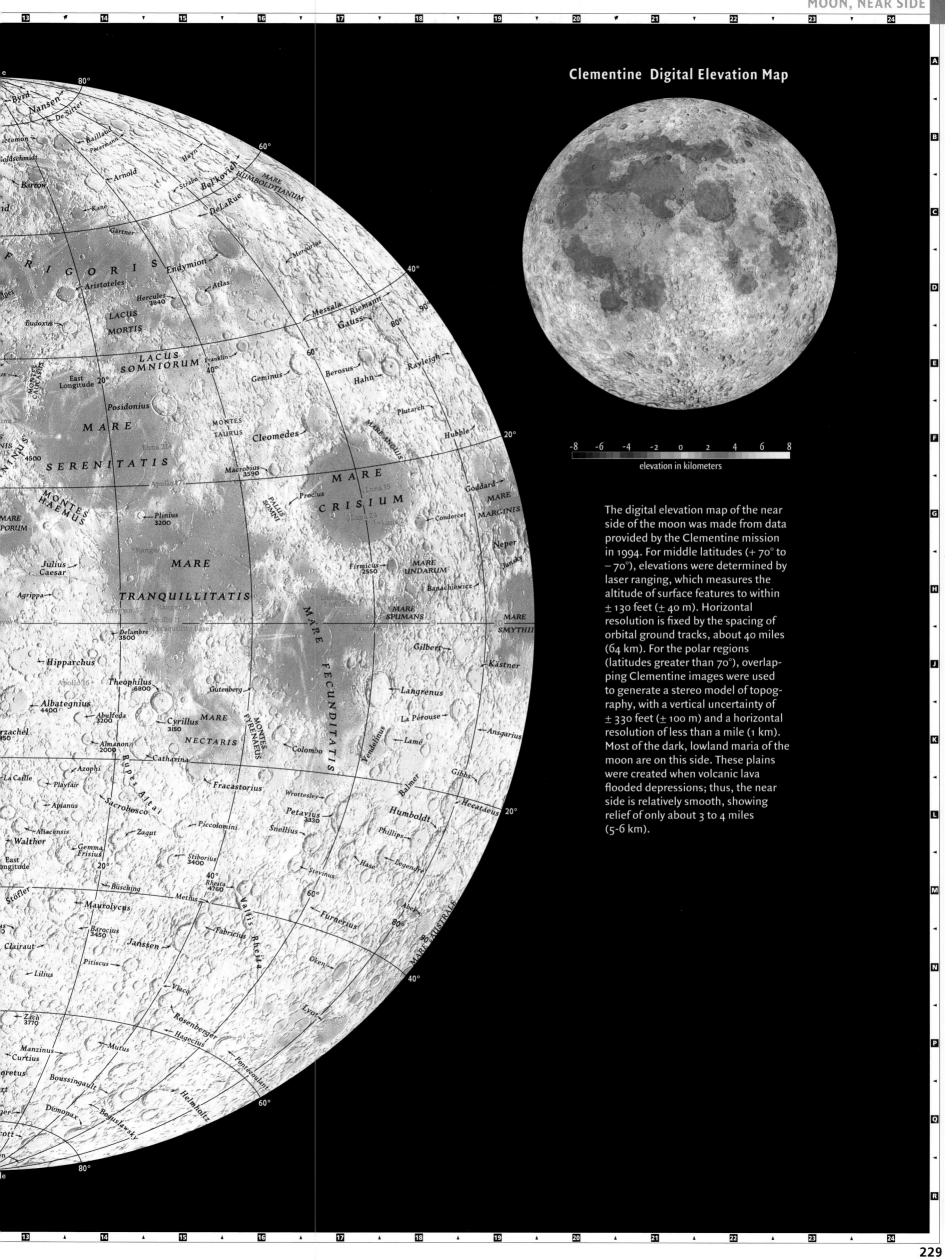

Clementine Digital Elevation Map

-8   -6   -4   -2   0   2   4   6   8
elevation in kilometers

The digital elevation map of the near side of the moon was made from data provided by the Clementine mission in 1994. For middle latitudes (+ 70° to – 70°), elevations were determined by laser ranging, which measures the altitude of surface features to within ± 130 feet (± 40 m). Horizontal resolution is fixed by the spacing of orbital ground tracks, about 40 miles (64 km). For the polar regions (latitudes greater than 70°), overlapping Clementine images were used to generate a stereo model of topography, with a vertical uncertainty of ± 330 feet (± 100 m) and a horizontal resolution of less than a mile (1 km). Most of the dark, lowland maria of the moon are on this side. These plains were created when volcanic lava flooded depressions; thus, the near side is relatively smooth, showing relief of only about 3 to 4 miles (5-6 km).

(Continued from page 228)

The rocks and soil brought back by Apollo missions are extremely dry; the moon has no indigenous water. However, it is bombarded by water-rich comets and meteoroids. Most of this water is lost to space, but some is trapped in permanently shadowed areas near both poles of the moon.

To the unaided eye, the bright lunar highlands and the dark maria (Latin for "seas") make up the "man in the moon." A telescope shows that they consist of a great variety of round impact features, scars left by objects that struck the moon long ago. In the highlands, craters are closely packed together. In the maria, they are fewer. The largest scars are the impact basins, ranging up to about 1,500 miles (2,400 km) across. The basin floors were flooded with lava some time after the titanic collisions that formed them. The dark lava flows are what the eye discerns as maria. Wrinkled ridges, domed hills, and fissures mark the maria, all familiar aspects of volcanic landscapes. Young craters are centers of radial patterns of bright ejecta, material thrown from the impacts that made them. Blocks of rock hurled from impacts traveled farther than they would on Earth because the force of gravity is weaker on the moon.

On the moon, there are no mountains like the Himalaya, produced by one tectonic plate bumping into another. There is no continental drift on the moon. Everywhere, the lunar surface is sheathed in regolith, rocky rubble created by constant bombardment by meteoroids, asteroids, and comets. Lunar mountains consist of volcanic domes and the central peaks and rims of impact craters.

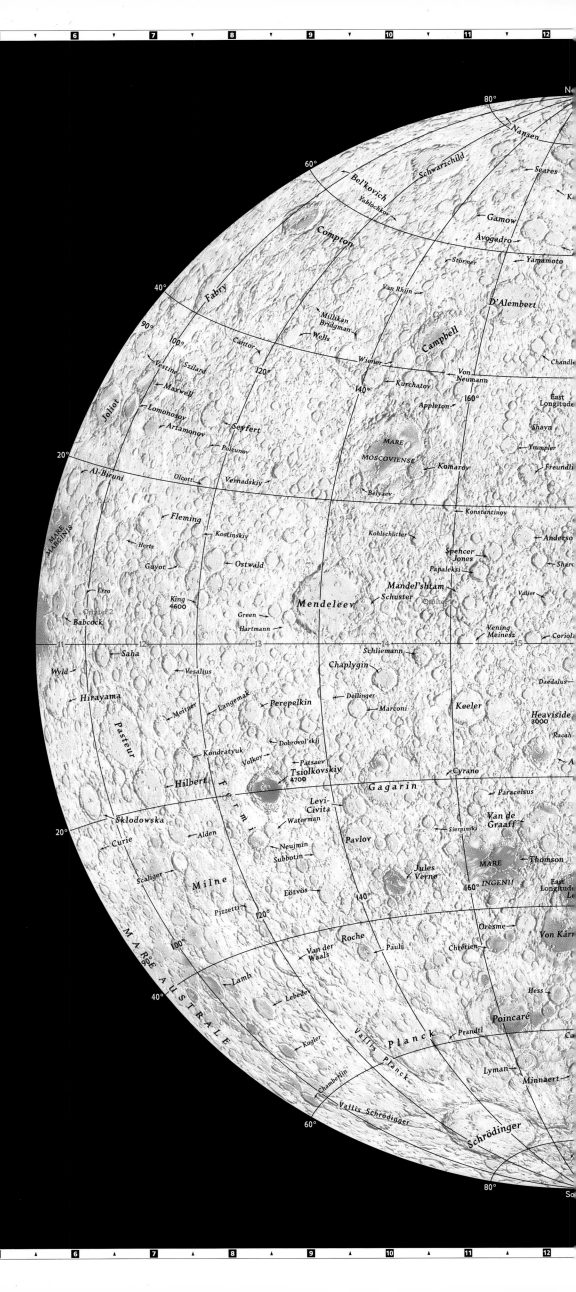

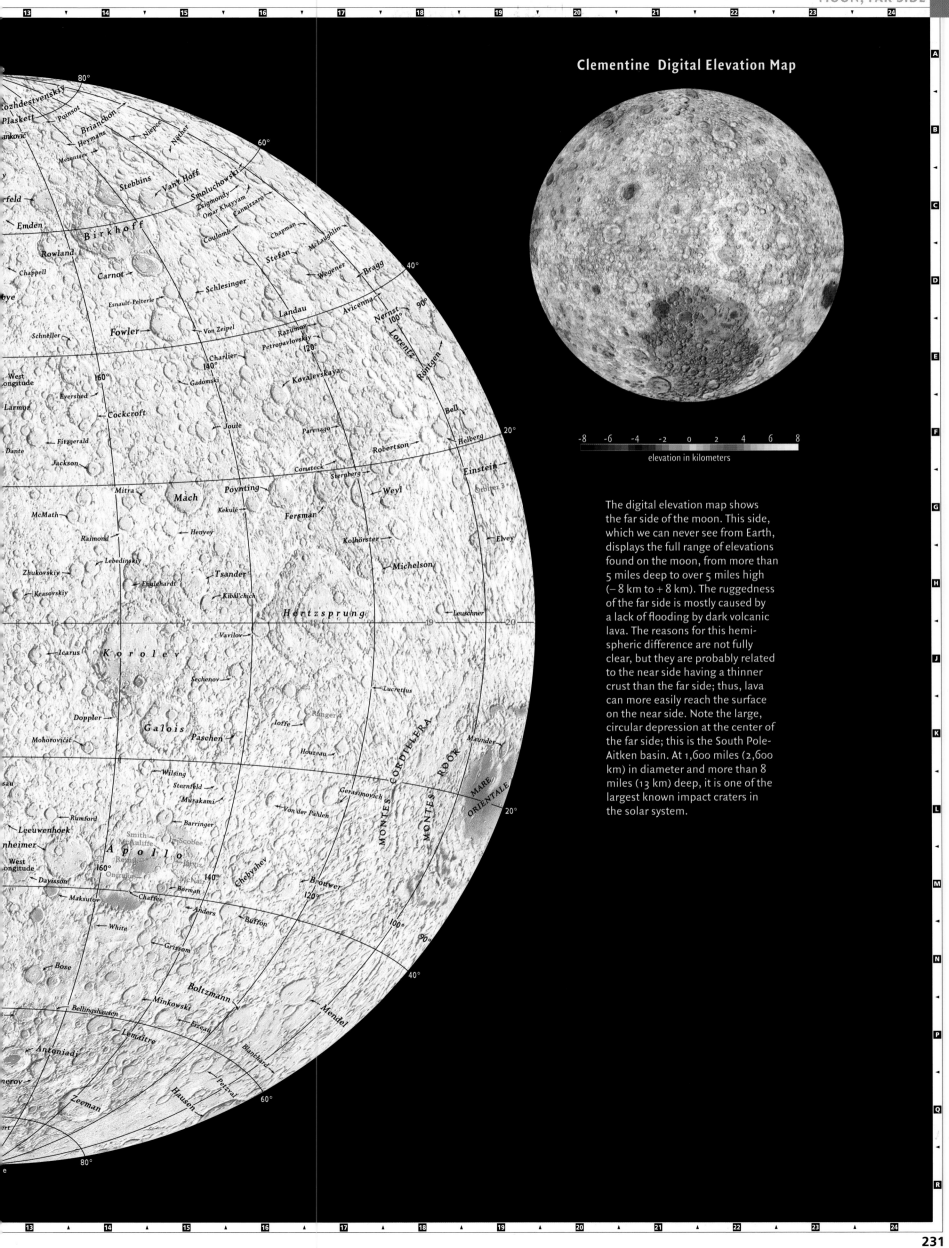

Clementine Digital Elevation Map

-8 -6 -4 -2 0 2 4 6 8
elevation in kilometers

The digital elevation map shows the far side of the moon. This side, which we can never see from Earth, displays the full range of elevations found on the moon, from more than 5 miles deep to over 5 miles high (– 8 km to + 8 km). The ruggedness of the far side is mostly caused by a lack of flooding by dark volcanic lava. The reasons for this hemispheric difference are not fully clear, but they are probably related to the near side having a thinner crust than the far side; thus, lava can more easily reach the surface on the near side. Note the large, circular depression at the center of the far side; this is the South Pole-Aitken basin. At 1,600 miles (2,600 km) in diameter and more than 8 miles (13 km) deep, it is one of the largest known impact craters in the solar system.

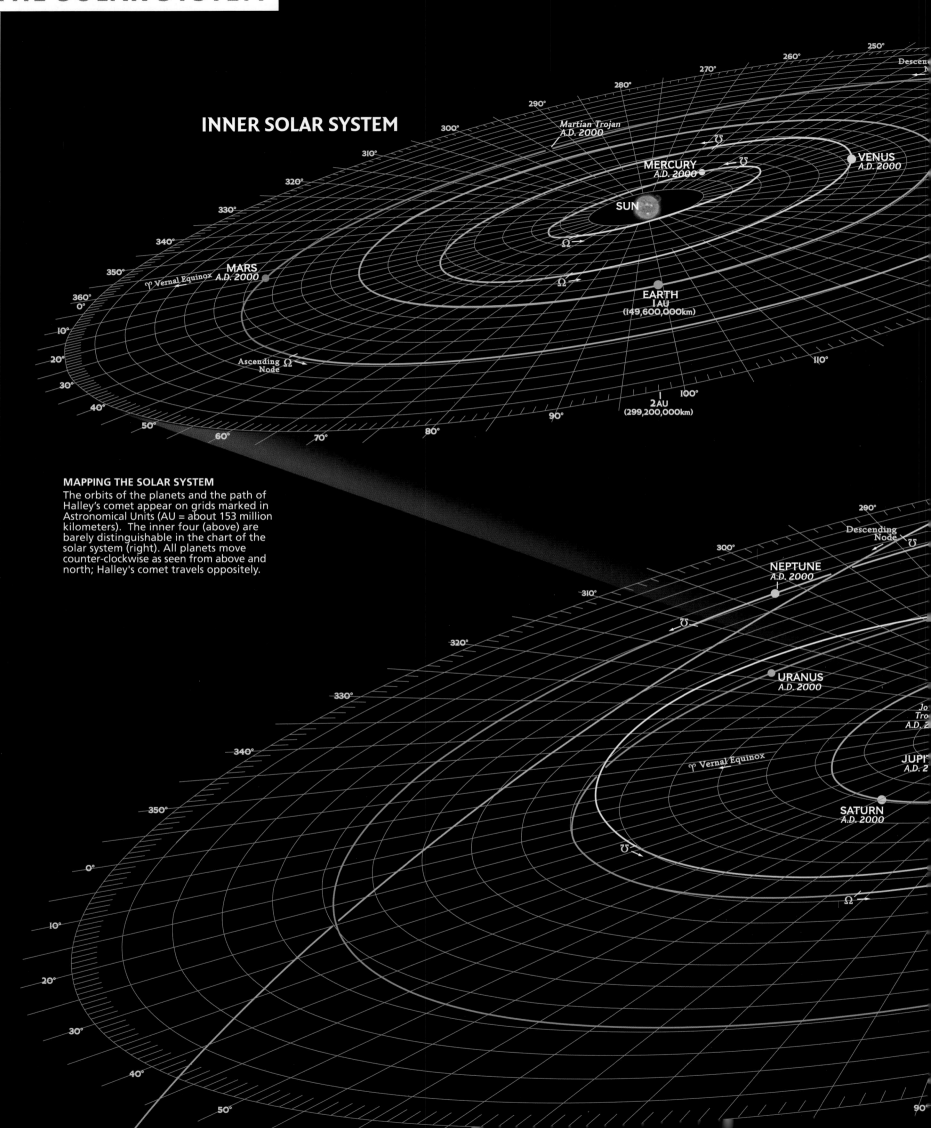

INNER SOLAR SYSTEM

250°
Descen...
260°
270°
280°
290°
300°
310°
320°
330°
340°
350°
360° 0°
10°
20°
30°
40°
50°
60°
70°
80°
90°
100°
110°

Martian Trojan A.D. 2000

VENUS *A.D. 2000*

MERCURY *A.D. 2000*

SUN

MARS *A.D. 2000*

♈ *Vernal Equinox*

EARTH 1 AU (149,600,000km)

Ascending Node ☊

℧

☊

2 AU (299,200,000km)

MAPPING THE SOLAR SYSTEM

The orbits of the planets and the path of
Halley's comet appear on grids marked in
Astronomical Units (AU = about 153 million
kilometers). The inner four (above) are
barely distinguishable in the chart of the
solar system (right). All planets move
counter-clockwise as seen from above and
north; Halley's comet travels oppositely.

290°
300°
310°
320°
330°
340°
350°
0°
10°
20°
30°
40°
50°
60°
90°

Descending Node ℧

NEPTUNE *A.D. 2000*

℧

URANUS *A.D. 2000*

Jo... Tro... *A.D. 2...*

JUPI... *A.D. 2...*

SATURN *A.D. 2000*

♈ *Vernal Equinox*

℧

☊

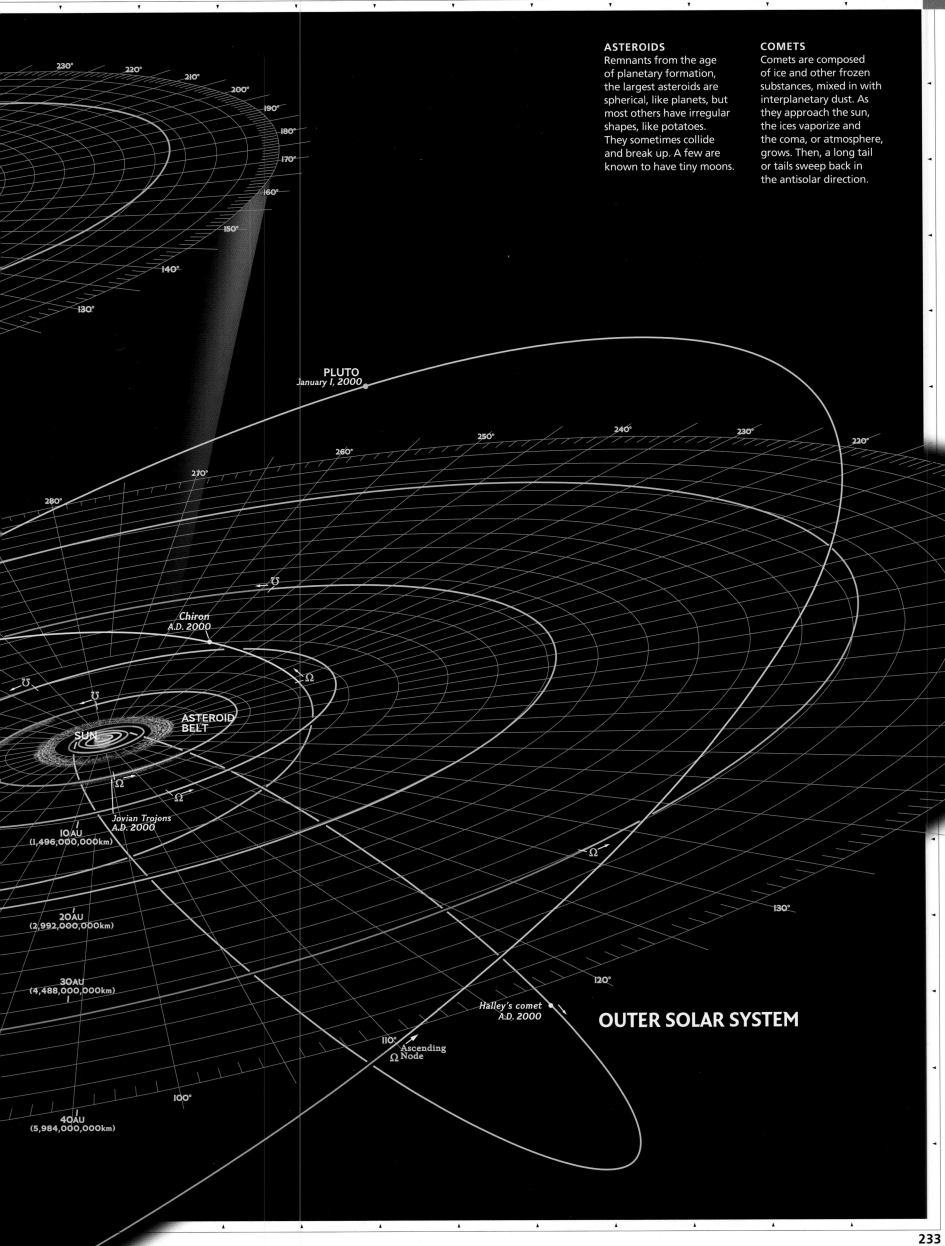

ASTEROIDS
Remnants from the age of planetary formation, the largest asteroids are spherical, like planets, but most others have irregular shapes, like potatoes. They sometimes collide and break up. A few are known to have tiny moons.

COMETS
Comets are composed of ice and other frozen substances, mixed in with interplanetary dust. As they approach the sun, the ices vaporize and the coma, or atmosphere, grows. Then, a long tail or tails sweep back in the antisolar direction.

230°
220°
210°
200°
190°
180°
170°
160°
150°
140°
130°

PLUTO
January 1, 2000

250°
240°
230°
220°
260°
270°
280°

☋

Chiron
A.D. 2000

Ω

☋

☊

☋

ASTEROID
BELT

SUN

Ω

Ω

Ω

IOAU
(1,496,000,000km)

Jovian Trojans
A.D. 2000

130°

20AU
(2,992,000,000km)

30AU
(4,488,000,000km)

120°

Halley's comet
A.D. 2000

OUTER SOLAR SYSTEM

110°
Ascending
Ω Node

100°

40AU
(5,984,000,000km)

JUPITER

SATURN

MERCURY

URANUS

NEPTUNE

SUN

Average Surface Temperature:	5,505 °C
Average Core Temperature	16,000,000 °C
Rotation:	25 days
Equatorial Diameter:	1,392,000 km
Mass (Earth=1):	332,950
Density:	1,408 kg/m³
Surface gravity (Earth=1):	28.0

MERCURY

Average distance from the sun:	58,000,000 km
Revolution:	88 days
Average orbital speed:	47.9 km/s
Average Temperature:	167 °C
Rotation:	58.8 days
Equatorial Diameter:	4,879 km
Mass (Earth=1):	0.055
Density:	5,427 kg/m³
Surface gravity (Earth=1):	0.38
Known satellites:	none

Imaged by: Mariner X

Mass and gravity data for each planet are expressed in proportional relation to Earth. Approximate values for Earth are given in both categories, allowing comparison between planets.

RELATIVE SCALE
The planets are shown here in proportionate size to one another. See the Orbital diagram in the upper right of this plate for their proper relationship to the Sun.

EARTH

VENUS

MARS

MERCURY

PLUTO

JUPITER

Average distance from the sun:	779,000,000 km
Revolution:	11.9 years
Average orbital speed:	13.1 km/s
Average Temperature:	-110 °C
Rotation:	9.9 hours
Equatorial Diameter:	142,984 km
Mass (Earth=1):	317.8
Density:	1,326 kg/m³
Surface gravity (Earth=1):	2.36
Known satellites:	39
Largest Satellites:	Io, Europa, Ganymede, Callisto

Imaged by: Cassini Orbiter

SATURN

Average distance from the sun:	1,434,000,000 km
Revolution:	29.4 years
Average orbital speed:	9.7 km/s
Average Temperature:	-140 °C
Rotation:	10.7 hours
Equatorial Diameter:	120,536 km
Mass (Earth=1):	95.2
Density:	687 kg/m³
Surface gravity (Earth=1):	0.92
Known satellites:	30
Largest Satellites:	Titan, Rhea, Iapetus, Dione, Tethys

Imaged by: Voyager I

PLANETARY ORBITS

Just an infinitesimal dot on the scale of the universe, the solar system measures nearly 49.5 Astronomical Units (AU) from the sun to the far end of Pluto's orbit. An AU, the average distance of the Earth from the sun, equals approximately 149,600,000 kilometers.

Sunlight reaches Earth in eight minutes and Jupiter in 43 minutes, but it takes almost seven hours to cross the orbit of Pluto. Beyond are small icy bodies, tens of kilometers in diameter, and millions of unseen comets.

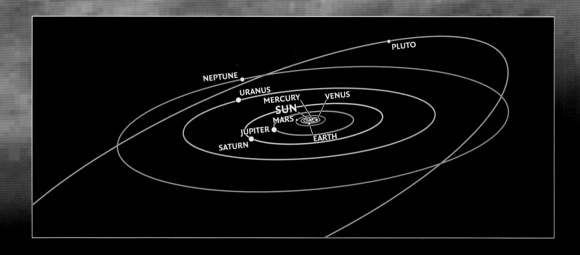

VENUS

Average distance from the sun:	108,000,000 km
Revolution:	225 days
Average orbital speed:	35 km/s
Average Temperature:	464 °C
Rotation:	244 days
Equatorial Diameter:	12,104 km
Mass (Earth=1):	0.815
Density:	5,243 kg/m³
Surface gravity (Earth=1):	0.91
Known satellites:	none

Imaged by: Magellan

EARTH

Average distance from the sun:	150,000,000 km
Revolution:	365 days
Average orbital speed:	29.8 km/s
Average Temperature:	15 °C
Rotation:	23.9 hours
Equatorial Diameter:	12,756 km
Mass:	5,974,000,000,000,000,000,000 metric tons
Density:	5,515 kg/m³
Surface gravity	9.81 m/s²
Known satellites:	1
Largest Satellite:	Earth's Moon

Imaged by: Galileo Orbiter

MARS

Average distance from the sun:	228,000,000 km
Revolution:	687 days
Average orbital speed:	24.1 km/s
Average Temperature:	-65 °C
Rotation:	24.6 hours
Equatorial Diameter:	6,794 km
Mass (Earth=1):	0.107
Density:	3,933 kg/m³
Surface gravity (Earth=1):	0.38
Known satellites:	2
Largest Satellites:	Phobos, Deimos

Imaged by: Mars Global Surveyor

URANUS

Average distance from the sun:	2,873,000,000 km
Revolution:	83.8 years
Average orbital speed:	6.8 km/s
Average Temperature:	-195 °C
Rotation:	17.2 hours
Equatorial Diameter:	51,118 km
Mass (Earth=1):	14.5
Density:	1,270 kg/m³
Surface gravity (Earth=1):	0.89
Known satellites:	20
Largest Satellites:	Oberon, Titania, Umbriel, Ariel

Imaged by: Hubble Space Telescope

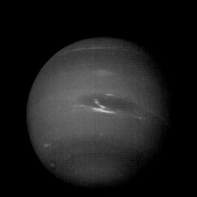

NEPTUNE

Average distance from the sun:	4,495,000,000 km
Revolution:	163.7 years
Average orbital speed:	5.4 km/s
Average Temperature:	-200 °C
Rotation:	16.1 hours
Equatorial Diameter:	49,528 km
Mass (Earth=1):	17.1
Density:	1,638 kg/m³
Surface gravity (Earth=1):	1.12
Known satellites:	8
Largest Satellite:	Triton

Imaged by: Voyager II

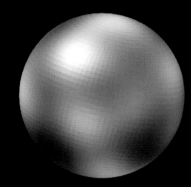

PLUTO

Average distance from the sun:	5,870,000,000 km
Revolution:	248 years
Average orbital speed:	4.7 km/s
Average Temperature:	-225 °C
Rotation:	6.4 days
Equatorial Diameter:	2,390 km
Mass (Earth=1):	0.002
Density:	1,750 kg/m³
Surface gravity (Earth=1):	0.06
Known satellites:	1
Largest Satellite:	Charon

Imaged by: Hubble Space Telescope

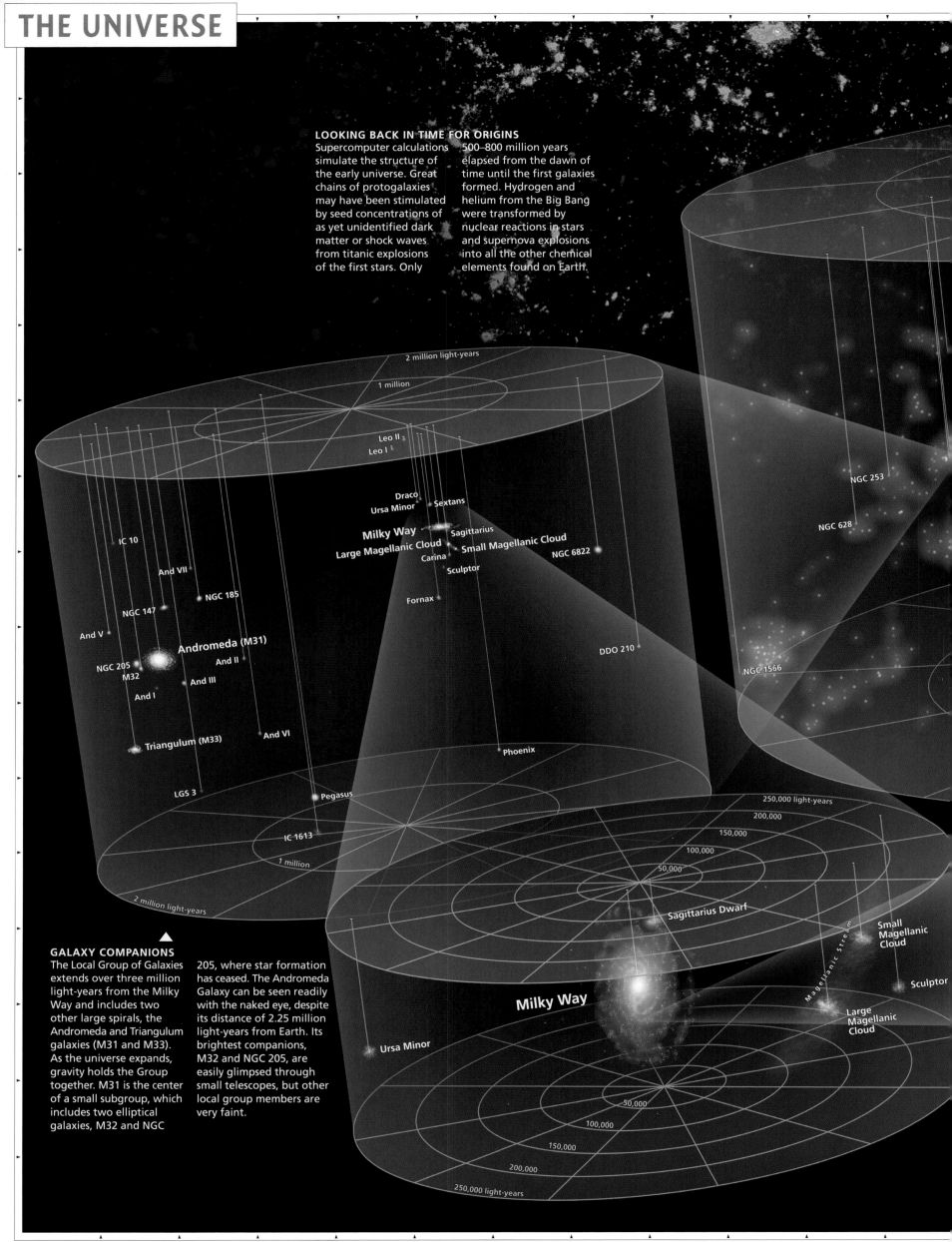

LOOKING BACK IN TIME FOR ORIGINS
Supercomputer calculations simulate the structure of the early universe. Great chains of protogalaxies may have been stimulated by seed concentrations of as yet unidentified dark matter or shock waves from titanic explosions of the first stars. Only 500–800 million years elapsed from the dawn of time until the first galaxies formed. Hydrogen and helium from the Big Bang were transformed by nuclear reactions in stars and supernova explosions into all the other chemical elements found on Earth.

▲
GALAXY COMPANIONS
The Local Group of Galaxies extends over three million light-years from the Milky Way and includes two other large spirals, the Andromeda and Triangulum galaxies (M31 and M33). As the universe expands, gravity holds the Group together. M31 is the center of a small subgroup, which includes two elliptical galaxies, M32 and NGC 205, where star formation has ceased. The Andromeda Galaxy can be seen readily with the naked eye, despite its distance of 2.25 million light-years from Earth. Its brightest companions, M32 and NGC 205, are easily glimpsed through small telescopes, but other local group members are very faint.

2 million light-years
1 million

Leo II
Leo I

Draco
Ursa Minor
Sextans

Milky Way
Sagittarius

Large Magellanic Cloud
Small Magellanic Cloud

Carina
NGC 6822

Sculptor

IC 10

Fornax

And VII

NGC 185

NGC 147

And V

DDO 210

Andromeda (M31)

NGC 205
M32
And II

And III

And I

Triangulum (M33)
And VI

Phoenix

LGS 3

Pegasus

IC 1613

1 million

2 million light-years

NGC 253

NGC 628

NGC 1566

250,000 light-years
200,000
150,000
100,000
50,000

Sagittarius Dwarf

Small Magellanic Cloud

Magellanic Stream

Sculptor

Milky Way

Large Magellanic Cloud

Ursa Minor

50,000
100,000
150,000
200,000
250,000 light-years

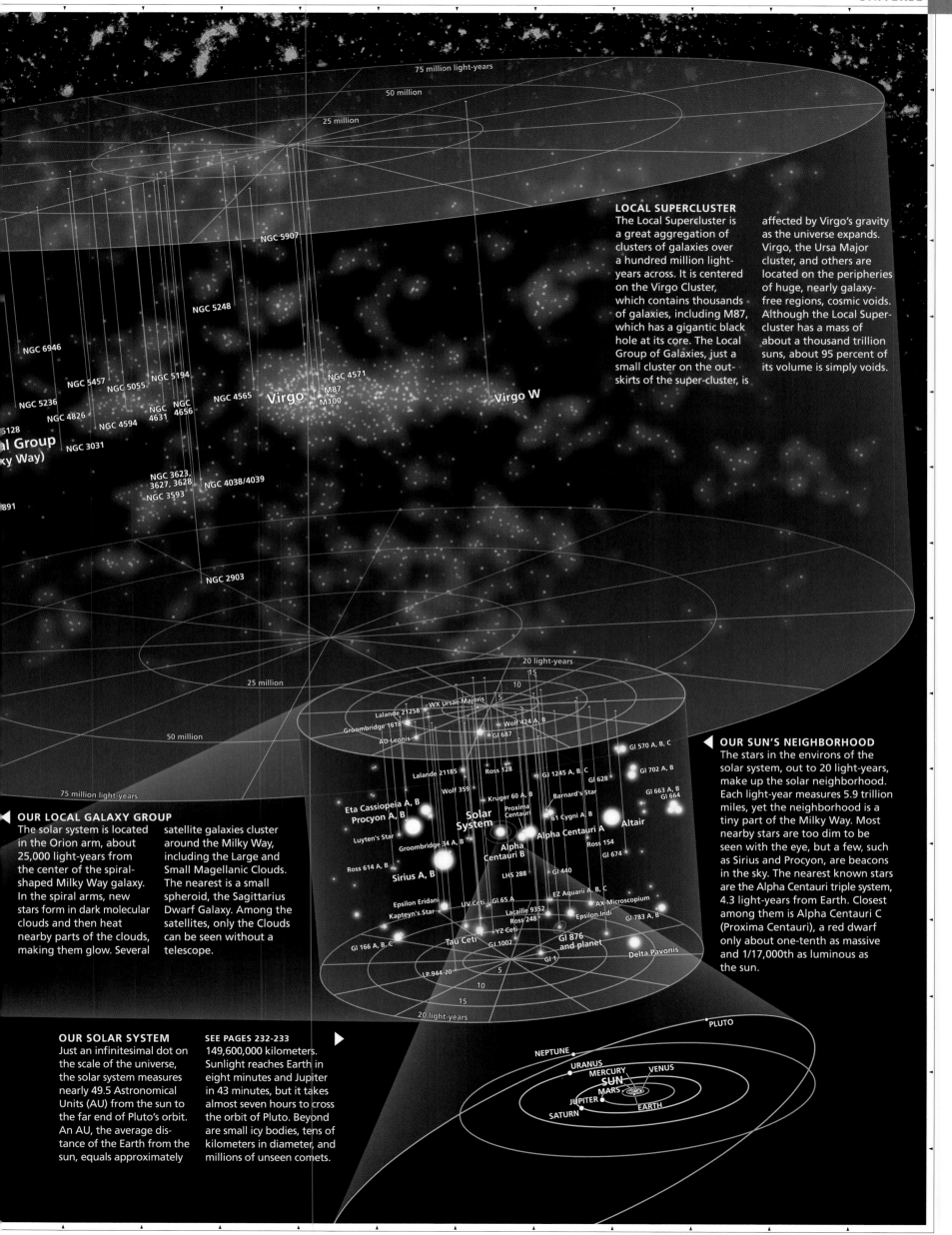

75 million light-years

50 million

25 million

NGC 5907

NGC 5248

NGC 6946

NGC 5457   NGC 5055   NGC 5194

NGC 5236   NGC 5194

NGC 4826

5128   NGC 4594   NGC   NGC
4631   4656

al Group   NGC 3031
ky Way)

891

NGC 3623,
3627, 3628   NGC 4038/4039
NGC 3593

NGC 2903

NGC 4565   Virgo   NGC 4571
M87
M100

Virgo W

LOCAL SUPERCLUSTER

The Local Supercluster is a great aggregation of clusters of galaxies over a hundred million light-years across. It is centered on the Virgo Cluster, which contains thousands of galaxies, including M87, which has a gigantic black hole at its core. The Local Group of Galaxies, just a small cluster on the outskirts of the super-cluster, is affected by Virgo's gravity as the universe expands. Virgo, the Ursa Major cluster, and others are located on the peripheries of huge, nearly galaxy-free regions, cosmic voids. Although the Local Super-cluster has a mass of about a thousand trillion suns, about 95 percent of its volume is simply voids.

25 million

50 million

75 million light-years

20 light-years
15
10
5

WX Ursae Majoris
Lalande 21258
Groombridge 1618   Wolf 424 A, B
AD Leonis   Gl 687

Lalande 21185   Ross 128   Gl 1245 A, B, C   Gl 702 A, B
Wolf 359   Gl 628   Gl 663 A, B
Kruger 60 A, B   Gl 664
Eta Cassiopeia A, B   Proxima   Barnard's Star
Procyon A, B   Solar   Centauri   61 Cygni A, B   Altair
System
Luyten's Star   Alpha Centauri A
Groombridge 34 A, B   Alpha   Ross 154
Ross 614 A, B   Centauri B   Gl 674
Sirius A, B   LHS 288   Gl 440
EZ Aquarii A, B, C
Epsilon Eridani   AX Microscopium
UV Ceti   Gl 65 A
Kapteyn's Star   Lacaille 9352   Epsilon Indi
Ross 248   Gl 783 A, B
YZ Ceti
Gl 166 A, B, C   Tau Ceti   Gl 1002   Gl 876
and planet
LP 944-20   Gl 1   Delta Pavonis

5
10
15
20 light-years

OUR LOCAL GALAXY GROUP

The solar system is located in the Orion arm, about 25,000 light-years from the center of the spiral-shaped Milky Way galaxy. In the spiral arms, new stars form in dark molecular clouds and then heat nearby parts of the clouds, making them glow. Several satellite galaxies cluster around the Milky Way, including the Large and Small Magellanic Clouds. The nearest is a small spheroid, the Sagittarius Dwarf Galaxy. Among the satellites, only the Clouds can be seen without a telescope.

OUR SUN'S NEIGHBORHOOD

The stars in the environs of the solar system, out to 20 light-years, make up the solar neighborhood. Each light-year measures 5.9 trillion miles, yet the neighborhood is a tiny part of the Milky Way. Most nearby stars are too dim to be seen with the eye, but a few, such as Sirius and Procyon, are beacons in the sky. The nearest known stars are the Alpha Centauri triple system, 4.3 light-years from Earth. Closest among them is Alpha Centauri C (Proxima Centauri), a red dwarf only about one-tenth as massive and 1/17,000th as luminous as the sun.

OUR SOLAR SYSTEM

Just an infinitesimal dot on the scale of the universe, the solar system measures nearly 49.5 Astronomical Units (AU) from the sun to the far end of Pluto's orbit. An AU, the average distance of the Earth from the sun, equals approximately

SEE PAGES 232-233
149,600,000 kilometers. Sunlight reaches Earth in eight minutes and Jupiter in 43 minutes, but it takes almost seven hours to cross the orbit of Pluto. Beyond are small icy bodies, tens of kilometers in diameter, and millions of unseen comets.

PLUTO
NEPTUNE
URANUS   MERCURY   VENUS
SUN
MARS
JUPITER   EARTH
SATURN

SPACE EXPLORATION TIME LINE

1955 | 1956 | 1957 | 1958 | 1959

FIRST ARTIFICIAL SATELLITE
U.S.S.R.
OCT. 4, 1957
Sputnik I was launched; it transmitted radio signals back to Earth for a short time.

FIRST LIVE ANIMAL IN SPACE
U.S.S.R.
NOV. 3, 1957
Dog named Laika lived eight days in space aboard Sputnik 2.

FIRST AMERICAN SATELLITE
U.S.
JAN. 31, 1958
Explorer I discovered radiation belts around the Earth.

CREATION OF NASA
U.S.
OCT. 1, 1958
National Aeronautics and Space Administration was established.

FIRST MAN-MADE OBJECT TO ACHIEVE SOLAR ORBIT
U.S.S.R.
JAN. 4, 1959
Luna 1

FIRST SPACECRAFT TO IMPACT ON THE MOON
U.S.S.R.
SEPT. 14, 1959
Luna 2

FIRST VIEW OF MOON'S FAR SIDE
U.S.S.R.
OCT. 7, 1959
Luna 3 photographed 70 percent of the far side.

1965 | 1966 | 1967 | 1968 | 1969

FIRST SPACE WALK
U.S.S.R.
MAR. 18, 1965
Alexei Leonov's tethered space walk lasted 12 minutes.

FIRST IMAGES OF MARS
U.S.
JULY 14, 1965
Pictures from Mariner 4 showed no evidence of life on Mars.

FIRST SPACECRAFT TO LAND ON THE MOON
U.S.S.R.
FEB. 3, 1966
Luna 9 demonstrated moon's surface strong enough to support large spacecraft.

FIRST AMERICAN SPACECRAFT ON THE MOON
U.S.
JUNE 2, 1966
Surveyor I soft-landed on the moon and transmitted photographs.

FIRST U.S. SPACE TRAGEDY
U.S.
JAN. 27, 1967
Three astronauts were killed in a fire during a test.

FIRST SPACE-FLIGHT CASUALTY
U.S.S.R.
APR. 24, 1967
Soyuz 1 crashed, killing one.

FIRST VENUS PROBE LAUNCHED
U.S.S.R.
JUNE 12, 1967
Venera 4 compiled data on Venusian atmosphere.

FIRST MOON ORBIT
U.S.S.R.
SEPT. 15, 1968
Zond 5

FIRST MANNED APOLLO MISSION
U.S.
OCT. 11, 1968
Apollo 7 orbited Earth once.

FIRST MANNED MOON ORBIT
U.S.
DEC. 24, 1968
Apollo 8 made ten orbits on six-day mission.

FIRST MANNED MOON LANDING
U.S.
JULY 20, 1969
Neil Armstrong and Edwin Aldrin Jr. were first to set foot on the moon.

1975 | 1976 | 1977 | 1978 | 1979

FIRST INTERNATIONAL SPACE RENDEZVOUS
U.S. - U.S.S.R.
JULY 17, 1975
American Apollo 18 and Soviet Soyuz 19 docked together.

FIRST SURFACE IMAGES OF VENUS
U.S.S.R.
OCT. 1975
Venera 9 and 10

FIRST SURFACE IMAGES OF MARS
U.S.
JULY 20, 1976
Viking 1 represented first U.S. attempt at landing on another planet.

DISCOVERY OF WATER FROST ON MARS
U.S.
SEPT. 1976
Viking 2 found water frost on Utopia Planitia.

LAUNCH OF VOYAGER MISSIONS
U.S.
AUG.- SEPT. 1977
Voyager I and II traveled to Jupiter and Saturn; they were the first spacecraft sent to explore these planets.

ARRIVAL OF U.S. PROBES AT VENUS
U.S.
DEC. 1978
U.S. probes obtained data on the atmosphere and mapped the surface.

ARRIVAL OF VOYAGER 1 AT JUPITER
U.S.
MAR. 5, 1979
Voyager 1 transmitted pictures of the planet and its moons.

ARRIVAL OF VOYAGER 2 AT JUPITER
U.S.
JULY 9, 1979
Voyager 2 transmitted images of the planet and its moons.

FIRST IMAGES OF SATURN
U.S.
SEPT. 1, 1979
Space probe Pioneer 11

1985 | 1986 | 1987 | 1988 | 1989

MAIDEN VOYAGE OF *ATLANTIS*
U.S.
OCT. 3, 1985
America's fourth space shuttle

ARRIVAL OF VOYAGER 2 AT URANUS
U.S.
JAN. 24, 1986
Captured the first close-up views of Uranus and its moons

CHALLENGER TRAGEDY
U.S.
JAN. 28, 1986
Shuttle's crew of seven were killed in an explosion when a leak ignited the fuel tank shortly after liftoff.

LAUNCH OF *MIR* SPACE STATION
U.S.S.R.
FEB. 20, 1986
First module successfully launched into orbit.

NEW SPACE ENDURANCE RECORD
U.S.S.R.
DEC. 29, 1987
Yuri Romanenko inhabited *Mir* for 326 days.

ARRIVAL OF VOYAGER 2 AT NEPTUNE
U.S.
AUG. 25, 1989
First close-up images of Neptune and its moons were transmitted.

1995 | 1996 | 1997 | 1998 | 1999

FIRST FEMALE SHUTTLE PILOT
U.S.
FEB. 3, 1995
Eileen M. Collins piloted *Discovery* on mission STS-63.

NEW SPACE ENDURANCE RECORD
RUSSIA
MAR. 22, 1995
Valeriy Polyakov spent 438 days aboard *Mir*.

FIRST SHUTTLE DOCKING WITH *MIR*
U.S.- RUSSIA
JUNE 29, 1995
American space shuttle *Atlantis* rendezvoused with the Russian space station.

ARRIVAL OF GALILEO AT JUPITER
U.S.
DEC. 7, 1995
Studies were made of the planet and its atmosphere.

75th SPACE SHUTTLE MISSION
U.S.
FEB. 22, 1996
The 19th *Columbia* mission

RETURN OF SHANNON LUCID FROM *MIR*
U.S.- RUSSIA
SEPT. 26, 1996
Lucid set U.S. space endurance record of 188 days aboard *Mir*.

LANDING OF MARS PATHFINDER ON MARS
U.S.
JULY 4, 1997
Spacecraft examined terrain and returned images of the planet's surface.

RETURN OF JOHN GLENN TO SPACE
U.S.
OCT. 29, 1998
Glenn returned to space for first time in 36 years.

LAUNCH OF FIRST MODULE OF I.S.S.
(INTERNATIONAL SPACE STATION)
RUSSIA
NOV. 20, 1998
Russian rocket carried first component of I.S.S.

FIRST AMERICAN I.S.S. MODULE
U.S.
DEC. 4, 1998
New module was attached to Russian module.

1960

FIRST WEATHER SATELLITE

U.S.

APR. 1, 1960

Tiros 1 established satellites as a useful tool for studying weather conditions.

1961

FIRST MAN IN SPACE

U.S.S.R.

APR. 12, 1961

Yuri Gagarin orbited Earth once in Vostok I, completing the trip in 108 minutes.

FIRST AMERICAN IN SPACE

U.S.

MAY 5, 1961

Alan Shepard's Freedom 7 flight lasted 15 minutes and did not reach orbit.

1962

PRESIDENT JOHN F. KENNEDY'S HISTORIC SPEECH

U.S.

MAY 25, 1961

Kennedy challenged nation to land man on moon by end of decade.

FIRST AMERICAN IN ORBIT

U.S.

FEB. 20, 1962

John Glenn orbited the Earth three times on Friendship 7.

1963

FIRST WOMAN IN SPACE

U.S.S.R.

JUNE 16, 1963

Valentina Tereshkova

1964

1970

APOLLO 13 LAUNCH

U.S.

APR. 11, 1970

After oxygen tanks exploded three astronauts were nearly killed; mission control coordinated their dramatic rescue.

FIRST AUTOMATED RETURN OF LUNAR SOIL

U.S.S.R.

SEPT. 12, 1970

Luna 16, an automated spacecraft, returned lunar soil samples.

FIRST ROBOTIC LUNAR MISSION

U.S.S.R.

NOV. 10, 1970

Robot controlled from Earth

1971

FIRST LANDING ON VENUS

U.S.S.R.

DEC. 15, 1970

Venera 7 transmitted from Venus' surface for 23 minutes.

FIRST SPACE STATION

U.S.S.R.

APR. 19, 1971

Salyut I orbited for more than two years.

FIRST OCCUPATION OF SPACE STATION

U.S.S.R.

JUNE 7, 1971

Three cosmonauts occupied Salyut 1 for several weeks.

1972

FIRST LUNAR ROVER MISSION

U.S.

JULY 30, 1971

Astronauts explored the moon's surface with a rover.

FIRST SPACECRAFT TO ORBIT ANOTHER PLANET

U.S.

NOV. 13, 1971

Mariner 9 orbited Mars and mapped the surface.

1973

FIRST BLACK HOLE CANDIDATE

U.S.

DEC. 1972

Cignus X-1 was designated as first probable black hole.

FIRST U.S. SPACE STATION

U.S.

MAY 14, 1973

Skylab was launched for science experiments.

1974

FIRST SKYLAB CREW

U.S.

MAY 25, 1973

Crew repaired damage to Skylab sustained during launch.

1980

ARRIVAL OF VOYAGER 1 AT SATURN

U.S.

NOV. 12, 1980

Probe transmitted images of the planet and its moons.

1981

FIRST SPACE SHUTTLE LAUNCH

U.S.

APR. 12, 1981

First mission of the Space Transportation System (STS-1)

ARRIVAL OF VOYAGER 2 AT SATURN

U.S.

AUG. 25, 1981

Probe transmitted images of the planet and its moons.

1982

FIRST VENUS SOIL SAMPLES

U.S.S.R.

MAR. 1, 1982

Venera 13

FIRST OPERATIONAL SPACE SHUTTLE MISSION

U.S.

NOV. 11, 1982

Space shuttle Columbia deployed two satellites.

1983

NEW SPACE ENDURANCE RECORD

U.S.S.R.

DEC. 11, 1982

Two Soviet cosmonauts inhabited space station Salyut 7 for 211 days.

MAIDEN VOYAGE OF CHALLENGER

U.S.

APR. 4, 1983

America's second space shuttle

FIRST AMERICAN WOMAN IN SPACE

U.S.

JUNE 18, 1983

Sally Ride traveled on Challenger mission STS-7.

1984

FIRST UNTETHERED SPACE WALK

U.S.

FEB. 3, 1984

Astronaut Bruce McCandless used the new Manned Maneuvering Unit.

MAIDEN VOYAGE OF DISCOVERY

U.S.

AUG. 30, 1984

America's third space shuttle

1990

LAUNCH OF HUBBLE SPACE TELESCOPE

U.S.

APR. 24, 1990

Telescope was successfully deployed, but a flawed mirror resulted in fuzzy images.

ARRIVAL OF MAGELLAN AT VENUS

U.S.

AUG. 10, 1990

Magellan used radar to map the Venusian surface.

1991

1992

MAIDEN VOYAGE OF ENDEAVOUR

U.S.

MAY 7, 1992

Launch brought the number of orbiters in the shuttle fleet back to four.

50th SPACE SHUTTLE MISSION

U.S.

SEPT. 12, 1992

The second Endeavour mission

1993

FIRST H.S.T. SERVICING MISSION

U.S.

DEC. 2, 1993

Endeavour began the first servicing mission of the Hubble Space Telescope.

1994

FIRST RUSSIAN COSMONAUT ABOARD SHUTTLE

U.S.- RUSSIA

FEB. 3, 1994

Sergei Krikalev flew aboard Discovery.

2000

100th SPACE SHUTTLE MISSION

U.S.

OCT. 11, 2000

The 28th Discovery mission

FIRST LANDING ON AN ASTEROID

U.S.

FEB. 12, 2001

NEAR spacecraft landed on asteroid Eros and sent back images.

2001

100th U.S. SPACE WALK

U.S.

FEB. 14, 2001

Space walk was necessary to install a new module for the I.S.S.

NEW SPACE WALK RECORD

U.S.

MAR. 11, 2001

Susan Helms and Jim Voss spent 8 hours, 56 minutes installing new I.S.S. module.

2002

FIRST TOURIST IN SPACE

U.S.- RUSSIA

APR. 28, 2001

Dennis Tito paid 20 million dollars to fly in a Russian Soyuz space capsule and board the I.S.S.

FUTURE

THE FUTURE

A new era in space exploration is under way as the new millennium begins to unfold. The U.S., Europe, and Japan are designing and deploying comet chasers, robotic rovers, and space stations. Missions to Mars will search for liquid water and establish networks of long-term laboratories. Asteroids and comets will be photographed and probed. A comet will even be pounded with copper projectiles at 20,000 miles per hour. By penetrating the deep interiors of such objects, scientists hope to learn more about the origins of the solar system. An orbiter and lander will journey to Mercury, the planet closest to the sun, and specialized spacecraft will scan for other Earthlike planets and life.

Airline Distances in Kilometers

	BEIJING	CAIRO	CAPE TOWN	CARACAS	HONG KONG	HONOLULU	LONDON	MELBOURNE	MEXICO	MONTRÉAL	MOSCOW	NEW DELHI	NEW YORK	PARIS	RIO DE JANEIRO	ROME	SAN FRANCISCO	SINGAPORE	STOCKHOLM	TOKYO
BEIJING		7557	12947	14411	1972	8171	8160	9093	12478	10490	5809	3788	11012	8236	17325	8144	9524	4465	6725	2104
CAIRO	7557		7208	10209	8158	14239	3513	13966	12392	8733	2899	4436	9042	3215	9882	2135	12015	8270	3404	9587
CAPE TOWN	12947	7208		10232	11867	18562	9635	10338	13703	12744	10101	9284	12551	9307	6075	8417	16487	9671	10334	14737
CARACAS	14411	10209	10232		16380	9694	7500	15624	3598	3932	9940	14221	3419	7621	4508	8363	6286	18361	8724	14179
HONG KONG	1972	8158	11867	16380		8945	9646	7392	14155	12462	7158	3770	12984	9650	17710	9300	11121	2575	8243	2893
HONOLULU	8171	14239	18562	9694	8945		11653	8862	6098	7915	11342	11930	7996	11988	13343	12936	3857	10824	11059	6208
LONDON	8160	3513	9635	7500	9646	11653		16902	8947	5240	2506	6724	5586	341	9254	1434	8640	10860	1436	9585
MELBOURNE	9093	13966	10338	15624	7392	8862	16902		13557	16730	14418	10192	16671	16793	13227	15987	12644	6050	15593	8159
MEXICO	12478	12392	13703	3598	14155	6098	8947	13557		3728	10740	14679	3362	9213	7669	10260	3038	16623	9603	11319
MONTRÉAL	10490	8733	12744	3932	12462	7915	5240	16730	3728		7077	11286	533	5522	8175	6601	4092	14816	5900	10409
MOSCOW	5809	2899	10101	9940	7158	11342	2506	14418	10740	7077		4349	7530	2492	11529	2378	9469	8426	1231	7502
NEW DELHI	3788	4436	9284	14221	3770	11930	6724	10192	14679	11286	4349		11779	6601	14080	5929	12380	4142	5579	5857
NEW YORK	11012	9042	12551	3419	12984	7996	5586	16671	3362	533	7530	11779		5851	7729	6907	4140	15349	6336	10870
PARIS	8236	3215	9307	7621	9650	11988	341	16793	9213	5522	2492	6601	5851		9146	1108	8975	10743	1546	9738
RIO DE JANEIRO	17325	9882	6075	4508	17710	13343	9254	13227	7669	8175	11529	14080	7729	9146		9181	10647	15740	10682	18557
ROME	8144	2135	8417	8363	9300	12936	1434	15987	10260	6601	2378	5929	6907	1108	9181		10071	10030	1977	9881
SAN FRANCISCO	9524	12015	16487	6286	11121	3857	8640	12644	3038	4092	9469	12380	4140	8975	10647	10071		13598	8644	8284
SINGAPORE	4465	8270	9671	18361	2575	10824	10860	6050	16623	14816	8426	4142	15349	10743	15740	10030	13598		9646	5317
STOCKHOLM	6725	3404	10334	8724	8243	11059	1436	15593	9603	5900	1231	5579	6336	1546	10682	1977	8644	9646		8193
TOKYO	2104	9587	14737	14179	2893	6208	9585	8159	11319	10409	7502	5857	10870	9738	18557	9881	8284	5317	8193	

Abbreviations

Adm.	Administrative	Kyrg.	Kyrgyzstan
Af.	Africa	L.	Lac, Lago, Lake, Límni, Loch, Lough
Afghan.	Afghanistan	La.	Louisiana
Agr.	Agriculture	Lab.	Labrador
Ala.	Alabama	Lag.	Laguna
Alas.	Alaska	Latv.	Latvia
Alban.	Albania	Leb.	Lebanon
Alg.	Algeria	Lib.	Libya
Alta.	Alberta	Liech.	Liechtenstein
Arch.	Archipelago, Archipiélago	Lith.	Lithuania
Arg.	Argentina	Lux.	Luxembourg
Ariz.	Arizona	m	meters
Ark.	Arkansas	Maced.	Macedonia
Arm.	Armenia	Madag.	Madagascar
Atl. Oc.	Atlantic Ocean	Maurit.	Mauritius
Aust.	Austria	Mass.	Massachusetts
Austral.	Australia	Md.	Maryland
Azerb.	Azerbaijan	Me.	Maine
B.	Baai, Baía, Baie, Bahía, Bay, Buḩayrat	Medit. Sea	Mediterranean Sea
B.C.	British Columbia	Mex.	Mexico
Belg.	Belgium	Mich.	Michigan
Bol.	Bolivia	Minn.	Minnesota
Bosn. Herzg.	Bosnia and Herzegovina	Miss.	Mississippi
Braz.	Brazil	Mo.	Missouri
Bulg.	Bulgaria	Mon.	Monument
C.	Cabo, Cap, Cape, Capo	Mont.	Montana
Calif.	California	Mor.	Morocco
Can.	Canada	Mt.-s.	Mont-s, Mount-ain-s
Cen. Af. Rep.	Central African Republic	N.	North-ern
C.H.	Court House	Nat.	National
Chan.	Channel	Nat. Mem.	National Memorial
Chap.	Chapada	Nat. Mon.	National Monument
Cmte.	Comandante	N.B.	National Battlefield
Cnel.	Coronel	N.B.	New Brunswick
Co.-s.	Cerro-s	N.C.	North Carolina
Col.	Colombia	N. Dak.	North Dakota
Colo.	Colorado	N.E.	Northeast
Conn.	Connecticut	Nebr.	Nebraska
Cord.	Cordillera	Neth.	Netherlands
C.R.	Costa Rica	Nev.	Nevada
Cr.	Creek, Crique	Nfld.	Newfoundland
C.S.I. Terr.	Coral Sea Islands Territory	N.H.	New Hampshire
D.C.	District of Columbia	Nicar.	Nicaragua
Del.	Delaware	Nig.	Nigeria
Den.	Denmark	N. Ire.	Northern Ireland
Dom. Rep.	Dominican Republic	N.J.	New Jersey
D.R.C.	Democratic Republic of the Congo	N. Mex.	New Mexico
		N.M.P.	National Military Park
		N.M.S.	National Marine Sanctuary

E.	East-ern	Nor.	Norway
Ecua.	Ecuador	N.P.	National Park
El Salv.	El Salvador	N.S.	Nova Scotia
Eng.	England	N.S.W.	New South Wales
Ens.	Ensenada	N.V.M.	National Volcanic Monument
Eq.	Equatorial	N.W.T.	Northwest Territories
Est.	Estonia	N.Y.	New York
Eth.	Ethiopia	N.Z.	New Zealand
Exp.	Exports	O.	Ostrov, Oued
Falk. Is.	Falkland Islands	Oc.	Ocean
Fd.	Fiord, Fiordo, Fjord	Okla.	Oklahoma
Fin.	Finland	Ont.	Ontario
Fk.	Fork	Oreg.	Oregon
Fla.	Florida	Oz.	Ozero
Fn.	Fortín	Pa.	Pennsylvania
Fr.	France, French	Pac. Oc.	Pacific Ocean
F.S.M.	Federated States of Micronesia	Pak.	Pakistan
ft	feet	Pan.	Panama
Ft.	Fort	Para.	Paraguay
G.	Golfe, Golfo, Gulf	Pass.	Passage
Ga.	Georgia	Peg.	Pegunungan
Ger.	Germany	P.E.I.	Prince Edward Island
Gl.	Glacier	Pen.	Peninsula, Péninsule
Gr.	Greece	Pk.	Peak
Gral.	General	P.N.G.	Papua New Guinea
Hbr.	Harbor, Harbour	Pol.	Poland
Hist.	Historic, -al	Pol.	Poluostrov
Hond.	Honduras	Port.	Portugal, Portuguese
Hts.	Heights	P.R.	Puerto Rico
Hung.	Hungary	Prov.	Province, Provincial
Hwy.	Highway	Pt.-e.	Point-e
I.-s.	Île-s, Ilha-s, Isla-s, Island-s, Isle, Isol-a, -e	Pta.	Ponta, Punta
Ice.	Iceland	Qnsld.	Queensland
I.H.S.	International Historic Site	Que.	Quebec
Ill.	Illinois	R.	Río, River, Rivière
Ind.	Indiana	Ra.-s.	Range-s
Ind.	Industry	Rec.	Recreation
Ind. Oc.	Indian Ocean	Rep.	Republic
Intl.	International	Res.	Reservoir, Reserve, Reservation
Ire.	Ireland	R.I.	Rhode Island
It.	Italy	Rom.	Romania
Jap.	Japan	Russ.	Russia
Jct.	Jonction, Junction	S.	South-ern
Kans.	Kansas	Sa.-s.	Serra, Sierra-s
Kaz.	Kazakhstan	S. Af.	South Africa
Kep.	Kepulauan	Sask.	Saskatchewan
Ky.	Kentucky	S.C.	South Carolina
		Scot.	Scotland

Sd.	Sound
S. Dak.	South Dakota
Sev.	Severn-yy, -aya, -oye
Sk.	Shankou
Slov.	Slovenia
Sp.	Spain, Spanish
Spr.-s.	Spring-s
St.-e.	Saint-e, Sankt, Sint
Str.-s.	Strait-s
Switz.	Switzerland
Syr.	Syria
Taj.	Tajikistan
Tas.	Tasmania
Tenn.	Tennessee
Terr.	Territory
Tex.	Texas
Tg.	Tanjung
Thai.	Thailand
Trin.	Trinidad
Tun.	Tunisia
Turk.	Turkey
Turkm.	Turkmenistan
U.A.E.	United Arab Emirates
U.K.	United Kingdom
Ukr.	Ukraine
U.N.	United Nations
Uru.	Uruguay
U.S.	United States
Uzb.	Uzbekistan
Va.	Virginia
Vdkhr.	Vodokhranilishche
Vdskh.	Vodoskhovyshche
Venez.	Venezuela
V.I.	Virgin Islands
Vic.	Victoria
Viet.	Vietnam
Vol.	Volcán, Volcano
Vt.	Vermont
W.	Wadi, Wādī, Webi
W.	West-ern
Wash.	Washington
Wis.	Wisconsin
W. Va.	West Virginia
Wyo.	Wyoming
Yug.	Yugoslavia
Zakh.	Zakhod-ni, -nyaya, -nye
Zimb.	Zimbabwe

Metric Conversions

QUICK REFERENCE CHART FOR METRIC TO ENGLISH CONVERSION

| 1 METER | 1 METER = 100 CENTIMETERS |
| 1 FOOT | 1 FOOT = 12 INCHES |

| 1 KILOMETER | 1 KILOMETER = 1,000 METERS |
| 1 MILE | 1 MILE = 5,280 FEET |

METERS	1	10	20	50	100	200	500	1,000	2,000	5,000	10,000
FEET	3.281	32.81	65.62	164.05	328.1	656.2	1,640.5	3,281.0	6,562.0	16,405.0	32,810.0
KILOMETERS	1	10	20	50	100	200	500	1,000	2,000	5,000	10,000
MILES	0.621	6.21	12.42	31.05	62.1	124.2	310.5	621.0	1,242.0	3,105.0	6,210.0

CONVERSION FROM METRIC MEASURES

SYMBOL	WHEN YOU KNOW	MULTIPLY BY	TO FIND	SYMBOL
LENGTH				
cm	centimeters	0.39	inches	in
m	meters	3.28	feet	ft
m	meters	1.09	yards	yd
km	kilometers	0.62	miles	mi
AREA				
cm^2	square centimeters	0.16	square inches	in^2
m^2	square meters	10.76	square feet	ft^2
m^2	square meters	1.20	square yards	yd^2
km^2	square kilometers	0.39	square miles	mi^2
ha	hectares	2.47	acres	—
MASS				
g	grams	0.04	ounces	oz
kg	kilograms	2.20	pounds	lb
t	metric tons	1.10	short tons	—
VOLUME				
mL	milliliters	0.06	cubic inches	in^3
mL	milliliters	0.03	liquid ounces	liq oz
L	liters	2.11	pints	pt
L	liters	1.06	quarts	qt
L	liters	0.26	gallons	gal
m^3	cubic meters	35.31	cubic feet	ft^3
m^3	cubic meters	1.31	cubic yards	yd^3
TEMPERATURE				
°C	degrees Celsius (centigrade)	9/5 then add 32	degrees Fahrenheit	°F

CONVERSION TO METRIC MEASURES

SYMBOL	WHEN YOU KNOW	MULTIPLY BY	TO FIND	SYMBOL
LENGTH				
in	inches	2.54	centimeters	cm
ft	feet	0.30	meters	m
yd	yards	0.91	meters	m
mi	miles	1.61	kilometers	km
AREA				
in^2	square inches	6.45	square centimeters	cm^2
ft^2	square feet	0.09	square meters	m^2
yd^2	square yards	0.84	square meters	m^2
mi^2	square miles	2.59	square kilometers	km^2
—	acres	0.40	hectares	ha
MASS				
oz	ounces	28.35	grams	g
lb	pounds	0.45	kilograms	kg
—	short tons	0.91	metric tons	t
VOLUME				
in^3	cubic inches	16.39	milliliters	mL
liq oz	liquid ounces	29.57	milliliters	mL
pt	pints	0.47	liters	L
qt	quarts	0.95	liters	L
gal	gallons	3.79	liters	L
ft^3	cubic feet	0.03	cubic meters	m^3
yd^3	cubic yards	0.76	cubic meters	m^3
TEMPERATURE				
°F	degrees Fahrenheit	5/9 after subtracting 32	degrees Celsius (centigrade)	°C

THE EARTH

Mass 5,974,000,000,000,000,000,000 (5.974 sextillion) metric tons

Total Area 510,066,000 sq km (196,938,000 sq mi)

Land Area 148,647,000 sq km (57,393,000 sq mi), 29.1% of total

Water Area 361,419,000 sq km (139,545,000 sq mi), 70.9% of total

Population 6,215,431,000

THE EARTH'S EXTREMES

Hottest Place: Dalol, Denakil Depression, Ethiopia; annual average temperature 34°C (93°F)

Coldest Place: Plateau Station, Antarctica; annual average temperature -56.7°C (-70°F)

Hottest Recorded Temperature: Al Aziziyah, Libya; 58°C (136.4°F), September 3, 1922

Coldest Recorded Temperature: Vostok, Antarctica; -89.2°C (-128.6°F), July 21, 1983

Wettest Place: Mawsynram, Assam, India; annual average rainfall 1,187 cm (467 in)

Driest Place: Arica, Atacama Desert, Chile; rainfall barely mesurable

Highest Waterfall: Angel Falls, Venezuela; 979 m (3,212 ft)

Largest Desert: Sahara, Africa; 9,000,000 sq km (3,475,000 sq mi)

Largest Canyon: Grand Canyon, Colorado River, Arizona; 446 km (277 mi) long along river, 549 m (1,801 ft) to 29 km (18 mi) wide, about 1.6 km (1 mi) deep

Largest Cave Chamber: Sarawak Cave, Gunung Mulu National Park, Malaysia; 40.2 acres and 260 feet high

Largest Cave System: Mammoth Cave, Kentucky; over 330 miles of passageways mapped

Most Predictable Geyser: Old Faithful, Wyoming; annual average interval 75 to 79 minutes

Longest Reef: Great Barrier Reef, Australia; 2,012 km (1,250 mi)

Greatest Tides: Bay of Fundy, Nova Scotia; 16 m (52 ft)

AREA OF EACH CONTINENT

	SQ KM	SQ MI	PERCENT OF EARTH'S LAND
Asia	44,579,000	17,212,000	30.0
Africa	30,065,000	11,608,000	20.2
North America	24,474,000	9,449,000	16.5
South America	17,819,000	6,880,000	12.0
Antarctica	13,209,000	5,100,000	8.9
Europe	9,938,000	3,837,000	6.7
Australia	7,687,000	2,968,000	5.2

HIGHEST POINT ON EACH CONTINENT

	METERS	FEET
Mount Everest, Asia	8,850	29,035
Cerro Aconcagua, South America	6,960	22,834
Mount McKinley (Denali), North America	6,194	20,320
Kilimanjaro, Africa	5,895	19,340
El'brus, Europe	5,642	18,510
Vinson Massif, Antarctica	4,897	16,067
Mount Kosciuszko, Australia	2,228	7,310

LOWEST SURFACE POINT ON EACH CONTINENT

	METERS	FEET
Dead Sea, Asia	-411	-1,349
Lake Assal, Africa	-156	-512
Death Valley, North America	-86	-282
Valdés Peninsula, South America	-40	-131
Caspian Sea, Europe	-28	-92
Lake Eyre, Australia	-16	-52
Antarctica (ice covered)	-2,550	-8,366

LARGEST ISLANDS

		AREA	
		SQ KM	SQ MI
1	Greenland	2,175,600	840,000
2	New Guinea	792,500	306,000
3	Borneo	725,100	280,100
4	Madagascar	587,000	226,600
5	Baffin Island	507,500	196,000
6	Sumatra	427,300	165,000
7	Honshu	227,400	87,800
8	Great Britain	218,100	84,200
9	Victoria Island	217,300	83,900
10	Ellesmere Island	196,200	75,800
11	Celebes	178,700	69,000
12	South Island (New Zealand)	151,000	58,300
13	Java	126,700	48,900
14	North Island (New Zealand)	114,000	44,000
15	Island of Newfoundland	108,900	42,000

LARGEST DRAINAGE BASINS

		AREA	
		SQ KM	SQ MI
1	Amazon, South America	7,050,000	2,721,000
2	Congo, Africa	3,700,000	1,428,000
3	Mississippi-Missouri, North America	3,250,000	1,255,000
4	Paraná, South America	3,100,000	1,197,000
5	Yenisey-Angara, Asia	2,700,000	1,042,000
6	Ob-Irtysh, Asia	2,430,000	938,000
7	Lena, Asia	2,420,000	934,000
8	Nile, Africa	1,900,000	733,400
9	Amur, Asia	1,840,000	710,000
10	Mackenzie-Peace, North America	1,765,000	681,000
11	Ganges-Brahmaputra, Asia	1,730,000	668,000
12	Volga, Europe	1,380,000	533,000
13	Zambezi, Africa	1,330,000	513,000
14	Niger, Africa	1,200,000	463,000
15	Chang Jiang (Yangtze), Asia	1,175,000	454,000

Longitude East of Greenwich

Molloy Deep
608 m (-18,399 ft)
Arctic Ocean's deepest point

El'brus
(18,510 ft) 5,642 m
Europe's highest point

Caspian Sea
-92 m (-28 ft)
Europe's lowest point

Dead Sea
-411 m (-1,349 ft)
World's lowest point

Mount Everest
(29,035 ft) 8,850 m
World's highest point

Al Aziziyah, Libya
World's hottest
recorded temperature

Mawsynram, Assam, India
World's wettest place

Dalol, Ethiopia
Denakil Depression
World's hottest place

Lake Assal
-156 m (-512 ft)
Africa's lowest point

Challenger Deep
-10,920 m (-35,827 ft)
World's greatest ocean depth

Sarawak Cave
Gunung Mulu National Park, Malaysia
World's largest cave chamber

Kilimanjaro 5,895 m (19,340 ft)
Africa's highest point

Java Trench
-7,125 m (-23,376 ft)
Indian Ocean's deepest point

Great Barrier Reef
World's longest reef

Lake Eyre
(-52 ft) -16 m
Australia's lowest point

Mount Kosciuszko
2,228 m (7,310 ft)
Australia's highest point

NORTH ISLAND
(NEW ZEALAND)

SOUTH ISLAND
(NEW ZEALAND)

Winkel Tripel Projection, Central Meridian 0°

SCALE 1:122,700,000
1 CENTIMETER = 1270 KILOMETERS; 1 INCH = 1940 MILES

KILOMETERS
STATUTE MILES

Plateau Station, U.S.
World's coldest place

Vostok, Russia
World's coldest recorded
temperature

Largest Country Russia: 17,074,993 sq km (6,592,692 sq mi)

Smallest Country Vatican City: 0.4 sq km (0.2 sq mi)

Most Populous Country China: 1,280,712,000 people

Least Populous Country Vatican City: 1,000 people

Most Crowded Country Monaco: 17,500 per sq km (45,300 per sq mi)

Least Crowded Country Mongolia: 1.56 per sq km (4 per sq mi)

Largest Metropolitan Area Tokyo: 26,546,000 people

Country with the Greatest Number of Bordering countries: China, Russia: 14

ENGINEERING WONDERS

Tallest Office Building: Petronas Towers, Kuala Lumpur, Malaysia; 452 meters, 1483 feet

Tallest Tower (Freestanding): CN Tower, Toronto, Canada; 553 meters, 1,815 feet

Tallest Manmade Structure: KVLY TV tower, near Fargo, North Dakota; 629 meters, 2,063 feet

Longest wall: Great Wall of China; approx. 3,460 km (2,150 miles)

Longest Road: Pan-American highway (not including gap in Panama and Colombia); more than 24,140 km (15,000 miles)

Longest Railroad: Trans-Siberian Railroad, Russia; 9,286 km (5,770 miles)

Longest Road Tunnel: Laerdal Tunnel, Norway; 24.5 km, 15.2 miles

Longest Rail Tunnel: Seikan rail tunnel, Japan; 53.9 km (33.5 miles)

Highest Bridge (over water): Royal Gorge Bridge, Colorado; 321 meters, 1,053 feet above water

Longest Highway Bridge: Lake Pontchartrain Causeway, Louisiana; 38.4 km (23.9 miles)

Longest Suspension Bridge: Akashi-Kaikyo Bridge, Japan; 3,911 meters (12,831 feet)

Longest Boat Canal: Grand Canal, China; over 1,770 km (1,100 miles)

Longest irrigation canal: Karakum Canal, Turkmenistan; nearly 1,100 km (700 miles)

Largest artificial lake: Lake Volta, Volta River, Ghana; 9,065 sq km (3,500 sq mi)

Tallest Dam: Nurek Dam, Vakhsh River, Tajikistan; 300 meters (984 feet)

Tallest Pyramid: Great Pyramid of Khufu, Egypt; 137 meters, 450 feet

Deepest Mine: Western Deep Levels Mine, South Africa; Approx. 4 km (2.5 miles) deep

Longest submarine cable: Sea-Me-We 3 cable, connects 34 countries on four continents; 39,000 km (24,200 miles) long

AREA OF EACH OCEAN

	SQ KM	SQ MI	PERCENT OF EARTH'S WATER AREA
Pacific	166,241,000	64,186,000	46.0
Atlantic	86,557,000	33,420,000	23.9
Indian	73,427,000	28,350,000	20.3
Arctic	9,485,000	3,662,000	2.6

LONGEST RIVERS

		KM	MI
1	Nile, Africa	6,825	4,241
2	Amazon, South America	6,437	4,000
3	Chang Jiang (Yangtze), Asia	6,380	3,964
4	Mississippi-Missouri, North America	5,971	3,710
5	Yenisey-Angara, Asia	5,536	3,440
6	Huang (Yellow), Asia	5,464	3,395
7	Ob-Irtysh, Asia	5,410	3,362
8	Amur, Asia	4,416	2,744
9	Lena, Asia	4,400	2,734
10	Congo, Africa	4,370	2,715
11	Mackenzie-Peace, North America	4,241	2,635
12	Mekong, Asia	4,184	2,600
13	Niger, Africa	4,170	2,591
14	Paraná-Río de la Plata, S. America	4,000	2,485
15	Murray-Darling, Australia	3,718	2,310
16	Volga, Europe	3,685	2,290
17	Purus, South America	3,380	2,100

DEEPEST POINT IN EACH OCEAN

	METERS	FEET
Challenger Deep, Pacific Ocean	-10,920	-35,827
Puerto Rico Trench, Atlantic Ocean	-8,605	-28,232
Java Trench, Indian Ocean	-7,125	-23,376
Molloy Deep, Arctic Ocean	-5,608	-18,399

LARGEST LAKES BY AREA

		AREA SQ KM	SQ MI	MAXIMUM DEPTH METERS	FEET
1	Caspian Sea	371,000	143,200	1,025	3,363
2	Lake Superior	82,100	31,700	406	1,332
3	Lake Victoria	69,500	26,800	82	269
4	Lake Huron	59,600	23,000	229	751
5	Lake Michigan	57,800	22,300	281	922
6	Lake Tanganyika	32,600	12,600	1,470	4,823
7	Lake Baikal	31,500	12,200	1,637	5,371
8	Great Bear Lake	31,300	12,100	446	1,463
9	Aral Sea	30,700	11,900	51	167
10	Lake Malawi	28,900	11,200	695	2,280

LARGEST SEAS BY AREA

		AREA SQ KM	SQ MI	AVGERAGE DEPTH METERS	FEET
1	South China Sea	2,974,600	1,148,500	1,464	4,803
2	Caribbean Sea	2,515,900	971,400	2,575	8,448
3	Mediterranean Sea	2,510,000	969,100	1,501	4,925
4	Bering Sea	2,261,100	873,000	1,491	4,892
5	Gulf of Mexico	1,507,600	582,100	1,615	5,299
6	Sea of Okhotsk	1,392,100	537,500	973	3,192
7	Sea of Japan	1,012,900	391,100	1,667	5,469
8	Hudson Bay	730,100	281,900	93	305
9	East China Sea	664,600	256,600	189	620
10	Andaman Sea	564,900	218,100	1,118	3,668
11	Black Sea	507,900	196,100	1,191	3,907
12	Red Sea	453,000	174,900	538	1,765

Pages 244 through 247 group all of Earth's lands into four categories: independent states, dependencies, areas of special status, and areas geographically separated from their mainland countries. At right, a world map uses different colors to show the distribution of lands within each category.

Each of the 192 countries listed in the independent states category (below) is a recognized territory whose government is the highest legal authority over the land and people within its boundaries.

A dependency, on the other hand, is a region whose territory is controlled by another, often very distant, country; it is not, however, considered an inherent part of the controlling country. Most dependencies are inhabited and have some form of local government with limited autonomy.

An area of special status is a region of ambiguous political status. Most of these areas can be described as disputed territory, territory not recognized as independent by other countries, or territory leased by one government to another.

In the fourth category are populated lands considered integral parts of independent states, but they are separated from the rest of their countries by a significant distance.

Independent States of the World

COUNTRY	CAPITAL	2002 POPULATION	DATE OF INDEPENDENCE
AFGHANISTAN	Kabul	27,756,000	Aug. 19, 1919
ALBANIA	Tirana	3,134,000	Nov. 28, 1912
ALGERIA	Algiers	31,382,000	July 5, 1962
ANDORRA	Andorra la Vella	66,000	1278
ANGOLA	Luanda	12,714,000	Nov. 11, 1975
ANTIGUA AND BARBUDA	St. John's	67,000	Nov. 1, 1981
ARGENTINA	Buenos Aires	36,518,000	July 9, 1816
ARMENIA	Yerevan	3,799,000	Sept. 21, 1991
AUSTRALIA	Canberra	19,731,000	Jan. 1, 1901
AUSTRIA	Vienna	8,149,000	1156
AZERBAIJAN	Baku	8,172,000	Aug. 30, 1991
BAHAMAS	Nassau	312,000	July 10, 1973
BAHRAIN	Manama	670,000	Aug. 15, 1971
BANGLADESH	Dhaka	133,603,000	Mar. 26, 1971
BARBADOS	Bridgetown	269,000	Nov. 30, 1966
BELARUS	Minsk	9,936,000	Aug. 25, 1991
BELGIUM	Brussels	10,299,000	July 21, 1831
BELIZE	Belmopan	255,000	Sept. 21, 1981
BENIN	Porto-Novo	6,629,000	Aug. 1, 1960
BHUTAN	Thimphu	922,000	Aug. 8, 1949
BOLIVIA	La Paz, Sucre	8,760,000	Aug. 6, 1825
BOSNIA AND HERZEGOVINA	Sarajevo	3,409,000	Mar. 1, 1992
BOTSWANA	Gaborone	1,591,000	Sept. 30, 1966
BRAZIL	Brasília	173,816,000	Sept. 7, 1822
BRUNEI	Bandar Seri Begawan	355,000	Jan. 1, 1984
BULGARIA	Sofia	7,822,000	Mar. 3, 1878
BURKINA FASO	Ouagadougou	12,603,000	Aug. 5, 1960
BURUNDI	Bujumbura	6,688,000	July 1, 1962
CAMBODIA	Phnom Penh	12,295,000	Nov. 9, 1953
CAMEROON	Yaoundé	16,185,000	Jan. 1, 1960
CANADA	Ottawa	31,333,000	July 1, 1867
CAPE VERDE	Praia	460,000	July 5, 1975
CENTRAL AFRICAN REPUBLIC	Bangui	3,643,000	Aug. 13, 1960
CHAD	N'Djamena	8,997,000	Aug. 11, 1960
CHILE	Santiago	15,589,000	Sept. 18, 1810
CHINA	Beijing	1,280,712,000	221 B.C.
COLOMBIA	Bogotá	43,792,000	July 20, 1810
COMOROS	Moroni	614,000	July 6, 1975
CONGO	Brazzaville	3,206,000	Aug. 15, 1960
CONGO, DEMOCRATIC REPUBLIC OF THE	Kinshasa	55,225,000	June 30, 1960
COSTA RICA	San José	3,944,000	Sept. 15, 1821
CÔTE D'IVOIRE	Yamoussoukro, Abidjan	16,805,000	Aug. 7, 1960
CROATIA	Zagreb	4,320,000	June 25, 1991
CUBA	Havana	11,332,000	May 20, 1902
CYPRUS	Nicosia	893,000	Aug. 16, 1960
CZECH REPUBLIC	Prague	10,276,000	Jan. 1, 1993
DENMARK	Copenhagen	5,378,000	10th century
DJIBOUTI	Djibouti	652,000	June 27, 1977

COUNTRY	CAPITAL	2002 POPULATION	DATE OF INDEPENDENCE
DOMINICA	Roseau	76,000	Nov. 3, 1978
DOMINICAN REPUBLIC	Santo Domingo	8,782,000	Feb. 27, 1844
EAST TIMOR	Dili	779,000	May 20, 2002
ECUADOR	Quito	13,000,000	May 24, 1822
EGYPT	Cairo	71,244,000	Feb. 28, 1922
EL SALVADOR	San Salvador	6,551,000	Sept. 15, 1821
EQUATORIAL GUINEA	Malabo	483,000	Oct. 12, 1968
ERITREA	Asmara	4,466,000	May 24, 1993
ESTONIA	Tallinn	1,358,000	Sept. 6, 1991
ETHIOPIA	Addis Ababa	67,673,000	circa 1 A.D.
FIJI ISLANDS	Suva	852,000	Oct. 10, 1970
FINLAND	Helsinki	5,196,000	Dec. 6, 1917
FRANCE	Paris	59,498,000	486
GABON	Libreville	1,233,000	Aug. 17, 1960
GAMBIA	Banjul	1,456,000	Feb. 18, 1965
GEORGIA	T'bilisi	4,400,000	April 9, 1991
GERMANY	Berlin	82,406,000	Jan. 18, 1871
GHANA	Accra	20,244,000	Mar. 6, 1957
GREECE	Athens	10,968,000	1829
GRENADA	St. George's	104,000	Feb. 7, 1974
GUATEMALA	Guatemala	12,063,000	Sept. 15, 1821
GUINEA	Conakry	8,381,000	Oct. 2, 1958
GUINEA-BISSAU	Bissau	1,257,000	Sept. 24, 1973
GUYANA	Georgetown	765,000	May 26, 1966
HAITI	Port-au-Prince	7,064,000	Jan. 1, 1804
HONDURAS	Tegucigalpa	6,732,000	Sept. 15, 1821
HUNGARY	Budapest	10,146,000	1001
ICELAND	Reykjavík	288,000	June 17, 1944
INDIA	New Delhi	1,049,464,000	Aug. 15, 1947
INDONESIA	Jakarta	216,983,000	Aug. 17, 1945
IRAN	Tehran	65,554,000	Apr. 1, 1979
IRAQ	Baghdad	23,605,000	Oct. 3, 1932
IRELAND	Dublin	3,787,000	Dec. 6, 1921
ISRAEL	Jerusalem	6,603,000	May 14, 1948
ITALY	Rome	58,091,000	Mar. 17, 1861
JAMAICA	Kingston	2,629,000	Aug. 6, 1962
JAPAN	Tokyo	127,378,000	660 B.C.
JORDAN	Amman	5,323,000	May 25, 1946
KAZAKHSTAN	Astana	14,809,000	Dec. 16, 1991
KENYA	Nairobi	31,139,000	Dec. 12, 1963
KIRIBATI	Tarawa	95,000	July 12, 1979
KOREA, NORTH	Pyongyang	23,154,000	Aug. 15, 1945
KOREA, SOUTH	Seoul	48,360,000	Aug. 15, 1945
KUWAIT	Kuwait	2,269,000	June 19, 1961
KYRGYZSTAN	Bishkek	4,994,000	Aug. 31, 1991
LAOS	Vientiane	5,465,000	July 19, 1949
LATVIA	Rīga	2,345,000	Nov. 18, 1991
LEBANON	Beirut	4,345,000	Nov. 22, 1943
LESOTHO	Maseru	2,208,000	Oct. 4, 1966
LIBERIA	Monrovia	3,288,000	July 26, 1847
LIBYA	Tripoli	5,369,000	Dec. 24, 1951
LIECHTENSTEIN	Vaduz	34,000	Jan. 23, 1719

COUNTRY	CAPITAL	2002 POPULATION	DATE OF INDEPENDENCE
LITHUANIA	Vilnius	3,477,000	Mar. 11, 1990
LUXEMBOURG	Luxembourg	450,000	1839
MACEDONIA	Skopje	2,045,000	Sept. 17, 1991
MADAGASCAR	Antananarivo	16,913,000	June 26, 1960
MALAWI	Lilongwe	10,917,000	July 6, 1964
MALAYSIA	Kuala Lumpur	24,370,000	Aug. 31, 1957
MALDIVES	Male	281,000	July 26, 1965
MALI	Bamako	11,340,000	Sept. 22, 1960
MALTA	Valletta	380,000	Sept. 21, 1964
MARSHALL ISLANDS	Majuro	54,000	Oct. 21, 1986
MAURITANIA	Nouakchott	2,635,000	Nov. 28, 1960
MAURITIUS	Port Louis	1,213,000	Mar. 12, 1968
MEXICO	Mexico	101,743,000	Sept. 16, 1810
MICRONESIA	Palikir	108,000	Nov. 3, 1986
MOLDOVA	Chişinău	4,258,000	Aug. 27, 1991
MONACO	Monaco	34,000	1419
MONGOLIA	Ulaanbaatar	2,447,000	July 11, 1921
MOROCCO	Rabat	29,662,000	Mar. 2, 1956
MOZAMBIQUE	Maputo	19,608,000	June 25, 1975
MYANMAR (Burma)	Yangon (Rangoon)	48,956,000	Jan. 4, 1948
NAMIBIA	Windhoek	1,821,000	Mar. 21, 1990
NAURU	Yaren	12,000	Jan. 31, 1968
NEPAL	Kathmandu	23,862,000	1768
NETHERLANDS	Amsterdam	16,125,000	1579

■ / ◇		Independent state
□ / ◇		Dependency
■ / ◆		Area of special status
■ / ◆		Area geographically separated from mainland country

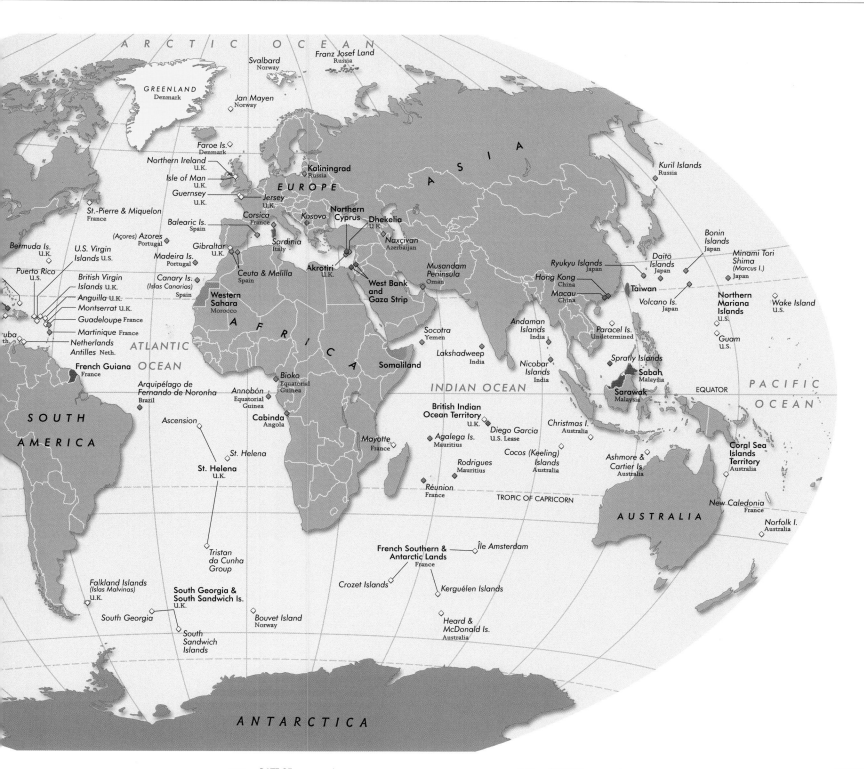

COUNTRY	CAPITAL	2002 POPULATION	DATE OF INDEPENDENCE
NEW ZEALAND	Wellington	3,867,000	Sept. 26, 1907
NICARAGUA	Managua	5,354,000	Sept. 15, 1821
NIGER	Niamey	11,641,000	Aug. 3, 1958
NIGERIA	Abuja	129,935,000	Oct. 1, 1960
NORWAY	Oslo	4,534,000	June 7, 1905
OMAN	Muscat	2,564,000	1650
PAKISTAN	Islamabad	143,481,000	Aug. 14, 1947
PALAU	Koror	20,000	Oct. 1, 1994
PANAMA	Panama	2,939,000	Nov. 3, 1903
PAPUA NEW GUINEA			
	Port Moresby	5,016,000	Sept. 16, 1975
PARAGUAY	Asunción	6,026,000	May 14, 1811
PERU	Lima	26,749,000	July 28, 1821
PHILIPPINES	Manila	80,025,000	July 4, 1946
POLAND	Warsaw	38,629,000	Nov. 11, 1918
PORTUGAL	Lisbon	10,438,000	1140
QATAR	Doha	618,000	Sept. 3, 1971
ROMANIA	Bucharest	22,382,000	1881
RUSSIA	Moscow	143,524,000	Aug. 24, 1991
RWANDA	Kigali	7,398,000	July 1, 1962
ST. KITTS AND NEVIS			
	Basseterre	39,000	Sept. 19, 1983
ST. LUCIA	Castries	166,000	Feb. 22, 1979
ST. VINCENT AND THE GRENADINES			
	Kingstown	116,000	Oct. 27, 1979
SAMOA	Apia	171,000	Jan. 1, 1962

COUNTRY	CAPITAL	2002 POPULATION	DATE OF INDEPENDENCE
SAN MARINO	San Marino	27,000	Sept. 3, 301
SAO TOME AND PRINCIPE			
	São Tomé	170,000	July 12, 1975
SAUDI ARABIA	Riyadh	23,965,000	Sept. 23, 1932
SENEGAL	Dakar	9,908,000	Apr. 4, 1960
SEYCHELLES	Victoria	85,000	June 29, 1976
SIERRA LEONE	Freetown	5,615,000	Apr. 27, 1961
SINGAPORE	Singapore	4,248,000	Aug. 9, 1965
SLOVAKIA	Bratislava	5,367,000	Jan. 1, 1993
SLOVENIA	Ljubljana	1,994,000	June 25, 1991
SOLOMON ISLANDS			
	Honiara	479,000	July 7, 1978
SOMALIA	Mogadishu	7,753,000	July 1, 1960
SOUTH AFRICA	Pretoria, Cape Town,		
	Bloemfontein	43,648,000	May 31, 1910
SPAIN	Madrid	41,298,000	1492
SRI LANKA	Colombo	18,947,000	Feb. 4, 1948
SUDAN	Khartoum	32,559,000	Jan. 1, 1956
SURINAME	Paramaribo	436,000	Nov. 25, 1975
SWAZILAND	Mbabane	1,124,000	Sept. 6, 1968
SWEDEN	Stockholm	8,922,000	June 6, 1523
SWITZERLAND	Bern	7,286,000	Aug. 1, 1291
SYRIA	Damascus	17,522,000	Apr. 17, 1946
TAJIKISTAN	Dushanbe	6,326,000	Sept. 9, 1991
TANZANIA	Dar es Salaam,		
	Dodoma	37,188,000	Apr. 26, 1964

COUNTRY	CAPITAL	2002 POPULATION	DATE OF INDEPENDENCE
THAILAND	Bangkok	62,626,000	1238
TOGO	Lomé	5,268,000	Apr. 27, 1960
TONGA	Nuku'alofa	101,000	June 4, 1970
TRINIDAD AND TOBAGO			
	Port-of-Spain	1,306,000	Aug. 31, 1962
TUNISIA	Tunis	9,782,000	Mar. 20, 1956
TURKEY	Ankara	67,264,000	Oct. 29, 1923
TURKMENISTAN	Ashgabat	5,567,000	Oct. 27, 1991
TUVALU	Funafuti	10,000	Oct. 1, 1978
UGANDA	Kampala	24,699,000	Oct. 9, 1962
UKRAINE	Kiev	48,225,000	Aug. 24, 1991
UNITED ARAB EMIRATES			
	Abu Dhabi	3,483,000	Dec. 2, 1971
UNITED KINGDOM			
	London	60,224,000	10th century
UNITED STATES	Washington	287,494,000	July 4, 1776
URUGUAY	Montevideo	3,361,000	Aug. 25, 1825
UZBEKISTAN	Tashkent	25,400,000	Sept. 1, 1991
VANUATU	Port-Vila	212,000	July 30, 1980
VATICAN CITY	Vatican City	1,000	Feb. 11, 1929
VENEZUELA	Caracas	25,093,000	July 5, 1811
VIETNAM	Hanoi	79,707,000	Sept. 2, 1945
YEMEN	Sanaa	18,607,000	May 22, 1990
YUGOSLAVIA	Belgrade	10,670,000	Apr. 27, 1992
ZAMBIA	Lusaka	9,959,000	Oct. 24, 1964
ZIMBABWE	Harare	12,341,000	Apr. 18, 1980

Dependencies of the World

DEPENDENCY	POPULATION	LOCATION	CAPITAL OR CHIEF CITY	DEPENDENCY OF	POLITICAL STATUS (SYSTEM)*
AMERICAN SAMOA	61,000	South Pacific Ocean	Pago Pago	United States	Unincorporated territory
ANGUILLA	13,000	Caribbean Sea	The Valley	United Kingdom	Overseas territory
ARUBA	96,000	Caribbean Sea	Oranjestad	Netherlands	Part of the Netherlands (parliamentary democracy)
ASHMORE AND CARTIER ISLANDS	no indigenous inhabitants	Indian Ocean	Administered from Canberra	Australia	Territory
BAKER ISLAND	uninhabited	North Pacific Ocean	Administered from Washington, D.C.	United States	Unincorporated territory
BERMUDA	64,000	North Atlantic Ocean	Hamilton	United Kingdom	Overseas territory (parliamentary government)
BOUVET ISLAND	uninhabited	South Atlantic Ocean	Administered from Oslo	Norway	Territory
BRITISH INDIAN OCEAN TERRITORY [1]	no indigenous inhabitants	Indian Ocean	Administered from London	United Kingdom	Overseas territory
BRITISH VIRGIN ISLANDS	21,000	Caribbean Sea	Road Town	United Kingdom	Overseas territory
CAYMAN ISLANDS	41,000	Caribbean Sea	George Town	United Kingdom	Overseas territory (British crown colony)
CHRISTMAS ISLAND	2,000	Indian Ocean	The Settlement	Australia	Territory
CLIPPERTON	uninhabited	North Pacific Ocean	Administered from French Polynesia	France	Possession of France
COCOS (KEELING) ISLANDS	1,000	Indian Ocean	West Island	Australia	Territory
COOK ISLANDS	19,000	South Pacific Ocean	Avarua	New Zealand	Free association with New Zealand (parliamentary democracy)
CORAL SEA ISLANDS TERRITORY	no indigenous inhabitants	South Pacific Ocean	Administered from Canberra	Australia	Territory
FALKLAND ISLANDS [2]	3,000	South Atlantic Ocean	Stanley	United Kingdom	Overseas territory
FAROE ISLANDS	47,000	North Atlantic Ocean	Tórshavn	Denmark	Part of Denmark (self-governing overseas division)
FRENCH POLYNESIA	241,000	South Pacific Ocean	Papeete	France	Overseas territory
FRENCH SOUTHERN AND ANTARCTIC LANDS [3]	no indigenous inhabitants	Indian Ocean	Administered from Paris	France	Overseas territory
GIBRALTAR	27,000	Europe	Gibraltar	United Kingdom	Overseas territory
GREENLAND (KALAALLIT NUNAAT)	56,000	North Atlantic Ocean	Nuuk (Godthåb)	Denmark	Part of Denmark (self-governing overseas division)
GUAM	158,000	North Pacific Ocean	Hagåtña (Agana)	United States	Unincorporated territory
GUERNSEY (Channel Islands)[4]	64,000	English Channel	St. Peter Port	United Kingdom	British crown dependency
HEARD AND MCDONALD ISLANDS	uninhabited	Indian Ocean	Administered from Canberra	Australia	Territory
HOWLAND ISLAND	uninhabited	North Pacific Ocean	Administered from Washington, D.C.	United States	Unincorporated territory
ISLE OF MAN	72,000	Irish Sea	Douglas	United Kingdom	British crown dependency (parliamentary democracy)
JAN MAYEN [5]	no indigenous inhabitants	Norwegian Sea	Administered from Oslo	Norway	Territory
JARVIS ISLAND	uninhabited	South Pacific Ocean	Administered from Washington, D.C.	United States	Unincorporated territory
JERSEY (Channel Islands)	89,000	English Channel	St. Helier	United Kingdom	British crown dependency
JOHNSTON ATOLL	no indigenous inhabitants	North Pacific Ocean	Administered from Washington, D.C.	United States	Unincorporated territory
KINGMAN REEF	uninhabited	North Pacific Ocean	Administered from Washington, D.C.	United States	Unincorporated territory
MAYOTTE	174,000	Mozambique Channel	Mamoudzou	France	Territorial collectivity
MIDWAY ISLANDS	no indigenous inhabitants	North Pacific Ocean	Administered from Washington, D.C.	United States	Unincorporated territory
MONTSERRAT	4,000	Caribbean Sea	Plymouth	United Kingdom	Overseas territory
NAVASSA ISLAND	uninhabited	Caribbean Sea	Administered from Washington, D.C.	United States	Unincorporated territory
NETHERLANDS ANTILLES [6]	225,000	Caribbean Sea	Willemstad	Netherlands	Part of the Netherlands (parliamentary government)
NEW CALEDONIA	220,000	South Pacific Ocean	Nouméa	France	Overseas territory
NIUE	2,000	South Pacific Ocean	Alofi	New Zealand	Free association with New Zealand (parliamentary democracy)
NORFOLK ISLAND	2,000	South Pacific Ocean	Kingston	Australia	Territory
NORTHERN MARIANA ISLANDS	78,000	North Pacific Ocean	Saipan	United States	Commonwealth in political union with the U.S. (commonwealth government)
PALMYRA ATOLL	no indigenous inhabitants	North Pacific Ocean	Administered from Washington, D.C.	United States	Incorporated territory
PARACEL ISLANDS [7]	no indigenous inhabitants	South China Sea	Administered from China	undetermined	NA
PITCAIRN ISLANDS	50	South Pacific Ocean	Adamstown	United Kingdom	Overseas territory
PUERTO RICO	3,858,000	Caribbean Sea	San Juan	United States	Commonwealth associated with the U.S. (commonwealth government)
ST. HELENA [8]	7,000	South Atlantic Ocean	Jamestown	United Kingdom	Overseas territory
ST.-PIERRE AND MIQUELON	7,000	North Atlantic Ocean	St.-Pierre	France	Self-governing territorial collectivity
SOUTH GEORGIA AND SOUTH SANDWICH ISLANDS [2]	no indigenous inhabitants	South Atlantic Ocean	Administered from Stanley	United Kingdom	Overseas territory
SVALBARD	2,000	Arctic Ocean	Longyearbyen	Norway	Territory
TOKELAU	2,000	South Pacific Ocean	Administered from Wellington	New Zealand	Territory
TURKS AND CAICOS ISLANDS	18,000	North Atlantic Ocean	Grand Turk	United Kingdom	Overseas territory
U.S. VIRGIN ISLANDS	110,000	Caribbean Sea	Charlotte Amalie	United States	Unincorporated territory
WAKE ISLAND	no indigenous inhabitants	North Pacific Ocean	Administered from Washington	United States	Unincorporated territory
WALLIS AND FUTUNA ISLANDS	15,000	South Pacific Ocean	Matâ'utu	France	Overseas territory

NOTES TO DEPENDENCIES OF THE WORLD

* **The political status of dependencies is based on the designation provided by the administering country. The variety of political designations reflects the diverse nature of the relationship dependencies have with their controlling countries.**

[1] Chagos Archipelago

[2] Dependent territory of the United Kingdom (also claimed by Argentina).

[3] The "French Southern and Antarctic Lands" dependency includes Île Amsterdam, Île Saint-Paul, the Crozet Islands, and the Kerguélen Islands in the southern Indian Ocean. It also includes Terre Adélie, the French-claimed sector of Antarctica; the French claim to this region is not internationally recognized, however (see "Areas of Special Status," below, for information on claims to Antarctica).

[4] The Bailiwick of Guernsey includes the islands of Alderney, Guernsey, Herm, and Sark, as well as smaller islands nearby.

[5] Jan Mayen is administered from Oslo, Norway, through a governor resident in Longyearbyen, Svalbard.

[6] Netherlands Antilles comprises two groupings of islands: Curaçao and Bonaire are located off the coast of Venezuela; Saba, Sint Eustatius, and Sint Maarten (the Dutch two-fifths of the island of Saint Martin) lie 500 miles (800 km) to the north.

[7] South China Sea islands are occupied by China but claimed by Vietnam.

[8] The territory of Saint Helena includes the island group of Tristan da Cunha, far to the southwest; Saint Helena also administers Ascension Island, lying to the northwest.

Areas of Special Status

AREA	POPULATION	LOCATION
ANTARCTICA	no indigenous inhabitants	Territory south of 60 degrees south latitude

Seven countries claim Antarctic territory, but these claims are not legally recognized by the Antarctic Treaty of 1959. This treaty prohibits military activities and dedicates Antarctica to peaceful use and free exchange of scientific information. Individual nations maintain bases, and the research projects they support typically involve collaborators from many countries.

DIEGO GARCIA	military base	Indian Ocean

Diego Garcia constitutes the southernmost island of the British Indian Ocean Territory, a dependency of Great Britain. In 1966, the United States leased Diego Garcia for 50 years and established a joint military base with Great Britain on the island. The U.S. lease will expire in 2016. Diego Garcia, along with the Chagos Archipelago, is claimed by Mauritius.

GUANTÁNAMO BAY	military base	Cuba

After helping Cuba gain independence in 1902, the United States leased 45 square miles (116 sq km) of territory around Guantánamo Bay. This lease was reaffirmed in a 1934 treaty stipulating that the return of Guantánamo Bay to Cuba could only be arranged through the mutual consent of the U.S. and Cuba. Though Guantánamo Bay remains sovereign Cuban territory, the American lease does not have a termination date.

HONG KONG	6,783,000	Part of China

Hong Kong became a Special Administrative Region (SAR) of China on July 1, 1997. China has promised that under its "one country, two systems" formula, China's socialist economic system will not be practiced in Hong Kong and that Hong Kong will enjoy a high degree of autonomy in all matters, except foreign and defense affairs, for the next 50 years.

KOSOVO	2,000,000	Part of Yugoslavia

Hostilities broke out in Kosovo in 1998. Ethnic Albanians, who make up 90 percent of the local population, sought an independent state, while Serbs fought to keep Kosovo part of Yugoslavia. NATO air strikes helped bring about an agreement to end the fighting, and the UN began administering Kosovo in June 1999.

MACAU	443,000	Part of China

After more than 400 years as a Portuguese outpost, Macau reverted to China in December 1999 as a Special Administrative Region, a status it will maintain for 50 years. Like Hong Kong, it enjoys a high degree of autonomy in all matters except foreign and defense affairs.

AREA	POPULATION	LOCATION
NORTHERN CYPRUS	160,000	Eastern Mediterranean Sea

Following a Greek-led coup and the landing of Turkish forces on the island in 1974, Cyprus split into two hostile territories. The internationally recognized Greek Cypriot government controls the southern portion of the island while Turkish Cypriots, bolstered by a Turkish military force, control the northern portion. Turkish Cypriots unilaterally declared independence in 1983, but their claims have not been recognized by any nation other than Turkey.

SOMALILAND	3,000,000	Horn of Africa

The government of Somalia collapsed in 1991, after a bloody civil war. Somaliland claims independence and governs some three million people in the north—an area that roughly corresponds to the former British Somaliland. The United Nations does not recognize Somaliland as an independent state.

SPRATLY ISLANDS	No indigenous inhabitants	South China Sea

The scattered islands and reefs known as the Spratly Islands are claimed by Brunei, China, Malaysia, the Philippines, Taiwan, and Vietnam.

TAIWAN	22,463,000	Southeast of China

The People's Republic of China claims the island of Taiwan as its 23rd province. The government of Taiwan (Republic of China) maintains that there is one China—but two political entities.

WEST BANK AND GAZA STRIP	3,465,000	Adjacent to Israel

The West Bank and Gaza Strip were captured by Israel in the 1967 Six Day War. In 1993 a peace agreement gave areas of the West Bank and Gaza Strip limited Palestinian autonomy. The future of these autonomous regions and three million Palestinians is subject to Israeli-Palestinian negotiations.

WESTERN SAHARA	256,000	Southwest of Morocco

Formerly Spanish Sahara, Western Sahara was annexed by Morocco in the late 1970s and brought under Moroccan administration. The Polisario Front, a resistance group that repudiated Moroccan sovereignty, fought a guerrilla war that ended in a 1991 cease-fire administered by the United Nations. A referendum on the final status of Western Sahara has repeatedly been postponed.

Areas Geographically Separated from Mainland Countries

REGION	POPULATION	COUNTRY	LOCATION	REGION	POPULATION	COUNTRY	LOCATION
AGALEGA ISLANDS	300	Mauritius	Indian Ocean	FRENCH GUIANA	174,000	France	South America
AKROTIRI	military base	United Kingdom	Cyprus	GALÁPAGOS ISLANDS	19,000	Ecuador	Pacific Ocean
ALASKA	635,000	United States	North America	GUADELOUPE	461,000	France	Caribbean Sea
ANDAMAN ISLANDS	314,000	India	Indian Ocean	HAWAII	1,224,000	United States	North Pacific Ocean
ANNOBÓN	2,400	Equatorial Guinea	Gulf of Guinea	KALININGRAD	951,000	Russia	Europe
ARQUIPÉLAGO DE FERNANDO DE NORONHA				KURIL ISLANDS	7,900	Russia	North Pacific Ocean
	2,100	Brazil	South Atlantic Ocean	LAKSHADWEEP	61,000	India	Indian Ocean
AZORES	245,000	Portugal	North Atlantic Ocean	MADEIRA ISLANDS	251,000	Portugal	North Atlantic Ocean
BALEARIC ISLANDS	846,000	Spain	Mediterranean Sea	MARTINIQUE	384,000	France	Caribbean Sea
BIOKO	100,000	Equatorial Guinea	Gulf of Guinea	MUSANDAM PENINSULA	30,000	Oman	Arabian Peninsula
BONIN ISLANDS	1,400	Japan	North Pacific Ocean	NAXÇIVAN	363,000	Azerbaijan	Asia
CABINDA	100,000	Angola	Africa	NICOBAR ISLANDS	42,000	India	Indian Ocean
CANARY ISLANDS	1,716,000	Spain	North Atlantic Ocean	NORTHERN IRELAND	1,698,000	United Kingdom	Ireland
CEUTA AND MELILLA	142,000	Spain	North Africa	RÉUNION	742,000	France	Indian Ocean
CHATHAM ISLANDS	700	New Zealand	South Pacific Ocean	RODRIGUES	36,000	Mauritius	Indian Ocean
CORSICA	260,000	France	Mediterranean Sea	RYUKYU ISLANDS	1,318,000	Japan	North Pacific Ocean
DAITO ISLANDS	2,100	Japan	North Pacific Ocean	SABAH AND SARAWAK	4,675,000	Malaysia	Borneo
DHEKELIA	military base	United Kingdom	Cyprus	SARDINIA	1,658,000	Italy	Mediterranean Sea
EASTER ISLAND	3,600	Chile	South Pacific Ocean	SOCOTRA	80,000	Yemen	Indian Ocean
FRANZ JOSEF LAND	not permanently inhabited	Russia	Arctic Ocean	VOLCANO ISLANDS	2,800	Japan	North Pacific Ocean

DISCLAIMER

The list of geographically separate areas includes places that do not fit conveniently into any of the three previous categories. Politically, these areas are integral parts of independent countries; thus, they are not dependencies. Nor are they areas of special status. They warrant inclusion in this category simply because they lie a significant distance, across either land or water, from the rest of their countries' land areas. In compiling this list, we chose to include only the areas that are populated at least part of the year. This means that we have not listed myriad uninhabited islands. Determining exactly what constitutes sufficient geographical separation to justify inclusion involves a certain degree of subjectivity. For this reason, the fourth category of Earth's lands should not be considered an official grouping. Instead, it should be viewed only as one way of classifying areas that do not fall neatly into the three other categories—but which are significant enough to deserve special attention.

If we could bring a snapshot back from the future, few images would tell us more about what lies ahead than a flag chart showing the banners of all countries. The independence of new nations, the breakup of empires, even changing political and religious currents—all would be reflected in the symbols and colors of the national flags. This is dramatically evident in the changing flag of the United States (below), but similar visual statements could be made for most countries.

Germany provides another example. In the Middle Ages a gold banner with a black eagle proclaimed its Holy Roman Emperor a successor to the Caesars. A united 19th-century German Empire adopted a black-white-red tricolor for Bismarck's "blood and iron" policies. The liberal Weimar and Federal Republics (1919-1933 and since 1949) hailed a black-red-gold tricolor. The dark years from 1933 to 1945 were under the swastika flag of the Nazi regime. These and similar flags in other countries are more than visual aids to history: Their development and use are a fundamental part of the political and social life of a community.

Like maps, flags are ways to communicate information in condensed form. The study of geography is paralleled by the study of flags, known as vexillology (from the Latin word vexillum, for "small sail" or flag). Books, journals, Web sites, and other sources convey information on vexillology; there are also organizations and institutions around the world linked by the International Federation of Vexillological Associations. Even very young students can gain understanding of countries, populations, political changes, religious movements, and historical events by learning about flags.

All flags embody myths and historical facts, whether they are displayed at the Olympic Games, carried by protesters, placed at a roadside shrine, or arrayed at a ceremony of national significance, such as a presidential inauguration. Flags are powerful symbols, attractive to groups of all kinds; hence their once prominent display by Nazis and Communists to manipulate the masses, their recent waving by the East Timorese after a successful struggle for independence, and their spontaneous use by people in the United States after September 11, 2001.

Flags of nations may be the most significant flags today, but they are far from the only ones. Sport teams, business enterprises, religious groups, ethnic groups, schools, and international organizations frequently rally, reward, and inspire people through the use of flags. An observant person will also notice advertising banners, nautical signals, warning flags, decorative pennants, the rank flags of important individuals, and many related symbols such as coats of arms and logos.

Examples of flags, as presented on these two pages, only hint at the rich possibilities of design, usage, and symbolism. The vexillophile (flag hobbyist) can easily and inexpensively acquire a substantial collection of flags and flag-related items. The vexillographer (flag designer) can create flags for self or family, club or team, or even for a city or county. The vexillologist (flag scholar) will find endless connections between flags and history, political science, communications theory, social behavior, and other areas. As with geography, the knowledge gained by a study of flags can be a richly rewarding personal experience.

Development of the Stars and Stripes

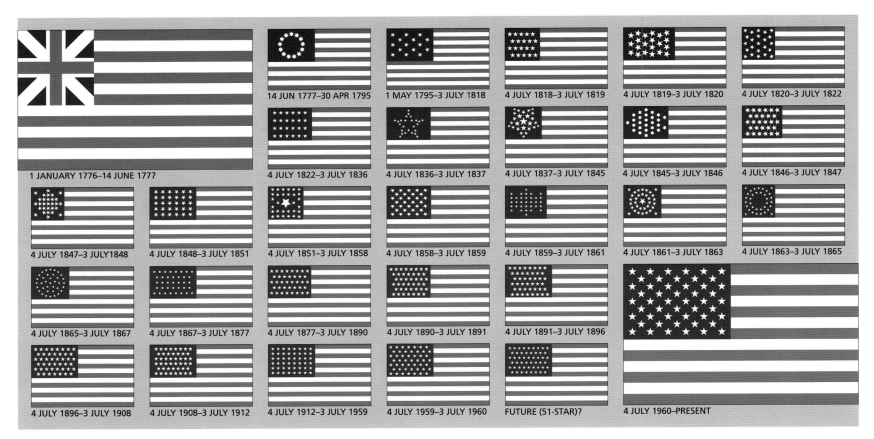

	14 JUN 1777–30 APR 1795	1 MAY 1795–3 JULY 1818	4 JULY 1818–3 JULY 1819	4 JULY 1819–3 JULY 1820	4 JULY 1820–3 JULY 1822
1 JANUARY 1776–14 JUNE 1777	4 JULY 1822–3 JULY 1836	4 JULY 1836–3 JULY 1837	4 JULY 1837–3 JULY 1845	4 JULY 1845–3 JULY 1846	4 JULY 1846–3 JULY 1847
4 JULY 1847–3 JULY1848	4 JULY 1848–3 JULY 1851	4 JULY 1851–3 JULY 1858	4 JULY 1858–3 JULY 1859	4 JULY 1859–3 JULY 1861	4 JULY 1861–3 JULY 1863	4 JULY 1863–3 JULY 1865
4 JULY 1865–3 JULY 1867	4 JULY 1867–3 JULY 1877	4 JULY 1877–3 JULY 1890	4 JULY 1890–3 JULY 1891	4 JULY 1891–3 JULY 1896	
4 JULY 1896–3 JULY 1908	4 JULY 1908–3 JULY 1912	4 JULY 1912–3 JULY 1959	4 JULY 1959–3 JULY 1960	FUTURE (51-STAR)?	4 JULY 1960–PRESENT

No country has changed its flag as frequently as the United States. The Continental Colors (top left) represented the Colonies during the early years of the American Revolution. Its British Union Jack, which signified loyalty to the crown, was replaced on June 14, 1777, by "13 stars...representing a new constellation." Congressman Francis Hopkinson was the designer.

The number of stars and stripes was increased to 15 in 1795. In 1817 Congressman Peter Wendover wrote the current flag law. The number of stripes was permanently limited to 13; the stars were to correspond to the number of states, with new stars added to the flag the following Fourth of July.

Star arrangement was not specified, however, and throughout the 19th century a variety of exuberant

star designs—"great luminaries," rings, ovals, and diamonds—were actually used. With the increasing number of states, the modern alternating rows of stars became standard. Finally, in 1912, President Taft set forth exact regulations for all flag details.

If a new state joins the Union, a 51-star flag will be needed. There is a logical design for it: alternating rows of nine and eight stars, as shown above.

International Flags

MOURNING
The black flag signals death, piracy, protest, and danger. It is also a symbol of mourning for the dead.

OLYMPIC GAMES
The colors refer to those in the national flags of participating countries. The Olympic flag was created in 1913.

RED CRESCENT
In Muslim nations, Geneva Convention organizations rejected the red cross in favor of a red crescent, officially recognized in 1906.

RED CROSS
The Geneva Convention chose its symbol and flag in 1864 to identify people, vehicles, and buildings protected during wartime.

TRUCE/PEACE
For a thousand years a white flag has served as a symbol of truce, surrender, noncombatant status, neutrality, and peace.

UNITED NATIONS
Olive branches of peace and a world map form the symbol adopted by the United Nations in 1946. The flag dates from 1947.

Regional Flags

ARAB LEAGUE
The color green and the crescent are often symbols in member countries of the League of Arab States, founded in 1945.

ASEAN
A stylized bundle of rice, the principal local crop, appears on the flag of the Association of South East Asian Nations (ASEAN).

COMMONWEALTH
Once the British Empire, the modern Commonwealth under this flag informally links countries with common goals.

EUROPEAN UNION
The number of stars for this flag, adopted in 1955, is permanently set at 12. The ring is a symbol for unity.

OAS
Flags of member nations appear on the flag of the Organization of American States; each new member prompts a flag change.

PACIFIC COMMISSION
The palm tree, surf, and sailboat are found in all of the member nations; each star on the flag represents a country.

Religious Flags

BUDDHISM
Designed in 1885 by Henry Olcott of the United States, the Buddhist flag features the auras associated with the Buddha.

CHRISTIANITY
The sacrifice of Christ on the Cross is heralded in this 1897 flag, which features a white field for purity.

ISLAM
"There Is No God But Allah and Muhammad Is the Prophet of Allah" is written on this widely used but unofficial flag.

Ethnic Flags

LA RAZA
Crosses for the ships of Columbus and a golden Inca sun recall the Spanish and Indian heritage of Latin Americans.

PALESTINIANS
Since 1922 Palestinians have used this flag, with traditional Arab dynastic colors, as a symbol of the statehood they desire.

ROMA (GYPSIES)
Against a background of blue sky and green grass, a wheel represents the vehicles (and homes) of the nomadic Roma people.

Specialized Flags

ANARCHISTS
Opposition to all forms of authority is hinted at in the "hand-drawn" rendition of an encircled A in the anarchist flag.

BLUE FLAG
The campaign for the improvement of the environment presents this flag as an award for success.

BOY SCOUTS
Created in 1961, this flag shows the traditional Boy Scout fleur-de-lis within a rope tied with a reef knot.

CIRCLE CROSS
This ancient religious symbol, related to the swastika, is widely used as a neo-Nazi symbol in Europe and North America.

CONFEDERATE BATTLE FLAG
In many countries this flag represents protest against established authority in culture, politics, and lifestyle.

DIVERS FLAG
As a warning signal to other boats, this flag flies wherever divers are underwater nearby—and at divers' clubhouses.

ESPERANTO
On the flag promoting Esperanto as a world language, a star signifies unity; green, traditionally, is a symbol of hope.

FRANCOPHONIE
French speakers share their common language and culture in periodic conferences and activities held under this flag.

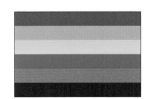

GAY PRIDE
The Rainbow Flag, in various configurations, has been flown since 1978 by the gay and lesbian community and their families.

GIRL SCOUTS
The trefoil with a compass needle adorns the World Flag of Girl Guides and Girl Scouts, which was adopted in May 1991.

GREEN CROSS
Organizations that display this flag promote public safety in natural disasters, transportation, and the workplace.

MASONS
The unofficial flag of the Masons displays their traditional logo with symbolic square and compass.

FOREIGN TERMS

Aaglet *well*
Aain *spring*
Aauinat *spring*
Āb *river, water*
Ache *stream*
Açude *reservoir*
Ada,-si *island*
Adrar *mountain-s, plateau*
Aguada *dry lake bed*
Aguelt *water hole, well*
'Ain, Aïn *spring, well*
Aïoun-et *spring-s, well*
Aivi *mountain*
Ákra, Akrotírion *cape, promontory*
Alb *mountain, ridge*
Alföld *plain*
Alin' *mountain range*
Alpe-n *mountain-s*
Altiplanicie *high-plain, plateau*
Alto *hill-s, mountain-s, ridge*
Älv-en *river*
Āmba *hill, mountain*
Anou *well*
Anse *bay, inlet*
Ao *bay, cove, estuary*
Ap *cape, point*
Archipel, Archipiélago *archipelago*
Arcipelago, Arkhipelag *archipelago*
Arquipélago *archipelago*
Arrecife-s *reef-s*
Arroio, Arroyo *brook, gully, rivulet, stream*
Ås *ridge*
Ava *channel*
Aylagy *gulf*
'Ayn *spring, well*

Ba *intermittent stream, river*
Baai *bay, cove, lagoon*
Bāb *gate, strait*
Badia *bay*
Bælt *strait*
Bagh *bay*
Bahar *drainage basin*
Bahía *bay*
Bahr, Baḥr *bay, lake, river, sea, wadi*
Baía, Baie *bay*
Bajo-s *shoal-s*
Ban *village*
Bañado-s *flooded area, swamp-s*
Banc, Banco-s *bank-s, sandbank-s, shoal-s*
Band *lake*
Bandao *peninsula*
Baño-s *hot spring-s, spa*
Baraj-ı *dam, reservoir*
Barra *bar, sandbank*
Barrage, Barragem *dam, lake, reservoir*
Barranca *gorge, ravine*
Bazar *marketplace*
Ben, Benin *mountain*
Belt *strait*
Bereg *bank, coast, shore*
Berg-e *mountain-s*
Bil *lake*
Biq'at *plain, valley*
Bir, Bîr, Bi'r *spring, well*
Birket *lake, pool, swamp*
Bjerg-e *mountain-s, range*
Boca, Bocca *channel, river, mouth*
Bocht *bay*
Bodden *bay*
Boğaz, -i *strait*
Bögeni *reservoir*
Boka *gulf, mouth*
Bol'sh-oy, -aya, -oye *big*
Bolsón *inland basin*
Boubairet *lagoon, lake*
Bras *arm, branch of a stream*
Braţ, -ul *arm, branch of a stream*
Bre, -en *glacier, ice cap*

Bredning *bay, broad water*
Bruch *marsh*
Bucht *bay*
Bugt-en *bay*
Buḥayrat, Buheirat *lagoon, lake, marsh*
Bukhta, Bukta, Bukt-en *bay*
Bulak, Bulaq *spring*
Bum *hill, mountain*
Burnu, Burun *cape, point*
Busen *gulf*
Buuraha *hill-s, mountain-s*
Buyuk *big, large*

Cabeza-s *head-s, summit-s*
Cabo *cape*
Cachoeira *rapids, waterfall*
Cal *hill, peak*
Caleta *cove, inlet*
Campo-s *field-s, flat country*
Canal *canal, channel, strait*
Caño *channel, stream*
Cao Nguyen *mountain, plateau*
Cap, Capo *cape*
Capitán *captain*
Càrn *mountain*
Castillo *castle, fort*
Catarata-s *cataract-s, waterfall-s*
Causse *upland*
Çay *brook, stream*
Cay-s, Cayo-s *island-s, key-s, shoal-s*
Cerro-s *hill-s, peak-s*
Chaîne, Chaînons *mountain chain, range*
Chapada-s *plateau, upland-s*
Chedo *archipelago*
Chenal *river channel*
Chersónisos *peninsula*
Chhung *bay*
Chi *lake*
Chiang *bay*
Chiao *cape, point, rock*
Ch'ih *lake*
Chink *escarpment*
Chott *intermittent salt lake, salt marsh*
Chou *island*
Ch'ü *canal*
Ch'üntao *archipelago, islands*
Chute-s *cataract-s, waterfall-s*
Chyrvony *red*
Cima *mountain, peak, summit*
Ciudad *city*
Co *lake*
Col *pass*
Collina, Colline *hill, mountains*
Con *island*
Cordillera *mountain chain*
Corno *mountain, peak*
Coronel *colonel*
Corredeira *cascade, rapids*
Costa *coast*
Côte *coast, slope*
Coxilha, Cuchilla *range of low hills*
Crique *creek, stream*
Csatorna *canal, channel*
Cul de Sac *bay, inlet*

Da *great, greater*
Daban *pass*
Dağ, -ı, Dagh *mountain*
Dağlar, -ı *mountains*
Dahr *cliff, mesa*
Dake *mountain, peak*
Dal-en *valley*
Dala *steppe*
Dan *cape, point*
Danau *lake*
Dao *island*
Dar'ya *lake, river*
Daryācheh *lake, marshy lake*
Dasht *desert, plain*
Dawan *pass*

Dawḩat *bay, cove, inlet*
Deniz, -i *sea*
Dent-s *peak-s*
Deo *pass*
Desēt *hummock, island, land-tied island*
Desierto *desert*
Détroit *channel, strait*
Dhar *hills, ridge, tableland*
Ding *mountain*
Distrito *district*
Djebel *mountain, range*
Do *island-s, rock-s*
Doi *hill, mountain*
Dome *ice dome*
Dong *village*
Dooxo *floodplain*
Dzong *castle, fortress*

Eiland-en *island-s*
Eilean *island*
Ejland *island*
Elv *river*
Embalse *lake, reservoir*
Emi *mountain, rock*
Enseada, Ensenada *bay, cove*
Ér *rivulet, stream*
Erg *sand dune region*
Est *east*
Estación *railroad station*
Estany *lagoon, lake*
Estero *estuary, inlet, lagoon, marsh*
Estrecho *strait*
Étang *lake, pond*
Eylandt *island*
Ežeras *lake*
Ezers *lake*

Falaise *cliff, escarpment*
Farvand-et *channel, sound*
Fell *mountain*
Feng *mount, peak*
Fiord-o *inlet, sound*
Fiume *river*
Fjäll-et *mountain*
Fjällen *mountains*
Fjärd-en *fjord*
Fjarðar, Fjörður *fjord*
Fjeld *mountain*
Fjell-ene *mountain-s*
Fjöll *mountain-s*
Fjord-en *inlet, fjord*
Fleuve *river*
Fljót *large river*
Flói *bay, marshland*
Foci *river mouths*
Főcsatorna *principal canal*
Förde *fjord, gulf, inlet*
Forsen *rapids, waterfall*
Fortaleza *fort, fortress*
Fortín *fortified post*
Foss-en *waterfall*
Foum *pass, passage*
Foz *mouth of a river*
Fuerte *fort, fortress*
Fwafwate *waterfalls*

Gacan-ka *hill, peak*
Gal *pond, spring, waterhole, well*
Gang *harbor*
Gangri *peak, range*
Gaoyuan *plateau*
Garaet, Gara'et *lake, lake bed, salt lake*
Gardaneh *pass*
Garet *hill, mountain*
Gat *channel*
Gata *bay, inlet, lake*
Gattet *channel, strait*
Gaud *depression, saline tract*
Gave *mountain stream*
Gebel *mountain-s, range*

Gebergte *mountain range*
Gebirge *mountains, range*
Geçidi *mountain pass, passage*
Geçit *mountain pass, passage*
Gezâir *islands*
Gezîra-t, Gezîret *island, peninsula*
Ghats *mountain range*
Ghubb-at, -et *bay, gulf*
Giri *mountain*
Gletscher *glacier*
Gobernador *governor*
Gobi *desert*
Gol *river, stream*
Göl, -ü *lake*
Golets *mountain, peak*
Golf, -e, -o *gulf*
Gor-a, -y, Gór-a, -y *mountain,-s*
Got *point*
Gowd *depression*
Goz *sand ridge*
Gran, -de *great, large*
Gryada *mountains, ridge*
Guan *pass*
Guba *bay, gulf*
Guelta *well*
Guntō *archipelago*
Gunung *mountain*
Gura *mouth, passage*
Guyot *table mount*

Haḑabat *plateau*
Haehyŏp *strait*
Haff *lagoon*
Hai *lake, sea*
Haihsia *strait*
Haixia *channel, strait*
Hakau *reef, rock*
Hakuchi *anchorage*
Halvø, Halvøy-a *peninsula*
Hama *beach*
Hamada, Ḥammādah *rocky desert*
Hamn *harbor, port*
Hāmūn, Hamun *depression, lake*
Hana *cape, point*
Hantō *peninsula*
Har *hill, mound, mountain*
Ḥarrat *lava field*
Hasi, Hassi *spring, well*
Hauteur *elevation, height*
Hav-et *sea*
Havn, Havre *harbor, port*
Hawr *lake, marsh*
Hāyk' *lake, reservoir*
Hegy, -ség *mountain, -s, range*
Heiau *temple*
Ho *canal, lake, river*
Hoek *hook, point*
Hög-en *high, hill*
Höhe, -n *height, high*
Høj *height, hill*
Holm, -e, Holmene *island-s, islet -s*
Ḥolot *dunes*
Hon *island-s*
Hor-a, -y *mountain, -s*
Horn *horn, peak*
Houma *point*
Hoved *headland, peninsula, point*
Hraun *lava field*
Hsü *island*
Hu *lake, reservoir*
Huk *cape, point*
Hüyük *hill, mound*

Idehan *sand dunes*
Île-s, Ilha-s, Illa-s, Îlot-s *island-s, islet-s*
Îlet, Ilhéu-s *islet, -s*
Irhil *mountain-s*
'Irq *sand dune-s*
Isblink *glacier, ice field*
Is-en *glacier*

Isla-s, Islote *island-s, islet*
Isol-a, -e *island, -s*
Istmo *isthmus*
Iwa *island, islet, rock*

Jabal, Jebel *mountain-s, range*
Järv, -i, Jaure, Javrre *lake*
Jazā'ir, Jazīrat, Jazīreh *island-s*
Jehīl *lake*
Jezero, Jezioro *lake*
Jiang *river, stream*
Jiao *cape*
Jibāl *hill, mountain, ridge*
Jima *island-s, rock-s*
Jøkel, Jökull *glacier, ice cap*
Joki, Jokka *river*
Jökulsá *river from a glacier*
Jūn *bay*

Kaap *cape*
Kafr *village*
Kaikyō *channel, strait*
Kaise *mountain*
Kaiwan *bay, gulf, sea*
Kanal *canal, channel*
Kangri *mountain, peak*
Kap, Kapp *cape*
Kavīr *salt desert*
Kefar *village*
Kënet' *lagoon, lake*
Kep *cape, point*
Kepulauan *archipelago, islands*
Khalîg, Khalīj *bay, gulf*
Khirb-at, -et *ancient site, ruins*
Khrebet *mountain range*
Kinh *canal*
Klint *bluff, cliff*
Kō *bay, cove, harbor*
Ko *island, lake*
Koh *island, mountain, range*
Köl-i *lake*
Kólpos *gulf*
Kong *mountain*
Körfez, -i *bay, gulf*
Kosa *spit of land*
Kou *estuary, river mouth*
Kowtal-e *pass*
Krasn-yy, -aya, -oye *red*
Kryazh *mountain range, ridge*
Kuala *estuary, river mouth*
Kuan *mountain pass*
Kūh, Kūhhā *mountain-s, range*
Kul', Kuli *lake*
Kum *sandy desert*
Kundo *archipelago*
Kuppe *hill-s, mountain-s*
Kust *coast, shore*
Kyst *coast*
Kyun *island*

La *pass*
Lac, Lac-ul, -us *lake*
Lae *cape, point*
Lago, -a *lagoon, lake*
Lagoen, Lagune *lagoon*
Laguna-s *lagoon-s, lake-s*
Laht *bay, gulf, harbor*
Laje *reef, rock ledge*
Laut *sea*
Lednik *glacier*
Leida *channel*
Lhari *mountain*
Li *village*
Liedao *archipelago, islands*
Liehtao *archipelago, islands*
Liman-ı *bay, estuary*
Límni *lake*
Ling *mountain-s, range*
Linn *pool, waterfall*
Lintasan *passage*
Liqen *lake*
Llano-s *plain-s*
Loch, Lough *lake, arm of the sea*
Loma-s *hill-s, knoll-s*

M

Mal *mountain, range*
Mal-yy, -aya, -oye *little, small*
Mamarr *pass, path*
Man *bay*
Mar, Mare *large lake, sea*
Marsa, Marsá *bay, inlet*
Masabb *mouth of river*
Massif *massif, mountain-s*
Mauna *mountain*
Mēda *plain*
Meer *lake, sea*
Melkosopochnik *undulating plain*
Mesa, Meseta *plateau, tableland*
Mierzeja *sandspit*
Minami *south*
Mios *island*
Misaki *cape, peninsula, point*
Mochun *passage*
Mong *town, village*
Mont-e, -i, -s *mount, -ain, -s*
Montagne, -s *mount, -ain, -s*
Montaña, -s *mountain, -s*
More *sea*
Morne *hill, peak*
Morro *bluff, headland, hill*
Motu, -s *islands*
Mouïet *well*
Mouillage *anchorage*
Muang *town, village*
Mui *cape, point*
Mull *headland, promontory*
Munkhafad *depression*
Munte *mountain*
Munţi-i *mountains*
Muong *town, village*
Mynydd *mountain*
Mys *cape*

N

Nacional *national*
Nada *gulf, sea*
Næs, Näs *cape, point*
Nafūd *area of dunes, desert*
Nagor'ye *mountain range, plateau*
Nahar, Nahr *river, stream*
Nakhon *town*
Namakzār *salt waste*
Ne *island, reef, rock-s*
Neem *cape, point, promontory*
Nes, Ness *peninsula, point*
Nevado-s *snow-capped mountain-s*
Nez *cape, promontory*
Ni *village*
Nísi, Nísia, Nisís, Nísoi *island-s, islet-s*
Nisídhes *islets*
Nizhn-iy, -yaya, -eye *lower*
Nizmennost' *low country*
Noord *north*
Nord-re *north-ern*
Nørre *north-ern*
Nos *cape, nose, point*
Nosy *island, reef, rock*
Nov-yy, -aya, -oye *new*
Nudo *mountain*
Numa *lake*
Nunatak, -s, -ker *peak-s surrounded by ice cap*
Nur *lake, salt lake*
Nuruu *mountain range, ridge*
Nut-en *peak*
Nuur *lake*

Ö-n, Ø-er *island-s*

Oblast' *administrative division, province, region*
Oceanus *ocean*
Odde-n *cape, point*
Øer-ne *islands*
Oglat *group of wells*
Oguilet *well*
Ór-os, -i *mountain, -s*
Órmos *bay, port*

Ort *place, point*
Øst-er *east*
Ostrov, -a, Ostrv-o, -a *island, -s*
Otoci, Otok *islands, island*
Ouadi, Oued *river, watercourse*
Øy-a *island*
Øyane *islands*
Ozer-o, -a *lake, -s*

P

Pää *mountain, point*
Palus *marsh*
Pampa-s *grassy plain-s*
Pantà *lake, reservoir*
Pantanal *marsh, swamp*
Pao, P'ao *lake*
Parbat *mountain*
Parque *park*
Pas, -ul *pass*
Paso, Passo *pass*
Passe *channel, pass*
Pasul *pass*
Pedra *rock*
Pegunungan *mountain range*
Pellg *bay, bight*
Peña *cliff, rock*
Pendi *basin*
Penedo-s *rock-s*
Péninsule *peninsula*
Peñón *point, rock*
Pereval *mountain pass*
Pertuis *strait*
Peski *sands, sandy region*
Phnom *hill, mountain, range*
Phou *mountain range*
Phu *mountain*
Piana-o *plain*
Pic, Pik, Piz *peak*
Picacho *mountain, peak*
Pico-s *peak-s*
Pistyll *waterfall*
Piton-s *peak-s*
Pivdennyy *southern*
Plaja, Playa *beach, inlet, shore*
Planalto, Plato *plateau*
Planina *mountain, plateau*
Plassen *lake*
Ploskogor'ye *plateau, upland*
Pointe *point*
Polder *reclaimed land*
Poluostrov *peninsula*
Pongo *water gap*
Ponta, -l *cape, point*
Ponte *bridge*
Poolsaar *peninsula*
Portezuelo *pass*
Porto *port*
Poulo *island*
Praia *beach, seashore*
Presa *reservoir*
Presidente *president*
Presqu'île *peninsula*
Prokhod *pass*
Proliv *strait*
Promontorio *promontory*
Průsmyk *mountain pass*
Przylądek *cape*
Puerto *bay, pass, port*
Pulao *island-s*
Pulau, Pulo *island*
Puncak *peak, summit, top*
Punt, Punta, -n *point, -s*
Pun *peak*
Puu *hill, mountain*
Puy *peak*

Q, Qal'eh *castle, fort*
Qā' *depression, marsh, mud flat*
Qal'at *fort*
Qanā *canal*
Qārat *hill-s, mountain-s*
Qaşr *castle, fort, hill*

Qila *fort*
Qiryat *settlement, suburb*
Qolleh *peak*
Qooriga *anchorage, bay*
Qoz *dunes, sand ridge*
Qu *canal*
Quebrada *ravine, stream*
Qullai *peak, summit*
Qum *desert, sand*
Qundao *archipelago, islands*
Qurayyāt *hills*

R

Raas *cape, point*
Rabt *hill*
Rada *roadstead*
Rade *anchorage, roadstead*
Rags *point*
Ramat *hill, mountain*
Rand *ridge of hills*
Rann *swamp*
Raqaba *wadi, watercourse*
Ras, Râs, Ra's *cape*
Ravnina *plain*
Récif-s *reef-s*
Regreg *marsh*
Represa *reservoir*
Reservatório *reservoir*
Restinga *barrier, sand area*
Rettō *chain of islands*
Ri *mountain range, village*
Ría *estuary*
Ribeirão *stream*
Río, Rio *river*
Roca-s *cliff, rock-s*
Roche-r, -s *rock-s*
Rosh *mountain, point*
Rt *cape, point*
Rubha *headland*
Rupes *scarp*

S

Saar *island*
Saari, Sari *island*
Sabkha-t, Sabkhet *lagoon, marsh, salt lake*
Sagar *lake, sea*
Sahara, Şaḥrā' *desert*
Sahl *plain*
Saki *cape, point*
Salar *salt flat*
Salina *salt pan*
Salin-as, -es *salt flat-s, salt marsh-es*
Salto *waterfall*
Sammyaku *mountain range*
San *hill, mountain*
San, -ta, -to *saint*
Sandur *sandy area*
Sankt *saint*
Sanmaek *mountain range*
São *saint*
Sarīr *gravel desert*
Sasso *mountain, stone*
Savane *savanna*
Scoglio *reef, rock*
Se *reef, rock-s, shoal-s*
Sebjet *salt lake, salt marsh*
Sebkha *salt lake, salt marsh*
Sebkhet *lagoon, salt lake*
See *lake, sea*
Selat *strait*
Selkä *lake, ridge*
Semenanjung *peninsula*
Sen *mountain*
Seno *bay, gulf*
Serra, Serranía *range of hills or mountains*
Severn-yy, -aya, -oye *northern*
Sgùrr *peak*
Sha *island, shoal*
Sha'ib *ravine, watercourse*
Shamo *desert*
Shan *island-s, mountain-s, range*
Shankou *mountain pass*

Shanmo *mountain range*
Sharm *cove, creek, harbor*
Shaṭṭ *large river*
Shi *administrative division, municipality*
Shima *island-s, rock-s*
Shō *island, reef, rock*
Shotō *archipelago*
Shott *intermittent salt lake*
Shuiku *reservoir*
Shuitao *channel*
Shyghanaghy *bay, gulf*
Sierra *mountain range*
Silsilesi *mountain chain, ridge*
Sint *saint*
Sinus *bay, sea*
Sjö-n *lake*
Skarv-et *barren mountain*
Skerry *rock*
Slieve *mountain*
Sø *lake*
Sønder, Søndre *south-ern*
Sopka *conical mountain, volcano*
Sor *lake, salt lake*
Sør, Sör *south-ern*
Sory *salt lake, salt marsh*
Spitz-e *peak, point, top*
Sredn-iy, -yaya, -eye *central, middle*
Stagno *lake, pond*
Stantsiya *station*
Stausee *reservoir*
Stenón *channel, strait*
Step'-i *steppe-s*
Štít *summit, top*
Stor-e *big, great*
Straat *strait*
Straum-en *current-s*
Strelka *spit of land*
Stretet, Stretto *strait*
Su *reef, river, rock, stream*
Sud *south*
Sudo *channel, strait*
Suidō *channel, strait*
Şummān *rocky desert*
Sund *sound, strait*
Sunden *channel, inlet, sound*
Svyat-oy, -aya, -oye *holy, saint*
Sziget *island*

T

Tagh *mountain-s*
Tall *hill, mound*
T'an *lake*
Tanezrouft *desert*
Tang *plain, steppe*
Tangi *peninsula, point*
Tanjong, Tanjung *cape, point*
Tao *island-s*
Tarso *hill-s, mountain-s*
Tassili *plateau, upland*
Tau *mountain-s, range*
Taūy *hills, mountains*
Tchabal *mountain-s*
Te Ava *tidal flat*
Tel-l *hill, mound*
Telok, Teluk *bay*
Tepe, -si *hill, peak*
Tepuí *mesa, mountain*
Terara *hill, mountain, peak*
Testa *bluff, head*
Thale *lake*
Thang *plain, steppe*
Tien *lake*
Tierra *land, region*
Ting *hill, mountain*
Tir'at *canal*
Tó *lake, pool*
To, Tō *island-s, rock-s*
Tonle *lake*
Tope *hill, mountain, peak*

Top-pen *peak-s*
Träsk *bog, lake*
Tso *lake*
Tsui *cape, point*
Tübegi *peninsula*
Tulu *hill, mountain*
Tunturi-t *hill-s, mountain-s*

U

Uad *wadi, watercourse*
Udde-m *point*
Ujong, Ujung *cape, point*
Umi *bay, lagoon, lake*
Ura *bay, inlet, lake*
'Urūq *dune area*
Uul, Uula *mountain, range*
'Uyūn *springs*

V

Vaara *mountain*
Vaart *canal*
Vær *fishing station*
Vaïn *channel, strait*
Valle, Vallée *valley, wadi*
Vallen *waterfall*
Valli *lagoon, lake*
Vallis *valley*
Vanua *land*
Varre *mountain*
Vatn, Vatten, Vatnet *lake, water*
Veld *grassland, plain*
Verkhn-iy, -yaya, -eye *higher, upper*
Vesi *lake, water*
Vest-er *west*
Via *road*
Vidda *plateau*
Vig, Vík, Vik, -en *bay, cove*
Vinh *bay, gulf*
Vodokhranilishche *reservoir*
Vodoskhovyshche *reservoir*
Volcan, Volcán *volcano*
Vostochn-yy, -aya, -oye *eastern*
Vötn *stream*
Vozvyshennost' *plateau, upland*
Vozyera *lake-s*
Vrchovina *mountains*
Vrch-y *mountain-s*
Vrh *hill, mountain*
Vrŭkh *mountain*
Vyaliki *big, large*
Vysočina *highland*

W

Wabē *stream*
Wadi, Wâdi, Wādī *valley, watercourse*
Wâhât, Wāḥat *oasis*
Wald *forest, wood*
Wan *bay, gulf*
Water *harbor*
Webi *stream*
Wiek *cove, inlet*

X

Xia *gorge, strait*
Xiao *lesser, little*

Y

Yanchi *salt lake*
Yang *ocean*
Yarymadasy *peninsula*
Yazovir *reservoir*
Yŏlto *island group*
Yoma *mountain range*
Yü *island*
Yumco *lake*
Yunhe *canal*
Yuzhn-yy, -aya, -oye *southern*

Z

Zaki *cape, point*
Zaliv *bay, gulf*
Zan *mountain, ridge*
Zangbo *river, stream*
Zapadn-yy, -aya, -oye *western*
Zatoka *bay, gulf*
Zee *bay, sea*
Zemlya *land*

WORLD TIME ZONES

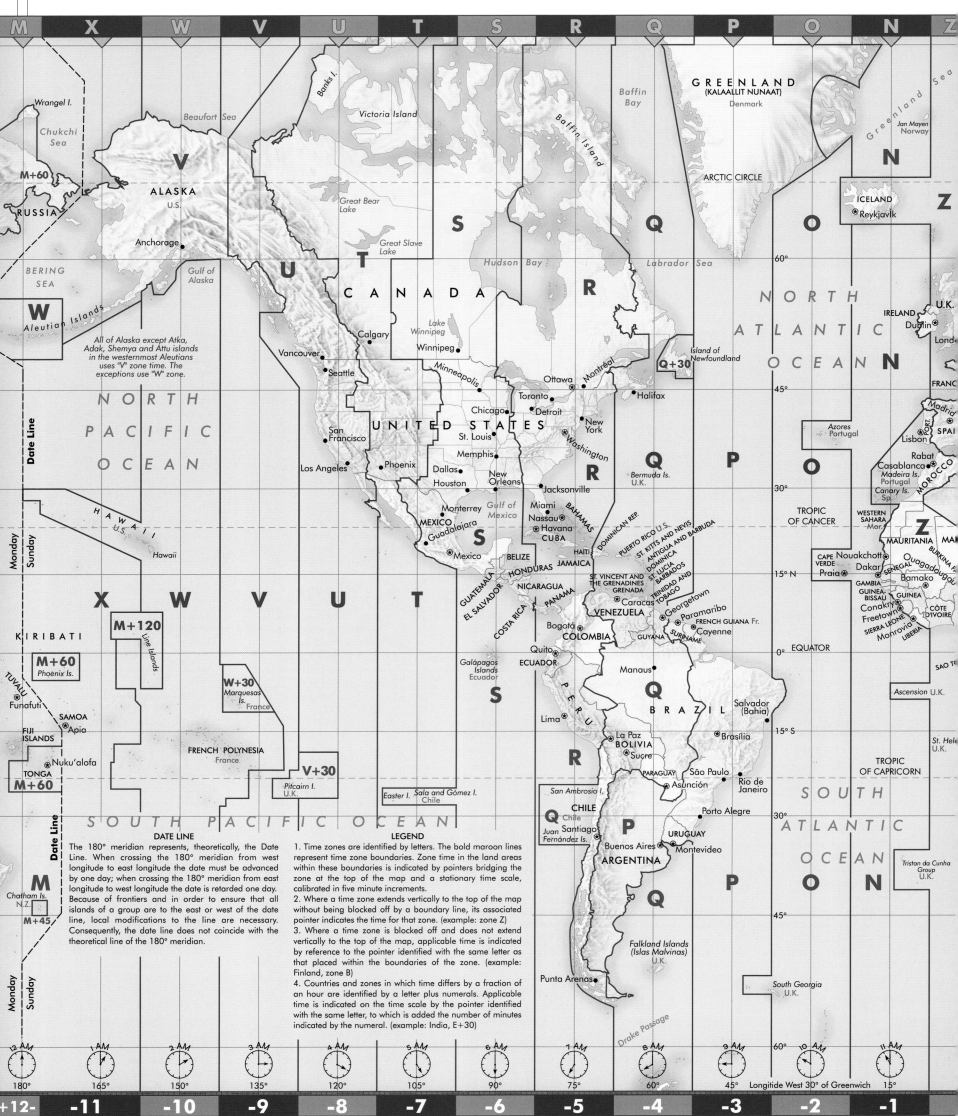

| M | X | W | V | U | T | S | R | Q | P | O | N | Z |

V ALASKA U.S.

All of Alaska except Atka, Adak, Shemya and Attu islands in the westernmost Aleutians uses "V" zone time. The exceptions use "W" zone.

W Aleutian Islands

GREENLAND (KALAALLIT NUNAAT) Denmark

ARCTIC CIRCLE

ICELAND ⊛Reykjavik

Wrangel I.

Chukchi Sea

M+60

RUSSIA

BERING SEA

Beaufort Sea

Banks I.

Victoria Island

Great Bear Lake

Great Slave Lake

Hudson Bay

Labrador Sea

Baffin Bay

Baffin Island

Greenland Sea

Jan Mayen Norway

Anchorage⊛

Gulf of Alaska

CANADA

60°

NORTH ATLANTIC OCEAN **N**

IRELAND
Dublin⊛ U.K.
Lond

Date Line

NORTH PACIFIC OCEAN

Calgary⊛
Vancouver⊛
Seattle⊛

Winnipeg⊛
Lake Winnipeg

Minneapolis⊛

Ottawa⊛ Montreal⊛
Toronto⊛ ⊛Halifax
Chicago⊛ Detroit⊛

Q+30 Island of Newfoundland

45°

Azores Portugal

FRANC
Madrid⊛ SPAI
PORT.
Lisbon⊛

San Francisco⊛

UNITED STATES
St. Louis⊛
Memphis⊛

New York⊛
Washington⊛

Bermuda Is. U.K.

Rabat⊛
Casablanca⊛ MOROCCO
Madeira Is. Portugal

HAWAII U.S.

Los Angeles⊛
Phoenix⊛
Dallas⊛
Houston⊛

New Orleans⊛
Jacksonville⊛
Miami⊛
Nassau⊛

Canary Is. Sp.

30°

TROPIC OF CANCER

WESTERN SAHARA Mor.

Hawaii

Monterrey⊛
Gulf of Mexico

Havana⊛
CUBA

BAHAMAS

DOMINICAN REP.
PUERTO RICO U.S.

Z
MAURITANIA
CAPE VERDE
Nouakchott⊛
Praia⊛ Dakar⊛ SENEGAL

MAL

MEXICO **S**
Guadalajara⊛
Mexico⊛

BELIZE
GUATEMALA HONDURAS
EL SALVADOR NICARAGUA

HAITI JAMAICA
ST. KITTS AND NEVIS
ANTIGUA AND BARBUDA
DOMINICA
ST. LUCIA
BARBADOS
ST. VINCENT AND THE GRENADINES GRENADA
TRINIDAD AND TOBAGO

15° N

GAMBIA
GUINEA-BISSAU
Conakry⊛ GUINEA
Freetown⊛ SIERRA LEONE
Monrovia⊛ CÔTE D'IVOIRE
LIBERIA

Ouagadougou⊛ BURKINA F.
Bamako⊛

X
KIRIBATI
M+120
Line Islands

W
M+60
Phoenix Is.

V

U

T

Caracas⊛
VENEZUELA
COSTA RICA PANAMA
Bogotá⊛
COLOMBIA

Georgetown⊛
Paramaribo⊛ FRENCH GUIANA Fr.
Cayenne⊛
GUYANA SURINAME

0° EQUATOR

SAO T

TUVALU
Funafuti⊛

SAMOA
⊛Apia

Quito⊛
ECUADOR
Galápagos Islands Ecuador

PERU
Manaus⊛

Q
BRAZIL

S

Ascension U.K.

FIJI ISLANDS

W+30 Marquesas Is. France

Lima⊛

La Paz⊛
BOLIVIA
Sucre⊛

Salvador (Bahia)⊛
Brasília⊛

15° S

St. Hele U.K.

Nuku'alofa⊛

TONGA
M+60

FRENCH POLYNESIA France

V+30

Pitcairn I. U.K.

Easter I. Sala and Gómez I. Chile

San Ambrosio I.

PARAGUAY
Asunción⊛

São Paulo⊛
Rio de Janeiro⊛
Porto Alegre⊛

TROPIC OF CAPRICORN

SOUTH ATLANTIC OCEAN

30°

Tristan da Cunha Group U.K.

M
Chatham Is. N.Z.
M+45

Date Line

SOUTH PACIFIC OCEAN

Q Chile
Juan
Santiago⊛ Fernández Is.

CHILE

URUGUAY
Buenos Aires⊛ Montevideo⊛
ARGENTINA

R **P**

45°

Q

P

O **N**

Falkland Islands (Islas Malvinas) U.K.

South Georgia U.K.

Punta Arenas⊛

Drake Passage

DATE LINE

The 180° meridian represents, theoretically, the Date Line. When crossing the 180° meridian from west longitude to east longitude the date must be advanced by one day; when crossing the 180° meridian from east longitude to west longitude the date is retarded one day. Because of frontiers and in order to ensure that all islands of a group are to the east or west of the date line, local modifications to the line are necessary. Consequently, the date line does not coincide with the theoretical line of the 180° meridian.

LEGEND

1. Time zones are identified by letters. The bold maroon lines represent time zone boundaries. Zone time in the land areas within these boundaries is indicated by pointers bridging the zone at the top of the map and a stationary time scale, calibrated in five minute increments.
2. Where a time zone extends vertically to the top of the map without being blocked off by a boundary line, its associated pointer indicates the time for that zone. (example: zone Z)
3. Where a time zone is blocked off and does not extend vertically to the top of the map, applicable time is indicated by reference to the pointer identified with the same letter as that placed within the boundaries of the zone. (example: Finland, zone B)
4. Countries and zones in which time differs by a fraction of an hour are identified by a letter plus numerals. Applicable time is indicated on the time scale by the pointer identified with the same letter, to which is added the number of minutes indicated by the numeral. (example: India, E+30)

| 12 AM | 1 AM | 2 AM | 3 AM | 4 AM | 5 AM | 6 AM | 7 AM | 8 AM | 9 AM | 10 AM | 11 AM |
| 180° | 165° | 150° | 135° | 120° | 105° | 90° | 75° | 60° | 45° | Longitide West 30° of Greenwich | 15° |

| +12- | -11 | -10 | -9 | -8 | -7 | -6 | -5 | -4 | -3 | -2 | -1 |

The numeral in each tab directly above shows the number of hours to be added to, or subtracted from, Greenwich time (Z).

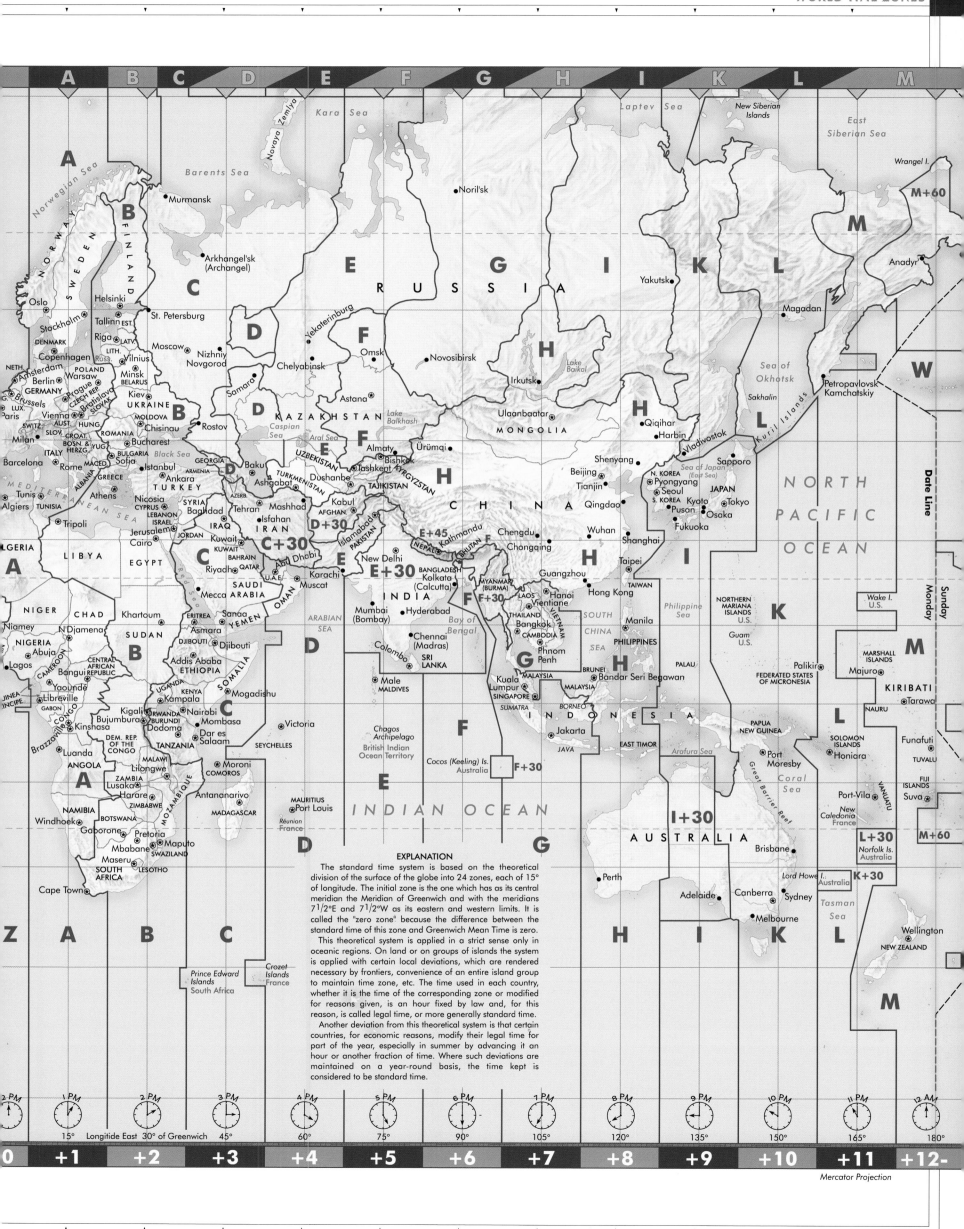

EXPLANATION

The standard time system is based on the theoretical division of the surface of the globe into 24 zones, each of 15° of longitude. The initial zone is the one which has as its central meridian the Meridian of Greenwich and with the meridians 7 1/2°E and 7 1/2°W as its eastern and western limits. It is called the "zero zone" because the difference between the standard time of this zone and Greenwich Mean Time is zero.

This theoretical system is applied in a strict sense only in oceanic regions. On land or on groups of islands the system is applied with certain local deviations, which are rendered necessary by frontiers, convenience of an entire island group to maintain time zone, etc. The time used in each country, whether it is the time of the corresponding zone or modified for reasons given, is an hour fixed by law and, for this reason, is called legal time, or more generally standard time.

Another deviation from this theoretical system is that certain countries, for economic reasons, modify their legal time for part of the year, especially in summer by advancing it an hour or another fraction of time. Where such deviations are maintained on a year-round basis, the time kept is considered to be standard time.

Mercator Projection

MAJOR CITIES OF THE WORLD

NOTES ON MAJOR CITY DATA

The population figures in the following list are from *World Urbanization Prospects: the 2001 Revision*, prepared by the United Nations. The list shows urban agglomerations with at least 750,000 inhabitants in the year 2000. An "urban agglomeration" is a contiguous territory with an urban level of population density; it includes one or more cities or towns and adjacent thickly settled areas. Thus, its geographic extent roughly coincides with the limits of a built-up urban area as seen from on high. Because an urban agglomeration is basically a metropolitan area, the population figure given for each area on the list will naturally be greater than the city-proper population figure cited in many other publications.

It is difficult to compare city populations because definitions of cities and metropolitan areas, as well as the availability of statistics, vary widely among countries. Also, the names given to metropolitan areas and the regions that comprise them may vary. As a result, some of the urban agglomeration names and population figures used in this atlas differ from names and figures given for the same general areas included on lists in other publications.

Spellings may vary, too. The UN list sometimes uses spellings that do not agree with ones used on National Geographic maps. In such cases, we have listed the place-names as they appear in the *Family Reference Atlas*. We did not change a UN spelling if we included it in the atlas as a parenthetical name or used it as a conventional name on world or physical maps.

Some of the names on the following list do not appear at all on maps in the atlas because they are regions rather than cities (Germany's Rhein-Ruhr South, for example). Others (some cities in China, for instance) were not included because of space limitations due to map scale.

CITY	COUNTRY	POPULATION
AACHEN	Germany	1,060,000
ABIDJAN	Côte d'Ivoire	3,790,000
ACCRA	Ghana	1,868,000
ADANA	Turkey	1,091,000
AD DAMMAM	Saudi Arabia	764,000
ADDIS ABABA	Ethiopia	2,645,000
ADELAIDE	Australia	1,064,000
AGRA	India	1,293,000
AHMADABAD	India	4,427,000
AHVAZ	Iran	871,000
AL MAWSIL	Iraq	1,131,000
ALEPPO	Syria	2,229,000
ALEXANDRIA	Egypt	3,506,000
ALGIERS	Algeria	2,761,000
ALLAHABAD	India	1,035,000
ALMATY	Kazakhstan	1,130,000
AMMAN	Jordan	1,148,000
AMRITSAR	India	955,000
AMSTERDAM	Netherlands	1,105,000
ANKARA	Turkey	3,155,000
ANSAN	South Korea	984,000
ANSHAN	China	1,453,000
ANSHUN	China	789,000
ANTANANARIVO	Madagascar	1,603,000
ASANSOL	India	1,065,000
ASUNCIÓN	Paraguay	1,262,000
ATHENS	Greece	3,116,000
ATLANTA	United States	2,706,000
AUCKLAND	New Zealand	1,102,000
AURANGABAD	India	868,000
AUSTIN	United States	759,000
BAGHDAD	Iraq	4,865,000
BAKU	Azerbaijan	1,948,000
BALTIMORE	United States	2,053,000
BAMAKO	Mali	1,114,000
BANDAR LAMPUNG	Indonesia	915,000
BANDUNG	Indonesia	3,409,000
BANGALORE	India	5,567,000
BANGKOK	Thailand	7,372,000
BAOTOU	China	1,319,000
BARCELONA	Spain	2,729,000
BARQUISIMETO	Venezuela	923,000
BARRANQUILLA	Colombia	1,683,000
BEIJING	China	10,839,000
BEIRUT	Lebanon	2,070,000
BELÉM	Brazil	1,658,000
BELGRADE	Yugoslavia	1,673,000
BELO HORIZONTE	Brazil	4,224,000
BENGHAZI	Libya	829,000
BENXI	China	957,000
BERLIN	Germany	3,319,000
BHOPAL	India	1,425,000
BIELEFELD	Germany	1,294,000
BIRMINGHAM	U.K.	2,272,000
BOGOTÁ	Colombia	6,771,000
BOSTON	United States	2,934,000
BRASÍLIA	Brazil	2,016,000
BRAZZAVILLE	Congo	1,306,000
BREMEN	Germany	880,000
BRISBANE	Australia	1,622,000
BRUSSELS	Belgium	1,135,000
BUCARAMANGA	Colombia	937,000
BUCHAREST	Romania	2,001,000
BUDAPEST	Hungary	1,819,000
BUENOS AIRES	Argentina	12,024,000
BUFFALO-NIAGARA FALLS	United States	990,000
BULAWAYO	Zimbabwe	824,000
BURSA	Turkey	1,166,000
CAIRO	Egypt	9,462,000
CALCUTTA	India	13,058,000
CALGARY	Canada	953,000
CALI	Colombia	2,233,000
CAMPINAS	Brazil	1,895,000
CAMPO GRANDE	Brazil	821,000
CAPE TOWN	South Africa	2,930,000
CARACAS	Venezuela	3,153,000
CARTAGENA	Colombia	845,000
CASABLANCA	Morocco	3,357,000
CHANDIGARH	India	791,000
CHANGCHUN	China	3,093,000
CHANGDE	China	1,374,000
CHANGSHA	China	1,775,000
CHANGZHOU	China	886,000
CHELYABINSK	Russia	1,045,000
CHENGDU	China	3,294,000
CHIFENG	China	1,087,000
CHITTAGONG	Bangladesh	3,651,000
CHONGQING	China	4,900,000
CINCINNATI	United States	1,323,000
CIUDAD GUAYANA	Venezuela	799,000
CIUDAD JUÁREZ	Mexico	1,239,000
CLEVELAND	United States	1,735,000
COIMBATORE	India	1,420,000
COLUMBUS, OHIO	United States	1,067,000
CONAKRY	Guinea	1,232,000
COPENHAGEN	Denmark	1,332,000
CÓRDOBA	Argentina	1,368,000
CÚCUTA	Colombia	772,000
CULIACÁN	Mexico	750,000
CURITIBA	Brazil	2,562,000
DAKAR	Senegal	2,078,000
DALIAN	China	2,628,000
DALLAS-FORT WORTH	United States	3,937,000
DAMASCUS	Syria	2,144,000
DAQING	China	1,076,000
DAR ES SALAM	Tanzania	2,115,000
DATONG	China	1,165,000
DAVAO	Philippines	1,146,000
DELHI	India	12,441,000
DENVER	United States	1,698,000
DETROIT	United States	3,809,000
DHAKA	Bangladesh	12,519,000
DHANBAD	India	1,046,000
DNIPROPETROVSK	Ukraine	1,069,000
DONETSK	Ukraine	1,007,000
DONGGUAN	China	1,319,000
DOUALA	Cameroon	1,642,000
DUBAYY	U.A.E.	886,000
DUBLIN	Ireland	985,000
DURBAN	South Africa	2,391,000
DURG-BHILAI	India	906,000
EAST RAND	South Africa	1,552,000
EDMONTON	Canada	944,000
ESFAHAN	Iran	1,381,000
FAISALABAD	Pakistan	2,142,000
FARIDABAD	India	1,018,000
FES	Morocco	907,000
FLORENCE	Italy	778,000
FORT LAUDERDALE-HOLLYWOOD-POMPANO BEACH	United States	1,471,000
FORTALEZA	Brazil	3,066,000
FREETOWN	Sierra Leone	800,000
FUSHUN	China	1,413,000
FUXIN	China	785,000
FUYU	China	1,025,000
FUZHOU	China	1,397,000
GAZIANTEP	Turkey	757,000
GDANSK	Poland	893,000
GENOA	Italy	890,000
GHAZIABAD	India	928,000
GOIÂNIA	Brazil	1,117,000
GÖTEBORG	Sweden	778,000
GUADALAJARA	Mexico	3,697,000
GUANGZHOU	China	3,893,000
GUATEMALA CITY	Guatemala	3,242,000
GUAYAQUIL	Ecuador	2,118,000
GUIYANG	China	2,533,000
GUJRANWALA	Pakistan	1,325,000
GUWAHATI	India	797,000
GWALIOR	India	855,000
HAIPHONG	Vietnam	1,676,000
HAMBURG	Germany	2,664,000
HANDAN	China	1,996,000
HANGZHOU	China	1,780,000
HANNOVER	Germany	1,283,000
HANOI	Vietnam	3,751,000
HARARE	Zimbabwe	1,791,000
HARBIN	China	2,928,000
HAVANA	Cuba	2,256,000
HEFEI	China	1,242,000
HELSINKI	Finland	937,000
HENGYANG	China	799,000
HEZE	China	1,600,000
HIROSHIMA	Japan	866,000
HO CHI MINH CITY	Vietnam	4,619,000
HOHHOT	China	978,000
HOMS	Syria	811,000
HONG KONG	China	6,860,000
HOUSTON	United States	3,386,000
HUAIBEI	China	814,000
HUAINAN	China	1,354,000
HUAIYIN	China	1,232,000
HUBLI-DHARWAD	India	776,000
HUNJIANG	China	772,000
HUZHOU	China	1,077,000
HYDERABAD	India	5,445,000
HYDERABAD	Pakistan	1,221,000
IBADAN	Nigeria	1,549,000
INCHON	South Korea	2,884,000
INDIANAPOLIS	United States	1,008,000
INDORE	India	1,597,000
ISTANBUL	Turkey	8,953,000
IZMIR	Turkey	2,214,000
JABALPUR	India	1,100,000
JACKSONVILLE	United States	883,000
JAIPUR	India	2,259,000
JAKARTA	Indonesia	11,018,000
JAMSHEDPUR	India	1,081,000
JEDDAH	Saudi Arabia	3,192,000
JIAMUSI	China	874,000
JIAXING	China	791,000
JILIN	China	1,435,000
JINAN	China	2,568,000
JINGMEN	China	1,153,000
JINING	China	1,019,000
JINXI	China	1,821,000
JINZHOU	China	834,000
JIXI	China	949,000
JODHPUR	India	833,000
JOHANNESBURG	South Africa	2,950,000
KABUL	Afghanistan	2,602,000
KAIFENG	China	769,000
KAMPALA	Uganda	1,213,000
KANPUR	India	2,641,000
KANSAS CITY	United States	1,460,000
KAOHSIUNG	China	1,463,000
KARACHI	Pakistan	10,032,000
KARAJ	Iran	1,044,000
KARLSRUHE	Germany	977,000
KATOWICE	Poland	3,494,000
KAZAN	Russia	1,063,000
KHARKIV	Ukraine	1,416,000
KHARTOUM	Sudan	2,742,000
KHULNA	Bangladesh	1,442,000
KIEV	Ukraine	2,499,000
KINSHASA	Dem. Rep. of the Congo	5,054,000
KITAKYUSHU	Japan	2,750,000
KOCHI (COCHIN)	India	1,340,000
KOZHIKODE (CALICUT)	India	875,000
KRAKÓW	Poland	859,000
KRASNOYARSK	Russia	840,000
KUALA LUMPUR	Malaysia	1,379,000
KUNMING	China	1,701,000
KUWAIT CITY	Kuwait	879,000
KWANGJU	South Korea	1,379,000
KYOTO	Japan	1,849,000
LA PAZ	Bolivia	1,460,000
LAGOS	Nigeria	8,665,000
LAHORE	Pakistan	5,452,000
LANZHOU	China	1,730,000
LAS VEGAS	United States	995,000
LEEDS	U.K.	1,433,000
LEÓN	Mexico	1,293,000
LESHAN	China	1,137,000
LILLE	France	991,000
LIMA	Peru	7,443,000
LINQING	China	891,000
LINYI	China	2,498,000
LISBON	Portugal	3,861,000

CITY	COUNTRY	POPULATION
LIUZHOU	China	928,000
LIVERPOOL	U.K.	915,000
LODZ	Poland	1,053,000
LONDON	U.K.	7,640,000
LOS ANGELES	United States	13,213,000
LOUISVILLE	United States	785,000
LUAN	China	1,818,000
LUANDA	Angola	2,697,000
LUBUMBASHI	Dem. Rep. of the Congo	965,000
LUCKNOW	India	2,221,000
LUDHIANA	India	1,368,000
LUOYANG	China	1,451,000
LUPANSHUI	China	2,023,000
LUSAKA	Zambia	1,653,000
LVIV	Ukraine	764,000
LYON	France	1,353,000
MACEIÓ	Brazil	886,000
MADRAS	India	6,353,000
MADRID	Spain	3,976,000
MADURAI	India	1,187,000
MALANG	Indonesia	787,000
MANAGUA	Nicaragua	1,009,000
MANAUS	Brazil	1,467,000
MANCHESTER	U.K.	2,252,000
MANDALAY	Myanmar	770,000
MAPUTO	Mozambique	1,094,000
MARACAIBO	Venezuela	1,901,000
MARACAY	Venezuela	1,100,000
MARRAKECH	Morocco	822,000
MARSEILLE	France	1,290,000
MASHHAD	Iran	1,990,000
MECCA	Saudi Arabia	1,335,000
MEDAN	Indonesia	1,879,000
MEDELLÍN	Colombia	2,866,000
MEDINA	Saudi Arabia	891,000
MEERUT	India	1,143,000
MELBOURNE	Australia	3,232,000
MEMPHIS	United States	894,000
MENDOZA	Argentina	934,000
MÉRIDA	Mexico	849,000
METRO MANILA	Philippines	9,950,000
MEXICALI	Mexico	771,000
MEXICO CITY	Mexico	18,066,000
MIAMI-HIALEAH	United States	2,224,000
MIANYANG	China	1,065,000
MILAN	Italy	4,251,000
MILWAUKEE	United States	1,285,000
MINNEAPOLIS-ST. PAUL	United States	2,378,000
MINSK	Belarus	1,667,000
MOGADISHU	Somalia	1,157,000
MONTERREY	Mexico	3,267,000
MONTEVIDEO	Uruguay	1,324,000
MONTRÉAL	Canada	3,480,000
MOSCOW	Russia	8,367,000
MUDANJIANG	China	801,000
MULTAN	Pakistan	1,263,000
MUMBAI (BOMBAY)	India	16,086,000
MUNICH	Germany	2,291,000
MYSORE	India	776,000
NAGOYA	Japan	3,157,000
NAGPUR	India	2,089,000
NAIROBI	Kenya	2,233,000
NAMPO	North Korea	1,022,000
NANCHANG	China	1,722,000
NANCHONG	China	1,055,000
NANJING	China	2,740,000
NANNING	China	1,311,000
NAPLES	Italy	3,012,000
NASIK	India	1,117,000
NATAL	Brazil	806,000
NEIJIANG	China	1,393,000
NEW ORLEANS	United States	1,079,000
NEW YORK	U.S.	16,732,000
NIAMEY	Niger	775,000
NINGBO	China	1,173,000
NIZHNIY NOVGOROD	Russia	1,332,000

CITY	COUNTRY	POPULATION
NORFOLK-VIRGINIA BEACH-NEWPORT NEWS	United States	1,963,000
NOVOSIBIRSK	Russia	1,321,000
NÜRNBERG	Germany	1,189,000
ODESA	Ukraine	931,000
OGBOMOSHO	Nigeria	809,000
OKLAHOMA CITY	United States	901,000
OMSK	Russia	1,174,000
ORLANDO	United States	1,226,000
OSAKA	Japan	11,013,000
OSLO	Norway	779,000
OTTAWA	Canada	1,081,000
OUAGADOUGOU	Burkina Faso	831,000
POHANG	South Korea	790,000
PALEMBANG	Indonesia	1,422,000
PANAMA CITY	Panama	1,173,000
PARIS	France	9,630,000
PATNA	India	1,658,000
PERM	Russia	991,000
PERTH	Australia	1,329,000
PESHAWAR	Pakistan	1,066,000
PHILADELPHIA	United States	4,427,000
PHNOM PENH	Cambodia	1,070,000
PHOENIX	United States	2,623,000
PINGXIANG	China	1,502,000
PITTSBURGH	United States	1,735,000
PORT ELIZABETH	South Africa	1,006,000
PORT-AU-PRINCE	Haiti	1,769,000
PORTLAND-VANCOUVER	United States	1,328,000
PORTO	Portugal	1,940,000
PORTO ALEGRE	Brazil	3,757,000
PRAGUE	Czech Republic	1,203,000
PRETORIA	South Africa	1,590,000
PROVIDENCE-PAWTUCKET	United States	916,000
PUCHON	South Korea	900,000
PUEBLA	Mexico	1,888,000
PUNE (POONA)	India	3,655,000
PUSAN	South Korea	3,830,000
P'YONGYANG	North Korea	3,124,000
QINGDAO	China	2,316,000
QIQIHAR	China	1,435,000
QOM	Iran	888,000
QUERÉTARO	Mexico	798,000
QUITO	Ecuador	1,616,000
RABAT	Morocco	1,616,000
RAJKOT	India	974,000
RAJSHAHI	Bangladesh	1,035,000
RANCHI	India	844,000
RAWALPINDI	Pakistan	1,521,000
RECIFE	Brazil	3,346,000
RHEIN-MAIN	Germany	3,681,000
RHEIN-NECKAR	Germany	1,605,000
RHEIN-RUHR MIDDLE	Germany	3,233,000
RHEIN-RUHR NORTH	Germany	6,531,000
RHEIN-RUHR SOUTH	Germany	3,050,000
RIGA	Latvia	761,000
RIO DE JANEIRO	Brazil	10,652,000
RIVERSIDE-SAN BERNARDINO	United States	1,699,000
RIYADH	Saudi Arabia	4,549,000
ROME	Italy	2,649,000
ROSARIO	Argentina	1,279,000
ROSTOV-NA-DONU	Russia	1,012,000
ROTTERDAM	Netherlands	1,078,000
SAARLAND	Germany	891,000
SACRAMENTO	United States	1,408,000
SALT LAKE CITY	United States	911,000
SALVADOR	Brazil	3,238,000
SAMARA	Russia	1,132,000

CITY	COUNTRY	POPULATION
SAN ANTONIO	United States	1,318,000
SAN DIEGO	United States	3,002,000
SAN FRANCISCO-OAKLAND	United States	4,077,000
SAN JOSE	United States	1,635,000
SAN JOSÉ	Costa Rica	961,000
SAN JUAN	Puerto Rico	1,388,000
SAN LUIS POTOSÍ	Mexico	857,000
SAN MIGUEL DE TUCUMÁN	Argentina	792,000
SAN SALVADOR	El Salvador	1,341,000
SANAA	Yemen	1,327,000
SANTA CRUZ	Bolivia	1,062,000
SANTIAGO	Chile	5,467,000
SANTIAGO	Dominican Republic	804,000
SANTO DOMINGO	Dominican Republic	2,563,000
SANTOS	Brazil	1,270,000
SÃO JOSÉ DOS CAMPOS	Brazil	972,000
SÃO LUÍS	Brazil	968,000
SÃO PAULO	Brazil	17,962,000
SAPPORO	Japan	1,813,000
SARATOV	Russia	881,000
SEATTLE	United States	2,097,000
SEMARANG	Indonesia	787,000
SENDAI	Japan	953,000
SEOUL	South Korea	9,888,000
SHANGHAI	China	12,887,000
SHANTOU	China	1,176,000
SHENYANG	China	4,828,000
SHENZHEN	China	1,131,000
SHIJIAZHUANG	China	1,603,000
SHIRAZ	Iran	1,124,000
SHOLAPUR	India	853,000
SHUBRA EL KHEIMA	Egypt	937,000
SINGAPORE	Singapore	4,018,000
SOFIA	Bulgaria	1,187,000
SONGNAM	South Korea	1,353,000
SRINAGAR	India	954,000
ST. LOUIS	United States	2,084,000
ST. PETERSBURG	Russia	4,635,000
STOCKHOLM	Sweden	1,612,000
STUTTGART	Germany	2,672,000
SUINING	China	1,428,000
SUQIAN	China	1,189,000
SURABAYA	Indonesia	2,461,000
SURAT	India	2,699,000
SUWON	South Korea	876,000
SUZHOU	China	1,183,000
SYDNEY	Australia	3,907,000
TABRIZ	Iran	1,274,000
TAEGU	South Korea	2,675,000
TAEJON	South Korea	1,522,000
TAIAN	China	1,503,000
TAICHUNG	China	950,000
TAIPEI	China	2,550,000
TAIYUAN	China	2,415,000
TAMPA-ST. PETERSBURG-CLEARWATER	United States	2,064,000
TANGSHAN	China	1,671,000
TASHKENT	Uzbekistan	2,148,000
TBILISI	Georgia	1,406,000
TEGAL	Indonesia	762,000
TEGUCIGALPA	Honduras	949,000
TEHRAN	Iran	6,979,000
TEL AVIV-YAFO	Israel	2,001,000
TERESINA	Brazil	848,000
THESSALONÍKI	Greece	789,000
THIRUVANANTHAPURAM	India	885,000
TIANJIN	China	9,156,000
TIANMEN	China	1,779,000
TIANSHUI	China	1,187,000
TIJUANA	Mexico	1,297,000
TIRUCHIRAPPALLI	India	837,000
TOGLIATTI	Russia	771,000

CITY	COUNTRY	POPULATION
TOKYO	Japan	26,444,000
TOLUCA	Mexico	1,455,000
TONGLIAO	China	785,000
TORONTO	Canada	4,752,000
TORREÓN	Mexico	1,012,000
TOULOUSE	France	761,000
TRIPOLI	Libya	1,733,000
TUNIS	Tunisia	1,892,000
TURIN	Italy	1,294,000
TYNESIDE (NEWCASTLE)	U.K.	981,000
UFA	Russia	1,102,000
UJUNGPANDANG	Indonesia	1,051,000
ULAANBAATAR	Mongolia	764,000
ULSAN	South Korea	1,340,000
ULYANOVSK	Russia	864,000
URUMQI	China	1,415,000
VADODARA	India	1,465,000
VALENCIA	Venezuela	1,893,000
VANCOUVER	Canada	2,049,000
VARANASI (BENARES)	India	1,199,000
VIENNA	Austria	2,065,000
VIJAYAWADA	India	999,000
VISHAKHAPATNAM	India	1,309,000
VOLGOGRAD	Russia	1,000,000
VORONEZH	Russia	918,000
WANXIAN	China	1,759,000
WARSAW	Poland	2,274,000
WASHINGTON, D.C.	United States	3,952,000
WEIFANG	China	1,287,000
WENZHOU	China	1,269,000
WEST PALM BEACH-BOCA RATON-DELRAY BEACH	United States	1,143,000
WUHAN	China	5,169,000
WUXI	China	1,127,000
XIAN	China	3,123,000
XIANGXIANG	China	908,000
XIANTAO	China	1,614,000
XIANYANG	China	896,000
XIAOSHAN	China	1,124,000
XINGHUA	China	1,556,000
XINTAI	China	1,325,000
XINYI	China	973,000
XINYU	China	808,000
XUANZHOU	China	823,000
XUZHOU	China	1,636,000
YANCHENG	China	1,562,000
YANGON	Myanmar	4,393,000
YANTAI	China	1,681,000
YAOUNDÉ	Cameroon	1,420,000
YEKATERINBURG	Russia	1,218,000
YEREVAN	Armenia	1,407,000
YICHUN (HEILONGJIANG)	China	904,000
YICHUN (JIANGXI)	China	871,000
YIXING	China	1,108,000
YIYANG	China	1,343,000
YONGZHOU	China	1,097,000
YUEYANG	China	1,213,000
YULIN	China	1,558,000
YUYAO	China	848,000
YUZHOU	China	1,173,000
ZAGREB	Croatia	1,067,000
ZAOYANG	China	1,121,000
ZAOZHUANG	China	2,048,000
ZAPORIZHZHYA	Ukraine	813,000
ZHANGJIAKOU	China	880,000
ZHANGJIAGANG	China	886,000
ZHANJIANG	China	1,368,000
ZHAODONG	China	851,000
ZHENGZHOU	China	2,070,000
ZIBO	China	2,675,000
ZIGONG	China	1,072,000
ZÜRICH	Switzerland	939,000

WORLD TEMPERATURE AND RAINFALL

Average daily high and low temperatures and monthly rainfall for selected world locations:

	JAN.			FEB.			MARCH			APRIL			MAY			JUNE			JULY			AUG.			SEPT.			OCT.			NOV.			DEC.		
CANADA																																				
CALGARY, Alberta	-4	-16	14	-2	-14	15	3	-9	20	11	-3	27	17	3	54	20	7	82	24	9	65	23	8	57	18	3	40	12	-1	18	3	-9	16	-2	-13	14
CHARLOTTETOWN, P.E.I.	-3	-11	100	-3	-12	83	1	-7	83	7	-1	77	14	4	79	20	10	75	24	14	78	23	14	86	18	10	91	13	5	106	6	0	106	0	-7	111
CHURCHILL, Manitoba	-23	-31	15	-22	-30	12	-15	-25	18	-6	-15	23	2	-5	27	11	1	43	17	7	55	16	7	62	9	2	53	2	-4	44	-9	-16	31	-18	-26	18
EDMONTON, Alberta	-9	-18	23	-5	-15	18	0	-9	19	10	-1	24	17	5	45	21	9	79	23	12	87	22	10	64	17	5	36	11	0	20	0	-8	18	-6	-15	22
FORT NELSON, B.C.	-18	-27	23	-11	-23	21	-2	-15	21	8	-4	20	16	3	44	21	8	65	23	10	76	21	8	58	15	3	39	6	-4	28	-9	-17	26	-16	-24	23
GOOSE BAY, Nfld.	-12	-22	1	-10	-21	4	-4	-15	4	3	-7	15	10	0	46	17	5	97	21	10	119	19	9	98	14	4	87	6	-2	58	0	-8	21	-9	-18	7
HALIFAX, Nova Scotia	0	-8	139	0	-9	121	3	-5	123	8	0	109	14	5	110	18	9	96	22	13	93	22	14	103	19	10	93	13	5	127	8	1	142	2	-5	141
MONTRÉAL, Quebec	-6	-15	71	-4	-13	66	2	-7	71	11	1	74	18	8	69	24	13	84	26	16	87	25	14	91	20	10	84	13	4	76	5	-2	90	-3	-11	85
MOOSONEE, Ontario	-14	-27	39	-12	-25	32	-5	-19	37	3	-8	36	11	0	55	18	5	72	22	9	79	20	8	78	15	5	77	8	0	66	-1	-9	53	-11	-21	41
OTTAWA, Ontario	-6	-16	67	-5	-15	59	1	-8	67	11	0	60	19	7	72	24	12	82	27	15	86	25	13	80	20	9	77	13	3	69	4	-3	70	-4	-12	74
PRINCE RUPERT, B.C.	4	-3	237	6	-1	198	7	0	202	9	2	179	12	5	133	14	8	110	16	10	115	16	10	149	15	8	218	11	5	345	7	1	297	5	-1	275
QUÉBEC, Quebec	-7	-17	85	-6	-16	75	0	-9	79	8	-1	76	17	5	93	22	10	108	25	13	112	23	12	109	18	7	113	11	2	89	3	-4	100	-5	-13	104
REGINA, Saskatchewan	-12	-23	17	-9	-21	13	-2	-13	18	10	-3	20	18	3	45	23	9	77	26	11	59	25	10	44	19	4	35	11	-2	20	0	-11	16	-8	-19	14
SAINT JOHN, N.B.	-3	-14	141	-2	-14	115	3	-7	111	10	-1	111	17	4	116	22	9	103	25	12	100	24	11	100	19	7	108	14	2	118	6	-3	149	-1	-10	157
ST. JOHN'S, Nfld.	-1	-8	69	-1	-9	69	1	-6	74	5	-2	80	10	1	91	16	6	95	20	11	78	20	11	122	16	8	125	11	3	147	6	0	122	2	-5	91
TORONTO, Ontario	-1	-8	68	-1	-9	60	3	-4	66	11	2	65	17	7	71	23	13	68	26	16	77	25	15	70	21	11	73	14	5	62	7	0	70	1	-6	67
VANCOUVER, B.C.	5	0	146	8	1	121	10	2	102	13	5	69	17	8	56	19	11	47	22	13	31	22	13	37	19	10	60	14	6	116	9	3	155	6	1	172
WHITEHORSE, Yukon Terr.	-14	-23	17	-9	-18	13	-2	-13	13	5	-5	9	13	1	14	18	5	30	20	8	37	18	6	39	12	3	31	4	-3	21	-6	-13	20	-12	-20	19
WINNIPEG, Manitoba	-13	-23	21	-10	-21	19	-2	-13	26	9	-2	34	18	5	55	23	10	81	26	14	74	25	12	66	19	6	55	12	1	35	-1	-9	26	-9	-18	22
YELLOWKNIFE, N.W.T.	-24	-32	14	-20	-30	12	-12	-24	11	-1	-13	10	10	0	16	18	8	20	21	12	35	18	10	39	10	4	29	1	-4	32	-10	-18	23	-20	-28	17
UNITED STATES																																				
ALBANY, New York	-1	-12	61	1	-10	59	7	-4	76	14	2	77	21	7	86	26	13	83	29	15	80	27	14	87	23	10	78	17	4	77	9	-1	80	2	-8	74
AMARILLO, Texas	9	-6	13	12	-4	14	16	0	23	22	6	28	26	11	71	31	16	88	33	19	70	32	18	74	28	14	50	23	7	35	15	0	15	10	-5	15
ANCHORAGE, Alaska	-6	-13	20	-3	-11	21	1	-8	17	6	-2	15	12	4	17	16	8	26	18	11	47	17	10	62	13	5	66	5	-2	47	-3	-9	29	-5	-12	28
ASPEN, Colorado	0	-18	32	2	-16	26	5	-11	35	10	-6	28	16	-2	39	22	1	34	26	5	44	25	4	45	21	0	34	15	-5	36	6	-10	31	1	-15	32
ATLANTA, Georgia	10	0	117	13	1	117	18	6	139	23	10	103	26	15	100	30	19	92	31	21	134	31	21	93	28	18	91	23	11	77	17	6	95	12	2	105
ATLANTIC CITY, N.J.	5	-6	83	6	-5	78	11	0	98	16	4	86	22	10	82	27	15	63	29	18	103	29	18	103	25	13	78	19	7	72	13	2	84	7	-3	81
AUGUSTA, Maine	-2	-11	76	0	-10	71	4	-5	84	11	1	92	19	7	95	23	12	85	26	16	85	25	15	84	20	10	80	14	4	92	7	-1	114	0	-8	93
BIRMINGHAM, Alabama	11	0	128	14	1	114	19	6	150	24	10	114	27	14	112	31	18	97	32	21	132	32	20	95	29	17	105	24	10	75	18	5	103	13	2	120
BISMARCK, N. Dak.	-7	-19	12	-3	-15	11	4	-8	20	13	-1	37	20	6	56	25	11	74	29	14	59	28	12	44	22	6	38	15	0	21	4	-8	14	-4	-16	12
BOISE, Idaho	2	-6	38	7	-3	28	12	0	32	16	3	31	22	7	31	27	11	22	32	14	8	31	14	9	25	9	16	18	4	18	9	-1	35	3	-5	35
BOSTON, Massachusetts	2	-6	95	3	-5	91	8	0	100	13	5	93	19	10	84	25	15	79	28	18	73	27	18	92	23	14	82	17	8	87	11	4	110	5	-3	105
BROWNSVILLE, Texas	21	10	37	22	11	36	26	15	16	29	19	41	31	22	64	33	24	74	34	24	39	34	24	69	32	23	134	30	19	89	26	15	41	22	11	30
BURLINGTON, Vermont	-4	-14	46	-3	-13	44	4	-6	55	12	1	71	20	7	78	24	13	85	27	15	90	26	14	101	21	9	85	14	4	77	7	-1	76	-1	-9	59
CHARLESTON, S.C.	14	3	88	16	4	80	20	9	114	24	12	71	28	17	97	31	21	155	32	23	180	32	22	176	29	20	135	25	14	77	21	8	63	16	5	82
CHARLESTON, W. Va.	5	-5	87	7	-4	82	14	2	100	19	6	85	24	11	99	28	15	92	30	18	126	29	17	102	26	14	81	20	7	67	14	2	85	8	-2	85
CHEYENNE, Wyoming	3	-9	10	5	-8	11	7	-6	26	13	-1	35	18	4	64	24	9	56	28	13	51	27	12	42	22	7	31	16	1	19	8	-5	15	4	-9	10
CHICAGO, Illinois	-1	-10	48	1	-7	42	8	-1	72	15	5	97	22	10	83	27	16	103	29	19	103	28	18	89	24	14	79	18	7	70	9	1	73	2	-6	65
CINCINNATI, Ohio	3	-6	89	5	-4	67	12	1	97	18	7	94	24	12	101	28	17	99	30	19	102	30	18	86	26	14	75	19	8	62	12	3	81	5	-3	75
CLEVELAND, Ohio	1	-7	62	2	-6	58	8	-2	78	15	4	85	21	9	90	26	14	89	28	17	88	27	16	86	23	12	80	17	7	65	10	2	80	3	-4	70
DALLAS, Texas	13	1	47	15	4	58	20	8	74	25	13	105	29	18	125	33	22	86	35	24	56	35	24	60	31	20	82	26	14	100	19	8	64	14	3	60
DENVER, Colorado	6	-9	14	8	-7	16	11	-3	34	17	1	45	22	6	63	27	11	43	31	15	47	30	14	38	25	9	28	19	2	26	11	-4	23	7	-8	15
DES MOINES, Iowa	-2	-12	26	1	-9	30	8	-2	57	17	4	85	23	11	103	28	16	108	30	19	97	29	18	105	24	13	80	18	6	58	9	-1	46	0	-9	31
DETROIT, Michigan	-1	-7	42	1	-7	43	7	-2	62	14	4	75	21	10	69	26	15	85	29	18	86	27	18	87	23	14	78	16	7	55	9	2	67	2	-4	67
DULUTH, Minnesota	-9	-19	31	-6	-16	21	1	-9	44	9	-2	59	17	4	84	22	9	105	25	13	102	23	12	101	18	7	95	11	2	62	2	-6	48	-6	-15	32
EL PASO, Texas	13	-1	11	17	1	11	21	5	8	26	9	7	31	14	9	36	18	17	36	20	38	34	19	39	31	16	34	26	10	20	19	4	11	14	-1	14
FAIRBANKS, Alaska	-19	-28	14	-14	-26	11	-5	-19	9	5	-6	7	15	3	15	21	10	35	22	11	45	19	8	46	13	2	28	0	-8	21	-12	-21	18	-17	-26	19
HARTFORD, Connecticut	1	-9	83	2	-7	79	8	-2	97	16	3	97	22	9	95	27	14	85	29	17	86	28	16	104	24	11	101	18	5	96	11	0	105	3	-6	99
HELENA, Montana	-1	-12	15	3	-9	12	7	-5	18	13	-1	24	19	4	45	24	9	53	29	12	28	28	11	27	21	5	28	15	0	19	6	-6	14	0	-12	16
HONOLULU, Hawaii	27	19	80	27	19	68	28	20	72	28	20	32	29	21	25	30	22	10	31	23	15	32	23	14	31	23	18	31	22	53	29	21	67	27	19	89
HOUSTON, Texas	16	4	98	19	6	75	22	10	88	26	15	91	29	18	142	32	21	133	34	22	85	34	22	95	31	20	106	28	14	120	22	10	97	18	6	91
INDIANAPOLIS, Indiana	1	-8	69	4	-6	61	11	0	92	17	5	94	23	11	98	28	16	98	30	18	111	29	17	88	25	13	74	19	6	69	11	1	89	4	-5	77
JACKSONVILLE, Florida	18	5	83	19	6	89	23	10	100	26	13	77	29	17	92	32	21	140	33	22	164	33	22	186	31	21	199	27	15	99	23	10	52	19	6	65
JUNEAU, Alaska	-1	-7	139	1	-5	116	4	-3	113	8	0	105	13	4	109	16	7	88	18	9	120	17	8	160	13	6	217	8	3	255	3	-2	186	0	-5	153
KANSAS CITY, Missouri	2	-9	30	5	-6	32	12	0	67	18	7	88	24	12	138	29	17	102	32	20	115	30	19	99	26	14	120	20	8	83	11	1	56	4	-6	43
LAS VEGAS, Nevada	14	0	14	17	4	12	20	7	13	25	10	5	31	16	5	38	21	3	41	25	9	40	23	13	35	19	7	28	12	6	20	6	11	14	1	10
LITTLE ROCK, Arkansas	9	-1	85	12	1	88	17	6	120	23	11	134	26	15	141	31	20	84	33	22	83	32	21	80	28	18	85	23	11	102	16	6	153	10	1	123
LOS ANGELES, California	19	9	70	19	10	61	19	10	51	20	12	20	21	14	3	22	15	1	24	17	1	25	18	2	25	17	5	24	15	7	21	12	38	19	9	43
LOUISVILLE, Kentucky	5	-5	85	7	-3	88	14	2	113	20	7	101	24	13	114	29	17	90	31	20	106	30	19	84	27	15	76	21	8	68	14	3	92	7	-2	89
MEMPHIS, Tennessee	9	-1	118	12	2	114	17	6	136	23	11	142	27	16	126	32	21	98	34	23	101	33	22	87	29	18	83	24	11	74	17	6	124	11	2	135
MIAMI, Florida	24	15	52	25	16	53	26	18	63	28	20	82	30	22	150	31	24	227	32	25	152	32	25	198	31	24	215	29	22	178	27	19	80	25	16	47
MILWAUKEE, Wisconsin	-3	-11	32	-1	-8	31	5	-3	54	12	2	87	18	7	73	24	13	87	27	17	85	26	16	94	22	12	95	15	6	66	7	-1	65	0	-7	53
MINNEAPOLIS, Minnesota	-6	-16	21	-3	-13	22	4	-5	45	14	2	58	21	9	80	26	14	103	29	17	97	27	16	95	22	10	70	15	4	49	5	-4	37	-4	-12	24
NASHVILLE, Tennessee	8	-3	108	10	-1	100	16	4	127	22	9	104	26	14	118	30	18	99	32	21	99	31	20	85	28	16	89	23	9	67	16	4	101	10	-1	112
NEW ORLEANS, Louisiana	16	5	136	18	7	147	22	11	124	26	15	119	29	18	135	32	22	147	33	23	167	32	23	157	30	21	138	26	15	76	22	11	101	18	7	132
NEW YORK, New York	3	-4	80	4	-3	76	9	1	99	15	7	94	21	12	93	26	17	80	29	21	101	28	20	107	24	16	85	18	10	81	12	5	96	6	-1	90
OKLAHOMA CITY, Okla.	8	-4	28	11	-1	36	17	4	61	22	9	76	26	14	145	31	19	107	34	21	74	34	21	65	29	17	97	23	10	80	16	4	43	10	-2	37
OMAHA, Nebraska	-1	-12	18	2	-9	21	9	-2	61	17	5	73	23	11	118	28	16	105	30	19	96	29	18	95	24	13	90	18	6	60	9	-1	35	1	-9	23
PENSACOLA, Florida	15	5	109	17	7	126	21	11	150	25	15	112	28	19	105	32	22	168	32	23	187	32	23	176	30	21	166	26	15	102	21	11	91	17	7	105
PHILADELPHIA, Pa.	3	-5	82	5	-4	70	11	1	95	17	6	88	23	12	94	28	17	87	30	20	108	29	19	97	25	15	86	19	8	67	13	3	85	6	-2	86
PHOENIX, Arizona	19	3	21	22	5	21	25	7	30	29	9	7	33	13	5	38	18	3	39	23	21	38	22	30	36	18	23	30	12	14	23	7	18	19	3	28
PITTSBURGH, Pa.	1	-8	66	3	-7	60	9	-1	85	16	4	80	21	9	92	26	14	91	28	16	98	27	16	83	24	12	74	17	6	61	10	1	69	4	-4	71
PORTLAND, Oregon	7	1	133	11	2	105	13	4	92	16	5	61	20	8	53	23	12	38	27	14	15	27	14	23	24	11	41	18	7	76	11	4	135	8	2	149
PROVIDENCE, R.I.	3	-7	101	4	-6	91	8	-2	111	14	3	102	20	9	89	25	14	77	28	17	77	27	17	102	24	12	88	18	6	93	12	2	117	5	-4	110
RALEIGH, N.C.	9	-2	89	11	0	88	17	4	94	22	8	70	26	13	96	29	18	91	31	20	111	30	20	110	27	16	79	22	9	77	17	4	76	12	0	79
RAPID CITY, S. Dak.	2	-12	10	4	-10	12	8	-6	26	14	0	52	20	6	84	25	12	89	30	15	63	29	13	43	23	7	32	17	1	26	8	-5	12	3	-11	10
RENO, Nevada	7	-6	28	11	-4	24	14	-2	20	18	1	11	23	5	17	28	8	11	33	11	7	32	10	6	26	5	9	20	1	10	12	-3	19	8	-7	27
ST. LOUIS, Missouri	3	-6	50	6	-4	54	13	2	84	19	8	97	25	13	100	30	19	103	32	21	92	31	20	76	27	16	73	20	9	70	13	3	78	5	-3	64
SALT LAKE CITY, Utah	2	-7	32	6	-4	30	11	0	45	16	3	52	22	8	46	28	13	23	33	18	18	32	17	21	26	11	27	19	5	34	10	-1	34	3	-6	34
SAN DIEGO, California	19	9	56	19	10	41	19	12	50	20	13	20	21	15	5	22	17	2	25	19	1	25	20	2	25	19	5	24	16	9	21	12	30	19	9	35
SAN FRANCISCO, Calif.	14	8	112	16	9	77	16	9	78	17	10	34	17	10	10	18	11	4	18	12	1	19	13	2	20	13	7	20	13	28	17	11	73	14	8	91

RED FIGURES: Average daily high temperature (°C)   **BLUE FIGURES:** Average daily low temperature (°C)   **BLACK FIGURES:** Average monthly rainfall (mm)

(Left margin: vertical FAHRENHEIT temperature scale — 20°, 10°, 00°, 90°, 80°, 70°, 60°, 50°, 40°, 30°, 20°, 10°, 0°, 10°, 20°, 30°, 40°, 50°, 60°)

Each monthly cell lists three values: average daily high (°C), average daily low (°C), average monthly rainfall (mm).

	JAN.	FEB.	MARCH	APRIL	MAY	JUNE	JULY	AUG.	SEPT.	OCT.	NOV.	DEC.
UNITED STATES												
SANTA FE, New Mexico	6 -10 11	9 -7 9	13 -5 12	18 -1 13	24 4 23	29 9 31	31 12 52	29 11 64	25 7 38	20 1 32	13 -5 14	7 -9 12
SEATTLE, Washington	7 2 141	10 3 107	12 4 94	14 5 64	18 8 42	21 11 38	24 13 20	24 13 27	21 11 47	15 8 89	10 5 149	7 2 149
SPOKANE, Washington	1 -6 52	5 -3 39	9 -1 37	14 2 28	20 6 35	24 10 33	28 12 15	28 12 16	22 8 20	15 2 31	5 -2 51	1 -6 57
TAMPA, Florida	21 10 54	22 11 73	25 14 90	28 16 44	31 20 76	32 23 143	32 24 189	32 24 196	32 23 160	29 18 60	25 14 46	22 11 54
VICKSBURG, Mississippi	14 2 155	16 3 131	21 8 160	25 12 147	29 16 130	32 20 88	33 22 106	33 21 80	30 18 85	26 12 106	20 8 126	16 4 168
WASHINGTON, D.C.	6 -3 71	8 -2 66	14 3 90	19 8 72	25 14 94	29 19 80	31 22 97	31 21 104	27 17 84	21 10 78	15 5 76	8 0 79
WICHITA, Kansas	4 -7 19	8 -5 23	14 1 57	20 7 57	25 12 99	30 18 105	34 21 82	33 20 78	27 15 85	21 8 62	13 1 37	6 -5 29
MIDDLE AMERICA												
ACAPULCO, Mexico	29 21 8	31 21 1	31 21 0	31 22 1	32 23 36	32 24 325	32 24 231	32 24 236	31 24 353	31 23 170	31 22 30	31 21 10
BALBOA, Panama	31 22 34	32 22 16	32 22 14	32 23 73	31 23 198	30 23 203	31 23 176	31 23 200	30 23 197	29 23 271	29 23 260	31 23 133
CHARLOTTE AMALIE, V.I.	28 23 50	27 22 41	28 23 49	28 23 63	29 24 105	30 25 67	31 26 71	31 26 112	31 26 132	31 25 139	29 24 131	28 23 69
GUATEMALA, Guatemala	23 12 4	25 12 5	27 14 10	28 14 32	29 16 110	27 16 257	26 16 197	26 16 193	26 16 235	24 16 98	24 13 33	23 13 13
GUAYMAS, Mexico	23 13 17	24 14 6	26 16 5	29 18 1	31 21 2	34 24 1	34 27 46	35 27 71	35 26 28	32 22 17	28 18 8	23 13 18
HAVANA, Cuba	26 18 71	26 18 46	27 19 46	29 21 58	30 22 119	31 23 165	32 24 124	32 24 135	31 24 150	29 23 173	27 21 79	26 19 58
KINGSTON, Jamaica	30 19 29	30 19 24	30 20 23	31 21 39	31 22 104	32 23 96	32 23 46	32 23 107	31 23 127	31 23 181	31 22 95	31 21 41
MANAGUA, Nicaragua	33 21 2	33 21 3	35 22 4	36 23 3	35 24 136	32 23 237	32 22 132	32 22 132	32 22 121	33 22 213	33 22 315	32 22 42
MÉRIDA, Mexico	28 17 30	29 17 23	32 19 18	33 21 20	34 22 81	33 23 142	33 23 132	33 22 142	32 22 173	32 22 97	29 19 33	28 18 33
MEXICO, Mexico	19 6 8	21 6 5	24 8 11	25 11 19	26 12 49	24 13 106	23 12 129	23 12 121	23 12 110	21 10 44	20 8 15	19 6 7
MONTERREY, Mexico	20 9 18	22 11 23	24 14 16	29 17 29	31 20 40	33 22 68	32 22 62	33 22 76	30 21 151	27 18 78	22 13 26	18 10 20
NASSAU, Bahamas	25 18 48	25 18 43	26 19 41	27 21 65	29 22 132	31 23 178	31 24 153	32 24 170	29 23 171	27 21 71	26 19 43	
PORT-AU-PRINCE, Haiti	31 20 32	31 20 50	32 21 79	32 22 156	32 22 218	33 23 96	34 23 73	34 23 139	33 23 166	32 22 164	31 22 84	31 21 35
PORT OF SPAIN, Trinidad	29 19 69	30 19 41	31 19 46	31 21 53	31 22 94	31 22 193	31 21 218	31 22 246	31 22 193	31 22 170	31 21 183	30 21 124
SAN JOSÉ, Costa Rica	24 14 11	24 14 5	26 15 14	26 17 46	27 17 224	26 17 276	25 17 215	26 16 243	26 16 326	25 16 323	25 16 148	24 14 42
SAN JUAN, Puerto Rico	27 21 75	27 21 56	27 21 59	28 22 95	29 23 156	29 24 112	29 24 115	29 24 133	30 24 136	29 24 140	29 23 148	27 22 118
SAN SALVADOR, El Salv.	32 16 7	33 16 7	34 17 13	34 18 53	33 19 179	31 19 315	32 18 312	32 19 307	31 19 317	31 18 230	31 17 40	32 16 12
SANTO DOMINGO, Dom. R.	29 19 57	29 19 43	29 19 49	29 21 77	30 22 179	31 22 154	31 22 155	31 23 162	31 22 173	31 22 164	30 21 111	29 19 63
TEGUCIGALPA, Honduras	25 13 9	27 14 4	29 14 8	30 17 32	29 18 151	28 18 159	28 17 82	28 17 87	28 17 185	27 16 135	26 16 38	25 15 12
SOUTH AMERICA												
ANTOFAGASTA, Chile	24 17 0	24 17 0	23 16 0	21 14 0	19 13 0	18 11 1	17 11 1	17 11 1	18 12 0	19 13 0	21 14 0	22 16 0
ASUNCIÓN, Paraguay	35 22 150	34 22 133	33 21 142	29 18 145	25 14 120	22 12 73	23 12 51	26 14 48	28 16 83	30 17 136	32 18 144	34 21 142
BELÉM, Brazil	31 22 351	30 22 412	31 23 441	31 23 370	31 23 282	31 22 164	31 22 154	31 22 122	32 22 129	32 22 105	32 22 101	32 22 202
BOGOTÁ, Colombia	19 9 48	20 9 52	19 10 81	19 11 119	19 11 103	18 11 61	18 10 47	18 10 48	19 9 58	19 10 142	19 10 115	19 9 67
BRASÍLIA, Brazil	27 18 262	27 18 213	28 18 202	28 17 103	26 13 20	25 11 4	26 11 4	28 13 6	31 16 35	28 18 140	28 19 238	26 18 329
BUENOS AIRES, Arg.	29 17 93	28 17 81	26 16 117	22 12 90	18 8 77	14 5 64	14 6 59	16 6 65	18 8 78	21 10 97	24 13 89	28 16 96
CARACAS, Venezuela	24 13 41	25 13 27	26 14 22	27 16 20	27 17 36	26 17 52	26 16 53	26 16 53	27 16 48	26 16 47	25 16 50	24 14 58
COM. RIVADAVIA, Arg.	26 13 16	25 13 11	22 11 21	18 8 21	14 6 34	11 3 21	11 3 25	12 3 22	14 5 13	19 9 13	22 10 13	24 12 15
CÓRDOBA, Argentina	31 16 110	30 16 102	28 14 96	24 11 45	21 7 25	18 3 10	18 3 10	21 4 13	23 7 27	25 11 69	28 13 97	30 16 118
GUAYAQUIL, Ecuador	31 21 224	31 22 278	31 22 287	32 22 180	31 20 53	31 20 17	29 19 2	30 18 0	31 19 2	30 20 3	31 20 3	31 21 30
LA PAZ, Bolivia	17 6 130	17 6 105	18 6 72	18 4 47	18 3 13	17 1 6	17 1 9	17 2 14	18 3 29	19 4 40	19 6 50	18 6 93
LIMA, Peru	28 19 1	28 19 1	28 19 1	27 17 0	23 16 1	20 14 2	19 14 4	19 13 3	20 14 3	22 14 2	23 16 1	26 17 1
MANAUS, Brazil	31 24 264	31 24 262	31 24 298	31 24 283	31 24 204	31 24 103	32 24 46	33 24 46	33 24 63	33 24 111	33 24 161	32 24 220
MARACAIBO, Venezuela	32 23 5	32 23 5	33 23 6	33 24 39	33 25 65	34 25 55	34 25 25	34 25 53	34 25 76	33 24 119	33 24 55	33 24 22
MONTEVIDEO, Uruguay	28 17 95	28 16 100	26 15 111	22 12 83	18 9 76	15 6 74	14 6 86	15 6 84	17 8 90	20 9 98	23 12 78	26 15 84
PARAMARIBO, Suriname	29 22 209	29 22 149	29 22 168	30 23 219	30 23 307	30 23 302	31 23 227	32 23 163	33 23 80	33 23 82	32 23 117	30 22 204
PUNTA ARENAS, Chile	14 7 35	14 7 28	12 5 39	10 4 41	7 2 42	5 1 32	4 -1 34	6 1 33	8 2 28	11 3 24	12 4 29	14 6 32
QUITO, Ecuador	22 8 113	22 8 128	22 8 154	21 8 176	21 8 124	22 7 48	22 7 20	23 7 24	23 7 78	22 8 127	22 7 109	22 8 103
RECIFE, Brazil	30 25 62	30 25 102	30 24 197	29 24 252	29 23 301	28 22 302	27 22 254	27 22 156	28 22 78	29 24 36	29 24 39	29 25 40
RIO DE JANEIRO, Brazil	29 23 135	29 23 124	28 22 134	27 21 109	25 19 78	24 18 52	24 17 45	24 18 46	24 18 62	25 19 82	26 20 100	28 22 137
SANTIAGO, Chile	29 12 3	29 11 3	27 9 5	23 7 13	18 5 64	14 3 84	15 3 76	17 4 56	19 6 30	22 7 15	26 9 8	28 11 5
SÃO PAULO, Brazil	27 17 225	28 18 208	27 17 160	26 14 71	23 12 67	22 11 54	22 9 35	23 11 48	23 12 77	24 14 117	26 15 139	27 16 185
VALPARAÍSO, Chile	22 13 0	22 13 0	21 12 0	19 11 22	17 10 38	16 9 100	16 8 111	16 8 42	17 9 27	18 10 15	21 11 15	22 12 1
EUROPE												
AJACCIO, Corsica	13 3 76	14 4 58	16 5 66	18 7 56	21 10 41	25 14 23	27 16 71	28 16 18	26 15 43	22 11 97	18 7 112	15 4 79
AMSTERDAM, Neth.	4 1 79	5 1 44	8 3 89	11 6 39	16 10 50	18 13 60	21 15 73	20 15 60	18 13 80	13 9 104	8 5 76	5 2 72
ATHENS, Greece	13 6 48	14 7 41	16 8 41	20 11 23	25 16 18	30 20 7	33 23 5	33 23 8	29 19 10	24 15 53	19 12 55	15 8 62
BARCELONA, Spain	13 6 38	14 7 38	16 9 47	18 11 47	21 14 44	25 18 38	28 21 28	28 21 44	25 19 76	21 15 96	16 11 51	13 8 44
BELFAST, N. Ireland	6 2 83	7 2 55	9 3 59	12 4 51	15 6 56	18 9 65	18 11 79	18 11 78	16 9 82	13 7 85	9 4 75	7 3 84
BELGRADE, Yugoslavia	3 -3 42	5 -2 39	11 2 43	18 7 57	23 12 73	26 15 84	28 17 63	28 17 53	24 13 47	18 8 50	11 4 55	5 0 52
BERLIN, Germany	2 -3 43	3 -3 38	8 0 38	13 4 41	19 8 49	22 12 64	24 14 71	23 13 62	20 10 44	13 6 44	7 2 46	3 -1 48
BIARRITZ, France	11 4 106	12 4 93	15 6 92	16 8 95	18 11 97	21 14 93	23 16 64	23 16 74	22 15 102	19 11 129	15 7 135	12 5 134
BORDEAUX, France	9 2 76	11 2 65	15 4 66	17 6 65	20 9 71	24 12 65	26 14 52	26 14 59	23 12 70	18 8 87	13 5 88	9 3 86
BRINDISI, Italy	12 6 57	13 7 61	15 8 67	18 11 35	22 14 26	26 18 20	29 21 9	29 21 25	26 18 47	22 15 71	18 11 72	14 8 65
BRUSSELS, Belgium	4 -1 82	7 0 51	10 2 81	14 5 53	18 8 74	22 11 74	23 12 58	22 12 42	21 11 69	15 7 85	9 3 61	6 0 68
BUCHAREST, Romania	1 -7 44	4 -5 37	10 -1 35	18 5 46	23 10 65	27 14 86	30 16 56	30 15 56	25 11 35	18 6 28	10 2 45	4 -3 42
BUDAPEST, Hungary	1 -4 41	4 -2 36	10 2 41	17 7 49	22 11 69	26 15 71	28 16 53	27 16 53	23 12 45	16 7 52	8 3 58	4 -1 49
CAGLIARI, Sardinia	14 7 53	15 7 52	17 9 45	19 11 35	23 14 27	27 18 10	30 21 3	30 21 10	27 19 27	23 15 57	19 11 56	16 9 55
CANDIA, Crete	16 9 94	16 9 76	17 10 41	20 12 23	23 15 18	27 19 3	29 21 1	29 22 3	27 19 18	24 17 43	21 14 69	18 11 102
COPENHAGEN, Denmark	2 -2 42	2 -3 25	5 -1 35	10 3 40	16 8 42	19 11 52	22 14 67	21 14 75	18 11 51	12 7 53	7 3 52	4 1 51
DUBLIN, Ireland	7 2 64	8 2 51	10 3 52	12 5 49	14 7 56	18 9 55	19 11 65	19 11 77	17 10 62	14 7 73	10 4 69	8 3 69
DURAZZO, Albania	11 6 76	12 6 84	13 8 99	17 13 56	22 17 41	25 21 48	28 23 13	28 22 48	24 18 43	20 14 180	14 11 216	12 8 185
EDINBURGH, Scotland	6 1 55	6 1 41	8 2 47	11 4 39	14 6 50	17 9 48	18 11 79	18 11 78	16 9 62	13 7 62	8 4 62	7 3 61
FLORENCE, Italy	9 2 64	11 3 62	14 5 69	19 8 71	23 12 73	27 15 56	30 18 34	30 17 47	26 15 99	20 11 99	14 7 103	11 4 79
GENEVA, Switzerland	4 -2 55	6 -1 53	10 2 60	15 5 63	19 9 76	23 13 81	25 15 72	24 14 90	21 12 90	14 7 91	8 3 81	4 0 66
HAMBURG, Germany	2 -2 61	3 -2 40	7 -1 52	13 3 47	18 7 55	21 11 74	22 13 81	22 12 79	19 10 68	13 6 62	7 3 65	4 0 71
HELSINKI, Finland	-3 -9 46	-4 -9 37	0 -7 35	6 -1 37	14 4 42	19 9 46	22 13 62	20 12 75	15 8 67	8 3 69	3 -1 66	-1 -5 55
LISBON, Portugal	14 8 95	15 8 87	17 10 85	20 12 60	21 13 43	25 15 16	27 17 4	28 17 7	26 17 33	22 14 75	17 11 100	15 9 97
LIVERPOOL, England	7 2 69	7 2 48	9 3 38	12 5 41	16 8 56	19 11 51	20 13 79	19 13 79	18 11 66	14 8 76	9 5 76	7 3 64
LONDON, England	7 2 62	7 2 36	11 3 50	14 4 43	17 7 45	21 11 46	23 13 46	22 12 44	19 11 43	14 7 73	9 4 45	7 2 50
LUXEMBOURG, Lux.	3 -1 66	4 -1 54	10 1 55	14 4 53	18 8 66	21 11 65	23 12 70	22 12 69	19 10 62	13 6 70	7 3 71	4 0 74
MADRID, Spain	9 2 45	11 2 43	15 5 37	18 7 45	21 10 40	27 15 25	31 17 9	30 17 10	25 14 29	19 10 46	13 5 64	9 2 47
MARSEILLE, France	10 2 49	12 2 40	15 5 45	18 8 46	22 11 46	26 15 26	29 17 15	28 17 24	25 14 63	20 10 94	15 6 76	11 3 59

WORLD TEMPERATURE AND RAINFALL

Average daily high and low temperatures and monthly rainfall for selected world locations:

EUROPE	JAN.			FEB.			MARCH			APRIL			MAY			JUNE			JULY			AUG.			SEPT.			OCT.			NOV.			DEC.		
MILAN, Italy	5	0	61	8	2	58	13	6	72	18	10	85	23	14	98	27	17	81	29	20	68	28	19	81	24	16	82	17	11	116	10	6	106	6	2	75
MUNICH, Germany	1	-5	49	3	-5	43	9	-1	52	14	3	70	18	7	101	21	11	123	23	13	127	23	12	112	20	9	83	13	4	62	7	0	54	2	-4	51
NANTES, France	8	2	79	9	2	62	13	4	62	15	6	54	19	9	61	22	12	55	24	14	50	24	13	54	21	12	70	16	8	89	11	5	91	8	3	86
NAPLES, Italy	12	4	94	13	5	81	15	6	76	18	9	66	22	12	46	26	16	46	29	18	15	29	18	18	26	16	71	22	12	130	17	9	114	14	6	137
NICE, France	13	4	77	13	5	73	15	7	73	17	9	64	20	13	49	24	16	37	27	18	19	27	18	32	25	16	65	21	12	111	17	8	117	13	5	88
OSLO, Norway	-2	-7	41	-1	-7	31	4	-4	34	10	1	36	16	6	45	20	10	59	22	13	75	21	12	86	16	8	72	9	3	71	3	-1	57	0	-4	49
PALERMO, Sicily	16	8	44	16	8	35	17	9	30	20	11	29	24	14	14	27	18	9	30	21	2	30	21	8	28	19	28	25	16	59	21	12	66	18	10	68
PALMA, Majorca	14	6	39	15	6	35	17	8	37	19	10	35	22	13	34	26	17	20	29	20	8	29	20	18	27	18	52	23	14	77	18	10	54	15	8	54
PARIS, France	6	1	46	7	1	39	12	4	41	16	6	44	20	10	56	23	13	57	25	15	57	24	14	55	21	12	53	16	8	57	10	5	54	7	2	49
PRAGUE, Czech. Rep.	1	-4	21	3	-2	19	7	1	26	13	4	36	18	9	59	22	13	68	23	14	67	23	14	62	18	11	41	12	7	30	5	2	27	1	-2	23
RIGA, Latvia	-4	10	32	-3	-10	24	2	-7	26	10	1	35	16	6	42	21	9	58	22	11	72	21	11	68	17	8	66	11	4	54	4	-1	52	-2	-7	39
ROME, Italy	11	5	80	13	5	71	15	7	69	19	10	67	23	13	52	28	17	34	30	20	16	30	19	24	26	17	69	22	13	113	16	9	111	13	6	97
SEVILLE, Spain	15	6	56	17	7	74	20	9	84	24	11	58	27	13	33	32	17	23	36	20	3	36	20	3	32	18	28	26	14	66	20	10	94	16	7	71
SOFIA, Bulgaria	2	-4	34	4	-3	34	10	1	38	16	5	54	21	10	69	24	14	78	27	16	56	26	15	43	22	11	40	17	8	35	9	3	52	4	-2	44
SPLIT, Croatia	10	5	80	11	5	65	14	7	65	18	11	62	23	16	62	27	19	48	30	22	28	30	22	43	26	19	66	20	14	87	15	10	111	12	7	113
STOCKHOLM, Sweden	-1	-5	31	-1	-5	25	3	-4	26	8	1	29	14	6	34	19	11	44	22	14	64	20	13	66	15	9	49	9	5	51	5	1	44	2	-2	39
VALENCIA, Spain	15	6	23	16	6	38	18	8	23	20	10	30	23	13	28	26	17	33	29	20	10	29	20	13	27	18	56	23	13	41	19	10	64	16	7	33
VALETTA, Malta	14	10	84	15	10	58	16	11	38	18	13	20	22	16	10	26	19	3	29	22	1	29	23	5	27	22	33	24	19	69	20	16	91	16	12	99
VENICE, Italy	6	1	51	8	2	53	12	5	61	17	10	71	21	14	81	25	17	84	27	19	66	27	18	66	24	16	66	19	11	94	12	7	89	8	3	66
VIENNA, Austria	1	-4	38	3	-3	36	8	1	46	15	6	51	19	10	71	23	14	69	25	15	76	24	15	69	20	11	51	14	7	25	7	3	48	3	-1	46
WARSAW, Poland	0	-6	28	0	-6	26	6	-2	31	12	3	37	20	9	50	23	12	66	24	15	77	23	14	72	19	10	47	13	5	41	6	1	38	2	-3	35
ZÜRICH, Switzerland	2	-3	61	5	-2	61	10	1	68	15	4	85	19	8	101	23	12	127	25	14	128	24	13	124	20	11	98	14	6	83	7	2	71	3	-2	72
ASIA																																				
ADEN, Yemen	27	23	8	27	23	7	29	24	8	31	26	4	34	28	3	35	29	1	34	28	2	33	27	3	34	28	4	32	26	2	29	24	2	27	23	4
ALMATY, Kazakhstan	-5	-14	33	-3	13	23	4	-6	56	13	3	102	20	10	94	24	14	66	27	16	36	27	14	30	22	8	25	13	2	51	4	-5	48	-2	-9	33
ANKARA, Turkey	4	-4	49	6	-3	52	11	-1	45	17	4	44	23	9	56	26	12	37	30	15	13	31	15	8	26	11	28	21	7	21	14	3	28	6	-2	63
ARKHANGEL'SK, Russia	-12	-20	30	-10	-18	28	-4	-13	28	5	-4	18	12	2	33	17	6	48	20	10	66	19	10	69	12	5	56	4	-1	48	-2	-7	41	-8	-15	33
BAGHDAD, Iraq	16	4	27	18	6	28	22	9	27	29	14	19	36	19	7	41	23	0	43	24	0	43	24	0	40	21	0	33	16	3	25	11	20	18	6	26
BALIKPAPAN, Indonesia	29	23	243	30	23	221	30	23	249	29	23	226	29	23	258	29	23	252	28	23	259	29	23	257	29	23	201	29	23	186	29	23	176	29	23	245
BANGKOK, Thailand	32	20	11	33	22	28	34	24	31	35	25	72	34	25	189	33	24	152	32	24	158	32	24	187	32	24	320	31	24	231	31	22	57	31	20	9
BEIJING, China	2	-9	4	5	-7	5	12	-1	8	20	7	18	27	13	33	31	18	78	32	22	224	31	21	170	27	14	58	21	7	18	10	-1	9	3	-7	3
BEIRUT, Lebanon	17	11	187	17	11	151	19	12	96	22	14	51	26	18	19	28	21	2	31	23	0	32	23	0	30	23	6	27	21	48	23	16	119	18	13	176
BOMBAY, India	28	19	3	28	19	1	30	22	1	32	24	2	33	27	14	32	26	518	29	25	647	29	24	384	29	24	276	32	24	55	32	23	15	31	21	2
BRUNEI	30	24	371	30	24	193	31	24	198	32	24	249	32	24	277	31	24	241	31	25	229	31	24	185	31	24	300	31	24	368	31	24	386	30	24	330
CALCUTTA, India	27	13	12	29	15	25	34	21	32	36	24	53	36	25	129	33	26	291	32	26	329	32	26	338	32	26	266	32	23	131	29	18	21	26	13	7
CHONGQING, China	9	5	18	13	7	21	18	11	38	23	16	94	27	19	148	29	22	174	34	24	151	35	25	128	28	22	144	22	16	103	16	12	49	13	8	23
COLOMBO, Sri Lanka	30	22	84	31	22	64	31	23	114	31	24	255	31	26	335	29	25	190	29	25	129	29	25	96	29	25	158	29	24	353	29	23	308	29	22	152
DAMASCUS, Syria	12	2	39	14	4	32	18	6	23	24	9	13	29	13	5	33	16	1	36	18	0	37	18	0	33	16	0	27	12	9	19	8	26	13	4	42
DAVAO, Philippines	31	22	117	32	22	110	32	22	109	33	22	149	32	23	223	31	23	205	31	22	171	31	22	161	32	22	177	32	22	184	32	22	139	31	22	139
DHAKA, Bangladesh	26	13	8	28	15	21	32	20	58	33	23	116	33	24	267	32	26	358	31	26	399	31	26	317	32	26	256	31	24	164	29	19	30	26	14	6
HANOI, Vietnam	20	13	20	21	14	30	23	17	64	28	21	91	32	23	104	33	26	284	33	26	302	32	26	386	31	24	254	29	22	89	26	18	66	22	15	71
HO CHI MINH CITY, Viet.	32	21	14	33	22	4	34	23	9	35	24	51	33	24	213	32	24	309	31	24	295	31	24	271	31	23	342	31	23	261	31	23	119	31	22	47
HONG KONG, China	18	13	27	17	13	44	19	16	75	24	19	140	28	23	298	29	26	399	31	26	371	31	26	377	29	25	297	27	23	119	23	18	38	20	15	25
IRKUTSK, Russia	-16	-26	13	-12	-25	10	-4	-17	8	6	-7	15	13	1	33	20	7	56	21	10	79	20	9	71	14	2	43	5	-6	18	-7	-17	15	-16	-24	15
ISTANBUL, Turkey	8	3	91	9	2	69	11	3	62	16	7	42	21	12	30	25	16	28	28	18	24	28	19	31	24	16	48	20	13	66	15	9	92	11	5	114
JAKARTA, Indonesia	29	23	342	29	23	302	30	23	210	31	24	135	31	24	108	31	23	90	31	23	59	31	23	48	31	23	69	31	23	106	30	23	139	29	23	208
JEDDAH, Saudi Arabia	29	19	5	29	18	1	29	19	1	33	21	1	35	23	1	36	24	0	37	23	1	37	27	1	36	25	1	35	23	1	33	22	25	30	19	30
JERUSALEM, Israel	13	5	140	13	6	111	18	8	116	23	10	17	27	14	6	29	16	0	31	17	0	31	18	0	29	17	0	27	15	11	21	12	68	15	7	129
KABUL, Afghanistan	2	-8	33	4	-6	54	12	1	70	19	6	66	26	11	21	31	13	1	33	16	5	33	15	1	29	11	2	23	6	4	17	1	11	8	-3	21
KARACHI, Pakistan	25	13	7	26	14	10	29	19	10	32	23	3	34	26	0	34	28	10	33	27	90	31	26	58	31	25	27	33	22	3	31	18	3	27	14	5
KATHMANDU, Nepal	18	2	17	19	4	15	25	7	30	28	12	37	30	16	102	29	19	201	29	20	375	28	20	325	28	19	189	27	13	56	23	7	2	19	3	10
KUNMING, China	16	3	11	18	4	14	21	7	17	24	11	20	26	14	90	25	17	175	25	17	205	25	17	203	24	15	126	21	12	78	18	7	40	17	3	13
LAHORE, Pakistan	21	4	25	22	7	24	28	12	27	35	17	15	40	22	17	41	26	39	38	27	155	36	26	135	36	23	63	35	15	10	28	8	3	23	4	14
LHASA, China	7	-10	0	9	-7	3	12	-2	4	16	1	6	19	5	24	24	9	72	23	9	132	22	9	128	21	7	58	17	1	9	13	-5	1	9	-9	1
MADRAS, India	29	19	29	31	20	9	33	22	9	35	26	17	38	28	44	38	27	52	36	26	99	35	26	124	34	25	125	32	24	285	29	22	345	29	21	138
MANAMA, Bahrain	30	14	14	21	15	16	24	17	11	29	21	8	33	26	1	36	28	0	37	29	0	38	29	0	36	27	0	32	24	0	28	21	7	22	16	17
MANDALAY, Myanmar	28	13	2	31	15	13	36	19	7	38	25	35	37	26	142	34	26	124	34	26	83	33	25	113	33	24	155	32	23	125	29	19	45	27	14	10
MANILA, Philippines	30	21	21	31	21	10	33	22	15	34	23	30	34	24	123	33	24	262	31	24	423	31	24	421	31	24	353	31	23	197	31	22	135	30	21	65
MOSCOW, Russia	-9	16	38	-6	-14	36	0	-8	28	10	1	46	19	8	56	21	11	74	23	13	76	22	12	74	16	7	48	9	3	69	2	-3	43	-5	-10	41
MUSCAT, Oman	25	19	28	25	19	18	28	22	10	32	26	10	37	30	1	38	31	3	36	31	1	33	29	1	34	28	0	34	27	3	30	23	10	26	20	18
NAGASAKI, Japan	9	2	75	10	2	87	14	5	124	19	10	190	23	14	191	26	18	326	29	23	284	31	23	187	27	20	236	22	14	108	17	9	89	12	4	80
NEW DELHI, India	21	7	23	24	9	20	31	14	15	36	20	10	41	26	15	39	28	68	36	27	200	34	26	200	34	24	123	34	18	19	29	11	3	23	8	10
NICOSIA, Cyprus	15	5	70	16	5	50	19	7	35	24	10	21	29	14	26	34	18	9	37	21	1	37	21	2	33	18	6	28	14	23	22	10	41	17	7	74
ODESA, Ukraine	0	-6	25	2	-4	18	5	-1	18	12	6	28	19	12	28	23	16	48	26	18	41	26	18	36	21	14	28	16	9	36	10	4	28	4	-2	28
PHNOM PENH, Cambodia	31	21	7	32	22	9	34	23	32	34	24	73	33	24	149	33	24	149	32	24	151	32	24	157	31	24	231	31	24	259	30	23	129	30	22	38
PONTIANAK, Indonesia	31	23	275	32	23	213	32	23	242	33	23	280	33	23	279	32	23	228	32	23	178	32	23	206	32	23	245	32	23	356	31	23	385	31	23	321
RIYADH, Saudi Arabia	21	8	14	23	9	10	28	13	30	32	18	30	38	22	13	42	25	0	42	26	0	42	24	0	39	22	0	34	16	1	29	13	5	21	9	11
ST. PETERSBURG, Russia	-7	-13	25	-5	-12	23	0	-8	23	8	4	25	15	6	41	20	11	51	21	13	64	20	13	71	15	9	53	9	4	46	2	-2	36	-3	-8	30
SANDAKAN, Malaysia	29	23	454	29	23	271	30	23	200	31	23	118	32	23	153	32	23	196	32	23	185	32	23	205	32	23	240	31	23	263	31	23	356	30	23	470
SAPPORO, Japan	-2	-12	100	-1	-11	79	2	-7	70	11	0	61	16	4	59	21	10	65	24	14	86	26	16	117	22	11	136	16	4	114	8	-2	106	1	-8	102
SEOUL, South Korea	0	-9	21	3	-7	28	8	-2	49	17	5	105	22	11	88	27	16	151	29	21	384	31	22	263	26	15	160	19	7	49	11	0	43	3	-7	24
SHANGHAI, China	8	1	47	8	1	61	13	4	85	19	10	95	25	15	104	28	19	174	32	23	145	32	23	137	28	19	138	23	14	69	17	7	52	12	2	37
SINGAPORE, Singapore	30	23	239	31	23	165	31	24	174	31	24	166	32	24	171	31	24	163	31	24	150	31	24	171	31	24	164	31	23	191	31	23	250	31	23	269
TAIPEI, China	19	12	95	18	12	141	21	14	162	25	17	167	28	21	209	32	23	280	33	24	248	33	24	277	31	23	201	27	19	112	24	17	76	21	14	76
T'BILISI, Georgia	6	-2	16	7	-1	21	12	2	30	18	7	52	23	12	83	27	16	73	31	19	49	31	19	40	26	15	44	20	9	39	13	4	32	8	0	21
TEHRAN, Iran	7	-3	42	10	0	37	15	4	39	22	9	33	28	14	15	34	19	3	37	22	2	36	22	2	32	18	2	24	12	9	17	6	24	11	1	32
TEL AVIV-YAFO, Israel	17	9	165	18	9	64	19	10	58	23	12	13	27	16	3	29	18	0	31	21	0	31	21	0	30	20	1	29	18	14	25	15	85	19	11	144
TOKYO, Japan	8	-2	50	9	-1	72	12	2	106	17	8	129	22	12	144	24	17	176	28	21	136	30	22	149	26	19	216	21	13	194	16	6	96	11	1	54
ULAANBAATAR, Mongolia	-19	-32	1	-13	-29	1	-4	-22	3	7	-8	5	13	-2	8	21	7	25	22	11	74	21	8	48	14	2	20	6	-8	5	-6	20	5	-16	-28	3
VIENTIANE, Laos	28	14	7	30	17	18	33	19	41	34	23	88	32	23	212	32	24	216	31	24	209	31	24	254	31	24	244	31	21	81	29	18	16	28	16	5
VLADIVOSTOK, Russia	-11	-18	8	-6	-14	10	1	-7	18	8	1	30	13	6	53	17	11	74	22	16	84	24	18	119	20	13	109	13	5	48	2	-4	30	-7	-13	15

RED FIGURES: Average daily high temperature (°C) BLUE FIGURES: Average daily low temperature (°C) BLACK FIGURES: Average monthly rainfall (mm)

(Each cell lists three values: daily high temperature / daily low temperature / monthly rainfall.)

	JAN.	FEB.	MARCH	APRIL	MAY	JUNE	JULY	AUG.	SEPT.	OCT.	NOV.	DEC.
ASIA												
WUHAN, China	8 1 41	9 2 57	14 6 92	21 13 136	26 18 165	31 23 212	34 26 165	34 26 114	29 21 73	23 16 74	17 9 49	11 3 30
YAKUTSK, Russia	-43 -47 8	-33 -40 5	-18 -29 3	-3 -14 8	9 -1 10	19 9 28	23 12 41	19 9 33	10 1 28	-5 12 13	-26 31 10	-39 -43 8
YANGON, Myanmar	32 18 4	33 19 4	36 22 17	36 24 47	33 25 307	30 24 478	29 24 535	29 24 511	30 24 368	31 24 183	31 23 62	31 19 11
YEKATERINBURG, Russia	-14 -21 8	-10 -17 10	-4 -12 5	6 -3 8	14 4 15	18 9 48	21 12 38	18 10 53	12 5 46	3 -2 23	-7 12 10	-12 -18 8
AFRICA												
ABIDJAN, Côte d'Ivoire	31 23 22	32 24 47	32 24 110	32 24 142	31 24 309	29 23 543	28 23 238	28 22 36	28 23 74	29 23 172	31 23 168	31 23 85
ACCRA, Ghana	31 23 15	31 24 29	31 24 57	31 24 90	31 24 136	29 23 199	27 23 50	27 22 19	27 23 43	29 23 64	31 24 34	31 24 20
ADDIS ABABA, Ethiopia	24 6 17	24 8 38	25 9 68	25 10 86	25 10 86	23 9 132	21 10 268	21 10 281	22 9 186	24 7 28	23 6 11	23 5 10
ALEXANDRIA, Egypt	18 11 52	19 11 28	21 13 13	23 15 4	26 18 1	28 21 0	31 23 0	30 23 1	28 20 8	25 17 35	21 13 55	
ALGIERS, Algeria	15 9 93	16 9 73	17 11 67	20 13 52	23 15 34	26 18 14	28 21 2	29 22 5	27 21 33	23 17 77	19 13 96	16 11 114
ANTANANARIVO, Madag.	26 16 287	26 16 262	26 16 194	24 14 57	23 12 18	21 10 9	20 9 8	21 9 10	23 11 16	27 12 61	27 14 153	27 16 290
ASMARA, Eritrea	23 7 0	24 8 0	25 9 1	26 11 7	26 12 23	26 12 48	22 12 114	22 12 123	23 13 49	22 12 4	22 10 3	22 9 0
BAMAKO, Mali	33 16 0	36 19 0	39 22 3	39 24 19	39 24 59	34 23 131	32 22 229	31 22 307	32 22 198	34 22 63	34 18 7	33 17 0
BANGUI, Cen. Af. Rep.	32 20 20	34 21 39	33 22 107	33 22 133	32 21 163	31 21 143	29 21 181	29 21 225	31 21 190	31 21 202	31 20 93	32 19 29
BEIRA, Mozambique	32 24 267	32 24 259	31 23 263	30 22 117	28 18 67	26 16 40	25 16 34	26 17 33	28 18 25	31 22 34	31 22 121	31 23 243
BENGHAZI, Libya	17 10 66	18 11 41	21 12 20	23 14 5	26 17 3	28 20 1	29 22 1	29 22 1	28 21 3	27 19 18	23 16 46	19 12 66
BUJUMBURA, Burundi	29 20 97	29 20 97	29 20 126	29 20 129	29 20 64	29 19 11	30 19 3	30 19 17	31 20 43	31 20 62	29 20 98	29 20 100
CAIRO, Egypt	18 8 5	21 9 4	24 11 4	28 14 2	33 17 1	35 20 0	36 21 0	35 22 0	32 20 0	30 18 1	24 14 3	20 10 6
CAPE TOWN, S. Africa	26 16 16	26 16 15	25 14 22	22 12 50	19 9 92	18 8 105	17 7 91	18 8 83	18 9 54	21 11 40	23 13 24	24 14 19
CASABLANCA, Morocco	17 7 57	18 8 53	19 9 51	21 11 38	22 13 21	24 16 6	26 18 0	27 19 1	26 17 6	24 14 34	21 11 65	18 8 73
CONAKRY, Guinea	31 22 1	31 23 1	32 23 6	32 23 21	32 24 141	30 23 503	28 22 1210	28 22 1016	29 23 664	31 23 318	31 24 106	31 23 14
DAKAR, Senegal	26 18 1	27 17 1	27 18 0	27 18 0	29 20 1	31 23 15	31 24 75	31 24 215	32 24 146	32 24 42	30 23 3	27 19 4
DAR ES SALAAM, Tanzania	31 25 66	31 25 66	31 24 130	30 23 290	29 22 188	29 20 33	28 19 31	28 19 30	29 19 30	29 21 41	30 22 74	31 24 91
DURBAN, S. Africa	27 21 119	27 21 126	27 20 132	26 18 84	24 14 56	23 12 34	22 11 35	22 13 49	23 15 73	24 17 110	25 18 118	26 19 120
HARARE, Zimbabwe	26 16 190	26 16 177	26 14 107	26 13 33	23 9 10	21 7 3	21 7 1	23 8 2	26 12 7	28 14 32	27 16 93	26 16 173
JOHANNESBURG, S. Africa	26 14 150	25 14 129	24 13 110	22 10 48	19 6 24	17 4 6	17 4 10	20 6 10	23 9 25	25 12 65	25 13 126	26 14 141
KAMPALA, Uganda	28 18 58	28 18 68	27 18 128	26 18 185	26 17 134	25 17 71	25 17 55	26 16 87	27 17 100	27 17 119	27 17 142	27 17 95
KHARTOUM, Sudan	32 15 0	34 16 0	38 19 0	41 22 0	42 25 4	41 26 7	38 25 49	37 24 69	39 25 21	40 24 5	36 20 0	33 17 0
KINSHASA, D.R.C.	31 21 138	31 22 148	32 22 184	32 22 220	31 22 145	29 19 5	27 18 3	29 18 4	31 20 40	31 21 133	31 22 235	30 21 156
KISANGANI, D.R.C.	31 21 97	31 21 107	31 21 172	31 21 190	31 21 162	30 21 128	29 19 114	28 20 178	29 20 164	30 20 233	29 20 207	30 20 105
LAGOS, Nigeria	31 23 27	32 25 44	32 26 98	32 25 146	31 24 252	29 23 414	28 23 253	28 23 69	28 23 153	29 23 197	31 24 66	31 24 25
LIBREVILLE, Gabon	31 23 164	31 22 137	32 23 248	32 23 232	31 22 181	29 21 24	28 20 3	29 21 6	29 22 69	30 22 332	30 22 378	31 22 197
LIVINGSTONE, Zambia	29 19 175	29 19 160	29 18 95	30 15 25	28 11 5	25 7 1	25 7 0	28 10 0	32 15 2	34 19 26	33 19 78	31 19 176
LUANDA, Angola	28 23 34	29 24 35	30 24 90	29 24 127	28 23 18	25 20 0	23 18 0	23 18 1	24 19 2	26 22 6	28 23 32	28 23 23
LUBUMBASHI, D.R.C.	28 16 253	28 17 256	28 16 210	28 14 51	27 10 4	27 7 1	26 6 0	28 8 0	32 11 6	33 14 31	31 16 150	28 17 272
LUSAKA, Zambia	26 17 213	26 17 172	26 17 104	26 15 22	25 12 3	23 10 0	23 9 0	25 12 0	29 15 1	31 18 14	29 18 86	27 17 200
LUXOR, Egypt	23 6 0	26 7 0	30 10 0	35 15 0	40 21 0	41 21 0	42 23 0	41 23 0	39 22 0	37 18 1	31 12 0	26 7 0
MAPUTO, Mozambique	30 22 153	31 22 134	29 21 99	28 19 52	27 16 29	25 13 18	24 13 15	26 14 13	27 16 32	28 18 51	28 19 78	29 21 94
MARRAKECH, Morocco	18 4 27	20 6 31	23 9 36	26 11 32	29 14 17	33 17 7	38 19 2	38 20 3	33 17 7	28 14 20	23 9 37	19 6 28
MOGADISHU, Somalia	30 23 0	30 23 0	31 24 8	32 26 58	32 25 59	29 23 78	28 23 67	28 23 42	29 23 21	30 24 30	31 24 40	30 24 9
MONROVIA, Liberia	30 23 5	29 23 3	31 23 112	31 23 297	30 22 340	27 22 917	27 22 615	27 22 472	27 22 759	28 22 640	29 23 208	30 23 74
NAIROBI, Kenya	25 12 45	26 13 43	25 14 73	24 14 160	22 13 119	21 12 30	21 11 13	21 11 13	24 11 26	24 13 42	23 13 121	23 13 77
N'DJAMENA, Chad	34 14 0	37 16 0	40 21 0	42 23 8	40 25 31	38 24 62	33 22 150	31 22 215	33 22 91	36 21 22	36 17 0	33 14 0
NIAMEY, Niger	34 14 0	37 18 0	41 22 3	42 25 6	41 27 35	38 25 75	34 23 143	32 23 187	34 23 90	38 23 16	38 18 1	34 15 0
NOUAKCHOTT, Maurit.	29 14 1	31 15 3	32 17 1	32 18 1	34 21 1	33 23 3	32 23 13	32 24 104	34 24 23	33 22 10	32 18 3	28 13 1
TIMBUKTU, Mali	31 13 0	34 14 0	38 19 0	42 22 1	43 26 4	43 27 19	39 25 62	36 24 79	39 24 33	40 23 3	37 18 0	32 13 0
TRIPOLI, Libya	16 8 69	17 9 40	19 11 27	22 14 13	24 16 5	27 19 1	29 22 0	30 22 1	29 21 11	27 18 38	23 14 60	18 9 81
TUNIS, Tunisia	14 6 62	16 7 52	18 8 46	21 11 38	24 13 22	29 17 10	32 20 3	33 21 7	31 19 32	25 15 55	20 11 54	16 7 63
WADI HALFA, Sudan	24 9 0	27 10 0	31 14 0	36 18 0	40 22 1	41 24 0	41 25 1	41 25 0	40 24 0	37 21 0	30 15 0	25 11 0
YAOUNDÉ, Cameroon	29 19 26	29 19 55	29 19 140	29 19 193	28 19 216	27 19 163	27 19 62	27 18 80	27 19 216	27 18 292	28 19 120	28 19 28
ZANZIBAR, Tanzania	32 24 75	33 24 61	33 25 150	30 25 350	29 24 251	28 23 54	28 22 44	28 22 39	29 22 48	30 23 86	32 24 201	32 24 145
ZOMBA, Malawi	27 18 299	27 18 269	26 18 230	26 17 85	24 14 23	22 12 13	22 12 8	24 13 8	27 15 8	29 18 29	29 19 124	27 18 281
ATLANTIC LANDS												
ASCENSION ISLAND	29 23 4	31 23 8	31 24 23	31 24 27	31 23 10	29 23 14	29 22 12	28 22 10	28 22 8	28 22 7	28 22 4	29 22 3
FALKLAND ISLANDS	13 6 71	13 5 58	12 4 64	9 3 66	7 1 66	5 -1 53	5 -1 51	7 1 38	9 2 41	11 3 51	12 4 71	
FUNCHAL, Madeira Is.	19 13 87	18 13 88	19 13 79	19 14 43	21 16 22	22 17 9	24 19 2	24 19 3	24 19 27	23 18 85	22 16 106	19 14 87
HAMILTON, Bermuda Is.	20 14 112	20 14 119	20 14 122	22 15 104	24 18 117	27 21 112	29 23 114	30 23 137	29 22 132	26 21 147	23 17 127	21 16 119
LAS PALMAS, Canary Is.	21 14 28	22 14 21	22 15 15	22 16 10	23 17 3	24 18 1	25 19 1	26 21 0	26 21 6	26 19 18 (-3)	24 18 37	22 16 32
NUUK, Greenland	-7 -12 36	-7 -13 43	-4 -11 41	-1 -7 30	4 -2 43	8 1 36	11 3 56	11 3 79	6 1 84	2 -1 64	-2 -7 48	-5 -10 38
PONTA DELGADA, Azores	17 12 105	17 11 91	17 12 87	18 12 62	20 13 57	22 15 36	25 17 25	26 18 34	25 17 75	22 24 97	20 14 108	18 12 98
PRAIA, Cape Verde	25 20 1	25 19 2	26 20 0	26 21 0	27 21 0	28 22 0	28 24 7	29 24 63	29 25 88	29 23 44	28 23 15	26 21 5
REYKJAVÍK, Iceland	2 -2 86	3 -2 75	4 -1 76	6 1 56	10 4 42	12 7 45	14 9 51	14 8 62	11 6 71	7 -13 88	4 0 83	2 -2 84
THULE, Greenland	-17 -27 7	-20 -29 8	-19 -28 4	-13 -23 4	-2 -9 5	5 -1 6	8 2 14	6 1 17	1 -6 13	-5 11	-11 -19 11	-18 -27 5
TRISTAN DA CUNHA	19 15 103	20 16 110	19 14 133	18 14 137	16 12 153	14 11 153	14 10 54	13 9 162	13 9 157	15 11 148	16 12 124	18 14 131
PACIFIC LANDS												
APIA, Samoa	30 24 437	29 24 360	30 23 356	30 24 236	29 23 174	29 23 135	29 23 100	29 23 111	29 23 144	29 24 206	30 23 259	29 23 374
AUCKLAND, New Zealand	23 16 70	23 16 86	22 15 77	19 13 96	17 11 115	14 9 126	13 8 131	14 8 112	16 9 94	17 11 93	19 12 82	21 14 78
DARWIN, Australia	32 25 396	32 25 331	33 25 282	33 24 97	32 23 18	31 21 3	31 19 1	32 21 4	33 23 15	34 25 60	34 26 130	33 26 239
DUNEDIN, New Zealand	19 10 81	19 10 70	17 9 78	15 7 75	12 5 78	9 4 78	9 3 70	11 3 61	13 5 61	15 6 70	17 7 79	18 9 81
GALÁPAGOS IS., Ecuador	30 22 20	30 24 36	31 24 28	31 24 18	30 23 1	28 22 1	27 21 1	27 19 1	27 19 1	27 19 1	27 20 1	28 21 1
GUAM, Mariana Is.	29 24 138	29 23 116	29 24 121	31 24 108	31 25 164	31 25 150	30 24 274	30 24 368	30 24 374	30 24 334	30 24 231	29 24 160
HOBART, Tasmania	22 12 51	22 12 38	20 11 46	17 9 51	14 7 46	12 5 51	11 4 51	13 5 48	15 6 47	17 8 60	19 9 52	21 11 57
MELBOURNE, Australia	26 14 48	26 14 47	24 13 52	20 11 57	17 8 58	14 7 49	13 6 49	15 6 50	17 8 59	19 9 67	22 11 60	24 12 59
NAHA, Okinawa	19 13 125	19 13 126	21 15 159	24 18 165	27 20 252	29 24 280	32 25 178	31 25 270	31 24 175	27 21 165	24 18 133	21 14 111
NOUMÉA, N. Caledonia	30 22 111	29 23 130	29 22 155	28 21 121	26 19 106	25 18 107	24 17 91	24 16 73	26 17 56	27 18 53	28 20 55	30 21 77
PAPEETE, Tahiti	32 22 335	32 22 292	32 22 165	32 22 173	31 21 124	30 21 81	30 20 66	30 20 48	30 21 58	31 21 86	31 22 165	31 22 302
PERTH, Australia	29 17 9	29 17 13	27 16 19	24 14 45	21 12 122	18 10 182	17 9 174	18 9 136	19 10 80	21 12 53	24 14 21	27 16 13
PORT MORESBY, P.N.G.	32 24 179	32 24 196	31 24 190	31 24 120	30 24 65	29 23 39	28 23 27	28 23 28	29 23 30	30 24 35	31 24 56	32 24 125
SUVA, Fiji Islands	30 23 305	30 23 293	30 23 367	29 23 342	28 22 261	27 21 166	26 20 142	26 20 184	27 21 200	28 21 217	28 22 266	29 23 296
SYDNEY, Australia	26 18 103	26 18 111	24 17 131	22 14 130	19 11 123	16 9 129	16 8 103	17 9 80	19 11 69	22 13 83	23 16 81	25 17 78
WELLINGTON, N.Z.	21 13 79	21 13 80	19 12 85	17 11 98	14 8 121	13 7 124	12 6 139	12 6 121	14 8 99	16 9 105	17 10 88	19 12 90

(Left margin Fahrenheit scale: 120°, 110°, 100°, 90°, 80°, 70°, 60°, 50°, 40°, 30°, 20°, 10°, 0°, -10°, -20°, -30°, -40°, -50°, -60°)

GLOSSARY OF GEOGRAPHIC TERMS

A

abyssal plain a flat, relatively featureless region of the deep ocean floor extending from the Mid-Ocean Ridge to a continental rise or deep-sea trench

acculturation the process of losing the traits of one cultural group while assimilating with another cultural group

alluvial fan a depositional, fan-shaped feature found where a stream or channel gradient levels out at the base of a mountain

antipode a point that lies diametrically opposite any given point on the surface of the Earth

Archean eon the earliest eon of Earth's geologic history

archipelago an associated group of scattered islands in a large body of water

asthenosphere the uppermost zone of Earth's mantle; it consists of rocks in a "plastic" state, immediately below the lithosphere

atmosphere the thin envelope of gases surrounding the solid Earth and comprising mostly nitrogen, oxygen, and various trace gases

atoll a circular coral reef enclosing a lagoon

B

barrier island a low-lying, sandy island parallel to a shoreline but separated from the mainland by a lagoon

basin a low-lying depression in the Earth's surface; some basins are filled with water and sediment, while others are dry most of the time.

biodiversity a broad concept that refers to the variety and range of species (flora and fauna) present in an ecosystem

biogeography the study of the distribution patterns of plants and animals and the processes that produce those patterns

biome a very large ecosystem made up of specific plant and animal communities interacting with the physical environment (climate and soil)

biosphere the realm of Earth that includes all plant and animal life-forms

bluff a steep slope or wall of consolidated sediment adjacent to a river or its floodplain

bog soft, spongy, waterlogged ground consisting chiefly of partially decayed plant matter (peat)

butte a tall, steep-sided, flat-topped tower of rock that is a remnant of extensive erosional processes

C

caldera a large, crater-like feature with steep, circular walls and a central depression resulting from the explosion and collapse of a volcano

capitalism an economic system characterized by resource allocation primarily through market mechanisms; means of production are privately owned (by either individuals or corporations), and production is organized around profit maximization

carbon cycle one of the several geochemical cycles by which matter is recirculated through the lithosphere, hydrosphere, atmosphere, and biosphere

carrying capacity the maximum number of animals and/or people a given area can support at a given time under specified levels of consumption

cartographer a person who interprets, designs, and creates maps and other modes of geographic representations

civilization a cultural concept suggesting substantial development in the form of agriculture, cities, food and labor surplus, labor specialization, social stratification, and state organization

climate the long-term behavior of the atmosphere; it includes measures of average weather conditions (e.g., temperature, humidity, precipitation, and pressure), as well as trends, cycles, and extremes

continental drift a theory that suggests the continents were at one time all part of a prehistoric supercontinent that broke apart; according to the theory, the continents slowly "drifted" across the Earth's surface to their present positions

continental shelf the submerged, offshore extension of a continent

Coriolis effect the deflection of wind systems and ocean currents (as well as freely moving objects not in contact with the solid Earth) toward the right in the Northern Hemisphere and to the left in the Southern Hemisphere as a consequence of the Earth's rotation on its axis

cultural diffusion the spread of cultural elements from one group to another

culture the "way of life" for a group; it is transmitted from generation to generation and involves a shared system of meanings, beliefs, values, and social relations; it also includes language, religion, clothing, music, laws, and entertainment

D

delta a flat, low-lying, often fan-shaped region at the mouth of a river; it is composed of sediment deposited by a river entering a lake, an ocean, or another large body of water

demography the study of population statistics, changes, and trends based on various measures of fertility, mortality, and migration

desertification the spread of desert conditions in arid and semiarid regions; desertification results from a combination of climatic changes and increasing human pressures in the form of overgrazing, removal of natural vegetation, and cultivation of marginal land

dialect a regional variation of one language, with differences in vocabulary, accent, pronunciation, and syntax

E

earthquake vibrations and shock waves caused by volcanic eruptions or the sudden movement of Earth's crustal rocks along fracture zones called faults

ecosystem a group of organisms and the environment with which they interact

elevation the height of a point or place above an established datum, sometimes mean sea level

El Niño a pronounced warming of the surface waters along the coast of Peru and the equatorial region of the east Pacific Ocean; it is caused by weakening (sometimes reversal) of the trade winds, with accompanying changes in ocean circulation (including cessation of upwelling in coastal waters).

emigrant a person migrating away from a country or area; an out-migrant

endangered species species at immediate risk of extinction

environment the sum of the conditions and stimuli that influence an organism

Equator latitude 0°; an imaginary line running east and west around the Earth and dividing it into two equal parts known as the Northern and Southern Hemispheres; the Equator always has approximately 12 hours of daylight and 12 hours of darkness.

equinox the time of year (usually September 22-23 and March 21-22) when all latitudes have 12 hours of daylight and darkness, and the sun is directly overhead at the Equator

erosion the general term for the removal of surface rocks and sediment by the action of water, air, ice, or gravity

estuary a broadened seaward end or extension of a river (usually a drowned river mouth), characterized by tidal influences and the mixing of fresh and saline water

ethnocentrism a belief in the inherent superiority of one's own ethnic group and culture; a tendency to view all other groups or cultures in terms of one's own

eutrophication the process that occurs when large amounts of nutrients from fertilizers or animal wastes enter a water body and bacteria break down the nutrients; the bacterial action causes depletion of dissolved oxygen

Exclusive Economic Zone (EEZ) an oceanic zone extending up to 200 nautical miles (370 km) from a shoreline, within which a coastal state claims jurisdiction over fishing, mineral exploration, and other economically important activities

F

fault a fracture or break in rock where the opposite sides are displaced relative to each other

fjord a coastal inlet that is narrow and deep and reaches far inland; it is usually formed by the sea filling in a glacially scoured valley or trough

flood basalt a huge lava flow that produces thick accumulations of basalt layers over a large area

floodplain a wide, relatively flat area that borders a stream or river and is subject to flooding and sedimentation; it is the most preferred land area for human settlement and agriculture

food chain the feeding pattern of organisms in an ecosystem, through which energy from food passes from one level to another in a sequence

fossil fuel fuel in the form of coal, petroleum, and natural gas derived from the remains of ancient plants and animals trapped and preserved in sedimentary rocks

G

geographic information system (GIS) an integrated hardware-software system used to store, organize, analyze, manipulate, model, and display geographic information or data

geography literally means "Earth description"; as a modern academic discipline, geography is concerned with the explanation of the physical and human characteristics of Earth's surface

geomorphology the study of planetary surface features, especially the processes of landform evolution on Earth

glaciation a period of glacial advancement through the growth of continental ice sheets and/or mountain glaciers

glacier a large, natural accumulation of ice that spreads outward on the land or moves slowly down a slope or valley

global positioning system (GPS) a space-based system of satellites that provides information on three-dimensional position and velocity to users at or near the Earth's surface

global warming the warming of Earth's average global temperature due to a buildup of "greenhouse gases" (e.g., carbon dioxide and methane) released by human activities; increased levels of these gases cause enhanced heat absorption by the atmosphere

globe a scale model of the Earth that correctly represents not only the area, relative size, and shape of physical features but also the distance between points and true compass directions

great circle the largest circle that can be drawn around a sphere such as a globe; a great circle route is the shortest route between two points

greenhouse effect an enhanced near-surface warming that is due to certain atmospheric gases absorbing and re-radiating long-wave radiation that might otherwise have escaped to space had those gases not been present in the atmosphere

gyre a large, semicontinuous system of major ocean currents flowing around the outer margins of every major ocean basin

H

habitat the natural environment (including controlling physical factors) in which a plant or animal is usually found or prefers to exist

hemisphere half a sphere; cartographers and geographers, by convention, divide the Earth into the Northern and Southern Hemispheres at the Equator and the Eastern and Western Hemispheres at the prime meridian (longitude 0°) and 180° meridian.

hot spot a localized and intensely hot region or mantle plume beneath the lithosphere; it tends to stay relatively fixed geographically as a lithospheric plate migrates over it

human geography one of the two major divisions of systematic geography; it is concerned with the spatial analysis of human population, cultures, and social, political, and economic activities

hurricane a large, rotating storm system that forms over tropical waters, with very low atmospheric pressure in the central region and winds in excess of 74 mph (119km/h); it is called a typhoon over the western Pacific Ocean and a cyclone over the northern Indian Ocean

hydrologic cycle the continuous recirculation of

water from the oceans, through the atmosphere, to the continents, through the biosphere and lithosphere, and back to the sea

I

ice age a period of pronounced glaciation usually associated with worldwide cooling, a greater proportion of global precipitation falling as snow, and a shorter snowmelt period

immigrant a person migrating into a particular country or area; an in-migrant

International Date Line an imaginary line that roughly follows the 180° meridian in the Pacific Ocean; immediately west of the date line the calendar date is one day ahead of the calendar date east of the line; people crossing the date line in a westward direction lose one calendar day, while those crossing eastward gain one calendar day

intertropical convergence zone (ITCZ) a zone of low atmospheric pressure created by intense solar heating, thereby leading to rising air and horizontal convergence of northeast and southeast trade winds; over the oceans, the ITCZ is usually found between 10° N and 10° S, and over continents the seasonal excursion of the ITCZ is much greater

J

jet stream a high-speed west-to-east wind current; jet streams flow in narrow corridors within upper-air westerlies, usually at the interface of polar and tropical air

K

karst a region underlain by limestone and characterized by extensive solution features such as sinkholes, underground streams, and caves

L

lagoon a shallow, narrow water body located between a barrier island and the mainland, with freshwater contributions from streams and salt-water exchange through tidal inlets or breaches throughout the barrier system

La Niña the pronounced cooling of equatorial waters in the eastern Pacific Ocean

latitude the distance north or south of the Equator; lines of latitude, called parallels, are evenly spaced from the Equator to the North and South Poles (from 0° to 90° N and S latitude); latitude and longitude (see below) are measured in terms of the 360 degrees of a circle and are expressed in degrees, minutes, and seconds.

lithosphere the rigid outer layer of the Earth, located above the asthenosphere and comprising the outer crust and the upper, rigid portion of the mantle

longitude the distance measured in degrees east or west of the prime meridian (0° longitude) up to 180°; lines of longitude are called meridians (compare with latitude, above)

M

magma molten, pressurized rock in the mantle that is occasionally intruded into the lithosphere or extruded to the surface of the Earth by volcanic activity

map projection the geometric system of transferring information about a round object, such as a globe, to a flat piece of paper or other surface for the purpose of producing a map with known properties and quantifiable distortion

meridian a north-south line of longitude used to reference time and distance east and west of the prime meridian (longitude 0°)

mesa a broad, flat-topped hill or mountain with marginal cliffs and/or steep slopes formed by progressive erosion of horizontally bedded sedimentary rocks

migration the movement of people across a specified boundary for the purpose of establishing a new place of residence

mineral an inorganic solid with a distinctive chemical composition and a specific crystal structure that affect its physical characteristics

monsoon a seasonal reversal of prevailing wind patterns, often associated with pronounced changes in moisture

N

nation a cultural concept for a group of people bound together by a strong sense of shared values and cultural characteristics, including language, religion, and common history

North Pole the most northerly geographic point on the Earth; the northern end of the Earth's axis of rotation

O

ocean current the regular and persistent flow of water in the oceans, usually driven by atmospheric wind and pressure systems or by regional differences in water density (temperature, salinity)

oxbow lake a crescent-shaped lake or swamp occupying a channel abandoned by a meandering river

ozone layer an ozone-enriched region of the stratosphere where ozone production and destruction are pronounced, thereby filtering out harmful ultraviolet rays from the sun

P

Pangaea the supercontinent from which today's continents are thought to have originated

Phanerozoic eon an eon of Earth's geologic history that comprises the Paleozoic, Mesozoic, and Cenozoic eras

physical geography one of the two major divisions of systematic geography; the spatial analysis of the structure, process, and location of Earth's natural phenomena, such as climate, soil, plants, animals, water, and topography

plain an extensive, flat-lying area characterized generally by the absence of local relief features

plate tectonics the theory that Earth's lithospheric plates slide or shift slowly over the asthenosphere and that their interactions cause earthquakes, volcanic eruptions, movement of landmasses, and other geologic events

plateau a landform feature characterized by high elevation and gentle upland slopes

pollution a direct or indirect process resulting from human activity; part of the environment is made potentially or actually unsafe or hazardous to the welfare of the organisms that live in it

prime meridian the line of 0° longitude that runs through Greenwich, England

Proterozoic eon the eon of geologic time that includes the interval between the Archean and Phanerozoic eons and is marked by rocks that contain fossils indicating the first appearance of eukaryotic organisms (as algae)

R

rain shadow the dry region on the downwind (leeward) side of a mountain range

regolith a layer of disintegrated or partly decomposed rock overlying unweathered parent materials; regolith is usually found in areas of low relief where the physical transport of debris is weak.

remote sensing the measurement of some property of an object by means other than direct contact, usually from aircraft or satellites

renewable resource a resource that can be regenerated or maintained if used at rates that do not exceed natural replenishment

Richter scale a logarithmic scale devised to represent the relative amount of energy released by an earthquake

rift valley a long, structural valley formed by the lowering of a block between two parallel faults

Ring of Fire (also Rim of Fire) an arc of volcanoes and tectonic activity along the perimeter of the Pacific Ocean

S

savanna a tropical grassland with widely spaced trees; it experiences distinct wet and dry seasons.

seamount a submerged volcano rising from the ocean floor

solstice a celestial event that occurs twice a year, when the sun appears directly overhead to observers at the Tropic of Cancer or the Tropic of Capricorn

South Pole the most southerly geographic point on the Earth; the southern end of the Earth's axis of rotation

state an area with defined and internationally acknowledged boundaries; a political unit

strait a narrow passage of water that connects two larger bodies of water

subduction the tectonic process by which the down-bent edge of one lithospheric plate is forced underneath another plate

T

tectonic plates (also lithospheric or crustal plates) sections of the Earth's rigid outer layer that move as distinct units upon the plastic-like mantle materials in the asthenosphere

threatened species species at some, but not immediate, risk of extinction

tide the regular rise and fall of the ocean, caused by the mutual gravitational attraction between the Earth, moon, and sun, as well as the rotation of the Earth-moon system around its center of gravity

topography the relief features that are evident on a planetary surface

tornado a violently rotating column of air characterized by extremely low atmospheric pressures and exceptional wind speeds generated within intense thunderstorms

Tropic of Cancer latitude 23.5° N; the farthest northerly excursion of the sun when it is directly overhead

Tropic of Capricorn latitude 23.5° S; the farthest southerly excursion of the sun when it is directly overhead

tsunami a series of ocean waves, often very destructive along coasts, caused by the vertical displacement of the seafloor during an earthquake, submarine landslide, or volcanic eruption

tundra a zone in cold, polar regions (mostly in the Northern Hemisphere) that is transitional between the zone of polar ice and the limit of tree growth; it is usually characterized by low-lying vegetation, with extensive permafrost and waterlogged soils

U

upwelling the process by which water rich in nutrients rises from depth toward the ocean surface; it is usually the result of diverging surface waters.

urbanization a process in which there is an increase in the percentage of people living and working in urban places as compared to rural places; a process of change from a rural to urban lifestyle

V

volcanism the upward movement and expulsion of molten (melted) material and gases from within the Earth's mantle onto the surface where it cools and hardens, producing characteristic terrain

W

watershed the drainage area of a river and its tributaries

weathering the processes or actions that cause the physical disintegration and chemical decomposition of rock and minerals

wetland an area of land covered by water or saturated by water sufficiently enough to support vegetation adapted to wet conditions

wilderness a natural environment that has remained essentially undisturbed by human activities and, increasingly, is protected by government or non-government organizations

X

xerophyte a plant that survives in a dry environment

Y

yazoo a tributary stream that runs parallel to the main river for some distance

Z

zenith a point in the sky that is immediately overhead; also the highest point above the observer's horizon obtained by a celestial body

zoning the process of subdividing urban areas as a basis for land-use planning and policy

PLACE-NAME INDEX

The following system is used to locate a place on a map in the *National Geographic Family Reference Atlas of the World.* The boldface type after an entry refers to the plate on which the map is found. The letter-number combination refers to the grid on which the particular place-name is located. The edge of each map is marked horizontally with numbers and vertically with letters. In between, at equally spaced intervals, are index ticks (▲). If these ticks were connected with lines, each page would be divided into a 12- by 16-square grid. Take Abilene, Kansas, for example. The index entry reads "**Abilene, *Kans., U.S.* 99 S8.**" On page 99, Abilene is located within the grid square where row S and column 8 intersect.

A place-name may appear on several maps, but the index lists only the best presentation. Usually, this means that a feature is indexed to the largest-scale map on which it appears in its entirety. (Note: Rivers are often labeled multiple times even on a single map. In such cases, the rivers are indexed to labels that are closest to their mouths.) The name of the country or continent in which a feature lies is shown in italic type and is usually abbreviated. (A full list of abbreviations appears on page 240.)

The index lists more than proper names. Some entries include a description, as in "**Elba, island, *It.* 136 G8**" and "**Amazon, river, *S. Amer.* 118 D7.**" In languages other than English, the description of a physical feature may be part of the name; e.g., the "Berg" in "**Swart Berg, *Af.* 174 R7,**" means "mountain." The Glossary of Foreign Terms on page 250 translates such terms into English.

When a feature or place can be referred to by more than one name, both may appear in the index with cross-references. These are especially useful for finding major cities in China, where the phonetic Pinyin system has replaced the Wade-Giles system (except in Taiwan) for the romanization of the Chinese language. For example, the entry for Canton reads "**Canton *see* Guangzhou, *China* 163 R4.**" That entry is "**Guangzhou (Canton), *China* 163 R4.**"

A

Aachen, *Ger.* **132** G4
Aansluit, *S. Af.* **182** J8
Aasu, *Tutuila, Amer. Samoa, U.S.* **198** M7
Aba, *China* **160** K11
Aba, *Dem. Rep. of the Congo* **178** H12
Aba, *Nig.* **181** H14
Abā as Sa'ūd, *Saudi Arabia* **152** N9
Abaco Island, *Bahamas* **110** C12
Ābādān, *Iran* **152** F11
Ābādeh, *Iran* **153** F13
Abadla, *Alg.* **176** C9
Abaetetuba, *Braz.* **123** D13
Abaiang, island, *Tarawa, Kiribati* **197** E17
Abaji, *Nig.* **181** G14
Abajo Peak, *Utah, U.S.* **101** P9
Abakan, *Russ.* **141** L13
Abancay, *Peru* **122** H5
Abaokoro, island, *Tarawa, Kiribati* **197** F17
Abashiri, *Jap.* **164** E15
Abashiri Wan, *Jap.* **164** E15
Abay, *Kaz.* **155** E14
Abaya, Lake, *Af.* **174** H10
Ābaya Hāyk', *Eth.* **179** G14
Abbaye, Point, *Mich., U.S.* **92** E7
Abbeville, *Ala., U.S.* **95** M17
Abbeville, *Fr.* **138** J10
Abbeville, *La., U.S.* **94** Q8
Abbeville, *S.C., U.S.* **90** K7
Abbot Ice Shelf, *Antarctica* **206** J6
Abbotsford, *Wis., U.S.* **92** H4
Abbottabad, *Pak.* **156** M11
'Abda (Eboda), ruins, *Israel* **151** P5
'Abd al Kūrī, island, *Yemen* **153** R13
Abéché, *Chad* **177** H16
Ab-e Istadeh-ye Moqor, lake, *Afghan.* **157** P7
Abemama, island, *Kiribati* **194** G8
Abengourou, *Côte d'Ivoire* **180** H9
Åbenrå, *Den.* **134** P11
Abeokuta, *Nig.* **180** G12
Aberdeen, *Idaho, U.S.* **100** H6
Aberdeen, *Md., U.S.* **90** C14
Aberdeen, *Miss., U.S.* **95** J13
Aberdeen, *N.C., U.S.* **90** J11
Aberdeen, *S. Dak., U.S.* **98** J6
Aberdeen, *Scot., U.K.* **138** D8
Aberdeen, *Wash., U.S.* **102** D2
Aberdeen Lake, *Nunavut, Can.* **77** H14
Abernathy, *Tex., U.S.* **96** J5
Abert, Lake, *Oreg., U.S.* **102** K6
Aberystwyth, *Wales, U.K.* **138** G7
Abhā, *Saudi Arabia* **152** N8
Abidjan, *Côte d'Ivoire* **180** H9
Abilene, *Kans., U.S.* **99** S8
Abilene, *Tex., U.S.* **96** L8
Abingden Downs, *Qnsld., Austral.* **191** R12
Abingdon, *Ill., U.S.* **93** Q4
Abingdon, *Va., U.S.* **90** G8
Abiquiu, *N. Mex., U.S.* **101** R12
Abisko, *Sw.* **135** D13
Abitibi, river, *N. Amer.* **74** H7
Abitibi, Lake, *N. Amer.* **74** H8
Abkhazia, republic, *Rep. of Georgia* **149** A15
Åbo *see* Turku, *Fin.* **135** K15
Abohar, *India* **158** E4
Abomey, *Benin* **180** G11
Abou Deïa, *Chad* **177** J15
Abraham Lincoln Birthplace National Historic Site, *Ky., U.S.* **95** C16
Abraham's Bay, *Bahamas* **111** H16
Abrantes, *Port.* **138** F5
Abra Pampa, *Arg.* **124** E9
Abreú, *Dom. Rep.* **111** L19
Abrolhos, Arquipélago dos, *Braz.* **123** K16
Absalom, Mount, *Antarctica* **206** E11
Absaroka Range, *Wyo., U.S.* **100** F9
Absarokee, *Mont., U.S.* **100** E9
Absheron Yarymadasy, *Azerb.* **149** D23
Abū al Abyaḑ, island, *U.A.E.* **153** J14
Abu al Ḩuşayn, Qā', *Jordan* **150** M10
Abū 'Alī, island, *Saudi Arabia* **152** H12
Abū Bahr, plain, *Saudi Arabia* **152** L11
Abu Ballâs, peak, *Af.* **174** E8
Abū Daghmah, *Syr.* **150** D10
Abu Dhabi *see* Abū Z̧aby, *U.A.E.* **153** J14
Abu Durba, *Egypt* **151** T2
Abu Hamed, *Sudan* **179** C13
Abuja, *Nig.* **181** G14
Abū Kamāl, *Syr.* **150** H14
Abū Madd, Ra's, *Saudi Arabia* **152** J5
Abu Matariq, *Sudan* **178** F11
Abunã, river, *Bol.-Braz.* **122** G7
Abunã, *Braz.* **122** G7
Abū Qumayyiş, Ra's, *Saudi Arabia* **153** J13
Abu Rudeis, *Egypt* **151** S2
Abu Shagara, Ras, *Sudan* **179** C14
Abu Simbel, site, *Egypt* **177** F18
Abuta, *Jap.* **164** G13
Ābuyē Mēda, peak, *Eth.* **179** F15
Abu Zabad, *Sudan* **178** F12
Abū Z̧aby (Abu Dhabi), *U.A.E.* **153** J14
Abu Zenîma, *Egypt* **151** S2
Abwong, *Sudan* **179** G13
Abyad, El Bahr el (White Nile), river, *Sudan* **179** F13
Abyek, *Iran* **152** C12
Academy Glacier, *Antarctica* **206** H10
Acadia National Park, *Me., U.S.* **89** F18
Acaponeta, *Mex.* **108** G9
Acapulco, *Mex.* **108** K11
Acaraú, *Braz.* **123** D16
Acarigua, *Venez.* **120** C8
Acatlán, *Mex.* **108** J12
Accomac, *Va., U.S.* **90** E15
Accra, *Ghana* **180** H11
Achach, island, *Chuuk, F.S.M.* **197** C14
Achayvayam, *Russ.* **141** D22
Achill Island, *Ire.* **138** F5
Achinsk, *Russ.* **141** K13
Achna, *Cyprus* **148** L9
Acıgöl, *Turk.* **148** G5
Acıpayam, *Turk.* **148** H5
Ackerman, *Miss., U.S.* **94** K12
Ackley, *Iowa, U.S.* **99** N12
Acklins, The Bight of, *Bahamas* **111** H15
Acklins Island, *Bahamas* **111** H15
Acoma Pueblo, *N. Mex., U.S.* **101** S11
Aconcagua, Cerro, *Arg.* **124** K7
Aconcagua, Río, *Chile* **124** K6
Açores *see* Azores, islands, *Atl. Oc.* **184** C3
A Coruña, *Sp.* **139** N5
Acraman, Lake, *Austral.* **190** J9
Acre, river, *Braz.* **122** G6
Acre *see* 'Akko, *Israel* **150** K5
Acteon, Groupe, *Fr. Polynesia, Fr.* **199** G22
Açu, *Braz.* **123** F17
Ada, *Ghana* **180** H11
Ada, *Minn., U.S.* **98** G8
Ada, *Ohio, U.S.* **93** Q12
Ada, *Okla., U.S.* **96** H12
Adair, Cape, *Nunavut, Can.* **77** E17
Adak Island, *Alas., U.S.* **104** Q5
Adam, *Oman* **153** K16
Adams, *Minn., U.S.* **98** L12
Adams, *Wis., U.S.* **92** K5
Adams, Mount, *Wash., U.S.* **102** E5
Adam's Peak, *Sri Lanka* **159** T7
Adam's Rock, *Pitcairn I., U.K.* **199** Q23
Adamstown, *Pitcairn I., U.K.* **199** Q23
Adamsville, *Tenn., U.S.* **95** G13
'Adan (Aden), *Yemen* **152** R9
Adana, *Turk.* **148** J10
'Adan aş Şughrá, peninsula, *Yemen* **152** R9
Adang, Teluk, *Indonesia* **168** K12
Adapazarı, *Turk.* **148** D6
Adare, Cape, *Antarctica* **207** R14
Adavale, *Qnsld., Austral.* **191** U12
Ad Dahnā', desert, *Saudi Arabia* **152** K11
Ad Dakhla, *W. Sahara, Mor.* **176** E5
Ad Dammām, *Saudi Arabia* **152** H12
Ad Dār al Ḩamrā', *Saudi Arabia* **152** H6
Ad Darb, *Saudi Arabia* **152** N8
Ad Dawādimī, *Saudi Arabia* **152** J9
Ad Dawḩah (Doha), *Qatar* **153** J13
Ad Dibdibah, region, *Asia* **152** G10
Ad Dilam, *Saudi Arabia* **152** K11
Addis Ababa *see* Ādīs Ābeba, *Eth.* **179** G15
Ad Dīwānīyah, *Iraq* **152** E10
Addu Atoll, *Maldives* **159** X3
Ad Duwayd, *Saudi Arabia* **152** F8
Addy, *Wash., U.S.* **102** B8
Adel, *Ga., U.S.* **91** P6
Adel, *Iowa, U.S.* **99** P11
Adel, *Oreg., U.S.* **102** L6
Adelaide, *Bahamas* **110** E11
Adelaide, *S. Austral., Austral.* **191** Y10
Adelaide Island, *Antarctica* **206** E4
Adelaide Peninsula, *Nunavut, Can.* **77** F14
Adelaide River, *N. Terr., Austral.* **191** P7
Adélie Coast, *Antarctica* **207** Q18
Aden *see* 'Adan, *Yemen* **152** R9
Aden, Gulf of, *Af.-Asia* **146** J3
Aderbissinat, *Niger* **176** H12
Adieu, Cape, *Austral.* **190** J8
Adige, river, *It.* **136** F9
Ādīgrat, *Eritrea* **179** E15
Adilabad, *India* **158** L6
Adin, *Calif., U.S.* **102** M5
Adirondack Mountains, *N.Y., U.S.* **88** G10
Ādīs Ābeba (Addis Ababa), *Eth.* **179** G15
Adi Ugri, *Eritrea* **179** E15
Adıyaman, *Turk.* **149** H13
Adlavik Islands, *Nfld., Can.* **77** K22
Admiralty Inlet, *Wash., U.S.* **102** B4
Admiralty Inlet, *Nunavut, Can.* **77** E16
Admiralty Island, *U.S.* **78** Q7
Admiralty Island National Monument, *Alas., U.S.* **105** K22
Admiralty Islands, *P.N.G.* **193** B19
Admiralty Mountains, *Antarctica* **207** Q14
Adour, river, *Fr.* **139** N9
Adrar, region, *Mauritania* **176** F6
Adrar, *Alg.* **176** D10
Adraskan, *Afghan.* **157** N2
Adrian, *Mich., U.S.* **93** N11
Adrian, *Minn., U.S.* **98** L9
Adrian, *Tex., U.S.* **96** G4
Adrianople *see* Edirne, *Turk.* **148** B3
Adriatic Sea, *Eur.* **130** J7
Adun Gol, *China* **162** B2
Ādwa, *Eth.* **179** E15
Aegean Sea, *Eur.* **130** K9
Aegir Ridge, *Norwegian Sea* **223** J20
Aej, island, *Enewetak Atoll, Marshall Is.* **196** G8
Aeon Point, *Kiritimati, Kiribati* **197** C24
Afaahiti, *Tahiti, Fr. Polynesia, Fr.* **199** P17
Afar, region, *Eth.* **179** E15
Afareaitu, *Moorea, Fr. Polynesia, Fr.* **199** N14
Afghanistan, *Asia* **157** N5
'Afīf, *Saudi Arabia* **152** K8
Afiq, *Israel* **150** K6
Afmadow, *Somalia* **179** J16
Afobaka, *Suriname* **121** E16
Afognak Island, *Alas., U.S.* **105** L16
Afono Bay, *Tutuila, Amer. Samoa, U.S.* **198** L8
'Afrīn, *Syr.* **150** D8
Afşin, *Turk.* **148** G12
Afton, *Okla., U.S.* **96** E14
Afton, *Wyo., U.S.* **100** H8
Afuefuniya Point, *Rota I., N. Mariana Is., U.S.* **196** E7
'Afula, *Israel* **150** L5
Afyon, *Turk.* **148** F6
Agadez, *Niger* **176** G12
Agadir, *Mor.* **176** C7
Agaete, *Canary Is., Sp.* **184** Q6
Agafo Gumas, *Guam, U.S.* **196** B11
Agana *see* Hagåtña, *Guam, U.S.* **196** C10
Agana Bay, *Guam, U.S.* **196** C10
Agana Heights, *Guam, U.S.* **196** C10
Agano, river, *Jap.* **164** M12
Aga Point, *Guam, U.S.* **196** E10
Agar, *India* **158** H5
Agartala, *India* **158** H13
Agassiz Fracture Zone, *Pac. Oc.* **219** P14
Agat, *Guam, U.S.* **196** D10
Agata, *Russ.* **141** G13
Agat Bay, *Guam, U.S.* **196** C10
Agate, *Colo., U.S.* **100** M14
Agate Fossil Beds National Monument, *Nebr., U.S.* **99** N1
Agats, *Indonesia* **169** L20
Agatti Island, *India* **159** R2
Agattu Island, *Alas., U.S.* **104** N1
Agattu Strait, *Alas., U.S.* **104** N1
Agboville, *Côte d'Ivoire* **180** H9
Ağdam, *Azerb.* **149** E21
Agen, *Fr.* **139** N9
Agfayan Bay, *Guam, U.S.* **196** E10
Aghdash, *Azerb.* **149** D21
Aghjabädi, *Azerb.* **149** E21
Aghsu, *Azerb.* **149** D22
Agidyem, island, *Jaluit Atoll, Marshall Is.* **196** L8
Agingan, Puntan, *Saipan, N. Mariana Is., U.S.* **196** C4
Aginskoye, *Russ.* **141** L17
Ágios Nikólaos, *Gr.* **137** N16
Agios Theodoros, *Cyprus* **148** K9
Agnes Creek, *S. Austral., Austral.* **191** U8
Agness, *Oreg., U.S.* **102** K2
Agnew, *W. Austral., Austral.* **191** V4
Agordat, *Eritrea* **179** D14
Agra, *India* **158** G6
Ağrı, *Turk.* **149** E17
Ağrı Dağı (Mount Ararat), *Turk.* **149** E18
Agrihan, island, *N. Mariana Is., U.S.* **196** A2
Agrínio, *Gr.* **137** K14
Ağstafa, *Azerb.* **149** C19
Aguada de Pasajeros, *Cuba* **110** H8
Aguadilla, *P.R., U.S.* **111** M22
Agua Fria National Monument, *Ariz., U.S.* **101** T7
Aguán, river, *N. Amer.* **74** P7
Aguapeí, *Braz.* **122** J9
Agua Prieta, *Mex.* **108** C8
Aguas Blancas, *Chile* **124** E7
Aguascalientes, *Mex.* **108** G10
Águas Formosas, *Braz.* **123** K16
Aguelhok, *Mali* **176** G10
Aguijan, island, *N. Mariana Is., U.S.* **196** C2
Aguila, *Ariz., U.S.* **101** T6
Aguilar, *Colo., U.S.* **101** P14
Aguilas, *Sp.* **139** S8
Aguja, Cabo de la, *Col.* **120** B5
Aguja, Punta, *Peru* **122** F1
Aguja Point, *S. Amer.* **118** E1
Agulhas, Cape, *S. Af.* **182** M8
Agulhas Bank, *Atl. Oc.-Ind. Oc.* **217** T15
Agulhas Basin, *Ind. Oc.* **220** Q1
Agulhas Plateau, *Ind. Oc.* **220** N2
Aguni Jima, *Jap.* **165** Y1
Ahaggar (Hoggar), plateau, *Alg.* **176** E11
Ahaggar Mountains, *Af.* **174** F5
Ahar, *Iran* **152** A11
Ahe, island, *Fr. Polynesia, Fr.* **199** D17
Ahiri, *India* **158** L7
Ahlat, *Turk.* **149** F17
Ahlatlıbel, ruins, *Turk.* **148** E8
Ahmadabad, *India* **158** J3
Ahmadnagar, *India* **158** L4
Ahmadpur East, *Pak.* **157** S9
Ahmad Wal, *Pak.* **157** S5
Ahoa, *Wallis and Futuna, Fr.* **198** B11
Ahoskie, *N.C., U.S.* **90** G13
Ahram, *Iran* **153** G13

Ahua, *Tubuai, Fr. Polynesia, Fr.* **199** K20
Ahu-a-miria Islands, *Penrhyn, Cook Is., N.Z.* **199** B18
Ahu a Umi Heiau, *Hawaii, U.S.* **107** M19
Ahumoa, peak, *Hawaii, U.S.* **107** L19
Ahuna, Motu, *Bora-Bora, Fr. Polynesia, Fr.* **199** K13
Ahunui, island, *Fr. Polynesia, Fr.* **199** G20
Ahvenanmaa *see* Åland, island, *Fin.* **135** K14
Ahvāz, *Iran* **152** F11
Aḩwar, *Yemen* **152** R10
Ai, island, *Jaluit Atoll, Marshall Is.* **196** M7
Aiea, *Hawaii, U.S.* **106** E11
Aigialousa, *Cyprus* **148** K9
Aiguá, *Uru.* **124** L15
Aikawa, *Jap.* **164** M11
Aiken, *S.C., U.S.* **90** L8
Aileron, *N. Terr., Austral.* **191** T8
Ailinginae Atoll, *Marshall Is.* **196** F3
Ailinglapalap Atoll, *Marshall Is.* **196** H4
Ailuk Atoll, *Marshall Is.* **196** F4
Aimere, *Indonesia* **169** M13
Ainaži, *Latv.* **135** L16
Aineman, island, *Jaluit Atoll, Marshall Is.* **196** M9
'Aïn Sefra, *Alg.* **176** B10
Ainsworth, *Nebr., U.S.* **99** N5
Aiquile, *Bol.* **122** K7
Aiquina, *Chile* **124** D8
Aïr (Azbine), region, *Niger* **176** G12
Airai, *Palau* **196** N11
Airão, *Braz.* **122** D8
Air Force Island, *Nunavut, Can.* **77** F18
Aitape, *P.N.G.* **193** C18
Aitkin, *Minn., U.S.* **98** G11
Aitutaki, island, *Aitutaki Atoll, Cook Is., N.Z.* **198** P11
Aitutaki Atoll, *Cook Is., N.Z.* **194** K12
Aiud, *Rom.* **137** E15
Aiurua, Passe, *Tahiti, Fr. Polynesia, Fr.* **199** Q18
Aiwa, island, *Fiji* **198** J9
Aiwo, *Nauru* **197** F22
Aiwokako Passage, *Palau* **196** M11
Aix-en- Provence, *Fr.* **139** N11
Aiyon Mountain, *Palau* **196** M12
Aiyura, *P.N.G.* **193** D19
Aizawl, *India* **158** H14
Aizpute, *Latv.* **135** M15
Aizuwakamatsu, *Jap.* **164** M12
Ajaccio, *Fr.* **139** P13
Ajajú, river, *Col.* **120** H6
Ajaria, republic, *Rep. of Georgia* **149** C16
Ajax Peak, *Idaho, U.S.* **100** E6
Ajayan Bay, *Guam, U.S.* **196** E10
Ajbağ, *Afghan.* **156** K7
Ajdābiyā, *Lib.* **177** C15
Ajigasawa, *Jap.* **164** J12
'Ajlūn, *Jordan* **150** L6
'Ajmān, *U.A.E.* **153** J15
Ajmer, *India* **158** G4
Ajo, *Ariz., U.S.* **101** V6
Ajokwola, island, *Majuro Atoll, Marshall Is.* **196** G10
Ajrestan, *Afghan.* **157** N6
Akabira, *Jap.* **164** F14
Akaiami, island, *Aitutaki Atoll, Cook Is., N.Z.* **198** Q12
Akaka Falls, *Hawaii, U.S.* **107** L21
Akamaru, island, *Gambier Is., Fr. Polynesia, Fr.* **199** R21
Akankohan, *Jap.* **164** F15
Akanthou, *Cyprus* **148** K9
Akashi, *Jap.* **165** Q8
Akaska, *S. Dak., U.S.* **98** J5
Akbulak, *Russ.* **140** J7
Akçaabat, *Turk.* **149** D14
Akçadağ, *Turk.* **149** G13
Akçakale, *Turk.* **149** J13
Akçakışla, *Turk.* **148** E11
Akçakoca, *Turk.* **148** C7
Akçay, *Turk.* **148** E3
Akçay, *Turk.* **148** J5
Akchâr, region, *Mauritania* **176** F5
Akdağ, *Turk.* **148** F2
Akdağ, *Turk.* **148** J7
Ak Dağlar, *Turk.* **148** J5
Akdağmadeni, *Turk.* **148** E11
Akeley, *Minn., U.S.* **98** G10
Akera, river, *Azerb.* **149** E20
Aketi, *Dem. Rep. of the Congo* **178** J10
Akhalts'ikhe, *Rep. of Georgia* **149** C17
Akhḑar, Jabal al, *Af.* **174** D7
Akhiok, *Alas., U.S.* **105** M15
Akhisar, *Turk.* **148** F3
Akhnur, *India* **157** N12
Akhtopol, *Bulg.* **137** H17
Akhtuba, river, *Eur.* **130** F13
Akhtubinsk, *Russ.* **140** J5
Aki, *Jap.* **165** R7
Akiachak, *Alas., U.S.* **104** J12
Akiaki, island, *Fr. Polynesia, Fr.* **199** F21
Akimiski Island, *Nunavut, Can.* **77** M17
Akita, *Jap.* **164** K12
Akitua, island, *Aitutaki Atoll, Cook Is., N.Z.* **198** P11
Akjoujt, *Mauritania* **176** F5
Akkarga, *Kaz.* **154** D10
Akkeshi, *Jap.* **164** F16
Akkeshi Wan, *Jap.* **164** F16
'Akko (Acre), *Israel* **150** K5
Akkol', *Kaz.* **155** J14
Akkuş, *Turk.* **148** D12
Aklavik, *N.W.T., Can.* **76** E9
Aklera, *India* **158** H5
Akoakoa Point, *Hawaii, U.S.* **107** K19
Akobo, *Sudan* **179** G13
Akobo, river, *Eth.-Sudan* **179** G13
Akola, *India* **158** K5
Akosombo Dam, *Ghana* **180** H11
Akpatok Island, *Nunavut, Can.* **77** J19
Akqi, *China* **160** F5
Akranes, *Ice.* **134** F2
Ákra Ténaro, *Gr.* **137** M14
Akron, *Colo., U.S.* **100** L15
Akron, *Iowa, U.S.* **98** M8
Akron, *Ohio, U.S.* **93** P14
Akrotiri, *Cyprus* **148** L8
Akrotiri Bay, *Cyprus* **148** L8
Aksai Chin, region, *China* **160** H4
Aksaray, *Turk.* **148** G9
Aksay, *China* **160** G9
Akşehir, *Turk.* **148** G7
Akşehir Gölü, *Turk.* **148** G7
Akseki, *Turk.* **148** H7
Aksu, river, *Turk.* **148** H6
Aksu, *China* **160** F5
Aksu, *Kaz.* **154** J6
Āksum, *Eth.* **179** E15
Aktag, peak, *China* **160** H6
Akto, *China* **160** F4
Akune, *Jap.* **165** S4
Akureyri, *Ice.* **134** E3
Akuse, *Ghana* **180** H11
Akuseki Shima, *Jap.* **165** V3
Akutan, *Alas., U.S.* **104** P10
Akyab *see* Sittwe, *Myanmar* **166** H4
Akyaka, *Turk.* **149** D17
Akyazı, *Turk.* **148** D6
Alabama, river, *Ala., U.S.* **95** M14
Alabama, *U.S.* **95** K14
Alabaster, *Ala., U.S.* **95** K15
Alaca, *Turk.* **148** E10
Alaca Dağ, *Turk.* **148** H7
Alacahöyük, ruins, *Turk.* **148** E10
Alaçam, *Turk.* **148** C10
Alachua, *Fla., U.S.* **91** R7
Alacránes, Arrecife, *Mex.* **109** G16
Aladağ, *Turk.* **148** G7
Aladağ, *Turk.* **148** H10
Aladzha, *Turkm.* **154** L6
Al Aflāj, region, *Saudi Arabia* **152** L10
Alagoinhas, *Braz.* **123** H17
Alagón, *Sp.* **139** P8
Al Aḩmadī, *Kuwait* **152** G11
Alajuela, *C.R.* **109** N19
Alakai Swamp, *Hawaii, U.S.* **106** B5
Alakanuk, *Alas., U.S.* **104** H11
Al Akhḑar, *Saudi Arabia* **152** G6
Alaköl, lake, *Kaz.* **155** F18
Alalakeiki Channel, *Hawaii, U.S.* **107** H16
Alalakh, ruins, *Turk.* **148** K11
Alamagan, island, *N. Mariana Is., U.S.* **196** B2
Al 'Amārah, *Iraq* **152** E11
Alameda, *Calif., U.S.* **103** S3
Alameda, *N. Mex., U.S.* **101** S12
'Alam Lek, *Afghan.* **156** K5
Alamo, *Nev., U.S.* **103** S12
Alamo, *Tenn., U.S.* **94** F12
Alamogordo, *N. Mex., U.S.* **101** U13
Alamo Heights, *Tex., U.S.* **97** R9
Alamosa, *Colo., U.S.* **101** P12
Åland (Ahvenanmaa), island, *Fin.* **135** K14
Alandar, *Afghan.* **156** M4
Åland Islands, *Eur.* **130** D8
Alanya, *Turk.* **148** J7
Alao, *Tutuila, Amer. Samoa, U.S.* **198** M9
Alaotra, Lac, *Madagascar* **183** F18
Alappuzha *see* Alleppey, *India* **159** R5
Al'Aqabah (Aqaba), *Jordan* **151** R5
Al 'Aqīq, *Saudi Arabia* **152** L8
Alara, river, *Turk.* **148** J7
Al 'Armah, plateau, *Saudi Arabia* **152** H10
Al Arţāwīyah, *Saudi Arabia* **152** H10
Al As'ad, *Saudi Arabia* **152** G6
Alaşehir, *Turk.* **148** F4
Al Ashkharah, *Oman* **153** L17
Alaska, *U.S.* **105** G14
Alaska, Gulf of, *Alas., U.S.* **105** L17
Alaska Highway, *Can.-U.S.* **105** G17
Alaska Peninsula, *Alas., U.S.* **105** N13
Alaska Range, *Alas., U.S.* **105** J15
Ālāt, *Azerb.* **149** E23
Al 'Athāmīn, peak, *Iraq* **152** F9
Alausí, *Ecua.* **120** K3
Alava, Cape, *Wash., U.S.* **102** B1
Alaverdi, *Arm.* **149** D18
Alāyat Samā'il, *Oman* **153** K16
'Ālayh, *Leb.* **150** J6
Alazani, river, *Azerb.-Rep. of Georgia* **149** C20
Al Bāb, *Syr.* **150** D9
Albacete, *Sp.* **139** R8
Al Bad', *Saudi Arabia* **152** G5
Al Badī', *Saudi Arabia* **152** L10
Al Bāḩah, *Saudi Arabia* **152** M8
Albanel, Lac, *Que., Can.* **77** M19
Albania, *Eur.* **137** H13
Albany, river, *Ont., Can.* **77** N17
Albany, *Ga., U.S.* **91** P5
Albany, *Ky., U.S.* **95** D17
Albany, *Mo., U.S.* **99** R11
Albany, *N.Y., U.S.* **88** K11
Albany, *Oreg., U.S.* **102** G3
Albany, *Tex., U.S.* **96** L8
Albany, *W. Austral., Austral.* **191** Y3
Al Bardī, *Lib.* **177** C17
Albardón, *Arg.* **124** J8
Al Başrah, *Iraq* **152** F11
Albatross Bay, *Austral.* **190** B12
Al Bayāḑ, plain, *Saudi Arabia* **152** L10
Al Bayḑāh (Beida), *Lib.* **177** B16
Albemarle Sound, *N.C., U.S.* **90** G14
Albenga, *It.* **136** F7
Albert, Lake, *Austral.* **190** L10
Albert, Lake, *Dem. Rep. of the Congo* **178** J12
Alberta, *Can.* **76** L10
Albert Lea, *Minn., U.S.* **98** L11
Albert Nile, river, *Af.* **174** J9
Albert Town, *Bahamas* **111** H14
Albertville, *Ala., U.S.* **95** H16
Albertville, *Fr.* **138** M12
Albi, *Fr.* **139** N10
Albia, *Iowa, U.S.* **99** Q12
Albin, *Wyo., U.S.* **100** K14
Albina Point, *Af.* **174** M6
Albion, *Ill., U.S.* **93** T7
Albion, *Mich., U.S.* **92** M11
Albion, *N.Y., U.S.* **88** H6
Albion, *Nebr., U.S.* **99** P7
Al Bi'r, *Saudi Arabia* **152** G5
Al Birk, *Saudi Arabia* **152** N8
Alborán, island, *Sp.* **139** T7
Alboran Sea, *Sp.* **139** T7
Ålborg, *Den.* **134** N11
Albuquerque, *N. Mex., U.S.* **101** S12
Al Buraymī, *U.A.E.* **153** J15
Albury, *N.S.W., Austral.* **191** Y13
Alcácer do Sal, *Port.* **139** R4
Alcamo, *It.* **136** L9
Alcántara, *Sp.* **139** R5
Alcaraz, *Sp.* **139** R8
Alcázar de San Juan, *Sp.* **139** R7
Alcoa, *Tenn., U.S.* **95** F18
Alcoota, *N. Terr., Austral.* **191** T9
Alcoy, *Sp.* **139** R9
Aldabra Islands, *Seychelles* **183** C17
Aldama, *Mex.* **108** D9
Aldan, river, *Russ.* **141** G18
Aldan, *Russ.* **141** J18
Aldanskoye Nagor'ye, *Russ.* **141** J18
Alderney, island, *Channel Is., U.K.* **138** J8
Aledo, *Ill., U.S.* **93** P3
Aleg, *Mauritania* **176** G5
Alegranza, island, *Canary Is., Sp.* **184** P8
Alegrete, *Braz.* **122** P10
Alejandro Selkirk, Isla, *Pac. Oc.* **195** M22
Aleksandrovsk Sakhalinskiy, *Russ.* **141** J21
Alekseyevka, *Kaz.* **155** E19
Aleksinac, *Yug.* **137** G14
Alemania, *Arg.* **124** F9
Alembel, island, *Enewetak Atoll, Marshall Is.* **196** H8
Alençon, *Fr.* **138** K9
Alenquer, *Braz.* **122** D11
Alenuihaha Channel, *Hawaii, U.S.* **107** J17
Aleppo *see* Ḩalab, *Syr.* **150** D9
Aléria, *Fr.* **139** P13
Alert, *Nunavut, Can.* **77** A16
Alert Point, *Tabuaeran, Kiribati* **197** B21
Alès, *Fr.* **139** N11
Ålesund, *Nor.* **134** J10
Aleutian Basin, *Pac. Oc.* **218** B9
Aleutian Islands, *Alas., U.S.* **104** N3
Aleutian Range, *Alas., U.S.* **105** M14
Aleutian Trench, *Pac. Oc.* **218** C9
Alevina, Mys, *Russ.* **141** F21
Alexander, *N. Dak., U.S.* **98** F2
Alexander, Cape, *Solomon Is.* **197** K15
Alexander Archipelago, *Alas., U.S.* **105** K21
Alexander Bay, *S. Af.* **182** K6
Alexander City, *Ala., U.S.* **95** K16
Alexander Island, *Antarctica* **206** F5
Alexandra, *N.Z.* **193** Q16
Alexandra, Zemlya, *Russ.* **140** B12
Alexandria *see* El Iskandarîya, *Egypt* **177** C18
Alexandria, *Ind., U.S.* **93** Q10
Alexandria, *La., U.S.* **94** N8
Alexandria, *Minn., U.S.* **98** H9
Alexandria, *Rom.* **137** G16
Alexandria, *S. Dak., U.S.* **98** L7
Alexandria, *Va., U.S.* **90** D13
Alexandria Bay, *N.Y., U.S.* **88** G9
Alexandrina, Lake, *Austral.* **190** L10
Alexandroúpoli (Dedéagach), *Gr.* **137** J16
Aleysk, *Russ.* **140** L11
Al Fallūjah, *Iraq* **152** D9
Al Farciya, *W. Sahara, Mor.* **176** D7
Alfaro, *Sp.* **139** P8
Al Fāw, *Iraq* **152** F11
Al Fujayrah, *U.A.E.* **153** J15
Al Fuqahā', *Lib.* **177** D14
Al Furāt (Euphrates), river, *Iraq* **152** E10
Algabas, *Kaz.* **154** D6
Algarrobal, *Arg.* **124** F10
Algarrobo, *Chile* **124** G7
Algeciras, *Sp.* **139** T6
Algena, *Eritrea* **179** D15
Alger (Algiers), *Alg.* **176** A11
Algeria, *Af.* **176** D9
Algha, *Kaz.* **154** D8
Al Ghayḑah, *Yemen* **153** P13
Al Ghayl, *Saudi Arabia* **152** K10
Al Ghazālah, *Saudi Arabia* **152** H8
Alghero, *It.* **136** J7
Algiers *see* Alger, *Alg.* **176** A11
Algoa Bay, *Af.* **174** R8
Algoma, *Wis., U.S.* **92** J7
Algona, *Iowa, U.S.* **98** M11
Algorta, *Uru.* **124** K13
Al Ḩadīdah, crater, *Saudi Arabia* **152** L12
Al Ḩadīthah, *Iraq* **152** D8
Al Ḩaffah, *Syr.* **150** F7
Al Ḩamād, plain, *Jordan* **150** L11
Al Hamād, plain, *Saudi Arabia* **152** E7
Alhambra, *Calif., U.S.* **103** X8
Al Ḩamīdīyah, *Syr.* **150** G7
Al Ḩamrā', desert, *Lib.* **177** C13
Al Ḩamrā', *Saudi Arabia* **152** J6
Al Ḩanākīyah, *Saudi Arabia* **152** J7
Al Ḩarīq, *Saudi Arabia* **152** K10
Al Harūj al Aswad, hills, *Lib.* **177** D15
Al Ḩasakah, *Syr.* **150** D14
Al Ḩawrah, *Yemen* **152** Q11
Al Hījānah, *Syr.* **150** K8
Al Ḩijāz (Hejaz), region, *Saudi Arabia* **152** H6
Al Ḩillah, *Iraq* **152** E9
Al Ḩillah, *Saudi Arabia* **152** K10
Al Hirmil, *Leb.* **150** H7
Al Ḩudaydah, *Yemen* **152** Q8
Al Hufūf, *Saudi Arabia* **152** J12
Aliabad, *Iran* **153** G15
Alibates Flint Quarries National Monument, *Tex., U.S.* **96** G5
Āli Bayramlı, *Azerb.* **149** E22
Alicante (Alacant), *Sp.* **139** R9
Alice, *Qnsld., Austral.* **191** T13
Alice, *Tex., U.S.* **97** U10
Alice, Punta, *It.* **136** K12
Alice Downs, *W. Austral., Austral.* **191** R6
Alice Springs, *N. Terr., Austral.* **191** T8
Alice Town, *Bahamas* **110** D12
Alice Town, *Bahamas* **110** D9
Aliceville, *Ala., U.S.* **95** K13
Aligarh, *India* **158** F6
Alijos, Rocas, *Mex.* **108** E4
Alijos Rocks, *N. Amer.* **74** M2
Alika Cone, *Hawaii, U.S.* **107** N19
Al Ikhwān (The Brothers), islands, *Yemen* **153** R14
Alindau, *Indonesia* **169** J13
Alingsås, *Sw.* **134** M12
Alipur, *Pak.* **157** S9
Alipur Duar, *India* **158** G12
Aliquippa, *Pa., U.S.* **88** N3
Al 'Irqah, *Yemen* **152** R11
Alişar Hüyük, ruins, *Turk.* **148** E10
Al 'Īsāwīyah, *Saudi Arabia* **152** F6
Aliwal North, *S. Af.* **182** L10
Alizai, *Pak.* **157** N9
Al Jabal ash Sharqī (Anti-Lebanon), mountains, *Syr.* **150** J7
Al Jafr, *Jordan* **151** Q7
Al Jāfūrah, desert, *Saudi Arabia* **152** J12
Al Jaghbūb, *Lib.* **177** C16
Al Jahrah, *Kuwait* **152** G11
Al Jawf, *Saudi Arabia* **152** F7
Al Jawf (Kufra Oasis), *Lib.* **177** E16
Al Jifārah, *Saudi Arabia* **152** K10
Al Jīzah, *Jordan* **150** M6
Al Jubayl, *Saudi Arabia* **152** H12
Al Jumaylīyah, *Qatar* **153** J13
Al Junaynah, *Saudi Arabia* **152** M8
Al Junaynah *see* Geneina, *Sudan* **178** E10
Al Kahfah, *Saudi Arabia* **152** H9
Al Karak, *Jordan* **151** N6
Al Kawm, *Syr.* **150** F11
Al Khābūrah, *Oman* **153** K16
Al Khalīl (Hebron), *West Bank* **151** N5
Al Kharfah, *Saudi Arabia* **152** L10
Al Kharj, *Saudi Arabia* **152** K11
Al Khāşirah, *Saudi Arabia* **152** K9
Al Khawr, *Qatar* **153** J13
Al Khīrān, *Kuwait* **152** G11

Al Khufayfīyah, Saudi Arabia 152 J9
Al Khums, Lib. 177 B14
Al Khunn, Saudi Arabia 152 K12
Al Khuraybah, Yemen 152 Q11
Al Khurmah, Saudi Arabia 152 L8
Al Kiswah, Syr. 150 J7
Al Kūfah, Iraq 152 E9
Al Kufrah, oasis, Lib. 177 E16
Al Kūt, Iraq 152 E10
Al Kuwayt (Kuwait), Kuwait 152 G11
Al Labwah, Leb. 150 H7
Al Lādhiqīyah (Latakia), Syr. 150 F7
Allagash, river, Me., U.S. 89 B16
Allahabad, India 158 H8
Allahüekber Dağı, Turk. 149 D17
Al Lajā, lava field, Syr. 150 K7
Allakaket, Alas., U.S. 105 E15
All American Canal, Calif., U.S. 103 Z12
Allan Hills, Antarctica 207 N14
Allan Mountain, Idaho, U.S. 100 E5
Allanmyo, Myanmar 166 J5
Allanton, N.Z. 193 R16
Allegan, Mich., U.S. 92 M9
Allegheny, river, Pa., U.S. 88 L5
Allegheny Mountains, U.S. 79 H18
Allegheny Reservoir, Pa., U.S. 88 L5
Allen, Arg. 125 P8
Allendale, S.C., U.S. 90 M9
Allende, Mex. 108 D11
Allentown, Pa., U.S. 88 N9
Alleppey (Alappuzha), India 159 R5
Alliance, Nebr., U.S. 99 N2
Alliance, Ohio, U.S. 93 P15
Al Lidām, Saudi Arabia 152 M9
Allinge, Den. 135 P13
Allison Peninsula, Antarctica 206 H6
Al Līth, Saudi Arabia 152 M7
Al Luḩayyah, Yemen 152 P8
Al Luwaymī, Saudi Arabia 152 G8
Alma, Ark., U.S. 94 F6
Alma, Ga., U.S. 91 P7
Alma, Kans., U.S. 99 S9
Alma, Mich., U.S. 92 L11
Alma, Nebr., U.S. 99 R5
Almaden, Qnsld., Austral. 191 R13
Al Madīnah (Medina), Saudi Arabia 152 J7
Al Mafraq, Jordan 150 L7
Al Majma'ah, Saudi Arabia 152 J10
Al Mālikīyah, Syr. 150 C16
Al Manāmah (Manama), Bahrain 152 H12
Almanor, Lake, Calif., U.S. 103 N5
Almansa, Sp. 139 R8
Almar, Afghan. 156 L4
Al Marj, Lib. 177 C15
Al Ma'shūqah, Saudi Arabia 152 M8
Almaty, Kaz. 155 H16
Al Mawşil (Mosul), Iraq 152 C9
Al Mayādīn, Syr. 150 G14
Al Mayyāh, Saudi Arabia 152 G9
Almazán, Sp. 139 Q8
Almeirim, Braz. 122 D12
Almena, Kans., U.S. 99 R5
Almenara, Braz. 123 J16
Almendralejo, Sp. 139 R6
Almería, Sp. 139 S8
Al'met'yevsk, Russ. 140 H7
Al Mīnā', Leb. 150 H6
Al Mintirib, Oman 153 K16
Almira, Wash., U.S. 102 C7
Almirantazgo, Seno, Chile 125 X8
Almirante, Pan. 109 N20
Al Mismīyah, Syr. 150 K7
Almo, Idaho, U.S. 100 J6
Al Mubarraz, Saudi Arabia 152 J12
Al Mudawwarah, Jordan 151 S7
Al Mughayrā', U.A.E. 153 K14
Al Mukallā, Yemen 152 Q12
Al Mukhā, Yemen 152 R8
Almus, Turk. 148 E12
Almus Barajı, Turk. 148 D12
Al Muwassam, Saudi Arabia 152 P8
Al Muwayh, Saudi Arabia 152 K8
Alnwick, Eng., U.K. 138 F8
Alo, Wallis and Futuna, Fr. 198 E11
Alo, Pointe d', Wallis and Futuna, Fr. 198 E11
Alofau, Tutuila, Amer. Samoa, U.S. 198 M8
Alofi, island, Wallis and Futuna, Fr. 198 F11
Alofi, Niue, N.Z. 199 B20
Alofi Bay, Niue, N.Z. 199 B20
Alokan, island, Solomon Is. 197 N18
Along, India 158 F15
Alor, island, Indonesia 169 M15
Alor, Kepulauan, Indonesia 169 M15
Alor Setar, Malaysia 167 S8
Aloysius, Mount, Austral. 190 G7
Alpena, Mich., U.S. 92 H12
Alpha Cordillera, Arctic Oc. 222 J10
Alpine, Tex., U.S. 97 Q2
Alpine Junction, Wyo., U.S. 100 H8
Alps, mountains, Eur. 130 H6
Al Qā', Leb. 150 H7
Al Qābil, Oman 153 K15
Al Qaḑīmah, Saudi Arabia 152 K7
Al Qadmūs, Syr. 150 F7
Al Qā'im, Iraq 152 D8
Al Qa'īyah, Saudi Arabia 152 J9
Al Qāmishlī, Syr. 150 C15
Al Qārah, Yemen 152 Q9
Al Qaryah ash Sharqīyah, Lib. 177 C13
Al Qaryatayn, Syr. 150 H9
Al Qaşīm, region, Saudi Arabia 152 H9
Al Qaţīf, Saudi Arabia 152 H12
Al Qaţrānah, Jordan 151 N7
Al Qaţrūn, Lib. 177 E14
Al Qayşūmah, Saudi Arabia 152 G10
Al Qunayţirah (El Quneitra), Syr. 150 K6
Al Qunfudhah, Saudi Arabia 152 M7
Al Qurnah, Iraq 152 F11
Al Quşayr, Syr. 150 G8
Al Quşūrīyah, Saudi Arabia 152 K9
Al Quţayfah, Syr. 150 J8
Al Quway'īyah, Saudi Arabia 152 K10
Al Quwayrah, Jordan 151 R5
Alroy Downs, N. Terr., Austral. 191 S9
Alsask, Sask., Can. 76 M11
Alta, Iowa, U.S. 99 N9
Alta, Nor. 135 C14
Alta Floresta, Braz. 122 G10
Alta Gracia, Arg. 124 K10
Altagracia, Venez. 120 B7
Altagracia de Orituco, Venez. 120 B10
Altamaha, river, Ga., U.S. 91 P8
Altamira, Braz. 122 D12
Altamira, Chile 124 F7
Altanbulag, Mongolia 160 C12
Altan Xiret see Ejin Horo Qi, China 162 D3
Altar Desert, N. Amer. 74 L3
Altata, Mex. 108 F8
Altavista, Va., U.S. 90 F11
Altay, China 160 D8
Altay, Mongolia 160 D10
Altay Mountains, Asia 146 F9
Altayskiy, Russ. 140 L12
Altıağac, Azerb. 149 C22
Altinekin, Turk. 148 G8
Altınhisar, Turk. 148 G9
Altıntaş, Turk. 148 F6
Altınyayla, Turk. 148 H5
Altiplano, plateau, S. Amer. 118 H4
Alto, Tex., U.S. 97 N14
Alto Araguaia, Braz. 122 K11
Alto Garças, Braz. 122 J11
Alto Molócuè, Mozambique 183 E14
Alton, Ill., U.S. 93 S4
Altoona, Pa., U.S. 88 N5
Alto Paraguai, Braz. 122 H10
Alto Parnaíba, Braz. 123 G14
Alto Purús, river, Peru 122 G5
Alto Río Senguerr, Arg. 125 S7
Altun Shan, China 160 H7
Alturas, Calif., U.S. 102 L5
Altus, Okla., U.S. 96 H8
Al 'Ubaylah, Saudi Arabia 153 L13
Al Ubayyiḑ see El Obeid, Sudan 178 E12
Alucra, Turk. 149 E13
Al 'Ulá, Saudi Arabia 152 H6
Al'Unnāb, site, Jordan 151 R8
Alupka, Ukr. 133 M16
Al Uqaylah, Lib. 177 C15
Aluta, Dem. Rep. of the Congo 178 K11
Al' Uwaynat see 'Uweinat, Jebel, Af. 174 F8
Al'Uwaynāt, Lib. 177 E13
Al 'Uwaynid, Saudi Arabia 152 J10
Al 'Uwayqīlah, Saudi Arabia 152 F8
Al 'Uyūn, Saudi Arabia 152 J7
Alva, Okla., U.S. 96 E9
Alvarado, Tex., U.S. 96 M11
Älvdalen, Sw. 134 J12
Alvesta, Sw. 135 M13
Alvin, Tex., U.S. 97 R14
Älvkarleby, Sw. 135 K13
Alvorada, Braz. 123 H13
Alvord, Tex., U.S. 96 K10
Alvord Desert, Oreg., U.S. 102 K8
Alvord Lake, Oreg., U.S. 102 K8
Älvsbyn, Sw. 135 F14
Al Wajh, Saudi Arabia 152 H5
Al Wannān, Saudi Arabia 152 H11
Alwar, India 158 F5
Al Warī'ah, Saudi Arabia 152 H11
Alxa Zuoqi, China 160 H12
Alytus, Lith. 135 N17
Alzada, Mont., U.S. 100 F13
Alzamay, Russ. 141 K14
Alzira, Sp. 139 R9
Ama, Jap. 165 N6
Amadeus, Lake, Austral. 190 F7
Amadeus Depression, Austral. 190 F7
Amadi, Sudan 178 H12
Amadjuak Lake, Nunavut, Can. 77 G18
Amagi, Jap. 165 R4
Amahai, Indonesia 169 K16
Amakusa Shotō, Jap. 165 S3
Åmål, Sw. 134 L12
Amamapare, Indonesia 169 L20
Amamapare, Indonesia 193 C16
Amambaí, Braz. 122 M11
Amamiō Shima, Jap. 165 W3
Amamula, Dem. Rep. of the Congo 178 K11
Amanave, Tutuila, Amer. Samoa, U.S. 198 M6
Amangeldi, Kaz. 154 D11
Amanu, island, Fr. Polynesia, Fr. 199 F20
Amapá, Braz. 122 B12
Amarante, Braz. 123 F15
Amargosa Range, Nev., U.S. 103 U10
Amarillo, Tex., U.S. 96 G5
Amarkantak, India 158 J8
Amarwara, India 158 J7
Amasa, Mich., U.S. 92 F6
Amasra, Turk. 148 C8
Amasya, Turk. 148 D11
Amata, S. Austral., Austral. 191 U7
Amatari, Braz. 122 D9
Amatuku, island, Funafuti, Tuvalu 197 J23
Amavon Islands, Solomon Is. 197 L16
Amazon, river, S. Amer. 118 D7
Amazon, Mouths of the, S. Amer. 118 C8
Amazon, Source of the, S. Amer. 118 G3
Amazonas (Amazon), river, Peru 122 E5
Amazon Basin, S. Amer. 118 D3
Ambajogai, India 158 L5
Ambala, India 158 E6
Ambalangoda, Sri Lanka 159 T7
Ambalantota, Sri Lanka 159 T8
Ambanja, Madagascar 183 E18
Ambarchik, Russ. 141 C19
Ambargasta, Salinas de, Arg. 124 H10
Ambato, Ecua. 120 J3
Ambatondrazaka, Madagascar 183 F18
Ambelau, island, Indonesia 169 K16
Amberg, Ger. 132 J6
Ambergris Cay, Belize 109 J17
Ambergris Cays, Turks and Caicos Is., U.K. 111 J17
Ambi, Santa Cruz Is., Solomon Is. 197 R23
Ambikapur, India 158 J9
Ambilobe, Madagascar 183 D18
Ambler, Alas., U.S. 105 E13
Ambo, Peru 122 G3
Ambo Channel, Kwajalein Atoll, Marshall Is. 196 M5
Amboise, Fr. 138 L9
Ambon, island, Indonesia 169 K16
Ambon, Indonesia 169 K16
Ambositra, Madagascar 183 G17
Ambovombe, Madagascar 183 J16
Amboy, Calif., U.S. 103 W11
Amboy Crater, Calif., U.S. 103 W11
Ambre, Cap d', Madagascar 183 D18
Ambriz, Angola 182 C5
Ambrym, island, Vanuatu 198 D3
Ambunti, P.N.G. 193 C18
Amburan Burnu, Azerb. 149 D23
Amchitka Island, Alas., U.S. 104 P3
Amchitka Pass, Alas., U.S. 104 P4
Am Dam, Chad 177 J15
Amderma, Russ. 140 E11
Amdi, India 158 H8
Ameca, Mex. 108 H9
Amelia Island, Fla., U.S. 91 Q8
America-Antarctic Ridge, Southern Oc. 224 D10
American Falls, Idaho, U.S. 100 H6
American Falls Reservoir, Idaho, U.S. 100 H6
American Fork, Utah, U.S. 100 L7
American Highland, Antarctica 207 G18
American Samoa, Pac. Oc. 194 J10
Americus, Ga., U.S. 91 N5
Amery, Wis., U.S. 92 H2
Amery Ice Shelf, Antarctica 207 F19
Ames, Iowa, U.S. 99 N11
Amga, river, Russ. 141 H18
Amga, Russ. 141 H18
Amguema, Russ. 141 B20
Amguid, Alg. 176 D11
Amhara, region, Eth. 179 F15
Amherst, N.S., Can. 77 P22
Amherst, N.Y., U.S. 88 J5
Amherst, Tex., U.S. 96 J4
Amherst, Va., U.S. 90 E11
Ami, Île, New Caledonia, Fr. 198 E9
Amidon, N. Dak., U.S. 98 G2
Amiens, Fr. 138 J10
Amik Gölü, Turk. 148 J11
Amindivi Islands, India 159 Q3
Amino, Jap. 165 P8
Aminuis, Namibia 182 H7
Amir, river, Afghan. 156 L6
Amirante Trench, Ind. Oc. 220 H6
Amir Chah, Pak. 157 S2
Amistad National Recreation Area, Tex., U.S. 97 R6
Amistad Reservoir, Tex., U.S. 97 R5
Amite, La., U.S. 94 P10
Amity, Ark., U.S. 94 H7
Åmli, Nor. 134 L11
Amlia Island, Alas., U.S. 104 Q7
'Ammān (Philadelphia), Jordan 150 M7
Ammaroo, N. Terr., Austral. 191 S9
Ammochostos (Famagusta), Cyprus 148 L9
Ammochostos Bay, Cyprus 148 L9
'Amol, Iran 153 C13
Amolar, Braz. 122 K10
Amory, Miss., U.S. 95 J13
Amos, Que., Can. 77 P18
Amoy see Xiamen, China 163 Q8
Ampani, India 158 L8
Ampanihy, Madagascar 183 J16
Ampere Seamount, Atl. Oc. 216 H11
Amphitrite Group, Paracel Is. 168 B10
'Amrān, Yemen 152 P9
Amravati, India 158 K6
Amreli, India 158 J2
'Amrīt (Marathus), ruins, Syr. 150 G7
Amritsar, India 157 Q12
Amsā ad, Lib. 177 C17
Amsterdam, N.Y., U.S. 88 J11
Amsterdam, Neth. 138 G11
Amsterdam, Île, Ind. Oc. 184 J10
Am Timan, Chad 177 J15
'Āmūdah, Syr. 150 C14
Amu Darya, river, Asia 146 F6
Amukta Island, Alas., U.S. 104 Q8
Amun, P.N.G. 197 K13
Amund Ringnes Island, Nunavut, Can. 77 C15
Amundsen Bay, Antarctica 207 C19
Amundsen Gulf, N.W.T., Can. 76 E11
Amundsen-Scott South Pole, station, Antarctica 206 J12
Amuntai, Indonesia 168 K11
Amur, river, Asia 146 D12
Amurang, Indonesia 169 H15
Amuri, Aitutaki Atoll, Cook Is., N.Z. 198 P11
Amur-Onon, Source of the, Asia 146 F10
Amursk, Russ. 141 K21
Amyūn, Leb. 150 H6
An, Myanmar 166 H5
Anaa, island, Fr. Polynesia, Fr. 199 E18
Anabar, Nauru 197 E23
Anabar, river, Russ. 141 F15
Anabarskiy Zaliv, Russ. 141 E15
Anacapa Islands, Calif., U.S. 103 X7
Anaco, Venez. 120 C11
Anacoco, La., U.S. 94 N7
Anaconda, Mont., U.S. 100 D6
Anacortes, Wash., U.S. 102 B4
Anadarko, Okla., U.S. 96 H10
Anadyr', river, Asia 146 B12
Anadyr', Russ. 141 B21
Anadyr, Gulf of, Asia 146 A12
Anadyrskiy Zaliv, Russ. 141 B21
Anadyrskoye Ploskogor'ye, Russ. 141 C20
Anae, island, Guam, U.S. 196 D9
Anaehoomalu Bay, Hawaii, U.S. 107 L18
'Ānah, Iraq 152 D8
Anaheim, Calif., U.S. 103 X9
Anahola, Hawaii, U.S. 106 B6
Anahuac, Tex., U.S. 97 Q15
Anai Mudi, peak, India 159 R5
Anak, N. Korea 162 E12
Anakapalle, India 158 M9
Anaktuvuk Pass, Alas., U.S. 105 D15
Analalava, Madagascar 183 E17
Anamã, Braz. 122 D8
Ana María, Cayos, Cuba 110 J10
Ana María, Golfo de, Cuba 110 J10
Anambas, Kepulauan, Indonesia 168 H8
Anamoose, N. Dak., U.S. 98 F5
Anamosa, Iowa, U.S. 99 N14
Anamur, Turk. 148 J8
Anamur Burnu, Turk. 148 K8
Anan, Jap. 165 R8
Anand, India 158 J3
Anangenimon, island, Chuuk, F.S.M. 197 B16
Ananij, island, Enewetak Atoll, Marshall Is. 196 H9
Anantapur, India 159 P6
Anantnag (Islamabad), India 157 N12
Anan'yevo, Kyrg. 156 D13
Anápolis, Braz. 123 J13
Anār, Iran 153 F14
Anārak, Iran 153 D14
Anar Darreh, Afghan. 157 P2
Anatahan, island, N. Mariana Is., U.S. 196 C2
Anatolia (Asia Minor), region, Turk. 148 F5
Anatom (Kéamu), island, Vanuatu 198 H4
Anatone, Wash., U.S. 102 E9
Añatuya, Arg. 124 H11
Anboru, island, Jaluit Atoll, Marshall Is. 196 L8
Anbyŏn, N. Korea 162 D13
Anchorage, Alas., U.S. 105 J16
Anchor Bay, Calif., U.S. 103 Q2
Anclitas, Cayo, Cuba 110 K10
Ancona, It. 136 G10
Ancón de Sardinas, Bahía de, Col.-Ecua. 120 H3
Ancud, Chile 125 R6

Andacollo, Arg. 125 N7
Andalgalá, Arg. 124 G9
Åndalsnes, Nor. 134 J10
Andalusia, Ala., U.S. 95 N16
Andaman and Nicobar Islands, India 159 Q15
Andaman Basin, Ind. Oc. 220 E12
Andaman Islands, India 159 Q15
Andaman Sea, India 159 P15
Andamooka, S. Austral., Austral. 191 W10
Andapa, Madagascar 183 E18
Andenes, Nor. 134 D12
Anderson, river, N.W.T., Can. 76 E11
Anderson, Alas., U.S. 105 G16
Anderson, Calif., U.S. 103 N3
Anderson, Ind., U.S. 93 R9
Anderson, Mo., U.S. 99 V11
Anderson, S.C., U.S. 90 K7
Andes, mountains, S. Amer. 118 E2
Andfjorden, Nor. 134 D12
Andijon, Uzb. 155 K14
Ándikíthira, island, Gr. 137 M15
Andırın, Turk. 148 H11
Andkhvoy, Afghan. 156 K4
Andoany (Hell-Ville), Madagascar 183 D18
Andoas, Peru 122 D3
Andorra, Eur. 139 P9
Andorra, Andorra 139 P10
Andover, Me., U.S. 89 F15
Andovoranto, Madagascar 183 G18
Andøya, island, Nor. 134 D12
Andradina, Braz. 122 L12
Andreanof Islands, Alas., U.S. 104 Q5
Andrew Johnson National Historic Site, Tenn., U.S. 95 E20
Andrews, N.C., U.S. 90 J5
Andrews, S.C., U.S. 90 L11
Andrews, Tex., U.S. 96 M4
Androka, Madagascar 183 J16
Ándros, island, Gr. 137 L16
Andros Island, Bahamas 110 E11
Andros Town, Bahamas 110 E11
Androth Island, India 159 R3
Andryushkino, Russ. 141 D19
Andselv, Nor. 135 D13
Andújar, Sp. 139 S7
Anefis I-n-Darane, Mali 176 G10
Anegada, island, British Virgin Is., U.K. 113 E14
Anegada, Bahía, Arg. 125 P11
Anécho, Togo 180 H11
Aneju, island, Majuro Atoll, Marshall Is. 196 G10
Anelghowhat, Vanuatu 198 H4
Anelghowhat Bay, Vanuatu 198 J4
Anemwanot, island, Majuro Atoll, Marshall Is. 196 G11
Anenelibw, island, Majuro Atoll, Marshall Is. 196 H11
Anengenipuan, island, Chuuk, F.S.M. 197 B16
Aneta, N. Dak., U.S. 98 F7
Anetan, Nauru 197 E23
Aneto, peak, Sp. 139 P9
Aney, Niger 177 G13
Anfu, China 163 N5
Angamos, Punta, Chile 124 E7
Angara, river, Russ. 141 K14
Angarei, island, Aitutaki Atoll, Cook Is., N.Z. 198 Q11
Angarsk, Russ. 141 L15
Angaur (Ngeaur), island, Palau 196 R10
Ånge, Sw. 135 J13
Ángel de la Guarda, Isla, Mex. 108 C6
Angeles, Philippines 169 C13
Angel Falls, Venez. 120 E12
Angelina, river, Tex., U.S. 97 N14
Angels Camp, Calif., U.S. 103 R5
Ångermanälven, river, Sw. 135 G13
Angers, Fr. 138 L9
Angkor, ruins, Cambodia 166 M11
Angle Inlet, Minn., U.S. 98 D9
Anglem, Mount, N.Z. 193 R15
Anglesey, island, U.K. 138 G7
Angleton, Tex., U.S. 97 R14
Ango, Dem. Rep. of the Congo 178 H11
Angoche, Mozambique 183 F15
Angoche, Ilha, Mozambique 183 F15
Angohrān, Iran 153 H16
Angol, Chile 125 N6
Angola, Af. 182 D7
Angola, Ind., U.S. 93 N10
Angola Plain, Atl. Oc. 217 Q13
Angoon, Alas., U.S. 105 K22
Angora see Ankara, Turk. 148 E8
Angoram, P.N.G. 193 C18
Angostura, Presa de la, Mex. 109 K14
Angoulême, Fr. 138 M9
Angren, Uzb. 155 K14
Angtassom, Cambodia 167 P11
Anguilla, island, Leeward Is. 113 F15
Anguilla Cays, Bahamas 110 F9
Angul, India 158 K10
Anguo, China 162 E6
Angvik, Nor. 134 J10
Anhai, China 163 Q8
Anholt, island, Den. 134 N12
Anhua, China 162 M3
Ani, Jap. 164 K13
Aniak, Alas., U.S. 105 J13
Aniakchak National Monument and Preserve, Alas., U.S. 105 M14
Anibare, Nauru 197 F23
Anibare Bay, Nauru 197 F23
Animas, river, Colo., U.S. 101 P11
Animas, N. Mex., U.S. 101 V10
Animas Peak, N. Mex., U.S. 101 W10
Anin, Myanmar 166 L7
Anina, Rom. 137 F14
Anipemza, Arm. 149 D18
Aniwa, island, Vanuatu 198 G4
Anixab, Namibia 182 G6
Anjar, India 158 J2
Anjira, Pak. 157 T5
Anjouan see Nzwani, island, Comoros 185 N16
Anju, N. Korea 162 D12
Ankang, China 162 J2
Ankara, river, Turk. 148 E7
Ankara (Angora), Turk. 148 E8
Ankeny, Iowa, U.S. 99 P11
An Khe, Vietnam 166 M14
Anklam, Ger. 132 F7
Ankola, India 159 P4
Anlu, China 162 K5
Ann, Cape, Antarctica 207 C19
Ann, Cape, Mass., U.S. 89 J15
Anna, Ill., U.S. 93 V5
Anna, Lake, Va., U.S. 90 E12
Annaba, Alg. 176 A12
An Nabk, Syr. 150 H8
An Nafūd, desert, Saudi Arabia 152 G7
An Najaf, Iraq 152 E9
Annam Cordillera, Laos-Vietnam 166 J11
Anna Pink, Bahía, Chile 125 T6
Anna Plains, W. Austral., Austral. 191 S4
Anna Point, Nauru 197 E23
Annapolis, Md., U.S. 90 C13
Annapurna, peak, Nepal 158 F9
An Nāqūrah, Leb. 150 K5
Ann Arbor, Mich., U.S. 92 M12
An Nashshāsh, U.A.E. 153 K14
An Nāşirīyah, Iraq 152 F10
An Nawfalīyah, Lib. 177 C15
Annean, Lake, Austral. 190 H3
Annecy, Fr. 138 M12
Annigeri, India 159 N4
An Nimāş, Saudi Arabia 152 M8
Anningie, N. Terr., Austral. 191 S8
Anniston, Ala., U.S. 95 J16
Annitowa, N. Terr., Austral. 191 S9
Annobón, island, Eq. Guinea 181 L13
Annotto Bay, Jam. 110 M12
An Nu'ayrīyah, Saudi Arabia 152 H11
Anoano, Solomon Is. 197 N19
Anoka, Minn., U.S. 98 J11
Anpu, China 163 S2
Anqing, China 162 L7
Anren, China 163 P4
Ansai, China 162 F2
Ansbach, Ger. 132 J6
Anse-à-Foleur, Haiti 111 L16
Anse-à-Galets, Haiti 111 M16
Anse-à-Pitre, Haiti 111 N17
Anse-à-Veau, Haiti 111 M15
Anse Boileau, Seychelles 185 P20
Anse d'Hainault, Haiti 111 M14
Anselmo, Nebr., U.S. 99 P5
Anse-Rouge, Haiti 111 L16
Anshan, China 162 C10
Ansley, Nebr., U.S. 99 P5
Anson, Me., U.S. 89 F16
Anson, Tex., U.S. 96 L7
Anson Bay, Austral. 190 B7
Anson Bay, Norfolk I., Austral. 197 F20
Ansŏng, S. Korea 162 F13
Ansongo, Mali 176 H9
Anson Point, Norfolk I., Austral. 197 F20
Ansted, W. Va., U.S. 90 E9
Ansudu, Indonesia 169 K21
Ansudu, Indonesia 193 B17
Antakya (Antioch), Turk. 148 J11
Antalaha, Madagascar 183 E18
Antalya, Turk. 148 H6
Antalya Körfezi, Turk. 148 J6
Antananarivo, Madagascar 183 G17
Antarctic Peninsula, Antarctica 206 D4
Ant Atoll, Pohnpei, F.S.M. 197 G13
Antelope, Oreg., U.S. 102 G5
Antelope Reservoir, Oreg., U.S. 102 K9
Antequera, Sp. 139 S7
Anthony, Kans., U.S. 99 V7
Anthony, N. Mex., U.S. 101 V12
Anthony Lagoon, N. Terr., Austral. 191 R9
Anticosti, Île d', Que., Can. 77 M22
Antigo, Wis., U.S. 92 H6
Antigonish, N.S., Can. 77 P22
Antigua, island, Leeward Is. 113 G16
Antigua, Canary Is., Sp. 184 Q7
Antigua, Guatemala 109 L15
Antigua and Barbuda, N. Amer. 113 G16
Anti-Lebanon see Al Jabal ash Sharqī, mountains, Syr. 150 J7
Antilla, Cuba 111 J13
Antimony, Utah, U.S. 101 N7
Antioch, Calif., U.S. 103 R4
Antioch see Antakya, Turk. 148 J11
Antipayuta, Russ. 140 F12
Antipodes Islands, Pac. Oc. 194 Q9
Antlers, Okla., U.S. 96 J13
Antofagasta, Chile 124 E7
Antofalla, Salar de, Arg. 124 F8
Anton, Tex., U.S. 96 J4
Anton Chico, N. Mex., U.S. 101 S13
Antongila, Baie d', Madagascar 183 F18
Antongila Bay, Af. 174 M12
Antónia, Pico da, Cape Verde 185 D16
Antonito, Colo., U.S. 101 Q12
Antsirabe, Madagascar 183 G17
Antsirañana, Madagascar 183 D18
Antu, China 162 A14
Antufash, Jazīrat, Yemen 152 P8
Antwerpen, Belg. 138 H11
Anuanu Raro, island, Fr. Polynesia, Fr. 199 G19
Anuanu Runga, island, Fr. Polynesia, Fr. 199 G19
Anupgarh, India 158 E4
Anuradhapura, Sri Lanka 159 S7
Anuta, island, Solomon Is. 197 P20
Anvers Island, Antarctica 206 D4
Anvik, Alas., U.S. 105 H13
Anvil see El Yunque, peak, Cuba 111 K14
Anxi, China 160 G9
Anxi, China 163 Q8
Anxiang, China 162 M4
Anxin, China 162 D6
Anyang, China 162 G5
Anyang, S. Korea 162 F13
A'nyêmaqên Shan, China 160 J10
Anyi, China 162 G3
Anyi, China 162 M6
Anyou, China 163 V1
Anyuan, China 163 Q5
Anzhero Sudzhensk, Russ. 140 K12
Anzhu, Ostrova, Russ. 141 D16
Anzio, It. 136 H9
Aoa Bay, Tutuila, Amer. Samoa, U.S. 198 L8
Aoba (Omba), island, Vanuatu 198 C2
Aoga Shima, Jap. 165 S12
Aohan Qi, China 162 B9
Aojing, China 161 M17
Aola, Solomon Is. 197 N19
Aoloautuai, Tutuila, Amer. Samoa, U.S. 198 M7
Aomon, island, Enewetak Atoll, Marshall Is. 196 G8
Aomori, Jap. 164 J13
Aonae, Jap. 164 H12
A'opo, Samoa 198 K2
Aorai, Mount, Tahiti, Fr. Polynesia, Fr. 199 P16
Aóre, island, Vanuatu 198 D2
Aosta, It. 136 E7
Aoulef, Alg. 176 D10
Aoumou, New Caledonia, Fr. 198 D8
Aoya, Jap. 165 P7
Aozi, Chad 177 F15
Aozou, Chad 177 F14
Aozou Strip, region, Chad 177 F15
Apa, river, Braz.-Para. 122 L10
Apache, Okla., U.S. 96 H9
Apakho, Santa Cruz Is., Solomon Is. 197 Q23
Apalachee Bay, U.S. 79 M18
Apalachicola, river, Fla., U.S. 91 R4
Apalachicola, Fla., U.S. 91 R4
Apalachicola Bay, Fla., U.S. 91 R4
Apamea, ruins, Syr. 150 F7
Apaora, Solomon Is. 197 P20
Apaporis, river, Col. 120 H7
Aparri, Philippines 169 B14
Apataki, island, Fr. Polynesia, Fr. 199 D18
Apatin, Yug. 137 F13
Apatity, Russ. 140 D8
Apatzingán, Mex. 108 J10
Apennines, mountains, It. 136 F8
Apia, Samoa 198 L3
Apia Harbour, Samoa 198 L3
Apishapa, river, Colo., U.S. 101 P14
Ap Iwan, Cerro, Arg. 125 T7
Apolima, island, Samoa 198 L2
Apolima Strait, Samoa 198 L2
Apollo Bay, Vic., Austral. 191 Z12
Apollonia see Suşah, Lib. 177 B16
Apolo, Bol. 122 J6
Apopka, Lake, Fla., U.S. 91 T8
Aporema, Braz. 122 C12
Apostle Islands, Wis., U.S. 92 E4
Apostle Islands National Lakeshore, Wis., U.S. 92 E3
Apóstoles, Arg. 124 H14
Apostolos Andreas, Cape, Cyprus 148 K9
Apostolos Andreas Monastery, Cyprus 148 K9
Apoteri, Guyana 121 F14
Appalachian Mountains, U.S. 79 J17
Appalachian Plateau, U.S. 79 J17
Appleton, Minn., U.S. 98 J9
Appleton, Wis., U.S. 92 J6
Appleton City, Mo., U.S. 99 T11
Apple Valley, Calif., U.S. 103 W9
Appomattox, Va., U.S. 90 F11
Apra Harbor, Guam, U.S. 196 C10
Apra Heights, Guam, U.S. 196 C10
Apua Point, Hawaii, U.S. 107 N21
Apucarana, Braz. 122 M12
Apurashokoru, island, Palau 196 P10
Apure, river, S. Amer. 118 B4
Apurímac, river, Peru 122 H4
Aqaba see Al'Aqabah, Jordan 151 R5
Aqaba, Gulf of, Saudi Arabia 152 F4
Aqadyr, Kaz. 155 F14
Aqchan, Afghan. 156 K5
Aqiq, Sudan 179 D14
Aqköl, Kaz. 155 C13
Aqköl, Kaz. 155 G16
Aq Kopruk, Afghan. 156 L6
Aqmola see Astana, Kaz. 155 D14
Aqqikkol Hu, China 160 H7
Aqqystaū, Kaz. 154 F6
Aqsay, Kaz. 154 C7
Aqshataū, Kaz. 155 F15
Aqsū, river, Kaz. 155 G17
Aqsū, Kaz. 155 C14
Aqtaū, Kaz. 154 H5
Aqtöbe, Kaz. 154 D8
Aqtoghay, Kaz. 155 F17
Aquidauana, Braz. 122 L10
Aquin, Haiti 111 M15
Aquitaine Basin, Eur. 130 H4
Ara, India 158 G9
Araara, Motu, Huahine, Fr. Polynesia, Fr. 199 H14
Araara, Passe, Huahine, Fr. Polynesia, Fr. 199 H14
Arab, Ala., U.S. 95 H15
'Arabah, Wādī al, Isreal-Jordan 151 Q5
Arabian Basin, Ind. Oc. 220 E8
Arabian Peninsula, Asia 146 G3
Arabian Sea, Asia 146 J5
Arabs Gulf, Af. 174 D8
Araç, river, Turk. 148 C9
Araç, Turk. 148 C9
Aracaju, Braz. 123 H17
Aracati, Braz. 123 E17
Araçatuba, Braz. 122 L12
Aracides, Cape, Solomon Is. 197 M20
Araçuaí, Braz. 123 K15
Arad, Rom. 137 E14
Arada, Chad 177 H15
Arafura Sea, Asia 146 L16
Aragarças, Braz. 122 J12
Aragats, peak, Arm. 149 D18
Arago, Cape, Oreg., U.S. 102 J1
Araguacema, Braz. 123 F13
Aragua de Barcelona, Venez. 120 C11
Araguaia, river, Braz. 123 F13
Araguaína, Braz. 123 F13
Araguari, Braz. 123 K13
Araguatins, Braz. 123 E13
Arai, Jap. 165 N11
Arak, Alg. 176 E11
Arāk, Iran 152 D12
Arakabesan, island, Palau 196 N11
Arakan Yoma, Myanmar 166 H5
Arakht, Afghan. 156 K9
Aral, Kaz. 154 F10
Aral, Kyrg. 156 E11
Aral Mangy Qaraqumy, Kaz. 154 F10
Aral Sea, Asia 154 G9
Aralsor, Lake, Eur. 130 F13
Aralsor Köli, Kaz. 154 D5
Aralsul'fat, Kaz. 154 F10
Araltobe, Kaz. 154 D9
Aramac, Qnsld., Austral. 191 T13
Ārān, Iran 153 D13
Aranda de Duero, Sp. 139 P7
Arandu, Afghan. 156 L9
Aran Islands, Ire. 138 G5
Aranjuez, Sp. 139 Q7
Aransas, river, Tex., U.S. 97 T11
Aransas Pass, Tex., U.S. 97 T11
Araouane, Mali 176 G8
Arapahoe, Nebr., U.S. 99 R5
Arapaho National Recreation Area, Colo., U.S. 100 L12
Arapiraca, Braz. 123 G17
Arapkir, Turk. 149 F13
'Ar'ar, Saudi Arabia 152 F8
Araraquara, Braz. 123 L13
Ararat, Arm. 149 E19
Ararat, Mount see Ağrı Dağı, Turk. 149 E18
Araria, India 158 G11
Aras, river, Azerb. 149 E21
Aras, river, Iran 152 A11
Aratika, island, Fr. Polynesia, Fr. 199 E18
Aratsu Bay, Rota I., N. Mariana Is., U.S. 196 E8
Arauá, river, Braz. 122 E7
Arauca, river, Col.-Venez. 120 D7
Arauca, Col. 120 D7

Arauco Gulf, S. Amer. 118 M4
Aravalli Range, India 158 H3
Araxá, Braz. 123 KI3
Araxes see Aras, river, Turk. 149 EI7
Arayit Daği, Turk. 148 F7
Ārba Minch', Eth. 179 HI4
Arbela see Irbid, Jordan 150 L6
Arbīl, Iraq 152 C9
Arborea, It. 136 J7
Arcadia, Fla., U.S. 91 V8
Arcadia, La., U.S. 94 L7
Arcadia, Mich., U.S. 92 J9
Arcadia, Wis., U.S. 92 J3
Arcata, Calif., U.S. 102 M2
Archangel see Arkhangel'sk, Russ. 140 E8
Archbald, Pa., U.S. 88 M9
Archer City, Tex., U.S. 96 K9
Arches National Park, Utah, U.S. 101 N9
Archman, Turkm. 154 L7
Arckaringa Creek, Austral. 190 H9
Arco, Idaho, U.S. 100 G6
Arco Pass, S. Amer. 118 N4
Arcoverde, Braz. 123 GI7
Arctic Bay, Nunavut, Can. 77 EI6
Arctic Ocean 74 A6
Arctic Red, river, N.W.T., Can. 76 E9
Arctic Village, Alas., U.S. 105 DI7
Arctowski, station, Antarctica 206 C3
Ardabīl, Iran 152 BII
Ardahan, Turk. 149 DI7
Ardakān, Iran 153 EI4
Ardanuç, Turk. 149 CI6
Arḑ aṣ Ṣawwān, plain, Jordan 151 P8
Ardennes, mountains, Belg. 138 JII
Ardestān, Iran 153 DI3
Ardmore, Okla., U.S. 96 JII
Ardmore, S. Dak., U.S. 98 MI
Åre, Sw. 134 HI2
Arecibo, P.R., U.S. III M22
Arei, Pointe, Rurutu, Fr. Polynesia, Fr. 199 K23
Areia Branca, Braz. 123 EI7
Arekalong Peninsula (Ngerchelong), Palau 196 MI2
Arena, Point, U.S. 78 F2
Arenápolis, Braz. 122 HIO
Arenas, Cayo, Mex. 109 GI5
Arenas, Punta de, Arg. 125 X9
Arendal, Nor. 134 MII
Arequipa, Peru 122 J5
Arethusa see Ar Rastan, Syr. 150 G8
Arezzo, It. 136 G9
Argadargada, N. Terr., Austral. 191 TIO
Argakhtakh, Russ. 141 DI9
Argentina, S. Amer. 124 S8
Argentina Range, Antarctica 206 FIO
Argentine Plain, Atl. Oc. 217 V6
Argentino, Lago, Arg. 125 V7
Argenton, Fr. 138 LIO
Arghandab, river, Afghan. 157 P5
Arghandab, Band-e, Afghan. 157 P5
Arghastan, river, Afghan. 157 Q5
Arghestan, Afghan. 157 Q6
Argo, Sudan 178 CI2
Árgos, Gr. 137 LI5
Argostóli, Gr. 137 LI3
Argoub, W. Sahara, Mor. 176 E5
Arguello, Point, Calif., U.S. 103 W5
Argun, river, Asia 146 EII
Argus, Dome, Antarctica 207 HI6
Arguut, Mongolia 160 EII
Argyle, Minn., U.S. 98 E8
Argyle, Lake, Austral. 190 C7
Ar Horqin Qi (Tianshan), China 162 A9
Arhrījīt, Mauritania 176 G7
Århus, Den. 134 NII
Ari, Motu, Gambier Is., Fr. Polynesia, Fr. 199 Q2O
Ariari, river, Col. 120 G6
Ari Atoll, Maldives 159 V3
Arica, Chile 124 B7
Arid, Cape, Austral. 190 K5
Arida, Jap. 165 R8
Aride, Seychelles 185 M2O
Arifwala, Pak. 157 RII
Arīḥā, Syr. 150 E8
Arīḥā (Jericho), West Bank 150 M6
Arikaree, river, Colo., U.S. 100 LI5
Arikawa, Jap. 165 R3
Arimã, Braz. 122 E8
Arima, Trin. & Tobago 113 PI7
Arimo, Idaho, U.S. 100 J7
Arinos, river, Braz. 122 HIO
Aripeka, Fla., U.S. 91 T7
Ariporo, river, Col. 120 E7
Aripuanã, river, Braz. 122 F9
Aripuanã, Braz. 122 G9
Ariquemes, Braz. 122 G8
'Arīsh, Wādi el, Egypt 151 Q3
Aristizábal, Cabo, Arg. 125 S9
Ariyalur, India 159 R6
Arizaro, Salar de, Arg. 124 F8
Arizona, U.S. 101 T6

Arizona, Arg. 124 M9
Arjeplog, Sw. 135 FI3
Arjona, Col. 120 C4
Arkadelphia, Ark., U.S. 94 H7
Arkagala, Russ. 141 FI9
Arkansas, river, U.S. 79 KI4
Arkansas, U.S. 94 G7
Arkansas City, Ark., U.S. 94 JIO
Arkansas City, Kans., U.S. 99 V8
Arkansas Post National Memorial, Ark., U.S. 94 H9
Arkhangel'sk (Archangel), Russ. 140 E8
Arkítsa, Gr. 137 KI5
Arklow, Ire. 138 G6
Arkona, Kap, Ger. 132 E7
Arkonam, India 159 P7
Arktícheskiy, Mys, Russ. 141 CI4
Arlap, island, Jaluit Atoll, Marshall Is. 196 L7
Arles, Fr. 139 NII
Arlington, Ga., U.S. 91 P4
Arlington, Oreg., U.S. 102 F6
Arlington, S. Dak., U.S. 98 K8
Arlington, Tex., U.S. 96 LII
Arlington, Va., U.S. 90 CI3
Arlington, Wash., U.S. 102 A4
Arlington Heights, Ill., U.S. 93 N7
Arlon, Belg. 138 JII
Arma, Kans., U.S. 99 UIO
Armagh, N. Ire., U.K. 138 F6
Armavir, Arm. 149 EI8
Armavir, Russ. 140 H4
Armells Creek, Mont., U.S. 100 C9
Armenia, Asia 149 DI8
Armenia, region, Iran 152 A9
Armenia, region, Turk. 149 EI5
Armenia, Col. 120 F4
Armidale, N.S.W., Austral. 191 WI5
Armijo, N. Mex., U.S. 101 SI2
Armorican Massif, Eur. 130 G3
Armour, S. Dak., U.S. 98 M6
Armstrong, Ont., Can. 77 NI6
Armur, India 158 L6
Armutcuk, Turk. 148 C7
Arnaoutis, Cape, Cyprus 148 L7
Årnes, Nor. 134 HII
Arnett, Okla., U.S. 96 F8
Arnhem, Neth. 138 HII
Arnhem, Cape, Austral. 190 BIO
Arnhem Land, N. Terr., Austral. 191 P9
Arniel, island, Majuro Atoll, Marshall Is. 196 GI2
Arno Atoll, Marshall Is. 196 H5
Arno Bay, S. Austral., Austral. 191 X9
Arnold, Nebr., U.S. 99 P5
Arney, island, Nor. 135 CI3
Aroab, Namibia 182 K8
Arock, Oreg., U.S. 102 J9
Arorae, island, Kiribati 194 G8
Arorangi, Rarotonga, Cook Is., N.Z. 198 Q9
Arowhana, peak, N.Z. 193 K2O
Arpa, river, Arm.-Turk. 149 DI8
Arpaçay, Turk. 149 DI7
Arqalyq, Kaz. 154 DI2
Ar Rabbah, Jordan 151 N6
Arrabury, Qnsld., Austral. 191 VII
Arraias, Braz. 123 HI4
Ar Ramādī, Iraq 152 D9
Ar Ramlah, Jordan 151 R6
Ar Ramthā, Jordan 150 L7
Ar Raqqah (Nicephorium), Syr. 150 EII
Arras, Fr. 138 JIO
Ar Rashādīyah, Jordan 151 P6
Ar Rastan (Arethusa), Syr. 150 G8
Ar Rawḑah, Saudi Arabia 152 L8
Arrecife, Canary Is., Sp. 184 P8
Ar Riyāḑ (Riyadh), Saudi Arabia 152 JIO
Ar Riyān, Yemen 152 QI2
Arrowrock Reservoir, Idaho, U.S. 100 G4
Arroyo Grande, Calif., U.S. 103 V5
Arroyos de Mantua, Cuba IIO H4
Arroyos y Esteros, Para. 122 MIO
Ar Rub' al Khālī, desert, Saudi Arabia 152 MII
Ar Ruṣāfah (Risāfe), ruins, Syr. 150 EII
Ar Ruṣayfah, Jordan 150 M7
Ar Ruṭbah, Iraq 152 D7
Ar Ruwayshid, Jordan 150 LIO
Arsen'yev, Russ. 141 L2I
Arsikere, India 159 P5
Arsuk, Greenland, Den. 75 D22
Art, Île, New Caledonia, Fr. 198 B6
Art Shīdīyan, Jordan 151 R6
Árta, Gr. 137 KI4
Artà, Sp. 139 RII
Artashat, Arm. 149 EI8
Artem, Russ. 141 M2I
Artemisa, Cuba IIO G6
Artemovsk, Russ. 141 LI3
Artesia, N. Mex., U.S. 101 UI4
Artesian, S. Dak., U.S. 98 L7
Arthur, Nebr., U.S. 99 P3
Arthur's Pass, N.Z. 193 NI7
Arthur's Town, Bahamas III EI3
Artigas, Uru. 124 JI4

Art'ik, Arm. 149 DI8
Artova, Turk. 148 EII
Artvin, Turk. 149 CI6
Artyk, Turkm. 154 M8
Artyk Yuryakh, Russ. 141 FI7
Artyom, Azerb. 149 D23
Aru, Kepulauan, Indonesia 169 LI9
Aruanã, Braz. 122 JI2
Aruba, island, Lesser Antilles 112 M8
Aruboe, island, Jaluit Atoll, Marshall Is. 196 M7
Arucas, Canary Is., Sp. 184 Q6
Arue, Tahiti, Fr. Polynesia, Fr. 199 NI6
Aru Islands, Asia 146 LI5
Arumã, Braz. 122 E8
Aru Passage, Pohnpei, F.S.M. 197 FI4
Arusha, Tanzania 179 LI4
Arutanga, Aitutaki Atoll, Cook Is., N.Z. 198 QII
Arutanga Passage, Aitutaki Atoll, Cook Is., N.Z. 198 QII
Arutua, island, Fr. Polynesia, Fr. 199 DI7
Aruwimi, river, Dem. Rep. of the Congo 178 JIO
Arvada, Colo., U.S. 100 MI3
Arvayheer, Mongolia 160 DII
Arviat, Nunavut, Can. 77 JI5
Arvidsjaur, Sw. 135 FI3
Arvika, Sw. 134 LI2
Arvon, Mount, Mich., U.S. 92 F7
Arwād, Jazīrat, Syr. 150 G6
Arxan, China 161 DI3
Ary, Russ. 141 EI6
Arys, Kaz. 155 JI3
Arys Kӧli, Kaz. 154 GI2
Arzamas, Russ. 140 G6
Asad, Afghan. 157 P5
Asad, Buḩayrat al, Syr. 150 EII
Asadabad, Afghan. 156 M9
Asaga Strait, Manua Is., Amer. Samoa, U.S. 198 N2
Aşağıpınarbaşı, Turk. 148 G8
Asahi, river, Jap. 165 Q7
Asahi Dake, Jap. 164 FI4
Asahikawa, Jap. 164 FI4
Asan, Guam, U.S. 196 CIO
Asansol, India 158 HII
Asatdas, Guam, U.S. 196 BII
Asau, Samoa 198 KI
Asau Harbour, Samoa 198 KI
Asbury Park, N.J., U.S. 88 PII
Ascención, Bol. 122 J8
Ascensión, Mex. 108 C8
Ascension, island, Atl. Oc. 184 F4
Ascension Fracture Zone, Atl. Oc. 217 PIO
Ascoli Piceno, It. 136 GIO
Āsela, Eth. 179 GI5
Ashāqif, Jabal al, Jordan 150 M9
Ashburn, Ga., U.S. 91 P6
Ashburton, river, Austral. 190 F2
Ashburton, N.Z. 193 PI7
Ashburton Downs, W. Austral., Austral. 191 T2
Ashchykӧl, lake, Kaz. 154 HI2
Ashdod, Israel 150 M4
Ashdown, Ark., U.S. 94 J6
Asherton, Tex., U.S. 97 T8
Asheville, N.C., U.S. 90 H7
Ashford, Wash., U.S. 102 D4
Ash Fork, Ariz., U.S. 101 S6
Ashgabat, Turkm. 154 M8
Ash Grove, Mo., U.S. 99 UI2
Ashibe, Jap. 165 R4
Ashikaga, Jap. 165 NI2
Ashizuri Misaki, Jap. 165 S6
Ashland, Kans., U.S. 99 V5
Ashland, Ky., U.S. 95 A2O
Ashland, Me., U.S. 89 BI7
Ashland, Mont., U.S. 100 EI2
Ashland, Nebr., U.S. 99 Q8
Ashland, Ohio, U.S. 93 PI4
Ashland, Oreg., U.S. 102 K3
Ashland, Va., U.S. 90 EI2
Ashland, Wis., U.S. 92 F4
Ashley, river, S.C., U.S. 90 MIO
Ashley, N. Dak., U.S. 98 H6
Ashmore Islands, Austral. 190 B4
Ashmyany, Belarus 132 EI2
Ashoro, Jap. 164 FI5
Ashqelon, Israel 150 M4
Ash Shabakah, Iraq 152 F9
Ash Sharqāt, Iraq 152 C9
Ash Shawbak, Jordan 151 Q6
Ash Shiḩḩ, Jordan 151 R6
Ash Shiḩr, Yemen 152 QI2
Ash Shiṣar, Oman 153 NI4
Ash Shumlūl, Saudi Arabia 152 HII
Ash Shuqayq, Saudi Arabia 152 N8
Ash Shurayf, Saudi Arabia 152 H7
Ashtabula, Ohio, U.S. 93 NI5
Ashtabula, Lake, N. Dak., U.S. 98 G7
Ashton, Idaho, U.S. 100 G7
'Āṣī (Orontes), river, Syr. 150 F7
Asia Minor see Anatolia, region, Turk. 148 F5
Asifabad, India 158 L7
Asiga, Puntan, Tinian, N. Mariana Is., U.S. 196 A8

Asika, India 158 LIO
Asinara, island, It. 136 H7
Asipovichy, Belarus 133 FI3
'Asīr, region, Saudi Arabia 152 M8
Aşkale, Turk. 149 EI5
Askole, Pak. 156 LI3
Asl, Egypt 151 RI
Asmar, Afghan. 156 M9
Asmara, Eritrea 179 EI5
Aso, peak, Jap. 165 S5
Āsosa, Eth. 179 FI3
Aspen, Colo., U.S. 100 MI2
Aspermont, Tex., U.S. 96 K7
Aspiring, Mount, N.Z. 193 PI5
As Sa'an, Syr. 150 F9
Assab, Eritrea 179 EI6
As Sabkhah, Syr. 150 EI2
Aş Şafā, lava field, Syr. 150 K8
As Safīrah, Syr. 150 E9
Aş Şa'īd, Yemen 152 QIO
Assal, Lake, Djibouti 179 FI6
Aş Şāliḩīyah (Dura Europus) see Aş Şāliḩīyah, Syr. 150 GI4
As Salṭ, Jordan 150 M6
As Salwá, Saudi Arabia 152 JI2
As Samāwah, Iraq 152 FIO
As Sanām, desert, Saudi Arabia 153 KI3
Aş Şarafand, Leb. 150 J6
Assateague Island National Seashore, Md., U.S. 90 DI5
Aş Şawrah, Saudi Arabia 152 G5
Assen, Neth. 138 GII
As Sidr, Lib. 177 CI5
As Sidr, Saudi Arabia 152 K7
Assis, Braz. 122 LI2
Assos, ruins, Turk. 148 E2
As Sukhnah, Syr. 150 GII
As Sulaymānīyah, Iraq 152 CIO
As Sulayyil, Saudi Arabia 152 MIO
Aş Şulb, region, Saudi Arabia 152 HII
Aş Şummān, plateau, Saudi Arabia 152 HIO
Assumption Island, Seychelles 183 CI7
Aş Şurrah, Yemen 152 QIO
Aş Şuwār, Syr. 150 FI4
As Suwaydāʾ, Syr. 150 L8
As Suwayḩ, Oman 153 KI7
Astana (Aqmola), Kaz. 155 DI4
Astara, Azerb. 149 F22
Āstārā, Iran 152 AII
Asti, It. 136 F7
Astola Island, Pak. 157 W3
Astor, Pak. 156 LI2
Astorga, Sp. 139 P6
Astoria, Oreg., U.S. 102 E2
Astove Island, Seychelles 183 CI7
Astra, Arg. 125 S9
Astrakhan', Russ. 140 J5
Astrolabe, Cape, Solomon Is. 197 MI9
Asuisui, Cape, Samoa 198 L2
Asunción, Para. 122 MIO
Asunción, Punta, Arg. 125 PI2
Asuncion, island, N. Mariana Is., U.S. 196 A2
Asuzudo Point, Rota I., N. Mariana Is., U.S. 196 D8
Aswān, Egypt 177 EI9
Aswān High Dam, Egypt 177 EI9
Asyût, Egypt 177 DI8
Ata, island, Tongatapu, Tonga 198 HI2
Atacama, Puna de, S. Amer. 118 J4
Atacama, Salar de, Chile 124 E8
Atacama Desert, S. Amer. 118 J4
Atafu, island, Kiribati 194 HIO
Atakpamé, Togo 180 GII
Atapupu, E. Timor 169 MI5
Atar, Mauritania 176 F6
Atascadero, Calif., U.S. 103 V5
Atascosa, river, Tex., U.S. 97 SIO
Atasu, Kaz. 155 EI4
Atata, island, Tongatapu, Tonga 198 HII
Atauro, island, E. Timor 169 MI5
Atbara, river, Sudan 179 DI3
Atbara, Sudan 179 DI3
At Bashy, Kyrg. 156 FI2
Atchafalaya, river, La., U.S. 94 P9
Atchafalaya Bay, La., U.S. 94 R9
Atchison, Kans., U.S. 99 SIO
Athabasca, river, Alta., Can. 76 KII
Athabasca, Alta., Can. 76 LII
Athabasca, Lake, Alta.-Sask., Can. 76 KI2
Athena, Oreg., U.S. 102 E8
Athens, Ala., U.S. 95 GI5
Athens, Ga., U.S. 90 L6
Athens see Athína, Gr. 137 LI5
Athens, Ohio, U.S. 93 SI4
Athens, Tenn., U.S. 95 FI8
Athens, Tex., U.S. 96 MI3
Atherton Tableland, Austral. 190 DI3
Athfālah, Saudi Arabia 152 M8
Athína (Athens), Gr. 137 LI5
Ati, Chad 177 JI5
Atico, Peru 122 J4
Atikokan, Ont., Can. 77 PI5
Atimoono, island, Manihiki Atoll, Cook Is., N.Z. 199 BI5

Atiti, *Afghan.* 156 L9
Atitue, *Tahiti, Fr. Polynesia, Fr.* 199 P15
Atiu, *island, Cook Is., N.Z.* 194 K12
Atka, *Alas., U.S.* 104 Q6
Atka, *Russ.* 141 F2O
Atka Island, *Alas., U.S.* 104 Q6
Atkins, *Ark., U.S.* 94 F8
Atkinson, *Nebr., U.S.* 99 N6
Atlanta, *Ga., U.S.* 90 L5
Atlanta, *Mich., U.S.* 92 H11
Atlanta, *Tex., U.S.* 96 K15
Atlantic, *Iowa, U.S.* 99 P1O
Atlantic, *N.C., U.S.* 90 J14
Atlantic Beach, *Fla., U.S.* 91 Q9
Atlantic Beach, *N.C., U.S.* 90 J14
Atlantic City, *N.J., U.S.* 88 Q1O
Atlantic City, *Wyo., U.S.* 100 J1O
Atlantic-Indian Ridge, *Atl. Oc.–Ind. Oc.* 220 R1
Atlantis Fracture Zone, *Atl. Oc.* 216 J7
Atlantis II Fracture Zone, *Ind. Oc.* 220 N6
Atlas Mountains, *Alg.–Mor.* 176 C8
Atlin, *B.C., Can.* 76 G8
'Atlit, *Israel* 150 L5
Atmautluak, *Alas., U.S.* 104 J12
Atmore, *Ala., U.S.* 95 N14
Atoka, *Okla., U.S.* 96 H12
Atoyac, *Mex.* 108 K11
Atrak (Etrek), *river, Iran* 153 B14
Atrato, *river, Col.* 120 D4
Atsumi, *Jap.* 165 Q1O
Atsunai, *Jap.* 164 G15
Atsutoko, *Jap.* 164 F16
Aţ Ţafilah, *Jordan* 151 P6
Aţ Ţā'if, *Saudi Arabia* 152 L7
Attalla, *Ala., U.S.* 95 H16
Attapu, *Laos* 166 M12
Attawapiskat, *river, N. Amer.* 74 G7
Attawapiskat, *Ont., Can.* 77 M17
At Taysīyah, *plateau, Saudi Arabia* 152 G9
At Tibnī, *Syr.* 150 F13
Attica, *Ind., U.S.* 93 Q8
Attica, *Kans., U.S.* 99 V6
Attleboro, *Mass., U.S.* 89 L14
Attu, *Greenland, Den.* 75 D21
Aţ Ţubayq, *region, Saudi Arabia* 152 F6
Attu Island, *Alas., U.S.* 104 M1
At Turbah, *Yemen* 152 R9
At Turbah, *Yemen* 152 R9
Atuel, *river, Arg.* 124 M8
Atuona, *Hiva Oa, Fr. Polynesia, Fr.* 199 M2O
Atutahi, *island, Penrhyn, Cook Is., N.Z.* 199 C18
Atwater, *Calif., U.S.* 103 S5
Atwood *see* Samana Cay, *island, Bahamas* 111 G15
Atwood, *Kans., U.S.* 99 R4
Atyraū, *Kaz.* 154 F6
Aua, *Tutuila, Amer. Samoa, U.S.* 198 M8
Auas Mountains, *Af.* 174 P7
Auau Channel, *Hawaii, U.S.* 107 G15
Aube, *river, Fr.* 138 K11
Aubry Lake, *N.W.T., Can.* 76 E1O
Auburn, *Qnsld., Austral.* 191 U15
Auburn, *Ala., U.S.* 95 L17
Auburn, *Calif., U.S.* 103 Q5
Auburn, *Ill., U.S.* 93 R5
Auburn, *Ind., U.S.* 93 P1O
Auburn, *Me., U.S.* 89 G15
Auburn, *N.Y., U.S.* 88 J8
Auburn, *Nebr., U.S.* 99 R9
Auburn, *Wash., U.S.* 102 C4
Auburndale, *Fla., U.S.* 91 U8
Auce, *Latv.* 135 M16
Auch, *Fr.* 139 N9
Auckland, *N.Z.* 193 J19
Auckland Islands, *N.Z.* 194 Q7
Audubon, *Iowa, U.S.* 99 P1O
Augathella, *Qnsld., Austral.* 191 U13
Augsburg, *Ger.* 132 J6
Augusta, *Ark., U.S.* 94 F9
Augusta, *Ga., U.S.* 90 L8
Augusta, *It.* 136 L11
Augusta, *Kans., U.S.* 99 U8
Augusta, *Ky., U.S.* 95 A18
Augusta, *Me., U.S.* 89 F16
Augusta, *Mont., U.S.* 100 C7
Augusta, *Wis., U.S.* 92 J3
Augusta Victoria, *Chile* 124 E7
Augustów, *Pol.* 132 F11
Augustus, Mount, *Austral.* 190 F2
Augustus Downs, *Qnsld., Austral.* 191 R11
Aukena, *island, Gambier Is., Fr. Polynesia, Fr.* 199 Q21
Auki, *Solomon Is.* 197 M19
Auld, Lake, *Austral.* 190 F5
Aulong, *island, Palau* 196 P1O
Auluptagel, *island, Palau* 196 P11
Aunuu, *island, Tutuila, Amer. Samoa, U.S.* 198 M9
Aunuu, *Tutuila, Amer. Samoa, U.S.* 198 M9
Auob, *river, Namibia* 182 J8
Auponhia, *Indonesia* 169 K15
Aur, *island, Malaysia* 167 U11

Auraiya, *India* 158 G7
Aurangabad, *India* 158 H9
Aurangabad, *India* 158 L4
Aur Atoll, *Marshall Is.* 196 G5
Auray, *Fr.* 138 L7
Aurillac, *Fr.* 138 M1O
Aurora, *Colo., U.S.* 100 M13
Aurora, *Ill., U.S.* 93 N6
Aurora, *Ind., U.S.* 93 S1O
Aurora, *Minn., U.S.* 98 F12
Aurora, *Mo., U.S.* 99 V11
Aurora, *Nebr., U.S.* 99 Q7
Aurukun, *Qnsld., Austral.* 191 P12
Aus, *Namibia* 182 J6
Au Sable, *river, Mich., U.S.* 92 J11
Au Sable, *Mich., U.S.* 92 J12
Au Sable Point, *Mich., U.S.* 92 F9
Austin, *Ind., U.S.* 93 T9
Austin, *Minn., U.S.* 98 L12
Austin, *Nev., U.S.* 103 P9
Austin, *Pa., U.S.* 88 L6
Austin, *Tex., U.S.* 97 Q1O
Austin, Lake, *Austral.* 190 H3
Austral, Chaco, *S. Amer.* 118 K6
Australian Alps, *mountains, Austral.* 190 M13
Australian Capital Territory, *Austral.* 191 Y14
Austral Islands (Tubuai Islands), *Fr. Polynesia, Fr.* 195 K13
Austria, *Eur.* 132 K6
Austvågøy, *island, Nor.* 134 E12
Autazes, *Braz.* 122 D9
Autlán, *Mex.* 108 H9
Aux Barques, Pointe, *Mich., U.S.* 92 K13
Auxerre, *Fr.* 138 K1O
Ava, *Mo., U.S.* 99 V13
Avaavaroa Passage, *Rarotonga, Cook Is., N.Z.* 198 Q9
Avaha, *island, Solomon Is.* 197 J18
Avalau, *island, Funafuti, Tuvalu* 197 L22
Avalon, *Calif., U.S.* 103 Y8
Avalon, Lake, *N. Mex., U.S.* 101 V14
Avalon Peninsula, *Nfld., Can.* 77 M24
Avanavero, *Suriname* 121 E15
Avanos, *Turk.* 148 F1O
Avapeihi, Passe, *Huahine, Fr. Polynesia, Fr.* 199 G13
Avarapa, Passe, *Moorea, Fr. Polynesia, Fr.* 199 P14
Avarua, *Rarotonga, Cook Is., N.Z.* 198 Q9
Avarua Harbour, *Rarotonga, Cook Is., N.Z.* 198 Q9
Avatele, *Niue, N.Z.* 199 B2O
Avatele Bay, *Niue, N.Z.* 199 B2O
Avatiu, *Rarotonga, Cook Is., N.Z.* 198 Q9
Avatiu Harbour, *Rarotonga, Cook Is., N.Z.* 198 Q9
Avatolu, Passe, *Wallis and Futuna, Fr.* 198 B11
Avatoru, *Rangiroa, Fr. Polynesia, Fr.* 199 K16
Āvāz, *Iran* 153 D17
Avea, *island, Fiji* 198 H9
Avea, Baie d', *Huahine, Fr. Polynesia, Fr.* 199 H14
Avea, Baie d', *Rurutu, Fr. Polynesia, Fr.* 199 K23
Aveiro, *Braz.* 122 D11
Aveiro, *Port.* 139 Q5
Āvej, *Iran* 152 C12
Avenal, *Calif., U.S.* 103 U6
Avera, *Raiatea, Fr. Polynesia, Fr.* 199 B23
Avera, *Rurutu, Fr. Polynesia, Fr.* 199 K23
Aves (Bird Island), *Venez.* 113 J15
Aves, Islas de, *Venez.* 120 A9
Aves Ridge, *Atl. Oc.* 216 L5
Avesta, *Sw.* 135 K13
Aviator Glacier, *Antarctica* 207 Q14
Avignon, *Fr.* 139 N11
Ávila, *Sp.* 139 Q7
Avilés, *Sp.* 139 N6
Avire, *Vanuatu* 198 B2
Avissawella, *Sri Lanka* 159 T7
Avita, *Santa Cruz Is., Solomon Is.* 197 Q23
Avoca, *Iowa, U.S.* 99 P9
Avon, *N.C., U.S.* 90 H15
Avondale, *Ariz., U.S.* 101 U6
Avon Downs, *N. Terr., Austral.* 191 S1O
Avon Park, *Fla., U.S.* 91 U8
Avu Avu, *Solomon Is.* 197 P19
Awaji Shima, *Jap.* 165 Q8
Awa Shima, *Jap.* 164 L11
Awarua Bay, *N.Z.* 193 P15
Awa Shima, *Jap.* 164 L11
Awat, *China* 160 F5
Awbārī, Şahrā', *Lib.* 177 D13
Aweil, *Sudan* 178 G11
Awini Plateau, *Hawaii, U.S.* 107 K19
Awjilah, *Lib.* 177 D16
Awsard, *W. Sahara, Mor.* 176 E5
Axel Heiberg Island, *Nunavut, Can.* 77 B15
Axim, *Ghana* 180 H1O
Axinim, *Braz.* 122 E9
Axtell, *Nebr., U.S.* 99 Q6
Ayabe, *Jap.* 165 P8
Ayacucho, *Arg.* 125 N13
Ayacucho, *Peru* 122 H4
Ayakkum Hu, *China* 160 H7
Ayaköz, *Kaz.* 155 E17
Ayamonte, *Sp.* 139 S5
Ayan, *Russ.* 141 H2O

Ayan, *Russ.* 141 J15
Ayancık, *Turk.* 148 C1O
Ayapel, *Col.* 120 D5
Ayaş, *Turk.* 148 E8
Ayat, *river, Kaz.* 154 C1O
Ayaviri, *Peru* 122 J5
Aybak (Samangan), *Afghan.* 156 L7
Aydarkul, lake, *Uzb.* 154 K12
Ayden, *N.C., U.S.* 90 H13
Aydere, *Turkm.* 154 L7
'Ayn al'Arab, *Syr.* 150 C1O
'Ayn al Baydā', *Syr.* 150 G1O
'Ayn an Nabk al Gharbī, *Saudi Arabia* 152 E6
'Ayn Dīwār, *Syr.* 150 B16
Ayní, *Taj.* 156 H7
'Aynūnah, *Saudi Arabia* 152 G5
Ayon, Ostrov, *Russ.* 141 C19
Ayorou, *Niger* 176 H1O
'Ayoûnel el 'Atroûs, *Mauritania* 176 G6
Aypolovo, *Russ.* 140 J11
Ayr, *Qnsld., Austral.* 191 S14
Ayr, *Scot., U.K.* 138 E7
Ayrancı, *Turk.* 148 H9
Ayteke Bi, *Kaz.* 154 G1O
Aytos, *Bulg.* 137 G17
Ayutla, *Mex.* 108 K11
Ayutthaya, *Thai.* 166 M9
Ayvacık, *Turk.* 148 E2
Ayvalık, *Turk.* 148 E2
Āzād Shahr, *Iran* 153 B14
Azamgarh, *India* 158 G9
Azapa, *Chile* 124 B7
Azare, *Nig.* 181 E15
Azaw, *Afghan.* 157 N3
A'zāz, *Syr.* 150 D8
Azbine *see* Aïr, *region, Niger* 176 G12
Azdavay, *Turk.* 148 C9
Azerbaijan, *Asia* 149 D21
Azerbaijan, *region, Iran* 152 C1O
Azle, *Tex., U.S.* 96 L11
Azogues, *Ecua.* 120 K3
Azores (Açores), *islands, Atl. Oc.* 184 C3
Azov, *Russ.* 140 H4
Azov, Sea of, *Ukr.* 133 L17
Azov Upland, *Eur.* 130 G11
Azraq, El Bahr al (Blue Nile), *river, Sudan* 179 E13
Azraq, Qaşr al, *Jordan* 150 M8
Aztec, *N. Mex., U.S.* 101 Q1O
Aztec Ruins National Monument, *N. Mex., U.S.* 101 Q1O
Azua, *Dom. Rep.* 111 M18
Azuero, Peninsula de, *Pan.* 109 P21
Azul, *Arg.* 124 M12
Azurduy, *Bol.* 122 L8
Az Zabadānī, *Syr.* 150 J7
Aẕ Ẕāhirīyah, *West Bank* 151 N5
'Azzān, *Yemen* 152 Q11
Az Zarqā', *Jordan* 150 M7
Azzel Matti, Sebkha, *Alg.* 176 E1O
Az Zilfī, *Saudi Arabia* 152 H9
Az Zubayr, *Iraq* 152 F11

B

Ba, *Fiji* 198 H6
Baaba, Île, *New Caledonia, Fr.* 198 B6
Baalbek *see* Ba'labakk, *Leb.* 150 H7
Baardheere, *Somalia* 179 J16
Baba Burnu, *Turk.* 148 C7
Baba Burnu, *Turk.* 148 E2
Baba Dağ, *Turk.* 148 J4
Babadag, peak, *Azerb.* 149 C22
Babaeski, *Turk.* 148 C3
Babahoyo, *Ecua.* 120 K2
Bāb al Mandab, strait, *Yemen* 152 R8
Babanūsah, *Sudan* 178 E12
Babati, *Tanzania* 179 L14
B'abdā, *Leb.* 150 J6
Babe Island, *Guam, U.S.* 196 E1O
Babeldaob *see* Babelthuap, *island, Palau* 196 N11
Babelthuap (Babeldaob), *island, Palau* 196 N11
Babi, *island, Indonesia* 168 H4
Babo, *Indonesia* 169 K18
Baboquivari Peak, *Ariz., U.S.* 101 W7
Babruysk, *Belarus* 133 F14
Babusar Pass, *Pak.* 158 B4
Babuyan, *island, Philippines* 169 A14
Babuyan Channel, *Philippines* 169 B14

Babuyan Islands, *Philippines* 169 A13
Babylon, ruins, *Iraq* 152 E9
Bacaadweyn, *Somalia* 179 G18
Bacabal, *Braz.* 123 E14
Bacan, *island, Indonesia* 169 J16
Bacău, *Rom.* 137 E16
Bachelor, Mount, *Oreg., U.S.* 102 H4
Bachu, *China* 160 F5
Back, *river, Nunavut, Can.* 77 G14
Backbone Mountain, *Md., U.S.* 90 C1O
Bac Lieu, *Vietnam* 167 Q12
Bac Ninh, *Vietnam* 166 H12
Bacolod, *Philippines* 169 E14
Bad, *river, S. Dak., U.S.* 98 L4
Badain Jaran Shamo, *China* 160 G1O
Badajoz, *Sp.* 139 R5
Badalona, *Sp.* 139 P1O
Badanah, *Saudi Arabia* 152 F8
Bad Axe, *Mich., U.S.* 92 K13
Baddeck, *N.S., Can.* 77 N22
Baddo, *river, Pak.* 157 T4
Baden, *Aust.* 132 K8
Badgah, *Afghan.* 156 M5
Badgastein, *Aust.* 132 K7
Badger, *Minn., U.S.* 98 E9
Badin, *Pak.* 157 W7
Badlands, *N. Dak., U.S.* 98 G2
Badlands National Park, *S. Dak., U.S.* 98 L3
Badogo, *Mali* 176 J7
Ba Dong, *Vietnam* 167 Q12
Badong, *China* 162 K3
Badrah, *Iraq* 152 D1O
Badr Ḥunayn, *Saudi Arabia* 152 K6
Badulla, *Sri Lanka* 159 T8
Badupi, *Myanmar* 166 G4
Baena, *Sp.* 139 S7
Baetic Mountains, *Eur.* 130 K2
Bafa Gölü, *Turk.* 148 G3
Bafatá, *Guinea-Bissau* 180 E4
Baffin Bay, *Nunavut, Can.* 77 D17
Baffin Bay, *Tex., U.S.* 97 U11
Baffin Island, *Nunavut, Can.* 77 E16
Bafia, *Cameroon* 181 H16
Bafing, *river, Mali* 176 H6
Bafoulabé, *Mali* 176 H6
Bafra, *Turk.* 148 C11
Bafra Burnu, *Turk.* 148 C11
Bäft, *Iran* 153 G15
Bafwasende, *Dem. Rep. of the Congo* 178 J11
Baga, *island, Solomon Is.* 197 L15
Bagamoyo, *Tanzania* 179 M15
Bagana, Mount, *P.N.G.* 197 K14
Bagan Serai, *Malaysia* 167 T9
Bagansiapiapi, *Indonesia* 168 H6
Bagdad, *Ariz., U.S.* 101 S6
Bagdarin, *Russ.* 141 K17
Bagé, *Braz.* 122 Q11
Baggs, *Wyo., U.S.* 100 K11
Baghdād, *Iraq* 152 D9
Bāghīn, *Iran* 153 F15
Baghlan, *Afghan.* 156 L7
Baghran Khowleh, *Afghan.* 157 N4
Bağırpaşa Dağı, *Turk.* 149 F14
Bağışlı, *Turk.* 149 G18
Bagley, *Minn., U.S.* 98 F9
Bago, *Myanmar* 166 K6
Bago Yoma, *Myanmar* 166 J6
Bagram, *Afghan.* 156 M8
Bagrimi, *Afghan.* 156 M8
Baguio, *Philippines* 169 B13
Bagzane, Mount, *Af.* 174 F5
Bahama Islands, *Atl. Oc.* 74 M9
Bahamas, *Atl. Oc.* 110 C11
Bahau, *Malaysia* 167 U1O
Bahawalnagar, *Pak.* 157 R11
Bahawalpur, *Pak.* 157 S1O
Bahçe, *Turk.* 148 H11
Bahçesaray, *Turk.* 149 G17
Bäherden, *Turkm.* 154 L8
Bahia *see* Salvador, *Braz.* 123 H17
Bahía, Islas de la, *Hond.* 109 K17
Bahía Blanca, *Arg.* 125 N11
Bahía de Caráquez, *Ecua.* 120 J2
Bahia Honda Key, *Fla., U.S.* 91 Y9
Bahía Laura, *Arg.* 125 U9
Bahir Dar, *Eth.* 179 F14
Bahlah, *Oman* 153 K16
Bahraich, *India* 158 F8
Bahrain, *Asia* 152 J12
Bahr el 'Arab, *river, Af.* 174 H8
Bāhū Kalāt, *Iran* 153 H18
Baía dos Tigres, *Angola* 182 F5
Baïbokoum, *Chad* 177 K14
Bai Bung, Mui, *Vietnam* 167 R11
Baichuan, *China* 160 F6
Baidoa *see* Baydhabo, *Somalia* 179 J16
Baihe, *China* 162 B13
Baihe, *China* 162 J2
Ba'jī, *Iraq* 152 C9

Baikal, Lake, Asia 146 E10
Baikha, Russ. 141 H13
Baikonur Cosmodrome, Kaz. 154 G11
Baikunthpur, India 158 J8
Baile Átha Cliath (Dublin), Ire. 138 G6
Baileys Harbor, Wis., U.S. 92 H8
Bailique, Braz. 123 C13
Bailong, river, China 160 K11
Bailundo, Angola 182 D6
Baima, China 160 K10
Bainbridge, Ga., U.S. 91 Q5
Bainet, Haiti 111 N16
Baing, Indonesia 169 N13
Bainville, Mont., U.S. 100 B13
Bā'ir, Jordan 151 P8
Baird, Tex., U.S. 96 M8
Baird Inlet, Alas., U.S. 104 J11
Baird Mountains, Alas., U.S. 105 D13
Bairiki see Tarawa, Kiribati 197 G17
Bairin Youqi, China 161 E15
Bairin Zouqi, China 162 A8
Bairnsdale, Vic., Austral. 191 Z13
Bairoil, Wyo., U.S. 100 J11
Baisha, China 162 M8
Baiti, Nauru 197 E23
Baixo, Ilhéu de, Madeira Is., Port. 184 L5
Baiyin, China 160 J12
Baja, Hung. 132 L9
Baja California, peninsula, Mex. 108 B5
Bajag, India 158 J8
Bājgīrān, Iran 153 B16
Bājil, Yemen 152 Q8
Bajitpur, Bangladesh 158 H13
Bajo, Indonesia 169 J13
Bajo Nuevo, cayo, Mex. 109 H15
Bakchar, Russ. 140 K12
Bakel, Senegal 176 H5
Baker, river, Chile 125 U7
Baker, Calif., U.S. 103 V11
Baker, Mont., U.S. 100 D13
Baker, Nev., U.S. 103 Q13
Baker, Mount, Wash., U.S. 102 A4
Baker City, Oreg., U.S. 102 G8
Baker Foreland, Nunavut, Can. 77 H15
Baker Island, Pac. Oc. 194 G9
Baker Lake, Austral. 190 G6
Baker Lake, Nunavut, Can. 77 H15
Baker Lake, Nunavut, Can. 77 H14
Bakersfield, Calif., U.S. 103 V7
Bakhchysaray, Ukr. 133 M16
Bakhmach, Ukr. 133 G15
Bakhta, Russ. 141 H13
Bakhtegān, Daryācheh-ye, Iran 153 G14
Bakı (Baku), Azerb. 149 D23
Bakırdağı, Turk. 148 G11
Bakkafjördur, Ice. 134 E4
Bakkagerđi, Ice. 134 F4
Bako, Eth. 179 H14
Bakony, mountains, Eur. 130 H7
Baku see Bakı, Azerb. 149 D23
Bakuriani, Rep. of Georgia 149 C17
Bakutis Coast, Antarctica 206 L7
Bâlâ, Turk. 148 E8
Balabac, island, Philippines 168 F12
Balabac, Philippines 168 F12
Balabac Strait, Malaysia-Philippines 168 F12
Ba'labakk (Baalbek), Leb. 150 H7
Balabat, Yap Is., F.S.M. 197 D18
Balabio, Île, New Caledonia, Fr. 198 B6
Bala Boluk, Afghan. 157 P2
Balagansk, Russ. 141 L15
Balaghat, India 158 K7
Balaghat Range, India 158 L4
Balakän, Azerb. 149 C20
Balaklava, S. Austral., Austral. 191 X10
Balaklava, Ukr. 133 M16
Balakot, Pak. 156 M11
Balakovo, Russ. 140 H6
Balancán, Mex. 109 J15
Balangir, India 158 K9
Balaözen, river, Kaz. 154 D5
Balaton, lake, Hung. 132 L9
Balbi, Mount, P.N.G. 197 J13
Balbina, Represa da, Braz. 122 D9
Balcarce, Arg. 125 N13
Balchik, Bulg. 137 G17
Balclutha, N.Z. 193 R16
Bald Knob, Ark., U.S. 94 F9
Bald Mountain, Idaho, U.S. 100 F5
Bald Mountain, Nev., U.S. 103 S11
Baldwin, Fla., U.S. 91 Q8
Baldwin City, Kans., U.S. 99 T10
Baldwinsville, N.Y., U.S. 88 J8
Baldwyn, Miss., U.S. 95 H13
Baldy, Mount, Ariz., U.S. 101 T9
Baldy Peak, U.S. 78 K7
Balearic Islands, Sp. 139 R10
Balearic Sea, Sp. 139 R9
Baleia, Ponta da, Braz. 123 K16
Balembangan, island, Malaysia 168 F12
Baleshwar, India 158 K11
Baley, Russ. 141 L17
Balfes Creek, Qnsld., Austral. 191 S13
Balfour Channel, Solomon Is. 197 M16
Balfour Downs, W. Austral., Austral. 191 T4
Balgazyn, Russ. 141 M13
Balgo, W. Austral., Austral. 191 S6
Balguerie, Cap, Hiva Oa, Fr. Polynesia, Fr. 199 M21
Balḩāf, Yemen 152 Q11
Bali, island, Indonesia 168 M11
Bali, India 158 G3
Bali, Selat, Indonesia 168 M11
Baliapal, India 158 K11
Balıkesir, Turk. 148 E3
Balık Göl, Turk. 148 C11
Balīkh, river, Syr. 150 D11
Balikpapan, Indonesia 168 J12
Balimo, P.N.G. 193 D18
Balingian, Malaysia 167 U16
Balintang Channel, Philippines 169 A13
Bali Sea, Indonesia 168 M11
Balkan Mountains, Bulg. 137 G15
Balkan Peninsula, Eur. 130 J9
Balkh, Afghan. 156 K6
Balkhab, Afghan. 156 L6
Balkhash, Lake, Asia 146 F7
Balladonia, W. Austral., Austral. 191 X5
Ballalae, island, Solomon Is. 197 L14
Ballantyne Strait, N.W.T., Can. 77 B13
Ballarat, Vic., Austral. 191 Z12
Ballard, Lake, Austral. 190 J4
Ball Bay, Norfolk I., Austral. 197 G20
Ballenas, Bahía, Mex. 108 E5
Ballenero, Canal, Chile 125 Y8
Ballina, Ire. 138 F5
Ballina, N.S.W., Austral. 191 W15
Ballinger, Tex., U.S. 97 N7
Ball's Pyramid, island, Coral Sea 194 M6
Balmaceda, Chile 125 T7
Balmorhea, Tex., U.S. 97 P2
Balod, India 158 K8
Baloeri de Cristo Rey, Bioko, Eq. Guinea 184 L7
Balotra, India 158 G3
Balqash, Kaz. 155 F15
Balqash Köli, Kaz. 155 G15
Balrampur, India 158 F8
Balranald, N.S.W., Austral. 191 Y12
Balsas, river, Mex. 108 K11
Balsas, Braz. 123 F14
Balta, N. Dak., U.S. 98 E5
Balta, Ukr. 133 K14
Baltasar Brum, Uru. 124 J13
Bălţi, Mold. 133 K13
Baltic Plains, Eur. 130 E8
Baltic Sea, Eur. 130 E7
Baltimore, Md., U.S. 90 C13
Baltistan, region, Pak. 156 L13
Baltit, Pak. 156 K12
Baluchistan, region, Iran 153 H18
Baluchistan, region, Pak. 157 U3
Balurghat, India 158 H12
Balya, Turk. 148 E3
Balykchy (Ysyk-Köl), Kyrg. 156 E12
Balyqshi, Kaz. 154 F6
Bam, Iran 153 G16
Bama, Nig. 181 E17
Bamaga, Qnsld., Austral. 191 N12
Bamako, Mali 176 J7
Bambari, Cen. Af. Rep. 178 H9
Bambaroo, Qnsld., Austral. 191 R13
Bamberg, S.C., U.S. 90 L9
Bamboo, W. Austral., Austral. 191 S3
Bam Co, China 160 K8
Bamenda, Cameroon 181 H15
Bamian, Afghan. 156 M6
Bamingui, Cen. Af. Rep. 178 G9
Bampūr, river, Iran 153 H17
Bampūr, Iran 153 H17
Bamy, Turkm. 154 L7
Bamyili-Beswick, N. Terr., Austral. 191 Q8
Banaba (Ocean Island), Kiribati 194 G7
Banalia, Dem. Rep. of the Congo 178 J11
Banam, Cambodia 167 P12
Banana, river, Fla., U.S. 91 T10
Banana, Kiritimati, Kiribati 197 A23
Banana, Qnsld., Austral. 191 U14
Bananal, Ilha do, Braz. 122 G12
Bananga, Nicobar Is., India 159 T15
Banaras see Varanasi, India 158 H9
Bânaş, Râs, Egypt 177 E20
Banas, river, India 158 G5
Banaz, Turk. 148 F5
Ban Ban, Laos 166 J10
Ban Bang Hin, Thai. 167 Q7
Bancroft, Iowa, U.S. 98 M11
Banda, India 158 H7
Banda, Kepulauan, Indonesia 169 L17
Banda, Pointe, Gabon 181 M15
Banda Aceh, Indonesia 168 G3
Banda Besar, island, Indonesia 169 L17
Banda Elat, Indonesia 169 L18
Bandanaira, Indonesia 169 L17
Bandar see Machilipatnam, India 159 N8
Bandarban, Bangladesh 158 J14
Bandarbeyla, Somalia 179 F18
Bandar-e 'Abbās, Iran 153 H15
Bandar-e Anzalī, Iran 152 B12
Bandar-e Būshehr, Iran 152 G12
Bandar-e Chārak, Iran 153 H14
Bandar-e Deylam, Iran 152 F12
Bandar-e Khoemir, Iran 153 H15
Bandar-e Māh Shahr, Iran 152 F12
Bandar-e Maqām, Iran 153 H14
Bandar-e Mollaha, Afghan. 156 L4
Bandar Seri Begawan, Brunei 168 G11
Banda Sea, Indonesia 169 L15
Bandau, Malaysia 168 F12
Bandeira, peak, Braz. 123 L15
Bandeira, Pico de la, S. Amer. 118 H10
Bandeirante, Braz. 122 H12
Bandelier National Monument, N. Mex., U.S. 101 R12
Bandera, Arg. 124 H11
Bandera, Tex., U.S. 97 R9
Banderas Bay, N. Amer. 74 N4
Bandiagara, Mali 176 H8
Bandikui, India 158 G5
Bandırma, Turk. 148 D4
Ban Don, Vietnam 167 N13
Ban Don, Ao, Thai. 167 Q8
Bandon, Oreg., U.S. 102 J1
Bändovan Burnu, Azerb. 149 E23
Bandundu, Dem. Rep. of the Congo 178 L8
Bandung, Indonesia 168 M8
Banes, Cuba 111 J13
Banff, Alta., Can. 76 M10
Banff, Scot., U.K. 138 D8
Banfora, Burkina Faso 180 F9
Bangalore, India 159 P6
Bangassou, Cen. Af. Rep. 178 H10
Banggai, Kepulauan, Indonesia 169 K14
Banggi, island, Malaysia 168 F12
Banggong Co, China 158 C7
Banghāzī (Benghazi), Lib. 177 C15
Banghiang, river, Laos 166 L12
Bangi Island, Guam, U.S. 196 D10
Bangka, island, Indonesia 168 K8
Bangka, island, Indonesia 169 H15
Bangkaru, island, Indonesia 168 H4
Bangkok see Krung Thep, Thai. 166 M9
Bangladesh, Asia 158 H12
Bangor, Me., U.S. 89 F17
Bangs, Tex., U.S. 97 N8
Bang Saphan, Thai. 167 P8
Bangui, Cen. Af. Rep. 178 H8
Bangui, Philippines 169 B13
Bangweulu, Lake, Zambia 182 D11
Bani, river, Mali 176 H8
Baní, Dom. Rep. 111 M18
Banihal Pass, India 157 N12
Banī Sharfā, Saudi Arabia 152 M8
Banī Walīd, Lib. 177 C14
Bāniyās, Syr. 150 F7
Banja Luka, Bosn. and Herzg. 136 F12
Banjarmasin, Indonesia 168 K11
Banjul, Gambia 176 H4
Bankä, Azerb. 149 E23
Banka, India 158 H11
Banka Banka, N. Terr., Austral. 191 R9
Banks Island, B.C., Can. 76 K7
Banks Island, N.W.T., Can. 76 D12
Banks Islands, Vanuatu 198 B2
Banks Lake, Wash., U.S. 102 C7
Banks Peninsula, N.Z. 193 P18
Banmauk, Myanmar 166 F6
Bannu, Pak. 157 P9
Banow, Afghan. 156 L8
Ban Phai, Thai. 166 L10
Banreaba, Tarawa, Kiribati 197 G17
Ban Sanam Chai, Thai. 167 R9
Banswara, India 158 J4
Bantabaré Pequeño, Bioko, Eq. Guinea 184 M7
Ban Taphan, Laos 166 L12
Bantry, Ire. 138 H5
Bantva, India 158 K2
Bantval, India 159 Q4
Ban Xénô, Laos 166 K11
Banyak, Kepulauan, Indonesia 168 H4
Banyas, Israel 150 K6
Banzare Coast, Antarctica 207 P19
Baochang see Taibus Qi, China 162 B6
Baode, China 162 D3
Baoding, China 162 D6
Baofeng, China 162 H4
Baó Grande, Bioko, Eq. Guinea 184 M8
Baoji, China 160 J12
Baoji, China 162 G1
Baojing, China 162 M2
Bao Lac, Vietnam 166 G12
Baoro, Cen. Af. Rep. 178 H8
Baoshan, China 160 N10
Baoting, China 163 U1
Baotou, China 162 C3
Baoying, China 162 J8
Bapatla, India 159 N7
Baqbaqty, Kaz. 155 H16
Baqty, Kaz. 155 F18
Ba'qūbah, Iraq 152 D10
Baquedano, Chile 124 E7
Bara, Indonesia 169 K15
Bara, Sudan 178 E12
Baraawe, Somalia 179 J16
Baraboo, Wis., U.S. 92 L5
Baracaldo, Sp. 139 N7
Baracoa, Cuba 111 K14
Baraga, Mich., U.S. 92 E6
Baragoi, Kenya 179 J14
Barahona, Dom. Rep. 111 M18
Bara Hoti, India 158 E7
Barak, Turk. 148 J12
Baraki, Afghan. 157 N7
Baramula, India 156 M12
Baran, India 158 H5
Baranavichy, Belarus 132 F12
Barangbarang, Indonesia 169 L13
Baranof Island, Alas., U.S. 105 L22
Barão de Melgaço, Braz. 122 J10
Barataria Bay, La., U.S. 94 R11
Barat Daya, Kepulauan, Indonesia 169 M15
Barate, Indonesia 169 N14
Barbacena, Braz. 123 L14
Barbacoas, Col. 120 H3
Barbados, N. Amer. 113 L19
Barbados, island, N. Amer. 74 P12
Barberton, Ohio, U.S. 93 P14
Barbourville, Ky., U.S. 95 D18
Barbuda, island, Leeward Is. 113 F16
Barcaldine, Qnsld., Austral. 191 T13
Barcellona Pozzo di Gotto, It. 136 L11
Barcelona, Sp. 139 Q10
Barcelona, Venez. 120 B11
Barcelos, Braz. 122 C8
Barco, N.C., U.S. 90 G14
Barcoo, river, Austral. 190 G12
Bärdä, Azerb. 149 D21
Barda del Medio, Arg. 125 N8
Barda Hills, India 158 J1
Bardaï, Chad 177 F14
Bardas Blancas, Arg. 124 M7
Bardawîl, Sabkhet el, Egypt 151 N2
Barddhaman, India 158 J11
Bardejov, Slovakia 132 J10
Bardoc, W. Austral., Austral. 191 W4
Bardstown, Ky., U.S. 95 C17
Bardwell, Ky., U.S. 94 D12
Bareilly, India 158 F7
Barents Plain, Arctic Oc. 223 G13
Barents Sea, Russ. 140 B10
Barfak, Afghan. 156 L7
Barga, China 160 K5
Bargaal, Somalia 179 F18
Bargarh, India 158 K9
Barg-e Matal, Afghan. 156 L9
Bar Harbor, Me., U.S. 89 F18
Barhi, India 158 H10
Barhi, India 158 H7
Bari, It. 136 J12
Ba Ria, Vietnam 167 P13
Barikowt, Afghan. 156 L9
Barīm (Perim), island, Yemen 152 R9
Barima, river, Guyana 121 D14
Barinas, Venez. 120 C7
Baripada, India 158 J11
Bārīs, Egypt 177 E18
Barisal, Bangladesh 158 J13
Barisan, Pegunungan, Indonesia 168 K6
Barisan Mountains, Asia 146 M11
Barkā', Oman 153 K16
Barka Kana, India 158 J10
Barkhan, Pak. 157 R8
Barkley, Lake, Ky., U.S. 95 D14
Barkly Tableland, Austral. 190 D10
Barkol, China 160 E9
Barkol Hu, China 160 E9
Barla Dağı, Turk. 148 G6
Barlee, Lake, Austral. 190 J3
Barletta, It. 136 J11
Barmer, India 158 G2
Barnaul, Russ. 140 L12
Barnegat, N.J., U.S. 88 Q11
Barnegat Light, N.J., U.S. 88 Q11
Barnes Ice Cap, Nunavut, Can. 77 E17
Barnesville, Ga., U.S. 90 M5
Barnesville, Minn., U.S. 98 G8
Barnhart, Tex., U.S. 97 P6
Barnsdall, Okla., U.S. 96 E12
Barnstaple, Eng., U.K. 138 H7
Barnum Bay, Palau 196 Q10
Barnwell, S.C., U.S. 90 L8
Baro, Nig. 181 G13
Baroghil Pass, Afghan.-Pak. 156 K11

Barora Fa, island, *Solomon Is.* **197** L17
Barora Ite, island, *Solomon Is.* **197** L17
Barpeta, *India* **158** G13
Barquisimeto, *Venez.* **120** B8
Barra, island, *Scot., U.K.* **138** D6
Barra, *Braz.* **123** G15
Barra, Ponta da, *Mozambique* **183** H13
Barra do Bugres, *Braz.* **122** J10
Barra do Corda, *Braz.* **123** E14
Barra do São Manuel, *Braz.* **122** F10
Barra Head, *Scot., U.K.* **138** E6
Barrancabermeja, *Col.* **120** D5
Barrancas, *Venez.* **120** C12
Barranqueras, *Arg.* **124** G13
Barranquilla, *Col.* **120** B5
Barra Point, *Af.* **174** P10
Barras, *Braz.* **123** E15
Barre, *Vt., U.S.* **89** G13
Barreiras, *Braz.* **123** H14
Barreirinha, *Braz.* **122** D10
Barreirinhas, *Braz.* **123** D15
Barreiro, *Port.* **139** R4
Barren, river, *Ky., U.S.* **95** D16
Barren, Nosy, *Madagascar* **183** F16
Barrie, *Ont., Can.* **77** Q18
Barrigada, *Guam, U.S.* **196** C11
Barringun, *N.S.W., Austral.* **191** W13
Barron, *Wis., U.S.* **92** H2
Barrow, *Alas., U.S.* **105** B14
Barrow, Point, *Alas., U.S.* **105** B14
Barrow Canyon, *Arctic Oc.* **222** L5
Barrow Creek, *N. Terr., Austral.* **191** S8
Barrow Island, *Austral.* **190** E1
Barry, *Ill., U.S.* **93** R3
Barrytown, *N.Z.* **193** N17
Barşa, *Rom.* **137** D15
Barshatas, *Kaz.* **155** E17
Barstow, *Calif., U.S.* **103** W10
Bartholomew, Bayou, *Ark., U.S.* **94** K9
Bartica, *Guyana* **121** D14
Bartın, *Turk.* **148** C8
Bartle Frere, peak, *Austral.* **190** D13
Bartlesville, *Okla., U.S.* **96** E12
Bartlett, *Nebr., U.S.* **99** P6
Bartlett, *Tex., U.S.* **97** P11
Bartlett Reservoir, *Ariz., U.S.* **101** T7
Bartolomeu Dias, *Mozambique* **183** G13
Barton, *N. Dak., U.S.* **98** E5
Barton, *Vt., U.S.* **89** F13
Barton Siding, *S. Austral., Austral.* **191** W8
Bartow, *Fla., U.S.* **91** U8
Barú, Volcán, *Pan.* **109** N20
Baruunharaa, *Mongolia* **160** C12
Baruunsuu, *Mongolia* **160** E12
Baruun Urt, *Mongolia* **161** D14
Barwani, *India* **158** J4
Barwon, river, *Austral.* **190** J14
Barykova, Mys, *Russ.* **141** B21
Barysaw, *Belarus* **133** F13
Basacato del Este, *Bioko, Eq. Guinea* **184** M8
Basacato del Oeste, *Bioko, Eq. Guinea* **184** M7
Basankusu, *Dem. Rep. of the Congo* **178** J9
Basargech'ar, *Arm.* **149** D19
Basaseachic Falls, *N. Amer.* **74** M4
Basco, *Philippines* **169** A14
Bascuñán, Cabo, *Chile* **124** H6
Basel, *Switz.* **132** K4
Basilan, island, *Philippines* **169** F14
Basilé, *Bioko, Eq. Guinea* **184** L8
Basile, *La., U.S.* **94** P8
Basilisk Harbor, *Santa Cruz Is., Solomon Is.* **197** Q23
Basin, *Wyo., U.S.* **100** G10
Basīt, Ra's al, *Syr.* **150** E6
Başkale, *Turk.* **149** G18
Baskil, *Turk.* **149** G13
Basmat, *India* **158** L5
Basoko, *Dem. Rep. of the Congo* **178** J10
Bass, Îlots de *see* Marotiri, *Fr. Polynesia, Fr.* **195** L14
Bassas da India, island, *Mozambique Channel* **183** H14
Basseterre, *St. Kitts and Nevis* **113** G15
Basse-Terre, island, *Guadeloupe, Fr.* **113** H16
Basse-Terre, *Guadeloupe, Fr.* **113** H16
Bassett, *Nebr., U.S.* **99** N5
Bassett, *Va., U.S.* **90** G10
Bassikounou, *Mauritania* **176** H8
Bass Islands, *Santa Cruz Is., Solomon Is.* **197** N24
Bass Strait, *Austral.* **190** L15
Bastak, *Iran* **153** H14
Basti, *India* **158** G8
Bastia, *Fr.* **139** N13
Bastogne, *Belg.* **138** J11
Bastrop, *La., U.S.* **94** K9
Bastrop, *Tex., U.S.* **97** Q11
Bastuträsk, *Sw.* **135** G14
Basu, island, *Indonesia* **168** J7
Basuo *see* Dongfang, *China* **163** U1
Basupú, *Bioko, Eq. Guinea* **184** L7
Bata, *Eq. Guinea* **181** K15
Bataan Peninsua, *Philippines* **169** C13
Batabanó, Golfo de, *Cuba* **110** H6
Batagay, *Russ.* **141** F18
Batala, *India* **157** P12
Batamay, *Russ.* **141** G18
Batamorghab, *Afghan.* **156** L3
Batan, island, *Philippines* **169** A14
Batang, *China* **160** L10
Batangafo, *Cen. Af. Rep.* **178** G8
Batangas, *Philippines* **169** C13
Batan Islands, *Philippines* **169** A14
Batanta, island, *Indonesia* **169** J17
Batavia, *N.Y., U.S.* **88** J6
Bates, Mount, *Norfolk I., Austral.* **197** F20
Batesburg, *S.C., U.S.* **90** L8
Batesville, *Ark., U.S.* **94** F9
Batesville, *Ind., U.S.* **93** S10
Batesville, *Miss., U.S.* **94** H11
Batesville, *Tex., U.S.* **97** S8
Batete, *Bioko, Eq. Guinea* **184** M7
Bath, *Me., U.S.* **89** G16
Bath, *N.Y., U.S.* **88** K7
Bath, *Eng., U.K.* **138** H8
Bathurst, *N.B., Can.* **77** N21
Bathurst, *N.S.W., Austral.* **191** X14
Bathurst, Cape, *N.W.T., Can.* **76** D11
Bathurst Inlet, *Nunavut, Can.* **77** F13
Bathurst Island, *Austral.* **190** A7
Bathurst Island, *Nunavut, Can.* **77** D14
Batié, *Burkina Faso* **180** F9
Batiki, island, *Fiji* **198** H7
Batista, Serra da, *Braz.* **123** F16
Batman, *Turk.* **149** G15
Batna, *Alg.* **176** A12
Batoicopo, *Bioko, Eq. Guinea* **184** L7
Baton Rouge, *La., U.S.* **94** P10
Batouri, *Cameroon* **181** J17
Batsfjord, *Nor.* **135** B15
Battambang, *Cambodia* **167** N10
Batteau, *Nfld., Can.* **77** K22
Batticaloa, *Sri Lanka* **159** S8
Battle Creek, *Idaho, U.S.* **100** J3
Battle Creek, *Mont., U.S.* **100** A9
Battle Creek, *Mich., U.S.* **92** M10
Battle Harbour, *Nfld., Can.* **77** L23
Battle Mountain, *Nev., U.S.* **103** N9
Batu, peak, *Eth.* **179** G15
Batu, Kepulauan, *Indonesia* **168** J5
Batukelau, *Indonesia* **168** J11
Bat'umi, *Rep. of Georgia* **149** C16
Batu Pahat, *Malaysia* **167** V10
Batuputih, *Indonesia* **168** H12
Baturaja, *Indonesia* **168** L7
Baturité, *Braz.* **123** E17
Bat Yam, *Israel* **150** M5
Bau, island, *Fiji* **198** J7
Baubau, *Indonesia* **169** L14
Baucau, *E. Timor* **169** M15
Bauchi, *Nig.* **181** F15
Bauchi Plateau, *Af.* **174** H5
Baudette, *Minn., U.S.* **98** E10
Baudó, Serranía de, *S. Amer.* **118** B2
Baun, *Indonesia* **169** N14
Baures, river, *Bol.* **122** H8
Bauru, *Braz.* **123** L13
Baús, *Braz.* **122** K11
Bautino, *Kaz.* **154** G5
Bawal, island, *Indonesia* **168** K9
Bawean, island, *Indonesia* **168** L10
Bawku, *Ghana* **180** F11
Baxkorgan, *China* **160** G8
Baxley, *Ga., U.S.* **91** P7
Baxoi, *China* **160** L9
Baxter, *Minn., U.S.* **98** H10
Baxter Springs, *Kans., U.S.* **99** V10
Bay'ah, *Oman* **153** J15
Bayamo, *Cuba* **110** K12
Bayamón, *P.R., U.S.* **111** M23
Bayan, *Mongolia* **160** D9
Bayanauyl, *Kaz.* **155** D15
Bayandalay, *Mongolia* **160** F11
Bayanga, *Cen. Af. Rep.* **178** J8
Bayan Gol *see* Dengkou, *China* **162** C1
Bayan Har Shan, *China* **160** J9
Bayan Har Shankou, *China* **160** J10
Bayanhongor, *Mongolia* **160** E11
Bayanmönh, *Mongolia* **161** D13
Bayano, Lago, *Pan.* **109** N22
Bayan Obo, *China* **162** B3
Bayan Range, *Afghan.* **156** M5
Bayard, *N. Mex., U.S.* **101** V10
Bayard, *Nebr., U.S.* **99** P1
Bayat, *Turk.* **148** F6
Bayāz, *Iran* **153** F15
Bayboro, *N.C., U.S.* **90** J14
Bayburt, *Turk.* **149** E15
Bay City, *Mich., U.S.* **92** K12
Bay City, *Tex., U.S.* **97** S13
Baydaratskaya Guba, *Russ.* **140** F11
Baydhabo (Baidoa), *Somalia* **179** J16
Bayès, Cap, *New Caledonia, Fr.* **198** C7
Bayfield, *Wis., U.S.* **92** E4
Bayghanin, *Kaz.* **154** E8
Bayḩān al Qişāb, *Yemen* **152** Q10
Bayındır, *Turk.* **148** F3
Bay Islands, *N. Amer.* **74** P7
Baykal, Ozero, *Russ.* **141** L16
Baykan, *Turk.* **149** G16
Baykurt, *China* **160** F4
Bay Minette, *Ala., U.S.* **95** N14
Bay of Whales, station, *Antarctica* **206** N11
Bayonne, *Fr.* **139** N8
Bayramaly, *Turkm.* **154** M10
Bayramiç, *Turk.* **148** D2
Bayreuth, *Ger.* **132** H6
Bayrūt (Beirut), *Leb.* **150** J6
Bay Saint Louis, *Miss., U.S.* **94** P12
Bay Springs, *Miss., U.S.* **94** M12
Bayt ad Dīn, *Leb.* **150** J6
Bayt al Faqīh, *Yemen* **152** Q8
Bayt Laḩm (Bethlehem), *West Bank* **150** M5
Baytown, *Tex., U.S.* **97** R14
Baza, *Sp.* **139** S7
Baza'i Gonbad, *Afghan.* **156** K11
Bazar Dyuzi, peak, *Azerb.* **149** C21
Bazar-e Panjva'i, *Afghan.* **157** Q5
Bazar-e Taleh, *Afghan.* **156** L7
Bazar-Kurgan, *Kyrg.* **156** F10
Bazartobe, *Kaz.* **154** D6
Bazmān, Kūh-e, *Iran* **153** G17
Be, Nosy, *Madagascar* **183** D18
Beach, *N. Dak., U.S.* **98** G1
Beach Haven, *N.J., U.S.* **88** Q11
Beagle Bay, *W. Austral., Austral.* **191** R4
Bear Creek, *Colo., U.S.* **101** P15
Bearden, *Ark., U.S.* **94** J8
Beardmore Glacier, *Antarctica* **207** L13
Beardstown, *Ill., U.S.* **93** R4
Bear Islands *see* Medvezh'i Ostrova, *Russ.* **141** C18
Bear Lake, *Utah, U.S.* **100** J8
Bear Paw Mountains, *U.S.* **78** C8
Bear River City, *Utah, U.S.* **100** K7
Bear River Range, *Utah, U.S.* **100** J7
Bears Paw Mountains, *Mont., U.S.* **100** B9
Beata, Cabo, *Dom. Rep.* **111** N17
Beata, Isla, *Dom. Rep.* **111** N17
Beata Ridge, *Atl. Oc.* **216** L4
Beatrice, *Nebr., U.S.* **99** R8
Beatrice, Cape, *Austral.* **190** B10
Beatton River, *B.C., Can.* **76** J9
Beatty, *Nev., U.S.* **103** T10
Beau Bassin, *Mauritius* **185** G19
Beauchêne Island, *Falk. Is., U.K.* **125** X12
Beaufort, *Malaysia* **168** G11
Beaufort, *N.C., U.S.* **90** J14
Beaufort, *S.C., U.S.* **90** M9
Beaufort Sea, *N. Amer.* **74** C4
Beaufort Shelf, *Arctic Oc.* **222** N5
Beaufort Slope, *Arctic Oc.* **222** N5
Beaufort West, *S. Af.* **182** L9
Beaumanoir, Port du, *Tahiti, Fr. Polynesia, Fr.* **199** Q17
Beaumont, *Tex., U.S.* **97** Q15
Beautemps Beaupré, Île, *New Caledonia, Fr.* **198** C8
Beauvais, *Fr.* **138** J10
Beaver, river, *Okla., U.S.* **96** E6
Beaver, *Alas., U.S.* **105** E16
Beaver, *Okla., U.S.* **96** E7
Beaver, *Oreg., U.S.* **102** F2
Beaver, *Utah, U.S.* **101** N6
Beaver Bay, *Minn., U.S.* **98** F13
Beaver City, *Nebr., U.S.* **99** R5
Beaver Creek, *Kans., U.S.* **99** R4
Beaver Creek, *Mont., U.S.* **100** C10
Beaver Dam, *Ky., U.S.* **95** C15
Beaver Dam, *Wis., U.S.* **92** L6
Beaver Falls, *Pa., U.S.* **88** N3
Beaver Glacier, *Antarctica* **207** C19
Beaverhead, river, *Mont., U.S.* **100** F6
Beaverhead Mountains, *Mont., U.S.* **100** F6
Beaver Island, *Mich., U.S.* **92** G9
Beaver Lake, *Ark., U.S.* **94** E6
Beaverton, *Oreg., U.S.* **102** F3
Beawar, *India* **158** G4
Bebar, *India* **158** H1
Bebiram, *Indonesia* **193** B14
Béchar, *Alg.* **176** C9
Becharof Lake, *Alas., U.S.* **105** L14
Beckley, *W. Va., U.S.* **90** E8
Beddouza, Cap, *Mor.* **176** B7
Bedford, *Ind., U.S.* **93** T9
Bedford, *Iowa, U.S.* **99** Q10
Bedford, *Pa., U.S.* **88** P5
Bedford, *Va., U.S.* **90** F10
Bedford, Cape, *Austral.* **190** C13
Bedourie, *Qnsld., Austral.* **191** U11
Beebe, *Ark., U.S.* **94** G9
Beech Grove, *Ind., U.S.* **93** R9
Beenleigh, *Qnsld., Austral.* **191** V15
Be'er Nenuḩa, *Israel* **151** Q5
Be'er Ora, *Israel* **151** R5
Beersheba *see* Be'ér Sheva', *Israel* **151** N5
Be'ér Sheva' (Beersheba), *Israel* **151** N5
Beetaloo, *N. Terr., Austral.* **191** R8
Beethoven Peninsula, *Antarctica* **206** F6
Beeville, *Tex., U.S.* **97** T10
Bega, *N.S.W., Austral.* **191** Z14
Begusarai, *India* **158** H10
Behagle *see* Laï, *Chad* **177** K14
Behbehān, *Iran* **152** F12
Behring Point, *Bahamas* **110** E11
Behshahr, *Iran* **153** B14
Bei, river, *China* **161** N14
Bei'an, *China* **161** C17
Beida *see* Al Bayḑāḩ, *Lib.* **177** B16
Beihai, *China* **163** S1
Beijing (Peking), *China* **162** D7
Beiliu, *China* **163** R2
Beilul, *Eritrea* **179** E16
Beipiao, *China* **162** B9
Beira, *Mozambique* **183** G13
Beirut *see* Bayrūt, *Leb.* **150** J6
Bei Shan, *China* **160** F9
Beitbridge, *Zimb.* **182** H11
Beiuş, *Rom.* **137** E14
Beizhen, *China* **162** B10
Beja, *Port.* **139** S5
Beja, *Tun.* **176** A12
Bejaïa, *Alg.* **176** A11
Bejestān, *Iran* **153** D16
Bekaa Valley, *Leb.* **150** J7
Bekdash, *Turkm.* **154** J6
Békés, *Hung.* **132** L10
Békéscsaba, *Hung.* **132** L10
Bekily, *Madagascar* **183** J16
Bekja, island, *Jaluit Atoll, Marshall Is.* **196** K8
Bekkai, *Jap.* **164** F16
Bekobod, *Taj.* **156** G8
Bekobod, *Uzb.* **155** L13
Bekoropoka-Antongo, *Madagascar* **183** H16
Bekwai, *Ghana* **180** H10
Bela, *India* **158** G8
Bela, *Pak.* **157** V5
Belaga, *Malaysia* **168** H11
Belarus, *Eur.* **133** F13
Bela Vista, *Braz.* **122** L10
Belaya, river, *Eur.* **130** D14
Belaya Gora, *Russ.* **141** E18
Belaya Zemlya, Ostrova, *Russ.* **141** C13
Belcheragh, *Afghan.* **156** L5
Belcher Islands, *Nunavut, Can.* **77** L17
Belcik, *Turk.* **148** E11
Belding, *Mich., U.S.* **92** L10
Beledweyne, *Somalia* **179** H17
Belele, *W. Austral., Austral.* **191** V3
Belém, *Braz.* **123** D13
Belén, *Arg.* **124** G8
Belen, *N. Mex., U.S.* **101** S12
Bélep, Îles, *New Caledonia, Fr.* **198** B6
Belfast, *Me., U.S.* **89** F17
Belfast, *N. Ire., U.K.* **138** F7
Belfield, *N. Dak., U.S.* **98** G2
Belfort, *Fr.* **138** K12
Belgaum, *India* **159** N4
Belgica Bank, *Arctic Oc.* **223** J15
Belgica Mountains, *Antarctica* **207** C16
Belgium, *Eur.* **138** J11
Belgorod, *Russ.* **140** G5
Belgrade, *Mont., U.S.* **100** E8
Belgrade *see* Beograd, *Yug.* **137** F13
Belgrano II, station, *Antarctica* **206** E10
Belhaven, *N.C., U.S.* **90** H14
Beliliou *see* Peleliu, island, *Palau* **196** Q10
Belinyu, *Indonesia* **168** K8
Belitung (Billiton), island, *Indonesia* **168** K9
Belize, *N. Amer.* **109** K17
Belize City, *Belize* **109** K16
Bel'kachi, *Russ.* **141** H19
Bel'kovskiy, Ostrov, *Russ.* **141** D16
Bella Bella, *B.C., Can.* **76** K7
Bellac, *Fr.* **138** M9
Bella Coola, *B.C., Can.* **76** K8
Bellaire, *Mich., U.S.* **92** H10
Bellaire, *Ohio, U.S.* **93** R15
Bellaire, *Tex., U.S.* **97** R14
Bellary, *India* **159** N5
Bella Unión, *Uru.* **124** J13
Bella Vista, *Arg.* **124** G9
Bella Vista, *Arg.* **124** H13
Bellavista, *Peru* **122** F2
Belle-Anse, *Haiti* **111** M17
Bellefontaine, *Ohio, U.S.* **93** Q12
Bellefonte, *Pa., U.S.* **88** N6
Belle Fourche, river, *Wyo., U.S.* **100** G13
Belle Fourche, *S. Dak., U.S.* **98** K1
Belle Fourche Reservoir, *S. Dak., U.S.* **98** K1
Belle Glade, *Fla., U.S.* **91** V10
Belle-Île, *Fr.* **138** L7
Belle Isle, *Nfld., Can.* **77** L23
Belle Isle, Strait of, *Nfld., Can.* **77** L22
Belle Plaine, *Iowa, U.S.* **99** N13
Belle Plaine, *Minn., U.S.* **98** K11
Belleville, *Ill., U.S.* **93** T4

Belleville, *Kans., U.S.* **99** R7
Bellevue, *Idaho, U.S.* **100** G5
Bellevue, *Iowa, U.S.* **99** N14
Bellevue, *Nebr., U.S.* **99** Q9
Bellevue, *Ohio, U.S.* **93** P13
Bellevue, *Tex., U.S.* **96** K10
Bellevue, *Wash., U.S.* **102** C4
Bellingham, *Wash., U.S.* **102** A4
Bellingshausen, station, *Antarctica* **206** C3
Bellingshausen Plain, *Southern Oc.* **224** J7
Bellinzona, *Switz.* **132** L5
Bello, *Col.* **120** E4
Bellona Island, *Solomon Is.* **197** Q18
Bellows Falls, *Vt., U.S.* **89** J13
Bellpat, *Pak.* **157** S7
Bell Peninsula, *Nunavut, Can.* **77** H17
Bells, *Tenn., U.S.* **94** F12
Belluno, *It.* **136** E9
Bell Ville, *Arg.* **124** K11
Bellville, *Tex., U.S.* **97** Q12
Belmond, *Iowa, U.S.* **98** M11
Belmont, *Miss., U.S.* **95** H13
Belmont, *N.C., U.S.* **90** J9
Belmonte, *Braz.* **123** J16
Belmopan, *Belize* **109** K16
Belogorsk, *Russ.* **141** K19
Belo Horizonte, *Braz.* **123** L14
Beloit, *Kans., U.S.* **99** S7
Beloit, *Wis., U.S.* **92** M6
Belomorsk, *Russ.* **140** D8
Belo-Tsiribihina, *Madagascar* **183** G16
Beloye, Lake, *Eur.* **130** C10
Beloye More, *Russ.* **140** D8
Belpre, *Ohio, U.S.* **93** S15
Belt, *Mont., U.S.* **100** C8
Belterra, *Braz.* **122** D11
Belton, *S.C., U.S.* **90** K7
Belton, *Tex., U.S.* **97** P11
Belton Lake, *Tex., U.S.* **97** N11
Belukha, peak, *Asia* **146** F8
Belush'ya Guba, *Russ.* **140** D10
Belūsovka, *Kaz.* **155** D18
Belvidere, *Ill., U.S.* **92** M6
Belvidere, *S. Dak., U.S.* **98** L4
Belyando, river, *Austral.* **190** F13
Belyy, Ostrov, *Russ.* **140** E12
Belzoni, *Miss., U.S.* **94** K10
Bemaraha, plateau, *Madagascar* **183** G16
Bembe, *Angola* **182** B6
Bemidji, *Minn., U.S.* **98** F10
Benāb, *Iran* **152** B10
Benadir, region, *Af.* **174** J11
Benavente, *Sp.* **139** P6
Benavides, *Tex., U.S.* **97** U10
Bend, *Oreg., U.S.* **102** H5
Bendena, *Qnsld., Austral.* **191** V13
Bender, *Mold.* **133** L14
Bender Cassim *see* Boosaaso, *Somalia* **179** F18
Bendigo, *Vic., Austral.* **191** Z12
Bené Beraq, *Israel* **150** M5
Benevento, *It.* **136** J10
Bengal, Bay of, *Asia* **146** K8
Bengara, *Indonesia* **168** H12
Bengbu, *China* **162** J7
Benghazi *see* Banghāzī, *Lib.* **177** C15
Bengkalis, island, *Indonesia* **168** H6
Bengkalis, *Indonesia* **168** H6
Bengkayang, *Indonesia* **168** J9
Bengkulu, *Indonesia* **168** K6
Bengo, Baía do, *Angola* **182** C5
Bengo Bay, *Af.* **174** L6
Benguela, *Angola* **182** D5
Benguerir, *Mor.* **176** B8
Beni, river, *S. Amer.* **118** F4
Beni Abbes, *Alg.* **176** C9
Beni Mazâr, *Egypt* **177** D18
Benin, *Af.* **180** G12
Benin, Bight of, *Af.* **180** J12
Benin City, *Nig.* **181** H13
Beni Ounif, *Alg.* **176** B9
Beni Suef, *Egypt* **177** D18
Benjamin, *Tex., U.S.* **96** K8
Benjamin Constant, *Braz.* **122** E5
Benjamín Hill, *Mex.* **108** C7
Benkelman, *Nebr., U.S.* **99** R3
Benlidi, *Qnsld., Austral.* **191** U13
Bennett, Ostrov, *Russ.* **141** C17
Bennett Peak, *N. Mex., U.S.* **101** Q10
Bennettsville, *S.C., U.S.* **90** K10
Ben Nevis, peak, *Scot., U.K.* **138** E7
Benneydale, *N.Z.* **193** K19
Bennington, *Vt., U.S.* **88** J12
Benoud, *Alg.* **176** B10
Bensbach, *P.N.G.* **193** E17
Benson, *Minn., U.S.* **98** J9
Benson, *N.C., U.S.* **90** H12
Benson Point, *Kiritimati, Kiribati* **197** B22
Bent, *Iran* **153** H17
Benta, *Malaysia* **168** G6
Bentinck Island, *Myanmar* **167** P7
Bentiu, *Sudan* **178** G12
Benton, *Ark., U.S.* **94** H8
Benton, *Ill., U.S.* **93** U6
Benton, *Ky., U.S.* **95** D13
Benton, *La., U.S.* **94** K6
Bentong, *Indonesia* **169** L13
Bentong, *Malaysia* **167** U9
Benton Harbor, *Mich., U.S.* **93** N9
Benton Lake, *Mont., U.S.* **100** C8
Bentonville, *Ark., U.S.* **94** E6
Bent's Old Fort National Historic Site, *Colo., U.S.* **101** N15
Benua, *Indonesia* **169** L14
Benue, river, *Nig.* **181** G15
Benxi, *China* **162** C11
Beograd (Belgrade), *Yug.* **137** F13
Beohari, *India* **158** H8
Beowawe, *Nev., U.S.* **103** N10
Beppu, *Jap.* **165** R5
Beqa, island, *Fiji* **198** J6
Bequia, island, *St. Vincent and the Grenadines* **113** L17
Bera Ndjoko, *Congo* **181** J18
Berard, *Kosrae, F.S.M.* **197** B18
Berard, Port, *Kosrae, F.S.M.* **197** B18
Berat, *Alban.* **137** J13
Berau, Telak, *Indonesia* **169** K18
Berau, Teluk, *Indonesia* **193** B14
Berber, *Sudan* **179** D13
Berbera, *Somalia* **179** F17
Berbérati, *Cen. Af. Rep.* **178** H8
Berbice, river, *Guyana* **121** E15
Berchtesgaden, *Ger.* **132** K7
Berdyans'k, *Ukr.* **133** K17
Berdychiv, *Ukr.* **133** J13
Berea, *Ky., U.S.* **95** C18
Bereina, *P.N.G.* **193** E19
Berenice, *Egypt* **177** E20
Berens River, *Man., Can.* **77** M14
Beresford, *S. Dak., U.S.* **98** M8
Berezniki, *Russ.* **140** G9
Berga, *Sp.* **139** P10
Bergama, *Turk.* **148** E3
Bergamo, *It.* **136** E8
Bergen, *Nor.* **134** K9
Bergerac, *Fr.* **138** M9
Berhala, Selat, *Indonesia* **168** J7
Bering, Ostrov, *Russ.* **141** E23
Bering Glacier, *Alas., U.S.* **105** J18
Bering Land Bridge National Preserve, *Alas., U.S.* **104** F11
Beringovskiy, *Russ.* **141** B21
Bering Sea, *N. Amer.* **74** Q3
Bering Strait, *N. Amer.* **74** P4
Berkeley, *Calif., U.S.* **103** S3
Berkner Island, *Antarctica* **206** F9
Berlevåg, *Nor.* **135** B15
Berlin, *Ger.* **132** G7
Berlin, *Md., U.S.* **90** D15
Berlin, *N.H., U.S.* **89** F14
Berlin, *Wis., U.S.* **92** K6
Berlin, Mount, *Antarctica* **206** M9
Bermejo, river, *Arg.* **124** E11
Bermuda Island, *Atl. Oc.* **111** G18
Bermuda Rise, *Atl. Oc.* **216** K4
Bern, *Switz.* **132** K4
Bernalillo, *N. Mex., U.S.* **101** S12
Bernardo de Irigoyen, *Arg.* **124** G15
Bernasconi, *Arg.* **125** N10
Berne, *Ind., U.S.* **93** Q10
Bernice, *La., U.S.* **94** K8
Bernie, *Mo., U.S.* **99** V15
Bernier Bay, *Nunavut, Can.* **77** E15
Beroroha, *Madagascar* **183** H16
Berrechid, *Mor.* **176** B8
Berry Islands, *Bahamas* **110** D11
Berryville, *Ark., U.S.* **94** E7
Bertam, *Malaysia* **167** T10
Berthold, *N. Dak., U.S.* **98** E3
Bertholet, Cape, *Austral.* **190** D4
Berthoud, *Colo., U.S.* **100** L13
Berthoud Pass, *Colo., U.S.* **100** M12
Bertoua, *Cameroon* **181** H17
Bertrand, *Nebr., U.S.* **99** Q5
Beru, island, *Kiribati* **194** G8
Beruniy, *Uzb.* **154** K9
Beruri, *Braz.* **122** E9
Beruwala, *Sri Lanka* **159** T7
Berwick, *La., U.S.* **94** Q9
Berwick upon Tweed, *Eng., U.K.* **138** E8
Berwyn, *Ill., U.S.* **93** N7
Beryslav, *Ukr.* **133** K16
Besalampy, *Madagascar* **183** F16
Besançon, *Fr.* **138** L12
Beserah, *Malaysia* **167** T10
Besham Qala, *Pak.* **156** M10
Besikama, *Indonesia* **169** N15
Beşiri, *Turk.* **149** G16
Beskol', *Kaz.* **155** F18
Besni, *Turk.* **148** H12
Beşparmak Dağı, *Turk.* **148** G3
Bessemer, *Ala., U.S.* **95** J15
Bessemer, *Mich., U.S.* **92** F5
Bestobe, *Kaz.* **155** C14
Bestyakh, *Russ.* **141** H18
Bethanie, *Namibia* **182** J7
Bethany, *Mo., U.S.* **99** R11
Bethany, *Okla., U.S.* **96** G10
Bethany Beach, *Del., U.S.* **90** D15
Bethel, *Alas., U.S.* **104** J12
Bethel Park, *Pa., U.S.* **88** N3
Bethesda, *Md., U.S.* **90** C13
Bethlehem, *Pa., U.S.* **88** N9
Bethlehem, *S. Af.* **182** K10
Bethlehem *see* Bayt Laḩm, *West Bank* **150** M5
Beth-shan *see* Bét She'an, *Israel* **150** L6
Betio, *Tarawa, Kiribati* **197** G17
Betong, *Malaysia* **167** S9
Betoota, *Qnsld., Austral.* **191** U11
Bétou, *Congo* **181** J19
Betpaqdala, desert, *Kaz.* **155** G13
Betroka, *Madagascar* **183** H17
Bét She'an (Beth-shan), *Israel* **150** L6
Betsiboka, river, *Af.* **174** N12
Bettendorf, *Iowa, U.S.* **99** P14
Betul, *India* **158** J6
Beulah, *Colo., U.S.* **101** N13
Beulah, *N. Dak., U.S.* **98** F3
Beycesultan, ruins, *Turk.* **148** G5
Bey Dağı, *Turk.* **148** E12
Bey Dağı, *Turk.* **148** G11
Beykoz, *Turk.* **148** C5
Beyla, *Guinea* **180** G7
Beyneu, *Kaz.* **154** G7
Beypazarı, *Turk.* **148** D7
Beyşehir, *Turk.* **148** H7
Beyşehir Gölü, *Turk.* **148** G7
Beytüşşebap, *Turk.* **149** H17
Béziers, *Fr.* **139** N10
Bhadarwah, *India* **157** N13
Bhadra, *India* **158** E5
Bhadrakh, *India* **158** K11
Bhag, *Pak.* **157** S6
Bhagalpur, *India* **158** H11
Bhakkar, *Pak.* **157** Q9
Bhaktapur, *Nepal* **158** F10
Bhamo, *Myanmar* **166** F7
Bhandara, *India* **158** K7
Bhanpura, *India* **158** H5
Bharatpur, *India* **158** F6
Bharatpur, *India* **158** H8
Bharuch, *India* **158** K3
Bhatapara, *India* **158** K8
Bhatinda, *India* **158** E5
Bhatkal, *India* **159** P4
Bhatpara, *India* **158** J12
Bhavnagar, *India* **158** J3
Bhawanipatna, *India* **158** L9
Bhera, *Pak.* **157** P11
Bhilai, *India* **158** K8
Bhilwara, *India* **158** H4
Bhima, river, *India* **158** M4
Bhimbar, *Pak.* **157** P11
Bhind, *India* **158** G6
Bhinmal, *India* **158** H3
Bhola, *Bangladesh* **158** J13
Bholari, *Pak.* **157** W7
Bhongir, *India* **158** M6
Bhopal, *India* **158** J6
Bhubaneshwar, *India* **158** K10
Bhuj, *India* **158** H1
Bhusawal, *India* **158** K5
Bhutan, *Asia* **158** F12
Biak, island, *Indonesia* **169** J19
Biak, *Indonesia* **169** J19
Białowieża, *Pol.* **132** G11
Białystok, *Pol.* **132** F11
Biaora, *India* **158** H5
Bīārjomand, *Iran* **153** C15
Biaro, island, *Indonesia* **169** H15
Biarritz, *Fr.* **139** N8
Biau, *Indonesia* **169** H14
Bibala, *Angola* **182** E5
Biberach, *Ger.* **132** J5
Bibi Nani, *Pak.* **157** S6
Bichänäk Ashyrymy, *Arm.* **149** E19
Bichvint'a, *Rep. of Georgia* **149** A15
Bickleton, *Wash., U.S.* **102** E6
Bicknell, *Ind., U.S.* **93** T8
Bicknell, *Utah, U.S.* **101** N7
Bida, *Nig.* **181** F13
Biddeford, *Me., U.S.* **89** H15
Bieber, *Calif., U.S.* **102** M5
Biei, *Jap.* **164** F14
Biel, *Switz.* **132** K4
Bielefeld, *Ger.* **132** G5
Bien Hoa, *Vietnam* **167** P13
Bienville, Lac, *Que., Can.* **77** L19
Bié Plateau, *Af.* **174** M6
Big, river, *N.W.T., Can.* **76** D12
Biga, *Turk.* **148** D3
Bigadiç, *Turk.* **148** E4
Big Baldy, peak, *Idaho, U.S.* **100** F4
Big Bay, *Espiritu Santu, Vanuatu* **198** C1
Big Bay, *Mich., U.S.* **92** F7
Big Bay (Drummond Bay), *Epi, Vanuatu* **198** E3
Big Bell, *W. Austral., Austral.* **191** V3
Big Belt Mountains, *Mont., U.S.* **100** D7
Big Bend National Park, *Tex., U.S.* **97** S3
Big Black, river, *Miss., U.S.* **94** L11
Big Blue, river, *Nebr., U.S.* **99** Q8
Big Canyon, river, *Tex., U.S.* **97** Q3
Big Creek, *Calif., U.S.* **103** S7
Big Cypress National Preserve, *Fla., U.S.* **91** W9
Big Cypress Swamp, *Fla., U.S.* **91** W9
Bigej, island, *Kwajalein Atoll, Marshall Is.* **196** M6
Bigej Channel, *Kwajalein Atoll, Marshall Is.* **196** M6
Big Falls, *Minn., U.S.* **98** E11
Big Fork, river, *Minn., U.S.* **98** F11
Bigfork, *Minn., U.S.* **98** F11
Bigfork, *Mont., U.S.* **100** B6
Biggar, *Sask., Can.* **76** M11
Biggarenn, island, *Kwajalein Atoll, Marshall Is.* **196** K3
Biggerann, island, *Kwajalein Atoll, Marshall Is.* **196** K2
Big Hatchet Peak, *N. Mex., U.S.* **101** W10
Big Hole, river, *Mont., U.S.* **100** E6
Big Hole National Battlefield, *Mont., U.S.* **100** E6
Bighorn, river, *Wyo., U.S.* **100** G10
Bighorn Canyon National Recreation Area, *Mont., U.S.* **100** F10
Bighorn Lake, *Mont., U.S.* **100** F10
Bighorn Mountains, *Wyo., U.S.* **100** F10
Bigi, island, *Kwajalein Atoll, Marshall Is.* **196** K3
Big Island, *Nunavut, Can.* **77** H19
Big Lake, *Tex., U.S.* **97** N5
Big Pine, *Calif., U.S.* **103** T8
Big Pine, *Fla., U.S.* **91** Y9
Big Piney, *Wyo., U.S.* **100** J9
Big Rapids, *Mich., U.S.* **92** K10
Big Sandy, river, *Wyo., U.S.* **100** J9
Big Sandy, *Mont., U.S.* **100** B9
Big Sioux, river, *S. Dak., U.S.* **98** L8
Big Snowy Mountains, *Mont., U.S.* **100** D9
Big South Fork National River and Recreation Area, *Tenn., U.S.* **95** E18
Big Spring, *Tex., U.S.* **96** M5
Big Springs, *Nebr., U.S.* **99** Q3
Big Stone City, *S. Dak., U.S.* **98** J8
Big Stone Gap, *Va., U.S.* **90** G7
Big Stone Lake, *Minn., U.S.* **98** J8
Big Sur, *Calif., U.S.* **103** U4
Big Thicket National Preserve, *Tex., U.S.* **97** P15
Big Timber, *Mont., U.S.* **100** E9
Big Trout Lake, *Ont., Can.* **77** M16
Big Trout Lake, *Ont., Can.* **77** M15
Big Wells, *Tex., U.S.* **97** S8
Big Wood, river, *Idaho, U.S.* **100** H5
Big Wood Cay, *Bahamas* **110** E11
Bihar Sharif, *India* **158** H10
Bihoro, *Jap.* **164** F15
Bijagós, Arquipélago dos, *Guinea-Bissau* **180** E4
Bijapur, *India* **158** L7
Bijapur, *India* **158** M5
Bījār, *Iran* **152** C11
Bijie, *China* **160** M12
Bijire, island, *Enewetak Atoll, Marshall Is.* **196** G8
Bijnor, *India* **158** E6
Bikaner, *India* **158** F4
Bikar Atoll, *Marshall Is.* **196** F5
Bikeman, island, *Tarawa, Kiribati* **197** G17
Biken, island, *Enewetak Atoll, Marshall Is.* **196** H7
Bikenibeu, *Tarawa, Kiribati* **197** G18
Bikennel, island, *Kwajalein Atoll, Marshall Is.* **196** L3
Bikenubati, island, *Tarawa, Kiribati* **197** F17
Bikin, *Russ.* **141** L21
Bikini Atoll, *Marshall Is.* **196** F3
Bīkkū Bīttī, peak, *Lib.* **177** F15
Bikoro, *Dem. Rep. of the Congo* **178** K8
Biläcäri, *Azerb.* **149** D23
Bilād Banī Bū'Alī, *Oman* **153** L17
Bilaspur, *India* **158** J8
Biläsuvar, *Azerb.* **149** E22
Bila Tserkva, *Ukr.* **133** J14
Bilauktaung Range, *Thai.* **166** M8
Bilbao (Bilbo), *Sp.* **139** N7
Bilecik, *Turk.* **148** D6
Bilhorod- Dnistrovs'kyy, *Ukr.* **133** L14
Bilibino, *Russ.* **141** C20
Bilican Dağları, *Turk.* **149** F16
Bilin, *Myanmar* **166** K7
Bill, *Wyo., U.S.* **100** H13
Billae, island, *Enewetak Atoll, Marshall Is.* **196** H8
Bill Baileys Bank, *Atl. Oc.* **216** C11
Billiluna, *W. Austral., Austral.* **191** S6
Billings, *Mont., U.S.* **100** E10
Billings, *Okla., U.S.* **96** E11
Billings, *Russ.* **141** B19
Billiton *see* Belitung, island, *Indonesia* **168** K9
Bill Williams, river, *Ariz., U.S.* **101** T5
Billy Chinook, Lake, *Oreg., U.S.* **102** G5
Bilma, *Niger* **177** G13
Biloela, *Qnsld., Austral.* **191** U15
Bilopillya, *Ukr.* **133** G16

Biloxi, Miss., U.S. 94 P12
Biltine, Chad 177 H16
Bilto, Nor. 135 C13
Bilüü, Mongolia 160 C8
Bimini Islands, Bahamas 110 D9
Bindle, Qnsld., Austral. 191 V14
Bindura, Zimb. 182 F12
Binford, N. Dak., U.S. 98 F7
Bingara, Qnsld., Austral. 191 V12
Bingara, N.S.W., Austral. 191 W14
Bing Bong, N. Terr., Austral. 191 Q9
Binger, Okla., U.S. 96 G9
Bingham, Me., U.S. 89 E16
Bingham Channel, Tarawa, Kiribati 197 E17
Binghamton, N.Y., U.S. 88 K9
Bingöl, Turk. 149 F15
Bingöl Dağları, Turk. 149 F16
Binhai (Dongkan), China 162 H9
Binh Khe, Vietnam 166 M14
Binh Lieu, Vietnam 166 G13
Binjai, Indonesia 168 G5
Binjai, Indonesia 168 G9
Binongko, island, Indonesia 169 L15
Bintan, island, Indonesia 168 H7
Bintuhan, Indonesia 168 L7
Bintulu, Malaysia 168 H10
Binxian, China 161 D17
Binxian, China 162 G1
Binyang, China 161 P13
Binzhou, China 162 F8
Bio-Bío, river, Chile 125 N6
Bioko, island, Eq. Guinea 184 F5
Bir, India 158 L5
Birāk, Lib. 177 D14
Bîr 'Alî, Yemen 152 Q11
Birao, Cen. Af. Rep. 178 F10
Biratnagar, Nepal 158 G11
Birchip, Vic., Austral. 191 Y11
Birch Mountains, Alta., Can. 76 K11
Bird, island, Seychelles 185 L19
Bird City, Kans., U.S. 99 R3
Bird Island see Aves, Venez. 113 J15
Bird Island, Minn., U.S. 98 K10
Birdsville, Qnsld., Austral. 191 U10
Birecik, Turk. 149 H13
Bîr el'Abd, Egypt 151 N2
Bireun, Indonesia 168 G4
Birganj, Nepal 158 G10
Bîr Ḥasana, Egypt 151 P3
Bîrjand, Iran 153 D16
Bîrlad, Rom. 137 E17
Birmingham, Ala., U.S. 95 J15
Birmingham, Eng., U.K. 138 G8
Bir Mogreïn (Fort Trinquet), Mauritania 176 D6
Birnie Island, Kiribati 194 H10
Birnin Kebbi, Nig. 180 E12
Birni Nkonni, Niger 176 H11
Birobidzhan, Russ. 141 K20
Birong, Philippines 168 E12
Birrindudu, N. Terr., Austral. 191 R7
Birshoghyr, Kaz. 154 E9
Birsilpur, India 158 F3
Birufu, Indonesia 169 L20
Biruli, Russ. 141 E14
Bisa, island, Indonesia 169 J16
Bisbee, Ariz., U.S. 101 W9
Bisbee, N. Dak., U.S. 98 E6
Biscay, Bay of, Eur. 130 G3
Biscayne Bay, Fla., U.S. 91 X10
Biscayne National Park, Fla., U.S. 91 X10
Biscay Plain, Atl. Oc. 216 G3
Biscoe Islands, Antarctica 206 E4
Bishkek, Kyrg. 156 D11
Bisho, S. Af. 182 M10
Bishop, Calif., U.S. 103 S8
Bishop, Tex., U.S. 97 U10
Bishop Rock, Eng., U.K. 138 J6
Bishopville, S.C., U.S. 90 K10
Bishrī, Jabal, Syr. 150 F12
Biskra, Alg. 176 B11
Bislig, Philippines 169 F15
Bismarck, N. Dak., U.S. 98 G4
Bismarck Archipelago, P.N.G. 193 C20
Bismarck Range, P.N.G. 193 C19
Bismarck Sea, P.N.G. 193 C20
Bismil, Turk. 149 G15
Bison, S. Dak., U.S. 98 J3
Bissagos Islands, Af. 174 G1
Bissameuttack, India 158 L9
Bissau, Guinea-Bissau 180 E4
Bistcho Lake, Alta., Can. 76 J10
Bistineau, Lake, La., U.S. 94 L7
Bistrița, Rom. 137 D15
Bitam, Gabon 181 K16
Bitlis, Turk. 149 G16
Bitola, Maced. 137 J14
Bitra Island, India 159 Q2
Bitterfontein, S. Af. 182 L7
Bitterroot, river, Mont., U.S. 100 D5
Bitterroot Range, U.S. 78 C6

Biu, Nig. 181 F16
Biwa Ko, Jap. 165 P9
Bixby, Okla., U.S. 96 F13
Biyang, China 162 J5
Biysk, Russ. 140 L12
Bizerte, Tun. 177 A13
Bjøllånes, Nor. 134 F12
Bjørnafjorden, Nor. 134 K9
Black, river, Ariz., U.S. 101 U8
Black, river, N.Y., U.S. 88 H9
Black, river, Ark.-Mo., U.S. 79 J14
Black see Da, river, Vietnam 166 H11
Black, river, Wis., U.S. 92 J4
Blackall, Qnsld., Austral. 191 U13
Blackball, N.Z. 193 N17
Blackbeard Island, Ga., U.S. 91 P9
Black Belt, region, U.S. 79 K16
Blackburn, Mount, Alas., U.S. 105 H18
Black Canyon, Ariz., U.S. 101 T7
Black Canyon of the Gunnison National Park, Colo., U.S. 101 N11
Black Coast, Antarctica 206 E6
Blackduck, Minn., U.S. 98 F10
Black Eagle, Mont., U.S. 100 C8
Blackfoot, river, Mont., U.S. 100 C6
Blackfoot, Idaho, U.S. 100 H7
Blackfoot Reservoir, Idaho, U.S. 100 H7
Black Forest, Ger. 132 J5
Black Hills, S. Dak., U.S. 98 K1
Black Irtysh, river, Asia 146 F8
Black Lake, Mich., U.S. 92 H11
Black Mesa, Okla., U.S. 96 E4
Black Mountain, Ky., U.S. 95 D20
Black Mountains, Ariz., U.S. 101 R4
Black Point see Kupikipikio, Hawaii, U.S. 106 F11
Blackpool, Eng., U.K. 138 G8
Black Range, N. Mex., U.S. 101 U11
Black River Falls, Wis., U.S. 92 J4
Black Rock, S. Amer. 118 R9
Black Rock Desert, Nev., U.S. 102 M7
Blacksburg, Va., U.S. 90 F9
Black Sea, Eur. 130 H11
Black Sea Lowland, Eur. 130 H10
Blacks Fork, river, Wyo., U.S. 100 K8
Blackshear, Ga., U.S. 91 P7
Blackstone, Va., U.S. 90 F12
Blackville, S.C., U.S. 90 L9
Black Volta, river, Af. 174 H3
Blackwater, Qnsld., Austral. 191 T14
Blackwell, Okla., U.S. 96 E11
Blackwell, Tex., U.S. 96 M7
Blagoevgrad, Bulg. 137 H15
Blagoveshchensk, Russ. 141 L19
Blaine, Wash., U.S. 102 A3
Blair, Nebr., U.S. 99 P9
Blair Athol, Qnsld., Austral. 191 T14
Blake-Bahama Ridge, Atl. Oc. 216 J3
Blakely, Ga., U.S. 91 P4
Blake Plateau, Atl. Oc. 216 J3
Blake Point, Mich., U.S. 92 C6
Blanc, Cap, Mauritania 176 F4
Blanc, Mont, Fr. 138 M12
Blanca, Sierra, Tex., U.S. 97 V3
Blanca Bay, S. Amer. 118 N6
Blanca Peak, Colo., U.S. 101 P13
Blanchard, Okla., U.S. 96 G10
Blanche, Lake, Austral. 190 H11
Blanche Channel, Solomon Is. 197 M16
Blanchisseuse, Trin. & Tobago 113 P17
Blanco, river, Bol. 122 J8
Blanco, river, Tex., U.S. 97 Q10
Blanco, Tex., U.S. 97 Q9
Blanco, Cape, Oreg., U.S. 102 J1
Blanding, Utah, U.S. 101 P9
Blanquilla, Isla, Venez. 120 A11
Blantyre, Malawi 183 F13
Blaze, Point, Austral. 190 B7
Blenheim, N.Z. 193 M18
Blida, Alg. 176 A11
Bligh Water, Fiji 198 H6
Blind River, Ont., Can. 77 Q17
Blinman, S. Austral., Austral. 191 W10
Blitar, Indonesia 168 M10
Block Island, R.I., U.S. 89 M14
Bloemfontein, S. Af. 182 K10
Blois, Fr. 138 L9
Blönduós, Ice. 134 E3
Bloomer, Wis., U.S. 92 H3
Bloomfield, Ind., U.S. 93 S8
Bloomfield, Iowa, U.S. 99 Q12
Bloomfield, Mo., U.S. 99 V15
Bloomfield, N. Mex., U.S. 101 Q10
Bloomfield, Nebr., U.S. 99 N7
Blooming Prairie, Minn., U.S. 98 L12
Bloomington, Ill., U.S. 93 Q6
Bloomington, Ind., U.S. 93 S8
Bloomington, Minn., U.S. 98 K11
Bloomington, Tex., U.S. 97 S12
Bloomsburg, Pa., U.S. 88 M8
Blossom, Mys, Russ. 141 B19

Blouberg, peak, Af. 174 P9
Blower Rock, Jam. 110 P11
Blue Earth, Minn., U.S. 98 L12
Bluefield, W. Va., U.S. 90 F8
Bluefields, Nicar. 109 M19
Blue Hill, Nebr., U.S. 99 R6
Blue Hills, Turks and Caicos Is., U.K. 111 H16
Bluejoint Lake, Oreg., U.S. 102 K7
Blue Lake, Calif., U.S. 102 M2
Blue Mountain, Ark., U.S. 94 G6
Blue Mountains, Oreg.-Wash., U.S. 102 F8
Blue Nile see Azraq, El Bahr el, river, Sudan 179 E13
Blue Nile Falls see Tis Isat Falls, Eth. 179 F14
Blue Rapids, Kans., U.S. 99 R8
Blue Ridge, Ga., U.S. 90 J6
Blue Ridge, Ga., U.S. 90 J5
Bluff, N.Z. 193 R15
Bluff, Utah, U.S. 101 P9
Bluff Knoll, Austral. 190 K3
Bluff Point, Austral. 190 H1
Bluffton, Ind., U.S. 93 Q10
Blumenau, Braz. 123 N13
Blunt, S. Dak., U.S. 98 K5
Bly, Oreg., U.S. 102 K5
Blythe, Calif., U.S. 103 X13
Blytheville, Ark., U.S. 94 F11
Bø, Nor. 134 D12
Bø, Nor. 134 K9
Bo, Sierra Leone 180 G6
Boaco, Nicar. 109 M18
Boano, island, Indonesia 169 K16
Boardman, Ohio, U.S. 93 P16
Boatman, Qnsld., Austral. 191 V13
Boa Vista, island, Cape Verde 185 C17
Boa Vista, Braz. 122 B9
Boaz, Ala., U.S. 95 H16
Bobai, China 163 S2
Bobbili, India 158 L14
Bobo Dioulasso, Burkina Faso 180 E9
Boby, peak, Madagascar 183 H17
Boby Peak, Af. 174 P11
Boca Chica, Dom. Rep. 111 M19
Boca Chica Key, Fla., U.S. 91 Y8
Bôca do Acre, Braz. 122 F6
Bôca do Jari, Braz. 122 C12
Bocage, Cap, New Caledonia, Fr. 198 C7
Boca Grande, Fla., U.S. 91 V8
Boca Raton, Fla., U.S. 91 W10
Bocas del Toro, Pan. 109 N20
Bocay, Nicar. 109 L18
Bochum, Ger. 132 G5
Böda, Sw. 135 M14
Bodaybo, Russ. 141 J16
Bodden Town, Cayman Is., U.K. 110 L7
Bodega Bay, Calif., U.S. 103 R2
Bodega Head, Calif., U.S. 103 R2
Bodele Depression, Af. 174 G6
Boden, Sw. 135 F14
Bodensee, lake, Eur. 132 K5
Bogda Shan, Asia 146 F9
Bodī, Mongolia 160 E11
Bodi, Indonesia 169 H14
Bodmin, Eng., U.K. 138 J7
Bodø, Nor. 134 E12
Bodrum, Turk. 148 H3
Bo Duc, Vietnam 167 N13
Boe, Nauru 197 F22
Boende, Dem. Rep. of the Congo 178 K9
Boerne, Tex., U.S. 97 R9
Boffa, Guinea 180 E5
Bogalusa, La., U.S. 94 N11
Bogan, river, Austral. 190 J13
Bogantungan, Qnsld., Austral. 191 U13
Boğazkale, Turk. 148 E10
Boğazlıyan, Turk. 148 F10
Bogdanovka, Rep. of Georgia 149 C17
Bogda Shan, China 160 E7
Bogenaga, island, Jaluit Atoll, Marshall Is. 196 K7
Boggabilla, N.S.W., Austral. 191 W14
Boggenadick, island, Jaluit Atoll, Marshall Is. 196 K7
Boggenatjen, island, Kwajalein Atoll, Marshall Is. 196 L3
Boggerik, island, Kwajalein Atoll, Marshall Is. 196 K4
Boggerik Passage, Kwajalein Atoll, Marshall Is. 196 K3
Boggerlapp, island, Kwajalein Atoll, Marshall Is. 196 K4
Bogia, P.N.G. 193 C19
Bognes, Nor. 134 E12
Bogor, Indonesia 168 M8
Bogotá, Col. 120 F5
Bogotol, Russ. 141 K13
Bogra, Bangladesh 158 H12
Bogué, Mauritania 176 G5
Bo Hai, China 162 E8
Bohé, Bioko, Eq. Guinea 184 N7
Bohe, China 163 S2
Bohemian Forest, Ger. 132 J6
Bohol, island, Philippines 169 E15
Bohol Sea, Philippines 169 E15
Boiaçu, Braz. 122 C8
Boim, Braz. 122 D11

Bois Blanc Island, Mich., U.S. 92 G11
Boisé, Port, New Caledonia, Fr. 198 E9
Boise, Idaho, U.S. 100 G4
Boise City, Okla., U.S. 96 E4
Bojnūrd, Iran 153 B15
Bokalijman, island, Jaluit Atoll, Marshall Is. 196 M7
Boké, Guinea 180 E5
Boken, island, Enewetak Atoll, Marshall Is. 196 G8
Boken, island, Enewetak Atoll, Marshall Is. 196 J8
Boken, island, Majuro Atoll, Marshall Is. 196 G10
Bokenelab, island, Enewetak Atoll, Marshall Is. 196 G8
Bokoluo, island, Enewetak Atoll, Marshall Is. 196 G7
Bokombako, island, Enewetak Atoll, Marshall Is. 196 G7
Bokpyinn, Myanmar 167 P7
Boku, P.N.G. 197 K14
Bokungu, Dem. Rep. of the Congo 178 K10
Bokurdak, Turkm. 154 L8
Bolaang, Indonesia 169 J14
Bolan Pass, Pak. 157 R6
Bole, Ghana 180 F10
Bolesławiec, Pol. 132 H8
Bolgatanga, Ghana 180 F10
Bolhrad, Ukr. 133 L14
Bolívar, Mo., U.S. 99 U12
Bolivar, Tenn., U.S. 94 G12
Bolívar, Cerro, Venez. 120 D11
Bolivia, S. Amer. 122 J8
Bolivia, Cuba 110 J12
Bolkar Dağları, Turk. 148 H9
Bollnäs, Sw. 135 J13
Bollon, Qnsld., Austral. 191 V13
Bollons Tablemount, Pac. Oc. 218 R10
Bolluk Gölü, Turk. 148 G8
Bologna, It. 136 F9
Bolognesi, Peru 122 G4
Bolovens Plateau, Laos 166 L12
Bol'shaya Bicha, Russ. 140 J10
Bol'sheretsk, Russ. 141 G22
Bol'shevik, Ostrov, Russ. 141 D14
Bol'shevik Island, Asia 146 B9
Bol'shezemel'skaya Tundra, Russ. 140 F10
Bol'shoy Begichev, Ostrov, Russ. 141 E15
Bol'shoy Lyakhovskiy, Ostrov, Russ. 141 D17
Bol'shoy Patom, Russ. 141 J17
Bol'shoy Shantar, Ostrov, Russ. 141 H20
Bolton Point, Tarawa, Kiribati 197 E17
Bolu, Turk. 148 D7
Boluntay, China 160 H8
Boluo, China 163 R5
Bolvadin, Turk. 148 F6
Bolzano, It. 136 E9
Boma, Dem. Rep. of the Congo 178 L7
Bomba, Gulf of, Af. 174 D7
Bombala, N.S.W., Austral. 191 Z13
Bombardopolis, Haiti 111 L15
Bombay see Mumbai, India 158 L3
Bombom, Ilhéu, São Tomé and Príncipe 185 A20
Bomdila, India 158 F14
Bomdo, India 158 E15
Bomi, China 160 L9
Bom Jesus da Lapa, Braz. 123 H15
Bomongo, Dem. Rep. of the Congo 178 J8
Bomu, river, Cen. Af. Rep.–Dem. Rep. of the Congo 178 H10
Bona, Mount, Alas., U.S. 105 H19
Bonaire, island, Lesser Antilles 112 M10
Bonang, Vic., Austral. 191 Z13
Bonanza, Oreg., U.S. 102 K5
Bonanza, Utah, U.S. 100 L9
Bonao, Dom. Rep. 111 M18
Bonaparte Archipelago, Austral. 190 B5
Bonasse, Trin. & Tobago 113 P16
Bonavista, Nfld., Can. 77 M24
Bonavista Bay, N. Amer. 74 G11
Bon Bon, S. Austral., Austral. 191 W9
Bondo, Dem. Rep. of the Congo 178 H10
Bondoukou, Côte d'Ivoire 180 G9
Bonds Cay, Bahamas 110 D11
Bonerate, island, Indonesia 169 M13
Bonesteel, S. Dak., U.S. 98 M6
Bonete, Cerro, S. Amer. 124 H8
Bongandanga, Dem. Rep. of the Congo 178 J9
Bongaree, Qnsld., Austral. 191 V15
Bongo Lava, Af. 174 N11
Bongor, Chad 177 K14
Bonham, Tex., U.S. 96 K12
Bonifacio, Fr. 139 P13
Bonifacio, Strait of, Fr.–It. 136 H8
Bonifay, Fla., U.S. 91 Q3
Bonin Islands (Ogasawara Guntō), Jap. 194 C4
Bonin Trench, Pac. Oc. 218 G6
Bonita Springs, Fla., U.S. 91 W8
Bonito, Braz. 122 L10
Bonito, Pueblo, N. Mex., U.S. 101 R10
Bonn, Ger. 132 G4
Bonners Ferry, Idaho, U.S. 100 A4

Bonne Terre, Mo., U.S. 99 T15
Bonneville Dam, Oreg.-Wash., U.S. 102 F4
Bonneville Salt Flats, Utah, U.S. 100 K5
Bonney Downs, W. Austral., Austral. 191 T3
Bonnie Rock, W. Austral., Austral. 191 W3
Bonriki, island, Tarawa, Kiribati 197 G18
Bonriki, Tarawa, Kiribati 197 G18
Bontang, Indonesia 168 J12
Bontoc, Philippines 169 B13
Bonvouloir Islands, P.N.G. 193 E21
Bookabie, S. Austral., Austral. 191 W8
Booker, Tex., U.S. 96 E7
Booker T. Washington National Monument, Va., U.S. 90 F10
Booligal, N.S.W., Austral. 191 X12
Boonah, Qnsld., Austral. 191 V15
Boonderoo, Qnsld., Austral. 191 S12
Boone, Colo., U.S. 101 N14
Boone, Iowa, U.S. 99 N11
Boone, N.C., U.S. 90 G8
Booneville, Ark., U.S. 94 G6
Booneville, Miss., U.S. 95 H13
Bööntsagaan Nuur, Mongolia 160 E10
Boonville, Ind., U.S. 93 U8
Boonville, Mo., U.S. 99 S12
Boonville, N.Y., U.S. 88 H9
Boorama, Somalia 179 F16
Boorara, Qnsld., Austral. 191 V12
Booroorban, N.S.W., Austral. 191 Y12
Boosaaso (Bender Cassim), Somalia 179 F18
Boothbay Harbor, Me., U.S. 89 G16
Boothia, Gulf of, Nunavut, Can. 77 F15
Boothia Peninsula, Nunavut, Can. 77 F15
Booué, Gabon 181 L16
Bopeechee, S. Austral., Austral. 191 W10
Bor, Turk. 148 G9
Bor, Yug. 137 G14
Bora-Bora, island, Fr. Polynesia, Fr. 199 K14
Boracho Peak, Tex., U.S. 97 P1
Borah Peak, Idaho, U.S. 100 G6
Boran, region, Eth. 179 H15
Boran, Kaz. 155 E19
Borås, Sw. 134 M12
Borāzjān, Iran 153 G13
Borba, Braz. 122 E9
Borborema, Planalto da, Braz. 123 F17
Borchgrevink Coast, Antarctica 207 Q14
Borçka, Turk. 149 C16
Bordeaux, Fr. 138 M9
Borden, W. Austral., Austral. 191 Y3
Borden Island, N.W.T., Can. 77 B13
Borden Peninsula, Nunavut, Can. 77 E16
Bordertown, S. Austral., Austral. 191 Y11
Bordj Flye Sainte Marie, Alg. 176 D9
Bordj Messouda, Alg. 176 C12
Bordj Omar Driss, Alg. 176 D12
Boré, Mali 176 H8
Boreal, Chaco, S. Amer. 118 J6
Boreas Plain, Arctic Oc. 223 H16
Bordeyri, Ice. 134 E2
Borgarnes, Ice. 134 F2
Borger, Tex., U.S. 96 G6
Borgholm, Sw. 135 M14
Borgne, Lake, La., U.S. 94 Q12
Borhoyn Tal, Mongolia 161 E13
Borisoglebsk, Russ. 140 G5
Borjomi, Rep. of Georgia 149 C17
Borkou, region, Chad 177 G15
Borlänge, Sw. 135 K13
Borneo, island, Asia 168 J10
Bornholm, island, Den. 135 P13
Bornova, Turk. 148 F3
Boro, river, Sudan 178 G11
Boroko, Indonesia 169 J14
Boromo, Burkina Faso 180 E9
Boronga Islands, Myanmar 166 H4
Borotou, Côte d'Ivoire 180 G7
Borovichi, Russ. 140 E6
Borovskoy, Kaz. 154 B11
Borroloola, N. Terr., Austral. 191 Q9
Børselv, Nor. 135 C14
Borūjerd, Iran 152 D11
Borzya, Russ. 141 L17
Bosa, It. 136 J7
Bosaga, Turkm. 154 M11
Boscobel, Wis., U.S. 92 L4
Bose, China 160 P12
Boshan, China 162 F7
Bosnia and Herzegovina, Eur. 136 F12
Bosobolo, Dem. Rep. of the Congo 178 H9
Bōsō Hantō, Jap. 165 P13
Bosporus see İstanbul Boğazi, strait, Turk. 148 C5
Bossangoa, Cen. Af. Rep. 178 G8
Bossembélé, Cen. Af. Rep. 178 H8
Bossier City, La., U.S. 94 L6
Bossut, Cape, Austral. 190 D4
Bostan, Pak. 157 R6
Bosten Hu, China 160 F7
Boston, Ga., U.S. 91 Q6
Boston, Mass., U.S. 89 K15
Boston Mountains, Ark., U.S. 94 F7
Boswell, Okla., U.S. 96 J13
Botany Bay, Austral. 190 L14
Botevgrad, Bulg. 137 G15
Bothnia, Gulf of, Fin.-Sw. 135 J14
Botoşani, Rom. 137 D16
Botswana, Af. 182 H9
Bottineau, N. Dak., U.S. 98 D5
Bottle Creek, Turks and Caicos Is., U.K. 111 H17
Botwood, Nfld., Can. 77 M23
Bouaflé, Côte d'Ivoire 180 G8
Bouaké, Côte d'Ivoire 180 G9
Bouar, Cen. Af. Rep. 178 H8
Boû Djébéha, Mali 176 G9
Bougainville, island, P.N.G. 197 K13
Bougainville, Cape, Austral. 190 B5
Bougainville, Mouillage de, Tahiti, Fr. Polynesia, Fr. 199 P17
Bougainville, Mount, Wallis and Futuna, Fr. 198 F12
Bougainville Strait, Solomon Is. 197 K15
Bougainville Strait, Vanuatu 198 D2
Bougouni, Mali 176 J7
Bouira, Alg. 176 A11
Boujdour, Cape, Af. 174 E1
Boulari, Passe de, New Caledonia, Fr. 198 E8
Boulder, Colo., U.S. 100 L13
Boulder, Mont., U.S. 100 D7
Boulder City, Nev., U.S. 103 U12
Boulia, Qnsld., Austral. 191 T11
Boulogne, Fr. 138 J10
Bouloupari, New Caledonia, Fr. 198 D8
Bouna, Côte d'Ivoire 180 F9
Boundary Peak, Nev., U.S. 103 S8
Boundiali, Côte d'Ivoire 180 F8
Bountiful, Utah, U.S. 100 K7
Bounty Bay, Pitcairn I., U.K. 199 Q23
Bounty Islands, Pac. Oc. 194 Q9
Bounty Trough, Pac. Oc. 218 Q9
Bourail, New Caledonia, Fr. 198 D7
Bouraké, New Caledonia, Fr. 198 D8
Bourayne, Port, Huahine, Fr. Polynesia, Fr. 199 H14
Bourem, Mali 176 G9
Bourges, Fr. 138 L10
Boû Rjeïmât, Mauritania 176 F5
Bourke, N.S.W., Austral. 191 W13
Bournemouth, Eng., U.K. 138 J8
Bousso, Chad 177 K14
Boutilimit, Mauritania 176 G5
Bouvard, Cape, Austral. 190 K2
Bovey, Minn., U.S. 98 F11
Bovill, Idaho, U.S. 100 D4
Bovina, Tex., U.S. 96 H4
Bowbells, N. Dak., U.S. 98 D3
Bowdle, S. Dak., U.S. 98 J5
Bowdoin, Lake, Mont., U.S. 100 B11
Bowen, Qnsld., Austral. 191 S14
Bowers Ridge, Pac. Oc. 218 C10
Bowie, Md., U.S. 90 C13
Bowie, Tex., U.S. 96 K10
Bowie Seamount, Pac. Oc. 219 C14
Bowling Green, Ky., U.S. 95 D15
Bowling Green, Mo., U.S. 99 S14
Bowling Green, Ohio, U.S. 93 P12
Bowling Green, Va., U.S. 90 E13
Bowman, N. Dak., U.S. 98 H2
Bowman Bay, Nunavut, Can. 77 G17
Bowman Glacier, Antarctica 206 K12
Box Butte Reservoir, Nebr., U.S. 99 N2
Box Elder Creek, Mont., U.S. 100 C10
Boxelder Creek, Mont., U.S. 100 E13
Boxing, China 162 F8
Boyabat, Turk. 148 C10
Boýadumasaz, Turkm. 154 J9
Boyang, China 162 M7
Boyarka, Russ. 141 F14
Boyce, La., U.S. 94 M8
Boyer, river, Iowa, U.S. 99 P9
Boyne City, Mich., U.S. 92 H10
Boynton Beach, Fla., U.S. 91 W10
Boyoma Falls, Dem. Rep. of the Congo 178 J11
Boysen Reservoir, Wyo., U.S. 100 H10
Bozashchy Tübegi, Kaz. 154 G6
Boz Burun, Turk. 148 D4
Bozburun, Turk. 148 H3
Bozburun Dağı, Turk. 148 H6
Bozcaada, island, Turk. 148 D2
Boz Dağ, Turk. 148 H4
Bozdoğan, Turk. 148 G4
Bozeman, Mont., U.S. 100 E8
Bozhou, China 162 H6
Bozkır, Turk. 148 H7
Bozkurt, Turk. 148 B9
Bozoum, Cen. Af. Rep. 178 G8
Bozova, Turk. 149 H13
Bozüyük, Turk. 148 E5
Brabant Island, Antarctica 206 D3
Brač, island, Croatia 136 G11
Brackettville, Tex., U.S. 97 R7
Bradenton, Fla., U.S. 91 U7
Bradford, Pa., U.S. 88 L5
Bradford, Eng., U.K. 138 G8
Bradley, Ill., U.S. 93 P7
Bradley, S. Dak., U.S. 98 J7
Brady, Nebr., U.S. 99 Q4
Brady, Tex., U.S. 97 P8
Braga, Port. 139 P5
Bragado, Arg. 124 L12
Bragança, Port. 139 P5
Braham, Minn., U.S. 98 H11
Brahmanbaria, Bangladesh 158 H13
Brahmapur, India 158 L10
Brahmaputra, river, Asia 146 H9
Brahmaur, India 157 P13
Brăila, Rom. 137 F17
Brainerd, Minn., U.S. 98 H10
Branchville, S.C., U.S. 90 L9
Branco, island, Cape Verde 185 B15
Branco, river, Braz. 122 C8
Brandberg, peak, Af. 174 N6
Brandenburg, Ger. 132 G7
Brandfort, S. Af. 182 K10
Brandon, Fla., U.S. 91 U8
Brandon, Man., Can. 77 N13
Brandon, Miss., U.S. 94 L11
Brandon, S. Dak., U.S. 98 L8
Brandvlei, S. Af. 182 L8
Brandy Peak, Oreg., U.S. 102 K2
Branford, Fla., U.S. 91 R7
Bransby, Qnsld., Austral. 191 V11
Bransfield Strait, Antarctica 206 C4
Branson, Colo., U.S. 101 Q14
Branson, Mo., U.S. 99 V12
Brantley, Ala., U.S. 95 M16
Brantley Lake, N. Mex., U.S. 101 V14
Bras d'Or Lake, N.S., Can. 77 N23
Brasil, Planalto do, Braz. 123 J14
Brasília, Braz. 123 J13
Brasília Legal, Braz. 122 E11
Braşov, Rom. 137 E16
Brasstown Bald, peak, Ga., U.S. 90 J5
Bratislava (Pressburg), Slovakia 132 K8
Bratsk, Russ. 141 K15
Bratskoye Vodokhranilishche, Russ. 141 K15
Bratsk Reservoir, Asia 146 E9
Brattleboro, Vt., U.S. 89 J13
Braunschweig, Ger. 132 G6
Brava, island, Cape Verde 185 E15
Brawley, Calif., U.S. 103 Y11
Bray, Ire. 138 G6
Bray Island, Nunavut, Can. 77 F17
Brazil, S. Amer. 123 G10
Brazil, Ind., U.S. 93 S8
Brazilian Highlands, S. Amer. 118 F8
Brazoria, Tex., U.S. 97 S13
Brazos, river, Tex., U.S. 97 P12
Brazzaville, Congo 181 M17
Breadalbane, Qnsld., Austral. 191 T11
Breakfast Island, Jaluit Atoll, Marshall Is. 196 M8
Breaux Bridge, La., U.S. 94 P9
Breckenridge, Colo., U.S. 100 M12
Breckenridge, Minn., U.S. 98 H8
Breckenridge, Tex., U.S. 96 L9
Brecknock, Península, Chile 125 Y8
Břeclav, Czech Rep. 132 J8
Bredasdorp, S. Af. 182 M8
Breezewood, Pa., U.S. 88 P5
Breiðafjörður, Ice. 134 E2
Breid Bay, Antarctica 207 B15
Brejo, Braz. 123 E15
Bremen, Ga., U.S. 90 L4
Bremen, Ger. 132 F5
Bremen, Ind., U.S. 93 P9
Bremerhaven, Ger. 132 F5
Bremerton, Wash., U.S. 102 C3
Bremond, Tex., U.S. 97 N12
Brenham, Tex., U.S. 97 Q12
Brenner Pass, Aust.-It. 132 K6
Brentwood, N.Y., U.S. 88 N12
Brescia, It. 136 E9
Brest, Belarus 132 G11
Brest, Fr. 138 K7
Bretón, Cayo, Cuba 110 J9
Breton Islands, La., U.S. 94 Q12
Breton Sound, La., U.S. 94 Q12
Brett, Cape, N.Z. 193 H18
Breu, river, Braz.-Peru 122 G5
Brevard, N.C., U.S. 90 J7
Breves, Braz. 122 D12
Brevoort Island, Nunavut, Can. 77 G19
Brewarrina, N.S.W., Austral. 191 W13
Brewer, Me., U.S. 89 F17
Brewster, Kans., U.S. 99 S3
Brewster, Nebr., U.S. 99 N5
Brewster, Wash., U.S. 102 B6
Brewton, Ala., U.S. 95 N15
Bria, Cen. Af. Rep. 178 G10
Bridgeport, Ala., U.S. 95 G16
Bridgeport, Calif., U.S. 103 R7
Bridgeport, Conn., U.S. 88 M12
Bridgeport, Ill., U.S. 93 T7
Bridgeport, Nebr., U.S. 99 P2
Bridgeport, Tex., U.S. 96 K10
Bridgeport, W. Va., U.S. 90 C9
Bridgeport, Lake, Tex., U.S. 96 K10
Bridger, Mont., U.S. 100 E10
Bridger Peak, Wyo., U.S. 100 K11
Bridgeton, N.J., U.S. 88 Q9
Bridgetown, Barbados 113 L19
Bridgetown, W. Austral., Austral. 191 Y3
Bridgewater, N.S., Can. 77 P22
Bridgton, Me., U.S. 89 G15
Brig, Switz. 132 L4
Brigham City, Utah, U.S. 100 K7
Brighton, Colo., U.S. 100 L13
Brighton, Eng., U.K. 138 J9
Brindisi, It. 136 J12
Brinkley, Ark., U.S. 94 G10
Brinkworth, S. Austral., Austral. 191 X10
Brisbane, Qnsld., Austral. 191 V15
Bristol, Conn., U.S. 88 L12
Bristol, Pa., U.S. 88 P10
Bristol, S. Dak., U.S. 98 J7
Bristol, Tenn., U.S. 95 D20
Bristol, Eng., U.K. 138 H8
Bristol, Va., U.S. 90 G7
Bristol Channel, U.K. 138 H8
Bristol Bay, Alas., U.S. 105 M13
Bristol Lake, Calif., U.S. 103 W11
Bristow, Okla., U.S. 96 F12
British Columbia, Can. 76 J8
British Isles, Eur. 130 D3
British Mountains, Can.-U.S. 78 M5
Britstown, S. Af. 182 L9
Britt, Iowa, U.S. 98 M11
Britton, S. Dak., U.S. 98 J7
Britton Hill, Fla., U.S. 91 Q3
Brive, Fr. 138 M10
Brno, Czech Rep. 132 J8
Broa, Ensenada de la, Cuba 110 G7
Broad, river, S.C., U.S. 90 J8
Broadus, Mont., U.S. 100 E12
Broadview, Sask., Can. 76 N12
Broadwater, Nebr., U.S. 99 P2
Brochet, Man., Can. 77 K13
Brock Island, N.W.T., Can. 77 B13
Brockport, N.Y., U.S. 88 H6
Brockton, Mass., U.S. 89 K15
Brockway, Mont., U.S. 100 C12
Brockway, Pa., U.S. 88 M5
Brodeur Peninsula, Nunavut, Can. 77 E15
Brogan, Oreg., U.S. 102 H9
Broken Arrow, Okla., U.S. 96 F13
Broken Bow, Nebr., U.S. 99 P5
Broken Bow, Okla., U.S. 96 J14
Broken Bow Lake, Okla., U.S. 96 J14
Broken Hill, N.S.W., Austral. 191 X11
Broken Ridge, Ind. Oc. 220 M12
Brokopondo, Suriname 121 E16
Brønnøysund, Nor. 134 G11
Bronson, Fla., U.S. 91 S7
Bronte, Tex., U.S. 96 M7
Brookfield, Mo., U.S. 99 R12
Brookfield, Wis., U.S. 92 L7
Brookhaven, Miss., U.S. 94 M10
Brookings, Oreg., U.S. 102 L1
Brookings, S. Dak., U.S. 98 K8
Brooklyn, Iowa, U.S. 99 P12
Brooklyn Center, Minn., U.S. 98 J11
Brookport, Ill., U.S. 93 V6
Brooks, Alta., Can. 76 M10
Brooks Banks, Hawaii, U.S. 106 M6
Brooks Range, Alas., U.S. 105 D13
Brooksville, Fla., U.S. 91 T7
Brookville, Ind., U.S. 93 S10
Brookville, Pa., U.S. 88 M4
Broome, W. Austral., Austral. 191 R4
Brosse, Île, New Caledonia, Fr. 198 E9
Brothers, Oreg., U.S. 102 H5
Broughton Islands, Austral. 190 K15
Browerville, Minn., U.S. 98 H10
Brown, Point, Austral. 190 K8
Brownfield, Tex., U.S. 96 K4
Browning, Mont., U.S. 100 B6
Brownlee Dam, Idaho-Oreg., U.S. 100 F3
Browns Town, Jam. 110 M11
Brownstown, Ind., U.S. 93 T9
Browns Valley, Minn., U.S. 98 J8
Brownsville, Oreg., U.S. 102 G3
Brownsville, Tenn., U.S. 94 F12
Brownsville, Tex., U.S. 97 X11
Brownsweg, Suriname 121 E16
Brownwood, Tex., U.S. 97 N9
Brownwood, Lake, Tex., U.S. 96 M9
Browse Island, Austral. 190 B4
Bruce, Miss., U.S. 94 J12
Bruce Rock, W. Austral., Austral. 191 X3
Brugge, Belg. 138 H10
Bruini, India 158 E15
Brule, river, Wis., U.S. 92 G6
Brumado, Braz. 123 J15
Brundidge, Ala., U.S. 95 M16
Bruneau, river, Idaho, U.S. 100 H4

Bruneau, Idaho, U.S. 100 H4
Brunei, Asia 168 G11
Brunei Bay, Malaysia 168 G11
Brunette Downs, N. Terr., Austral. 191 R9
Brunner, Lake, N.Z. 193 N17
Brunswick, Ga., U.S. 91 P8
Brunswick, Me., U.S. 89 G16
Brunswick, Mo., U.S. 99 S12
Brunswick, Ohio, U.S. 93 P14
Brunswick Bay, Austral. 190 C5
Brush, Colo., U.S. 100 L14
Brus Laguna, Hond. 109 K18
Brusque, Braz. 123 N13
Brussels see Bruxelles, Belg. 138 H11
Bruxelles (Brussels), Belg. 138 H11
Bruzual, Venez. 120 D8
Bryan, Ohio, U.S. 93 P11
Bryan, Tex., U.S. 97 P12
Bryan Coast, Antarctica 206 H6
Bryansk, Russ. 140 F5
Bryant, Ark., U.S. 94 G8
Bryant, S. Dak., U.S. 98 K7
Bryce Canyon National Park, Utah, U.S. 101 P7
Bryson City, N.C., U.S. 90 J6
Bua, Fiji 198 G7
Bua Bay, Fiji 198 H7
Buache, Mount, Kosrae, F.S.M. 197 A18
Buada, Nauru 197 F23
Buada Lagoon, Nauru 197 F23
Buala, Solomon Is. 197 M18
Buariki, island, Tarawa, Kiribati 197 F17
Buariki, Tarawa, Kiribati 197 F17
Bua Yai, Thai. 166 L10
Buḩayrāt al Ḩasūn, Lib. 177 C14
Buba, Guinea-Bissau 180 E4
Būbiyān, island, Kuwait 152 F11
Bucak, Turk. 148 H6
Bucakkışla, Turk. 148 H8
Bucaramanga, Col. 120 D6
Buccaneer Archipelago, Austral. 190 C4
Buchanan, Liberia 180 H6
Buchanan, Mich., U.S. 93 N9
Buchanan, Lake, Tex., U.S. 97 P9
Buchan Gulf, Nunavut, Can. 77 E17
Bucharest see Bucureşti, Rom. 137 F16
Buchon, Point, Calif., U.S. 103 V5
Buckeye, Ariz., U.S. 101 U6
Buckhannon, W. Va., U.S. 90 D9
Buck Island, Virgin Is., U.S. 113 F14
Buckland Tableland, Austral. 190 G13
Buckley, Wash., U.S. 102 C4
Bucklin, Kans., U.S. 99 U5
Buckner Bay see Nakagusuku Wan, Jap. 165 Y1
Bucksport, Me., U.S. 89 F17
Bu Craa, W. Sahara, Mor. 176 D6
Bucureşti (Bucharest), Rom. 137 F16
Bucyrus, Ohio, U.S. 93 Q13
Bud, Nor. 134 J10
Buda, Tex., U.S. 97 Q10
Budalin, Myanmar 166 G5
Budapest, Hung. 132 K9
Búdardalur, Ice. 134 E2
Budaun, India 158 F7
Budd Coast, Antarctica 207 M21
Buddhas of Bamian, ruins, Afghan. 156 M6
Bude, Miss., U.S. 94 M10
Budgewoi, N.S.W., Austral. 191 X14
Búđir, Ice. 134 F4
Budjala, Dem. Rep. of the Congo 178 J9
Budū', Sabkhat al, Saudi Arabia 152 K12
Buena Esperanza, Arg. 124 L9
Buenaventura, Col. 120 F4
Buenaventura, Mex. 108 C8
Buenaventura Bay, S. Amer. 118 C2
Buena Vista, Colo., U.S. 101 N12
Buena Vista, Ga., U.S. 91 N5
Buena Vista, Va., U.S. 90 E10
Buenavista, Canary Is., Sp. 184 Q5
Buena Vista Lake Bed, Calif., U.S. 103 V7
Buenos Aires, Arg. 124 L13
Buenos Aires, Lago, Arg. 125 T7
Buen Tiempo, Cabo, Arg. 125 W8
Bufareh, Indonesia 169 K20
Buffalo, river, Ark., U.S. 94 E8
Buffalo, Minn., U.S. 98 J11
Buffalo, Mo., U.S. 99 U12
Buffalo, N.Y., U.S. 88 J5
Buffalo, Okla., U.S. 96 E8
Buffalo, S. Dak., U.S. 98 J2
Buffalo, Tex., U.S. 97 N13
Buffalo, Wyo., U.S. 100 G11
Buffalo Bill Reservoir, Wyo., U.S. 100 F9
Buffalo Hump, peak, Idaho, U.S. 100 E4
Buffalo Lake, Tex., U.S. 96 H4
Buffalo National River, Ark., U.S. 94 E8
Buford, Ga., U.S. 90 K5
Bug, river, Belarus-Pol. 132 G11
Buga, Col. 120 F4
Bugio, Ilhéu do, Madeira Is., Port. 184 N4
Bugsuk, island, Philippines 168 F12
Bugt, China 161 C16
Buhl, Idaho, U.S. 100 H5
Buhl, Minn., U.S. 98 F12
Buin, P.N.G. 197 K14
Bujumbura, Burundi 178 L12
Buka, island, P.N.G. 197 J13
Bukachacha, Russ. 141 L17
Bukama, Dem. Rep. of the Congo 178 N11
Buka Passage, P.N.G. 197 J13
Bukavu, Dem. Rep. of the Congo 178 K12
Bukhara see Buxoro, Uzb. 154 L11
Bukittinggi, Indonesia 168 J5
Bukoba, Tanzania 179 K13
Bula, Indonesia 169 K17
Būlaevo, Kaz. 155 A13
Bulan, Philippines 169 D14
Bulancak, Turk. 149 D13
Bulandshahr, India 158 F6
Bulanık, Turk. 149 F16
Bulawayo, Zimb. 182 G11
Buldan, Turk. 148 G4
Buldir Island, Alas., U.S. 104 N2
Bulgan, Mongolia 160 C11
Bulgan, Mongolia 160 C11
Bulgan, Mongolia 160 E10
Bulgaria, Eur. 137 H15
Buli, Teluk, Indonesia 169 J16
Buliluyan, Cape, Philippines 168 F12
Buliya, island, Fiji 198 K7
Bullara, W. Austral., Austral. 191 T1
Bullfinch, W. Austral., Austral. 191 W3
Bull Mountains, Mont., U.S. 100 D10
Bulloo Downs, Qnsld., Austral. 191 V12
Bulloo Downs, W. Austral., Austral. 191 U3
Bullo River, N. Terr., Austral. 191 Q7
Bulls Bay, S.C., U.S. 90 M11
Bull Shoals Lake, Ark., U.S. 94 E8
Bulun, Russ. 141 E16
Bulung'ur, Uzb. 154 L12
Bumba, Dem. Rep. of the Congo 178 J10
Bumbat, Mongolia 160 D12
Bum La, India 158 F13
Buna, Kenya 179 J15
Bunbury, W. Austral., Austral. 191 X2
Bundaberg, Qnsld., Austral. 191 U15
Bundaleer, Qnsld., Austral. 191 V13
Bundi, India 158 G5
Bundooma, N. Terr., Austral. 191 U9
Bungalaut, Selat, Indonesia 168 K5
Bungku, Indonesia 169 K14
Bungo Suidō, Jap. 165 S6
Bungotakada, Jap. 165 R5
Bunia, Dem. Rep. of the Congo 178 J12
Bunji, Pak. 156 L12
Bunker, Mo., U.S. 99 U14
Bunkie, La., U.S. 94 N8
Bunnell, Fla., U.S. 91 S9
Buntok, Indonesia 168 K11
Bünyan, Turk. 148 F11
Bunyu, island, Indonesia 168 H12
Buol, Indonesia 169 H14
Buon Me Thuot, Vietnam 167 N13
Buqūm, Harrat al, Saudi Arabia 152 L8
Bur, Russ. 141 J15
Bura, Kenya 179 K15
Burakin, W. Austral., Austral. 191 W3
Burang, China 160 K5
Burao see Burco, Somalia 179 F17
Buras, La., U.S. 94 R12
Buraydah, Saudi Arabia 152 H9
Burbank, Calif., U.S. 103 X8
Burco (Burao), Somalia 179 F17
Burdalyk, Turkm. 154 M11
Burdekin, river, Austral. 190 E13
Burdur, Turk. 148 G5
Burdur Gölü, Turk. 148 G5
Bûr Fu'ad, Egypt 151 N1
Burgas, Bulg. 137 H17
Burgaw, N.C., U.S. 90 J12
Burghūth, Sabkhat al, Syr. 150 G15
Burgos, Sp. 139 P7
Burgsvik, Sw. 135 M14
Burhaniye, Turk. 148 E3
Burhanpur, India 158 K5
Burias, island, Philippines 169 D14
Burica, Punta, C.R.-Pan. 109 P19
Buriram, Thai. 166 L10
Burkburnett, Tex., U.S. 96 J9
Burke, S. Dak., U.S. 98 M6
Burke Island, Antarctica 206 K6
Burkesville, Ky., U.S. 95 D17
Burketown, Qnsld., Austral. 191 R11
Bur Khaybyt, Russ. 141 E18
Burkina Faso, Af. 180 E10
Burle, island, Kwajalein Atoll, Marshall Is. 196 L4
Burleson, Tex., U.S. 96 L11
Burley, Idaho, U.S. 100 H5
Burlingame, Kans., U.S. 99 T9
Burlington, Colo., U.S. 100 M16
Burlington, Iowa, U.S. 99 Q14
Burlington, Kans., U.S. 99 T9
Burlington, N.C., U.S. 90 G10
Burlington, Vt., U.S. 88 F12
Burlington, Wash., U.S. 102 A4
Burlington, Wis., U.S. 92 M6
Burma see Myanmar, Asia 166 H6
Burma Road, China 160 N10
Burnet, Tex., U.S. 97 P10
Burnett Bay, N.W.T., Can. 76 C12
Burney, Calif., U.S. 102 M4
Burnie, Tas., Austral. 191 Y16
Burns, Oreg., U.S. 102 J7
Burns, Wyo., U.S. 100 K14
Burnside, Lake, Austral. 190 G5
Burns Lake, B.C., Can. 76 K8
Burnsville, Minn., U.S. 98 K11
Burnt, river, Oreg., U.S. 102 G8
Burnt Pine, Norfolk I., Austral. 197 F20
Burqin, China 160 D7
Burqu', Qaşr al, Jordan 150 L10
Burrendong Reservoir, Austral. 190 K14
Burren Junction, N.S.W., Austral. 191 W14
Burrton, Kans., U.S. 99 U7
Burrundie, N. Terr., Austral. 191 P8
Burrwood, La., U.S. 94 R12
Bursa, Turk. 148 D5
Bûr Safâga, Egypt 177 D19
Bûr Sa'îd (Port Said), Egypt 151 N1
Būr Sūdān (Port Sudan), Sudan 179 C14
Burt Lake, Mich., U.S. 92 H11
Burton, Mich., U.S. 92 L12
Burton, Nebr., U.S. 98 M5
Buru, island, Indonesia 169 K15
Burūm, Yemen 152 Q11
Burundi, Af. 178 L12
Bururi, Burundi 178 L12
Burwash Landing, Yukon Terr., Can. 76 F7
Burwell, Nebr., U.S. 99 P6
Burylbaytal, Kaz. 155 H15
Burzil Pass, Pak. 156 M12
Busanga Swamp, Af. 174 M8
Buşayrah, Syr. 150 F14
Bushnell, Ill., U.S. 93 Q4
Bushnell, Nebr., U.S. 99 P1
Bushy Park, N. Terr., Austral. 191 T8
Businga, Dem. Rep. of the Congo 178 H9
Buşrá ash Shām, Syr. 150 L7
Busselton, W. Austral., Austral. 191 Y2
Bussol', Proliv, Russ. 141 J23
Bustamante, Bahía, Arg. 125 S9
Busuanga, island, Philippines 169 D13
Busu-Djanoa, Dem. Rep. of the Congo 178 J9
Buta, Dem. Rep. of the Congo 178 J10
Butaritari, island, Kiribati 194 G8
Butchers Hill, Qnsld., Austral. 191 Q13
Butembo, Dem. Rep. of the Congo 178 K12
Buthidaung, Myanmar 166 H4
Butler, Ala., U.S. 95 L13
Butler, Ga., U.S. 90 M5
Butler, Mo., U.S. 99 T11
Butler, Pa., U.S. 88 N3
Butner, N.C., U.S. 90 G11
Buton, island, Indonesia 169 L14
Butte, Mont., U.S. 100 E7
Butte, Nebr., U.S. 98 M6
Butterworth, Malaysia 167 S9
Button Islands, Nunavut, Can. 77 H20
Butuan, Philippines 169 E15
Butwal, Nepal 158 F9
Buulobarde, Somalia 179 H17
Buur Gaabo, Somalia 179 K16
Buurhakaba, Somalia 179 J16
Buxoro (Bukhara), Uzb. 154 L11
Buxton, Guyana 121 D15
Buxton, N.C., U.S. 90 H15
Buy, Russ. 140 F7
Buyanbat, Mongolia 160 D10
Buyant, Mongolia 161 D13
Buyant-Uhaa, Mongolia 161 E13
Buyr Nuur, China-Mongolia 161 D15
Büyük Menderes, river, Turk. 148 G4
Buzău, Rom. 137 F16
Buzaymah, Lib. 177 E16
Búzi, river, Mozambique 182 G12
Büzmeyin, Turkm. 154 M8
Buzul Daği, Turk. 149 H18
Buzuluk, Kaz. 154 C12
Buzzards Bay, Mass., U.S. 89 M15
Bwokworlap, island, Majuro Atoll, Marshall Is. 196 G11
Byam Martin, Cape, Nunavut, Can. 77 D17
Byam Martin Island, Nunavut, Can. 77 D14
Byaroza, Belarus 132 G12
Byblos see Jubayl, Leb. 150 H6
Bydgoszcz, Pol. 132 F9
Byers, Colo., U.S. 100 M14
Byfield, Qnsld., Austral. 191 T15
Bylas, Ariz., U.S. 101 U8
Bylot Island, Nunavut, Can. 77 D16
Bynum Reservoir, Mont., U.S. 100 B7
Byrdbreen, glacier, Antarctica 207 B15
Byrd Glacier, Antarctica 207 M14
Byrock, N.S.W., Austral. 191 W13
Byron, Wyo., U.S. 100 F10
Byron, Cape, Austral. 190 J15
Byron, Isla, Chile 125 U6
Bytom, Pol. 132 H9

C

C, Dome, Antarctica 207 M17
Caála, Angola 182 D6
Caazapá, Para. 122 N10
Cabaiguán, Cuba 110 H9
Caballones, Cayo, Cuba 110 J10
Caballo Reservoir, N. Mex., U.S. 101 U11
Cabanatuan, Philippines 169 C13
Cabezas, Bol. 122 K8
Cabimas, Venez. 120 B7
Cabinda, district, Angola 182 B4
Cabinda, Angola 182 B5
Cabinet Mountains, Mont., U.S. 100 B4
Cable, Wis., U.S. 92 F3
Cabo, Braz. 123 G18
Cabo Blanco, Arg. 125 T10
Cabo Frio, Braz. 123 M15
Cabonga, Réservoir, Que., Can. 77 P19
Cabool, Mo., U.S. 99 V13
Caboolture, Qnsld., Austral. 191 V15
Caborca, Mex. 108 C6
Cabo San Lucas, Mex. 108 G7
Cabot, Ark., U.S. 94 G9
Cabot Strait, Nfld.-N.S., Can. 77 N22
Cabral, Dom. Rep. 111 M18
Cabras Island, Guam, U.S. 196 C10
Cabrera, island, Sp. 139 R10
Cabrera, Dom. Rep. 111 L19
Cabrobó, Braz. 123 G16
Cabrón, Cabo, Dom. Rep. 111 L20
Čačak, Yug. 137 G13
Cáceres, Braz. 122 J10
Cáceres, Sp. 139 R6
Cache, river, Ark., U.S. 94 E10
Cache Creek, Calif., U.S. 103 Q3
Cachimbo, Braz. 122 G11
Cachoeira, Braz. 123 H16
Cachoeira do Sul, Braz. 122 P11
Cachoeiro do Itapemirim, Braz. 123 L15
Cacine, Guinea-Bissau 180 E4
Cacolo, Angola 182 C7
Cactus, Tex., U.S. 96 F5
Caçu, Braz. 122 K12
Caculé, Braz. 123 J15
Cacuri, Venez. 120 E10
Caddo, Okla., U.S. 96 J12
Caddo Lake, La.-Tex., U.S. 94 K6
Cadillac, Mich., U.S. 92 J10
Çadır Dağı, Turk. 149 G17
Cádiz, Sp. 139 T6
Cádiz, Golfo de, Sp. 139 S5
Cadiz, Calif., U.S. 103 W11
Cadiz, Ky., U.S. 95 D14
Cadiz, Ohio, U.S. 93 Q15
Cadiz, Philippines 169 E14
Cadiz Lake, Calif., U.S. 103 W12
Caen, Fr. 138 K9
Caesarea, ruins, Israel 150 L5
Cafayate, Arg. 124 F9
Cagayan de Oro, Philippines 169 F15
Cagayan Islands, Philippines 169 E13
Cagayan Sulu Island, Philippines 168 F12
Cagliari, It. 136 K7
Cagliari, Golfo de, It. 136 K8
Caguán, river, Col. 120 H5
Caguas, P.R., U.S. 111 M23
Cahora Bossa, Lago de, Mozambique 182 E12
Cahors, Fr. 139 N10
Cahul, Mold. 133 L14
Caia, Mozambique 183 F13
Caiapônia, Braz. 122 J12
Caibarién, Cuba 110 H9
Caicara, Venez. 120 D10
Caicó, Braz. 123 F17
Caicos Islands, Turks and Caicos Is., U.K. 111 J17
Caicos Passage, Bahamas 111 H16
Caijiapo, China 162 H1
Cainsville, Mo., U.S. 99 Q11
Caird Coast, Antarctica 206 D10
Cairns, Qnsld., Austral. 191 R13
Cairo see El Qâhira, Egypt 177 C18
Cairo, Ga., U.S. 91 Q5
Cairo, Ill., U.S. 93 V5
Caixão Grande, São Tomé and Príncipe 185 D20
Cajamarca, Peru 122 F2
Cajàzeiras, Braz. 123 F17
Çakırgöl Dağı, Turk. 149 D14
Cakit, river, Turk. 148 H10
Çakmak, Turk. 148 F7
Çakmak Dağı, Turk. 149 E16

Çal, Turk. 148 G5
Calabar, Nig. 181 H14
Calabó, Bioko, Eq. Guinea 184 M7
Calabozo, Venez. 120 C9
Calabria, peninsula, Eur. 130 K7
Calafat, Rom. 137 G15
Calais, Fr. 138 H10
Calais, Me., U.S. 89 E19
Calalaste, Sierra de, Arg. 124 F8
Calalin, island, Majuro Atoll, Marshall Is. 196 G11
Calalin Channel, Majuro Atoll, Marshall Is. 196 G11
Calama, Braz. 122 F8
Calama, Chile 124 D7
Calamar, Col. 120 B5
Calamar, Col. 120 G6
Calamian Group, Philippines 169 D13
Calamocha, Sp. 139 Q8
Calanscio, Sand Sea of, Af. 174 E7
Calanscio, Sarīr, Af. 174 E7
Calapan, Philippines 169 D13
Călărași, Rom. 137 F17
Calatayud, Sp. 139 Q8
Calayan, island, Philippines 169 A13
Calbayog, Philippines 169 D15
Calcanhar, Ponta do, Braz. 123 E18
Calcasieu, river, La., U.S. 94 N7
Calcasieu Lake, La., U.S. 94 Q7
Calçoene, Braz. 122 B12
Calcutta see Kolkata, India 158 J12
Caldera, peak, Bioko, Eq. Guinea 184 N7
Caldera, Chile 124 G7
Çaldıran, Turk. 149 F18
Caldwell, Idaho, U.S. 100 G3
Caldwell, Kans., U.S. 99 V7
Caldwell, Tex., U.S. 97 P12
Caledonia, Minn., U.S. 98 L13
Calexico, Calif., U.S. 103 Z12
Calgary, Alta., Can. 76 M10
Calheta, Madeira Is., Port. 184 M2
Calhoun, Ga., U.S. 90 K4
Calhoun City, Miss., U.S. 94 J12
Calhoun Falls, S.C., U.S. 90 K7
Cali, Col. 120 G4
Calico Rock, Ark., U.S. 94 E9
Calicut see Kozhikode, India 159 Q5
Caliente, Nev., U.S. 103 S12
California, U.S. 103 N4
California, Mo., U.S. 99 T12
California, Golfo de, Mex. 108 B6
California Aqueduct, Calif., U.S. 103 V6
Calilegua, Arg. 124 E10
Cälilibad, Azerb. 149 E22
Calipatria, Calif., U.S. 103 Y11
Calistoga, Calif., U.S. 103 R3
Callabonna, Lake, Austral. 190 H11
Callao, Peru 122 H3
Callaway, Nebr., U.S. 99 P5
Calliope, Qnsld., Austral. 191 U15
Calliope Range, Austral. 190 G15
Caloosahatchee, river, Fla., U.S. 91 V8
Caloundra, Qnsld., Austral. 191 V15
Caltagirone, It. 136 L10
Caltanissetta, It. 136 L10
Çaltı Burnu, Turk. 148 C12
Calulo, Angola 182 C6
Calumet, Mich., U.S. 92 E6
Caluula, Somalia 179 F18
Calvert, Tex., U.S. 97 P12
Calvi, Fr. 139 P13
Calvinia, S. Af. 182 L8
Calwa, Calif., U.S. 103 T6
Camabatela, Angola 182 C6
Camacupa, Angola 182 D7
Camagüey, Cuba 110 J11
Camagüey, Archipiélago de, Cuba 110 G10
Camajuaní, Cuba 110 H9
Camaná, Peru 122 J5
Camanche Reservoir, Calif., U.S. 103 R5
Camapuã, Braz. 122 K11
Câmara de Lobos, Madeira Is., Port. 184 M3
Çamardı, Turk. 148 G10
Camargo, Bol. 122 L7
Camargo, Okla., U.S. 96 F8
Camarón, Cape, N. Amer. 74 P8
Camarones, Arg. 125 S9
Camarones, Bahía, Arg. 125 S10
Camas, Wash., U.S. 102 F4
Camas Creek, Idaho, U.S. 100 G7
Camas Valley, Oreg., U.S. 102 J2
Ca Mau, Vietnam 167 Q12
Camballin, W. Austral., Austral. 191 R5
Cambodia, Asia 167 N11
Cambrai, Fr. 138 J10
Cambria, Calif., U.S. 103 V5
Cambrian Mountains, Eur. 130 E4
Cambridge, Idaho, U.S. 100 F3
Cambridge, Jam. 110 M11
Cambridge, Mass., U.S. 89 K15
Cambridge, Md., U.S. 90 D14
Cambridge, Minn., U.S. 98 J11
Cambridge, Nebr., U.S. 99 R5
Cambridge, Ohio, U.S. 93 R14
Cambridge, Eng., U.K. 138 H9
Cambridge Bay, Nunavut, Can. 77 F13
Cambridge Downs, Qnsld., Austral. 191 S12
Cambridge Springs, Pa., U.S. 88 L3
Cambundi-Catembo, Angola 182 C7
Çam Burnu, Turk. 148 D12
Camden, Ala., U.S. 95 M14
Camden, Ark., U.S. 94 J8
Camden, Me., U.S. 89 G17
Camden, N.J., U.S. 88 P9
Camden, N.Y., U.S. 88 H9
Camden, S.C., U.S. 90 K9
Camden, Tenn., U.S. 95 E13
Camden, Tex., U.S. 97 P14
Camden Bay, U.S. 78 L5
Camdenton, Mo., U.S. 99 T12
Çameli, Turk. 148 H5
Cameron, La., U.S. 94 Q7
Cameron, Mo., U.S. 99 R11
Cameron, Tex., U.S. 97 P11
Cameroon, Af. 181 H16
Cameroon Mountain, Cameroon 181 J15
Cametá, Braz. 123 D13
Camiguin, island, Philippines 169 A14
Camiguin, island, Philippines 169 E15
Camilla, Ga., U.S. 91 P5
Camiri, Bol. 122 L8
Camissombo, Angola 182 C8
Camocim, Braz. 123 D16
Camooweal, Qnsld., Austral. 191 S10
Camorta Island, Nicobar Is., India 159 S15
Campana, Arg. 124 L13
Campana, Isla, Chile 125 U6
Campanario, Cerro, Arg. 124 M7
Campbell, Mo., U.S. 99 V15
Campbell, Cape, N.Z. 193 N18
Campbell Hill, Ohio, U.S. 93 Q12
Campbell Island, Pac. Oc. 194 R7
Campbell Plateau, Pac. Oc. 218 Q8
Campbell River, B.C., Can. 76 L7
Campbellsville, Ky., U.S. 95 C17
Camp Crook, S. Dak., U.S. 98 J1
Campeche, Mex. 109 J15
Campeche Bank, Mex. 109 H15
Campechuela, Cuba 110 K11
Cam Pha, Vietnam 166 H13
Campina Grande, Braz. 123 F18
Campinas, Braz. 123 M13
Campo, Cameroon 181 J15
Campo, Colo., U.S. 101 P15
Campoalegre, Col. 120 G5
Campobasso, It. 136 H10
Campo Gallo, Arg. 124 G11
Campo Grande, Braz. 122 L11
Campo Mourão, Braz. 122 M12
Campos, region, S. Amer. 118 G9
Campos, Braz. 123 L15
Camp Point, Ill., U.S. 93 R3
Campti, La., U.S. 94 M7
Camp Verde, Ariz., U.S. 101 S7
Camp Wood, Tex., U.S. 97 R7
Cam Ranh, Vietnam 167 N14
Cam Ranh, Vung, Vietnam 167 N14
Camrose, Alta., Can. 76 L10
Camsell Portage, Sask., Can. 76 J12
Çan, Turk. 148 D3
Ca Na, Vietnam 167 P14
Ca Na, Mui, Vietnam 167 P14
Canaan, Trin. & Tobago 113 N17
Canacona, India 159 N4
Canada Basin, Arctic Oc. 222 M6
Cañada de Gómez, Arg. 124 K11
Cañada Honda, Arg. 124 K8
Canada Plain, Arctic Oc. 222 L6
Canadian, river, Okla., U.S. 96 H12
Canadian, Tex., U.S. 96 F7
Canadian Shield, region, N. Amer. 74 E5
Çanakkale, Turk. 148 D2
Çanakkale Boğazi (Dardanelles), Turk. 148 D2
Canala, New Caledonia, Fr. 198 D8
Canala, Baie de, New Caledonia, Fr. 198 D8
Canandaigua, N.Y., U.S. 88 J7
Cananea, Mex. 108 C7
Canarias, Islas see Canary Islands, Atl. Oc. 184 C4
Canarreos, Archipiélago de los, Cuba 110 H6
Canary Islands (Islas Canarias), Atl. Oc. 184 C4
Cañas, C.R. 109 N18
Canastota, N.Y., U.S. 88 J9
Canatlán, Mex. 108 F9
Canaveral, Cape, Fla., U.S. 91 T10
Canaveral National Seashore, Fla., U.S. 91 S9
Canavieiras, Braz. 123 J16
Canberra, Austral. 191 Y14
Canby, Calif., U.S. 102 M5
Canby, Minn., U.S. 98 K9
Cancún, Mex. 109 H17
Çandarlı, Turk. 148 F3
Çandarli Körfezi, Turk. 148 F3
Candia see Iráklio, Gr. 137 N16
Cando, N. Dak., U.S. 98 E6
Candon, Philippines 169 B13
Canea see Haniá, Gr. 137 M15
Caney, Kans., U.S. 99 V9
Cangamba, Angola 182 E8
Canguaretama, Braz. 123 F18
Cangwu, China 163 R3
Cangzhou, China 162 E7
Caniapiscau, river, Que., Can. 77 K19
Caniapiscau, Réservoir, Que., Can. 77 L19
Canindé, Braz. 123 E16
Canipaan, Philippines 168 F12
Canisteo, N.Y., U.S. 88 K6
Canjilon, N. Mex., U.S. 101 Q12
Çankırı, Turk. 148 D9
Cannanore, India 159 Q4
Cannelton, Ind., U.S. 93 U8
Cannes, Fr. 139 N12
Canning Hill, Austral. 190 H3
Cannonball, river, N. Dak., U.S. 98 H4
Cannon Beach, Oreg., U.S. 102 E2
Cannon Falls, Minn., U.S. 98 K12
Cann River, Vic., Austral. 191 Z13
Canoas, Braz. 122 P12
Canobie, Qnsld., Austral. 191 S11
Canoe Passage, Tabuaeran, Kiribati 197 B20
Canon City, Colo., U.S. 101 N13
Canonniers Point, Mauritius 185 F20
Canouan, island, St. Vincent and the Grenadines 113 M17
Canso, Strait of, N.S., Can. 77 P22
Cantabrian Mountains, Eur. 130 H2
Canterbury Bight, N.Z. 193 P17
Can Tho, Vietnam 167 Q12
Cantiles, Cayo, Cuba 110 J7
Canto do Buriti, Braz. 123 F15
Canton see Guangzhou, China 163 R4
Canton, Ga., U.S. 90 K5
Canton, Ill., U.S. 93 Q4
Canton, Miss., U.S. 94 L11
Canton, Mo., U.S. 99 R13
Canton, N.C., U.S. 90 H7
Canton, N.Y., U.S. 88 F9
Canton, Ohio, U.S. 93 P15
Canton, Okla., U.S. 96 F9
Canton, Pa., U.S. 88 L7
Canton, S. Dak., U.S. 98 M8
Canton Lake, Okla., U.S. 96 F9
Cantwell, Alas., U.S. 105 G16
Canumã, Braz. 122 E9
Canutama, Braz. 122 F7
Canutillo, Tex., U.S. 97 U1
Canyon, Tex., U.S. 96 H5
Canyon City, Oreg., U.S. 102 G7
Canyon de Chelly National Monument, Ariz., U.S. 101 R9
Canyon Ferry Lake, Mont., U.S. 100 D7
Canyon Lake, Tex., U.S. 97 Q10
Canyonlands National Park, Utah, U.S. 101 N9
Canyons of the Ancients National Monument, Colo., U.S. 101 P10
Canyonville, Oreg., U.S. 102 J3
Cao Bang, Vietnam 166 G12
Caoxian, China 162 H6
Capanema, Braz. 123 D14
Capayán, Arg. 124 H9
Cap Barbas, W. Sahara, Mor. 176 E5
Cap-Chat, Que., Can. 77 N21
Cape Barren Island, Austral. 190 L16
Cape Breton Island, N.S., Can. 77 N23
Cape Charles, Va., U.S. 90 F14
Cape Coast, Ghana 180 H10
Cape Cod Bay, Mass., U.S. 89 L16
Cape Cod National Seashore, Mass., U.S. 89 L16
Cape Coral, Fla., U.S. 91 W8
Cape Dorset, Nunavut, Can. 77 H17
Cape Fear, river, N.C., U.S. 90 K12
Cape Girardeau, Mo., U.S. 99 U16
Cape Hatteras National Seashore, N.C., U.S. 90 H15
Cape Krusenstern National Monument, Alas., U.S. 104 D12
Capel, W. Austral., Austral. 191 Y2
Cape Lookout National Seashore, N.C., U.S. 90 J14
Cape Lookout Shoals, N.C., U.S. 90 J14
Cape May, N.J., U.S. 88 R10
Cape Plain, Atl. Oc. 217 T14
Cape Rodney, P.N.G. 193 E20
Cape Town, S. Af. 182 M7
Cape Verde, Atl. Oc. 184 D3
Cape Verde Plain, Atl. Oc. 216 K10
Cape Vincent, N.Y., U.S. 88 G8
Cape York Peninsula, Austral. 190 B12
Cap-Haïtien, Haiti 111 L17
Capitan, N. Mex., U.S. 101 U13
Capitán Arturo Prat, station, Antarctica 206 C3
Capitán Pablo Lagerenza, Para. 122 K9
Capitan Peak, N. Mex., U.S. 101 T13
Capitão, Ponta, São Tomé and Príncipe 185 A21
Capitol Hill, Saipan, N. Mariana Is., U.S. 196 B5
Capitol Reef National Park, Utah, U.S. 101 N7
Capoeira, Corredeira, Braz. 122 F10
Cappadocia, region, Turk. 148 G10
Capraia, island, It. 136 G8
Capreol, Ont., Can. 77 P18
Capri, island, It. 136 J10
Capricorn Channel, Austral. 190 F15
Capricorn Group, Austral. 190 F15
Caprivi Strip, region, Namibia 182 F9
Cap Rock Escarpment, U.S. 78 K10
Captain Cook, Hawaii, U.S. 107 M18
Captain Cook's Landing, Hawaii, U.S. 106 C5
Captain Cook's Monument, Hawaii, U.S. 107 N18
Captiva, Fla., U.S. 91 W8
Capulin, N. Mex., U.S. 101 Q14
Capulin Volcano National Monument, N. Mex., U.S. 101 Q14
Caquetá, river, Col. 120 H4
Caracal, Rom. 137 G15
Caracaraí, Braz. 122 B9
Caracas, Venez. 120 B9
Caracol, Braz. 123 G15
Carahue, Chile 125 P6
Carajás, Serra dos, Braz. 122 E12
Caratasca, Laguna de, Hond. 109 K20
Carauari, Braz. 122 E7
Caraúbas, Braz. 123 F17
Caravelas, Braz. 123 K16
Carbonara, Capo, It. 136 K8
Carbondale, Colo., U.S. 100 M11
Carbondale, Ill., U.S. 93 U5
Carbondale, Pa., U.S. 88 L9
Carbon Hill, Ala., U.S. 95 J14
Carbonia, It. 136 K7
Carcajou, Alta., Can. 76 J10
Carcasse, Cap, Haiti 111 M14
Carcross, Yukon Terr., Can. 76 G8
Cardabia, W. Austral., Austral. 191 U1
Cardamom Mountains, Cambodia 167 N10
Cardamum Island see Kadmat Island, India 159 Q3
Cárdenas, Cuba 110 G7
Cárdenas, Mex. 108 G11
Cardiff, Wales, U.K. 138 H8
Cardoso y Pinto, Bioko, Eq. Guinea 184 M7
Cardwell, Qnsld., Austral. 191 R13
Carei, Rom. 137 D14
Carey, Ohio, U.S. 93 P12
Carey, Lake, Austral. 190 H4
Carey Downs, W. Austral., Austral. 191 U2
Cargados Carajos Bank, Ind. Oc. 220 J7
Carhué, Arg. 125 N11
Caribbean Sea, N. Amer. 74 P8
Caribou, Me., U.S. 89 B18
Caribou Mountains, N. Amer. 74 F4
Carinda, N.S.W., Austral. 191 W13
Carinhanha, Braz. 123 J15
Caripará, Braz. 123 H14
Caripito, Venez. 120 B12
Carlin, Nev., U.S. 103 N10
Carlinville, Ill., U.S. 93 S4
Carlisle, Ark., U.S. 94 G9
Carlisle, Ky., U.S. 95 B18
Carlisle, Pa., U.S. 88 P7
Carlisle, Eng., U.K. 138 F8
Carlos, Isla, Chile 125 X7
Carlow, Ire. 138 G6
Carlsbad, Calif., U.S. 103 Y9
Carlsbad, N. Mex., U.S. 101 V14
Carlsbad, Tex., U.S. 97 N6
Carlsbad Caverns National Park, N. Mex., U.S. 101 V14
Carlsberg Ridge, Ind. Oc. 220 F7
Carlton, Minn., U.S. 98 G12
Carlyle, Ill., U.S. 93 T5
Carlyle Lake, Ill., U.S. 93 T5
Carmacks, Yukon Terr., Can. 76 F8
Carmel-by-the-Sea, Calif., U.S. 103 T4
Carmelo, Uru. 124 L13
Carmen, Idaho, U.S. 100 E5
Carmen, Okla., U.S. 96 E9
Carmen, Isla, Mex. 108 E7
Carmen de Bolívar, Col. 120 C5
Carmen de Patagones, Arg. 125 Q11
Carmi, Ill., U.S. 93 U6
Carmona, Sp. 139 S6
Carnamah, W. Austral., Austral. 191 W2
Carnarvon, S. Af. 182 L8
Carnarvon, W. Austral., Austral. 191 U1
Carnegie, W. Austral., Austral. 191 U5
Carnegie, Okla., U.S. 96 G9
Carnegie, Lake, Austral. 190 G4
Carnegie Ridge, Pac. Oc. 219 K19
Carney Island, Antarctica 206 M7
Car Nicobar, island, Nicobar Is., India 159 S14
Carnot, Cen. Af. Rep. 178 H8
Carnot, Cape, Austral. 190 K9
Caro, Mich., U.S. 92 K12
Caroço, Ilhéu, São Tomé and Príncipe 185 B21
Carol City, Fla., U.S. 91 X10
Carolina, Braz. 123 F14
Carolina Beach, N.C., U.S. 90 K12
Carolinas, Puntan, Tinian, N. Mariana Is., U.S. 196 C8
Caroline Island, Kiribati 195 H13
Caroline Islands, F.S.M. 196 Q2
Caroní, river, Venez. 120 D12

Carora, *Venez.* **120** B8
Carp, *Nev., U.S.* **103** T12
Carpathian Mountains, *Eur.* **130** G8
Carpenteria, Gulf of, *Austral.* **190** B10
Carpina, *Braz.* **123** F18
Carpio, *N. Dak., U.S.* **98** E3
Carrabelle, *Fla., U.S.* **91** R4
Carrantuohill, peak, *Ire.* **138** G5
Carrara, *It.* **136** F8
Carrarang, *W. Austral., Austral.* **191** V1
Carrboro, *N.C., U.S.* **90** H11
Carriacou, island, *Grenada* **113** M17
Carrieton, *S. Austral., Austral.* **191** X10
Carrington, *N. Dak., U.S.* **98** F6
Carrizal Bajo, *Chile* **124** H6
Carrizo Creek, *N. Mex., U.S.* **101** Q15
Carrizo Plain National Monument, *Calif., U.S.* **103** W6
Carrizo Springs, *Tex., U.S.* **97** T7
Carrizozo, *N. Mex., U.S.* **101** T13
Carroll, *Iowa, U.S.* **99** N10
Carrollton, *Ga., U.S.* **90** L4
Carrollton, *Ill., U.S.* **93** S4
Carrollton, *Ky., U.S.* **95** A17
Carrollton, *Mo., U.S.* **99** S11
Çarşamba, river, *Turk.* **148** H7
Çarşamba, *Turk.* **148** D11
Carson, *N. Dak., U.S.* **98** H4
Carson City, *Nev., U.S.* **103** Q6
Carson Sink, *Nev., U.S.* **103** P8
Carsonville, *Mich., U.S.* **92** L13
Cartagena, *Col.* **120** B4
Cartagena, *Sp.* **139** S8
Cartago, *C.R.* **109** N19
Cartago, *Col.* **120** F4
Cartersville, *Ga., U.S.* **90** K4
Carthage, *Ark., U.S.* **94** H8
Carthage, *Ill., U.S.* **93** Q3
Carthage, *Miss., U.S.* **94** K12
Carthage, *Mo., U.S.* **99** V11
Carthage, *N.C., U.S.* **90** H11
Carthage, *N.Y., U.S.* **88** G9
Carthage, *S. Dak., U.S.* **98** L7
Carthage, *Tenn., U.S.* **95** E16
Carthage, *Tex., U.S.* **96** M15
Cartier Island, *Austral.* **190** B4
Cartwright, *Nfld., Can.* **77** K22
Caruaru, *Braz.* **123** G17
Carúpano, *Venez.* **120** B12
Carutapera, *Braz.* **123** D14
Caruthersville, *Mo., U.S.* **99** W16
Carvoeiro, *Braz.* **122** D8
Cary, *N.C., U.S.* **90** H11
Caryapundy Swamp, *Austral.* **190** H12
Casablanca, *Mor.* **176** B8
Casa Grande Ruins National Monument, *Ariz., U.S.* **101** U7
Casamance, region, *Senegal* **176** H5
Casanare, river, *Col.* **120** E7
Cascade, *Idaho, U.S.* **100** F4
Cascade, *Mont., U.S.* **100** C7
Cascade, *Norfolk I., Austral.* **197** F20
Cascade, *Seychelles* **185** P20
Cascade Bay, *Norfolk I., Austral.* **197** F20
Cascade Head, *Oreg., U.S.* **102** F2
Cascade Locks, *Oreg., U.S.* **102** F4
Cascade Range, *U.S.* **102** M4
Cascade Reservoir, *Idaho, U.S.* **100** F4
Cascade-Siskiyou National Monument, *Oreg., U.S.* **102** L3
Cascadia Basin, *Pac. Oc.* **219** D15
Cascavel, *Braz.* **122** M11
Cascorro, *Cuba* **110** J11
Caserta, *It.* **136** J10
Casey, station, *Antarctica* **207** M21
Casey, *Ill., U.S.* **93** S7
Casey Bay, *Antarctica* **207** C19
Cashmere, *Wash., U.S.* **102** C6
Casiguran, *Philippines* **169** B14
Casilda, *Arg.* **124** K11
Casiquiare, river, *Venez.* **120** G10
Casma, *Peru* **122** G3
Casmalia, *Calif., U.S.* **103** W5
Caspar, *Calif., U.S.* **103** P2
Casper, *Wyo., U.S.* **100** H12
Caspian Depression, *Asia-Eur.* **146** E5
Caspian Sea, *Asia-Eur.* **146** F5
Cass, *W. Va., U.S.* **90** D10
Cass City, *Mich., U.S.* **92** K12
Casselton, *N. Dak., U.S.* **98** G8
Cassiar Mountains, *B.C., Can.* **76** H8
Cassino, *It.* **136** H10
Cass Lake, *Minn., U.S.* **98** F10
Cassville, *Mo., U.S.* **99** V11
Cassville, *Wis., U.S.* **92** M3
Castaño Nuevo, *Arg.* **124** J7
Castelló de la Plana, *Sp.* **139** Q9
Castelo Branco, *Port.* **139** Q5
Casterton, *Vic., Austral.* **191** Z11
Castilhiano, *Cape Verde* **185** B16
Castillo, Pampa del, *Arg.* **125** T8
Castillo de San Marcos National Monument, *Fla., U.S.* **91** R9
Castillos, *Uru.* **124** L15
Castle Dale, *Utah, U.S.* **100** M8
Castle Island, *Bahamas* **111** H14
Castlemaine, *Vic., Austral.* **191** Z12
Castle Peak, *Idaho, U.S.* **100** G5
Castlereagh, river, *Austral.* **190** J14
Castle Rock, *Colo., U.S.* **100** M13
Castle Rock, *Wash., U.S.* **102** E3
Castlevale, *Qnsld., Austral.* **191** U13
Castlewood, *S. Dak., U.S.* **98** K8
Castres, *Fr.* **139** N10
Castries, *St. Lucia* **113** K17
Castro, *Braz.* **122** M12
Castro, *Chile* **125** R6
Castrovillari, *It.* **136** K11
Castroville, *Tex., U.S.* **97** R9
Çat, *Turk.* **149** E15
Catahoula Lake, *La., U.S.* **94** M8
Çatak, *Turk.* **149** G17
Catalão, *Braz.* **123** K13
Çatalca, *Turk.* **148** C4
Catalina, *Chile* **124** F7
Catalina Point, *Guam, U.S.* **196** B12
Catamarca, *Arg.* **124** H9
Catanduanes, island, *Philippines* **169** C15
Catania, *It.* **136** L11
Catanzaro, *It.* **136** K11
Catarina, *Tex., U.S.* **97** T8
Catarman, *Philippines* **169** D15
Catawba, river, *U.S.* **79** J18
Cat Cays, *Bahamas* **110** D9
Cateel, *Philippines* **169** F15
Catete, *Angola* **182** C5
Cathedral Mountain, *Tex., U.S.* **97** Q2
Cathlamet, *Wash., U.S.* **102** E3
Catingas, region, *S. Amer.* **118** E8
Cat Island, *Bahamas* **111** E13
Cat Island, *Miss., U.S.* **94** P12
Cat Lake, *Ont., Can.* **77** N15
Catlettsburg, *Ky., U.S.* **95** B20
Catlow Valley, *Oreg., U.S.* **102** K7
Catoche, Cape, *N. Amer.* **74** N7
Cato Island, *Austral.* **190** F16
Catonsville, *Md., U.S.* **90** C13
Catriló, *Arg.* **124** M10
Catrimani, river, *Braz.* **122** C8
Catrimani, *Braz.* **122** C8
Catskill, *N.Y., U.S.* **88** K11
Catskill Mountains, *N.Y., U.S.* **88** K10
Čatyrtaš, *Kyrg.* **156** F13
Cauca, river, *Col.* **120** D5
Caucasus Mountains, *Asia-Eur.* **146** E4
Caucete, *Arg.* **124** K8
Caungula, *Angola* **182** C7
Cauquenes, *Chile* **124** M6
Caura, river, *Venez.* **120** E11
Cauterets, *Fr.* **139** P9
Cauto, river, *Cuba* **110** K12
Cavalcante, *Braz.* **123** H13
Cavalier, *N. Dak., U.S.* **98** E7
Cavalla (Cavally), river, *Liberia* **180** H7
Cavally (Cavalla), river, *Côte d'Ivoire* **180** H7
Cavan, *Ire.* **138** F6
Cave Creek, *Ariz., U.S.* **101** T7
Cave Junction, *Oreg., U.S.* **102** K2
Caviana, Ilha, *Braz.* **123** C13
Çavuş Burnu, *Turk.* **148** J6
Çavuşçu Gölü, *Turk.* **148** G7
Cawker City, *Kans., U.S.* **99** S6
Caxias, *Braz.* **122** E5
Caxias, *Braz.* **123** E15
Caxias do Sul, *Braz.* **122** P12
Caxito, *Angola* **182** C5
Çay, *Turk.* **148** F6
Cayambe, *Ecua.* **120** J3
Cayce, *S.C., U.S.* **90** K9
Çaycuma, *Turk.* **148** C7
Çayeli, *Turk.* **149** D15
Cayenne, *Fr. Guiana* **121** E18
Cayey, *P.R., U.S.* **111** M23
Çayıralan, *Turk.* **148** F10
Cayman Brac, island, *Cayman Is., U.K.* **110** L9
Cayman Islands, *Caribbean Sea* **110** L8
Cayman Trench, *Atl. Oc.* **216** L2
Caynabo, *Somalia* **179** G17
Cay Sal Bank, *Bahamas* **110** F9
Cayucos, *Calif., U.S.* **103** V5
Cayuga Lake, *N.Y., U.S.* **88** K8
Cazombo, *Angola* **182** D9
Ceara Plain, *Atl. Oc.* **217** N8
Cebollar, *Arg.* **124** H9
Cebu, island, *Philippines* **169** E14
Cebu, *Philippines* **169** E14
Cedar, river, *Iowa, U.S.* **99** P13
Cedar Bluff Reservoir, *Kans., U.S.* **99** T4
Cedar Breaks National Monument, *Utah, U.S.* **101** P6
Cedar City, *Utah, U.S.* **101** P6
Cedar Creek Reservoir, *Tex., U.S.* **96** M12
Cedar Falls, *Iowa, U.S.* **99** N12
Cedar Key, *Fla., U.S.* **91** S6
Cedar Lake, *Ind., U.S.* **93** P7
Cedar Rapids, *Iowa, U.S.* **99** N13
Cedar River, *Mich., U.S.* **92** H8
Cedartown, *Ga., U.S.* **90** K4
Cedar Vale, *Kans., U.S.* **99** V8
Cedarville, *Calif., U.S.* **102** L6
Cedros, Isla, *Mex.* **108** D5
Cedros Trench, *Pac. Oc.* **219** G16
Ceel Buur, *Somalia* **179** H17
Ceerigaabo (Erigavo), *Somalia* **179** F17
Cegléd, *Hung.* **132** L10
Cejal, *Col.* **120** G9
Çekerek, river, *Turk.* **148** E10
Çekerek, *Turk.* **148** E10
Celaya, *Mex.* **108** H11
Celebes *see* Sulawesi, island, *Indonesia* **169** K13
Celebes Basin, *Pac. Oc.* **218** J3
Celebes Sea, *Indonesia* **169** H14
Celina, *Ohio, U.S.* **93** Q11
Celje, *Slov.* **136** E11
Celle, *Ger.* **132** F6
Celtic Sea, *Eur.* **130** F3
Cement, *Okla., U.S.* **96** H10
Çemişgezek, *Turk.* **149** F13
Cenderawasih, Teluk, *Indonesia* **169** K19
Center, *Colo., U.S.* **101** P12
Center, *N. Dak., U.S.* **98** G4
Center, *Tex., U.S.* **96** M15
Center Hill Lake, *Tenn., U.S.* **95** E16
Center Mountain, *Idaho, U.S.* **100** F4
Center Point, *Ala., U.S.* **95** J15
Center Point, *Tex., U.S.* **97** Q9
Centerville, *Iowa, U.S.* **99** Q12
Centerville, *S. Dak., U.S.* **98** M8
Centerville, *Tenn., U.S.* **95** F14
Centerville, *Tex., U.S.* **97** N13
Centerville, *Utah, U.S.* **100** M7
Central, *Alas., U.S.* **105** F17
Central, *N. Mex., U.S.* **101** U10
Central, Cordillera, *Dom. Rep.* **111** L17
Central, Cordillera, *S. Amer.* **118** C2
Central, Massif, *Eur.* **130** H4
Central African Republic, *Af.* **178** G9
Central America, *N. Amer.* **74** P7
Central Brahul Range, *Pak.* **157** S6
Central City, *Ky., U.S.* **95** C15
Central City, *Nebr., U.S.* **99** Q7
Central Highlands, *Vietnam* **166** M13
Centralia, *Ill., U.S.* **93** T5
Centralia, *Mo., U.S.* **99** S13
Centralia, *Wash., U.S.* **102** D3
Central Lowland, *U.S.* **79** F14
Central Lowlands, *Austral.* **190** E10
Central Makran Range, *Pak.* **157** U4
Central Pacific Basin, *Pac. Oc.* **218** J9
Central Point, *Oreg., U.S.* **102** K3
Central Range, *P.N.G.* **193** C18
Central Russian Upland, *Eur.* **130** E11
Central Siberian Plateau, *Asia* **146** C9
Central Valley, *Calif., U.S.* **103** N3
Centre, *Ala., U.S.* **95** H16
Centre de Flacq, *Mauritius* **185** G20
Centreville, *Miss., U.S.* **94** N10
Cenxi, *China* **163** R2
Cephalonia *see* Kefaloniá, island, *Gr.* **137** L13
Ceram, island, *Indonesia* **169** K16
Ceram Sea, *Indonesia* **169** K16
Ceres, *Arg.* **124** J11
Ceres, *Braz.* **123** J13
Cerf Island, *Seychelles* **183** C19
Çerkeş, *Turk.* **148** D8
Çermik, *Turk.* **149** G14
Cernavodă, *Rom.* **137** F17
Cerralvo, Isla, *Mex.* **108** F7
Cerrillos, *Arg.* **124** F9
Cerrillos, *N. Mex., U.S.* **101** R12
Cerro de Pasco, *Peru* **122** G3
Cesar, river, *Col.* **120** C5
Cēsis, *Latv.* **135** L17
České Budějovice, *Czech Rep.* **132** J7
Çeşme, *Turk.* **148** F2
Céspedes, *Cuba* **110** J10
Cessnock, *N.S.W., Austral.* **191** X14
Cetti Bay, *Guam, U.S.* **196** D10
Ceuta, *Sp.* **139** T6
Ceuta, *Sp.* **176** A9
Cévennes, mountains, *Eur.* **130** H4
Ceyhan, river, *Turk.* **148** H11
Ceyhan, *Turk.* **148** H11
Ceylanpınar, *Turk.* **149** J14
Ceylon *see* Sri Lanka, *Asia* **159** U6
Chābahār, *Iran* **153** J17
Chabana, *Jap.* **165** X2
Chacabuco, *Arg.* **124** L12
Chacao, Canal de, *Chile* **125** Q6
Chachapoyas, *Peru* **122** F3
Chacharan, *Pak.* **157** S9
Chachersk, *Belarus* **133** F14
Chachora, *India* **158** H5
Chachro, *Pak.* **157** W9
Chaco Culture National Historical Park, *N. Mex., U.S.* **101** R11
Chad, *Af.* **177** H15
Chad, Lake, *Af.* **174** G6
Chadan, *Russ.* **141** L13
Chadbourn, *N.C., U.S.* **90** K11
Chadron, *Nebr., U.S.* **98** M2
Chadwick, *Mo., U.S.* **99** V12
Chaffee, *Mo., U.S.* **99** U16
Chagai, *Pak.* **157** S4
Chagai Hills, *Pak.* **157** S3
Chagda, *Russ.* **141** H18
Chagdo Kangri, *China* **160** J6
Chaghcharan, *Afghan.* **156** M5
Chagos Archipelago, *Asia* **146** M6
Chagos-Laccadive Plateau, *Ind. Oc.* **220** E9
Chagos Trench, *Ind. Oc.* **220** H9
Chagyl, *Turkm.* **154** K7
Chahar Bagh, *Afghan.* **156** K5
Chahar Borj, *Afghan.* **156** M2
Chah-e Ab, *Afghan.* **156** K8
Chah-e Kerteh, *Afghan.* **157** P2
Chaibasa, *India* **158** J10
Chai-Nat, *Thai.* **166** L8
Chain Fracture Zone, *Atl. Oc.* **217** N10
Chain of Craters, *Hawaii, U.S.* **107** N21
Chajarí, *Arg.* **124** J13
Chakar, river, *Pak.* **157** S7
Chakaria, *Bangladesh* **158** J14
Chake Chake, *Tanzania* **179** L15
Chakhansur, *Afghan.* **157** Q2
Chakwal, *Pak.* **157** N11
Chalan Kanoa, *Saipan, N. Mariana Is., U.S.* **196** C4
Chalan Pago, *Guam, U.S.* **196** C11
Chalap Dalan Range, *Afghan.* **157** N3
Chalbi Desert, *Af.* **174** J10
Chaleur Bay, *N.B.-Que., Can.* **77** N21
Chalhuanca, *Peru* **122** J4
Chaling, *China* **163** P4
Chalisgaon, *India* **158** K4
Chalkhi, *Afghan.* **156** L2
Chalkidikí, peninsula, *Gr.* **137** J15
Chalkyitsik, *Alas., U.S.* **105** E17
Challenger Deep (World's greatest ocean depth), *Pac. Oc.* **218** H6
Challenger Fracture Zone, *Pac. Oc.* **219** N16
Challis, *Idaho, U.S.* **100** F5
Chālmeh, *Iran* **152** A11
Chalon, *Fr.* **138** L11
Châlons, *Fr.* **138** K11
Chama, *N. Mex., U.S.* **101** Q12
Chamah, peak, *Malaysia* **167** T9
Chaman, *Pak.* **157** Q5
Chaman Bid, *Iran* **153** B15
Chamatang, *India* **157** N15
Chamba, *India* **157** P13
Chambal, river, *India* **158** G5
Chamberlain, *S. Dak., U.S.* **98** L6
Chamberlain Lake, *Me., U.S.* **89** C17
Chamberlin, Mount, *Alas., U.S.* **105** C17
Chambers, *Ariz., U.S.* **101** S9
Chambersburg, *Pa., U.S.* **88** P6
Chambers Creek, *Tex., U.S.* **96** M12
Chambéry, *Fr.* **138** M12
Chambeshi, river, *Af.* **174** M9
Chamburi Kalat, *Pak.* **157** V4
Chamical, *Arg.* **124** J9
Chamizal National Memorial, *Tex., U.S.* **97** U2
Chamkani, *Afghan.* **157** N8
Ch'amo Hāyk', *Eth.* **179** H14
Chamoli, *India* **158** E7
Chamonix, *Fr.* **138** L12
Champaign, *Ill., U.S.* **93** R6
Champasak, *Laos* **166** M12
Champlain, Lake, *N.Y.-Vt., U.S.* **88** F12
Champotón, *Mex.* **109** J15
Chamrajnagar, *India* **159** Q5
Chañaral, *Chile* **124** G7
Chanārān, *Iran* **153** B16
Chandalar, river, *Alas., U.S.* **105** E16
Chandeleur Islands, *La., U.S.* **95** Q13
Chandeleur Sound, *La., U.S.* **94** Q12
Chandigarh, *India* **158** E5
Chandler, *Okla., U.S.* **96** G11
Chandless, river, *Braz.-Peru* **122** G5
Chandpur, *Bangladesh* **158** J13
Chandrapur, *India* **158** L7
Chang, Ko, *Thai.* **167** N10
Changanacheri, *India* **159** S5
Changane, river, *Mozambique* **182** H12
Changbai Shan, *China* **162** B13
Chang Chenmo Range, *China-India* **156** M15
Changchun, *China* **162** A12
Changde, *China* **162** M3
Changhua, *Taiwan, China* **163** R9
Changhŭng, *S. Korea* **162** H13
Changji, *China* **160** E7
Chang Jiang (Yangtze), river, *China* **162** L6
Changjiang (Shiliu), *China* **163** U1
Changjin Reservoir, *N. Korea* **162** C13
Changle, *China* **163** P8
Changli, *China* **162** D8

Changling, China 161 E16
Changmar, China 160 J5
Changning, China 163 P4
Changping, China 162 D7
Changsha, China 162 M4
Changshan, China 162 M8
Changshu, China 162 K9
Changting, China 163 P6
Changyŏn, N. Korea 162 E12
Changzhi, China 162 F5
Changzhou, China 162 K9
Channapatna, India 159 Q5
Channel Country, Austral. 190 G11
Channel Islands, Calif., U.S. 103 Y6
Channel Islands, U.K. 138 K8
Channel Islands National Park, Calif., U.S. 103 X6
Channel-Port aux Basques, Nfld., Can. 77 N23
Channel Rock, Bahamas 110 G12
Chanthaburi, Thai. 167 N10
Chantrey Inlet, Nunavut, Can. 77 G15
Chanute, Kans., U.S. 99 U9
Chão, Ilhéu, Madeira Is., Port. 184 N4
Chao Hu, China 162 K7
Chao Phraya, river, Thai. 166 L8
Chaoyang, China 162 B9
Chaoyang, China 163 R6
Chaozhou, China 163 R6
Chapadinha, Braz. 123 E15
Chapaev, Kaz. 154 D6
Chapak Gozar, Afghan. 156 K4
Chapala, Lago de, Mex. 108 H10
Chapcha, Bhutan 158 F12
Chapel Hill, N.C., U.S. 90 H11
Chapleau, Ont., Can. 77 P17
Chapman, Ala., U.S. 95 M15
Chapman, Kans., U.S. 99 S8
Chappaquiddick Island, Mass., U.S. 89 M15
Chappell, Nebr., U.S. 99 P2
Char, India 157 N14
Chara, river, Russ. 141 J17
Chara, Russ. 141 J17
Charadai, Arg. 124 G12
Charagua, Bol. 122 K8
Charambirá, Punta, Col. 120 F3
Charcot Island, Antarctica 206 G5
Chardonnières, Haiti 111 M14
Charduar, India 158 F14
Chari, river, Af. 174 H7
Charikar, Afghan. 156 M8
Chariton, river, Mo., U.S. 99 Q12
Chariton, Iowa, U.S. 99 Q12
Charity, Guyana 121 D14
Chärjew, Turkm. 154 L10
Charleroi, Belg. 138 J11
Charles, Cape, Va., U.S. 90 F14
Charles City, Iowa, U.S. 98 M12
Charles Island, Nunavut, Can. 77 H18
Charles Mound, Ill., U.S. 92 M4
Charles Point, Austral. 190 B7
Charleston, Ill., U.S. 93 S7
Charleston, Miss., U.S. 94 H11
Charleston, Mo., U.S. 99 V16
Charleston, N.Z. 193 N17
Charleston, Oreg., U.S. 102 J1
Charleston, S.C., U.S. 90 M10
Charleston, W. Va., U.S. 90 D8
Charles Town, W. Va., U.S. 90 C12
Charlestown, Ind., U.S. 93 T10
Charlestown, St. Kitts and Nevis 113 G16
Charleville, Qnsld., Austral. 191 U13
Charlevoix, Mich., U.S. 92 H10
Charlie-Gibbs Fracture Zone, Atl. Oc. 216 F8
Charlotte, Mich., U.S. 92 M10
Charlotte, N.C., U.S. 90 J9
Charlotte, Tex., U.S. 97 S9
Charlotte Amalie, Virgin Is., U.S. 113 F13
Charlotte Harbor, Fla., U.S. 91 V8
Charlottenberg, Sw. 134 K12
Charlottesville, Va., U.S. 90 E11
Charlottetown, P.E.I., Can. 77 N22
Charlotteville, Trin. & Tobago 113 N18
Charlton Island, Nunavut, Can. 77 M18
Charsadda, Pak. 156 M10
Charşaňňy, Turkm. 154 M12
Chartres, Fr. 138 K9
Chascomús, Arg. 124 M13
Chase, Kans., U.S. 99 T6
Chase City, Va., U.S. 90 F12
Chaska, Minn., U.S. 98 K11
Chassahowitzka, Fla., U.S. 91 T7
Chasseloup, Baie, New Caledonia, Fr. 198 C6
Chateaubriand, Baie du, New Caledonia, Fr. 198 C9
Châteaubriant, Fr. 138 L8
Châteauroux, Fr. 138 L10
Chatfield, Minn., U.S. 98 L12
Chatham, Ill., U.S. 93 R5
Chatham, Mass., U.S. 89 L16
Chatham, N.B., Can. 77 N21
Chatham, N.Y., U.S. 88 K11
Chatham, Va., U.S. 90 F10
Chatham Island, Pac. Oc. 194 P9
Chatham Islands, Pac. Oc. 194 P9
Chatham Rise, Pac. Oc. 218 Q9
Chatham Strait, Alas., U.S. 105 K22
Chatom, Ala., U.S. 95 M13
Chatra, India 158 H10
Chatsworth, Qnsld., Austral. 191 T11
Chatsworth, Ga., U.S. 90 J4
Chattahoochee, river, U.S. 79 K17
Chattahoochee, Fla., U.S. 91 Q4
Chattanooga, Tenn., U.S. 95 G17
Chau Doc, Vietnam 167 P11
Chauk, Myanmar 166 H5
Chaukan Pass, India 158 F16
Chaumont, Fr. 138 K11
Chaunskaya Guba, Russ. 141 C19
Chavé, Baie, Ua Huka, Fr. Polynesia, Fr. 199 N23
Chaves, Braz. 123 C13
Chaves, Port. 139 P5
Chayek, Kyrg. 156 E11
Cheaha Mountain, Ala., U.S. 95 J16
Cheboksary, Russ. 140 G7
Cheboygan, Mich., U.S. 92 G11
Chech, Erg, Alg.-Mali 176 E9
Chechaktu, Afghan. 156 L4
Checotah, Okla., U.S. 96 G13
Cheduba Island, Myanmar 166 J4
Cheektowaga, N.Y., U.S. 88 J5
Cheepie, Qnsld., Austral. 191 V12
Chehalis, Wash., U.S. 102 D3
Chehar Borjak, Afghan. 157 R2
Cheju, S. Korea 162 H13
Cheju Do (Quelpart), S. Korea 162 J13
Chekichler, Turkm. 154 M6
Chelan, Wash., U.S. 102 B6
Chelan, Lake, Wash., U.S. 102 B6
Cheleken, Turkm. 154 L6
Chelforó, Arg. 125 P9
Chełm, Pol. 132 H11
Chełmno, Pol. 132 F9
Chelsea, Okla., U.S. 96 E13
Chelyabinsk, Russ. 140 J8
Chelyuskin, Russ. 141 D14
Chemin Grenier, Mauritius 185 H19
Chemnitz, Ger. 132 H7
Chemult, Oreg., U.S. 102 J4
Chemung, river, N.Y., U.S. 88 L7
Chenab, river, Pak. 157 R10
Cheney, Wash., U.S. 102 C9
Cheney Reservoir, Kans., U.S. 99 U7
Chengalpattu, India 159 Q7
Chengbu, China 163 P2
Chengchow see Zhengzhou, China 162 H5
Chengde, China 161 F15
Chengde, China 162 C8
Chengdu, China 160 L11
Chengele, India 158 E15
Chenggu, China 162 H1
Chenghai, China 163 R7
Chengkou, China 162 J1
Ch'engkung, Taiwan, China 163 R10
Chenglingji, China 162 M4
Chengshan Jiao, China 162 F10
Chennai (Madras), India 159 P7
Chenxi, China 162 M2
Chenzhou, China 163 P4
Cheom Ksan, Cambodia 166 M11
Chepén, Peru 122 F2
Chépénéhe, New Caledonia, Fr. 198 C9
Chepes, Arg. 124 J9
Chequamegon Bay, Wis., U.S. 92 F4
Cher, river, Fr. 138 L9
Cheraw, S.C., U.S. 90 J10
Cherbourg, Fr. 138 J8
Cherepovets, Russ. 140 E7
Chergui, Chott ech, Alg. 176 B10
Cherkasy, Ukr. 133 J15
Cherkessk, Russ. 140 J4
Cherlak, Russ. 140 K10
Chernaya, Russ. 140 E10
Chernihiv, Ukr. 133 G15
Chernivtsi, Ukr. 132 K12
Chernogorsk, Russ. 141 L13
Chernyayevo, Russ. 141 K19
Chernyshevskiy, Russ. 141 H16
Cherokee, Iowa, U.S. 98 M9
Cherokee, Okla., U.S. 96 E9
Cherokees, Lake O' The, Okla., U.S. 96 E14
Cherokee Sound, Bahamas 110 C12
Cherrabun, W. Austral., Austral. 191 R5
Cherryfield, Me., U.S. 89 F18
Cherry Island see Anuta, Solomon Is. 194 J7
Cherskiy, Russ. 141 D19
Cherskiy Range, Asia 146 C11
Cherskogo, Khrebet, Russ. 141 F18
Chervonohrad, Ukr. 132 H12
Chesaning, Mich., U.S. 92 L11
Chesapeake, Va., U.S. 90 F14
Chesapeake Bay, Md., U.S. 90 D14
Chesha Bay, Eur. 130 A11
Cheshskaya Guba, Russ. 140 E9
Chesht-e Sharif, Afghan. 156 M3
Chester, Calif., U.S. 103 N5
Chester, Ill., U.S. 93 U4
Chester, Mont., U.S. 100 B8
Chester, Pa., U.S. 88 Q9
Chester, S.C., U.S. 90 J9
Chester, Eng., U.K. 138 G8
Chesterfield, Îles, Coral Sea 194 K6
Chesterfield Inlet, Nunavut, Can. 77 H15
Chesterfield Inlet, Nunavut, Can. 77 H15
Chestertown, Md., U.S. 90 C14
Chesuncook Lake, Me., U.S. 89 C16
Chetamale, Andaman Is., India 159 R14
Chetek, Wis., U.S. 92 H3
Chetlat Island, India 159 Q3
Chetumal, Mex. 109 J16
Chetumal Bay, N. Amer. 74 P7
Chetvertyy Kuril'skiy Proliv, Russ. 141 G24
Chevak, Alas., U.S. 104 J11
Chevelon Butte, Ariz., U.S. 101 S8
Ch'ew Bahir, lake, Eth.-Kenya 179 H14
Chewelah, Wash., U.S. 102 B8
Cheyenne, river, S. Dak., U.S. 98 K3
Cheyenne, Okla., U.S. 96 G8
Cheyenne, Wyo., U.S. 100 K13
Cheyenne Bottoms, Kans., U.S. 99 T6
Cheyenne Wells, Colo., U.S. 101 N16
Chhapra, India 158 G10
Chhatarpur, India 158 H7
Chhep, Cambodia 166 M12
Chhindwara, India 158 J6
Chhukha, Bhutan 158 F12
Chi, river, Thai. 166 L11
Chiai, Taiwan, China 163 R9
Chiang Mai, Thai. 166 J8
Chiang Rai, Thai. 166 H8
Chiat'ura, Rep. of Georgia 149 B17
Chiba, Jap. 165 P12
Chibemba, Angola 182 E6
Chibia, Angola 182 E5
Chibougamau, Que., Can. 77 N19
Chiburi Shima, Jap. 165 P6
Chicago, Ill., U.S. 93 N7
Chicago Heights, Ill., U.S. 93 P7
Chicapa, river, Angola 182 C8
Chichagof Island, Alas., U.S. 105 K21
Chichawatni, Pak. 157 R10
Chichén Itzá, ruins, Mex. 109 H16
Chichester Range, Austral. 190 F3
Chichibu, Jap. 165 P12
Chichi Jima Rettō, Jap. 194 C4
Chickamauga, Ga., U.S. 90 J4
Chickamauga Lake, Tenn., U.S. 95 F17
Chickasawhay, river, Miss., U.S. 95 M13
Chickasaw National Recreation Area, Okla., U.S. 96 H11
Chickasha, Okla., U.S. 96 H10
Chicken, Alas., U.S. 105 F18
Chiclayo, Peru 122 F2
Chico, river, Arg. 125 S9
Chico, river, Arg. 125 V8
Chico, river, Arg. 125 W8
Chico, Calif., U.S. 103 P4
Chicoma Mountain, N. Mex., U.S. 101 R12
Chicomo, Mozambique 182 J12
Chicopee, Mass., U.S. 89 K13
Chicoutimi, Que., Can. 77 N20
Chief Joseph Dam, Wash., U.S. 102 B6
Chiefland, Fla., U.S. 91 S7
Chifeng (Ulanhad), China 162 B8
Chignik Lagoon, Alas., U.S. 105 N13
Chihuahua, Mex. 108 D9
Chikan, Russ. 141 K15
Chikhli, India 158 K5
Chilas, Pak. 156 L11
Chilaw, Sri Lanka 159 T7
Chilca, Peru 122 H3
Childers, Qnsld., Austral. 191 U15
Childersburg, Ala., U.S. 95 K16
Childress, Tex., U.S. 96 J7
Chile, S. Amer. 125 T6
Chile Basin, Pac. Oc. 219 M20
Chilecito, Arg. 124 H8
Chile Rise, Pac. Oc. 219 P19
Chililabombwe, Zambia 182 D10
Chilka Lake, India 158 L10
Chillán, Chile 125 N6
Chillicothe, Ill., U.S. 93 P5
Chillicothe, Mo., U.S. 99 R11
Chillicothe, Ohio, U.S. 93 S13
Chillicothe, Tex., U.S. 96 J8
Chiloquin, Oreg., U.S. 102 K4
Chilpancingo, Mex. 108 K11
Chilton, Wis., U.S. 92 K7
Chilumba, Malawi 183 C13
Chilung (Keelung), Taiwan, China 163 Q10
Chilwa, Lake, Af. 174 M10
Chimacum, Wash., U.S. 102 B3
Chimborazo, peak, Ecua. 120 K3
Chimbote, Peru 122 G2
Chimboy, Uzb. 154 J9
Chimney Rock National Historic Site, Nebr., U.S. 99 P1
Chimoio, Mozambique 182 G12
China, Asia 160 K8
China Lake, Calif., U.S. 103 V9
Chinandega, Nicar. 109 M17
China Point, Calif., U.S. 103 Z8
Chinati Peak, Tex., U.S. 97 Q1
Chincha Islands, S. Amer. 118 G2
Chincha Alta, Peru 122 H3
Chinchilla, Qnsld., Austral. 191 V15
Chincoteague, Va., U.S. 90 E15
Chincoteague Bay, Md., U.S. 90 D15
Chinde, Mozambique 183 F13
Chindwin, river, Myanmar 166 E5
Chingola, Zambia 182 D10
Chingoni, Mayotte, Fr. 185 P17
Chinguetti, Mauritania 176 F6
Chin Hills, Myanmar 166 G5
Chinhoyi, Zimb. 182 F11
Chiniot, Pak. 157 Q11
Chinju, S. Korea 162 G14
Chino, Jap. 165 P11
Chinook, Mont., U.S. 100 B9
Chinook Trough, Pac. Oc. 218 E10
Chino Valley, Ariz., U.S. 101 S6
Chinsali, Zambia 182 C12
Chinta, S. Austral., Austral. 191 W8
Chios see Hios, island, Gr. 137 L16
Chipata, Zambia 182 E12
Chipley, Fla., U.S. 91 Q3
Chiplun, India 158 M3
Chippewa, river, Wis., U.S. 92 G3
Chippewa, Lake, Wis., U.S. 92 G3
Chippewa Falls, Wis., U.S. 92 H3
Chiquián, Peru 122 G3
Chiquimula, Guatemala 109 L16
Chiquinquirá, Col. 120 E5
Chirchiq, Uzb. 155 K13
Chiredzi, Zimb. 182 G12
Chiricahua National Park, Ariz., U.S. 101 V9
Chiricahua Peak, Ariz., U.S. 101 V9
Chirikof Island, Alas., U.S. 105 N14
Chirinda, Russ. 141 G14
Chiriquí, Golfo de, Pan. 109 P20
Chiromo, Malawi 183 F13
Chirripo, Cerro, C.R. 109 N19
Chisasibi, Que., Can. 77 M18
Ch'ishan, Taiwan, China 163 S9
Chisholm, Minn., U.S. 98 F12
Chishtian Mandi, Pak. 157 R11
Chisimayu see Kismaayo, Somalia 179 K16
Chişinău, Mold. 133 L14
Chisos Mountains, Tex., U.S. 97 R2
Chita, Russ. 141 L17
Chitado, Angola 182 F5
Chitato, Angola 182 B8
Chitembo, Angola 182 E7
Chitipa, Malawi 182 C12
Chitose, Jap. 164 G13
Chitradurga, India 159 P5
Chitral, Pak. 156 L10
Chitré, Pan. 109 P21
Chittagong, Bangladesh 158 J13
Chittaurgarh, India 158 H4
Chittoor, India 159 P6
Chitungwiza, Zimb. 182 F11
Chiumbe, river, Angola 182 C8
Chivilcoy, Arg. 124 L12
Chizu, Jap. 165 P7
Chlef, Alg. 176 A10
Chloride, Ariz., U.S. 101 R5
Chobe, river, Af. 174 N8
Choch'iwŏn, S. Korea 162 F13
Chocolate Mountans, Calif., U.S. 103 Y12
Choctawhatchee, river, Fla., U.S. 91 Q3
Choctawhatchee Bay, Fla., U.S. 91 Q2
Choele Choel, Arg. 125 P9
Choirokoitia, Cyprus 148 L8
Choiseul, island, Solomon Is. 197 K15
Choiseul Sound, Falk. Is., U.K. 125 W12
Choke Canyon Reservoir, Tex., U.S. 97 T9
Chokoloskee, Fla., U.S. 91 X9
Chokurdakh, Russ. 141 D18
Cholet, Fr. 138 L8
Cholpon-Ata, Kyrg. 156 D13
Choluteca, Hond. 109 M17
Choma, Zambia 182 F10
Ch'ŏnan, S. Korea 162 F13
Chon Buri, Thai. 167 N9
Chonchi, Chile 125 R6
Chone, Ecua. 120 J2
Chong'an, China 163 N7
Ch'ŏngjin, N. Korea 162 B14
Chŏngju, S. Korea 162 G13
Ch'ŏngju, S. Korea 162 F13
Chong Kal, Cambodia 166 M10
Chongming, China 162 K10
Chongming Dao, China 162 K10
Chongqing, China 160 L12

Chongxin, *China* **162** G1
Chongyi, *China* **163** P5
Chŏnju, *S. Korea* **162** G13
Chonogol, *Mongolia* **161** D14
Chonos, Archipiélago, *Chile* **125** S6
Chop, *Ukr.* **132** K11
Chornobyl', *Ukr.* **133** H14
Chornomors'ke, *Ukr.* **133** L16
Chorregon, *Qnsld., Austral.* **191** T12
Chorrillos, *Peru* **122** H3
Ch'ŏrwŏn, *S. Korea* **162** E13
Ch'osan, *N. Korea* **162** C12
Chōshi, *Jap.* **165** P13
Chos Malal, *Arg.* **125** N7
Choszczno, *Pol.* **132** F8
Chota Nagpur Plateau, *Asia* **146** J8
Choteau, *Mont., U.S.* **100** C7
Chotila, *India* **158** J2
Chowan, river, *N.C., U.S.* **90** G14
Chowchilla, *Calif., U.S.* **103** T6
Choybalsan, *Mongolia* **161** D14
Choyr, *Mongolia* **161** D13
Christchurch, *N.Z.* **193** P17
Christian, Point, *Pitcairn I., U.K.* **199** Q23
Christiansburg, *Va., U.S.* **90** F9
Christiansted, *Virgin Is., U.S.* **113** F13
Christmas Creek, *W. Austral., Austral.* **191** R5
Christmas Island, *Ind. Oc.* **168** N8
Christmas Island *see* Kiritimati, *Kiribati* **194** G12
Christmas Lake Valley, *Oreg., U.S.* **102** J6
Christopher, *Ill., U.S.* **93** U5
Christoval, *Tex., U.S.* **97** N7
Chrysochou Bay, *Cyprus* **148** L7
Chubb Crater *see* Nouveau-Québec, Cratère du, *Que., Can.* **77** J18
Chubbuck, *Idaho, U.S.* **100** H7
Chub Cay, *Bahamas* **110** D11
Chubut, river, *Arg.* **125** R8
Chukchi Range, *Asia* **146** A12
Chudleigh Park, *Qnsld., Austral.* **191** S12
Chudskoye Ozero *see* Peipus, Lake, *Estonia* **135** K17
Chugach Mountains, *Alas., U.S.* **105** J17
Chugwater, *Wyo., U.S.* **100** J13
Chuhuyiv, *Ukr.* **133** H17
Chukai, *Malaysia* **167** T10
Chukchi Peninsula, *Asia* **146** A12
Chukchi Plain, *Arctic Oc.* **222** J6
Chukchi Plateau, *Arctic Oc.* **222** J6
Chukchi Sea, *Asia* **146** A12
Chukotskiy Poluostrov, *Russ.* **141** A21
Chukotskoye Nagor'ye, *Russ.* **141** B20
Chula Vista, *Calif., U.S.* **103** Z10
Chumar, *India* **157** N15
Chumbicha, *Arg.* **124** H9
Chumikan, *Russ.* **141** J20
Chumphon, *Thai.* **167** P8
Chumunjin, *S. Korea* **162** E14
Chun'an, *China* **162** M8
Ch'unch'ŏn, *S. Korea* **162** E13
Chungli, *Taiwan, China* **163** Q10
Chunhua, *China* **162** G2
Chunya, *Tanzania* **179** M13
Chuquibamba, *Peru* **122** J5
Chuquicamata, *Chile* **124** D7
Chur, *Switz.* **132** K5
Churachandpur, *India* **158** H14
Churchill, river, *Man., Can.* **77** K14
Churchill, *Man., Can.* **77** K15
Churchill, Cape, *Man., Can.* **77** K15
Churchill Falls, *Nfld., Can.* **77** L21
Churchill Lake, *Me., U.S.* **89** C16
Churchill Lake, *Sask., Can.* **76** L12
Churchill Mountains, *Antarctica* **207** L13
Church Point, *La., U.S.* **94** P8
Churuguara, *Venez.* **120** B8
Chushul, *India* **157** N15
Chuska Mountains, *N. Mex., U.S.* **101** R10
Chusovoy, *Russ.* **140** H9
Chuuk (Truk Is.), islands, *F.S.M.* **196** Q6
Chuuk Lagoon (Truk Lagoon), *Chuuk, F.S.M.* **197** B15
Chuxiong, *China* **160** N11
Cianjur, *Indonesia* **168** M8
Ciaravuti, *Taj.* **156** J7
Cibecue, *Ariz., U.S.* **101** T8
Çiçekdağı, *Turk.* **148** E9
Cicero, *Ill., U.S.* **93** N7
Cicia, island, *Fiji* **198** H9
Cidade Velha, *Cape Verde* **185** D16
Cide, *Turk.* **148** C8
Ciechanów, *Pol.* **132** G10
Ciego de Ávila, *Cuba* **110** H10
Ciénaga, *Col.* **120** B5
Cienfuegos, *Cuba* **110** H8
Cieza, *Sp.* **139** S8
Çiftlik, *Turk.* **148** G9
Cihanbeyli, *Turk.* **148** F8
Cikobia, island, *Fiji* **198** F8
Cilacap, *Indonesia* **168** M9
Cilaos, *Réunion, Fr.* **185** G16
Çıldır, *Turk.* **149** C17
Çıldır Gölü, *Turk.* **149** D17
Cilician Gates, *Turk.* **148** H10
Cimarron, river, *U.S.* **78** J11
Cimarron, *Kans., U.S.* **99** V3
Cimarron, *N. Mex., U.S.* **101** Q13
Cîmpulung Moldovenesc, *Rom.* **137** D15
Çınar, *Turk.* **149** H15
Cinaruco, river, *Venez.* **120** D9
Cincinnati, *Ohio, U.S.* **93** S11
Cinco Balas, Cayos, *Cuba* **110** J9
Çine, *Turk.* **148** G3
Cinnabar Mountain, *Idaho, U.S.* **100** H3
Cinto, Monte, *Fr.* **139** P13
Çırçır, *Turk.* **148** E12
Circle, *Alas., U.S.* **105** E17
Circle, *Mont., U.S.* **100** C12
Circleville, *Ohio, U.S.* **93** R13
Cirebon, *Indonesia* **168** M9
Ciscaucasia, region, *Eur.* **130** G12
Cisco, *Tex., U.S.* **96** M9
Cisco, *Utah, U.S.* **101** N9
Cisneros, *Col.* **120** E5
Cistern Point, *Bahamas* **110** F11
Citronelle, *Ala., U.S.* **95** N13
City of Refuge National Historical Park *see* Puuhonua o Honaunau National Historical Park, *Hawaii, U.S.* **107** N18
City of Rocks National Reserve, *Idaho, U.S.* **100** J5
Ciudad Acuña, *Mex.* **108** D11
Ciudad Altamirano, *Mex.* **108** J11
Ciudad Bolívar, *Venez.* **120** C11
Ciudad Camargo, *Mex.* **108** E9
Ciudad Cortés, *C.R.* **109** N19
Ciudad del Carmen, *Mex.* **109** J15
Ciudad del Este, *Para.* **122** N11
Ciudad Guayana, *Venez.* **120** C12
Ciudad Guerrero, *Mex.* **108** D8
Ciudad Guzmán, *Mex.* **108** H10
Ciudad Hidalgo, *Mex.* **109** L15
Ciudad Juárez, *Mex.* **108** C9
Ciudad Madero, *Mex.* **108** G12
Ciudad Mante, *Mex.* **108** G12
Ciudad Obregón, *Mex.* **108** D7
Ciudad Piar, *Venez.* **120** D12
Ciudad Real, *Sp.* **139** R7
Ciudad-Rodrigo, *Sp.* **139** Q6
Ciudad Sandino, *Cuba* **110** H4
Ciudad Valles, *Mex.* **108** G12
Ciudad Victoria, *Mex.* **108** G12
Ciutadella, *Sp.* **139** Q11
Civa Burnu, *Turk.* **148** C11
Civitanova Marche, *It.* **136** G10
Civitavecchia, *It.* **136** H9
Çivril, *Turk.* **148** G5
Cixian, *China* **162** F5
Cizre, *Turk.* **149** H16
Clair Engle Lake, *Calif., U.S.* **102** M3
Clairton, *Pa., U.S.* **88** P3
Clairview, *Qnsld., Austral.* **191** T14
Clam Lake, *Wis., U.S.* **92** F4
Clanton, *Ala., U.S.* **95** K15
Clare, *Mich., U.S.* **92** K10
Claremont, *N.H., U.S.* **89** H13
Claremore, *Okla., U.S.* **96** F13
Clarence, river, *N.Z.* **193** N18
Clarence Island, *Antarctica* **206** B3
Clarence Strait, *Austral.* **190** A7
Clarence Town, *Bahamas* **111** G14
Clarendon, *Ark., U.S.* **94** G10
Clarendon, *Tex., U.S.* **96** H6
Clarie Coast, *Antarctica* **207** Q19
Clarinda, *Iowa, U.S.* **99** Q10
Clarión, Isla, *Mex.* **108** H4
Clarion, *Iowa, U.S.* **98** M11
Clarion, *Pa., U.S.* **88** M4
Clarion Fracture Zone, *Pac. Oc.* **219** H13
Clarión Island, *N. Amer.* **74** N2
Clark, *S. Dak., U.S.* **98** K7
Clark, Lake, *Alas., U.S.* **105** K15
Clarkdale, *Ariz., U.S.* **101** S7
Clarke Range, *Austral.* **190** E14
Clark Fork, river, *Mont., U.S.* **100** D6
Clark Fork, *Idaho, U.S.* **100** B4
Clark Mountain, *Calif., U.S.* **103** V11
Clarks, *La., U.S.* **94** L8
Clarksburg, *W. Va., U.S.* **90** C9
Clarksdale, *Miss., U.S.* **94** H10
Clarks Fork, river, *Wyo., U.S.* **100** F9
Clarks Hill Lake, *Ga.-S.C., U.S.* **90** L7
Clarkson, *Nebr., U.S.* **99** P8
Clarkston, *Wash., U.S.* **102** D9
Clarksville, *Ark., U.S.* **94** F7
Clarksville, *Tenn., U.S.* **95** E14
Clarksville, *Tex., U.S.* **96** K14
Clatskanie, *Oreg., U.S.* **102** E3
Claude, *Tex., U.S.* **96** G6
Claxton, *Ga., U.S.* **91** N8
Clay, *Ky., U.S.* **95** C14
Clay Center, *Kans., U.S.* **99** S8
Claypool, *Ariz., U.S.* **101** U8
Clayton, *Ala., U.S.* **95** M17
Clayton, *Ga., U.S.* **90** J6
Clayton, *Idaho, U.S.* **100** F5
Clayton, *La., U.S.* **94** M9
Clayton, *N. Mex., U.S.* **101** Q15
Clayton, *N.Y., U.S.* **88** G8
Clayton, *Okla., U.S.* **96** H13
Clayton Lake, *Me., U.S.* **89** B16
Clearbrook, *Minn., U.S.* **98** F9
Clear Creek, *Tex., U.S.* **96** K11
Clearfield, *Pa., U.S.* **88** M5
Clearfield, *Utah, U.S.* **100** K7
Clear Lake, *Calif., U.S.* **103** Q3
Clear Lake, *Iowa, U.S.* **98** M11
Clear Lake, *S. Dak., U.S.* **98** K8
Clear Lake, *Wash., U.S.* **102** B4
Clear Lake, *Wis., U.S.* **92** H2
Clear Lake Reservoir, *Calif., U.S.* **102** L5
Clearmont, *Wyo., U.S.* **100** F12
Clearwater, river, *Alta.-Sask., Can.* **76** K11
Clearwater, river, *Idaho, U.S.* **100** D3
Clearwater, *Fla., U.S.* **91** U7
Clearwater, *Wash., U.S.* **102** C2
Clearwater Mountains, *Idaho, U.S.* **100** D4
Cleburne, *Tex., U.S.* **96** M11
Cle Elum, *Wash., U.S.* **102** C5
Clemson, *S.C., U.S.* **90** K7
Clendenin, *W. Va., U.S.* **90** D8
Cleopatra Needle, peak, *Philippines* **169** E13
Clermont, *Qnsld., Austral.* **191** T14
Clermont- Ferrand, *Fr.* **138** M10
Cleveland, *Miss., U.S.* **94** J10
Cleveland, *Ohio, U.S.* **93** N14
Cleveland, *Okla., U.S.* **96** F12
Cleveland, *Tenn., U.S.* **95** G17
Cleveland, *Tex., U.S.* **97** Q14
Cleveland, *Wis., U.S.* **92** K7
Cleveland, Mount, *Mont., U.S.* **100** A6
Clewiston, *Fla., U.S.* **91** V9
Clifden, *Ire.* **138** F5
Cliff, *N. Mex., U.S.* **101** U10
Clifton, *Kans., U.S.* **99** S8
Clifton, *Tex., U.S.* **97** N11
Clifton Forge, *Va., U.S.* **90** E10
Clifton Hills, *S. Austral., Austral.* **191** V10
Clinch, river, *Tenn., U.S.* **95** E19
Clingmans Dome, *N.C.-Tenn., U.S.* **90** H6
Clint, *Tex., U.S.* **97** U2
Clinton, *Ark., U.S.* **94** F8
Clinton, *Ill., U.S.* **93** R6
Clinton, *Ind., U.S.* **93** R7
Clinton, *Iowa, U.S.* **99** N15
Clinton, *Ky., U.S.* **94** D12
Clinton, *Miss., U.S.* **94** L11
Clinton, *Mo., U.S.* **99** T11
Clinton, *N.C., U.S.* **90** J12
Clinton, *Okla., U.S.* **96** G9
Clinton, *S.C., U.S.* **90** K8
Clintonville, *Wis., U.S.* **92** J6
Clipperton, island, *Pac. Oc.* **195** F19
Clipperton Fracture Zone, *Pac. Oc.* **219** J13
Cliza, *Bol.* **122** K7
Cloates, Point, *Austral.* **190** F1
Clodomira, *Arg.* **124** G10
Cloncurry, river, *Austral.* **190** D11
Cloncurry, *Qnsld., Austral.* **191** S11
Cloncurry Plateau, *Austral.* **190** E11
Clonmel, *Ire.* **138** G6
Cloquet, *Minn., U.S.* **98** G12
Cloudcroft, *N. Mex., U.S.* **101** U13
Cloud Peak, *Wyo., U.S.* **100** F11
Clover, *S.C., U.S.* **90** J8
Cloverdale, *Calif., U.S.* **103** Q3
Cloverport, *Ky., U.S.* **95** C15
Clovis, *Calif., U.S.* **103** T6
Clovis, *N. Mex., U.S.* **101** S15
Cluj-Napoca, *Rom.* **137** E15
Cluny, *Qnsld., Austral.* **191** U11
Clutha, river, *N.Z.* **193** R16
Clyde, *Kans., U.S.* **99** S7
Clyde, *Ohio, U.S.* **93** P13
Clyde, *Tex., U.S.* **96** M8
Clyde Inlet, *Nunavut, Can.* **77** E18
Clyde River, *Nunavut, Can.* **77** E18
Coachella, *Calif., U.S.* **103** X11
Coachella Canal, *Calif., U.S.* **103** Y12
Coahoma, *Tex., U.S.* **96** M6
Coalcomán, *Mex.* **108** J10
Coal Creek, *N.Z.* **193** Q16
Coaldale, *Nev., U.S.* **103** R8
Coalgate, *Okla., U.S.* **96** H12
Coalinga, *Calif., U.S.* **103** U6
Coamo, *P.R., U.S.* **111** N23
Coari, river, *Braz.* **122** E8
Coari, *Braz.* **122** E8
Coastal Plain, *U.S.* **78** N12
Coast Mountains, *N. Amer.* **74** F3
Coast Range, *S. Amer.* **118** A4
Coast Ranges, *Calif.-Oreg., U.S.* **102** E3
Coats Island, *Nunavut, Can.* **77** H16
Coats Land, *Antarctica* **206** E10
Coatzacoalcos, *Mex.* **109** J14
Cobalt, *Ont., Can.* **77** P18
Cobán, *Guatemala* **109** L16
Cobar, *N.S.W., Austral.* **191** X13
Cobh, *Ire.* **138** H5
Cobia, island, *Fiji* **198** G8
Cobija, *Bol.* **122** G6
Cobourg Peninsula, *Austral.* **190** A8
Cobre, *Nev., U.S.* **102** M12
Cóbuè, *Mozambique* **183** D13
Coburg, *Ger.* **132** H6
Coburg Island, *Nunavut, Can.* **77** C16
Cocanada *see* Kakinada, *India* **158** M8
Cochabamba, *Bol.* **122** K7
Cochin (Kochi), *India* **159** R5
Cochinoca, *Arg.* **124** E9
Cochinos, Bahía de (Bay of Pigs), *Cuba* **110** H7
Cochise Head, peak, *Ariz., U.S.* **101** V9
Cochran, *Ga., U.S.* **91** N6
Cochrane, *Ont., Can.* **77** N17
Cockburn, *S. Austral., Austral.* **191** X11
Cockburn Harbour, *Turks and Caicos Is., U.K.* **111** J17
Cockburn Town, *Bahamas* **111** F14
Cocklebiddy Motel, *W. Austral., Austral.* **191** X6
Cockscomb Point, *Tutuila, Amer. Samoa, U.S.* **198** L8
Coco, river, *Hond.-Nicar.* **109** L19
Coco, Cayo, *Cuba* **110** H10
Coco, Isla del, *C.R.* **109** Q17
Cocoa, *Fla., U.S.* **91** T9
Cocoa Island, *Mauritius* **185** J19
Coco Channel, *India-Myanmar* **159** P15
Coco-de-Mer Seamounts, *Ind. Oc.* **220** G6
Coconut Point, *Tutuila, Amer. Samoa, U.S.* **198** M7
Cocos Island, *Guam, U.S.* **196** E10
Cocos Island, *N. Amer.* **74** R7
Cocos Lagoon, *Guam, U.S.* **196** E10
Cocos Ridge, *Pac. Oc.* **219** J19
Cod, Cape, *Mass., U.S.* **89** L16
Codajás, *Braz.* **122** D8
Cod Island, *Nfld., Can.* **77** J21
Codó, *Braz.* **123** E15
Codrington, *Barbuda* **113** F16
Codrington, Mount, *Antarctica* **207** C19
Cody, *Nebr., U.S.* **98** M4
Cody, *Wyo., U.S.* **100** F9
Coeburn, *Va., U.S.* **90** F7
Coen, *Qnsld., Austral.* **191** P12
Coëtlogon, Passe du, *New Caledonia, Fr.* **198** C8
Coeur d'Alene, *Idaho, U.S.* **100** C3
Coeur d'Alene Lake, *Idaho, U.S.* **100** C3
Coffeyville, *Kans., U.S.* **99** V9
Coffs Harbour, *N.S.W., Austral.* **191** W15
Cognac, *Fr.* **138** M9
Cohagen, *Mont., U.S.* **100** C11
Cohoes, *N.Y., U.S.* **88** J11
Coiba, Isla de, *Pan.* **109** P20
Coig, river, *Arg.* **125** W8
Coihaique, *Chile* **125** S7
Coimbatore, *India* **159** R5
Coimbra, *Port.* **139** Q5
Coipasa, Salar de, *Bol.* **122** K6
Cojimíes, Boca de, *Ecua.* **120** J2
Cokato, *Minn., U.S.* **98** J10
Cokeville, *Wyo., U.S.* **100** J8
Colac, *Vic., Austral.* **191** Z12
Colatina, *Braz.* **123** L16
Colby, *Kans., U.S.* **99** S4
Colchester, *Eng., U.K.* **138** H9
Cold Bay, *Alas., U.S.* **104** N11
Cold Spring, *Minn., U.S.* **98** J10
Coldwater, river, *Miss., U.S.* **94** H11
Coldwater, *Kans., U.S.* **99** V5
Coldwater, *Mich., U.S.* **93** N10
Coldwater Creek, *Tex., U.S.* **96** E4
Colebrook, *N.H., U.S.* **89** F14
Coleman, *Mich., U.S.* **92** K11
Coleman, *Tex., U.S.* **96** M8
Coleraine, *Minn., U.S.* **98** F11
Coleraine, *N. Ire., U.K.* **138** F6
Coles, Punta, *Peru* **122** K5
Colesberg, *S. Af.* **182** L9
Colfax, *Calif., U.S.* **103** Q5
Colfax, *Iowa, U.S.* **99** P12
Colfax, *La., U.S.* **94** M8
Colfax, *Wash., U.S.* **102** D9
Colhué Huapí, Lago, *Arg.* **125** S8
Colídor, *Braz.* **122** G11
Colima, *Mex.* **108** J9
Colinas, *Braz.* **123** E15
College, *Alas., U.S.* **105** F16
College Park, *Ga., U.S.* **90** L5
College Station, *Tex., U.S.* **97** P12
Collerina, *N.S.W., Austral.* **191** W13
Collie, *W. Austral., Austral.* **191** X2
Collier Bay, *Austral.* **190** C5
Collier Range, *Austral.* **190** G3
Colliers Point, *Cayman Is., U.K.* **110** L7
Collierville, *Tenn., U.S.* **94** G12
Collingwood, *N.Z.* **193** M17
Collins, *Miss., U.S.* **94** M12

Collins Head, Norfolk I., Austral. 197 G20
Collinson Peninsula, Nunavut, Can. 77 F14
Collinsville, Ill., U.S. 93 T4
Collinsville, Okla., U.S. 96 E13
Collinsville, Qnsld., Austral. 191 S14
Collinsville, Va., U.S. 90 G10
Collipulli, Chile 125 N6
Colmar, Fr. 138 K12
Cologne see Köln, Ger. 132 G4
Colômbia, Braz. 123 L13
Colombia, S. Amer. 120 F6
Colombo, Sri Lanka 159 T7
Colón, Cuba 110 G8
Colón, Pan. 109 N21
Colón, Archipiélago de see Galápagos Islands, Pac. Oc. 195 G21
Colonel Hill, Bahamas 111 G14
Colonet, Cabo, Mex. 108 B5
Colonia, Yap Is., F.S.M. 197 D18
Colonia Dora, Arg. 124 H11
Colonial Beach, Va., U.S. 90 D13
Colonial Heights, Va., U.S. 90 F13
Colonial National Historical Park, Va., U.S. 90 F14
Colonia 25 de Mayo, Arg. 125 N8
Colon Ridge, Pac. Oc. 219 J18
Colophon, ruins, Turk. 148 G3
Colorado, river, Arg. 125 P10
Colorado, river, Tex., U.S. 97 R12
Colorado, river, U.S. 78 K5
Colorado, U.S. 100 M12
Colorado City, Tex., U.S. 96 M6
Colorado National Monument, Colo., U.S. 100 M10
Colorado Plateau, Ariz., U.S. 101 Q8
Colorado River Aqueduct, Calif., U.S. 103 X12
Colorado Springs, Colo., U.S. 101 N13
Colotepec, Mex. 109 L13
Colquitt, Ga., U.S. 91 P4
Colstrip, Mont., U.S. 100 E11
Columbia, river, N. Amer. 74 H3
Columbia, Ky., U.S. 95 D17
Columbia, La., U.S. 94 L8
Columbia, Md., U.S. 90 C13
Columbia, Miss., U.S. 94 N11
Columbia, Mo., U.S. 99 S13
Columbia, N.C., U.S. 90 G14
Columbia, Pa., U.S. 88 P8
Columbia, S.C., U.S. 90 K9
Columbia, Tenn., U.S. 95 F15
Columbia, Cape, Nunavut, Can. 77 A16
Columbia, District of, U.S. 90 C13
Columbia, Mount, Alta.-B.C., Can. 76 L9
Columbia City, Ind., U.S. 93 P10
Columbia Falls, Mont., U.S. 100 B5
Columbia Mountains, B.C., Can. 76 L9
Columbia Plateau, U.S. 78 C5
Columbia Seamount, Atl. Oc. 217 R9
Columbine, Cape, S. Af. 182 M7
Columbus, Ga., U.S. 91 N4
Columbus, Ind., U.S. 93 S9
Columbus, Kans., U.S. 99 V10
Columbus, Miss., U.S. 95 J13
Columbus, Mont., U.S. 100 E9
Columbus, N. Dak., U.S. 98 D3
Columbus, N. Mex., U.S. 101 W11
Columbus, Nebr., U.S. 99 P7
Columbus, Ohio, U.S. 93 R13
Columbus, Tex., U.S. 97 R12
Columbus, Wis., U.S. 92 L6
Columbus Monument, Bahamas 111 F14
Colusa, Calif., U.S. 103 Q4
Colville, river, Alas., U.S. 105 C15
Colville, N.Z. 193 J19
Colville, Wash., U.S. 102 A8
Colville Channel, N.Z. 193 J19
Colville Lake, N.W.T., Can. 76 F10
Colwich, Kans., U.S. 99 U7
Comacchio, It. 136 F9
Comallo, Arg. 125 Q7
Comanche, Okla., U.S. 96 J10
Comanche, Tex., U.S. 96 M9
Comandante Ferraz, station, Antarctica 206 C3
Comandante Fontana, Arg. 124 F12
Comandante Luis Piedrabuena, Arg. 125 V8
Comayagua, Hond. 109 L17
Combarbalá, Chile 124 J7
Combermere Bay, Myanmar 166 J4
Comboyne, N.S.W., Austral. 191 X15
Comet, Qnsld., Austral. 191 T14
Comfort, Tex., U.S. 97 Q9
Comino, Capo, It. 136 J8
Commandant Charcot Glacier, Antarctica 207 Q18
Commander Islands see Komandorskiye Ostrova, Russ. 141 E23
Commerce, Ga., U.S. 90 K6
Commerce, Tex., U.S. 96 K13
Committee Bay, Nunavut, Can. 77 F16
Commonwealth Bay, Antarctica 207 R18
Communism Peak see Imeni Ismail Sumani Peak, Kyrg.-Taj. 156 H10
Como, It. 136 E8
Como, Lake, Eur. 130 H6
Comodoro Rivadavia, Arg. 125 T9
Comondú, Mex. 108 E6
Comorin, Cape, India 159 S6
Comoro Islands, Af. 174 M11
Comoros, Ind. Oc. 183 D16
Compiègne, Fr. 138 J10
Compostela, Mex. 108 H9
Comrat, Mold. 133 L14
Comstock Seamount, Pac. Oc. 218 D12
Cona, China 160 M8
Conakry, Guinea 180 F5
Conara Junction, Tas., Austral. 191 Z16
Concarneau, Fr. 138 K7
Conceição, Braz. 123 F17
Conceição do Araguaia, Braz. 123 F13
Conceição do Maú, Braz. 122 B9
Concepción, Arg. 124 G9
Concepción, Bol. 122 J8
Concepción, Chile 125 N6
Concepción del Uruguay, Arg. 124 K13
Conception, Point, Calif., U.S. 103 W5
Conception Bay, Nfld., Can. 77 M24
Concepción del Oro, Mex. 108 F11
Conception Island, Bahamas 111 F14
Conchas, river, N. Mex., U.S. 101 R13
Conchas Dam, N. Mex., U.S. 101 R14
Conchas Lake, N. Mex., U.S. 101 R14
Concho, river, Tex., U.S. 97 N7
Concho, Ariz., U.S. 101 T9
Conchos, river, Mex. 108 D8
Conchos, river, N. Amer. 74 M4
Con Co, Dao, Vietnam 166 K13
Conconully, Wash., U.S. 102 A6
Concord, Calif., U.S. 103 R4
Concord, N.C., U.S. 90 H9
Concord, N.H., U.S. 89 J14
Concordia, station, Antarctica 207 M17
Concordia, Arg. 124 J13
Concordia, Kans., U.S. 99 S7
Concrete, Wash., U.S. 102 A4
Condamine, Qnsld., Austral. 191 V14
Conde, S. Dak., U.S. 98 J7
Condeúba, Braz. 123 J15
Condobolin, N.S.W., Austral. 191 X13
Condon, Oreg., U.S. 102 F6
Conecuh, river, Ala., U.S. 95 M16
Conflict Group, islands, P.N.G. 193 E21
Conghua, China 163 R4
Congjiang, China 163 P1
Congo, Af. 181 K18
Congo, river, Af. 174 K6
Congo, Source of the, Af. 174 M8
Congo Basin, Af. 174 J7
Congo Canyon, Atl. Oc. 217 P14
Congress, Ariz., U.S. 101 T6
Cónico, Cerro, Arg. 125 R7
Conneaut, Ohio, U.S. 93 N15
Connecticut, river, N.H.-Vt., U.S. 89 J13
Connecticut, U.S. 89 L13
Connell, Wash., U.S. 102 D7
Connellsville, Pa., U.S. 88 P4
Connersville, Ind., U.S. 93 R10
Connmara, Qnsld., Austral. 191 T12
Connors Range, Austral. 190 F14
Cononaco, Ecua. 120 J5
Conrad, Mont., U.S. 100 B7
Conroe, Tex., U.S. 97 Q14
Conselheiro Lafaiete, Braz. 123 L14
Consolación del Sur, Cuba 110 G5
Con Son, island, Vietnam 167 Q13
Con Son, Vietnam 167 Q13
Constance, Lake, Eur. 130 G6
Constância dos Baetas, Braz. 122 E8
Constanţa, Rom. 137 F17
Constantine, Alg. 176 A12
Constantinople see İstanbul, Turk. 148 C5
Constellation Inlet, Antarctica 206 H8
Constitución, Chile 124 M6
Contact, Nev., U.S. 102 L12
Contai, India 158 K11
Contamana, Peru 122 F4
Contramaestre, Cuba 110 J11
Contreras, Isla, Chile 125 W6
Contwoyto Lake, Nunavut, Can. 76 G12
Conway, Ark., U.S. 94 G8
Conway, N.H., U.S. 89 G14
Conway, S.C., U.S. 90 K11
Conway Springs, Kans., U.S. 99 U7
Coober Pedy, S. Austral., Austral. 191 V9
Cook, Minn., U.S. 98 F12
Cook, S. Austral., Austral. 191 W7
Cook, Bahía, Chile 125 Y8
Cook, Baie de, Moorea, Fr. Polynesia, Fr. 199 N14
Cook, Mouillage de, Tahiti, Fr. Polynesia, Fr. 199 P17
Cook, Mount, N.Z. 193 P16
Cook Bay, Vanuatu 198 G4
Cookes Peak, N. Mex., U.S. 101 V11
Cookeville, Tenn., U.S. 95 E17
Cook Ice Shelf, Antarctica 207 R16
Cook Inlet, Alas., U.S. 105 K15
Cook Island, Kiritimati, Kiribati 197 B22
Cook Island Passage, Kiritimati, Kiribati 197 B22
Cook Islands, Pac. Oc. 194 J11
Cook Strait, N.Z. 193 M18
Cooktown, Qnsld., Austral. 191 Q13
Coolabah, N.S.W., Austral. 191 W13
Coolabri, Qnsld., Austral. 191 U13
Cooladdi, Qnsld., Austral. 191 V13
Coolah, N.S.W., Austral. 191 X14
Coolatai, N.S.W., Austral. 191 W14
Coolgardie, W. Austral., Austral. 191 W4
Coolidge, Tex., U.S. 97 N12
Coolidge Dam, Ariz., U.S. 101 U8
Coonabarabran, N.S.W., Austral. 191 X14
Coonamble, N.S.W., Austral. 191 W14
Coonana, W. Austral., Austral. 191 W5
Coonbah, N.S.W., Austral. 191 X11
Coondambo, S. Austral., Austral. 191 W9
Coondapoor see Kundapura, India 159 P4
Coongoola, Qnsld., Austral. 191 V13
Coon Rapids, Iowa, U.S. 99 P10
Coon Rapids, Minn., U.S. 98 J11
Cooper, Tex., U.S. 96 K13
Cooper Creek, Austral. 190 H10
Cooper's Town, Bahamas 110 C11
Cooperstown, N. Dak., U.S. 98 F7
Cooperstown, N.Y., U.S. 88 J10
Coorow, W. Austral., Austral. 191 W2
Coosa, river, Ala., U.S. 95 H16
Coos Bay, Oreg., U.S. 102 J2
Cootamundra, N.S.W., Austral. 191 Y13
Copaipó, Chile 124 G7
Copano Bay, Tex., U.S. 97 T11
Cope, Colo., U.S. 100 M15
Copenhagen see København, Den. 134 N12
Copiapó, Río, Chile 124 G6
Copper, river, Alas., U.S. 105 H18
Copperas Cove, Tex., U.S. 97 P10
Copper Butte, Wash., U.S. 102 A8
Copper Center, Alas., U.S. 105 H17
Copper Harbor, Mich., U.S. 92 D7
Copulhue Pass, S. Amer. 118 M4
Coqên, China 160 K6
Coquille, Oreg., U.S. 102 J2
Coquille Harbor, Kosrae, F.S.M. 197 A18
Coquimbo, Chile 124 J6
Coracora, Peru 122 J4
Corail, Haiti 111 M15
Coral Gables, Fla., U.S. 91 X10
Coral Harbour, Nunavut, Can. 77 H16
Coral Island see Far'ûn, Egypt 151 R5
Coral Sea, Pac. Oc. 194 J5
Coral Sea Basin, Pac. Oc. 218 L7
Coral Sea Islands Territory, Austral. 191 R14
Coral Springs, Fla., U.S. 91 W10
Corangamite, Lake, Austral. 190 M12
Corantijn, river, Guyana-Suriname 121 E15
Corbin, Ky., U.S. 95 D18
Corcoran, Calif., U.S. 103 U6
Corcovado, Golfo, Chile 125 R6
Cordele, Ga., U.S. 91 N5
Cordell, Okla., U.S. 96 G9
Cordillo Downs, S. Austral., Austral. 191 U11
Córdoba, Arg. 124 J10
Córdoba, Mex. 109 J13
Córdoba, Sp. 139 S6
Córdoba, Sierras de, Arg. 124 K10
Cordova, Ala., U.S. 95 J15
Cordova, Alas., U.S. 105 J18
Corfu see Kérkira, island, Gr. 137 K13
Corguinho, Braz. 122 K11
Coribe, Braz. 123 H14
Corigliano Calabro, It. 136 K11
Coringa Islets, C.S.I. Terr., Austral. 191 R15
Corinna, Tas., Austral. 191 Z15
Corinth see Kórinthos, Gr. 137 L15
Corinth, Miss., U.S. 95 G13
Corinth, N.Y., U.S. 88 J11
Cork, Ire. 138 H5
Çorlu, Turk. 148 C4
Cornelia, Ga., U.S. 90 K6
Cornell, Wis., U.S. 92 H3
Corner Brook, Nfld., Can. 77 M23
Corner Seamounts, Atl. Oc. 216 H7
Corning, Ark., U.S. 94 E10
Corning, Calif., U.S. 103 P4
Corning, Iowa, U.S. 99 Q10
Corning, N.Y., U.S. 88 K7
Corno Grande, peak, Eur. 130 J6
Cornwall, Ont., Can. 77 Q19
Cornwallis, Port, Andaman Is., India 159 P14
Cornwallis Island, Nunavut, Can. 77 D15
Cornwall Island, Nunavut, Can. 77 C15
Coro, Venez. 120 B8
Coroa, Tope de, Cape Verde 185 B14
Coroatá, Braz. 123 E15
Corocoro, Bol. 122 K6
Coroico, Bol. 122 J6
Corolla, N.C., U.S. 90 G15
Coromandel Coast, India 159 R8
Coromandel Peninsula, N.Z. 193 J19
Corona, N. Mex., U.S. 101 T13
Coronado, Calif., U.S. 103 Z9
Coronado Bay, N. Amer. 74 Q8
Coronado National Memorial, Ariz., U.S. 101 W8
Coronation Gulf, Nunavut, Can. 76 F12
Coronation Island, Antarctica 206 A4
Coronel, Chile 125 N6
Coronel Bogado, Para. 122 N10
Coronel Dorrego, Arg. 125 P11
Coronel Francisco Sosa, Arg. 125 P10
Coronel Oviedo, Para. 122 N10
Coronel Pringles, Arg. 125 N11
Coronel Suárez, Arg. 125 N11
Coropuna, Nevado, Peru 122 J5
Corozal, Belize 109 J16
Corozal, Col. 120 C5
Corpus Christi, Tex., U.S. 97 U11
Corpus Christi, Lake, Tex., U.S. 97 T10
Corpus Christi Bay, U.S. 78 N12
Corral, Chile 125 P6
Corralillo, Cuba 110 G8
Corrientes, Arg. 124 G13
Corrientes, Bahía de, Cuba 110 H4
Corrientes, Cabo, Col. 120 E3
Corrientes, Cabo, Cuba 110 H4
Corrientes, Cabo, Mex. 108 H9
Corrigan, Tex., U.S. 97 P14
Corrigin, W. Austral., Austral. 191 X3
Corriverton, Guyana 121 E15
Corry, Pa., U.S. 88 L4
Corryong, Vic., Austral. 191 Y13
Corse (Corsica), island, Fr. 139 P13
Corse, Cap, Fr. 139 N13
Corsica see Corse, island, Fr. 139 P13
Corsica, S. Dak., U.S. 98 M6
Corsicana, Tex., U.S. 96 M12
Corte, Fr. 139 P13
Cortez, Colo., U.S. 101 P10
Cortland, N.Y., U.S. 88 K8
Çoruh, river, Turk. 149 D15
Çorum, Turk. 148 D10
Corumbá, Braz. 122 K10
Corumbau, Ponta de, Braz. 123 K16
Corvallis, Oreg., U.S. 102 G3
Corydon, Iowa, U.S. 99 Q12
Cosenza, It. 136 K11
Coshocton, Ohio, U.S. 93 Q14
Cosmoledo Group, Seychelles 183 C17
Cosmo Newberry, W. Austral., Austral. 191 V5
Cosmopolis, Wash., U.S. 102 D2
Cosquín, Arg. 124 J10
Costa Rica, N. Amer. 75 Q20
Costa del Silencio, Canary Is., Sp. 184 Q5
Costa Rica, N. Amer. 109 N18
Costilla, N. Mex., U.S. 101 Q13
Cotabato, Philippines 169 F15
Cotagaita, Bol. 122 L7
Coteaux, Haiti 111 N15
Côte d'Ivoire, Af. 180 G8
Côtes-de-Fer, Haiti 111 N16
Coton, Pointe, Mauritius 185 J21
Cotonou, Benin 180 H12
Cotopaxi, peak, Ecua. 120 J3
Cottage Grove, Oreg., U.S. 102 H3
Cottbus, Ger. 132 G7
Cotter, Ark., U.S. 94 E8
Cotton Plant, Ark., U.S. 94 G10
Cotton Valley, La., U.S. 94 K7
Cottonwood, Ariz., U.S. 101 S7
Cottonwood, Idaho, U.S. 100 D4
Cotulla, Tex., U.S. 97 T8
Coudersport, Pa., U.S. 88 L6
Coulee City, Wash., U.S. 102 C7
Coulee Dam, Wash., U.S. 102 B7
Council, Idaho, U.S. 100 F3
Council Bluffs, Iowa, U.S. 99 P9
Council Grove, Kans., U.S. 99 T8
Courantyne, river, Guyana 121 F15
Courtenay, B.C., Can. 76 M7
Coushatta, La., U.S. 94 L7
Coutances, Fr. 138 K8
Cove, Oreg., U.S. 102 F8
Covelo, Calif., U.S. 103 P2
Coventry, Eng., U.K. 138 G8
Covilhã, Port. 139 Q5
Covington, Ga., U.S. 90 L5
Covington, Ind., U.S. 93 R7
Covington, Ky., U.S. 95 A18
Covington, La., U.S. 94 P11
Covington, Okla., U.S. 96 F10
Covington, Tenn., U.S. 94 F12
Covington, Va., U.S. 90 E10
Cowal, Lake, Austral. 190 K13
Cowan, Lake, Austral. 190 J4
Cow and Calf Islands, Myanmar 159 N15
Cowaramup, W. Austral., Austral. 191 Y2
Cowarie, S. Austral., Austral. 191 V10
Cowell, S. Austral., Austral. 191 X9
Coweta, Okla., U.S. 96 F13
Cowley, Wyo., U.S. 100 F10

Cowlitz, river, Wash., U.S. 102 D4
Coxim, river, Braz. 122 KII
Coxim, Braz. 122 KII
Cox's Bazar, Bangladesh 158 KI4
Coyanosa Draw, Tex., U.S. 97 P3
Cozad, Nebr., U.S. 99 Q5
Cozumel, Mex. 109 HI7
Cozumel, Isla, Mex. 109 HI7
Crab Island, Mauritius 185 K2O
Cradock, S. Af. 182 LIO
Crafers, S. Austral., Austral. 191 YIO
Craig, Alas., U.S. 105 L23
Craig, Colo., U.S. 100 LII
Craigmont, Idaho, U.S. 100 D4
Craiova, Rom. 137 FI5
Cranberry Lake, N.Y., U.S. 88 GIO
Cranbourne, Vic., Austral. 191 ZI2
Cranbrook, B.C., Can. 76 M9
Crandon, Wis., U.S. 92 G6
Crane, Oreg., U.S. 102 J8
Crane, Tex., U.S. 97 N4
Crane Lake, Minn., U.S. 98 EI2
Crary Mountains, Antarctica 206 L8
Crater Lake, Oreg., U.S. 102 J4
Crater Lake National Park, Oreg., U.S. 102 J4
Craters of the Moon National Monument, Idaho, U.S. 100 H6
Crateús, Braz. 123 EI6
Crato, Braz. 123 FI6
Crawford, Nebr., U.S. 98 MI
Crawfordsville, Ind., U.S. 93 R8
Crawfordville, Fla., U.S. 91 R5
Crazy Mountains, Mont., U.S. 100 E9
Cree, river, Sask., Can. 76 KI2
Creede, Colo., U.S. 101 PII
Cree Lake, Sask., Can. 76 KI2
Creighton, Nebr., U.S. 99 N7
Cremona, It. 136 F8
Cres, island, Croatia 136 FIO
Cresbard, S. Dak., U.S. 98 J6
Crescent, Okla., U.S. 96 FIO
Crescent, Oreg., U.S. 102 J4
Crescent City, Calif., U.S. 102 LI
Crescent City, Fla., U.S. 91 S8
Crescent Group, Paracel Is. 168 BIO
Crescent Junction, Utah, U.S. 101 N9
Crescent Lake, Fla., U.S. 91 S8
Crescent Lake, Oreg., U.S. 102 J4
Cresco, Iowa, U.S. 98 MI3
Crested Butte, Colo., U.S. 101 NII
Creston, Iowa, U.S. 99 QIO
Crestview, Fla., U.S. 91 Q2
Creswell, Oreg., U.S. 102 H3
Crete, Nebr., U.S. 99 Q8
Crete (Kríti), island, Gr. 137 NI6
Crete, Sea of, Gr. 137 MI6
Creus, Cap de, Sp. 139 PIO
Creuse, river, Fr. 138 L9
Crevasse Valley Glacier, Antarctica 206 N9
Crewe, Va., U.S. 90 FI2
Criciúma, Braz. 122 PI2
Crimea, region, Ukr. 133 LI6
Crimean Mountains, Eur. 130 HII
Cripple Creek, Colo., U.S. 101 NI3
Crisfield, Md., U.S. 90 EI4
Cristalina, Braz. 123 JI3
Croatia, Eur. 136 FII
Crocker Range, Malaysia 168 GII
Crockett, Tex., U.S. 97 NI3
Crofton, Nebr., U.S. 98 M7
Croix des Bouquets, Haiti III MI7
Croker Island, Austral. 190 A8
Crook, Colo., U.S. 100 KI5
Crooked, river, Oreg., U.S. 102 H6
Crooked Island, Bahamas III GI5
Crooked Island Passage, Bahamas III HI4
Crook Point, Oreg., U.S. 102 KI
Crookston, Minn., U.S. 98 F8
Crosby, Minn., U.S. 98 HII
Crosby, N. Dak., U.S. 98 D2
Crosbyton, Tex., U.S. 96 K6
Cross City, Fla., U.S. 91 R6
Crossett, Ark., U.S. 94 K9
Crossing Rocks, Bahamas IIO CII
Cross Plains, Tex., U.S. 96 M8
Cross Sound, Alas., U.S. 105 K2I
Crossville, Tenn., U.S. 95 EI7
Croswell, Mich., U.S. 92 LI3
Crotone, It. 136 KI2
Crow Agency, Mont., U.S. 100 EII
Crowell, Tex., U.S. 96 J8
Crowley, La., U.S. 94 P8
Crown King, Ariz., U.S. 101 T6
Crownpoint, N. Mex., U.S. 101 RIO
Crown Prince Christian Land, N. Amer. 74 A8
Croydon, Qnsld., Austral. 191 RI2
Crozer, Mount, Kosrae, F.S.M. 197 BI8
Crozet Islands, Ind. Oc. 184 K8
Crozet Plateau, Southern Oc. 225 DI6
Cruces, Cuba IIO H8
Crump Lake, Oreg., U.S. 102 K6

Cruz, Cabo, Cuba IIO LII
Cruz Alta, Braz. 122 PII
Cruz del Eje, Arg. 124 JIO
Cruz del Padre, Cayo, Cuba IIO G8
Cruzeiro, Ponta, São Tomé and Príncipe 185 C2O
Cruzeiro do Sul, Braz. 122 F4
Cruz Grande, Chile 124 H6
Crystal City, Mo., U.S. 99 TI5
Crystal City, Tex., U.S. 97 S8
Crystal Falls, Mich., U.S. 92 G6
Crystal Lake, Ill., U.S. 92 M6
Crystal Mountains, Af. 174 K6
Crystal River, Fla., U.S. 91 S7
Crystal Springs, Miss., U.S. 94 MII
Ctesiphon, ruins, Iraq 152 EIO
Ču, Kaz. 155 HI5
Cuamba, Mozambique 183 EI3
Cuando, river, Angola 182 E8
Cuangar, Angola 182 F7
Cuango, river, Angola 182 C7
Cuanza, river, Angola 182 C6
Cuauhtémoc, Mex. 108 D8
Cuba, N. Amer. IIO G8
Cuba, island, N. Amer. 74 N9
Cuba, Mo., U.S. 99 TI4
Cubal, Angola 182 D6
Cubango, river, Angola 182 F7
Çubuk, Turk. 148 D8
Cuchilla Grande, S. Amer. 118 L7
Cucuí, Braz. 122 C7
Cúcuta, Col. 120 D6
Cudahy, Wis., U.S. 92 L7
Cuddalore, India 159 Q7
Cuddapah, India 159 P6
Cuenca, Ecua. 120 K3
Cuenca, Sp. 139 Q8
Cuencamé, Mex. 108 FIO
Cuernavaca, Mex. 108 JII
Cuero, Tex., U.S. 97 SII
Cuervo, N. Mex., U.S. 101 SI4
Cuevo, Bol. 122 L8
Cuiabá, Braz. 122 JIO
Cuito, river, Angola 182 F7
Cuito Cuanavale, Angola 182 E7
Çukurca, Turk. 149 HI8
Culbertson, Mont., U.S. 100 BI3
Culbertson, Nebr., U.S. 99 R4
Culebra, island, P.R., U.S. III M24
Culfa, Azerb. 149 FI9
Culiacán, Mex. 108 F8
Culion, island, Philippines 169 DI3
Cullera, Sp. 139 R9
Cullman, Ala., U.S. 95 HI5
Culpataro, N.S.W., Austral. 191 XI2
Culpeper, Va., U.S. 90 DI2
Culuene, river, Braz. 122 HII
Culver, Point, Austral. 190 K5
Culverden, N.Z. 193 NI7
Cumalı, Turk. 148 H3
Cumaná, Venez. 120 BII
Cumanayagua, Cuba IIO H8
Cumberland, river, Tenn., U.S. 95 EI4
Cumberland, Ky., U.S. 95 DI9
Cumberland, Md., U.S. 90 CII
Cumberland, Wis., U.S. 92 G2
Cumberland, Cape, Vanuatu 198 CI
Cumberland, Lake, Ky., U.S. 95 DI7
Cumberland Gap National Historical Park, Ky.-Tenn.-Va., U.S. 95 DI9
Cumberland Island National Seashore, Ga., U.S. 91 Q8
Cumberland Islands, Austral. 190 G5
Cumberland Peninsula, Nunavut, Can. 77 FI9
Cumberland Plateau, U.S. 79 JI7
Cumberland Sound, Nunavut, Can. 77 GI9
Cumborah, N.S.W., Austral. 191 WI3
Cumbrera, Cerro, Chile 125 U7
Cumbres Pass, Colo., U.S. 101 QI2
Cuminá, Braz. 122 DIO
Cumina see Paru de Oeste, river, Braz. 122 CII
Cúmpas, Mex. 108 C7
Çumra, Turk. 148 H8
Cunaviche, Venez. 120 D9
Cunco, Chile 125 P7
Cunene (Kunene), river, Angola 182 F5
Cuneo, It. 136 F7
Cunnamulla, Qnsld., Austral. 191 VI3
Cunyu, W. Austral., Austral. 191 U3
Cupica, Col. 120 E3
Cupica, Golfo de, Col. 120 E3
Curaçao, island, Lesser Antilles 112 M9
Curanilahue, Chile 125 N6
Curaray, river, Ecua. 120 K4
Curbur, W. Austral., Austral. 191 V2
Curecanti National Recreation Area, Colo., U.S. 101 NII
Curepipe, Mauritius 185 G2O
Curiapo, Venez. 121 CI3
Curicó, Chile 124 L7
Curieuse, island, Seychelles 185 N2O
Curitiba, Braz. 122 NI2
Curley Cut Cays, Bahamas IIO FII

Curral Velho, Cape Verde 185 CI7
Current, river, Mo., U.S. 99 VI4
Current, Bahamas IIO DI2
Currie, Tas., Austral. 191 YI5
Currituck, N.C., U.S. 90 GI4
Currituck Sound, N.C., U.S. 90 GI5
Curtin Springs, N. Terr., Austral. 191 U8
Curtis, Nebr., U.S. 99 Q4
Curtis Island, Kermadec Is., N.Z. 194 L9
Curuá, river, Braz. 122 FII
Curuaés, river, Braz. 122 FII
Curuçá, river, Braz. 122 E5
Curuçá, Braz. 123 CI3
Cururupu, Braz. 123 DI5
Curuzú Cuatiá, Arg. 124 HI3
Curvelo, Braz. 123 KI4
Cusco, Peru 122 H5
Cushing, Okla., U.S. 96 FII
Cusson, Pointe, Que., Can. 77 JI7
Custer, Mont., U.S. 100 EII
Custer, S. Dak., U.S. 98 LI
Cut, island, Indonesia 169 LI8
Cut Bank, Mont., U.S. 100 B7
Cuthbert, Ga., U.S. 91 N4
Cutler Ridge, Fla., U.S. 91 XIO
Cutral Có, Arg. 125 P8
Cuttack, India 158 KIO
Cuvier, Cape, Austral. 190 GI
Cuvier Plateau, Ind. Oc. 221 LI4
Cuxhaven, Ger. 132 E5
Cuya, Chile 124 C7
Cuyahoga Falls, Ohio, U.S. 93 PI5
Cuyahoga Valley National Recreation Area, Ohio, U.S. 93 PI4
Cuyama, river, Calif., U.S. 103 W7
Cuyo Islands, Philippines 169 EI3
Cuyuni, river, Guyana-Venez. 121 DI3
Cyangugu, Rwanda 178 KI2
Cyclades see Kikládes, islands, Gr. 137 LI6
Cynthiana, Ky., U.S. 95 BI8
Cyprus, Asia 148 L8
Cyprus, island, Asia 146 F3
Cyrenaica, region, Lib. 177 CI5
Cyrene see Shaḥḥāt, Lib. 177 BI6
Cyrus Field Bay, Nunavut, Can. 77 HI9
Czech Republic, Eur. 132 J7
Czestochowa, Pol. 132 H9

D

Da (Black), river, Vietnam 166 HII
Da'an, China 161 DI6
Ḍab'ah, Jordan 151 N7
Dabakala, Côte d'Ivoire 180 G9
Daba Shan, China 162 JI
Dabie Shan, China 162 K5
Dabola, Guinea 180 F6
Dabqig see Uxin Qi, China 162 E2
Dachau, Ger. 132 J6
Dac To, Vietnam 166 MI3
Dadale, Solomon Is. 197 MI8
Daday, Turk. 148 C9
Dade City, Fla., U.S. 91 T8
Dadeville, Ala., U.S. 95 KI6
Dadhar, Pak. 157 S6
Dadu, river, China 160 LII
Dadu, Pak. 157 U6
Dafeng (Dazhongji), China 162 J9
Dafoe, Sask., Can. 76 MI2
Dagana, Senegal 180 F5
Dagcanglhamo, China 160 KII
Dagelet see Ullŭng Do, island, S. Korea 162 EI5
Dagupan, Philippines 169 CI3
Dahab, Egypt 151 T4
Dahanu, India 158 K3
Da Hinggan Ling, China 161 EI5
Dahla, Afghan. 157 Q5
Dahlak Archipelago, Af. 174 GIO
Dahlonega, Ga., U.S. 90 K5
Dahod, India 158 J4
Dahongliutan, China 156 KI5
Dahūk, Iraq 152 B9
Dai (Ndai), island, Solomon Is. 197 MI9
Daigo, Jap. 165 NI3
Dailekh, Nepal 158 F8
Daimiel, Sp. 139 R7
Daingerfield, Tex., U.S. 96 KI4
Daiō, Jap. 165 QIO
Dair, Jebel ed, Af. 174 G9
Dairen see Dalian, China 162 DIO
Dairy Creek, W. Austral., Austral. 191 U2
Dai Senga Dake, Jap. 164 HI2
Daisetta, Tex., U.S. 97 QI5
Daitō, Jap. 164 LI3
Daitō Islands, Jap. 194 C2
Daixian, China 162 D5
Dajabón, Dom. Rep. III LI7
Dajarra, Qnsld., Austral. 191 SII
Dakar, Senegal 176 H4

Dakhla Oasis, Egypt 177 EI8
Dakoank, Nicobar Is., India 159 TI5
Dakoro, Niger 176 HII
Dakota City, Nebr., U.S. 99 N8
Dala, Solomon Is. 197 MI9
Dalai Nur, China 162 A7
Dalaman, river, Turk. 148 H4
Dalandzadgad, Mongolia 160 FI2
Dalap, island, Majuro Atoll, Marshall Is. 196 HI2
Da Lat, Vietnam 167 NI4
Dalbandin, Pak. 157 S4
Dalbeg, Qnsld., Austral. 191 SI4
Dalby, Qnsld., Austral. 191 VI5
Dale, Nor. 134 KIO
Daleville, Ala., U.S. 95 NI6
Dalgonally, Qnsld., Austral. 191 SII
Dalhart, Tex., U.S. 96 F4
Dali, China 160 NIO
Dali, China 162 G2
Dalian (Dairen), China 162 DIO
Dalidag, peak, Azerb. 149 E2O
Dalkhaki, Afghan. 156 K7
Dallas, Oreg., U.S. 102 G3
Dallas, Tex., U.S. 96 LI2
Dall Island, U.S. 78 R7
Dalmatia, region, Eur. 130 J7
Dal'negorsk, Russ. 141 L2I
Dal'nerechensk, Russ. 141 L2I
Daloa, Côte d'Ivoire 180 G8
Daltenganj, India 158 H9
Dalton, Ga., U.S. 90 J4
Dalton, Nebr., U.S. 99 P2
Dalton Highway, Alas., U.S. 105 CI6
Dalupiri, island, Philippines 169 AI3
Daly, river, Austral. 190 B7
Daly Bay, Nunavut, Can. 77 HI5
Daly Waters, N. Terr., Austral. 191 Q8
Daman (Damão), India 158 K3
Damanhûr, Egypt 177 CI8
Damão see Daman, India 158 K3
Damar, island, Indonesia 169 JI6
Damar, island, Indonesia 169 MI6
Damas Cays, Bahamas IIO F9
Damascus see Dimashq, Syr. 150 J7
Damāvand, Qolleh-ye, Iran 153 CI3
Damboa, Nig. 181 EI6
Dambulla, Sri Lanka 159 S7
Dame-Marie, Haiti III MI4
Dam Ha, Vietnam 166 HI3
Daming, China 162 F6
Damīr Qābū, Syr. 150 CI5
Damoh, India 158 H7
Damongo, Ghana 180 FIO
Dampar, Tasek, Malaysia 167 UIO
Dampier, Selat, Indonesia 169 JI7
Dampier Archipelago, Austral. 190 E2
Dampier Downs, W. Austral., Austral. 191 R4
Dampier Land, Austral. 190 D4
Damqawt, Yemen 153 PI4
Damroh, India 158 EI5
Damxung, China 160 L8
Dan, river, N.C., U.S. 90 GIO
Danakil Desert, Eth. 182 EI5
Da Nang, Vietnam 166 LI3
Dana Point, Calif., U.S. 103 Y9
Danbury, Conn., U.S. 88 MI2
Danby Lake, Calif., U.S. 103 XI2
Dancheng, China 162 H6
Dancheng see Xiangshan, China 162 MIO
Danco Coast, Antarctica 206 D4
Dandan, Puntan, Saipan, N. Mariana Is., U.S. 196 C5
Dandong, China 162 DII
Daneborg, Greenland, Den. 75 A2I
Danfeng, China 162 H3
Danforth, Me., U.S. 89 DI8
Dang, river, China 160 G9
Dangara, Taj. 156 J8
Danger Islands see Pukapuka Atoll, Cook Is., N.Z. 194 JII
Dangrek Range, Thai. 166 MIO
Dangriga, Belize 109 KI7
Dangshan, China 162 H6
Dangtu, China 162 K8
Daniel, Wyo., U.S. 100 H9
Daning, China 162 F3
Danjiangkou, China 162 J3
Danjo Guntō, Jap. 165 S2
Ḏank, Oman 153 KI5
Dankhar Gömpa, India 157 PI5
Danmark Havn, Greenland, Den. 75 A2I
Dannemora, N.Y., U.S. 88 FII
Dansville, N.Y., U.S. 88 K6
Danube (Donau, Duna), river, Eur. 130 H9
Danube, Mouths of the, Rom. 137 EI8
Danube, Source of the, Eur. 130 G6
Danube River Delta, Eur. 130 HIO
Danville, Ill., U.S. 93 R7
Danville, Ky., U.S. 95 CI7
Danville, Va., U.S. 90 GIO
Danxian (Nada), China 163 UI

Dao, Mui, Vietnam 166 K12
Daos du Sud, Îles, New Caledonia, Fr. 198 B6
Daoxian, China 163 P3
Daphne, Ala., U.S. 95 P14
Da Qaidam, China 160 H9
Daqing, China 161 D17
Dar'ā (Edrei), Syr. 150 L7
Dārāb, Iran 153 G14
Daraban, Pak. 157 Q9
Darakht-e Yahya, Afghan. 157 Q7
Ḑarbat 'Alī, Ra's, Oman 153 P14
Darbhanga, India 158 G10
Darby, Mont., U.S. 100 E5
Dardanelle, Ark., U.S. 94 G7
Dardanelle, Lake, Ark., U.S. 94 F7
Dardanelles see Çanakkale Boğazi, strait, Turk. 148 D2
Darende, Turk. 148 G12
Dar Es Salaam, Tanzania 179 M15
Dargai, Pak. 156 M10
Darganata, Turkm. 154 K10
Dargaville, N.Z. 193 H18
Dargeçit, Turk. 149 H16
Darhan, Mongolia 160 C12
Darien, Ga., U.S. 91 P8
Daringali, Solomon Is. 197 M19
Darjiling, India 158 G11
Darling, river, Austral. 190 K11
Darling, Lake, N. Dak., U.S. 98 E4
Darling, Source of the, Austral. 190 H15
Darling Downs, region, Austral. 190 H14
Darling Range, Austral. 190 K3
Darlington, S.C., U.S. 90 K10
Darlington, Eng., U.K. 138 F8
Darlot, Lake, Austral. 190 H4
Darmstadt, Ger. 132 H5
Darnah, Lib. 177 B16
Darnley, Cape, Antarctica 207 F20
Daroot-Korgon, Kyrg. 156 H10
Darregueira, Arg. 125 N11
Darreh Gaz, Iran 153 B16
Darreh-ye Awd, Afghan. 156 M6
Darreh-ye Bum, Afghan. 156 L3
Darrington, Wash., U.S. 102 B5
Darrouzett, Tex., U.S. 96 E7
Dartmouth, N.S., Can. 77 P22
Daru, P.N.G. 193 E18
Darwaji-e Bala, Afghan. 157 N2
Darwha, India 158 K6
Darwin, Falk. Is., U.K. 125 W12
Darwin, N. Terr., Austral. 191 P7
Darwin, Isla, Galapagos Is., Ecua. 195 G21
Darwin Glacier, Antarctica 207 M14
Darya Khan, Pak. 157 Q9
Das, Pak. 158 B5
Dashitou, China 162 A13
Dashkäsän, Azerb. 149 D20
Daşhowuz, Turkm. 154 J9
Dasht, river, Pak. 157 V2
Daska, Pak. 157 P12
Datça, Turk. 148 H3
Datia, India 158 G6
Datian, China 163 Q7
Datong, river, China 160 H10
Datong, China 162 C5
Datu Piang, Philippines 169 F15
Da Ty, Hon, Vietnam 167 Q14
Daud Khel, Pak. 157 P10
Daudnagar, India 158 H9
Daugava, river, Latv. 135 M17
Daugavpils, Latv. 135 M17
Dauphin, Man., Can. 77 N13
Dauphin Island, Ala., U.S. 95 P13
Däväçi, Azerb. 149 C22
Davangere, India 159 P5
Davao, Philippines 169 F15
Davao Gulf, Philippines 169 F15
Davenport, Iowa, U.S. 99 P14
Davenport, Wash., U.S. 102 C8
Davenport Downs, Qnsld., Austral. 191 T11
Davenport Range, Austral. 190 E9
David, Pan. 109 P20
David City, Nebr., U.S. 99 P8
Davidson Mountains, U.S. 78 M5
Davis, station, Antarctica 207 G20
Davis, Calif., U.S. 103 R4
Davis, Okla., U.S. 96 H11
Davis, Mount, Pa., U.S. 88 Q4
Davis Dam, Ariz.-Nev., U.S. 101 S4
Davis Inlet, Nfld., Can. 77 K21
Davis Mountains, Tex., U.S. 97 P2
Davis Strait, Nunavut, Can. 77 F20
Davos, Switz. 132 K5
Davyhurst, W. Austral., Austral. 191 W4
Dawa, river, Af. 174 J10
Dawei, Myanmar 166 M7
Dawkah, Oman 153 N14
Dawna Range, Myanmar 166 K7
Dawāsir, Wādī ad, Saudi Arabia 152 M9
Dawqah, Saudi Arabia 152 M7
Dawra, W. Sahara, Mor. 176 D6
Dawson, river, Austral. 190 G14
Dawson, Ga., U.S. 91 P5
Dawson, Minn., U.S. 98 K9
Dawson, N. Dak., U.S. 98 G5
Dawson, Tex., U.S. 96 M12
Dawson, Yukon Terr., Can. 76 E8
Dawson, Isla, Chile 125 X8
Dawson Creek, B.C., Can. 76 K9
Dawson Springs, Ky., U.S. 95 D14
Dawu, China 162 K5
Dawwah, Oman 153 L17
Dax, Fr. 139 N8
Daxing, China 162 D7
Daxinggou, China 162 A14
Daxue Mountains, Asia 146 H10
Daydawn, W. Austral., Austral. 191 V3
Dayong, China 162 M2
Dayr az Zawr, Syr. 150 F13
Dayr Sim'ān, Syr. 150 D8
Dayton, Ohio, U.S. 93 R11
Dayton, Tenn., U.S. 95 F17
Dayton, Tex., U.S. 97 Q14
Dayton, Wash., U.S. 102 E8
Dayton, Wyo., U.S. 100 F11
Daytona Beach, Fla., U.S. 91 S9
Dayu, China 163 Q5
Da Yunhe (Grand Canal), China 162 J8
Dayushan, island, China 163 S4
Dayville, Oreg., U.S. 102 G7
Dazhongji see Dafeng, China 162 J9
Dazkırı, Turk. 148 G5
De Aar, S. Af. 182 L9
Deadhorse, Alas., U.S. 105 B16
Deadmans Cay, Bahamas 111 G14
Deadman's Cays, Bahamas 110 F8
Dead Sea, Asia 151 N6
Deadwood, S. Dak., U.S. 98 K1
Deakin, W. Austral., Austral. 191 W7
De'an, China 162 M6
Deán Funes, Arg. 124 J10
Dean Passage, Santa Cruz Is., Solomon Is. 197 R24
Dearborn, Mich., U.S. 92 M12
Dease Arm, N.W.T., Can. 76 F11
Dease Inlet, Alas., U.S. 105 B14
Dease Lake, B.C., Can. 76 H8
Dease Strait, Nunavut, Can. 77 F13
Death Valley, Calif., U.S. 103 U10
Death Valley, Calif., U.S. 103 T9
Death Valley National Park, Calif.-Nev., U.S. 103 T9
Deauville, Fr. 138 J9
Debar, Maced. 137 H13
DeBeque, Colo., U.S. 100 M10
Debin, Russ. 141 F20
Debir, ruins, Israel 151 N5
Débo, Lake, Mali 176 H8
Debrecen, Hung. 132 K11
Debre Mark'os, Eth. 179 F14
Debuu, island, Kwajalein Atoll, Marshall Is. 196 K4
Decatur, Ala., U.S. 95 H15
Decatur, Ga., U.S. 90 L5
Decatur, Ill., U.S. 93 R6
Decatur, Ind., U.S. 93 Q10
Decatur, Nebr., U.S. 99 N9
Decatur, Tex., U.S. 96 K11
Deccan, plateau, India 159 P5
Deception Island, Antarctica 206 D3
Dechu, India 158 G3
Decorah, Iowa, U.S. 98 M13
Dedéagach see Alexandroúpoli, Gr. 137 J16
Dededo, Guam, U.S. 196 B11
Dedegöl Dağı, Turk. 148 H6
Dédougou, Burkina Faso 180 E9
Dee, river, Scot., U.K. 138 E8
Deep, river, N. Dak., U.S. 98 E4
Deep Creek, Bahamas 110 E12
Deep Creek Lake, Md., U.S. 90 C10
Deep Creek Range, Utah, U.S. 100 M5
Deep Well, N. Terr., Austral. 191 U9
Deering, Alas., U.S. 104 F12
Deer Isle, Me., U.S. 89 G17
Deer Lodge, Mont., U.S. 100 D7
Deer Park, Wash., U.S. 102 B9
Deer River, Minn., U.S. 98 F11
Deerton, Mich., U.S. 92 F8
Deer Trail, Colo., U.S. 100 M14
Deeth, Nev., U.S. 102 M11
Defiance, Ohio, U.S. 93 P11
De Funiak Springs, Fla., U.S. 91 Q3
Deganya, Israel 150 L6
Dêgê, China 160 K10
Degeh Bur, Eth. 179 G16
Deggendorf, Ger. 132 J7
DeGrey, W. Austral., Austral. 191 S3
DeGrey, river, Austral. 190 E3
Deh Bīd, Iran 153 F13
Deh Khavak, Afghan. 156 L8
Dehqonobod, Uzb. 154 M12
Dehra Dun, India 158 E6
Deh Rawod, Afghan. 157 P5
Deh Shu, Afghan. 157 R3
Dehui, China 161 D17
Deim Zubeir, Sudan 178 G11
Dej, Rom. 137 D15
Dejiang, China 162 M1
De Jongs, Tanjung, Indonesia 193 D16
De Kalb, Ill., U.S. 93 N6
De Kalb, Miss., U.S. 95 K13
De Kalb, Tex., U.S. 96 K14
Dekese, Dem. Rep. of the Congo 178 L9
Dekle Beach, Fla., U.S. 91 R6
Delamere, N. Terr., Austral. 191 Q8
De Land, Fla., U.S. 91 S9
Delano, Calif., U.S. 103 V7
Delano Peak, Utah, U.S. 101 N6
Delaram, Afghan. 157 P3
Delarof Islands, Alas., U.S. 104 Q4
Delavan, Wis., U.S. 92 M6
Delaware, river, N.Y.-Pa., U.S. 88 L9
Delaware, U.S. 90 C14
Delaware, Ohio, U.S. 93 Q13
Delaware Bay, U.S. 79 G20
Delaware Water Gap National Recreation Area, N.J.-Pa., U.S. 88 M10
De Leon, Tex., U.S. 96 M9
Delgado, Cabo, Mozambique 183 D15
Delgo, Sudan 178 C12
Delhi, India 158 F6
Delhi, La., U.S. 94 L9
Delhi, N.Y., U.S. 88 K10
Delice, river, Turk. 148 E9
Delicias, Mex. 108 D9
Deliktaş, Turk. 148 F12
Délı̨ne, N.W.T., Can. 76 F10
Delingha, China 160 H9
Delissaville, N. Terr., Austral. 191 P7
Dell Rapids, S. Dak., U.S. 98 L8
Delmar, Del., U.S. 90 D15
Delmenhorst, Ger. 132 F5
Del Norte, Colo., U.S. 101 P12
De Long Mountains, Alas., U.S. 104 D12
Deloraine, Tas., Austral. 191 Z16
Delphi, Ind., U.S. 93 Q8
Delphos, Ohio, U.S. 93 Q11
Delray Beach, Fla., U.S. 91 W10
Del Rio, Tex., U.S. 97 R6
Delta, Colo., U.S. 101 N10
Delta, Utah, U.S. 100 M6
Delta Downs, Qnsld., Austral. 191 R11
Delta Junction, Alas., U.S. 105 G17
Deltona, Fla., U.S. 91 S9
Demagiri, India 158 J14
Demarcation Point, U.S. 78 L5
Demba, Dem. Rep. of the Congo 178 L9
Demchok, India 157 N16
Demerara Plain, Atl. Oc. 216 M6
Deming, N. Mex., U.S. 101 V11
Demini, river, Braz. 122 C8
Demirci, Turk. 148 F4
Demirköprü Baraji, Turk. 148 F4
Demirköy, Turk. 148 B4
Demirtaş, Turk. 148 J7
Democratic Republic of the Congo, Af. 178 J10
Demopolis, Ala., U.S. 95 L14
Dempster Highway, Yukon Terr., Can. 76 E9
Demta, Indonesia 193 B17
Denali see McKinley, Mount, peak, Alas., U.S. 105 H16
Denali Highway, Alas., U.S. 105 G17
Denali National Park and Preserve, Alas., U.S. 105 G16
Denali Park, Alas., U.S. 105 G16
Denges Passage, Palau 196 Q11
Dengkou, China 160 G12
Dengkou (Bayan Gol), China 162 C1
Dêngqên, China 160 L9
Dengxian, China 162 J4
Denham, W. Austral., Austral. 191 V1
Denham Springs, La., U.S. 94 P10
Den Helder, Neth. 138 G11
Denia, Sp. 139 R9
Denigomodu, Nauru 197 E22
Deniliquin, N.S.W., Austral. 191 Y12
Denio, Nev., U.S. 102 L8
Denis, island, Seychelles 185 L20
Denison, Iowa, U.S. 99 N9
Denison, Tex., U.S. 96 J12
Denizli, Turk. 148 G4
Denmark, Eur. 134 N9
Denmark, S.C., U.S. 90 L9
Denmark, W. Austral., Austral. 191 Y3
Denmark Strait, N. Amer. 74 B10
Denow, Uzb. 154 M12
Denpasar, Indonesia 168 M11
Denton, Md., U.S. 90 C14
Denton, Tex., U.S. 96 K11
D'Entrecasteaux, Point, Austral. 190 L3
D'Entrecasteaux Islands, P.N.G. 193 E21
Denver, Colo., U.S. 100 M13
Denver City, Tex., U.S. 96 L3
Deobhog, India 158 L8
Deoghar, India 158 H11
Deora, India 158 G2
Deoria, India 158 G9
Deosai Mountains, Pak. 156 L12
Deosri, India 158 G13
De Pere, Wis., U.S. 92 J7
Depoe Bay, Oreg., U.S. 102 G2
Deposit, N.Y., U.S. 88 L9
Depósito, Braz. 122 A9
Deputatskiy, Russ. 141 E18
Deqing, China 162 L9
Deqing, China 163 R3
De Queen, Ark., U.S. 94 H6
De Quincy, La., U.S. 94 P7
Dera Ghazi Khan, Pak. 157 R9
Dera Ismail Khan, Pak. 157 Q9
Dera Murad Jamali, Pak. 157 T7
Derbent, Russ. 140 K4
Derby, Kans., U.S. 99 U8
Derby, Eng., U.K. 138 G8
Derby, W. Austral., Austral. 191 R5
Dergaon, India 158 G14
De Ridder, La., U.S. 94 N7
Derik, Turk. 149 H15
Dermott, Ark., U.S. 94 J9
Dernberg, Cape, Namibia 182 K6
Dernieres, Isles, La., U.S. 94 R10
Derry see Londonderry, N. Ire., U.K. 138 F6
Derudeb, Sudan 179 D14
Derweza, Turkm. 154 K8
Derzhavīnsk, Kaz. 154 D12
Désappointement, Îles du, Fr. Polynesia, Fr. 199 D20
Des Arc, Ark., U.S. 94 G9
Deschutes, river, Oreg., U.S. 102 G5
Desē, Eth. 179 F15
Deseado, river, Arg. 125 T8
Desecheo, island, P.R., U.S. 111 M21
Desengaño, Punta, Arg. 125 U9
Deseret, Utah, U.S. 100 M6
Deserta Grande, island, Madeira Is., Port. 184 N4
Desertas, Ilhas, Madeira Is., Port. 184 N4
Desert Center, Calif., U.S. 103 X12
Deshler, Nebr., U.S. 99 R7
Des Lacs, river, N. Dak., U.S. 98 E3
Desloge, Mo., U.S. 99 T15
De Smet, S. Dak., U.S. 98 K7
Des Moines, river, Iowa, U.S. 99 Q12
Des Moines, Iowa, U.S. 99 P11
Des Moines, N. Mex., U.S. 101 Q14
Desna, river, Ukr. 133 H14
Desnudez, Punta, Arg. 125 P12
Desolación, Isla, Chile 125 X7
De Soto, Mo., U.S. 99 T15
Des Plaines, Ill., U.S. 93 N7
Dessalines, Haiti 111 L16
Dessau, Ger. 132 G7
Destruction Island, Wash., U.S. 102 C2
De Tour Village, Mich., U.S. 92 G11
Detroit, Mich., U.S. 92 M13
Detroit Lake, Oreg., U.S. 102 G4
Detroit Lakes, Minn., U.S. 98 G9
Detroit Seamount, Pac. Oc. 218 C8
Deveci Dağı, Turk. 148 E11
Develi, Turk. 148 G10
Devils, river, Tex., U.S. 97 Q6
Devils Cataract see Raudal Yupurari, Col. 120 H7
Devils Hole, Atl. Oc. 216 E13
Devils Hole, Death Valley National Park, Nev., U.S. 103 U10
Devil's Island, S. Amer. 118 B8
Devils Lake, N. Dak., U.S. 98 F6
Devils Lake, N. Dak., U.S. 98 E6
Devils Paw, peak, Alas., U.S. 105 J22
Devil's Point, Vanuatu 198 F3
Devil's Point, Bahamas 111 F13
Devils Postpile National Monument, Calif., U.S. 103 S7
Devils Tower National Monument, Wyo., U.S. 100 F13
Devine, Tex., U.S. 97 S9
Devon Island, Nunavut, Can. 77 D15
Devonport, Tas., Austral. 191 Z16
Devrek, Turk. 148 C7
Devrekâni, Turk. 148 C9
Devrukh, India 158 M3
Dewas, India 158 J5
Dewey, Okla., U.S. 96 E12
De Witt, Ark., U.S. 94 H9
De Witt, Iowa, U.S. 99 N14
Dexter, Me., U.S. 89 E17
Dexter, Mo., U.S. 99 V15
Dexter, N. Mex., U.S. 101 U14
Dey Dey, Lake, Austral. 190 H7
Deyhūk, Iran 153 D15
Deynau, Turkm. 154 L10
Dezfūl, Iran 152 E11
Dezhou, China 162 F7
Dhaka, Bangladesh 158 H13
Dhamār, Yemen 152 Q9
Dhamtari, India 158 K8
Dhanbad, India 158 H10
D'Hanis, Tex., U.S. 97 R8
Dhanushkodi, India 159 S7
Dhar, India 158 J4
Dharan, Nepal 158 G11

Dharapuram, *India* **159** R6
Dharmjaygarh, *India* **158** J9
Dharmsala, *India* **157** P13
Dharwad, *India* **159** N4
Dhaulagiri, peak, *Nepal* **158** F9
Dhekelia, *Cyprus* **148** L9
Dhenkanal, *India* **158** K10
Dhībān, *Jordan* **151** N6
Dhone, *India* **159** N6
Dhuburi, *India* **158** G12
Dhule, *India* **158** K4
Dhupgarh, peak, *India* **158** J6
Dhuusamarreeb, *Somalia* **179** H17
Diable, Île du (Devil's I.), *Fr. Guiana* **121** E18
Diablo Range, *Calif., U.S.* **103** T5
Diamante, river, *Arg.* **124** L8
Diamante, *Arg.* **124** K12
Diamantina, river, *Austral.* **190** F11
Diamantina, *Braz.* **123** K15
Diamantina, Chapada, *Braz.* **123** H15
Diamantina Fracture Zone, *Ind. Oc.* **221** M13
Diamantina Lakes, *Qnsld., Austral.* **191** T11
Diamantino, *Braz.* **122** H10
Diamond Harbour, *India* **158** J12
Diamond Head, *Hawaii, U.S.* **106** E11
Diamond Mountains, *Nev., U.S.* **103** P11
Diamond Peak, *Oreg., U.S.* **102** J4
Diamond Shoals, *N.C., U.S.* **90** H15
Diamondville, *Wyo., U.S.* **100** J8
Dianbai, *China* **163** S2
Dian Chi, lake, *China* **160** N11
Dianópolis, *Braz.* **123** G14
Diapaga, *Burkina Faso* **180** E12
Diavolo, Mount, *Andaman Is., India* **159** Q14
Dībā al Ḩişn, *U.A.E.* **153** J15
Dibai, *India* **158** F6
Diboll, *Tex., U.S.* **97** N14
Dibrugarh, *India* **158** F15
Dibsī Faraj, *Syr.* **150** E10
Dickens, *Tex., U.S.* **96** K6
Dickinson, *N. Dak., U.S.* **98** G2
Dickson, *Russ.* **141** E13
Dickson, *Tenn., U.S.* **95** E14
Dickson City, *Pa., U.S.* **88** M9
Dicle, *Turk.* **149** G14
Dicle (Tigris), river, *Turk.* **149** H15
Didwana, *India* **158** F4
Diego de Almagro, *Chile* **124** G7
Diego de Almagro, Isla, *Chile* **125** W6
Diemal Find, *W. Austral., Austral.* **191** W3
Dien Bien, *Vietnam* **166** H10
Dien Chau, *Vietnam* **166** J12
Dieppe, *Fr.* **138** J9
Dierks, *Ark., U.S.* **94** H6
Dif, *Kenya* **179** J15
Diffa, *Niger* **177** J13
Digboi, *India* **158** F15
Digby, *N.S., Can.* **77** P21
Dighton, *Kans., U.S.* **99** T4
Digne, *Fr.* **139** N12
Digor, *Turk.* **149** D17
Digri, *Pak.* **157** W8
Digul, river, *Indonesia* **169** M21
Digura, island, *Maldives* **159** V3
Dijlah (Tigris), river, *Iraq* **152** E11
Dijon, *Fr.* **138** L11
Dika, Mys, *Russ.* **141** D15
Dikili, *Turk.* **148** E3
Dikwa, *Nig.* **181** E17
Dīla, *Eth.* **179** H15
Dildarde Burnu, *Turk.* **148** J7
Dili, *E. Timor* **169** M15
Dilijan, *Arm.* **149** D19
Di Linh, *Vietnam* **167** P13
Dilley, *Tex., U.S.* **97** S8
Dilling, *Sudan* **178** F12
Dillingham, *Alas., U.S.* **105** L13
Dillon, *Mont., U.S.* **100** F7
Dillon, *S.C., U.S.* **90** K11
Dillon's Bay, *Vanuatu* **198** G3
Dilolo, *Dem. Rep. of the Congo* **178** N9
Dilworth, *Minn., U.S.* **98** G8
Dimas, *Mex.* **108** F8
Dimashq (Damascus), *Syr.* **150** J7
Dimitrovgrad, *Bulg.* **137** H16
Dimmitt, *Tex., U.S.* **96** H4
Dinagat, island, *Philippines* **169** E15
Dinajpur, *Bangladesh* **158** G12
Dinar, *Turk.* **148** G5
Dīnār, Kūh-e, *Iran* **153** F13
Dinaric Alps, *Eur.* **130** H7
Dindigul, *India* **159** R6
Ding'an, *China* **163** U2
Dingbian, *China* **162** E1
Dingnan, *China* **163** Q5
Dingo, *Qnsld., Austral.* **191** T14
Dingtao, *China* **162** G6
Dinguiraye, *Guinea* **180** E6
Dingwall, *Scot., U.K.* **138** D7
Dingxiang, *China* **162** E5
Dingxing, *China* **162** D6
Dingzhou, *China* **162** E6
Dingzi Gang, *China* **162** F9
Dinosaur, *Colo., U.S.* **100** L10
Dinosaur National Monument, *Colo., U.S.* **100** L10
Dinuba, *Calif., U.S.* **103** T7
Diomede Islands, *Russ.-U.S.* **141** A21
Dios, *P.N.G.* **197** J13
Dios, Cayos de, *Cuba* **110** J7
Diourbel, *Senegal* **176** H4
Diphu Pass, *India-Myanmar* **158** F16
Diplo, *Pak.* **157** W8
Dir, *Pak.* **156** M10
Diré, *Mali* **176** H8
Dirē Dawa, *Eth.* **179** F16
Dirico, *Angola* **182** F8
Dirj, *Lib.* **177** C13
Dirk Hartog Island, *Austral.* **190** H1
Dirranbandi, *Qnsld., Austral.* **191** V14
Dirty Devil, river, *Utah, U.S.* **101** N8
Disa, *India* **158** H3
Disappointment, Cape, *Wash., U.S.* **102** E2
Disappointment, Lake, *Austral.* **190** F4
Discovery Bay, *Austral.* **190** M11
Discovery Bay, *Jam.* **110** M11
Discovery Tablemount, *Atl. Oc.* **217** U13
Disney Cay, *Bahamas* **110** D11
Dispur, *India* **158** G13
Disteghil Sar, *Pak.* **156** K12
Diu, *India* **158** K2
Divalak, *Afghan.* **157** Q3
Dīvāndarreh, *Iran* **152** C11
Divinhe, *Mozambique* **183** G13
Divinópolis, *Braz.* **123** L14
Diviso, *Col.* **120** H3
Divo, *Côte d'Ivoire* **180** H8
Divriği, *Turk.* **149** F13
Diwana, *Pak.* **157** V6
Dixie, *Idaho, U.S.* **100** E4
Dixon, *Calif., U.S.* **103** R4
Dixon, *Ill., U.S.* **93** N5
Dixon, *Ky., U.S.* **95** C14
Dixon, *Mo., U.S.* **99** T13
Dixon, *Mont., U.S.* **100** C5
Dixon, *N. Mex., U.S.* **101** R12
Dixon Entrance, *Alas., U.S.* **105** M24
Diyadin, *Turk.* **149** E18
Diyālá, river, *Iraq* **152** D10
Diyarbakır, *Turk.* **149** G15
Dja, river, *Cameroon* **181** J16
Djado, *Niger* **177** F13
Djado, Plateau du, *Niger* **177** F13
Djamaa, *Alg.* **176** B11
Djambala, *Congo* **181** M17
Djanet, *Alg.* **176** E12
Djarrit, island, *Majuro Atoll, Marshall Is.* **196** G12
Djelfa, *Alg.* **176** B11
Djénné, *Mali* **176** H8
Djibouti, *Af.* **179** F16
Djibouti, *Djibouti* **179** F16
Djougou, *Benin* **180** F11
Djoum, *Cameroon* **181** J16
Djúpavík, *Ice.* **134** E2
Djúpivogur, *Ice.* **134** F4
Dmitriya Lapteva, Proliv, *Russ.* **141** D17
Dnieper, river, *Belarus* **133** E14
Dnieper, Source of the, *Eur.* **130** E10
Dnieper Lowland, *Eur.* **130** F10
Dnieper Upland, *Eur.* **130** G10
Dniester, river, *Eur.* **130** G10
Dnipro (Dnieper), river, *Ukr.* **133** K16
Dniprodzerzhyns'k, *Ukr.* **133** J16
Dnipropetrovs'k, *Ukr.* **133** J16
Dnister (Dniester), river, *Mold.-Ukr.* **133** K13
Do Ab-e Mikh-e Zarrin, *Afghan.* **156** M7
Doba, *Chad* **177** K14
Dobane, *Cen. Af. Rep.* **178** G10
Dobbs, Cape, *Nunavut, Can.* **77** H16
Dobrich, *Bulg.* **137** G17
Dobrush, *Belarus* **133** G14
Dobson, *N.Z.* **193** N17
Docampadó, Ensenada, *Col.* **120** F3
Doce, river, *Braz.* **123** L15
Docker River, *N. Terr., Austral.* **191** U7
Dock Junction, *Ga., U.S.* **91** P8
Doctor David Douglas Historical Monument (Kaluakauka), *Hawaii, U.S.* **107** L21
Dodecanese *see* Dodekánissa, islands, *Gr.* **137** M17
Dodekánissa (Dodecanese), islands, *Gr.* **137** M17
Dodge, *Nebr., U.S.* **99** P8
Dodge City, *Kans., U.S.* **99** U5
Dodgeville, *Wis., U.S.* **92** L4
Dodoma, *Tanzania* **179** M14
Dodson, *Mont., U.S.* **100** B10
Dodson, *Tex., U.S.* **96** H7
Doerun, *Ga., U.S.* **91** P5
Dogai Coring, lake, *China* **160** J7
Doğanşehir, *Turk.* **148** G12
Dog Creek, *B.C., Can.* **76** L8
Dōgo, island, *Jap.* **165** N7
Dogondoutchi, *Niger* **176** H10
Dog Rocks, *Bahamas* **110** F9
Doğruyol, *Turk.* **149** D17
Doğubayazıt, *Turk.* **149** E18
Doha *see* Ad Dawḩah, *Qatar* **153** J13
Dois Irmãos, Serra, *Braz.* **123** G16
Dolak, island, *Asia* **146** L16
Dolak (Yos Sudarso), island, *Indonesia* **169** M20
Doland, *S. Dak., U.S.* **98** K7
Dolbeau, *Que., Can.* **77** N19
Doldrums Fracture Zone, *Atl. Oc.* **216** M7
Dole, *Fr.* **138** L11
Dolgiy Most, *Russ.* **141** K14
Dolinsk, *Russ.* **141** K22
Dolly Cays, *Bahamas* **110** F11
Dolo Bay, *Eth.* **179** H16
Dolonnur *see* Duolun, *China* **162** B7
Dolores, river, *Colo., U.S.* **101** N10
Dolores, *Arg.* **124** M13
Dolores, *Colo., U.S.* **101** P10
Dolores, *Uru.* **124** L13
Dolphin, Cape, *Falk. Is., U.K.* **125** W12
Do Luong, *Vietnam* **166** J11
Dom, peak, *Indonesia* **193** B16
Domaniç, *Turk.* **148** E5
Dombås, *Nor.* **134** J11
Domett, *N.Z.* **193** N18
Domeyko, *Chile* **124** H7
Domeyko, Cordillera, *Chile* **124** E7
Dominica, *N. Amer.* **113** J17
Dominica, island, *N. Amer.* **74** N12
Dominican Republic, *N. Amer.* **111** K19
Dominica Passage, *Dominica-Guadeloupe, Fr.* **113** J17
Dominion, Cape, *Nunavut, Can.* **77** G17
Dom Pedro, *Braz.* **123** E15
Domuyo, Volcán, *Arg.* **124** M7
Dôn, river, *Laos* **166** L12
Don, river, *Russ.* **140** H5
Donaldson, *Minn., U.S.* **98** E8
Donaldsonville, *La., U.S.* **94** P10
Donalsonville, *Ga., U.S.* **91** Q4
Donau (Danube), river, *Ger.* **132** J5
Dondo, *Angola* **182** C6
Dondo, *Indonesia* **169** J14
Dondo, *Mozambique* **183** G13
Donegal, *Ire.* **138** F6
Donegal Bay, *Ire.* **138** F6
Donets, river, *Eur.* **130** G11
Donets'k, *Ukr.* **133** J18
Donets Ridge, *Eur.* **130** G11
Donga, *Nig.* **181** G15
Dong'an, *China* **163** P3
Dongara, *W. Austral., Austral.* **191** W2
Dongfang (Basuo), *China* **163** U1
Dongfeng, *China* **162** B12
Donggou, *China* **162** D11
Dongguang, *China* **162** E7
Donghai, *China* **161** J16
Dong Hoi, *Vietnam* **166** K12
Dongkalang, *Indonesia* **169** J13
Dongkan *see* Binhai, *China* **162** H9
Dong Khe, *Vietnam* **166** G12
Dongning, *China* **161** D18
Dongo, *Dem. Rep. of the Congo* **178** J8
Dongola, *Sudan* **178** C12
Dongou, *Congo* **181** K18
Dongping, *China* **162** G7
Dongping, *China* **163** S3
Dongqiao, *China* **160** K7
Dongshan, *China* **163** R7
Dongsheng, *China* **162** D3
Dongtai, *China* **162** J9
Dongting Hu, *China* **162** M4
Dong Ujimqin Qi, *China* **161** D15
Dong Van, *Vietnam* **166** F11
Dongxiang, *China* **163** N6
Dongyztaū, *Kaz.* **154** F8
Doniphan, *Mo., U.S.* **99** V14
Dønna, island, *Nor.* **134** F11
Donnelly, *Idaho, U.S.* **100** F4
Donnellys Crossing, *N.Z.* **193** H18
Donner Pass, *Calif., U.S.* **103** Q6
Donors Hill, *Qnsld., Austral.* **191** R11
Donostia-San Sebastián, *Sp.* **139** N8
Doomadgee, *Qnsld., Austral.* **191** R10
Door Peninsula, *Wis., U.S.* **92** H8
Dora, *Ala., U.S.* **95** J15
Dora, *N. Mex., U.S.* **101** T15
Dora, Lake, *Austral.* **190** F4
Dorah Pass, *Afghan.-Pak.* **156** L9
Dorchester, Cape, *Nunavut, Can.* **77** G17
Dordogne, river, *Fr.* **138** M9
Dori, *Burkina Faso* **180** D11
Dornbirn, *Aust.* **132** K5
Dorohoi, *Rom.* **137** D16
Dorris, *Calif., U.S.* **102** L4
Dortmund, *Ger.* **132** G5
Dörtyol, *Turk.* **148** J11
Dos Bahías, Cabo, *Arg.* **125** S10
Do Shakh, *Afghan.* **156** L6
Dosso, *Niger* **176** J10
Dossor, *Kaz.* **154** F6
Dostyq, *Kaz.* **155** G19
Dothan, *Ala., U.S.* **95** N17
Douala, *Cameroon* **181** J15
Douarnenez, *Fr.* **138** K7
Double Island Point, *Austral.* **190** G15
Double Mountain Fork Brazos, river, *Tex., U.S.* **96** L6
Double Point, *Austral.* **190** D13
Doubtless Bay, *N.Z.* **193** H18
Douentza, *Mali* **176** H8
Douéoulou, *New Caledonia, Fr.* **198** C9
Douglas, *Ariz., U.S.* **101** W9
Douglas, *Ga., U.S.* **91** P7
Douglas, *Mich., U.S.* **92** M9
Douglas, *I. of Man, U.K.* **138** F7
Douglas, *Wyo., U.S.* **100** H13
Douglas Lake, *Tenn., U.S.* **95** E19
Douglass, *Kans., U.S.* **99** U8
Douglasville, *Ga., U.S.* **90** L4
Doura, *Mali* **176** H7
Dourada, Serra, *S. Amer.* **118** G8
Dourados, *Braz.* **122** L11
Douro, river, *Port.-Sp.* **139** P6
Dove Creek, *Colo., U.S.* **101** P10
Dover, *Del., U.S.* **90** C15
Dover, *N.H., U.S.* **89** J15
Dover, *Ohio, U.S.* **93** Q15
Dover, *Eng., U.K.* **138** H9
Dover, Strait of, *Fr.-U.K.* **138** J9
Dover-Foxcroft, *Me., U.S.* **89** E17
Dowagiac, *Mich., U.S.* **93** N9
Dowlatabad, *Afghan.* **156** K4
Dowlatābād, *Iran* **153** G15
Dowlat Yar, *Afghan.* **156** M5
Downey, *Calif., U.S.* **103** X8
Downey, *Idaho, U.S.* **100** J7
Downieville, *Calif., U.S.* **103** P5
Downs, *Kans., U.S.* **99** S6
Dowshi, *Afghan.* **156** L7
Dōzen, island, *Jap.* **165** P7
Drâa, Hamada du, *Alg.* **176** C8
Drâa, Oued, *Alg.-Mor.* **176** C8
Dragon's Mouths, channel, *Trin. & Tobago* **113** P16
Drain, *Oreg., U.S.* **102** H3
Drake, *N. Dak., U.S.* **98** F5
Drakensberg, mountains, *S. Af.* **182** K11
Drake Peak, *Oreg., U.S.* **102** K6
Dráma, *Gr.* **137** J15
Drammen, *Nor.* **134** L11
Dran, *Vietnam* **167** N14
Dras, *India* **156** M13
Drasan, *Pak.* **156** K10
Drau, river, *Aust.* **132** L7
Drava, river, *Eur.* **130** H7
Drayton, *N. Dak., U.S.* **98** E8
Dresden, *Ger.* **132** H7
Drevsjø, *Nor.* **134** J12
Drew, *Miss., U.S.* **94** J10
Drewsey, *Oreg., U.S.* **102** H8
Drews Reservoir, *Oreg., U.S.* **102** L5
Driggs, *Idaho, U.S.* **100** G8
Drina, river, *Bons. and Herzg.-Yug.* **137** G13
Driskill Mountain, *La., U.S.* **94** L7
Drøbak, *Nor.* **134** L11
Drobeta-Turnu Severin, *Rom.* **137** F14
Drogheda, *Ire.* **138** G6
Drohobych, *Ukr.* **132** J11
Drosh, *Pak.* **156** L10
Drovyanoy, *Russ.* **140** E12
Drua, island, *Fiji* **198** G8
Drumheller, *Alta., Can.* **76** M10
Drummond, *Mont., U.S.* **100** D6
Drummond Bay *see* Big Bay, *Vanuatu* **198** E3
Drummond Island, *Mich., U.S.* **92** G12
Drummond Range, *Austral.* **190** F13
Drumright, *Okla., U.S.* **96** F12
Druskininkai, *Lith.* **135** P17
Druya, *Belarus* **133** E13
Drvar, *Bosn. and Herzg.* **136** F11
Dryden, *Ont., Can.* **77** N15
Dryden, *Tex., U.S.* **97** Q4
Drygalski Ice Tongue, *Antarctica* **207** P14
Drygalski Island, *Antarctica* **207** J21
Drygalski Mountains, *Antarctica* **207** B13
Drysdale, river, *Austral.* **190** C6
Dry Tortugas, islands, *U.S.* **79** P18
Dry Tortugas National Park, *Fla., U.S.* **91** Y7
Dschang, *Cameroon* **181** H15
Duaringa, *Qnsld., Austral.* **191** U14
Duarte, Pico, *Dom. Rep.* **111** M18
Ḑubā, *Saudi Arabia* **152** G5
Dubăsari, *Mold.* **133** K14
Dubawnt, river, *N.W.T., Can.* **77** J13
Dubawnt Lake, *N.W.T.-Nunavut, Can.* **77** H13
Dubayy, *U.A.E.* **153** J15
Dubbo, *N.S.W., Austral.* **191** X14
Dublin *see* Baile Átha Cliath, *Ire.* **138** G6
Duvergé, *Dom. Rep.* **111** M17
Dublin, *Ga., U.S.* **90** M7

Dublin, Tex., U.S. 96 M10
Dublon see Tonoas, island, Chuuk, F.S.M. 197 C15
Dubno, Ukr. 132 H12
Du Bois, Pa., U.S. 88 M5
Dubois, Idaho, U.S. 100 G7
Dubois, Wyo., U.S. 100 G9
Dubrovnik, Croatia 136 H12
Dubrovytsya, Ukr. 133 G13
Dubuque, Iowa, U.S. 99 N14
Duc de Gloucester, Îles, Fr. Polynesia, Fr. 199 G19
Duchesne, river, Utah, U.S. 100 L8
Duchesne, Utah, U.S. 100 L8
Duchess, Qnsld., Austral. 191 S11
Ducie Island, Pac. Oc. 195 L16
Duck, river, Tenn., U.S. 95 F15
Duck Hill, Miss., U.S. 94 J11
Ducktown, Tenn., U.S. 95 G18
Ducos, Île, New Caledonia, Fr. 198 D8
Duc Tho, Vietnam 166 J12
Dudinka, Russ. 141 F13
Dudleyville, Ariz., U.S. 101 U8
Dudune, Île, New Caledonia, Fr. 198 D9
Dufek Coast, Antarctica 206 L12
Duffield, N. Terr., Austral. 191 U9
Duff Islands, Santa Cruz Is., Solomon Is. 197 N24
Dufur, Oreg., U.S. 102 F5
Dugi Otok, island, Croatia 136 G11
Dugway, Utah, U.S. 100 L6
Duifken Point, Austral. 190 B12
Duisburg, Ger. 132 G4
Duitama, Col. 120 E6
Dulan (Qagan Us), China 160 J10
Dulce, river, Arg. 124 J11
Dulce, N. Mex., U.S. 101 Q11
Dulce, Golfo, C.R. 109 P19
Dulovo, Bulg. 137 G17
Duluth, Minn., U.S. 98 G12
Dūmā, Syr. 150 J7
Dumai, Indonesia 168 H6
Dumaran, island, Philippines 169 E13
Dumas, Ark., U.S. 94 J9
Dumas, Tex., U.S. 96 F5
Dumbéa, New Caledonia, Fr. 198 E8
Dumfries, Scot., U.K. 138 F7
Dumka, India 158 H11
Dumoga Kecil, Indonesia 169 J15
Dumont d'Urville, station, Antarctica 207 Q18
Dumra, India 158 G10
Dumshaf Plain, Atl. Oc. 216 A13
Dumyât, Egypt 177 C18
Duna (Danube), river, Hung. 132 L9
Dunărea (Danube), river, Bulg.-Rom. 137 G15
Dunav, river, Yug. 137 F13
Dunbar, Qnsld., Austral. 191 Q12
Dunbar, W. Va., U.S. 90 D8
Duncan, Okla., U.S. 96 H10
Duncan Passage, Andaman Is., India 159 Q14
Duncan Town, Bahamas 111 H13
Duncombe Bay, Norfolk I., Austral. 197 F20
Dundalk, Ire. 138 F6
Dundalk, Md., U.S. 90 C13
Dundas, Lake, Austral. 190 K4
Dundas Peninsula, N.W.T., Can. 77 D13
Dundee, Scot., U.K. 138 E8
Dundee Island, Antarctica 206 C4
Dund-Urt, Mongolia 160 D12
Dund-Us, Mongolia 160 D9
Dunedin, Fla., U.S. 91 U7
Dunedin, N.Z. 193 R16
Dunedoo, N.S.W., Austral. 191 X14
Dunes City, Oreg., U.S. 102 H2
Dunfermline, Scot., U.K. 138 E8
Dungarpur, India 158 H4
Dungarvan, Ire. 138 H6
Dungeness, Punta, Arg. 125 W9
Dunhua, China 162 A13
Dunhuang, China 160 G9
Dunkirk, Ind., U.S. 93 Q10
Dunkirk, N.Y., U.S. 88 K4
Dunkwa, Ghana 180 H10
Dunlap, Iowa, U.S. 99 P9
Dunmore, Pa., U.S. 88 M9
Dunmore Town, Bahamas 110 D12
Dunn, N.C., U.S. 90 H12
Dunnellon, Fla., U.S. 91 S7
Dunning, Nebr., U.S. 99 P5
Dunolly, Vic., Austral. 191 Z12
Dunsborough, W. Austral., Austral. 191 Y2
Dunseith, N. Dak., U.S. 98 E5
Dunsmuir, Calif., U.S. 102 M4
Duntroon, N.Z. 193 Q16
Duolun (Dolonnur), China 162 B7
Dupree, S. Dak., U.S. 98 J3
Dupuyer, Mont., U.S. 100 B7
Duqm, Oman 153 M16
Duque de Caxias, Braz. 123 M15
Duque de York, Isla, Chile 125 V6
Duquesne, Pa., U.S. 88 N3
Du Quoin, Ill., U.S. 93 U5
Dura Europus, Syr. 150 G14
Durand, Wis., U.S. 92 J2
Durango, Colo., U.S. 101 P11
Durango, Mex. 108 F9
Durant, Miss., U.S. 94 K11
Durant, Okla., U.S. 96 J12
Durazno, Uru. 124 L14
Durban, S. Af. 182 L11
Dureji, Pak. 157 V6
Durg, India 158 K8
Durham, N.C., U.S. 90 G11
Durham, N.H., U.S. 89 J15
Durham Downs, Qnsld., Austral. 191 V11
Ḑurmā, Saudi Arabia 152 J10
Durmitor, peak, Eur. 130 J8
Durong, Qnsld., Austral. 191 V15
Duroy, Russ. 141 L18
Durrës, Alban. 137 J13
Dursunbey, Turk. 148 E4
Durusu Gölü, Turk. 148 C4
Durūz, Jabal ad, Syr. 150 L8
D'Urville, Tanjung, Indonesia 193 B15
D'Urville Channel, Fiji 198 J7
D'Urville Island, N.Z. 193 M18
Duşak, Turkm. 154 M9
Dûsh, Egypt 177 E18
Dushanbe, Taj. 156 H7
Dushanzi, China 160 E7
Düsseldorf, Ger. 132 G4
Dutch John, Utah, U.S. 100 K9
Dutton, Mount, Utah, U.S. 101 P7
Duyun, China 160 N12
Düzce, Turk. 148 D7
Dvina Bay, Eur. 130 B10
Dwarka, India 158 J1
Dwight, Ill., U.S. 93 P6
Dworshak Reservoir, Idaho, U.S. 100 D4
Dyer, Cape, Nunavut, Can. 77 F19
Dyer Bay, N.W.T., Can. 76 C12
Dyersburg, Tenn., U.S. 94 E12
Dysart, Qnsld., Austral. 191 T14
Dzaanhushuu, Mongolia 160 D11
Dzag, Mongolia 160 D10
Dzangali, Afghan. 157 P6
Dzaoudzi, Mayotte, Fr. 185 P17
Dzavhan, river, Mongolia 160 D9
Dzhagdy, Khrebet, Russ. 141 J19
Dzhankoy, Ukr. 133 L16
Dzhardzhan, Russ. 141 F16
Dzhartyrabot, Taj. 156 J11
Dzhilandy, Taj. 156 J10
Dzhugdzhur, Khrebet, Russ. 141 H20
Dzhunkun, Russ. 141 H16
Dzibilchaltún, ruins, Mex. 109 H16
Džirgatal', Taj. 156 H9
Dzöölön, Mongolia 160 B10
Dzungarian Basin see Junggar Pendi, China 160 E7
Dzungarian Gate, China-Kaz. 160 D6

E

Eads, Colo., U.S. 101 N15
Eagan, Ariz., U.S. 101 T9
Eagle, Alas., U.S. 105 F18
Eagle, Colo., U.S. 100 M11
Eagle Butte, S. Dak., U.S. 98 K4
Eagle Grove, Iowa, U.S. 99 N11
Eagle Harbor, Mich., U.S. 92 D7
Eagle Lake, Calif., U.S. 103 N5
Eagle Lake, Me., U.S. 89 B17
Eagle Lake, Tex., U.S. 97 R12
Eagle Mountain, Minn., U.S. 98 F14
Eagle Mountain, Calif., U.S. 103 X11
Eagle Mountain Lake, Tex., U.S. 96 L11
Eagle Nest Lake, N. Mex., U.S. 101 Q13
Eagle Pass, Tex., U.S. 97 S7
Eagle Peak, Calif., U.S. 102 M6
Eagle Peak, N. Mex., U.S. 101 T10
Eagle Peak, Tex., U.S. 97 W3
Eagle River, Mich., U.S. 92 E7
Eagle River, Wis., U.S. 92 G5
Eagles Mere, Pa., U.S. 88 M8
Earle, Ark., U.S. 94 G11
Earlimart, Calif., U.S. 103 U7
Earlington, Ky., U.S. 95 D14
Earp, Calif., U.S. 103 X13
Earth, Tex., U.S. 96 J4
Easley, S.C., U.S. 90 J7
East Antarctica, Antarctica 207 H16
East Aurora, N.Y., U.S. 88 J5
East Bay, La., U.S. 94 R12
East Caicos, island, Turks and Caicos Is., U.K. 111 H17
East Cape, Asia 146 A12
East Cape, N.Z. 193 K21
East Carbon, Utah, U.S. 100 M8
East Caroline Basin, Pac. Oc. 218 J6
East Channel, Enewetak Atoll, Marshall Is. 196 H9
East Chicago, Ind., U.S. 93 N7
East China Sea, Asia 146 G13
East Coast Bays, N.Z. 193 J19
East Cote Blanche Bay, La., U.S. 94 Q9
East Dubuque, Ill., U.S. 92 M4
East Entrance, Palau 196 L12
Easter Fracture Zone, Pac. Oc. 219 M16
Easter Island see Pascua, Isla de, Pac. Oc. 195 L19
Eastern Channel, Jap. 165 Q3
Eastern Desert, Egypt 177 C18
Eastern Ghats, mountains, India 159 Q6
Eastern Island, Hawaii, U.S. 106 K2
Eastern Sayan Mountains, Asia 146 E9
East Falkland, island, Falk. Is., U.K. 125 W13
East Fayu, island, F.S.M. 196 P6
East Fork Bruneau, river, Idaho, U.S. 100 J4
East Fork White, river, U.S. 79 G16
East Glacier Park, Mont., U.S. 100 B6
East Grand Forks, Minn., U.S. 98 F8
East Helena, Mont., U.S. 100 D7
East Indiaman Ridge, Ind. Oc. 221 L13
East Isaac, island, Bahamas 110 D10
East Jordan, Mich., U.S. 92 H10
East Lake, Mich., U.S. 92 J9
Eastland, Tex., U.S. 96 M9
East Lansing, Mich., U.S. 92 M11
East Liverpool, Ohio, U.S. 93 Q16
East London, S. Af. 182 M10
Eastmain, river, Que., Can. 77 M19
Eastmain, Que., Can. 77 M18
Eastman, Ga., U.S. 91 N6
East Mariana Basin, Pac. Oc. 218 H7
East Millinocket, Me., U.S. 89 D17
East Moline, Ill., U.S. 93 P4
East Novaya Zemlya Trough, Arctic Oc. 223 C13
Easton, Md., U.S. 90 C14
Easton, Pa., U.S. 88 N9
East Orange, N.J., U.S. 88 N11
East Pacific Rise, Pac. Oc. 219 R16
East Pen Island, Ont., Can. 77 L16
East Peoria, Ill., U.S. 93 Q5
East Point, Jaluit Atoll, Marshall Is. 196 M9
East Point, Ga., U.S. 90 L5
Eastpoint, Fla., U.S. 91 R4
Eastport, Me., U.S. 89 E19
East Prairie, Mo., U.S. 99 V16
East Prussia, region, Russ. 140 D4
East Ridge, Tenn., U.S. 95 G17
East Saint Louis, Ill., U.S. 93 T4
East Sea see Japan, Sea of, Asia 146 F13
East Siberian Sea, Russ. 141 C18
East Tasman Plateau, Pac. Oc. 218 Q7
East Tawas, Mich., U.S. 92 J12
East Timor, Asia 169 N14
Eastville, Va., U.S. 90 E14
Eaton, Colo., U.S. 100 L13
Eaton, Ohio, U.S. 93 R11
Eaton Rapids, Mich., U.S. 92 M11
Eatonton, Ga., U.S. 90 L6
Eatonville, Wash., U.S. 102 D4
Eau Claire, Wis., U.S. 92 H3
Eau Claire, Lac à l', Que., Can. 77 L19
Eauripik Atoll, F.S.M. 196 Q4
Eauripik Rise, Pac. Oc. 218 J6
Ebadon, island, Kwajalein Atoll, Marshall Is. 196 K1
Ebagoola, Qnsld., Austral. 191 Q12
Eber Gölü, Turk. 148 F6
Eberswalde, Ger. 132 F7
Ebeye, island, Kwajalein Atoll, Marshall Is. 196 N5
Ebino, Jap. 165 S4
Ebinur Hu, China 160 D6
Ebjapik, island, Kwajalein Atoll, Marshall Is. 196 N5
Eboda see 'Abda, ruins, Israel 151 P5
Ebolowa, Cameroon 181 J16
Ebon Atoll, Marshall Is. 196 J4
Ebro, river, Sp. 139 P8
Ebwaj, island, Kwajalein Atoll, Marshall Is. 196 N5
Eceabat, Turk. 148 D2
Echo, Oreg., U.S. 102 E7
Echo Bay, N.W.T., Can. 76 F11
Echuca, Vic., Austral. 191 Y12
Écija, Sp. 139 S6
Ecuador, S. Amer. 120 J3
Edah, W. Austral., Austral. 191 V3
Edcouch, Tex., U.S. 97 W10
Ed Damer, Sudan 179 D13
Ed Debba, Sudan 178 D12
Eddyville, Ky., U.S. 95 D13
Edéa, Cameroon 181 J15
Eden, N.C., U.S. 90 G10
Eden, Tex., U.S. 97 N7
Eden, Wyo., U.S. 100 J9
Edenburg, S. Af. 182 L10
Edenton, N.C., U.S. 90 G14
Edgar, Nebr., U.S. 99 R7
Edgartown, Mass., U.S. 89 M15
Edgefield, S.C., U.S. 90 L8
Edgeley, N. Dak., U.S. 98 H6
Edgell Island, Nunavut, Can. 77 H20
Edgemont, S. Dak., U.S. 98 M1
Edgerton, Minn., U.S. 98 L9
Edgerton, Wis., U.S. 92 M6
Edgerton, Wyo., U.S. 100 H12
Edgigen, island, Kwajalein Atoll, Marshall Is. 196 K4
Edina, Mo., U.S. 99 R13
Edinburg, Tex., U.S. 97 W10
Edinburgh, Ind., U.S. 93 S9
Edinburgh, Scot., U.K. 138 E8
Edirne (Adrianople), Turk. 148 B3
Edison, Ga., U.S. 91 P4
Edison, N.J., U.S. 88 N10
Edisto, river, S.C., U.S. 90 M9
Edisto Island, S.C., U.S. 90 M10
Edithburgh, S. Austral., Austral. 191 Y10
Edjell, island, Kwajalein Atoll, Marshall Is. 196 K4
Edmond, Okla., U.S. 96 G11
Edmonds, Wash., U.S. 102 B4
Edmonton, Alta., Can. 76 L10
Edmore, N. Dak., U.S. 98 E6
Edmundston, N.B., Can. 77 N21
Edna, Tex., U.S. 97 S12
Edrei see Dar'ā, Syr. 150 L7
Edremit, Turk. 148 E3
Edremit Körfezi, Turk. 148 E3
Edrengiyn Nuruu, Mongolia 160 E10
Eduardo Castex, Arg. 124 M10
Edward, river, Austral. 190 L12
Edward, Lake, Dem. Rep. of the Congo 178 K12
Edward River, Qnsld., Austral. 191 Q12
Edwards, Calif., U.S. 103 W8
Edwards Plateau, Tex., U.S. 97 P7
Edwardsville, Ill., U.S. 93 T4
Edward VIII Bay, Antarctica 207 D20
Edward VII Peninsula, Antarctica 206 N10
Ee, island, Aitutaki Atoll, Cook Is., N.Z. 198 Q12
Eek, Alas., U.S. 104 K12
Eel, river, Calif., U.S. 103 N2
Éfaté (Île Vaté), island, Vanuatu 198 F3
Effigy Mounds National Monument, Iowa, U.S. 98 M14
Effingham, Ill., U.S. 93 S6
Eflâni, Turk. 148 C8
Efuenaarukosu Point, Rota I., N. Mariana Is., U.S. 196 D8
Egan Range, Nev., U.S. 103 Q12
Egegik, Alas., U.S. 105 L14
Eger, Hung. 132 K10
Egeria Fracture Zone, Ind. Oc. 220 K8
Egersund, Nor. 134 M10
Egg Lagoon, Tas., Austral. 191 Y15
Eğil, Turk. 149 G14
Egilsstadir, Ice. 134 F4
Égio, Gr. 137 L14
Egiyn, river, Mongolia 160 C11
Eglinton Fiord, Nunavut, Can. 77 E18
Egmont, Mount see Taranaki, Mount, N.Z. 193 L18
Eğridir, Turk. 148 G6
Eğridir Gölü, Turk. 148 G6
Eğrigöz Dağı, Turk. 148 E5
Egvekinot, Russ. 141 B20
Egypt, Af. 177 D18
Ehrenberg, Ariz., U.S. 101 T4
Ei, Jap. 165 T4
Eiao, island, Fr. Polynesia, Fr. 195 H14
Eickelberg Seamount, Pac. Oc. 219 D14
Eidsvold, Qnsld., Austral. 191 U15
Eight Degree Channel, Maldives 159 S2
Eight Mile Rock, Bahamas 110 C10
Eights Coast, Antarctica 206 J6
Eighty Mile Beach, Austral. 190 E3
Eildon, Lake, Austral. 190 M12
Eil Malk (Macharchar), island, Palau 196 P11
Einasleigh, Qnsld., Austral. 191 R12
Eindhoven, Neth. 138 H11
Eirik Ridge, Atl. Oc. 216 D7
Eirunepé, Braz. 122 F5
Eisenach, Ger. 132 H6
Eita, island, Tarawa, Kiribati 197 G17
Eita, Tarawa, Kiribati 197 G17
Eivissa, Sp. 139 R10
Ejin Horo Qi (Altan Xiret), China 162 D3
Ejin Qi, China 160 F11
Ejmiatsin, Arm. 149 E18
Ekalaka, Mont., U.S. 100 E13
Ekarma, island, Russ. 141 H23
Ekerem, Turkm. 154 L6
Ekiatapskiy Khrebet, Russ. 141 B20
Ekibastuz, Kaz. 155 C15
Ekonda, Russ. 141 G15
Ekström Ice Shelf, Antarctica 206 A11
Ekwan, river, Ont., Can. 77 M17
El Salvador, N. Amer. 75 Q19
Elaia, Cape, Cyprus 148 K9
El Alamein, Egypt 177 C18
Elamanchili, India 158 M9
El'Arîsh (Rhinocolura), Egypt 151 N3
Elat, Israel 151 R5
Elath see Ezion-geber, ruins, Jordan 151 R5
Elato Atoll, F.S.M. 196 Q4
El'Auja see Nizzana, Israel 151 P4
Elâzığ, Turk. 149 G14
Elba, island, It. 136 G8
Elba, Ala., U.S. 95 M16
Elba, Cape (Ras Hadarba), Af. 174 F10

El Banco, Col. 120 C5
Elbasan, Alban. 137 J13
El Baúl, Venez. 120 C9
El Bayadh, Alg. 176 B10
Elbe, river, Ger. 132 F6
Elbert, Mount, Colo., U.S. 100 M12
Elberta, Mich., U.S. 92 J9
Elberton, Ga., U.S. 90 K7
Elbistan, Turk. 148 G12
Elbląg, Pol. 132 F10
Elbow Cays, Bahamas 110 F8
Elbow Lake, Minn., U.S. 98 H9
El'brus, peak, Eur. 130 H13
El Bureij, Gaza Strip 151 N4
Elburz Mountains see Reshteh-ye Alborz, Iran 152 B11
El Cajon, Calif., U.S. 103 Z10
El Calafate (Lago Argentino), Arg. 125 V7
El Callao, Venez. 120 D12
El Calvario, Venez. 120 C9
El Campo, Tex., U.S. 97 R12
El Carmen, Arg. 124 E9
El Ceibo, Guatemala 109 K15
El Ceibo, Mex. 109 H16
El Centro, Calif., U.S. 103 Z11
El Cerro, Bol. 122 K9
Elchi see Wādī Mūsá, Jordan 151 Q6
El Cuyo, Mex. 109 H17
Elda, Sp. 139 R9
El'dikan, Russ. 141 G19
El Djouf, desert, Mali-Mauritania 176 F7
Eldon, Iowa, U.S. 99 Q13
Eldon, Mo., U.S. 99 T12
Eldora, Iowa, U.S. 99 N12
El Dorado, Ark., U.S. 94 K8
El Dorado, Kans., U.S. 99 U8
El Dorado, Venez. 120 D12
Eldorado, Arg. 124 G15
Eldorado, Ill., U.S. 93 U6
Eldorado, Mex. 108 F8
Eldorado, Okla., U.S. 96 H8
Eldorado, Tex., U.S. 97 P6
El Dorado Springs, Mo., U.S. 99 U11
Eldoret, Kenya 179 J14
Electra, Tex., U.S. 96 J9
Electric Mills, Miss., U.S. 95 K13
Elephant Butte Reservoir, N. Mex., U.S. 101 U11
Elephant Island, Antarctica 206 B3
Eleşkirt, Turk. 149 E17
Eleuthera Island, Bahamas 111 E13
El Faiyûm, Egypt 177 C18
El Fasher, Sudan 178 E11
El Fifi, Sudan 178 F10
Elfrida, Ariz., U.S. 101 W9
El Fuerte, Mex. 108 E8
El Galpón, Arg. 124 F10
El Gassi, Alg. 176 C11
El Gezira, region, Af. 174 G9
Elgin, Ill., U.S. 93 N6
Elgin, N. Dak., U.S. 98 H3
Elgin, Nebr., U.S. 99 N7
Elgin, Nev., U.S. 103 S12
Elgin, Oreg., U.S. 102 F8
Elgin, Tex., U.S. 97 Q11
Elgin, Scot., U.K. 138 D8
El Gîza, Egypt 177 C18
El Golea, Alg. 176 C11
Elgon, Mount, Af. 174 J9
El Hadjira, Alg. 176 B11
El Hobra, Alg. 176 C11
El Homeur, Alg. 176 C10
Eliase, Indonesia 193 D14
Elida, N. Mex., U.S. 101 T15
Elim, Alas., U.S. 104 G12
El Iskandarîya (Alexandria), Egypt 177 C18
Elista, Russ. 140 J5
Elizabeth, La., U.S. 94 N7
Elizabeth, N.J., U.S. 88 N11
Elizabeth, Cape, Me., U.S. 89 H16
Elizabeth City, N.C., U.S. 90 G14
Elizabeth Island, Jaluit Atoll, Marshall Is. 196 M8
Elizabethton, Tenn., U.S. 95 E20
Elizabethtown, Ky., U.S. 95 C16
Elizabethtown, N.C., U.S. 90 J12
El Jadida (Mazagan), Mor. 176 B8
Ełk, Pol. 132 F11
Elk, river, W. Va., U.S. 90 D9
Elk, Calif., U.S. 103 Q2
Elkader, Iowa, U.S. 98 M13
Elk City, Idaho, U.S. 100 E4
Elk City, Okla., U.S. 96 G8
Elkedra, N. Terr., Austral. 191 S9
El Kef, Tun. 176 A12
Ēl Kerē, Eth. 179 H16
El Khandaq, Sudan 178 D12
El Khârga, Egypt 177 E18
Elkhart, Ind., U.S. 93 N9
Elkhart, Kans., U.S. 99 V3
Elkhorn, river, Nebr., U.S. 99 N6
Elkhorn, river, U.S. 78 F12
Elkhorn City, Ky., U.S. 95 C20
Elkhorn Ranch Site, Theodore Roosevelt National Park, N. Dak., U.S. 98 F2
Elkhovo, Bulg. 137 H16
Elkin, N.C., U.S. 90 G9
Elkins, N. Mex., U.S. 101 T14
Elkins, W. Va., U.S. 90 D10
Elkland, Pa., U.S. 88 L7
Elk Mountain, N. Mex., U.S. 101 R13
Elk Mountain, Wyo., U.S. 100 K12
Elko, Nev., U.S. 102 M11
Elk Point, S. Dak., U.S. 99 N8
Elk River, Idaho, U.S. 100 D4
Elk River, Minn., U.S. 98 J11
Elkton, Ky., U.S. 95 D15
Elkton, Md., U.S. 90 B14
El Kûbri, Egypt 151 Q1
El Kuntilla, Egypt 151 Q4
Elle, island, Enewetak Atoll, Marshall Is. 196 G8
Ellef Ringnes Island, Nunavut, Can. 77 B14
Ellen, Mount, Utah, U.S. 101 P8
Ellendale, N. Dak., U.S. 98 H6
Ellensburg, Wash., U.S. 102 D6
Ellep, island, Kwajalein Atoll, Marshall Is. 196 M5
Ellep Passage, Kwajalein Atoll, Marshall Is. 196 L5
Ellesmere, Lake, N.Z. 193 P17
Ellesmere Island, Nunavut, Can. 77 C16
Ellijay, Ga., U.S. 90 J5
Ellington, Mo., U.S. 99 U14
Ellinwood, Kans., U.S. 99 T6
Elliot Lake, Ont., Can. 77 P17
Elliott, N. Terr., Austral. 191 R8
Elliott Key, Fla., U.S. 91 X10
Ellis, Idaho, U.S. 100 F5
Ellis, Kans., U.S. 99 S5
Ellisburg, N.Y., U.S. 88 H8
Elliston, S. Austral., Austral. 191 X9
Ellisville, Miss., U.S. 94 M12
Ellsworth, Kans., U.S. 99 T7
Ellsworth, Me., U.S. 89 F18
Ellsworth Land, Antarctica 206 J6
Ellsworth Mountains, Antarctica 206 J8
Elma, Wash., U.S. 102 D3
El Macao, Dom. Rep. 111 M20
Elma Dağı, Turk. 148 E8
Elmadağı, Turk. 148 E8
El Maitén, Arg. 125 R7
Elmalı, Turk. 148 H5
El Malpais National Monument, N. Mex., U.S. 101 S10
El Mazâr, Egypt 151 N3
Elm Creek, Tex., U.S. 97 S7
Elm Creek, Nebr., U.S. 99 Q5
El Milagro, Arg. 124 J9
El Minya, Egypt 177 D18
Elmira, N.Y., U.S. 88 L7
El Morro National Monument, N. Mex., U.S. 101 S10
El Mreyyé, region, Mauritania 176 G8
El Nido, Philippines 169 E13
El Obeid (Al Ubayyiḍ), Sudan 178 E12
El Odaiya, Sudan 178 F11
Elorza, Venez. 120 D8
El Oued, Alg. 176 B12
El Palito, Venez. 120 B9
El Pao, Venez. 120 C12
El Paso, Ill., U.S. 93 Q6
El Paso, Tex., U.S. 97 U1
El Portal, Calif., U.S. 103 S6
El Qâhira (Cairo), Egypt 177 C18
El Qanṭara, Egypt 151 P1
El Qaṣr, Egypt 177 E18
El Quṣeima, Egypt 151 P4
El Quneitra see Al Qunayṭirah, Syr. 150 K6
El Reno, Okla., U.S. 96 G10
El Rito, N. Mex., U.S. 101 Q12
El Rosario, Mex. 108 C5
Elroy, Wis., U.S. 92 K4
Elsa, Tex., U.S. 97 W10
El Salto, Mex. 108 F9
El Salvador, N. Amer. 109 M16
Elsberry, Mo., U.S. 99 S14
El Seibo, Dom. Rep. 111 M20
El Sharana, N. Terr., Austral. 191 P8
Elsinore, Utah, U.S. 101 N7
El Sombrero, Venez. 120 C9
El Suweis (Suez), Egypt 151 Q1
Eltanin Bay, Antarctica 206 H6
Eltanin Fracture Zone, Pac. Oc. 219 R13
Eltham, N.Z. 193 L18
El Thamad, Egypt 151 R4
El Tigre, Venez. 120 C11
El Tofo, Chile 124 H6
Eltopia, Wash., U.S. 102 D7
El Ṭûr, Egypt 151 T3
El Turbio, Arg. 125 W7
Eluru, India 158 M8
Elvas, Port. 139 R5
El Vendrell, Sp. 139 Q10
Elverum, Nor. 134 K11
El Wak, Kenya 179 J15
Elwell, Lake, Mont., U.S. 100 B8
Elwood, Ind., U.S. 93 Q9
Elwood, Mo., U.S. 99 R10
Elwood, Nebr., U.S. 99 Q5
Elx (Elche), Sp. 139 S9
Ely, Minn., U.S. 98 F12
Ely, Nev., U.S. 103 Q12
Elyria, Ohio, U.S. 93 P14
El Yunque (Anvil), peak, Cuba 111 K14
Émaé, island, Vanuatu 198 E3
Emam Saheb, Afghan. 156 K7
Émao, island, Vanuatu 198 F3
Emba, Kaz. 154 E9
Embarcación, Arg. 124 E10
Embetsu, Jap. 164 E13
Emden, Ger. 132 F5
Emerald, Qnsld., Austral. 191 T14
Emerald Basin, Pac. Oc. 218 R8
Emerald Island, N.W.T., Can. 77 C13
Emery, Utah, U.S. 101 N8
Emet, Turk. 148 E5
Emidj, island, Jaluit Atoll, Marshall Is. 196 M9
Emigrant Pass, Nev., U.S. 103 N10
Emi Koussi, peak, Af. 174 F7
Emily, Minn., U.S. 98 G11
Emin, China 160 D6
Emirau, island, P.N.G. 193 B20
Emirdağ, Turk. 148 F6
Emir Dağları, Turk. 148 F6
Emita, Tas., Austral. 191 Y16
Emmaus, Pa., U.S. 88 N9
Emmetsburg, Iowa, U.S. 98 M10
Emmett, Idaho, U.S. 100 G3
Emmonak, Alas., U.S. 104 H11
Emory Peak, Tex., U.S. 97 R3
Empedrado, Arg. 124 G13
Emperor Trough, Pac. Oc. 218 D9
Empire, Mich., U.S. 92 J9
Emporia, Kans., U.S. 99 T9
Emporia, Va., U.S. 90 F13
Emporium, Pa., U.S. 88 L5
Empress Augusta Bay, P.N.G. 197 K14
Emu Park, Qnsld., Austral. 191 T15
Ena, Jap. 165 P10
'En Boqeq, Israel 151 N6
Encampment, Wyo., U.S. 100 K11
Encarnación, Para. 122 N10
Encinal, Tex., U.S. 97 T8
Encinitas, Calif., U.S. 103 Y9
Encino, N. Mex., U.S. 101 S13
Encino, Tex., U.S. 97 V10
Encontrados, Venez. 120 C6
Encounter Bay, Austral. 190 L10
Ende, Indonesia 169 M14
Endeavour Hill, Austral. 190 C7
Endeavour Strait, Austral. 190 A12
Enderbury Island, Kiribati 194 G10
Enderby Land, Antarctica 207 C18
Enderby Plain, Southern Oc. 225 E14
Enderlin, N. Dak., U.S. 98 G7
Endicott, N.Y., U.S. 88 L8
Endicott Mountains, Alas., U.S. 105 D15
Eneeldak, island, Jaluit Atoll, Marshall Is. 196 N8
Enengeseiru, island, Chuuk, F.S.M. 197 C14
Enengonomei, island, Chuuk, F.S.M. 197 C14
Enewetak (Eniwetok), island, Enewetak Atoll, Marshall Is. 196 J8
Enewetak Atoll, Marshall Is. 196 F1
Enewetak Lagoon, Enewetak Atoll, Marshall Is. 196 H8
Enez, Turk. 148 C2
Enfer, Pointe d', Martinique, Fr. 113 K17
Enfield, N.C., U.S. 90 G13
Engaño, Cabo, Dom. Rep. 111 M21
Engaru, Jap. 164 E15
Engelhard, N.C., U.S. 90 H15
Engels, Russ. 140 H6
Engenenimo, island, Chuuk, F.S.M. 197 C16
Enggano, island, Indonesia 168 L6
England, U.K. 138 G9
England, Ark., U.S. 94 H9
Englewood, Colo., U.S. 100 M13
Englewood, Fla., U.S. 91 V7
Englewood, Kans., U.S. 99 V5
English Channel, Eur. 130 F4
English Coast, Antarctica 206 G6
English Harbor, Tabuaeran, Kiribati 197 B20
English Roads, channel, Tonga 198 J12
Enid, Okla., U.S. 96 E10
Enigu, island, Majuro Atoll, Marshall Is. 196 G11
Eniwa, Jap. 164 G13
Eniwetak, island, Kwajalein Atoll, Marshall Is. 196 M5
Eniwetak Passage, Kwajalein Atoll, Marshall Is. 196 M6
Eniwetok see Enewetak, island, Enewetak Atoll, Marshall Is. 196 J8
Enjebi, island, Enewetak Atoll, Marshall Is. 196 G8
Enna, It. 136 L10
En Nahud, Sudan 178 F11
Ennedi, plateau, Chad 177 G16
Enngonia, N.S.W., Austral. 191 W13
Enning, S. Dak., U.S. 98 K2
Ennis, Mont., U.S. 100 E7
Ennis, Tex., U.S. 96 M12
Ennuebing, island, Kwajalein Atoll, Marshall Is. 196 K4
Ennugarret, island, Kwajalein Atoll, Marshall Is. 196 K4
Ennugenliggelap, island, Kwajalein Atoll, Marshall Is. 196 M4
Ennumennet, island, Kwajalein Atoll, Marshall Is. 196 K4
Ennumet, island, Kwajalein Atoll, Marshall Is. 196 L3
Ennylabegan, island, Kwajalein Atoll, Marshall Is. 196 N5
Enontekiö, Fin. 135 D14
Enriquillo, Dom. Rep. 111 N18
Enriquillo, Lago, Dom. Rep. 111 M17
Enschede, Neth. 138 G12
Ensenada, Mex. 108 B5
Enshi, China 162 L2
Enterprise, Ala., U.S. 95 N16
Enterprise, Miss., U.S. 95 L13
Enterprise, Oreg., U.S. 102 F9
Enterprise, Utah, U.S. 101 P5
Entrada, Punta, Arg. 125 V9
Entre Ríos, region, S. Amer. 118 K6
Enugu, Nig. 181 H14
Enumclaw, Wash., U.S. 102 C4
Enurmino, Russ. 141 A20
Envira, Braz. 122 F5
'En Yahav, Israel 151 P5
Enybor, island, Jaluit Atoll, Marshall Is. 196 M8
Eo, Îlot, New Caledonia, Fr. 198 C8
Eori, Bioko, Eq. Guinea 184 N7
Eot, island, Chuuk, F.S.M. 197 B15
Eparit, island, Chuuk, F.S.M. 197 A15
Eparit, Mochun, Chuuk, F.S.M. 197 A15
Epéna, Congo 181 K18
Epeti, Roches, Ua Huka, Fr. Polynesia, Fr. 199 M23
Ephesus, ruins, Turk. 148 G3
Ephraim, Utah, U.S. 100 M7
Ephrata, Wash., U.S. 102 C7
Epi, island, Vanuatu 198 E3
Épinal, Fr. 138 K12
Episkopi, Cyprus 148 L8
Episkopi Bay, Cyprus 148 L8
Epsilon, Qnsld., Austral. 191 V11
Epukiro, Namibia 182 H7
Epu Pel, Arg. 125 N10
Equatorial Channel, Maldives 159 X3
Equatorial Guinea, Af. 181 J14
Erbaa, Turk. 148 D11
Erçek, Turk. 149 G18
Erçek Gölü, Turk. 149 F18
Erciş, Turk. 149 F17
Erciyeş Dağı, Turk. 148 G10
Erdek, Turk. 148 D4
Erdemli, Turk. 148 J9
Ere, island, Kwajalein Atoll, Marshall Is. 196 L3
Erebus, Mount, Antarctica 207 N13
Ereğli, Turk. 148 C7
Ereğli, Turk. 148 H9
Erenhot, China 162 A4
Erexim, Braz. 122 N12
Ereymentaū, Kaz. 155 C14
Erfoud, Mor. 176 C9
Erfurt, Ger. 132 H6
Ergani, Turk. 149 G14
Ergedzhey, Russ. 141 H17
Ergene, river, Turk. 148 C4
Ergun, river, China 161 B15
Ergun Youqi, China 161 B15
Ergun Zuoqi, China 161 B15
Er Hai, lake, China 160 N10
Erick, Okla., U.S. 96 G7
Erie, Pa., U.S. 88 K3
Erie, Lake, Can.-U.S. 79 F18
Erigavo see Ceerigaabo, Somalia 179 F17
Erikub Atoll, Marshall Is. 196 G5
Erimi, Cyprus 148 L8
Erimo, Jap. 164 G15
Erimo Misaki, Jap. 164 H15
Erin, Tenn., U.S. 95 E14
Eritrea, Af. 179 D14
Erkilet, Turk. 148 F10
Erlanger, Ky., U.S. 95 A17
Erldunda, N. Terr., Austral. 191 U8
Erling, Lake, Ark., U.S. 94 K7
Ermenek, Turk. 148 J8
Ermoúpoli, Gr. 137 L16
Ernabella, S. Austral., Austral. 191 U8
Ernakulam, India 159 R5
Erode, India 159 Q6
Eroj, island, Majuro Atoll, Marshall Is. 196 G11
Eromanga, Qnsld., Austral. 191 U12
Er Rachidia, Mor. 176 B9
Er Rahad, Sudan 178 E12
Er Rif, Af. 174 C3
Erris Head, Ire. 138 F5
Erromango, island, Vanuatu 198 G3
Error Tablemount, Ind. Oc. 220 E6
Erskine, Minn., U.S. 98 F9
Ertai, China 160 D8
Ertis, Kaz. 155 B15
Ertis (Irtysh), river, Kaz. 155 C16
Ertix, river, China 160 D8
Eru, island, Kwajalein Atoll, Marshall Is. 196 L3
Eruh, Turk. 149 H16

Erwin, N.C., U.S. **90** H11
Erwin, Tenn., U.S. **95** E20
Erzin, Russ. **141** M13
Erzincan, Turk. **149** E14
Erzurum, Turk. **149** E16
Esan Misaki, Jap. **164** H13
Esashi, Jap. **164** E14
Esashi, Jap. **164** H12
Esbjerg, Den. **134** P11
Escalante, river, Utah, U.S. **101** P8
Escalante, Utah, U.S. **101** P7
Escambia, river, Fla., U.S. **91** Q1
Escanaba, river, Mich., U.S. **92** F7
Escanaba, Mich., U.S. **92** G8
Escárcego, Mex. **109** J15
Esch, Lux. **138** J11
Escocesa, Bahía, Dom. Rep. **111** L19
Escondido, Calif., U.S. **103** Y10
Escuinapa, Mex. **108** G9
Escuintla, Guatemala **109** L15
Escuintla, Mex. **109** L15
Eséka, Cameroon **181** J15
Esenguly, Turkm. **154** M6
Eşfahān, Iran **153** E13
Esfandak, Iran **153** H18
Eshkamesh, Afghan. **156** K8
Eshkashem, Afghan. **156** K9
Esil, river, Kaz. **154** B12
Esil, Kaz. **154** C12
Esker, Nfld., Can. **77** L20
Eskifjördur, Ice. **134** F4
Eskilstuna, Sw. **135** L13
Eskimo Lakes, N.W.T., Can. **76** E10
Eskipazar, Turk. **148** D8
Eskişehir, Turk. **148** E6
Esla, river, Sp. **139** P6
Eslāmābād, Iran **152** D10
Eslam Qal'eh, Afghan. **156** M1
Eşler Dağı, Turk. **148** G5
Eşme, Turk. **148** F4
Esmeralda, Qnsld., Austral. **191** R12
Esmeralda, Cuba **110** H10
Esmeralda, Isla, Chile **125** V6
Esmeraldas, Ecua. **120** H2
Esmeraldas, Río, Ecua. **120** H2
Espakeh, Iran **153** H17
Espanola, N. Mex., U.S. **101** R12
Esperance, W. Austral., Austral. **191** X4
Esperance, Cape, Solomon Is. **197** N18
Esperanza, station, Antarctica **206** C4
Esperanza, Arg. **124** J12
Esperanza, Mex. **108** D7
Esperanza, Peru **122** G5
Espiègle Bay, Vanuatu **198** D1
Espigão Mestre, mountains, S. Amer. **118** G9
Espinhaço, Serra do, Braz. **123** K15
Espiritu Santo, island, Vanuatu **198** C2
Espíritu Santo, Isla, Mex. **108** F7
Espungabera, Mozambique **182** G12
Esquel, Arg. **125** R7
Esquina, Arg. **124** J12
Essaouira, Mor. **176** B7
Essen, Ger. **132** G4
Essendon, Mount, Austral. **190** G4
Essequibo, river, Guyana **121** E14
Essexville, Mich., U.S. **92** K12
Essington, Port, Austral. **190** A8
Esso, Russ. **141** F22
Es Suki, Sudan **179** E13
Estacado, Llano, Tex., U.S. **96** J4
Estados, Isla de los (Staten Island), Arg. **125** Y10
Eşţahbānāt, Iran **153** G14
Estância, Braz. **123** H17
Estancia, N. Mex., U.S. **101** S12
Este, Punta del, S. Amer. **118** M7
Estelí, Nicar. **109** M18
Estelline, S. Dak., U.S. **98** K8
Estelline, Tex., U.S. **96** H7
Estepona, Sp. **139** T6
Estes Park, Colo., U.S. **100** L13
Estevan, Sask., Can. **76** N12
Estherville, Iowa, U.S. **98** M10
Estill, S.C., U.S. **90** M9
Estonia, Eur. **135** L16
Estrella Bay, Solomon Is. **197** M18
Estremoz, Port. **139** R5
Etadunna, S. Austral., Austral. **191** V10
Etal Atoll, F.S.M. **196** Q7
Étang-Sale, Réunion, Fr. **185** H15
Étarik see Monument, island, Vanuatu **198** E3
Etawah, India **158** G7
Etcharai, island, Kwajalein Atoll, Marshall Is. **196** K2
Etena, Swains I., Amer. Samoa, U.S. **198** R4
Ethiopia, Af. **179** G15
Ethiopian Highlands, Af. **174** H10
Etna, peak, It. **136** L10
Etna, Wyo., U.S. **100** H8
Etorofu see Iturup, island, Russ. **141** J23
Etosha Pan, Namibia **182** F6
Etoumbi, Congo **181** L17
Etowah, Tenn., U.S. **95** F18
Etrek see Atrak, river, Iran **153** B14
Etrek, river, Turkm. **154** M6
Etten, island, Chuuk, F.S.M. **197** B16
Etten, island, Chuuk, F.S.M. **197** C15
Ettrick, N.Z. **193** Q16
'Eua, island, Tonga **194** K10
'Eua, island, Tonga **198** K12
'Euaiki, island, Tongatapu, Tonga **198** H12
'Euaiki, island, Vava'u Group, Tonga **198** M11
'Euakafa, island, Vava'u Group, Tonga **198** M11
Euboea see Évia, island, Gr. **137** K15
Eucla Basin, Austral. **190** K5
Eucla Motel, W. Austral., Austral. **191** W7
Euclid, Ohio, U.S. **93** N14
Eucumbene, Lake, Austral. **190** L13
Eudora, Ark., U.S. **94** K9
Eudunda, S. Austral., Austral. **191** X10
Eufaula, Ala., U.S. **95** M17
Eufaula, Okla., U.S. **96** G13
Eufaula Lake, Okla., U.S. **96** G13
Eugene, Oreg., U.S. **102** H3
Eugenio Bustos, Arg. **124** L8
Euginia, Punta, Mex. **108** D5
Eunice, La., U.S. **94** P8
Eunice, N. Mex., U.S. **101** V15
Euphrates, river, Asia **146** F3
Eupora, Miss., U.S. **94** J12
Eurardy, W. Austral., Austral. **191** V2
Eureka, Calif., U.S. **102** M1
Eureka, Ill., U.S. **93** Q5
Eureka, Kans., U.S. **99** U9
Eureka, Mont., U.S. **100** A5
Eureka, Nev., U.S. **103** P11
Eureka, Nunavut, Can. **77** B15
Eureka, S. Dak., U.S. **98** J5
Eureka, Utah, U.S. **100** L7
Eureka Springs, Ark., U.S. **94** E7
Europa, Picos D', Sp. **139** N7
Europa, Île, Mozambique Channel **184** H8
Eustis, Fla., U.S. **91** S8
Eutaw, Ala., U.S. **95** K14
Eva Downs, N. Terr., Austral. **191** R9
Evans, Mount, Mont., U.S. **100** E6
Evanston, Ill., U.S. **93** N7
Evanston, Wyo., U.S. **100** K8
Evansville, Alas., U.S. **105** E15
Evansville, Ind., U.S. **93** U7
Evansville, Wyo., U.S. **100** H12
Evart, Mich., U.S. **92** K10
Eveleth, Minn., U.S. **98** F12
Evensk, Russ. **141** E21
Everard, Lake, Austral. **190** J9
Everard Park, S. Austral., Austral. **191** V8
Everest, Mount, Asia **146** H8
Everett, Wash., U.S. **102** B4
Everglades City, Fla., U.S. **91** X9
Everglades National Park, Fla., U.S. **91** X9
Evergreen, Ala., U.S. **95** M15
Évia (Euboea), island, Gr. **137** K15
Évora, Port. **139** R5
Évreux, Fr. **138** K9
Évros, river, Gr.-Turk. **148** B3
Ewa, Nauru **197** E23
Ewa, Hawaii, U.S. **106** E10
Ewab see Kai, Kepulauan, island, Indonesia **169** L18
Ewaninga, N. Terr., Austral. **191** T8
Ewing, Nebr., U.S. **99** N6
Ewo, Congo **181** L17
Excelsior Springs, Mo., U.S. **99** S11
Executive Committee Range, Antarctica **206** M8
Exeter, Calif., U.S. **103** U7
Exeter, N.H., U.S. **89** J15
Exeter, Eng., U.K. **138** J7
Exeter Sound, Nunavut, Can. **77** F19
Exmouth, W. Austral., Austral. **191** T1
Exmouth Gulf, Austral. **190** F1
Exmouth Plateau, Ind. Oc. **221** K15
Exploring Balavu Isles, Fiji **198** H9
Exu, Braz. **123** F16
Exuma Sound, Bahamas **110** E12
Eyl, river, Somalia **179** G17
Eyl, Somalia **179** G18
Eyrarbakki, Ice. **134** F2
Eyre, Lake, Austral. **190** H10
Eyre North, Lake, Austral. **190** H10
Eyre Peninsula, Austral. **190** K9
Eyre South, Lake, Austral. **190** H10
Eysturoy, island, Faroe Is., Den. **134** J6
Ezequiel Ramos Mexia, Embalse, Arg. **125** P8
Ezine, Turk. **148** E2
Ezion-geber (Elath), ruins, Jordan **151** R5

F

Faaa, Tahiti, Fr. Polynesia, Fr. **199** N15
Faaaha, Tahaa, Fr. Polynesia, Fr. **199** A23
Faaite, island, Fr. Polynesia, Fr. **199** E18
Faanui, Bora-Bora, Fr. Polynesia, Fr. **199** K14
Faanui, Baie de, Bora-Bora, Fr. Polynesia, Fr. **199** K14
Faaone, Tahiti, Fr. Polynesia, Fr. **199** P17
Faaroa, Baie de, Raiatea, Fr. Polynesia, Fr. **199** B23
Fabala, Guinea **180** F7
Fabens, Tex., U.S. **97** V2
Faber Lake, N.W.T., Can. **76** G11
Facatativá, Col. **120** F5
Fachi, Niger **177** G13
Facho, Pico do, Madeira Is., Port. **184** L5
Facpi Point, Guam, U.S. **196** D9
Fada, Chad **177** G16
Fada N'Gourma, Burkina Faso **180** E11
Faddeyevskiy, Ostrov, Russ. **141** C17
Fadghamī, Syr. **150** E14
Fadian Point, Guam, U.S. **196** C11
Fadiffolu Atoll, Maldives **159** U3
Fafa, island, Tongatapu, Tonga **198** H11
Fagaitua, Tutuila, Amer. Samoa, U.S. **198** M8
Fagaitua Bay, Tutuila, Amer. Samoa, U.S. **198** M8
Fagaloa Bay, Samoa **198** L4
Fagamalo, Samoa **198** K2
Fagamalo, Tutuila, Amer. Samoa, U.S. **198** M6
Făgăraş, Rom. **137** E15
Fagasa, Tutuila, Amer. Samoa, U.S. **198** M7
Fagatele Bay, Tutuila, Amer. Samoa, U.S. **198** N7
Fagatogo, Tutuila, Amer. Samoa, U.S. **198** M7
Fagernes, Nor. **134** K11
Fagnano, Lago, Chile **125** Y8
Faguibine, Lake, Af. **174** G3
Fagurhólsmýri, Ice. **134** G3
Fahala, island, Maldives **159** V3
Fahefa, Tongatapu, Tonga **198** H10
Fahraj, Iran **153** G16
Faibus Point, Tinian, N. Mariana Is., U.S. **196** B7
Faichuk, islands, Chuuk, F.S.M. **197** B14
Faie, Huahine, Fr. Polynesia, Fr. **199** G14
Faie, Baie de, Huahine, Fr. Polynesia, Fr. **199** G14
Faihava Passage, Vava'u Group, Tonga **198** L11
Faioa, island, Vava'u Group, Tonga **198** L12
Faïoa, island, Wallis and Futuna, Fr. **198** C11
Fairacres, N. Mex., U.S. **101** V12
Fairbanks, Alas., U.S. **105** F16
Fairborn, Ohio, U.S. **93** R12
Fairburn, Ga., U.S. **90** L5
Fairbury, Ill., U.S. **93** Q6
Fairbury, Nebr., U.S. **99** R8
Fairfax, Okla., U.S. **96** E11
Fairfax, S.C., U.S. **90** M9
Fairfield, Ala., U.S. **95** J15
Fairfield, Calif., U.S. **103** R4
Fairfield, Idaho, U.S. **100** H5
Fairfield, Ill., U.S. **93** T6
Fairfield, Iowa, U.S. **99** Q13
Fairfield, Mont., U.S. **100** C7
Fairfield, Ohio, U.S. **93** S11
Fairfield, Tex., U.S. **97** N13
Fair Haven, Vt., U.S. **88** H12
Fairhope, Ala., U.S. **95** P14
Fair Isle, Scot., U.K. **138** C8
Fairmont, Minn., U.S. **98** L10
Fairmont, W. Va., U.S. **90** C9
Fairport, Mich., U.S. **92** G8
Fairport, N.Y., U.S. **88** J7
Fairview, Qnsld., Austral. **191** Q12
Fairview, Mont., U.S. **100** B13
Fairview, Okla., U.S. **96** F9
Fairview, Tenn., U.S. **95** E15
Fairview, Utah, U.S. **100** M7
Fairweather, Mount, Alas., U.S. **105** K21
Fais, island, F.S.M. **194** F3
Faisalabad, Pak. **157** Q11
Faith, S. Dak., U.S. **98** J3
Faizabad, India **158** G8
Fajardo, P.R., U.S. **111** M23
Fakahiku, island, Ha'apai Group, Tonga **198** Q6
Fakahina, island, Fr. Polynesia, Fr. **199** E20
Fakakakai, Ha'apai Group, Tonga **198** P7
Fakaofu, island, Kiribati **194** H10
Fakarava, island, Fr. Polynesia, Fr. **199** E18
Fakfak, Indonesia **169** K18
Faku, China **162** B11
Fala Ane Point, Swains I., Amer. Samoa, U.S. **198** Q3
Falamae, Solomon Is. **197** L14
Falcon, Cape, Oreg., U.S. **102** E2
Falconer, N.Y., U.S. **88** K4
Falcon Lake, Tex., U.S. **97** V8
Falealupo, Samoa **198** K1
Faleasao, Manua Is., Amer. Samoa, U.S. **198** P3
Falefatu, island, Funafuti, Tuvalu **197** L23
Falelatie, Samoa **198** L3
Falelima, Samoa **198** K1
Falémé, river, Mali-Senegal **176** H6
Faleniu, Tutuila, Amer. Samoa, U.S. **198** M7
Falfurrias, Tex., U.S. **97** V10
Falkenberg, Sw. **134** N12
Falkland Escarpment, Atl. Oc. **217** V6
Falkland Islands (Islas Malvinas), Falk. Is., U.K. **125** X12
Falkland Plateau, Atl. Oc. **217** V6
Falkland Sound, Falk. Is., U.K. **125** W12
Falköping, Sw. **134** M12
Fallbrook, Calif., U.S. **103** Y9
Fallières Coast, Antarctica **206** E5
Fallon, Nev., U.S. **103** P7
Fall River, Mass., U.S. **89** L15
Fall River Lake, Kans., U.S. **99** U9
Fall River Mills, Calif., U.S. **102** M4
Falls City, Nebr., U.S. **99** R9
Falls City, Oreg., U.S. **102** G2
Falmouth, Antigua **113** G16
Falmouth, Jam. **110** M11
Falmouth, Ky., U.S. **95** A18
Falmouth, Me., U.S. **89** H16
Falmouth, Eng., U.K. **138** J7
False Bay, Af. **174** R7
False Cape, N. Amer. **74** N3
False Divi Point, India **159** N8
False Pass, Alas., U.S. **104** P11
False Point, India **158** K11
Falso, Cabo, Dom. Rep. **111** N17
Falso, Cabo, Mex. **108** G7
Falster, island, Den. **134** P12
Fălticeni, Rom. **137** D16
Falun, Sw. **135** K13
Famagusta see Ammochostos, Cyprus **148** L9
Fanaik, island, Chuuk, F.S.M. **197** D16
Fanan, island, Chuuk, F.S.M. **197** C16
Fanananei, Mochun, Chuuk, F.S.M. **197** B14
Fanangat, island, Chuuk, F.S.M. **197** B15
Fanannon, island, Chuuk, F.S.M. **197** C15
Fanapanges, island, Chuuk, F.S.M. **197** C14
Fanasich, island, Chuuk, F.S.M. **197** C14
Fanchang, China **162** K8
Fanemoch, island, Chuuk, F.S.M. **197** B15
Faneno, island, Chuuk, F.S.M. **197** B15
Fanew, island, Chuuk, F.S.M. **197** C15
Fanew, Mochun, Chuuk, F.S.M. **197** C15
Fangak, Sudan **178** G12
Fangale'ounga, Ha'apai Group, Tonga **198** P7
Fangasito, island, Vava'u Group, Tonga **198** M11
Fangatau, island, Fr. Polynesia, Fr. **199** E20
Fangataufa, island, Fr. Polynesia, Fr. **199** H21
Fangcheng, China **162** J4
Fangshan, China **162** E4
Fangxian, China **162** K3
Fanning Island see Tabuaeran, Kiribati **194** F12
Fanos, island, Chuuk, F.S.M. **197** B15
Fanshan, China **163** N9
Fanshi, China **162** D5
Fanūdah, Saudi Arabia **152** J7
Fañunchuluyan, Bahia, Saipan, N. Mariana Is., U.S. **196** B6
Fanurmot, island, Chuuk, F.S.M. **197** C14
Fanxian, China **162** G6
Farafangana, Madagascar **183** H17
Farâfra Oasis, Egypt **177** D17
Farah, river, Afghan. **157** P2
Farah, Afghan. **157** P2
Farallon de Medinilla, island, N. Mariana Is., U.S. **196** C2
Farallon de Pajaros, island, N. Mariana Is., U.S. **194** D4
Farallon Islands, U.S. **78** G2
Faranah, Guinea **180** F6
Farasān, Jazā'ir, Saudi Arabia **152** P8
Faraulep Atoll, F.S.M. **196** Q4
Fare, Huahine, Fr. Polynesia, Fr. **199** G14
Fareara, Pointe, Tahiti, Fr. Polynesia, Fr. **199** Q17
Fareera, Passe, Huahine, Fr. Polynesia, Fr. **199** G14
Farewell, Cape, N. Amer. **74** D10
Farewell, Cape, N.Z. **193** M17
Fargo, N. Dak., U.S. **98** G8
Fargona, Uzb. **155** K14
Faribault, Minn., U.S. **98** K11
Faridkot, India **158** D4
Faridpur, Bangladesh **158** H12
Farim, Guinea-Bissau **180** E4
Farīmān, Iran **153** C16
Fariones, Punta, Canary Is., Sp. **184** P8
Farmersville, Tex., U.S. **96** K12
Farmerville, La., U.S. **94** K8
Farmington, Ill., U.S. **93** Q4
Farmington, Me., U.S. **89** F16
Farmington, Mo., U.S. **99** U15
Farmington, N. Mex., U.S. **101** Q10
Farmington, Utah, U.S. **100** K7
Farmville, Va., U.S. **90** F12
Farnham, N.Y., U.S. **88** K4
Fårö, island, Sw. **135** L14
Faro, Port. **139** S5
Faroe Bank, Atl. Oc. **216** C11
Faroe-Iceland Ridge, Atl. Oc. **216** C11
Faroe Islands (Føroyar), Norwegian Sea **134** J5
Farquhar Group, Seychelles **183** C19
Farrell, Pa., U.S. **88** M3
Fārs, region, Iran **153** G14
Farsund, Nor. **134** M10
Fartak, Ra's, Yemen **153** P13
Far'ūn (Coral Island), Egypt **151** R5
Farwell, Tex., U.S. **96** H3
Fasā, Iran **153** G14
Fastiv, Ukr. **133** H14
Fastnet Rock, Ire. **138** H5

Fataka (Mitre Island), *Solomon Is.* **194** J8
Fatato, island, *Funafuti, Tuvalu* **197** K23
Fatehabad, *India* **158** E5
Fatehgarh, *India* **158** F7
Fatehpur, *India* **158** G7
Fátima, *Port.* **139** Q4
Fatsa, *Turk.* **148** D12
Fatumanini, Passe, *Wallis and Futuna, Fr.* **198** B11
Fatumanongi, island, *Ha'apai Group, Tonga* **198** P6
Fatumu, *Tongatapu, Tonga* **198** J12
Faulkton, *S. Dak., U.S.* **98** J6
Fauna Nui, Lac, *Huahine, Fr. Polynesia, Fr.* **199** G14
Făurei, *Rom.* **137** F17
Fauro, island, *Solomon Is.* **197** L15
Fauske, *Nor.* **134** E12
Faxaflói, bay, *Ice.* **134** F2
Faya-Largeau, *Chad* **177** G15
Fayaoué, *New Caledonia, Fr.* **198** C8
Fayaoué, Baie de, *New Caledonia, Fr.* **198** C8
Fayd, *Saudi Arabia* **152** H8
Fayette, *Ala., U.S.* **95** J14
Fayette, *Miss., U.S.* **94** M10
Fayette, *Mo., U.S.* **99** S12
Fayetteville, *Ark., U.S.* **94** E6
Fayetteville, *N.C., U.S.* **90** J11
Fayetteville, *Tenn., U.S.* **95** G15
Fayetteville, *W. Va., U.S.* **90** E8
Fazilka, *India* **158** E4
Fdérik, *Mauritania* **176** E6
Fear, Cape, *N.C., U.S.* **90** K12
Federal, *Arg.* **124** J13
Federated States of Micronesia, *Pac. Oc.* **196** P4
Fedorovka, *Kaz.* **154** B10
Fefen, island, *Chuuk, F.S.M.* **197** C15
Fehmarn, island, *Ger.* **132** E6
Feijó, *Braz.* **122** F5
Feilding, *N.Z.* **193** L19
Feira de Santana, *Braz.* **123** H16
Feixi, *China* **162** K7
Feke, *Turk.* **148** G11
Félicité, island, *Seychelles* **185** N21
Felidu Atoll, *Maldives* **159** V3
Felipe Carrillo Puerto, *Mex.* **109** J17
Femund, lake, *Nor.* **134** J11
Fen, river, *China* **162** F4
Fena Valley Reservoir, *Guam, U.S.* **196** D10
Feneppi, island, *Chuuk, F.S.M.* **197** D15
Fengcheng, *China* **162** C11
Fengcheng, *China* **163** N6
Fenghuang, *China* **163** N2
Fengjie, *China* **162** K2
Fengkai, *China* **163** R3
Fenglin, *Taiwan, China* **163** R10
Fengning, *China* **162** C7
Fengshan, *Taiwan, China* **163** S9
Fengtai, *China* **162** J7
Fengxian, *China* **160** K12
Fengyüan, *Taiwan, China* **163** R9
Fengzhen, *China* **162** C5
Feni Islands, *P.N.G.* **193** C22
Fenua Fu, island, *Wallis and Futuna, Fr.* **198** C11
Fenualoa, island, *Santa Cruz Is., Solomon Is.* **197** P23
Fenua Roa, island, *Rangiroa, Fr. Polynesia, Fr.* **199** K16
Fenxi, *China* **162** F4
Fenyang, *China* **162** F4
Feodosiya, *Ukr.* **133** M17
Fer, Point au, *La., U.S.* **94** R9
Fera, island, *Solomon Is.* **197** M18
Férai, *Gr.* **137** J16
Ferdows, *Iran* **153** D16
Fērfēr, *Eth.* **179** H17
Fergana Valley, *Uzb.* **155** K14
Fergus Falls, *Minn., U.S.* **98** H9
Ferguson Seamount, *Pac. Oc.* **218** F8
Fergusson Island, *P.N.G.* **193** E21
Feridu, island, *Maldives* **159** U3
Ferit, island, *Chuuk, F.S.M.* **197** B16
Ferkéssédougou, *Côte d'Ivoire* **180** F8
Fermont, *Que., Can.* **77** L20
Fernandina, Isla, *Galapagos Is., Ecua.* **195** G21
Fernandina Beach, *Fla., U.S.* **91** Q8
Fernando de Noronha, Arquipélago de, *Braz.* **123** E19
Fernan Vaz *see* Omboué, *Gabon* **181** L15
Ferndale, *Calif., U.S.* **103** N1
Ferndale, *Wash., U.S.* **102** A4
Fern Grotto, *Hawaii, U.S.* **106** B6
Fernlee, *Qnsld., Austral.* **191** V13
Fernley, *Nev., U.S.* **103** P7
Fern Ridge Lake, *Oreg., U.S.* **102** H2
Ferrara, *It.* **136** F9
Ferreñafe, *Peru* **122** F2
Ferreira Gomes, *Braz.* **122** C12
Ferriday, *La., U.S.* **94** M9
Ferro *see* Hierro, island, *Canary Is., Sp.* **184** R3
Ferro, Ilhéu de, *Madeira Is., Port.* **184** L5
Ferrol, *Sp.* **139** N5
Ferrolana, *Bioko, Eq. Guinea* **184** M6
Ferron, *Utah, U.S.* **100** M8
Ferrysburg, *Mich., U.S.* **92** L9
Fertile, *Minn., U.S.* **98** F8
Fès (Fez), *Mor.* **176** B9
Feshi, *Dem. Rep. of the Congo* **178** M8
Fessenden, *N. Dak., U.S.* **98** F5
Festus, *Mo., U.S.* **99** T15
Feteşti, *Rom.* **137** F17
Fethiye, *Turk.* **148** J4
Fethiye Körfezi, *Turk.* **148** J4
Fetlar, island, *Scot., U.K.* **138** B9
Fetoa, island, *Ha'apai Group, Tonga* **198** Q6
Fetokopunga, island, *Ha'apai Group, Tonga* **198** Q7
Fetuna, *Raiatea, Fr. Polynesia, Fr.* **199** C23
Feuet, *Lib.* **176** E12
Feuilles, Rivière aux, *Que., Can.* **77** K18
Fevzipaşa, *Turk.* **148** H11
Feyzabad, *Afghan.* **156** K9
Fez *see* Fès, *Mor.* **176** B9
Fezzan, region, *Lib.* **177** E13
Fianarantsoa, *Madagascar* **183** H17
Fieberling Tablemount, *Pac. Oc.* **219** F15
Fields Find, *W. Austral., Austral.* **191** W3
Fife Lake, *Mich., U.S.* **92** J10
Fifth Cataract, *Sudan* **179** D13
Figueira da Foz, *Port.* **139** Q4
Figueres, *Sp.* **139** P10
Figuig, *Mor.* **176** B9
Fiji Islands, *Pac. Oc.* **198** J8
Fiji Plateau, *Pac. Oc.* **218** L10
Filadelfia, *Para.* **122** L9
Filchner Ice Sheet, *Antarctica* **206** F10
Filer, *Idaho, U.S.* **100** H5
Filipstad, *Sw.* **134** L12
Fillmore, *Calif., U.S.* **103** W7
Fillmore, *Utah, U.S.* **101** N7
Filyos, river, *Turk.* **148** C8
Fimbul Ice Shelf, *Antarctica* **206** A12
Fimi, river, *Dem. Rep. of the Congo* **178** K8
Fındıklı, *Turk.* **149** C15
Findlay, *Ohio, U.S.* **93** P12
Fineveke, *Wallis and Futuna, Fr.* **198** B11
Finger Lakes, *N.Y., U.S.* **88** K7
Fingoè, *Mozambique* **182** E12
Finike, *Turk.* **148** J5
Finisterre, Cape, *Eur.* **130** H2
Finke, river, *Austral.* **190** G8
Finke, *N. Terr., Austral.* **191** U9
Finland, *Eur.* **135** H16
Finland, *Minn., U.S.* **98** F13
Finland, Gulf of, *Estonia-Fin.* **135** K16
Finlay, river, *B.C., Can.* **76** J9
Finley, *N. Dak., U.S.* **98** F7
Finnmark Plateau, *Eur.* **130** A8
Finschhafen, *P.N.G.* **193** D20
Firat (Euphrates), river, *Turk.* **149** G14
Fire Island National Seashore, *N.Y., U.S.* **88** N12
Firenze (Florence), *It.* **136** G9
Firmat, *Arg.* **124** L11
Firozabad, *India* **158** G6
Firozkoh, region, *Afghan.* **156** M4
First Cataract, *Egypt* **177** E19
First Sugar Mill, *Hawaii, U.S.* **106** C5
Fīrūzābād, *Iran* **153** G13
Fish, river, *Namibia* **182** J7
Fisher, river, *Mont., U.S.* **100** B5
Fisher, *S. Austral., Austral.* **191** W7
Fisher Glacier, *Antarctica* **207** F18
Fisher Strait, *Nunavut, Can.* **77** H16
Fish Lake, *Utah, U.S.* **101** N7
Fisterra, Cabo, *Sp.* **139** N4
Fitchburg, *Mass., U.S.* **89** K14
Fitii, *Huahine, Fr. Polynesia, Fr.* **199** G14
Fitii, Baie de, *Huahine, Fr. Polynesia, Fr.* **199** G14
Fitiuta, *Manua Is., Amer. Samoa, U.S.* **198** P4
Fito, Mount, *Samoa* **198** L3
Fitri, Lac, *Chad* **177** J15
Fitzgerald, *Alta., Can.* **76** J11
Fitzgerald, *Ga., U.S.* **91** P6
Fitzroy, river, *Austral.* **190** D5
Fitzroy, river, *Austral.* **190** F15
Fitzroy Crossing, *W. Austral., Austral.* **191** R5
Fivaku, island, *Maldives* **159** T3
Flagler, *Colo., U.S.* **100** M15
Flagstaff, *Ariz., U.S.* **101** S7
Flagstaff Lake, *Oreg., U.S.* **102** K6
Flåm, *Nor.* **134** K10
Flambeau, river, *Wis., U.S.* **92** G4
Flaming Gorge National Recreation Area, *Wyo., U.S.* **100** K9
Flaming Gorge Reservoir, *Wyo., U.S.* **100** K9
Flamingo, *Fla., U.S.* **91** Y9
Flamingo, Teluk, *Indonesia* **193** C16
Flamingo Cay, *Bahamas* **111** G13
Flamingo Point, *Bahamas* **111** E13
Flandreau, *S. Dak., U.S.* **98** L8
Flathead Lake, *Mont., U.S.* **100** B6
Flat Island, *Mauritius* **185** F20
Flat Island, *Spratly Is.* **168** E11
Flatonia, *Tex., U.S.* **97** R11
Flat River, *Mo., U.S.* **99** U15
Flattery, Cape, *Austral.* **190** C13
Flattery, Cape, *Wash., U.S.* **102** B1
Flatts Village, *Bermuda, U.K.* **111** F17
Flatwoods, *Ky., U.S.* **95** A20
Flaxton, *N. Dak., U.S.* **98** D3
Flekkefjord, *Nor.* **134** M10
Fleming Glacier, *Antarctica* **206** E5
Flemingsburg, *Ky., U.S.* **95** B18
Flemish Cap, *Atl. Oc.* **216** F7
Flensburg, *Ger.* **132** E6
Flers, *Fr.* **138** K9
Fletcher Peninsula, *Antarctica* **206** H6
Fletcher Plain, *Arctic Oc.* **222** H10
Flinders, river, *Austral.* **190** D11
Flinders Bay, *W. Austral., Austral.* **191** Y2
Flinders Island, *Austral.* **190** L16
Flinders Ranges, *Austral.* **190** J10
Flin Flon, *Man., Can.* **77** L13
Flint, river, *Ga., U.S.* **91** P5
Flint, *Mich., U.S.* **92** L12
Flint Hills, *Kans., U.S.* **99** U8
Flint Hills, *U.S.* **78** H12
Flint Island, *Kiribati* **195** J13
Flipper Point, *Wake I., U.S.* **196** F8
Flisa, *Nor.* **134** K12
Flomaton, *Ala., U.S.* **95** N14
Flood Range, *Antarctica* **206** M8
Floodwood, *Minn., U.S.* **98** G12
Flora, *Ill., U.S.* **93** T6
Flora, *Ind., U.S.* **93** Q9
Flora, *Oreg., U.S.* **102** E9
Florac, *Fr.* **139** N11
Florala, *Ala., U.S.* **95** N16
Florence, *Ala., U.S.* **95** G14
Florence, *Ariz., U.S.* **101** U7
Florence, *Colo., U.S.* **101** N13
Florence *see* Firenze, *It.* **136** G9
Florence, *Kans., U.S.* **99** T8
Florence, *Ky., U.S.* **95** A17
Florence, *Oreg., U.S.* **102** H2
Florence, *S.C., U.S.* **90** K10
Florence, *Wis., U.S.* **92** G7
Florencia, *Col.* **120** H4
Flores, island, *Indonesia* **169** M14
Flores, *Guatemala* **109** K16
Flores Sea, *Indonesia* **168** M12
Floresville, *Tex., U.S.* **97** S10
Floriano, *Braz.* **123** F15
Floriano Peixoto, *Braz.* **122** G6
Florianópolis, *Braz.* **123** N13
Florida, *U.S.* **91** S8
Florida, *Cuba* **110** J10
Florida, Straits of, *N. Amer.* **74** M8
Florida Bay, *Fla., U.S.* **91** Y10
Florida City, *Fla., U.S.* **91** X10
Florida Islands, *Solomon Is.* **197** N18
Florida Keys, *Fla., U.S.* **91** Y9
Florissant, *Mo., U.S.* **99** S15
Florissant Fossil Beds National Monument, *Colo., U.S.* **101** N13
Florø, *Nor.* **134** J9
Flotte, Cap de, *New Caledonia, Fr.* **198** C9
Floyd, *N. Mex., U.S.* **101** T15
Floydada, *Tex., U.S.* **96** J6
Fly, river, *P.N.G.* **193** D17
Foa, island, *Ha'apai Group, Tonga* **198** P7
Foça, *Turk.* **148** F2
Focşani, *Rom.* **137** E16
Fofoa, island, *Vava'u Group, Tonga* **198** L11
Fogang, *China* **163** R4
Fogausa, Cape, *Tutuila, Amer. Samoa, U.S.* **198** M8
Foggia, *It.* **136** H11
Fogo, island, *Cape Verde* **185** E15
Fogo Island, *Nfld., Can.* **77** L23
Foix, *Fr.* **139** P10
Foko Malsu, point, *Kosrae, F.S.M.* **197** A18
Folda, bay, *Nor.* **134** G11
Folégandros, island, *Gr.* **137** M16
Foley, *Ala., U.S.* **95** P14
Foley, *Minn., U.S.* **98** J11
Foley Island, *Nunavut, Can.* **77** F17
Foligno, *It.* **136** G9
Folkston, *Ga., U.S.* **91** Q8
Follett, *Tex., U.S.* **96** E7
Folly Beach, *S.C., U.S.* **90** M10
Foloha, *Tongatapu, Tonga* **198** J11
Folsom, *Calif., U.S.* **103** Q5
Fomboni, *Comoros* **185** N15
Fomento, *Cuba* **110** H9
Fond du Lac, *Sask., Can.* **76** J12
Fond du Lac, *Wis., U.S.* **92** K6
Fongafale *see* Funafuti, *Tuvalu* **197** K24
Fono, island, *Chuuk, F.S.M.* **197** B15
Fonoifua, island, *Ha'apai Group, Tonga* **198** Q7
Fononuk, island, *Chuuk, F.S.M.* **197** D16
Fonou, island, *Chuuk, F.S.M.* **197** C15
Fonseca, Golfo de, *El Salv.-Hond.-Nicar.* **109** M17
Fontana Lake, *N.C., U.S.* **90** J6
Fonte Boa, *Braz.* **122** D7
Fontenelle Reservoir, *Wyo., U.S.* **100** J8
Fonuafo'ou, island, *Vava'u Group, Tonga* **198** M12
Fonuaika, island, *Ha'apai Group, Tonga* **198** Q6
Fonuakula, *Niue, N.Z.* **199** B20
Fonua'one'one, island, *Vava'u Group, Tonga* **198** M11
Fonua'unga, island, *Vava'u Group, Tonga* **198** M12
Fonua'unga, Ava, *Vava'u Group, Tonga* **198** M12
Fonuchu, island, *Chuuk, F.S.M.* **197** A15
Foping, *China* **162** H1
Forbesganj, *India* **158** G11
Ford, Cape, *Austral.* **190** B7
Fordate, island, *Indonesia* **193** D14
Førde, *Nor.* **134** K10
Ford Ranges, *Antarctica* **206** N9
Fords Bridge, *N.S.W., Austral.* **191** W12
Fordyce, *Ark., U.S.* **94** J8
Forécariah, *Guinea* **180** F5
Forel, Mont, *N. Amer.* **74** C10
Foreman, *Ark., U.S.* **94** J6
Forest, *Miss., U.S.* **94** L12
Forest City, *Iowa, U.S.* **98** M11
Forest City, *N.C., U.S.* **90** J8
Forest Grove, *Oreg., U.S.* **102** F3
Forest Home, *Qnsld., Austral.* **191** R12
Forest Park, *Ga., U.S.* **90** L5
Forestville, *Mich., U.S.* **92** K13
Forestville, *Que., Can.* **77** N20
Forgan, *Okla., U.S.* **96** E7
Forks, *Wash., U.S.* **102** B2
Forlì, *It.* **136** F9
Forman, *N. Dak., U.S.* **98** H7
Formentera, island, *Sp.* **139** R10
Formentor, Cap de, *Sp.* **139** Q11
Formiga, *Braz.* **123** L14
Formosa, *Arg.* **124** F13
Formosa, *Braz.* **123** J13
Formosa, Serra, *Braz.* **122** G11
Formosa do Rio Prêto, *Braz.* **123** G14
Føroyar *see* Faroe Islands, *Norwegian Sea* **134** J5
Forrest, *W. Austral., Austral.* **191** W6
Forrestal Range, *Antarctica* **206** G10
Forrest City, *Ark., U.S.* **94** G10
Forrest River, *W. Austral., Austral.* **191** Q6
Forsayth, *Qnsld., Austral.* **191** R12
Forssa, *Fin.* **135** J15
Forst, *Ger.* **132** G8
Forster-Tuncurry, *N.S.W., Austral.* **191** X15
Forsyth, *Ga., U.S.* **90** M5
Forsyth, *Mo., U.S.* **99** V12
Forsyth, *Mont., U.S.* **100** D11
Fort Abbas, *Pak.* **157** S11
Fort Albany, *Ont., Can.* **77** M17
Fortaleza, *Braz.* **123** E17
Fort Atkinson, *Wis., U.S.* **92** L6
Fort Benton, *Mont., U.S.* **100** C8
Fort Bowie National Historic Site, *Ariz., U.S.* **101** V9
Fort Bragg, *Calif., U.S.* **103** P2
Fort Caroline National Memorial, *Fla., U.S.* **91** Q8
Fort Chipewyan, *Alta., Can.* **76** J11
Fort Clatsop National Memorial, *Oreg., U.S.* **102** E2
Fort Cobb Reservoir, *Okla., U.S.* **96** G9
Fort Collins, *Colo., U.S.* **100** L13
Fort Davis, *Tex., U.S.* **97** P2
Fort Davis National Historic Site, *Tex., U.S.* **97** P2
Fort Defiance, *Ariz., U.S.* **101** R9
Fort-de- France, *Martinique, Fr.* **113** K17
Fort Deposit, *Ala., U.S.* **95** M15
Fort Dick, *Calif., U.S.* **102** L1
Fort Dodge, *Iowa, U.S.* **99** N11
Forteau, *Nfld., Can.* **77** L22
Fortescue, river, *Austral.* **190** F2
Fort Fairfield, *Me., U.S.* **89** B18
Fort Frances, *Ont., Can.* **77** P14
Fort Fraser, *B.C., Can.* **76** K8
Fort Frederica National Monument, *Ga., U.S.* **91** P9
Fort Gaines, *Ga., U.S.* **91** P4
Fort Gibson, *Okla., U.S.* **96** F13
Fort Gibson Lake, *Okla., U.S.* **96** F13
Fort Good Hope, *N.W.T., Can.* **76** F10
Forth, Firth of, *Eur.* **130** D4
Fort Hall, *Idaho, U.S.* **100** H7
Fort Hancock, *Tex., U.S.* **97** V2
Fort Hope, *Ont., Can.* **77** N16
Fortín General Díaz, *Para.* **122** M9
Fortín Infante Rivarola, *Para.* **122** L8
Fortín Madrejón, *Para.* **122** L9
Fortín May Alberto Gardel, *Para.* **122** L8
Fortín Presidente Ayala, *Para.* **122** M9
Fortín Suárez Arana, *Bol.* **122** K9
Fort Jones, *Calif., U.S.* **102** L3
Fort Kent, *Me., U.S.* **89** A17
Fort Klamath, *Oreg., U.S.* **102** K4
Fort Laramie, *Wyo., U.S.* **100** J13
Fort Laramie National Historic Site, *Wyo., U.S.* **100** J13
Fort Larned National Historic Site, *Kans., U.S.* **99** T5
Fort Lauderdale, *Fla., U.S.* **91** W10
Fort Liard, *N.W.T., Can.* **76** H9
Fort-Liberté, *Haiti* **111** L17
Fort Lupton, *Colo., U.S.* **100** L13
Fort Madison, *Iowa, U.S.* **99** Q14
Fort Matanzas National Monument, *Fla., U.S.* **91** R9
Fort McMurray, *Alta., Can.* **76** K11
Fort McPherson, *N.W.T., Can.* **76** E9
Fort Meade, *Fla., U.S.* **91** U8
Fort Mill, *S.C., U.S.* **90** J9

Fort Miribel, *Alg.* **176** C11
Fort Morgan, *Colo., U.S.* **100** L14
Fort Munro, *Pak.* **157** R8
Fort Myers, *Fla., U.S.* **91** W8
Fort Myers Beach, *Fla., U.S.* **91** W8
Fort Nelson, *B.C., Can.* **76** J9
Fort Payne, *Ala., U.S.* **95** H16
Fort Peck, *Mont., U.S.* **100** B12
Fort Peck Dam, *Mont., U.S.* **100** B12
Fort Peck Lake, *Mont., U.S.* **100** C11
Fort Pierce, *Fla., U.S.* **91** U10
Fort Pierre, *S. Dak., U.S.* **98** K5
Fort Providence, *N.W.T., Can.* **76** H11
Fort Pulaski National Monument, *Ga., U.S.* **91** N9
Fort Raleigh National Historic Site, *N.C., U.S.* **90** G15
Fort Randall Dam, *S. Dak., U.S.* **98** M6
Fort Resolution, *N.W.T., Can.* **76** H11
Fort Rock, *Oreg., U.S.* **102** J5
Fort Saint John, *B.C., Can.* **76** K9
Fort Scott, *Kans., U.S.* **99** U10
Fort Scott National Historic Site, *Kans., U.S.* **99** U10
Fort Severn, *Ont., Can.* **77** L16
Fort Shafter, *Hawaii, U.S.* **106** E11
Fort Shevchenko, *Kaz.* **154** G5
Fort Simpson, *N.W.T., Can.* **76** H10
Fort Smith, *Ark., U.S.* **94** F6
Fort Smith, *N.W.T., Can.* **76** J11
Fort Stanwix National Monument, *N.Y., U.S.* **88** J9
Fort Stockton, *Tex., U.S.* **97** P3
Fort Sumner, *N. Mex., U.S.* **101** S14
Fort Sumter National Monument, *S.C., U.S.* **90** M10
Fort Supply, *Okla., U.S.* **96** E8
Fort Thompson, *S. Dak., U.S.* **98** L5
Fort Trinquet *see* Bir Mogreïn, *Mauritania* **176** D6
Fortuna, *Calif., U.S.* **103** N1
Fortuna, *N. Dak., U.S.* **98** D2
Fortune Island *see* Long Cay, *Bahamas* **111** H14
Fort Union National Monument, *N. Mex., U.S.* **101** R13
Fort Union Trading Post National Historic Site, *N. Dak., U.S.* **98** E1
Fort Valley, *Ga., U.S.* **90** M5
Fort Vermilion, *Alta., Can.* **76** J10
Fort Walton Beach, *Fla., U.S.* **91** Q2
Fort Wayne, *Ind., U.S.* **93** P10
Fort William, *Scot., U.K.* **138** E7
Fort Wingate, *N. Mex., U.S.* **101** R10
Fort Worth, *Tex., U.S.* **96** L11
Fort Yates, *N. Dak., U.S.* **98** H4
Fort Yukon, *Alas., U.S.* **105** E17
Foshan, *China* **163** R4
Fosheim Peninsula, *Nunavut, Can.* **77** B16
Fossil, *Oreg., U.S.* **102** G6
Fossil Butte National Monument, *Wyo., U.S.* **100** J8
Fosston, *Minn., U.S.* **98** F9
Foster, Mount, *Alas., U.S.* **105** J21
Fostoria, *Ohio, U.S.* **93** P12
Fotuha'a, island, *Ha'apai Group, Tonga* **198** P6
Fougères, *Fr.* **138** K8
Foula, island, *Scot., U.K.* **138** C8
Foulweather, Cape, *Oreg., U.S.* **102** G1
Foulwind, Cape, *N.Z.* **193** N17
Foumban, *Cameroon* **181** H15
Foumbouni, *Comoros* **185** M14
Foundation Ice Stream, *Antarctica* **206** G10
Fountain, *Colo., U.S.* **101** N13
Fountain City, *Wis., U.S.* **92** J3
Fourche, Île, *St.-Barthélemy, Fr.* **113** F15
Four Corners, *Wyo., U.S.* **100** G14
Fourcroy, Cape, *Austral.* **190** A7
Four Mountains, Islands of, *Alas., U.S.* **104** Q8
Fournaise, Piton de la, *Réunion, Fr.* **185** H17
Fourth Cataract, *Sudan* **179** D13
Fourup, island, *Chuuk, F.S.M.* **197** C15
Fouta Djallon, hills, *Guinea* **180** E5
Foux, Cap-à-, *Haiti* **111** L15
Foveaux Strait, *N.Z.* **193** R15
Fowler, *Colo., U.S.* **101** N14
Fowler, *Ind., U.S.* **93** Q8
Fowler, *Kans., U.S.* **99** U4
Fowlers Bay, *S. Austral., Austral.* **191** X8
Fox, river, *Ill., U.S.* **93** P6
Fox, river, *Wis., U.S.* **92** J7
Foxe Basin, *Nunavut, Can.* **77** G17
Foxe Channel, *Nunavut, Can.* **77** H17
Foxe Peninsula, *Nunavut, Can.* **77** H17
Fox Glacier, *N.Z.* **193** P16
Fox Islands, *Alas., U.S.* **104** P9
Foxpark, *Wyo., U.S.* **100** K12
Foyn Coast, *Antarctica* **206** E4
Foz do Cunene, *Angola* **182** F5
Foz do Iguaçu, *Braz.* **122** N11
Fram Basin, *Arctic Oc.* **222** H11
Framnes Mountains, *Antarctica* **207** D20
Fram Peak, *Antarctica* **207** D19
Franca, *Braz.* **123** L13
France, *Eur.* **138** L9
Francés, Cabo, *Cuba* **110** H4
Francés, Punta, *Cuba* **110** H5
Frances Lake, *Yukon Terr., Can.* **76** G9
Francés Viejo, Cabo, *Dom. Rep.* **111** L19
Franceville, *Gabon* **181** L17
Francis Case, Lake, *S. Dak., U.S.* **98** L5
Francistown, *Botswana* **182** G10
Francs Peak, *Wyo., U.S.* **100** G9
Frankfort, *Ind., U.S.* **93** Q8
Frankfort, *Kans., U.S.* **99** R8
Frankfort, *Ky., U.S.* **95** B17
Frankfort, *Mich., U.S.* **92** J9
Frankfurt, *Ger.* **132** G8
Frankfurt, *Ger.* **132** H5
Franklin, *Idaho, U.S.* **100** J7
Franklin, *Ind., U.S.* **93** S9
Franklin, *Ky., U.S.* **95** D15
Franklin, *La., U.S.* **94** Q9
Franklin, *N.C., U.S.* **90** J6
Franklin, *N.H., U.S.* **89** H14
Franklin, *Nebr., U.S.* **99** R6
Franklin, *Pa., U.S.* **88** M3
Franklin, *Tenn., U.S.* **95** F15
Franklin, *Va., U.S.* **90** F13
Franklin Bay, *N.W.T., Can.* **76** E11
Franklin D. Roosevelt Lake, *Wash., U.S.* **102** B8
Franklin Lake, *Nev., U.S.* **103** N11
Franklin Mountains, *N. Amer.* **74** D4
Franklin Strait, *Nunavut, Can.* **77** E14
Franklinton, *La., U.S.* **94** N11
Franklinville, *N.Y., U.S.* **88** K5
Frankston, *Tex., U.S.* **96** M13
Frantsa Iosifa, Zemlya (Franz Josef Land), *Russ.* **140** C12
Franz, *Ont., Can.* **77** P17
Franz Josef Glacier, *N.Z.* **193** P16
Franz Josef Land *see* Frantsa Iosifa, Zemlya, *Russ.* **140** C12
Fraser, river, *B.C., Can.* **76** L8
Fraserburg, *S. Af.* **182** L8
Fraserburgh, *Scot., U.K.* **138** D8
Fraser Island (Great Sandy I.), *Austral.* **190** G16
Fraser Range, *W. Austral., Austral.* **191** X5
Frasertown, *N.Z.* **193** L20
Frazee, *Minn., U.S.* **98** G9
Frederick, *Md., U.S.* **90** C12
Frederick, *Okla., U.S.* **96** J9
Frederick, *S. Dak., U.S.* **98** H6
Frederick, Mount, *Austral.* **190** D7
Fredericksburg, *Tex., U.S.* **97** Q9
Fredericksburg, *Va., U.S.* **90** D12
Fredericktown, *Mo., U.S.* **99** U15
Fredericton, *N.B., Can.* **77** P21
Frederikshavn, *Den.* **134** M11
Frederiksted, *Virgin Is., U.S.* **113** F13
Fredonia, *Ariz., U.S.* **101** Q6
Fredonia, *Kans., U.S.* **99** U9
Fredonia, *N.Y., U.S.* **88** K4
Fredrikstad, *Nor.* **134** L11
Freedom, *Okla., U.S.* **96** E8
Freehold, *N.J., U.S.* **88** P11
Freeman, *S. Dak., U.S.* **98** M7
Freeport, *Bahamas* **110** C10
Freeport, *Ill., U.S.* **92** M5
Freeport, *Me., U.S.* **89** G16
Freeport, *N.Y., U.S.* **88** N11
Freeport, *Tex., U.S.* **97** S14
Freer, *Tex., U.S.* **97** U9
Freetown, *Sierra Leone* **180** G5
Freiburg, *Ger.* **132** J4
Freirina, *Chile* **124** H6
Freising, *Ger.* **132** J6
Fréjus, *Fr.* **139** N12
Fremantle, *W. Austral., Austral.* **191** X2
Fremont, river, *Utah, U.S.* **101** N7
Fremont, *Calif., U.S.* **103** S4
Fremont, *Mich., U.S.* **92** L9
Fremont, *Nebr., U.S.* **99** P8
Fremont, *Ohio, U.S.* **93** P13
Fremont Lake, *Wyo., U.S.* **100** H9
Fremont Mountains, *Oreg., U.S.* **102** K4
French Broad, river, *Tenn., U.S.* **95** E19
French Cays *see* Plana Cays, *Bahamas* **111** G15
French Frigate Shoals, *Hawaii, U.S.* **106** M7
French Guiana, *S. Amer.* **121** F17
Frenchman Creek, *Nebr., U.S.* **99** Q3
Frenchman Flat, *Nev., U.S.* **103** T11
French Polynesia, *Pac. Oc.* **199** F18
Frenchville, *Me., U.S.* **89** A18
Fresh Water Lagoons, *Kiritimati, Kiribati* **197** C23
Fresnillo, *Mex.* **108** G10
Fresno, *Calif., U.S.* **103** T6
Fresno Reservoir, *Mont., U.S.* **100** B9
Frewena, *N. Terr., Austral.* **191** S9
Fria, *Guinea* **180** F5
Friars Point, *Miss., U.S.* **94** H10
Frías, *Arg.* **124** H10
Fribourg, *Switz.* **132** K4
Fridtjof Nansen, Mount, *Antarctica* **206** K12
Friedrichshafen, *Ger.* **132** K5
Friend, *Nebr., U.S.* **99** Q7
Frigate, island, *Seychelles* **185** P21
Friiser-Larsen Ice Shelf, *Antarctica* **206** C10
Frio, river, *Tex., U.S.* **97** S8
Frio, Cape, *S. Amer.* **118** J10
Friona, *Tex., U.S.* **96** H4
Frisan Islands, *Neth.* **138** G11
Frisco, *Colo., U.S.* **100** M12
Frisco City, *Ala., U.S.* **95** M14
Frisian Islands, *Eur.* **130** F5
Frissel, Mount, *Conn., U.S.* **88** L12
Fritch, *Tex., U.S.* **96** G5
Friza, Proliv, *Russ.* **141** J23
Frobisher Bay, *Nunavut, Can.* **77** H19
Frolovo, *Russ.* **140** H5
Fromberg, *Mont., U.S.* **100** E10
Frome, Lake, *Austral.* **190** J11
Frome Downs, *S. Austral., Austral.* **191** W11
Frontenac, *Kans., U.S.* **99** U10
Frontera, *Mex.* **108** E11
Frontera, *Mex.* **109** J15
Front Range, *Colo., U.S.* **100** L12
Frostburg, *Md., U.S.* **90** C11
Frostproof, *Fla., U.S.* **91** U8
Frøya, island, *Nor.* **134** H10
Fruita, *Colo., U.S.* **100** M10
Fruitland, *Idaho, U.S.* **100** G3
Fruitland, *N. Mex., U.S.* **101** Q10
Fryeburg, *Me., U.S.* **89** G15
Frying Pan Shoals, *N.C., U.S.* **90** L13
Fu, river, *China* **160** L12
Fu, river, *China* **163** N6
Fua'amotu, island, *Vava'u Group, Tonga* **198** M11
Fua'amotu, *Tongatapu, Tonga* **198** J11
Fuafatu, island, *Funafuti, Tuvalu* **197** K22
Fuagea, island, *Funafuti, Tuvalu* **197** L22
Fuagea, Te Ava, *Funafuti, Tuvalu* **197** K22
Fualifexe, island, *Funafuti, Tuvalu* **197** J23
Fualopa, island, *Funafuti, Tuvalu* **197** K22
Fua Mulaku, island, *Maldives* **159** X3
Fu'an, *China* **163** N9
Fuding, *China* **163** N9
Fuencaliente, *Canary Is., Sp.* **184** Q4
Fuencaliente, Punta de, *Canary Is., Sp.* **184** Q3
Fuerte Olimpo, *Para.* **122** L10
Fuerteventura, island, *Canary Is., Sp.* **184** Q8
Fuga, island, *Philippines* **169** A13
Fugauvea, Passe, *Wallis and Futuna, Fr.* **198** B11
Fugou, *China* **162** H5
Fugu, *China* **162** D3
Fuhai, *China* **160** D7
Fuji, peak, *Jap.* **165** P11
Fujisawa, *Jap.* **165** P12
Fukagawa, *Jap.* **164** F14
Fukave, island, *Tongatapu, Tonga* **198** H12
Fukuchiyama, *Jap.* **165** P8
Fukue, *Jap.* **165** S3
Fukue Jima, *Jap.* **165** S2
Fukui, *Jap.* **165** P9
Fukuoka, *Jap.* **165** R4
Fukura, *Jap.* **164** K12
Fukushima, *Jap.* **164** H12
Fukushima, *Jap.* **164** M13
Fukushima, Mount, *Antarctica* **207** C16
Fukuyama, *Jap.* **165** Q7
Fulaga, island, *Fiji* **198** K9
Fulaga Passage, *Fiji* **198** K9
Fulda, *Ger.* **132** H5
Fulda, *Minn., U.S.* **98** L9
Fuling, *China* **160** L12
Fullerton, *Nebr., U.S.* **99** P7
Fulton, *Ill., U.S.* **93** N4
Fulton, *Ky., U.S.* **94** E12
Fulton, *Miss., U.S.* **95** H13
Fulton, *Mo., U.S.* **99** S13
Fulton, *N.Y., U.S.* **88** H8
Funabashi, *Jap.* **165** P12
Funadomari, *Jap.* **164** D13
Funafara, island, *Funafuti, Tuvalu* **197** L23
Funafuti, island, *Funafuti, Tuvalu* **197** K24
Funafuti (Fongafale), *Funafuti, Tuvalu* **197** K24
Funamanu, island, *Funafuti, Tuvalu* **197** K23
Funan, *China* **162** J6
Funangongo, island, *Funafuti, Tuvalu* **197** K23
Funchal, *Madeira Is., Port.* **184** M3
Fundo de Figueiras, *Cape Verde* **185** C17
Fundy, Bay of, *N.B.-N.S., Can.* **77** P21
Funhalouro, *Mozambique* **183** H13
Funiya Point, *Rota I., N. Mariana Is., U.S.* **196** E8
Funtanasupanie Point, *Rota I., N. Mariana Is., U.S.* **196** E8
Funtua, *Nig.* **181** E14
Fuping, *China* **162** G2
Fuqing, *China* **163** Q8
Furano, *Jap.* **164** F14
Furneaux Group, islands, *Austral.* **190** L16
Furqlus, *Syr.* **150** G8
Fürth, *Ger.* **132** J6
Furukawa, *Jap.* **164** L13
Fuse, *Jap.* **165** N7
Fushan, *China* **162** F9
Fushun, *China* **162** B11
Fusong, *China* **161** E18
Fusong, *China* **162** B13
Futiga, *Tutuila, Amer. Samoa, U.S.* **198** N7
Futuna, island, *Vanuatu* **198** H5
Futuna, island, *Wallis and Futuna, Fr.* **198** E11
Fuwwah, *Yemen* **152** Q12
Fuxian, *China* **162** F2
Fuxin, *China* **162** B10
Fuya, *Jap.* **164** L12
Fuyang, river, *China* **162** F6
Fuyang, *China* **162** J6
Fuyu, *China* **161** C16
Fuyun, *China* **160** D8
Fuzhou, *China* **163** P8
Füzuli, *Azerb.* **149** E21
Fyn, island, *Den.* **134** P11

G

Gaalkacyo, *Somalia* **179** G17
Gabbs, *Nev., U.S.* **103** Q8
Gabela, *Angola* **182** D6
Gabert Island, *Kosrae, F.S.M.* **197** A18
Gabes, *Tun.* **177** B13
Gabes, Gulf of, *Tun.* **177** B13
Gabon, *Af.* **181** L16
Gaborone, *Botswana* **182** J10
Gabras, *Sudan* **178** F11
Gabriel Vera, *Bol.* **122** K7
Gabrovo, *Bulg.* **137** G16
Gackle, *N. Dak., U.S.* **98** G6
Gădăbăy, *Azerb.* **149** D19
Gadag, *India* **159** N5
Gadarwara, *India* **158** J6
Gäddede, *Sw.* **134** G12
Gadifuri, island, *Maldives* **159** V3
Gadrut, *Azerb.* **149** E21
Gadsden, *Ala., U.S.* **95** H16
Gadsden, *Ariz., U.S.* **101** V4
Gadwal, *India* **159** N6
Găeşi, *Rom.* **137** F16
Gaferut, island, *F.S.M.* **196** P4
Gaffney, *S.C., U.S.* **90** J8
Gafsa, *Tun.* **176** B12
Gagan, island, *Kwajalein Atoll, Marshall Is.* **196** K4
Gagan, *P.N.G.* **197** J13
Gagil-Tomil, island, *Yap Is., F.S.M.* **197** D18
Gagnoa, *Côte d'Ivoire* **180** H8
Gagra, *Rep. of Georgia* **149** A15
Gahi, *Wallis and Futuna, Fr.* **198** C11
Gahnpa, *Liberia* **180** G7
Gaimán, *Arg.* **125** R9
Gainesville, *Fla., U.S.* **91** R7
Gainesville, *Ga., U.S.* **90** K5
Gainesville, *Mo., U.S.* **99** V13
Gainesville, *Tex., U.S.* **96** K11
Gairdner, Lake, *Austral.* **190** J9
Gaixian, *China* **162** C10
Gaja Shima, *Jap.* **165** V3
Gakona, *Alas., U.S.* **105** H17
Gakuch, *Pak.* **156** L11
Galan, Cerro, *S. Amer.* **118** J5
Galap, *Palau* **196** M12
Galápagos Fracture Zone, *Pac. Oc.* **219** K13
Galápagos Islands (Archipiélago de Colón), *Pac. Oc.* **195** G21
Galápagos Rift, *Pac. Oc.* **219** J18
Galápagos Rise, *Pac. Oc.* **219** L18
Galaţi, *Rom.* **137** E17
Galax, *Va., U.S.* **90** G9
Galbraith, *Qnsld., Austral.* **191** Q11
Gáldar, *Canary Is., Sp.* **184** Q6
Galdhøpiggen, peak, *Nor.* **134** J10
Galegu, *Sudan* **179** E14
Galela, *Indonesia* **169** H16
Galena, *Alas., U.S.* **105** F14
Galena, *Ill., U.S.* **92** M4
Galena, *Kans., U.S.* **99** V10
Galena Park, *Tex., U.S.* **97** Q14
Galera, Punta, *Chile* **125** P6
Galera, Punta, *Ecua.* **120** H2
Galera Point, *Trin. & Tobago* **113** P17
Galesburg, *Ill., U.S.* **93** P4
Galesville, *Wis., U.S.* **92** K3
Galeton, *Pa., U.S.* **88** L6
Galets, Pointe des, *Réunion, Fr.* **185** F15
Gali, *Rep. of Georgia* **149** B16
Galich, *Russ.* **140** F7
Galilee, Lake, *Austral.* **190** F13
Galilee, Sea of, *Israel* **150** K6
Galina Mine, *W. Austral., Austral.* **191** V2
Galion, *Ohio, U.S.* **93** Q13
Galiuro Mountains, *Ariz., U.S.* **101** V8
Galiwinku, *N. Terr., Austral.* **191** P9
Gallatin, river, *Mont., U.S.* **100** E8
Gallatin, *Mo., U.S.* **99** R11
Gallatin, *Tenn., U.S.* **95** E15
Galle, *Sri Lanka* **159** T7
Gállego, river, *Sp.* **139** P8
Gallinas, Punta, *Col.* **120** A7
Gallinas Peak, *N. Mex., U.S.* **101** T13
Gallipoli, *N. Terr., Austral.* **191** R10
Gallipoli, *It.* **136** J12
Gallipolis, *Ohio, U.S.* **93** S14

Gällivare, *Sw.* **135** E13
Gallup, *N. Mex., U.S.* **101** R10
Galoa, *Fiji* **198** J6
Galt, *Calif., U.S.* **103** R4
Galva, *Ill., U.S.* **93** P4
Galveston, *Tex., U.S.* **97** R15
Galveston Bay, *Tex., U.S.* **97** R15
Galveston Island, *Tex., U.S.* **97** R14
Gálvez, *Arg.* **124** K11
Galwa, *Nepal* **158** E8
Galway, *Ire.* **138** G5
Gambaga, *Ghana* **180** F10
Gambēla, *Eth.* **179** G13
Gambell, *Alas., U.S.* **104** G9
Gambia, *Af.* **176** H4
Gambia, river, *Af.* **174** G1
Gambia Plain, *Atl. Oc.* **216** L9
Gambia Shoal, *Hawaii, U.S.* **106** K2
Gambier, Îles, *Fr. Polynesia, Fr.* **199** Q21
Gamboma, *Congo* **181** L18
Gamboula, *Cen. Af. Rep.* **178** H7
Gamerco, *N. Mex., U.S.* **101** R10
Gamkonora, peak, *Indonesia* **169** H16
Gamlaha, *Indonesia* **169** H16
Gamleby, *Sw.* **135** M13
Gamua, *Wallis and Futuna, Fr.* **198** B11
Gan, island, *Maldives* **159** X3
Gan, island, *Maldives* **159** X3
Gan, river, *China* **161** B16
Gan, river, *China* **163** P5
Gana, river, *Af.* **174** H5
Ganado, *Ariz., U.S.* **101** R9
Ganado, *Tex., U.S.* **97** S12
Ganāveh, *Iran* **152** F12
Gäncä, *Azerb.* **149** D20
Gandajika, *Dem. Rep. of the Congo* **178** M10
Gandava, *Pak.* **157** T6
Gander, *Nfld., Can.* **77** M23
Gandesa, *Sp.* **139** Q9
Gandhinagar, *India* **158** J3
Gang, island, *Maldives* **159** W3
Ganga (Ganges), river, *India* **158** G7
Gan Gan, *Arg.* **125** R8
Ganganagar, *India* **158** E4
Gangapur, *India* **158** G5
Gangawati, *India* **159** N5
Gangca, *China* **160** H10
Gangdise Range, *Asia* **146** H8
Gangdisê Shan, *China* **160** K5
Ganges, river, *Asia* **146** J8
Ganges, Mouths of the, *Bangladesh* **158** K12
Ganges Fan, *Ind. Oc.* **220** D11
Ganges Plain, *Asia* **146** H8
Gangtok, *India* **158** F12
Gannett Peak, *Wyo., U.S.* **100** H9
Ganongga *see* Ranongga, island, *Solomon Is.* **197** M15
Ganquan, *China* **162** F2
Gantgaw, *Myanmar* **166** G5
Ganyu, *China* **162** H8
Ganyushkino, *Kaz.* **154** F5
Ganzhou, *China* **163** P5
Gao, *Mali* **176** H9
Gaoligong Shan, *Myanmar* **166** D8
Gaoping, *China* **162** G4
Gaotai, *China* **160** G10
Gaotang, *China* **162** F6
Gaoua, *Burkina Faso* **180** F9
Gaoual, *Guinea* **180** E5
Gaoyang, *China* **162** E6
Gaoyi, *China* **162** E5
Gaoyou Hu, *China* **162** J8
Gap, *Fr.* **138** M12
Garabil Plateau, *Turkm.* **154** N10
Garabogaz Aylagy, *Turkm.* **154** J6
Garabogaz Bay, *Asia* **146** F5
Garabogazköl, *Turkm.* **154** K6
Garacad, *Somalia* **179** G18
Garagum, desert, *Turkm.* **154** K8
Garagum Canal, *Turkm.* **154** M10
Garaina, *P.N.G.* **193** D19
Garanhuns, *Braz.* **123** G17
Garapan, *Saipan, N. Mariana Is., U.S.* **196** B4
Garapan, Lagunan, *Saipan, N. Mariana Is., U.S.* **196** C4
Garber, *Okla., U.S.* **96** E10
Garberville, *Calif., U.S.* **103** N2
Garbyang, *India* **158** E8
Garda, Lake, *Eur.* **130** H6
Gardaneh-ye Asadābād, pass, *Iran* **152** C11
Gardar Ridge, *Atl. Oc.* **216** D10
Garden City, *Ga., U.S.* **91** N9
Garden City, *Kans., U.S.* **99** U4
Garden Island Bay, *La., U.S.* **94** R12
Garden of the Gods, *Hawaii, U.S.* **107** G14
Garden Point, *N. Terr., Austral.* **191** N7
Gardiner, *Me., U.S.* **89** G16
Gardiner, *Mont., U.S.* **100** F8
Gardiz, *Afghan.* **157** N8
Gardner Pinnacles, *Hawaii, U.S.* **106** L6
Gardnerville, *Nev., U.S.* **103** Q6
Garfield, *Wash., U.S.* **102** D9
Garhakota, *India* **158** H7
Garibaldi, *Oreg., U.S.* **102** F2
Garies, *S. Af.* **182** L7
Garim Island, *Yap Is., F.S.M.* **197** D18
Garissa, *Kenya* **179** K15
Garland, *Tex., U.S.* **96** L12
Garland, *Utah, U.S.* **100** J7
Garm, *Taj.* **156** H8
Garm Ab, *Afghan.* **157** N4
Garner, *Iowa, U.S.* **98** M11
Garnett, *Kans., U.S.* **99** T10
Garonne, river, *Fr.* **139** N9
Garoowe, *Somalia* **179** G18
Garoua, *Cameroon* **181** F16
Garreru, island, *Palau* **196** N11
Garrison, *N. Dak., U.S.* **98** F4
Garrison, *Utah, U.S.* **101** N5
Garrucha, *Sp.* **139** S8
Garrygala, *Turkm.* **154** L7
Garry Lake, *Nunavut, Can.* **77** G14
Garsen, *Kenya* **179** K15
Garshy, *Turkm.* **154** K6
Garu, *India* **158** J9
Garub, *Namibia* **182** J6
Garusuun, *Palau* **196** N11
Garut, *Indonesia* **168** M8
Garwa, *India* **158** H9
Gary, *Ind., U.S.* **93** N8
Garyarsa, *China* **160** K4
Garzón, *Col.* **120** G4
Gasa, *Bhutan* **158** F12
Gas City, *Ind., U.S.* **93** Q10
Gasconade, river, *Mo., U.S.* **99** U13
Gascoyne, river, *Austral.* **190** G2
Gascoyne Junction, *W. Austral., Austral.* **191** U2
Gascoyne Tablemount, *Pac. Oc.* **218** P7
Gashagar, *Nig.* **181** E16
Gas Hu, *China* **160** H8
Gashua, *Nig.* **181** E15
Gaspé, *Que., Can.* **77** N21
Gaspé Peninsula, *Que., Can.* **77** N21
Gassaway, *W. Va., U.S.* **90** D9
Gaston, Lake, *N.C.-Va., U.S.* **90** G12
Gastonia, *N.C., U.S.* **90** J9
Gastre, *Arg.* **125** R8
Gata, Cabo de, *Sp.* **139** T8
Gata, Cape, *Cyprus* **148** L8
Gataivai, *Samoa* **198** L2
Gatayake, Baie de, *Gambier Is., Fr. Polynesia, Fr.* **199** Q20
Gate, *Okla., U.S.* **96** E7
Gate City, *Va., U.S.* **90** G7
Gates of the Arctic National Park and Preserve, *Alas., U.S.* **105** D15
Gatesville, *Tex., U.S.* **97** N10
Gateway, *Colo., U.S.* **101** N10
Gatjapar, *Yap Is., F.S.M.* **197** D18
Gatlinburg, *Tenn., U.S.* **95** F19
Gau, island, *Fiji* **198** J7
Gausta, peak, *Nor.* **134** L10
Gavāter, *Iran* **153** J18
Gāvbandī, *Iran* **153** H14
Gávdos, island, *Gr.* **137** N15
Gaviota, *Calif., U.S.* **103** W6
Gävle, *Sw.* **135** K13
Gawachab, *Namibia* **182** K7
Gawai, *Myanmar* **166** C7
Gawler, *S. Austral., Austral.* **191** Y10
Gawler Ranges, *Austral.* **190** J9
Gaxun Nur, *China* **160** F10
Gaya, *India* **158** H10
Gaya, *Nig.* **181** E15
Gaya, *Niger* **176** J10
Gaylord, *Mich., U.S.* **92** H11
Gaylord, *Minn., U.S.* **98** K10
Gaza, *Gaza Strip* **151** N4
Gazak, *Afghan.* **156** L5
Gazak, *Iran* **153** G17
Gazanjyk, *Turkm.* **154** L7
Gaza Strip, *Asia* **151** N4
Gaziantep, *Turk.* **148** H12
Gazipaşa, *Turk.* **148** J7
Gazojak, *Turkm.* **154** K10
Gbadolite, *Dem. Rep. of the Congo* **178** H9
Gcuwa, *S. Af.* **182** L10
Gdańsk, *Pol.* **132** F9
Gdańsk, Gulf of, *Pol.* **132** E10
Gdynia, *Pol.* **132** E9
Gea, island, *Kwajalein Atoll, Marshall Is.* **196** N5
Gea Pass, *Kwajalein Atoll, Marshall Is.* **196** N5
Geary, *Okla., U.S.* **96** G9
Gebe, island, *Indonesia* **169** J17
Gebiz, *Turk.* **148** H6
Gebze, *Turk.* **148** D5
Gedaref, *Sudan* **179** E14
Geddes, *S. Dak., U.S.* **98** M6
Gediz, river, *Turk.* **148** F3
Gediz, *Turk.* **148** F5
Gedser, *Den.* **134** P12
Geelong, *Vic., Austral.* **191** Z12
Geelvink Channel, *Austral.* **190** J2
Geeveston, *Tas., Austral.* **191** Z16
Gefara, plain, *Af.* **174** D6
Gegibu, island, *Kwajalein Atoll, Marshall Is.* **196** L3
Gê'gyai, *China* **160** J5
Gehh, island, *Kwajalein Atoll, Marshall Is.* **196** N5
Geidam, *Nig.* **181** E16
Geiga, island, *Kwajalein Atoll, Marshall Is.* **196** K2
Geilo, *Nor.* **134** K10
Geita, *Tanzania* **179** L13
Gejiu, *China* **160** P11
Gelam, island, *Indonesia* **168** K9
Gelasa, Selat, *Indonesia* **168** K8
Gelibolu, *Turk.* **148** D3
Gellinam, island, *Kwajalein Atoll, Marshall Is.* **196** L5
Gemena, *Dem. Rep. of the Congo* **178** J9
Gemerek, *Turk.* **148** F11
Gemlik, *Turk.* **148** D5
Gemlik Körfezi, *Turk.* **148** D5
Gemsa, *Egypt* **177** D19
Gen, river, *China* **161** B15
Genalē, river, *Eth.* **179** H15
Genç, *Turk.* **149** F15
Geneina (Al Junaynah), *Sudan* **178** E10
General Acha, *Arg.* **125** N10
General Alvear, *Arg.* **124** L8
General Bernardo O'Higgins, station, *Antarctica* **206** C4
General Carrera, Lago, *Chile* **125** T7
General Conesa, *Arg.* **125** P10
General Eugenio A. Garay, *Para.* **122** L8
General Güemes, *Arg.* **124** F10
General Guido, *Arg.* **124** M13
General Juan Madariage, *Arg.* **125** N13
General La Madrid, *Arg.* **125** N11
General Levalle, *Arg.* **124** L10
General Lorenzo Vintter, *Arg.* **125** Q10
General Paz, *Arg.* **124** G13
General Pico, *Arg.* **124** M10
General Pinedo, *Arg.* **124** G11
General Roca, *Arg.* **125** P9
General San Martín, *Arg.* **125** N10
General San Martín, *Arg.* **125** S8
General Santos, *Philippines* **169** F15
Genesee, river, *N.Y., U.S.* **88** K6
Genesee, *Idaho, U.S.* **100** D3
Geneseo, *Ill., U.S.* **93** P4
Geneseo, *N.Y., U.S.* **88** J6
Geneva, *Ala., U.S.* **95** N16
Geneva, *Idaho, U.S.* **100** J8
Geneva, *N.Y., U.S.* **88** J7
Geneva, *Nebr., U.S.* **99** Q7
Geneva, *Ohio, U.S.* **93** N15
Geneva *see* Genève, *Switz.* **132** K3
Geneva, Lake of, *Eur.* **130** H5
Genève (Geneva), *Switz.* **132** K3
Genoa *see* Genova, *It.* **136** F8
Genoa, *Nebr., U.S.* **99** P7
Genova (Genoa), *It.* **136** F8
Gent, *Belg.* **138** H10
Geographe Bay, *Austral.* **190** K2
Geographe Channel, *Austral.* **190** G1
George, river, *Que., Can.* **77** K20
George, *S. Af.* **182** M8
George, Lake, *Austral.* **190** L14
George, Lake, *Fla., U.S.* **91** S8
George, Lake, *N.Y., U.S.* **88** H11
George, Zemlya, *Russ.* **140** B12
George Bligh Bank, *Atl. Oc.* **216** D11
George Town, *Cayman Is., U.K.* **110** L7
George Town, *Malaysia* **167** S8
George Town, *Tas., Austral.* **191** Y16
Georgetown, *Del., U.S.* **90** D15
Georgetown, *Gambia* **176** H5
Georgetown, *Guyana* **121** D15
Georgetown, *Ill., U.S.* **93** R7
Georgetown, *Ky., U.S.* **95** B18
Georgetown, *Ohio, U.S.* **93** T12
Georgetown, *Qnsld., Austral.* **191** R12
Georgetown, *S.C., U.S.* **90** L11
Georgetown, *St. Vincent and the Grenadines* **113** L17
Georgetown, *Tex., U.S.* **97** P10
George-Town, *Bahamas* **111** F13
Georve V Coast, *Antarctica* **207** R16
George VI Sound, *Antarctica* **206** F6
George Washington Birthplace National Monument, *Va., U.S.* **90** D13
George Washington Carver National Monument, *Mo., U.S.* **99** V11
George West, *Tex., U.S.* **97** T10
Georgia, *Asia* **149** B17
Georgia, *U.S.* **90** M6
Georgia, Strait of, *B.C., Can.* **76** M8
Georgiana, *Ala., U.S.* **95** M15
Georgian Bay, *Ont., Can.* **77** Q18
Georgievka, *Kaz.* **155** J15
Georgīevka, *Kaz.* **155** D18
Georgina, river, *Austral.* **190** F11
Gera, *Ger.* **132** H7
Geral de Goiás, Serra, *Braz.* **123** H14
Geraldine, *Mont., U.S.* **100** C9
Geraldine, *N.Z.* **193** P17
Geraldton, *Ont., Can.* **77** N16
Geraldton, *W. Austral., Austral.* **191** W2
Gerasa *see* Jarash, *Jordan* **150** L6
Gerber, *Calif., U.S.* **103** N4
Gercüş, *Turk.* **149** H16
Gerdine, Mount, *U.S.* **78** P4
Gerede, *Turk.* **148** D8
Gereshk, *Afghan.* **157** Q4
Gering, *Nebr., U.S.* **99** N1
Gerlach, peak, *Eur.* **130** G8
Gerlach, *Nev., U.S.* **103** N7
Germantown, *Tenn., U.S.* **94** G11
Germany, *Eur.* **132** G5
Germfask, *Mich., U.S.* **92** F9
Germī, *Iran* **152** A11
Gêrzê, *China* **160** K6
Gerze, *Turk.* **148** C10
Gesoa, *P.N.G.* **193** D18
Gestro, Wabē, *Eth.* **179** H16
Gettysburg, *Pa., U.S.* **88** Q7
Gettysburg, *S. Dak., U.S.* **98** J5
Getz Ice Shelf, *Antarctica* **206** M7
Geumpang, *Indonesia* **168** G4
Gevaş, *Turk.* **149** G17
Geylegphug, *Bhutan* **158** G13
Geyve, *Turk.* **148** D6
Ghadāmis, *Alg.* **176** C12
Ghaddūwah, *Lib.* **177** D14
Ghaghe, island, *Solomon Is.* **197** L17
Ghana, *Af.* **180** G10
Ghanzi, *Botswana* **182** H8
Gharandal, *Jordan* **151** Q5
Ghardaïa, *Alg.* **176** B11
Gharo, *Pak.* **157** W6
Gharyān, *Lib.* **177** C13
Ghatere, *Solomon Is.* **197** M18
Ghazal, Bahr el, *Chad* **177** H14
Ghaziabad, *India* **158** F6
Ghazipur, *India* **158** G9
Ghazīr, *Leb.* **150** H6
Ghazni, *Afghan.* **157** N7
Gheorghieni, *Rom.* **137** E16
Ghisonaccia, *Fr.* **139** P13
Ghormach, *Afghan.* **156** L3
Ghotki, *Pak.* **157** T8
Ghow Gardan Pass, *Afghan.* **156** M6
Ghurian, *Afghan.* **156** M2
Gia Nghia, *Vietnam* **167** N13
Gia Rai, *Vietnam* **167** Q12
Gibara, *Cuba* **110** J12
Gibbon, *Nebr., U.S.* **99** Q6
Gibbonsville, *Mont., U.S.* **100** E6
Gibb River, *W. Austral., Austral.* **191** Q5
Gibeon, *Namibia* **182** J7
Gibraltar, *Eur.* **139** T6
Gibraltar, Strait of, *Af.-Eur.* **130** K2
Gibsland, *La., U.S.* **94** L7
Gibson, *W. Austral., Austral.* **191** X4
Gibson City, *Ill., U.S.* **93** Q6
Gibson Desert, *Austral.* **190** F5
Gidar, *Pak.* **157** T5
Giddalur, *India* **159** N6
Giddings, *Tex., U.S.* **97** Q12
Gīdolē, *Eth.* **179** H14
Gien, *Fr.* **138** L10
Giessen, *Ger.* **132** H5
Gifford, river, *Nunavut, Can.* **77** E16
Gifford, *Fla., U.S.* **91** U10
Gifu, *Jap.* **165** P10
G'ijduvon, *Uzb.* **154** L11
Gijón, *Sp.* **139** N6
Gila, river, *Ariz., U.S.* **101** U5
Gila, *N. Mex., U.S.* **101** U10
Gila Bend, *Ariz., U.S.* **101** U6
Gila Bend Mountains, *Ariz., U.S.* **101** U6
Gila Cliff Dwellings National Monument, *N. Mex., U.S.* **101** U10
Gilbert, river, *Austral.* **190** C12
Gilbert, *Ariz., U.S.* **101** U7
Gilbert, *Minn., U.S.* **98** F12
Gilbert Islands, *Kiribati* **194** G8
Gilbert River, *Qnsld., Austral.* **191** R12
Gilbert Seamount, *Pac. Oc.* **219** C13
Gilbués, *Braz.* **123** G14
Gilchrist, *Oreg., U.S.* **102** J4
Gildford, *Mont., U.S.* **100** B9
Gilf Kebir Plateau, *Egypt* **177** E17
Gilgandra, *N.S.W., Austral.* **191** X14
Gilgit, region, *Pak.* **156** L11
Gilgit, river, *Pak.* **156** L11
Gilgit, *Pak.* **156** L11
Gillam, *Man., Can.* **77** L14
Gillen, Lake, *Austral.* **190** G5
Gilles, Lake, *Austral.* **190** K9
Gillespie, *Ill., U.S.* **93** S4
Gillett, *Ark., U.S.* **94** H9
Gillette, *Wyo., U.S.* **100** G12
Gills Rock, *Wis., U.S.* **92** H8
Gilman, *Ill., U.S.* **93** Q7
Gilmer, *Tex., U.S.* **96** L14
Gilmore Hut, *Qnsld., Austral.* **191** U12

Gilpeppee, *Qnsld., Austral.* **191** U11
Gilroy, *Calif., U.S.* **103** T4
Gima, *Jap.* **165** Y1
Gimli, *Man., Can.* **77** N14
Gingoog, *Philippines* **169** E15
Gīnīr, *Eth.* **179** G15
Ginowan, *Jap.* **165** Y1
Gippsland, region, *Austral.* **190** M13
Girab, *India* **158** G2
Girard, *Kans., U.S.* **99** U10
Girard, *Pa., U.S.* **88** K3
Girardot, *Col.* **120** F5
Giresun, *Turk.* **149** D13
Girga, *Egypt* **177** D19
Gir Hills, *India* **158** K2
Giridih, *India* **158** H10
Girona, *Sp.* **139** P10
Gisborne, *N.Z.* **193** K20
Gitega, *Burundi* **178** L12
Githio, *Gr.* **137** M15
Giurgiu, *Rom.* **137** G16
Gizab, *Afghan.* **157** N5
Gizo, *Solomon Is.* **197** M15
Gjirokastër, *Alban.* **137** J13
Gjoa Haven, *Nunavut, Can.* **77** F14
Gjøvik, *Nor.* **134** K11
Gkreko, Cape, *Cyprus* **148** L9
Glace Bay, *N.S., Can.* **77** N23
Glacier Bay, *Alas., U.S.* **105** K21
Glacier Bay National Park and Preserve, *Alas., U.S.* **105** K21
Glacier National Park, *Mont., U.S.* **100** A6
Glacier Peak, *Wash., U.S.* **102** B5
Gladewater, *Tex., U.S.* **96** L14
Gladstone, *Mich., U.S.* **92** G8
Gladstone, *Qnsld., Austral.* **191** U15
Gladstone, *S. Austral., Austral.* **191** X10
Gladwin, *Mich., U.S.* **92** K11
Glåma, river, *Nor.* **134** J11
Glasco, *Kans., U.S.* **99** S7
Glasgow, *Ky., U.S.* **95** D16
Glasgow, *Mo., U.S.* **99** S12
Glasgow, *Mont., U.S.* **100** B11
Glasgow, *Scot., U.K.* **138** E7
Glassboro, *N.J., U.S.* **88** Q9
Glass Buttes, *Oreg., U.S.* **102** J6
Glass Mountain, *Calif., U.S.* **102** L4
Glass Mountains, *Tex., U.S.* **97** Q3
Glazov, *Russ.* **140** G8
Glen Arbor, *Mich., U.S.* **92** H9
Glenavy, *N.Z.* **193** Q17
Glenayle, *W. Austral., Austral.* **191** U4
Glen Canyon Dam, *Ariz., U.S.* **101** Q7
Glen Canyon National Recreation Area, *Utah, U.S.* **101** P8
Glencoe, *Minn., U.S.* **98** K11
Glendale, *Ariz., U.S.* **101** U6
Glendale, *Calif., U.S.* **103** X8
Glendale, *Oreg., U.S.* **102** K2
Glendive, *Mont., U.S.* **100** C13
Glendo, *Wyo., U.S.* **100** J13
Glendo Reservoir, *Wyo., U.S.* **100** H13
Glengyle, *Qnsld., Austral.* **191** U11
Glen Innes, *N.S.W., Austral.* **191** W15
Glenmora, *La., U.S.* **94** N8
Glennallen, *Alas., U.S.* **105** H17
Glenn Highway, *Alas., U.S.* **105** H17
Glenns Ferry, *Idaho, U.S.* **100** H4
Glennville, *Ga., U.S.* **91** N8
Glenormiston, *Qnsld., Austral.* **191** T10
Glenreagh, *N.S.W., Austral.* **191** W15
Glenrock, *Wyo., U.S.* **100** H12
Glen Rose, *Tex., U.S.* **96** M10
Glenroy, *W. Austral., Austral.* **191** R5
Glens Falls, *N.Y., U.S.* **88** H11
Glen Ullin, *N. Dak., U.S.* **98** G3
Glenwood, *Ark., U.S.* **94** H7
Glenwood, *Iowa, U.S.* **99** Q9
Glenwood, *Minn., U.S.* **98** J9
Glenwood, *N. Mex., U.S.* **101** U10
Glenwood Springs, *Colo., U.S.* **100** M11
Glidden, *Wis., U.S.* **92** F4
Gliwice, *Pol.* **132** H9
Globe, *Ariz., U.S.* **101** U8
Gloria, Puntan, *Saipan, N. Mariana Is., U.S.* **196** B5
Gloria Ridge, *Atl. Oc.* **216** E7
Glorieuses, Îles, *Ind. Oc.* **183** D17
Gloster, *Miss., U.S.* **94** N10
Gloucester, *Mass., U.S.* **89** K15
Gloucester, *N.S.W., Austral.* **191** X15
Gloucester, *P.N.G.* **193** C20
Gloversville, *N.Y., U.S.* **88** J10
Glübokoe, *Kaz.* **155** D18
Gmünd, *Aust.* **132** J8
Gnaraloo, *W. Austral., Austral.* **191** U1
Goa, *India* **159** N4
Goalpara, *India* **158** G13
Goba, *Eth.* **179** G15
Gobabis, *Namibia* **182** H7
Gobernador Duval, *Arg.* **125** P9
Gobernador Gregores, *Arg.* **125** U8
Gobi, desert, *Asia* **146** F11
Gobō, *Jap.* **165** R8
Go Cong, *Vietnam* **167** P13
Godavari, river, *India* **158** M8
Godavari, Mouths of the, *India* **159** N8
Godhavn *see* Qeqertarsuaq, *Greenland, Den.* **75** C21
Godhra, *India* **158** J4
Godoy Cruz, *Arg.* **124** K8
Gods, river, *Man., Can.* **77** L15
Gods Lake, *Man., Can.* **77** L14
Godthåb *see* Nuuk, *Greenland, Den.* **75** D21
Godwin Austen *see* K2, peak, *Asia* **146** G7
Goélands, Lac aux, *Que., Can.* **77** K20
Gogebic, Lake, *Mich., U.S.* **92** F5
Gogebic Range, *U.S.* **79** D14
Gogrial, *Sudan* **178** G11
Goianésia, *Braz.* **123** J13
Goiânia, *Braz.* **123** J13
Goikul, *Palau* **196** N12
Gojōme, *Jap.* **164** K12
Gojra, *Pak.* **157** Q10
Gök, river, *Turk.* **148** C10
Goka, *Jap.* **165** N7
Gokak, *India* **159** N4
Gökçeada (İmroz), island, *Turk.* **148** D2
Gökdepe, *Turkm.* **154** M8
Gökova Körfezi, *Turk.* **148** H3
Göksu, river, *Turk.* **148** G11
Göksu, river, *Turk.* **148** J8
Göksun, *Turk.* **148** G11
Golaghat, *India* **158** G14
Golan Heights, *Israel* **150** K6
Golbahar, *Afghan.* **156** M8
Gölbaşı, *Turk.* **148** E8
Gölbaşı, *Turk.* **148** H12
Golconda, *Nev., U.S.* **102** M9
Gölcük, *Turk.* **148** D5
Gold Beach, *Oreg., U.S.* **102** K1
Gold Coast, *Ghana* **180** J10
Gold Coast, *Qnsld., Austral.* **191** V15
Golden, *Colo., U.S.* **100** M13
Golden Bay, *N.Z.* **193** M17
Goldendale, *Wash., U.S.* **102** E5
Golden Gate, strait, *Calif., U.S.* **103** S3
Golden Gate National Recreation Area, *Calif., U.S.* **103** R3
Golden Meadow, *La., U.S.* **94** R11
Golden Ridge, *W. Austral., Austral.* **191** W4
Golden Spike National Historic Site, *Utah, U.S.* **100** K6
Goldfield, *Nev., U.S.* **103** S9
Goldsboro, *N.C., U.S.* **90** H12
Goldsmith, *Tex., U.S.* **96** M4
Goldsworthy, *W. Austral., Austral.* **191** S3
Goldthwaite, *Tex., U.S.* **97** N9
Göle, *Turk.* **149** D17
Golela, *Swaziland* **182** K12
Goleta, *Calif., U.S.* **103** W6
Golfito, *C.R.* **109** P19
Golfo Aranci, *It.* **136** J8
Goliad, *Tex., U.S.* **97** S11
Gölköy, *Turk.* **148** D12
Golmud, *China* **160** J9
Gölören, *Turk.* **148** G9
Golovin, *Alas., U.S.* **104** G12
Gölpazarı, *Turk.* **148** D6
Golubovka, *Kaz.* **155** B15
Goma, *Dem. Rep. of the Congo* **178** K12
Gombe, *Nig.* **181** F15
Gombrani Island, *Mauritius* **185** J20
Gomera, island, *Canary Is., Sp.* **184** Q4
Gómez Palacio, *Mex.* **108** F10
Gonaïves, *Haiti* **111** L16
Gonam, river, *Russ.* **141** J18
Gonam, *Russ.* **141** H19
Gonâve, Golfe de la, *Haiti* **111** L15
Gonâve, Île de la, *Haiti* **111** M15
Gonbad-e Kāvūs, *Iran* **153** B14
Gonda, *India* **158** G8
Gonder, *Eth.* **179** E14
Gondia, *India* **158** K7
Gönen, *Turk.* **148** D3
Gong'an, *China* **162** L4
Gongbo'gyamda, *China* **160** L8
Gongcheng, *China* **163** Q2
Gonggar, *China* **160** L7
Gongga Shan, *China* **160** L11
Gonglee, *Liberia* **180** H7
Gongola, river, *Nig.* **181** F16
Gongolgon, *N.S.W., Austral.* **191** W13
Gongxi, *China* **163** N6
Gongzhuling, *China* **162** A11
Gōno, river, *Jap.* **165** Q6
Gōnoura, *Jap.* **165** R3
Gonzales, *Calif., U.S.* **103** T4
Gonzales, *Tex., U.S.* **97** R11
González Chaves, *Arg.* **125** N12
Goodenough Island, *P.N.G.* **193** E21
Good Hope, Cape of, *S. Af.* **182** M7
Goodhouse, *S. Af.* **182** K7
Gooding, *Idaho, U.S.* **100** H5
Goodland, *Kans., U.S.* **99** S3
Goodlands, *Mauritius* **185** F20
Goodlettsville, *Tenn., U.S.* **95** E15
Goodman, *Miss., U.S.* **94** K11
Goodman, *Wis., U.S.* **92** G6
Goodnews Bay, *Alas., U.S.* **104** L12
Goodooga, *N.S.W., Austral.* **191** W13
Goodparla, *N. Terr., Austral.* **191** P8
Goodridge, *Minn., U.S.* **98** E9
Goodwell, *Okla., U.S.* **96** E5
Goofnuw Inlet, *Yap Is., F.S.M.* **197** D18
Goolgowi, *N.S.W., Austral.* **191** X12
Goomalling, *W. Austral., Austral.* **191** X3
Goondiwindi, *Qnsld., Austral.* **191** V14
Goongarrie, Lake, *Austral.* **190** J4
Goonyella, *Qnsld., Austral.* **191** T14
Goose Creek, *S.C., U.S.* **90** M10
Goose Lake, *Calif.-Oreg., U.S.* **102** L6
Gora, *Russ.* **141** L17
Gora Belukha, peak, *Kaz.* **155** D20
Gorakhpur, *India* **158** G9
Goraklbad Passage, *Palau* **196** P12
Gördes, *Turk.* **148** F4
Gordion, ruins, *Turk.* **148** E7
Gordo, *Ala., U.S.* **95** K14
Gordon, *Ga., U.S.* **90** M6
Gordon, *Nebr., U.S.* **98** M3
Gordon, *Wis., U.S.* **92** F3
Gordon, Lake, *Austral.* **190** M16
Gordon Downs, *W. Austral., Austral.* **191** R6
Gordon's, *Bahamas* **111** G14
Gordonsville, *Va., U.S.* **90** E12
Goré, *Chad* **177** K14
Gore, *N.Z.* **193** R16
Gorē, *Eth.* **179** G14
Goreda, *Indonesia* **193** C15
Goree, *Tex., U.S.* **96** K8
Görele, *Turk.* **149** D13
Gorgān, *Iran* **153** B14
Gorgona, Isla, *Col.* **120** G3
Gorham, *N.H., U.S.* **89** F14
Gori, *Rep. of Georgia* **149** B18
Goris, *Arm.* **149** E20
Gorizia, *It.* **136** E10
Gor'kiy Reservoir, *Eur.* **130** D11
Görlitz, *Ger.* **132** H8
Gorman, *Tex., U.S.* **96** M9
Gorno Altaysk, *Russ.* **140** L12
Gornozavodsk, *Russ.* **141** K22
Gornyak, *Russ.* **140** L11
Gornyatskiy, *Russ.* **140** F11
Goroka, *P.N.G.* **193** D19
Gorong, Kepulauan, *Indonesia* **169** L17
Gorongosa, Serra da, *Af.* **174** N9
Gorontalo, *Indonesia* **169** J14
Gorror, *Yap Is., F.S.M.* **197** D18
Gorzów Wielkopolski, *Pol.* **132** G8
Goschen Strait, *P.N.G.* **193** E21
Gosen, *Jap.* **164** M12
Gosford, *N.S.W., Austral.* **191** X14
Goshen, *Ind., U.S.* **93** N9
Goshen, *Utah, U.S.* **100** L7
Goshogawara, *Jap.* **164** J12
Gosnel, *Ark., U.S.* **94** E11
Gospić, *Croatia* **136** F11
Göteborg, *Sw.* **134** M12
Gotha, *Ger.* **132** H6
Gothenburg, *Nebr., U.S.* **99** Q5
Gothèye, *Niger* **176** H10
Gotland, island, *Sw.* **135** M14
Gotō Rettō, *Jap.* **165** R2
Gotska Sandön, island, *Sw.* **135** L14
Gōtsu, *Jap.* **165** Q6
Gouaro, Baie de, *New Caledonia, Fr.* **198** D7
Gouin, Réservoir, *Que., Can.* **77** N19
Gould, *Ark., U.S.* **94** H9
Gould Bay, *Antarctica* **206** E9
Gould Coast, *Antarctica* **206** K11
Gouldsboro, *Me., U.S.* **89** F18
Goulimine, *Mor.* **176** C7
Goulvain, Cap, *New Caledonia, Fr.* **198** D7
Goumbou, *Mali* **176** H7
Goundam, *Mali* **176** G8
Gouré, *Niger* **176** H12
Gouro, *Chad* **177** G15
Gouverneur, *N.Y., U.S.* **88** G9
Gove, *Kans., U.S.* **99** S4
Govena, Mys, *Russ.* **141** D22
Govenlock, *Sask., Can.* **76** N11
Gove Peninsula, *Austral.* **190** B9
Governador Valadares, *Braz.* **123** K15
Governor Generoso, *Philippines* **169** F15
Governor's Harbour, *Bahamas* **110** E12
Govindgarh, *India* **158** H8
Govorovo, *Russ.* **141** F16
Gowanda, *N.Y., U.S.* **88** K5
Gowd-e Zereh, Dasht-e, *Afghan.* **157** R2
Gowmal Kalay, *Afghan.* **157** P7
Gowrzanak, *Afghan.* **157** P3
Goya, *Arg.* **124** H13
Göyçay, *Azerb.* **149** D21
Göynük, *Turk.* **148** D6
Gozha Co, *China* **160** H5
Gozo, island, *Malta* **136** M10
Graaff-Reinet, *S. Af.* **182** L9
Grace, *Idaho, U.S.* **100** J7
Graceville, *Fla., U.S.* **91** Q3
Graceville, *Minn., U.S.* **98** J8
Gracias a Dios, Cabo, *Nicar.* **109** K19
Graciosa, island, *Canary Is., Sp.* **184** P8
Graciosa Bay, *Santa Cruz Is., Solomon Is.* **197** P22
Gradaús, *Braz.* **122** F12
Graford, *Tex., U.S.* **96** L10
Grafton, *N. Dak., U.S.* **98** E7
Grafton, *N.S.W., Austral.* **191** W15
Grafton, *W. Va., U.S.* **90** C10
Grafton, *Wis., U.S.* **92** L7
Grafton, Mount, *Nev., U.S.* **103** Q12
Graham, *N.C., U.S.* **90** G11
Graham, *Ont., Can.* **77** N15
Graham, *Tex., U.S.* **96** L9
Graham, Mount, *Ariz., U.S.* **101** V9
Graham Bell, Ostrov, *Russ.* **141** C13
Graham Island, *B.C., Can.* **76** J6
Graham Island, *Nunavut, Can.* **77** C15
Graham Lake, *Me., U.S.* **89** F18
Graham land, *Antarctica* **206** D4
Grahamstown, *S. Af.* **182** M10
Grain Coast, *Liberia* **180** H6
Grajaú, *Braz.* **123** E14
Grampian Mountains, *Eur.* **130** D4
Granada, *Colo., U.S.* **101** N16
Granada, *Nicar.* **109** M18
Granada, *Sp.* **139** S7
Granadilla, *Canary Is., Sp.* **184** Q5
Gran Altiplanicie Central, *Arg.* **125** U8
Granbury, *Tex., U.S.* **96** L10
Granby, *Colo., U.S.* **100** L12
Granby, *Que., Can.* **77** P20
Gran Canaria, island, *Canary Is., Sp.* **184** R6
Gran Chaco, *S. Amer.* **118** J6
Grand, river, *Mich., U.S.* **92** L10
Grand, river, *Mo., U.S.* **99** R12
Grand, river, *S. Dak., U.S.* **98** J3
Grand Bahama Island, *Bahamas* **110** C10
Grand-Bassam, *Côte d'Ivoire* **180** H9
Grand Bay, *Mauritius* **185** J20
Grand-Bourg, *Guadeloupe, Fr.* **113** H17
Grand Caicos, island, *Turks and Caicos Is., U.K.* **111** H17
Grand Canal *see* Da Yunhe, *China* **162** J8
Grand Canyon, *Ariz., U.S.* **101** R6
Grand Canyon, *Ariz., U.S.* **101** R7
Grand Canyon National Park, *Ariz., U.S.* **101** Q6
Grand Canyon-Parashant National Monument, *Ariz., U.S.* **101** Q5
Grand Cayman, island, *Cayman Is., U.K.* **110** L7
Grand Cess, *Liberia* **180** H7
Grand Coulee, *Wash., U.S.* **102** B7
Grand Coulee Dam, *Wash., U.S.* **102** B7
Grande, river, *Arg.* **124** M7
Grande, river, *Arg.* **125** X9
Grande, river, *Bol.* **122** J8
Grande, river, *Bol.* **122** K7
Grande, river, *Braz.* **123** G15
Grande, river, *Braz.* **123** L13
Grande, river, *Chile* **125** X9
Grande, river, *Oreg., U.S.* **102** E8
Grande, Bahía, *Arg.* **125** V9
Grande, Boca, *Venez.* **121** C13
Grande, Cayo, *Cuba* **110** J9
Grande, Cuchilla, *Uru.* **124** L14
Grande, Salina, *Arg.* **125** N8
Grande Cayemite, island, *Haiti* **111** M15
Grande Comore *see* Njazidja, *Comoros* **183** D16
Grande de Chiloé, Isla, *Chile* **125** R6
Grande de Tierra del Fuego, Isla, *Arg.-Chile* **125** X9
Grande Prairie, *Alta., Can.* **76** K10
Grande Rivière du Nord, *Haiti* **111** L17
Grande Rivière Sud Est, *Mauritius* **185** G21
Grandes, Salinas, *Arg.* **124** H10
Grande-Terre, island, *Guadeloupe, Fr.* **113** H17
Grande 2, Réservoir de La, *Que., Can.* **77** L18
Grandfalls, *Tex., U.S.* **97** N3
Grand Falls-Windsor, *Nfld., Can.* **77** M23
Grandfather Mountain, *N.C., U.S.* **90** H8
Grandfield, *Okla., U.S.* **96** J9
Grand Forks, *N. Dak., U.S.* **98** F8
Grand-Gosier, *Haiti* **111** N17
Grand Haven, *Mich., U.S.* **92** L9
Grand Island, *Mich., U.S.* **92** F8
Grand Island, *Nebr., U.S.* **99** Q6
Grand Isle, *La., U.S.* **94** R11
Grand Junction, *Colo., U.S.* **100** M10
Grand Lake, *La., U.S.* **94** Q8
Grand Lake, *Ohio, U.S.* **93** Q11
Grand Ledge, *Mich., U.S.* **92** M11
Grand Marais, *Mich., U.S.* **92** F9
Grand Marais, *Minn., U.S.* **98** F14
Grand Mountain, *Mauritius* **185** J20
Grand Passage, *New Caledonia, Fr.* **198** A5
Grand Portage, *Minn., U.S.* **98** E14
Grand Portage National Monument, *Minn., U.S.* **98** E15

Grand Prairie, *Tex., U.S.* **96** L11
Grand Rapids, *Man., Can.* **77** M13
Grand Rapids, *Mich., U.S.* **92** L10
Grand Rapids, *Minn., U.S.* **98** G11
Grand Saline, *Tex., U.S.* **96** L13
Grand Staircase-Escalante National Monument, *Utah, U.S.* **101** P7
Grand Teton, *Wyo., U.S.* **100** G8
Grand Teton National Park, *Wyo., U.S.* **100** G8
Grand Traverse Bay, *Mich., U.S.* **92** H9
Grand Turk, *Turks and Caicos Is., U.K.* **111** J18
Grandview, *Wash., U.S.* **102** E6
Granger, *Tex., U.S.* **97** P11
Granger, *Wash., U.S.* **102** E6
Granger, *Wyo., U.S.* **100** K9
Grangeville, *Idaho, U.S.* **100** E4
Granite, *Okla., U.S.* **96** H8
Granite, *Oreg., U.S.* **102** G8
Granite City, *Ill., U.S.* **93** T4
Granite Falls, *Minn., U.S.* **98** K9
Granite Mountains, *Calif., U.S.* **103** V10
Granite Peak, *W. Austral., Austral.* **191** U4
Granite Peak, *Mont., U.S.* **100** F9
Granite Peak, *Nev., U.S.* **102** M7
Granite Peak, *Utah, U.S.* **100** L6
Granja, *Braz.* **123** E16
Gran Quivira *see* Salinas Pueblo Missions National Monument, *N. Mex., U.S.* **101** T12
Grant, *Nebr., U.S.* **99** Q3
Grant, Mount, *Nev., U.S.* **103** R7
Gran Tarajal, *Canary Is., Sp.* **184** Q7
Grant City, *Mo., U.S.* **99** Q10
Grant Island, *Antarctica* **206** N8
Grant-Kohrs Ranch National Historic Site, *Mont., U.S.* **100** D6
Grant Range, *Nev., U.S.* **103** R11
Grants, *N. Mex., U.S.* **101** S11
Grantsburg, *Wis., U.S.* **92** G2
Grants Pass, *Oreg., U.S.* **102** K2
Grantville, *Ga., U.S.* **90** M4
Granville, *Fr.* **138** K8
Granville, *N. Dak., U.S.* **98** E4
Granville, *N.Y., U.S.* **88** H12
Granville Lake, *Man., Can.* **77** L13
Grão Mogol, *Braz.* **123** J15
Grapeland, *Tex., U.S.* **97** N13
Grapevine Lake, *Tex., U.S.* **96** L11
Grassmere, *Qnsld., Austral.* **191** V13
Grass Patch, *W. Austral., Austral.* **191** X4
Grassrange, *Mont., U.S.* **100** D10
Grass Valley, *Calif., U.S.* **103** Q5
Grassy Butte, *N. Dak., U.S.* **98** F2
Grassy Key, *Fla., U.S.* **91** Y9
Gravelbourg, *Sask., Can.* **76** N11
Grave Peak, *Idaho, U.S.* **100** D5
Gravette, *Ark., U.S.* **94** E6
Gravois, Pointe-à-, *Haiti* **111** N15
Grayland, *Wash., U.S.* **102** D2
Grayling, *Alas., U.S.* **105** H13
Grayling, *Mich., U.S.* **92** J11
Grays Harbor, *Wash., U.S.* **102** D2
Grays Lake, *Idaho, U.S.* **100** H7
Grayson, *Ky., U.S.* **95** B19
Grayville, *Ill., U.S.* **93** T7
Graz, *Aust.* **132** K8
Great, river, *Myanmar* **167** N8
Great Artesian Basin, *Austral.* **190** F11
Great Australian Bight, *Austral.* **190** K7
Great Bahama Bank, *Bahamas* **110** E10
Great Barrier Island, *N.Z.* **193** J19
Great Barrier Reef, *Austral.* **190** E15
Great Basin, *U.S.* **78** G5
Great Basin National Park, *Nev., U.S.* **103** Q12
Great Bear Lake, *N. Amer.* **74** D4
Great Bear Lake, *N.W.T., Can.* **76** F11
Great Bend, *Kans., U.S.* **99** T6
Great Bitter Lake *see* Murrat el Kubra, Buheirat, *Egypt* **151** Q1
Great Britain, island, *U.K.* **138** F9
Great Channel, *India* **159** T15
Great Channel, *Indonesia* **168** F3
Great Coco Island, *Myanmar* **159** P15
Great Crack, *Hawaii, U.S.* **107** N20
Great Crater, *Israel* **151** P5
Great Dismal Swamp, *N.C.-Va., U.S.* **90** G14
Great Divide Basin, *U.S.* **78** F8
Great Dividing Range, *Austral.* **190** C12
Great Eastern Erg, *Af.* **174** D5
Greater Antilles, islands, *N. Amer.* **74** N9
Greater Khingan Range, *Asia* **146** F11
Greater Sunda Islands, *Indonesia* **168** K10
Great Exuma, island, *Bahamas* **111** F13
Great Fall, *Guyana* **121** E13
Great Falls, *Mont., U.S.* **100** C8
Great Falls, *S.C., U.S.* **90** K9
Great Guana Cay, *Bahamas* **110** C12
Great Guana Cay, *Bahamas* **110** F12
Great Harbour Cay, *Bahamas* **110** D11
Great Hungarian Plain, *Eur.* **130** H8
Great Inagua Island, *Bahamas* **111** J15
Great Indian Desert (Thar Desert), *India-Pak.* **157** S9
Great Isaac, island, *Bahamas* **110** D9
Great Karroo, region, *Af.* **174** Q7
Great Meteor Tablemount, *Atl. Oc.* **216** J9
Great Miami, river, *U.S.* **79** G17
Great Namaland, region, *Namibia* **182** J7
Great Nicobar, island, *Nicobar Is., India* **159** T15
Great Pedro Bluff, *Jam.* **110** N11
Great Pee Dee, river, *S.C., U.S.* **90** L11
Great Plains, *U.S.* **78** D9
Great Rift Valley, *Af.* **174** J10
Great Ruaha, river, *Tanzania* **179** M13
Great Sacandaga Lake, *N.Y., U.S.* **88** J11
Great Salt Lake, *Utah, U.S.* **100** K6
Great Salt Lake Desert, *Utah, U.S.* **100** L6
Great Salt Plains Lake, *Okla., U.S.* **96** E10
Great Sand Dunes National Monument, *Colo., U.S.* **101** P13
Great Sandy Desert, *Austral.* **190** E5
Great Sandy Desert, *U.S.* **78** D4
Great Sandy Island *see* Fraser Island, *Austral.* **190** G16
Great Sitkin Island, *Alas., U.S.* **104** Q6
Great Slave Lake, *N.W.T., Can.* **76** H11
Great Smoky Mountains, *U.S.* **79** J18
Great Smoky Mountains National Park, *N.C.-Tenn., U.S.* **90** H6
Great Sound, *Bermuda, U.K.* **111** G17
Great Stirrup Cay, *Bahamas* **110** D11
Great Victoria Desert, *Austral.* **190** H6
Great Wall, station, *Antarctica* **206** C3
Great Wall, *China* **161** H13
Great Western Erg, *Af.* **174** D4
Great Western Tiers, *Austral.* **190** L16
Great Zab, river, *Turk.* **149** G18
Great Zimbabwe, ruins, *Zimb.* **182** G11
Greece, *Eur.* **131** X8
Greece, *N.Y., U.S.* **88** H6
Greeley, *Colo., U.S.* **100** L13
Greeley, *Nebr., U.S.* **99** P6
Greely Fjord, *Nunavut, Can.* **77** B16
Green, river, *Ky., U.S.* **95** D15
Green, river, *Utah, U.S.* **100** L9
Green Bay, *Wis., U.S.* **92** H7
Green Bay, *Wis., U.S.* **92** J7
Greenbrier, river, *W. Va., U.S.* **90** E10
Greenbush, *Mich., U.S.* **92** J12
Greenbush, *Minn., U.S.* **98** E9
Greencastle, *Ind., U.S.* **93** R8
Greencastle, *Pa., U.S.* **88** Q6
Green Cay, *Bahamas* **110** F11
Green Cove Springs, *Fla., U.S.* **91** R8
Greeneville, *Tenn., U.S.* **95** E20
Greenfield, *Calif., U.S.* **103** U5
Greenfield, *Ind., U.S.* **93** R9
Greenfield, *Iowa, U.S.* **99** P10
Greenfield, *Mass., U.S.* **89** K13
Greenfield, *Mo., U.S.* **99** U11
Greenfield, *Ohio, U.S.* **93** S12
Greenfield, *Tenn., U.S.* **95** E13
Greenfield, *Wis., U.S.* **92** L7
Green Head, *Austral.* **190** J2
Green Island, *P.N.G.* **193** C22
Green Island, *Jam.* **110** M10
Green Islands, *P.N.G.* **197** H13
Greenland (Kalaallit Nunaat), *N. Amer.* **75** B20
Greenland Fracture Zone, *Arctic Oc.* **223** H16
Greenland Plain, *Arctic Oc.* **223** J17
Greenland Sea, *N. Amer.* **74** A10
Green Mountains, *Vt., U.S.* **88** J12
Green Mountains, *Wyo., U.S.* **100** J11
Greenock, *Scot., U.K.* **138** E7
Greenport, *N.Y., U.S.* **89** M13
Green River, *Utah, U.S.* **100** M9
Green River, *Wyo., U.S.* **100** K9
Greensboro, *Ala., U.S.* **95** L14
Greensboro, *Ga., U.S.* **90** L6
Greensboro, *N.C., U.S.* **90** G10
Greensburg, *Ind., U.S.* **93** S10
Greensburg, *Kans., U.S.* **99** U5
Greensburg, *Ky., U.S.* **95** C17
Greensburg, *Pa., U.S.* **88** P4
Greens Peak, *Ariz., U.S.* **101** T9
Green Valley, *Ariz., U.S.* **101** V8
Greenville, *Ala., U.S.* **95** M15
Greenville, *Calif., U.S.* **103** N5
Greenville, *Fla., U.S.* **91** Q6
Greenville, *Ill., U.S.* **93** T5
Greenville, *Ky., U.S.* **95** D15
Greenville, *Liberia* **180** H7
Greenville, *Me., U.S.* **89** D16
Greenville, *Mich., U.S.* **92** L10
Greenville, *Miss., U.S.* **94** J10
Greenville, *N.C., U.S.* **90** H13
Greenville, *Ohio, U.S.* **93** R11
Greenville, *Pa., U.S.* **88** M3
Greenville, *S.C., U.S.* **90** J7
Greenville, *Tex., U.S.* **96** K12
Greenwood, *Ark., U.S.* **94** F6
Greenwood, *Ind., U.S.* **93** R9
Greenwood, *Miss., U.S.* **94** J11
Greenwood, *S.C., U.S.* **90** K7
Greer, *Ariz., U.S.* **101** T9
Greer, *S.C., U.S.* **90** J7
Greers Ferry Lake, *Ark., U.S.* **94** F8
Gregory, river, *Austral.* **190** D11
Gregory, *S. Dak., U.S.* **98** M5
Gregory, Lake, *Austral.* **190** H10
Gregory Downs, *Qnsld., Austral.* **191** R10
Gregory Range, *Austral.* **190** D12
Greifswald, *Ger.* **132** F7
Grenada, *N. Amer.* **113** M17
Grenada, island, *N. Amer.* **74** P12
Grenada, *Calif., U.S.* **102** L3
Grenada, *Miss., U.S.* **94** J11
Grenoble, *Fr.* **138** M12
Grenora, *N. Dak., U.S.* **98** E2
Grenville, *Grenada* **113** M17
Grenville, Cape, *Austral.* **190** A12
Grenville, Point, *Wash., U.S.* **102** C2
Gresham, *Oreg., U.S.* **102** F4
Gretna, *La., U.S.* **94** Q11
Grey, Mount, *Austral.* **190** J3
Greybull, river, *Wyo., U.S.* **100** G10
Greybull, *Wyo., U.S.* **100** F10
Grey Islands, *Nfld., Can.* **77** L23
Greylock, Mount, *Mass., U.S.* **88** K12
Grey Range, *Austral.* **190** H12
Gridley, *Calif., U.S.* **103** P4
Grieg Point, *Tabuaeran, Kiribati* **197** B20
Griffin, *Ga., U.S.* **90** M5
Griffith, *N.S.W., Austral.* **191** Y13
Griggsville, *Ill., U.S.* **93** R3
Grimault, Île, *New Caledonia, Fr.* **198** D7
Grímsey, island, *Ice.* **134** E3
Grimshaw, *Alta., Can.* **76** K10
Grimstad, *Nor.* **134** M11
Grinnell, *Iowa, U.S.* **99** P12
Grinnell Peninsula, *Nunavut, Can.* **77** C15
Grise Fiord, *Nunavut, Can.* **77** C16
Grishkino, *Russ.* **140** J12
Grisslehamn, *Sw.* **135** K14
Groesbeck, *Tex., U.S.* **97** N12
Grójec, *Pol.* **132** G10
Groningen, *Neth.* **138** G11
Groom, *Tex., U.S.* **96** G6
Groote Eylandt, *Austral.* **190** B10
Grootfontein, *Namibia* **182** G7
Gros-Morne, *Haiti* **111** L16
Grosseto, *It.* **136** G9
Grossglockner, peak, *Eur.* **130** H6
Grosvenor Downs, *Qnsld., Austral.* **191** T14
Grosvenor Mountains, *Antarctica* **206** K12
Grosvenor Seamount, *Pac. Oc.* **218** G8
Gros Ventre Range, *Wyo., U.S.* **100** H8
Grotli, *Nor.* **134** J10
Groton, *S. Dak., U.S.* **98** J7
Grouse Creek, *Utah, U.S.* **100** J5
Grove City, *Pa., U.S.* **88** M3
Grove Hill, *Ala., U.S.* **95** M14
Grove Mountains, *Antarctica* **207** G18
Grover, *Colo., U.S.* **100** K14
Grover Beach, *Calif., U.S.* **103** W5
Groves, *Tex., U.S.* **97** Q16
Groveton, *N.H., U.S.* **89** F14
Groveton, *Tex., U.S.* **97** P14
Groznyy, *Russ.* **140** J4
Grudziądz, *Pol.* **132** F9
Grundy, *Va., U.S.* **90** F7
Grundy Center, *Iowa, U.S.* **99** N12
Gruver, *Tex., U.S.* **96** F5
Grygla, *Minn., U.S.* **98** E9
Guacanayabo, Golfo de, *Cuba* **110** K11
Gu Achi *see* Santa Rosa, *Ariz., U.S.* **101** V7
Guadalajara, *Mex.* **108** H10
Guadalajara, *Sp.* **139** Q7
Guadalcanal, island, *Solomon Is.* **197** N18
Guadalquivir, river, *Sp.* **139** S6
Guadalupe, river, *Tex., U.S.* **97** S11
Guadalupe, *Calif., U.S.* **103** W5
Guadalupe, Isla de, *Mex.* **108** C4
Guadalupe Mountains, *U.S.* **78** L9
Guadalupe Mountains National Park, *Tex., U.S.* **97** U4
Guadalupe Peak, *Tex., U.S.* **97** U4
Guadalupita, *N. Mex., U.S.* **101** R13
Guadeloupe, island, *Guadeloupe, Fr.* **113** H17
Guadeloupe Passage, *Guadeloupe, Fr.* **113** H16
Guadeloupe Passage, *Montserrat, U.K.* **113** H16
Guadiana, river, *Eur.* **130** J1
Guadiana, Bahía, *Cuba* **110** H4
Guadix, *Sp.* **139** S7
Guafo, Boca del, *Chile* **125** S6
Guafo, Isla, *Chile* **125** S6
Guai, *Indonesia* **169** K21
Guáimaro, *Cuba* **110** J11
Guainía, river, *Col.* **120** G8
Guaíra, *Braz.* **122** M11
Guajaba, Cayo, *Cuba* **110** H11
Guajará-Mirim, *Braz.* **122** G7
Guajira, Península de la, *Col.* **120** A7
Gualala, *Calif., U.S.* **103** Q2
Gualeguay, *Arg.* **124** K12
Gualeguaychú, *Arg.* **124** K13
Gualicho, Salina, *Arg.* **125** P9
Guallatiri, Volcán, *Chile* **124** B7
Guam, island, *Asia* **146** H16
Guamúchil, *Mex.* **108** E8
Gua Musang, *Malaysia* **167** T10
Guanajay, *Cuba* **110** G6
Guanajuato, *Mex.* **108** H11
Guanal, Punta del, *Cuba* **110** J6
Guanambi, *Braz.* **123** J15
Guanare, river, *Venez.* **120** C8
Guanare, *Venez.* **120** C8
Guandacol, *Arg.* **124** H8
Guane, *Cuba* **110** H4
Guangchang, *China* **163** P6
Guangfeng, *China* **162** M8
Guanghai, *China* **163** S4
Guangning, *China* **163** R3
Guangrao, *China* **162** F8
Guangshan, *China* **162** K5
Guangshui, *China* **162** K5
Guangyuan, *China* **160** K12
Guangzhou (Canton), *China* **163** R4
Guanipa, river, *Venez.* **120** C12
Guano, Cayo, *Cuba* **110** J8
Guano Lake, *Nev.-Oreg., U.S.* **102** L7
Guantánamo, *Cuba* **111** K13
Guantánamo, Bahía de (Guantánamo Bay), *Cuba* **111** L13
Guantánamo Bay *see* Guantánamo, Bahía de, *Cuba* **111** L13
Guanyan, *China* **162** H8
Guanyang, *China* **163** P3
Guapí, *Col.* **120** G3
Guaporé, river, *S. Amer.* **118** G6
Guaporé (Iténez), river, *Braz.* **122** H9
Guaranda, *Ecua.* **120** K3
Guarapuava, *Braz.* **122** N12
Guaratinguetá, *Braz.* **123** M14
Guarda, *Port.* **139** Q5
Guardalauaca, *Cuba* **111** J13
Guarda Mor, *Braz.* **123** K13
Guárico, river, *Venez.* **120** C9
Guarico, Punta, *Cuba* **111** K14
Guasave, *Mex.* **108** E8
Guascama, Punta, *Col.* **120** G3
Guasdualito, *Venez.* **120** D7
Guatemala, *N. Amer.* **109** K16
Guatemala, *Guatemala* **109** L16
Guatemala Basin, *Pac. Oc.* **219** J18
Guaviare, river, *Col.* **120** F8
Guayabal, *Cuba* **110** K11
Guayaguayare, *Trin. & Tobago* **113** P17
Guayama, *P.R., U.S.* **111** N23
Guayaquil, *Ecua.* **120** K2
Guayaquil, Gulf of, *S. Amer.* **118** D1
Guaymas, *Mex.* **108** D7
Gûbâl, Strait of, *Egypt* **151** U3
Gucheng, *China* **162** J3
Gudalur, *India* **159** Q5
Gudaut'a, *Rep. of Georgia* **149** A15
Gudgeon Bay, *Pitcairn I., U.K.* **199** Q23
Gudur, *India* **159** P7
Güeppí, *Peru* **122** C3
Guéra Massif, *Af.* **174** G7
Guéret, *Fr.* **138** M10
Guernsey, island, *Channel Is., U.K.* **138** J8
Guernsey, *Wyo., U.S.* **100** J13
Guernsey Reservoir, *Wyo., U.S.* **100** J13
Gueydan, *La., U.S.* **94** P8
Gugegwe, island, *Kwajalein Atoll, Marshall Is.* **196** N5
Guguan, island, *N. Mariana Is., U.S.* **196** B2
Gui, river, *China* **163** Q2
Guía de Isora, *Canary Is., Sp.* **184** Q5
Guiana Highlands, *S. Amer.* **118** B5
Guichi, *China* **162** L7
Guide, *China* **160** J11
Guiglo, *Côte d'Ivoire* **180** G7
Guijá, *Mozambique* **182** J12
Guildford, *Eng., U.K.* **138** H9
Guilford, *Me., U.S.* **89** E16
Guilin, *China* **163** Q2
Guillaume-Delisle, Lac, *Que., Can.* **77** K18
Guimarães, *Braz.* **123** D15
Guimarães, *Port.* **139** P5
Guin, *Ala., U.S.* **95** J14
Guinchos Cay, *Cuba* **110** G11
Guinea, *Af.* **180** F6
Guinea, Gulf of, *Nig.* **180** J12
Guinea-Bissau, *Af.* **180** E4
Güines, *Cuba* **110** G6
Guingamp, *Fr.* **138** K7
Guiping, *China* **163** R2
Güira de Melena, *Cuba* **110** G6
Güiria, *Venez.* **120** B12
Guixi, *China* **163** N7
Guixian, *China* **163** R1
Guiyang, *China* **160** N12
Guiyang, *China* **163** P4
Gujar Khan, *Pak.* **157** N11
Gujranwala, *Pak.* **157** P12
Gujrat, *Pak.* **157** P11
Gulang, *China* **160** H11

Gulbarga, India 158 M5
Gulbene, Latv. 135 L17
Gul'cha, Kyrg. 156 G11
Gulf Islands National Seashore, Fla., U.S. 91 Q2
Gulf Islands National Seashore, Miss., U.S. 95 P13
Gulfport, Miss., U.S. 94 P12
Gulf Shores, Ala., U.S. 95 P14
Gulgong, N.S.W., Austral. 191 X14
Guling, China 162 M6
Guliston, Uzb. 155 K13
Gulitel, Mount, Palau 196 M12
Gulja see Yining, China 160 E6
Gulkana, Alas., U.S. 105 H17
Güllük, Turk. 148 H3
Gülnar, Turk. 148 J8
Gülşehir, Turk. 148 F9
Gulya, Russ. 141 K18
Guma see Pishan, China 160 G4
Gumdag, Turkm. 154 L6
Gumla, India 158 J9
Gummi, Nig. 181 E13
Gümüşdere, Turk. 149 G17
Gümüşhacıköy, Turk. 148 D10
Gümüşhane, Turk. 149 D14
Gümüşören, Turk. 148 G10
Gumzai, Indonesia 169 L19
Gumzai, Indonesia 193 C15
Guna, India 158 H6
Guna Terara, peak, Af. 174 G10
Gun Cay, Bahamas 110 D9
Gundagai, N.S.W., Austral. 191 Y13
Gundlupet, India 159 Q5
Gündoğmuş, Turk. 148 J7
Güney, Turk. 148 G4
Gungu, Dem. Rep. of the Congo 178 L9
Gunnbjørn, peak, N. Amer. 74 B10
Gunnedah, N.S.W., Austral. 191 W14
Gunners Quoin, island, Mauritius 185 F20
Gunnewin, Qnsld., Austral. 191 U14
Gunnison, Colo., U.S. 101 N11
Gunnison, Utah, U.S. 100 M7
Gunt, river, Taj. 156 J10
Guntersville, Ala., U.S. 95 H16
Guntersville Lake, Ala., U.S. 95 H16
Guntur, India 159 N7
Gunungsugih, Indonesia 168 L7
Guoyang, China 162 J6
Gupis, Pak. 156 L11
Gurage, peak, Af. 174 H10
Gurban Obo, China 161 F14
Gurdaspur, India 157 P13
Gurdon, Ark., U.S. 94 H7
Güre, Turk. 148 F5
Gurer, island, Kwajalein Atoll, Marshall Is. 196 L3
Gurguan Point, Tinian, N. Mariana Is., U.S. 196 B7
Guri Dam, Venez. 120 D12
Gurimatu, P.N.G. 193 D19
Gurney, P.N.G. 193 E21
Gürün, Turk. 148 G12
Gurupá, Braz. 122 D12
Gurupá Island, S. Amer. 118 D8
Gurupi, river, Braz. 123 D14
Gurupi, Braz. 123 G13
Gurupi, Cape, S. Amer. 118 D9
Gurupi, Serra do, Braz. 123 E13
Gusau, Nig. 181 E14
Gushan, China 162 D11
Guşhgy, Turkm. 154 P10
Gushgy, river, Turkm. 154 N10
Gushi, China 162 K6
Gushikawa, Jap. 165 Y1
Gusikha, Russ. 141 E15
Gusinaya Bank, Arctic Oc. 223 C16
Gusinoozersk, Russ. 141 L16
Gustavia, St.-Barthélemy, Fr. 113 F15
Gustine, Calif., U.S. 103 S5
Guthrie, Ky., U.S. 95 D15
Guthrie, Okla., U.S. 96 F11
Guthrie, Tex., U.S. 96 K7
Guthrie Center, Iowa, U.S. 99 P10
Gutian, China 163 P8
Guttenberg, Iowa, U.S. 98 M14
Güvem, Turk. 148 D8
Guwahati, India 158 G13
Guwlymayak, Turkm. 154 K6
Guyana, S. Amer. 121 E14
Guyandotte, river, W. Va., U.S. 90 E7
Guyang, China 162 C3
Guymon, Okla., U.S. 96 E5
Guyra, N.S.W., Austral. 191 W15
Guyuan, China 162 B6
Güzeloluk, Turk. 148 J9
Güzelyurt, Turk. 148 G9
Guzhang, China 162 M2
G'uzor, Uzb. 154 M12
Gwa, Myanmar 166 K5
Gwadar, Pak. 157 W2
Gwai, Zimb. 182 G10
Gwalior, India 158 G6
Gwanda, Zimb. 182 G11
Gwardafuy, Cape, Af. 174 G12
Gwatar Bay, Pak. 157 W1
Gweru, Zimb. 182 G11
Gwinn, Mich., U.S. 92 F7
Gwinner, N. Dak., U.S. 98 H7
Gwoza, Nig. 181 F16
Gwydir, river, Austral. 190 J14
Gyamysh, peak, Azerb. 149 D20
Gyangzê, China 160 L7
Gyaring, Co, China 160 K7
Gyaring Hu, China 160 J9
Gydan see Kolymskoye Nagor'ye, Russ. 141 F20
Gydanskiy Poluostrov, Russ. 140 F12
Gyda Peninsula, Asia 146 C8
Gyêgu, China 160 K9
Gympie, Qnsld., Austral. 191 V15
Győr, Hung. 132 K9
Gypsum, Kans., U.S. 99 T7
Gyumri, Arm. 149 D18
Gyzylarbat, Turkm. 154 L7
Gyzyletrek, Turkm. 154 M6
Gyzylgaya, Turkm. 154 K7
Gyzylsuw, Turkm. 154 K6

H

Ha'afeva, island, Ha'apai Group, Tonga 198 Q6
Ha'akame, Tongatapu, Tonga 198 J11
Ha'alaufuli, Vava'u Group, Tonga 198 L12
Haamaire, Baie, Bora-Bora, Fr. Polynesia, Fr. 199 K14
Haamene, Baie de, Tahaa, Fr. Polynesia, Fr. 199 A23
Ha'ano, island, Ha'apai Group, Tonga 198 P7
Ha'apai Group, Tonga 198 K10
Haapamäki, Fin. 135 H15
Haapiti, Moorea, Fr. Polynesia, Fr. 199 N14
Haapsalu, Estonia 135 K16
Haapu, Huahine, Fr. Polynesia, Fr. 199 H14
Ha'asini, Tongatapu, Tonga 198 J12
Haast, N.Z. 193 P16
Haast Bluff, N. Terr., Austral. 191 T8
Haava, Canal, Hiva Oa, Fr. Polynesia, Fr. 199 N20
Hab, river, Pak. 157 V6
Habahe, China 160 C7
Ḩabarūt, Yemen 153 N13
Habomai, Jap. 164 F16
Habomai Islands, Russ. 141 K23
Haboro, Jap. 164 E13
Hachijō Jima, Jap. 165 S12
Hachiman, Jap. 165 P10
Hachinohe, Jap. 164 J13
Hachiōji, Jap. 165 P12
Hachirō Gata, lake, Jap. 164 J12
Hachita, N. Mex., U.S. 101 V10
Hacıbektaş, Turk. 148 F10
Hadarba, Ras, Sudan 179 B14
Ḩadd, Ra's al, Oman 153 K17
Haddummati Atoll, Maldives 159 W3
Hadejia, river, Af. 174 G5
Ḩadera, Israel 150 L5
Hadhramaut, region, Asia 146 J3
Hadīboh (Tamrida), Yemen 153 R14
Ḩadīdah, Syr. 150 D10
Hadım, Turk. 148 H7
Hadja, Solomon Is. 197 P20
Hadley Bay, Nunavut, Can. 77 E13
Ha Dong, Vietnam 166 H12
Ḩaḑramawt, region, Yemen 152 Q11
Hadyach, Ukr. 133 H16
Haedo, Cuchilla de, Uru. 124 K14
Haeju, N. Korea 162 E12
Haena, Hawaii, U.S. 107 M22
Haenam, S. Korea 162 H13
Ḩafar al Bāţin, Saudi Arabia 152 G10
Hafik, Turk. 148 E12
Ḩafīt, Jabal, U.A.E. 153 K15
Hafizabad, Pak. 157 P11
Hagåtña (Agana), Guam, U.S. 196 C10
Hagemeister Island, Alas., U.S. 104 L12
Hagerman, N. Mex., U.S. 101 U14
Hagerman Fossil Beds National Monument, Idaho, U.S. 100 H4
Hagerstown, Md., U.S. 90 B12
Häggenås, Sw. 134 H12
Hagi, Jap. 165 Q5
Ha Giang, Vietnam 166 G11
Hagman, Puntan, Saipan, N. Mariana Is., U.S. 196 C5
Hagoi Susupe, lake, Saipan, N. Mariana Is., U.S. 196 C4
Hague, Cap de la, Fr. 138 J8
Haha Jima Rettō, Jap. 194 C4
Hai, Hon, Vietnam 167 Q14
Hai'an, China 161 Q13
Hai'an, China 162 J9
Haicheng, China 162 C10
Hai Duong, Vietnam 166 H12
Haifa see Ḩefa, Israel 150 K5
Haifeng, China 163 S6
Haig, W. Austral., Austral. 191 W6
Haikang, China 163 T1
Haikou, China 163 T2
Haiku, Hawaii, U.S. 107 G17
Ḩā'il, Saudi Arabia 152 H8
Hailar, China 161 C15
Hailey, Idaho, U.S. 100 G5
Hails, China 162 B1
Hailuoto, island, Fin. 135 F15
Haimen see Jiaojiang, China 162 M10
Haimen Wan, China 163 S6
Hainan, island, China 163 U2
Haines, Alas., U.S. 105 J21
Haines, Oreg., U.S. 102 G8
Haines City, Fla., U.S. 91 U8
Haines Junction, Yukon Terr., Can. 76 G7
Hainiya Point, Rota I., N. Mariana Is., U.S. 196 E8
Haiphong, Vietnam 166 H12
Haiti, N. Amer. 111 L15
Haiya, Sudan 179 D14
Haiyan, China 160 H11
Haiyan, China 162 L9
Haizhou Wan, China 162 H8
Hajiki Saki, Jap. 164 L11
Haji Pir Pass, India-Pak. 157 N11
Ḩajjah, Yemen 152 P9
Ḩājjīābād, Iran 153 G15
Hakalau, Hawaii, U.S. 107 L21
Hakamaru, island, Manihiki Atoll, Cook Is., N.Z. 199 B15
Hakataramea, N.Z. 193 Q16
Hakauata, island, Ha'apai Group, Tonga 198 P7
Hakha, Myanmar 166 G4
Hakkâri, Turk. 149 H18
Hakken San, peak, Jap. 165 Q9
Hakodate, Jap. 164 H13
Hakui, Jap. 165 N10
Hakupa Pass, Solomon Is. 197 J18
Hala, Pak. 157 V7
Halaaniyaat, Juzor al (Kuria Muria Islands), Oman 153 N15
Ḩalab (Aleppo), Syr. 150 D9
Ḩalabān, Saudi Arabia 152 K9
Halachó, Mex. 109 H16
Halaib, Sudan 179 B14
Halalii Lake, Hawaii, U.S. 106 C3
Halalo, Pointe, Wallis and Futuna, Fr. 198 C11
Halaula (Kohala Mill), Hawaii, U.S. 107 J19
Halawa, Hawaii, U.S. 107 K19
Halawa, Cape, Hawaii, U.S. 107 F15
Halawa Bay, Hawaii, U.S. 107 F15
Halayeb, Egypt 177 F20
Ḩalbā, Leb. 150 G7
Halban, Mongolia 160 C10
Halcon, Mount, Philippines 169 D13
Haldwani, India 158 E7
Hale, Mich., U.S. 92 J12
Haleakala Crater, Hawaii, U.S. 107 H17
Haleakala National Park, Hawaii, U.S. 107 H18
Haleakala Observatories, Hawaii, U.S. 107 H17
Hale Center, Tex., U.S. 96 J5
Haleiwa, Hawaii, U.S. 106 D10
Halekii-Pihana Heiaus, Hawaii, U.S. 107 G16
Haleyville, Ala., U.S. 95 H14
Halfeti, Turk. 148 H12
Halfway, Oreg., U.S. 102 G9
Halgan, Cape, Kosrae, F.S.M. 197 A19
Halifax, N.S., Can. 77 P22
Halifax, Qnsld., Austral. 191 R13
Halifax, Va., U.S. 90 G11
Haliimaile, Hawaii, U.S. 107 G17
Halkída, Gr. 137 K15
Hallandale, Fla., U.S. 91 W10
Hall Basin, Nunavut, Can. 77 A17
Hall Beach, Nunavut, Can. 77 F16
Hallettsville, Tex., U.S. 97 R12
Halley, station, Antarctica 206 D10
Halliday, N. Dak., U.S. 98 F3
Hallim, S. Korea 162 J13
Hall Islands, F.S.M. 196 Q6
Hällnäs, Sw. 135 G14
Hallock, Minn., U.S. 98 E8
Hall Peninsula, Nunavut, Can. 77 H19
Halls, Tenn., U.S. 94 F12
Halls Creek, W. Austral., Austral. 191 R6
Halmahera, island, Indonesia 169 H16
Halmahera Sea, Indonesia 169 J16
Halmstad, Sw. 134 N12
Halola, Solomon Is. 197 L14
Halsa, Nor. 134 H10
Halstead, Kans., U.S. 99 U7
Haltdalen, Nor. 134 H11
Halten Bank, Atl. Oc. 216 C14
Halulu Heiau, Hawaii, U.S. 107 G14
Ḩaluza, Ḩolot, Israel 151 N4
Halys see Kızılırmak, river, Turk. 148 D9
Hamada, Jap. 165 Q6
Hamadān, Iran 152 D11
Hamaguir, Alg. 176 C9
Ḩamāh (Hamath), Syr. 150 F8
Hamakua, region, Hawaii, U.S. 107 M20
Hamamatsu, Jap. 165 Q10
Hamamet, Gulf of, Af. 174 C6
Hamar, Nor. 134 K11
Hamasaka, Jap. 165 P8
Hamâta, Gebel, Egypt 177 E20
Hamath see Ḩamāh, Syr. 150 F8
Hamatombetsu, Jap. 164 D14
Hamburg, Ark., U.S. 94 K9
Hamburg, Ger. 132 F6
Hamburg, Iowa, U.S. 99 Q9
Hamburg, N.Y., U.S. 88 J5
Ḩamḑah, Saudi Arabia 152 M9
Ḩamdānah, Saudi Arabia 152 M7
Hamden, Conn., U.S. 88 M12
Hämeenlinna, Fin. 135 J16
Hamelin, W. Austral., Austral. 191 V1
Hamersley Range, Austral. 190 F2
Hamhŭng, N. Korea 162 D13
Hami (Kumul), China 160 F9
Hamilton, Ala., U.S. 95 H14
Hamilton, Bermuda, U.K. 111 F17
Hamilton, Ill., U.S. 93 Q3
Hamilton, Mo., U.S. 99 R11
Hamilton, Mont., U.S. 100 D5
Hamilton, N.Y., U.S. 88 J9
Hamilton, N.Z. 193 K19
Hamilton, Ohio, U.S. 93 S11
Hamilton, Ont., Can. 77 R18
Hamilton, Tas., Austral. 191 Z16
Hamilton, Tex., U.S. 97 N10
Hamilton, Vic., Austral. 191 Z11
Hamilton, Lake, Ark., U.S. 94 H7
Hamilton Inlet, Nfld., Can. 77 K22
Hamina, Fin. 135 J17
Hamirpur, India 158 G7
Hamlet, N.C., U.S. 90 J10
Hamlin, Tex., U.S. 96 L7
Ḩammār, Hawr al, Asia 146 G4
Hammerfest, Nor. 135 C14
Hammon, Okla., U.S. 96 G8
Hammond, Ind., U.S. 93 N7
Hammond, La., U.S. 94 P10
Hammond, Mont., U.S. 100 E13
Hammonton, N.J., U.S. 88 Q10
Hampden, N.Z. 193 Q16
Hampton, Ark., U.S. 94 J8
Hampton, Iowa, U.S. 98 M12
Hampton, S.C., U.S. 90 M9
Hampton, Va., U.S. 90 F14
Hampton Bays, N.Y., U.S. 89 N13
Hampton Butte, Oreg., U.S. 102 H6
Hampton Tableland, Austral. 190 J6
Hamp'yŏng, S. Korea 162 G13
Ḩamrīn, Jabal, Iraq 152 C9
Hāmūn-e Jaz Mūrīān, dry lake, Iran 153 H16
Hāmūn-e Şāberī, lake, Iran 153 E17
Ham Yen, Vietnam 166 G11
Han, river, China 162 K4
Hana, Hawaii, U.S. 107 G18
Hanahan, P.N.G. 197 J13
Hanahe, Baie, Ua Huka, Fr. Polynesia, Fr. 199 M23
Hana Highway, Hawaii, U.S. 107 G18
Hanahupe, Baie, Hiva Oa, Fr. Polynesia, Fr. 199 N21
Hanaiapa, Baie, Hiva Oa, Fr. Polynesia, Fr. 199 M20
Hanaiapaoa, Baie, Hiva Oa, Fr. Polynesia, Fr. 199 M20
Hanalei, Hawaii, U.S. 106 B5
Hanalei Bay, Hawaii, U.S. 106 A5
Hanamaki, Jap. 164 K13
Hanamalo Point, Hawaii, U.S. 107 P18
Hanamaulu, Hawaii, U.S. 106 B6
Hanamenu, Baie, Hiva Oa, Fr. Polynesia, Fr. 199 M20
Hanaoo, Hiva Oa, Fr. Polynesia, Fr. 199 N20
Hanapepe, Hawaii, U.S. 106 C5
Hana Teio, Hiva Oa, Fr. Polynesia, Fr. 199 N20
Hana Tetena, Hiva Oa, Fr. Polynesia, Fr. 199 N20
Hana Tuuna, Hiva Oa, Fr. Polynesia, Fr. 199 N20
Hanaui, Hiva Oa, Fr. Polynesia, Fr. 199 M20
Hanawa, Jap. 164 J13
Hancheng, China 162 G3
Hanchuan, China 162 L5
Hancock, Md., U.S. 90 B12
Hancock, Mich., U.S. 92 E6
Hancock, Minn., U.S. 98 J9
Handan, China 162 F5
Hane, Ua Huka, Fr. Polynesia, Fr. 199 N23
Hane, Baie d', Ua Huka, Fr. Polynesia, Fr. 199 N23
Hanford, Calif., U.S. 103 U6
Hanford Site, Wash., U.S. 102 E7
Hangayn Nuruu, Mongolia 160 D10
Hanggin Houqi, China 160 G12
Hanggin Houqi, China 162 C1
Hanggin Qi, China 162 C2
Hangö (Hanko), Fin. 135 K15
Hangu, China 162 D7
Hangu, Pak. 157 N9
Hangzhou, China 162 L9
Hani, Turk. 149 G15
Hānī, Ra's Ibn, Syr. 150 E6
Haniá (Canea), Gr. 137 M15
Hanimadu, island, Maldives 159 T3
Ḩanīsh al Kabīr, island, Yemen 152 Q8
Hankinson, N. Dak., U.S. 98 H8
Hanko see Hangö, Fin. 135 K15

Hanksville, Utah, U.S. 101 N8
Hanle, India 157 N15
Hanna, Alta., Can. 76 M10
Hanna, Wyo., U.S. 100 J12
Hannibal, Mo., U.S. 99 R14
Hannover, Ger. 132 F6
Hanoi, Vietnam 166 H12
Hanover, Kans., U.S. 99 R8
Hanover, N. Mex., U.S. 101 U10
Hanover, N.H., U.S. 89 H13
Hanover, Pa., U.S. 88 Q7
Hanover, Isla, Chile 125 W6
Hanpan, Cape, P.N.G. 197 J13
Hansen Mountains, Antarctica 207 D19
Hanumangarh, India 158 E4
Hanuy, river, Mongolia 160 D11
Hanyang, China 162 L5
Hanzhong, China 160 K12
Hao, island, Fr. Polynesia, Fr. 199 F20
Haora, India 158 J11
Haou, Hawaii, U.S. 107 H18
Hapai, Solomon Is. 197 M16
Haparanda, Sw. 135 F15
Hapatoni, Baie, Hiva Oa, Fr. Polynesia, Fr. 199 N20
Hapo, Indonesia 169 H16
Happy, Tex., U.S. 96 H5
Happy Camp, Calif., U.S. 102 L2
Happy Valley-Goose Bay, Nfld., Can. 77 L21
Ḩaql, Saudi Arabia 152 F5
Har, Indonesia 169 L18
Ḩaraḑ, Saudi Arabia 152 K12
Haraiki, island, Fr. Polynesia, Fr. 199 E19
Haranomachi, Jap. 164 M13
Harappa, ruins, Pak. 157 R11
Harare, Zimb. 182 F12
Haratini, island, Manihiki Atoll, Cook Is., N.Z. 199 C15
Har Ayrag, Mongolia 161 E13
Harbin, China 161 D17
Harbor Beach, Mich., U.S. 92 K13
Harbor Springs, Mich., U.S. 92 H10
Harbours, Bay of, Falk. Is., U.K. 125 W12
Harda, India 158 J5
Hardangerfjorden, Nor. 134 L9
Hardin, Ill., U.S. 93 S3
Hardin, Mont., U.S. 100 E11
Harding, S. Af. 182 L11
Hardman, Oreg., U.S. 102 F6
Hardwick, Ga., U.S. 90 M6
Hardy, Ark., U.S. 94 E9
Hardy, Península, Chile 125 Y9
Härer, Eth. 179 G16
Hargeysa, Somalia 179 F16
Harguš, Afghan. 156 J11
Har Hu, China 160 H10
Haría, Canary Is., Sp. 184 P8
Haridwar, India 158 E6
Harihari, N.Z. 193 P16
Harij, India 158 H3
Ḩārim, Syr. 150 D8
Haripur, Pak. 157 N11
Harirud, river, Afghan. 156 L1
Harirud, river, Iran 153 C17
Harlan, Iowa, U.S. 99 P10
Harlan, Ky., U.S. 95 D19
Harlem, Mont., U.S. 100 B10
Harlingen, Tex., U.S. 97 W11
Harlowton, Mont., U.S. 100 D9
Harmancık, Turk. 148 E5
Harmony, Minn., U.S. 98 L13
Harnai, Pak. 157 R7
Harney Basin, Oreg., U.S. 102 J7
Harney Lake, Oreg., U.S. 102 J7
Harney Peak, S. Dak., U.S. 98 L1
Härnösand, Sw. 135 H13
Har Nuur, Mongolia 160 D9
Haro, Sp. 139 P7
Harpanahalli, India 159 N5
Harper, Kans., U.S. 99 V7
Harper, Liberia 180 J7
Harper Lake, Calif., U.S. 103 W9
Harpers Ferry, W. Va., U.S. 90 C12
Harput, Turk. 149 F14
Harqin, China 162 C9
Harqin Qi, China 162 B8
Ḩarrah, Yemen 152 Q12
Harrai, India 158 J7
Har Ramon, peak, Israel 151 Q4
Harran, Turk. 149 J14
Harricana, river, Que., Can. 77 N18
Harriman, Tenn., U.S. 95 E18
Harrington, Wash., U.S. 102 C8
Harrington Harbour, Que., Can. 77 M22
Harrington Sound, Bermuda, U.K. 111 F18
Harris, Lake, Austral. 190 J9
Harrisburg, Ark., U.S. 94 F10
Harrisburg, Ill., U.S. 93 U6
Harrisburg, Nebr., U.S. 99 P1
Harrisburg, Oreg., U.S. 102 G3
Harrisburg, Pa., U.S. 88 P7
Harrison, Ark., U.S. 94 E7
Harrison, Idaho, U.S. 100 C3
Harrison, Mich., U.S. 92 K10
Harrison, Nebr., U.S. 98 M1
Harrison, Cape, Nfld., Can. 77 K22
Harrison Bay, Alas., U.S. 105 B15
Harrisonburg, La., U.S. 94 M9
Harrisonburg, Va., U.S. 90 D11
Harrisonville, Mo., U.S. 99 T11
Harris Seamount, Pac. Oc. 218 D12
Harrisville, Mich., U.S. 92 J12
Harrodsburg, Ky., U.S. 95 C17
Harrogate, U.K. 138 F8
Harry S. Truman Reservoir, Mo., U.S. 99 T11
Harşit, river, Turk. 149 D13
Harstad, Nor. 134 D12
Hart, Mich., U.S. 92 K9
Hart, Tex., U.S. 96 H5
Hartford, Ala., U.S. 95 N17
Hartford, Ark., U.S. 94 G6
Hartford, Conn., U.S. 89 L13
Hartford, Mich., U.S. 93 N9
Hartford, S. Dak., U.S. 98 L8
Hartford, Wis., U.S. 92 L6
Hartford City, Ind., U.S. 93 Q10
Hartington, Nebr., U.S. 99 N8
Hart Lake, Oreg., U.S. 102 K6
Hartlepool, Eng., U.K. 138 F8
Hartley, Iowa, U.S. 98 M9
Hartley, Tex., U.S. 96 F4
Hart Mountain, Oreg., U.S. 102 K6
Hartselle, Ala., U.S. 95 H15
Hartshorne, Okla., U.S. 96 H13
Hartsville, S.C., U.S. 90 K10
Hartsville, Tenn., U.S. 95 E16
Hartwell, Ga., U.S. 90 K6
Hartwell Lake, Ga.-S.C., U.S. 90 K7
Har Us Nuur, Mongolia 160 C9
Harut, river, Afghan. 157 P1
Harūz-e Bālā, Iran 153 F15
Harvard, Ill., U.S. 92 M6
Harvard, Nebr., U.S. 99 Q7
Harvard, Mount, Colo., U.S. 101 N12
Harvest Home, Qnsld., Austral. 191 S13
Harvey, N. Dak., U.S. 98 F5
Harz, mountains, Eur. 130 F6
Ḩaşānah, Yemen 152 Q12
Hasan Dağı, Turk. 148 G9
Ḩasan Langī, Iran 153 H15
Hasa Plain, Asia 146 G4
Hashaat, Mongolia 160 E12
Ḩāsik, Oman 153 N15
Hasil, island, Indonesia 169 J16
Hasilpur, Pak. 157 S10
Haskell, Okla., U.S. 96 F13
Haskell, Tex., U.S. 96 K8
Hassel Sound, Nunavut, Can. 77 C14
Hassi Messaoud, Alg. 176 C11
Hassi R'mel, Alg. 176 B11
Hässleholm, Sw. 135 N13
Hastings, Mich., U.S. 92 M10
Hastings, Minn., U.S. 98 K12
Hastings, N.Z. 193 L20
Hastings, Nebr., U.S. 99 Q6
Hastings, Eng., U.K. 138 H9
Hasvik, Nor. 135 C13
Haswell, Colo., U.S. 101 N15
Hat see Teuaua, island, Fr. Polynesia, Fr. 199 N23
Hatch, N. Mex., U.S. 101 V11
Hatches Creek, N. Terr., Austral. 191 S9
Hatchie, river, Tenn., U.S. 94 F12
Haţeg, Rom. 137 F14
Hatgal, Mongolia 160 C11
Ḩāţibah, Ra's, Saudi Arabia 152 L6
Ha Tien, Vietnam 167 P11
Ha Tinh, Vietnam 166 J12
Hato Mayor, Dom. Rep. 111 M20
Ha Trung, Vietnam 166 H12
Hatteras, N.C., U.S. 90 H15
Hatteras, Cape, N.C., U.S. 90 H15
Hatteras Plain, Atl. Oc. 216 J4
Hattiesburg, Miss., U.S. 94 N12
Ḩaţţīyah, Jordan 151 R6
Hatton, N. Dak., U.S. 98 F7
Hatunuru, Indonesia 169 K16
Hatutu, island, Fr. Polynesia, Fr. 195 H14
Hat Yai, Thai. 167 S9
Haud, region, Af. 174 H11
Haugesund, Nor. 134 L9
Haukeligrend, Nor. 134 L10
Haukipudas, Fin. 135 F15
Haukivesi, lake, Fin. 135 H17
Haunanu, Pointe, Ua Huka, Fr. Polynesia, Fr. 199 M23
Hauraki Gulf, N.Z. 193 J19
Hauser, Oreg., U.S. 102 J2
Haut, Isle au, Me., U.S. 89 G18
Hauti, Rurutu, Fr. Polynesia, Fr. 199 K23
Hauula, Hawaii, U.S. 106 D11
Havana see La Habana, Cuba 110 G6
Havana, Fla., U.S. 91 Q5
Havana, Ill., U.S. 93 Q4
Havannah, Canal de la, New Caledonia, Fr. 198 E9
Havasu, Lake, Ariz.-Calif., U.S. 101 T5
Haveli, Pak. 157 R11
Havelock, N.C., U.S. 90 J14
Haveluloto, Tongatapu, Tonga 198 H11
Haven, Kans., U.S. 99 U7
Haverhill, Mass., U.S. 89 J15
Haveri, India 159 N4
Haviland, Kans., U.S. 99 U6
Havre, Mont., U.S. 100 B9
Havre de Grace, Md., U.S. 90 B14
Havre-Saint-Pierre, Que., Can. 77 M21
Havza, Turk. 148 D11
Hawaii, island, Hawaii, U.S. 107 M17
Hawaiian Ridge, Pac. Oc. 218 G10
Hawaii Belt Road, Hawaii, U.S. 107 N20
Hawaii Volcanoes National Park, Hawaii, U.S. 107 N20
Hawarden, Iowa, U.S. 98 M8
Hawea, Lake, N.Z. 193 Q16
Ḩawf, Yemen 153 P14
Hawi, Hawaii, U.S. 107 K19
Hawick, Scot., U.K. 138 F8
Hawke Bay, N.Z. 193 L20
Hawker, S. Austral., Austral. 191 W10
Hawkinsville, Ga., U.S. 91 N6
Hawley, Minn., U.S. 98 G8
Hawr as Suwayqīyah, lake, Iraq 152 E10
Hawthorne, Nev., U.S. 103 R8
Haxtun, Colo., U.S. 100 K15
Hay, river, Alta., Can. 76 J10
Hay, river, Austral. 190 F10
Hay, N.S.W., Austral. 191 Y12
Hayden, Ariz., U.S. 101 U8
Hayden, Colo., U.S. 100 L11
Hayes, river, Man., Can. 77 L15
Hayes, S. Dak., U.S. 98 K4
Hayes, Mount, Alas., U.S. 105 G17
Hayes Center, Nebr., U.S. 99 Q4
Hayes Peninsula, N. Amer. 74 B7
Hayfork, Calif., U.S. 103 N2
Haymā', Oman 153 M15
Haymana, Turk. 148 E8
Haynesville, La., U.S. 94 K7
Hayneville, Ala., U.S. 95 L15
Haynin, Yemen 152 P11
Hayrabolu, Turk. 148 C3
Ḩayr al Gharbī, Qaşr al, Syr. 150 H9
Hay River, N.W.T., Can. 76 H11
Hays, Kans., U.S. 99 S5
Hays, Mont., U.S. 100 B10
Hay Springs, Nebr., U.S. 98 M2
Haysville, Kans., U.S. 99 U7
Haysyn, Ukr. 133 J14
Hayti, Mo., U.S. 99 W16
Hayvoron, Ukr. 133 K14
Hayward, Calif., U.S. 103 S4
Hayward, Wis., U.S. 92 G3
Hazarajat, region, Afghan. 157 N6
Hazārān, Kūh-e, Iran 153 F15
Hazard, Ky., U.S. 95 C19
Hazar Gölü, Turk. 149 G14
Hazar Qadam, Afghan. 157 P6
Ḩaẕawẕā', Sabkhat, Saudi Arabia 152 F6
Hazelton, B.C., Can. 76 J8
Hazelton, N. Dak., U.S. 98 H5
Hazen, Ark., U.S. 94 G9
Hazen, N. Dak., U.S. 98 F4
Hazen, Nev., U.S. 103 P7
Ḩaẕeva, Israel 151 P5
Hazlehurst, Ga., U.S. 91 N7
Hazlehurst, Miss., U.S. 94 M11
Hazleton, Pa., U.S. 88 N8
Hazro, Turk. 149 G15
Healdsburg, Calif., U.S. 103 Q3
Healdton, Okla., U.S. 96 J11
Healy, Alas., U.S. 105 G16
Healy, Kans., U.S. 99 T4
Héani, Mount, Hiva Oa, Fr. Polynesia, Fr. 199 M20
Hearne, Tex., U.S. 97 P12
Hearst, Ont., Can. 77 N17
Hearst Island, Antarctica 206 E5
Heart, river, N. Dak., U.S. 98 G4
Heart, river, U.S. 78 D10
Heath, Pointe, Que., Can. 77 M22
Heavener, Okla., U.S. 96 H14
Hebbronville, Tex., U.S. 97 U9
Heber, Ariz., U.S. 101 T8
Heber City, Utah, U.S. 100 L7
Heber Springs, Ark., U.S. 94 F9
Hebgen Lake, Mont., U.S. 100 F8
Hebi, China 162 G5
Hebron, N. Dak., U.S. 98 G3
Hebron, Nebr., U.S. 99 R7
Hebron see Al Khalīl, West Bank 151 N5
Hecate Strait, B.C., Can. 76 K7
Hechi, China 161 N13
Hechuan, China 160 L12
Hecla, S. Dak., U.S. 98 H7
Hecla, Cape, Nunavut, Can. 77 A16
Heddal, Nor. 134 L11
Hede see Sheyang, China 162 H9
Hede, Sw. 134 J12
He Devil Mountain, Idaho, U.S. 100 E3
Hedley, Tex., U.S. 96 H6
Hedo Misaki, Jap. 165 Y2
Heel Point, Wake I., U.S. 196 F8
Ḩefa (Haifa), Israel 150 K5
Hefei, China 162 K7
Hefeng, China 162 L2
Heflin, Ala., U.S. 95 J17
Hegang, China 161 C18
Hegura Jima, Jap. 164 M10
Heicheng (Khara Khoto), ruins, China 160 F11
Heidelberg, Ger. 132 H5
Heidelberg, Miss., U.S. 94 M12
Heidenheim, Ger. 132 J5
Heihe, China 161 B17
Heilbronn, Ger. 132 J5
Heilong, river, Russ. 141 L20
Heilong Jiang, river, China 161 A16
Heimaey, island, Ice. 134 G2
Heinola, Fin. 135 J16
Heishan, China 162 B10
Hejaz see Al Ḩijāz, region, Saudi Arabia 152 H6
Hejian, China 162 E6
Hejing, China 160 F7
Hekimhan, Turk. 148 F12
Hekla, peak, Ice. 134 F2
Hekou, China 160 P11
Helagsfjället, peak, Sw. 134 H12
Hele Islands, Solomon Is. 197 M16
Helena, Ark., U.S. 94 H10
Helena, Ga., U.S. 91 N7
Helena, Mont., U.S. 100 D7
Helena, Okla., U.S. 96 E10
Helengili, island, Maldives 159 U3
Helen Island, Palau 194 G2
Helen Springs, N. Terr., Austral. 191 R8
Helgoland, island, Ger. 132 E5
Helgoländer Bucht, Ger. 132 E5
Hell, Nor. 134 H11
Hellín, Sp. 139 R8
Hellissandur, Ice. 134 E1
Hells Canyon, Idaho-Oreg., U.S. 100 E3
Hells Canyon Dam, Idaho-Oreg., U.S. 100 E3
Hells Canyon National Recreation Area, Idaho-Oreg., U.S. 100 E3
Hell-Ville see Andoany, Madagascar 183 D18
Helmand, river, Afghan. 157 R2
Helmsdale, Scot., U.K. 138 D8
Helong, China 162 B14
Helper, Utah, U.S. 100 M8
Helsingborg, Sw. 134 N12
Helsingfors see Helsinki, Fin. 135 J16
Helsinki (Helsingfors), Fin. 135 J16
Hemet, Calif., U.S. 103 X10
Hemingford, Nebr., U.S. 99 N2
Hempstead, N.Y., U.S. 88 N11
Hempstead, Tex., U.S. 97 Q13
Henashi Zaki, Jap. 164 J12
Henbury, N. Terr., Austral. 191 U8
Hendek, Turk. 148 D6
Henderson, Ky., U.S. 95 C14
Henderson, N.C., U.S. 90 G12
Henderson, Nev., U.S. 103 U12
Henderson, Tenn., U.S. 95 F13
Henderson, Tex., U.S. 96 M14
Henderson Island, Pac. Oc. 195 L16
Henderson Seamount, Pac. Oc. 219 G16
Hendersonville, N.C., U.S. 90 J7
Hendersonville, Tenn., U.S. 95 E15
Hengch'un, Taiwan, China 163 S9
Hengduan Shan, China 160 M9
Hengshan, China 162 E2
Hengshan, China 163 N4
Hengshui, China 162 E6
Hengxian, China 163 R1
Hengyang, China 163 N4
Heniches'k, Ukr. 133 L17
Henlopen, Cape, Del., U.S. 90 C15
Hennessey, Okla., U.S. 96 F10
Henning, Minn., U.S. 98 H9
Henrietta, Tex., U.S. 96 J10
Henrietta, Ostrov, Russ. 141 C17
Henrietta Maria, Cape, Ont., Can. 77 L17
Henrieville, Utah, U.S. 101 P7
Henry, Cape, Va., U.S. 90 F14
Henryetta, Okla., U.S. 96 G12
Henry Kater Peninsula, Nunavut, Can. 77 E18
Henrys Fork, river, Idaho, U.S. 100 G7
Henslow, Cape, Solomon Is. 197 P19
Hentiyn Nuruu, Mongolia 161 C13
Heping, China 163 Q5
Heppner, Oreg., U.S. 102 F7
Hepu, China 163 S1
Hequ, China 162 D4
Herald, Ostrov, Russ. 141 A19
Herald Cays, Austral. 190 D14
Herat (Hirat), Afghan. 156 M2
Herbert, river, Austral. 190 D13

Herbert, Sask., Can. 76 N11
Herceg-Novi, Yug. 136 H12
Hercules Dome, Antarctica 206 J11
Herdman Seamount, Atl. Oc. 217 U13
Hereford, Tex., U.S. 96 H4
Hereheretue, island, Fr. Polynesia, Fr. 199 G18
Herford, Ger. 132 G5
Herington, Kans., U.S. 99 T8
Heritage Range, Antarctica 206 H8
Herkimer, N.Y., U.S. 88 J10
Herlacher, Cape, Antarctica 206 L7
Herlen, river, Mongolia 161 D14
Herman, Minn., U.S. 98 J9
Hermann, Mo., U.S. 99 T14
Hermannsburg, N. Terr., Austral. 191 T8
Hermansville, Mich., U.S. 92 G7
Hermanus, S. Af. 182 M7
Hermidale, N.S.W., Austral. 191 X13
Hermiston, Oreg., U.S. 102 E7
Hermit Island, P.N.G. 193 B19
Hermleigh, Tex., U.S. 96 L6
Hermosa, S. Dak., U.S. 98 L2
Hermosa, Punta, Bioko, Eq. Guinea 184 L8
Hermosillo, Mex. 108 C7
Hernando, Arg. 124 K10
Hernando, Miss., U.S. 94 G11
Herreid, S. Dak., U.S. 98 H5
Herrera, Arg. 124 H11
Herrin, Ill., U.S. 93 U5
Herschel Island, Yukon Terr., Can. 76 D10
Hershey, Nebr., U.S. 99 P4
Hertford, N.C., U.S. 90 G14
Hervey Bay, Austral. 190 G15
Hervey Islands, Cook Is., N.Z. 194 K12
Hesar Range, Afghan. 156 M5
Heshui, China 162 F1
Hess Rise, Pac. Oc. 218 E9
Hettinger, N. Dak., U.S. 98 H2
Heuru, Solomon Is. 197 P20
Hexian, China 162 K8
Hexian, China 163 Q3
Hexigten Qi (Jingpeng), China 162 A7
Heyuan, China 163 R5
Heze, China 162 G6
Hialeah, Fla., U.S. 91 X10
Hiawatha, Kans., U.S. 99 R9
Hiawatha, Utah, U.S. 100 M8
Hibbing, Minn., U.S. 98 F11
Hicacos, Peninsula de, Cuba 110 G7
Hickam Air Force Base, Hawaii, U.S. 106 E11
Hickiwan, Ariz., U.S. 101 V6
Hickman, Ky., U.S. 94 E12
Hickmann, Arg. 124 E10
Hickory, N.C., U.S. 90 H8
Hicks Bay, N.Z. 193 K20
Hicksville, Ohio, U.S. 93 P11
Hico, Tex., U.S. 96 M10
Hidaka Sammyaku, mountains, Jap. 164 G14
Hidalgo del Parral, Mex. 108 E9
Hienghène, New Caledonia, Fr. 198 C7
Hienghène, Baie de, New Caledonia, Fr. 198 C7
Hierro, island, Canary Is., Sp. 176 C5
Hierro, island, Canary Is., Sp. 184 R3
Higgins, Tex., U.S. 96 F7
Higgins Lake, Mich., U.S. 92 J10
Higginsville, Mo., U.S. 99 S11
High Atlas, mountains, Af. 174 D3
High Island, Tex., U.S. 97 R15
Highland, Ill., U.S. 93 T5
Highland Park, Ill., U.S. 93 N7
Highlands, Eur. 130 D4
Highmore, S. Dak., U.S. 98 K5
High Plains, U.S. 78 J10
High Point, N.J., U.S. 88 M10
High Point, N.C., U.S. 90 H10
High Red Rock, Norfolk I., Austral. 197 G20
High Rock, Bahamas 110 C10
High Springs, Fla., U.S. 91 R7
Higüero, Punta, P.R., U.S. 111 M22
Higüey, Dom. Rep. 111 M20
Hiiumaa, island, Estonia 135 L15
Hijāz, Jabal al, Saudi Arabia 152 M8
Hikari, Jap. 165 R5
Hikiau Heiau, Hawaii, U.S. 107 N18
Hiko, Nev., U.S. 103 S12
Hikueru, island, Fr. Polynesia, Fr. 199 F19
Hikurangi, peak, N.Z. 193 K20
Hikutavake, Niue, N.Z. 199 A20
Hilāl, Ras al, Af. 174 D7
Hilina Pali, Hawaii, U.S. 107 N20
Hillary Coast, Antarctica 207 N14
Hill City, Kans., U.S. 99 S5
Hill City, Minn., U.S. 98 G11
Hill City, S. Dak., U.S. 98 L1
Hillman, Mich., U.S. 92 H11
Hillsboro, Ill., U.S. 93 S5
Hillsboro, Kans., U.S. 99 T8
Hillsboro, N. Dak., U.S. 98 F8
Hillsboro, N. Mex., U.S. 101 U11
Hillsboro, Ohio, U.S. 93 S12
Hillsboro, Oreg., U.S. 102 F3
Hillsboro, Tex., U.S. 96 M11
Hillsborough, Grenada 113 M17
Hillsdale, Mich., U.S. 93 N11
Hillside, W. Austral., Austral. 191 T3
Hillston, N.S.W., Austral. 191 X12
Hillsville, Va., U.S. 90 G9
Hilo, region, Hawaii, U.S. 107 L21
Hilo, Hawaii, U.S. 107 M21
Hilo Bay, Hawaii, U.S. 107 L21
Hilton Head Island, S.C., U.S. 91 N9
Hilvan, Turk. 149 H13
Himalaya, mountains Asia 146 H8
Ḩimar, Wādī al, Syr. 150 D12
Himatnagar, India 158 H3
Himeji, Jap. 165 Q8
Ḩimş (Homs), Syr. 150 G8
Hinako, Kepulauan, Indonesia 168 J4
Hinche, Haiti 111 L17
Hinchinbrook Island, Alas., U.S. 105 J17
Hinchinbrook Island, Austral. 190 D13
Hinckley, Minn., U.S. 98 H12
Hinckley, Utah, U.S. 100 M6
Hindaun, India 158 G6
Hindmarsh, Lake, Austral. 190 L11
Hindu Kush, mountains, Asia 146 G6
Hines, Oreg., U.S. 102 J7
Hines Creek, Alta., Can. 76 K10
Hinesville, Ga., U.S. 91 N8
Hinganghat, India 158 K6
Hingol, river, Pak. 157 V4
Hingorja, Pak. 157 U7
Hinidan, Pak. 157 V6
Hınıs, Turk. 149 F16
Hinnøya, island, Nor. 134 D12
Hino, Jap. 165 P7
Hinoemata, Jap. 165 N12
Hinomi Saki, Jap. 165 P6
Hinthada, Myanmar 166 K5
Hinton, Okla., U.S. 96 G9
Hinton, W. Va., U.S. 90 E9
Híos, Gr. 137 K16
Híos (Chios), island, Gr. 137 L16
Ḩīr, Qaşr al, Syr. 150 G11
Hirado, Jap. 165 R3
Hirado Shima, Jap. 165 R3
Hiranai, Jap. 164 J13
Hira Se, Jap. 165 U3
Hirat see Herat, Afghan. 156 M2
Hirata, Jap. 165 P6
Hirfanlı Barajı, Turk. 148 F9
Hiroo, Jap. 164 G15
Hirosaki, Jap. 164 J12
Hiroshima, Jap. 165 Q6
Hisarönü, Turk. 148 C7
Ḩismá, plain, Jordan 151 S6
Hismá, plain, Saudi Arabia 152 G5
Hispaniola, island, Dom. Rep.-Haiti 111 M18
Ḩisyah, Syr. 150 H8
Hita, Jap. 165 R5
Hitachi, Jap. 165 N13
Hitadu, island, Maldives 159 W3
Hitadu, island, Maldives 159 X3
Hiti, island, Fr. Polynesia, Fr. 199 E18
Hitiaa, Tahiti, Fr. Polynesia, Fr. 199 P17
Hitoyoshi, Jap. 165 S4
Hitra, island, Nor. 134 H10
Hiu, island, Vanuatu 198 A1
Hiva Oa, island, Hiva Oa, Fr. Polynesia, Fr. 199 M21
Hiwasa, Jap. 165 R8
Hiwassee, river, Tenn., U.S. 95 F18
Hizan, Turk. 149 G17
Hjälmaren, lake, Sw. 135 L13
Hjørring, Den. 134 M11
Hkakabo Razi, peak, Myanmar 166 C7
Hlukhiv, Ukr. 133 G16
Hlybokaye, Belarus 133 E13
Ho, Ghana 180 H11
Hoa Binh, Vietnam 166 H11
Hoai An, Vietnam 166 M14
Hoanib, river, Namibia 182 G5
Hoare Bay, Nunavut, Can. 77 G19
Hobart, Ind., U.S. 93 P8
Hobart, Okla., U.S. 96 H8
Hobart, Tas., Austral. 191 Z16
Hobbs, N. Mex., U.S. 101 U15
Hobbs, Mount, Austral. 190 M16
Hobe Sound, Fla., U.S. 91 V10
Hoboksar, China 160 D7
Hobot Xar see Xianghuang Qi, China 162 B5
Hobro, Den. 134 N11
Hobucken, N.C., U.S. 90 H14
Hobyo, Somalia 179 H18
Ho Chi Minh City (Saigon), Vietnam 167 P13
Hodge, La., U.S. 94 L8
Hodgenville, Ky., U.S. 95 C16
Hodgson, river, Austral. 190 C9
Hódmezővásárhely, Hung. 132 L10
Hödrögö, Mongolia 160 C10
Hoedspruit, S. Af. 182 J11
Hoeryŏng, N. Korea 162 B14
Hof, Ger. 132 H6
Höfdakaupstadur, Ice. 134 E3
Hoffman, Minn., U.S. 98 H9
Höfn, Ice. 134 G4
Hofsjökull, Ice. 134 F3
Hogansville, Ga., U.S. 90 M4
Hog Cay, Bahamas 111 G13
Hoggar see Ahaggar, plateau, Alg. 176 E11
Hog Island, Va., U.S. 90 E15
Hohenwald, Tenn., U.S. 95 F14
Hohhot, China 162 C4
Hohonu, island, Manihi, Fr. Polynesia, Fr. 199 K17
Hoh Xil Shan, China 160 J7
Hoi An, Vietnam 166 L13
Hoisington, Kans., U.S. 99 T6
Hokatu, Ua Huka, Fr. Polynesia, Fr. 199 N23
Hokitika, N.Z. 193 N17
Hokkaidō, island, Jap. 164 G15
Hokukano Heiau, Hawaii, U.S. 107 F15
Hokula, Ha'apai Group, Tonga 198 P6
Hola Prystan', Ukr. 133 L15
Holbrook, Ariz., U.S. 101 S8
Holbrook, Idaho, U.S. 100 J6
Holden, Mo., U.S. 99 T11
Holden, Utah, U.S. 100 M7
Holdenville, Okla., U.S. 96 G12
Holdrege, Nebr., U.S. 99 Q5
Holei Pali, Hawaii, U.S. 107 N21
Holguín, Cuba 110 J12
Holland, Mich., U.S. 92 M9
Hollandale, Miss., U.S. 94 K10
Hollandsbird Island, Namibia 182 K6
Hollick-Kenyon Plateau, Antarctica 206 K8
Hollidaysburg, Pa., U.S. 88 N5
Hollis, Okla., U.S. 96 H7
Hollister, Calif., U.S. 103 T4
Holly, Colo., U.S. 101 N16
Holly Hill, S.C., U.S. 90 L10
Holly Ridge, N.C., U.S. 90 J13
Holly Springs, Miss., U.S. 94 G12
Hollywood, Calif., U.S. 103 X8
Hollywood, Fla., U.S. 91 W10
Holman, N. Mex., U.S. 101 R13
Holman, N.W.T., Can. 76 E12
Hólmavík, Ice. 134 E2
Holme Bay, Antarctica 207 E20
Holonga, Vava'u Group, Tonga 198 L12
Holopaw, Fla., U.S. 91 T9
Holstebro, Den. 134 N11
Holstein, Iowa, U.S. 99 N9
Holston, river, Tenn., U.S. 95 E20
Holt, Ala., U.S. 95 K14
Holton, Kans., U.S. 99 S9
Holtville, Calif., U.S. 103 Z12
Holualoa, Hawaii, U.S. 107 M18
Holy Cross, Alas., U.S. 105 H13
Holyoke, Colo., U.S. 100 L15
Holyoke, Mass., U.S. 89 K13
Hombetsu, Jap. 164 F15
Hombori, Mali 176 H9
Home Bay, Banaba, Kiribati 197 E20
Home Bay, Nunavut, Can. 77 F18
Homedale, Idaho, U.S. 100 G3
Homer, Alas., U.S. 105 K16
Homer, La., U.S. 94 K7
Homer, Mich., U.S. 93 N11
Homer, N.Y., U.S. 88 K8
Homerville, Ga., U.S. 91 Q7
Homestead, Fla., U.S. 91 X10
Homestead National Monument of America, Nebr., U.S. 99 R8
Homewood, Ala., U.S. 95 J15
Hominy, Okla., U.S. 96 E12
Hommalinn, Myanmar 166 E5
Hommura, Jap. 165 Q12
Homnabad, India 158 M5
Homo Bay, Vanuatu 198 D3
Homosassa Springs, Fla., U.S. 91 T7
Homs see Ḩimş, Syr. 150 G8
Homyel', Belarus 133 G14
Honaunau, Hawaii, U.S. 107 N18
Honavar, India 159 P4
Honaz, Turk. 148 G5
Honda, Col. 120 E5
Hondo, Jap. 165 S4
Hondo, N. Mex., U.S. 101 U13
Hondo, Tex., U.S. 97 R8
Honduras, N. Amer. 109 L17
Honduras, Golfo de, Belize-Guatemala-Hond. 109 K17
Honea Path, S.C., U.S. 90 K7
Hønefoss, Nor. 134 K11
Honesdale, Pa., U.S. 88 L9
Honey Grove, Tex., U.S. 96 K13
Honey Lake, Calif., U.S. 103 N6
Hong (Red), river, Vietnam 166 G10
Hong'an, China 162 K5
Hong Gai, Vietnam 166 H13
Hong Hu, China 162 L4
Honghu, China 162 L4
Hongjiang, China 163 N2
Hong Kong, China 163 S5
Hongliuyuan, China 160 G9
Hongor, Mongolia 161 E14
Hongshui, river, China 163 Q1
Hongsŏng, S. Korea 162 F13
Hongtong, China 162 F4
Hongū, Jap. 165 R9
Hongwŏn, N. Korea 162 C13
Hongze Hu, China 162 J8
Honiara, Solomon Is. 197 N18
Honikulu, Passe, Wallis and Futuna, Fr. 198 C11
Honjō, Jap. 164 K12
Honokaa, Hawaii, U.S. 107 K20
Honokahua, Hawaii, U.S. 107 F16
Honokohau Settlement, Hawaii, U.S. 107 M18
Honokowai, Hawaii, U.S. 107 G15
Honolulu, Hawaii, U.S. 106 E11
Honomanu Bay, Hawaii, U.S. 107 G17
Honomu, Hawaii, U.S. 107 L21
Hon Quan, Vietnam 167 P12
Honshu, island, Jap. 165 P5
Honuapo Bay, Hawaii, U.S. 107 P20
Hood, Mount, Oreg., U.S. 102 F4
Hood River, Oreg., U.S. 102 E5
Hoodsport, Wash., U.S. 102 C3
Hookena, Hawaii, U.S. 107 N18
Hooker, Okla., U.S. 96 E6
Hoolehua, Hawaii, U.S. 107 F14
Hoonah, Alas., U.S. 105 K22
Hooper, Cape, Nunavut, Can. 77 F18
Hooper Bay, Alas., U.S. 104 J11
Hoopeston, Ill., U.S. 93 Q7
Hoover, Ala., U.S. 95 J15
Hoover Dam, Ariz.-Nev., U.S. 101 R4
Hopa, Turk. 149 C16
Hope, Ark., U.S. 94 J7
Hope, N. Dak., U.S. 98 G7
Hope, Lake, Austral. 190 K4
Hope, Point, U.S. 78 M2
Hopedale, Nfld., Can. 77 K21
Hopelchén, Mex. 109 J16
Hope Mills, N.C., U.S. 90 J11
Hope Point, Myanmar 166 L7
Hopetoun, W. Austral., Austral. 191 Y4
Hope Town, Bahamas 110 C12
Hopetown, S. Af. 182 L9
Hopewell, Va., U.S. 90 F13
Hopewell Culture National Historical Park, Ohio, U.S. 93 S13
Hopewell Islands, Nunavut, Can. 77 K18
Hopkins, Mount, Ariz., U.S. 101 W8
Hopkinsville, Ky., U.S. 95 D14
Hoquiam, Wash., U.S. 102 D2
Horasan, Turk. 149 E16
Horicon, Wis., U.S. 92 L6
Horinger, China 162 C4
Horki, Belarus 133 E14
Horlick Mountains, Antarctica 206 J11
Horlivka, Ukr. 133 J18
Ḩormak, Iran 153 F17
Hormuz, Strait of, Asia 153 H15
Horn, Aust. 132 J8
Horn, Cape see Hornos, Cabo de, Chile 125 Y9
Hornavan, lake, Sw. 135 F13
Hornbeck, La., U.S. 94 M7
Hornbrook, Calif., U.S. 102 L3
Horne, Îles de, Pac. Oc. 194 J9
Hornell, N.Y., U.S. 88 K6
Horn Island, Miss., U.S. 95 P13
Hornos, Cabo de (Cape Horn) see (Horn, Cape), Chile 125 Y9
Horodnya, Ukr. 133 G15
Horqin Zuoyi Houqi, China 162 A10
Horqueta, Para. 122 M10
Horse Cave, Ky., U.S. 95 D16
Horse Creek, river, Wyo., U.S. 100 K13
Horsehead Lake, N. Dak., U.S. 98 G5
Horseheads, N.Y., U.S. 88 K7
Horse Mountain, N. Mex., U.S. 101 T10
Horseshoe Beach, Fla., U.S. 91 S6
Horseshoe Bend, Ark., U.S. 94 E9
Horseshoe Bend, Idaho, U.S. 100 G4
Horseshoe Canyon, Canyonlands National Park, Utah, U.S. 101 N8
Horseshoe Reservoir, Ariz., U.S. 101 T7
Horsham, Vic., Austral. 191 Y11
Horten, Nor. 134 L11
Horton, river, N.W.T., Can. 76 E11
Horton, Kans., U.S. 99 R9
Hosdrug, India 159 Q4
Hoshab, Pak. 157 V3
Hoshangabad, India 158 J6
Hosmer, S. Dak., U.S. 98 J5
Hosta Butte, N. Mex., U.S. 101 R10
Hoste, Isla, Chile 125 Y9
Hosur, India 159 Q6
Hot, Thai. 166 K7
Hotan, river, China 160 G5
Hotan, China 160 G5
Hotchkiss, Colo., U.S. 101 N11
Hot Creek Range, Nev., U.S. 103 R10
Hotevilla, Ariz., U.S. 101 R8

Hot Springs, Ark., U.S. 94 H7
Hot Springs, Mont., U.S. 100 C5
Hot Springs, S. Dak., U.S. 98 L1
Hot Springs, Va., U.S. 90 E10
Hot Springs National Park, Ark., U.S. 94 H7
Hotspur Seamount, Atl. Oc. 217 Q8
Hot Sulphur Springs, Colo., U.S. 100 L12
Hottah Lake, N.W.T., Can. 76 G11
Hotte, Massif de la, Haiti 111 M14
Hottentot Bay, Namibia 182 J6
Houaïlou, New Caledonia, Fr. 198 D7
Houayxay, Laos 166 H9
Houghton, Mich., U.S. 92 E6
Houlton, Me., U.S. 89 C18
Houma, China 162 G3
Houma, La., U.S. 94 Q10
Houma, Tongatapu, Tonga 198 J11
Houma Toloa, point, Tongatapu, Tonga 198 J11
Houston, Minn., U.S. 98 L13
Houston, Miss., U.S. 94 J12
Houston, Mo., U.S. 99 U13
Houston, Tex., U.S. 97 R14
Houtman Abrolhos, islands, Austral. 190 J1
Hoven, S. Dak., U.S. 98 J5
Hovenweep National Monument, Utah, U.S. 101 P9
Hövsgöl, Mongolia 161 E13
Hövsgöl Nuur, Mongolia 160 C11
Howar, Wadi, Sudan 178 D11
Howard, Kans., U.S. 99 U9
Howard, S. Dak., U.S. 98 L7
Howard City, Mich., U.S. 92 L10
Howard Lake, N.W.T.-Nunavut, Can. 77 H13
Howe, Idaho, U.S. 100 G6
Howe, Cape, Austral. 190 M14
Howe, Point, Norfolk I., Austral. 197 F20
Howland, Me., U.S. 89 E17
Howland Island, Pac. Oc. 194 G9
Ho Xa, Vietnam 166 K13
Hoxie, Ark., U.S. 94 E10
Hoxie, Kans., U.S. 99 S4
Hoy, island, Scot., U.K. 138 C8
Høyanger, Nor. 134 K10
Hoyos, Sp. 139 Q6
Hoyt Lakes, Minn., U.S. 98 F12
Hozat, Turk. 149 F14
Hpa-an, Myanmar 166 K7
Hradec Králové, Czech Rep. 132 H8
Hrazdan, river, Arm. 149 D18
Hrodna, Belarus 132 F11
Hsi-hseng, Myanmar 166 H7
Hsinchu, Taiwan, China 163 Q9
Hsinying, Taiwan, China 163 R9
Hsipaw, Myanmar 166 G7
Huachi, China 162 F1
Huacho, Peru 122 H3
Huade, China 162 B5
Huadian, China 162 A12
Hua Hin, Thai. 167 N8
Huahine, island, Fr. Polynesia, Fr. 199 E15
Huahine, Tubuai, Fr. Polynesia, Fr. 199 K20
Huahine Iti, island, Huahine, Fr. Polynesia, Fr. 199 H14
Huahine Nui, island, Huahine, Fr. Polynesia, Fr. 199 G14
Huaibei, China 162 H7
Huaibin, China 162 J6
Huaiji, China 163 R3
Huailai, China 162 C6
Huainan, China 162 J7
Huaining, China 162 L6
Huairen, China 162 D5
Huai Yang, Thai. 167 P8
Huaiyin, China 162 J8
Huajuapan de León, Mex. 108 K12
Hualalai, peak, Hawaii, U.S. 107 M19
Hualapai Peak, Ariz., U.S. 101 S5
Hualfín, Arg. 124 G9
Hualien, Taiwan, China 163 R10
Huallaga, river, Peru 122 F3
Huambo, Angola 182 D6
Huancané, Peru 122 J6
Huancavelica, Peru 122 H4
Huancayo, Peru 122 H4
Huang (Yellow), river, China 160 K10
Huangchuan, China 162 K6
Huanggang, China 162 L5
Huanggangliang, China 162 A7
Huanghua, China 162 E7
Huangling, China 162 G2
Huangliu, China 163 U1
Huangnihe, China 162 A13
Huangquqiao, China 162 D1
Huangshan, China 162 M8
Huangshi, China 162 L5
Huangxian, China 162 D9
Huangyan, China 162 M10
Huanren, China 162 C12
Huanta, Peru 122 H4
Huantai, China 162 F8
Huánuco, Peru 122 G3
Huanxian, China 162 F1
Huara, Chile 124 C7
Huaral, Peru 122 H3
Huaraz, Peru 122 G3
Huarmey, Peru 122 G3
Huarong, China 162 M4
Huascarán, Nevado, S. Amer. 118 F2
Huasco, Chile 124 H6
Huatabampo, Mex. 108 E7
Huaura, Peru 122 H3
Huaxian, China 162 G5
Huayuan, China 162 M2
Huazhou, China 163 S2
Hubbard, Tex., U.S. 96 M12
Hubbard Lake, Mich., U.S. 92 J12
Hubbell Trading Post National Historic Site, Ariz., U.S. 101 R9
Hubli, India 159 N4
Huch'ang, N. Korea 162 B13
Hudiksvall, Sw. 135 J13
Hudson, river, N.Y., U.S. 88 L11
Hudson, Fla., U.S. 91 T7
Hudson, Mich., U.S. 93 N11
Hudson, N.Y., U.S. 88 K11
Hudson, Wyo., U.S. 100 H10
Hudson Bay, N. Amer. 74 F7
Hudson Bay, Sask., Can. 77 M13
Hudson Canyon, Atl. Oc. 216 H4
Hudson Strait, N. Amer. 74 E8
Hue, Vietnam 166 L13
Huedin, Rom. 137 E14
Huehue Ranch, Hawaii, U.S. 107 L18
Huehuetenango, Guatemala 109 L15
Huelva, Sp. 139 S5
Huerfano, river, Colo., U.S. 101 P13
Huesca, Sp. 139 P9
Huff, N. Dak., U.S. 98 G4
Hughenden, Qnsld., Austral. 191 S12
Hughes, Alas., U.S. 105 F15
Hughes, Ark., U.S. 94 G11
Hughes, S. Austral., Austral. 191 W7
Hughes Bay, Antarctica 206 D3
Hugli, estuary, India 158 J11
Hugo, Okla., U.S. 96 J13
Hugon, Île, New Caledonia, Fr. 198 D8
Hugoton, Kans., U.S. 99 V3
Hui'an, China 163 Q8
Huichang, China 163 Q6
Hüich'ŏn, N. Korea 162 C12
Huilai, China 163 R6
Huila Plateau, Af. 174 M6
Huimin, China 162 F7
Huinan, China 162 B12
Huinca Renancó, Arg. 124 L10
Huitong, China 163 N2
Huize, China 160 N11
Huizhou, China 163 R5
Hukawng Valley, Myanmar 166 D6
Hŭksan Chedo, S. Korea 162 H12
Hulan, China 161 D17
Hulan Ergi, China 161 C16
Ḩulayfā', Saudi Arabia 152 H7
Hulbert, Mich., U.S. 92 F10
Hulett, Wyo., U.S. 100 F13
Hull, Ill., U.S. 93 R3
Hulu, river, China 162 F2
Hulun Nur, China 161 C15
Huma, river, China 161 A16
Huma, China 161 A16
Humacao, P.R., U.S. 111 M23
Humahuaca, Arg. 124 E9
Humaitá, Braz. 122 F8
Humansdorp, S. Af. 182 M9
Humansville, Mo., U.S. 99 U11
Ḩumar, U.A.E. 153 K14
Humbe, Angola 182 F6
Humberstone, Chile 124 C7
Humberto de Campos, Braz. 123 D15
Humble, Tex., U.S. 97 Q14
Humboldt, river, Nev., U.S. 102 M9
Humboldt, Ariz., U.S. 101 S6
Humboldt, Iowa, U.S. 98 M11
Humboldt, Kans., U.S. 99 U10
Humboldt, Nebr., U.S. 99 R9
Humboldt, Sask., Can. 76 M12
Humboldt, Tenn., U.S. 94 F12
Humboldt Bay, Calif., U.S. 102 M1
Humboldt Plain, Pac. Oc. 219 R19
Hūmedān, Iran 153 J17
Humphreys Peak, Ariz., U.S. 101 S7
Humpty Doo, N. Terr., Austral. 191 P7
Humuula Saddle, Hawaii, U.S. 107 M20
Hūn, Lib. 177 D14
Húnaflói, bay, Ice. 134 E2
Hunchun, China 162 A15
Hunedoara, Rom. 137 F14
Hunga, island, Vava'u Group, Tonga 198 L11
Hunga Ha'apai, island, Ha'apai Group, Tonga 198 R5
Hungary, Eur. 132 L9
Hunga Tonga, island, Ha'apai Group, Tonga 198 R5
Hungerford, N.S.W., Austral. 191 V12
Hŭngnam, N. Korea 162 D13
Hungry Horse Reservoir, Mont., U.S. 100 B6
Hungund, India 159 N5
Hunjiang, China 162 B12
Huns Mountains, Af. 174 Q6
Hunsur, India 159 Q5
Hunt, Mongolia 160 D10
Hunter, island, Vanuatu 194 K8
Hunter, N. Dak., U.S. 98 G8
Hunter, Cape, Solomon Is. 197 P18
Hunter Islands, Austral. 190 L15
Huntingburg, Ind., U.S. 93 T8
Huntingdon, Pa., U.S. 88 N6
Huntingdon, Tenn., U.S. 95 E13
Huntington, Ind., U.S. 93 Q10
Huntington, Oreg., U.S. 102 G9
Huntington, Tex., U.S. 97 N15
Huntington, Utah, U.S. 100 M8
Huntington, W. Va., U.S. 90 D7
Huntington Beach, Calif., U.S. 103 X8
Huntly, N.Z. 193 K19
Huntsville, Ala., U.S. 95 G15
Huntsville, Ark., U.S. 94 E7
Huntsville, Mo., U.S. 99 S12
Huntsville, Tex., U.S. 97 P13
Huntsville, Utah, U.S. 100 K7
Hunucmá, Mex. 109 H16
Hunyuan, China 162 D5
Hunza, region, Pak. 156 K12
Huocheng, China 160 E6
Huolu, China 162 E5
Huon, Île, Coral Sea 194 K6
Huong Hoa, Vietnam 166 K12
Huon Gulf, P.N.G. 193 D19
Huon Peninsula, P.N.G. 193 D19
Huoqiu, China 162 J6
Huoshan, China 162 K6
Huoxian, China 162 F4
Hurdiyo, Somalia 179 F19
Hure Qi, China 161 E16
Hure Qi, China 162 B10
Hurghada, Egypt 177 D19
Hurley, N. Mex., U.S. 101 V10
Hurley, Wis., U.S. 92 F4
Hurmagai, Pak. 157 T4
Huron, S. Dak., U.S. 98 K7
Huron, Lake, N. Amer. 74 J8
Huron Mountain, Mich., U.S. 92 E7
Hurricane, Utah, U.S. 101 P6
Hurtsboro, Ala., U.S. 95 L17
Húsavík, Ice. 134 E3
Huşi, Rom. 137 E17
Huslia, Alas., U.S. 105 F14
Hutag, Mongolia 160 C11
Hutchinson, Kans., U.S. 99 U7
Hutchinson, Minn., U.S. 98 K10
Hutch Mountain, Ariz., U.S. 101 S7
Huthi, Myanmar 166 L8
Huttig, Ark., U.S. 94 K8
Hutuo Ziya, river, China 162 E6
Huvadu see Suvadiva Atoll, atoll, Maldives 159 W3
Huxian, China 162 H2
Hüyük, Turk. 148 G7
Huzhou, China 162 L9
Hvammstangi, Ice. 134 E2
Hvannadalshnúkur, peak, Eur. 130 A3
Hvar, island, Croatia 136 G11
Hveragerði, Ice. 134 F2
Hvítá, river, Ice. 134 F2
Hwange, Zimb. 182 F10
Hyannis, Mass., U.S. 89 L16
Hyannis, Nebr., U.S. 99 N3
Hyargas Nuur, Mongolia 160 C9
Hyden, W. Austral., Austral. 191 X3
Hyde Park, N.Y., U.S. 88 L11
Hyder, Alas., U.S. 105 L24
Hyderabad, India 158 M6
Hyderabad, Pak. 157 V7
Hydro, Okla., U.S. 96 G9
Hyères, Fr. 139 N12
Hyères, Îles d', Fr. 139 N12
Hyesan, N. Korea 162 B13
Hyndman Peak, Idaho, U.S. 100 G5
Hyrra Banda, Cen. Af. Rep. 178 H10
Hyrynsalmi, Fin. 135 F16
Hysham, Mont., U.S. 100 D11
Hyūga, Jap. 165 S5

I

Iaco, river, Braz. 122 G6
Iaeger, W. Va., U.S. 90 F8
Iamara, P.N.G. 193 E18
Iaşi, Rom. 137 D17
Iauaretê, Braz. 122 C6
Ibadan, Nig. 180 G12
Ibagué, Col. 120 F5
Ibapah, Utah, U.S. 100 L5
Ibarra, Ecua. 120 H3
Ibb, Yemen 152 Q9
Iberá, Laguna, Arg. 124 H14
Iberia, Peru 122 G6
Iberian Mountains, Eur. 130 H3
Iberian Peninsula, Eur. 130 H2
Ibiapaba, Serra da, S. Amer. 118 E10
Irbid (Arbela), Jordan 150 L6
Ibipetuba, Braz. 123 G14
Ibiza (Iviza), island, Sp. 139 R10
Ibo, Mozambique 183 D15
Iboperenda, Bol. 122 K8
Ibotirama, Braz. 123 H15
Ibra, Wadi, Sudan 178 F10
Ibrā', Oman 153 K16
'Ibrī, Oman 153 K15
Ibusuki, Jap. 165 T4
Içá, river, Braz. 122 D6
Ica, river, Peru 122 J4
Ica, Peru 122 J4
Içana, river, Braz. 122 C6
Içana, Braz. 122 C6
İçel see Mersin, Turk. 148 J9
Iceland, Eur. 134 F2
Iceland, island, Eur. 130 A3
Iceland Plateau, Arctic Oc. 223 K19
Ichchapuram, India 158 L10
Ichikawa, Jap. 165 P12
Ichinohe, Jap. 164 J13
Ichinomiya, Jap. 165 P10
Ichinoseki, Jap. 164 L13
Ichinskiy, Russ. 141 F22
Ichnya, Ukr. 133 H15
Ich'ŏn, N. Korea 162 E13
Icó, Braz. 123 F17
Icoraci, Braz. 123 D13
Icy Cape, Alas., U.S. 104 B12
Idabel, Okla., U.S. 96 J14
Ida Grove, Iowa, U.S. 99 N9
Idah, Nig. 181 G14
Idaho, U.S. 100 D4
Idaho City, Idaho, U.S. 100 G4
Idaho Falls, Idaho, U.S. 100 G7
Idaho Springs, Colo., U.S. 100 M13
Idalou, Tex., U.S. 96 K5
Idanha, Oreg., U.S. 102 G4
'Idd el Ghanam, Sudan 178 F10
Ideriyn, river, Mongolia 160 C10
Idfu, Egypt 177 E19
Idi, Indonesia 168 G4
İdil, Turk. 149 H16
Idiofa, Dem. Rep. of the Congo 178 L9
Idlib, Syr. 150 E8
Ierápetra, Gr. 137 N16
Ieta, P.N.G. 197 J13
Ifalik Atoll, F.S.M. 196 Q4
Ife, Nig. 181 G13
Iferouâne, Niger 176 G12
Ifjord, Nor. 135 B14
Iforas, Adrar des, Mali 176 F10
Igan, Malaysia 167 U16
Igara Paraná, river, Col. 120 J6
Igarka, Russ. 141 G13
Igatpuri, India 158 L3
Iğdır, Turk. 149 E18
Igikpak, Mount, Alas., U.S. 105 E14
Iglesias, It. 136 K7
Igli, Alg. 176 C9
Igloolik, Nunavut, Can. 77 F16
Igma, Gebel el', Egypt 151 S3
Ignacio, Colo., U.S. 101 Q11
Ignalina, Lith. 135 N17
İğneada, Turk. 148 B4
İğneada Burnu, Turk. 148 B4
Igrim, Russ. 140 G10
Iguala, Mex. 108 J11
Iguatu, Braz. 123 F16
Iguazú Falls, S. Amer. 118 J7
Igué, Île, New Caledonia, Fr. 198 B5
Iguéla, Gabon 181 L15
Iguidi, Erg, Alg.-Mauritania 176 D8
Iharaña (Vohemar), Madagascar 183 D18
Ihavandiffulu Atoll, Maldives 159 T3
Ihavandu, island, Maldives 159 T3
Iheya Rettō, Jap. 165 X1
Iheya Shima, Jap. 165 X1
Ihosy, Madagascar 183 H17
Ihu, P.N.G. 193 D19
Ii, Fin. 135 F15
Iida, Jap. 165 P11
Iisalmi, Fin. 135 G16
Iittuarmiit, Greenland, Den. 75 D22
Ijevan, Arm. 149 D19
Ijill, Sebkhet, Mauritania 176 E6
IJsselmeer, Neth. 138 G11
Ijuí, Braz. 122 P11
Ijuw, Nauru 197 E23
Ikanbujmal, China 160 G7
Ikare, Nig. 181 G13
Ikaría, island, Gr. 137 L16
Ikeda, Jap. 164 F15
Ikela, Dem. Rep. of the Congo 178 K10

Iki, island, Jap. 165 R3
İkizdere, Turk. 149 D15
Ikopa, river, Madagascar 183 F17
Iku, island, Tarawa, Kiribati 197 F17
Ikuren, island, Enewetak Atoll, Marshall Is. 196 J8
Ilab, Ţurāq al', hills, Syr. 150 J10
Ilagan, Philippines 169 B14
Ilave, Peru 122 J6
Ilbilbie, Qnsld., Austral. 191 T14
Ilbunga, S. Austral., Austral. 191 U9
Ile see Ili, river, Kaz. 155 H16
Île-à-la-Crosse, Sask., Can. 76 L12
Ilebo, Dem. Rep. of the Congo 178 L9
Ilfracombe, Qnsld., Austral. 191 T12
Ilgaz, Turk. 148 D9
Ilgaz Dağları, Turk. 148 C9
Ilgın, Turk. 148 G7
Ilhéus, Braz. 123 J16
Ili (Ile), river, Kaz. 155 H16
Iliamna Lake, Alas., U.S. 105 K15
İliç, Turk. 149 F13
Ilıca, Turk. 149 E15
Iligan, Philippines 169 F15
Iliili, Tutuila, Amer. Samoa, U.S. 198 M7
Iliiliopae Heiau, Hawaii, U.S. 107 F15
Ilion, N.Y., U.S. 88 J10
Ilio Point, Hawaii, U.S. 107 F13
Illampu, peak, S. Amer. 118 G4
Illapel, Chile 124 K6
Illeginni, island, Kwajalein Atoll, Marshall Is. 196 L4
Illéla, Niger 176 H11
Illichivs'k, Ukr. 133 L15
Illimani, peak, S. Amer. 118 G4
Illinois, river, Ill., U.S. 93 Q4
Illinois, river, Oreg., U.S. 102 K2
Illinois, U.S. 93 Q4
Illinois Peak, U.S. 78 C6
Illizi, Alg. 176 D12
Il'men', Lake, Eur. 130 D10
Ilo, Peru 122 K5
Iloilo, Philippines 169 E14
Ilorin, Nig. 181 G13
Il'pyrskiy, Russ. 141 E21
Ilulissat, Greenland, Den. 75 C21
Ilwaco, Wash., U.S. 102 E2
Imabari, Jap. 165 R6
Imabetsu, Jap. 164 H12
I Maddock, Puntan, Saipan, N. Mariana Is., U.S. 196 B6
Imaichi, Jap. 165 N12
Imajō, Jap. 165 P9
Imandra, Lake, Eur. 130 A9
Imarssuak Seachannel, Atl. Oc. 216 E7
Imatra, Fin. 135 H17
Imbert, Dom. Rep. 111 L18
Imeni Ismail Sumani Peak (Communism Peak), Kyrg.-Taj. 156 H10
Imese, Dem. Rep. of the Congo 178 J8
Īmī, Eth. 179 G16
Imías, Cuba 111 K14
Imieji Anchorage, Jaluit Atoll, Marshall Is. 196 M8
İmişli, Azerb. 149 E21
Imjun, river, N. Korea 162 E13
Imlay, Nev., U.S. 103 N8
Imlay City, Mich., U.S. 92 L12
Immarna, S. Austral., Austral. 191 W8
Immokalee, Fla., U.S. 91 W9
Imnaha, Oreg., U.S. 102 F9
Imola, It. 136 F9
Imotski, Croatia 136 G12
Imperatriz, Braz. 123 E13
Imperia, It. 136 F7
Imperial, Calif., U.S. 103 Z11
Imperial, Nebr., U.S. 99 Q3
Imperial Beach, Calif., U.S. 103 Z9
Imperial Dam, Ariz.-Calif., U.S. 101 U4
Imperial Valley, Calif., U.S. 103 Z11
Impfondo, Congo 181 K18
Imphal, India 158 H14
İmralı, island, Turk. 148 D4
İmranlı, Turk. 149 E13
Imrodj, island, Jaluit Atoll, Marshall Is. 196 L8
İmroz see Gökçeada, island, Turk. 148 D2
Imtān, Syr. 150 L8
Ina, Jap. 165 P11
Inaccessible Island, Atl. Oc. 174 R2
I Naftan, Puntan, Saipan, N. Mariana Is., U.S. 196 D5
Inamba Jima, Jap. 165 R12
I-n-Amenas, Alg. 176 D12
I-n-Amguel, Alg. 176 E11
Inanwatan, Indonesia 169 K18
Inarajan, Guam, U.S. 196 D10
Inari, lake, Fin. 135 C15
Inari, Fin. 135 D15
Inca de Oro, Chile 124 G7
İnce Burun, Turk. 148 B10
İncekum Burnu, Turk. 148 J9
İncesu, Turk. 148 G10
Inch'ŏn, S. Korea 162 F13
Indalsälven, river, Eur. 130 C7
Indawgyi Lake, Myanmar 166 E6
Independence, Calif., U.S. 103 T8
Independence, Iowa, U.S. 99 N13
Independence, Kans., U.S. 99 V9
Independence, Mo., U.S. 99 S10
Independence Mountains, Nev., U.S. 102 M10
India, Asia 158 H6
Indian, river, Fla., U.S. 91 U10
Indiana, U.S. 93 R8
Indiana, Pa., U.S. 88 N4
Indianapolis, Ind., U.S. 93 R9
Indian Harbour, Nfld., Can. 77 K22
Indianola, Iowa, U.S. 99 P11
Indianola, Miss., U.S. 94 J10
Indianola, Nebr., U.S. 99 R4
Indian Peak, Utah, U.S. 101 N5
Indian Springs, Nev., U.S. 103 T11
Indiantown, Fla., U.S. 91 V10
Indigirka, river, Russ. 141 D18
Indio, Calif., U.S. 103 X11
Indira Point, Nicobar Is., India 159 T15
Indispensable Strait, Solomon Is. 197 M19
Indochina Peninsula, Asia 146 J10
Indomed Fracture Zone, Ind. Oc. 220 P5
Indonesia, Asia 168 L9
Indore, India 158 J5
Indravati, river, India 158 L7
Indus, river, Asia 146 H6
Indus, Mouths of the, Pak. 157 W6
Indus Fan, Ind. Oc. 220 D8
İnebolu, Turk. 148 B9
İnegöl, Turk. 148 E5
I-n-Eker, Alg. 176 E11
Inez, Ky., U.S. 95 B20
Infante D. Henrique, São Tomé and Príncipe 185 B21
Ingal, Niger 176 H11
Ingende, Dem. Rep. of the Congo 178 K9
Ingeniero Guillermo N. Juárez, Arg. 124 E11
Ingeniero Jacobacci, Arg. 125 Q8
Ingeniero Luiggi, Arg. 124 M10
Ingettolgoy, Mongolia 160 C11
Ingleside, Tex., U.S. 97 U11
Inglis, Fla., U.S. 91 S7
Ingolstadt, Ger. 132 J6
Ingomar, S. Austral., Austral. 191 W9
Ingraj Bazar, India 158 H11
Ingram, Tex., U.S. 97 Q8
Ingrid Christensen Coast, Antarctica 207 G19
Inhambane, Mozambique 183 H13
Inharrime, Mozambique 183 J13
Inhul, river, Ukr. 133 K15
Inírida, river, Col. 120 G8
Inkerman, Qnsld., Austral. 191 Q11
Inland Sea, Jap. 165 R6
Inn, river, Aust. 132 K6
Innamincka, S. Austral., Austral. 191 V11
Inner Hebrides, islands, Scot., U.K. 138 E6
Inner Mongolia, region, China 162 C1
Innesowen, N.S.W., Austral. 191 W12
Innisfail, Qnsld., Austral. 191 R13
Innoko, river, Alas., U.S. 105 G14
Innsbruck, Aust. 132 K6
Inongo, Dem. Rep. of the Congo 178 K8
İnönü, Turk. 148 E6
Inowrocław, Pol. 132 G9
I-n-Salah, Alg. 176 D10
Inscription, Cape, Austral. 190 G1
Insein, Myanmar 166 K6
Insiaf, Kosrae, F.S.M. 197 B18
Inta, Russ. 140 F10
Intendente Alvear, Arg. 124 M10
Interior, S. Dak., U.S. 98 L3
International Falls, Minn., U.S. 98 E11
Interview Island, Andaman Is., India 159 P14
Inthanon, Doi, Thai. 166 J7
Intiyaco, Arg. 124 H12
Inubō Zaki, Jap. 165 P13
Inukjuak, Que., Can. 77 K18
Inuvik, N.W.T., Can. 76 E10
Inuya, river, Peru 122 G4
Invercargill, N.Z. 193 R15
Inverness, Fla., U.S. 91 T7
Inverness, Scot., U.K. 138 D7
Inverway, N. Terr., Austral. 191 R7
Investigator Ridge, Ind. Oc. 221 H13
Investigator Strait, Austral. 190 L9
Inyokern, Calif., U.S. 103 V9
Inyo Mountains, Calif., U.S. 103 T8
Inzia, river, Dem. Rep. of the Congo 178 L8
Ioánina, Gr. 137 K14
Iō Jima, Jap. 165 U4
Iola, Kans., U.S. 99 U10
Iolkós see Vólos, Gr. 137 K15
Ioma, P.N.G. 193 D20
Iona, Idaho, U.S. 100 G7
Ione, Calif., U.S. 103 R5
Ione, Nev., U.S. 103 Q9
Ione, Oreg., U.S. 102 F6
Ione, Wash., U.S. 102 A9
Ionia, Mich., U.S. 92 L10
Ionian Islands, Eur. 130 K8
Ionian Sea, Eur. 130 K7
Iony, Ostrov (Saint Jona Island), Russ. 141 H20
Iori, river, Azerb. 149 C20
Iori, river, Rep. of Georgia 149 B19
Íos, island, Gr. 137 M16
Iotori Shima, Jap. 165 W1
Iowa, river, Iowa, U.S. 99 P12
Iowa, river, U.S. 79 F14
Iowa, U.S. 99 N10
Iowa City, Iowa, U.S. 99 P13
Iowa Falls, Iowa, U.S. 99 N12
Iowa Park, Tex., U.S. 96 J9
Ipiales, Col. 120 H3
Ipis, island, Chuuk, F.S.M. 197 D16
Ipixuna, river, Braz. 122 F4
Ipixuna, Braz. 122 F5
Ipoh, Malaysia 167 T9
Iporá, Braz. 122 J12
İpsala, Turk. 148 C2
Ipswich, Qnsld., Austral. 191 V15
Ipswich, S. Dak., U.S. 98 J6
Ipswich, Eng., U.K. 138 H9
Iqaluit, Nunavut, Can. 77 H19
Iquique, Chile 124 C7
Iquitos, Peru 122 E4
Iraan, Tex., U.S. 97 P5
Iracoubo, Fr. Guiana 121 E17
Īrafshān, Iran 153 H18
Iráklio (Candia), Gr. 137 N16
Iran, Asia 152 E12
Īrānshahr, Iran 153 H17
Irapuata, Mex. 108 H10
Iraq, Asia 152 E9
Irayel', Russ. 140 F9
Irazú, Volcán, C.R. 109 N19
Ireland, Eur. 138 G6
Ireland, island, Eur. 130 E3
Iret', Russ. 141 F21
Iri, S. Korea 162 G13
Irian Jaya, Indonesia 169 K20
Irimi, Indonesia 193 B14
Iringa, Tanzania 179 M14
Iriri, river, Braz. 122 E11
Iriri, river, Braz. 122 G11
Iriru, Passe, Raiatea, Fr. Polynesia, Fr. 199 B23
Irish Sea, Eur. 130 E4
Irkeshtam, Kyrg. 156 G11
Irkutsk, Russ. 141 L15
Irmauw, Indonesia 169 M17
Irondequoit, N.Y., U.S. 88 H6
Iron Gate, valley, Eur. 130 H8
Iron Knob, S. Austral., Austral. 191 X10
Iron Mountain, Mich., U.S. 92 G7
Iron River, Mich., U.S. 92 G6
Iron River, Wis., U.S. 92 F3
Ironton, Mo., U.S. 99 U15
Ironton, Ohio, U.S. 93 T13
Ironwood, Mich., U.S. 92 F4
Ironwood Forest National Monument, Ariz., U.S. 101 V7
Iroquois, S. Dak., U.S. 98 K7
Irō Zaki, Jap. 165 Q11
Irrawaddy see Ayeyarwady, river, Myanmar 166 G6
Irtysh, river, Asia 146 D7
Irún, Sp. 139 N8
Irvine, Ky., U.S. 95 C18
Irving, Tex., U.S. 96 L11
Irwin, Idaho, U.S. 100 H8
Isabel, S. Dak., U.S. 98 J4
Isabela, P.R., U.S. 111 M22
Isabela, Philippines 169 F14
Isabela, Cabo, Dom. Rep. 111 K18
Isabela, Isla, Galapagos Is., Ecua. 195 G21
Isabela de Sagua, Cuba 110 G9
Isabella, Minn., U.S. 98 F13
Isabelle, Point, Mich., U.S. 92 E7
Isachsen Mountain, Antarctica 207 B15
Ísafördur, Ice. 134 E2
Isahaya, Jap. 165 S4
Isa Khel, Pak. 157 P9
Isakov Seamount, Pac. Oc. 218 F7
Isangel, Vanuatu 198 H4
Ischia, island, It. 136 J10
Isdu, island, Maldives 159 W3
Ise, Jap. 165 Q10
Isen Saki, Jap. 165 X2
Isère, river, Fr. 138 M11
Isère, Pointe, Fr. Guiana 121 E17
Ise Wan, Jap. 165 Q10
Ishikari Wan, Jap. 164 F13
Ishim, river, Russ. 140 J10
Ishim, Russ. 140 J10
Ishim Steppe, Kaz. 154 A12
Ishinomaki, Jap. 164 L13
Ishinomaki Wan, Jap. 164 L13
Ishioka, Jap. 165 N13
Ishkuman, Pak. 156 K11
Ishpeming, Mich., U.S. 92 F7
Işık Dağı, Turk. 148 D8
Isikveren, Turk. 149 H17
Isimu, Indonesia 169 J14
Isiro, Dem. Rep. of the Congo 178 J11
Isisford, Qnsld., Austral. 191 U12
Iskandar, Uzb. 155 K13
İskenderun, Turk. 148 J11
İskenderun Körfezi, Turk. 148 J11
İskilip, Turk. 148 D9
Iskushuban, Somalia 179 F18
İslâhiye, Turk. 148 H11
Islamabad see Anantnag, India 157 N12
Islamabad, Pak. 157 N11
Islamkot, Pak. 157 W9
Islamorada, Fla., U.S. 91 Y10
Isla Mujeres, Mex. 109 H17
Island Falls, Me., U.S. 89 C18
Island Lagoon, Austral. 190 J9
Island Lake, Man., Can. 77 M14
Island Park, Idaho, U.S. 100 F8
Island Park Reservoir, Idaho, U.S. 100 G7
Island Pond, Vt., U.S. 89 F13
Islands, Bay of, N.Z. 193 H18
Islas Orcadas Rise, Atl. Oc. 217 V9
Islay, island, Scot., U.K. 138 E6
Isle Royale National Park, Mich., U.S. 92 D6
Ismâ'ilîya, Egypt 151 P1
Isna, Egypt 177 E19
Isoka, Zambia 182 C12
Isparta, Turk. 148 G6
Ispas, Turkm. 154 L10
Ispikan, Pak. 157 V2
İspir, Turk. 149 D15
Israel, Asia 150 L4
Isrīyah, ruins, Syr. 150 F9
Issano, Guyana 121 E14
İstanbul (Constantinople), Turk. 148 C5
İstanbul Boğazi (Bosporus), Turk. 148 C5
Isto, Mount, Alas., U.S. 105 C17
Istokpoga, Lake, Fla., U.S. 91 V9
Itabaianinha, Braz. 123 H17
Itaberaba, Braz. 123 H16
Itabuna, Braz. 123 J16
Itacoatiara, Braz. 122 D10
Itaetê, Braz. 123 H16
Itaituba, Braz. 122 E10
Itajaí, Braz. 123 N13
Italia, Monte, Chile 125 Y9
Italy, Eur. 136 G9
Itambé, Pico de, Braz. 123 K15
Itanagar, India 158 F14
Itapetinga, Braz. 123 J16
Itapipoca, Braz. 123 E16
Itasca, Tex., U.S. 96 M11
Itasca, Lake, Minn., U.S. 98 G9
Itatupã, Braz. 122 C12
Itbayat, island, Philippines 169 A14
Iténez (Guaporé), river, Bol. 122 H9
Itezhi-Tezhi, Lake, Zambia 182 F10
Ithaca, Mich., U.S. 92 L11
Ithaca, N.Y., U.S. 88 K8
Iti, Motu see Tupai, Fr. Polynesia, Fr. 199 E15
Itimbiri, river, Af. 174 J8
Itiquira, river, Braz. 122 K10
Itō, Jap. 165 Q12
Itoman, Jap. 165 Y1
Itta Bena, Miss., U.S. 94 J11
Ittoqqortoormiit, Greenland, Den. 75 B22
Itu Aba Island, Spratly Is. 168 E11
Ituí, river, Braz. 122 E5
Ituiutaba, Braz. 123 K13
Ituni, Guyana 121 E14
Iturama, Braz. 122 K12
Iturup (Etorofu), island, Russ. 141 J23
Ituxi, river, Braz. 122 F7
Ituzaingó, Arg. 124 G14
Iuka, Miss., U.S. 95 G13
Iul'tin, Russ. 141 B20
Ivaí, river, Braz. 122 M11
Ivalo, Fin. 135 D15
Ivanhoe, W. Austral., Austral. 191 Q6
Ivanhoe, N.S.W., Austral. 191 X12
Ivano-Frankivs'k, Ukr. 132 J12
Ivanovo, Russ. 140 F6
Ivdel', Russ. 140 G9
Ivirairai, Mount, Tahiti, Fr. Polynesia, Fr. 199 P16
Iviza see Ibiza, island, Sp. 139 R10
Ivory Coast, Côte d'Ivoire 180 J8
Ivujivik, Que., Can. 77 H17
Iwadate, Jap. 164 J12
Iwaizumi, Jap. 164 K14
Iwaki, Jap. 165 N13
Iwakuni, Jap. 165 Q6
Iwamizawa, Jap. 164 F13
Iwanuma, Jap. 164 L13
Iwate, Jap. 164 K13
Iwembere Steppe, Af. 174 K9
Iwo, Nig. 180 G12
Iwo Jima, Jap. 194 C4
Ixtapa, Mex. 108 K10
Iyo, Jap. 165 R6
Īzad Khvāst, Iran 153 E13
Izamal, Mex. 109 H16

Izena Shima, *Jap.* 165 XI
Izhevsk, *Russ.* 140 H8
Izhma, river, *Eur.* 130 BI2
Izmayil, *Ukr.* 133 MI4
İzmir (Smyrna), *Turk.* 148 F3
İzmit, *Turk.* 148 D6
İznik, *Turk.* 148 D5
İznik Gölü, *Turk.* 148 D5
Izozog, Bañados del, *S. Amer.* 118 H5
Izra', *Syr.* 150 K7
Izu Hantō, *Jap.* 165 QII
Izuhara, *Jap.* 165 Q3
Izu Islands, *Asia* 146 FI4
Izumo, *Jap.* 165 P6
Izu Shichitō, *Jap.* 165 QI2
Izu Trench, *Pac. Oc.* 218 F6
Izyum, *Ukr.* 133 JI7

J

Jaba, *P.N.G.* 197 KI4
Jabalpur, *India* 158 J7
Jabal Zuqar, Jazīrat, *Yemen* 152 Q8
Jabbūl, *Syr.* 150 E9
Jabbūl, Sabkhat al, *Syr.* 150 E9
Jabel Abyad Plateau, *Af.* 174 F8
Jabiru, *N. Terr., Austral.* 191 P8
Jablah, *Syr.* 150 F7
Jabnoren, island, *Jaluit Atoll, Marshall Is.* 196 K7
Jaboatão, *Braz.* 123 GI8
Jabor, *Jaluit Atoll, Marshall Is.* 196 M8
Jäbrayyl, *Azerb.* 149 E2I
Jabwot Island, *Marshall Is.* 196 H4
Jaca, *Sp.* 139 P9
Jacareacanga, *Braz.* 122 EIO
Jaciparaná, *Braz.* 122 G7
Jackman, *Me., U.S.* 89 DI5
Jackpot, *Nev., U.S.* 102 LI2
Jacksboro, *Tex., U.S.* 96 KIO
Jackson, *Ala., U.S.* 95 MI4
Jackson, *Calif., U.S.* 103 R5
Jackson, *Ga., U.S.* 90 L5
Jackson, *La., U.S.* 94 N9
Jackson, *Mich., U.S.* 92 MII
Jackson, *Minn., U.S.* 98 LIO
Jackson, *Miss., U.S.* 94 LII
Jackson, *Mo., U.S.* 99 UI6
Jackson, *Ohio, U.S.* 93 SI3
Jackson, *S.C., U.S.* 90 L8
Jackson, *Tenn., U.S.* 95 FI3
Jackson, *Wyo., U.S.* 100 H8
Jackson, Ostrov, *Russ.* 140 CI2
Jackson Bay, *N.Z.* 193 PI5
Jackson Lake, *Ga., U.S.* 90 L5
Jackson Lake, *Wyo., U.S.* 100 G8
Jacksonport, *Wis., U.S.* 92 HI4
Jacksonville, *Ala., U.S.* 95 JI6
Jacksonville, *Ark., U.S.* 94 G9
Jacksonville, *Fla., U.S.* 91 Q8
Jacksonville, *Ill., U.S.* 93 R4
Jacksonville, *N.C., U.S.* 90 JI3
Jacksonville, *Oreg., U.S.* 102 K3
Jacksonville, *Tex., U.S.* 96 MI4
Jacksonville Beach, *Fla., U.S.* 91 R9
Jacmel, *Haiti* III MI6
Jacobabad, *Pak.* 157 T7
Jacob Lake, *Ariz., U.S.* 101 Q7
Jacquinot Bay, *P.N.G.* 193 C2I
Jacumba, *Calif., U.S.* 103 ZII
J.A.D. Jensen Nunatakker, peak, *N. Amer.* 74 DIO
Jaén, *Peru* 122 F2
Jaén, *Sp.* 139 S7
Jaffa, Cape, *Austral.* 190 LIO
Jaffna, *Sri Lanka* 159 R7
Jafr, Qā' al, *Jordan* 151 Q7
Jagdalpur, *India* 158 L8
Jāghir Bāzār, *Syr.* 150 CI4
Jaghjagh, river, *Syr.* 150 DI4
Jagraon, *India* 158 D5
Jagtial, *India* 158 L6
Jaguaquara, *Braz.* 123 HI6
Jaguarão, *Braz.* 122 QII
Jahanabad, *India* 158 HIO
Jahrom, *Iran* 153 GI4
Jaicós, *Braz.* 123 FI6
Jaigarh, *India* 158 M3
Jaintiapur, *Bangladesh* 158 HI3
Jaipur, *India* 158 G5
Jaisalmer, *India* 158 F2
Jājarm, *Iran* 153 BI5
Jajpur, *India* 158 KIO
Jakar, *Bhutan* 158 FI3
Jakarta, *Indonesia* 168 L8
Jakeru, island, *Kwajalein Atoll, Marshall Is.* 196 L3
Jakhau, *India* 158 HI
Jakobstad (Pietarsaari), *Fin.* 135 GI5
Jal, *N. Mex., U.S.* 101 VI5
Jalaihai Point, *Guam, U.S.* 196 DII

Jalalabad, *Afghan.* 156 M9
Jalal-Abad, *Kyrg.* 156 FIO
Jalasjärvi, *Fin.* 135 HI5
Jalaun, *India* 158 G7
Jaldak, *Afghan.* 157 P6
Jaleswar, *India* 158 KII
Jalgaon, *India* 158 K5
Jalgaon, *India* 158 K5
Jalingo, *Nig.* 181 GI6
Jalkot, *Pak.* 156 LII
Jaloklab, island, *Majuro Atoll, Marshall Is.* 196 GIO
Jalón, river, *Sp.* 139 Q8
Jalor, *India* 158 G3
Jalpaiguri, *India* 158 GI2
Jālq, *Iran* 156 EI4
Jáltipan, *Mex.* 109 KI4
Jaluit, island, *Jaluit Atoll, Marshall Is.* 196 M8
Jaluit Atoll, *Marshall Is.* 196 H4
Jaluit Lagoon, *Jaluit Atoll, Marshall Is.* 196 M8
Jamaame, *Somalia* 179 KI6
Jamaica, *N. Amer.* 110 MIO
Jamaica, island, *N. Amer.* 74 N9
Jamaica Cay, *Bahamas* III GI3
Jamalpur, *Bangladesh* 158 HI2
Jaman Pass, *Afghan.-Taj.* 156 JI2
Jambi, *Indonesia* 168 K7
Jambusar, *India* 158 J3
James, river, *S. Dak., U.S.* 98 M7
James, river, *Va., U.S.* 90 EII
James Bay, *N. Amer.* 74 G8
James Range, *Austral.* 190 F8
James Ross Island, *Antarctica* 206 C4
Jamestown, *N. Dak., U.S.* 98 G6
Jamestown, *N.Y., U.S.* 88 K4
Jamestown, *S. Af.* 182 LIO
Jamestown National Historic Site, *Va., U.S.* 90 FI3
Jamestown Reservoir, *N. Dak., U.S.* 98 G6
Jammu, *India* 157 PI2
Jamnagar, *India* 158 J2
Jampur, *Pak.* 157 S9
Jämsä, *Fin.* 135 HI5
Jamshedpur, *India* 158 JIO
Jamuna, river, *Bangladesh* 158 HI2
Janaúba, *Braz.* 123 JI5
Jan Bulaq, *Afghan.* 156 K6
Jand, *Pak.* 157 NIO
Jandaq, *Iran* 153 DI4
Jandia, Punta de, *Canary Is., Sp.* 184 R7
Jandiatuba, river, *Braz.* 122 E5
Jandola, *Pak.* 157 P8
Janesville, *Wis., U.S.* 92 M6
Jangain, island, *P.N.G.* 197 HI4
Jangaon, *India* 158 M7
Jangeru, *Indonesia* 168 KI2
Jangipur, *India* 158 HII
Jani Kheyl, *Afghan.* 157 P7
Janīn, *West Bank* 150 L6
Jan Mayen Fracture Zone, *Arctic Oc.* 223 JI8
Jan Mayen Ridge, *Atl. Oc.* 216 BI2
Jansenville, *S. Af.* 182 M9
Januária, *Braz.* 123 JI4
Jaora, *India* 158 H4
Japan, *Asia* 165 T7
Japan, *Asia* 146 FI4
Japan, Sea of (East Sea), *Asia* 146 FI3
Japan Trench, *Pac. Oc.* 218 E6
Japtan, island, *Enewetak Atoll, Marshall Is.* 196 H9
Japurá, *Braz.* 122 D7
Jarābulus, *Syr.* 150 CIO
Jarales, *N. Mex., U.S.* 101 SI2
Jaramillo, *Arg.* 125 T9
Jaranwala, *Pak.* 157 QII
Jarash (Gerasa), *Jordan* 150 L6
Jarbidge, river, *Idaho, U.S.* 100 J4
Jarbidge, *Nev., U.S.* 102 LII
Jardim, *Braz.* 122 LIO
Jardines de la Reina, island, *Cuba* 110 J9
Jargalant, *Mongolia* 160 EIO
Jargalant, *Mongolia* 161 DI4
Jarghan, *Afghan.* 156 L5
Jari, river, *Braz.* 122 CII
Jarud Qi, *China* 161 EI6
Järvenpää, *Fin.* 135 JI6
Jarvis Island, *Pac. Oc.* 194 GI2
Järvsö, *Sw.* 135 JI3
Jashpurnagar, *India* 158 J9
Jāsk, *Iran* 153 JI6
Jason Islands, *Falk. Is., U.K.* 125 VII
Jason Peninsula, *Antarctica* 206 D4
Jasonville, *Ind., U.S.* 93 S8
Jasper, *Ala., U.S.* 95 JI4
Jasper, *Alta., Can.* 76 L9
Jasper, *Ark., U.S.* 94 E7
Jasper, *Fla., U.S.* 91 Q7
Jasper, *Ga., U.S.* 90 K5
Jasper, *Ind., U.S.* 93 T8
Jasper, *Tex., U.S.* 97 PI5
Jataí, *Braz.* 122 KI2
Jati, *Pak.* 157 W7
Jatibonico, *Cuba* 110 H9

Jatobal, *Braz.* 123 EI3
Jaú, river, *Braz.* 122 D8
Jauaperi, river, *Braz.* 122 C9
Jaunpur, *India* 158 G8
Java (Jawa), island, *Indonesia* 168 M8
Javan, *Taj.* 156 J7
Javari, river, *Peru-Braz.* 122 E4
Java Ridge, *Ind. Oc.* 221 HI5
Java Sea, *Indonesia* 168 L9
Java Trench, *Ind. Oc.* 221 HI4
Javhlant *see* Uliastay, *Mongolia* 160 DIO
Jawa *see* Java, island, *Indonesia* 168 M8
Jawhar, *Somalia* 179 JI7
Jawi, *Indonesia* 168 J9
Jay, *Okla., U.S.* 96 EI4
Jaya, Puncak, *Indonesia* 193 CI6
Jaya Peak, *Asia* 146 LI6
Jayapura, *Indonesia* 169 K2I
Jayawijaya, Pegunungan, *Indonesia* 169 L2O
Jay Em, *Wyo., U.S.* 100 JI4
Jayton, *Tex., U.S.* 96 K7
Jazzīn, *Leb.* 150 J6
Jeanerette, *La., U.S.* 94 Q9
Jeanette, Ostrov, *Russ.* 141 CI7
Jean Marie River, *N.W.T., Can.* 76 HIO
Jean-Rabel, *Haiti* III LI6
Jebba, *Nig.* 181 FI3
Jebel, Bahr el (Mountain Nile), *Sudan* 179 HI3
Jebri, *Pak.* 157 U5
Jebus, *Indonesia* 168 K7
Jeddah, *Saudi Arabia* 152 L7
Jedrol, island, *Enewetak Atoll, Marshall Is.* 196 H8
Jędrzejów, *Pol.* 132 HIO
Jefferson, river, *Mont., U.S.* 100 E7
Jefferson, *Ga., U.S.* 90 K6
Jefferson, *Iowa, U.S.* 99 NIO
Jefferson, *Tex., U.S.* 96 LI5
Jefferson, *Wis., U.S.* 92 L6
Jefferson, Mount, *Nev., U.S.* 103 QIO
Jefferson, Mount, *Oreg., U.S.* 102 G4
Jefferson City, *Mo., U.S.* 99 TI3
Jefferson City, *Tenn., U.S.* 95 EI9
Jeffersonville, *Ind., U.S.* 93 TIO
Jeffrey City, *Wyo., U.S.* 100 JII
Jef Jef el Kebir, peak, *Chad* 177 FI5
Jekyll Island, *Ga., U.S.* 91 P8
Jelbart Ice Shelf, *Antarctica* 206 AI2
Jelenia Góra, *Pol.* 132 H8
Jelgava, *Latv.* 135 MI6
Jellico, *Tenn., U.S.* 95 DI8
Jemaja, island, *Indonesia* 168 H8
Jember, *Indonesia* 168 MII
Jembongan, island, *Malaysia* 168 FI2
Jemez Pueblo, *N. Mex., U.S.* 101 RI2
Jeminay, *China* 160 D7
Jemo Island, *Marshall Is.* 196 F4
Jena, *Fla., U.S.* 91 R6
Jena, *Ger.* 132 H6
Jena, *La., U.S.* 94 M8
Jenkins, *Ky., U.S.* 95 C2O
Jennings, *La., U.S.* 94 P8
Jensen, *Utah, U.S.* 100 L9
Jensen Beach, *Fla., U.S.* 91 VIO
Jens Munk Island, *Nunavut, Can.* 77 FI6
Jenu, *Indonesia* 168 J9
Jequié, *Braz.* 123 JI6
Jequitinhonha, river, *Braz.* 123 JI6
Jerantut, *Malaysia* 167 TIO
Jerba Island, *Tun.* 177 BI3
Jérémie, *Haiti* III MI5
Jeremoabo, *Braz.* 123 GI7
Jerez de la Frontera, *Sp.* 139 T6
Jericho *see* Arīḥā, *West Bank* 150 M6
Jericoacoara, Point, *S. Amer.* 118 DII
Jerid, Shott el, *Af.* 174 D5
Jerilderie, *N.S.W., Austral.* 191 YI2
Jerimoth Hill, *R.I., U.S.* 89 LI4
Jerome, *Ariz., U.S.* 101 S7
Jerome, *Idaho, U.S.* 100 H5
Jerramungup, *W. Austral., Austral.* 191 Y3
Jersey, island, *Channel Is., U.K.* 138 K8
Jersey City, *N.J., U.S.* 88 NII
Jersey Shore, *Pa., U.S.* 88 M7
Jerseyside, *Nfld., Can.* 77 M24
Jerseyville, *Ill., U.S.* 93 S4
Jerusalem, *Israel* 150 M5
Jervis Bay, *Austral.* 190 LI4
Jessore, *Bangladesh* 158 JI2
Jesup, *Ga., U.S.* 91 P8
Jesús María, *Arg.* 124 JIO
Jetmore, *Kans., U.S.* 99 T5
Jetpur, *India* 158 J2
Jewel Cave National Monument, *S. Dak., U.S.* 98 LI
Jewell, *Iowa, U.S.* 99 NII
Jewett, *Tex., U.S.* 97 NI2
Jeypore, *India* 158 L8
Jhalawar, *India* 158 H5
Jhal Jhao, *Pak.* 157 V5
Jhang Sadr, *Pak.* 157 QIO
Jhansi, *India* 158 H6

Jharsuguda, *India* 158 K9
Jhatpat, *Pak.* 157 T7
Jhelum, river, *Pak.* 157 QIO
Jhelum, *Pak.* 157 PII
Jhimpir, *Pak.* 157 W7
Jhudo, *Pak.* 157 W8
Jhunjhunun, *India* 158 F5
Jiahe, *China* 163 P3
Jiaji *see* Qionghai, *China* 163 U2
Jiamusi, *China* 161 CI8
Ji'an, *China* 162 CI2
Ji'an, *China* 163 N5
Jianchang, *China* 162 C9
Jianchuan, *China* 160 NIO
Jiande, *China* 161 LI6
Jianghua, *China* 163 Q3
Jiangjunmiao, *China* 160 E8
Jiangle, *China* 163 P7
Jiangling, *China* 162 L4
Jiangmen, *China* 163 S4
Jiangshan, *China* 162 M8
Jianli, *China* 162 L4
Jianning, *China* 163 P7
Jian'ou, *China* 163 P8
Jianping, *China* 162 C9
Jianshi, *China* 162 L2
Jianyang, *China* 163 N7
Jiaohe, *China* 162 AI3
Jiaojiang (Haimen), *China* 162 MIO
Jiaokou, *China* 162 F3
Jiaonan, *China* 162 G9
Jiaozhou, *China* 162 F9
Jiaozhou Wan, *China* 162 G9
Jiaozuo, *China* 162 G4
Jiawang, *China* 162 H7
Jiaxian, *China* 162 E3
Jiaxing, *China* 162 L9
Jiayin, *China* 161 BI7
Jiayu, *China* 162 L5
Jiayuguan, *China* 160 GIO
Jibsh, Ra's, *Oman* 153 LI7
Jiddat al Ḥarāsīs, desert, *Oman* 153 MI6
Jido, *India* 158 EI5
Jieshou, *China* 162 J6
Jiesjavrre, lake, *Nor.* 135 CI4
Jiexiu, *China* 162 F4
Jieyang, *China* 163 R6
Jiggalong, *W. Austral., Austral.* 191 T4
Jigüey, Bahía de, *Cuba* 110 HIO
Jihlava, *Czech Rep.* 132 J8
Jijiga, *Eth.* 179 GI6
Jilib, *Somalia* 179 JI6
Jilin, *China* 162 AI2
Jiloy, *Azerb.* 149 D24
Jīma, *Eth.* 179 GI4
Jimaní, *Dom. Rep.* III MI7
Jiménez, *Mex.* 108 E9
Jimo, *China* 162 F9
Jinan, *China* 162 F7
Jinbal, island, *Jaluit Atoll, Marshall Is.* 196 L8
Jinchang, *China* 160 HII
Jincheng, *China* 162 G4
Jinedrol, island, *Enewetak Atoll, Marshall Is.* 196 H9
Jingbian, *China* 162 E2
Jingde, *China* 162 L8
Jingdezhen, *China* 162 M7
Jinggu, *China* 160 PIO
Jinghai, *China* 162 D7
Jinghong, *China* 160 QIO
Jingle, *China* 162 E4
Jingmen, *China* 162 K4
Jingpeng *see* Hexigten Qi, *China* 162 A7
Jingpo Hu, *China* 161 EI8
Jingxi, *China* 160 PI2
Jingxian, *China* 163 P2
Jingxing, *China* 162 E5
Jingyu, *China* 162 BI3
Jinhua, *China* 162 M9
Jinimi, island, *Enewetak Atoll, Marshall Is.* 196 H9
Jining, *China* 162 C5
Jining, *China* 162 G7
Jinjiang, *China* 163 Q8
Jinmen Dao (Quemoy), *Taiwan, China* 163 R8
Jinmu Jiao, *China* 161 RI3
Jinping, *China* 163 NI
Jinsha *see* Nantong, *China* 162 K9
Jinsha (Yangtze), river, *China* 160 NII
Jinshan, *China* 162 L9
Jinshi, *China* 162 L3
Jinxi, *China* 162 C9
Jinxiang, *China* 162 G6
Jinzhai, *China* 162 K6
Jinzhou, *China* 162 C9
Jinzhou, *China* 162 DIO
Jiparaná, river, *Braz.* 122 F8
Ji-Paraná (Rondônia), *Braz.* 122 G8
Jipijapa, *Ecua.* 120 K2
Jīroft, *Iran* 153 GI6
Jishou, *China* 162 M2
Jishui, *China* 163 N5

Jisr ash Shughūr, Syr. 150 E7
Jiujiang, China 162 M6
Jiulong (Kowloon), China 163 S5
Jiuquan, China 160 G10
Jiutai, China 161 E17
Jiwani, Pak. 157 W1
Jixi, China 161 D18
Jixi, China 162 L8
Jixian, China 162 D7
Jixian, China 162 F3
Jiyuan, China 162 G4
Jīzān, Saudi Arabia 152 P8
Jizzax, Uzb. 154 L12
Joaçaba, Braz. 122 N12
João Pessoa, Braz. 123 F18
Joaquín V. González, Arg. 124 F10
Jodhpur, India 158 G3
Joensuu, Fin. 135 G17
Joe's Hill, Kiritimati, Kiribati 197 B23
Jōetsu, Jap. 164 M11
Jogindarnagar, India 157 P14
Jogipet, India 158 M6
Johannesburg, Calif., U.S. 103 V9
Johannesburg, S. Af. 182 J10
John Day, river, Oreg., U.S. 102 G6
John Day, Oreg., U.S. 102 G7
John Day Dam, Oreg.-Wash., U.S. 102 E5
John Day Fossil Beds National Monument, Oreg., U.S. 102 G6
John D. Rockefeller Junior Memorial Parkway, Wyo., U.S. 100 G8
John Eyre Motel, W. Austral., Austral. 191 X6
John F. Kennedy Space Center, Fla., U.S. 91 T10
John H. Kerr Reservoir, N.C.-Va., U.S. 90 G12
John Martin Reservoir, Colo., U.S. 101 N15
John Redmond Reservoir, Kans., U.S. 99 T9
Johnson, Kans., U.S. 99 U3
Johnsonburg, Pa., U.S. 88 M5
Johnson City, N.Y., U.S. 88 K8
Johnson City, Tenn., U.S. 95 E20
Johnson City, Tex., U.S. 97 Q9
Johnson Draw, Tex., U.S. 97 Q6
Johnston Atoll, Pac. Oc. 194 E10
Johnston, S.C., U.S. 90 L8
Johnston, Lake, Austral. 190 K4
Johnston, Mount, Antarctica 207 F19
Johnston City, Ill., U.S. 93 U6
Johnstown, N.Y., U.S. 88 J10
Johnstown, Pa., U.S. 88 P4
Johor Baharu, Malaysia 167 V11
Joinville, Braz. 123 N13
Joinville Island, Antarctica 206 C4
Jokaj, island, Pohnpei, F.S.M. 197 F14
Jokkmokk, Sw. 135 F13
Joliet, Ill., U.S. 93 P7
Joliette, Que., Can. 77 P19
Jolo, island, Philippines 169 G14
Jolo, Philippines 169 F13
Jomda, China 160 L10
Jonesboro, Ark., U.S. 94 F10
Jonesboro, La., U.S. 94 L8
Jonesport, Me., U.S. 89 F19
Jones Sound, Nunavut, Can. 77 D15
Jonesville, La., U.S. 94 M9
Jonesville, S.C., U.S. 90 J8
Jönköping, Sw. 135 M13
Jonuta, Mex. 109 J15
Jonzac, Fr. 138 M9
Joplin, Mo., U.S. 99 V11
Joplin, Mont., U.S. 100 B8
Jordan, Asia 151 P7
Jordan, river, Jordan-W. Bank 150 M6
Jordan, river, Utah, U.S. 100 L7
Jordan, Minn., U.S. 98 K11
Jordan, Mont., U.S. 100 C11
Jordan Creek, Idaho, U.S. 100 H3
Jordan Valley, Oreg., U.S. 102 J9
Jorge Montt, Isla, Chile 125 W6
Jorhat, India 158 G15
Jorm, Afghan. 156 K9
Jörn, Sw. 135 G14
Jornada del Muerto, desert, N. Mex., U.S. 101 U12
Jorong, Indonesia 168 K11
Jørpeland, Nor. 134 L10
Jos, Nig. 181 F14
José Batlle-y-Ordóñez, Uru. 124 L14
Joseph, Oreg., U.S. 102 F9
Joseph Bonaparte Gulf, Austral. 190 B6
Joseph City, Ariz., U.S. 101 S8
Josephine Seamount, Atl. Oc. 216 H11
José Rodrigues, Braz. 122 E12
Joshimath, India 158 E7
Joshua Tree National Park, Calif., U.S. 103 X11
Jotunheimen, mountains, Nor. 134 K10
Jou, São Tomé and Príncipe 185 D19
Joulter Cays, Bahamas 110 D11
Jourdanton, Tex., U.S. 97 S9
Joutsa, Fin. 135 H16
Jovellanos, Cuba 110 G7
J. Percy Priest Lake, Tenn., U.S. 95 E15
Ju, river, China 162 K3
Juan Aldama, Mex. 108 F10
Juan de Fuca, Strait of, U.S. 78 B3
Juan de Fuca Ridge, Pac. Oc. 219 D15
Juan de Nova, Île, Mozambique Channel 183 F15
Juan Fernández, Islas, Pac. Oc. 195 M22
Juan José Castelli, Arg. 124 F12
Juanjuí, Peru 122 F3
Juan Stuven, Isla, Chile 125 U6
Juárez, Arg. 125 N12
Juàzeiro, Braz. 123 G16
Juàzeiro do Norte, Braz. 123 F16
Juba, Sudan 179 H13
Jubany, station, Antarctica 206 C3
Jubayl (Byblos), Leb. 150 H6
Jubba, river, Af. 174 J11
Jubba, Webi, Somalia 179 J16
Jubbah, Saudi Arabia 152 G8
Jubb al Jarrāḩ, Syr. 150 G9
Juby, Cap, Mor. 176 C6
Júcar, river, Sp. 139 R8
Júcaro, Cuba 110 J10
Juchitán, Mex. 109 K13
Judayyidat'Ar'ar, Saudi Arabia 152 E8
Judge Seamount, Pac. Oc. 218 F9
Judith, river, Mont., U.S. 100 C9
Judith Basin, Mont., U.S. 100 C9
Judith Gap, Mont., U.S. 100 D9
Judsonia, Ark., U.S. 94 F9
Juegang see Rudong, China 162 K10
Juifang, Taiwan, China 163 Q10
Juigalpa, Nicar. 109 M18
Juiling Shan, China 162 M5
Juiz de Fora, Braz. 123 L15
Julesburg, Colo., U.S. 100 K15
Juliaca, Peru 122 J5
Julia Creek, Qnsld., Austral. 191 S11
Julian, Calif., U.S. 103 Y10
Jullundur, India 158 D5
Julu, China 162 F6
Jumla, Nepal 158 E8
Junan, China 162 G8
Juncos, P.R., U.S. 111 M23
Junction, Tex., U.S. 97 Q8
Junction, Utah, U.S. 101 N7
Junction City, Ark., U.S. 94 K8
Junction City, Kans., U.S. 99 S8
Junction City, Oreg., U.S. 102 H3
Jundah, Qnsld., Austral. 191 U12
Juneau, Alas., U.S. 105 K22
Jungar Qi, China 162 D3
Junggar Pendi (Dzungarian Basin), China 160 E7
Jungshahi, Pak. 157 W7
Juniata, river, Pa., U.S. 88 N7
Junín, Arg. 124 L12
Junín, Peru 122 H3
Junín de los Andes, Arg. 125 P7
Juniper Mountain, Oreg., U.S. 102 J6
Jūniyah, Leb. 150 H6
Junlian, China 160 M12
Junnar, India 158 L4
Juno Beach, Fla., U.S. 91 V10
Juntura, Oreg., U.S. 102 H8
Jupaguá, Braz. 123 H14
Jupiter, Fla., U.S. 91 V10
Jura, island, Scot., U.K. 138 E7
Juradó, Col. 120 D3
Jura Mountains, Eur. 130 G5
Jurien, W. Austral., Austral. 191 W2
Juruá, river, Braz. 122 F4
Juruá, Braz. 122 D7
Juruena, river, Braz. 122 F10
Juruti, Braz. 122 D10
Justo Daract, Arg. 124 L10
Jutaí, river, Braz. 122 E6
Jutaí, Braz. 122 E6
Jutiapa, Guatemala 109 L16
Juticapla, Hond. 109 L18
Jutland see Jylland, region, Den. 134 N11
Juventud, Isla de la (Isle of Youth), Cuba 110 J5
Juxian, China 162 G8
Juye, China 162 G6
Jūymand, Iran 153 D16
Juzzak, Pak. 157 S1
Jylland (Jutland), region, Den. 134 N11
Jyväskylä, Fin. 135 H16

K

Kaaawa, Hawaii, U.S. 106 D11
Kaala-Gomén, New Caledonia, Fr. 198 C6
Kaalualu Bay, Hawaii, U.S. 107 Q20
Kaamanen, Fin. 135 C15
Kaambooni, Somalia 179 K16
Kaambooni, Raas, Af. 174 K11
Kaanapali, Hawaii, U.S. 107 G15
Kaap Plateau, Af. 174 Q8
Kabaena, island, Indonesia 169 L14
Kabala, Sierra Leone 180 F6
Kabalo, Dem. Rep. of the Congo 178 M11
Kabambare, Dem. Rep. of the Congo 178 L11
Kabara, island, Fiji 198 K9
Kabarei, Indonesia 169 J17
Kabbenbock, island, Jaluit Atoll, Marshall Is. 196 M8
Kabinda, Dem. Rep. of the Congo 178 M10
Kabīr, river, Leb.-Syr. 150 G7
Kabol (Kabul), Afghan. 156 M7
Kabong, Malaysia 168 H10
Kabongo, Dem. Rep. of the Congo 178 M11
Kabūd Gombad, Iran 153 B16
Kabul, river, Afghan. 156 M8
Kabul see Kabol, Afghan. 156 M7
Kabuli, P.N.G. 193 B19
Kabumbé, Pico, São Tomé and Príncipe 185 D20
Kaburuang, island, Indonesia 169 G16
Kabwe, Zambia 182 E11
Kachīry, Kaz. 155 B15
Kachreti, Rep. of Georgia 149 C19
Kaçkar Dağı, Turk. 149 D15
Kadaingti, Myanmar 166 K7
Kadan Kyun, Myanmar 167 N7
Kadavu, island, Fiji 198 K6
Kadavu Passage, Fiji 198 J6
Kadé, Guinea 180 E5
Kadıköy, Turk. 148 D3
Kading, river, Laos 166 K11
Kadınhanı, Turk. 148 G7
Kadiri, India 159 P6
Kadirli, Turk. 148 H11
Kadmat Island (Cardamum Island), India 159 Q3
Kadoka, S. Dak., U.S. 98 L3
Kadokura Zaki, Jap. 165 U4
Kadoma, Zimb. 182 F11
Kadugli, Sudan 178 F12
Kaduna, Nig. 181 F14
Kadur, India 159 P5
Kadzhi-Say, Kyrg. 156 E13
Kaédi, Mauritania 176 G5
Kaélé, Cameroon 181 F17
Kaena Point, Hawaii, U.S. 106 D10
Kaeo, peak, Hawaii, U.S. 106 C3
Kaeo, N.Z. 193 H18
Kaesŏng, N. Korea 162 E13
Kāf, Saudi Arabia 152 E6
Kafar Jar Ghar Range, Afghan. 157 P6
Kafia Kingi, Sudan 178 G10
Kafue, river, Zambia 182 E10
Kafue, Zambia 182 E10
Kafuka, Jap. 164 D13
Kaga, Jap. 165 N9
Kagan, Pak. 156 M11
Kağızman, Turk. 149 E17
Kagmar, Sudan 178 E12
Kagoshima, Jap. 165 T4
Kahakuloa, Hawaii, U.S. 107 F16
Kahaluu, Hawaii, U.S. 106 E11
Kahaluu, Hawaii, U.S. 107 M18
Kahama, Tanzania 179 L13
Kahan, Pak. 157 S7
Kahana, Hawaii, U.S. 107 G15
Kahea Heiau and Petroglyphs, Hawaii, U.S. 107 G15
Kahei Homesteads, Hawaii, U.S. 107 K19
Kahemba, Dem. Rep. of the Congo 178 M8
Kahili, peak, Hawaii, U.S. 106 B5
Kahlotus, Wash., U.S. 102 D8
Kahnūj, Iran 153 G16
Kahoka, Mo., U.S. 99 Q13
Kahoolawe, island, Hawaii, U.S. 107 H15
Kâhta, Turk. 149 H13
Kahuku, Hawaii, U.S. 106 D11
Kahuku, Hawaii, U.S. 107 P19
Kahuku Point, Hawaii, U.S. 106 D11
Kahului, Hawaii, U.S. 107 G16
Kahului Harbor, Hawaii, U.S. 107 G16
Kai, Kepulauan (Ewab), Indonesia 169 L18
Kaiama, Nig. 180 F12
Kaibab Plateau, U.S. 78 H6
Kaibara, Jap. 165 Q8
Kaibito, Ariz., U.S. 101 Q8
Kaieteur Fall, Guyana 121 E14
Kaifeng, China 162 H5
Kaifu, Jap. 165 R7
Kaiholena, peak, Hawaii, U.S. 107 P20
Kai Kecil, island, Indonesia 169 L18
Kaikoura, N.Z. 193 N18
Kailu, China 162 A9
Kailua, Hawaii, U.S. 106 E12
Kailua, Hawaii, U.S. 107 M18
Kaimana, Indonesia 193 C15
Kainji Reservoir, Nig. 181 F13
Kaipara Harbour, N.Z. 193 J18
Kaishantun, China 162 A14
Kaitaia, N.Z. 193 H18
Kaiwaloa Heiau and Olowalu Petroglyphs, Hawaii, U.S. 107 G16
Kaiwi Channel, Hawaii, U.S. 106 F12
Kaixian, China 162 K1
Kaiyuan, China 160 P11
Kaiyuan, China 162 B11
Kaiyuh Mountains, Alas., U.S. 105 G13
Kajaani, Fin. 135 G16
Kajabbi, Qnsld., Austral. 191 S11
Kajaki, Afghan. 157 P4
Kajaki, Band-e, Afghan. 157 P4
Kajang, Malaysia 167 U9
Kajiki, Jap. 165 T4
Kaka, Sudan 179 F13
Kaka, Turkm. 154 M9
Kakamas, S. Af. 182 K8
Kakana, Nicobar Is., India 159 S14
Kaka Point, Hawaii, U.S. 107 H16
Kakaramea, N.Z. 193 L18
Kakdwip, India 158 J11
Kake, Alas., U.S. 105 K22
Kake, Jap. 165 Q6
Kakeroma Jima, Jap. 165 W2
Kākhk, Iran 153 D16
Kakhovka Reservoir, Eur. 130 G11
Kakinada (Cocanada), India 158 M8
Kakogawa, Jap. 165 Q8
Kakshaal Range, China-Kyrg. 156 F14
Kaktovik, Alas., U.S. 105 B17
Kakuda, Jap. 164 M13
Kala, Azerb. 149 D23
Kalaallit Nunaat see Greenland, N. Amer. 75 B20
Kalabagh, Pak. 157 P9
Kalabakan, Malaysia 168 G12
Kalabo, Zambia 182 E9
Kalach na Donu, Russ. 140 H5
Ka Lae (South Cape), Hawaii, U.S. 107 Q19
Kalaeloa Harbor, Hawaii, U.S. 107 F15
Kalahari Desert, Botswana 182 H8
Kalaheo, Hawaii, U.S. 106 C5
Kal'ai Khumb, Taj. 156 J9
Kala-I-Mor, Turkm. 154 N10
Kalalea, Heiau o, Hawaii, U.S. 107 Q19
Kalalua, peak, Hawaii, U.S. 107 N21
Kalam, Pak. 156 L10
Kalama, Wash., U.S. 102 E3
Kalamáta, Gr. 137 L14
Kalamazoo, river, Mich., U.S. 92 M9
Kalamazoo, Mich., U.S. 92 M10
Kalannie, W. Austral., Austral. 191 W3
Kalao, island, Indonesia 169 M13
Kalaoa, Hawaii, U.S. 107 M18
Kalaotoa, island, Indonesia 169 M13
Kalasin, Thai. 166 L10
Kalat see Qalat, Afghan. 157 P6
Kalat, Pak. 157 S5
Kálathos, Gr. 137 M18
Kalaupapa, Hawaii, U.S. 107 F14
Kalaupapa National Historical Park, Hawaii, U.S. 107 F14
Kalawao, Hawaii, U.S. 107 F14
Kalay-wa, Myanmar 166 F5
Kalb, Ra's al, Yemen 152 Q11
Kälbäjär, Azerb. 149 E20
Kalbān, Oman 153 M17
Kalbarri, W. Austral., Austral. 191 V1
Kaldar, Afghan. 156 K6
Kale, Turk. 148 J5
Kalealoa, Hawaii, U.S. 106 E10
Kale Burnu, Turk. 149 D14
Kalecik, Turk. 148 E9
Kaledupa, island, Indonesia 169 L14
Kalemie, Dem. Rep. of the Congo 178 M12
Kalemyo, Myanmar 166 F5
Kalenyy, Kaz. 154 D6
Kaleybar, Iran 152 A11
Kalgoorlie, W. Austral., Austral. 191 W4
Kalianda, Indonesia 168 L7
Kalihiwai, Hawaii, U.S. 106 B5
Kalihiwai Bay, Hawaii, U.S. 106 A6
Kalima, Dem. Rep. of the Congo 178 K11
Kalimantan, Indonesia 168 J10
Kálimnos, Gr. 137 L17
Kalimpang, India 158 G11
Kaliningrad, Russ. 140 D4
Kaliningrad Oblast, Russ. 140 C4
Kalinino, Arm. 149 D18
Kalinkavichy, Belarus 133 G14
Kalispell, Mont., U.S. 100 B5
Kalisz, Pol. 132 G9
Kalix, Sw. 135 F14
Kalkan, Turk. 148 J5
Kalkaska, Mich., U.S. 92 J10
Kallsjön, lake, Sw. 134 H12
Kalmar, Sw. 135 N13
Kalnai, India 158 J9
Kalohi Channel, Hawaii, U.S. 107 G14
Kaloko-Honokahau National Historical Park, Hawaii, U.S. 107 M18
Kaloli Point, Hawaii, U.S. 107 M22
Kalpa, India 158 D6
Kalpeni Island, India 159 R3
Kalpi, India 158 G7
Kalpitiya, Sri Lanka 159 S7
Kalskag, Alas., U.S. 105 J13
Kalsubai, peak, India 158 L4
Kaltag, Alas., U.S. 105 G13
Kaluakauka see Doctor David Douglas Historical Monument, Hawaii, U.S. 107 L21

Kaluga, *Russ.* **140** F6
Kalumburu, *W. Austral., Austral.* **191** Q6
Kal'ya, *Russ.* **140** G9
Kalyan, *India* **158** L3
Kama, river, *Russ.* **140** H7
Kamaing, *Myanmar* **166** E6
Kamaishi, *Jap.* **164** K14
Kamakal, island, *Gambier Is., Fr. Polynesia, Fr.* **199** R20
Kamakou, peak, *Hawaii, U.S.* **107** F15
Kamalino, *Hawaii, U.S.* **106** C2
Kaman, *Turk.* **148** F9
Kamarān, island, *Yemen* **152** P8
Kama Reservoir, *Eur.* **130** C13
Kamarod, *Pak.* **157** U3
Kamar Zard, *Afghan.* **157** N2
Kambang, *Indonesia* **168** K6
Kambove, *Dem. Rep. of the Congo* **178** N11
Kamchatka, Poluostrov, *Russ.* **141** F22
Kamchatskiy Poluostrov, *Russ.* **141** E22
Kamdesh, *Afghan.* **156** L9
Kamehameha I Birthplace, *Hawaii, U.S.* **107** J18
Kamenka, *Kaz.* **154** C6
Kamenka, *Russ.* **140** E9
Kamensk Ural'skiy, *Russ.* **140** J9
Kamiagata, *Jap.* **165** Q3
Kamiah, *Idaho, U.S.* **100** D4
Kamieskroon, *S. Af.* **182** L7
Kamileroi, *Qnsld., Austral.* **191** S11
Kamiloloa, *Hawaii, U.S.* **107** F14
Kamina, *Dem. Rep. of the Congo* **178** M10
Kamin'-Kashyrs'kyy, *Ukr.* **132** G12
Kaminone Shima, *Jap.* **165** W3
Kamino Shima, *Jap.* **165** Q3
Kamioka, *Jap.* **165** N10
Kamitsuki, *Jap.* **165** R12
Kamitsushima, *Jap.* **165** Q3
Kamiyaku, *Jap.* **165** U4
Kamkhat Muḩaywir, peak, *Jordan* **151** N7
Kamloops, *B.C., Can.* **76** M9
Kammuri, peak, *Jap.* **165** Q6
Kamo, *Arm.* **149** D19
Kamoenai, *Jap.* **164** F12
Kamohio Bay, *Hawaii, U.S.* **107** H16
Kamoke, *Pak.* **157** P12
Kamooloa, *Hawaii, U.S.* **106** D10
Kampar, *Malaysia* **167** T9
Kamphaeng Phet, *Thai.* **166** L8
Kâmpóng Cham, *Cambodia* **167** N12
Kampong Kuala Besut, *Malaysia* **167** S10
Kampot, *Cambodia* **167** P11
Kamrau, Teluk, *Indonesia* **193** C15
Kamsack, *Sask., Can.* **77** M13
Kamsar, *Guinea* **180** F4
Kamuela *see* Waimea, *Hawaii, U.S.* **107** K19
Kamui Misaki, *Jap.* **164** F12
Kam'yanets'-Podil's'kyy, *Ukr.* **133** K13
Kamyshin, *Russ.* **140** H6
Kanab, *Utah, U.S.* **101** Q6
Kanab Creek, *Ariz., U.S.* **101** Q6
Kanacea, island, *Fiji* **198** H9
Kanaga Island, *Alas., U.S.* **104** Q5
Kanak, river, *Turk.* **148** E10
Kananga, *Dem. Rep. of the Congo* **178** L9
Kanapou Bay, *Hawaii, U.S.* **107** H16
Kanarraville, *Utah, U.S.* **101** P6
Kanatea, island, *Tongatapu, Tonga* **198** J11
Kanawha, river, *W. Va., U.S.* **90** D7
Kanazawa, *Jap.* **165** N9
Kanbalu, *Myanmar* **166** F6
Kanchenjunga, peak, *Nepal* **158** F11
Kanchipuram, *India* **159** Q7
Kandahar, *Afghan.* **157** Q5
Kandalaksha, *Russ.* **140** D8
Kandalakshskiy Zaliv, *Russ.* **140** D8
Kandangan, *Indonesia* **168** K11
Kandhkot, *Pak.* **157** T8
Kandi, *Benin* **180** F12
Kandi, *India* **158** H11
Kandiaro, *Pak.* **157** U7
Kandıra, *Turk.* **148** C6
Kandrach, *Pak.* **157** V5
Kandrian, *P.N.G.* **193** D20
Kandudu, island, *Maldives* **159** W3
Kandudu, island, *Maldives* **159** X3
Kandu-ye Bala, *Afghan.* **157** N5
Kandy, *Sri Lanka* **159** T7
Kane, *Pa., U.S.* **88** L5
Kane Basin, *Nunavut, Can.* **77** B16
Kane Fracture Zone, *Atl. Oc.* **216** K7
Kanengo, Note, *Santa Cruz Is., Solomon Is.* **197** P22
Kaneohe, *Hawaii, U.S.* **106** E11
Kang, *Afghan.* **157** Q2
Kangaamiut, *Greenland, Den.* **75** D21
Kangal, *Turk.* **148** F12
Kangan, *Iran* **153** G13
Kangān, *Iran* **153** H16
Kanganpur, *Pak.* **157** Q12
Kangar, *Malaysia* **167** S8
Kangaroo Island, *Austral.* **190** L10
Kangbao, *China* **162** B6
Kangding, *China* **160** L11
Kangean, Kepulauan, *Indonesia* **168** L11
Kangeeak Point, *Nunavut, Can.* **77** F19
Kangerlussuaq, *Greenland, Den.* **75** D21
Kangertittivaq, glacier, *N. Amer.* **74** B10
Kanggava Bay, *Solomon Is.* **197** Q19
Kanggye, *N. Korea* **162** C13
Kanggyŏng, *S. Korea* **162** F13
Kangiqsualujjuaq, *Que., Can.* **77** J20
Kangiqsujuaq, *Que., Can.* **77** J18
Kangirsuk, *Que., Can.* **77** J19
Kangmar, *China* **160** M7
Kangnŭng, *S. Korea* **162** E14
Kango, *Gabon* **181** K14
Kangping, *China* **162** B11
Kangpokpi, *India* **158** G14
Kangrinboqê Feng, *China* **160** K5
Kangto, peak, *China* **160** M8
Kangto, peak, *India* **158** F14
Kaniama, *Dem. Rep. of the Congo* **178** M10
Kaniere, *N.Z.* **193** N17
Kanif, *Yap Is., F.S.M.* **197** D18
Kanigiri, *India* **159** N7
Kanin, Poluostrov, *Russ.* **140** E9
Kanin Nos, Mys, *Russ.* **140** D9
Kanin Peninsula, *Eur.* **130** A11
Kanish, ruins, *Turk.* **148** F10
Kanita, *Jap.* **164** J13
Kanjarkot, site, *Pak.* **157** W8
Kankakee, river, *Ind., U.S.* **93** P8
Kankakee, *Ill., U.S.* **93** P7
Kankan, *Guinea* **180** F7
Kanker, *India* **158** K8
Kanmaw Kyun, *Myanmar* **167** P7
Kanmen, *China* **163** N10
Kannapolis, *N.C., U.S.* **90** H9
Kannari, *Jap.* **164** L13
Kannauj, *India* **158** G7
Kano, *Nig.* **181** E14
Kanokupolu, *Tongatapu, Tonga* **198** H11
Kanopolis, *Kans., U.S.* **99** T7
Kanorado, *Kans., U.S.* **99** S3
Kanosh, *Utah, U.S.* **101** N6
Kanoya, *Jap.* **165** T4
Kanpur, *India* **158** G7
Kansas, river, *Kans., U.S.* **99** S8
Kansas, *U.S.* **99** T5
Kansas City, *Kans., U.S.* **99** S10
Kansas City, *Mo., U.S.* **99** S10
Kansk, *Russ.* **141** K14
Kansŏng, *S. Korea* **162** E14
Kant, *Kyrg.* **156** D11
Kantankufri, *Ghana* **180** G11
Kanton, island, *Kiribati* **194** G10
Kanuku Mountains, *Guyana* **121** F14
Kanye, *Botswana* **182** J9
Kao, island, *Ha'apai Group, Tonga* **198** P6
Kaohsiung, *Taiwan, China* **163** S9
Kaoka Bay, *Solomon Is.* **197** N19
Kaokoveld, plain, *Namibia* **182** F5
Kaolack, *Senegal* **176** H4
Kaoma, *Zambia* **182** E9
Kapa, island, *Vava'u Group, Tonga* **198** M11
Kapaa, *Hawaii, U.S.* **106** B6
Kapaau (Kohala), *Hawaii, U.S.* **107** J19
Kapadvanj, *India* **158** J3
Kapan, *Arm.* **149** F20
Kapanga, *Dem. Rep. of the Congo* **178** M10
Kapıdağı, *Turk.* **148** D4
Kapingamarangi Atoll, *F.S.M.* **194** G5
Kapiri Mposhi, *Zambia* **182** E11
Kapisillit, *Greenland, Den.* **75** D22
Kapiskau, river, *Ont., Can.* **77** M17
Kapit, *Malaysia* **168** H10
Kaplan, *La., U.S.* **94** Q8
Kapoeta, *Sudan* **179** H13
Kapoho Crater, *Hawaii, U.S.* **107** M22
Kaposvár, *Hung.* **132** L9
Kappar, *Pak.* **157** V2
Kapuaiwa Coconut Grove, *Hawaii, U.S.* **107** F14
Kapue Stream, *Hawaii, U.S.* **107** L21
Kapulena, *Hawaii, U.S.* **107** K20
Kapunda, *S. Austral., Austral.* **191** X10
Kapurthala, *India* **158** D5
Kapuskasing, *Ont., Can.* **77** N17
Kapydzhik, *Arm.* **149** F20
Kara Balta, *Kyrg.* **156** E11
Karabiga, *Turk.* **148** D3
Karabük, *Turk.* **148** C8
Kara Burun, *Turk.* **148** J7
Karaburun, *Turk.* **148** F2
Karacabey, *Turk.* **148** D4
Karaca Dağ, *Turk.* **149** H14
Karacadağ, *Turk.* **149** H14
Karacaköy, *Turk.* **148** C4
Karachala, *Azerb.* **149** E22
Karachi, *Pak.* **157** W6
Karad, *India* **158** M4
Kara Dağ, *Turk.* **148** H8
Kara Dağ, *Turk.* **149** H18
Karadag, *Azerb.* **149** D23
Karaginskiy, Ostrov, *Russ.* **141** E22
Karahallı, *Turk.* **148** G5
Karahüyük, *Turk.* **148** G7
Karaisalı, *Turk.* **148** H10
Karaj, *Iran* **152** C12
Karakeçi, *Turk.* **149** H14
Karakelong, island, *Indonesia* **169** G16
Karakoçan, *Turk.* **149** F14
Karakol (Przheval'sk), *Kyrg.* **156** E14
Karakoram Pass, *China-Pak.* **156** L14
Karakoram Range, *Asia* **146** G7
Karakul', *Taj.* **156** H11
Karakuwisa, *Namibia* **182** G8
Karam, *Russ.* **141** K15
Karaman, *Turk.* **148** H8
Karamay, *China* **160** D7
Karamea, *N.Z.* **193** M17
Karamea Bight, *N.Z.* **193** M17
Karamürsel, *Turk.* **148** D5
Karanja, *India* **158** K6
Karapınar, *Turk.* **148** H9
Kara-Say, *Kyrg.* **156** E14
Karasburg, *Namibia* **182** K7
Kara Sea, *Russ.* **140** E11
Karasjok, *Nor.* **135** C14
Karas Mountains, *Af.* **174** P7
Karasu, river, *Turk.* **149** E15
Karasu, river, *Turk.* **149** F18
Karasu, *Turk.* **148** C6
Karasuk, *Russ.* **140** K11
Karataş, *Turk.* **148** J10
Karatepe, *Turk.* **148** H11
Karathuri, *Myanmar* **167** P7
Karatsu, *Jap.* **165** R4
Karatung, island, *Indonesia* **169** G16
Karaul, *Russ.* **141** F13
Karayazı, *Turk.* **149** E16
Karayün, *Turk.* **148** E12
Karbalā', *Iraq* **152** E9
Karcag, *Hung.* **132** K10
Karditsa, *Gr.* **137** K14
Kardiva (Karidu), island, *Maldives* **159** U3
Kardiva Channel, *Maldives* **159** U3
Kärdla, *Estonia* **135** K15
Karesuando, *Sw.* **135** D14
Kargalik *see* Yecheng, *China* **160** G4
Kargı, *Turk.* **148** C10
Kargil, *India* **156** M13
Kari, *Nig.* **181** F15
Kariba, *Zimb.* **182** F11
Kariba, Lake, *Zambia-Zimb.* **182** F11
Karidu *see* Kardiva, island, *Maldives* **159** U3
Karikari, Cape, *N.Z.* **193** H18
Karimata, island, *Indonesia* **168** K9
Karimata, Kepulauan, *Indonesia* **168** J9
Karimganj, *India* **158** H14
Karimnagar, *India* **158** L7
Karimunjawa, Kepulauan, *Indonesia* **168** L9
Karitane, *N.Z.* **193** Q16
Karizak, *Afghan.* **157** P1
Karkar, island, *P.N.G.* **193** C19
Karkas, Kūh-e, *Iran* **153** D13
Karkinits'ka Zatoka, *Ukr.* **133** L16
Karlıova, *Turk.* **149** F15
Karlovac, *Croatia* **136** F11
Karlovy Vary, *Czech Rep.* **132** H7
Karlshamn, *Sw.* **135** N13
Karlskrona, *Sw.* **135** N13
Karlsruhe, *Ger.* **132** J5
Karlstad, *Minn., U.S.* **98** E8
Karlstad, *Sw.* **134** L12
Karmala, *India* **158** L4
Karmir Blur, ruins, *Arm.* **149** E18
Karnali, river, *Nepal* **158** E8
Karnaphuli Reservoir, *Bangladesh* **158** J14
Karnes City, *Tex., U.S.* **97** S10
Karoi, *Zimb.* **182** F11
Karokh, *Afghan.* **156** M2
Karoko, *Fiji* **198** G8
Karompa, island, *Indonesia* **169** M14
Karonga, *Malawi* **183** C13
Karonie, *W. Austral., Austral.* **191** W5
Karosa, *Indonesia* **169** K13
Kárpathos, island, *Gr.* **137** M17
Karratha, *W. Austral., Austral.* **191** S2
Karre Mountains, *Af.* **174** H6
Karridale, *W. Austral., Austral.* **191** Y2
Kars, *Turk.* **149** D17
Kartal, *Turk.* **148** C5
Karumba, *Qnsld., Austral.* **191** R11
Kārūn, river, *Iran* **152** F11
Karunjie, *W. Austral., Austral.* **191** Q6
Karwar, *India* **159** N4
Karwi, *India* **158** H8
Kar'yepol'ye, *Russ.* **140** E9
Karynzharyk, desert, *Kaz.* **154** J6
Kaş, *Turk.* **148** J5
Kas, *Sudan* **178** E10
Kasai, river, *Af.* **174** K7
Kasaji, *Dem. Rep. of the Congo* **178** N10
Kasama, *Zambia* **182** C12
Kasane, *Botswana* **182** F9
Kasar, Ras, *Sudan* **179** D15
Kasaragod, *India* **159** Q4
Kasari, *Jap.* **165** W3
Kasari Saki, *Jap.* **165** W3
Kasba Lake, *N.W.T.-Nunavut, Can.* **77** J13
Kasempa, *Zambia* **182** E10
Kasenga, *Dem. Rep. of the Congo* **178** N11
Kasese, *Dem. Rep. of the Congo* **178** K11
Kasganj, *India* **158** F6
Kasha-Katuwe Tent Rocks National Monument, *N. Mex., U.S.* **101** R12
Kāshān, *Iran* **153** D13
Kashgar *see* Kashi, *China* **160** F4
Kashi (Kashgar), *China* **160** F4
Kashiwazaki, *Jap.* **164** M11
Kashkandyow, *Afghan.* **156** K10
Kāshmar, *Iran* **153** C16
Kashmir, region, *Asia* **146** G7
Kashmir, Vale of, *India* **156** M12
Kashmor, *Pak.* **157** T8
Kasiruta, island, *Indonesia* **169** J16
Kaskaskia, river, *Ill., U.S.* **93** S6
Kaskö, *Fin.* **135** H14
Kasongo, *Dem. Rep. of the Congo* **178** L11
Kasongo-Lunda, *Dem. Rep. of the Congo* **178** M8
Kaspiyskiy, *Russ.* **140** J5
Kassala, *Sudan* **179** E14
Kassel, *Ger.* **132** G5
Kasson, *Minn., U.S.* **98** L12
Kássos, island, *Gr.* **137** M17
Kastamonu, *Turk.* **148** C9
Kastellórizon *see* Megisti, island, *Turk.* **148** J5
Kastsyukovichy, *Belarus* **133** F15
Kasumiga Ura, lake, *Jap.* **165** P13
Kasur, *Pak.* **157** Q12
Katafaga, island, *Fiji* **198** H9
Katahdin, Mount, *Me., U.S.* **89** D17
Katanga, plateau, *Dem. Rep. of the Congo* **178** N10
Katanning, *W. Austral., Austral.* **191** Y3
Katchall Island, *Nicobar Is., India* **159** S15
Katerini, *Gr.* **137** J14
Kates Needle, *Alas., U.S.* **105** K23
Katha, *Myanmar* **166** F6
Katherîna, Gebel, *Egypt* **151** T3
Katherine, river, *Austral.* **190** B8
Katherine, *N. Terr., Austral.* **191** Q8
Kathiawar, peninsula, *India* **158** J2
Kathmandu, *Nepal* **158** F10
Kathua, *India* **157** P13
Katiu, island, *Fr. Polynesia, Fr.* **199** E18
Katmai, Mount, *Alas., U.S.* **105** L14
Katmai National Park and Preserve, *Alas., U.S.* **105** L15
Katohau, Baie, *Ua Huka, Fr. Polynesia, Fr.* **199** M23
Katoomba, *N.S.W., Austral.* **191** Y14
Katowice, *Pol.* **132** H9
Katrancık Dağı, *Turk.* **148** H5
Katsina, *Nig.* **181** E14
Katsumoto, *Jap.* **165** R3
Katsuyama, *Jap.* **165** P9
Katsuyama, *Jap.* **165** Q7
Kattankudi, *Sri Lanka* **159** T8
Kattaqo'rg'on, *Uzb.* **154** L12
Kattavía, *Gr.* **137** M17
Kattegat, strait, *Den.-Sw.* **134** N11
Katun', river, *Russ.* **140** L12
Kau, region, *Hawaii, U.S.* **107** P20
Kau, *Indonesia* **169** H16
Kauai, island, *Hawaii, U.S.* **106** C5
Kauai Channel, *Hawaii, U.S.* **106** D8
Kauakaiakaola Heiau, *Hawaii, U.S.* **107** M18
Kauehi, island, *Fr. Polynesia, Fr.* **199** E18
Kaufman, *Tex., U.S.* **96** L12
Kauhako Crater, *Hawaii, U.S.* **107** F14
Kaukauai, *P.N.G.* **197** K14
Kaukauna, *Wis., U.S.* **92** J6
Kaukau Veld, *Botswana-Namibia* **182** G8
Kaukura, island, *Fr. Polynesia, Fr.* **199** E17
Kaula, island, *Hawaii, U.S.* **106** N9
Kaula Gulch, *Hawaii, U.S.* **107** L21
Kaulakahi Channel, *Hawaii, U.S.* **106** B3
Kauluapaoa Heiau Wet and Dry Caves, *Hawaii, U.S.* **106** B5
Kauluoa Point, *Hawaii, U.S.* **107** N18
Kaumakani, *Hawaii, U.S.* **106** C5
Kaumalapau, *Hawaii, U.S.* **107** G14
Kaumana Cave, *Hawaii, U.S.* **107** M21
Kaumu o Kaleihoohie, peak, *Hawaii, U.S.* **107** K19
Kaunakakai, *Hawaii, U.S.* **107** F14
Kaunakakai Harbour, *Hawaii, U.S.* **107** F14
Kauna Point, *Hawaii, U.S.* **107** P18
Kaunas, *Lith.* **135** N16
Kaunolu, site, *Hawaii, U.S.* **107** H15
Kaupakulua, *Hawaii, U.S.* **107** G17
Kaupo, *Hawaii, U.S.* **107** H18
Kaupulehu, site, *Hawaii, U.S.* **107** L18
Kaura-Namoda, *Nig.* **181** E14
Kautokeino, *Nor.* **135** D14

Kavacha, *Russ.* 141 D22
Kavak, *Turk.* 148 D11
Kavála (Neapolis), *Gr.* 137 J15
Kavalerovo, *Russ.* 141 L21
Kavali, *India* 159 N7
Kavaratti, *India* 159 R3
Kavieng, *P.N.G.* 193 B21
Kavír, Dasht-e, *Iran* 153 D14
Kavír-e Namak, dry lake, *Iran* 153 D15
Kawagoe, *Jap.* 165 P12
Kawaihae, *Hawaii, U.S.* 107 K19
Kawaihae Bay, *Hawaii, U.S.* 107 L18
Kawaihoa Point, *Hawaii, U.S.* 106 C3
Kawaikini, peak, *Hawaii, U.S.* 106 B5
Kawakawa, *N.Z.* 193 H18
Kawambwa, *Zambia* 182 C11
Kawasaki, *Jap.* 165 P12
Kawasaki, *Jap.* 165 P12
Kawashiri Misaki, *Jap.* 165 Q4
Kawe, island, *Indonesia* 169 J17
Kawela, site, *Hawaii, U.S.* 107 F14
Kawela, *Hawaii, U.S.* 106 D11
Kawela, *Hawaii, U.S.* 107 F14
Kawhia, *N.Z.* 193 K19
Kawich Peak, *Nev., U.S.* 103 R11
Kawthoung, *Myanmar* 167 Q7
Kaya, *Burkina Faso* 180 E10
Kaya, *Indonesia* 168 H12
Kayan, river, *Indonesia* 168 H12
Kayangel Islands (Ngcheangel), *Palau* 196 K12
Kayangel Passage, *Palau* 196 K12
Kayapınar, *Turk.* 149 H15
Kaycee, *Wyo., U.S.* 100 G12
Kayenta, *Ariz., U.S.* 101 Q8
Kayes, *Congo* 181 M16
Kayes, *Mali* 176 H6
Kaymaz, *Turk.* 148 E7
Kaynar, *Turk.* 148 F11
Kayseri, *Turk.* 148 F10
Kaysville, *Utah, U.S.* 100 K7
Kazach'ye, *Russ.* 141 E17
Kazakhstan, *Asia* 154 E8
Kazakh Uplands, *Kaz.* 155 D13
Kazan, *Nunavut, Can.* 77 H14
Kazan', *Russ.* 140 G7
Kazanlŭk, *Bulg.* 137 H16
Kazan Rettō *see* Volcano Islands, *Jap.* 194 C4
Kazarman, *Kyrg.* 156 F11
Kazbek, peak, *Rep. of Georgia* 149 B18
Kāzerūn, *Iran* 153 G13
Kazi Ahmad, *Pak.* 157 V7
Kaztalovka, *Kaz.* 154 D5
Kazym Mys, *Russ.* 140 G10
Kéa (Tziá), island, *Gr.* 137 L15
Keaau, *Hawaii, U.S.* 107 M22
Keaau Ranch, *Hawaii, U.S.* 107 M22
Keadu, island, *Maldives* 159 V3
Keahole Point, *Hawaii, U.S.* 107 M18
Kealaikahiki Channel, *Hawaii, U.S.* 107 H15
Kealaikahiki Point, *Hawaii, U.S.* 107 H15
Kealakekua, *Hawaii, U.S.* 107 M18
Kealia, *Hawaii, U.S.* 106 B6
Kealia, *Hawaii, U.S.* 107 N18
Keams Canyon, *Ariz., U.S.* 101 R8
Kéamu *see* Anatom, island, *Vanuatu* 198 H4
Keanae, *Hawaii, U.S.* 107 G17
Keanapapa Point, *Hawaii, U.S.* 107 G14
Kearney, *Nebr., U.S.* 99 Q6
Kearny, *Ariz., U.S.* 101 U8
Keauhou, *Hawaii, U.S.* 107 M18
Keauhou Holua Slide, *Hawaii, U.S.* 107 M18
Keauhou Landing, *Hawaii, U.S.* 107 N21
Ke Avainiu Pass, *Solomon Is.* 197 J18
Keawanui Bay, *Hawaii, U.S.* 106 C3
Keban, *Turk.* 149 F13
Kebnekaise, peak, *Sw.* 135 E13
Kech, river, *Pak.* 157 V3
Keçiborlu, *Turk.* 148 G6
Kecil, Kai, *Indonesia* 193 D14
Kecskemét, *Hung.* 132 L10
Kediri, *Indonesia* 168 M10
Kédougou, *Senegal* 176 J6
Keei, *Hawaii, U.S.* 107 N18
Keele, river, *N.W.T., Can.* 76 G10
Keele Peak, *Yukon Terr., Can.* 76 F9
Keeler, *Calif., U.S.* 103 U9
Keelung *see* Chilung, *Taiwan, China* 163 Q10
Keene, *N.H., U.S.* 89 J13
Keer-weer, Cape, *Austral.* 190 B11
Keetmanshoop, *Namibia* 182 J7
Keewatin, *Minn., U.S.* 98 F11
Kefaloniá (Cephalonia), island, *Gr.* 137 L13
Kefaluka, *Turk.* 148 H3
Keflavík, *Ice.* 134 F1
Kegen, *Kaz.* 155 H17
Keg River, *Alta., Can.* 76 J10
Keheili, *Sudan* 179 C13
Ke Ila, island, *Solomon Is.* 197 J18
Keila, *Estonia* 135 K16

Kéita, *Bahr, Chad* 177 K15
Keitele, lake, *Fin.* 135 H16
Keith, *S. Austral., Austral.* 191 Y11
Keith Arm, *N.W.T., Can.* 76 F10
Keithsburg, *Ill., U.S.* 93 P3
Kekaha, *Hawaii, U.S.* 106 B4
Kékes, peak, *Hung.* 132 K10
Kekirawa, *Sri Lanka* 159 S7
Keklau, *Palau* 196 M12
Kekra, *Russ.* 141 H20
Kekri, *India* 158 G4
K'elafo, *Eth.* 179 H16
Kelai, island, *Maldives* 159 T3
Kelan, *China* 162 D4
Kelang, island, *Indonesia* 169 K16
Kelang, *Malaysia* 167 U9
Kelefesia, island, *Ha'apai Group, Tonga* 198 R6
Keleft, *Afghan.* 156 K5
Kelkit, river, *Turk.* 148 D12
Kelkit, *Turk.* 148 E14
Keller Lake, *N.W.T., Can.* 76 G10
Kellet, Cape, *N.W.T., Can.* 76 D11
Kellogg, *Idaho, U.S.* 100 C4
Kélo, *Chad* 177 K14
Ke Loma, island, *Solomon Is.* 197 J18
Kelowna, *B.C., Can.* 76 M9
Kelso, *Calif., U.S.* 103 W11
Kelso, *Wash., U.S.* 102 E3
Keluang, *Malaysia* 167 V10
Kelvin Seamount, *Atl. Oc.* 216 H5
Kem', *Russ.* 140 D8
Kema, *Indonesia* 169 H15
Kemah, *Turk.* 149 E13
Kemaliye, *Turk.* 149 F13
Kemasik, *Malaysia* 167 T10
Kembanye, Note, *Santa Cruz Is., Solomon Is.* 197 Q22
Kemer, *Turk.* 148 D3
Kemer, *Turk.* 148 G4
Kemer, *Turk.* 148 J5
Kemer, *Turk.* 148 J6
Kemerovo, *Russ.* 140 K12
Kemi, river, *Eur.* 130 B8
Kemi, *Fin.* 135 F15
Kemijärvi, lake, *Fin.* 135 E15
Kemijärvi, *Fin.* 135 E15
Kemijoki, river, *Fin.* 135 D15
Kemmerer, *Wyo., U.S.* 100 J8
Kemp, Lake, *Tex., U.S.* 96 J8
Kemp Coast, *Antarctica* 207 D20
Kempendyay, *Russ.* 141 H17
Kempopla, Note, *Santa Cruz Is., Solomon Is.* 197 Q22
Kemp Peninsula, *Antarctica* 206 E7
Kemps Bay, *Bahamas* 110 F11
Kempsey, *N.S.W., Austral.* 191 X15
Kenai, *Alas., U.S.* 105 J16
Kenai Fjords National Park, *Alas., U.S.* 105 K16
Kenai Peninsula, *Alas., U.S.* 105 K16
Kendall, *Fla., U.S.* 91 X10
Kendall, *N.S.W., Austral.* 191 X15
Kendall, *N.Y., U.S.* 88 H6
Kendall, Cape, *Nunavut, Can.* 77 H16
Kendallville, *Ind., U.S.* 93 P10
Kendari, *Indonesia* 169 K14
Kendawangan, *Indonesia* 168 K9
Kendikolu, island, *Maldives* 159 T3
Kendrapara, *India* 158 K11
Kendrick, *Idaho, U.S.* 100 D3
Kenedy, *Tex., U.S.* 97 S10
Kenema, *Sierra Leone* 180 G6
Kêngkok, *Laos* 166 L11
Kengtung, *Myanmar* 166 H8
Kenhardt, *S. Af.* 182 K8
Kenitra, *Mor.* 176 B8
Kenli, *China* 162 F8
Kenmare, *Ire.* 138 H5
Kenmare, N. Dak., *U.S.* 98 E3
Kenna, N. Mex., *U.S.* 101 T15
Kennebec, river, *Me., U.S.* 89 D16
Kennebec, S. Dak., *U.S.* 98 L5
Kennebunk, *Me., U.S.* 89 H15
Kennedy, Cape *see* Canaveral, Cape, *N. Amer.* 74 M8
Kennedy Channel, *Nunavut, Can.* 77 B16
Kenner, *La., U.S.* 94 Q11
Kennett, *Mo., U.S.* 99 W15
Kennewick, *Wash., U.S.* 102 E7
Keno Hill, *Yukon Terr., Can.* 76 F8
Kenora, *Ont., Can.* 77 N14
Kenosha, *Wis., U.S.* 92 M7
Kenova, *W. Va., U.S.* 90 D7
Kent, *Ohio, U.S.* 93 P15
Kent, *Oreg., U.S.* 102 F5
Kent, *Tex., U.S.* 97 P2
Kent, *Wash., U.S.* 102 C4
Kentland, *Ind., U.S.* 93 Q7
Kenton, *Ohio, U.S.* 93 Q12
Kent Peninsula, *Nunavut, Can.* 77 F13
Kentucky, river, *U.S.* 79 H17
Kentucky, *U.S.* 95 C14
Kentucky Lake, *Ky., U.S.* 95 D13

Kentwood, La., *U.S.* 94 N10
Kentwood, Mich., *U.S.* 92 L10
Kenutu, island, *Vava'u Group, Tonga* 198 L12
Kenya, *Af.* 179 J14
Kenya, Mount, *Kenya* 179 K14
Kenya Highlands, *Af.* 174 K10
Keokea, *Hawaii, U.S.* 107 H17
Keokea, *Hawaii, U.S.* 107 N18
Keokeo, Puu o, *Hawaii, U.S.* 107 P19
Keokuk, *Iowa, U.S.* 99 Q14
Keomuku, site, *Hawaii, U.S.* 107 G15
Keonjhargarh, *India* 158 K10
Kep, *Cambodia* 167 P11
Kepi, *Indonesia* 169 M21
Kępno, *Pol.* 132 H9
Kepsut, *Turk.* 148 E4
Keran, *India* 156 M11
Kerby, *Oreg., U.S.* 102 K2
Kerch, *Ukr.* 133 L17
Kerchenskiy Proliv, *Ukr.* 133 L18
Kerempe Burnu, *Turk.* 148 B9
Keren, *Eritrea* 179 D15
Kerens, *Tex., U.S.* 96 M12
Kerguélen Plateau, *Southern Oc.* 225 G16
Kerikeri, *N.Z.* 193 H18
Kerinci, peak, *Indonesia* 168 J6
Kerki, *Turkm.* 156 M11
Kérkira, *Gr.* 137 K13
Kérkira (Corfu), island, *Gr.* 137 K13
Kermadec Islands, *Pac. Oc.* 194 L9
Kermadec Trench, *Pac. Oc.* 218 P10
Kermān, *Iran* 153 F15
Kermānshāh, *Iran* 152 D11
Kermānshāhān, *Iran* 153 F14
Kermit, *Tex., U.S.* 96 M3
Kern, river, *Calif., U.S.* 103 V7
Kernersville, *N.C., U.S.* 90 G10
Kernville, *Calif., U.S.* 103 V8
Kerrobert, *Sask., Can.* 76 M11
Kerrville, *Tex., U.S.* 97 Q8
Kershaw, *S.C., U.S.* 90 K9
Kertamulia, *Indonesia* 168 J9
Keryneia, *Cyprus* 148 K8
Keşan, *Turk.* 148 C3
Keşap, *Turk.* 149 D13
Kesennuma, *Jap.* 164 L13
Keshem, *Afghan.* 156 K8
Keshīt, *Iran* 153 F16
Keshod, *India* 158 K2
Keşiş Dağı, *Turk.* 149 E14
Keskal, *India* 158 L8
Keskin, *Turk.* 148 E9
Ketanda, *Russ.* 141 G19
Ketaun, *Indonesia* 168 K6
Ketchikan, *Alas., U.S.* 105 L24
Ketchum, *Idaho, U.S.* 100 G5
Ketchum Mountain, *Tex., U.S.* 97 N6
Keti Bandar, *Pak.* 157 X6
Kettering, *Ohio, U.S.* 93 R11
Kettle Falls, *Wash., U.S.* 102 A8
Kettle River Range, *Wash., U.S.* 102 A8
Keul', *Russ.* 141 K15
Kewanee, *Ill., U.S.* 93 P4
Kewaunee, *Wis., U.S.* 92 J7
Keweenaw Bay, *Mich., U.S.* 92 E7
Keweenaw National Historical Park, *Mich., U.S.* 92 E6
Keweenaw Peninsula, *Mich., U.S.* 92 E7
Keweenaw Point, *Mich., U.S.* 92 E7
Keyano, *Que., Can.* 77 L19
Key Colony Beach, *Fla., U.S.* 91 Y9
Keyes, *Okla., U.S.* 96 E4
Keyhole Reservoir, *Wyo., U.S.* 100 F13
Key Largo, *Fla., U.S.* 91 Y10
Keyser, *W. Va., U.S.* 90 C11
Keystone, *S. Dak., U.S.* 98 L2
Keystone, *W. Va., U.S.* 90 F8
Keystone Lake, *U.S.* 78 J12
Key West, *Fla., U.S.* 91 Z8
Khabarovsk, *Russ.* 141 K21
Khābūr, river, *Syr.* 150 D14
Khada Hills, *India* 157 Q5
Khailino, *Russ.* 141 D21
Khairpur, *Pak.* 157 S10
Khairpur, *Pak.* 157 U7
Khakhar', *Russ.* 141 H19
Khalatse, *India* 156 M14
Khalîg el Tîna, bay, *Egypt* 151 N1
Khalīj Maşīrah, *Oman* 153 M16
Khalūf, *Oman* 153 L16
Khambhaliya, *India* 158 J1
Khambhat, Gulf of, *India* 158 K3
Khamgaon, *India* 158 K5
Khamīs Mushayţ, *Saudi Arabia* 152 N8
Kham Khowrki, *Afghan.* 157 N3
Khammouan, *Laos* 166 K11
Khamr, *Yemen* 152 P9
Khanabad, *Afghan.* 156 K8
Khān Abū Shāmāt, *Syr.* 150 J8
Khanai, *Pak.* 157 R6
Khanaqa, *Afghan.* 156 K5

Khānaqīn, *Iraq* 152 D10
Khān az Zābīb, *Jordan* 151 N7
Khanderi Island, *India* 158 L3
Khandwa, *India* 158 J5
Khandyga, *Russ.* 141 G18
Khanewal, *Pak.* 157 R10
Khangarh, *Pak.* 157 T10
Khaniadhana, *India* 158 H6
Khanka, Lake, *Asia* 146 E12
Khanlar, *Azerb.* 149 D20
Khanozai, *Pak.* 157 R6
Khanpur, *Pak.* 157 T9
Khān Shaykhūn, *Syr.* 150 F8
Khan Tängiri (Lord of the Sky), *China-Kyrg.* 156 E15
Khantayskoye, Ozero, *Russ.* 141 G13
Khanty Mansiysk, *Russ.* 140 H10
Khān Yūnis, *Gaza Strip* 151 N4
Khapalu, *Pak.* 156 L13
Kharagpur, *India* 158 J11
Khara Khoto *see* Heicheng, ruins, *China* 160 F11
Kharan, *Pak.* 157 T4
Kharānaq, *Iran* 153 E14
Kharasavey, Mys, *Russ.* 140 E11
Khārga Oasis, *Egypt* 177 E18
Khargon, *India* 158 J5
Kharian, *Pak.* 157 P11
Khariar, *India* 158 K8
Kharimkotan, island, *Russ.* 141 H23
Khārk, island, *Iran* 152 G12
Kharkiv, *Ukr.* 133 H17
Kharlovka, *Russ.* 140 D9
Kharovsk, *Russ.* 140 F7
Khartoum, *Sudan* 179 E13
Khartoum North, *Sudan* 179 D13
Kharyyalakh, *Russ.* 141 G15
Khash, river, *Afghan.* 157 P4
Khash, *Afghan.* 157 Q3
Khāsh, *Iran* 153 G17
Khash Desert, *Afghan.* 157 P2
Khashuri, *Rep. of Georgia* 149 C17
Khasi Hills, *India* 158 G13
Khaskovo, *Bulg.* 137 H16
Khatanga, *Russ.* 141 F14
Khan Tängiri (Lord of the Sky), peak, *Kaz.* 155 J18
Khatangskiy Zaliv, *Russ.* 141 E15
Khātūnīyah, *Syr.* 150 D15
Khatyrka, *Russ.* 141 C21
Khaval, *Afghan.* 156 L5
Khavda, *India* 158 H2
Khawr Duwayhin, gulf, *Saudi Arabia* 153 J13
Khaybar, Harrat, *Saudi Arabia* 152 H7
Khaydarken, *Kyrg.* 156 G9
Khemmarat, *Thai.* 166 L11
Khenjan, *Afghan.* 156 L7
Kherson, *Ukr.* 133 L15
Kherwara, *India* 158 H4
Kheta, *Russ.* 141 F14
Khewari, *Pak.* 157 U7
Kheyrabad, *Afghan.* 156 K6
Khipro, *Pak.* 157 V8
Khiri Ratthanikhom, *Thai.* 167 Q8
Khizy, *Azerb.* 149 C22
Khmel'nyts'kyy, *Ukr.* 133 J13
Khoai, Hon, *Vietnam* 167 R11
Khocho, *Russ.* 141 G18
Khodja Bahauddin *see* Khvajeh Baha od Din, *Afghan.* 156 K8
Khojagala, *Turkm.* 154 L7
Khojak Pass, *Pak.* 157 R5
Khokhropar, *Pak.* 157 V9
Khok Kloi, *Thai.* 167 R7
Kholm, *Afghan.* 156 K6
Kholmsk, *Russ.* 141 K22
Khõng, *Laos* 166 M12
Khõngxédôn, *Laos* 166 L12
Khon Kaen, *Thai.* 166 L10
Khoper, river, *Eur.* 130 F12
Khorāsān, region, *Iran* 153 C15
Khormaleq, *Afghan.* 157 P2
Khorramābād, *Iran* 152 D11
Khorugh, *Taj.* 156 J9
Khost, *Pak.* 157 R6
Khost (Khowst), *Afghan.* 157 N8
Khowst *see* Khost, *Afghan.* 157 N8
Khoyniki, *Belarus* 133 G14
Khromtaū, *Kaz.* 154 D9
Khudabad, *Pak.* 156 K12
Khuiala, *India* 158 F2
Khujand, *Taj.* 156 G8
Khulna, *Bangladesh* 158 J12
Khunjerab Pass, *China-Pak.* 156 K12
Khunti, *India* 158 J10
Khurda, *India* 158 K10
Khushab, *Pak.* 157 P10
Khust, *Ukr.* 132 K11
Khuzdar, *Pak.* 157 T5
Khvāf, *Iran* 153 C17
Khvajeh Baha od Din (Khodja Bahauddin), *Afghan.* 156 K8
Khvajeh Mohammad Range, *Afghan.* 156 L8
Khvor, *Iran* 153 D14
Khvoy, *Iran* 152 A10

Khwazagak, *Afghan.* 156 M5
Khyber Pass, *Afghan.-Pak.* 156 M9
Kia, island, *Fiji* 198 G7
Kia, *Solomon Is.* 197 L17
Kiakeana Point, *Hawaii, U.S.* 107 H17
Kiama, *N.S.W., Austral.* 191 Y14
Kiamichi, river, *Okla., U.S.* 96 H13
Kiana, *Alas., U.S.* 105 E13
Kibombo, *Dem. Rep. of the Congo* 178 L11
Kibwezi, *Kenya* 179 K14
Kickapoo, Lake, *Tex., U.S.* 96 K9
Kidal, *Mali* 176 G10
Kidnappers, Cape, *N.Z.* 193 L20
Kidrenen, island, *Enewetak Atoll, Marshall Is.* 196 G8
Kidrinen, island, *Enewetak Atoll, Marshall Is.* 196 J8
Kiel, *Ger.* 132 E6
Kiel, *Wis., U.S.* 92 K7
Kielce, *Pol.* 132 H10
Kieler Bucht, *Ger.* 132 E6
Kien An, *Vietnam* 166 H12
Kien Duc, *Vietnam* 167 N13
Kieta, *P.N.G.* 197 K14
Kiev see Kyyiv, *Ukr.* 133 H14
Kiffa, *Mauritania* 176 G6
Kifrī, *Iraq* 152 D10
Kigali, *Rwanda* 178 K12
Kiğı, *Turk.* 149 F15
Kigoma, *Tanzania* 178 L12
Kihei, *Hawaii, U.S.* 107 G16
Kiholo Bay, *Hawaii, U.S.* 107 L18
Kii Landing, *Hawaii, U.S.* 106 B3
Kii Suidō, *Jap.* 165 R8
Kikaiga Shima, *Jap.* 165 W3
Kikiakki, *Russ.* 140 H12
Kikki, *Pak.* 157 V2
Kikládes (Cyclades), islands, *Gr.* 137 L16
Kikori, river, *P.N.G.* 193 D18
Kikori, *P.N.G.* 193 D18
Kikwit, *Dem. Rep. of the Congo* 178 L8
Kil, river, *Pak.* 157 V3
Kilafors, *Sw.* 135 J13
Kilakkarai, *India* 159 S6
Kilar, *India* 157 N13
Kilauea, peak, *Hawaii, U.S.* 107 N21
Kilauea, *Hawaii, U.S.* 106 B6
Kilauea Lighthouse, *Hawaii, U.S.* 106 A6
Kilbuck Mountains, *U.S.* 78 Q2
Kilchu, *N. Korea* 162 C14
Kilcowera, *Qnsld., Austral.* 191 V12
Kilgore, *Nebr., U.S.* 98 M4
Kilgore, *Tex., U.S.* 96 L14
Kılıçkaya, *Turk.* 149 D16
Kili Island, *Marshall Is.* 196 H4
Kilimanjaro, peak, *Tanzania* 179 L14
Kilinailau Islands, *P.N.G.* 197 H14
Kılınç Tepesi, *Turk.* 149 D13
Kilinochchi, *Sri Lanka* 159 S7
Kilis, *Turk.* 148 J12
Kiliya, *Ukr.* 133 M14
Kilkenny, *Ire.* 138 G6
Killarney, *Ire.* 138 G5
Killdeer, *N. Dak., U.S.* 98 F2
Killeen, *Tex., U.S.* 97 P10
Killiniq Island, *Nunavut, Can.* 77 H20
Kilmarnock, *Scot., U.K.* 138 E7
Kilombero, river, *Tanzania* 179 N14
Kilosa, *Tanzania* 179 M14
Kiltan Island, *India* 159 Q3
Kilwa Kivinje, *Tanzania* 179 N15
Kim, *Colo., U.S.* 101 P15
Kimaam, *Indonesia* 169 M20
Kimball, *Nebr., U.S.* 99 P1
Kimball, *S. Dak., U.S.* 98 L6
Kimbe Bay, *P.N.G.* 193 C21
Kimberley, region, *W. Austral., Austral.* 191 R5
Kimberley, *B.C., Can.* 76 M9
Kimberley, *S. Af.* 182 K9
Kimberley, Cape, *Austral.* 190 C13
Kimberley Plateau, *Austral.* 190 C6
Kimberly, *Idaho, U.S.* 100 H5
Kimch'aek, *N. Korea* 162 C14
Kimch'ŏn, *S. Korea* 162 F14
Kimje, *S. Korea* 162 G13
Kimmirut, *Nunavut, Can.* 77 H19
Kimobetsu, *Jap.* 164 G13
Kinabalu, peak, *Malaysia* 168 G12
Kinadyeng, island, *Jaluit Atoll, Marshall Is.* 196 L8
Kindadal, *Indonesia* 169 K14
Kinder, *La., U.S.* 94 P7
Kindia, *Guinea* 180 F5
Kindu, *Dem. Rep. of the Congo* 178 L11
Kineshma, *Russ.* 140 F7
King Christian IX Land, *N. Amer.* 74 C10
King Christian X Land, *N. Amer.* 74 B9
King City, *Calif., U.S.* 103 U5
King City, *Mo., U.S.* 99 R10
King Cove, *Alas., U.S.* 104 P12
Kingfisher, *Okla., U.S.* 96 F10
Kingfisher Lake, *Ont., Can.* 77 M15
King Frederik VI Coast, *N. Amer.* 74 D10
King Frederik VIII Land, *N. Amer.* 74 A8
King George Bay, *Falk. Is., U.K.* 125 W12
King George Island, *Antarctica* 206 C3
King George Islands, *Nunavut, Can.* 77 K17
King George Sound, *Austral.* 190 L3
King Island, *Alas., U.S.* 104 F10
King Island, *Austral.* 190 L15
King Khalid Military City, *Saudi Arabia* 152 G10
King Lear Peak, *Nev., U.S.* 102 M8
King Leopold Ranges, *Austral.* 190 D5
Kingman, *Ariz., U.S.* 101 S5
Kingman, *Kans., U.S.* 99 U7
King Mountain, *Tex., U.S.* 97 N4
Kingoonya, *S. Austral., Austral.* 191 W9
King Peak, *Antarctica* 206 J11
Kingri, *Pak.* 157 R8
Kings, river, *Calif., U.S.* 103 T7
King Salmon, *Alas., U.S.* 105 L14
Kingsburg, *Calif., U.S.* 103 T6
Kings Canyon National Park, *Calif., U.S.* 103 T7
Kingscote, *S. Austral., Austral.* 191 Y10
King Sejong, station, *Antarctica* 206 C3
Kingsford, *Mich., U.S.* 92 G7
Kingsland, *Ga., U.S.* 91 Q8
Kings Mountain, *N.C., U.S.* 90 J8
King Sound, *Austral.* 190 C4
Kings Peak, *Utah, U.S.* 100 L8
Kingsport, *Tenn., U.S.* 95 D20
Kingston, *Jam.* 110 N12
Kingston, *N.Y., U.S.* 88 L11
Kingston, *Norfolk I., Austral.* 197 G20
Kingston, *Ont., Can.* 77 Q19
Kingston, *Pa., U.S.* 88 M8
Kingston, *Tas., Austral.* 191 Z16
Kingston South East, *S. Austral., Austral.* 191 Y10
Kingston upon Hull, *Eng., U.K.* 138 G9
Kingstown, *St. Vincent and the Grenadines* 113 L17
Kingstree, *S.C., U.S.* 90 L10
Kingsville, *Tex., U.S.* 97 U10
King Wilhelm Land, *N. Amer.* 74 B9
King William Island, *Nunavut, Can.* 77 F14
Kiniama, *Dem. Rep. of the Congo* 178 N11
Kinniyai, *Sri Lanka* 159 S8
Kino, river, *Jap.* 165 Q9
Kinsale, *Ire.* 138 H5
Kinshasa, *Dem. Rep. of the Congo* 178 L7
Kinsley, *Kans., U.S.* 99 U5
Kinston, *N.C., U.S.* 90 H13
Kintyre, peninsula, *Scot., U.K.* 138 E7
Kinyeti, peak, *Sudan* 179 H13
Kinzua, *Oreg., U.S.* 102 G6
Kioa, island, *Fiji* 198 G8
Kiokluk Mountains, *Alas., U.S.* 105 J13
Kiowa, *Colo., U.S.* 100 M14
Kiowa, *Kans., U.S.* 99 V6
Kipahulu, *Hawaii, U.S.* 107 H18
Kipili, *Tanzania* 178 M12
Kipini, *Kenya* 179 K15
Kipnuk, *Alas., U.S.* 104 K11
Kirakira, *Solomon Is.* 197 P20
Kiraz, *Turk.* 148 G4
Kirbey, *Russ.* 141 G15
Kirbyville, *Tex., U.S.* 97 P16
Kirensk, *Russ.* 141 K15
Kiri, *Dem. Rep. of the Congo* 178 K9
Kiribati, *Pac. Oc.* 194 G9
Kırıkhan, *Turk.* 148 J11
Kırıkkale, *Turk.* 148 E9
Kiritimati (Christmas Island), *Kiribati* 194 G12
Kiriwina, island, *P.N.G.* 193 E21
Kırka, *Turk.* 148 E6
Kirkağaç, *Turk.* 148 E3
Kirkcaldy, *Scot., U.K.* 138 E8
Kirkenes, *Nor.* 135 C15
Kırkgeçit, *Turk.* 149 G18
Kirkjubæjarklaustur, *Ice.* 134 G3
Kirkland, *Tex., U.S.* 96 J7
Kirkland Lake, *Ont., Can.* 77 P18
Kırklar Dağı, *Turk.* 149 D15
Kırklareli, *Turk.* 148 B3
Kirksville, *Mo., U.S.* 99 R12
Kirkūk, *Iraq* 152 C9
Kirkwall, *Scot., U.K.* 138 C8
Kirkwood, *Mo., U.S.* 99 T15
Kirov, *Kyrg.* 156 E9
Kirov, *Russ.* 140 G8
Kirova, island, *Russ.* 141 D13
Kirovohrad, *Ukr.* 133 J15
Kirovskiy, *Kaz.* 155 G17
Kırşehir, *Turk.* 148 F9
Kirthar Range, *Pak.* 157 U6
Kirtland, *N. Mex., U.S.* 101 Q10
Kiruna, *Sw.* 135 E13
Kirunu, island, *Enewetak Atoll, Marshall Is.* 196 G7
Kirwan Escarpment, *Antarctica* 206 B12
Kirwin Reservoir, *Kans., U.S.* 99 S5
Kiryū, *Jap.* 165 N12
Kisangani, *Dem. Rep. of the Congo* 178 J10
Kishanganj, *India* 158 G11
Kishangarh, *India* 158 F2
Kishangarh, *India* 158 G4
Kishb, Harrat al, *Saudi Arabia* 152 K8
Kishiga Zaki, *Jap.* 165 U5
Kishiwada, *Jap.* 165 Q8
Kisigo, river, *Af.* 174 L10
Kısır Dağı, *Turk.* 149 D17
Kiska Island, *Alas., U.S.* 104 P3
Kismaayo (Chisimayu), *Somalia* 179 K16
Kiso, river, *Jap.* 165 P10
Kissidougou, *Guinea* 180 F6
Kissimmee, river, *Fla., U.S.* 91 U9
Kissimmee, *Fla., U.S.* 91 T9
Kissimmee, Lake, *Fla., U.S.* 91 U9
Kistrand, *Nor.* 135 C14
Kisumu, *Kenya* 179 K13
Kita, *Mali* 176 H6
Kita Daitō Jima, *Jap.* 194 C2
Kitaibaraki, *Jap.* 165 N13
Kita Iwo Jima, *Jap.* 194 C4
Kitakami, *Jap.* 164 K13
Kitakata, *Jap.* 164 M12
Kitakyūshū, *Jap.* 165 R4
Kitale, *Kenya* 179 J14
Kitami, *Jap.* 164 F15
Kitami Sanchi, *Jap.* 164 E14
Kitaura, *Jap.* 164 K12
Kit Carson, *Colo., U.S.* 101 N15
Kitchener, *Ont., Can.* 77 R18
Kitchener, *W. Austral., Austral.* 191 W5
Kíthira, island, *Gr.* 137 M15
Kiti, Cape, *Cyprus* 148 L8
Kitimat, *B.C., Can.* 76 K7
Kiti Point, *Pohnpei, F.S.M.* 197 G14
Kitiu, Motu, *Aitutaki Atoll, Cook Is., N.Z.* 198 R12
Kitob, *Uzb.* 154 L12
Kittanning, *Pa., U.S.* 88 N4
Kittery, *Me., U.S.* 89 J15
Kittilä, *Fin.* 135 D14
Kittitas, *Wash., U.S.* 102 D6
Kitt Peak, *Ariz., U.S.* 101 V7
Kitty Hawk, *N.C., U.S.* 90 G15
Kitwe, *Zambia* 182 D10
Kiukiu, Pointe, *Hiva Oa, Fr. Polynesia, Fr.* 199 M20
Kiunga, *P.N.G.* 193 D17
Kivalina, *Alas., U.S.* 104 D12
Kivu, Lac, *Dem. Rep. of the Congo-Rwanda* 178 K12
Kiyan Saki, *Jap.* 165 Y1
Kiyāt, *Saudi Arabia* 152 N8
Kıyıköy, *Turk.* 148 C4
Kizema, *Russ.* 140 F8
Kızılcahamam, *Turk.* 148 D8
Kızılin, *Turk.* 149 H13
Kızılırmak, *Turk.* 148 D9
Kızılırmak (Halys), river, *Turk.* 148 D9
Kızılliman Burnu, *Turk.* 148 K8
Kızıltepe, *Turk.* 149 H15
Klagenfurt, *Aust.* 132 L7
Klaipėda, *Lith.* 135 N15
Klaksvík, *Faroe Is., Den.* 134 J6
Klamath, river, *Calif., U.S.* 102 L2
Klamath, *Calif., U.S.* 102 L2
Klamath Falls, *Oreg., U.S.* 102 K4
Klamath Mountains, *Calif., U.S.* 102 M3
Klarälven, river, *Sw.* 134 K12
Klatovy, *Czech Rep.* 132 J7
Klawer, *S. Af.* 182 L7
Klawock, *Alas., U.S.* 105 L23
Kle, *Liberia* 180 G6
Klerksdorp, *S. Af.* 182 K10
Klickitat, *Wash., U.S.* 102 E5
Klintehamn, *Sw.* 135 M14
Klintsy, *Russ.* 140 F5
Kłodzko, *Pol.* 132 H8
Klong, river, *Thai.* 166 M8
Klyaz'ma, river, *Eur.* 130 D11
Klyuchevskaya Sopka, *Asia* 146 C13
Knife River, *Minn., U.S.* 98 G13
Knin, *Croatia* 136 G11
Knjaževac, *Yug.* 137 G14
Knob, Cape, *Austral.* 190 L4
Knotts Island, *N.C., U.S.* 90 G14
Knox, *Ind., U.S.* 93 P8
Knox, Fort, *Ky., U.S.* 95 C16
Knox Atoll, *Marshall Is.* 196 H5
Knox City, *Tex., U.S.* 96 K8
Knox Coast, *Antarctica* 207 L21
Knoxville, *Iowa, U.S.* 99 P11
Knoxville, *Tenn., U.S.* 95 E18
Knud Rasmussen Land, *N. Amer.* 74 B7
Knysna, *S. Af.* 182 M9
Ko, Motu, *Pukapuka Atoll, Cook Is., N.Z.* 198 R2
Koba, *Indonesia* 168 K8
Koba, *Indonesia* 169 M19
Kobayashi, *Jap.* 165 T4
Kōbe, *Jap.* 165 Q8
København (Copenhagen), *Den.* 134 N12
Koblenz, *Ger.* 132 H5
Kobo, *India* 158 F15
Kobroor, island, *Indonesia* 169 L19
Kobryn, *Belarus* 132 G12
Kobu, *Azerb.* 149 D23
Kobuk, river, *Alas., U.S.* 105 E14
Kobuk, *Alas., U.S.* 105 E14
Kobuk Valley National Park, *Alas., U.S.* 105 E13
K'obulet'i, *Rep. of Georgia* 149 C16
Koçarlı, *Turk.* 148 G3
Koçbaşı Tepe, *Turk.* 149 F17
Koch'ang, *S. Korea* 162 G13
Koch Bihar, *India* 158 G12
Kochi see Cochin, *India* 159 R5
Kōchi, *Jap.* 165 R7
Koch Island, *Nunavut, Can.* 77 F17
Koch Peak, *Mont., U.S.* 100 F8
Kočkorka, *Kyrg.* 156 E12
Kodari, *Nepal* 158 F10
Koddiyar Bay, *Sri Lanka* 159 S8
Kodiak, *Alas., U.S.* 105 M16
Kodiak Island, *Alas., U.S.* 105 M15
Kodiak Seamount, *Pac. Oc.* 219 B13
Kodinar, *India* 158 K2
Kodinskiy, *Russ.* 141 J14
Kodok, *Sudan* 179 F13
Kodomari, *Jap.* 164 H12
Köes, *Namibia* 182 J7
Koetoi, *Jap.* 164 D13
Koforidua, *Ghana* 180 H11
Kōfu, *Jap.* 165 P11
Koga, *Jap.* 165 N12
Ko Gaja Shima, *Jap.* 165 V3
Kogaluc, river, *Que., Can.* 77 K18
Kogon, *Uzb.* 154 L11
Kohala, region, *Hawaii, U.S.* 107 K19
Kohala see Kapaau, *Hawaii, U.S.* 107 J19
Kohala Mill see Halaula, *Hawaii, U.S.* 107 J19
Kohala Mountains, *Hawaii, U.S.* 107 K19
Kohat, *Pak.* 157 N9
Koh-e Baba Range, *Afghan.* 156 M6
Kohima, *India* 158 G15
Kohistan, region, *Pak.* 156 L11
Kohler Glacier, *Antarctica* 206 L7
Kohlu, *Pak.* 157 R8
Kohnieh, *Cambodia* 167 N13
Kohtla-Järve, *Estonia* 135 K17
Koilani, *Cyprus* 148 L8
Kŏje Do, *S. Korea* 162 H14
Ko Jima, *Jap.* 165 S12
Kok-Aigyr, *Kyrg.* 156 F12
Kök-Art, *Kyrg.* 156 G11
Kokas, *Indonesia* 169 K18
Kokee, *Hawaii, U.S.* 106 B5
Kokkola, *Fin.* 135 G15
Koko, *Nig.* 181 E13
Koko Crater, *Hawaii, U.S.* 106 E12
Koko Head, *Hawaii, U.S.* 106 E12
Kokomo, *Ind., U.S.* 93 Q9
Kokoolau, peak, *Hawaii, U.S.* 107 M20
Kökpekti, *Kaz.* 155 E18
Kökshetaū, *Kaz.* 155 C13
Kokubu, *Jap.* 165 T4
Kok Yangak, *Kyrg.* 156 F10
Kola, island, *Indonesia* 169 L19
Kolachi, river, *Pak.* 157 T6
Kolaka, *Indonesia* 169 K14
Kola Peninsula, *Eur.* 130 A10
Kolar, *India* 159 P6
Kolari, *Fin.* 135 E14
Kolayat, *India* 158 F3
Kolbano, *Indonesia* 169 N15
Kolbeinsey Ridge, *Atl. Oc.* 216 A10
Kolbio, *Kenya* 179 K16
Kolding, *Den.* 134 P11
Kolé, *Vanuatu* 198 C2
Kole, *Dem. Rep. of the Congo* 178 J11
Kole, *Dem. Rep. of the Congo* 178 L10
Kolekole Stream, *Hawaii, U.S.* 107 L20
Kolguyev, Ostrov, *Russ.* 140 E10
Kolguyev Island, *Eur.* 130 A11
Kolhapur, *India* 158 M4
Kolhozabad, *Taj.* 156 J7
Kolia, *Wallis and Futuna, Fr.* 198 E11
Koliganek, *Alas., U.S.* 105 K14
Kolkata (Calcutta), *India* 158 J12
Kollam see Quilon, *India* 159 S5
Kollidam, river, *India* 159 R6
Kolmogorovo, *Russ.* 141 J13
Köln (Cologne), *Ger.* 132 G4
Koloa, island, *Vava'u Group, Tonga* 198 L12
Koloa, *Hawaii, U.S.* 106 C5
Kołobrzeg, *Pol.* 132 F8
Kolokani, *Mali* 176 H7
Kolombangara, island, *Solomon Is.* 197 M16
Kolomna, *Russ.* 140 F6
Kolonga, *Tongatapu, Tonga* 198 H12
Kolonia, *Pohnpei, F.S.M.* 197 F14
Kolonodale, *Indonesia* 169 K14
Kolosovykh, *Russ.* 141 E13
Kolovai, *Tongatapu, Tonga* 198 H10
Kolowr va Dah Sil, *Afghan.* 156 L7
Kolpashevo, *Russ.* 140 J12
Kolpino, *Russ.* 140 D6

Ko'lquduq, Uzb. 154 J10
Kol'skiy Poluostrov, Russ. 140 D9
Kolufuri, island, Maldives 159 V3
Kolumadulu Atoll, Maldives 159 V3
Kolwezi, Dem. Rep. of the Congo 178 N10
Kolyma, river, Russ. 141 D19
Kolyma Lowland, Asia 146 B11
Kolyma Range, Asia 146 C12
Kolymskoye Nagor'ye (Gydan), Russ. 141 F20
Komagane, Jap. 165 P11
Komandorskiye Ostrova (Commander Islands), Russ. 141 E23
Komatsu, Jap. 165 N9
Komebail Lagoon (Ngertachebeab), Palau 196 N11
Komo, island, Fiji 198 J9
Komodo, island, Indonesia 169 M13
Komoé, river, Côte d'Ivoire 180 G9
Kôm Ombo, Egypt 177 E19
Komoran, island, Indonesia 169 M20
Komoro, Jap. 165 N11
Komotini, Gr. 137 J16
Kompong Chhnang, Cambodia 167 N11
Kompong Som, Cambodia 167 P11
Kompong Som, Chhung, Cambodia 167 P10
Kompong Speu, Cambodia 167 P11
Kompong Sralao, Cambodia 166 M12
Kompong Thom, Cambodia 167 N11
Komsomol, Kaz. 154 F7
Komsomolets, Kaz. 154 B10
Komsomolets, Ostrov, Russ. 141 C14
Komsomolets Island, Asia 146 B9
Komsomol'sk, Uzb. 154 H8
Komsomol'skiy, Russ. 141 B19
Komsomol'sk na Amure, Russ. 141 K20
Komusan, N. Korea 162 B14
Kona, region, Hawaii, U.S. 107 M19
Konakpınar, Turk. 148 F12
Konawa, Okla., U.S. 96 H11
Konda, Indonesia 169 K18
Kondagaon, India 158 L8
Kondinin, W. Austral., Austral. 191 X3
Kondoa, Tanzania 179 L14
Kondopoga, Russ. 140 E7
Kondoz (Kunduz), Afghan. 156 K7
Kondukur, India 159 N7
Konduz, river, Afghan. 156 K7
Koné, New Caledonia, Fr. 198 C7
Koné, Passe de, New Caledonia, Fr. 198 C6
Köneyurgenç, Turkm. 154 J9
Kong, river, Laos 166 L13
Kong, Koh, Cambodia 167 P10
Kongauru, island, Palau 196 Q10
Kongiganak, Alas., U.S. 104 K12
Konginskiy Khrebet, Russ. 141 D20
Konglu, Myanmar 166 D7
Kongolo, Dem. Rep. of the Congo 178 L11
Kongor, Sudan 178 G12
Kongou Falls, Gabon 181 K16
Kongsberg, Nor. 134 L11
Kongsvinger, Nor. 134 K12
Kongwa, Tanzania 179 M14
Konibodom, Taj. 156 G8
Konin, Pol. 132 G9
Konnongorring, W. Austral., Austral. 191 X3
Konosha, Russ. 140 E7
Konotop, Ukr. 133 G15
Konqi, river, China 160 G7
Konrai, Palau 196 M12
Konstanz, Ger. 132 K5
Konta, India 158 M8
Kontagora, Nig. 181 F13
Kon Tum, Vietnam 166 M13
Konya, Turk. 148 G8
Konza, Kenya 179 K14
Kookynie, W. Austral., Austral. 191 W4
Koolau Range, Hawaii, U.S. 106 D11
Koolburra, Qnsld., Austral. 191 Q12
Koonalda, S. Austral., Austral. 191 W7
Koonibba, S. Austral., Austral. 191 W8
Kópasker, Ice. 134 E4
Kopbirlik, Kaz. 155 F16
Köpekkayası Burnu, Turk. 148 B8
Kopervik, Nor. 134 L9
Köpetdag Dagerşi, mountains, Iran 153 A15
Köpetdag Dagerşi, mountains, Turkm. 154 L7
Kopet Mountains, Asia 146 G5
Koppal, India 159 N5
Koprivnica, Croatia 136 E12
Köprü, river, Turk. 148 H6
Kopylovka, Russ. 140 J12
K'orahē, Eth. 179 G16
Korak, island, Palau 196 N12
Korangi, Pak. 157 W6
Korba, India 158 J8
Korçë, Alban. 137 J14
Korčula, island, Croatia 136 G12
Korea, Asia 146 F12
Korea Bay, China 162 D11
Korea Strait, S. Korea 162 H14
Korem, Eth. 179 E15
Korf, Russ. 141 D21
Korhogo, Côte d'Ivoire 180 F8
Kori Creek, India 157 X7
Kori Creek, India 158 H1
Korido, Indonesia 169 J19
Kórinthos (Corinth), Gr. 137 L15
Kōriyama, Jap. 164 M13
Korkuteli, Turk. 148 H5
Korla, China 160 F7
Kormakitis, Cape, Cyprus 148 K8
Koro, island, Fiji 198 H7
Korolevu, Fiji 198 J6
Koromiri, island, Rarotonga, Cook Is., N.Z. 198 Q9
Koror, Palau 196 N11
Koror (Oreor), island, Palau 196 P11
Koro Sea, Fiji 198 H8
Korosten', Ukr. 133 H13
Korotkova, Russ. 141 K15
Koro Toro, Chad 177 H15
Korti, Sudan 178 D12
Koryak Range, Asia 146 B13
Koryakskoye Nagor'ye, Russ. 141 D21
Kos, Gr. 137 L17
Kosaka, Jap. 164 J13
Kō Saki, Jap. 165 Q3
Kosan, N. Korea 162 D13
Kosciusko, Miss., U.S. 94 K12
Kosciuszko, Mount, Austral. 190 L13
Koshikijima Rettō, Jap. 165 T3
Köshim, river, Kaz. 154 D6
Koshk, Afghan. 156 M2
Koshk-e Kohneh, Afghan. 156 M2
Košice, Slovakia 132 K10
Koson, Uzb. 154 L11
Kosŏng, S. Korea 162 G14
Kosovo, Yug. 137 H13
Kosovska Mitrovica, Yug. 137 G13
Kosrae (Kusaie), island, F.S.M. 196 Q9
Kossol Passage, Palau 196 L12
Kossou, Lac de, Côte d'Ivoire 180 G8
Kosti, Sudan 179 E13
Kostino, Russ. 141 H13
Kostroma, Russ. 140 F7
Kostrzyn, Pol. 132 G8
Koszalin, Pol. 132 F8
Kota, India 158 H5
Kotaagung, Indonesia 168 L7
Kota Baharu, Malaysia 167 S10
Kotabaru, Indonesia 168 K12
Kotabumi, Indonesia 168 L7
Kotabunan, Indonesia 169 J15
Kot Addu, Pak. 157 R9
Ko Takara Jima, Jap. 165 V3
Kota Kinabalu, Malaysia 168 G11
Kota Tinggi, Malaysia 167 V11
Kotawa, Motu, Pukapuka Atoll, Cook Is., N.Z. 198 R2
Kotel'nich, Russ. 140 G7
Kotel'nyy, Ostrov, Russ. 141 D16
Kotel'nyy Island, Asia 146 B10
Kotka, Fin. 135 J16
Kotlas, Russ. 140 F8
Kotlik, Alas., U.S. 104 H12
Kotooka, Jap. 164 K12
Kotovs'k, Ukr. 133 K14
Kotri, Pak. 157 V7
Kottayam, India 159 R5
Kotto, river, Cen. Af. Rep. 178 G10
Kotu, island, Ha'apai Group, Tonga 198 Q6
Kotu Group, Ha'apai Group, Tonga 198 Q6
Koturdepe, Turkm. 154 L6
Kotzebue, Alas., U.S. 104 E12
Kotzebue Sound, Alas., U.S. 104 E12
Koua, New Caledonia, Fr. 198 D8
Kouakou, island, Gambier Is., Fr. Polynesia, Fr. 199 R21
Kouango, Cen. Af. Rep. 178 U9
Koudougou, Burkina Faso 180 E10
Kouilou, river, Congo 181 M16
Koukdjuak, Great Plain of the, Nunavut, Can. 77 G18
Kouklia, Cyprus 148 L7
Koulamoutou, Gabon 181 L16
Koulen, Cambodia 166 M11
Koulikoro, Mali 176 H7
Koumac, New Caledonia, Fr. 198 C6
Koumra, Chad 177 K15
Kountze, Tex., U.S. 97 P15
Kourou, Fr. Guiana 121 E18
Kouroussa, Guinea 180 F7
Koussi, Emi, Chad 177 G15
Koutiala, Mali 176 J8
Koutomo, Île, New Caledonia, Fr. 198 E9
Kouvola, Fin. 135 J16
Kovel', Ukr. 132 H12
Kovic, Baie, Nunavut, Can. 77 J17
Kovrov, Russ. 140 F6
Kovur, India 159 P7
Kowanyama, Qnsld., Austral. 191 Q12
Kowloon see Jiulong, China 163 S5
Köyceğiz, Turk. 148 H4
Koyda, Russ. 140 E9
Koyuk, Alas., U.S. 104 F12
Koyukuk, river, Alas., U.S. 105 E15
Koyukuk, Alas., U.S. 105 F13
Koyulhisar, Turk. 148 E12
Kozan, Turk. 148 H11
Kozáni, Gr. 137 J14
Kozhasay, Kaz. 154 E8
Kozhikode (Calicut), India 159 Q5
Kozlu, Turk. 148 C7
Kozluk, Turk. 149 G16
Kōzu Shima, Jap. 165 Q12
Kozyatyn, Ukr. 133 J14
Kpalimé, Togo 180 G11
Kra, Isthmus of, Thai. 167 Q8
Krabi, Thai. 167 R8
Kra Buri, Thai. 167 P7
Kragerø, Nor. 134 L11
Kraków, Pol. 132 J10
Kralanh, Cambodia 166 M10
Kralendijk, Bonaire, Neth. 112 M10
Kramators'k, Ukr. 133 J17
Kramfors, Sw. 135 H13
Kranj, Slov. 136 E10
Krasavino, Russ. 140 F8
Krasnoarmeysk, Kaz. 155 B13
Krasnoarmeysk, Russ. 140 H6
Krasnodar, Russ. 140 H4
Krasnogorsk, Russ. 141 J22
Krasnokamensk, Russ. 141 L18
Krasnoperekops'k, Ukr. 133 L16
Krasnovishersk, Russ. 140 G9
Krasnoyarsk, Russ. 141 K13
Krasnyy Dolginets, Kaz. 154 G5
Kratie, Cambodia 167 N12
Kraul Mountains, Antarctica 206 B11
Kray Lesa, Russ. 141 D19
Krefeld, Ger. 132 G4
Kremenchuk, Ukr. 133 J16
Kremenchuk Reservoir, Eur. 130 G10
Kremenchuts'ke Vodokhovyshche, Ukr. 133 K16
Kremenets', Ukr. 132 J12
Kremmling, Colo., U.S. 100 L12
Kress, Tex., U.S. 96 J5
Kresty, Russ. 141 F13
Kretinga, Lith. 135 N15
Kribi, Cameroon 181 J15
Krishna, river, India 159 N5
Krishnagiri, India 159 Q6
Krishnanagar, India 158 J12
Kristiansand, Nor. 134 M10
Kristianstad, Sw. 135 N13
Kristiansund, Nor. 134 H10
Kristinestad, Fin. 135 H14
Kríti see Crete, island, Gr. 137 N16
Krk, island, Croatia 136 F11
Kroken, Nor. 134 G12
Krong Koh Kong, Cambodia 167 P10
Kroonstad, S. Af. 182 K10
Krui, Indonesia 168 L7
Krung Thep (Bangkok), Thai. 166 M9
Krupki, Belarus 133 E13
Kruševac, Yug. 137 G13
Kruzof Island, U.S. 78 R6
Krychaw, Belarus 133 F15
Krylov Seamount, Atl. Oc. 216 L9
Kryvyy Rih, Ukr. 133 K16
Ksar el Kebir, Mor. 176 A8
K2 (Godwin Austen), China-Pak. 156 L13
Kuala Abang, Brunei 168 G11
Kuala Belait, Brunei 168 G11
Kuala Berang, Malaysia 167 T10
Kuala Dungun, Malaysia 167 T10
Kualakapuas, Indonesia 168 K11
Kuala Kerai, Malaysia 167 S10
Kualakurun, Indonesia 168 J11
Kuala Lumpur, Malaysia 167 U9
Kualamanjual, Indonesia 168 J10
Kuala Nerang, Malaysia 168 F6
Kualapuu, Hawaii, U.S. 107 F14
Kuala Rompin, Malaysia 167 U10
Kuala Terengganu, Malaysia 167 T10
Kualatungkal, Indonesia 168 J7
Kuancheng, China 162 C8
Kuandian, China 162 C11
Kuanshan, Taiwan, China 163 S10
Kuantan, Malaysia 167 T10
Kuban', river, Eur. 130 H12
Kuban Lowland, Eur. 130 G12
Kubbum, Sudan 178 F10
Kubeno, Lake, Eur. 130 D11
Kubokawa, Jap. 165 R6
Kubonitu, Mount, Solomon Is. 197 M18
Kuchaman, India 158 F4
Kuching, Malaysia 168 H9
Kuchinoerabu Jima, Jap. 165 U4
Kuchino Shima, Jap. 165 V4
Kuchnay Darvishan, Afghan. 157 Q3
Küçüksu, Turk. 149 G16
Kud, river, Pak. 157 U5
Kudara, Taj. 156 J10
Kudat, Malaysia 168 F12
Kudgee, N.S.W., Austral. 191 X11
Kudremukh, peak, India 159 P4
Kudu Kyuyel', Russ. 141 J17
Kuee Ruins, Hawaii, U.S. 107 P20
Kufra Oasis see Al Jawf, Lib. 177 E16
Kugluktuk, Nunavut, Can. 76 F12
Kūhak, Iran 153 H18
Kūhak, Pak. 157 U3
Kuh-e Sangan, peak, Afghan. 157 N4
Kuh-e Sayyad, Afghan. 156 L4
Kūhhā-ye Zāgros (Zagros Mountains), Iran 152 D11
Kuhmo, Fin. 135 F16
Kui Buri, Thai. 167 N8
Kuikuina, Nicar. 109 L18
Kuikui Point, Hawaii, U.S. 107 H16
Kuiseb, river, Namibia 182 H6
Kuitan, China 163 R6
Kuito, Angola 182 D7
Kuiu Island, U.S. 78 R7
Kuivaniemi, Fin. 135 F15
Kuizhuang, China 162 D8
Kujang-ŭp, N. Korea 162 D12
Kuji, Jap. 164 J14
Kuju, peak, Jap. 165 R5
Kukolu, island, Solomon Is. 197 J18
Kukpowruk, river, Alas., U.S. 104 C12
Kukui, Hawaii, U.S. 107 M21
Kukuihaele, Hawaii, U.S. 107 K20
Kukuiula, Hawaii, U.S. 106 C5
Kuku Point, Wake I., U.S. 196 F7
Kula see Waiakoa, Hawaii, U.S. 107 G17
Kula, Turk. 148 F4
Kula Gangri, peak, Bhutan 158 F13
Kulagino, Kaz. 154 E6
Kula Gulf, Solomon Is. 197 M16
Kulani, peak, Hawaii, U.S. 107 M21
Kulaura, Bangladesh 158 H13
Kul'chi, Russ. 141 J20
Kuldīga, Latv. 135 M15
Kule, Botswana 182 H8
Kulgera, N. Terr., Austral. 191 U8
Kulin, W. Austral., Austral. 191 X3
Kullorsuaq, Greenland, Den. 75 C20
Kulm, N. Dak., U.S. 98 H6
Kulob, Taj. 156 J8
Kuloy, river, Eur. 130 B11
Kulp, Turk. 149 G15
Kulu, Turk. 148 F8
Kulua, Puu, Hawaii, U.S. 107 M20
Kulumadau, P.N.G. 193 E21
Kulunda, Russ. 140 L11
Kuma, river, Eur. 130 G13
Kumagaya, Jap. 165 N12
Kumai, Indonesia 168 K10
Kumai, Teluk, Indonesia 168 K10
Kumamoto, Jap. 165 S4
Kumano, Jap. 165 R9
Kumano Nada, Jap. 165 R9
Kumara Junction, N.Z. 193 N17
Kumasi, Ghana 180 G10
Kumawa, Pegunungan, Indonesia 193 C14
Kumba, Cameroon 181 H15
Kumbakale, Solomon Is. 197 K15
Kumbakonam, India 159 R7
Kumbe, Indonesia 169 N21
Kume Shima, Jap. 165 Y1
Kŭmhwa, S. Korea 162 E13
Kumphawapi, Thai. 166 K10
Kŭmsan, S. Korea 162 G13
Kumta, India 159 P4
Kumul see Hami, China 160 F9
Kumzār, Oman 153 H15
Kunahandu, island, Maldives 159 W3
Kunashir, island, Russ. 141 K23
Kundapura (Coondapoor), India 159 P4
Kundar, river, Afghan.-Pak. 157 Q7
Kundian, Pak. 157 P9
Kundu, Solomon Is. 197 M15
Kunduz see Kondoz, Afghan. 156 K7
Kunene (Cunene), river, Namibia 182 F5
Kungsbacka, Sw. 134 M12
Kungurtug, Russ. 141 M14
Kunié see Île des Pins, island, New Caledonia, Fr. 198 E9
Kunlon, Myanmar 166 F7
Kunlun Shan, China 160 H4
Kunlun Shankou, China 160 J9
Kunming, China 160 N11
Kunnamkulam, India 159 R5
Kunsan, S. Korea 162 G13
Kunu, island, Chuuk, F.S.M. 197 B14
Kununurra, W. Austral., Austral. 191 Q6
Kuopio, Fin. 135 G16
Kupang, Indonesia 169 N14
Kupikipikio (Black Point), Hawaii, U.S. 106 F11
Kupino, Russ. 140 K11
Kupreanof Island, Alas., U.S. 105 K23
Kupupolo Heiau, Hawaii, U.S. 106 D10
Kup"yans'k, Ukr. 133 H17
Kuqa, China 160 F6
Kür (Kura), river, Azerb. 149 E22
Kura see Kür, river, Azerb. 149 E22

Kura Lowland, *Azerb.* **149** D21
Kūrān Dap, *Iran* **153** H17
Kurashassayskiy, *Kaz.* **154** D8
Kurashiki, *Jap.* **165** Q7
Kurayoshi, *Jap.* **165** P7
Kurbağa Gölü, *Turk.* **148** G10
Kurchatov, *Kaz.* **155** D16
Kürdämir, *Azerb.* **149** D22
Kur Dili, point, *Azerb.* **149** F23
Kurdistan, region, *Iran-Iraq* **152** B9
Kurdoğlu Burnu, *Turk.* **148** J4
Kurduna, *Pak.* **157** Q6
Kurduvadi, *India* **158** M4
Kŭrdzhali, *Bulg.* **137** H16
Küre, *Turk.* **148** C9
Kure, *Jap.* **165** Q6
Kure Atoll (Ocean Island), *Hawaii, U.S.* **106** K2
Kure Beach, *N.C., U.S.* **90** K12
Kuressaare, *Estonia* **135** L15
Kureyka, *Russ.* **141** G13
Kurgan, *Russ.* **140** J9
Kuria Muria Islands *see* Halaaniyaat, Juzor al, *Oman* **153** N15
Kuri Bay, *W. Austral., Austral.* **191** Q5
Kurikka, *Fin.* **135** H15
Kuril Basin, *Pac. Oc.* **218** D6
Kuril Islands *see* Kuril'skiye Ostrova, *Russ.* **141** K23
Kuril'sk, *Russ.* **141** J23
Kuril'skiye Ostrova (Kuril Islands), *Russ.* **141** K23
Kuril Trench, *Pac. Oc.* **218** E6
Kurio, *Jap.* **165** U4
Kurnool, *India* **159** N6
Kurobe, *Jap.* **165** N10
Kuroishi, *Jap.* **164** J13
Kuroiso, *Jap.* **165** N12
Kuro Shima, *Jap.* **165** U3
Kurshskiy Zaliv, *Lith.* **135** N15
Kursk, *Russ.* **140** F5
Kuršumlija, *Yug.* **137** G14
Kurşunlu, *Turk.* **148** D8
Kurtalan, *Turk.* **149** G16
Kurtistown, *Hawaii, U.S.* **107** M22
Kuru, river, *Sudan* **178** G11
Kuruçay, *Turk.* **149** E13
Kuruktag, *China* **160** F7
Kuruman, *S. Af.* **182** K9
Kurumdu, *Kyrg.* **156** F13
Kurume, *Jap.* **165** R4
Kurunegala, *Sri Lanka* **159** T7
Kurun Uryakh, *Russ.* **141** H19
Kuşadası, *Turk.* **148** G3
Kuşadasi Körfezi, *Turk.* **148** G3
Kusaie *see* Kosrae, island, *F.S.M.* **196** Q9
Kusakaki Guntō, *Jap.* **165** U3
Kus Gölü, *Turk.* **148** D4
Kushima, *Jap.* **165** T5
Kushimoto, *Jap.* **165** R9
Kushiro, *Jap.* **164** F15
Kushnīya, *Israel* **150** K6
Kushtia, *Bangladesh* **158** H12
Kuskokwim, river, *Alas., U.S.* **105** J13
Kuskokwim Bay, *Alas., U.S.* **104** K12
Kuskokwim Mountains, *Alas., U.S.* **105** H14
Kusŏng, *N. Korea* **162** D12
Kussharo Ko, *Jap.* **164** F15
Kut, Ko, *Thai.* **167** P10
Kütahya, *Turk.* **148** E5
K'ut'aisi, *Rep. of Georgia* **149** B17
Kutanibong, *Indonesia* **168** G4
Kutch, Gulf of, *India* **158** J1
Kutch, Rann of, *India-Pak.* **157** X8
Kutchan, *Jap.* **164** G13
Kutná Hora, *Czech Rep.* **132** H8
Kutno, *Pol.* **132** G10
Kutru, *India* **158** L7
Kutu, *Dem. Rep. of the Congo* **178** K8
Kutubdia, island, *Bangladesh* **158** J13
Kutum, *Sudan* **178** E10
Kutu-Puhi-Puhi, Pointe, *Gambier Is., Fr. Polynesia, Fr.* **199** Q20
Kuujjuaq, *Que., Can.* **77** K19
Kuujjuarapik, *Que., Can.* **77** L18
Kuŭm-ni, *N. Korea* **162** D13
Kuusamo, *Fin.* **135** E16
Kuvango, *Angola* **182** E6
Kuwaé *see* Tongoa, island, *Vanuatu* **198** E3
Kuwait, *Asia* **152** F11
Kuwait *see* Al Kuwayt, *Kuwait* **152** G11
Kuybyshev, *Russ.* **140** K11
Kuybyshev Reservoir, *Eur.* **130** D13
Kuybyshevskiy, *Kaz.* **154** C12
Kuybyshevskiy, *Taj.* **156** J7
Kuzey Anadolu Dağları, *Turk.* **148** C9
Kuznetsk, *Russ.* **140** H6
Kuzumaki, *Jap.* **164** K13
Kvænangen, bay, *Nor.* **135** C13
Kvaløy, island, *Nor.* **135** D13
Kvikkjokk, *Sw.* **135** E13
Kwa, river, *Dem. Rep. of the Congo* **178** L8
Kwadak, island, *Kwajalein Atoll, Marshall Is.* **196** M5
Kwailibesi, *Solomon Is.* **197** M19
Kwajalein, island, *Kwajalein Atoll, Marshall Is.* **196** N5
Kwajalein Atoll, *Marshall Is.* **196** G4
Kwajalein Lagoon, *Kwajalein Atoll, Marshall Is.* **196** L3
Kwale, *Kenya* **179** L15
Kwangju, *S. Korea* **162** G13
Kwango, river, *Af.* **174** L6
Kwanza, river, *Af.* **174** L6
Kwaos, *Indonesia* **169** K17
Kwekwe, *Zimb.* **182** G11
Kwenge, river, *Dem. Rep. of the Congo* **178** M8
Kwethluk, *Alas., U.S.* **104** J12
Kwigillingok, *Alas., U.S.* **104** K11
Kwilu, river, *Dem. Rep. of the Congo* **178** L8
Kwinana, *W. Austral., Austral.* **191** X2
Kwitaro, river, *Guyana* **121** F14
Kwoka, peak, *Indonesia* **169** J18
Kyaikkami, *Myanmar* **166** L7
Kyaikto, *Myanmar* **166** K6
Kyakhta, *Russ.* **141** M15
Kyaukkyi, *Myanmar* **166** J6
Kyaukme, *Myanmar* **166** G7
Kyaukphyu, *Myanmar* **166** J4
Kyauktaw, *Myanmar* **166** H4
Kybartai, *Lith.* **135** N16
Kyle, *Tex., U.S.* **97** Q10
Kyle, *Scot., U.K.* **138** D7
Kými, *Gr.* **137** K15
Kynuna, *Qnsld., Austral.* **191** S11
Kyōga Misaki, *Jap.* **165** P8
Kyŏngju, *S. Korea* **162** G14
Kyŏngsŏng, *N. Korea* **162** B14
Kyōto, *Jap.* **165** Q9
Kyparissía, *Gr.* **137** L14
Kyrgyz Range, *Kyrg.* **156** E10
Kyrgyzstan, *Asia* **156** E11
Kyshtovka, *Russ.* **140** K11
Ky Son, *Vietnam* **166** J11
Kythrea, *Cyprus* **148** L8
Kyubeyingde, *Russ.* **141** G16
Kyūroku Jima, *Jap.* **164** J12
Kyushe, *Kaz.* **154** G8
Kyushu, island, *Jap.* **165** S5
Kyushu-Palau Ridge, *Pac. Oc.* **218** H5
Kyustendil, *Bulg.* **137** H14
Kyyiv (Kiev), *Ukr.* **133** H14
Kyzyl, *Russ.* **141** L13
Kyzylkup, *Turkm.* **154** K6
Kyzyl-Kyya, *Kyrg.* **156** G10
Kyzyl-Ünkür, *Kyrg.* **156** F10

L

La Adela, *Arg.* **125** P10
Laascaanood, *Somalia* **179** G17
Laasqoray, *Somalia* **179** F18
Laau Point, *Hawaii, U.S.* **107** F13
Laayoune, *W. Sahara, Mor.* **176** D6
La Banda, *Arg.* **124** G10
La Barca, *Mex.* **108** H10
La Barge, *Wyo., U.S.* **100** J9
Labasa, *Fiji* **198** G7
Labé, *Guinea* **180** E6
La Belle, *Fla., U.S.* **91** V9
Labota, *Indonesia* **169** K14
Laboulaye, *Arg.* **124** L10
Labrador, *Nfld., Can.* **77** L21
Labrador City, *Nfld., Can.* **77** L20
Labrador Sea, *N. Amer.* **74** E10
Lábrea, *Braz.* **122** F7
Labuan, island, *Malaysia* **168** G11
Labuk Bay, *Malaysia* **168** F12
Labutta, *Myanmar* **166** L5
La Calera, *Chile* **124** K7
Laccadive Sea, *India* **159** Q3
Lac du Flambeau, *Wis., U.S.* **92** G5
La Ceiba, *Hond.* **109** K17
La Chaux-de-Fonds, *Switz.* **132** K4
Lachish, ruins, *Israel* **151** N5
Lachlan, river, *Austral.* **190** K12
Lachyn, *Azerb.* **149** E20
La Citadelle, *Haiti* **111** L16
Lackawanna, *N.Y., U.S.* **88** J5
Lac La Biche, *Alta., Can.* **76** L11
Lacon, *Ill., U.S.* **93** P5
Laconia, *N.H., U.S.* **89** H14
La Conner, *Wash., U.S.* **102** B4
Lacoochee, *Fla., U.S.* **91** T8
La Crosse, *Kans., U.S.* **99** T5
La Crosse, *Wash., U.S.* **102** D8
La Crosse, *Wis., U.S.* **92** K3
La Cruz, *C.R.* **109** M18
La Cruz, *Mex.* **108** F8
La Cygne, *Kans., U.S.* **99** T10
Ladakh, region, *China-India* **156** M14
Ladakh Range, *India* **156** M14
Ladd Seamount, *Hawaii, U.S.* **106** K2
La Désirade, island, *Guadeloupe, Fr.* **113** H17
La Digue, island, *Seychelles* **185** N21
Lâdik, *Turk.* **148** D11
Lādīz, *Iran* **153** G17
Ladnun, *India* **158** F4
Ladoga, Lake, *Eur.* **130** C9
La Dorada, *Col.* **120** E5
Ladozhskoye Ozero, *Russ.* **140** D7
Ladrillero, Golfo, *Chile* **125** V6
Ladron Peak, *N. Mex., U.S.* **101** T11
Lady Ann Strait, *Nunavut, Can.* **77** D16
Ladygin Yar, *Russ.* **141** F13
Ladysmith, *S. Af.* **182** K11
Ladysmith, *Wis., U.S.* **92** G3
Ladyzhenka, *Kaz.* **155** D13
Lae, *P.N.G.* **193** D19
Laea, *Indonesia* **169** L14
Lae Atoll, *Marshall Is.* **196** G3
Laem Ngop, *Thai.* **167** N10
La Esmeralda, *Venez.* **120** F10
Læsø, island, *Den.* **134** M11
La Esperanza, *Cuba* **110** G5
Lafayette, *Ala., U.S.* **95** K17
LaFayette, *Ga., U.S.* **90** J4
Lafayette, *Ind., U.S.* **93** Q8
Lafayette, *La., U.S.* **94** P8
Lafayette, *Tenn., U.S.* **95** E16
La Fe, *Cuba* **110** H4
La Fe, *Cuba* **110** H6
La Ferme, *Mauritius* **185** J20
La Flèche, *Fr.* **138** L9
La Foa, *New Caledonia, Fr.* **198** D8
La Follette, *Tenn., U.S.* **95** E18
Laga Bor, river, *Kenya* **179** J15
Lagan, river, *Sw.* **135** M13
Lagash (Telloh), ruins, *Iraq* **152** E10
Lagdo Reservoir, *Cameroon* **181** G17
Laghouat, *Alg.* **176** B11
Lago Argentino *see* El Calafate, *Arg.* **125** V7
Lagodekhi, *Rep. of Georgia* **149** C20
Lagos, *Port.* **139** S4
Lagos de Moreno, *Mex.* **108** H10
La Grande, *Oreg., U.S.* **102** F8
La Grange, *Ga., U.S.* **90** M4
La Grange, *Ky., U.S.* **95** B17
La Grange, *Mo., U.S.* **99** R13
La Grange, *N.C., U.S.* **90** H12
La Grange, *Tex., U.S.* **97** Q12
La Grange, *Wyo., U.S.* **100** J14
Lagrange, *Ind., U.S.* **93** N10
Lagrange, *W. Austral., Austral.* **191** R4
La Gran Sabana, *Venez.* **120** E12
La Grulla, *Tex., U.S.* **97** W9
La Guaira, *Venez.* **120** B9
Lagua Lichan, Puntan, *Saipan, N. Mariana Is., U.S.* **196** A6
Laguna, *N. Mex., U.S.* **101** S11
Laguna Beach, *Calif., U.S.* **103** Y9
Laguna Blanca, *Arg.* **124** F13
Laguna Dam, *Ariz.-Calif., U.S.* **101** U4
Laguna de Perlas, *Nicar.* **109** M19
Laguna Grande, *Arg.* **125** V8
Laguna Paiva, *Arg.* **124** J12
Lagunas, *Chile* **124** D7
Lagunas, *Peru* **122** E3
Lagunillas, *Bol.* **122** K8
Lagwira, *Mauritania* **176** F4
Laha, *China* **161** C16
La Habana (Havana), *Cuba* **110** G6
Lahad Datu, *Malaysia* **168** G12
Lahaina, *Hawaii, U.S.* **107** G15
Lahainaluna School, *Hawaii, U.S.* **107** G16
Laham, *Indonesia* **168** J11
La Harpe, *Ill., U.S.* **93** Q3
Lahat, *Indonesia* **168** K7
Lahıc, *Azerb.* **149** D22
Lahij, *Yemen* **152** R9
Lāhījān, *Iran* **152** B12
Lahi Passage, *Tongatapu, Tonga* **198** H11
Lahontan Reservoir, *Nev., U.S.* **103** P7
Lahore, *Pak.* **157** Q12
Lahri, *Pak.* **157** S7
Lahti, *Fin.* **135** J16
Laï (Behagle), *Chad* **177** K14
Laibin, *China* **163** R1
Lai Chau, *Vietnam* **166** G10
Laie, *Hawaii, U.S.* **106** D11
Laifeng, *China* **162** L2
Laïka, island, *Vanuatu* **198** E3
Laingsburg, *S. Af.* **182** M8
Laird, river, *N. Amer.* **74** E4
Laisamis, *Kenya* **179** J14
Laiwu, *China* **162** G7
Laiyang, *China* **162** F9
Laizhou Wan, *China* **162** E8
Lajamanu, *N. Terr., Austral.* **191** R7
La Jara, *Colo., U.S.* **101** P12
Lajes, *Braz.* **122** N12
Lajitas, *Tex., U.S.* **97** R2
La Junta, *Colo., U.S.* **101** P15
Lakatoro, *Vanuatu* **198** D2
Lakaträsk, *Sw.* **135** F14
Lake Andes, *S. Dak., U.S.* **98** M6
Lake Arthur, *La., U.S.* **94** P8
Lake Arthur, *N. Mex., U.S.* **101** U14
Lakeba, island, *Fiji* **198** J9
Lakeba Passage, *Fiji* **198** J9
Lake Butler, *Fla., U.S.* **91** R7
Lake Cargelligo, *N.S.W., Austral.* **191** X13
Lake Charles, *La., U.S.* **94** P7
Lake Chelan National Recreation Area, *Wash., U.S.* **102** B6
Lake City, *Colo., U.S.* **101** P11
Lake City, *Fla., U.S.* **91** R7
Lake City, *Iowa, U.S.* **99** N10
Lake City, *Mich., U.S.* **92** J10
Lake City, *Minn., U.S.* **98** K12
Lake City, *S.C., U.S.* **90** L10
Lake Clark National Park and Preserve, *Alas., U.S.* **105** J15
Lake Coleridge, *N.Z.* **193** P17
Lake Crystal, *Minn., U.S.* **98** L10
Lake Eyre Basin, *Austral.* **190** G10
Lakefield, *Minn., U.S.* **98** L10
Lake Geneva, *Wis., U.S.* **92** M6
Lake Grace, *W. Austral., Austral.* **191** X3
Lake Harbor, *Fla., U.S.* **91** V9
Lake Havasu City, *Ariz., U.S.* **101** S4
Lake Jackson, *Tex., U.S.* **97** S14
Lake King, *W. Austral., Austral.* **191** X4
Lakeland, *Fla., U.S.* **91** U8
Lakeland, *Ga., U.S.* **91** Q6
Lake Linden, *Mich., U.S.* **92** E6
Lake Louise, *Alta., Can.* **76** M10
Lake Mead National Recration Area, *Ariz.-Nev., U.S.* **101** R5
Lake Meredith National Recreation Area, *Tex., U.S.* **96** G5
Lake Mills, *Iowa, U.S.* **98** M11
Lake Murray, *P.N.G.* **193** D17
Lake Nash, *N. Terr., Austral.* **191** S10
Lake Oswego, *Oreg., U.S.* **102** F3
Lakepa, *Niue, N.Z.* **199** B21
Lake Placid, *N.Y., U.S.* **88** G11
Lakeport, *Calif., U.S.* **103** Q3
Lakeport, *Mich., U.S.* **92** L13
Lake Preston, *S. Dak., U.S.* **98** K7
Lake Providence, *La., U.S.* **94** K10
Lake Region, *Eur.* **130** C9
Lake Roosevelt National Recreation Area, *Wash., U.S.* **102** B8
Lakeside, *Nebr., U.S.* **99** N2
Lakeside, *Oreg., U.S.* **102** H2
Lake Stewart, *N.S.W., Austral.* **191** V11
Lakeview, *Mich., U.S.* **92** L10
Lakeview, *Oreg., U.S.* **102** K6
Lake Village, *Ark., U.S.* **94** J9
Lakeville, *Minn., U.S.* **98** K11
Lake Violet, *W. Austral., Austral.* **191** V4
Lake Wales, *Fla., U.S.* **91** U8
Lakewood, *Colo., U.S.* **100** M13
Lakewood, *N.J., U.S.* **88** P11
Lakewood, *Ohio, U.S.* **93** N14
Lake Worth, *Fla., U.S.* **91** W10
Lakhpat, *India* **158** H1
Lakin, *Kans., U.S.* **99** U3
Lakki, *Pak.* **157** P9
Lakonikós Kólpos, *Gr.* **137** M15
Lakota, *N. Dak., U.S.* **98** F7
Lakselv, *Nor.* **135** C14
Lakshadweep, islands, *India* **159** R2
La Laguna, *Canary Is., Sp.* **184** Q5
Lala Musa, *Pak.* **157** P11
La Leonesa, *Arg.* **124** G13
Lalibela, *Eth.* **179** F15
La Libertad, *Ecua.* **120** K1
La Libertad, *Guatemala* **109** K16
La Libertad, *Mex.* **108** C6
La Ligua, *Chile* **124** K7
La Línea, *Sp.* **139** T6
Lalitpur, *India* **158** H6
Lalitpur (Patan), *Nepal* **158** F10
Lalomanu, *Samoa* **198** L4
Lalona, island, *Ha'apai Group, Tonga* **198** R7
Laluai Point, *P.N.G.* **197** K14
La Madrid, *Arg.* **124** G9
Lamag, *Malaysia* **168** G12
La Malbaie, *Que., Can.* **77** N20
Lamap, *Vanuatu* **198** D2
Lamar, *Colo., U.S.* **101** N15
Lamar, *Mo., U.S.* **99** U11
La Marque, *Tex., U.S.* **97** R14
Lamas, *Peru* **122** F3
Lamas, *Turk.* **148** J9
Lambaréné, *Gabon* **181** L15
Lambert Glacier, *Antarctica* **207** F18
Lambert's Bay, *S. Af.* **182** L7
Lambertville, *Mich., U.S.* **93** N12
Lambton, Cape, *N.W.T., Can.* **76** D11
Lame Deer, *Mont., U.S.* **100** E11
La Mesa, *Calif., U.S.* **103** Z10
La Mesa, *N. Mex., U.S.* **101** V12
Lamesa, *Tex., U.S.* **96** L5
Lamía, *Gr.* **137** K14
Lamitan, *Philippines* **169** F14
Lamlam, Mount, *Guam, U.S.* **196** D10
Lamoille, *Nev., U.S.* **102** M11
Lamoni, *Iowa, U.S.* **99** Q11
Lamont, *Wyo., U.S.* **100** J11

La Montaña, S. Amer. 118 F3
Lamotrek Atoll, F.S.M. 196 Q5
LaMoure, N. Dak., U.S. 98 H7
Lampang, Thai. 166 J8
Lampasas, Tex., U.S. 97 P10
Lampedusa, island, It. 136 M9
Lamphun, Thai. 166 J8
Lampione, island, It. 136 M9
Lamu, Kenya 179 K15
Lamutskoye, Russ. 141 C20
Lanai, island, Hawaii, U.S. 107 G14
Lanai City, Hawaii, U.S. 107 G15
Lanaihale, peak, Hawaii, U.S. 107 G15
Lananibot, Puntan, Tinian, N. Mariana Is., U.S. 196 B7
La Nao, Cabo de, Sp. 139 R9
Lanbi Kyun, Myanmar 167 P7
Lancang, China 160 P10
Lancang (Mekong), river, China 160 P10
Lancaster, Calif., U.S. 103 W8
Lancaster, Mo., U.S. 99 Q12
Lancaster, N.H., U.S. 89 F14
Lancaster, Ohio, U.S. 93 R13
Lancaster, Pa., U.S. 88 P8
Lancaster, S.C., U.S. 90 J9
Lancaster, Tex., U.S. 96 L12
Lancaster, Wis., U.S. 92 L4
Lancaster Sound, N. Amer. 74 C7
Lance Creek, Wyo., U.S. 100 H13
Landay, Afghan. 157 R3
Lander, river, Austral. 190 E8
Lander, Wyo., U.S. 100 H10
Landing, Manihiki Atoll, Cook Is., N.Z. 199 B13
Land O'Lakes, Wis., U.S. 92 F5
Landor, W. Austral., Austral. 191 U2
Landrum, S.C., U.S. 90 J7
Landsborough Creek, Austral. 190 F12
Lands End, point, N.W.T., Can. 76 C12
Land's End, cape, Eng., U.K. 138 J6
Landshut, Ger. 132 J6
Landskrona, Sw. 134 N12
Lanett, Ala., U.S. 95 K17
Langanes, cape, Ice. 134 E4
Langao, China 162 J2
Langar, island, Pohnpei, F.S.M. 197 F14
Langdon, N. Dak., U.S. 98 E7
Langfang, China 162 D7
Langford, S. Dak., U.S. 98 J7
Langjökull, Ice. 134 F2
Langkawi, island, Malaysia 167 S8
Langlois, Oreg., U.S. 102 J1
Langøya, island, Nor. 134 D12
Langres, Fr. 138 K11
Langsa, Indonesia 168 G4
Lang Son, Vietnam 166 G12
Lang Suan, Thai. 167 Q8
Langting, India 158 G14
Langtry, Tex., U.S. 97 R5
Langu, Thai. 167 S8
Lankao, China 162 H5
Länkäran, Azerb. 149 F22
Lano, Wallis and Futuna, Fr. 198 B11
Lansdale, Pa., U.S. 88 P9
Lansdowne, W. Austral., Austral. 191 R6
Lansdowne House, Ont., Can. 77 M16
L'Anse, Mich., U.S. 92 F6
L'Anse aux Meadows, Nfld., Can. 77 L23
Lansing, Iowa, U.S. 98 L13
Lansing, Mich., U.S. 92 M11
Lanta Yai, Ko, Thai. 167 R8
Lanusei, It. 136 J8
Lanxian, China 162 E4
Lan Yü, Taiwan, China 163 S10
Lanzarote, island, Canary Is., Sp. 184 P7
Lanzhou, China 160 J11
Laoag, Philippines 169 B13
Lao Cai, Vietnam 166 G11
Laoha, river, China 161 F16
Laohekou, China 162 J3
Laojunguan see Yumen, China 160 G10
La Oliva, Canary Is., Sp. 184 Q8
Laona, Wis., U.S. 92 G6
Lao Re, Cu, Vietnam 166 L14
La Orotava, Canary Is., Sp. 184 Q5
La Oroya, Peru 122 H3
Laos, Asia 166 J11
Laoshan, China 162 G9
Lao Thu, Cu, Vietnam 167 P14
Laotougou, China 162 A14
Lapakahi State Historical Park, Hawaii, U.S. 107 K18
La Palma, island, Canary Is., Sp. 184 P3
La Palma, Pan. 109 N22
La Paloma, Uru. 124 L15
La Paragua, Venez. 120 D11
La Paz, Arg. 124 J12
La Paz, Arg. 124 L8
La Paz, Bol. 122 J6
La Paz, Mex. 108 F7
La Pedrera, Col. 120 J8
Lapeer, Mich., U.S. 92 L12
La Perouse Pinnacle, Hawaii, U.S. 106 M6
La Perouse Strait, Russ. 141 K22
La Pine, Oreg., U.S. 102 H5
Lapinlahti, Fin. 135 G16
Lapithos, Cyprus 148 K8
La Place, La., U.S. 94 Q10
La Plaine, Réunion, Fr. 185 G16
Lapland, region, Fin.-Sw. 135 F13
La Plant, S. Dak., U.S. 98 J4
La Plata, Arg. 124 L13
La Plata, Md., U.S. 90 D13
La Plata, Mo., U.S. 99 R12
La Porte, Tex., U.S. 97 R14
La Porte City, Iowa, U.S. 99 N13
La Possession, Réunion, Fr. 185 G15
Lappeenranta, Fin. 135 J17
La Pryor, Tex., U.S. 97 S8
Lâpseki, Turk. 148 D3
Laptev Sea, Russ. 141 D15
Lapthal, India 158 E7
Lapua, Fin. 135 H15
La Purísima, Mex. 108 E6
La Push, Wash., U.S. 102 B2
La Quiaca, Arg. 124 D9
L'Aquila, It. 136 H10
Lār, Iran 153 H14
Lara, Gabon 181 K16
Larache, Mor. 176 A8
Laramie, river, Wyo., U.S. 100 J12
Laramie, Wyo., U.S. 100 K13
Laramie Mountains, Wyo., U.S. 100 H12
Laramie Peak, U.S. 78 F9
Larantuka, Indonesia 169 M14
Larat, island, Indonesia 169 M18
Laredo, Tex., U.S. 97 U8
Largo, Fla., U.S. 91 U7
Largo, Cayo, Cuba 110 J7
Larimore, N. Dak., U.S. 98 F7
La Rioja, Arg. 124 H9
Lárissa, Gr. 137 K14
Larkana, Pak. 157 T7
Larnaka, Cyprus 148 L8
Larnaka Bay, Cyprus 148 L9
Larned, Kans., U.S. 99 T6
La Rochelle, Fr. 138 L8
La Roche-sur-Yon, Fr. 138 L8
La Roda, Sp. 139 R8
La Romana, Dom. Rep. 111 M20
La Ronge, Sask., Can. 76 L12
Larose, La., U.S. 94 Q10
Larrimah, N. Terr., Austral. 191 Q8
Lars Christensen Coast, Antarctica 207 F19
Larsen Bay, Alas., U.S. 105 M15
Larsen Ice Shelf, Antarctica 206 E5
La Rubia, Arg. 124 J11
Laruri, India 158 G15
Larvik, Nor. 134 L11
La Sal, Utah, U.S. 101 N9
La Salle, Ill., U.S. 93 P5
Lasan, Indonesia 168 H11
Las Animas, Colo., U.S. 101 N15
La Sarre, Que., Can. 77 N18
Lascahobas, Haiti 111 M17
Lascano, Uru. 124 L15
Lascelles, Vic., Austral. 191 Y11
La Scie, Nfld., Can. 77 L23
Las Cruces, N. Mex., U.S. 101 V12
Lasengmiao, China 162 D1
La Serena, Chile 124 J6
Las Flores, Arg. 124 M12
Lash-e Joveyn, Afghan. 157 P1
Las Heras, Arg. 124 K8
Las Heras, Arg. 125 T8
Lashio, Myanmar 166 G7
Lashkar, India 158 G6
Lashkar Gah, Afghan. 157 Q4
Lashkari Bazar, ruins, Afghan. 157 Q4
Lasia, island, Indonesia 168 H4
La Sila, peak, It. 136 K11
Las Lomitas, Arg. 124 F12
Las Martinas, Cuba 110 H4
Las Palmas, Canary Is., Sp. 184 Q6
La Spezia, It. 136 F8
Las Plumas, Arg. 125 R9
Lassen Peak, Calif., U.S. 103 N4
Lassen Volcanic National Park, Calif., U.S. 103 N5
Lassiter Coast, Antarctica 206 F7
Las Tablas, Pan. 109 P21
Las Toscas, Arg. 124 H13
Lastoursville, Gabon 181 L16
Lastovo, island, Croatia 136 H12
Las Tunas, Cuba 110 J12
Las Varillas, Arg. 124 K11
Las Vegas, N. Mex., U.S. 101 R13
Las Vegas, Nev., U.S. 103 U12
Lata, Samoa 198 K2
Latacunga, Ecua. 120 J3
Latady Island, Antarctica 206 G5
Latady Mountains, Antarctica 206 F7
Latakia see Al Lādhiqīyah, Syr. 150 F7
Lata Mountain, Manua Is., Amer. Samoa, U.S. 198 P4
Latehar, India 158 H9
Lathi see Sakao, island, Vanuatu 198 C2
Latina, It. 136 H10
La Tortuga, Isla, Venez. 120 B10
Latouche Treville, Cape, Austral. 190 D4
Latta, S.C., U.S. 90 K11
La Tuque, Que., Can. 77 P19
Latur, India 158 L5
Latvia, Eur. 135 M16
Lau Basin, Pac. Oc. 218 M10
Laucala, island, Fiji 198 G8
Laughlan Islands, P.N.G. 193 E22
Laughlin Peak, N. Mex., U.S. 101 Q14
Lau Group, islands, Fiji 198 H9
Lauhkaung, Myanmar 166 E7
Laula Katan, Puntan, Saipan, N. Mariana Is., U.S. 196 C5
Laulau, Bahia, Saipan, N. Mariana Is., U.S. 196 C5
Lauli'i, Samoa 198 L3
Lauliituai, Tutuila, Amer. Samoa, U.S. 198 M8
Launceston, Tas., Austral. 191 Z16
La Unión, Chile 125 Q6
La Unión, Peru 122 G3
La Unión, Sp. 139 S8
Laupahoehoe, Hawaii, U.S. 107 K21
Laura see Majuro, island, Marshall Is. 196 H10
Laura, Majuro Atoll, Marshall Is. 196 G10
Laura, Qnsld., Austral. 191 Q13
Laurel, Del., U.S. 90 D15
Laurel, Miss., U.S. 94 M12
Laurel, Mont., U.S. 100 E10
Laurel, Nebr., U.S. 99 N8
Laurens, Iowa, U.S. 98 M10
Laurens, S.C., U.S. 90 K8
Laurentian Fan, Atl. Oc. 216 G6
Laurentian Scarp, N. Amer. 74 H8
Laurentide Scarp, N. Amer. 74 H9
Lau Ridge, Pac. Oc. 218 N10
Laurie Island, Antarctica 206 A5
Laurinburg, N.C., U.S. 90 J11
Laurium, Mich., U.S. 92 E6
Laurot Islands see Laut Kecil, Kepulauan, Indonesia 168 M11
Lausanne, Switz. 132 K4
Laut, island, Indonesia 168 G8
Laut, island, Indonesia 168 K12
Lautaro, Volcán, Chile 125 V7
Laut Kecil, Kepulauan (Laurot Islands), Indonesia 168 M11
Lautoka, Fiji 198 H5
Lauvi Point, Solomon Is. 197 P19
Lava, Vanua, Vanuatu 198 B2
Lava Beds National Monument, Calif., U.S. 102 L4
Lavaca, river, Tex., U.S. 97 R12
Lavaca Bay, Tex., U.S. 97 S13
Lava Hot Springs, Idaho, U.S. 100 H7
Laval, Fr. 138 K8
Lāvān (Sheykh Sho'eyb), island, Iran 153 H13
L'Avedy, Cape, P.N.G. 197 J14
La Vega, Dom. Rep. 111 L18
La Venta, ruins, Mex. 109 K14
La Verkin, Utah, U.S. 101 P6
Laverne, Okla., U.S. 96 E7
Laverton, W. Austral., Austral. 191 V4
La Veta, Colo., U.S. 101 P13
Lavina, Mont., U.S. 100 D10
Lavonia, Ga., U.S. 90 K6
Lavrentiya, Russ. 141 A21
Lávrion, Gr. 137 L15
Lavruska, Vozvyshennost', Russ. 141 H15
Lawa, river, Fr. Guiana-Suriname 121 F17
Lawai, Hawaii, U.S. 106 C5
Lawdar, Yemen 152 Q10
Lawit, peak, Indonesia 168 H10
Lawqah, Saudi Arabia 152 F9
Lawra, Ghana 180 F10
Lawrence, Ind., U.S. 93 R9
Lawrence, Kans., U.S. 99 S10
Lawrence, Mass., U.S. 89 J14
Lawrenceburg, Ind., U.S. 93 S11
Lawrenceburg, Tenn., U.S. 95 G14
Lawrenceville, Ga., U.S. 90 L5
Lawrenceville, Ill., U.S. 93 T7
Lawrenceville, Va., U.S. 90 F12
Lawton, Okla., U.S. 96 H9
Lawz, Jabal al, Saudi Arabia 152 G5
Laylá, Saudi Arabia 152 L10
Laysan Island, Hawaii, U.S. 106 L4
Layshi, Myanmar 166 E5
Layton, Utah, U.S. 100 K7
Laytonville, Calif., U.S. 103 P2
Lázaro Cárdenas, Mex. 108 H10
Lazo, Russ. 141 F18
Leachville, Ark., U.S. 94 F11
Lead, S. Dak., U.S. 98 K1
Leadore, Idaho, U.S. 100 F6
Leadville, Colo., U.S. 100 M12
Leaf, river, Miss., U.S. 94 M12
Leakesville, Miss., U.S. 95 N13
Leakey, Tex., U.S. 97 R8
Leandro N. Alem, Arg. 124 G15
Learmonth, W. Austral., Austral. 191 T1
Leava see Sigavé, Wallis and Futuna, Fr. 198 E11
Leavenworth, Kans., U.S. 99 S10
Leavenworth, Wash., U.S. 102 C5
Łeba, Pol. 132 E9
Lebak, Philippines 169 F15
Lebanon, Asia 150 H6
Lebanon, mountains, Leb. 150 J6
Lebanon, Ind., U.S. 93 R9
Lebanon, Kans., U.S. 99 R6
Lebanon, Ky., U.S. 95 C17
Lebanon, Mo., U.S. 99 U12
Lebanon, N.H., U.S. 89 H13
Lebanon, Ohio, U.S. 93 S11
Lebanon, Oreg., U.S. 102 G3
Lebanon, Pa., U.S. 88 P8
Lebanon, Tenn., U.S. 95 E16
Lebap, Turkm. 154 K10
Lebec, Calif., U.S. 103 W7
Lebedyn, Ukr. 133 H16
Lebombo Mountains, Af. 174 P9
Le Borgne, Haiti 111 L16
Lębork, Pol. 132 E9
Lebu, Chile 125 N6
Lebyazh'e, Kaz. 155 C16
Le Cap, New Caledonia, Fr. 198 D7
Lecce, It. 136 J12
Lechang, China 163 Q4
Lecompte, La., U.S. 94 N8
Le Creusot, Fr. 138 L11
Ledong, China 163 U1
Lee, Nev., U.S. 103 N11
Leech Lake, Minn., U.S. 98 G10
Leedey, Okla., U.S. 96 F8
Leeds, Ala., U.S. 95 J15
Leeds, N. Dak., U.S. 98 E6
Leeds, Eng., U.K. 138 G8
Leeds, Utah, U.S. 101 P6
Leesburg, Fla., U.S. 91 T8
Leesburg, Va., U.S. 90 C12
Lees Summit, Mo., U.S. 99 S11
Leesville, La., U.S. 94 N7
Leeuwarden, Neth. 138 G11
Leeuwin, Cape, Austral. 190 L2
Leeward Islands, N. Amer. 74 N12
Lefka, Cyprus 148 L8
Lefkáda, island, Gr. 137 K13
Lefkáda, Gr. 137 K13
Lefkonoiko, Cyprus 148 K9
Lefkosia (Nicosia), Cyprus 148 L8
Lefroy, Lake, Austral. 190 J4
Legan, island, Kwajalein Atoll, Marshall Is. 196 M5
Legazpi, Philippines 169 D14
Leggett, Calif., U.S. 103 P2
Legionowo, Pol. 132 G10
Legnica, Pol. 132 H8
Legune, N. Terr., Austral. 191 Q7
Leh, India 156 M14
Le Havre, Fr. 138 J9
Lehr, N. Dak., U.S. 98 H6
Lehua, island, Hawaii, U.S. 106 B3
Lehua, Puu, Hawaii, U.S. 107 M19
Lehututu, Botswana 182 H8
Leiah, Pak. 157 Q9
Leicester, Eng., U.K. 138 G8
Leigh, N.Z. 193 J19
Leigh Creek, S. Austral., Austral. 191 W10
Leikanger, Nor. 134 K10
Leimatu'a, Vava'u Group, Tonga 198 L11
Leipzig, Ger. 132 G7
Leitchfield, Ky., U.S. 95 C16
Leiway, Myanmar 166 J6
Leiyang, China 163 P4
Leizhou Bandao (Luichow Peninsula), China 163 T1
Leizhou Wan, China 163 T2
Lekeleka, island, Ha'apai Group, Tonga 198 Q7
Lekitobi, Indonesia 169 K15
Leksula, Indonesia 169 K15
Le Lamentin, Martinique, Fr. 113 K17
Leland, Miss., U.S. 94 J10
Lele, Kosrae, F.S.M. 197 B19
Lele Harbor, Kosrae, F.S.M. 197 B19
Leleiwi Point, Hawaii, U.S. 107 M22
Lélépa, island, Vanuatu 198 F3
Leli, island, Solomon Is. 197 M20
Lelingluang, Indonesia 169 M17
Lelintah, Indonesia 169 K17
Lêliogat, Île, New Caledonia, Fr. 198 D9
Le Maire, Estrecho de, Arg. 125 Y10
Lemanmanu, P.N.G. 197 J13
Le Mans, Fr. 138 K9
Le Mars, Iowa, U.S. 98 M9
Lemei Rock, Wash., U.S. 102 E4
Lemesos (Limassol), Cyprus 148 L8
Lemhi, river, Idaho, U.S. 100 F6
Lemhi Range, Idaho, U.S. 100 F6
Lemieux Islands, Nunavut, Can. 77 G19
Lemitar, N. Mex., U.S. 101 T12
Lemmon, S. Dak., U.S. 98 H3
Lemmon, Mount, Ariz., U.S. 101 V8
Lemnos see Límnos, island, Gr. 137 J16
Lemoore, Calif., U.S. 103 U6

Lemotol, bay, Chuuk, F.S.M. 197 CI4
Lena, river, Russ. 141 EI6
Lena Tablemount, Southern Oc. 225 DI5
Lenger, Kaz. 155 JI3
Lenghu, China 160 G8
Lengua de Vaca Point, S. Amer. 118 L4
Lenin, Taj. 156 J7
Leningrad see Saint Petersburg, Russ. 140 D6
Leninogorsk, Kaz. 155 DI8
Lenin Peak, Kyrg.-Taj. 156 HIO
Leninsk, Kaz. 154 GIO
Leninsk Kuznetskiy, Russ. 140 KI2
Leninskoe, Kaz. 154 BII
Lennox, S. Dak., U.S. 98 M8
Lennox-King Glacier, Antarctica 207 LI3
Lenoir, N.C., U.S. 90 H8
Lenoir City, Tenn., U.S. 95 FI8
Lenora, Kans., U.S. 99 R5
Lenox, Iowa, U.S. 99 QIO
Lensk, Russ. 141 JI6
Lenya, Myanmar 167 P8
Léo, Burkina Faso 180 FIO
Leoben, Aust. 132 K8
Léogâne, Haiti III MI6
Leola, S. Dak., U.S. 98 J6
Leominster, Mass., U.S. 89 KI4
León, Mex. 108 HIO
León, Nicar. 109 MI7
León, Sp. 139 P6
Leon, river, Tex., U.S. 96 MIO
Leon, Iowa, U.S. 99 QII
Leonard, Tex., U.S. 96 KI2
Leone, Tutuila, Amer. Samoa, U.S. 198 M7
Leone Bay, Tutuila, Amer. Samoa, U.S. 198 M6
Leongatha, Vic., Austral. 191 ZI2
Leonora, W. Austral., Austral. 191 V4
Leopold and Astrid Coast, Antarctica 207 G2I
Leoti, Kans., U.S. 99 T3
Lepanto, Ark., U.S. 94 FII
Leping, China 162 M7
Le Port, Réunion, Fr. 185 GI5
Lepsi, Kaz. 155 FI7
Lepsinsk, Kaz. 155 GI8
Le Puy, Fr. 138 MII
Ler, Sudan 178 GI2
Léré, Chad 177 KI4
Lerida, Qnsld., Austral. 191 TI2
Lerik, Azerb. 149 F22
Lerma, river, N. Amer. 74 N5
Le Roy, N.Y., U.S. 88 J6
LeRoy, Kans., U.S. 99 T9
Lerwick, Scot., U.K. 138 B9
Lesbos see Lésvos, island, Gr. 137 KI6
Les Cayes, Haiti III MI5
Leshan, China 160 LII
Leskovac, Yug. 137 GI4
Leslie, Ark., U.S. 94 F8
Lesosibirsk, Russ. 141 KI3
Lesotho, Af. 182 LIO
Lesozavodsk, Russ. 141 L2I
Lesparre, Fr. 138 M8
L'Esperance Rock, Kermadec Is., N.Z. 194 M9
Les Sables-d'Olonne, Fr. 138 L8
Les Saintes, islands, Guadeloupe, Fr. 113 HI6
Lesser Antilles, islands, N. Amer. 74 NI2
Lesser Caucasus, Asia 149 CI7
Lesser Khingan Range, Asia 146 EI2
Lesser Slave Lake, Alta., Can. 76 KIO
Lesser Sunda Islands, Indonesia 168 MI2
Lesson, Point, Kosrae, F.S.M. 197 BI8
Le Sueur, Minn., U.S. 98 KII
Lésvos (Lesbos), island, Gr. 137 KI6
Leszno, Pol. 132 G8
Le Tampon, Réunion, Fr. 185 HI6
Lethbridge, Alta., Can. 76 NIO
Lethem, Guyana 121 FI4
Le Thuy, Vietnam 166 KI3
Leti, Kepulauan, Indonesia 169 MI6
Leticia, Col. 120 L8
Leting, China 162 D8
Letsôk-aw Kyun, Myanmar 167 P7
Leulumoega, Samoa 198 L3
Leuser, peak, Indonesia 168 G4
Leusoalii, Manua Is., Amer. Samoa, U.S. 198 P4
Levan, Utah, U.S. 100 M7
Levanger, Nor. 134 HII
Levant Coast, Asia 146 F3
Levelland, Tex., U.S. 96 K4
Leveque, Cape, Austral. 190 C4
Levin, N.Z. 193 MI9
Lévis, Que., Can. 77 P2O
Levittown, N.Y., U.S. 88 NII
Levittown, Pa., U.S. 88 PIO
Levu, Vanua, Fiji 198 G7
Levuka, Fiji 198 H7
Lewellen, Nebr., U.S. 99 P3
Lewes, Del., U.S. 90 CI5
Lewis, river, Wash., U.S. 102 E4
Lewis, Kans., U.S. 99 U5
Lewis, Butt of, Scot., U.K. 138 C7

Lewis, Isle of, Scot., U.K. 138 D7
Lewis and Clark Range, Mont., U.S. 100 C6
Lewisburg, Tenn., U.S. 95 FI5
Lewisburg, W. Va., U.S. 90 E9
Lewis Pass, N.Z. 193 NI7
Lewis Range, Austral. 190 E6
Lewis Smith Lake, Ala., U.S. 95 HI4
Lewiston, Idaho, U.S. 100 D3
Lewiston, Me., U.S. 89 GI6
Lewistown, Ill., U.S. 93 Q4
Lewistown, Mont., U.S. 100 C9
Lewistown, Pa., U.S. 88 N6
Lewisville, Ark., U.S. 94 J7
Lewisville Lake, Tex., U.S. 96 KII
Lexington, Ky., U.S. 95 BI8
Lexington, Miss., U.S. 94 KII
Lexington, Mo., U.S. 99 SII
Lexington, N.C., U.S. 90 HIO
Lexington, Nebr., U.S. 99 Q5
Lexington, Oreg., U.S. 102 F6
Lexington, Tenn., U.S. 95 FI3
Lexington, Va., U.S. 90 EIO
Lexington Park, Md., U.S. 90 DI4
Leydsdorp, S. Af. 182 HII
Leyte, island, Philippines 169 EI5
Leyte Gulf, Philippines 169 EI5
Lezhë, Alban. 137 HI3
L'gov, Russ. 140 F5
Lhasa, China 160 L8
Lhazê, China 160 L6
Lhokseumawe, Indonesia 168 G4
Li, river, China 162 M3
Lian, river, China 163 Q4
Liancheng, China 163 Q6
Liangbuaya, Indonesia 168 JI2
Liangcheng, China 162 C4
Liangping, China 162 KI
Lianjiang, China 163 P8
Lianjiang, China 163 S2
Lianping, China 163 Q5
Lianshan, China 163 Q3
Lianxian, China 163 Q3
Lianyun, China 162 H8
Lianyungang (Xinpu), China 162 H8
Liao, river, China 162 BII
Liaocheng, China 162 F6
Liaodong Bandao, China 162 DIO
Liaodong Wan, China 162 C9
Liaodun, China 160 F8
Liaoyang, China 162 CII
Liaoyuan, China 162 AI2
Liaozhong, China 162 CIO
Liaquatpur, Pak. 157 S9
Liard, river, N.W.T., Can. 76 HIO
Liari, Pak. 157 V5
Libby, Mont., U.S. 100 B4
Libenge, Dem. Rep. of the Congo 178 H8
Liberal, Kans., U.S. 99 V4
Liberec, Czech Rep. 132 H8
Liberia, Af. 180 H7
Liberia, C.R. 109 NI8
Libertador General San Martín, Arg. 124 EIO
Liberty, Mo., U.S. 99 SIO
Liberty, N.Y., U.S. 88 LIO
Liberty, S.C., U.S. 90 J7
Liberty, Tex., U.S. 97 QI4
Lib Island, Marshall Is. 196 G3
Libni, Gebel, Egypt 151 P3
Liboi, Kenya 179 KI5
Libreville, Gabon 181 KI5
Libya, Af. 177 DI3
Libyan Desert, Af. 174 E8
Libyan Plateau, Egypt-Lib. 177 CI6
Licantén, Chile 124 M6
Lice, Turk. 149 GI5
Lichinga, Mozambique 183 EI3
Lichuan, China 162 LI
Lichuan, China 163 N7
Licking, river, Ky., U.S. 95 BI9
Licking, Mo., U.S. 99 UI3
Licosa, Punta, It. 136 JII
Lida, Belarus 132 FI2
Lidgerwood, N. Dak., U.S. 98 H8
Lidköping, Sw. 134 LI2
Liechtenstein, Eur. 132 K5
Liège, Belg. 138 JII
Lieksa, Fin. 135 GI7
Liepāja, Latv. 135 MI5
Lifford, Ire. 138 F6
Lifou, Île (Lifu), New Caledonia, Fr. 198 C9
Lifu see Lifou, Île, island, New Caledonia, Fr. 198 C9
Lifuka, island, Ha'apai Group, Tonga 198 P7
Ligurian Sea, It. 136 G8
Liha Point, Niue, N.Z. 199 B2I
Lihir, island, P.N.G. 193 C2I
Lihir Group, P.N.G. 193 B2I
Lihue, Hawaii, U.S. 106 B6
Lijeron, island, Jaluit Atoll, Marshall Is. 196 L7
Lijiang, China 160 MIO

Likasi, Dem. Rep. of the Congo 178 NII
Likiep Atoll, Marshall Is. 196 G4
Likoma Island, Malawi 183 DI3
Liku, Niue, N.Z. 199 B2I
Likuone Bay, Vava'u Group, Tonga 198 LI2
Likupang, Indonesia 169 HI5
Lilbourn, Mo., U.S. 99 VI6
Lilian Point, Banaba, Kiribati 197 E2O
Liling, China 163 N4
Lille, Fr. 138 JIO
Lillehammer, Nor. 134 KII
Lillesand, Nor. 134 MIO
Lillie Glacier, Antarctica 207 QI4
Lillongwe, Malawi 182 EI2
Lilo Viejo, Arg. 124 GII
Lima, Mont., U.S. 100 F7
Lima, Ohio, U.S. 93 QII
Lima, Peru 122 H3
Lima Reservoir, Mont., U.S. 100 F7
Limari, Rio, Chile 124 J6
Limassol see Lemesos, Cyprus 148 L8
Limay, river, S. Amer. 118 N4
Limbdi, India 158 J3
Limbe, Haiti III LI6
Limbe, Cameroon 181 JI5
Limeira, Braz. 123 MI3
Limerick, Ire. 138 G5
Limestone, Me., U.S. 89 BI8
Limfjorden, bay, Den. 134 NII
Liminka, Fin. 135 FI5
Limmen Bight, Austral. 190 B9
Limnos (Lemnos), island, Gr. 137 JI6
Limoges, Fr. 138 M9
Limon, Colo., U.S. 100 MI4
Limon, Mount, Mauritius 185 J2O
Limoux, Fr. 139 PIO
Limpopo, river, Mozambique 182 HI2
Limu, island, Ha'apai Group, Tonga 198 Q7
Limufuafua Point, Niue, N.Z. 199 C2O
Līnah, Saudi Arabia 152 G9
Lin'an, China 162 L9
Linapacan, island, Philippines 169 DI3
Linares, Chile 124 M7
Linares, Mex. 108 FII
Linares, Sp. 139 S7
Lincang, China 160 PIO
Linchuan, China 163 N6
Lincoln, Arg. 124 LII
Lincoln, Calif., U.S. 103 Q5
Lincoln, Ill., U.S. 93 R5
Lincoln, Kans., U.S. 99 S7
Lincoln, Me., U.S. 89 DI8
Lincoln, Mich., U.S. 92 JI2
Lincoln, N. Mex., U.S. 101 UI3
Lincoln, N.H., U.S. 89 GI4
Lincoln, Nebr., U.S. 99 Q8
Lincoln City, Oreg., U.S. 102 F2
Lincoln Island, Paracel Is. 168 BIO
Lincoln Park, Colo., U.S. 101 NI3
Lincoln Park, Mich., U.S. 92 MI2
Lincoln Sea, N. Amer. 74 A7
Lincolnton, Ga., U.S. 90 L7
Lincolnton, N.C., U.S. 90 H8
Lind, Wash., U.S. 102 D8
Linda Downs, Qnsld., Austral. 191 TIO
Lindale, Ga., U.S. 90 K4
Lindale, Tex., U.S. 96 LI3
Linden, Ala., U.S. 95 LI4
Linden, Guyana 121 EI4
Linden, Tex., U.S. 96 KI5
Lindesnes, cape, Nor. 134 MIO
Lindi, Tanzania 179 NI5
Lindsay, Calif., U.S. 103 U7
Lindsay, Mont., U.S. 100 CI3
Lindsay, Okla., U.S. 96 HIO
Lindsborg, Kans., U.S. 99 T7
Line Islands, Pac. Oc. 194 GI2
Linfen, China 162 F4
Lingao, China 163 TI
Lingbao, China 162 H3
Lingbi, China 162 J7
Lingchuan, China 163 P2
Lingga, island, Indonesia 168 J7
Lingga, Kepulauan, Indonesia 168 J7
Lingle, Wyo., U.S. 100 JI4
Lingqiu, China 161 GI4
Lingshan, China 163 SI
Lingshui, China 163 VI
Lingtai, China 162 GI
Linguère, Senegal 176 G5
Lingui, China 163 Q2
Lingxian, China 163 P4
Lingyuan, China 162 C8
Linhai (Taizhou), China 162 MIO
Linhares, Braz. 123 LI6
Linhe, China 160 GI2
Linhe, China 162 CI
Linjiang, China 162 BI3
Linköping, Sw. 135 LI3

Linn, Tex., U.S. 97 VIO
Linosa, island, It. 136 M9
Linqing, China 162 F6
Linquan, China 162 J6
Linru, China 162 H4
Lintao, China 160 JII
Linton, Ind., U.S. 93 S8
Linton, N. Dak., U.S. 98 H5
Lintong, China 162 H2
Linxi, China 162 A8
Linxi, China 162 D8
Linxian, China 162 E3
Linyi, China 162 F7
Linyi, China 162 G8
Linz, Aust. 132 K7
Lio Matoh, Malaysia 168 HII
Lion, Golfe du, Fr. 139 NII
Lions Den, Zimb. 182 FII
Liot Point, N.W.T., Can. 76 DI2
Liouesso, Congo 181 KI7
Lipa, Philippines 169 CI3
Lipari, Isole, It. 136 KIO
Lipetsk, Russ. 140 G5
Liping, China 163 PI
Lipno, Pol. 132 GIO
Lipoa Point, Hawaii, U.S. 107 FI6
Lipscomb, Tex., U.S. 96 F7
Lipu, China 163 Q2
Lipu Lekh Pass, China-India 160 K4
Līsakovsk, Kaz. 154 CIO
Lisala, Dem. Rep. of the Congo 178 J9
Lisboa (Lisbon), Port. 139 R4
Lisbon, N. Dak., U.S. 98 H7
Lisbon Falls, Me., U.S. 89 GI6
Lisburne, Cape, Alas., U.S. 104 CII
Lishu, China 162 AII
Lishui, China 162 M9
Lisianski Island, Hawaii, U.S. 106 L3
Lismore, N.S.W., Austral. 191 WI5
Lister, Mount, Antarctica 207 NI4
Listowel Downs, Qnsld., Austral. 191 UI3
Litang, river, China 160 MIO
Litang, China 160 LIO
Litang, China 163 RI
Lītāni, river, Leb. 150 K6
Litani, river, Fr. Guiana-Suriname 121 FI7
Litchfield, Ill., U.S. 93 S5
Litchfield, Minn., U.S. 98 JIO
Lithgow, N.S.W., Austral. 191 XI4
Lithuania, Eur. 135 NI6
Little, river, La., U.S. 94 M8
Little, river, Okla., U.S. 96 JI4
Little, river, Tex., U.S. 97 PII
Little Abaco Island, Bahamas IIO CII
Little Andaman, island, Andaman Is., India 159 RI4
Little Barrier Island, N.Z. 193 JI9
Little Belt Mountains, Mont., U.S. 100 D8
Little Bighorn, river, Mont., U.S. 100 FII
Little Bighorn Battlefield National Monument, Mont., U.S. 100 EII
Little Bitter Lake see Murrat el Sughra, Buheirat, Egypt 151 QI
Little Blue, river, Nebr., U.S. 99 R7
Little Cayman, island, Cayman Is., U.K. IIO L8
Little Chute, Wis., U.S. 92 J6
Little Coco Island, Myanmar 166 M4
Little Exuma, island, Bahamas III GI3
Little Falls, Minn., U.S. 98 HIO
Little Falls, N.Y., U.S. 88 JIO
Littlefield, Ariz., U.S. 101 Q5
Littlefield, Tex., U.S. 96 J4
Little Fork, river, Minn., U.S. 98 EII
Littlefork, Minn., U.S. 98 EII
Little Inagua Island, Bahamas III JI6
Little Lost, river, Idaho, U.S. 100 G6
Little Marais, Minn., U.S. 98 FI3
Little Mecatina, river, Nfld.-Que., Can. 77 L22
Little Missouri, river, S. Dak., U.S. 98 JI
Little Nicobar, island, Nicobar Is., India 159 TI5
Little Powder, river, Mont., U.S. 100 FI3
Little Red, river, Ark., U.S. 94 F8
Little Rock, Ark., U.S. 94 G8
Little Salt Lake, Utah, U.S. 101 P6
Little San Salvador, island, Bahamas III EI3
Little Sioux, river, Iowa, U.S. 99 N9
Little Snake, river, Colo., U.S. 100 LIO
Little Suamico, Wis., U.S. 92 J7
Littleton, Colo., U.S. 100 MI3
Littleton, N.H., U.S. 89 GI4
Little Wabash, river, Ill., U.S. 93 S6
Liucheng, China 163 QI
Liuhe, China 161 EI7
Liuhe, China 162 BI2
Liuyang, China 163 N4
Liuzhai, China 160 NI2
Liuzhou, China 163 QI
Līvāni, Latv. 135 MI7
Live Oak, Fla., U.S. 91 R6
Livermore, Calif., U.S. 103 S4
Livermore, Ky., U.S. 95 CI5
Livermore, Mount, Tex., U.S. 97 PI

Liverpool, N.S., Can. 77 P22
Liverpool, Eng., U.K. 138 G8
Liverpool Bay, N.W.T., Can. 76 DIO
Liverpool Range, Austral. 190 KI4
Livingston, Ala., U.S. 95 LI3
Livingston, Mont., U.S. 100 E8
Livingston, Tenn., U.S. 95 EI7
Livingston, Tex., U.S. 97 PI4
Livingston, Guatemala 109 KI6
Livingston, Lake, Tex., U.S. 97 PI4
Livingstone, Zambia 182 FIO
Livingstone Island, Antarctica 206 D3
Livno, Bosn. and Herzg. 136 GI2
Livonia, Mich., U.S. 92 MI2
Livorno, It. 136 G8
Līwā, region, U.A.E. 153 KI4
Liwale, Tanzania 179 NI4
Liwonde, Malawi 183 EI3
Lixian, China 162 L3
Li Yubu, Sudan 178 HII
Ljubljana, Slov. 136 EII
Ljusdal, Sw. 135 JI3
Llaima Volcano, S. Amer. 118 N4
Llamara, Salar de, Chile 124 D7
Llanes, Sp. 139 N7
Llano, river, Tex., U.S. 97 P8
Llano, Tex., U.S. 97 P9
Llanos, region, S. Amer. 118 B4
Llanquihue, Lago, Chile 125 Q6
Lleida, Sp. 139 P9
Llica, Bol. 122 L6
Lliria, Sp. 139 R9
Llivia, Sp. 139 PIO
Lloydminster, Alta.-Sask., Can. 76 LII
Ló, Ponta do, São Tomé and Príncipe 185 D2O
Lo, river, Vietnam 166 GII
Loa, river, Chile 124 D7
Loa, Utah, U.S. 101 N7
Loaita Island, Spratly Is. 168 EII
Loaloa Heiau, Hawaii, U.S. 107 HI7
Lobatse, Botswana 182 JIO
Lobaya, river, Af. 174 J6
Lobería, Arg. 125 NI3
Lobería, Arg. 125 QIO
Lobikaere, island, Majuro Atoll, Marshall Is. 196 GII
Lobito, Angola 182 D5
Lobitos, Peru 122 EI
Lobo, Indonesia 169 KI9
Lobos, Arg. 124 MI3
Lobos, Cay, Cuba 110 HII
Lobos Islands, S. Amer. 118 EI
Lobuya, Russ. 141 DI9
Lochsa, river, Idaho, U.S. 100 D4
Lockesburg, Ark., U.S. 94 H6
Lockhart, Tex., U.S. 97 QIO
Lockhart River, Qnsld., Austral. 191 PI2
Lock Haven, Pa., U.S. 88 M6
Lockney, Tex., U.S. 96 J5
Lockport, N.Y., U.S. 88 J5
Lockwood Terrace, Guam, U.S. 196 CIO
Lod (Lydda), Israel 150 M5
Lodge Creek, Mont., U.S. 100 A9
Lodge Grass, Mont., U.S. 100 EII
Lodgepole, Nebr., U.S. 99 P2
Lodgepole Creek, Nebr., U.S. 99 PI
Lodhran, Pak. 157 SIO
Lodi, Calif., U.S. 103 R5
Lodja, Dem. Rep. of the Congo 178 LIO
Lodwar, Kenya 179 JI4
Łódź, Pol. 132 GIO
Loei, Thai. 166 K9
Lofanga, island, Ha'apai Group, Tonga 198 P7
Lofoten, islands, Nor. 134 EII
Lofty Range, Austral. 190 G3
Logan, Iowa, U.S. 99 P9
Logan, Kans., U.S. 99 R5
Logan, N. Mex., U.S. 101 RI5
Logan, Ohio, U.S. 93 R2
Logan, Utah, U.S. 100 J7
Logan, W. Va., U.S. 90 E8
Logan, Mount, Wash., U.S. 102 A5
Logan, Mount, Yukon Terr., Can. 76 F7
Logansport, Ind., U.S. 93 Q9
Logansport, La., U.S. 94 L6
Logashkino, Russ. 141 DI8
Logone, river, Af. 174 H6
Logoniégué, Burkina Faso 180 F9
Logroño, Sp. 139 P8
Loh, island, Vanuatu 198 AI
Lohardaga, India 158 JIO
Loharghat, India 158 GI3
Lohatlha, S. Af. 182 K9
Lohne, Ger. 132 F5
Loi, island, Kwajalein Atoll, Marshall Is. 196 N5
Loi Mwe, Myanmar 166 H8
Loir, river, Fr. 138 K9
Loire, river, Fr. 138 L8
Loja, Ecua. 120 L3
Loji, Indonesia 169 KI6
Lojjairok, island, Kwajalein Atoll, Marshall Is. 196 N5

Lojwa, island, Enewetak Atoll, Marshall Is. 196 G8
Lokhwabe, Botswana 182 J8
Lokitaung, Kenya 179 HI4
Lokoja, Nig. 181 GI4
Lokolama, Dem. Rep. of the Congo 178 K9
Lokomo, Cameroon 181 JI7
Lokoro, river, Dem. Rep. of the Congo 178 K9
Loks Land, island, Nunavut, Can. 77 H2O
Lokuru, Solomon Is. 197 MI6
Lol, river, Sudan 178 GII
Lolland, island, Den. 134 PI2
Lolo Pass, Idaho, U.S. 100 D5
Lolowaï, Vanuatu 198 C2
Lom, Bulg. 135 GI5
Lom, Nor. 134 JIO
Lomaloma, Fiji 198 H9
Lomami, river, Dem. Rep. of the Congo 178 KIO
Loma Mountains, Af. 174 H2
Lomawai, Fiji 198 J5
Lombadina, W. Austral., Austral. 191 R4
Lomblen, island, Indonesia 169 MI4
Lombok, island, Indonesia 168 MI2
Lombok, Selat, Indonesia 168 MII
Lomé, Togo 180 HII
Lomela, river, Dem. Rep. of the Congo 178 K9
Lomela, Dem. Rep. of the Congo 178 KIO
Lometa, Tex., U.S. 97 N9
Lomié, Cameroon 181 JI7
Lomlom, island, Santa Cruz Is., Solomon Is. 197 P23
Lomonosov Ridge, Arctic Oc. 222 F8
Lomphat, Cambodia 166 MI3
Lompoc, Calif., U.S. 103 W5
Łomża, Pol. 132 FII
Lon, Hon, Vietnam 167 NI4
Lonauli, India 158 L3
Loncoche, Chile 125 P6
Loncopué, Arg. 125 N7
London, Kiritimati, Kiribati 197 B22
London, Ky., U.S. 95 DI8
London, Ohio, U.S. 93 RI2
London, Ont., Can. 77 RI8
London, Eng., U.K. 138 H9
Londonderry (Derry), N. Ire., U.K. 138 F6
Londonderry, Cape, Austral. 190 B6
Londonderry, Isla, Chile 125 Y8
Londrina, Braz. 122 MI2
Lone Pine, Calif., U.S. 103 T8
Lonerock, Oreg., U.S. 102 F6
Longa, river, Angola 182 D6
Long Beach, Calif., U.S. 103 X8
Long Beach, Miss., U.S. 94 PI2
Long Beach, N.C., U.S. 90 KI2
Long Beach, Wash., U.S. 102 D2
Longboat Key, Fla., U.S. 91 V7
Long Branch, N.J., U.S. 88 PII
Long Cay (Fortune I.), Bahamas 111 HI4
Longchuan, China 163 R5
Long Creek, Oreg., U.S. 102 G7
Longford, Ire. 138 F6
Longglat, Indonesia 168 HI2
Longhai, China 163 R7
Longhua, China 162 C7
Longido, Tanzania 179 LI4
Longiram, Indonesia 168 JII
Long Island, Bahamas 111 GI4
Long Island, N.Y., U.S. 88 NI2
Long Island, Nunavut, Can. 77 LI7
Long Island, P.N.G. 193 CI9
Long Island Sound, N.Y., U.S. 89 MI3
Longjiang, China 161 CI6
Longju, India 158 EI4
Long Key, Fla., U.S. 91 YIO
Longkou, China 162 E9
Longlac, Ont., Can. 77 NI6
Long Lake, N. Dak., U.S. 98 G5
Longmen, China 163 R5
Longmont, Colo., U.S. 100 LI3
Longnan, China 163 Q5
Longnawan, Indonesia 168 HII
Longomapu, Vava'u Group, Tonga 198 LII
Long Pine, Nebr., U.S. 99 N5
Long Prairie, Minn., U.S. 98 HIO
Longquan, China 163 N8
Long Range Mountains, N. Amer. 74 GIO
Longreach, Qnsld., Austral. 191 TI2
Longshan, China 162 L2
Longsheng, China 163 P2
Longs Peak, Colo., U.S. 100 LI3
Longton, Qnsld., Austral. 191 SI3
Longview, Tex., U.S. 96 LI4
Longview, Wash., U.S. 102 E3
Longville, La., U.S. 94 P7
Longxi, China 160 JI2
Long Xuyen, Vietnam 167 PI2
Longyan, China 163 Q7
Long'yugan, Russ. 140 GII
Lonoke, Ark., U.S. 94 G9
Lonquimay, Chile 125 N7
Loogootee, Ind., U.S. 93 T8
Lookout, Cape, N.C., U.S. 90 JI4

Lookout, Cape, Oreg., U.S. 102 F2
Lookout, Point, Austral. 190 HI5
Lookout Mountain, N. Mex., U.S. 101 SIO
Lookout Mountain, Tenn., U.S. 95 GI7
Lookout Ridge, Alas., U.S. 105 CI3
Loongana, W. Austral., Austral. 191 W6
Loop Head, Ire. 138 G5
Lop, China 160 G5
Lopatka, Mys, Russ. 141 G23
Lopévi (Ulvéah), island, Vanuatu 198 E3
Lopez, Cap, Gabon 181 LI4
Lopez Point, Calif., U.S. 103 U4
Lop Nur, China 160 G8
Lopphavet, bay, Nor. 135 CI3
Lora, Hamun-i-, Pak. 157 S4
Lorain, Ohio, U.S. 93 PI4
Loraine, Tex., U.S. 96 M6
Loralai, Pak. 157 R7
Lorca, Sp. 139 S8
Lord Howe Atoll see Ontong Java Atoll, Solomon Is. 197 JI8
Lord Howe Island, Coral Sea 194 M6
Lord Howe Island see Tomotu Noi, Santa Cruz Is., Solomon Is. 197 Q22
Lord Howe Rise, Pac. Oc. 218 M8
Lord of the Sky see Khan Tängiri, peak, China-Kyrg. 156 EI5
Lordsburg, N. Mex., U.S. 101 VIO
Lorenzo, Tex., U.S. 96 K5
Loreto, Bol. 122 J7
Loreto, Braz. 123 FI4
Loreto, Mex. 108 E6
Loretto, Tenn., U.S. 95 GI4
Lorian Swamp, Af. 174 JIO
Lorica, Col. 120 C4
Lorient, Fr. 138 K7
Lorimers, Turks and Caicos Is., U.K. 111 HI7
Loris, S.C., U.S. 90 KII
Lormi, India 158 J8
Lorne, Qnsld., Austral. 191 UI3
Los Andes, Chile 124 K7
Los Blancos, Arg. 124 EII
Los Cerrillos, Arg. 124 K9
Los Lagos, Chile 125 P6
Los Loros, Chile 124 G7
Los Alamos, N. Mex., U.S. 101 RI2
Los Ángeles, Chile 125 N6
Los Angeles, Calif., U.S. 103 X8
Los Angeles Aqueduct, Calif., U.S. 103 V8
Los Banos, Calif., U.S. 103 T5
Los Gatos, Calif., U.S. 103 S4
Lošinj, island, Croatia 136 FIO
Los Llanos, Canary Is., Sp. 184 Q4
Los Lunas, N. Mex., U.S. 101 SI2
Los Mochis, Mex. 108 E7
Los Ojos, N. Mex., U.S. 101 QI2
Los Olmos Creek, Tex., U.S. 97 UIO
Los Osos, Calif., U.S. 103 V5
Los Palacios, Cuba 110 G5
Lospalos, E. Timor 169 MI6
Los Roques, Islas, Venez. 120 AIO
Los Teques, Venez. 120 B9
Lostine, Oreg., U.S. 102 F9
Lost River Range, Idaho, U.S. 100 G6
Lost Trail Pass, Idaho-Mont., U.S. 100 E5
Losuia, P.N.G. 193 E2I
Los Vilos, Chile 124 K6
Lot, Pohnpei, F.S.M. 197 GI4
Lota, Chile 125 N6
Lotagipi Swamp, Kenya 179 HI4
Lot Harbor, Pohnpei, F.S.M. 197 GI4
Lotofaga, Samoa 198 L3
Lot's Wife see Sōfu Gan, island, Jap. 194 C3
Lott, Tex., U.S. 97 NII
Lottin, Port, Kosrae, F.S.M. 197 BI8
Lou, island, P.N.G. 193 BI9
Louang-Namtha, Laos 166 H9
Louangphrabang, Laos 166 JIO
Loubomo, Congo 181 MI6
Loudonville, Ohio, U.S. 93 QI4
Loufan, China 162 E4
Louga, Senegal 176 G4
Lougheed Island, Nunavut, Can. 77 CI4
Louisa, Ky., U.S. 95 B2O
Louisburg, N.C., U.S. 90 GI2
Louisiade Archipelago, P.N.G. 193 E22
Louisiana, U.S. 94 L7
Louisiana, Mo., U.S. 99 SI4
Louisiana Point, La., U.S. 94 Q6
Louis Trichardt, S. Af. 182 HII
Louisville, Ga., U.S. 90 M7
Louisville, Ky., U.S. 95 BI6
Louisville, Miss., U.S. 94 KI2
Louisville, Nebr., U.S. 99 Q9
Louisville Ridge, Pac. Oc. 218 NIO
Louis-XIV, Point, Que., Can. 77 LI7
Louj, island, Enewetak Atoll, Marshall Is. 196 G8
Loukouo, Congo 181 MI7
Loulan Yiji, ruins, China 160 G8
Loup, river, Nebr., U.S. 99 P7
Loup City, Nebr., U.S. 99 P6

Lourdes, Fr. 139 N9
Lourdes-de-Blanc-Sablon, Que., Can. 77 L22
Louth, N.S.W., Austral. 191 WI2
Louxiao Shan, China 163 N4
Lovea, Cambodia 167 NIO
Loveland, Colo., U.S. 100 LI3
Loveland Pass, Colo., U.S. 100 MI2
Lovell, Wyo., U.S. 100 FIO
Lovelock, Nev., U.S. 103 N8
Loving, N. Mex., U.S. 101 VI4
Lovington, N. Mex., U.S. 101 UI5
Low, Cape, Nunavut, Can. 77 HI6
Lowell, Mass., U.S. 89 KI4
Lowell, Oreg., U.S. 102 H3
Lowell, Lake, Idaho, U.S. 100 G3
Lower Goose Creek Reservoir, Idaho, U.S. 100 J5
Lower Guinea, Af. 174 L6
Lower Hutt, N.Z. 193 MI9
Lower Lake, Calif., U.S. 102 M6
Lower Matecumbe Key, Fla., U.S. 91 YIO
Lower Paia, Hawaii, U.S. 107 GI7
Lower Peninsula, U.S. 79 EI6
Lower Post, B.C., Can. 76 H9
Lower Red Lake, Minn., U.S. 98 FIO
Lower Tunguska, river, Asia 146 DIO
Lowestoft, Eng., U.K. 138 G9
Lowital, Vanuatu 198 H4
Lowkhi, Afghan. 157 Q2
Lowville, N.Y., U.S. 88 H9
Loyalty Islands see Loyauté, Îles, New Caledonia, Fr. 198 D8
Loyauté, Îles (Loyalty Islands), New Caledonia, Fr. 198 D8
Loyola, Punta, Arg. 125 W9
Loznica, Yug. 137 FI3
Lozova, Ukr. 133 JI7
Luahiwa Petroglyphs, Hawaii, U.S. 107 GI5
Luahoko, island, Ha'apai Group, Tonga 198 P7
Luama, river, Dem. Rep. of the Congo 178 LII
Luamotu, island, Funafuti, Tuvalu 197 L23
Luan, river, China 162 C7
Lu'an, China 162 K6
Luanda, Angola 182 D8
Luang, Thale, Thai. 167 R8
Luang Prabang Range, Laos 166 K9
Luangwa, river, Zambia 182 EI2
Luangwa, Zambia 182 EII
Luaniua, island, Solomon Is. 197 JI8
Luaniva, island, Wallis and Futuna, Fr. 198 BI2
Luanping, China 162 C7
Luanshya, Zambia 182 DII
Luanxian, China 162 D8
Luapula, river, Af. 174 M8
Luarca, Sp. 139 N6
Luatefito, island, Vava'u Group, Tonga 198 MII
Luau, Angola 182 D8
Luba, Bioko, Eq. Guinea 184 M7
Lubang Island, Philippines 169 CI3
Lubango, Angola 182 E5
Lubao, Dem. Rep. of the Congo 178 LII
Lubbock, Tex., U.S. 96 K5
Lubec, Me., U.S. 89 EI9
Lübeck, Ger. 132 F6
Lubero, Dem. Rep. of the Congo 178 KI2
Lubin, Pol. 132 H8
Lublin, Pol. 132 HII
Lubny, Ukr. 133 HI5
Lubok Antu, Malaysia 168 HIO
Lubuagan, Philippines 169 BI3
Lubudi, Dem. Rep. of the Congo 178 NII
Lubuklinggau, Indonesia 168 K6
Lubumbashi, Dem. Rep. of the Congo 178 NII
Lucas, Kans., U.S. 99 S6
Lucaya, Bahamas 110 CIO
Lucaya, Jam. 110 MIO
Lucedale, Miss., U.S. 95 NI3
Lucena, Philippines 169 CI4
Lucena, Sp. 139 S7
Lučenec, Slovakia 132 KIO
Luchegorsk, Russ. 141 L2I
Luchuan, China 163 S2
Lucie, river, Suriname 121 FI5
Lucipara, Kepulauan, Indonesia 169 LI6
Lucira, Angola 182 E5
Luckenwalde, Ger. 132 G7
Lucknow, Qnsld., Austral. 191 TII
Lucknow, India 158 G8
Lucy Creek, N. Terr., Austral. 191 T9
Lüderitz, Namibia 182 J6
Ludhiana, India 158 D5
Ludington, Mich., U.S. 92 K9
Ludlow, Calif., U.S. 103 WII
Ludlow, Vt., U.S. 89 HI3
Ludogorie, plateau, Eur. 130 J9
Ludowici, Ga., U.S. 91 P8
Luebo, Dem. Rep. of the Congo 178 L9
Luena, Angola 182 D8
Lufeng, China 163 S6
Lufilufi, Samoa 198 L4
Lufkin, Tex., U.S. 97 NI4
Luga, Russ. 140 D6
Lugano, Switz. 132 L5

Luganville, Vanuatu 198 D2
Lugenda, river, Mozambique 183 D14
Lugo, Sp. 139 N5
Lugoj, Rom. 137 E14
Lūgovoy, Kaz. 155 J15
Lugovoy, Russ. 140 H10
Luhans'k, Ukr. 133 J18
Lui, river, China 163 Q1
Luiana, river, Angola 182 F8
Luichow Peninsula, China 163 T1
Luitpold Coast, Antarctica 206 E10
Luján, Arg. 124 L12
Lujor, island, Enewetak Atoll, Marshall Is. 196 G8
Lukachukai, Ariz., U.S. 101 Q9
Lukenie, river, Dem. Rep. of the Congo 178 L8
Lukeville, Ariz., U.S. 101 V6
Lukolela, Dem. Rep. of the Congo 178 K8
Lukulu, Zambia 182 E9
Lukunor Atoll, F.S.M. 196 Q7
Luleå, Sw. 135 F14
Luleälven, river, Eur. 130 B8
Lüleburgaz, Turk. 148 C3
Lules, Arg. 124 G9
Lüliang Shan, China 162 F3
Luling, Tex., U.S. 97 R11
Lulonga, river, Dem. Rep. of the Congo 178 J8
Lulua, river, Dem. Rep. of the Congo 178 N10
Lulu Fakahega, peak, Wallis and Futuna, Fr. 198 B11
Lumajangdong Co, China 160 J5
Luman, Afghan. 157 N6
Lumbala N'guimbo, Angola 182 E8
Lumber City, Ga., U.S. 91 N7
Lumberton, Miss., U.S. 94 N12
Lumberton, N. Mex., U.S. 101 Q11
Lumberton, N.C., U.S. 90 J11
Lumbo, Mozambique 183 E15
Lumding, India 158 G14
Lumi, P.N.G. 193 C18
Lumpkin, Ga., U.S. 91 N4
Lumu, Indonesia 169 K13
Lumut, Malaysia 167 T9
Luna, N. Mex., U.S. 101 T10
Lunavada, India 158 J4
Lund, Nev., U.S. 103 Q12
Lundazi, Zambia 182 D12
Lundu, Malaysia 168 H9
Lunglei, India 158 J14
Lungwebungu, river, Angola 182 D8
Luni, river, India 158 G3
Luni, India 158 G3
Luning, Nev., U.S. 103 R8
Luninyets, Belarus 133 G13
Luntai, China 160 F6
Lunyama, Dem. Rep. of the Congo 178 M11
Luo, river, China 162 H4
Luobei, China 161 C18
Luocheng, China 163 Q1
Luoding, China 163 S3
Luohe, China 162 H5
Luonan, China 162 H3
Luoqing, river, China 163 Q1
Luoshan, China 162 K5
Luoyang, China 162 H4
Luoyuan, China 163 P9
Lupanshui, China 160 N12
Luperón, Dom. Rep. 111 L18
Lupog, Guam, U.S. 196 B12
Luqu, China 160 J11
Lurah, river, Afghan. 157 Q6
Luray, Va., U.S. 90 D11
Lúrio, river, Mozambique 183 E14
Lúrio, Mozambique 183 E15
Lusaka, Zambia 182 E11
Lusambo, Dem. Rep. of the Congo 178 L10
Lusancay Island, P.N.G. 193 D21
Lushi, China 162 H3
Lushoto, Tanzania 179 L15
Lüshun (Port Arthur), China 162 E9
Lusk, Wyo., U.S. 100 H13
Lūt, Dasht-e, Iran 153 E15
Lūţak, Iran 153 F17
Lü Tao, Taiwan, China 163 S10
Lutcher, La., U.S. 94 Q10
Luti, Solomon Is. 197 L15
Luton, Eng., U.K. 138 H9
Łutselk'e, N.W.T., Can. 76 H12
Lutsen, Minn., U.S. 98 F14
Luts'k, Ukr. 132 H12
Lützow-Holm Bay, Antarctica 207 B17
Luuq, Somalia 179 H16
Luverne, Ala., U.S. 95 M16
Luverne, Minn., U.S. 98 L9
Luvua, river, Dem. Rep. of the Congo 178 M11
Luxembourg, Eur. 138 J11
Luxembourg, Lux. 138 J11
Luxi, China 160 N10
Luxi, China 162 M2
Luxor, Egypt 177 E19
Luxora, Ark., U.S. 94 F11
Luyi, China 162 H6
Luy Kalay, Afghan. 157 Q5
Luy Radzay, Afghan. 157 Q2
Luz, Braz. 123 L14
Luza, Russ. 140 F8
Luzern, Switz. 132 K4
Luzhai, China 163 Q2
Luzhou, China 160 M12
Luzon, island, Philippines 169 C14
Luzon Strait, Philippines 169 A13
L'viv, Ukr. 132 J12
Lyakhovskiye Ostrova, Russ. 141 D17
Lyaki, Azerb. 149 D21
Lyangar, Taj. 156 K10
Lycksele, Sw. 135 G13
Lycoming, N.Y., U.S. 88 H8
Lydda see Lod, Israel 150 M5
Lyddan Island, Antarctica 206 C10
Lyepyel', Belarus 133 E13
Lyford, Tex., U.S. 97 W10
Lyman, Wyo., U.S. 100 K8
Lynch, Ky., U.S. 95 D20
Lynch, Nebr., U.S. 98 M6
Lynchburg, Va., U.S. 90 F11
Lynden, Wash., U.S. 102 A4
Lyndhurst, S. Austral., Austral. 191 W10
Lyndon, W. Austral., Austral. 191 U2
Lyndon B. Johnson National Historical Park, Tex., U.S. 97 P9
Lyndonville, Vt., U.S. 89 F13
Lynn, Mass., U.S. 89 K15
Lynn Haven, Fla., U.S. 91 R3
Lynn Lake, Man., Can. 77 L13
Lynton, W. Austral., Austral. 191 W2
Lyon, Fr. 138 M11
Lyons, river, Austral. 190 G2
Lyons, Ga., U.S. 91 N7
Lyons, Kans., U.S. 99 T7
Lyons, N.Y., U.S. 88 J7
Lyons, Nebr., U.S. 99 P8
Lysychans'k, Ukr. 133 J18
Lytton, B.C., Can. 76 M8
Lyuboml', Ukr. 132 H12
Lyubotyn, Ukr. 133 H17

M

Maalaea, Hawaii, U.S. 107 G16
Maalaea Bay, Hawaii, U.S. 107 G16
Ma'ān, Jordan 151 Q6
Maan Ridge, Eur. 130 B9
Maanselkä, ridge, Fin. 135 D16
Ma'anshan, China 162 K8
Maarianhamina see Mariehamn, Fin. 135 K14
Ma'arrat an Nu'mān, Syr. 150 E8
Maastricht, Neth. 138 H11
Ma'bar, Yemen 152 Q9
Mabaruma, Guyana 121 C14
Mabiri, Cape, P.N.G. 197 K14
MacAlpine Lake, Nunavut, Can. 77 G13
Macapá, Braz. 122 C12
Macará, Ecua. 120 L2
Macaroni, Qnsld., Austral. 191 Q11
Macas, Ecua. 120 K3
Macau, Braz. 123 E17
Macau, China 163 S4
Macaúba, Braz. 122 G12
Macauley Island, Kermadec Is., N.Z. 194 L9
Macbride Head, Falk. Is., U.K. 125 W13
Macclenny, Fla., U.S. 91 R8
Macdonnell Ranges, Austral. 190 F8
Macedonia, Eur. 137 H14
Maceió, Braz. 123 G18
Maceió, Ponta do, Braz. 123 E17
Macenta, Guinea 180 G7
Macerata, It. 136 G10
Mach, Pak. 157 R6
Machagai, Arg. 124 G12
Machala, Ecua. 120 L2
Machanao, Mount, Guam, U.S. 196 A11
Macharchar see Eil Malk, island, Palau 196 P11
Macheng, China 162 K6
Macherla, India 159 N7
Machias, Me., U.S. 89 F19
Machico, Madeira Is., Port. 184 M4
Machilipatnam (Bandar), India 159 N8
Machiques, Venez. 120 B6
Machu Picchu, ruins, Peru 122 H5
Macinac, Straits of, Mich., U.S. 92 G10
Mack, Colo., U.S. 100 M10
Maçka, Turk. 149 D14
Mackay, Idaho, U.S. 100 G6
Mackay, Qnsld., Austral. 191 T14
Mackay, Lake, Austral. 190 E7
Mackenzie, river, Austral. 190 F14
Mackenzie, river, N.W.T., Can. 76 F10
Mackenzie, B.C., Can. 76 K9
Mackenzie Bay, N.W.T.-Yukon Terr., Can. 76 D10
Mackenzie King Island, N.W.T., Can. 77 B13
Mackenzie Mountains, N.W.T., Can. 76 F9
Mackenzie-Peace, Source of the, N. Amer. 74 F3
Mackenzie Trough, Arctic Oc. 222 N5
Mackinac, Straits of, U.S. 79 D16
Mackinac Island, Mich., U.S. 92 G11
Mackinaw City, Mich., U.S. 92 G10
Macknade, Qnsld., Austral. 191 R13
Macksville, Kans., U.S. 99 U6
Maclear, S. Af. 182 L10
Macleod, Lake, Austral. 190 G1
Macomb, Ill., U.S. 93 Q4
Macomer, It. 136 J7
Macon, Ga., U.S. 90 M6
Macon, Miss., U.S. 95 K13
Macon, Mo., U.S. 99 R13
Macondo, Angola 182 D9
Macovane, Mozambique 183 H13
Macpherson's Strait, Andaman Is., India 159 Q14
Macquarie, river, Austral. 190 J13
Macquarie, Port, Austral. 190 K15
Macquarie Island, Pac. Oc. 194 R6
Macquarie Ridge, Pac. Oc. 218 R8
Mac. Robertson Land, Antarctica 207 E18
Macurijes, Punta, Cuba 110 J10
Macuro, Venez. 120 B12
Macusani, Peru 122 H5
Mad, river, Calif., U.S. 103 N2
Ma'dabā, Jordan 150 M6
Madagascar, Ind. Oc. 183 H16
Madagascar, Af. 174 N11
Madagascar Basin, Ind. Oc. 220 L6
Madagascar Plateau, Ind. Oc. 220 M5
Madā'in Şāliḩ, Saudi Arabia 152 H6
Madalai, Palau 196 N11
Madalena, São Tomé and Príncipe 185 D20
Madanapalle, India 159 P6
Madang, P.N.G. 193 C19
Madaripur, Bangladesh 158 J13
Madawaska, Me., U.S. 89 A18
Madayar, Myanmar 166 G6
Maddock, N. Dak., U.S. 98 F5
Madeira, island, Atl. Oc. 184 M3
Madeira, river, S. Amer. 118 F5
Madeira Islands, Atl. Oc. 184 C4
Madeleine, Îles de la, Que., Can. 77 N22
Madelia, Minn., U.S. 98 L10
Madeline Island, Wis., U.S. 92 E4
Maden, Turk. 149 G14
Madera, Calif., U.S. 103 T6
Madgaon, India 159 N4
Madhubani, India 158 G10
Madidi, river, Bol. 122 H6
Madill, Okla., U.S. 96 J12
Madimba, Dem. Rep. of the Congo 178 L7
Madīnat ash Sha'b, Yemen 152 R9
Madīnat ath Thawrah, Syr. 150 E11
Madīnat Zāyid, U.A.E. 153 K14
Madison, Fla., U.S. 91 Q6
Madison, Ga., U.S. 90 L6
Madison, Ind., U.S. 93 T10
Madison, Kans., U.S. 99 T9
Madison, Me., U.S. 89 F16
Madison, Minn., U.S. 98 J9
Madison, N.C., U.S. 90 G10
Madison, Nebr., U.S. 99 P7
Madison, S. Dak., U.S. 98 L8
Madison, W. Va., U.S. 90 E8
Madison, Wis., U.S. 92 L5
Madisonville, Ky., U.S. 95 C14
Madisonville, Tex., U.S. 97 P13
Madiun, Indonesia 168 M10
Madley, Mount, Austral. 190 F5
Mado Gashi, Kenya 179 J15
Madoi, China 160 J10
Madona, Latv. 135 L17
Madrakah, Ra's al, Oman 153 M16
Madras see Chennai, India 159 P7
Madras, Oreg., U.S. 102 G5
Madre, Laguna, Mex. 108 F12
Madre, Laguna, Tex., U.S. 97 V11
Madre, Sierra, N. Amer. 74 P6
Madre de Dios, river, Bol.-Peru 122 H6
Madre de Dios, Isla, Chile 125 V6
Madre del Sur, Sierra, N. Amer. 74 P5
Madre Occidental, Sierra, N. Amer. 74 M4
Madre Oriental, Sierra, N. Amer. 74 M5
Madrid, Iowa, U.S. 99 P11
Madrid, Sp. 139 Q7
Madridejos, Sp. 139 R7
Madrid Point, S. Amer. 118 H4
Madura, W. Austral., Austral. 191 X6
Madura, island, Indonesia 168 M10
Madura, Selat, Indonesia 168 M11
Madurai, India 159 R6
Madurantakam, India 159 Q7
Madyan, Pak. 156 M10
Mae, river, Thai. 166 M8
Maebashi, Jap. 165 N12
Mae Hong Son, Thai. 166 J7
Mae Sariang, Thai. 166 K7
Maeser, Utah, U.S. 100 L9
Mae Sot, Thai. 166 K7
Maeva, Huahine, Fr. Polynesia, Fr. 199 G14
Maevatanana, Madagascar 183 F17
Maéwo, island, Vanuatu 198 C3
Mafia Island, Tanzania 179 M15
Mafikeng, S. Af. 182 J10
Maga, Tinian, N. Mariana Is., U.S. 196 B7
Magadan, Russ. 141 F20
Magadi, Kenya 179 K14
Magallanes, Estrecho de, Chile 125 X8
Magangué, Col. 120 C5
Magazine Mountain, Ark., U.S. 94 G7
Magdagachi, Russ. 141 K18
Magdalena, river, Col. 120 C5
Magdalena, river, N. Amer. 74 L3
Magdalena, Bol. 122 H8
Magdalena, Mex. 108 C7
Magdalena, N. Mex., U.S. 101 T11
Magdalena, Bahía, Mex. 108 F6
Magdalena, Isla, Chile 125 S6
Magdalena, Isla, Mex. 108 E6
Magdalena, Llano de la, Mex. 108 E6
Magdalena Bay, N. Amer. 74 M3
Magdeburg, Ger. 132 G6
Magdelaine Cays, Austral. 190 D15
Magee, Miss., U.S. 94 M11
Magelang, Indonesia 168 M9
Magellan, Strait of, S. Amer. 118 R4
Magellan Rise, Pac. Oc. 218 J10
Magellan Seamounts, Pac. Oc. 218 H7
Magerøya, island, Nor. 135 B14
Magic Reservoir, Idaho, U.S. 100 H5
Magnitogorsk, Russ. 140 J8
Magnolia, Ark., U.S. 94 J7
Magnolia, Miss., U.S. 94 N10
Mago, island, Fiji 198 H9
Magpi, Puntan, Saipan, N. Mariana Is., U.S. 196 A5
Magude, Mozambique 182 J12
Magway, Myanmar 166 H5
Mahābād, Iran 152 B10
Mahabharat Range, Nepal 158 F8
Mahabo, Madagascar 183 G16
Mahad, India 158 M3
Mahaena, Tahiti, Fr. Polynesia, Fr. 199 N17
Mahaena, Passe de, Tahiti, Fr. Polynesia, Fr. 199 N17
Mahagi, Dem. Rep. of the Congo 178 J12
Mahaiatea, Tahiti, Fr. Polynesia, Fr. 199 P16
Mahajamba, Baie de la, Madagascar 183 E17
Mahajan, India 158 F4
Mahajanga, Madagascar 183 E17
Mahalapye, Botswana 182 H10
Māhān, Iran 153 F15
Mahana Bay, Hawaii, U.S. 107 Q20
Mahanadi, river, India 158 K8
Mahanoro, Madagascar 183 G18
Mahasamund, India 158 K8
Mahavavy, river, Madagascar 183 F17
Mahbubnagar, India 158 M6
Mahd adh Dhahab, Saudi Arabia 152 K7
Mahdia, Guyana 121 E14
Mahébourg, Mauritius 185 G20
Mahé Island, Seychelles 185 P20
Mahendraganj, India 158 G12
Mahen dra Giri, peak, India 158 L9
Mahenge, Tanzania 179 N14
Maheno, N.Z. 193 Q16
Mahere Honae, island, Rangiroa, Fr. Polynesia, Fr. 199 K16
Mahesana, India 158 H3
Mahia Peninsula, N.Z. 193 L20
Mahige, island, Solomon Is. 197 M18
Mahilyow, Belarus 133 F14
Mahina, Tahiti, Fr. Polynesia, Fr. 199 N16
Mahinaakaka Heiau, Hawaii, U.S. 107 N22
Mahishadal, India 158 J11
Mahitu, island, Rangiroa, Fr. Polynesia, Fr. 199 K16
Mahmud-e Raqi, Afghan. 156 M8
Mahmudiye, Turk. 148 E6
Mahnomen, Minn., U.S. 98 G9
Mahoba, India 158 H7
Mahoe, Puu, Hawaii, U.S. 107 H17
Mahri, Pak. 157 U6
Mahu, Tubuai, Fr. Polynesia, Fr. 199 K20
Mahuti, Baie de, Huahine, Fr. Polynesia, Fr. 199 H14
Mahuva, India 158 K2
Maia, Manua Is., Amer. Samoa, U.S. 198 N4
Maiao, island, Fr. Polynesia, Fr. 199 F16
Maibong, India 158 G14
Maicuru, river, Braz. 122 C11
Maiduguri, Nig. 181 E16
Maigualida, Sierra, Venez. 120 E10
Maihar, India 158 H7
Maikoor, island, Indonesia 169 L18
Maili, Hawaii, U.S. 106 E10
Mailsi, Pak. 157 R10
Main, river, Ger. 132 H6
Maina, island, Aitutaki Atoll, Cook Is., N.Z. 198 Q11
Mai-Ndombe, Lac, Dem. Rep. of the Congo 178 K8
Maine, U.S. 89 E15
Maine, Gulf of, U.S. 79 D22
Maingkwan, Myanmar 166 D6
Mainland, island, Orkney Is., Scot., U.K. 138 C8

Mainland, island, Shetland Is., Scot., U.K. 138 B8
Mainoru, N. Terr., Austral. 191 P9
Maintirano, Madagascar 183 F16
Mainz, Ger. 132 H5
Maio, island, Cape Verde 185 D17
Maipo Volcano, S. Amer. 118 L4
Maiquetía, Venez. 120 B9
Mairenui, peak, Tahiti, Fr. Polynesia, Fr. 199 Q17
Maisí, Cuba 111 K15
Maisí, Punta de, Cuba 111 K15
Maiskhal, island, Bangladesh 158 K14
Maitland, N.S.W., Austral. 191 X14
Maitri, station, Antarctica 207 A14
Maíz, Islas del, Nicar. 109 M19
Maizuru, Jap. 165 P8
Majene, Indonesia 169 K13
Majī, Eth. 179 H14
Majli-Saj, Kyrg. 156 F10
Majorca see Mallorca, island, Sp. 139 R11
Majuro, Majuro Atoll, Marshall Is. 196 G12
Majuro, Marshall Is. 196 H5
Majuro (Laura), island, Majuro Atoll, Marshall Is. 196 H10
Majuro Lagoon, Majuro Atoll, Marshall Is. 196 G10
Makaala, Puu, Hawaii, U.S. 107 M21
Makaha, Hawaii, U.S. 106 E10
Makakilo City, Hawaii, U.S. 106 E10
Makale, Indonesia 169 K13
Makaleha Mountains, Hawaii, U.S. 106 B6
Makalu, peak, Nepal 158 F11
Makanaka, Puu, Hawaii, U.S. 107 L20
Makapala, Hawaii, U.S. 107 K19
Makapu Point, Niue, N.Z. 199 B20
Makaroa, island, Gambier Is., Fr. Polynesia, Fr. 199 R20
Makarov, Russ. 141 J22
Makarov Basin, Arctic Oc. 222 H8
Makarovo, Russ. 141 K15
Makarov Seamount, Pac. Oc. 218 F7
Makassar see Ujungpandang, Indonesia 169 L13
Makassar Strait, Indonesia 168 K12
Makatea, island, Fr. Polynesia, Fr. 199 E17
Makawao, peak, Hawaii, U.S. 107 G17
Makefu, Niue, N.Z. 199 B20
Make Jima, Jap. 165 U4
Makelulu, Mount, Palau 196 M12
Makemo, island, Fr. Polynesia, Fr. 199 E19
Makena, Hawaii, U.S. 107 H16
Makeni, Sierra Leone 180 F6
Makéone, Vanuatu 198 B2
Makgadikgadi Pans, Botswana 182 G9
Makhachkala, Russ. 140 K4
Makhad, Pak. 157 N10
Makhambet, Kaz. 154 E6
Makhfar al Buşayyah, Iraq 152 F10
Makhfar al Ḩammām (Sura), Syr. 150 E11
Maki, Indonesia 169 K19
Makinsk, Kaz. 155 C13
Makira Harbour, Solomon Is. 197 P20
Makiyivka, Ukr. 133 J18
Makkah (Mecca), Saudi Arabia 152 L7
Makkovik, Nfld., Can. 77 K21
Makó, Hung. 132 L10
Makogai, island, Fiji 198 H7
Makokou, Gabon 181 K16
Makolea Point, Hawaii, U.S. 107 L18
Makoua, Congo 181 L17
Makrana, India 158 G4
Makran Coast Range, Pak. 157 V3
Mākū, Iran 152 A10
Makung (Penghu), Taiwan, China 163 R8
Makunudu Atoll (Malcolm), Maldives 159 T3
Makura, island, Vanuatu 198 E3
Makurazaki, Jap. 165 T4
Makurdi, Nig. 181 G14
Mal, Mauritania 176 G5
Malabar Coast, India 159 Q3
Malabo, Bioko, Eq. Guinea 184 L7
Malabuñgan, Philippines 168 E12
Malacca, Malaysia 167 U10
Malacca, Strait of, Asia 146 L10
Malad City, Idaho, U.S. 100 J7
Maladzyechna, Belarus 133 F13
Málaga, Col. 120 D6
Málaga, Sp. 139 T7
Malaga, N. Mex., U.S. 101 V14
Malaita, island, Solomon Is. 197 N20
Malakal, Palau 196 N11
Malakal, Sudan 179 F13
Malakal Harbor, Palau 196 P11
Malakal Pass, Palau 196 P11
Malakanagiri, India 158 M8
Malakand, Pak. 156 M10
Malake, island, Fiji 198 H6
Malakoff, Tex., U.S. 96 M13
Malakula, island, Vanuatu 198 D2
Malam, Kosrae, F.S.M. 197 B19
Malang, Indonesia 168 M10
Malanje, Angola 182 C6
Malanville, Benin 180 E12
Malao, Vanuatu 198 C1
Malapo, Tongatapu, Tonga 198 J11
Malapu, Santa Cruz Is., Solomon Is. 197 P23
Malar, Pak. 157 V4
Mälaren, lake, Sw. 135 K14
Malargüe, Arg. 124 M8
Malaspina Glacier, Alas., U.S. 105 J19
Malatya, Turk. 149 G13
Malawi, Af. 183 D13
Malawi, Lake (Lake Nyasa), Malawi-Mozambique-Tanzania 183 D13
Malayagiri, peak, India 158 K10
Malaybalay, Philippines 169 F15
Malāyer, Iran 152 D11
Malay Peninsula, Malaysia-Thai. 167 Q8
Malaysia, Asia 167 T9
Malazgirt, Turk. 149 F17
Malbork, Pol. 132 F10
Malcolm see Makunudu Atoll, atoll, Maldives 159 T3
Malcolm, W. Austral., Austral. 191 V4
Malden, Mo., U.S. 99 V15
Malden Island, Kiribati 194 H12
Maldive Islands, Maldives 159 U2
Maldives, Asia 159 U4
Maldonado, Uru. 124 L15
Maldonado, Punta, Mex. 108 K12
Male, Maldives 159 U3
Male Atoll, Maldives 159 U3
Malebo, Pool, Dem. Rep. of the Congo 178 L7
Malegaon, India 158 K4
Malemba-Nkulu, Dem. Rep. of the Congo 178 M11
Malevangga, Solomon Is. 197 K15
Malhargarh, India 158 H4
Malheur, river, Oreg., U.S. 102 H9
Malheur Lake, Oreg., U.S. 102 J7
Mali, Af. 176 H7
Mali, island, Fiji 198 G7
Mali, river, Myanmar 166 D7
Mali Kyun, Myanmar 167 N7
Malili, Indonesia 169 K13
Malin, Oreg., U.S. 102 L5
Malindi, Kenya 179 L15
Malin Head, Ire. 138 E6
Malinoa, island, Tongatapu, Tonga 198 H11
Malkapur, India 158 K5
Malkara, Turk. 148 C3
Malki, Russ. 141 F22
Malko Tŭrnovo, Bulg. 137 H17
Mallacoota, Vic., Austral. 191 Z14
Mallawi, Egypt 177 D18
Mallawli, island, Malaysia 168 F12
Mallorca (Majorca), island, Sp. 139 R11
Malmand Range, Afghan. 157 N3
Malmberget, Sw. 135 E13
Malmesbury, S. Af. 182 M7
Malmö, Sw. 134 N12
Malo, island, Vanuatu 198 D2
Maloelap Atoll, Marshall Is. 196 G5
Malolo, island, Fiji 198 J5
Malone, N.Y., U.S. 88 F10
Maloshuyka, Russ. 140 E8
Måløy, Nor. 134 J9
Malozemel'skaya Tundra, Eur. 130 A11
Malpelo, Isla de, Pac. Oc. 195 G22
Malpelo Island, Col. 118 C1
Malta, Eur. 136 M10
Malta, island, Malta 136 M10
Malta, Idaho, U.S. 100 J6
Malta, Mont., U.S. 100 B10
Maltahöhe, Namibia 182 J7
Maltese Islands, Eur. 130 L6
Maluku see Moluccas, islands, Indonesia 169 J15
Ma'lūlā, Syr. 150 J8
Malung, Sw. 134 K12
Maluu, Solomon Is. 197 M19
Malvan, India 159 N3
Malvern, Ark., U.S. 94 H8
Malvern, Iowa, U.S. 99 Q9
Malvinas, Islas see Falkland Islands, Falk. Is., U.K. 125 X12
Malyye Karmakuly, Russ. 140 D11
Malyy Lyakhovskiy, Ostrov, Russ. 141 D17
Mamagota, P.N.G. 197 K14
Mamala Bay, Hawaii, U.S. 106 F11
Mamalahoa Highway, Hawaii, U.S. 107 L19
Mamalu Bay, Hawaii, U.S. 107 H17
Mamberamo, Indonesia 169 K20
Mamfé, Cameroon 181 H15
Mamiña, Chile 124 C7
Mammoth, Ariz., U.S. 101 V8
Mammoth, Wyo., U.S. 100 F8
Mammoth Cave National Park, Ky., U.S. 95 D16
Mammoth Spring, Ark., U.S. 94 E9
Mamoré, river, Bol. 122 G7
Mamoriá, Braz. 122 F7
Mamou, Guinea 180 F6
Mamou, La., U.S. 94 P8
Mamoudzou, Mayotte, Fr. 185 P17
Mampong, Ghana 180 G10
Mamuju, Indonesia 169 K13
Man, Côte d'Ivoire 180 G7
Man, Isle of, U.K. 138 F7
Mana, river, Fr. Guiana 121 E17
Mana, Fr. Guiana 121 E17
Mana, Hawaii, U.S. 106 B4
Manacapuru, Braz. 122 D9
Manacor, Sp. 139 R11
Manado, Indonesia 169 H15
Mañagaha Island, Saipan, N. Mariana Is., U.S. 196 B4
Managua, Nicar. 109 M18
Managua, Lago de, Nicar. 109 M17
Manaia, N.Z. 193 L18
Manakara, Madagascar 183 H17
Manakau, peak, N.Z. 193 N18
Manākhah, Yemen 152 Q9
Mana La, India 158 D7
Manam, island, P.N.G. 193 C19
Manama see Al Manāmah, Bahrain 152 H12
Manamadurai, India 159 R6
Mananjary, Madagascar 183 H17
Manantiales, Chile 125 W8
Manaoba, island, Solomon Is. 197 M19
Mana Point, Hawaii, U.S. 106 B4
Manapouri, Lake, N.Z. 193 Q15
Manas, China 160 E7
Manas Hu, China 160 D7
Manassa, Colo., U.S. 101 P12
Manassas, Va., U.S. 90 D12
Manatí, Cuba 110 J12
Manatí, P.R., U.S. 111 M22
Manaus, Braz. 122 D9
Manavgat, Turk. 148 J6
Manawai Harbour, Solomon Is. 197 N20
Manbij, Syr. 150 D10
Manchester, Conn., U.S. 89 L13
Manchester, Ga., U.S. 90 M5
Manchester, Iowa, U.S. 99 N13
Manchester, Ky., U.S. 95 D19
Manchester, N.H., U.S. 89 J14
Manchester, Tenn., U.S. 95 F16
Manchester, Eng., U.K. 138 G8
Manchhar Lake, Pak. 157 V6
Manchuria, region, China 161 D16
Manchurian Plain, Asia 146 F12
Mancos, Colo., U.S. 101 P10
Mand, river, Iran 153 G13
Mand, Pak. 157 V2
Manda, Tanzania 179 N13
Mandab, Bāb al, Af. 174 G11
Mandai, Pak. 157 S7
Mandal, Mongolia 160 D12
Mandal, Nor. 134 M10
Mandala, Puncak, Indonesia 193 C17
Mandalay, Myanmar 166 G6
Mandalgovĭ, Mongolia 160 E12
Mandalī, Iraq 152 D10
Mandalt see Sonid Zuoqi, China 162 A5
Mandan, N. Dak., U.S. 98 G4
Mandapeta, India 158 M8
Mandel, Afghan. 157 N2
Mandera, Kenya 179 H16
Mandeville, Jam. 110 N11
Mandi, India 157 P14
Mandi Burewala, Pak. 157 R10
Mandimba, Mozambique 183 E13
Mandioli, island, Indonesia 169 J16
Mandla, India 158 J7
Mandritsara, Madagascar 183 E18
Mandsaur, India 158 H4
Mandu, island, Maldives 159 V3
Mandurah, W. Austral., Austral. 191 X2
Mandvi, India 158 J1
Manga, region, Af. 174 G6
Manga, Braz. 123 J15
Mangabeiras, Chapada das, Braz. 123 G14
Mangaia, island, Cook Is., N.Z. 194 K12
Mangalia, Rom. 137 F17
Mangalore, India 159 Q4
Mangareva, island, Fr. Polynesia, Fr. 199 H23
Mangareva, island, Gambier Is., Fr. Polynesia, Fr. 199 Q20
Mangarongaro, island, Penrhyn, Cook Is., N.Z. 199 B17
Mangeigne, Chad 177 K16
Mangere, island, Aitutaki Atoll, Cook Is., N.Z. 198 Q12
Manggautu, Solomon Is. 197 Q18
Mangghyshlaq, Kaz. 154 H5
Mang'it, Uzb. 154 J9
Mangnai, China 160 H8
Mango, island, Ha'apai Group, Tonga 198 Q6
Mango, Togo 180 F11
Mangoche, Malawi 183 E13
Mangoky, river, Madagascar 183 H16
Mangole, island, Indonesia 169 K15
Mangqystaū Shyghanaghy, Kaz. 154 G5
Mangrol, India 158 K2
Manguchar, Pak. 157 S5
Mangueira, Lagoa, Braz. 122 Q11
Mangueni Plateau, Af. 174 F6
Manguinho, Ponta do, Braz. 123 G17
Manguinho Point, S. Amer. 118 F11
Mangum, Okla., U.S. 96 H8
Mangut, Russ. 141 M17
Manhattan, Kans., U.S. 99 S8
Manhattan, Nev., U.S. 103 R9
Mania, river, Madagascar 183 G17
Maniamba, Mozambique 183 D13
Manica, Mozambique 182 G12
Manicoré, Braz. 122 E9
Manicouagan, Réservoir, Que., Can. 77 M20
Manīfah, Saudi Arabia 152 H12
Manifold, Cape, Austral. 190 F15
Maniganggo, China 160 K10
Manihi, island, Fr. Polynesia, Fr. 199 D18
Manihiki Atoll, Cook Is., N.Z. 194 H11
Manihiki Plateau, Pac. Oc. 218 L12
Manila, Ark., U.S. 94 F11
Manila, Philippines 169 C13
Manila, Utah, U.S. 100 K9
Manila Bay, Philippines 169 C13
Manily, Russ. 141 D21
Maningrida, N. Terr., Austral. 191 P9
Manini, Motus, Bora-Bora, Fr. Polynesia, Fr. 199 J13
Maninita, island, Vava'u Group, Tonga 198 M11
Manipa, island, Indonesia 169 K16
Manisa, Turk. 148 F3
Manistee, river, Mich., U.S. 92 J9
Manistee, Mich., U.S. 92 J9
Manistique, Mich., U.S. 92 G9
Manistique Lake, Mich., U.S. 92 F9
Manitoba, Can. 77 L14
Manitoba, Lake, Man., Can. 77 N13
Manitou Island, Mich., U.S. 92 E7
Manitou Islands, Mich., U.S. 92 H9
Manitowoc, Wis., U.S. 92 K7
Manizales, Col. 120 E4
Manja, Madagascar 183 H16
Manjra, river, India 158 M6
Mankato, Kans., U.S. 99 R7
Mankato, Minn., U.S. 98 L11
Manley Hot Springs, Alas., U.S. 105 F16
Manly, Iowa, U.S. 98 M11
Manmad, India 158 K4
Mann, island, Kwajalein Atoll, Marshall Is. 196 M5
Manna, Indonesia 168 L6
Mannar, Gulf of, India 159 S6
Mannheim, Ger. 132 H5
Manning, Iowa, U.S. 99 P10
Manning, N. Dak., U.S. 98 G2
Manning, S.C., U.S. 90 L10
Manning, Cape, Kiritimati, Kiribati 197 A23
Manning Strait, Solomon Is. 197 L16
Mannington, W. Va., U.S. 90 C9
Mann Passage, Kwajalein Atoll, Marshall Is. 196 M5
Manoa, Bol. 122 G7
Man-of-War Cay, Bahamas 111 G13
Manokotak, Alas., U.S. 105 L13
Manokwari, Indonesia 169 J19
Manono, island, Samoa 198 L2
Manono, Dem. Rep. of the Congo 178 M11
Manoron, Myanmar 167 P8
Mano Wan, Jap. 164 M11
Man O'War Cay, Bahamas 110 C12
Manp'o, N. Korea 162 C12
Manra, island, Kiribati 194 H10
Manresa, Sp. 139 P10
Mansa, Zambia 182 D11
Mansehra, Pak. 156 M11
Mansel Island, Nunavut, Can. 77 J17
Manseriche, Pongo de, S. Amer. 118 D2
Mansfield, Ark., U.S. 94 G6
Mansfield, La., U.S. 94 L6
Mansfield, Mo., U.S. 99 V13
Mansfield, Ohio, U.S. 93 Q13
Mansfield, Pa., U.S. 88 L7
Mansfield, Vic., Austral. 191 Z12
Mansfield, Mount, Vt., U.S. 88 F12
Manson, Iowa, U.S. 99 N10
Manta, Ecua. 120 J2
Manteca, Calif., U.S. 103 S5
Manteo, N.C., U.S. 90 G15
Manti, Utah, U.S. 100 M7
Mantiqueira, Serra da, S. Amer. 118 J9
Mant Islands, Pohnpei, F.S.M. 197 F14
Manton, Mich., U.S. 92 J10
Mantova, It. 136 F9
Mant Passage, Pohnpei, F.S.M. 197 F14
Mantua, Cuba 110 H4
Mäntyluoto, Fin. 135 J15
Manú, Peru 122 H5
Manuae, island, Fr. Polynesia, Fr. 199 E14
Manua Islands, Amer. Samoa, U.S. 194 J10
Manuhangi, island, Fr. Polynesia, Fr. 199 F20
Manui, island, Gambier Is., Fr. Polynesia, Fr. 199 R20
Manui, island, Indonesia 169 K14
Manukau, N.Z. 193 J19
Manulu Lagoon, Kiritimati, Kiribati 197 B23
Manus, island, P.N.G. 193 B19
Manvers, Port, Nfld., Can. 77 J21
Manville, Wyo., U.S. 100 H13
Many, La., U.S. 94 M7
Manych Guidilo, Lake, Eur. 130 G12
Many Farms, Ariz., U.S. 101 Q9
Manzai, Pak. 157 P8
Manzanares, Sp. 139 R7

Manzanar National Historic Site, Calif., U.S. 103 T8
Manzanillo, Cuba 110 K11
Manzanillo, Mex. 108 J9
Manzanillo Bay, Dom. Rep.-Haiti 111 L17
Manzanola, Colo., U.S. 101 N14
Manzano Mountains, N. Mex., U.S. 101 S12
Manzano Peak, N. Mex., U.S. 101 S12
Manzhouli, China 161 C15
Manzil, Pak. 157 S3
Maó, Sp. 139 Q11
Mao, Chad 177 H14
Mao, Dom. Rep. 111 L18
Maoke, Pegunungan, Indonesia 169 K19
Maoming, China 163 S2
Map, island, Yap Is., F.S.M. 197 C18
Mapai, Mozambique 182 H12
Mapam Yumco, China 160 K5
Mapi, Indonesia 169 M21
Mapi, Indonesia 193 D17
Mapia, Kepulauan (Saint David Islands), Indonesia 169 J19
Mapimí, Bolsón de, N. Amer. 74 M4
Mapleton, Iowa, U.S. 99 N9
Mapleton, Oreg., U.S. 102 H2
Mapmaker Seamounts, Pac. Oc. 218 G8
Maprik, P.N.G. 193 C18
Mapuera, river, Braz. 122 C10
Maputo, Mozambique 182 J12
Maputo, Baía de, Mozambique 182 J12
Maqat, Kaz. 154 F7
Maqnā, Saudi Arabia 152 G5
Maqshūsh, Saudi Arabia 152 K6
Maquan, river, China 160 L6
Maquela do Zombo, Angola 182 B6
Maquinchao, Arg. 125 Q8
Maquoketa, Iowa, U.S. 99 N14
Mar, Russ. 141 H16
Mar, Serra do, S. Amer. 118 K8
Mara, Guyana 121 E15
Mara, India 158 F14
Maraã, Braz. 122 D7
Maraa, Tahiti, Fr. Polynesia, Fr. 199 P15
Maraa, Passe de, Tahiti, Fr. Polynesia, Fr. 199 P15
Marabá, Braz. 123 E13
Marabo, island, Fiji 198 K9
Maracá, Ilha de, Braz. 123 B13
Maracaibo, Venez. 120 B7
Maracaibo, Lago de, Venez. 120 C7
Maracaibo Basin, S. Amer. 118 A3
Maracá Island, S. Amer. 118 C8
Maracaju, Braz. 122 L11
Maracaju, Serra de, S. Amer. 118 H7
Maracanã, Braz. 123 C14
Maracay, Venez. 120 B9
Marādah, Lib. 177 D15
Maradi, Niger 176 J11
Marāghah, Sabkhat, Syr. 150 E9
Marāgheh, Iran 152 B10
Maragogipe, Braz. 123 H16
Marahuaca, Cerro, Venez. 120 F10
Marajó, Baía de, Braz. 123 C13
Marajó, Ilha de, Braz. 123 D13
Marakei, island, Kiribati 194 G8
Maralal, Kenya 179 J14
Maralinga, S. Austral., Austral. 191 W8
Maramasike, island, Solomon Is. 197 N20
Marambio, station, Antarctica 206 C4
Maran, Malaysia 167 U10
Marana, Ariz., U.S. 101 V7
Maranboy, N. Terr., Austral. 191 Q8
Marand, Iran 152 A10
Marang, Malaysia 167 T10
Marañón, river, S. Amer. 118 E2
Mara Rosa, Braz. 123 H13
Maraş, Turk. 148 H12
Marathon, Fla., U.S. 91 Y9
Marathon, Tex., U.S. 97 Q3
Marathus see 'Amrīt, ruins, Syr. 150 G7
Maraú, Braz. 123 J16
Maravae, Solomon Is. 197 M15
Marāveh Tappeh, Iran 153 B15
Maravillas Creek, Tex., U.S. 97 Q3
Maravovo, Solomon Is. 197 N18
Maraza, Azerb. 149 D22
Marble Bar, W. Austral., Austral. 191 S3
Marble Canyon, Ariz., U.S. 101 Q7
Marble Falls, Tex., U.S. 97 P10
Marceline, Mo., U.S. 99 R12
Mar Chiquita, Laguna, Arg. 124 J11
Marco, Fla., U.S. 91 X8
Marcola, Oreg., U.S. 102 H3
Marcos Juárez, Arg. 124 K11
Marcus see Minami Tori Shima, island, Pac. Oc. 194 C5
Marcus Baker, Mount, Alas., U.S. 105 J17
Marcy, Mount, N.Y., U.S. 88 G11
Mardan, Pak. 156 M10
Mar del Plata, Arg. 125 N13
Mardin, Turk. 149 H15
Maré, Île, New Caledonia, Fr. 198 D10
Marea del Portillo, Cuba 110 L11
Marechal Taumaturgo, Braz. 122 G4
Marenanuka, island, Tarawa, Kiribati 197 F17
Marengo, Iowa, U.S. 99 P13
Marennes, Fr. 138 M8
Marfa, Tex., U.S. 97 Q2
Marfa, Massif de, Chad 177 J16
Margai Caka, lake, China 160 J7
Margaret River, W. Austral., Austral. 191 R6
Margarita, Isla de, Venez. 120 B11
Margat (Marghab), ruins, Syr. 150 F7
Marghab see Margat, ruins, Syr. 150 F7
Margow Desert, Afghan. 157 R2
Marguerite Bay, Antarctica 206 F5
Marhanets', Ukr. 133 K16
Mari, ruins, Syr. 150 G14
Maria, island, Fr. Polynesia, Fr. 199 H22
Maria, Îles, Fr. Polynesia, Fr. 194 K12
Maria Bay, Tongatapu, Tonga 198 H11
María Elena, Chile 124 D7
Mariana Islands, Asia 146 G16
Mariana Trench, Pac. Oc. 218 H6
Mariana Trough, Pac. Oc. 218 H6
Marianna, Ark., U.S. 94 G10
Marianna, Fla., U.S. 91 Q4
Marias, river, Mont., U.S. 100 B8
Marías, Islas, Mex. 108 G8
Maria van Diemen, Cape, N.Z. 193 G17
Ma'rib, Yemen 152 P10
Maribor, Slov. 136 E11
Maricopa, Ariz., U.S. 101 U7
Maricopa, Calif., U.S. 103 W7
Maridi, Sudan 178 H12
Marié, river, Braz. 122 C6
Marie Anne, island, Seychelles 185 N21
Marie Byrd Land, Antarctica 206 K7
Marie-Galante, island, Guadeloupe, Fr. 113 H17
Mariehamn (Maarianhamina), Fin. 135 K14
Mariental, Namibia 182 J7
Marietta, Ga., U.S. 90 L5
Marietta, Ohio, U.S. 93 S15
Marietta, Okla., U.S. 96 J11
Marigot, Haiti 111 M16
Marigot, St. Martin, Fr.-Neth. 113 F15
Mariiru Point, Rota I., N. Mariana Is., U.S. 196 E8
Marijampolė, Lith. 135 N16
Marília, Braz. 122 L12
Marillana, W. Austral., Austral. 191 T3
Marinduque, island, Philippines 169 D14
Marine City, Mich., U.S. 92 M13
Marineland, Fla., U.S. 91 R9
Marinette, Wis., U.S. 92 H7
Maringá, Braz. 122 M12
Maringa, river, Dem. Rep. of the Congo 178 J9
Marino, Vanuatu 198 C3
Marion, Ala., U.S. 95 L14
Marion, Ark., U.S. 94 G11
Marion, Ill., U.S. 93 U6
Marion, Ind., U.S. 93 Q10
Marion, Iowa, U.S. 99 N13
Marion, Kans., U.S. 99 T8
Marion, Ky., U.S. 95 C13
Marion, Mich., U.S. 92 K10
Marion, N.C., U.S. 90 H7
Marion, Ohio, U.S. 93 Q13
Marion, S. Dak., U.S. 98 M8
Marion, S.C., U.S. 90 K11
Marion, Va., U.S. 90 G8
Marion, Lake, S.C., U.S. 90 L10
Marion Downs, Qnsld., Austral. 191 T11
Marionville, Mo., U.S. 99 V11
Maripaviche, Venez. 120 D10
Mariposa, Calif., U.S. 103 S6
Marisa, Indonesia 169 J14
Mariscal Estigarribia, Para. 122 L9
Maritsa, river, Eur. 130 J9
Mariupol', Ukr. 133 K18
Marivan, Iran 152 C10
Marj'Uyūn, Leb. 150 J6
Marka (Merca), Somalia 179 J17
Markam, China 160 L10
Markandeh, ruins, Afghan. 156 M6
Marked Tree, Ark., U.S. 94 F11
Markermeer, Neth. 138 G11
Markham, Mount, Antarctica 207 L13
Markham Bay, Nunavut, Can. 77 H18
Markit, China 160 G4
Markleeville, Calif., U.S. 103 Q6
Markovo, Russ. 141 C21
Marks, Miss., U.S. 94 H11
Marksville, La., U.S. 94 N8
Marlborough, Qnsld., Austral. 191 T14
Marlette, Mich., U.S. 92 L12
Marlin, Tex., U.S. 97 N12
Marlinton, W. Va., U.S. 90 E10
Marlow, Okla., U.S. 96 H10
Marmande, Fr. 139 N9
Marmara, island, Turk. 148 D3
Marmara Denizi, Turk. 148 D4
Marmaraereğlisi, Turk. 148 C4
Marmara Gölü, Turk. 148 F4
Marmaris, Turk. 148 H4
Marmarth, N. Dak., U.S. 98 H1
Marmelos, river, Braz. 122 F8
Marmet, W. Va., U.S. 90 E8
Marne, river, Fr. 138 K10
Maroa, Venez. 120 G9
Maroantsetra, Madagascar 183 E18
Marobee Range, Austral. 190 K13
Maroe, Huahine, Fr. Polynesia, Fr. 199 H14
Maroe, Baie de, Huahine, Fr. Polynesia, Fr. 199 G14
Marokau, island, Fr. Polynesia, Fr. 199 F19
Marol, Pak. 156 M13
Maromokotro, peak, Madagascar 183 E18
Maroni, river, S. Amer. 118 B7
Maroochydore, Qnsld., Austral. 191 V15
Maro Reef, Hawaii, U.S. 106 L5
Marotiri (Îlots de Bass), Fr. Polynesia, Fr. 195 L14
Maroua, Cameroon 181 F17
Maro'u Bay, Solomon Is. 197 P20
Marovoay, Madagascar 183 F17
Marpi Point, Saipan, N. Mariana Is., U.S. 196 A6
Marpo, Puntan, Tinian, N. Mariana Is., U.S. 196 C8
Marqaköl, lake, Kaz. 155 D19
Marquesas Fracture Zone, Pac. Oc. 219 L14
Marquesas Islands, Fr. Polynesia, Fr. 195 H14
Marquesas Keys, Fla., U.S. 91 Y8
Marquette, Mich., U.S. 92 F7
Marra, Jebel, Sudan 178 E10
Marrakech, Mor. 176 B8
Marra Mountains, Af. 174 G8
Marrawah, Tas., Austral. 191 Y15
Marree, S. Austral., Austral. 191 W10
Marrero, La., U.S. 94 Q11
Marromeu, Mozambique 183 F13
Marrupa, Mozambique 183 D14
Marsá al Burayqah, Lib. 177 C15
Marsabit, Kenya 179 J14
Marsa Fatma, Eritrea 179 E15
Marsala, It. 136 L9
Marseille, Fr. 139 N11
Marsfjället, peak, Sw. 134 G12
Marshall, river, Austral. 190 F9
Marshall, Alas., U.S. 104 J12
Marshall, Ark., U.S. 94 E8
Marshall, Ill., U.S. 93 S7
Marshall, Mich., U.S. 92 M10
Marshall, Minn., U.S. 98 K9
Marshall, Mo., U.S. 99 S12
Marshall, Tex., U.S. 96 L15
Marshall Islands, Pac. Oc. 196 F3
Marshalltown, Iowa, U.S. 99 N12
Marshfield, Mo., U.S. 99 U12
Marshfield, Wis., U.S. 92 J4
Marsh Harbour, Bahamas 110 C12
Mars Hill, Me., U.S. 89 B18
Mars Hill, N.C., U.S. 90 H7
Marsh Island, La., U.S. 94 Q8
Marsh Island, U.S. 79 M14
Marsland, Nebr., U.S. 99 N2
Marsugalt, island, Kwajalein Atoll, Marshall Is. 196 K2
Mart, Tex., U.S. 97 N12
Martaban, Gulf of, Myanmar 166 L6
Martapura, Indonesia 168 K11
Martha's Vineyard, island, Mass., U.S. 89 M15
Marti, Cuba 110 J11
Martin, S. Dak., U.S. 98 M3
Martin, Tenn., U.S. 95 E13
Martin, Lake, Ala., U.S. 95 K16
Martinez, Ga., U.S. 90 L7
Martinez Lake, Ariz., U.S. 101 U4
Martinique, island, Windward Is. 113 K17
Martinique Passage, Dominica-Martinique, Fr. 113 J17
Martinsburg, W. Va., U.S. 90 C12
Martins Ferry, Ohio, U.S. 93 Q15
Martinsville, Ind., U.S. 93 S9
Martinsville, Va., U.S. 90 G10
Martuni, Arm. 149 E19
Martuni, Azerb. 149 E21
Maru, island, Indonesia 193 D14
Ma'ruf, Afghan. 157 Q6
Marum Volcano, Vanuatu 198 D3
Marutea, island, Fr. Polynesia, Fr. 199 E19
Marutea, island, Fr. Polynesia, Fr. 199 G22
Marv Dasht, Iran 153 F13
Marvel Loch, W. Austral., Austral. 191 X4
Marvine, Mount, Utah, U.S. 101 N7
Marvin Spur, Arctic Oc. 222 J10
Marwah, Afghan. 156 M3
Mary, Turkm. 154 M10
Maryborough, Qnsld., Austral. 191 U15
Maryland, U.S. 90 C13
Marys, river, Nev., U.S. 102 M11
Marysvale, Utah, U.S. 101 N7
Marysville, Calif., U.S. 103 Q4
Marysville, Kans., U.S. 99 R8
Marysville, Ohio, U.S. 93 Q12
Marysville, Wash., U.S. 102 B4
Maryville, Mo., U.S. 99 R10
Maryville, Tenn., U.S. 95 F18
Marzo, Cabo, Col. 120 E3
Marzūq, Lib. 177 E13
Marzūq, Şaḩrā', Lib. 177 E13
Masada, ruins, Israel 151 N6
Masai Steppe, Tanzania 179 L14
Masallı, Azerb. 149 F22
Masalog, Puntan, Tinian, N. Mariana Is., U.S. 196 B8
Masamba, Indonesia 169 K13
Masan, S. Korea 162 G14
Masasi, Tanzania 179 N15
Masaya, Nicar. 109 M18
Masbate, island, Philippines 169 D14
Masbate, Philippines 169 D14
Mascara, Alg. 176 A10
Mascarene Basin, Ind. Oc. 220 J6
Mascarene Plain, Ind. Oc. 220 K6
Mascarene Plateau, Ind. Oc. 220 H7
Masefau Bay, Tutuila, Amer. Samoa, U.S. 198 L8
Masein, Myanmar 166 F5
Masela, island, Indonesia 169 M17
Maseru, Lesotho 182 K10
Mash'abbé Sade, Israel 151 P5
Mashhad, Iran 153 B17
Mashīz, Iran 153 F15
Mashkai, river, Pak. 157 U5
Mashkel, river, Pak. 157 T3
Mashkel, Hamun-i-, Pak. 157 T2
Mashki Chah, Pak. 157 S2
Mashuray, Afghan. 157 P7
Masi, Vanua, Fiji 198 J9
Masi-Manimba, Dem. Rep. of the Congo 178 L8
Masin, Indonesia 169 M21
Masira see Maşīrah, Jazīrat, Oman 153 M17
Masira, Gulf of, Asia 146 J5
Maşīrah, Jazīrat (Masira), Oman 153 M17
Masisea, Peru 122 G4
Masjed Soleymān, Iran 152 E12
Maskanah (Meskéné), Syr. 150 E10
Maskelynes Islands, Vanuatu 198 E2
Masoala, Presqu'île de, Madagascar 183 E18
Mason, Mich., U.S. 92 M11
Mason, Tex., U.S. 97 P8
Mason Bay, N.Z. 193 R15
Mason City, Iowa, U.S. 98 M12
Masontown, Pa., U.S. 88 P3
Maspalomas, Canary Is., Sp. 184 R6
Masqaţ (Muscat), Oman 153 K16
Massachusetts, U.S. 89 K13
Massachusetts Bay, Mass., U.S. 89 K16
Massacre Bay, Tutuila, Amer. Samoa, U.S. 198 M7
Massakory, Chad 177 J14
Massangena, Mozambique 182 H12
Massawa, Eritrea 179 D15
Mass City, Mich., U.S. 92 F6
Massena, N.Y., U.S. 88 F10
Massenya, Chad 177 J14
Masset, B.C., Can. 76 J7
Massif Central, Fr. 138 M10
Massillon, Ohio, U.S. 93 P14
Massinga, Mozambique 183 H13
Masson Island, Antarctica 207 K21
Mastābah, Saudi Arabia 152 L7
Maştağa, Azerb. 149 D23
Masterton, N.Z. 193 M19
Mastuj, Pak. 156 K10
Mastung, Pak. 157 R6
Mastūrah, Saudi Arabia 152 K6
Masuda, Jap. 165 Q5
Masvingo, Zimb. 182 G11
Maşyāf, Syr. 150 F7
Mataabé, Cape, Vanuatu 198 D1
Matacaw Levu, island, Fiji 198 H5
Matadi, Dem. Rep. of the Congo 178 L7
Matador, Tex., U.S. 96 J6
Matagalpa, Nicar. 109 M18
Matagami, Que., Can. 77 N18
Matagorda, Tex., U.S. 97 S13
Matagorda Bay, U.S. 78 N12
Matagorda Peninsula, Tex., U.S. 97 S13
Matah see Mataso, island, Vanuatu 198 E3
Matahiva see Mataiva, island, Fr. Polynesia, Fr. 199 D16
Mataiea, Tahiti, Fr. Polynesia, Fr. 199 P16
Mataigou see Taole, China 162 D1
Mataiva (Matahiva), island, Fr. Polynesia, Fr. 199 D16
Matak, island, Indonesia 168 H8
Matalaa, Pointe, Wallis and Futuna, Fr. 198 C11
Matale, Sri Lanka 159 T7
Matam, Senegal 176 G5
Mata Mata Vika, Ava, Ha'apai Group, Tonga 198 Q7
Matamoros, Mex. 108 F12
Matane, Que., Can. 77 N21
Matanzas, Cuba 110 G7
Mata Point, Niue, N.Z. 199 C20
Matara, Sri Lanka 159 T7
Mataram, Indonesia 168 M12
Mataranka, N. Terr., Austral. 191 Q8
Mataró, Sp. 139 P10
Matasiri, island, Indonesia 168 L11
Mataso (Matah), island, Vanuatu 198 E3
Matatépai, Pointe, Hiva Oa, Fr. Polynesia, Fr. 199 M20
Matatiele, S. Af. 182 L11
Matatula, Cape, Tutuila, Amer. Samoa, U.S. 198 L9

Mataura, *Tubuai, Fr. Polynesia, Fr.* **199** K20
Mataura, Mouillage de, *Tubuai, Fr. Polynesia, Fr.* **199** K20
Matā'utu, *Wallis and Futuna, Fr.* **198** B11
Matautu, *Samoa* **198** L3
Mata-Utu, Baie de, *Wallis and Futuna, Fr.* **198** B12
Matautulele Point, *Tutuila, Amer. Samoa, U.S.* **198** M7
Matauvau, Passe, *Moorea, Fr. Polynesia, Fr.* **199** N14
Matavai, Baie de, *Tahiti, Fr. Polynesia, Fr.* **199** N16
Matavanu, Mount, *Samoa* **198** K2
Matavera, *Rarotonga, Cook Is., N.Z.* **198** Q9
Matcha, *Taj.* **156** H8
Mateguá, *Bol.* **122** H8
Matehuala, *Mex.* **108** G11
Mateika, island, *Funafuti, Tuvalu* **197** L23
Mateika, Te Ava, *Funafuti, Tuvalu* **197** L23
Matema, island, *Santa Cruz Is., Solomon Is.* **197** P22
Matera, *It.* **136** J11
Matfors, *Sw.* **135** J13
Mathematicians Seamounts, *Pac. Oc.* **219** H17
Mather, *Calif., U.S.* **103** S6
Mathews, *Va., U.S.* **90** E14
Mathis, *Tex., U.S.* **97** T10
Mathura, *India* **158** F6
Mati, *Philippines* **169** F15
Matiere, *N.Z.* **193** K19
Matinicus Island, *Me., U.S.* **89** G17
Matira, Pointe, *Bora-Bora, Fr. Polynesia, Fr.* **199** L14
Matli, *Pak.* **157** W7
Matochkin Shar, *Russ.* **140** D11
Mato Grosso, *Braz.* **122** J9
Mato Grosso, Planalto do, *Braz.* **122** J10
Matopo Hills, *Af.* **174** N8
Matosinhos, *Port.* **139** P5
Maṭraḥ, *Oman* **153** K16
Maṭrûḥ, *Egypt* **177** C17
Matsu *see* Matsu Tao, island, *Taiwan, China* **163** P9
Matsubara, *Jap.* **165** X2
Matsue, *Jap.* **165** P6
Matsumae, *Jap.* **164** H12
Matsumoto, *Jap.* **165** N11
Matsu Tao (Matsu), *Taiwan, China* **163** P9
Matsuyama, *Jap.* **165** R6
Mattamuskeet, Lake, *N.C., U.S.* **90** H14
Mattaponi, river, *Va., U.S.* **90** E13
Mattawamkeag, *Me., U.S.* **89** D18
Matterhorn, peak, *Nev., U.S.* **102** L11
Matthew, island, *Vanuatu* **194** K8
Matthews Peak, *U.S.* **78** J7
Matthew's Ridge, *Guyana* **121** D13
Matthew Town, *Bahamas* **111** J15
Maṭṭī, Sabkhat, *Saudi Arabia-U.A.E.* **153** K13
Mattili, *India* **158** L8
Mattoon, *Ill., U.S.* **93** S6
Matu, *Malaysia* **167** U16
Matua, island, *Russ.* **141** H23
Matua, *Indonesia* **168** K9
Matuku, island, *Fiji* **198** K8
Matunga, island, *Penrhyn, Cook Is., N.Z.* **199** B17
Matunuck, *R.I., U.S.* **89** M14
Maturei Vavao, island, *Fr. Polynesia, Fr.* **199** G22
Maturín, *Venez.* **120** B12
Matxitxako, Cabo, *Sp.* **139** N7
Maúa, *Mozambique* **183** E14
Maubara, *E. Timor* **169** M15
Maudheim, station, *Antarctica* **206** A11
Maud Rise, *Southern Oc.* **224** E11
Maués, *Braz.* **122** D10
Maug Islands, *N. Mariana Is., U.S.* **196** A2
Maui, island, *Hawaii, U.S.* **107** G17
Mauke, island, *Cook Is., N.Z.* **194** K12
Maukme, *Myanmar* **166** H7
Maule, Río, *Chile* **124** M6
Maullín, *Chile* **125** Q6
Maumee, river, *Ohio, U.S.* **93** P12
Maumee, river, *U.S.* **79** F17
Maumee, *Ohio, U.S.* **93** N12
Maun, *Botswana* **182** G9
Mauna Iki, peak, *Hawaii, U.S.* **107** N20
Mauna Kea, peak, *Hawaii, U.S.* **107** L20
Mauna Kea Adz Quarry, *Hawaii, U.S.* **107** L20
Mauna Kea Observatory, *Hawaii, U.S.* **107** L20
Mauna Loa, peak, *Hawaii, U.S.* **107** M19
Maunaloa, *Hawaii, U.S.* **107** F14
Maunalua Bay, *Hawaii, U.S.* **106** E12
Mauna Ulu, peak, *Hawaii, U.S.* **107** N21
Maungapu, peak, *Aitutaki Atoll, Cook Is., N.Z.* **198** P11
Maungdaw, *Myanmar* **166** H4
Maunoir, Lac, *N.W.T., Can.* **76** F11
Maupihaa (Mopelia), island, *Fr. Polynesia, Fr.* **199** E14
Maupin, *Oreg., U.S.* **102** F5
Maupiti, island, *Fr. Polynesia, Fr.* **199** E15
Mau Ranipur, *India* **158** H7
Maurepas, Lake, *La., U.S.* **94** P10
Maurice, Lake, *Austral.* **190** H8
Mauritania, *Af.* **176** G6
Mauritius, *Ind. Oc.* **184** H9
Mauritius Trench, *Ind. Oc.* **220** K6
Maury Bay, *Antarctica* **207** P20
Maury Mountains, *Oreg., U.S.* **102** H5
Maury Seachannel, *Atl. Oc.* **216** E9
Mauston, *Wis., U.S.* **92** K4
Mautaro, Motu, *Tubuai, Fr. Polynesia, Fr.* **199** K21
Mautau, Pointe, *Hiva Oa, Fr. Polynesia, Fr.* **199** M20
Maverick, *Ariz., U.S.* **101** T9
Mavinga, *Angola* **182** E8
Mavrovouni Mine, *Cyprus* **148** L8
Mawlamyine, *Myanmar* **166** L7
Mawlite, *Myanmar* **166** F5
Mawlu, *Myanmar* **166** F6
Mawqaq, *Saudi Arabia* **152** H8
Mawshij, *Yemen* **152** Q8
Mawson, station, *Antarctica* **207** E20
Mawson Coast, *Antarctica* **207** D20
Mawson Escarpment, *Antarctica* **207** F18
Mawson Peninsula, *Antarctica* **207** R16
Max, *N. Dak., U.S.* **98** F4
Maxixe, *Mozambique* **183** H13
Maxton, *N.C., U.S.* **90** J11
Maxwell, *N. Mex., U.S.* **101** Q14
Mayabandar, *Andaman Is., India* **159** P14
Mayaguana Island, *Bahamas* **111** H16
Mayaguana Passage, *Bahamas* **111** H15
Mayagüez, *P.R., U.S.* **111** M22
Mayāmey, *Iran* **153** C15
Mayang, *China* **163** N2
Mayarí, *Cuba* **111** K13
Maydān Ikbiz, *Syr.* **150** C8
Maydh, *Somalia* **179** F17
Maydī, *Yemen* **152** P8
Mayer, *Ariz., U.S.* **101** T6
Mayfa'ah, *Yemen* **152** Q11
Mayfield, *Ky., U.S.* **95** D13
Mayhill, *N. Mex., U.S.* **101** U13
Maykop, *Russ.* **140** H4
Mayno Gytkino, *Russ.* **141** C21
Mayo, *Fla., U.S.* **91** R6
Mayo, *Yukon Terr., Can.* **76** F8
Mayo, Cerro, *Chile* **125** V7
Mayo Faran, *Nig.* **181** G16
Mayotte, island, *Ind. Oc.* **183** D16
Mayotte, Île de, *Mozambique Channel* **185** P17
May Pen, *Jam.* **110** N11
Mayreau, island, *St. Vincent and the Grenadines* **113** M17
Maysville, *Ky., U.S.* **95** A18
Maysville, *Mo., U.S.* **99** R11
Mayumba, *Gabon* **181** M15
Mayville, *N. Dak., U.S.* **98** F7
Mayville, *Wis., U.S.* **92** L6
Maywood, *Nebr., U.S.* **99** Q4
Mazabuka, *Zambia* **182** F10
Mazagan *see* El Jadida, *Mor.* **176** B8
Mazagão, *Braz.* **122** C12
Mazar, *China* **160** H4
Mazar-e Sharif, *Afghan.* **156** K6
Mazari Pass, *Pak.* **157** S3
Mazarrón, *Sp.* **139** S8
Mazaruni, river, *Guyana* **121** D13
Mazatenango, *Guatemala* **109** L15
Mazatán, *Mex.* **108** D7
Mazatlán, *Mex.* **108** G8
Mazgirt, *Turk.* **149** F14
Mazıdağı, *Turk.* **149** H15
Mazirbe, *Latv.* **135** L15
Mazowe, *Zimb.* **182** F11
Mazrub, *Sudan* **178** E12
Mazyr, *Belarus* **133** G14
Mbabane, *Swaziland* **182** J11
Mbaïki, *Cen. Af. Rep.* **178** H8
Mbakaou Reservoir, *Cameroon* **181** H16
Mbala, *Zambia* **182** C12
Mbalmayo, *Cameroon* **181** J16
Mbalo, *Solomon Is.* **197** P19
Mbamba Bay, *Tanzania* **179** N13
Mbandaka, *Dem. Rep. of the Congo* **178** K8
Mbang Mountains, *Af.* **174** H6
Mbanika, island, *Solomon Is.* **197** N18
M'banza Congo, *Angola* **182** B6
Mbanza-Ngungu, *Dem. Rep. of the Congo* **178** L7
Mbari, river, *Cen. Af. Rep.* **178** H10
Mbé, *Cameroon* **181** G16
M'Beni, *Comoros* **185** M14
Mbeya, *Tanzania* **179** N13
M'Binda, *Congo* **181** M16
Mbini, *Eq. Guinea* **181** K15
Mborokua, island, *Solomon Is.* **197** N17
Mbout, *Mauritania* **176** G6
Mbrés, *Cen. Af. Rep.* **178** G9
Mbuji-Mayi, *Dem. Rep. of the Congo* **178** M10
Mbulo, island, *Solomon Is.* **197** M17
Mburucuyá, *Arg.* **124** H13
Mbuyuni, *Tanzania* **179** M14
McAlester, *Okla., U.S.* **96** H13
McAllen, *Tex., U.S.* **97** W10
McArthur River, *N. Terr., Austral.* **191** Q9
McCall, *Idaho, U.S.* **100** F4
McCamey, *Tex., U.S.* **97** N4
McCammon, *Idaho, U.S.* **100** H7
McCaysville, *Ga., U.S.* **90** J5
McCleary, *Wash., U.S.* **102** D3
McClellanville, *S.C., U.S.* **90** M11
McCloud, *Calif., U.S.* **102** M4
McColl, *S.C., U.S.* **90** J10
McComb, *Miss., U.S.* **94** N10
McConaughy, Lake, *Nebr., U.S.* **99** P3
McCook, *Nebr., U.S.* **99** R4
McCormick, *S.C., U.S.* **90** L7
McCrory, *Ark., U.S.* **94** G10
McDermitt, *Nev., U.S.* **102** L9
McDonald, *Kans., U.S.* **99** R3
McDonald Peak, *Mont., U.S.* **100** C6
McDouall Peak, *S. Austral., Austral.* **191** W9
McGehee, *Ark., U.S.* **94** J9
McGill, *Nev., U.S.* **103** P12
McGrath, *Alas., U.S.* **105** H14
McGregor, *Minn., U.S.* **98** G11
McGregor, *Tex., U.S.* **97** N11
McGuire, Mount, *Idaho, U.S.* **100** E5
Mchinji, *Malawi* **182** E12
McIntosh, *Minn., U.S.* **98** F9
McIntosh, *S. Dak., U.S.* **98** H4
McKean Island, *Kiribati* **194** G10
McKeesport, *Pa., U.S.* **88** N3
McKees Rocks, *Pa., U.S.* **88** N3
McKenzie, *Tenn., U.S.* **95** E13
McKinlay, *Qnsld., Austral.* **191** S11
McKinley, Mount (Denali), *Alas., U.S.* **105** H16
McKinleyville, *Calif., U.S.* **102** M2
McKinney, *Tex., U.S.* **96** K12
McKinney, Lake, *Kans., U.S.* **99** T3
McKinnon, *Wyo., U.S.* **100** K9
McKittrick, *Calif., U.S.* **103** V6
McLaughlin, *S. Dak., U.S.* **98** H4
McLean, *Tex., U.S.* **96** G7
McLeansboro, *Ill., U.S.* **93** U6
McLeod Bay, *N.W.T., Can.* **76** H12
M'Clintock Channel, *Nunavut, Can.* **77** E14
M'Clintock Inlet, *Nunavut, Can.* **77** A16
McLoughlin, Mount, *Oreg., U.S.* **102** K4
M'Clure Strait, *N.W.T., Can.* **76** C12
McMinnville, *Oreg., U.S.* **102** F3
McMinnville, *Tenn., U.S.* **95** F16
McMurdo, station, *Antarctica* **207** N13
McMurdo Sound, *Antarctica* **207** N14
McNary, *Ariz., U.S.* **101** T9
McNary Dam, *Oreg.-Wash., U.S.* **102** E7
McPherson, *Kans., U.S.* **99** T7
McRae, *Ga., U.S.* **91** N7
McVeigh, *Ky., U.S.* **95** C20
McVille, *N. Dak., U.S.* **98** F7
Mdennah, region, *Af.* **176** E8
Mead, Lake, *U.S.* **78** H5
Meade, river, *Alas., U.S.* **105** C14
Meade, *Kans., U.S.* **99** V4
Meade Peak, *Idaho, U.S.* **100** J8
Meadow, *W. Austral., Austral.* **191** V2
Meadow, *Tex., U.S.* **96** K4
Meadow Lake, *Sask., Can.* **76** L11
Meadow Valley Wash, *Nev., U.S.* **103** T12
Meadville, *Pa., U.S.* **88** L3
Meandarra, *Qnsld., Austral.* **191** V14
Meander River, *Alta., Can.* **76** J10
Meares, Cape, *Oreg., U.S.* **102** F2
Mears, *Mich., U.S.* **92** K9
Meaux, *Fr.* **138** K10
Mebane, *N.C., U.S.* **90** G11
Mecca, *Calif., U.S.* **103** Y11
Mecca *see* Makkah, *Saudi Arabia* **152** L7
Mechanicsburg, *Pa., U.S.* **88** P7
Mechol, *Yap Is., F.S.M.* **197** C18
Mecitözü, *Turk.* **148** D10
Meck, island, *Kwajalein Atoll, Marshall Is.* **196** M5
Mecklenburger Bucht, *Ger.* **132** E7
Mecúfi, *Mozambique* **183** D15
Mecula, *Mozambique* **183** D14
Medan, *Indonesia* **168** G5
Médéa, *Alg.* **176** A11
Medellín, *Col.* **120** E4
Medford, *Okla., U.S.* **96** E10
Medford, *Oreg., U.S.* **102** K3
Medford, *Wis., U.S.* **92** H4
Media Luna, Cayo, *Cuba* **110** K11
Mediaş, *Rom.* **137** E15
Medical Lake, *Wash., U.S.* **102** C8
Medicine Bow, *Wyo., U.S.* **100** J12
Medicine Bow Mountains, *Colo., U.S.* **100** K12
Medicine Bow Peak, *Wyo., U.S.* **100** K12
Medicine Hat, *Alta., Can.* **76** N11
Medicine Lake, *Mont., U.S.* **100** B13
Medicine Lodge, *Kans., U.S.* **99** V6
Medina, river, *Tex., U.S.* **97** R9
Medina, *N. Dak., U.S.* **98** G6
Medina, *N.Y., U.S.* **88** H5
Medina *see* Al Madīnah, *Saudi Arabia* **152** J7
Medina, *Tex., U.S.* **97** R8
Medinaceli, *Sp.* **139** Q8
Medina del Campo, *Sp.* **139** Q6
Medina de Rioseco, *Sp.* **139** P6
Medina Lake, *Tex., U.S.* **97** R9
Medinipur, *India* **158** J11
Mediterranean Sea, *Eur.* **130** K4
Mednogorsk, *Russ.* **140** J7
Mednyy, Ostrov, *Russ.* **141** E23
Mêdog, *China* **160** L9
Medora, *N. Dak., U.S.* **98** G2
Medren, island, *Enewetak Atoll, Marshall Is.* **196** H8
Medvezh'i Ostrova (Bear Islands), *Russ.* **141** C18
Medvezh'yegorsk, *Russ.* **140** D7
Medyado, island, *Jaluit Atoll, Marshall Is.* **196** L8
Medyai, island, *Jaluit Atoll, Marshall Is.* **196** L8
Meekatharra, *W. Austral., Austral.* **191** V3
Meeker, *Colo., U.S.* **100** L10
Meerut, *India* **158** E6
Meeteetse, *Wyo., U.S.* **100** G10
Mega, *Indonesia* **169** J18
Mēga, *Eth.* **179** H15
Mégara, *Gr.* **137** L15
M̃égham, *Vanuatu* **198** D3
Meghri, *Arm.* **149** F20
Megiddo, *Israel* **150** L5
Megion, *Russ.* **140** H11
Megísti (Kastellórizon), island, *Turk.* **148** J5
Megísti Greece, island, *Gr.* **137** M18
Mehamn, *Nor.* **135** B14
Mehar, *Pak.* **157** U7
Meharry, Mount, *Austral.* **190** F3
Meherrin, river, *Va., U.S.* **90** F12
Mehetia, island, *Fr. Polynesia, Fr.* **199** F17
Mehrīz, *Iran* **153** E14
Mehtar Lam, *Afghan.* **156** M8
Meiganga, *Cameroon* **181** G17
Meighan Island, *Nunavut, Can.* **77** B14
Meigs, *Ga., U.S.* **91** Q5
Meihekou, *China* **162** B12
Meiktila, *Myanmar* **166** H6
Meizhou, *China* **163** R6
Mejatto, island, *Kwajalein Atoll, Marshall Is.* **196** K1
Mejillones, *Chile* **124** E7
Mejillones del Sur, Bahía de, *Chile* **124** E7
Mejit Island, *Marshall Is.* **196** F5
Mékambo, *Gabon* **181** K17
Mek'elē, *Eth.* **179** E15
Mekerrhane, Sebkha, *Alg.* **176** D10
Mekhtar, *Pak.* **157** R8
Mekiro, island, *Gambier Is., Fr. Polynesia, Fr.* **199** Q21
Meknès, *Mor.* **176** B8
Mekong, river, *Asia* **146** K11
Mekong River Delta, *Vietnam* **167** Q13
Mekoryuk, *Alas., U.S.* **104** J11
Melanesia, islands, *Pac. Oc.* **194** G4
Melbourne, *Fla., U.S.* **91** T10
Melbourne, *Vic., Austral.* **191** Z12
Melbourne, Mount, *Antarctica* **207** P14
Mélé Bay, *Vanuatu* **198** F3
Melekeiok, *Palau* **196** N12
Melekeiok Point, *Palau* **196** N12
Melfi, *Chad* **177** J15
Melfort, *Sask., Can.* **76** M12
Melilla, *Sp.* **139** T7
Melinka, *Chile* **125** S6
Melipilla, *Chile* **124** L7
Melitopol', *Ukr.* **133** K17
Mellansel, *Sw.* **135** H13
Mellen, *Wis., U.S.* **92** F4
Melo, *Uru.* **124** K15
Melolo, *Indonesia* **169** N13
Melozitna, river, *Alas., U.S.* **105** F14
Melrhir, Chott, *Alg.* **176** B12
Melrose, *W. Austral., Austral.* **191** V4
Melrose, *Minn., U.S.* **98** J10
Melrose, *N. Mex., U.S.* **101** S15
Meltaus, *Fin.* **135** E15
Melton, *Vic., Austral.* **191** Z12
Meluan, *Malaysia* **168** H10
Melun, *Fr.* **138** K10
Melville, *Sask., Can.* **76** N12
Melville, Lake, *Nfld., Can.* **77** K22
Melville Bay, *N. Amer.* **74** C8
Melville Hills, *N.W.T., Can.* **76** E11
Melville Island, *Austral.* **190** A7
Melville Island, *N.W.T.-Nunavut, Can.* **77** C13
Melville Peninsula, *Nunavut, Can.* **77** F16
Melvin, *Tex., U.S.* **97** N8
Mé Maoya, peak, *New Caledonia, Fr.* **198** D7
Memba, *Mozambique* **183** E15
Memboro, *Indonesia* **169** N13
Memmingen, *Ger.* **132** K5
Memphis, *Mo., U.S.* **99** Q13
Memphis, *Tenn., U.S.* **94** G11
Memphis, *Tex., U.S.* **96** H7
Mena, *Ark., U.S.* **94** G6
Menahga, *Minn., U.S.* **98** G10
Ménaka, *Mali* **176** H10
Menard, *Tex., U.S.* **97** P8
Menard Fracture Zone, *Pac. Oc.* **219** Q15
Menasha, *Wis., U.S.* **92** J6
Mendebo Mountains, *Af.* **174** H10
Mendeleyev Plain, *Arctic Oc.* **222** J7
Mendeleyev Ridge, *Arctic Oc.* **222** H6
Mendelssohn Seamount, *Pac. Oc.* **218** G12
Mendenhall, *Miss., U.S.* **94** M11

Mendi, P.N.G. 193 D18
Mendī, Eth. 179 F14
Mendocino, Calif., U.S. 103 P2
Mendocino, Cape, U.S. 78 E2
Mendocino Fracture Zone, Pac. Oc. 218 E12
Mendota, Calif., U.S. 103 T6
Mendota, Ill., U.S. 93 P5
Mendoza, Arg. 124 K8
Menehune Ditch, Hawaii, U.S. 106 B5
Menehune Fishpond, Hawaii, U.S. 106 C6
Meneng, Nauru 197 F23
Meneng Point, Nauru 197 F23
Menfi, It. 136 L9
Menge, island, Jaluit Atoll, Marshall Is. 196 M8
Mengen, Turk. 148 D7
Mengene Dağı, Turk. 149 G18
Menghai, China 160 Q10
Mengzi, China 160 P11
Meningie, S. Austral., Austral. 191 Y10
Menkere, Russ. 141 F16
Menno, S. Dak., U.S. 98 M7
Menominee, river, Wis., U.S. 92 G7
Menominee, Mich., U.S. 92 H7
Menomonee Falls, Wis., U.S. 92 L7
Menomonie, Wis., U.S. 92 H2
Menongue, Angola 182 E7
Menorca (Minorca), island, Sp. 139 Q11
Men'shikova, Mys, Russ. 140 E11
Mentasta Lake, Alas., U.S. 105 G18
Mentawai, Kepulauan, Indonesia 168 K5
Mentawai Islands, Asia 146 M10
Mentmore, N. Mex., U.S. 101 R10
Mentor, Ohio, U.S. 93 N15
Menyamya, P.N.G. 193 D19
Menzies, W. Austral., Austral. 191 W4
Menzies, Mount, Antarctica 207 F18
Me'ona, Israel 150 K6
Meramangye, Lake, Austral. 190 H8
Meramec, river, Mo., U.S. 99 T14
Merampit, island, Indonesia 169 G16
Merano, It. 136 E9
Meratus, Pegunungan, Indonesia 168 K11
Merauke, Indonesia 169 N21
Merca see Marka, Somalia 179 J17
Mercan Dağları, Turk. 149 F14
Mercara, India 159 Q5
Merced, Calif., U.S. 103 S5
Mercedario, Cerro, S. Amer. 118 L4
Mercedes, Arg. 124 H13
Mercedes, Arg. 124 L12
Mercedes, Arg. 124 L9
Mercedes, Tex., U.S. 97 W10
Mercedes, Uru. 124 K13
Merceditas, Chile 124 H7
Mercy, Cape, Nunavut, Can. 77 G19
Mercy Bay, N.W.T., Can. 76 D12
Meredith, Cape, Falk. Is., U.K. 125 W12
Meredith, Lake, Tex., U.S. 96 G5
Mereeg, Somalia 179 H17
Méré Lava, island, Vanuatu 198 B2
Mergenevo, Kaz. 154 D6
Mergui Archipelago, Myanmar 167 N7
Meriç, river, Gr.-Turk. 137 J16
Meriç, Turk. 148 C2
Mérida, Mex. 109 H16
Mérida, Sp. 139 R6
Mérida, Venez. 120 C7
Mérida, Cordillera de, Venez. 120 C7
Meriden, Conn., U.S. 88 M12
Meridian, Idaho, U.S. 100 G3
Meridian, Miss., U.S. 95 L13
Meridian, Tex., U.S. 96 M10
Mérig, island, Vanuatu 198 B2
Merimbula, N.S.W., Austral. 191 Z14
Merir, island, Palau 194 F2
Merizo, Guam, U.S. 196 E10
Merkel, Tex., U.S. 96 L7
Meroe, ruins, Sudan 179 D13
Merowe, Sudan 179 D13
Merredin, W. Austral., Austral. 191 X3
Merrick Mountains, Antarctica 206 G7
Merrill, Oreg., U.S. 102 L4
Merrill, Wis., U.S. 92 H5
Merrillville, Ind., U.S. 93 P8
Merrimack, river, N.H., U.S. 89 J14
Merriman, Nebr., U.S. 98 M3
Merritt Island, Fla., U.S. 91 T10
Mer Rouge, La., U.S. 94 K9
Merryville, La., U.S. 94 N6
Mersin (İçel), Turk. 148 J9
Mersing, Malaysia 167 U11
Merta Road, India 158 G4
Mertz Glacier, Antarctica 207 R17
Mertz Glacier Tongue, Antarctica 207 R17
Mertzon, Tex., U.S. 97 N6
Meru, Kenya 179 K14
Merzifon, Turk. 148 D10
Mesa, Ariz., U.S. 101 U7
Mesabi Range, U.S. 79 C14
Mesach Mellet, hills, Lib. 177 E13
Mesa Verde National Park, Colo., U.S. 101 Q10
Mescalero, N. Mex., U.S. 101 U13
Mescit Dağı, Turk. 149 D15
Meseong, island, Chuuk, F.S.M. 197 D16
Meseta, plateau, Eur. 130 H2
Me Shima, Jap. 165 S2
Mesilla, N. Mex., U.S. 101 V12
Meskéné see Maskanah, Syr. 150 E10
Mesopotamia, region, Iraq 152 C8
Mesquite, Nev., U.S. 103 T13
Mesquite, Tex., U.S. 96 L12
Messina, It. 136 L11
Messina, S. Af. 182 H11
Messina, Stretto di, It. 136 L11
Messiniakós Kólpos, Gr. 137 M14
Messolóngi, Gr. 137 L14
Mestia, Rep. of Georgia 149 A17
Mesudiye, Turk. 148 D12
Meta, river, Col.-Venez. 120 E8
Meta Incognita Peninsula, Nunavut, Can. 77 H19
Metairie, La., U.S. 94 Q11
Metalanim, Pohnpei, F.S.M. 197 F14
Metalanim Harbor, Pohnpei, F.S.M. 197 F14
Metaline Falls, Wash., U.S. 102 A9
Metán, Arg. 124 F10
Metaponto, It. 136 J11
Meteor Crater, Ariz., U.S. 101 S8
Meteor Seamount, Atl. Oc. 217 V14
Metković, Croatia 136 G12
Metlakatla, Alas., U.S. 105 L24
Metlili Chaamba, Alg. 176 B11
Metolius, Oreg., U.S. 102 G5
Métoma, island, Vanuatu 198 A1
Metropolis, Ill., U.S. 93 V6
Metter, Ga., U.S. 91 N8
Mettur Dam, India 159 Q6
Metz, Fr. 138 K11
Meuse, river, Fr. 138 J11
Mexia, Tex., U.S. 97 N12
Mexiana, Ilha, Braz. 123 C13
Mexicali, Mex. 108 A5
Mexican Hat, Utah, U.S. 101 Q9
México, Mex. 108 J11
Mexico, N. Amer. 108 F9
Mexico, Me., U.S. 89 F15
Mexico, Mo., U.S. 99 S13
Mexico, Gulf of, N. Amer. 74 M7
Meyanodas, Indonesia 193 D14
Meydan Shahr, Afghan. 156 M7
Meymaneh, Afghan. 156 L4
Mezen', river, Russ. 140 F9
Mezen', Russ. 140 E9
Mezen' Bay, Eur. 130 A11
Mezhdusharskiy, Ostrov, Russ. 140 E10
Miahuatlán, Mex. 109 K13
Miami, river, N. Amer. 74 K7
Miami, Ariz., U.S. 101 U8
Miami, Fla., U.S. 91 X10
Miami, Okla., U.S. 96 E14
Miami, Tex., U.S. 96 G7
Miami Beach, Fla., U.S. 91 X10
Miamisburg, Ohio, U.S. 93 R11
Mianchi, China 162 H4
Mīāndowāb, Iran 152 B10
Miandrivazo, Madagascar 183 G17
Mīāneh, Iran 152 B11
Miani Hor, lake, Pak. 157 V5
Mianrud, Pak. 157 T3
Mianwali, Pak. 157 P10
Mianyang, China 160 L12
Miaodao Qundao, China 162 E9
Miaoli, Taiwan, China 163 Q9
Miarinarivo, Madagascar 183 G17
Miass, Russ. 140 J8
Miches, Dom. Rep. 111 M20
Michigan, U.S. 92 F7
Michigan, Lake, U.S. 79 E16
Michigan City, Ind., U.S. 93 N8
Michurinsk, Russ. 140 G6
Micronesia, islands, Pac. Oc. 194 E4
Midai, island, Indonesia 168 H8
Mid-Atlantic Ridge, Atl. Oc. 216 K7
Middelburg, S. Af. 182 L9
Middle Alkali Lake, Calif., U.S. 102 M6
Middle America Trench, Pac. Oc. 219 H18
Middle Andaman, island, Andaman Is., India 159 Q14
Middle Bight, Bahamas 110 F11
Middlebury, Vt., U.S. 88 G12
Middlegate, Norfolk I., Austral. 197 F20
Middle Loup, river, Nebr., U.S. 99 P4
Middlemarch, N.Z. 193 Q16
Middle Park, Qnsld., Austral. 191 S12
Middleport, Ohio, U.S. 93 S14
Middle River, Minn., U.S. 98 E9
Middlesboro, Ky., U.S. 95 D19
Middlesbrough, Eng., U.K. 138 F8
Middleton, Wis., U.S. 92 L5
Middletown, Conn., U.S. 89 M13
Middletown, N.Y., U.S. 88 M10
Middletown, Ohio, U.S. 93 S11
Midelt, Mor. 176 B9
Mid-Indian Basin, Ind. Oc. 220 H10
Mid-Indian Ridge, Ind. Oc. 220 G8
Midland, Mich., U.S. 92 K11
Midland, S. Dak., U.S. 98 L4
Midland, Tex., U.S. 96 M5
Midlothian, Tex., U.S. 96 L11
Mid-Pacific Mountains, Pac. Oc. 218 G7
Midu, island, Maldives 159 X3
Midvale, Idaho, U.S. 100 F3
Midway Islands, Hawaii, U.S. 106 K2
Midwest, Wyo., U.S. 100 H12
Midwest City, Okla., U.S. 96 G11
Midyat, Turk. 149 H16
Mielec, Pol. 132 H10
Mieres, Sp. 139 N6
Miguel Calmon, Braz. 123 H16
Migyaunglaung, Myanmar 166 M7
Mihalıççık, Turk. 148 E7
Miho Wan, Jap. 165 P7
Mijdaḩah, Yemen 152 Q11
Mikkeli, Fin. 135 H16
Mikun', Russ. 140 F8
Mikura Jima, Jap. 165 R12
Milaca, Minn., U.S. 98 H11
Miladummadulu Atoll, Maldives 159 T3
Milagro, Ecua. 120 K2
Milan see Milano, It. 136 E8
Milan, Mo., U.S. 99 R12
Milan, Tenn., U.S. 95 F13
Milano (Milan), It. 136 E8
Milâs, Turk. 148 H3
Milbank, S. Dak., U.S. 98 J8
Milbridge, Me., U.S. 89 F18
Mildura, Vic., Austral. 191 X11
Mile, China 160 P11
Mil Entrance, Yap Is., F.S.M. 197 C18
Miles, Qnsld., Austral. 191 V14
Miles, Tex., U.S. 97 N7
Miles City, Mont., U.S. 100 D12
Miletus, ruins, Turk. 148 G3
Mileura, W. Austral., Austral. 191 V3
Milford, Del., U.S. 90 C15
Milford, Iowa, U.S. 98 M10
Milford, Mass., U.S. 89 K14
Milford, Nebr., U.S. 99 Q8
Milford, Utah, U.S. 101 N6
Milford Lake, Kans., U.S. 99 S8
Milford Sound, N.Z. 193 Q15
Milgarra, Qnsld., Austral. 191 R11
Milgun, W. Austral., Austral. 191 U3
Mili Atoll, Marshall Is. 196 H5
Milikapiti, N. Terr., Austral. 191 N7
Mililani Town, Hawaii, U.S. 106 E11
Milingimbi, N. Terr., Austral. 191 P9
Milk, river, Mont., U.S. 100 B11
Milk, Wadi el, Sudan 178 D12
Mil'kovo, Russ. 141 F22
Millau, Fr. 139 N10
Mill City, Oreg., U.S. 102 G4
Milledgeville, Ga., U.S. 90 M6
Mille Lacs Lake, Minn., U.S. 98 H11
Millen, Ga., U.S. 90 M8
Miller, S. Dak., U.S. 98 K6
Miller Peak, Ariz., U.S. 101 W8
Millersburg, Ohio, U.S. 93 Q14
Millers Creek, S. Austral., Austral. 191 W9
Millington, Tenn., U.S. 94 F11
Millinocket, Me., U.S. 89 D17
Mill Island, Antarctica 207 K21
Mill Island, Nunavut, Can. 77 H17
Millmerran, Qnsld., Austral. 191 V15
Mills, Wyo., U.S. 100 H12
Milltown, Mont., U.S. 100 D6
Millungera, Qnsld., Austral. 191 S11
Millville, N.J., U.S. 88 Q10
Milly Milly, W. Austral., Austral. 191 V2
Milnor, N. Dak., U.S. 98 H7
Milo, river, Guinea 180 F7
Milo, Me., U.S. 89 E17
Miloli'i, Hawaii, U.S. 107 P18
Mílos, island, Gr. 137 M15
Milpa, N.S.W., Austral. 191 W11
Milparinka, N.S.W., Austral. 191 W11
Milton, Fla., U.S. 91 Q2
Milton, Pa., U.S. 88 M7
Milton- Freewater, Oreg., U.S. 102 E8
Miltonvale, Kans., U.S. 99 S7
Milu, island, Kwajalein Atoll, Marshall Is. 196 K4
Milu Pass, Kwajalein Atoll, Marshall Is. 196 K4
Milwaukee, Wis., U.S. 92 L7
Mimizan, Fr. 139 N8
Mimot, Cambodia 167 N12
Mims, Fla., U.S. 91 T9
Min, river, China 160 K11
Min, river, China 163 P8
Mina, Nev., U.S. 103 R8
Mina Bazar, Pak. 157 Q8
Minahasa, Indonesia 169 H15
Mīnā' Jabal 'Alī, U.A.E. 153 J15
Minamata, Jap. 165 S4
Minami Iwo Jima, Jap. 194 D4
Minamitane, Jap. 165 U4
Minami Tori Shima (Marcus), Pac. Oc. 194 C5
Minas, Cuba 110 J11
Minas, Uru. 124 L14
Mīnā' Su'ūd, Kuwait 152 G11
Minatitlán, Mex. 109 K14
Minch, The, channel, Scot., U.K. 138 D7
Minco, Okla., U.S. 96 G10
Mindanao, island, Philippines 169 F14
Mindelo, Cape Verde 185 B15
Minden, La., U.S. 94 K7
Minden, Nebr., U.S. 99 Q6
Minden, Nev., U.S. 103 Q6
Mindon, Myanmar 166 J5
Mindoro, island, Philippines 169 D13
Mindoro Strait, Philippines 169 D13
Mindouli, Congo 181 M17
Mine, Jap. 165 Q3
Mine, Jap. 165 Q5
Mineiros, Braz. 122 K12
Mineloa, Tex., U.S. 96 L13
Mineral Point, Wis., U.S. 92 L4
Mineral Wells, Tex., U.S. 96 L10
Minersville, Utah, U.S. 101 N6
Mineyama, Jap. 165 P8
Minfeng (Niya), China 160 H5
Mingäçevir, Azerb. 149 D21
Mingäçevir Reservoir, Azerb. 149 C20
Mingan, Que., Can. 77 M21
Mingaora, Pak. 156 M10
Mingbuloq, Uzb. 154 J10
Mingenew, W. Austral., Austral. 191 W2
Mingin, Myanmar 166 G5
Mingteke, China 160 G3
Mingteke Pass, China-Pak. 158 A5
Minicoy Island, India 159 S3
Minidoka, Idaho, U.S. 100 H6
Minidoka Internment National Monument, Idaho, U.S. 100 H5
Minigwal, Lake, Austral. 190 J5
Minilya, W. Austral., Austral. 191 U1
Minimarg, Pak. 156 M12
Minjilang, N. Terr., Austral. 191 N8
Minna, Nig. 181 F13
Minneapolis, Kans., U.S. 99 S7
Minneapolis, Minn., U.S. 98 K11
Minnedosa, Man., Can. 77 N13
Minneola, Kans., U.S. 99 U5
Minneota, Minn., U.S. 98 K9
Minnesota, river, Minn., U.S. 98 K10
Minnesota, U.S. 98 H9
Minnewaukan, N. Dak., U.S. 98 E6
Miño, river, Sp. 139 P5
Minocqua, Wis., U.S. 92 G5
Minonk, Ill., U.S. 93 P6
Minorca see Menorca, island, Sp. 139 Q11
Minot, N. Dak., U.S. 98 E4
Minqing, China 163 P8
Minsk, Belarus 133 F13
Minsk Mazowiecki, Pol. 132 G10
Minto, N. Dak., U.S. 98 E7
Minto, Lac, Que., Can. 77 K18
Minto, Mount, Antarctica 207 R14
Minto Inlet, N.W.T., Can. 76 E12
Minturn, Colo., U.S. 100 M12
Minwakh, Yemen 152 P11
Minxian, China 160 J11
Mio, Mich., U.S. 92 J11
Mirabad, Afghan. 157 R2
Mirador, Braz. 123 F15
Miraflores, Col. 120 H7
Miragoâne, Haiti 111 M16
Miramar, Arg. 125 N13
Miram Shah, Pak. 157 P8
Miran, China 160 G7
Miranda, river, Braz. 122 K10
Miranda, Braz. 122 L10
Miranda de Ebro, Sp. 139 P7
Mirando City, Tex., U.S. 97 U9
Mira Por Vos, island, Bahamas 111 H14
Mir Bacheh Kowt, Afghan. 156 M8
Mirbashir, Azerb. 149 D20
Mirbāţ, Oman 153 P15
Mirbāţ, Ra's, Oman 153 P15
Mirebalais, Haiti 111 M17
Miri, Malaysia 168 G11
Mirialguda, India 158 M7
Miriam Vale, Qnsld., Austral. 191 U15
Mirik see Timiris, Cap, cape, Mauritania 176 F4
Mirim, Lagoa, Braz. 122 Q11
Mīrjāveh, Iran 153 G17
Mirnyy, station, Antarctica 207 J21
Mirnyy, Russ. 141 H16
Mirpur Khas, Pak. 157 V8
Mirpur Sakro, Pak. 157 W6
Mirzapur, India 158 H8
Misaki, Jap. 165 R6
Misawa, Jap. 164 J13

Misgar, Pak. 156 K12
Mish'āb, Ra's al, Saudi Arabia 152 G11
Mishawaka, Ind., U.S. 93 N9
Mi Shima, Jap. 165 Q5
Misima, island, P.N.G. 193 E21
Miskitos, Cayos, Nicar. 109 L19
Miskitos, Costa de, Nicar. 109 M19
Miskolc, Hung. 132 K10
Misool, island, Indonesia 169 K17
Mişrātah, Lib. 177 C14
Mission, S. Dak., U.S. 98 M4
Mission, Tex., U.S. 97 W10
Mississippi, river, U.S. 79 K15
Mississippi, U.S. 94 M11
Mississippi Fan, Atl. Oc. 216 K2
Mississippi River, Source of the, Minn., U.S. 98 G9
Mississippi River Delta, La., U.S. 95 R13
Mississippi Sound, Miss., U.S. 94 P12
Mississippi State, Miss., U.S. 95 J13
Missoula, Mont., U.S. 100 D6
Missouri, river, U.S. 79 H14
Missouri, U.S. 99 T12
Missouri-Red Rock, Source of the, N. Amer. 74 J4
Missouri Valley, Iowa, U.S. 99 P9
Mistassini, Que., Can. 77 N19
Mistassini, Lac, Que., Can. 77 N19
Misty Fjords National Monument, Alas., U.S. 105 L24
Misumi, Jap. 165 Q5
Misurata, Cape, Af. 174 D6
Mitai, Jap. 165 S5
Mitchell, river, Austral. 190 C12
Mitchell, Ind., U.S. 93 T9
Mitchell, Nebr., U.S. 99 N1
Mitchell, Oreg., U.S. 102 G6
Mitchell, Qnsld., Austral. 191 V14
Mitchell, S. Dak., U.S. 98 L7
Mitchell, Mount, N.C., U.S. 90 H7
Mitchell Lake, Ala., U.S. 95 K15
Mithankot, Pak. 157 S9
Mithi, Pak. 157 W8
Mitiaro, island, Cook Is., N.Z. 194 K12
Mitilíni, Gr. 137 K17
Mitla, Mex. 109 K13
Mitla Pass, Egypt 151 Q2
Mito, Jap. 165 N13
Mitre, peak, N.Z. 193 M19
Mitre Island see Fataka, Solomon Is. 194 J8
Mitsamiouli, Comoros 185 L14
Mitsio, Nosy, Madagascar 183 D18
Mitsoudjé, Comoros 185 M14
Mitsushima, Jap. 165 Q3
Mittelland Canal, Eur. 130 F6
Mitú, Col. 120 H8
Mitumba Mountains, Dem. Rep. of the Congo 178 N11
Mitwaba, Dem. Rep. of the Congo 178 M11
Mityushikha, Guba, Russ. 140 D11
Mitzic, Gabon 181 K16
Miura, Jap. 165 Q12
Mixian, China 162 H5
Miyake Jima, Jap. 165 R12
Miyako, Jap. 164 K14
Miyakonojō, Jap. 165 T5
Miyazaki, Jap. 165 T5
Miyazu, Jap. 165 P8
Miyoshi, Jap. 165 Q6
Miyun, China 162 C7
Mizdah, Lib. 177 C13
Mizhi, China 162 E3
Mizo Hills, India 158 H14
Mizusawa, Jap. 164 K13
Mjøsa, lake, Nor. 134 K11
Mladá Boleslav, Czech Rep. 132 H8
Mljet, island, Croatia 136 H12
Mmabatho, S. Af. 182 J10
Moa, island, Indonesia 169 M16
Moa, river, Sierra Leone 180 G6
Moa, Cuba 111 K14
Moab, Utah, U.S. 101 N9
Moaco, river, Braz. 122 F6
Moala, island, Fiji 198 J8
Moapa, Nev., U.S. 103 T12
Moaulanui, Puu, Hawaii, U.S. 107 H16
Mobayi-Mbongo, Dem. Rep. of the Congo 178 H9
Mobeetie, Tex., U.S. 96 G7
Moberly, Mo., U.S. 99 S13
Mobile, river, Ala., U.S. 95 N14
Mobile, Ala., U.S. 95 P13
Mobile Bay, Ala., U.S. 95 P14
Mobile Point, Ala., U.S. 95 P14
Mobridge, S. Dak., U.S. 98 J5
Moca, Dom. Rep. 111 L18
Mocajuba, Braz. 123 D13
Moçambique, Mozambique 183 E15
Moce, island, Fiji 198 J9
Moch, island, Chuuk, F.S.M. 197 B16
Mocha, Isla, Chile 125 P6
Mochenap, passage, Chuuk, F.S.M. 197 B16
Mochonap, passage, Chuuk, F.S.M. 197 A15
Mochon Point, Rota I., N. Mariana Is., U.S. 196 D8
Mochudi, Botswana 182 J10
Mocímboa da Praia, Mozambique 183 D15
Mocksville, N.C., U.S. 90 H9
Moclips, Wash., U.S. 102 C2
Mocoa, Col. 120 H4
Moctezuma, Mex. 108 C7
Mocuba, Mozambique 183 F14
Model, Colo., U.S. 101 P14
Modena, It. 136 F9
Modesto, Calif., U.S. 103 S5
Modica, It. 136 M10
Mo Duc, Vietnam 166 M14
Moe, Vic., Austral. 191 Z12
Moen see Weno, island, Chuuk, F.S.M. 197 B15
Moengo, Suriname 121 E17
Moenkopi, Ariz., U.S. 101 R7
Moerai, Rurutu, Fr. Polynesia, Fr. 199 K23
Moerai, Baie de, Rurutu, Fr. Polynesia, Fr. 199 K23
Mogadishu see Muqdisho, Somalia 179 J17
Mogalo, Dem. Rep. of the Congo 178 J9
Mogán, Canary Is., Sp. 184 R6
Mogaung, Myanmar 166 E7
Mogi das Cruzes, Braz. 123 M14
Mogincual, Mozambique 183 E15
Mogocha, Russ. 141 K18
Mogoi, Indonesia 169 K18
Mogok, Myanmar 166 G6
Mogollon Rim, Ariz., U.S. 101 T8
Mogotes, Punta, Arg. 125 N13
Mohács, Hung. 132 L9
Mohala, India 158 K7
Mohall, N. Dak., U.S. 98 E4
Mohammad Agha, Afghan. 156 M8
Mohana, India 158 L9
Mohave, Lake, Ariz.-Nev., U.S. 101 R4
Mohawk, river, N.Y., U.S. 88 J10
Mohe, China 161 A15
Mohéli see Mwali, island, Comoros 185 N15
Mohenjo Daro, ruins, Pak. 157 U7
Mohns Ridge, Arctic Oc. 223 G17
Mohnyin, Myanmar 166 E6
Mohon Peak, Ariz., U.S. 101 S5
Mohotani (Motane), island, Hiva Oa, Fr. Polynesia, Fr. 199 N21
Moindou, New Caledonia, Fr. 198 D7
Mo i Rana, Nor. 134 F12
Moirang, India 158 H14
Moisie, river, Que., Can. 77 M20
Moïssala, Chad 177 K15
Mojave, river, Calif., U.S. 103 W10
Mojave, Calif., U.S. 103 W8
Mojave Desert, Calif.-Nev., U.S. 103 V10
Mojave National Preserve, Calif., U.S. 103 V11
Mojokerto, Indonesia 168 M10
Mokdale, Indonesia 169 N14
Mokil Atoll, F.S.M. 196 Q8
Mokokchung, India 158 G15
Mokp'o, S. Korea 162 G13
Molde, Nor. 134 J10
Moldova, Eur. 133 K13
Molepolole, Botswana 182 J10
Môle Saint-Nicolas, Haiti 111 L15
Molesworth, N.Z. 193 N18
Molfetta, It. 136 J11
Molilele, Heiau o, Hawaii, U.S. 107 Q19
Molina, Chile 124 M7
Molina de Aragón, Sp. 139 Q8
Moline, Ill., U.S. 93 P4
Moline, Kans., U.S. 99 U9
Mollendo, Peru 122 K5
Molloy Deep (Arctic Ocean's deepest point), Arctic Oc. 223 H15
Moloaa Bay, Hawaii, U.S. 106 B6
Molodezhnaya, station, Antarctica 207 C18
Molokai, island, Fr. Polynesia, Fr. 195 H15
Molokai, island, Hawaii, U.S. 107 E14
Molokai Fracture Zone, Pac. Oc. 219 G13
Molopo, river, Botswana-S. Af. 182 J9
Moloundou, Cameroon 181 K17
Molson, Wash., U.S. 102 A7
Moltke, Cape, P.N.G. 197 K13
Molu, island, Indonesia 169 M17
Moluccas (Maluku), islands, Indonesia 169 J16
Molucca Sea, Indonesia 169 J15
Moma, river, Russ. 141 E19
Moma, Mozambique 183 F14
Mombasa, Kenya 179 L15
Mombetsu, Jap. 164 E14
Mombetsu, Jap. 164 G14
Momence, Ill., U.S. 93 P7
Momi, Fiji 198 J5
Momi, Ra's, Yemen 153 R15
Momote, P.N.G. 193 B20
Mompós, Col. 120 C5
Møn, island, Den. 134 P12
Mona, Isla, P.R., U.S. 111 N21
Monaco, Eur. 139 N12
Monahans, Tex., U.S. 97 N3
Mona Passage, Dom. Rep.-P.R., U.S. 111 M21
Mona Point (Monkey Point), N. Amer. 74 Q8
Monarch Pass, Colo., U.S. 101 N12
Mona Reservoir, Utah, U.S. 100 M7
Monari, Afghan. 157 P7
Monchegorsk, Russ. 140 D8
Monchique, Port. 139 S4
Moncks Corner, S.C., U.S. 90 L10
Monclova, Mex. 108 E11
Moncton, N.B., Can. 77 P21
Mondego, Cabo, Port. 139 Q4
Mondeodo, Indonesia 169 K14
Mondovi, Wis., U.S. 92 J3
Mondy, Russ. 141 L15
Monemvasía, Gr. 137 M15
Monero, N. Mex., U.S. 101 Q12
Monessen, Pa., U.S. 88 P3
Monett, Mo., U.S. 99 V11
Monforte, Sp. 139 P5
Mongalla, Sudan 179 H13
Mongbwalu, Dem. Rep. of the Congo 178 J12
Mong Cai, Vietnam 166 G13
Mongers Lake, Austral. 190 J2
Möng Hsu, Myanmar 166 G7
Möng Küng, Myanmar 166 G7
Mongmong, Guam, U.S. 196 C11
Möng Nawng, Myanmar 166 G7
Mongo, Chad 177 J15
Mongolia, Asia 160 D10
Mongolian Plateau, Asia 146 F10
Mongororo, Chad 177 J16
Mongos, Chaîne des, Af. 174 H7
Mongoy, Russ. 141 K17
Möng Pan, Myanmar 166 H7
Mongton, Myanmar 166 H8
Mongu, Zambia 182 E9
Moni, Cyprus 148 L8
Monito, island, P.R., U.S. 111 M21
Monitor Range, Nev., U.S. 103 Q10
Monkey Point see Mona Point, N. Amer. 74 Q8
Monkira, Qnsld., Austral. 191 U11
Monmouth, Ill., U.S. 93 P4
Monmouth, Oreg., U.S. 102 G3
Mono, island, Solomon Is. 197 L14
Mono, Punta, Nicar. 109 M19
Mono Lake, Calif., U.S. 103 R7
Monomoy Island, Mass., U.S. 89 L16
Monon, Ind., U.S. 93 Q8
Monona, Iowa, U.S. 98 M13
Monongahela, river, Pa., U.S. 88 P3
Monopoli, It. 136 J12
Monroe, Ga., U.S. 90 L6
Monroe, La., U.S. 94 L8
Monroe, Mich., U.S. 93 N12
Monroe, N.C., U.S. 90 J9
Monroe, Utah, U.S. 101 N7
Monroe, Wash., U.S. 102 B4
Monroe, Wis., U.S. 92 M5
Monroe City, Mo., U.S. 99 R13
Monroe Lake, Ind., U.S. 93 S9
Monroeville, Ala., U.S. 95 M14
Monrovia, Liberia 180 H6
Mons, Belg. 138 J10
Mönsterås, Sw. 135 M13
Montague, Calif., U.S. 102 L3
Montague Island, Alas., U.S. 105 K17
Montalbán, Sp. 139 Q8
Montana, U.S. 100 D7
Montana, Bulg. 137 G15
Montargis, Fr. 138 K10
Montauban, Fr. 139 N9
Montbard, Fr. 138 L11
Mont Belvieu, Tex., U.S. 97 Q14
Mont-de-Marsan, Fr. 139 N9
Mont-Dore, New Caledonia, Fr. 198 E8
Monteagle, Mount, Antarctica 207 Q14
Monte Azul, Braz. 123 J15
Monte Carlo, Monaco 139 N12
Monte Caseros, Arg. 124 J13
Montecito, Calif., U.S. 103 W7
Monte Comán, Arg. 124 L8
Monte Cristi, Dom. Rep. 111 L17
Montecristo, island, It. 136 H9
Monte Dinero, Arg. 125 W9
Montego Bay, Jam. 110 M10
Montego Bay, Jam. 110 M11
Monte Lindo, river, Para. 122 M9
Montello, Nev., U.S. 102 M12
Montemayor, Meseta de, Arg. 125 S9
Montemorelos, Mex. 108 F11
Montenegro, Yug. 137 H13
Monte Plata, Dom. Rep. 111 M19
Montepuez, Mozambique 183 D14
Monte Quemado, Arg. 124 F11
Monterey, Calif., U.S. 103 T4
Monterey, Tenn., U.S. 95 E17
Monterey Bay, Calif., U.S. 103 T4
Montería, Col. 120 C4
Monterrey, Mex. 108 F11
Montesano, Wash., U.S. 102 D3
Montes Claros, Braz. 123 J15
Montevallo, Ala., U.S. 95 K15
Montevideo, Minn., U.S. 98 K10
Montevideo, Uru. 124 L14
Monte Vista, Colo., U.S. 101 P12
Montezuma, Ga., U.S. 91 N5
Montezuma, Iowa, U.S. 99 P12
Montezuma, Kans., U.S. 99 U4
Montezuma Castle National Monument, Ariz., U.S. 101 S7
Montezuma Creek, Utah, U.S. 101 P9
Montgomery, Ala., U.S. 95 L16
Montgomery, W. Va., U.S. 90 E8
Montgomery City, Mo., U.S. 99 S14
Monticello, Ark., U.S. 94 J9
Monticello, Fla., U.S. 91 Q5
Monticello, Ga., U.S. 90 L6
Monticello, Ill., U.S. 93 R6
Monticello, Ind., U.S. 93 Q8
Monticello, Iowa, U.S. 99 N14
Monticello, Ky., U.S. 95 D17
Monticello, Me., U.S. 89 C18
Monticello, Minn., U.S. 98 J11
Monticello, Miss., U.S. 94 M11
Monticello, N. Mex., U.S. 101 U11
Monticello, N.Y., U.S. 88 L10
Monticello, Utah, U.S. 101 P9
Montijo, Port. 139 R4
Mont-Joli, Que., Can. 77 N20
Montluçon, Fr. 138 L10
Monto, Qnsld., Austral. 191 U15
Montoursville, Pa., U.S. 88 M7
Montpelier, Idaho, U.S. 100 J8
Montpelier, Ohio, U.S. 93 N11
Montpelier, Vt., U.S. 89 G13
Montpellier, Fr. 139 N11
Montréal, Que., Can. 77 P19
Montreal, Wis., U.S. 92 F4
Montrose, Colo., U.S. 101 N11
Montrose, Scot., U.K. 138 E8
Montserrat, island, Leeward Is. 113 G16
Monuafe, island, Tongatapu, Tonga 198 H11
Monument, Oreg., U.S. 102 G7
Monument (Étarik), island, Vanuatu 198 E3
Monumental Buttes, Idaho, U.S. 100 C4
Monument Valley, Ariz.-Utah, U.S. 101 Q9
Monveda, Dem. Rep. of the Congo 178 J9
Monywa, Myanmar 166 G5
Monza, It. 136 E8
Moody, Tex., U.S. 97 N11
Mookini Heiau, Hawaii, U.S. 107 J18
Moolawatana, S. Austral., Austral. 191 W11
Mooloogool, W. Austral., Austral. 191 U3
Moonless Mountains, Pac. Oc. 219 F14
Moora, W. Austral., Austral. 191 W2
Mooraberree, Qnsld., Austral. 191 U11
Moorcroft, Wyo., U.S. 100 G13
Moore, Okla., U.S. 96 G11
Moore, Tex., U.S. 97 S9
Moore, Lake, Austral. 190 J3
Moorea, island, Fr. Polynesia, Fr. 199 N14
Moorefield, W. Va., U.S. 90 C11
Moore Haven, Fla., U.S. 91 V9
Mooreland, Okla., U.S. 96 E8
Moore's Island, Bahamas 110 C11
Moorhead, Minn., U.S. 98 G8
Moorhead, Miss., U.S. 94 J10
Moosehead Lake, Me., U.S. 89 D16
Moose Jaw, Sask., Can. 76 N12
Moose Lake, Minn., U.S. 98 H12
Moosonee, Ont., Can. 77 N17
Mootwingee, N.S.W., Austral. 191 W11
Mopelia see Maupihaa, island, Fr. Polynesia, Fr. 199 E14
Mopti, Mali 176 H8
Moqor, Afghan. 157 P6
Moquegua, Peru 122 K5
Mora, Minn., U.S. 98 H11
Mora, N. Mex., U.S. 101 R13
Mora, Sw. 134 K12
Moradabad, India 158 F6
Moran, Tex., U.S. 96 L8
Moran, Wyo., U.S. 100 G8
Morane, island, Fr. Polynesia, Fr. 199 H22
Morant Cays, Jam. 111 N13
Morant Point, Jam. 111 N13
Morava, river, Eur. 130 H8
Morawhanna, Guyana 121 C14
Moray Firth, Scot., U.K. 138 D8
Morbi, India 158 J2
Mörbylånga, Sw. 135 N14
Morcenx, Fr. 139 N8
Mor Dağı, Turk. 149 G18
Mordyyakha, Russ. 140 F11
Moreau, river, S. Dak., U.S. 98 J2
Morehead, Ky., U.S. 95 B19
Morehead City, N.C., U.S. 90 J14
Morehouse, Mo., U.S. 99 V16
Morelia, Mex. 108 J11
Morella, Qnsld., Austral. 191 T12
Morella, Sp. 139 Q9
Morena, India 158 G6
Morena, Sierra, Sp. 139 S6
Morenci, Ariz., U.S. 101 U9
Moreno Valley, Calif., U.S. 103 X9
Morere, N.Z. 193 L20

Moresby Island, B.C., Can. 76 K7
Moreton, Qnsld., Austral. 191 P12
Moreton Island, Austral. 190 H15
Morgan, S. Austral., Austral. 191 X10
Morgan, Utah, U.S. 100 K7
Morgan City, La., U.S. 94 Q9
Morganfield, Ky., U.S. 95 C14
Morgan Hill, Calif., U.S. 103 T4
Morganito, Col. 120 E9
Morganito, Venez. 120 E9
Morganton, N.C., U.S. 90 H8
Morgantown, W. Va., U.S. 90 C10
Mori, Jap. 164 G13
Moriah, Mount, U.S. 78 G6
Moriarty, N. Mex., U.S. 101 S12
Morioka, Jap. 164 K13
Moriu, Vanuatu 198 E3
Morjärv, Sw. 135 F14
Mor Khun, Pak. 156 K12
Morkoka, river, Russ. 141 H16
Morlaix, Fr. 138 K7
Mormon Lake, Ariz., U.S. 101 S7
Mornington, Qnsld., Austral. 191 Q11
Mornington, Isla, Chile 125 V6
Mornington Island, Austral. 190 C11
Moro, Pak. 157 U7
Morocco, Af. 176 C7
Morogoro, Tanzania 179 M14
Moro Gulf, Philippines 169 F14
Morombe, Madagascar 183 H16
Mörön, Mongolia 160 C11
Morón, Cuba 110 H10
Morona, river, Peru 122 E3
Morondava, Madagascar 183 G16
Moroni, Comoros 185 M14
Moroni, Utah, U.S. 100 M7
Morotai, island, Indonesia 169 H16
Morpará, Braz. 123 H15
Morphou, Cyprus 148 L8
Morphou Bay, Cyprus 148 K8
Morrill, Nebr., U.S. 99 N1
Morrilton, Ark., U.S. 94 G8
Morrinhos, Braz. 123 K13
Morris, Ill., U.S. 93 P6
Morris, Minn., U.S. 98 J9
Morris, Okla., U.S. 96 G13
Morris Jesup, Cape, N. Amer. 74 A7
Morris Jesup Rise, Arctic Oc. 223 J13
Morrison, Ill., U.S. 93 N4
Morristown, N.J., U.S. 88 N10
Morristown, N.Y., U.S. 88 F9
Morristown, S. Dak., U.S. 98 H3
Morristown, Tenn., U.S. 95 E19
Morrisville, Vt., U.S. 89 F13
Morro Bay, Calif., U.S. 103 V5
Morros, Braz. 123 D15
Morrosquillo, Golfo de, Col. 120 C4
Morrumbene, Mozambique 183 H13
Morsi, India 158 K6
Morteros, Arg. 124 J11
Mortlake, Vic., Austral. 191 Z11
Mortlock Islands, F.S.M. 196 R7
Morton, Ill., U.S. 93 Q5
Morton, Miss., U.S. 94 L12
Morton, Tex., U.S. 96 K4
Morton, Wash., U.S. 102 D4
Mortyq, Kaz. 154 D8
Moruga, Trin. & Tobago 113 P17
Moruroa (Mururoa), island, Fr. Polynesia, Fr. 199 H21
Morven, Qnsld., Austral. 191 U13
Moscos Islands, Myanmar 166 M7
Moscow, river, Eur. 130 E11
Moscow, Idaho, U.S. 100 D3
Moscow see Moskva, Russ. 140 F6
Moscow University Ice Shelf, Antarctica 207 N20
Mose, Cape, Antarctica 207 P19
Moselle, river, Eur. 130 G5
Moses Lake, Wash., U.S. 102 C7
Moses Lake, Wash., U.S. 102 C7
Moshi, Tanzania 179 L14
Mosinee, Wis., U.S. 92 J5
Mosjøen, Nor. 134 F12
Moskva (Moscow), Russ. 140 F6
Moso, island, Vanuatu 198 F3
Mosquero, N. Mex., U.S. 101 R14
Mosquitia, region, Hond. 109 K19
Mosquito Coast, N. Amer. 74 Q8
Mosquito Lagoon, Fla., U.S. 91 S9
Mosquitos, Golfo de los, Pan. 109 N20
Moss, Nor. 134 L11
Mossaka, Congo 181 L18
Mossburn, N.Z. 193 Q15
Mossel Bay, S. Af. 182 M8
Mossendjo, Congo 181 M16
Mossgiel, N.S.W., Austral. 191 X12
Mossoró, Braz. 123 E17
Moss Point, Miss., U.S. 95 P13
Most, Czech Rep. 132 H7
Mostaganem, Alg. 176 A10
Mostar, Bosn. and Herzg. 136 G12
Mostardas, Braz. 122 Q12
Mosul see Al Mawşil, Iraq 152 C9
Mosŭlp'o, S. Korea 162 J13
Mota, island, Vanuatu 198 B2
Motaba, river, Congo 181 J18
Mota Khan, Afghan. 157 N7
Motala, Sw. 135 L13
Mota Lava, island, Vanuatu 198 B2
Motane see Mohotani, island, Hiva Oa, Fr. Polynesia, Fr. 199 N21
Motihia, Motu, Tubuai, Fr. Polynesia, Fr. 199 K21
Moto Piti Aau, island, Bora-Bora, Fr. Polynesia, Fr. 199 K14
Motopu, Hiva Oa, Fr. Polynesia, Fr. 199 N20
Motoyoshi, Jap. 164 L13
Motril, Sp. 139 T7
Mott, N. Dak., U.S. 98 H3
Motta Misaki, Jap. 164 G12
Motu, river, N.Z. 193 K20
Motueka, N.Z. 193 M18
Motul, Mex. 109 H16
Motuloa, island, Funafuti, Tuvalu 197 L22
Motupae, island, Manihiki Atoll, Cook Is., N.Z. 199 C14
Motupe, Peru 122 F2
Motupena Point, P.N.G. 197 K14
Moturakau, island, Aitutaki Atoll, Cook Is., N.Z. 198 Q11
Moturiki, island, Fiji 198 J7
Motutapu, island, Rarotonga, Cook Is., N.Z. 198 Q9
Motutapu, island, Tongatapu, Tonga 198 H12
Motutunga, island, Fr. Polynesia, Fr. 199 E18
Motykleyka, Russ. 141 F20
Mouchoir Passage, Turks and Caicos Is., U.K. 111 J17
Moudjéria, Mauritania 176 G6
Mouila, Gabon 181 L15
Moulamein, N.S.W., Austral. 191 Y12
Mould Bay, N.W.T., Can. 77 C13
Mòulede Gaesa, Bioko, Eq. Guinea 184 M7
Moulins, Fr. 138 L10
Moulton, Ala., U.S. 95 H14
Moultrie, Ga., U.S. 91 P6
Moultrie, Lake, S.C., U.S. 90 L10
Mouly, New Caledonia, Fr. 198 C8
Mound Bayou, Miss., U.S. 94 J10
Mound City, Ill., U.S. 93 V5
Mound City, Kans., U.S. 99 T10
Mound City, Mo., U.S. 99 R10
Moundou, Chad 177 K14
Moundsville, W. Va., U.S. 90 B9
Moundville, Ala., U.S. 95 K14
Mo'unga'one, island, Ha'apai Group, Tonga 198 P7
Mounlapamôk, Laos 166 M12
Mountainair, N. Mex., U.S. 101 S12
Mountain Brook, Ala., U.S. 95 J15
Mountain City, Nev., U.S. 102 L11
Mountain City, Tenn., U.S. 95 D21
Mountain Grove, Mo., U.S. 99 V13
Mountain Home, Ark., U.S. 94 E8
Mountain Home, Idaho, U.S. 100 H4
Mountain Lake, Minn., U.S. 98 L10
Mountain Nile see Jebel, Bahr el, river, Sudan 179 H13
Mountain View, Ark., U.S. 94 F9
Mountain View, Hawaii, U.S. 107 M21
Mountain View, Mo., U.S. 99 V14
Mountain View, Wyo., U.S. 100 K8
Mountain Village, Alas., U.S. 104 H11
Mount Airy, N.C., U.S. 90 G9
Mount Arrowsmith, N.S.W., Austral. 191 W11
Mount Ayr, Iowa, U.S. 99 Q11
Mount Barker, W. Austral., Austral. 191 Y3
Mount Barnett, W. Austral., Austral. 191 R5
Mount Carmel, Ill., U.S. 93 T7
Mount Carmel, Pa., U.S. 88 N8
Mount Cavenagh, N. Terr., Austral. 191 U8
Mount Cook, N.Z. 193 P16
Mount Coolon, Qnsld., Austral. 191 T14
Mount Desert Island, Me., U.S. 89 F18
Mount Dora, Fla., U.S. 91 T8
Mount Dora, N. Mex., U.S. 101 Q15
Mount Douglas, Qnsld., Austral. 191 T13
Mount Ebenezer, N. Terr., Austral. 191 U8
Mount Elsie, Qnsld., Austral. 191 S13
Mount Enterprise, Tex., U.S. 96 M14
Mount Gambier, S. Austral., Austral. 191 Z11
Mount Hagen, P.N.G. 193 D18
Mount Hope, N.S.W., Austral. 191 X13
Mount Hope, W. Va., U.S. 90 E8
Mount House, W. Austral., Austral. 191 R5
Mount Ida, W. Austral., Austral. 191 W4
Mount Isa, Qnsld., Austral. 191 S11
Mount Jewett, Pa., U.S. 88 L5
Mount Keith, W. Austral., Austral. 191 V4
Mount Lofty Ranges, Austral. 190 K10
Mount Magnet, W. Austral., Austral. 191 V3
Mount Maunganui, N.Z. 193 K19
Mount Molloy, Qnsld., Austral. 191 R13
Mount Morris, Ill., U.S. 93 N5
Mount Morris, Mich., U.S. 92 L12
Mount Mulgrave, Qnsld., Austral. 191 Q12
Mount Murchison, N.S.W., Austral. 191 W12
Mount Olive, Miss., U.S. 94 M11
Mount Olive, N.C., U.S. 90 J12
Mount Pleasant, Iowa, U.S. 99 Q13
Mount Pleasant, Mich., U.S. 92 K10
Mount Pleasant, Tenn., U.S. 95 F14
Mount Pleasant, Tex., U.S. 96 K14
Mount Pleasant, Utah, U.S. 100 M7
Mount Rainier National Park, Wash., U.S. 102 D4
Mount Riddock, N. Terr., Austral. 191 T9
Mount Rushmore National Memorial, S. Dak., U.S. 98 L2
Mount Saint Helens National Volcanic Monument, Wash., U.S. 102 E4
Mount Sanford, N. Terr., Austral. 191 R7
Mount Sarah, S. Austral., Austral. 191 U9
Mount Shasta, Calif., U.S. 102 M3
Mount Sterling, Ill., U.S. 93 R3
Mount Sterling, Ky., U.S. 95 B18
Mount Stuart, W. Austral., Austral. 191 T2
Mount Vernon, W. Austral., Austral. 191 U3
Mount Vernon, Ala., U.S. 95 N14
Mount Vernon, Ill., U.S. 93 T6
Mount Vernon, Ind., U.S. 93 U7
Mount Vernon, Ky., U.S. 95 C18
Mount Vernon, Mo., U.S. 99 V11
Mount Vernon, N.Y., U.S. 88 N11
Mount Vernon, Ohio, U.S. 93 Q13
Mount Vernon, Oreg., U.S. 102 G7
Mount Vernon, Tex., U.S. 96 K14
Mount Vernon, Wash., U.S. 102 B4
Mount Wedge, N. Terr., Austral. 191 T8
Mount Willoughby, S. Austral., Austral. 191 V9
Mount Zion, Ill., U.S. 93 R6
Moura, Braz. 122 D8
Mouroubra, W. Austral., Austral. 191 W3
Mouse see Souris, river, N. Dak., U.S. 98 E3
Moussoro, Chad 177 J14
Moweaqua, Ill., U.S. 93 R5
Mowshkheyl, Afghan. 157 N7
Moyale, Kenya 179 H15
Moyo, island, Indonesia 168 M12
Moyobamba, Peru 122 F3
Moyu, China 160 G5
Moyynqum, desert, Kaz. 155 H13
Moyynty, Kaz. 155 F15
Mozambique, Af. 182 H12
Mozambique Channel, Af. 174 N10
Mozambique Escarpment, Ind. Oc. 220 N3
Mozambique Plateau, Ind. Oc. 220 M3
Mozarlândia, Braz. 122 J12
Mozdūrān, Iran 153 C17
Mpanda, Tanzania 178 M12
Mpandamatenga, Botswana 182 F10
Mpika, Zambia 182 D12
M'Ramani, Comoros 185 N16
Msaken, Tun. 177 B13
Mt'a Didi Abuli, peak, Rep. of Georgia 149 C17
Mtkvari see Kura, river, Rep. of Georgia 149 C18
Mts'khet'a, Rep. of Georgia 149 C18
Mtwara, Tanzania 179 N15
Mua, Wallis and Futuna, Fr. 198 C11
Mua, Wallis and Futuna, Fr. 198 E12
Mua, Baie de, Wallis and Futuna, Fr. 198 C11
Mu'a, Tongatapu, Tonga 198 J12
Mualama, Mozambique 183 F14
Muang Bèng, Laos 166 H9
Muang Gnômmarat, Laos 166 K11
Muang Kao, Laos 166 M13
Muang Khamkeut, Laos 166 J11
Muang Khoa, Laos 166 H10
Muang Meung, Laos 166 H9
Muang Ngoy, Laos 166 H10
Muang Paklay, Laos 166 K9
Muang Phin, Laos 166 L12
Muang Sing, Laos 166 H9
Muang Xianghon, Laos 166 J9
Muang Xon, Laos 166 H10
Muar, Malaysia 167 V10
Muaraaman, Indonesia 168 K6
Muarabungo, Indonesia 168 J6
Muaraenim, Indonesia 168 K7
Muarakumpe, Indonesia 168 J7
Muaramawai, Indonesia 168 J12
Muaratewe, Indonesia 168 J11
Mubi, Nig. 181 F16
Mucajaí, river, Braz. 122 B8
Muchea, W. Austral., Austral. 191 X2
Muchinga Mountains, Zambia 182 D12
Muchot, Puntan, Saipan, N. Mariana Is., U.S. 196 B4
Muckety, N. Terr., Austral. 191 R8
Muconda, Angola 182 D8
Mucur, Turk. 148 F9
Mucuripe, Ponta de, Braz. 123 E17
Mucusso, Angola 182 F8
Mudamuckla, S. Austral., Austral. 191 X9
Mudan, river, China 161 D18
Mudanjiang, China 161 D18
Mudanya, Turk. 148 D5
Muḑayrib, Oman 153 K16
Muddy Gap, Wyo., U.S. 100 J11
Mudgee, N.S.W., Austral. 191 X14
Mudhol, India 159 N4
Mud Lake, Idaho, U.S. 100 G7
Mudurnu, Turk. 148 D7
Mueda, Mozambique 183 D15
Muéo, New Caledonia, Fr. 198 D7
Muertos Cays, Bahamas 110 F8
Mufulira, Zambia 182 D11
Mufu Shan, China 162 M5
Muganly, Azerb. 149 C20
Mughalzhar Taūy, mountains, Kaz. 154 F9
Mu Gia, Deo, Laos-Vietnam 166 K12
Muğla, Turk. 148 H4
Muglad, Sudan 178 F11
Mugu, Nepal 158 E8
Mūḩ, Sabkhat al, Syr. 150 H10
Muḩammad, Râs, Egypt 151 U4
Muhammad Qol, Sudan 179 C14
Muḩayy, Jordan 151 P6
Muhembo, Botswana 182 F8
Mühlig- Hofmann Mountains, Antarctica 207 A13
Mui Hopohoponga, point, Tongatapu, Tonga 198 J12
Muir Woods National Monument, Calif., U.S. 103 R3
Muisne, Ecua. 120 H2
Mukacheve, Ukr. 132 K11
Mukah, Malaysia 167 U16
Mukawa, Jap. 164 G14
Mukayris, Yemen 152 Q10
Mukeru, Palau 196 N11
Mukhtadir, Azerb. 149 B22
Mukinbudin, W. Austral., Austral. 191 W3
Muko Jima Rettō, Jap. 194 C4
Mukomuko, Indonesia 168 K6
Mukry, Turkm. 154 M12
Muktinath, Nepal 158 F9
Mul, India 158 L7
Mula, river, India 158 L4
Muladu, island, Maldives 159 T3
Mulaku Atoll, Maldives 159 V3
Mulberry, Ark., U.S. 94 F6
Mulberry Creek, Tex., U.S. 96 H6
Mulchatna, river, Alas., U.S. 105 K14
Mulchén, peak, Eur. 130 K2
Muldraugh, Ky., U.S. 95 B16
Mulegé, Mex. 108 D6
Mule Peak, N. Mex., U.S. 101 U13
Muleshoe, Tex., U.S. 96 J4
Mulgildie, Qnsld., Austral. 191 U15
Mulhacén, peak, Sp. 139 S7
Mulhouse, Fr. 138 K12
Muli, China 160 M11
Mulifanua, Samoa 198 L3
Muling, China 161 D18
Mulinu'u, Cape, Samoa 198 K1
Mulitapuili, Cape, Samoa 198 L3
Mulitefala, island, Funafuti, Tuvalu 197 J23
Mulka, S. Austral., Austral. 191 V10
Mull, island, Scot., U.K. 138 E7
Mullan, Idaho, U.S. 100 C4
Mullen, Nebr., U.S. 99 N4
Mullens, W. Va., U.S. 90 E8
Mullett Lake, Mich., U.S. 92 G11
Mullewa, W. Austral., Austral. 191 W2
Mullins, S.C., U.S. 90 K11
Mullumbimby, N.S.W., Austral. 191 W15
Mulobezi, Zambia 182 F9
Multan, Pak. 157 R9
Mulvane, Kans., U.S. 99 U8
Mumbai (Bombay), India 158 L3
Mumbwa, Zambia 182 E10
Mŭ'minobod, Taj. 156 J8
Muna, island, Indonesia 169 L14
Muna, river, Russ. 141 G16
Munaba, India 158 G2
Munan Pass, China-Vietnam 160 Q12
Munburra, Qnsld., Austral. 191 Q13
München (Munich), Ger. 132 J6
Muncie, Ind., U.S. 93 R10
Muncy, Pa., U.S. 88 M7
Munda, Solomon Is. 197 M16
Mundabullangana, W. Austral., Austral. 191 S2
Munday, Tex., U.S. 96 K8
Mundiwindi, W. Austral., Austral. 191 U3
Mundra, India 158 J1
Mundrabilla, W. Austral., Austral. 191 W6
Mundubbera, Qnsld., Austral. 191 U15
Mundul, Afghan. 156 L8
Mungana, Qnsld., Austral. 191 R13
Mungbere, Dem. Rep. of the Congo 178 J12
Mungeli, India 158 J8
Munger, India 158 H11
Mungindi, N.S.W., Austral. 191 W14
Munguba, Braz. 122 D12
Munia, island, Fiji 198 H9
Munich see München, Ger. 132 J6
Munising, Mich., U.S. 92 F8
Münster, Ger. 132 G5
Muntok, Indonesia 168 K7
Munzur Dağları, Turk. 149 F14
Mu'omu'a, island, Vava'u Group, Tonga 198 M11
Muong Te, Vietnam 166 G10
Muonio, Fin. 135 D14
Muping, China 162 F10

Muqdisho (Mogadishu), Somalia 179 J17
Muradiye, Turk. 149 F18
Murakami, Jap. 164 L12
Murang'a, Kenya 179 K14
Murashi, Russ. 140 G8
Murat, river, Turk. 149 F15
Murat Dağı, Turk. 148 F5
Muratlı, Turk. 148 C3
Murayama, Jap. 164 L13
Murchison, river, Austral. 190 G2
Murcia, Sp. 139 S8
Murdo, S. Dak., U.S. 98 L4
Mureş, river, Rom. 137 E14
Muret, Fr. 139 N9
Murfreesboro, Ark., U.S. 94 H7
Murfreesboro, N.C., U.S. 90 G13
Murfreesboro, Tenn., U.S. 95 F15
Murgha Kibzai, Pak. 157 R8
Murghob, river, Taj. 156 J11
Murghob, Taj. 156 J11
Murgoo, W. Austral., Austral. 191 V2
Murguz, peak, Arm. 149 D19
Muri, Rarotonga, Cook Is., N.Z. 198 Q9
Murihiti, island, Manihiki Atoll, Cook Is., N.Z. 199 A13
Murilo Atoll, F.S.M. 196 Q6
Murimaora, Motu, Huahine, Fr. Polynesia, Fr. 199 G14
Muritapua, island, Aitutaki Atoll, Cook Is., N.Z. 198 Q12
Murjek, Sw. 135 F14
Murman Coast, Eur. 130 A9
Murmansk, Russ. 140 C9
Murmansk Rise, Arctic Oc. 223 D16
Murom, Russ. 140 G6
Muroran, Jap. 164 G13
Muroto, Jap. 165 R7
Muroto Zaki, Jap. 165 R7
Murphy, Idaho, U.S. 100 H3
Murphy, N.C., U.S. 90 J5
Murphysboro, Ill., U.S. 93 U5
Murrat el Kubra, Buheirat (Great Bitter Lake), Egypt 151 Q1
Murrat el Sughra, Buheirat (Little Bitter Lake), Egypt 151 Q1
Murray, river, Austral. 190 K11
Murray, river, Austral. 190 K2
Murray, Ky., U.S. 95 E13
Murray, Lake, P.N.G. 193 D17
Murray, Lake, S.C., U.S. 90 K8
Murray, Source of the, Austral. 190 L13
Murray Bridge, S. Austral., Austral. 191 Y10
Murray Fracture Zone, Pac. Oc. 218 F12
Murray River Basin, Austral. 190 K11
Murrayville, Vic., Austral. 191 Y11
Murrells Inlet, S.C., U.S. 90 L11
Murrenja Hill, Austral. 190 B7
Murrin Murrin, W. Austral., Austral. 191 V4
Murrumbidgee, river, Austral. 190 K12
Murshidabad, India 158 H11
Murud, India 158 L3
Murud, Mount, Indonesia-Malaysia 168 G11
Murukta, Russ. 141 G14
Mururoa see Moruroa, island, Fr. Polynesia, Fr. 199 H21
Muş, Turk. 149 F16
Mûsa, Gebel (Mount Sinai), Egypt 151 T3
Musa Dağ, Turk. 148 K11
Musa Khel Bazar, Pak. 157 Q8
Musan, N. Korea 162 B14
Musandam, Ra's, Oman 153 H15
Musa Qal'eh, Afghan. 157 P4
Muşawwal, Jordan 151 Q6
Musaymīr, Yemen 152 R9
Muscat see Masqaţ, Oman 153 K16
Muscatine, Iowa, U.S. 99 P14
Muscle Shoals, Ala., U.S. 95 G14
Muse, Okla., U.S. 96 H14
Musgrave, Port, Austral. 190 A12
Musgrave Ranges, Austral. 190 G8
Mushie, Dem. Rep. of the Congo 178 L8
Musicians Seamounts, Pac. Oc. 218 F11
Music Mountains, Ariz., U.S. 101 R5
Muskegon, river, Mich., U.S. 92 K10
Muskegon, Mich., U.S. 92 L9
Muskegon Heights, Mich., U.S. 92 L9
Muskingum, river, Ohio, U.S. 93 R14
Muskogee, Okla., U.S. 96 F13
Muslimbagh, Pak. 157 R6
Muslimīyah, Syr. 150 D9
Musmar, Sudan 179 D14
Musoma, Tanzania 179 K13
Mussau Islands, P.N.G. 193 B20
Musselshell, river, Mont., U.S. 100 C10
Musselshell, Mont., U.S. 100 D10
Mussuma, Angola 182 E8
Mustafakemalpaşa, Turk. 148 E4
Mustahīl, Eth. 179 H17
Mustang, Nepal 158 E9
Musters, Lago, Arg. 125 S8
Mustique, island, St. Vincent and the Grenadines 113 L17
Muswellbrook, N.S.W., Austral. 191 X14
Mûţ, Egypt 177 E18
Mut, island, Enewetak Atoll, Marshall Is. 196 J8
Mut, Turk. 148 J8
Mutá, Ponta do, Braz. 123 J16
Mutalau, Niue, N.Z. 199 A20
Mutarara, Mozambique 183 F13
Mutare, Zimb. 182 G12
Mute, Motu, Bora-Bora, Fr. Polynesia, Fr. 199 J13
Muting, Indonesia 169 M21
Mutki, Turk. 149 G16
Mutok Harbor, Pohnpei, F.S.M. 197 G14
Mutoray, Russ. 141 J14
Mutsu, Jap. 164 H13
Mutsu Wan, Jap. 164 H13
Muttaburra, Qnsld., Austral. 191 T12
Muturi, Indonesia 169 K18
Mu Us Shamo (Ordos), desert, China 162 D2
Mŭynoq, Uzb. 154 H9
Muzaffarabad, Pak. 156 M11
Muzaffargarh, Pak. 157 R9
Muzaffarnagar, India 158 E6
Muzaffarpur, India 158 G10
Muztag, peak, China 160 H7
Mwali (Mohéli), island, Comoros 185 N15
Mwaniwowo, Solomon Is. 197 Q21
Mwanza, Tanzania 179 K13
Mweka, Dem. Rep. of the Congo 178 L9
Mwene-Ditu, Dem. Rep. of the Congo 178 M10
Mwenezi, Zimb. 182 G11
Mweru, Lake, Af. 174 L8
Mwinilunga, Zambia 182 D9
Myanaung, Myanmar 166 J5
Myanmar (Burma), Asia 166 H6
Myebon, Myanmar 166 H4
Myeik, Myanmar 167 N7
Myingyan, Myanmar 166 G6
Myitkyinā, Myanmar 166 E7
Myitta, Myanmar 166 M7
Mykhaylivka, Ukr. 133 K17
Mykolayiv, Ukr. 133 K15
Mymensingh, Bangladesh 158 H13
Myohaung, Myanmar 166 H4
Myoungmya, Myanmar 166 L5
Myrdal, Nor. 134 K10
Mýrdalsjökull, Ice. 134 G2
Myrtle Beach, S.C., U.S. 90 L11
Myrtle Creek, Oreg., U.S. 102 J3
Myrtle Grove, Fla., U.S. 91 Q1
Myrtle Point, Oreg., U.S. 102 J2
Mysore, India 159 Q5
Mysovaya, Russ. 141 D19
Mys Shmidta, Russ. 141 B20
Mystic, Conn., U.S. 89 M14
Mystic, Iowa, U.S. 99 Q12
Mys Zhelaniya, Russ. 140 D12
My Tho, Vietnam 167 P13
Myton, Utah, U.S. 100 L9
Mzuzu, Malawi 182 D12

N

Na, island, Pohnpei, F.S.M. 197 G14
Naalehu, Hawaii, U.S. 107 P20
Nabari, Tabuaeran, Kiribati 197 B20
Nabeina, Tarawa, Kiribati 197 F17
Nabeul, Tun. 177 A13
Nabire, Indonesia 169 K19
Nablus see Nābulus, West Bank 150 L6
Nabouwalu, Fiji 198 H7
Nabq, Egypt 151 U4
Nābulus (Nablus), West Bank 150 L6
Nacala, Mozambique 183 E15
Nacaome, Hond. 109 L17
Naches, Wash., U.S. 102 D5
Nachingwea, Tanzania 179 N15
Nachu, island, Chuuk, F.S.M. 197 C16
Nachvak Fjord, Nfld., Can. 77 J20
Nacimiento, Lake, Calif., U.S. 103 V5
Nacogdoches, Tex., U.S. 97 N15
Nacozari Viejo, Mex. 108 C7
Nacula, island, Fiji 198 H5
Nada see Danxian, China 163 U1
Nadale, island, Maldives 159 X3
Nadi, Fiji 198 J5
Nadiad, India 158 J3
Nadi Bay, Fiji 198 H5
Naduri, Fiji 198 G7
Nadvoitsy, Russ. 140 D8
Nadym, Russ. 140 G11
Náfplio, Gr. 137 L15
Nafūd ad Daḩy, desert, Saudi Arabia 152 L10
Nafūsah, Jabal, Lib. 177 C13
Nag, Pak. 157 U4
Naga, Indonesia 169 M13
Naga, Philippines 169 D14
Naga Hills, India 158 G15
Nagano, Jap. 165 N11
Naganuma, Jap. 164 M12
Nagaoka, Jap. 164 M11
Nagaon, India 158 G14
Nagar Parkar, Pak. 157 W9
Nagasaki, Jap. 165 S4
Nagato, Jap. 165 Q5
Nagaur, India 158 F4
Nagēlē, Eth. 179 H15
Nagercoil, India 159 S5
Nagir, Pak. 156 K12
Nago, Jap. 165 Y1
Nagorno-Karabakh, region, Azerb. 149 E20
Nagoya, Jap. 165 Q10
Nagpur, India 158 K7
Nagqu, China 160 K8
Nagykanizsa, Hung. 132 L8
Naha, Jap. 165 Y1
Nahanni Butte, N.W.T., Can. 76 H10
Nahari, Jap. 165 R7
Nahma, Mich., U.S. 92 G8
Nahoe, Hiva Oa, Fr. Polynesia, Fr. 199 M21
Nahuei Huapí, Lago, Arg. 125 Q7
Nailaga, Fiji 198 H6
Naiman Qi, China 162 B9
Nain, Nfld., Can. 77 K21
Nā'īn, Iran 153 E13
Nainpur, India 158 J7
Nairai, island, Fiji 198 J7
Nairiri, Tahiti, Fr. Polynesia, Fr. 199 P16
Nairobi, Kenya 179 K14
Naitaba, island, Fiji 198 H9
Naitonitoni, Fiji 198 J6
Najafābād, Iran 153 E13
Najd, region, Saudi Arabia 152 H8
Najin, N. Korea 162 B15
Najrān, oasis, Saudi Arabia 152 N9
Najrān, Saudi Arabia 152 N9
Naka, river, Jap. 165 R7
Nakadōri Jima, Jap. 165 R3
Nakagusuku Wan (Buckner Bay), Jap. 165 Y1
Naka Kharai, Pak. 157 W6
Nakalele Point, Hawaii, U.S. 107 F16
Nakamura, Jap. 165 S6
Nakano, Jap. 165 N11
Nakano Shima, Jap. 165 P7
Nakano Shima, Jap. 165 V4
Naka Shibetsu, Jap. 164 F16
Nakatane, Jap. 165 U4
Nakatombetsu, Jap. 164 D14
Nakatsu, Jap. 165 R5
Nakéty, New Caledonia, Fr. 198 D8
Nakfa, Eritrea 179 D15
Nakhl, Egypt 151 Q3
Nakhodka, Russ. 141 M21
Nakhon Phanom, Thai. 166 K11
Nakhon Ratchasima, Thai. 166 M10
Nakhon Sawan, Thai. 166 L8
Nakhon Si Thammarat, Thai. 167 R8
Nakina, Ont., Can. 77 N16
Naknek, Alas., U.S. 105 L14
Nakodar, India 158 D5
Nakodu, Fiji 198 H7
Nakuru, Kenya 179 K14
Nal, Pak. 157 T5
Nal'chik, Russ. 140 J4
Nalgonda, India 158 M7
Nallıhan, Turk. 148 D7
Nalogo, island, Santa Cruz Is., Solomon Is. 197 P22
Nālūt, Lib. 177 C13
Namai Bay, Palau 196 M12
Namaite, island, Rangiroa, Fr. Polynesia, Fr. 199 K16
Namak, Daryācheh-ye, Iran 153 D13
Namakzar, Lake, Afghan.-Iran 157 N1
Namakzār-e Shahdād, dry lake, Iran 153 F16
Namanga, Kenya 179 K14
Namangan, Uzb. 155 K14
Namapa, Mozambique 183 E15
Namaram, Vanuatu 198 D3
Namatanai, P.N.G. 193 C21
Nambour, Qnsld., Austral. 191 V15
Nam Can, Vietnam 167 Q11
Nam Co, China 160 L7
Nam Dinh, Vietnam 166 H12
Namekagon, river, Wis., U.S. 92 G3
Namelakl Passage, Palau 196 N12
Namenalala, island, Fiji 198 H7
Namgia, India 157 P15
Namib Desert, Namibia 182 H6
Namibe, Angola 182 E5
Namibia, Af. 182 H7
Namioka, Jap. 164 J13
Namiquipa, Mex. 108 D8
Namlea, Indonesia 169 K16
Nam Ngum Dam, Laos 166 J10
Namoi, river, Austral. 190 J14
Namolokama Mountain, Hawaii, U.S. 106 B5
Namoluk Atoll, F.S.M. 196 Q6
Namonuito Atoll, F.S.M. 196 P5
Namoren, island, Jaluit Atoll, Marshall Is. 196 K7
Namorik Atoll, Marshall Is. 196 H4
Nampa, Idaho, U.S. 100 G3
Nampala, Mali 176 H8
Namp'o, N. Korea 162 E12
Nampō Shotō, Jap. 194 B3
Nampula, Mozambique 183 E14
Namsen, river, Nor. 134 G12
Namsê Pass, Nepal 158 E8
Namsos, Nor. 134 G11
Nam Tok, Thai. 166 M8
Namtsy, Russ. 141 G18
Namtu, Myanmar 166 G7
Namu Atoll, Marshall Is. 196 H4
Namuka-i-Lau, island, Fiji 198 K9
Namukulu, Niue, N.Z. 199 B20
Namuli, peak, Af. 174 M10
Namur, Belg. 138 J11
Namutoni, Namibia 182 G7
Namwŏn, S. Korea 162 G13
Nan, river, Thai. 166 K9
Nan, Thai. 166 J9
Nanaimo, B.C., Can. 76 M8
Nanakuli, Hawaii, U.S. 106 E10
Nanam, N. Korea 162 B14
Nan'an, China 163 Q8
Nanao, Jap. 165 N10
Nanatsu Shima, Jap. 164 M10
Nanbu, China 160 L12
Nanchang, China 162 M6
Nancheng, China 163 N6
Nanchong, China 160 L12
Nancowry Island, Nicobar Is., India 159 S15
Nancy, Fr. 138 K11
Nanda Devi, peak, India 158 E7
Nanded, India 158 L6
Nandgaon, India 158 K4
Nandurbar, India 158 K4
Nandyal, India 159 N6
Nanfeng, China 163 N6
Nanga Parbat, peak, Pak. 156 L12
Nangapinoh, Indonesia 168 J10
Nangaraun, Indonesia 168 J10
Nangatayap, Indonesia 168 J9
Nangin, Myanmar 167 P7
Nangiré, Vanuatu 198 C2
Nangnim Sanmaek, N. Korea 162 C13
Nangong, China 162 F6
Nangtud, Mount, Philippines 169 D14
Nanij, island, Jaluit Atoll, Marshall Is. 196 K8
Nanjing, China 162 K8
Nanjing, China 163 R7
Nankang, China 163 Q5
Nankoku, Jap. 165 R7
Nan Ling, China 163 Q3
Nanliu, river, China 163 S1
Nanmatol, island, Pohnpei, F.S.M. 197 G14
Nanmatol Islands, Pohnpei, F.S.M. 197 G14
Nanning, China 163 R1
Nannup, W. Austral., Austral. 191 Y2
Nanortalik, Greenland, Den. 75 D22
Nanpan, river, China 160 N11
Nanping, China 163 P8
Nanri Dao, China 163 Q8
Nansan Dao, China 163 T2
Nansei Shotō see Ryukyu Islands, Jap. 165 Y1
Nansen Basin, Arctic Oc. 222 E9
Nansen Ridge, Arctic Oc. 222 F10
Nansen Sound, Nunavut, Can. 77 B15
Nanshan Island, Spratly Is. 168 E11
Nansio, Tanzania 179 K13
Nantes, Fr. 138 L8
Nanticoke, Pa., U.S. 88 M8
Nantong (Jinsha), China 162 K9
Nantucket, Mass., U.S. 89 M16
Nantucket Island, Mass., U.S. 89 M16
Nantucket Sound, Mass., U.S. 89 M16
Nantulo, Mozambique 183 D14
Nanualele Point, Hawaii, U.S. 107 G18
Nanukuloa, Fiji 198 H6
Nanuku Passage, Fiji 198 H8
Nanumanga, island, Tuvalu 194 H8
Nanumea, island, Tuvalu 194 H8
Nanuque, Braz. 123 K16
Nanusa, Kepulauan, Indonesia 169 G16
Nanutarra, W. Austral., Austral. 191 T2
Nanxian, China 162 M4
Nanxiong, China 163 Q5
Nanyang, China 162 J4
Nanzhang, China 162 K3
Naococane, Lac, Que., Can. 77 M19
Naomid Plain, Afghan. 157 N1
Nao Nao, island, Raiatea, Fr. Polynesia, Fr. 199 C23
Nao Nao, Passe, Raiatea, Fr. Polynesia, Fr. 199 C23
Naonao, Motu, Rangiroa, Fr. Polynesia, Fr. 199 K16
Naozhou Dao, China 163 T2
Napa, Calif., U.S. 103 R3
Na Pali Coast, Hawaii, U.S. 106 B4
Naperville, Ill., U.S. 93 N7
Napia, island, Tabuaeran, Kiribati 197 B20
Napier, N.Z. 193 L20
Napier Mountains, Antarctica 207 C19
Naples, Fla., U.S. 91 W8
Naples see Napoli, It. 136 J10
Naples, Tex., U.S. 96 K14
Napo, river, S. Amer. 118 D3
Napoleon, N. Dak., U.S. 98 H5

Napoleon, Ohio, U.S. 93 P11
Napoleonville, La., U.S. 94 Q10
Napoli (Naples), It. 136 J10
Napoli, Golfo di, It. 136 J10
Napuka, island, Fr. Polynesia, Fr. 199 D20
Na Puu Kulua, peak, Hawaii, U.S. 107 M19
Nara, river, India 158 H1
Nara, river, Pak. 157 V8
Nara, Jap. 165 Q9
Nara, Mali 176 H7
Nara Canal, Pak. 157 U7
Naracoorte, S. Austral., Austral. 191 Y11
Narang, Afghan. 156 M9
Narao, Jap. 165 S3
Narasannapeta, India 158 L9
Narathiwat, Thai. 167 S9
Nara Visa, N. Mex., U.S. 101 R15
Narayanganj, Bangladesh 158 H13
Narbonne, Fr. 139 N10
Nardoo, Qnsld., Austral. 191 R11
Narembeem, W. Austral., Austral. 191 X3
Nares Plain, Atl. Oc. 216 K5
Naretha, W. Austral., Austral. 191 W5
Narew, river, Pol. 132 F11
Narib, Namibia 182 H7
Narlı, Turk. 148 H12
Narmada, river, India 158 J4
Narmidj, island, Jaluit Atoll, Marshall Is. 196 K8
Narnaul, India 158 F5
Narndee, W. Austral., Austral. 191 W3
Narngulu, W. Austral., Austral. 191 W2
Narodnaya, peak, Asia 146 C7
Narooma, N.S.W., Austral. 191 Z14
Narovorovo, Vanuatu 198 C3
Narowal, Pak. 157 P12
Narrabri, N.S.W., Austral. 191 W14
Narragansett, R.I., U.S. 89 M14
Narrandera, N.S.W., Austral. 191 Y13
Narran Lake, Austral. 190 J13
Narrogin, W. Austral., Austral. 191 X3
Narrows, Va., U.S. 90 F9
Narsarsuaq, Greenland, Den. 75 D22
Narsinghgarh, India 158 H5
Narsipatnam, India 158 M8
Naruko, Jap. 164 L13
Naruto, Jap. 165 Q8
Narva, Estonia 135 K17
Narvik, Nor. 134 D12
Nar'yan Mar, Russ. 140 E10
Naryilco, Qnsld., Austral. 191 V11
Naryn, river, Kyrg. 156 F10
Naryn, Kyrg. 156 F12
Naryn, Russ. 141 M14
Narynkol, Kaz. 155 H18
Näs, Sw. 134 H12
Nasarawa, Nig. 181 G14
Nasca, Peru 122 J4
Nashua, river, Mass., U.S. 89 K14
Nashua, Iowa, U.S. 98 M12
Nashua, Mont., U.S. 100 B12
Nashua, N.H., U.S. 89 J14
Nashville, Ark., U.S. 94 H6
Nashville, Ga., U.S. 91 P6
Nashville, Ill., U.S. 93 T5
Nashville, Tenn., U.S. 95 E15
Nashwauk, Minn., U.S. 98 F11
Näsijärvi, lake, Fin. 135 H15
Nasik, India 158 K4
Nasir, Sudan 179 G13
Nasirabad, India 158 G4
Nassau, island, Cook Is., N.Z. 194 J11
Nassau, Bahamas 110 E11
Nassawadox, Va., U.S. 90 E14
Nasser, Lake, Egypt 177 E19
Nässjö, Sw. 135 M13
Nastapoka Islands, Nunavut, Can. 77 K18
Nata, Botswana 182 G10
Natal, Braz. 123 F18
Natal, Indonesia 168 J5
Natal Basin, Ind. Oc. 220 L4
Natal Downs, Qnsld., Austral. 191 S13
Natalia, Tex., U.S. 97 R9
Natal'inskiy, Russ. 141 C22
Natara, Russ. 141 F16
Natashquan, river, Nfld.-Que., Can. 77 L21
Natashquan, Que., Can. 77 M22
Natchez, Miss., U.S. 94 M9
Natchitoches, La., U.S. 94 M7
Natewa Bay, Fiji 198 G8
National City, Calif., U.S. 103 Z10
Natitingou, Benin 180 F11
Natividad, Isla, Mex. 108 D5
Natividade, Braz. 123 H13
Natkyizin, Myanmar 166 M7
Natoma, Kans., U.S. 99 S6
Nattavaara, Sw. 135 E14
Natuna Besar, island, Indonesia 168 G9
Natuna Besar, Kepulauan (Bunguran Utara), Indonesia 168 G8
Natuna Selatan, Kepulauan (Bunguran Selatan), Indonesia 168 H9
Natural Bridges National Monument, Utah, U.S. 101 P9
Naturaliste, Cape, Austral. 190 K2
Naturaliste Plateau, Ind. Oc. 221 M15
Naturita, Colo., U.S. 101 N10
Naubinway, Mich., U.S. 92 G10
Naukot, Pak. 157 W8
Naungpale, Myanmar 166 J7
Nauroz Kalat, Pak. 157 S5
Nauru, Pac. Oc. 197 F23
Naushahra, India 157 N12
Naushahro Firoz, Pak. 157 U7
Nausori, Fiji 198 J7
Nauta, Peru 122 E4
Nautla, Mex. 109 H13
Nauvoo, Ill., U.S. 93 Q3
Navabad, Taj. 156 H8
Navadwip, India 158 J11
Navai, Fiji 198 H6
Navajo Mountain, Utah, U.S. 101 Q8
Navajo National Monument, Ariz., U.S. 101 Q8
Navajo Reservoir, N. Mex., U.S. 101 Q11
Navapolatsk, Belarus 133 E13
Navarin, Mys, Russ. 141 B21
Navarino, Isla, Chile 125 Y9
Navasota, river, Tex., U.S. 97 N12
Navasota, Tex., U.S. 97 Q13
Navassa Island, U.S., Caribbean Sea 111 M14
Navidad, river, Tex., U.S. 97 R12
Naviti, island, Fiji 198 H5
Navoiy, Uzb. 154 L11
Navojoa, Mex. 108 E7
Navrongo, Ghana 180 F10
Navsari, India 158 K3
Navua, river, Fiji 198 J6
Navua, Fiji 198 J6
Nawá, Syr. 150 K7
Nawabshah, Pak. 157 V7
Nawada, India 158 H10
Nawah, Afghan. 157 P7
Nawalgarh, India 158 F5
Nawāṣīf, Harrat, Saudi Arabia 152 L8
Naxçıvan, region, Azerb. 149 F19
Naxçıvan, Azerb. 149 F19
Náxos, island, Gr. 137 L16
Nayak, Afghan. 156 M6
Nayau, island, Fiji 198 J9
Nāy Band, Iran 153 E16
Nāy Band, Iran 153 H13
Nayoro, Jap. 164 E14
Nazaré, Braz. 123 H16
Nazaré, Port. 139 R4
Nazareth see Nazerat, Israel 150 L6
Nazareth, Vanuatu 198 C3
Nazareth Bank, Ind. Oc. 220 J7
Nazas, Mex. 108 F9
Nazca Ridge, Pac. Oc. 219 M20
Naze, Jap. 165 W3
Nazerat (Nazareth), Israel 150 L6
Nāzīk, Iran 152 A10
Nazik Gölü, Turk. 149 F16
Nazilli, Turk. 148 G4
Nazımiye, Turk. 149 F14
Nazimovo, Russ. 141 J13
Nazrēt, Eth. 179 G15
Nazwá, Oman 153 K16
Ndaga, Nig. 181 G16
Ndai see Dai, island, Solomon Is. 197 M19
N'dalatando, Angola 182 C6
Ndélé, Cen. Af. Rep. 178 G9
Ndendé, Gabon 181 M16
Ndeni see Nendo, island, Solomon Is. 197 Q22
N'Djamena, Chad 177 J14
Ndola, Zambia 182 D11
Nduindui, Solomon Is. 197 P18
Nduindui, Vanuatu 198 C2
Neagh, Lake, Eur. 130 E3
Neah Bay, Wash., U.S. 102 B2
Neale, Lake, Austral. 190 F7
Neapolis see Kavála, Gr. 137 J15
Near Islands, Alas., U.S. 104 M1
Neba, Île, New Caledonia, Fr. 198 B6
Nebine Creek, Austral. 190 H13
Nebitdag, Turkm. 154 L6
Neblina, Pico da, Braz. 122 C7
Nebraska, U.S. 99 P2
Nebraska City, Nebr., U.S. 99 Q9
Nécé, New Caledonia, Fr. 198 D10
Necedah, Wis., U.S. 92 K4
Neches, river, Tex., U.S. 97 N15
Neckarboo Range, Austral. 190 K12
Necker Island, Hawaii, U.S. 106 M7
Necker Ridge, Pac. Oc. 218 G11
Necochea, Arg. 125 N13
Nederland, Tex., U.S. 97 Q16
Needles, Calif., U.S. 103 W12
Neenah, Wis., U.S. 92 K6
Neftçala, Azerb. 149 E23
Nefteyugansk, Russ. 140 H11
Negaunee, Mich., U.S. 92 F7
Negeribatin, Indonesia 168 L7
Negev, region, Israel 151 P5
Negomane, Mozambique 183 D14
Negombo, Sri Lanka 159 T7
Negonego, island, Fr. Polynesia, Fr. 199 F20
Negotin, Yug. 137 G14
Negra, Laguna, Uru. 124 L15
Negra, Punta, Peru 122 F1
Negril, Jam. 110 M10
Negritos, Peru 122 E1
Negro, river, Arg. 125 P9
Negro, river, Arg. 125 Q10
Negro, river, Bol. 122 J8
Negro, river, Braz. 122 C7
Negro, river, Braz. 122 D9
Negros, island, Philippines 169 E14
Nehbandān, Iran 153 E17
Nehe, China 161 C16
Néhoué, Baie de, New Caledonia, Fr. 198 C6
Nehus, Cape, P.N.G. 197 J14
Neiafu, Vava'u Group, Tonga 198 L11
Neiba, Dom. Rep. 111 M17
Neiba, Bahía de, Dom. Rep. 111 N18
Neiden, Nor. 135 C15
Neiges, Piton des, Réunion, Fr. 185 G16
Neihart, Mont., U.S. 100 D8
Neijiang, China 160 L12
Neillsville, Wis., U.S. 92 J4
Nei Mongol Gaoyuan, China 162 B1
Neiqiu, China 162 F5
Neiva, Col. 120 G5
Nekoosa, Wis., U.S. 92 J5
Neksø, Den. 135 P13
Nekurandu, island, Maldives 159 T3
Nelemnoye, Russ. 141 E19
Neligh, Nebr., U.S. 99 N7
Nel'kan, Russ. 141 H19
Nell, island, Kwajalein Atoll, Marshall Is. 196 L4
Nellore, India 159 P7
Nell Passage, Kwajalein Atoll, Marshall Is. 196 L3
Nelson, river, Man., Can. 77 L14
Nelson, B.C., Can. 76 M9
Nelson, N.Z. 193 M18
Nelson, Nebr., U.S. 99 R7
Nelson, Nev., U.S. 103 V12
Nelson, Cape, Austral. 190 M11
Nelson, Estrecho, Chile 125 W6
Nelson House, Man., Can. 77 L13
Nelson Island, Alas., U.S. 104 K11
Nelson Lagoon, Alas., U.S. 104 N12
Nelson Reservoir, Mont., U.S. 100 B10
Néma, Mauritania 176 G7
Neman, river, Eur. 130 E8
Nembrala, Indonesia 169 N14
Nemiscau, Que., Can. 77 M18
Nemrud Dagh, Turk. 149 G13
Nemrut Gölü, Turk. 149 G16
Nemunas, river, Lith. 135 N16
Nemuro, Jap. 164 F16
Nemuro Strait, Jap. 164 E16
Nen, river, China 161 B16
Nenana, Alas., U.S. 105 G16
Nendo (Ndeni), island, Santa Cruz Is., Solomon Is. 197 Q22
Nenjiang, China 161 C16
Nenom, Mochun, Chuuk, F.S.M. 197 B14
Neoch, atoll, Chuuk, F.S.M. 197 D15
Neodesha, Kans., U.S. 99 U9
Neola, Utah, U.S. 100 L9
Neosho, river, U.S. 79 H13
Neosho, Mo., U.S. 99 V11
Nepa, Russ. 141 J15
Nepal, Asia 158 F9
Nepalganj, India 158 F8
Nepean, island, Norfolk I., Austral. 197 G20
Nephi, Utah, U.S. 100 M7
Nepis, Mochun, Chuuk, F.S.M. 197 C15
Neptune Range, Antarctica 206 G10
Nerchinsk, Russ. 141 L17
Nerchinskiy Zavod, Russ. 141 L18
Neriquinha, Angola 182 F8
Nero Seamount, Hawaii, U.S. 106 K2
Nerpo, Russ. 141 J17
Nerrima, W. Austral., Austral. 191 R5
Nesika Beach, Oreg., U.S. 102 K1
Neskaupstadur, Ice. 134 F4
Nespelem, Wash., U.S. 102 B7
Ness, Loch, Scot., U.K. 138 D7
Ness City, Kans., U.S. 99 T5
Netanya, Israel 150 L5
Netherdale, Qnsld., Austral. 191 S14
Netherlands, Eur. 138 G12
Nettilling Lake, Nunavut, Can. 77 G18
Netzahualcóyotl, Mex. 108 J12
Neubrandenburg, Ger. 132 F7
Neuchâtel, Switz. 132 K4
Neumayer, station, Antarctica 206 A11
Neumünster, Ger. 132 E6
Neun, river, Laos 166 H11
Neuquén, river, Arg. 125 N8
Neuquén, Arg. 125 P8
Neuse, river, N.C., U.S. 90 H12
Neusiedler Lake, Eur. 130 G7
Neustrelitz, Ger. 132 F7
Nevada, U.S. 103 Q10
Nevada, Iowa, U.S. 99 N11
Nevada, Mo., U.S. 99 U11
Nevada, Sierra, U.S. 78 G4
Nevada City, Calif., U.S. 103 Q5
Nevada de Santa Marta, Serra, S. Amer. 118 A3
Nevea, Santa Cruz Is., Solomon Is. 197 P22
Nevel', Russ. 140 E5
Never, Russ. 141 K18
Nevers, Fr. 138 L10
Neves, São Tomé and Príncipe 185 C20
Nevinnomyssk, Russ. 140 J4
Nevis, island, St. Kitts and Nevis 113 G16
Nevşehir, Turk. 148 G10
New, river, N.C., U.S. 90 J13
New, river, Va., U.S. 90 F9
New Albany, Ind., U.S. 93 T9
New Albany, Miss., U.S. 94 H12
New Amsterdam, Guyana 121 D15
Newark, Ark., U.S. 94 F9
Newark, Del., U.S. 90 B14
Newark, N.J., U.S. 88 N11
Newark, N.Y., U.S. 88 J7
Newark, Ohio, U.S. 93 R13
Newaygo, Mich., U.S. 92 L9
New Bedford, Mass., U.S. 89 L15
Newberg, Oreg., U.S. 102 F3
New Bern, N.C., U.S. 90 J13
Newbern, Tenn., U.S. 94 E12
Newberry, Fla., U.S. 91 R7
Newberry, Mich., U.S. 92 F10
Newberry, S.C., U.S. 90 K8
New Bight, Bahamas 111 F13
New Boston, Ohio, U.S. 93 T13
New Boston, Tex., U.S. 96 K15
New Braunfels, Tex., U.S. 97 R10
New Britain, island, P.N.G. 193 C21
New Britain, Conn., U.S. 88 L12
New Brunswick, Can. 77 P21
New Brunswick, N.J., U.S. 88 N10
Newburg, Mo., U.S. 99 U13
Newburgh, N.Y., U.S. 88 M11
New Caledonia, island, Pac. Oc. 194 K7
New Caledonia Basin, Pac. Oc. 218 M8
New Castle, Ind., U.S. 93 R10
New Castle, Pa., U.S. 88 M3
Newcastle, Calif., U.S. 103 Q5
Newcastle, N.S.W., Austral. 191 X15
Newcastle, Tex., U.S. 96 K9
Newcastle, Eng., U.K. 138 F8
Newcastle, Wyo., U.S. 100 G14
Newcastle Waters, N. Terr., Austral. 191 R8
New City, N.Y., U.S. 88 M11
Newdegate, W. Austral., Austral. 191 X3
New Delhi, India 158 F6
Newell, S. Dak., U.S. 98 K2
New England, N. Dak., U.S. 98 G2
New England Range, Austral. 190 J15
New England Seamounts, Atl. Oc. 216 H5
Newenham, Cape, Alas., U.S. 104 L12
Newfoundland, Grand Banks of, Atl. Oc. 216 G6
Newfoundland, Island of, Nfld., Can. 77 M23
Newfoundland and Labrador, Can. 77 J20
Newfoundland Evaporation Basin, Utah, U.S. 100 K6
New Franklin, Mo., U.S. 99 S12
New Georgia, island, Solomon Is. 197 M16
New Georgia Group, Solomon Is. 197 M16
New Georgia Sound (The Slot), Solomon Is. 197 L16
New Glasgow, N.S., Can. 77 P22
New Guinea, island, Asia 146 K16
New Hampshire, U.S. 89 J14
New Hampton, Iowa, U.S. 98 M12
New Hanover, island, P.N.G. 193 B21
New Harbor, Me., U.S. 89 G16
New Harmony, Utah, U.S. 101 P6
New Haven, Conn., U.S. 88 M12
New Haven, Ind., U.S. 93 P10
New Hebrides Trench, Pac. Oc. 218 M9
New Iberia, La., U.S. 94 Q9
New Ireland, island, P.N.G. 193 C21
New Jersey, U.S. 88 P10
Newkirk, N. Mex., U.S. 101 S14
Newkirk, Okla., U.S. 96 E11
New Lexington, Ohio, U.S. 93 R14
New Lisbon, Wis., U.S. 92 K4
New Liskeard, Ont., Can. 77 P18
New London, Conn., U.S. 89 M13
New London, Iowa, U.S. 99 Q14
New London, Wis., U.S. 92 J6
New Madrid, Mo., U.S. 99 V16
Newman, Calif., U.S. 103 S5
Newman, W. Austral., Austral. 191 T3
Newman Grove, Nebr., U.S. 99 P7
New Market, Va., U.S. 90 D11
New Martinsville, W. Va., U.S. 90 C9
New Meadows, Idaho, U.S. 100 F4
New Mexico, U.S. 101 S11

New Mirpur, Pak. 157 N11
Newnan, Ga., U.S. 90 L4
New Orleans, La., U.S. 94 Q11
New Philadelphia, Ohio, U.S. 93 Q15
New Plymouth, N.Z. 193 L18
Newport, Ark., U.S. 94 F10
Newport, Ky., U.S. 95 A18
Newport, Me., U.S. 89 E17
Newport, Oreg., U.S. 102 G2
Newport, R.I., U.S. 89 M14
Newport, Tenn., U.S. 95 E19
Newport, Eng., U.K. 138 J8
Newport, Vt., U.S. 89 E13
Newport, Wash., U.S. 102 B9
Newport Beach, Calif., U.S. 103 Y9
Newport News, Va., U.S. 90 F14
New Port Richey, Fla., U.S. 91 T7
New Prague, Minn., U.S. 98 K11
New Providence, Bahamas 110 E11
New Richmond, Wis., U.S. 92 H2
New Roads, La., U.S. 94 N9
New Rochelle, N.Y., U.S. 88 N11
New Rockford, N. Dak., U.S. 98 F6
Newry, N. Terr., Austral. 191 Q7
Newry, N. Ire., U.K. 138 F6
New Salem, N. Dak., U.S. 98 G4
New Schwabenland, Antarctica 206 C11
New Siberian Islands see Novosibirskiye Ostrova, Russ. 141 D16
New Smyrna Beach, Fla., U.S. 91 S9
New South Wales, Austral. 191 W13
New Springs, W. Austral., Austral. 191 U3
New Stuyahok, Alas., U.S. 105 K14
Newton, Ill., U.S. 93 S7
Newton, Iowa, U.S. 99 P12
Newton, Kans., U.S. 99 U7
Newton, Mass., U.S. 89 K14
Newton, Miss., U.S. 94 L12
Newton, Tex., U.S. 97 P16
New Town, N. Dak., U.S. 98 F3
New Ulm, Minn., U.S. 98 K10
New Waverly, Tex., U.S. 97 P13
New York, U.S. 88 K7
New York, N.Y., U.S. 88 N11
Neyrīz, Iran 153 G14
Neyshābūr, Iran 153 C16
Nezperce, Idaho, U.S. 100 D4
Nez Perce National Historical Park, Idaho, U.S. 100 D3
Nez Perce Pass, Idaho-Mont., U.S. 100 E5
Ngabordamlu, Tanjung, Indonesia 193 D15
Ngain, island, Jaluit Atoll, Marshall Is. 196 K7
Ngajangel, island, Palau 196 K12
Ngake, island, Manihiki Atoll, Cook Is., N.Z. 199 B14
Ngake, Pukapuka Atoll, Cook Is., N.Z. 198 Q2
Ngalkol, Palau 196 Q10
Ngamegei Passage, Palau 196 L12
Ngami, Lake, Botswana 182 G8
Ngamring, China 160 L6
Ngangla Ringco, lake, China 160 K5
Nganglong Kangri, China 160 J5
Ngaoundéré, Cameroon 181 G16
Ngape, Myanmar 166 H5
Ngardmau, Palau 196 M12
Ngardmau Bay, Palau 196 M12
Ngardololok, Palau 196 Q10
Ngaregur, island, Palau 196 L12
Ngarekeklav, island, Palau 196 L12
Ngaremediu, island, Palau 196 P11
Ngaruangl Passage, Palau 196 J12
Ngaruawahia, N.Z. 193 K19
Ngatangiia, Rarotonga, Cook Is., N.Z. 198 Q9
Ngatik Atoll, F.S.M. 196 Q7
Ngauruhoe, Mount, N.Z. 193 L19
Ngcheangel see Kayangel Islands, islands, Palau 196 K12
Ngeaur see Angaur, island, Palau 196 R10
Ngemelis Islands, Palau 196 Q10
Ngerchelong see Arekalong Peninsula, Palau 196 M11
Ngeregong, island, Palau 196 Q11
Ngergoi, island, Palau 196 Q10
Ngertachebeab see Komebail Lagoon, Palau 196 N11
Ngeruktabel see Urukthapel, island, Palau 196 P11
Ngesebus, island, Palau 196 Q10
Nggatokae, island, Solomon Is. 197 N17
Nggela Pile, island, Solomon Is. 197 N19
Nggela Sule, island, Solomon Is. 197 N19
Ngobasangel, island, Palau 196 P10
Ngoko, river, Cameroon-Congo 181 K17
Ngoring Hu, China 160 J10
Ngorongoro Crater, Tanzania 179 L14
Ngounié, river, Gabon 181 L15
Ngourti, Niger 177 H13
Nguigmi, Niger 177 H13
Nguiu, N. Terr., Austral. 191 N7
Ngukurr, N. Terr., Austral. 191 Q9
Ngulu Atoll, F.S.M. 196 Q2
Nguna, island, Vanuatu 198 E3
Nguru, Nig. 181 E15
Nhamundá, Braz. 122 D10
Nha Trang, Vietnam 167 N14
Nhulunbuy, N. Terr., Austral. 191 P10
Niafounké, Mali 176 H8
Niagara, river, N.Y., U.S. 88 H5
Niagara, Wis., U.S. 92 G7
Niagara Falls, N.Y., U.S. 88 J5
Niah, Malaysia 168 G11
Niamey, Niger 176 J10
Niangara, Dem. Rep. of the Congo 178 H11
Niangua, river, Mo., U.S. 99 U12
Nianiau, Puu, Hawaii, U.S. 107 G17
Nianzishan, China 161 C16
Nias, island, Indonesia 168 H4
Niau, island, Fr. Polynesia, Fr. 199 E17
Nibok, Nauru 197 E23
Nicaragua, N. Amer. 109 M18
Nicaragua, Lago de, Nicar. 109 M18
Nicastro, It. 136 K11
Nice, Fr. 139 N12
Nicephorium see Ar Raqqah, Syr. 150 E11
Niceville, Fla., U.S. 91 Q2
Nichinan, Jap. 165 T5
Nicholas Channel, Bahamas-Cuba 110 F8
Nicholasville, Ky., U.S. 95 B18
Nicholls' Town, Bahamas 110 E11
Nicholson, W. Austral., Austral. 191 R7
Nicholson Range, Austral. 190 H2
Nickavilla, Qnsld., Austral. 191 U12
Nickerson, Kans., U.S. 99 T7
Nicobar Islands, India 159 S14
Nicosia see Lefkosia, Cyprus 148 L8
Nicosia, It. 136 L10
Nicotera, It. 136 K11
Nicoya, Península de, C.R. 109 N18
Nida, Lith. 135 N15
Nidzh, Azerb. 149 C21
Nidzica, Pol. 132 F10
Nienburg, Ger. 132 F6
Nieuw Amsterdam, Suriname 121 E16
Nieuw Nickerie, Suriname 121 E15
Nif, Yap Is., F.S.M. 197 D18
Nifiloli, island, Santa Cruz Is., Solomon Is. 197 P23
Niğde, Turk. 148 G10
Niger, Af. 176 H12
Niger, river, Af. 174 H5
Niger, Source of the, Af. 174 H2
Nigeria, Af. 181 F14
Niger River Delta, Af. 174 J5
Nightingale Island, Atl. Oc. 174 R2
Nihing, river, Pak. 157 V2
Nihiru, island, Fr. Polynesia, Fr. 199 E19
Nihoa, island, Hawaii, U.S. 106 M8
Nihonmatsu, Jap. 164 M13
Niigata, Jap. 164 M11
Niihama, Jap. 165 R7
Niihau, island, Hawaii, U.S. 106 C3
Niimi, Jap. 165 Q7
Nii Shima, Jap. 165 Q12
Nijmegen, Neth. 138 H11
Nikalap Aru, island, Pohnpei, F.S.M. 197 G13
Nikao, Rarotonga, Cook Is., N.Z. 198 Q9
Nikaupara, Aitutaki Atoll, Cook Is., N.Z. 198 Q11
Nikel', Russ. 140 C9
Nikiti Seamount, Ind. Oc. 220 G10
Nikolai, Alas., U.S. 105 H15
Nikolayevsk, Russ. 140 H6
Nikolayevskiy, Russ. 141 J19
Nikolayevsk na Amure, Russ. 141 J21
Nikolski, Alas., U.S. 104 Q9
Nikol'skoye, Russ. 141 E23
Nikopol', Ukr. 133 K16
Nīk Pey, Iran 152 B11
Niksar, Turk. 148 D12
Nīkshahr, Iran 153 H17
Nikšić, Yug. 137 H13
Nikumaroro, island, Kiribati 194 H10
Nil, Russ. 141 K18
Nilandu, island, Maldives 159 V3
Nilandu, island, Maldives 159 W3
Nilandu Atoll, Maldives 159 V3
Nile, river, Af. 174 E9
Nile, Sources of the, Af. 174 K9
Nile River Delta, Af. 174 D9
Niles, Mich., U.S. 93 N9
Niles, Ohio, U.S. 93 P15
Nilgiri Hills, India 159 Q5
Nimach, India 158 H4
Nimbahera, India 158 H4
Nimba Mountains, Côte d'Ivoire 180 G7
Nimbin, N.S.W., Austral. 191 W15
Nîmes, Fr. 139 N11
Nimrod Glacier, Antarctica 207 L13
Ninati, Indonesia 169 L21
Nine Degree Channel, India 159 S2
Ninety East Ridge, Ind. Oc. 220 K11
Ninety Mile Beach, Austral. 190 M13
Ninety Mile Beach, N.Z. 193 G18
Nineveh, ruins, Iraq 152 C9
Ninfas, Punta, Arg. 125 R10
Ningbo, China 162 L10
Ningcheng, China 162 C8
Ningde, China 163 P8
Ningdu, China 163 P6
Ningguo, China 162 L8
Ningshan, China 162 H1
Ningwu, China 162 D4
Ningyuan, China 163 P3
Ninh Binh, Vietnam 166 H12
Ninh Hoa, Vietnam 167 N14
Ninigo Group, islands, P.N.G. 193 B18
Ninilchik, Alas., U.S. 105 K16
Niniva, island, Ha'apai Group, Tonga 198 P6
Ninnescah, river, Kans., U.S. 99 U7
Ninni, island, Kwajalein Atoll, Marshall Is. 196 N5
Ninnis Glacier, Antarctica 207 R17
Ninole, Hawaii, U.S. 107 L21
Ninole, Hawaii, U.S. 107 P20
Nioaque, Braz. 122 L10
Niobrara, river, Nebr., U.S. 98 M5
Nioro du Sahel, Mali 176 H6
Niort, Fr. 138 L9
Nioumachoua, Comoros 185 N15
Nipawin, Sask., Can. 76 M12
Nipe, Bahía de, Cuba 111 K13
Nipigon, Ont., Can. 77 P16
Nipigon, Lake, Ont., Can. 77 N16
Nipton, Calif., U.S. 103 V12
Niquelândia, Braz. 123 J13
Niquero, Cuba 110 K11
Nīr, Iran 152 B11
Nirmal, India 158 L6
Niš, Yug. 137 G14
Nişāb, Saudi Arabia 152 G9
Nişāb, Yemen 152 Q10
Nishikō, Jap. 165 S4
Nishine, Jap. 164 K13
Nishinoomote, Jap. 165 U4
Nishino Shima, Jap. 165 P6
Nishtūn, Yemen 153 P13
Nissi, Estonia 135 K16
Nisswa, Minn., U.S. 98 H10
Niţā', Saudi Arabia 152 H11
Niterói, Braz. 123 M15
Nitro, W. Va., U.S. 90 D8
Niuafo'ou, island, Tonga 194 J9
Niuatoputapu, island, Tonga 194 J10
Niu Aunfo Point, point, Tongatapu, Tonga 198 H11
Niue, island, Pac. Oc. 194 K10
Niulakita, island, Tuvalu 194 J9
Niutao, island, Tuvalu 194 H9
Niutoua, Tongatapu, Tonga 198 H12
Niutou Shan, China 162 M10
Nixon, Tex., U.S. 97 R10
Niya see Minfeng, China 160 H5
Nizamabad, India 158 L6
Nizamghat, India 158 F15
Nizam Sagar, lake, India 158 M6
Nizao, Dom. Rep. 111 M19
Nizhneshadrino, Russ. 141 J13
Nizhneudinsk, Russ. 141 L14
Nizhnevartovsk, Russ. 140 H11
Nizhneyansk, Russ. 141 E17
Nizhniy Bestyakh, Russ. 141 G18
Nizhniy Lomov, Russ. 140 G6
Nizhniy Pyandzh see Panji Poyon, Afghan. 156 K7
Nizhniy Tagil, Russ. 140 H9
Nizhnyaya Tunguska, river, Russ. 141 H13
Nizhnyaya Tura, Russ. 140 H9
Nizhny Novgorod, Russ. 140 G7
Nizhyn, Ukr. 133 H15
Nizip, river, Turk. 148 H12
Nizip, Turk. 148 H12
Nizzana (El'Auja), Israel 151 P4
Njazidja (Grande Comore), island, Comoros 185 M14
Njombe, Tanzania 179 N13
Nkhata Bay, Malawi 183 D13
Nkongsamba, Cameroon 181 H15
Nmai, river, Myanmar 166 D7
Noakhali, Bangladesh 158 J13
Noatak, river, U.S. 78 M3
Noatak, Alas., U.S. 104 D12
Noatak National Preserve, Alas., U.S. 105 D13
Nobeoka, Jap. 165 S5
Noblesville, Ind., U.S. 93 R9
Nobo, Indonesia 169 M14
Noboribetsu, Jap. 164 G13
Nocona, Tex., U.S. 96 J10
Nodales, Bahía de los, Arg. 125 U10
Nodaway, river, Mo., U.S. 99 Q10
Nogales, Ariz., U.S. 101 W8
Nogales, Mex. 108 B7
Nōgata, Jap. 165 R4
Noginsk, Russ. 140 F6
Nogoyá, Arg. 124 K12
Nogu Dabu, island, P.N.G. 197 H18
Nohar, India 158 E4
Noheji, Jap. 164 J13
Nohili Point, Hawaii, U.S. 106 B4
Nohonaohae, peak, Hawaii, U.S. 107 L19
Nohta, India 158 J7
Noia, Sp. 139 N5
Nojima Zaki, Jap. 165 Q12
Noka, Santa Cruz Is., Solomon Is. 197 P22
Nokaneng, Botswana 182 G8
Nokia, Fin. 135 J15
Nok Kundi, Pak. 157 S2
Nokomis, Ill., U.S. 93 S5
Nokuku, Vanuatu 198 C1
Nola, Cen. Af. Rep. 178 H8
Noma Misaki, Jap. 165 T4
Nome, Alas., U.S. 104 G11
Nomgon, Mongolia 160 F12
Nomoneas, islands, Chuuk, F.S.M. 197 B15
Nomo Saki, Jap. 165 S3
Nomuka, island, Ha'apai Group, Tonga 198 Q6
Nomuka Group, Ha'apai Group, Tonga 198 Q6
Nomuka Iki, island, Ha'apai Group, Tonga 198 Q6
Nomwin Atoll, F.S.M. 196 P6
Nondalton, Alas., U.S. 105 K14
Nongjrong, India 158 G14
Nong Khai, Thai. 166 K10
Nonouti, island, Kiribati 194 G8
Nonthaburi, Thai. 166 M9
Nonume, Santa Cruz Is., Solomon Is. 197 Q22
Noole, Santa Cruz Is., Solomon Is. 197 Q22
Noonan, N. Dak., U.S. 98 D2
Noormarkku, Fin. 135 J15
Noorvik, Alas., U.S. 105 E13
Nóqui, Angola 182 B5
Norak, Taj. 156 J8
Norborne, Mo., U.S. 99 S11
Nord, Greenland, Den. 75 A20
Nord, Pointe, Wallis and Futuna, Fr. 198 E11
Norden, Ger. 132 E5
Nordfjordeid, Nor. 134 J10
Nordkapp, cape, Nor. 135 B14
Nordkjosbotn, Nor. 135 D13
Nordli, Nor. 134 G12
Nordoyar, island, Faroe Is., Den. 134 J6
Norfolk, Nebr., U.S. 99 N7
Norfolk, Va., U.S. 90 F14
Norfolk Island, Coral Sea 194 L7
Norfolk Lake, Ark., U.S. 94 E9
Norfolk Ridge, Pac. Oc. 218 M8
Noril'sk, Russ. 141 F13
Normal, Ill., U.S. 93 Q6
Norman, river, Austral. 190 D11
Norman, Ark., U.S. 94 H7
Norman, Okla., U.S. 96 G11
Norman, Lake, N.C., U.S. 90 H9
Normanby Island, P.N.G. 193 E21
Normanton, Qnsld., Austral. 191 R11
Norman Wells, N.W.T., Can. 76 F10
Nornalup, W. Austral., Austral. 191 Y3
Ñorquincó, Arg. 125 Q7
Norris Lake, Tenn., U.S. 95 E18
Norristown, Pa., U.S. 88 P9
Norrköping, Sw. 135 L13
Norrsundet, Sw. 135 J13
Norseman, W. Austral., Austral. 191 X4
Norsk, Russ. 141 K19
Norsup, Vanuatu 198 D2
Norte, Cabo, Braz. 123 C13
Norte, Canal do, Braz. 123 C13
Norte, Punta, Arg. 124 M14
Norte, Serra do, Braz. 122 G10
North, Cape, N.S., Can. 77 N22
North Adams, Mass., U.S. 88 J12
Northampton, Mass., U.S. 89 K13
Northampton, Eng., U.K. 138 H9
Northampton, W. Austral., Austral. 191 W2
Northampton Seamounts, Hawaii, U.S. 106 L4
North Andaman, island, Andaman Is., India 159 P14
North Arm, N.W.T., Can. 76 H11
North Augusta, S.C., U.S. 90 L8
North Aulatsivik Island, Nfld., Can. 77 J20
North Australian Basin, Ind. Oc. 221 J16
North Battleford, Sask., Can. 76 M11
North Bay, Mauritius 185 J20
North Bay, Ont., Can. 77 P18
North Belcher Islands, Nunavut, Can. 77 L17
North Bend, Oreg., U.S. 102 J2
North Branch, Minn., U.S. 98 J12
North Branch Potomac, river, Md.-W. Va., U.S. 90 C10
North Caicos, Turks and Caicos Is., U.K. 111 H17
North Canadian, river, Okla., U.S. 96 F9
North Cape, Eur. 130 A9
North Cape, N.Z. 193 G18
North Cape, Tabuaeran, Kiribati 197 A20
North Carolina, U.S. 90 H10
North Cascades National Park, Wash., U.S. 102 A5
North Channel, Mich., U.S. 92 G12
North Charleston, S.C., U.S. 90 M10
North Chicago, Ill., U.S. 92 M7
North China Plain, Asia 146 G11
Northcliffe, W. Austral., Austral. 191 Y3
North Dakota, U.S. 98 F2
North East, Pa., U.S. 88 K3
Northeast Cay, Jam. 110 P11
Northeast Pacific Basin, Pac. Oc. 218 D11
Northeast Pass, Jaluit Atoll, Marshall Is. 196 L8
Northeast Passage, Santa Cruz Is., Solomon Is. 197 R24

North East Point, Cayman Is., U.K. 110 L9
North East Point, Kiritimati, Kiribati 197 B23
Northeast Point, Bahamas 111 G15
Northeast Providence Channel, Bahamas 110 D12
North Entrance, Palau 196 K12
Northern Light Lake, Minn., U.S. 98 E14
Northern European Plain, Eur. 130 F5
Northern Ireland, U.K. 138 F6
Northern Karroo, region, Af. 174 Q7
Northern Mariana Islands, Pac. Oc. 196 B1
Northern Perimeter Highway, Braz. 122 C10
Northern Sporades, islands, Eur. 130 K9
Northern Territory, Austral. 191 R8
Northern Uvals, hills, Eur. 130 C12
Northfield, Minn., U.S. 98 K11
Northfield, Vt., U.S. 89 G13
North Fiji Basin, Pac. Oc. 218 L9
North Fond du Lac, Wis., U.S. 92 K6
North Fork, Calif., U.S. 103 S7
North Fork Clearwater, river, Idaho, U.S. 100 D4
North Fork Flathead, river, Mont., U.S. 100 A5
North Fork Payette, river, Idaho, U.S. 100 G4
North Fork Red, river, Okla., U.S. 96 H9
North Fork Salt, river, Mo., U.S. 99 R13
North Head, N.Z. 193 J18
North Island, N.Z. 193 K18
North Island, Seychelles 185 N19
North Korea, Asia 162 D14
North Lakhimpur, India 158 F14
North Land see Severnaya Zemlya, Russ. 141 C14
North Las Vegas, Nev., U.S. 103 U12
North Little Rock, Ark., U.S. 94 G8
North Loup, river, Nebr., U.S. 99 N5
North Magnetic Pole, Nunavut, Can. 77 A14
North Malosmadulu Atoll, Maldives 159 U3
North Manchester, Ind., U.S. 93 P9
North Myrtle Beach, S.C., U.S. 90 L12
North Naples, Fla., U.S. 91 W8
North Negril Point, Jam. 110 M10
North New Hebrides Trench, Pac. Oc. 218 L8
North Olmsted, Ohio, U.S. 93 P14
North Pacific Ocean, Pac. Oc. 194 B6
North Pass, Kwajalein Atoll, Marshall Is. 196 K4
North Perry, Ohio, U.S. 93 N15
North Pioa, peak, Tutuila, Amer. Samoa, U.S. 198 M8
North Platte, river, Nebr., U.S. 99 P2
North Platte, Nebr., U.S. 99 Q4
North Point, Manihiki Atoll, Cook Is., N.Z. 199 A14
North Point, Mich., U.S. 92 H12
North Point, Seychelles 185 N20
North Pole, Arctic Oc. 222 H11
Northport, Ala., U.S. 95 K14
Northport, Wash., U.S. 102 A8
North Powder, Oreg., U.S. 102 F8
North Raccoon, river, Iowa, U.S. 99 P11
North Saskatchewan, river, Alta.-Sask., Can. 76 L11
North Sea, Eur. 130 E5
North Sentinel Island, Andaman Is., India 159 Q14
North Siberian Lowland, Asia 146 C9
North Slope, Alas., U.S. 105 C14
North Sound, Cayman Is., U.K. 110 L7
North Springfield, Pa., U.S. 88 K3
North Stradbroke Island, Austral. 190 H15
North Taranaki Bight, N.Z. 193 K18
North Tipalao, Guam, U.S. 196 C10
North Tonawanda, N.Y., U.S. 88 J5
North Truchas Peak, N. Mex., U.S. 101 R13
North Uist, island, Scot., U.K. 138 D6
Northumberland, Cape, Austral. 190 M11
Northumberland Islands, Austral. 190 F15
North Vanlaiphai, India 158 J14
North Vernon, Ind., U.S. 93 S10
Northway, Alas., U.S. 105 G18
Northwest Atlantic Mid-Ocean Canyon, Atl. Oc. 216 D6
North West Basin, Austral. 190 G1
Northwest Bay, Seychelles 185 P19
North West Cape, Austral. 190 F1
Northwestern Hawaiian Islands, Hawaii, U.S. 106 K2
Northwest Hawaiian Ridge, Pac. Oc. 218 F10
Northwest Pacific Basin, Pac. Oc. 218 E7
North West Point, Kiritimati, Kiribati 197 A22
Northwest Providence Channel, Bahamas 110 C10
North West River, Nfld., Can. 77 L21
Northwest Territories, Can. 76 G11
North Wilkesboro, N.C., U.S. 90 G8
Northwind Escarpment, Arctic Oc. 222 K6
Northwind Plain, Arctic Oc. 222 K5
Northwind Ridge, Arctic Oc. 222 K5
Northwood, Iowa, U.S. 98 L12
Northwood, N. Dak., U.S. 98 F7
Norton, Kans., U.S. 99 R5
Norton, Va., U.S. 90 F7
Norton Bay, Alas., U.S. 104 G12
Norton Shores, Mich., U.S. 92 L9
Norton Sound, Alas., U.S. 104 G12
Northern Dvina, river, Eur. 130 B11
Norvegia, Cape, Antarctica 206 B11
Norwalk, Calif., U.S. 103 X8
Norwalk, Conn., U.S. 88 M12
Norwalk, Ohio, U.S. 93 P13
Norway, Eur. 134 K11
Norway, Me., U.S. 89 G15
Norway, Mich., U.S. 92 G7
Norway House, Man., Can. 77 M14
Norwegian Basin, Arctic Oc. 223 G18
Norwegian Bay, Nunavut, Can. 77 C15
Norwegian Sea, Eur. 130 B5
Norwich, Conn., U.S. 89 M13
Norwich, N.Y., U.S. 88 K9
Norwich, Eng., U.K. 138 G10
Norwood, Colo., U.S. 101 N10
Norwood, N.C., U.S. 90 J10
Norwood, N.Y., U.S. 88 F10
Norwood, Ohio, U.S. 93 S11
Noshiro, Jap. 164 J12
Noşratābād, Iran 153 F17
Nossob, river, Botswana-S. Af. 182 J8
Nosy-Varika, Madagascar 183 G17
Noteć, river, Pol. 132 F9
Noto, Jap. 164 M10
Noto Hantō, Jap. 164 M9
Notre Dame Bay, Nfld., Can. 77 L23
Nottaway, river, Que., Can. 77 N18
Nottingham, Eng., U.K. 138 G8
Nottingham Island, Nunavut, Can. 77 H17
Nottoway, river, Va., U.S. 90 F12
Nouadhibou, Mauritania 176 F4
Nouakchott, Mauritania 176 G5
Nouamrhar, Mauritania 176 F4
Nouméa, New Caledonia, Fr. 198 E8
Nouna, Burkina Faso 180 E9
Nouveau Québec, Que., Can. 77 K19
Nouveau-Québec, Cratère du (Chubb Crater), Que., Can. 77 J18
Nouvelle-Calédonie, island, New Caledonia, Fr. 198 C7
Nova Friburgo, Braz. 123 M15
Nova Iguaçu, Braz. 123 M14
Nova Kakhovka, Ukr. 133 L16
Novalukoml', Belarus 133 E13
Nova Mambone, Mozambique 183 G13
Nova Odesa, Ukr. 133 K15
Nova Olinda do Norte, Braz. 122 D9
Novara, It. 136 E8
Nova Scotia, peninsula, N. Amer. 74 H10
Nova Scotia, Can. 77 P22
Nova Sofala, Mozambique 183 G13
Nova Xavantina, Braz. 122 J12
Novaya Sibir', Ostrov, Russ. 141 C17
Novaya Zemlya, island, Russ. 140 D11
Nové Zámky, Slovakia 132 K9
Novhorod-Sivers'kyy, Ukr. 133 G15
Novi Pazar, Bulg. 137 G17
Novi Pazar, Yug. 137 G13
Novi Sad, Yug. 137 F13
Novo Aripuanã, Braz. 122 E9
Novo Cruzeiro, Braz. 123 K15
Novo Hamburgo, Braz. 122 P12
Novohrad-Volyns'kyy, Ukr. 133 H13
Novokuznetsk, Russ. 140 L12
Novolazarevskaya, station, Antarctica 207 A14
Novomoskovsk, Russ. 140 F6
Novomoskovs'k, Ukr. 133 J16
Novorossiysk, Russ. 140 H3
Novorybnoye, Russ. 141 F15
Novosibirsk, Russ. 140 K12
Novosibirskiye Ostrova (New Siberian Islands), Russ. 141 D16
Novotroitsk, Russ. 140 J7
Novotroitskoye, Kaz. 155 H15
Novouzensk, Russ. 140 H6
Novovolyns'k, Ukr. 132 H12
Novoye Ust'ye, Russ. 141 G20
Novozybkov, Russ. 140 F5
Novyy Buh, Ukr. 133 K15
Novyy Port, Russ. 140 F11
Novyy Urengoy, Russ. 140 G12
Nowabad-e Ish, Afghan. 156 J9
Nowa Nowa, Vic., Austral. 191 Z13
Nowata, Okla., U.S. 96 E13
Now Deh, Afghan. 157 P2
Nowood, river, Wyo., U.S. 100 G11
Nowra, N.S.W., Austral. 191 Y14
Nowrangapur, India 158 L8
Nowshak, peak, Afghan.-Pak. 156 K9
Nowshera, Pak. 157 N10
Nowy Sącz, Pol. 132 J10
Now Zad, Afghan. 157 P4
Noxon, Mont., U.S. 100 B4
Noyabr'sk, Russ. 140 H11
Nsukka, Nig. 181 G14
Ntem, river, Af. 174 J6
Ntomba, Lac, Dem. Rep. of the Congo 178 K8
Nu (Salween), river, China 160 N10
Nuapapu, island, Vava'u Group, Tonga 198 M11
Nuapapu, Vava'u Group, Tonga 198 L11
Nuatabu, Tarawa, Kiribati 197 F17
Nuba Mountains, Af. 174 H9
Nubia, Lake, Sudan 178 C12
Nubian Desert, Sudan 179 C13
Nucla, Colo., U.S. 101 N10
Nuclear Test Site, India 158 F3
Nuclear Test Site, Pak. 157 S4
Nuclear Test Site, Pak. 157 T3
Nueces, river, Tex., U.S. 97 T9
Nueltin Lake, Nunavut, Can. 77 J14
Nuestra Señora, Bahía, Chile 124 F7
Nueva Gerona, Cuba 110 H6
Nueva Imperial, Chile 125 P6
Nueva Rosita, Mex. 108 E11
9 de Julio, Arg. 124 M12
Nuevitas, Cuba 110 J11
Nuevo, Golfo, Arg. 125 R10
Nuevo Casas Grandes, Mex. 108 C8
Nuevo Laredo, Mex. 108 E11
Nuevo Rocafuerte, Ecua. 120 J5
Nuguria Islands, P.N.G. 193 C22
Nui, island, Tuvalu 194 H9
Nukapu, island, Santa Cruz Is., Solomon Is. 197 N22
Nukhayb, Iraq 152 E8
Nuku, island, Tongatapu, Tonga 198 H12
Nukuaeta, island, Wallis and Futuna, Fr. 198 C11
Nuku'alofa, Tongatapu, Tonga 198 H11
Nukubasaga, island, Fiji 198 G9
Nukudamu, Fiji 198 G8
Nukufetau, island, Tuvalu 194 H9
Nukufufulanoa, island, Wallis and Futuna, Fr. 198 A11
Nukufutu, island, Wallis and Futuna, Fr. 198 A11
Nukuhifala, island, Wallis and Futuna, Fr. 198 B12
Nuku Hiva, island, Fr. Polynesia, Fr. 195 H14
Nukuira, island, Fiji 198 G7
Nukulaelae, island, Tuvalu 194 H9
Nukuloa, island, Wallis and Futuna, Fr. 198 A11
Nukumanu Islands, P.N.G. 197 H18
Nukunono, island, Kiribati 194 H10
Nukuoro Atoll, F.S.M. 196 R7
Nukus, Uzb. 154 J9
Nukutapu, island, Wallis and Futuna, Fr. 198 B12
Nukutavake, island, Fr. Polynesia, Fr. 199 F21
Nukuteatea, island, Wallis and Futuna, Fr. 198 B11
Nukutipipi, island, Fr. Polynesia, Fr. 199 G19
Nulato, Alas., U.S. 105 G13
Nullagine, W. Austral., Austral. 191 T3
Nullarbor Plain, Austral. 190 J6
Num, island, Indonesia 169 K19
Numakawa, Jap. 164 D13
Numan, Nig. 181 F16
Numata, Jap. 164 F13
Numata, Jap. 165 N11
Numazu, Jap. 165 Q11
Numbulwar, N. Terr., Austral. 191 P9
Numfoor, island, Indonesia 169 J19
Numila, Hawaii, U.S. 106 C5
Numto, Russ. 140 G11
Nunavut, Can. 77 G15
Nunivak Island, Alas., U.S. 104 K10
Nunligran, Russ. 141 B21
Nuoro, It. 136 J8
Nupani, island, Santa Cruz Is., Solomon Is. 197 N22
Nuquí, Col. 120 E3
Nura, river, Kaz. 155 E14
Nur Gama, Pak. 157 T6
Nurina, W. Austral., Austral. 191 W6
Nurmes, Fin. 135 G16
Nürnberg, Ger. 132 J6
Nurpur, Pak. 157 Q10
Nurse Cay, Bahamas 111 H13
Nusaybin, Turk. 149 H16
Nuşayrīyah, Jabal an, Syr. 150 F7
Nushki, Pak. 157 S5
Nuttal, Pak. 157 S7
Nutwood Downs, N. Terr., Austral. 191 Q9
Nuuanu Pali Overlook, Hawaii, U.S. 106 E12
Nuuk (Godthåb), Greenland, Den. 75 D21
Nu'ulua, island, Samoa 198 L4
Nuupere, Pointe, Moorea, Fr. Polynesia, Fr. 199 P14
Nuusilaelae, island, Manua Is., Amer. Samoa, U.S. 198 N1
Nu'utele, island, Samoa 198 L4
Nuutele, island, Manua Is., Amer. Samoa, U.S. 198 N1
Nuuuli, Tutuila, Amer. Samoa, U.S. 198 M7
Nuweiba', Egypt 151 S4
Nyagan', Russ. 140 G10
Nyainqêntanglha Shan, China 160 L8
Nyala, Sudan 178 F10
Nyalam, China 160 L6
Nyamlell, Sudan 178 G11
Nyandoma, Russ. 140 E7
Nyasa, Lake see Malawi, Lake, Malawi-Mozambique-Tanzania 183 D13
Nyaunglebin, Myanmar 166 K6
Nybergsund, Nor. 134 K12
Nyborg, Den. 134 P11
Nyborg, Nor. 135 C15
Nyda, Russ. 140 G11
Nyeri, Kenya 179 K14
Nyerol, Sudan 179 G13
Nyeying, India 158 F15
Nyima, China 160 K7
Nyingchi, China 160 L8
Nyíregyháza, Hung. 132 K11
Nykarleby, Fin. 135 G15
Nykøbing, Den. 134 P12
Nyköping, Sw. 135 L13
Nymagee, N.S.W., Austral. 191 X13
Nyngan, N.S.W., Austral. 191 X13
Nyoman, river, Belarus 132 F12
Nyong, river, Cameroon 181 J15
Nysh, Russ. 141 J21
Nyssa, Oreg., U.S. 102 H9
Nyūdō Zaki, Jap. 164 K12
Nyunzu, Dem. Rep. of the Congo 178 M11
Nyurba, Russ. 141 H16
Nzega, Tanzania 179 L13
Nzérékoré, Guinea 180 G7
N'zeto, Angola 182 B5
Nzwani (Anjouan), island, Comoros 185 N16

O

Oacoma, S. Dak., U.S. 98 L5
Oahe, Lake, U.S. 78 D11
Oahu, island, Hawaii, U.S. 106 F11
Oak Creek, Colo., U.S. 100 L11
Oakdale, Calif., U.S. 103 S5
Oakdale, La., U.S. 94 N8
Oakes, N. Dak., U.S. 98 H7
Oakesdale, Wash., U.S. 102 C9
Oak Grove, La., U.S. 94 K9
Oak Harbor, Wash., U.S. 102 B4
Oak Hill, Ohio, U.S. 93 S13
Oak Hill, W. Va., U.S. 90 E8
Oakhurst, Calif., U.S. 103 S6
Oakland, Calif., U.S. 103 S3
Oakland, Iowa, U.S. 99 P9
Oakland, Md., U.S. 90 C10
Oakland, Nebr., U.S. 99 P8
Oakland, Oreg., U.S. 102 J3
Oakland City, Ind., U.S. 93 T8
Oak Lawn, Ill., U.S. 93 N7
Oakley, Idaho, U.S. 100 J5
Oakley, Kans., U.S. 99 S4
Oak Park, Ill., U.S. 93 N7
Oak Ridge, Tenn., U.S. 95 E18
Oakridge, Oreg., U.S. 102 H3
Oakvale, S. Austral., Austral. 191 X11
Oakwood, Qnsld., Austral. 191 U13
Ōamami Guntō, Jap. 165 X2
Oamaru, N.Z. 193 Q17
Oaro, N.Z. 193 N18
Oatara, island, Raiatea, Fr. Polynesia, Fr. 199 B24
Oates Coast, Antarctica 207 R15
Oatman, Ariz., U.S. 101 S4
Oaxaca, Mex. 109 K13
Ob', river, Russ. 140 G11
Ob, Gulf of, Asia 146 C8
Oba, Ont., Can. 77 P17
Obama, Jap. 165 P9
Oban, Qnsld., Austral. 191 S10
Oban, N.Z. 193 R15
Oban, Scot., U.K. 138 E7
Obanazawa, Jap. 164 L13
Obando, Col. 120 F9
Ob' Bank, Arctic Oc. 223 J15
Ob' Bay, Antarctica 207 R14
Obelisk Island, Santa Cruz Is., Solomon Is. 197 N24
Obella, island, Kwajalein Atoll, Marshall Is. 196 K4
Oberlin, Kans., U.S. 99 R4
Oberlin, La., U.S. 94 P7
Oberlin, Ohio, U.S. 93 P14
Obi, island, Indonesia 169 K16
Obi, Kepulauan, Indonesia 168 H9
Óbidos, Braz. 122 D11
Obigarm, Taj. 156 H8
Obihiro, Jap. 164 G14
Obilatu, island, Indonesia 169 J16
Obion, Tenn., U.S. 94 E12
Ob-Irtysh, Source of the, Asia 146 F9
Obluch'ye, Russ. 141 L20
Obo, Cen. Af. Rep. 178 H11
Obome, Indonesia 169 K18
O'Brien, Oreg., U.S. 102 L2
Obruk, Turk. 148 G8
Obshchiy Syrt, mountains, Eur. 130 E13
Obskaya Guba, Russ. 140 G11
Obstruccion, Fiordo, Chile 125 W7
Ob' Tablemount, Southern Oc. 225 D15
Ocala, Fla., U.S. 91 S8
Ocaña, Col. 120 D6
Occidental, Cordillera, S. Amer. 118 B2
Occidental, Grand Erg, Alg. 176 C10
Ocean Cay, Bahamas 110 D10
Ocean City, Md., U.S. 90 D15
Ocean City, N.J., U.S. 88 R10
Ocean Falls, B.C., Can. 76 K7
Ocean Island see Kure Atoll, Hawaii, U.S. 106 K2
Ocean Island see Banaba, Kiribati 194 G7
Oceanographer Fracture Zone, Atl. Oc. 216 H8
Ocean Park, Wash., U.S. 102 D2
Oceanside, Calif., U.S. 103 Y9
Ocean Springs, Miss., U.S. 95 P13

Oceanview, *Guam, U.S.* **196** B11
O.C. Fisher Lake, *Tex., U.S.* **97** N7
Ocha, island, *Chuuk, F.S.M.* **197** D15
Ocha, Mochun, *Chuuk, F.S.M.* **197** D15
Och'amch'ire, *Rep. of Georgia* **149** B16
Ocheyedan Mound, *U.S.* **79** E13
Ochiishi, *Jap.* **164** F16
Ochlockonee, river, *Ga., U.S.* **91** Q5
Ocilla, *Ga., U.S.* **91** P6
Ocmulgee, river, *Ga., U.S.* **91** N6
Ocmulgee National Monument, *Ga., U.S.* **90** M6
Ocoa, Bahía de, *Dom. Rep.* **111** M18
Oconee, river, *Ga., U.S.* **91** N7
Oconee, Lake, *Ga., U.S.* **90** L6
Oconomowoc, *Wis., U.S.* **92** L6
Oconto, *Wis., U.S.* **92** H7
Oconto Falls, *Wis., U.S.* **92** H7
Ocracoke, *N.C., U.S.* **90** H15
Ocracoke Inlet, *N.C., U.S.* **90** J15
October Revolution Island, *Asia* **146** B9
Ocumare del Tuy, *Venez.* **120** B10
Ōda, *Jap.* **165** P6
Ōdate, *Jap.* **164** J13
Odawara, *Jap.* **165** P12
Odda, *Nor.* **134** K10
Odebolt, *Iowa, U.S.* **99** N10
Odem, *Tex., U.S.* **97** T11
Odemira, *Port.* **139** S4
Ödemiş, *Turk.* **148** G3
Odense, *Den.* **134** P11
Oder (Odra), river, *Ger.* **132** F8
Odesa, *Ukr.* **133** L15
Odessa, *Mo., U.S.* **99** S11
Odessa, *Tex., U.S.* **96** M4
Odessa, *Wash., U.S.* **102** C7
Odienné, *Côte d'Ivoire* **180** F7
O'Donnell, *Tex., U.S.* **96** L5
Odra (Oder), river, *Pol.* **132** F8
Oecussi *see* Pante Macassar, *E. Timor* **169** N15
Oeiras, *Braz.* **123** F15
Oelrichs, *S. Dak., U.S.* **98** M2
Oelwein, *Iowa, U.S.* **98** M13
Oeno Island, *Pac. Oc.* **195** K16
Oenpelli, *N. Terr., Austral.* **191** P8
Of, *Turk.* **149** D15
O'Fallon Creek, *Mont., U.S.* **100** D13
Offenbach, *Ger.* **132** H5
Oficina Dominador, *Chile* **124** F7
Oficina Rica Aventura, *Chile* **124** D7
Ofolanga, island, *Ha'apai Group, Tonga* **198** P7
Ofu, island, *Manua Is., Amer. Samoa, U.S.* **198** N2
Ofu, island, *Vava'u Group, Tonga* **198** M12
Ofu, *Manua Is., Amer. Samoa, U.S.* **198** N1
Ōfunato, *Jap.* **164** K14
Oga, *Jap.* **164** K12
Ogachi, *Jap.* **164** L13
Ogaden, region, *Eth.* **179** G17
Ōgaki, *Jap.* **165** P9
Ogallala, *Nebr., U.S.* **99** Q3
Ogasawara Guntō *see* Bonin Islands, *Jap.* **194** C4
Ogawara Ko, *Jap.* **164** J13
Ogbomosho, *Nig.* **180** G12
Ogden, *Iowa, U.S.* **99** N11
Ogden, *Utah, U.S.* **100** K7
Ogdensburg, *N.Y., U.S.* **88** F9
Ogea Driki, island, *Fiji* **198** K9
Ogea Levu, island, *Fiji* **198** K9
Ogeechee, river, *Ga., U.S.* **91** N8
Ogi, *Jap.* **164** M11
Ogilvie Mountains, *Yukon Terr., Can.* **76** E8
Oglesby, *Ill., U.S.* **93** P5
Oglethorpe, *Ga., U.S.* **91** N5
Ogmore, *Qnsld., Austral.* **191** T14
Ognev Yar, *Russ.* **140** J11
Ogoja, *Nig.* **181** H14
Ogoki, river, *Ont., Can.* **77** N16
Ogoki, *Ont., Can.* **77** N16
Ogooué, river, *Gabon* **181** L15
Ogr, *Sudan* **178** F11
Ogulin, *Croatia* **136** F11
Ohau, Lake, *N.Z.* **193** P16
O'Higgins, Lago, *Chile* **125** U7
Ohio, river, *U.S.* **79** H15
Ohio, *U.S.* **93** Q12
Ohonua, *Tonga* **198** J12
Ohrid, Lake, *Alban.-Maced.* **137** J14
Ōi, river, *Jap.* **165** P11
Oiapoque, river, *Braz.* **122** B12
Oiapoque, river, *Fr. Guiana* **121** F18
Oiapoque, *Braz.* **122** B12
Oil City, *Pa., U.S.* **88** M4
Oildale, *Calif., U.S.* **103** V7
Oilton, *Okla., U.S.* **96** F12
Oise, river, *Fr.* **138** K10
Ōita, *Jap.* **165** R5
Ojika, *Jap.* **164** L13
Ojika Jima, *Jap.* **165** R3
Ojinaga, *Mex.* **108** D9
Ojiya, *Jap.* **164** M11
Ojo Caliente, *N. Mex., U.S.* **101** Q12
Ojo de Liebre, Laguna, *Mex.* **108** D5
Ojos del Salado, Cerro, *Arg.* **124** G8
Oka, river, *Russ.* **140** F6
Okaba, *Indonesia* **169** M21
Oka-Don Plain, *Eur.* **130** E12
Okahandja, *Namibia* **182** H7
Okak Islands, *Nfld., Can.* **77** J21
Okanogan, river, *U.S.* **78** B5
Okanogan, *Wash., U.S.* **102** B7
Okanogan Range, *Wash., U.S.* **102** A6
Okara, *Pak.* **157** Q11
Okau, *Yap Is., F.S.M.* **197** D18
Okaukuejo, *Namibia* **182** G6
Okavango, river, *Angola-Namibia* **182** F7
Okavango Delta, *Botswana* **182** G9
Okaya, *Jap.* **165** P11
Okayama, *Jap.* **165** Q7
Okazaki, *Jap.* **165** Q10
Okeechobee, *Fla., U.S.* **91** V9
Okeechobee, Lake, *Fla., U.S.* **91** V9
Okeene, *Okla., U.S.* **96** F9
Okefenokee Swamp, *Fla.-Ga., U.S.* **91** Q7
Okemah, *Okla., U.S.* **96** G12
Okha, *Russ.* **141** H21
Okhaldhunga, *Nepal* **158** F10
Okhotsk, *Russ.* **141** G20
Okhotsk, Sea of, *Asia* **146** D13
Okiep, *S. Af.* **182** K7
Okinawa, island, *Jap.* **165** Y2
Okinawa Shotō, *Jap.* **165** Y1
Okino Daitō Jima, *Jap.* **194** C2
Okino Erabu Shima, *Jap.* **165** X2
Okino Shima, *Jap.* **165** Q4
Okino Shima, *Jap.* **165** S6
Oki Shotou, *Jap.* **165** N6
Oklahoma, *U.S.* **96** G8
Oklahoma City, *Okla., U.S.* **96** G11
Okmulgee, *Okla., U.S.* **96** G12
Okolona, *Ky., U.S.* **95** B16
Okolona, *Miss., U.S.* **95** J13
Okoppe, *Jap.* **164** E14
Okoyo, *Congo* **181** L17
Okp'yŏng-ni, *N. Korea* **162** D13
Okso' Takpochao, peak, *Saipan, N. Mariana Is., U.S.* **196** B5
Oktyabr'sk, *Kaz.* **154** E8
Oktyabr'skiy, *Russ.* **140** H7
Oktyabr'skoy Revolyutsii, Ostrov, *Russ.* **141** D14
Ōkuchi, *Jap.* **165** S4
Okushiri Tō, *Jap.* **164** G11
Okwa, river, *Botswana* **182** H8
Okytyabr'skoye, *Russ.* **140** G10
Ola, *Ark., U.S.* **94** G7
Ólafsvík, *Ice.* **134** E1
Olancha Peak, *Calif., U.S.* **103** U8
Öland, island, *Sw.* **135** N14
Olary, *S. Austral., Austral.* **191** X11
Olathe, *Kans., U.S.* **99** S10
Olavarría, *Arg.* **124** M12
Olbia, *It.* **136** J8
Old Bahama Channel, *Cuba* **110** G10
Old Bight, *Bahamas* **111** F13
Old Cork, *Qnsld., Austral.* **191** T11
Old Crow, *Yukon Terr., Can.* **76** D9
Oldenburg, *Ger.* **132** F5
Old Forge, *Pa., U.S.* **88** M9
Old Harbor, *Alas., U.S.* **105** M15
Old Orchard Beach, *Me., U.S.* **89** H15
Old Sugar Mill, *Hawaii, U.S.* **106** D11
Old Town, *Me., U.S.* **89** E17
Olduvai Gorge, *Tanzania* **179** L14
Olean, *N.Y., U.S.* **88** K5
Olekma, river, *Russ.* **141** J17
Olekminsk, *Russ.* **141** H17
Oleksandriya, *Ukr.* **133** J16
Olenegorsk, *Russ.* **140** D8
Olenek, river, *Russ.* **141** F16
Olenek, *Russ.* **141** G15
Oleniy, Ostrov, *Russ.* **140** E12
Oléron, Île d', *Fr.* **138** M8
Olga, Mount, *Austral.* **190** G7
Olga Basin, *Arctic Oc.* **223** F14
Ölgiy, *Mongolia* **160** C8
Olimarao Atoll, *F.S.M.* **196** Q4
Olinda, *Braz.* **123** F18
Olio, *Qnsld., Austral.* **191** T12
Oliva, *Arg.* **124** K10
Olivia, *Minn., U.S.* **98** K10
Ölkeyek, river, *Kaz.* **154** E10
Olla, *La., U.S.* **94** M8
Olmos, *Peru* **122** F2
Olney, *Ill., U.S.* **93** T7
Olney, *Tex., U.S.* **96** K9
ђOlomburi, *Solomon Is.* **197** N20
Olomouc, *Czech Rep.* **132** J9
Olongapo, *Philippines* **169** C13
Oloron, *Fr.* **139** N9
Olorua, island, *Fiji* **198** J9
Olosega, island, *Manua Is., Amer. Samoa, U.S.* **198** N2
Olosega, *Manua Is., Amer. Samoa, U.S.* **198** N2
Olot, *Sp.* **139** P10
Olotania Crater, *Manua Is., Amer. Samoa, U.S.* **198** P3
Olovyannaya, *Russ.* **141** L17
Olowalu, *Hawaii, U.S.* **107** G16
Olpoï, *Vanuatu* **198** C1
Olsztyn, *Pol.* **132** F10
Olt, river, *Rom.* **137** E15
Olton, *Tex., U.S.* **96** J5
Oltu, river, *Turk.* **149** D16
Oltu, *Turk.* **149** D16
Oluan Pi, *Taiwan, China* **163** S9
Olympia, *Wash., U.S.* **102** D3
Olympic National Park, *Wash., U.S.* **102** B2
Olympos (Olympus), peak, *Gr.* **137** J14
Olympus, peak, *Cyprus* **148** L8
Olympus *see* Olympos, peak, *Gr.* **137** J14
Olympus, Mount *see* Ulu Dağ, *Turk.* **148** D5
Olympus, Mount, *Wash., U.S.* **102** B2
Olyutorskiy, Mys, *Russ.* **141** D22
Olyutorskiy Zaliv, *Russ.* **141** D22
Ōma, *Jap.* **164** H13
Omae Zaki, *Jap.* **165** Q11
Ōmagari, *Jap.* **164** K13
Omagh, *N. Ire., U.K.* **138** F6
Omaha, *Nebr., U.S.* **99** P9
Omaja, *Cuba* **110** K12
Omak, *Wash., U.S.* **102** B7
Omak Lake, *Wash., U.S.* **102** B7
Oman, *Asia* **153** M15
Oman, Gulf of, *Asia* **146** H5
Omaok, *Palau* **196** Q10
Ōma Zaki, *Jap.* **164** H13
Omba *see* Aoba, island, *Vanuatu* **198** C2
Omboué (Fernan Vaz), *Gabon* **181** L15
Ombu, *China* **160** K6
Omchak, *Russ.* **141** F20
Omdurman (Umm Durmān), *Sudan* **179** D13
Omelek, island, *Kwajalein Atoll, Marshall Is.* **196** M5
Ometepec, *Mex.* **108** K12
Omihi, *N.Z.* **193** P17
Omin, *Yap Is., F.S.M.* **197** C18
Omoka, island, *Penrhyn, Cook Is., N.Z.* **199** B17
Omoka, *Penrhyn, Cook Is., N.Z.* **199** B17
Omolon, river, *Russ.* **141** D20
Omolon, *Russ.* **141** D20
Omoto, *Jap.* **164** K14
Omsk, *Russ.* **140** K10
Omsukchan, *Russ.* **141** E20
Ōmu, *Jap.* **164** E14
Ōmuta, *Jap.* **165** R4
Onaf, island, *Chuuk, F.S.M.* **197** A15
Onaga, *Kans., U.S.* **99** S9
Onalaska, *Wis., U.S.* **92** K3
Onamia, *Minn., U.S.* **98** H11
Onamue, island, *Chuuk, F.S.M.* **197** C14
Onancock, *Va., U.S.* **90** E14
Onaram, island, *Chuuk, F.S.M.* **197** C16
Onarga, *Ill., U.S.* **93** Q7
Onawa, *Iowa, U.S.* **99** N9
Onaway, *Mich., U.S.* **92** H11
Oncativo, *Arg.* **124** K10
Ondangwa, *Namibia* **182** F6
Ondjiva, *Angola* **182** F6
Ondo, *Nig.* **181** G13
Öndörhaan, *Mongolia* **161** D13
Ondor Sum, *China* **162** B5
One, Motu, *Bora-Bora, Fr. Polynesia, Fr.* **199** J14
One, Motu, *Society Is., Fr. Polynesia, Fr.* **199** E14
One and Half Degree Channel, *Maldives* **159** W3
Oneata, island, *Fiji* **198** J9
Onega, river, *Russ.* **140** E7
Onega, *Russ.* **140** E8
Onega, Lake, *Eur.* **130** C10
Onega Bay, *Eur.* **130** B10
Oneida, *N.Y., U.S.* **88** J9
Oneida, *Tenn., U.S.* **95** E18
Oneida Lake, *N.Y., U.S.* **88** J8
O'Neill, *Nebr., U.S.* **99** N6
Onekama, *Mich., U.S.* **92** J9
Onekotan, island, *Russ.* **141** H23
Onemak, island, *Kwajalein Atoll, Marshall Is.* **196** L4
Onemak East Passage, *Kwajalein Atoll, Marshall Is.* **196** L4
Onemak West Passage, *Kwajalein Atoll, Marshall Is.* **196** L4
Oneonta, *Ala., U.S.* **95** J15
Oneonta, *N.Y., U.S.* **88** K10
Oneroa, island, *Rarotonga, Cook Is., N.Z.* **198** Q9
One Tree Peak, *N. Mex., U.S.* **101** U13
Onevai, island, *Tongatapu, Tonga* **198** H12
Onezhskoye Ozero, *Russ.* **140** E7
Ongarue, *N.Z.* **193** K19
Ongjin, *N. Korea* **162** E12
Ongniud Qi (Wudan), *China* **162** A8
Ongole, *India* **159** N7
Ongombua, Île, *New Caledonia, Fr.* **198** B6
Oni, *Rep. of Georgia* **149** B17
Onida, *S. Dak., U.S.* **98** K5
Onilahy, river, *Madagascar* **183** H16
Oniotto, island, *Kwajalein Atoll, Marshall Is.* **196** K3
Onishibetsu, *Jap.* **164** D13
Onishika, *Jap.* **164** E13
Onitsha, *Nig.* **181** H14
Oniwaki, *Jap.* **164** D13
Onnang, island, *Chuuk, F.S.M.* **197** C14
Ono, island, *Fiji* **198** K7
Ōno, *Jap.* **165** P9
Ono Channel, *Fiji* **198** K6
Onoheha, Pass d', *Tahiti, Fr. Polynesia, Fr.* **199** N17
Ono-i-Lau, island, *Fiji* **194** K9
Onomichi, *Jap.* **165** Q6
Onon, river, *Mongolia* **161** C13
Onon, *Mongolia* **161** C13
Onon, *Mongolia* **161** C14
Onsen, *Jap.* **165** P8
Onslow, *W. Austral., Austral.* **191** T1
Ontario, *Can.* **77** N15
Ontario, *Calif., U.S.* **103** X9
Ontario, *Oreg., U.S.* **102** H9
Ontario, Lake, *U.S.-Can.* **79** E19
Ontonagon, *Mich., U.S.* **92** E5
Ontong Java Atoll (Lord Howe Atoll), *Solomon Is.* **197** J18
Ōnuma, *Jap.* **164** H13
Ooa, island, *Jaluit Atoll, Marshall Is.* **196** N8
Oodnadatta, *S. Austral., Austral.* **191** V9
Ookala, *Hawaii, U.S.* **107** K21
Oologah Lake, *Okla., U.S.* **96** E13
Ooma, *Banaba, Kiribati* **197** D20
Oostende, *Belg.* **138** H10
Opal, *Wyo., U.S.* **100** J8
Opana Point, *Hawaii, U.S.* **107** G17
Opava, *Czech Rep.* **132** J9
Opelika, *Ala., U.S.* **95** L17
Opelousas, *La., U.S.* **94** P8
Open Bay, *P.N.G.* **193** C21
Opheim, *Mont., U.S.* **100** A12
Ophir, *Oreg., U.S.* **102** K1
Ophthalmia Range, *Austral.* **190** F3
Opihikao, *Hawaii, U.S.* **107** N22
Opinaca, river, *Que., Can.* **77** M18
Opoa, *Raiatea, Fr. Polynesia, Fr.* **199** B23
Opole, *Pol.* **132** H9
Opotiki, *N.Z.* **193** K20
Opp, *Ala., U.S.* **95** N16
Oppdal, *Nor.* **134** J11
Opportunity, *Wash., U.S.* **102** C9
Opunake, *N.Z.* **193** L18
Opunohu, Baie d', *Moorea, Fr. Polynesia, Fr.* **199** N14
Opuwo, *Namibia* **182** F6
Opyan, Puntan, *Saipan, N. Mariana Is., U.S.* **196** D4
Or, river, *Kaz.* **154** E9
Oracle, *Ariz., U.S.* **101** V8
Oradea, *Rom.* **137** E14
Orai, *India* **158** G7
Oral, *Kaz.* **154** C6
Oran, *Alg.* **176** A10
Orange, river, *Namibia-S. Af.* **182** K7
Orange, *Fr.* **139** N11
Orange, *N.S.W., Austral.* **191** X14
Orange, *Tex., U.S.* **97** Q16
Orange, *Va., U.S.* **90** D12
Orange, Cabo, *Braz.* **122** A12
Orangeburg, *S.C., U.S.* **90** L9
Orange Cay, *Bahamas* **110** E10
Orange City, *Iowa, U.S.* **98** M9
Orange Grove, *Tex., U.S.* **97** T10
Orange Park, *Fla., U.S.* **91** R8
Orange Walk, *Belize* **109** J16
Oranjemund, *Namibia* **182** K6
Oranjestad, *Aruba, Neth.* **112** M8
Oranjestad, *St. Eustatius, Neth.* **113** G15
Oravița, *Rom.* **137** F14
Orbetello, *It.* **136** H9
Orbost, *Vic., Austral.* **191** Z13
Orcadas, station, *Antarctica* **206** A4
Orchard City, *Colo., U.S.* **101** N10
Orchila, Isla, *Venez.* **120** A10
Ord, river, *Austral.* **190** C6
Ord, *Nebr., U.S.* **99** P6
Ord, Mount, *Austral.* **190** D5
Orderville, *Utah, U.S.* **101** P6
Ordos *see* Mu Us Shamo, desert, *China* **162** D2
Ordot, *Guam, U.S.* **196** C11
Ord River, *W. Austral., Austral.* **191** R7
Ordu, *Turk.* **148** D12
Ordubad, *Azerb.* **149** F20
Ordway, *Colo., U.S.* **101** N14
Oreba, island, *Kwajalein Atoll, Marshall Is.* **196** K1
Örebro, *Sw.* **135** L13
Oregon, *U.S.* **102** H6
Oregon, *Ill., U.S.* **93** N5
Oregon, *Ohio, U.S.* **93** N12
Oregon Caves National Monument, *Oreg., U.S.* **102** L2
Oregon City, *Oreg., U.S.* **102** F3
Oregon Dunes National Recreation Area, *Oreg., U.S.* **102** H2
Orel, *Russ.* **140** F5
Orellana, *Peru* **122** F4
Orem, *Utah, U.S.* **100** L7
Ore Mountains, *Eur.* **130** G6
Ören, *Turk.* **148** H3
Orenburg, *Russ.* **140** J7
Örenşehir, *Turk.* **148** F11
Oreor *see* Koror, island, *Palau* **196** P11

Orepuki, *N.Z.* **193** R15
Oreti, river, *N.Z.* **193** R15
Organ Pipe Cactus National Monument, *Ariz., U.S.* **101** V6
Orgun, *Afghan.* **157** P8
Orhangazi, *Turk.* **148** D5
Orhei, *Mold.* **133** K14
Orhon, river, *Mongolia* **160** C12
Orick, *Calif., U.S.* **102** M2
Orient, *Wash., U.S.* **102** A8
Oriental, Cordillera, *S. Amer.* **118** C2
Oriental, Grand Erg, *Alg.* **176** C11
Oriente, *Arg.* **125** P12
Orihuela, *Sp.* **139** S8
Orikhiv, *Ukr.* **133** K17
Orinduik, *Guyana* **121** E13
Orinoco, river, *S. Amer.* **118** A5
Orinoco, Source of the, *S. Amer.* **118** C5
Orinoco River Delta, *S. Amer.* **118** A6
Oristano, *It.* **136** J7
Oriximiná, *Braz.* **122** D11
Orizaba, Pico de, *Mex.* **108** J12
Orjonikidzeobod, *Taj.* **156** J8
Orkanger, *Nor.* **134** H11
Orkney Islands, *Scot., U.K.* **138** C8
Orland, *Calif., U.S.* **103** P4
Orlando, *Fla., U.S.* **91** T9
Orléans, *Fr.* **138** K10
Orleans, *Nebr., U.S.* **99** R5
Orleans, *Vt., U.S.* **89** F13
Ormara, *Pak.* **157** W4
Ormara, Ras, *Pak.* **157** W4
Ormoc, *Philippines* **169** E15
Ormond Beach, *Fla., U.S.* **91** S9
Örnsköldsvik, *Sw.* **135** H13
Orocué, *Col.* **120** F7
Orofino, *Idaho, U.S.* **100** D4
Oro Grande, *Calif., U.S.* **103** W9
Orohena, Mount, *Tahiti, Fr. Polynesia, Fr.* **199** P16
Oroluk Atoll, *F.S.M.* **196** Q7
Oromahana, island, *Tahaa, Fr. Polynesia, Fr.* **199** A23
Oromia, region, *Eth.* **179** G15
Orona, island, *Kiribati* **194** H10
Orono, *Me., U.S.* **89** E17
Orontes *see* 'Āṣī, river, *Syr.* **150** F7
Orós, *Braz.* **123** F17
Orote Peninsula, *Guam, U.S.* **196** C9
Oroville, *Calif., U.S.* **103** P4
Oroville, *Wash., U.S.* **102** A7
Oroville, Lake, *Calif., U.S.* **103** P4
Orphan Knoll, *Atl. Oc.* **216** F7
Orr, *Minn., U.S.* **98** E12
Orsa, *Sw.* **134** K12
Orsha, *Belarus* **133** E14
Orsk, *Russ.* **140** J7
Orşova, *Rom.* **137** F14
Orta, *Turk.* **148** D8
Ortaca, *Turk.* **148** H4
Ortegal, Cabo, *Sp.* **139** N5
Ortepah, *Afghan.* **156** L4
Ortigueira, *Sp.* **139** N5
Ortón, river, *Bol.* **122** G7
Ortonville, *Minn., U.S.* **98** J8
Orto Surt, *Russ.* **141** H17
Orukuizu, island, *Palau* **196** P10
Orūmīyeh, *Iran* **152** B10
Orūmīyeh, Daryācheh-ye (Lake Urmia), *Iran* **152** B10
Oruro, *Bol.* **122** K7
Oruzgan, *Afghan.* **157** P6
Osa, Peninsula de, *C.R.* **109** P19
Osage, river, *Mo., U.S.* **99** T13
Osage, *Iowa, U.S.* **98** M12
Osage, *Wyo., U.S.* **100** G13
Osage Beach, *Mo., U.S.* **99** T12
Osage City, *Kans., U.S.* **99** T9
Osaka, *Jap.* **165** P10
Ōsaka, *Jap.* **165** Q9
Osakarovka, *Kaz.* **155** D14
Ōsaka Wan, *Jap.* **165** Q8
Osakis, *Minn., U.S.* **98** H10
Osawatomie, *Kans., U.S.* **99** T10
Osborne, *Kans., U.S.* **99** S6
Osborn Plateau, *Ind. Oc.* **220** J11
Oscar II Coast, *Antarctica* **206** D4
Osceola, *Ark., U.S.* **94** F11
Osceola, *Iowa, U.S.* **99** Q11
Osceola, *Mo., U.S.* **99** T11
Osceola, *Nebr., U.S.* **99** Q7
Oscoda, *Mich., U.S.* **92** J12
Oscura Peak, *N. Mex., U.S.* **101** T12
Osen, *Nor.* **134** G11
Osgood Mountains, *Nev., U.S.* **102** M9
Osh, *Kyrg.* **156** G10
Oshawa, *Ont., Can.* **77** Q18
Oshidomari, *Jap.* **164** D13
O Shima, *Jap.* **165** S2
Ō Shima, *Jap.* **164** H12
Ō Shima, *Jap.* **165** Q12
Ō Shima, *Jap.* **165** R9
Ōshima, *Jap.* **165** Q12
Oshkosh, *Nebr., U.S.* **99** P2
Oshkosh, *Wis., U.S.* **92** K6
Oshogbo, *Nig.* **181** G13
Oshwe, *Dem. Rep. of the Congo* **178** L9
Osijek, *Croatia* **136** F12
Oskaloosa, *Iowa, U.S.* **99** P12
Oskarshamn, *Sw.* **135** M13
Öskemen (Ust' Kamenogorsk), *Kaz.* **155** D18
Oskoba, *Russ.* **141** J14
Oslo, *Minn., U.S.* **98** E8
Oslo, *Nor.* **134** L11
Osmanabad, *India* **158** M5
Osmancık, *Turk.* **148** D10
Osmaneli, *Turk.* **148** D6
Osmaniye, *Turk.* **148** H11
Osnabrück, *Ger.* **132** F5
Osorno, *Chile* **125** Q6
Osorno, Volcán, *Chile* **125** Q6
Osprey, *Fla., U.S.* **91** V7
Ossa, Mount, *Austral.* **190** M16
Ossabaw Island, *Ga., U.S.* **91** N9
Ossabaw Sound, *Ga., U.S.* **91** N9
Osseo, *Wis., U.S.* **92** J3
Ossineke, *Mich., U.S.* **92** H12
Østerdalen, valley, *Nor.* **134** J11
Östersund, *Sw.* **134** H12
Östhammar, *Sw.* **135** K14
Ostrava, *Czech Rep.* **132** J9
Ostróda, *Pol.* **132** F10
Ostrogozhsk, *Russ.* **140** G5
Ostrołęka, *Pol.* **132** F10
Ostrov, *Russ.* **140** D6
Ostrowiec Świętokrzyski, *Pol.* **132** H10
Ostrów Wielkopolski, *Pol.* **132** G9
O'Sullivan Dam, *Wash., U.S.* **102** D7
Ōsumi Kaikyō, *Jap.* **165** U4
Ōsumi Shotō, *Jap.* **165** U3
Osuna, *Sp.* **139** S6
Oswego, *N.Y., U.S.* **88** H8
Oswego, *N.Y., U.S.* **88** L8
Ōta, *Jap.* **165** N12
Otaki, *N.Z.* **193** M19
Otar, *Kaz.* **155** H16
Otare, Cerro, *Col.* **120** G6
Otaru, *Jap.* **164** F13
Otavalo, *Ecua.* **120** H3
Otavi, *Namibia* **182** G7
O.T. Downs, *N. Terr., Austral.* **191** Q9
Otepipi, island, *Rangiroa, Fr. Polynesia, Fr.* **199** L16
Othello, *Wash., U.S.* **102** D7
Otis, *Colo., U.S.* **100** L15
Otish, Monts, *N. Amer.* **74** G9
Otjiwarongo, *Namibia* **182** G7
Otobe, *Jap.* **164** H12
Otog Qi, *China* **162** D2
Otoineppu, *Jap.* **164** E14
Otradnoye, *Russ.* **141** G23
Otranto, Strait of, *It.* **136** J12
Otsego, *Mich., U.S.* **92** M9
Ōtsu, *Jap.* **164** G15
Ōtsu, *Jap.* **165** Q9
Ōtsuchi, *Jap.* **164** K14
Ottawa, river, *Ont.-Que., Can.* **77** P18
Ottawa, *Ill., U.S.* **93** P6
Ottawa, *Kans., U.S.* **99** T10
Ottawa, *Ohio, U.S.* **93** P11
Ottawa, *Ont., Can.* **77** Q19
Ottawa Islands, *Nunavut, Can.* **77** J17
Ottenby, *Sw.* **135** N14
Otter Creek, *Mont., U.S.* **100** E12
Otter Rapids, *Ont., Can.* **77** N17
Otter Tail Lake, *Minn., U.S.* **98** H9
Ottumwa, *Iowa, U.S.* **99** Q12
Otukpo, *Nig.* **181** G14
Otutéhé, *Hiva Oa, Fr. Polynesia, Fr.* **199** M20
Otuzco, *Peru* **122** F2
Otway, Bahía, *Chile* **125** X7
Otway, Cape, *Austral.* **190** M12
Otway, Seno de, *Chile* **125** X7
Ou, river, *China* **163** N9
Ou, river, *Laos* **166** G10
'O'ua, island, *Ha'apai Group, Tonga* **198** Q6
Oua, Île, *New Caledonia, Fr.* **198** D9
Ouachita, river, *La., U.S.* **94** L8
Ouachita, Lake, *Ark., U.S.* **94** G7
Ouachita Mountains, *U.S.* **79** K13
Ouaco, *New Caledonia, Fr.* **198** C6
Ouadane, *Mauritania* **176** F6
Ouadda, *Cen. Af. Rep.* **178** G10
Ouagadougou, *Burkina Faso* **180** E10
Ouahigouya, *Burkina Faso* **180** D10
Oualâta, *Mauritania* **176** G7
Ouanda Djallé, *Cen. Af. Rep.* **178** G10
Ouani, *Comoros* **185** N16
Ouargla, *Alg.* **176** C11
Ouarra, river, *Cen. Af. Rep.* **178** H11
Oubangui, river, *Cen. Af. Rep.-Dem. Rep. of the Congo* **178** H8
Oubatche, *New Caledonia, Fr.* **198** C6
Oudtshoorn, *S. Af.* **182** M8
Ouégoa, *New Caledonia, Fr.* **198** C6
Ouen, Île, *New Caledonia, Fr.* **198** E9
Ouessa, *Burkina Faso* **180** F10
Ouessant, Île d', *Fr.* **138** K7
Ouesso, *Congo* **181** K18
Ouest, Baie de l', *Wallis and Futuna, Fr.* **198** B11
Ouest, Pointe de l', *Que., Can.* **77** M21
Ouezzane, *Mor.* **176** A9
Oufrane, *Alg.* **176** D10
Ouinné, Baie, *New Caledonia, Fr.* **198** D8
Oujda, *Mor.* **176** B9
Oujeft, *Mauritania* **176** F6
Oulainen, *Fin.* **135** G15
Oulu, river, *Eur.* **130** B9
Oulu (Uleåborg), *Fin.* **135** F15
Oulujärvi, lake, *Eur.* **130** C9
Oulujoki, river, *Fin.* **135** F15
Oum Chalouba, *Chad* **177** H15
Oum Hadjer, *Chad* **177** J15
Oumm ed Drous Telli, Sebkhet, *Mauritania* **176** E6
Ounianga Kébir, *Chad* **177** G15
Ou Nua, *Laos* **166** G9
Ouray, *Colo., U.S.* **101** P11
Ouray, *Utah, U.S.* **100** L9
Ourense, *Sp.* **139** P5
Ourinhos, *Braz.* **122** M12
Ouse, *Tas., Austral.* **191** Z16
Outer Bailey, bank, *Atl. Oc.* **216** D11
Outer Hebrides, islands, *Scot., U.K.* **138** D6
Outjo, *Namibia* **182** G6
Outokumpu, *Fin.* **135** G17
Ouvéa, Baie d', *New Caledonia, Fr.* **198** C8
Ouvéa, Île (Uvéa), *New Caledonia, Fr.* **198** C8
Ouyen, *Vic., Austral.* **191** Y11
Ovacık, *Turk.* **148** J9
Ovaka, island, *Vava'u Group, Tonga* **198** M11
Ovalau, island, *Fiji* **198** H7
Ovalle, *Chile* **124** J6
Ovamboland, region, *Namibia* **182** F6
Ovar, *Port.* **139** Q5
Ovau, island, *Solomon Is.* **197** K15
Overland Park, *Kans., U.S.* **99** S10
Overton, *Nev., U.S.* **103** T12
Overton, *Tex., U.S.* **96** M14
Ovid, *Colo., U.S.* **100** K15
Oviedo, *Dom. Rep.* **111** N17
Oviedo, *Sp.* **139** N6
Ovoot, *Mongolia* **161** E14
Ovruch, *Ukr.* **133** H13
Ow, island, *Chuuk, F.S.M.* **197** C15
Owaka, *N.Z.* **193** R16
Owando, *Congo* **181** L18
Ōwani, *Jap.* **164** J13
Owatonna, *Minn., U.S.* **98** L11
Owbeh, *Afghan.* **156** M3
Owen, Mount, *N.Z.* **193** M17
Owen Fracture Zone, *Ind. Oc.* **220** F6
Owens, river, *Calif., U.S.* **103** T8
Owensboro, *Ky., U.S.* **95** C15
Owens Lake Bed, *Calif., U.S.* **103** U8
Owen Stanley Range, *P.N.G.* **193** E20
Owensville, *Mo., U.S.* **99** T14
Owl Creek Mountains, *Wyo., U.S.* **100** G10
Owo, *Nig.* **181** G13
Owosso, *Mich., U.S.* **92** L11
Owyhee, river, *Oreg., U.S.* **102** J9
Owyhee, *Nev., U.S.* **102** L10
Owyhee, Lake, *Oreg., U.S.* **102** J9
Owyhee Mountains, *Idaho, U.S.* **100** H3
Oxford, *Ala., U.S.* **95** J16
Oxford, *Kans., U.S.* **99** V8
Oxford, *Miss., U.S.* **94** H12
Oxford, *N.Z.* **193** P17
Oxford, *Nebr., U.S.* **99** R5
Oxford, *Ohio, U.S.* **93** S11
Oxford, *Eng., U.K.* **138** H8
Oxnard, *Calif., U.S.* **103** X7
Oyem, *Gabon* **181** K16
Oyo, *Congo* **181** L18
Oyo, *Nig.* **180** G12
Oyotung, *Russ.* **141** D18
Oyster Bay, *Mauritius* **185** J20
Oysterville, *Wash., U.S.* **102** D2
Oytal, *Kaz.* **155** J15
Oyyl, river, *Kaz.* **154** E7
Oyyl, *Kaz.* **154** E7
Özalp, *Turk.* **149** F18
Ozark, *Ala., U.S.* **95** M17
Ozark, *Ark., U.S.* **94** F7
Ozark, *Mo., U.S.* **99** V12
Ozark National Scenic Riverways, *Mo., U.S.* **99** U14
Ozark Plateau, *U.S.* **79** J13
Ozarks, Lake of the, *Mo., U.S.* **99** T12
Ózd, *Hung.* **132** K10
Özen, *Kaz.* **154** H6
Ozernovskiy, *Russ.* **141** G23
Ozernoy, Mys, *Russ.* **141** E22
Ozernoy, Zaliv, *Russ.* **141** E22
Ozette Lake, *Wash., U.S.* **102** B2
Ozieri, *It.* **136** J8
Ozona, *Tex., U.S.* **97** P6
Ōzu, *Jap.* **165** R6
Ozurget'i, *Rep. of Georgia* **149** C16

P

Paagoumène, *New Caledonia, Fr.* **198** C6
Paama, island, *Vanuatu* **198** D3
Paamiut, *Greenland, Den.* **75** D22
Paarl, *S. Af.* **182** M7
Paauhau, *Hawaii, U.S.* **107** K20
Paauilo, *Hawaii, U.S.* **107** K20
Paavola, *Fin.* **135** G15
Pabna, *Bangladesh* **158** H12
Pacaraima, Sierra, *S. Amer.* **118** C5
Pacasmayo, *Peru* **122** F2
Pachuca, *Mex.* **108** H12
Pacific-Antarctic Ridge, *Southern Oc.* **224** M9
Pacific Beach, *Wash., U.S.* **102** C2
Pacific City, *Oreg., U.S.* **102** F2
Pacific Grove, *Calif., U.S.* **103** T4
Padada, *Philippines* **169** F15
Padam, *India* **157** N14
Padang, island, *Indonesia* **168** H6
Padang, *Indonesia* **168** J5
Padang Endau, *Malaysia* **167** U11
Padangpanjang, *Indonesia* **168** J5
Padangsidempuan, *Indonesia* **168** H5
Padangtiji, *Indonesia* **168** G4
Padangtikar Maya, island, *Indonesia* **168** J9
Paden City, *W. Va., U.S.* **90** C9
Paderborn, *Ger.* **132** G5
Padloping Island, *Nunavut, Can.* **77** F19
Padma (Ganges), river, *Bangladesh* **158** H13
Padmanabhapuram, *India* **159** S5
Padova, *It.* **136** F9
Padrauna, *India* **158** G9
Padre Island, *U.S.* **78** P12
Padre Island National Seashore, *Tex., U.S.* **97** U11
Padrés Hanna-Karkur, *Israel* **150** L5
Paducah, *Ky., U.S.* **95** D13
Paducah, *Tex., U.S.* **96** J7
Paea, *Tahiti, Fr. Polynesia, Fr.* **199** P15
Paektu San, *China-N. Korea* **162** B13
Paengnyŏng Do, *S. Korea* **162** E11
Paeroa, *N.Z.* **193** J19
Paeu, *Santa Cruz Is., Solomon Is.* **197** R23
Paeua, island, *Manihi, Fr. Polynesia, Fr.* **199** K17
Pafos, *Cyprus* **148** L7
Pafúri, *Mozambique* **182** H12
Pag, island, *Croatia* **136** F11
Pagadian, *Philippines* **169** F14
Pagai Selatan, island, *Indonesia* **168** K5
Pagai Utara, island, *Indonesia* **168** K5
Pagan, island, *N. Mariana Is., U.S.* **196** B2
Pagatan, *Indonesia* **168** K11
Page, *Ariz., U.S.* **101** Q7
Page, *N. Dak., U.S.* **98** G7
Pageland, *S.C., U.S.* **90** J10
Pagnag, *China* **160** K8
Pago, river, *Guam, U.S.* **196** C10
Pago Bay, *Guam, U.S.* **196** C11
Pagoda Point, *Myanmar* **166** L5
Pago Pago, *Tutuila, Amer. Samoa, U.S.* **198** M7
Pago Pago Harbor, *Tutuila, Amer. Samoa, U.S.* **198** M8
Pagosa Springs, *Colo., U.S.* **101** P11
Pagri, *China* **160** M7
Paguate, *N. Mex., U.S.* **101** S11
Pahala, *Hawaii, U.S.* **107** P20
Paharpur, *Pak.* **157** P9
Pahoa, *Hawaii, U.S.* **107** M22
Pahokee, *Fla., U.S.* **91** V10
Pahrump, *Nev., U.S.* **103** U11
Pahsimeroi, river, *Idaho, U.S.* **100** F6
Pahute Mesa, *Nev., U.S.* **103** S10
Paia, *Hawaii, U.S.* **107** G17
Paige, *Tex., U.S.* **97** Q11
Päijänne, lake, *Fin.* **135** H16
Paili, *P.N.G.* **193** E20
Pailin City, *Cambodia* **167** N10
Pailolo Channel, *Hawaii, U.S.* **107** F15
Paine, Cerro, *Chile* **125** W7
Painesville, *Ohio, U.S.* **93** N15
Painted Desert, *Ariz., U.S.* **101** R7 - S9
Paint Rock, *Tex., U.S.* **97** N7
Paintsville, *Ky., U.S.* **95** B20
Paio, Motu, *Rangiroa, Fr. Polynesia, Fr.* **199** K16
Païromé, *New Caledonia, Fr.* **198** B6
Paisley, *Oreg., U.S.* **102** K6
Paistunturit, peak, *Fin.* **135** C14
Paita, *New Caledonia, Fr.* **198** D8
Paita, *Peru* **122** E1
Pajala, *Sw.* **135** E14
Pakala Village, *Hawaii, U.S.* **106** C5
Pakaraima Mountains, *Braz.* **122** A9
Pakbèng, *Laos* **166** H9
Pakin Atoll, *F.S.M.* **196** Q8
Pakistan, *Asia* **157** U5
Pak Nam Chumphon, *Thai.* **167** P8
Pakokku, *Myanmar* **166** G5

Pakpattan, *Pak.* **157** R11
Pak Phanang, *Thai.* **167** R8
Pakuru, island, *Chuuk, F.S.M.* **197** C15
Pakxan, *Laos* **166** J11
Pakxé, *Laos* **166** L12
Pala, *Chad* **177** K14
Pala, *Myanmar* **167** N7
Palacios, *Tex., U.S.* **97** S13
Palagruža, island, *Croatia* **136** H11
Palalankwe, *Andaman Is., India* **159** R14
Palana, *Russ.* **141** E21
Palanga, *Lith.* **135** N15
Palangkaraya, *Indonesia* **168** K11
Palanpur, *India* **158** H3
Palaoa Point, *Hawaii, U.S.* **107** H14
Palapye, *Botswana* **182** H10
Palatka, *Fla., U.S.* **91** R8
Palatka, *Russ.* **141** F20
Palau, *Pac. Oc.* **196** M10
Palauk, *Myanmar* **167** N7
Palauli Bay, *Samoa* **198** L2
Palau Trench, *Pac. Oc.* **218** J5
Palaw, *Myanmar* **167** N7
Palawan, island, *Philippines* **168** E12
Palawan Trough, *Pac. Oc.* **218** J3
Paldiski, *Estonia* **135** K16
Palel, *India* **158** H15
Palembang, *Indonesia* **168** K7
Palencia, *Sp.* **139** P7
Palermo, *Calif., U.S.* **103** P4
Palermo, *It.* **136** L10
Palestina, *Chile* **124** E7
Palestine, *Tex., U.S.* **96** M13
Paletwa, *Myanmar* **166** G4
Palghat, *India* **159** R5
Pali, *India* **158** G4
Palian, *Thai.* **167** R8
Palikir, *Pohnpei, F.S.M.* **197** F14
Palikir Passage, *Pohnpei, F.S.M.* **197** F13
Palisade, *Colo., U.S.* **100** M10
Palisade, *Nebr., U.S.* **99** R4
Palk Bay, *India* **159** R6
Palkonda, *India* **158** L9
Palk Strait, *India-Sri Lanka* **159** R7
Palliser, Cape, *N.Z.* **193** M19
Palma, *Mozambique* **183** C15
Palma de Mallorca, *Sp.* **139** R10
Palmares, *Braz.* **123** G18
Palmas, *Braz.* **122** N12
Palmas, Cape, *Liberia* **180** J7
Palma Soriano, *Cuba* **111** K13
Palm Bay, *Fla., U.S.* **91** U10
Palm Beach, *Fla., U.S.* **91** V10
Palm City, *Cuba* **110** H11
Palm Coast, *Fla., U.S.* **91** S9
Palmdale, *Calif., U.S.* **103** W8
Palmeira, *Cape Verde* **185** B17
Palmeira dosÍndios, *Braz.* **123** G17
Palmeirinhas, Ponta das, *Angola* **182** C5
Palmer, station, *Antarctica* **206** D4
Palmer, *Alas., U.S.* **105** J16
Palmer Archipelago, *Antarctica* **206** D4
Palmer Land, *Antarctica* **206** E5
Palmerston Atoll, *Cook Is., N.Z.* **194** K11
Palmerston North, *N.Z.* **193** M19
Palmer Valley, *N. Terr., Austral.* **191** U8
Palmerville, *Qnsld., Austral.* **191** Q12
Palmetto, *Fla., U.S.* **91** U7
Palmi, *It.* **136** L11
Palmira, *Col.* **120** F4
Palm Island (Prune Island), *St. Vincent and the Grenadines* **113** M17
Palm Point, *Nig.* **181** J13
Palm Springs, *Calif., U.S.* **103** X10
Palmyra, *Mo., U.S.* **99** R13
Palmyra, *N.Y., U.S.* **88** J7
Palmyra *see* Tadmur, *Syr.* **150** G10
Palmyra Atoll, *Pac. Oc.* **194** F11
Palmyras Point, *India* **158** K11
Palo Alto, *Calif., U.S.* **103** S4
Palo Alto Battlefield National Historic Site, *Tex., U.S.* **97** W11
Palo Duro Creek, *Tex., U.S.* **96** H4
Paloh, *Indonesia* **168** H9
Palomar Mountain, *Calif., U.S.* **103** Y10
Palopo, *Indonesia* **169** K13
Palouse, river, *Wash., U.S.* **102** D8
Palouse, *Wash., U.S.* **102** D9
Palpana, Cerro, *Chile* **124** D8
Palparara, *Qnsld., Austral.* **191** U11
Paltamo, *Fin.* **135** F16
Palu, *Indonesia* **169** J13
Palu, *Turk.* **149** F14
Palwal, *India* **158** F6
Pamir, river, *Afghan.-Taj.* **156** K10
Pamirs, mountains, *Taj.* **156** J10
Pamlico Sound, *N.C., U.S.* **90** H15
Pampa, *Tex., U.S.* **96** G6
Pampas, region, *S. Amer.* **118** M5
Pamplemousses, *Mauritius* **185** F20
Pamplona, *Col.* **120** D6
Pamplona (Iruña), *Sp.* **139** P8
Pamua, *Solomon Is.* **197** P20
Pamuk Imwintiati, island, *Pohnpei, F.S.M.* **197** G13
Pamzal, *India* **156** M15
Pana, *Ill., U.S.* **93** S5
Panaca, *Nev., U.S.* **103** S13
Panacea, *Fla., U.S.* **91** R5
Panadura, *Sri Lanka* **159** T7
Panahan, *Indonesia* **168** K10
Panaitan, island, *Indonesia* **168** M7
Panaji, *India* **159** N3
Panamá, *Pan.* **109** N21
Panamá, Golfo de, *Pan.* **109** P21
Panama, *N. Amer.* **109** N21
Panama, *Okla., U.S.* **96** G14
Panama, Isthmus of, *N. Amer.* **74** Q9
Panama Basin, *Pac. Oc.* **219** J20
Panama Canal, *Pan.* **109** N21
Panama City, *Fla., U.S.* **91** R3
Panamint Range, *Calif., U.S.* **103** T9
Panay, island, *Philippines* **169** E14
Pancake Range, *Nev., U.S.* **103** R11
Pandharkawada, *India* **158** L6
Pandharpur, *India* **158** M4
Pandhurna, *India* **158** K6
Pandie Pandie, *S. Austral., Austral.* **191** U10
Paneri, *India* **158** G13
Panevėžys, *Lith.* **135** M16
Panfilov, *Kaz.* **155** H18
Pangai, *Ha'apai Group, Tonga* **198** P7
Pangai, *Tonga* **198** K12
Pangaimoto, island, *Vava'u Group, Tonga* **198** M11
Pangaimotu, island, *Tongatapu, Tonga* **198** H11
Pangalanes, Canal des, *Madagascar* **183** G18
Pangani, river, *Tanzania* **179** L14
Panggoe, *Solomon Is.* **197** L16
Pangi, *Dem. Rep. of the Congo* **178** L11
Pangkajene, *Indonesia* **169** L13
Pangkalpinang, *Indonesia* **168** K8
Pangnirtung, *Nunavut, Can.* **77** G19
Panguitch, *Utah, U.S.* **101** P6
Pangutaran Group, *Philippines* **169** F13
Panhandle, *Tex., U.S.* **96** G6
Panian, island, *Pohnpei, F.S.M.* **197** G14
Paniau, peak, *Hawaii, U.S.* **106** C3
Panié, Mont, *New Caledonia, Fr.* **198** C7
Panj, river, *Afghan.-Taj.* **156** J9
Panj, *Taj.* **156** K8
Panjakent, *Taj.* **156** H6
Panjang, island, *Indonesia* **168** H9
Panjgur, *Pak.* **157** U3
Panji Poyon (Nizhniy Pyandzh), *Afghan.* **156** K7
Panjshir, river, *Afghan.* **156** L8
Panna, *India* **158** H7
Pannawonica, *W. Austral., Austral.* **191** T2
Pano Platres, *Cyprus* **148** L8
Panovo, *Russ.* **141** J15
Panruti, *India* **159** Q7
Panshi, *China* **162** A12
Pantanal, wetland, *Braz.* **122** K10
Pantelleria, island, *It.* **136** M9
Pante Macassar (Oecussi), *E. Timor* **169** N15
Panvel, *India* **158** L3
Panxian, *China* **160** N12
Panzhihua, *China* **160** N11
Pao, river, *Thai.* **166** K10
Paola, *It.* **136** K11
Paola, *Kans., U.S.* **99** T10
Paoli, *Ind., U.S.* **93** T9
Paonia, *Colo., U.S.* **101** N11
Paopao, *Moorea, Fr. Polynesia, Fr.* **199** N14
Papa, *Samoa* **198** K1
Papaaloa, *Hawaii, U.S.* **107** L21
Papa Bay, *Hawaii, U.S.* **107** P18
Papa Heiau, *Hawaii, U.S.* **107** F15
Papai, Mount, *Mauritius* **185** J20
Papaikou, *Hawaii, U.S.* **107** L21
Papakura, *N.Z.* **193** J19
Papara, *Tahiti, Fr. Polynesia, Fr.* **199** P16
Papau, island, *Aitutaki Atoll, Cook Is., N.Z.* **198** Q12
Papeari, *Tahiti, Fr. Polynesia, Fr.* **199** P17
Papeete, *Tahiti, Fr. Polynesia, Fr.* **199** N15
Papenoo, river, *Tahiti, Fr. Polynesia, Fr.* **199** N16
Papenoo, *Tahiti, Fr. Polynesia, Fr.* **199** N16
Papetoai, *Moorea, Fr. Polynesia, Fr.* **199** N14
Papohaku Beach, *Hawaii, U.S.* **107** F13
Papua, Gulf of, *Indonesia* **169** N23
Papua New Guinea, *Asia* **193** D18
Papua Passage, *Rarotonga, Cook Is., N.Z.* **198** Q9
Papun, *Myanmar* **166** K7
Papunya, *N. Terr., Austral.* **191** T8
Pará, river, *Braz.* **123** D13
Parabel', *Russ.* **140** J12
Paracatu, *Braz.* **123** K14
Paracel Islands, *S. China Sea* **169** B19
Parachilna, *S. Austral., Austral.* **191** W10
Parachinar, *Pak.* **157** N8
Parachute, *Colo., U.S.* **100** M10
Paracuru, *Braz.* **123** E17
Paradeep *see* Paradwip, *India* **158** K11
Paradise, *Calif., U.S.* **103** P4
Paradise, *Mich., U.S.* **92** F10
Paradise, *Mont., U.S.* **100** C5
Paradise Valley, *Nev., U.S.* **102** L9
Paradwip (Paradeep), *India* **158** K11
Paragould, *Ark., U.S.* **94** E11
Paraguá, river, *Bol.* **122** J9
Paragua, river, *Venez.* **120** E11
Paraguai, river, *Braz.* **122** K10
Paraguaipoa, *Venez.* **120** B6
Paraguaná, Península de, *Venez.* **120** A8
Paraguarí, *Para.* **122** N10
Paraguay, *S. Amer.* **122** L9
Paraguay, river, *Para.* **122** L10
Paraíso, *Mex.* **109** J14
Paraíso do Tocantins, *Braz.* **123** G13
Parakou, *Benin* **180** F12
Paralakhemundi, *India* **158** L9
Param, island, *Pohnpei, F.S.M.* **197** F14
Paramaribo, *Suriname* **121** E16
Paramushir, island, *Russ.* **141** G23
Paran, *Israel* **151** Q5
Paranã, *Braz.* **123** H13
Paraná, river, *S. Amer.* **118** J7
Paraná, *Arg.* **124** K12
Paraná, Source of the, *S. Amer.* **118** J9
Paranaguá, *Braz.* **123** N13
Paranaguá, Baía de, *Braz.* **123** N13
Paranaíba, river, *Braz.* **122** K12
Paranaíba, *Braz.* **122** K12
Paraoa, island, *Fr. Polynesia, Fr.* **199** F20
Pardo, river, *Braz.* **122** L11
Pardo, river, *Braz.* **123** J16
Pardoo, *W. Austral., Austral.* **191** S3
Pardubice, *Czech Rep.* **132** H8
Parea, *Huahine, Fr. Polynesia, Fr.* **199** H14
Parece Vela, island, *Jap.* **194** D3
Parecis, Serra dos, *Braz.* **122** G8
Paredón, *Mex.* **108** F11
Parem, island, *Chuuk, F.S.M.* **197** C15
Paren', *Russ.* **141** D21
Parepare, *Indonesia* **169** K13
Párga, *Gr.* **137** K13
Paria, river, *Utah, U.S.* **101** P7
Paria, Gulf of, *Trin. & Tobago* **113** P16
Pariaguánviche, *Venez.* **120** C11
Paria Peninsula, *S. Amer.* **118** A5
Parika, *Guyana* **121** D14
Parikkala, *Fin.* **135** H17
Parima, Sierra, *Braz.* **122** B8
Parima, Sierra, *Venez.* **120** F11
Pariñas, Punta, *Peru* **122** E1
Parintins, *Braz.* **122** D10
Paris, *Ark., U.S.* **94** F7
Paris, *Fr.* **138** K10
Paris, *Ill., U.S.* **93** R7
Paris, *Kiritimati, Kiribati* **197** B22
Paris, *Ky., U.S.* **95** B18
Paris, *Mo., U.S.* **99** S13
Paris, *Tenn., U.S.* **95** E13
Paris, *Tex., U.S.* **96** K13
Paris Basin, *Eur.* **130** G4
Parit Buntar, *Malaysia* **167** T9
Parker, *Ariz., U.S.* **101** T4
Parker, *S. Dak., U.S.* **98** M8
Parker Dam, *Ariz.-Calif., U.S.* **101** T5
Parker Ranch Headquarters, *Hawaii, U.S.* **107** K19
Parkersburg, *W. Va., U.S.* **90** C8
Parkes, *N.S.W., Austral.* **191** X13
Park Falls, *Wis., U.S.* **92** G4
Park Forest, *Ill., U.S.* **93** P7
Parkin, *Ark., U.S.* **94** G10
Parkland, *Wash., U.S.* **102** C4
Park Range, *Colo., U.S.* **100** L12
Park Rapids, *Minn., U.S.* **98** G10
Park River, *N. Dak., U.S.* **98** E7
Parksley, *Va., U.S.* **90** E15
Parkston, *S. Dak., U.S.* **98** M7
Park Valley, *Utah, U.S.* **100** J6
Parma, *Idaho, U.S.* **100** G3
Parma, *It.* **136** F8
Parma, *Ohio, U.S.* **93** P14
Parmakan, *Afghan.* **157** N2
Parnaguá, *Braz.* **123** G15
Parnaíba, river, *S. Amer.* **118** D10
Parnamirim, *Braz.* **123** F16
Parnassus, peak, *Eur.* **130** K8
Parnassus, *N.Z.* **193** N18
Pärnu, *Estonia* **135** L16
Paromay, *Russ.* **141** H21
Paroo, *W. Austral., Austral.* **191** V3
Paropamisus Range *see* Sefid Kuh Mountains, *Afghan.* **156** M3
Páros, island, *Gr.* **137** L16
Parowan, *Utah, U.S.* **101** P6
Parraburdoo, *W. Austral., Austral.* **191** T2
Parral, *Chile* **124** M6
Parras, *Mex.* **108** F10
Parry, Cape, *N.W.T., Can.* **76** E11
Parry Channel, *Nunavut, Can.* **77** D13
Parry Islands, *N.W.T.-Nunavut, Can.* **77** C13
Parshall, *N. Dak., U.S.* **98** F3
Parsons, *Kans., U.S.* **99** U10
Parsons, *Tenn., U.S.* **95** F13
Parsons, *W. Va., U.S.* **90** C10
Parsons Range, *Austral.* **190** B9
Partizansk, *Russ.* **141** M21
Paru, river, *Braz.* **122** C11
Paru de Oeste (Cumina), river, *Braz.* **122** C11
Paruru, *Solomon Is.* **197** P19
Parvatipuram, *India* **158** L9
Pasa, island, *Pohnpei, F.S.M.* **197** G13
Pasadena, *Calif., U.S.* **103** X8
Pasadena, *Tex., U.S.* **97** R14
Pasado, Cabo, *Ecua.* **120** J2
Pasaje, *Ecua.* **120** L2
P'asanauri, *Rep. of Georgia* **149** B18
Pasarseluma, *Indonesia* **168** L6
Pascagoula, *Miss., U.S.* **95** P13
Paşcani, *Rom.* **137** D16
Pasco, *Wash., U.S.* **102** E7
Pascua, Isla de (Easter Island), *Pac. Oc.* **195** L19
Pasewalk, *Ger.* **132** F7
Pasighat, *India* **158** F15
Pasinler, *Turk.* **149** E16
Pasir Mas, *Malaysia* **167** S10
Pasley, Cape, *Austral.* **190** K5
Pasni, *Pak.* **157** V3
Paso de Indios, *Arg.* **125** R8
Paso de los Toros, *Uru.* **124** K14
Paso Río Mayo, *Arg.* **125** T8
Paso Robles, *Calif., U.S.* **103** V5
Pasrur, *Pak.* **157** P12
Passau, *Ger.* **132** J7
Pass Christian, *Miss., U.S.* **94** P12
Passero, Capo, *It.* **136** M11
Passo Fundo, *Braz.* **122** P11
Passos, *Braz.* **123** L14
Passu Keah, island, *Paracel Is.* **168** C10
Pastavy, *Belarus* **133** E13
Pastaza, river, *Peru* **122** E3
Pasto, *Col.* **120** H3
Pastora Peak, *Ariz., U.S.* **101** Q9
Pastos Bons, *Braz.* **123** F15
Pasuruan, *Indonesia* **168** M10
Patagonia, region, *Arg.* **125** W8
Patagonia, *Ariz., U.S.* **101** W8
Patan, *India* **158** J7
Patan *see* Lalitpur, *Nepal* **158** F10
Patanga, island, *Penrhyn, Cook Is., N.Z.* **199** B18
Patani, *Indonesia* **169** J16
Patara Shiraki, *Rep. of Georgia* **149** C20
Patchogue, *N.Y., U.S.* **88** N12
Pate Island, *Kenya* **179** K16
Paterson, *N.J., U.S.* **88** N11
Pathankot, *India* **157** P13
Pathein, *Myanmar* **166** K5
Pathfinder Reservoir, *Wyo., U.S.* **100** J11
Patía, river, *Col.* **120** G3
Patiala, *India* **158** E5
Patio, *Tahaa, Fr. Polynesia, Fr.* **199** A23
Pati Point, *Guam, U.S.* **196** B12
Pativilca, *Peru* **122** G3
Pātkai Range, *India-Myanmar* **158** G15
Patna, *India* **158** G10
Patnos, *Turk.* **149** F17
Patos, *Braz.* **123** F17
Patos, Lagoa dos, *Braz.* **122** Q12
Patos de Minas, *Braz.* **123** K14
Patquía, *Arg.* **124** J9
Pátra (Patrae), *Gr.* **137** L14
Patrae *see* Pátra, *Gr.* **137** L14
Patricio Lynch, Isla, *Chile* **125** U6
Patrick, Port, *Vanuatu* **198** H4
Pattani, *Thai.* **167** S9
Patten, *Me., U.S.* **89** C18
Patterson, *Calif., U.S.* **103** S5
Patterson, *La., U.S.* **94** Q9
Patteson, Port, *Vanuatu* **198** B2
Patteson Passage, *Vanuatu* **198** C3
Pattoki, *Pak.* **157** Q11
Patton Escarpment, *Pac. Oc.* **219** F16
Patu, *Braz.* **123** F17
Patuakhali, *Bangladesh* **158** J13
Patuca, river, *Hond.* **109** K18
Patuxent Range, *Antarctica* **206** H11
Pátzcuaro, *Mex.* **108** J10
Pau, *Fr.* **139** N9
Pauini, river, *Braz.* **122** F6
Pauini, *Braz.* **122** F6
Pauktaw, *Myanmar* **166** H4
Paulatuk, *N.W.T., Can.* **76** E11
Paulding, *Ohio, U.S.* **93** P11
Paulistana, *Braz.* **123** F16
Paulo Afonso, *Braz.* **123** G17
Pauls Valley, *Okla., U.S.* **96** H11
Paungbyin, *Myanmar* **166** F5
Paungde, *Myanmar* **166** J6
Pauni, *India* **158** K7
Pauwela, *Hawaii, U.S.* **107** G17
Pava, island, *Funafuti, Tuvalu* **197** J23

Pavagada, *India* **159** P5
Pavaiai, *Tutuila, Amer. Samoa, U.S.* **198** M7
Pavia, *It.* **136** F8
Pavillion, *Wyo., U.S.* **100** H10
Pāvilosta, *Latv.* **135** M15
Pavlodar, *Kaz.* **155** C16
Pavlof Volcano, *Alas., U.S.* **104** N12
Pavuvu, island, *Solomon Is.* **197** N18
Pawarenga, *N.Z.* **193** H18
Pawhuska, *Okla., U.S.* **96** E12
Pawleys Island, *S.C., U.S.* **90** L11
Pawnee, *Okla., U.S.* **96** F11
Pawnee City, *Nebr., U.S.* **99** R9
Paw Paw, *Mich., U.S.* **92** M9
Pawtucket, *R.I., U.S.* **89** L14
Paxton, *Ill., U.S.* **93** Q7
Paxton, *Nebr., U.S.* **99** Q3
Payakumbuh, *Indonesia* **168** J6
Payer Mountains, *Antarctica* **207** B14
Payette, river, *Idaho, U.S.* **100** G3
Payette, *Idaho, U.S.* **100** G3
Payette Lake, *Idaho, U.S.* **100** F4
Payne, Lac, *Que., Can.* **77** J18
Paynes Find, *W. Austral., Austral.* **191** W3
Paynesville, *Minn., U.S.* **98** J10
Payong, Tanjong, *Malaysia* **168** G10
Paysandú, *Uru.* **124** K13
Payson, *Ariz., U.S.* **101** T7
Payson, *Utah, U.S.* **100** L7
Pazar, *Turk.* **148** D8
Pazar, *Turk.* **148** E11
Pazar, *Turk.* **149** D15
Pazarcık, *Turk.* **148** H12
Pea, *Tongatapu, Tonga* **198** J11
Peabody, *Kans., U.S.* **99** T8
Peace, river, *Alta., Can.* **76** J11
Peace, river, *Fla., U.S.* **91** V8
Peace River, *Alta., Can.* **76** K10
Peach Springs, *Ariz., U.S.* **101** R5
Peacock Point, *Wake I., U.S.* **196** G8
Peak Hill, *W. Austral., Austral.* **191** U3
Peale, Mount, *Utah, U.S.* **101** N9
Peale Island, *Wake I., U.S.* **196** F8
Peao, island, *Tabuaeran, Kiribati* **197** B20
Peard Bay, *Alas., U.S.* **105** B13
Pea Ridge National Military Park, *Ark., U.S.* **94** E6
Pearl *see* Zhu, river, *China* **163** S4
Pearl, river, *Miss., U.S.* **94** M11
Pearl, *Miss., U.S.* **94** L11
Pearl and Hermes Atoll, *Hawaii, U.S.* **106** K3
Pearl City, *Hawaii, U.S.* **106** E11
Pearl Harbor, *Hawaii, U.S.* **106** E11
Pearsall, *Tex., U.S.* **97** S9
Pearson, *Ga., U.S.* **91** P7
Peary Channel, *Nunavut, Can.* **77** B14
Peary Land, *N. Amer.* **74** A7
Pease, river, *Tex., U.S.* **96** J8
Peawanuk, *Ont., Can.* **77** L16
Pebane, *Mozambique* **183** F14
Pebas, *Peru* **122** D5
Pebble Island, *Falk. Is., U.K.* **125** W12
Peć, *Yug.* **137** H13
Pecan Island, *La., U.S.* **94** Q8
Pechora, river, *Russ.* **140** F9
Pechora, *Russ.* **140** F10
Pechora Basin, *Eur.* **130** A12
Pechorskoy More, *Russ.* **140** E10
Pecos, river, *U.S.* **78** M10
Pecos, *N. Mex., U.S.* **101** R13
Pecos, *Tex., U.S.* **97** N3
Pecos National Historical Park, *N. Mex., U.S.* **101** R13
Pécs, *Hung.* **132** L9
Peddapalli, *India* **158** L7
Peddler, Lake, *Austral.* **190** M16
Pedernales, river, *Tex., U.S.* **97** Q9
Pedernales, *Dom. Rep.* **111** N17
Pedra Azul, *Braz.* **123** J15
Pedra Lume, *Cape Verde* **185** B17
Pedras Negras, *Braz.* **122** H8
Pedro Afonso, *Braz.* **123** G13
Pedro Betancourt, *Cuba* **110** G7
Pedro Cays, *Jam.* **110** P11
Pedro de Valdivia, *Chile* **124** D7
Pedro Juan Caballero, *Para.* **122** L10
Pedro Luro, *Arg.* **125** P11
Pedro Osório, *Braz.* **122** Q11
Peebles, *Ohio, U.S.* **93** S12
Peedamulla, *W. Austral., Austral.* **191** T2
Peekskill, *N.Y., U.S.* **88** M11
Peel, river, *Yukon Terr., Can.* **76** E9
Pe Ell, *Wash., U.S.* **102** D3
Peel Sound, *Nunavut, Can.* **77** E15
Peetz, *Colo., U.S.* **100** K15
Pegasus Bay, *N.Z.* **193** P17
Pehuajó, *Arg.* **124** M11
Peipus, Lake (Chudskoye Ozero), *Estonia* **135** K17
Peixe, *Braz.* **123** H13
Pekalongan, *Indonesia* **168** M9
Pekan, *Malaysia* **167** U10
Pekanbaru, *Indonesia* **168** J6
Pekin, *Ill., U.S.* **93** Q5
Peking *see* Beijing, *China* **162** D7
Pelabuhanratu, Teluk, *Indonesia* **168** M8
Pelagie, Isole, *It.* **136** M9
Pelahatchie, *Miss., U.S.* **94** L11
Pelau, island, *Solomon Is.* **197** J18
Pelée, Montagne, *Martinique, Fr.* **113** J17
Peleliu (Beliliou), island, *Palau* **196** Q10
Peleng, island, *Indonesia* **169** J14
Pelham, *Ala., U.S.* **95** K15
Pelham, *Ga., U.S.* **91** P5
Pelican, *Alas., U.S.* **105** K21
Pelican Lake, *Minn., U.S.* **98** E12
Pelican Point, *Af.* **174** P6
Pelican Rapids, *Minn., U.S.* **98** G9
Péligre, Lago de, *Haiti* **111** M17
Pelješac, island, *Croatia* **136** H12
Pella, *Iowa, U.S.* **99** P12
Pellston, *Mich., U.S.* **92** G10
Pelly, river, *Yukon Terr., Can.* **76** G9
Pelly Bay, *Nunavut, Can.* **77** F15
Pelly Crossing, *Yukon Terr., Can.* **76** F8
Peloponnesus, peninsula, *Eur.* **130** K8
Peloponnisos, peninsula, *Gr.* **137** L14
Pelotas, *Braz.* **122** Q11
Pelusium, ruins, *Egypt* **151** N1
Pematang, *Indonesia* **168** J6
Pematangsiantar, *Indonesia* **168** H5
Pemba, *Mozambique* **183** D15
Pemba Bay, *Af.* **174** M11
Pemba Island, *Tanzania* **179** L15
Pemberton, *W. Austral., Austral.* **191** Y3
Pembina, *N. Dak., U.S.* **98** D7
Pembroke, *Ga., U.S.* **91** N8
Pembroke, *Ont., Can.* **77** Q18
Pembroke, *Wales, U.K.* **138** H7
Pen, *India* **158** L3
Penambulai, island, *Indonesia* **169** M19
Peñas, Cabo de, *Sp.* **139** N6
Penas, Golfo de, *Chile* **125** U6
Pendan, *Malaysia* **168** H10
Pendembu, *Sierra Leone* **180** G6
Pender, *Nebr., U.S.* **99** N8
Pendleton, *Oreg., U.S.* **102** F7
Pend Oreille, river, *Wash., U.S.* **102** B9
Pend Oreille, Lake, *Idaho, U.S.* **100** B4
Pendra, *India* **158** J8
Pendroy, *Mont., U.S.* **100** B7
Penedo, *Braz.* **123** G17
Pengcheng, *China* **161** H14
Penghu *see* Makung, *Taiwan, China* **163** R8
P'enghu Ch'üntao (Pescadores), islands, *Taiwan, China* **163** R9
Penglai, *China* **162** E9
Pengshui, *China* **162** L1
Penha do Tapauá, *Braz.* **122** E7
Peniche, *Port.* **139** R4
Penmarc'h, Pointe de, *Fr.* **138** K7
Pennell Coast, *Antarctica* **207** R14
Penner, river, *India* **159** P6
Penneshaw, *S. Austral., Austral.* **191** X10
Penn Hills, *Pa., U.S.* **88** N3
Pennington Gap, *Va., U.S.* **90** G6
Pennsylvania, *U.S.* **88** M3
Penn Yan, *N.Y., U.S.* **88** J7
Penobscot, river, *U.S.* **79** C22
Penobscot Bay, *Me., U.S.* **89** F17
Penola, *S. Austral., Austral.* **191** Z11
Penonomé, *Pan.* **109** N21
Pénot, Mount, *Vanuatu* **198** D2
Penrhyn Atoll (Tongareva), *Cook Is., N.Z.* **194** H12
Pensacola, *Fla., U.S.* **91** Q1
Pensacola Bay, *Fla., U.S.* **91** Q1
Pensacola Mountains, *Antarctica* **206** G11
Pentecost (Île Pentecote), island, *Vanuatu* **198** D3
Pentecote, Île *see* Pentecost, *Vanuatu* **198** D3
Penticton, *B.C., Can.* **76** M9
Pentland Firth, *Scot., U.K.* **138** C8
Pentwater, *Mich., U.S.* **92** K9
Penuguan, *Indonesia* **168** K7
Penunjok, Tanjong, *Malaysia* **167** T11
Penwell, *Tex., U.S.* **97** N4
Penza, *Russ.* **140** G6
Penzance, *Eng., U.K.* **138** J6
Penzhinskaya Guba, *Russ.* **141** E21
Peoples Creek, *Mont., U.S.* **100** B10
Peoria, *Ariz., U.S.* **101** U6
Peoria, *Ill., U.S.* **93** Q5
Pepeekeo, *Hawaii, U.S.* **107** L21
Pepillo Salcedo, *Dom. Rep.* **111** L17
Pepin, Lake, *Minn.-Wis., U.S.* **98** K13
Perabumulih, *Indonesia* **168** K7
Percival Lakes, *Austral.* **190** E5
Perdido, Arroyo, river, *Arg.* **125** R8
Pereira, *Col.* **120** F4
Peremul Par, island, *India* **159** Q2
Perenjori, *W. Austral., Austral.* **191** W2
Perga, ruins, *Turk.* **148** H6
Pergamino, *Arg.* **124** L12
Perham, *Minn., U.S.* **98** G9
Peri, river, *Turk.* **149** F15
Péribonka, river, *Que., Can.* **77** M20
Perico, *Arg.* **124** E10
Perigoso, Canal, *Braz.* **123** C13
Perigot *see* Puamau, Baie, *Fr. Polynesia, Fr.* **199** M21
Périgueux, *Fr.* **138** M9
Perijá, Sierra de, *Col.-Venez.* **120** B6
Peri Lake, *Austral.* **190** J12
Perim *see* Barīm, island, *Yemen* **152** R9
Perito Moreno, *Arg.* **125** T7
Perkins, *Okla., U.S.* **96** F11
Perky, *Fla., U.S.* **91** Y9
Perm', *Russ.* **140** H8
Pernambuco Plain, *Atl. Oc.* **217** P9
Pernik, *Bulg.* **137** H15
Peron, Cape, *Austral.* **190** K2
Peronit Burnu, *Turk.* **149** C15
Péronne, *Fr.* **138** J10
Perpetua, Cape, *Oreg., U.S.* **102** G2
Perpignan, *Fr.* **139** P10
Perros-Guirec, *Fr.* **138** K7
Perry, *Fla., U.S.* **91** R6
Perry, *Ga., U.S.* **91** N6
Perry, *Iowa, U.S.* **99** P11
Perry, *Okla., U.S.* **96** F11
Perrysburg, *Ohio, U.S.* **93** N12
Perryton, *Tex., U.S.* **96** E6
Perryville, *Alas., U.S.* **105** N13
Perryville, *Mo., U.S.* **99** U15
Persepolis, ruins, *Iran* **153** F13
Persian Gulf, *Asia* **146** G4
Pertek, *Turk.* **149** F14
Perth, *Scot., U.K.* **138** E8
Perth, *W. Austral., Austral.* **191** X2
Perth Basin, *Ind. Oc.* **221** M15
Peru, *S. Amer.* **122** F4
Peru, *Ill., U.S.* **93** P5
Peru, *Ind., U.S.* **93** Q9
Peru, *Nebr., U.S.* **99** Q9
Peru Basin, *Pac. Oc.* **219** L19
Perugia, *It.* **136** G9
Pervari, *Turk.* **149** G17
Pervomays'k, *Ukr.* **133** K15
Pervoural'sk, *Russ.* **140** H9
Pervyy Kuril'skiy Proliv, *Russ.* **141** G23
Pesaro, *It.* **136** G10
Pescadores *see* P'enghu Ch'üntao, islands, *Taiwan, China* **163** R9
Pescara, *It.* **136** H10
Peschici, *It.* **136** H11
Peshawar, *Pak.* **157** N9
Peshawarun, ruins, *Afghan.* **157** Q2
Peshin Jan, *Afghan.* **157** N1
Peshtigo, *Wis., U.S.* **92** H7
Pesu, *India* **158** G15
Petacalco, Bahía, *Mex.* **108** K10
Petacalco Bay, *N. Amer.* **74** P5
Petaḥ Tiqwa, *Israel* **150** M5
Petal, *Miss., U.S.* **94** N12
Petaluma, *Calif., U.S.* **103** R3
Petatlán, *Mex.* **108** K10
Petenwell Lake, *Wis., U.S.* **92** J5
Peterborough, *N.H., U.S.* **89** J13
Peterborough, *Ont., Can.* **77** Q18
Peterborough, *S. Austral., Austral.* **191** X10
Peterhead, *Scot., U.K.* **138** D8
Peter I Island, *Antarctica* **206** J4
Petermann Ranges, *Austral.* **190** G6
Peter Pond Lake, *Sask., Can.* **76** K11
Petersburg, *Alas., U.S.* **105** K23
Petersburg, *Ill., U.S.* **93** R4
Petersburg, *Ind., U.S.* **93** T8
Petersburg, *Tex., U.S.* **96** J5
Petersburg, *Va., U.S.* **90** F13
Petersburg, *W. Va., U.S.* **90** C11
Petit Bois Island, *Miss., U.S.* **95** P13
Petite Rivière del' Artibonite, *Haiti* **111** L16
Petit-Goâve, *Haiti* **111** M16
Petitot, river, *B.C., Can.* **76** J10
Petoskey, *Mich., U.S.* **92** H10
Petra, ruins, *Jordan* **151** Q6
Petrich, *Bulg.* **137** H15
Petrified Forest National Park, *Ariz., U.S.* **101** S9
Petro, *Pak.* **157** U8
Petroglyphs, *Hawaii, U.S.* **107** L18
Petroglyphs, *Hawaii, U.S.* **107** N21
Petroglyphs, *Hawaii, U.S.* **107** Q19
Petrolândia, *Braz.* **123** G17
Petrolia, *Calif., U.S.* **103** N1
Petrolia, *Tex., U.S.* **96** J10
Petrolina, *Braz.* **123** G16
Petropavl, *Kaz.* **155** B13
Petropavlovsk Kamchatskiy, *Russ.* **141** F23
Petroşani, *Rom.* **137** F15
Petrovsk Zabaykal'skiy, *Russ.* **141** L16
Petrozavodsk, *Russ.* **140** E7
Petukhovo, *Russ.* **140** J9
Pevek, *Russ.* **141** C19
Peywar Kandaw, pass, *Afghan.-Pak.* **157** N8
Phaeton, Port, *Tahiti, Fr. Polynesia, Fr.* **199** P17
Phalodi, *India* **158** F3
Phaltan, *India* **158** M4
Phan, *Thai.* **166** J8
Phangan, Ko, *Thai.* **167** Q8
Phangnga, *Thai.* **167** R7
Phan Ly, *Vietnam* **167** P14
Phan Rang, *Vietnam* **167** P14
Phan Thiet, *Vietnam* **167** P13
Pharr, *Tex., U.S.* **97** W10
Phatthalung, *Thai.* **167** R8
Phayao, *Thai.* **166** J8
Phelps, *Ky., U.S.* **95** C20
Phelps Lake, *N.C., U.S.* **90** H14
Phenix City, *Ala., U.S.* **95** L17
Phetchabun Range, *Thai.* **166** M9
Phetchaburi, *Thai.* **167** N8
Phiafai, *Laos* **166** M12
Phichai, *Thai.* **166** K8
Phichit, *Thai.* **166** L8
Philadelphia *see* 'Ammān, *Jordan* **150** M7
Philadelphia, *Miss., U.S.* **94** K12
Philadelphia, *Pa., U.S.* **88** P9
Philip, *S. Dak., U.S.* **98** L3
Philippi, *W. Va., U.S.* **90** C10
Philippi Glacier, *Antarctica* **207** H21
Philippine Islands, *Asia* **146** J13
Philippines, *Asia* **169** C14
Philippine Sea, *Pac. Oc.* **194** D2
Philippine Trench, *Pac. Oc.* **218** H4
Philippolis, *S. Af.* **182** L9
Philippopolis *see* Shahbā', *Syr.* **150** K8
Philipsburg, *Mont., U.S.* **100** D6
Philipsburg, *Pa., U.S.* **88** N5
Philipsburg, *St. Martin, Fr.-Neth.* **113** F15
Philip Smith Mountains, *Alas., U.S.* **105** C17
Phillip Island, *Coral Sea* **194** L7
Phillip Island, *Norfolk I., Austral.* **197** G20
Phillips, *Tex., U.S.* **96** G6
Phillips, *Wis., U.S.* **92** G4
Phillipsburg, *Kans., U.S.* **99** R5
Phillips Inlet, *Nunavut, Can.* **77** A15
Philmont, site, *N. Mex., U.S.* **101** Q13
Philomath, *Oreg., U.S.* **102** G3
Philpots Island, *Nunavut, Can.* **77** D16
Phippsburg, *Colo., U.S.* **100** L11
Phitsanulok, *Thai.* **166** K8
Phnom Penh, *Cambodia* **167** P11
Phoenix, *Ariz., U.S.* **101** U7
Phoenix Islands, *Kiribati* **194** H10
Phôngsali, *Laos* **166** G10
Phong Tho, *Vietnam* **166** G10
Phraaspa, ruins, *Iran* **152** B11
Phrae, *Thai.* **166** K8
Phrao, *Thai.* **166** J8
Phra Thong, Ko, *Thai.* **167** Q7
Phrom Phiram, *Thai.* **166** K8
Phu Cat, *Vietnam* **166** M14
Phuket, *Thai.* **167** R7
Phuket, Ko, *Thai.* **167** R7
Phulabani, *India* **158** K9
Phulad, *India* **158** G4
Phu Loc, *Vietnam* **166** L13
Phu My, *Vietnam* **166** M14
Phu Quoc, Dao, *Vietnam* **167** Q11
Phu Rieng, *Vietnam* **167** P13
Phu Tho, *Vietnam* **166** G11
Phyarpon, *Myanmar* **166** L6
Piacenza, *It.* **136** F8
Piamafua, peak, *Manua Is., Amer. Samoa, U.S.* **198** N2
Pianguan, *China* **162** D4
Pianu, island, *Chuuk, F.S.M.* **197** C14
Pianu, Mochun, *Chuuk, F.S.M.* **197** C13
Piatra Neamţ, *Rom.* **137** D16
Piauí, Serra do, *Braz.* **123** G15
Piave, river, *It.* **136** E10
Pibor Post, *Sudan* **179** G13
Picacho, *Ariz., U.S.* **101** V7
Picayune, *Miss., U.S.* **94** P11
Pichanal, *Arg.* **124** E10
Picher, *Okla., U.S.* **96** D14
Pichilemu, *Chile* **124** L6
Pickens, *Miss., U.S.* **94** K11
Pickle Lake, *Ont., Can.* **77** N15
Pickwick Lake, *Tenn., U.S.* **95** G13
Picos, *Braz.* **123** F16
Pico Truncado, *Arg.* **125** T9
Pictured Rocks National Lakeshore, *Mich., U.S.* **92** F9
Pidarak, *Pak.* **157** V3
Piedmont, region, *Eur.* **130** H5
Piedmont, region, *U.S.* **79** J18
Piedmont, *Ala., U.S.* **95** J17
Piedmont, *Mo., U.S.* **99** U15
Piedras, river, *Peru* **122** G5
Piedras Blancas, Point, *Calif., U.S.* **103** V4
Piedras Negras, *Mex.* **108** D11
Pieksämäki, *Fin.* **135** H16
Pielinen, lake, *Fin.* **135** G17
Pierce, *Idaho, U.S.* **100** D4
Pierce, *Nebr., U.S.* **99** N7
Pierre, *S. Dak., U.S.* **98** K5
Pierrot Island, *Mauritius* **185** K20

Pietarsaari see Jakobstad, Fin. 135 G15
Pietermaritzburg, S. Af. 182 K11
Pietersburg (Polokwane), S. Af. 182 H11
Pigailoe (West Fayu Atoll), F.S.M. 196 Q5
Pigeon, Mich., U.S. 92 K12
Piggott, Ark., U.S. 94 E11
Pigs, Bay of see Cochinos, Bahía de, Cuba 110 H7
Pigüé, Arg. 125 N11
Piha Passage, Tongatapu, Tonga 198 H12
Pihtipudas, Fin. 135 G15
Piilanihale Heiau, Hawaii, U.S. 107 G18
Piis-Panewu, island, Chuuk, F.S.M. 197 A15
Pijijiapan, Mex. 109 L14
Pikelot, island, F.S.M. 196 Q5
Pikes Peak, Colo., U.S. 101 N13
Pikeville, Ky., U.S. 95 C20
Pikijin, island, Jaluit Atoll, Marshall Is. 196 L8
Piła, Pol. 132 F9
Pilani, India 158 F5
Pilão Arcado, Braz. 123 G15
Pilar, Para. 122 N10
Pilar, Cabo, Chile 125 X6
Pilbarra Point, Vanuatu 198 G4
Pilcomayo, river, S. Amer. 118 J6
Pileni, island, Santa Cruz Is., Solomon Is. 197 P23
Pil'gyn, Russ. 141 B20
Pilibhit, India 158 F7
Pilliga, N.S.W., Austral. 191 W14
Pilón, Cuba 110 L11
Pílos, Gr. 137 M14
Pilot Knob, Idaho, U.S. 100 E4
Pilot Peak, Nev., U.S. 103 R8
Pilot Point, Alas., U.S. 105 M14
Pilot Rock, Oreg., U.S. 102 F7
Pilot Station, Alas., U.S. 104 H12
Pilottown, La., U.S. 94 R12
Pilsen see Plzeň, Czech Rep. 132 J7
Pima, Ariz., U.S. 101 U9
Pimba, S. Austral., Austral. 191 W9
Pimentel, Dom. Rep. 111 L19
Pinaki 2, island, Fr. Polynesia, Fr. 199 F21
Pinang, island, Malaysia 167 T8
Pinangah, Malaysia 168 G12
Pınarbaşı, Turk. 148 F11
Pinar del Río, Cuba 110 H5
Piñas, Ecua. 120 L2
Pinas, Arg. 124 J9
Pinckneyville, Ill., U.S. 93 U5
Pinconning, Mich., U.S. 92 K11
Pindaré, river, Braz. 123 E14
Pindi Bhattian, Pak. 157 P11
Pindi Gheb, Pak. 157 N10
Pindus Mountains, Alban.-Gr. 137 K14
Pine Barrens, region, U.S. 79 F20
Pine Bluff, Ark., U.S. 94 H9
Pine Bluffs, Wyo., U.S. 100 K14
Pine City, Minn., U.S. 98 H12
Pine Creek, N. Terr., Austral. 191 P8
Pinedale, Calif., U.S. 103 T6
Pinedale, Wyo., U.S. 100 H9
Pinega, river, Eur. 130 B11
Pinegrove, W. Austral., Austral. 191 V2
Pine Hill, N. Terr., Austral. 191 T8
Pinehill, Qnsld., Austral. 191 T13
Pine Hills, Fla., U.S. 91 T9
Pinehurst, Idaho, U.S. 100 C4
Pinehurst, N.C., U.S. 90 J11
Pine Island Bay, Antarctica 206 K7
Pine Island Glacier, Antarctica 206 J7
Pineland, Tex., U.S. 97 N16
Pinellas Park, Fla., U.S. 91 U7
Pine Point, N.W.T., Can. 76 J11
Pine Ridge, S. Dak., U.S. 98 M2
Pine River, Minn., U.S. 98 G10
Pines, Lake O' The, Tex., U.S. 96 L14
Pinetop-Lakeside, Ariz., U.S. 101 T9
Pineville, Ky., U.S. 95 D19
Pineville, La., U.S. 94 N8
Piney Buttes, Mont., U.S. 100 C11
Ping, river, Thai. 166 L8
Pingdingshan, China 162 H5
Pingdu, China 162 F9
Pingelap Atoll, F.S.M. 196 Q8
Pingelly, W. Austral., Austral. 191 X3
Pinghe, China 163 R7
Pingjiang, China 162 M5
Pinglap, island, Jaluit Atoll, Marshall Is. 196 M7
Pingle, China 163 Q2
Pingli, China 162 J2
Pingliang, China 160 J12
Pinglu, China 162 D4
Pinglu, China 162 G3
Pingluo, China 162 D1
Pingnan, China 163 R2
Pingquan, China 162 C8
Pingtan, China 163 Q9
P'ingtung, Taiwan, China 163 S9
Pingxiang, China 160 P12
Pingxiang, China 163 N5
Pingyang, China 163 N9
Pingyao, China 162 F4
Pingyi, China 162 G7
Pingyin, China 162 F7
Pingyuan, China 163 Q6
Pinheiro, Braz. 123 D14
Pinhel, Port. 139 Q5
Pini, island, Indonesia 168 J5
Pinjan, Indonesia 169 H13
Pinjarra, W. Austral., Austral. 191 X2
Pinlaung, Myanmar 166 H6
Pinleibu, Myanmar 166 F6
Pinnacles National Monument, Calif., U.S. 103 U5
Pinnaroo, S. Austral., Austral. 191 Y11
Pinos, Point, Calif., U.S. 103 T4
Pins, Île des (Kunié), New Caledonia, Fr. 198 E9
Pinsk, Belarus 132 G12
Pinsk Marshes, Belarus 132 G12
Pintados, Chile 124 C7
Pintharuka, W. Austral., Austral. 191 W2
Pioche, Nev., U.S. 103 R12
Piombino, It. 136 G8
Pioneer Fracture Zone, Pac. Oc. 219 E13
Pioneer Mountains, Mont., U.S. 100 E6
Pioneer Tablemount, Hawaii, U.S. 106 L4
Pioner, Ostrov, Russ. 141 D14
Piotrków Trybunalski, Pol. 132 H10
Pipanaco, Salar de, Arg. 124 H9
Pipar, India 158 G4
Piparia, India 158 J6
Piper Peak, Nev., U.S. 103 S8
Pipe Spring National Monument, Ariz., U.S. 101 Q6
Pipestem Creek, N. Dak., U.S. 98 G6
Pipestone, Minn., U.S. 98 L8
Pipestone National Monument, Minn., U.S. 98 L8
Pipinas, Arg. 124 M13
Piplan, Pak. 157 P9
Pippu, Jap. 164 F14
Piqua, Ohio, U.S. 93 R11
Piracicaba, Braz. 123 M13
Piracuruca, Braz. 123 E16
Pirae, Tahiti, Fr. Polynesia, Fr. 199 N16
Piraeus (Pireás), Gr. 137 L15
Pirané, Arg. 124 F13
Piranhas, Braz. 122 J12
Pirapora, Braz. 123 K14
Pirássununga, Braz. 123 L13
Pireás see Piraeus, Gr. 137 L15
Pírgos, Gr. 137 L14
Pirimapun, Indonesia 169 M20
Piripiri, Braz. 123 E16
Pirojpur, Bangladesh 158 J12
Pir Panjal Range, India 157 N12
Pirsagat, river, Azerb. 149 D22
Pirtleville, Ariz., U.S. 101 W9
Pisa, It. 136 G8
Pisagua, Chile 124 C7
Pisamwe, island, Chuuk, F.S.M. 197 A14
Pisco, Peru 122 H3
Písek, Czech Rep. 132 J7
Pisemew, island, Chuuk, F.S.M. 197 A15
Pishan (Guma), China 160 G4
Pishin, Pak. 157 R6
Pīshīn, Iran 153 H18
Pisininin, island, Chuuk, F.S.M. 197 A15
Pisinun, island, Chuuk, F.S.M. 197 C16
Pismo Beach, Calif., U.S. 103 V5
Piso Firme, Bol. 122 H8
Pistol River, Oreg., U.S. 102 K1
Pitaga, Nfld., Can. 77 L21
Pitanga, Braz. 122 M12
Pitav, Afghan. 156 L8
Pitcairn Island, Pac. Oc. 195 L16
Piteå, Sw. 135 F14
Piteşti, Rom. 137 F15
Pit Gorodok, Russ. 141 J13
Pithara, W. Austral., Austral. 191 W2
Piti, Guam, U.S. 196 C10
Piti U Tai, island, Bora-Bora, Fr. Polynesia, Fr. 199 L14
Piti U Uta, island, Bora-Bora, Fr. Polynesia, Fr. 199 L14
Piton, peak, Wallis and Futuna, Fr. 198 F11
Pitti Island, India 159 R3
Pitt Island, Pac. Oc. 194 P9
Pittsburg, Kans., U.S. 99 U10
Pittsburg, Tex., U.S. 96 L14
Pittsburgh, Pa., U.S. 88 N3
Pittsfield, Ill., U.S. 93 R3
Pittsfield, Mass., U.S. 88 K12
Pittsfield, Me., U.S. 89 F17
Pittston, Pa., U.S. 88 M9
Piura, Peru 122 F2
Pixian, China 162 H7
Pkulagalid, point, Palau 196 M11
Pkulagasemieg, island, Palau 196 Q11
Pkulngril, cape, Palau 196 M11
Pkurengel, point, Palau 196 N11
Placentia Bay, Nfld., Can. 77 M24
Placerville, Calif., U.S. 103 Q5
Placetas, Cuba 110 H9
Placida, Fla., U.S. 91 V8
Plain Dealing, La., U.S. 94 K6
Plainfield, Ind., U.S. 93 R9
Plainfield, N.J., U.S. 88 N10
Plains, Ga., U.S. 91 N5
Plains, Kans., U.S. 99 V4
Plains, Mont., U.S. 100 C5
Plains, Tex., U.S. 96 K4
Plainview, Minn., U.S. 98 L12
Plainview, Nebr., U.S. 99 N7
Plainview, Tex., U.S. 96 J5
Plainville, Kans., U.S. 99 S5
Plainwell, Mich., U.S. 92 M10
Plaisance, Haiti 111 L16
Plana Cays (French Cays), Bahamas 111 G15
Plankinton, S. Dak., U.S. 98 L6
Plano, Tex., U.S. 96 L12
Plantation, Fla., U.S. 91 W10
Plant City, Fla., U.S. 91 U8
Plantsite, Ariz., U.S. 101 U9
Plaquemine, La., U.S. 94 P9
Plata, Isla de la, Ecua. 120 K1
Plata, Río de la, Arg.-Uru. 124 M14
Plato, Col. 120 C5
Platte, river, U.S. 78 G11
Platteville, Wis., U.S. 92 M4
Plattsburg, Mo., U.S. 99 S10
Plattsburgh, N.Y., U.S. 88 F12
Plattsmouth, Nebr., U.S. 99 Q9
Plauen, Ger. 132 H6
Playa Blanca, Canary Is., Sp. 184 P8
Playa Dayaniguas, Cuba 110 H5
Playa Girón, Cuba 110 H8
Playas Lake, N. Mex., U.S. 101 W10
Play Ku, Vietnam 166 M13
Plaza Huincul, Arg. 125 P8
Pleasant, Lake, Ariz., U.S. 101 T6
Pleasant Grove, Utah, U.S. 100 L7
Pleasanton, Kans., U.S. 99 T10
Pleasanton, Tex., U.S. 97 S9
Pleasantville, N.J., U.S. 88 Q10
Pleasure Ridge Park, Ky., U.S. 95 B16
Plenty, river, Austral. 190 F9
Plenty, Bay of, N.Z. 193 K20
Plentywood, Mont., U.S. 100 A13
Plesetsk, Russ. 140 E8
Plétipi, Lac, Que., Can. 77 M20
Pleven, Bulg. 137 G15
Plevna, Mont., U.S. 100 D13
Ploče, Croatia 136 G12
Płock, Pol. 132 G10
Ploieşti, Rom. 137 F16
Płońsk, Pol. 132 G10
Plovdiv, Bulg. 137 H15
Plummer, Idaho, U.S. 100 C3
Plumtree, Zimb. 182 G10
Plymouth, Ind., U.S. 93 P9
Plymouth, Mass., U.S. 89 L15
Plymouth, Montserrat, U.K. 113 G16
Plymouth, N.C., U.S. 90 H14
Plymouth, N.H., U.S. 89 H14
Plymouth, Pa., U.S. 88 M8
Plymouth, Eng., U.K. 138 J7
Plymouth, Vt., U.S. 88 H12
Plymouth, Wis., U.S. 92 K7
Plzeň (Pilsen), Czech Rep. 132 J7
Pô, Burkina Faso 180 E10
Po, river, It. 136 F9
Pobedy Peak (Victory Peak), China-Kyrg. 156 E15
Pocahontas, Ark., U.S. 94 E10
Pocahontas, Iowa, U.S. 98 M10
Pocahontas, Va., U.S. 90 F8
Pocatello, Idaho, U.S. 100 H7
Pochutla, Mex. 109 L13
Pocomoke City, Md., U.S. 90 D15
Poconé, Braz. 122 J10
Poços de Caldas, Braz. 123 L14
Podgorica, Yug. 137 H13
Podil's'ka Vysochyna, Ukr. 132 J12
Podkamennaya Tunguska, river, Russ. 141 J13
Podkamennaya Tunguska, Russ. 141 J13
Podol'sk, Russ. 140 F6
Podporozh'ye, Russ. 140 E7
Poh, Indonesia 169 J14
Pohakueaea Point, Hawaii, U.S. 107 H17
P'ohang, S. Korea 162 F15
Pohnpei (Ponape), island, F.S.M. 196 Q8
Pohnpei Harbor, Pohnpei, F.S.M. 197 F14
Pohue Bay, Hawaii, U.S. 107 Q19
Pohuerahi, peak, Huahine, Fr. Polynesia, Fr. 199 H14
Poi, Wallis and Futuna, Fr. 198 E11
Poindimié, New Caledonia, Fr. 198 C7
Poinsett, Cape, Antarctica 207 M21
Point Arena, Calif., U.S. 103 Q2
Pointe a la Hache, La., U.S. 94 Q11
Pointe-à-Pitre, Guadeloupe, Fr. 113 H17
Pointe-Noire, Congo 181 N16
Point Fortin, Trin. & Tobago 113 P17
Point Hope, Alas., U.S. 104 D11
Point Lake, N.W.T., Can. 76 G12
Point Lay, Alas., U.S. 104 C12
Point Lilian, peak, Austral. 190 H6
Point Pedro, Sri Lanka 159 R7
Point Pleasant, N.J., U.S. 88 P11
Point Pleasant, W. Va., U.S. 90 D7
Point Reyes National Seashore, Calif., U.S. 103 R3
Point Samson, W. Austral., Austral. 191 S2
Point Sud, Comoros 185 M14
Point Washington, Fla., U.S. 91 R3
Poipu, Hawaii, U.S. 106 C5
Poitiers, Fr. 138 L9
Pok, Pohnpei, F.S.M. 197 G14
Pokataroo, N.S.W., Austral. 191 W14
Pokka, Fin. 135 D15
Poko, Dem. Rep. of the Congo 178 J11
Pola see Pula, Croatia 136 F10
Polacca, Ariz., U.S. 101 R8
Pola Island, Tutuila, Amer. Samoa, U.S. 198 L8
Polān, Iran 153 H17
Poland, Eur. 132 G8
Poland, Kiritimati, Kiribati 197 B22
Polar Plateau, Antarctica 206 G12
Polatlı, Turk. 148 E7
Polatsk, Belarus 133 E13
Pol-e'Alam, Afghan. 157 N7
Pol-e Khomri, Afghan. 156 L7
Pole Plain, Arctic Oc. 222 F9
Policastro, Golfo di, It. 136 K11
Polihale State Park and Heiau, Hawaii, U.S. 106 B4
Polis, Cyprus 148 L7
Polk, Pa., U.S. 88 M3
Pollock, S. Dak., U.S. 98 H5
Polnovat, Russ. 140 G10
Poloa Bay, Tutuila, Amer. Samoa, U.S. 198 M6
Polokwane see Pietersburg, S. Af. 182 H11
Polson, Mont., U.S. 100 C5
Poltava, Ukr. 133 H16
Polvadera, N. Mex., U.S. 101 T12
Polyarnyy, Russ. 140 C9
Polynesia, islands, Pac. Oc. 194 E10
Polynesian Cultural Center, Hawaii, U.S. 106 D11
Pom, Indonesia 193 B15
Pomabamba, Peru 122 G3
Pomene, Mozambique 183 H13
Pomeroy, Ohio, U.S. 93 S14
Pomeroy, Wash., U.S. 102 D9
Pomichna, Ukr. 133 K15
Pomona, Calif., U.S. 103 X9
Pompano Beach, Fla., U.S. 91 W10
Pompeiopolis, ruins, Turk. 148 J9
Pompeys Pillar National Monument, Mont., U.S. 100 E10
Ponape see Pohnpei, island, F.S.M. 196 Q8
Ponca City, Okla., U.S. 96 E11
Ponce, P.R., U.S. 111 N22
Ponce de Leon Bay, Fla., U.S. 91 X9
Poncha Springs, Colo., U.S. 101 N12
Ponchatoula, La., U.S. 94 P10
Ponch'on, S. Korea 162 F14
Pond Creek, Okla., U.S. 96 E10
Pondicherry (Puduchcheri), India 159 Q7
Pond Inlet, Nunavut, Can. 77 E17
Pondosa, Calif., U.S. 102 M4
Ponérihouen, New Caledonia, Fr. 198 C7
Pones, island, Chuuk, F.S.M. 197 C16
Ponferrada, Sp. 139 P6
Pong, Thai. 166 J8
Pongara, Pointe, Gabon 181 K15
Pongaroa, N.Z. 193 M19
Pongdu-ri, N. Korea 162 B14
Poniya Point, Rota I., N. Mariana Is., U.S. 196 E7
Ponnani, India 159 R5
Ponoy, Russ. 140 D9
Ponta do Pargo, Madeira Is., Port. 184 M2
Ponta do Sol, Madeira Is., Port. 184 M3
Ponta Grossa, Braz. 122 M12
Ponta Porã, Braz. 122 L10
Pontchartrain, Lake, La., U.S. 94 P11
Pontevedra, Sp. 139 P5
Ponte Vedra Beach, Fla., U.S. 91 R9
Pontiac, Ill., U.S. 93 Q6
Pontiac, Mich., U.S. 92 M12
Pontianak, Indonesia 168 J9
Pontotoc, Miss., U.S. 94 H12
Poochera, S. Austral., Austral. 191 X9
Poofai, Baie de, Bora-Bora, Fr. Polynesia, Fr. 199 K14
Pooncarie, N.S.W., Austral. 191 X11
Poopó, Bol. 122 K7
Poopó, Lago, Bol. 122 K7
Popayán, Col. 120 G4
Poplar, river, Man., Can. 77 M14
Poplar, river, Mont., U.S. 100 B12
Poplar, Mont., U.S. 100 B13
Poplar Bluff, Mo., U.S. 99 V15
Poplarville, Miss., U.S. 94 N12
Popocatépetl, peak, Mex. 108 J12
Popokabaka, Dem. Rep. of the Congo 178 L8
Popondetta, P.N.G. 193 E20
Poprad, Slovakia 132 J10
Porali, river, Pak. 157 U5
Porangahau, N.Z. 193 M20
Porbandar, India 158 J1
Porcupine, river, Alas., U.S. 105 D17

Porcupine Bank, *Atl. Oc.* **216** E11
Porcupine Creek, *Mont., U.S.* **100** B12
Porcupine Mountains, *Mich., U.S.* **92** F5
Porcupine Plain, *Atl. Oc.* **216** F11
Porea, island, *Manihiki Atoll, Cook Is., N.Z.* **199** C14
Porga, *Benin* **180** F11
Pori, *Fin.* **135** J15
Porirua, *N.Z.* **193** M19
Porlamar, *Venez.* **120** B11
Porongurup, *W. Austral., Austral.* **191** Y3
Porpoise Bay, *Antarctica* **207** P19
Porsangen, bay, *Nor.* **135** B14
Porsuk, river, *Turk.* **148** E6
Portage, *Ind., U.S.* **93** N8
Portage, *Mich., U.S.* **93** N10
Portage, *Wis., U.S.* **92** K5
Portage la Prairie, *Man., Can.* **77** N13
Portageville, *Mo., U.S.* **99** V16
Portal, *N. Dak., U.S.* **98** D3
Port Albert, *Vic., Austral.* **191** Z13
Portalegre, *Port.* **139** R5
Portales, *N. Mex., U.S.* **101** T15
Port Alfred, *S. Af.* **182** M10
Port Allegany, *Pa., U.S.* **88** L5
Port Allen, *La., U.S.* **94** P9
Port Angeles, *Wash., U.S.* **102** B3
Port Antonio, *Jam.* **110** N12
Port-à-Piment, *Haiti* **111** M15
Port Aransas, *Tex., U.S.* **97** U11
Port Arthur *see* Lüshun, *China* **162** E9
Port Arthur, *Tex., U.S.* **97** Q16
Port Augusta, *S. Austral., Austral.* **191** X10
Port-au-Prince, *Haiti* **111** M16
Port Austin, *Mich., U.S.* **92** K13
Port Beaufort, *S. Af.* **182** M8
Port Blair, *Andaman Is., India* **159** Q14
Port Bolivar, *Tex., U.S.* **97** R15
Portbou, *Sp.* **139** P10
Port Broughton, *S. Austral., Austral.* **191** X10
Port Burwell, *Nunavut, Can.* **77** J20
Port-Cartier, *Que., Can.* **77** M21
Port Charlotte, *Fla., U.S.* **91** V8
Port Clinton, *Ohio, U.S.* **93** N13
Port-de-Paix, *Haiti* **111** L16
Port Douglas, *Qnsld., Austral.* **191** R13
Port Eads, *La., U.S.* **94** R12
Port Edward, *S. Af.* **182** L11
Porteira, *Braz.* **122** D10
Portel, *Braz.* **122** D12
Port Elizabeth, *S. Af.* **182** M10
Port Elizabeth, *St. Vincent and the Grenadines* **113** L17
Porterdale, *Ga., U.S.* **90** L5
Porterville, *Calif., U.S.* **103** U7
Porterville, *S. Af.* **182** M7
Port Fairy, *Vic., Austral.* **191** Z11
Port-Gentil, *Gabon* **181** L14
Port Gibson, *Miss., U.S.* **94** M10
Port Graham, *Alas., U.S.* **105** K16
Port Harcourt, *Nig.* **181** H14
Port Hardy, *B.C., Can.* **76** L7
Port Hawkesbury, *N.S., Can.* **77** P22
Port Hedland, *W. Austral., Austral.* **191** S3
Port Heiden, *Alas., U.S.* **105** M13
Port Henry, *N.Y., U.S.* **88** G12
Port Hope, *Mich., U.S.* **92** K13
Port Hope Simpson, *Nfld., Can.* **77** L22
Port Howe, *Bahamas* **111** F13
Port Huron, *Mich., U.S.* **92** L13
Port-İliç, *Azerb.* **149** F22
Portimão, *Port.* **139** S4
Port Isabel, *Tex., U.S.* **97** W11
Port Jervis, *N.Y., U.S.* **88** M10
Port Kaituma, *Guyana* **121** D13
Portland, *Ind., U.S.* **93** Q10
Portland, *Me., U.S.* **89** H15
Portland, *Mich., U.S.* **92** L10
Portland, *N. Dak., U.S.* **98** F7
Portland, *Oreg., U.S.* **102** F3
Portland, *Tenn., U.S.* **95** E15
Portland, *Tex., U.S.* **97** T11
Portland, *Vic., Austral.* **191** Z11
Portland Bight, *Jam.* **110** N11
Portland Point, *Jam.* **110** N11
Portland Rock, *Jam.* **110** P11
Port Lavaca, *Tex., U.S.* **97** S12
Port Lincoln, *S. Austral., Austral.* **191** Y9
Port Lions, *Alas., U.S.* **105** L15
Port Loko, *Sierra Leone* **180** F5
Port Louis, *Mauritius* **185** F20
Port-Louis, *Guadeloupe, Fr.* **113** H17
Port Macquarie, *N.S.W., Austral.* **191** X15
Port Mansfield, *Tex., U.S.* **97** W11
Port Maria, *Jam.* **110** M12
Port Mathurin, *Mauritius* **185** J20
Port-Menier, *Que., Can.* **77** M21
Port Morant, *Jam.* **110** N12
Port Moresby, *P.N.G.* **193** E19
Port Neches, *Tex., U.S.* **97** Q16
Port Nelson, *Bahamas* **111** F14
Port Nolloth, *S. Af.* **182** K7
Pôrto, *Braz.* **123** E15
Porto, *Port.* **139** Q5
Porto Alegre, *Braz.* **122** P12
Porto Alegre, *São Tomé and Príncipe* **185** E20
Porto Amboim, *Angola* **182** D5
Pôrto Artur, *Braz.* **122** H11
Portobelo, *Pan.* **109** N21
Port O'Connor, *Tex., U.S.* **97** T12
Pôrto dos Gauchos, *Braz.* **122** G10
Porto Empedocle, *It.* **136** L10
Pôrto Esperidião, *Braz.* **122** J10
Portofino, *It.* **136** F8
Pôrto Franco, *Braz.* **123** F14
Port-of-Spain, *Trin. & Tobago* **113** P17
Pôrto Grande, *Braz.* **122** C12
Pôrto Inglês, *Cape Verde* **185** D17
Portola, *Calif., U.S.* **103** P6
Porto Moniz, *Madeira Is., Port.* **184** M2
Pôrto Murtinho, *Braz.* **122** L10
Pôrto Nacional, *Braz.* **123** G13
Porto Novo, *India* **159** Q7
Porto-Novo, *Benin* **180** H12
Port Ontario, *N.Y., U.S.* **88** H8
Port Orange, *Fla., U.S.* **91** S9
Port Orchard, *Wash., U.S.* **102** C3
Port Orford, *Oreg., U.S.* **102** K1
Porto Santo, island, *Madeira Is., Port.* **184** L5
Porto Santo, *Madeira Is., Port.* **184** L5
Pôrto Seguro, *Braz.* **123** K16
Porto Torres, *It.* **136** J7
Porto-Vecchio, *Fr.* **139** P13
Pôrto Velho, *Braz.* **122** F8
Portoviejo, *Ecua.* **120** J2
Port Phillip Bay, *Austral.* **190** M12
Port Pirie, *S. Austral., Austral.* **191** X10
Port Royal, *S.C., U.S.* **91** N9
Port Royal Sound, *S.C., U.S.* **91** N9
Port Said *see* Būr Sa'īd, *Egypt* **151** N1
Port Saint Joe, *Fla., U.S.* **91** R4
Port Saint Johns, *S. Af.* **182** L11
Port Saint Lucie, *Fla., U.S.* **91** V10
Port Salerno, *Fla., U.S.* **91** V10
Port-Salut, *Haiti* **111** N15
Port Saunders, *Nfld., Can.* **77** L23
Port Shepstone, *S. Af.* **182** L11
Portsmouth, *Dominica* **113** J17
Portsmouth, *N.C., U.S.* **90** J15
Portsmouth, *N.H., U.S.* **89** J15
Portsmouth, *Ohio, U.S.* **93** T13
Portsmouth, *Eng., U.K.* **138** J8
Portsmouth, *Va., U.S.* **90** F14
Port South East, *Mauritius* **185** J20
Port Sudan *see* Būr Sūdān, *Sudan* **179** C14
Port Sulphur, *La., U.S.* **94** Q11
Port Townsend, *Wash., U.S.* **102** B3
Portugal, *Eur.* **131** W1
Portugal, *Eur.* **139** S5
Portuguesa, river, *Venez.* **120** C9
Port-Vendres, *Fr.* **139** P10
Port-Vila, *Vanuatu* **198** F3
Port Vincent, *S. Austral., Austral.* **191** Y10
Port Warrender, *W. Austral., Austral.* **191** Q5
Port Washington, *Wis., U.S.* **92** L7
Porvenir, *Bol.* **122** G6
Porvenir, *Chile* **125** X8
Porvoo, *Fin.* **135** J16
Posadas, *Arg.* **124** G14
Posht-e Bādām, *Iran* **153** E14
Posio, *Fin.* **135** E16
Poso, *Indonesia* **169** J13
Posof, *Turk.* **149** C17
Posŏng, *S. Korea* **162** H13
Possum Kingdom Lake, *Tex., U.S.* **96** L9
Post, *Tex., U.S.* **96** K5
Post Falls, *Idaho, U.S.* **100** C3
Postville, *Iowa, U.S.* **98** M13
Poteau, *Okla., U.S.* **96** G14
Poteet, *Tex., U.S.* **97** S9
Potenza, *It.* **136** J11
Poth, *Tex., U.S.* **97** S10
Potholes Reservoir, *Wash., U.S.* **102** D7
P'ot'i, *Rep. of Georgia* **149** B16
Potiskum, *Nig.* **181** E15
Potlatch, *Idaho, U.S.* **100** C3
Pot Mountain, *Idaho, U.S.* **100** D4
Potnarvin, *Vanuatu* **198** G4
Potomac, river, *Md.-Va., U.S.* **90** D13
Potosi, *Mo., U.S.* **99** T14
Potosí, *Bol.* **122** K7
Potrerillos, *Chile* **124** G7
Potsdam, *Ger.* **132** G7
Potsdam, *N.Y., U.S.* **88** F10
Pott, Île, *New Caledonia, Fr.* **198** B5
Potter, *Nebr., U.S.* **99** P1
Pottstown, *Pa., U.S.* **88** P9
Pottsville, *Pa., U.S.* **88** N8
Poudre d'Or, *Mauritius* **185** F20
Pouébo, *New Caledonia, Fr.* **198** C6
Pouembout, *New Caledonia, Fr.* **198** C7
Poughkeepsie, *N.Y., U.S.* **88** L11
Poulsbo, *Wash., U.S.* **102** C4
Poum, *New Caledonia, Fr.* **198** C6
Pouoanuu, Mount, *Hiva Oa, Fr. Polynesia, Fr.* **199** M20
Poutasi, *Samoa* **198** L3
Poutoru, *Tahaa, Fr. Polynesia, Fr.* **199** B23
Povai, *Bora-Bora, Fr. Polynesia, Fr.* **199** K14
Póvoa de Varzim, *Port.* **139** P4
Povorino, *Russ.* **140** G5
Povungnituk, Baie de, *Nunavut, Can.* **77** K17
Powder, river, *Mont., U.S.* **100** D13
Powder, river, *Oreg., U.S.* **102** G9
Powder River, *Wyo., U.S.* **100** H11
Powell, *Wyo., U.S.* **100** F10
Powell, Lake, *Utah, U.S.* **101** Q7
Powell Butte, *Oreg., U.S.* **102** H5
Powell River, *B.C., Can.* **76** M8
Powers, *Oreg., U.S.* **102** J2
Powers Lake, *N. Dak., U.S.* **98** E3
Poxoréo, *Braz.* **122** J11
Poya, *New Caledonia, Fr.* **198** D7
Poyang Hu, *China* **162** M6
Poygan, Lake, *Wis., U.S.* **92** J6
Pozantı, *Turk.* **148** H10
Poza Rica, *Mex.* **108** H12
Poznań, *Pol.* **132** G9
Pozo Almonte, *Chile* **124** C7
Prachin Buri, *Thai.* **166** M9
Prachuap Khiri Khan, *Thai.* **167** P8
Prado, *Braz.* **123** K16
Prague *see* Praha, *Czech Rep.* **132** H7
Praha (Prague), *Czech Rep.* **132** H7
Praia, *Cape Verde* **185** D16
Prainha, *Braz.* **122** D11
Prainha, *Braz.* **122** F9
Prairie City, *Oreg., U.S.* **102** G7
Prairie Dog Creek, *Kans., U.S.* **99** R4
Prairie Dog Town Fork Red, river, *Tex., U.S.* **96** H6
Prairie du Chien, *Wis., U.S.* **92** L3
Prairie Grove, *Ark., U.S.* **94** E6
Pran Buri, *Thai.* **167** N8
Praslin, island, *Seychelles* **185** N20
Pratas Island *see* Tungsha Tao, *Taiwan, China* **163** T6
Prato, *It.* **136** G9
Pratt, *Kans., U.S.* **99** U6
Pratt Seamount, *Pac. Oc.* **219** B14
Prattville, *Ala., U.S.* **95** L15
Prazeres, *Madeira Is., Port.* **184** M2
Preguiça, *Cape Verde* **185** B15
Preguiça, *Cape Verde* **185** B17
Prehistoric Petroglyphs, *Afghan.* **156** K9
Premont, *Tex., U.S.* **97** U10
Prentice, *Wis., U.S.* **92** G4
Prentiss, *Miss., U.S.* **94** M11
Preobrazhenka, *Russ.* **141** J15
Preparis Island, *Myanmar* **166** M4
Preparis North Channel, *Myanmar* **166** L4
Preparis South Channel, *Myanmar* **166** M4
Přerov, *Czech Rep.* **132** J9
Prescott, *Ariz., U.S.* **101** S6
Prescott, *Ark., U.S.* **94** J7
Prescott, *Wash., U.S.* **102** E8
Presho, *S. Dak., U.S.* **98** L5
Presidencia Roca, *Arg.* **124** F12
Presidente Dutra, *Braz.* **123** E15
Presidente Eduardo Frei, station, *Antarctica* **206** C3
Presidente Prudente, *Braz.* **122** L12
Presidente Roque Sáenz Peña, *Arg.* **124** G12
President Thiers Bank, *Pac. Oc.* **219** M13
Presidio, *Tex., U.S.* **97** R1
Presidio, *Tex., U.S.* **97** Y4
Prešov, *Slovakia* **132** J10
Presque Isle, *Me., U.S.* **89** B18
Presque Isle, *Mich., U.S.* **92** H12
Pressburg *see* Bratislava, *Slovakia* **132** K8
Preston, *Idaho, U.S.* **100** J7
Preston, *Minn., U.S.* **98** L13
Preston, *Mo., U.S.* **99** U12
Prestonsburg, *Ky., U.S.* **95** C20
Pretoria, *S. Af.* **182** J10
Préveza, *Gr.* **137** K13
Pribilof Islands, *Alas., U.S.* **104** M9
Price, river, *Utah, U.S.* **100** M8
Price, *Utah, U.S.* **100** M8
Price, Cape, *Andaman Is., India* **159** P14
Prichard, *Ala., U.S.* **95** N13
Priekule, *Latv.* **135** M15
Prieska, *S. Af.* **182** L9
Priest Lake, *Idaho, U.S.* **100** B3
Priestley Glacier, *Antarctica* **207** P14
Priest River, *Idaho, U.S.* **100** B3
Prijedor, *Bosn. and Herzg.* **136** F11
Prilep, *Maced.* **137** J14
Prince Albert, *S. Af.* **182** M8
Prince Albert, *Sask., Can.* **76** M12
Prince Albert Mountains, *Antarctica* **207** N14
Prince Albert Peninsula, *N.W.T., Can.* **76** D12
Prince Albert Sound, *N.W.T., Can.* **76** E12
Prince Alfred, Cape, *N.W.T., Can.* **76** C12
Prince Charles Island, *Nunavut, Can.* **77** F17
Prince Charles Mountains, *Antarctica* **207** F18
Prince Edward Fracture Zone, *Ind. Oc.* **220** Q3
Prince Edward Island, *N. Amer.* **74** H10
Prince Edward Island, *Can.* **77** N22
Prince Edward Islands, *Ind. Oc.* **184** K7
Prince George, *B.C., Can.* **76** K9
Prince Gustaf Adolf Sea, *Nunavut, Can.* **77** C14
Prince Harald Coast, *Antarctica* **207** B17
Prince Kuhio Park, *Hawaii, U.S.* **106** C5
Prince of Wales, Cape, *Alas., U.S.* **104** F10
Prince of Wales Island, *Alas., U.S.* **105** M23
Prince of Wales Island, *Austral.* **190** A12
Prince of Wales Island, *Nunavut, Can.* **77** E14
Prince of Wales Strait, *N.W.T., Can.* **76** D12
Prince Olav Coast, *Antarctica* **207** B17
Prince Patrick Island, *N.W.T., Can.* **77** C13
Prince Regent Inlet, *Nunavut, Can.* **77** E15
Prince Rupert, *B.C., Can.* **76** J7
Princess Anne, *Md., U.S.* **90** D15
Princess Astrid Coast, *Antarctica* **207** A13
Princess Charlotte Bay, *Austral.* **190** B12
Princess Martha Coast, *Antarctica* **206** C11
Princess Ragnhild Coast, *Antarctica* **207** B15
Princeton, *B.C., Can.* **76** M8
Princeton, *Ill., U.S.* **93** P5
Princeton, *Ind., U.S.* **93** T7
Princeton, *Ky., U.S.* **95** D14
Princeton, *Minn., U.S.* **98** J11
Princeton, *Mo., U.S.* **99** Q11
Princeton, *N.J., U.S.* **88** P10
Princeton, *W. Va., U.S.* **90** F8
Princeville, *Hawaii, U.S.* **106** A5
Prince William Sound, *Alas., U.S.* **105** J17
Príncipe, island, *São Tomé and Príncipe* **185** B20
Príncipe da Beira, *Braz.* **122** H7
Prineville, *Oreg., U.S.* **102** G5
Pringle, *S. Dak., U.S.* **98** L1
Priština, *Yug.* **137** H14
Pritchett, *Colo., U.S.* **101** P15
Privol'noye, *Russ.* **141** G22
Probolinggo, *Indonesia* **168** M10
Proctor, *Minn., U.S.* **98** G12
Progreso Limitada, *Bioko, Eq. Guinea* **184** M8
Progress, station, *Antarctica* **207** G20
Progress, *Russ.* **141** K20
Prokop'yevsk, *Russ.* **140** L12
Prony, *New Caledonia, Fr.* **198** E9
Prony, Baie du, *New Caledonia, Fr.* **198** E9
Propriá, *Braz.* **123** G17
Proserpine, *Qnsld., Austral.* **191** S14
Prospect, *Oreg., U.S.* **102** K3
Prosser, *Wash., U.S.* **102** E6
Prostějov, *Czech Rep.* **132** J9
Protection, *Kans., U.S.* **99** V5
Providence, *Ky., U.S.* **95** C14
Providence, *R.I., U.S.* **89** L14
Providence Island, *Seychelles* **183** C19
Providence Mountains, *Calif., U.S.* **103** W11
Providencia, Isla de, *Col.* **109** L20
Providenciales, island, *Turks and Caicos Is., U.K.* **111** H16
Provideniya, *Russ.* **141** A21
Provincetown, *Mass., U.S.* **89** K16
Provo, *Utah, U.S.* **100** L7
Prudhoe Bay, *Alas., U.S.* **105** B16
Prüm, *Ger.* **132** H4
Prune Island *see* Palm Island, *St. Vincent and the Grenadines* **113** M17
Prut, river, *Eur.* **130** G9
Prydz Bay, *Antarctica* **207** F20
Pryluky, *Ukr.* **133** H15
Pryor, *Okla., U.S.* **96** E13
Pryor Creek, *Mont., U.S.* **100** E10
Prypyats, river, *Belarus-Ukr.* **133** G14
Przemyśl, *Pol.* **132** J11
Przheval'sk *see* Karakol, *Kyrg.* **156** E14
Pskov, *Russ.* **140** D6
Pskov, Lake, *Eur.* **130** D9
Pskovskoye Ozero, *Estonia* **135** L17
Ps'ol, river, *Ukr.* **133** H16
Pua, *Thai.* **166** J9
Puako, *Hawaii, U.S.* **107** L19
Puakonikai, *Banaba, Kiribati* **197** D20
Puamau, Baie (Perigot), *Hiva Oa, Fr. Polynesia, Fr.* **199** M21
Puán, *Arg.* **125** N11
Pua Pua, Te Ava, *Funafuti, Tuvalu* **197** L23
Pu'apu'a, *Samoa* **198** K2
Puaumu Nord, island, *Gambier Is., Fr. Polynesia, Fr.* **199** Q20
Puava, Cape, *Samoa* **198** K1
Pubei, *China* **163** S1
Pucallpa, *Peru* **122** F4
Puca Urco, *Peru* **122** D5
Pucheng, *China* **162** G2
Pucheng, *China* **163** N8
Puck, *Pol.* **132** E9
Pudasjärvi, *Fin.* **135** F15
Pudu, *Indonesia* **168** J6
Puduchcheri *see* Pondicherry, *India* **159** Q7
Pudukkottai, *India* **159** R6
Puebla, *Mex.* **108** J12
Pueblo, *Colo., U.S.* **101** N14
Pueo Point, *Hawaii, U.S.* **106** C3

Pu'er, China 160 P10
Puerco, river, Ariz., U.S. 101 S9
Puerto Acosta, Bol. 122 J6
Puerto Aisén, Chile 125 S7
Puerto América, Peru 122 E3
Puerto Ángel, Mex. 109 L13
Puerto Armuelles, Pan. 109 P19
Puerto Ayacucho, Venez. 120 E9
Puerto Bahía Negra, Para. 122 L10
Puerto Barrios, Guatemala 109 K16
Puerto Belgrano, Arg. 125 P11
Puerto Berrío, Col. 120 E5
Puerto Cabello, Venez. 120 B9
Puerto Cabezas, Nicar. 109 L19
Puerto Carreño, Col. 120 E9
Puerto Chicama, Peru 122 F2
Puerto Coig, Arg. 125 V8
Puerto Colombia, Col. 120 B5
Puerto Cortés, Hond. 109 K17
Puerto Cumarebo, Venez. 120 B8
Puerto de la Cruz, Canary Is., Sp. 184 Q5
Puerto del Rosario, Canary Is., Sp. 184 Q8
Puerto de Luna, N. Mex., U.S. 101 S14
Puerto de Nutrias, Venez. 120 C8
Puerto Deseado, Arg. 125 U9
Puerto Etén, Peru 122 F2
Puerto Heath, Bol. 122 H6
Puerto Jiménez, C.R. 109 P19
Puerto La Concordia, Col. 120 G6
Puerto La Cruz, Venez. 120 B11
Puerto La Paz, Arg. 124 D11
Puerto Leguízamo, Col. 120 J5
Puerto Limón, C.R. 109 N19
Puertollano, Sp. 139 R7
Puerto Lobos, Arg. 125 Q10
Puerto López, Col. 120 F6
Puerto Madryn, Arg. 125 R10
Puerto Maldonado, Peru 122 H6
Puerto Manatí, Cuba 110 J12
Puerto Montt, Chile 125 Q6
Puerto Morelos, Mex. 109 H17
Puerto Natales, Chile 125 W7
Puerto Obaldía, Pan. 109 N22
Puerto Padre, Cuba 110 J12
Puerto Páez, Venez. 120 E9
Puerto Peñasco, Mex. 108 B6
Puerto Pinasco, Para. 122 L10
Puerto Pirámides, Arg. 125 R10
Puerto Plata, Dom. Rep. 111 L18
Puerto Portillo, Peru 122 G4
Puerto Princesa, Philippines 168 E12
Puerto Rico, island, N. Amer. 74 N11
Puerto Rico, N. Amer. 111 M23
Puerto Rico Trench, Atl. Oc. 216 K4
Puerto San Carlos, Chile 125 U7
Puerto San Julián, Arg. 125 U9
Puerto Santa Cruz, Arg. 125 V9
Puerto Suárez, Bol. 122 K10
Puerto Tres Palmas, Para. 122 L10
Puerto Vallarta, Mex. 108 H9
Puerto Wilches, Col. 120 D5
Puerto Williams, Chile 125 Y9
Puetton Tanapag, bay, Saipan, N. Mariana Is., U.S. 196 B4
Pueu, Tahiti, Fr. Polynesia, Fr. 199 P17
Pueyrredón, Lago, Arg. 125 U7
Puget Sound, U.S. 78 B4
Puhi, Hawaii, U.S. 106 C6
Puigcerdà, Sp. 139 P10
Pujehun, Sierra Leone 180 G6
Pujiang, China 162 M9
Pukaki, Lake, N.Z. 193 P16
Pukalani, Hawaii, U.S. 107 G17
Pukapuka Atoll (Danger Islands), Cook Is., N.Z. 194 J11
Pukarua, island, Fr. Polynesia, Fr. 199 F22
Pukch'ŏng, N. Korea 162 C14
Pukp'yŏng-ni, S. Korea 162 E14
Pula (Pola), Croatia 136 F10
Pulap Atoll, F.S.M. 196 Q5
Pulaski, N.Y., U.S. 88 H8
Pulaski, Tenn., U.S. 95 G15
Pulaski, Va., U.S. 90 F9
Puli, Taiwan, China 163 R9
Pulicat Lake, India 159 P7
Puliyangudi, India 159 S5
Puliyankulam, Sri Lanka 159 S7
Pullman, Wash., U.S. 102 D9
Pulo Anna, island, Palau 194 F2
Pulog, Mount, Philippines 169 B13
Pułtusk, Pol. 132 G10
Pülümür, Turk. 149 E14
Pulusuk, island, F.S.M. 196 Q5
Puluwat Atoll, F.S.M. 196 Q5
Pumpkin Creek, Mont., U.S. 100 E12
Puná, Isla, Ecua. 120 K2
Puna, region, Hawaii, U.S. 107 N21
Punaauia, Tahiti, Fr. Polynesia, Fr. 199 P15
Punaauia, Pointe, Tahiti, Fr. Polynesia, Fr. 199 P15
Punaeroa, Passe, Raiatea, Fr. Polynesia, Fr. 199 C23
Punakha, Bhutan 158 F12
Punalu'u, Hawaii, U.S. 106 D11

Punalu'u, Hawaii, U.S. 107 P20
Punan, Indonesia 168 H11
Puncak Jaya, peak, Indonesia 169 L20
Punch, India 157 N11
Pune, India 158 L4
P'ungsan, N. Korea 162 C13
Punitaqui, Chile 124 J6
Puno, Peru 122 J6
Punta Alta, Arg. 125 P11
Punta Arenas, Chile 125 X8
Punta del Este, Uru. 124 M15
Punta Delgada, Arg. 125 R10
Punta Gorda, Belize 109 K16
Punta Gorda, Fla., U.S. 91 V8
Punta Prieta, Mex. 108 C5
Puntarenas, C.R. 109 N18
Puntland, region, Somalia 179 G18
Punto Fijo, Venez. 120 A7
Puntudo, Cerro, S. Amer. 118 Q4
Punxsutawney, Pa., U.S. 88 M5
Puohine, Raiatea, Fr. Polynesia, Fr. 199 C23
Puqi, China 162 M4
Puquio, Peru 122 J4
Puranpur, India 158 F7
Purari, river, P.N.G. 193 D19
Purcell, Okla., U.S. 96 H11
Purcell Mountains, Mont., U.S. 100 A4
Purdy Islands, P.N.G. 193 B19
Purgatoire, river, Colo., U.S. 101 P14
Puri, India 158 L10
Purna, river, India 158 K5
Purnia, India 158 G11
Pursat, Cambodia 167 N11
Purus, river, S. Amer. 118 F4
Purvis, Miss., U.S. 94 N12
Pusad, India 158 L6
Pusan, S. Korea 162 G14
Pusht-i-Rud, region, Afghan. 157 P3
Puta, Azerb. 149 D23
Putangaroa, island, Manihiki Atoll, Cook Is., N.Z. 199 C15
Putao, Myanmar 166 D7
Putian, China 163 Q8
Putina, Peru 122 J6
Puting, Tanjung, Indonesia 168 K10
Puto, P.N.G. 197 J13
Putorana, Plato, Russ. 141 G13
Putrachoique, Cerro, Arg. 125 R7
Puttalam, Sri Lanka 159 S7
Puttur, India 159 P7
Putumayo, river, Col.-Ecua. 120 H4
Putumayo, river, Peru 122 D4
Pütürge, Turk. 149 G13
Puuanahulu, Hawaii, U.S. 107 L19
Puuhonua o Honaunau National Historical Park (City of Refuge National Historical Park), Hawaii, U.S. 107 N18
Puukohola Heiau National Historic Site, Hawaii, U.S. 107 K19
Puunene, Hawaii, U.S. 107 G16
Puuwai, Hawaii, U.S. 106 C3
Puwe, island, Chuuk, F.S.M. 197 B15
Puxian, China 162 F3
Puyallup, Wash., U.S. 102 C4
Puyang, China 162 G6
Puysegur Point, N.Z. 193 R14
Puzak, Hamun-e, Afghan. 157 Q2
Pweto, Dem. Rep. of the Congo 178 M12
Pya, Lake, Eur. 130 B9
P'yagina, Poluostrov, Russ. 141 F21
Pyasinskiy Zaliv, Russ. 141 E13
Pyatigorsk, Russ. 140 J4
Pyay, Myanmar 166 J5
Pyhäjoki, Fin. 135 G15
Pyinkayaing, Myanmar 166 L5
Pyinmanaa, Myanmar 166 J6
Pyin-U-Lwin, Myanmar 166 G6
Pymatuning Reservoir, Ohio-Pa., U.S. 93 N16
Pyŏnggok, N. Korea 162 F14
P'yŏnghae, S. Korea 162 F14
P'yŏng-song, N. Korea 162 D12
P'yŏngyang, N. Korea 162 D12
Pyote, Tex., U.S. 97 N3
Pyramides, Pointe, Wallis and Futuna, Fr. 198 E11
Pyramid Lake, Nev., U.S. 103 P6
Pyramid Rock, Paracel Is. 168 B10
Pyramids, ruins, Egypt 177 C18
Pyrenees, mountains, Fr. 139 P9
Pyryatyn, Ukr. 133 H15
Pyu, Myanmar 166 J6

Q

Qabqa, China 160 J10
Qāḍub, Yemen 153 R14
Qāʻemābād, Iran 153 E17
Qāḥemshahr, Iran 153 C13
Qagan Nur, China 162 A6
Qagan Nur, China 162 A5
Qagan Us see Dulan, China 160 J10
Qahar Youyi Houqi, China 162 B5

Qahar Youyi Zhongqi, China 162 C5
Qaidam Basin, Asia 146 G9
Qaidam Pendi, China 160 H9
Qairouan, Tun. 177 A13
Qalamcheshmeh, Afghan. 157 N4
Qalansīyah, Yemen 153 R14
Qalat (Kalat), Afghan. 157 P6
Qalʻat al Azlam, ruins, Saudi Arabia 152 H5
Qalʻat Bīshah, Saudi Arabia 152 M8
Qalʻeh Shahr, Afghan. 156 L5
Qalʻeh-ye Fath, Afghan. 157 R2
Qalʻeh-ye Gaz, Afghan. 157 P4
Qalʻeh-ye Now, Afghan. 156 M3
Qalʻeh-ye Sarkari, Afghan. 156 L6
Qalhāt, Oman 153 K17
Qallabat, Sudan 179 E14
Qamar, Ghubbat al, Yemen 153 P13
Qamdo, China 160 L9
Qamea, island, Fiji 198 G8
Qamīnis, Lib. 177 C15
Qamystybas, Kaz. 154 G10
Qandala, Somalia 179 F18
Qapshaghay, Kaz. 155 H16
Qapshaghay Reservoir, Kaz. 155 H17
Qarabutaq, Kaz. 154 D9
Qaraghandy, Kaz. 155 E14
Qaraghayly, Kaz. 155 E15
Qarah Bagh, Afghan. 157 N7
Qaraqoynn Köli, Kaz. 155 G13
Qarataī Zhotasy, Kaz. 154 H12
Qaratal, river, Kaz. 155 G16
Qarataū, Kaz. 155 J14
Qaratobe, Kaz. 154 D7
Qaraton, Kaz. 154 F7
Qaraūyl, Kaz. 155 E17
Qarazhal, Kaz. 155 F14
Qarchi Gak, Afghan. 156 K6
Qardho, Somalia 179 F18
Qarokūl, lake, Taj. 156 H11
Qarqan, river, China 160 G6
Qarqaraly, Kaz. 155 E15
Qarqin, Afghan. 156 K5
Qarsaqbay, Kaz. 154 F12
Qarshi, Uzb. 154 L12
Qaryat al ʻUlyā, Saudi Arabia 152 H11
Qaryat az Zuwaytīnah, Lib. 177 C15
Qaṣr-e Qand, Iran 153 H17
Qaṣr Farāfra, Egypt 177 D17
Qaṣr Ḩamām, Saudi Arabia 152 L10
Qaʻṭabah, Yemen 152 Q9
Qaṭanā, Syr. 150 J7
Qatar, Asia 153 H13
Qattara Depression, Egypt 177 C17
Qax, Azerb. 149 C20
Qāyen, Iran 153 D16
Qayghy, Kaz. 154 D11
Qaynar, Kaz. 155 E16
Qazakh, Azerb. 149 C19
Qazaly, Kaz. 154 G10
Qazaq Shyghanaghy, Kaz. 154 J6
Qazi Deh, Afghan. 156 K10
Qazimämmäd, Azerb. 149 D22
Qazvīn, Iran 152 C12
Qeissan, Sudan 179 F13
Qele Levu, island, Fiji 198 G9
Qena, Egypt 177 D19
Qeqertarsuaq (Godhavn), Greenland, Den. 75 C21
Qeqertarsuatsiaat, Greenland, Den. 75 D22
Qerqertarsuaq, island, N. Amer. 74 C8
Qeshm, island, Iran 153 H15
Qeshm, Iran 153 H15
Qeys, island, Iran 153 H14
Qeysar, Afghan. 156 L4
Qianjiang, China 161 L13
Qianxian, China 162 G1
Qianxian, China 162 G1
Qianyang, China 162 G1
Qianyang, China 163 N2
Qidong, China 162 K10
Qidong, China 163 P3
Qiemo, China 160 G6
Qijiaojing, China 160 E8
Qikiqtarjuaq, Nunavut, Can. 77 F19
Qila Ladgasht, Pak. 157 T2
Qila Safed, Pak. 157 S1
Qila Saifullah, Pak. 157 R7
Qilian Shan, China 160 G9
Qimantag, mountains, China 160 H7
Qimen, China 162 L7
Qing, river, China 162 L3
Qingdao, China 162 G9
Qinghai Hu, China 160 H10
Qingjian, China 162 F3
Qingjiang, China 163 N6
Qingshuihe, China 162 D4
Qingtian, China 163 N9
Qingxu, China 162 E4
Qingyang, China 162 F1
Qingyuan, China 162 B12
Qingyuan, China 163 R4

Qingzhou, China 162 F8
Qinhuangdao, China 162 D8
Qin Lin, mountains, Asia 146 G11
Qin Ling, China 162 H1
Qinxian, China 162 F4
Qinzhou, China 161 P13
Qionghai (Jiaji), China 163 U2
Qiongshan, China 163 U2
Qiongzhou Haixia, China 163 T1
Qiqian, China 161 B15
Qiqihar, China 161 C16
Qishn, Yemen 153 P13
Qitai, China 160 E8
Qitaihe, China 161 D18
Qixia, China 162 F9
Qiyang, China 161 M14
Qiyang, China 163 P3
Qiyl, river, Kaz. 154 D7
Qızılağac Körfäzi, Azerb. 149 F22
Qizilqum, desert, Uzb. 154 J10
Qom, river, Iran 152 D12
Qom, Iran 152 D12
Qomolangma Feng (Mount Everest), China 160 M6
Qomsheh, Iran 153 E13
Qonaqkänd, Azerb. 149 C22
Qoʻngʻirot, Uzb. 154 J8
Qongyrat, Kaz. 155 F15
Qoʻqon, Uzb. 155 K14
Qorakūl, Uzb. 154 L11
Qoraqalpogʻiston, region, Uzb. 154 H8
Qosköl, Kaz. 154 E12
Qosshaghyl, Kaz. 154 F7
Qostanay, Kaz. 154 B11
Qowryah, Afghan. 157 Q4
Quairading, W. Austral., Austral. 191 X3
Quamby, Qnsld., Austral. 191 S11
Quanah, Tex., U.S. 96 J8
Quan Dao Nam Du, island, Vietnam 167 Q11
Quang Ngai, Vietnam 166 L14
Quang Tri, Vietnam 166 K13
Quannan, China 163 Q5
Quanshuigou, China 156 L15
Quanzhou, China 163 P3
Quanzhou, China 163 Q8
Quaraí, Braz. 122 P10
Quartzsite, Ariz., U.S. 101 T4
Quatre Bornes, Mauritius 185 G20
Quba, Azerb. 149 C22
Qūchān, Iran 153 B16
Queanbeyan, N.S.W., Austral. 191 Y14
Québec, Que., Can. 77 P20
Quebec, Can. 77 M19
Quebracho Coto, Arg. 124 G10
Queen Adelaida Archipelago, S. Amer. 118 R4
Queen Alexandra Range, Antarctica 207 L13
Queen Charlotte Islands, B.C., Can. 76 J6
Queen Charlotte Sound, B.C., Can. 76 K7
Queen Elizabeth Islands, Nunavut, Can. 77 B15
Queen Elizabeth Range, Antarctica 207 L13
Queen Fabiola Mountains (Yamato Mountains), Antarctica 207 C16
Queen Kaahumanu Highway, Hawaii, U.S. 107 L18
Queen Mary Coast, Antarctica 207 J21
Queen Maud Gulf, Nunavut, Can. 77 F14
Queen Maud Land, Antarctica 206 C11
Queen Maud Mountains, Antarctica 206 K12
Queensland, Austral. 191 T11
Queenstown, N.Z. 193 Q15
Queenstown, S. Af. 182 L10
Queenstown, Tas., Austral. 191 Z15
Queen Victoria's Profile, Hawaii, U.S. 106 C6
Queets, Wash., U.S. 102 C2
Queiros, Cape, Vanuatu 198 C1
Quelimane, Mozambique 183 F14
Quellón, Chile 125 R6
Quelpart see Cheju Do, island, S. Korea 162 J13
Quemado, N. Mex., U.S. 101 T10
Quemado, Tex., U.S. 97 S6
Quemoy see Jinmen Dao, island, Taiwan, China 163 R8
Quemú Quemú, Arg. 124 M10
Quequén, Arg. 125 N13
Querétaro, Mex. 108 H11
Quesada, C.R. 109 N19
Queshan, China 162 J5
Quesnel, B.C., Can. 76 L8
Que Son, Vietnam 166 L13
Questa, N. Mex., U.S. 101 Q13
Quetta, Pak. 157 R6
Quetzaltenango, Guatemala 109 L15
Quezon City, Philippines 169 C13
Qufu, China 162 G7
Quibala, Angola 182 D6
Quibdó, Col. 120 E4
Quilá, Mex. 108 F8
Quilcene, Wash., U.S. 102 B3
Quillota, Chile 124 K7
Quilon (Kollam), India 159 S5
Quilpie, Qnsld., Austral. 191 V12
Quimilí, Arg. 124 G11

Quimper, *Fr.* **138** K7
Quinault, river, *Wash., U.S.* **102** C2
Quinault, *Wash., U.S.* **102** C2
Quince Mil, *Peru* **122** H5
Quincy, *Calif., U.S.* **103** P5
Quincy, *Fla., U.S.* **91** Q5
Quincy, *Ill., U.S.* **93** R3
Quincy, *Mass., U.S.* **89** K15
Quines, *Arg.* **124** K9
Quinhagak, *Alas., U.S.* **104** K12
Qui Nhon, *Vietnam* **166** M14
Quinn, river, *Nev., U.S.* **102** L8
Quinter, *Kans., U.S.* **99** S4
Quipungo, *Angola* **182** E6
Quirindi, *N.S.W., Austral.* **191** X14
Quissanga, *Mozambique* **183** D15
Quitaque, *Tex., U.S.* **96** J6
Quitilipi, *Arg.* **124** G12
Quitman, *Ga., U.S.* **91** Q6
Quitman, *Miss., U.S.* **95** M13
Quito, *Ecua.* **120** J3
Quixadá, *Braz.* **123** E17
Qujiang, *China* **163** Q4
Qujing, *China* **160** N11
Qulandy, *Kaz.* **154** G9
Qulbān Banī Murrah, ruins, *Jordan* **151** Q8
Qulsary, *Kaz.* **154** F7
Quobba, *W. Austral., Austral.* **191** U1
Qurayyāt, *Oman* **153** K16
Qurghonteppa, *Taj.* **156** J7
Quryq, *Kaz.* **154** H5
Qusar, *Azerb.* **149** C22
Quṣeir, *Egypt* **177** D19
Qusmuryn, *Kaz.* **154** C11
Qusmuryn Köli, *Kaz.* **154** C11
Quwo, *China* **162** G3
Quxian, *China* **160** L12
Qüxü, *China* **160** L7
Quy Chau, *Vietnam* **166** J11
Quyghan, *Kaz.* **155** G15
Quy Hop, *Vietnam* **166** J11
Quzhou, *China* **162** F6
Quzhou, *China* **162** M8
Qvareli, *Rep. of Georgia* **149** B19
Qyzan, *Kaz.* **154** G6
Qyzylorda, *Kaz.* **154** H11
Qyzyltū, *Kaz.* **155** B14

R

Raahe, *Fin.* **135** G15
Raas, island, *Indonesia* **168** M11
Raba, *Indonesia* **169** M13
Rabat, *Mor.* **176** B8
Rabaul, *P.N.G.* **193** C21
Rabga Pass, *Nepal* **158** F11
Rabi (Rambi), island, *Fiji* **198** G8
Rābigh, *Saudi Arabia* **152** K7
Raccoon Cay, *Bahamas* **111** H13
Raccoon Point, *La., U.S.* **94** R10
Race, Cape, *Nfld., Can.* **77** M24
Raceland, *La., U.S.* **94** Q10
Rach Gia, *Vietnam* **167** Q11
Racine, *Wis., U.S.* **92** M7
Raco, *Mich., U.S.* **92** F10
Rădăuţi, *Rom.* **137** D16
Radcliff, *Ky., U.S.* **95** C16
Radford, *Va., U.S.* **90** F9
Radhanpur, *India* **158** H3
Radisson, *Que., Can.* **77** M18
Radom, *Pol.* **132** H10
Radomsko, *Pol.* **132** H10
Radviliškis, *Lith.* **135** N16
Raḍwá, Jabal, *Saudi Arabia* **152** J6
Rae, *N.W.T., Can.* **76** H11
Rae Bareli, *India* **158** G8
Raeford, *N.C., U.S.* **90** J11
Rae Isthmus, *Nunavut, Can.* **77** G16
Rae Lakes, *N.W.T., Can.* **76** G11
Raeside, Lake, *Austral.* **190** H4
Raetihi, *N.Z.* **193** L19
Rāf, Jabal, *Saudi Arabia* **152** G7
Rafaela, *Arg.* **124** J11
Rafaḩ, *Gaza Strip* **151** N4
Rafaï, *Cen. Af. Rep.* **178** H10
Rafḩā', *Saudi Arabia* **152** F9
Rafsanjān, *Iran* **153** F15
Raga, *Sudan* **178** G11
Ragged, Mount, *Austral.* **190** K5
Ragged Island, *Bahamas* **111** H13
Ragged Island, *Me., U.S.* **89** G17
Ragusa, *It.* **136** M10
Raha, *Indonesia* **169** L14
Rahimyar Khan, *Pak.* **157** T9
Raiatea, island, *Fr. Polynesia, Fr.* **199** B23
Raijua, island, *Indonesia* **169** N14
Rainbow Bridge National Monument, *Utah, U.S.* **101** Q8
Rainbow City, *Ala., U.S.* **95** J16
Rainbow Falls, *Hawaii, U.S.* **107** M21
Rainier, *Oreg., U.S.* **102** E3
Rainier, Mount, *Wash., U.S.* **102** D4
Rainy, river, *Minn., U.S.* **98** E10 - E11
Rainy Lake, *U.S.-Can.* **79** C14
Raipur, *India* **158** K8
Rairakhol, *India* **158** K9
Rairik, island, *Majuro Atoll, Marshall Is.* **196** H12
Ra'īs, *Saudi Arabia* **152** K6
Raisinghnagar, *India* **158** E4
Raita Bank, *Hawaii, U.S.* **106** L5
Raititi, Pointe, *Bora-Bora, Fr. Polynesia, Fr.* **199** K14
Raivavae (Vavitu), island, *Fr. Polynesia, Fr.* **199** J17
Raiwind, *Pak.* **157** Q12
Rajahmundry, *India* **158** M8
Rajampet, *India* **159** P6
Rajang, river, *Malaysia* **168** H10
Rajang, *Malaysia* **168** H10
Rajanpur, *Pak.* **157** S9
Rajapalaiyam, *India* **159** S6
Rajasthan Canal, *India* **158** F3
Rajgarh, *India* **158** F5
Rajkot, *India* **158** J2
Raj Nandgaon, *India* **158** K8
Rajpura, *India* **158** E5
Raj Samund, *India* **158** H4
Rakahanga Atoll, *Cook Is., N.Z.* **194** H11
Rakaia, *N.Z.* **193** P17
Rakaposhi, peak, *Pak.* **156** L12
Rakhiv, *Ukr.* **132** K12
Rakhman Qaynary, *Kaz.* **155** D20
Rakhshan, river, *Pak.* **157** U4
Rakhyūt, *Oman* **153** P14
Rakiraki, *Fiji* **198** H6
Rakops, *Botswana* **182** G9
Rakvere, *Estonia* **135** K16
Raleigh, *Miss., U.S.* **94** M12
Raleigh, *N.C., U.S.* **90** H11
Ralik Chain, *Marshall Is.* **196** G3
Ralls, *Tex., U.S.* **96** K5
Ramah, *N. Mex., U.S.* **101** S10
Rām Allāh, *West Bank* **150** M5
Raman, *Thai.* **167** S9
Ramanum, island, *Chuuk, F.S.M.* **197** B14
Ramat Gan, *Israel* **150** M5
Rambi *see* Rabi, island, *Fiji* **198** G8
Rambu, *Indonesia* **169** J14
Rambutyo, island, *P.N.G.* **193** B20
Ramgarh, *India* **158** F2
Ramla, *Israel* **150** M5
Ramnagar, *India* **158** E7
Ramona, *Calif., U.S.* **103** Y10
Ramos Island, *Solomon Is.* **197** M19
Rampart, *Alas., U.S.* **105** F16
Rampur, *India* **158** D6
Rampur, *India* **158** F7
Rampur Hat, *India* **158** H11
Ramree, *Myanmar* **166** J4
Ramree Island, *Myanmar* **166** J4
Ramsay, *Mich., U.S.* **92** F5
Ramu, river, *P.N.G.* **193** C18
Ramu, *Bangladesh* **158** K14
Ramvik, *Sw.* **135** H13
Rancagua, *Chile* **124** L7
Ranchester, *Wyo., U.S.* **100** F11
Ranchi, *India* **158** J10
Rancho Cordova, *Calif., U.S.* **103** R5
Ranchos de Taos, *N. Mex., U.S.* **101** Q13
Ranco, Lago, *Chile* **125** P6
Randers, *Den.* **134** N11
Randolph, *Nebr., U.S.* **99** N7
Randolph, *Utah, U.S.* **100** K8
Randolph, *Vt., U.S.* **89** G13
Rangahoe, island, *Manihiki Atoll, Cook Is., N.Z.* **199** B13
Rangamati, *Bangladesh* **158** J14
Rangeley, *Me., U.S.* **89** E15
Rangely, *Colo., U.S.* **100** L10
Ranger, *Tex., U.S.* **96** L9
Rangiroa, island, *Fr. Polynesia, Fr.* **199** D17
Rangitaiki, river, *N.Z.* **193** K20
Rangkasbitung, *Indonesia* **168** L8
Rang-Kul', *Taj.* **156** H11
Rangoon *see* Yangon, *Myanmar* **166** K6
Rangpur, *Bangladesh* **158** G12
Rangsang, island, *Indonesia* **168** H6
Raniganj, *India* **158** J11
Ranikhet, *India* **158** E7
Ranikot, ruins, *Pak.* **157** V7
Rankin, *Tex., U.S.* **97** N5
Rankin Inlet, *Nunavut, Can.* **77** H15
Ranong, *Thai.* **167** Q7
Ranongga (Ganongga), island, *Solomon Is.* **197** M15
Ransiki, *Indonesia* **169** J19
Rantauprapat, *Indonesia* **168** H5
Rantekombola, peak, *Indonesia* **169** K13
Rantoul, *Ill., U.S.* **93** Q7
Ranwas, *Vanuatu* **198** D3
Raohe, *China* **161** C19
Raoping, *China* **163** R7
Raoul Island (Sunday), *Kermadec Is., N.Z.* **194** L9
Rap, *India* **157** N15
Rapa, island, *Fr. Polynesia, Fr.* **195** L14
Rapa Passage, *Tabuaeran, Kiribati* **197** B21
Rapar, *India* **158** H2
Raper, Cape, *Nunavut, Can.* **77** E18
Rapid, river, *Minn., U.S.* **98** E10
Rapid City, *S. Dak., U.S.* **98** L2
Rapid River, *Mich., U.S.* **92** G8
Rapota, island, *Aitutaki Atoll, Cook Is., N.Z.* **198** Q11
Rápulo, river, *Bol.* **122** H7
Raquette Lake, *N.Y., U.S.* **88** G10
Raraka, island, *Fr. Polynesia, Fr.* **199** E18
Raroia, island, *Fr. Polynesia, Fr.* **199** E19
Rarotonga, island, *Cook Is., N.Z.* **194** K12
Rasa, Punta, *Arg.* **125** Q11
Ra's al'Ayn, *Syr.* **150** C13
Ra's al Khaymah, *U.A.E.* **153** J15
Ra's an Naqb, *Jordan* **151** Q6
Rasa Point, *S. Amer.* **118** N6
Ras Dashen Terara, peak, *Eth.* **179** E15
Rashad, *Sudan* **178** F12
Rāshayyā, *Leb.* **150** J6
Rashîd, *Egypt* **177** C18
Rasht, *Iran* **152** B12
Ras Koh Range, *Pak.* **157** S4
Rason Lake, *Austral.* **190** H5
Ra's Shamrah (Ugarit), ruins, *Syr.* **150** E6
Râs Sharâtîb, *Egypt* **151** T2
Rasshua, island, *Russ.* **141** H23
Rasua Garhi, *Nepal* **158** F10
Ratak Chain, *Marshall Is.* **196** F4
Ratangarh, *India* **158** F4
Rathdrum, *Idaho, U.S.* **100** B3
Rathenow, *Ger.* **132** F7
Rat Island, *Alas., U.S.* **104** P3
Rat Islands, *Alas., U.S.* **104** P3
Ratlam, *India* **158** J4
Ratnagiri, *India* **158** M3
Ratnapura, *Sri Lanka* **159** T7
Ratodero, *Pak.* **157** T7
Raton, *N. Mex., U.S.* **101** Q14
Raton Pass, *Colo.-N. Mex., U.S.* **101** Q14
Rattlesnake Creek, *Oreg., U.S.* **102** K9
Rattlesnake Hills, *Wash., U.S.* **102** D6
Rattlesnake National Recreation Area, *Mont., U.S.* **100** C6
Rattray Head, *Scot., U.K.* **138** D8
Rau, island, *Indonesia* **169** H16
Raub, *Malaysia* **167** U9
Rauch, *Arg.* **124** M12
Raudal Yupurari (Devils Cataract), *Col.* **120** H7
Raufarhöfn, *Ice.* **134** E4
Raukotaha, island, *Manihiki Atoll, Cook Is., N.Z.* **199** C14
Rauma, *Fin.* **135** J15
Raurkela, *India* **158** J10
Rausu, *Jap.* **164** E16
Rausu Dake, *Jap.* **164** E16
Ravahere, island, *Fr. Polynesia, Fr.* **199** F19
Rāvar, *Iran* **153** E15
Ravena, *N.Y., U.S.* **88** K11
Ravenna, *It.* **136** F9
Ravenna, *Nebr., U.S.* **99** Q6
Ravenna, *Ohio, U.S.* **93** P15
Ravensburg, *Ger.* **132** K5
Ravenshoe, *Qnsld., Austral.* **191** R13
Ravensthorpe, *W. Austral., Austral.* **191** X4
Ravenswood, *Qnsld., Austral.* **191** S13
Ravenswood, *W. Va., U.S.* **90** D8
Ravi, river, *Pak.* **157** Q11
Ravnina, *Turkm.* **154** M10
Rāwah, *Iraq* **152** D8
Rawaki, island, *Kiribati* **194** H10
Rawalpindi, *Pak.* **157** N11
Rawāndūz, *Iraq* **152** B10
Rawḑah, lake, *Syr.* **150** F14
Rawḩah, *Saudi Arabia* **152** M8
Rawi, Ko, *Thai.* **167** S8
Rawlinna, *W. Austral., Austral.* **191** W5
Rawlins, *Wyo., U.S.* **100** J11
Rawson, *Arg.* **125** R10
Rawu, *China* **160** L9
Ray, *N. Dak., U.S.* **98** E1
Ray, Cape, *Nfld., Can.* **77** N22
Raya, peak, *Indonesia* **168** J10
Rayachoti, *India* **159** P6
Raychikhinsk, *Russ.* **141** L19
Raydā', plain, *Saudi Arabia* **152** M11
Raymond, *Alta., Can.* **76** N10
Raymond, *Calif., U.S.* **103** S6
Raymond, *Wash., U.S.* **102** D2
Raymond Terrace, *N.S.W., Austral.* **191** X15
Raymondville, *Tex., U.S.* **97** W10
Ray Mountains, *U.S.* **78** N4
Rayne, *La., U.S.* **94** P8
Rayner Glacier, *Antarctica* **207** C18
Rayoke, island, *Russ.* **141** H23
Rayong, *Thai.* **167** N9
Raysūt, *Oman* **153** P14
Rayville, *La., U.S.* **94** L9
Raz, Pointe du, *Fr.* **138** K7
Razelm, Lacul, *Rom.* **137** F17
Razgrad, *Bulg.* **137** G16
Razmak, *Pak.* **157** P8
Razo, island, *Cape Verde* **185** B15
Razzaza Lake, *Iraq* **152** E9
Reading, *Pa., U.S.* **88** P8
Reading, *Eng., U.K.* **138** H8
Realicó, *Arg.* **124** L10
Ream, *Cambodia* **167** P11
Reao, island, *Fr. Polynesia, Fr.* **199** F22
Rebecca, Lake, *Austral.* **190** J4
Rebiana Sand Sea, *Af.* **174** E7
Rebola, *Bioko, Eq. Guinea* **184** L8
Rebun Tō, *Jap.* **164** D13
Recherche, Archipelago of the, *Austral.* **190** K5
Rechytsa, *Belarus* **133** G14
Recife, *Braz.* **123** G18
Recife, Cape, *S. Af.* **182** M10
Reconquista, *Arg.* **124** H12
Recreo, *Arg.* **124** H9
Rector, *Ark., U.S.* **94** E11
Red *see* Yuan, river, *China* **160** P10
Red, river, *La., U.S.* **94** N9
Red, river, *Man., Can.* **77** N14
Red, river, *U.S.* **79** L14
Red *see* Hong, river, *Vietnam* **166** G10
Redang, island, *Malaysia* **167** S10
Red Bank, *Tenn., U.S.* **95** G17
Red Bay, *Ala., U.S.* **95** H13
Red Bluff, *Calif., U.S.* **103** N4
Red Bluff Lake, *Tex., U.S.* **96** M2
Red Butte, *Ariz., U.S.* **101** R7
Redcliffe, Mount, *Austral.* **190** H4
Red Cloud, *Nebr., U.S.* **99** R6
Red Deer, *Alta., Can.* **76** M10
Red Devil, *Alas., U.S.* **105** J14
Redding, *Calif., U.S.* **103** N3
Redfield, *S. Dak., U.S.* **98** K6
Red Hill, *Hawaii, U.S.* **107** H17
Red Hills, *Kans., U.S.* **99** V5
Redig, *S. Dak., U.S.* **98** J2
Red Lake, *Minn., U.S.* **98** F10
Red Lake, *Ont., Can.* **77** N14
Red Lake, *W. Austral., Austral.* **191** X4
Red Lake Falls, *Minn., U.S.* **98** F8
Redlands, *Calif., U.S.* **103** X9
Red Lodge, *Mont., U.S.* **100** F9
Redmond, *Oreg., U.S.* **102** H5
Red Mountain, *Mont., U.S.* **100** C7
Red Oak, *Iowa, U.S.* **99** Q10
Redonda, island, *Leeward Is.* **113** G16
Redoubt Volcano, *Alas., U.S.* **105** K15
Red River of the North, *U.S.* **78** C12
Red Rock, river, *Mont., U.S.* **100** F6
Red Rocks Point, *Austral.* **190** J6
Red Sea, *Af.-Asia* **146** G2
Red Springs, *N.C., U.S.* **90** J11
Redwater, river, *Mont., U.S.* **100** C12
Red Wing, *Minn., U.S.* **98** K12
Redwood Empire, region, *Calif., U.S.* **102** M2
Redwood Falls, *Minn., U.S.* **98** K10
Redwood National Park, *Calif., U.S.* **102** L1
Reed City, *Mich., U.S.* **92** K10
Reeder, *N. Dak., U.S.* **98** H2
Reedley, *Calif., U.S.* **103** T7
Reeds, Plain of, *Vietnam* **167** P12
Reedsburg, *Wis., U.S.* **92** K4
Reedsport, *Oreg., U.S.* **102** H2
Reedville, *Va., U.S.* **90** E14
Reedy Glacier, *Antarctica* **206** K11
Reef Islands, *Santa Cruz Is., Solomon Is.* **197** P22
Reef Islands (Rowa Islands), *Vanuatu* **198** A2
Reefton, *N.Z.* **193** N17
Reese, river, *Nev., U.S.* **103** N9
Refahiye, *Turk.* **149** E13
Reform, *Ala., U.S.* **95** J14
Refuge, Temple of, *Hawaii, U.S.* **106** B6
Refugio, *Tex., U.S.* **97** T11
Regensburg, *Ger.* **132** J6
Reggane, *Alg.* **176** D10
Reggio di Calabria, *It.* **136** L11
Régina, *Fr. Guiana* **121** F18
Regina, *Sask., Can.* **76** N12
Rehoboth, *Namibia* **182** H7
Rehoboth Beach, *Del., U.S.* **90** C15
Reid, *W. Austral., Austral.* **191** W7
Reid River, *Qnsld., Austral.* **191** S13
Reidsville, *Ga., U.S.* **91** N8
Reidsville, *N.C., U.S.* **90** G10
Reims, *Fr.* **138** J11
Reina Adelaida, Archipiélago de los, *Chile* **125** W6
Reindeer Lake, *Man., Can.* **77** K13
Reinga, Cape, *N.Z.* **193** G17
Reitoru, island, *Fr. Polynesia, Fr.* **199** F19
Rekareka *see* Tehuata, island, *Fr. Polynesia, Fr.* **199** E19
Rekata Bay, *Solomon Is.* **197** L17
Reliance, *N.W.T., Can.* **76** H12
Reliance, *Wyo., U.S.* **100** K9
Remada, *Tun.* **177** C13
Remanso, *Braz.* **123** G15
Remedios, *Cuba* **110** H9

Remer, *Minn., U.S.* 98 G11
Remeshk, *Iran* 153 H16
Rémire, *Fr. Guiana* 121 E18
Ren, island, *Jaluit Atoll, Marshall Is.* 196 K7
Rend Lake, *Ill., U.S.* 93 U6
Rendova, island, *Solomon Is.* 197 M16
Rendsburg, *Ger.* 132 E6
Rengat, *Indonesia* 168 J6
Reni, *Ukr.* 133 M14
Renmark, *S. Austral., Austral.* 191 X11
Rennell, island, *Solomon Is.* 197 R19
Rennes, *Fr.* 138 K8
Rennick Glacier, *Antarctica* 207 R15
Reno, *Nev., U.S.* 103 P6
Renovo, *Pa., U.S.* 88 M6
Rensselaer, *Ind., U.S.* 93 P8
Renton, *Wash., U.S.* 102 C4
Renville, *Minn., U.S.* 98 K9
Repetek, *Turkm.* 154 M10
Republic, *Mich., U.S.* 92 F7
Republic, *Wash., U.S.* 102 A7
Republican, river, *Nebr., U.S.* 99 R6
Repulse Bay, *Austral.* 190 E14
Repulse Bay, *Nunavut, Can.* 77 G16
Requena, *Peru* 122 E4
Requena, *Sp.* 139 R8
Reşadiye, *Turk.* 148 E12
Researcher Ridge, *Atl. Oc.* 216 L7
Reserve, river, *La., U.S.* 94 Q10
Reserve, *N. Mex., U.S.* 101 T10
Reshteh-ye Alborz (Elburz Mountains), *Iran* 152 B11
Resistencia, *Arg.* 124 G13
Reşiţa, *Rom.* 137 F14
Resolute, *Nunavut, Can.* 77 D15
Resolution Island, *N.Z.* 193 R14
Resolution Island, *Nunavut, Can.* 77 H20
Restinga, Punta, *Canary Is., Sp.* 184 R4
Réthimno, *Gr.* 137 N16
Reti, *Pak.* 157 T8
Réunion, island, *Ind. Oc.* 184 H9
Reus, *Sp.* 139 Q9
Reva, *S. Dak., U.S.* 98 J2
Reval *see* Tallinn, *Estonia* 135 K16
Revelstoke, *B.C., Can.* 76 M9
Revillagigedo, Islas, *Mex.* 108 H5
Revillagigedo Island, *Alas., U.S.* 105 L24
Revsbotn, *Nor.* 135 C14
Rewa, river, *Fiji* 198 J6
Rewa, *India* 158 H8
Rexburg, *Idaho, U.S.* 100 G7
Rexford, *Mont., U.S.* 100 A5
Rexton, *Mich., U.S.* 92 F10
Rey, *Iran* 153 C13
Rey, Isla del, *Pan.* 109 N21
Rey Bouba, *Cameroon* 181 G17
Reyes, *Bol.* 122 H6
Reyes, Point, *U.S.* 78 G2
Reyhanlı, *Turk.* 148 J11
Reykjanes, cape, *Eur.* 130 A3
Reykjanes Ridge, *Atl. Oc.* 216 D9
Reykjavík, *Ice.* 134 F2
Reynosa, *Mex.* 108 F12
Rēzekne, *Latv.* 135 M17
Rhame, *N. Dak., U.S.* 98 H2
Rhein (Rhine), river, *Ger.* 132 J4
Rheine, *Ger.* 132 F5
Rhin, river, *Ger.* 132 J4
Rhin (Rhine), river, *Fr.* 138 K12
Rhine, river, *Eur.* 130 F5
Rhine, Sources of the, *Eur.* 130 H6
Rhinelander, *Wis., U.S.* 92 G5
Rhinocolura *see* El'Arîsh, *Egypt* 151 N3
Rhir, Cape, *Af.* 174 D2
Rhode Island, *U.S.* 89 L14
Rhodes *see* Ródos, island, *Gr.* 137 M18
Rhodes Peak, *Idaho, U.S.* 100 D5
Rhodope Mountains, *Bulg.* 137 H15
Rhône, river, *Eur.* 130 H5
Rhum, island, *Scot., U.K.* 138 D7
Riaba, *Bioko, Eq. Guinea* 184 M7
Riachão, *Braz.* 123 F14
Riang, *India* 158 F14
Riasi, *India* 157 N12
Riau, Kepulauan, *Indonesia* 168 J7
Ribadeo, *Sp.* 139 N5
Ribáuè, *Mozambique* 183 E14
Ribeira Afonso, *São Tomé and Príncipe* 185 D20
Ribeira Brava, *Madeira Is., Port.* 184 M3
Ribeira da Cruz, *Cape Verde* 185 A14
Ribeira Grande, *Cape Verde* 185 A14
Ribeirão Prêto, *Braz.* 123 L13
Riberalta, *Bol.* 122 G7
Ribewon, island, *Enewetak Atoll, Marshall Is.* 196 J8
Riblah, *Syr.* 150 H8
Rib Lake, *Wis., U.S.* 92 H4
Rib Mountain, *Wis., U.S.* 92 H5
Ribniţa, *Mold.* 133 K14
Rice Lake, *Wis., U.S.* 92 G3
Richardson, *Tex., U.S.* 96 L12
Richardson Highway, *Alas., U.S.* 105 G17
Richardson Mountains, *Yukon Terr., Can.* 76 E9
Richardton, *N. Dak., U.S.* 98 G3
Richey, *Mont., U.S.* 100 C13
Richfield, *Utah, U.S.* 101 N7
Richford, *Vt., U.S.* 89 E13
Rich Hill, *Mo., U.S.* 99 T11
Richland, *Ga., U.S.* 91 N4
Richland, *Mo., U.S.* 99 U13
Richland, *Oreg., U.S.* 102 G9
Richland, *Wash., U.S.* 102 E7
Richland Center, *Wis., U.S.* 92 L4
Richland Chambers Reservoir, *Tex., U.S.* 96 M12
Richlands, *Va., U.S.* 90 F8
Richland Springs, *Tex., U.S.* 97 N9
Richmond, *Calif., U.S.* 103 R3
Richmond, *Ind., U.S.* 93 R10
Richmond, *Ky., U.S.* 95 C18
Richmond, *Me., U.S.* 89 G16
Richmond, *Mo., U.S.* 99 S11
Richmond, *N.S.W., Austral.* 191 Y14
Richmond, *Qnsld., Austral.* 191 S12
Richmond, *S. Af.* 182 L9
Richmond, *Tex., U.S.* 97 R13
Richmond, *Utah, U.S.* 100 J7
Richmond, *Va., U.S.* 90 E13
Rich Square, *N.C., U.S.* 90 G13
Richton, *Miss., U.S.* 94 N12
Richwood, *W. Va., U.S.* 90 E9
Rico, *Colo., U.S.* 101 P10
Ridā', *Yemen* 152 Q9
Riddle, *Idaho, U.S.* 100 J3
Riddle, *Oreg., U.S.* 102 J2
Ridgecrest, *Calif., U.S.* 103 V9
Ridgefield, *Wash., U.S.* 102 E3
Ridgeland, *S.C., U.S.* 90 M9
Ridgway, *Colo., U.S.* 101 N11
Ridgway, *Pa., U.S.* 88 M5
Riding Rocks, *Bahamas* 110 D10
Rifle, *Colo., U.S.* 100 M11
Rifstangi, cape, *Eur.* 130 A4
Rīga, *Latv.* 135 M16
Riga, Gulf of, *Estonia-Latv.* 135 L16
Rīgān, *Iran* 153 G16
Rigby, *Idaho, U.S.* 100 G7
Rigestan, region, *Afghan.* 157 R4
Riggins, *Idaho, U.S.* 100 E4
Rigo, *P.N.G.* 193 E20
Rigolet, *Nfld., Can.* 77 K22
Rig Rig, *Chad* 177 H14
Riiser-Larsen Peninsula, *Antarctica* 207 B17
Rijeka, *Croatia* 136 F10
Rikitea, *Gambier Is., Fr. Polynesia, Fr.* 199 Q20
Rikubetsu, *Jap.* 164 F15
Rikuzentakata, *Jap.* 164 L14
Riley, *Kans., U.S.* 99 S8
Rimāḩ, Jabal ar, *Jordan* 150 L8
Rimah, Wādī ar, *Saudi Arabia* 152 H8
Rimatara, island, *Fr. Polynesia, Fr.* 195 K13
Rimini, *It.* 136 G10
Rîmnicu Vîlcea, *Rom.* 137 F15
Rimouski, *Que., Can.* 77 N20
Rincon, *Ga., U.S.* 91 N9
Rincon, *N. Mex., U.S.* 101 V11
Rinconada, *Arg.* 124 D9
Rincón del Bonete, Lago, *Uru.* 124 K14
Ringdom Gompa, *India* 156 M13
Ringdove Passage, *Santa Cruz Is., Solomon Is.* 197 Q23
Ringgold, *La., U.S.* 94 L7
Ringgold Isles, island, *Fiji* 198 G9
Ringkøbing, *Den.* 134 N10
Ringling, *Okla., U.S.* 96 J10
Ringvassøy, island, *Nor.* 135 C13
Ringwood, *N. Terr., Austral.* 191 T9
Riobamba, *Ecua.* 120 K3
Rio Branco, *Braz.* 122 G6
Rio Brilhante, *Braz.* 122 L11
Río Bueno, *Chile* 125 Q6
Río Cauto, *Cuba* 110 K12
Rio Chama, *N. Mex., U.S.* 101 Q12
Río Cuarto, *Arg.* 124 K10
Rio de Janeiro, *Braz.* 123 M15
Rio Dell, *Calif., U.S.* 103 N1
Rio Do Ouro, *São Tomé and Príncipe* 185 C20
Río Gallegos, *Arg.* 125 W8
Rio Grande, *N. Amer.* 74 M5
Rio Grande, *Braz.* 122 Q12
Río Grande, *Mex.* 108 C9
Río Grande, *Arg.* 125 X9
Rio Grande, Source of the, *N. Amer.* 74 K4
Rio Grande City, *Tex., U.S.* 97 W9
Rio Grande Rise, *Atl. Oc.* 217 S8
Rio Grande Wild and Scenic River, *Tex., U.S.* 97 Q3
Riohacha, *Col.* 120 B6
Rio Hondo, *N. Mex., U.S.* 101 U13
Rio Largo, *Braz.* 123 G18
Riom, *Fr.* 138 M10
Río Mulatos, *Bol.* 122 K7
Río Muni, region, *Eq. Guinea* 181 K15
Rioni, river, *Rep. of Georgia* 149 B17
Rio Peñasco, *N. Mex., U.S.* 101 U14
Rio Puerco, *N. Mex., U.S.* 101 S11
Rio Rancho, *N. Mex., U.S.* 101 S12
Rio Verde, *Braz.* 122 K12
Río Verde, *Chile* 125 W8
Río Verde, *Mex.* 108 H11
Rio Verde de Mato Grosso, *Braz.* 122 K11
Ripley, *Calif., U.S.* 103 Y13
Ripley, *Miss., U.S.* 94 G12
Ripley, *Ohio, U.S.* 93 T12
Ripley, *Tenn., U.S.* 94 F12
Ripley, *W. Va., U.S.* 90 D8
Ripon, *Wis., U.S.* 92 K6
Risāfe *see* Ar Ruşāfah, ruins, *Syr.* 150 E11
Rishikesh, *India* 158 E6
Rishiri Tō, *Jap.* 164 D13
Rishon LeZiyyon, *Israel* 150 M5
Rising Star, *Tex., U.S.* 96 M9
Rison, *Ark., U.S.* 94 H8
Risør, *Nor.* 134 L11
Rita Blanca Creek, *Tex., U.S.* 96 E4
Ritchie's Archipelago, *Andaman Is., India* 159 Q14
Ritidian Point, *Guam, U.S.* 196 A11
Ritscher Upland, *Antarctica* 206 C11
Ritzville, *Wash., U.S.* 102 D8
Rivadavia, *Arg.* 124 K8
Rivadavia, *Chile* 124 J7
Rivas, *Nicar.* 109 M18
Rivera, *Uru.* 124 J14
River Cess, *Liberia* 180 H7
Riverdale, *N. Dak., U.S.* 98 F4
River des Anguilles, *Mauritius* 185 H20
Riverhead, *N.Y., U.S.* 89 N13
Riverina, *W. Austral., Austral.* 191 W4
Riverina, region, *Austral.* 190 L12
Riverside, *Calif., U.S.* 103 X9
Riverside, *Wash., U.S.* 102 B7
Riversleigh, *Qnsld., Austral.* 191 R10
Riverton, *Man., Can.* 77 N14
Riverton, *Wyo., U.S.* 100 H10
Riviera, coast, *Eur.* 130 H5
Rivière-du-Loup, *Que., Can.* 77 N20
Rivière du Rempart, *Mauritius* 185 F20
Rivière Noire, Piton de la, *Mauritius* 185 G19
Rivne, *Ukr.* 133 H13
Riwoqê, *China* 160 L9
Riyadh *see* Ar Riyāḑ, *Saudi Arabia* 152 J10
Rize, *Turk.* 149 D15
Rizhao, *China* 162 G8
Rizokarpaso, *Cyprus* 148 K9
Ro, *New Caledonia, Fr.* 198 D10
Road Town, *British Virgin Is., U.K.* 113 F14
Roan Cliffs, *U.S.* 78 G7
Roanne, *Fr.* 138 M11
Roanoke, river, *N.C., U.S.* 90 G13
Roanoke, *Ala., U.S.* 95 K17
Roanoke, *Va., U.S.* 90 F10
Roanoke Island, *N.C., U.S.* 90 G15
Roanoke Rapids, *N.C., U.S.* 90 G12
Roan Plateau, *Colo., U.S.* 100 M10
Robāt-e Khān, *Iran* 153 D15
Robāt-e Khoshk Aveh, *Afghan.* 157 P2
Robe, *S. Austral., Austral.* 191 Z10
Robersonville, *N.C., U.S.* 90 H13
Robert Glacier, *Antarctica* 207 D19
Robert Lee, *Tex., U.S.* 96 M7
Roberts, *Idaho, U.S.* 100 G7
Roberts Butte, *Antarctica* 207 Q15
Roberts Creek Mountain, *Nev., U.S.* 103 P10
Robert S. Kerr Reservoir, *Okla., U.S.* 96 G14
Roberts Mountain, *U.S.* 78 Q1
Robertsport, *Liberia* 180 G6
Robeson Channel, *Nunavut, Can.* 77 A17
Robinson, *Ill., U.S.* 93 S7
Róbinson Crusoe, Isla, *Pac. Oc.* 195 M23
Robinson Range, *Austral.* 190 G3
Robinson River, *N. Terr., Austral.* 191 Q10
Robinvale, *Vic., Austral.* 191 Y11
Robokaere, island, *Majuro Atoll, Marshall Is.* 196 G11
Roboré, *Bol.* 122 K9
Rob Roy, island, *Solomon Is.* 197 L16
Robson, Mount, *B.C., Can.* 76 L9
Robstown, *Tex., U.S.* 97 U11
Roby, *Tex., U.S.* 96 L7
Rocamadour, *Fr.* 138 M9
Roca Partida, Isla, *Mex.* 108 H6
Roca Partida Island, *N. Amer.* 74 N3
Rocas, Atol das, *Braz.* 123 E18
Rocha, *Uru.* 124 L15
Rochedo, *Braz.* 122 K11
Rochefort, *Fr.* 138 M8
Rochelle, *Ga., U.S.* 91 N6
Rochelle, *Ill., U.S.* 93 N5
Roches Noires, Mouillage des, *Tubuai, Fr. Polynesia, Fr.* 199 J20
Rochester, *Ind., U.S.* 93 P9
Rochester, *Minn., U.S.* 98 L12
Rochester, *N.H., U.S.* 89 H15
Rochester, *N.Y., U.S.* 88 J6
Rock, river, *Ill., U.S.* 93 N5
Rockall, bank, *Atl. Oc.* 216 D11
Rockaway, *Oreg., U.S.* 102 F2
Rock Creek, *Mont., U.S.* 100 E9
Rock Creek Butte, *Oreg., U.S.* 102 G8
Rockdale, *Tex., U.S.* 97 P11
Rockefeller Plateau, *Antarctica* 206 L10
Rock Falls, *Ill., U.S.* 93 N5
Rockford, *Ill., U.S.* 92 M5
Rockhampton, *Qnsld., Austral.* 191 T15
Rockhampton Downs, *N. Terr., Austral.* 191 R9
Rock Hill, *S.C., U.S.* 90 J9
Rockingham, *N.C., U.S.* 90 J10
Rockingham, *W. Austral., Austral.* 191 X2
Rockingham Bay, *Austral.* 190 D13
Rock Island, *Ill., U.S.* 93 P4
Rock Lake, *N. Dak., U.S.* 98 E6
Rockland, *Idaho, U.S.* 100 H6
Rockland, *Me., U.S.* 89 G17
Rockland, *Mich., U.S.* 92 F6
Rocklea, *W. Austral., Austral.* 191 T2
Rockledge, *Fla., U.S.* 91 T9
Rockmart, *Ga., U.S.* 90 K4
Rock Port, *Mo., U.S.* 99 Q9
Rockport, *Calif., U.S.* 103 P2
Rockport, *Ind., U.S.* 93 U8
Rockport, *Tex., U.S.* 97 T11
Rock Rapids, *Iowa, U.S.* 98 M9
Rock River, *Wyo., U.S.* 100 J12
Rock Springs, *Mont., U.S.* 100 D12
Rock Springs, *Wyo., U.S.* 100 K9
Rocksprings, *Tex., U.S.* 97 Q7
Rockton, *Ill., U.S.* 92 M6
Rockville, *Ind., U.S.* 93 R8
Rockville, *Md., U.S.* 90 C13
Rockwell City, *Iowa, U.S.* 99 N10
Rockwood, *Me., U.S.* 89 D16
Rockwood, *Tenn., U.S.* 95 F18
Rocky Ford, *Colo., U.S.* 101 N14
Rocky Mount, *N.C., U.S.* 90 G12
Rocky Mount, *Va., U.S.* 90 F10
Rocky Mountain National Park, *Colo., U.S.* 100 L12
Rocky Mountains, *N. Amer.* 74 F3
Rocky Point, *Norfolk I., Austral.* 197 G20
Rodanthe, *N.C., U.S.* 90 H15
Roddickton, *Nfld., Can.* 77 L23
Rodeo, *Arg.* 124 J7
Rodeo, *N. Mex., U.S.* 101 W10
Rodez, *Fr.* 139 N10
Rodinga, *N. Terr., Austral.* 191 U9
Ródós, *Gr.* 137 M18
Ródos (Rhodes), island, *Gr.* 137 M18
Rodrigues, island, *Ind. Oc.* 184 H10
Rodrigues Fracture Zone, *Ind. Oc.* 220 K7
Roebourne, *W. Austral., Austral.* 191 S2
Roebuck Bay, *Austral.* 190 D4
Roebuck Plains, *W. Austral., Austral.* 191 R4
Roes Welcome Sound, *Nunavut, Can.* 77 H16
Rogagua, Lago, *Bol.* 122 H7
Rogers, *Ark., U.S.* 94 E6
Rogers, *Tex., U.S.* 97 P11
Rogers, Mount, *Va., U.S.* 90 G8
Rogers City, *Mich., U.S.* 92 H11
Rogers Lake, *Calif., U.S.* 103 W9
Rogerson, *Idaho, U.S.* 100 J5
Rogersville, *Tenn., U.S.* 95 E19
Roggan, river, *Que., Can.* 77 L18
Rognan, *Nor.* 134 E12
Rogue, river, *Oreg., U.S.* 102 K2
Rogue River, *Oreg., U.S.* 102 K3
Roguron, island, *Majuro Atoll, Marshall Is.* 196 G10
Rohri, *Pak.* 157 T7
Rohtak, *India* 158 F5
Roi, *Pohnpei, F.S.M.* 197 G14
Roi Anchorage, *Kwajalein Atoll, Marshall Is.* 196 K4
Roi Et, *Thai.* 166 L11
Roi-Namur, island, *Kwajalein Atoll, Marshall Is.* 196 K4
Rojas, *Arg.* 124 L12
Rojhan, *Pak.* 157 S8
Rojo, Cabo, *P.R., U.S.* 111 N22
Rokera, *Solomon Is.* 197 N20
Rokiškis, *Lith.* 135 M17
Rôlas, Ilhéu das, *São Tomé and Príncipe* 185 E20
Rolette, *N. Dak., U.S.* 98 E5
Rolla, *Mo., U.S.* 99 U13
Rolla, *N. Dak., U.S.* 98 D5
Rolleston, *N.Z.* 193 P17
Rolleston, *Qnsld., Austral.* 191 U14
Rolleville, *Bahamas* 111 F13
Rolling Fork, *Miss., U.S.* 94 K10
Rollins, *Mont., U.S.* 100 B5
Rolvsøya, island, *Nor.* 135 B14
Roma, *Qnsld., Austral.* 191 V14
Roma (Rome), *It.* 136 H9
Romain, Cape, *S.C., U.S.* 90 M11
Romaine, river, *Que., Can.* 77 M21
Roma-Los Saenz, *Tex., U.S.* 97 W9
Roman, *Rom.* 137 D16
Romanche Fracture Zone, *Atl. Oc.* 217 N11
Romanche Gap, *Atl. Oc.* 217 N10
Romang, island, *Indonesia* 169 M16
Romāni, *Egypt* 151 N1

Romania, *Eur.* **137** E15
Romano, Cape, *Fla., U.S.* **91** X8
Romano, Cayo, *Cuba* **110** H10
Romanovka, *Russ.* **141** L16
Romanzof, Cape, *U.S.* **78** P1
Rombo, Ilhéus do *see* Secos, Ilhéus, *Cape Verde* **185** D15
Rome, *Ga., U.S.* **90** K4
Rome *see* Roma, *It.* **136** H9
Rome, *N.Y., U.S.* **88** J9
Rommani, *Mor.* **176** B8
Romney, *W. Va., U.S.* **90** C11
Romny, *Ukr.* **133** H15
Rona, island, *Scot., U.K.* **138** C7
Ronan, *Mont., U.S.* **100** C5
Roncador, Serra do, *Braz.* **122** H12
Roncador Cay, *N. Amer.* **74** P9
Ronceverte, *W. Va., U.S.* **90** E9
Ronchamp, *Fr.* **138** K12
Ronde, island, *Grenada* **113** M17
Ronde, river, *Oreg., U.S.* **102** F8
Rondônia *see* Ji-Paraná, *Braz.* **122** G8
Rondonópolis, *Braz.* **122** J11
Rondu, *Pak.* **156** L12
Rong, Koh, *Cambodia* **167** P10
Rong'an, *China* **163** P1
Rongcheng, *China* **162** F10
Ronge, Lac la, *N. Amer.* **74** G5
Rongelap Atoll, *Marshall Is.* **196** F3
Rongerik Atoll, *Marshall Is.* **196** F3
Rongjiang, *China* **163** P1
Rong Kwang, *Thai.* **166** J8
Rongshui, *China* **163** Q1
Rongxian, *China* **163** R2
Ronkiti, *Pohnpei, F.S.M.* **197** G14
Ronkiti Harbor, *Pohnpei, F.S.M.* **197** G14
Rønne, *Den.* **135** P13
Ronne Entrance, *Antarctica* **206** G6
Ronne Ice Shelf, *Antarctica* **206** F8
Roodhouse, *Ill., U.S.* **93** S4
Roof Butte, *Ariz., U.S.* **101** Q9
Roonui, Mount, *Tahiti, Fr. Polynesia, Fr.* **199** Q17
Roorkee, *India* **158** E6
Roosevelt, *Utah, U.S.* **100** L9
Roosevelt, Mount, *B.C., Can.* **76** J9
Roosevelt Island, *Antarctica* **206** M11
Root, river, *Minn., U.S.* **98** L13
Roper Valley, *N. Terr., Austral.* **191** Q9
Ropesville, *Tex., U.S.* **96** K4
Roraima, Mount, *S. Amer.* **118** B6
Røros, *Nor.* **134** J11
Rørvik, *Nor.* **134** G11
Rosa, Lake, *Bahamas* **111** J15
Rosalia, *Wash., U.S.* **102** C9
Rosário, *Braz.* **123** D15
Rosario, *Arg.* **124** K12
Rosario, *Mex.* **108** G9
Rosario, *Para.* **122** M10
Rosario, Cayo del, *Cuba* **110** J7
Rosario de la Frontera, *Arg.* **124** F10
Rosario de Lerma, *Arg.* **124** F9
Rosarno, *It.* **136** L11
Roscoe, *S. Dak., U.S.* **98** J6
Roscoe, *Tex., U.S.* **96** L7
Roscommon, *Mich., U.S.* **92** J11
Rose Atoll, *Amer. Samoa, U.S.* **194** J11
Roseau, river, *Minn., U.S.* **98** D8
Roseau, *Dominica* **113** J17
Roseau, *Minn., U.S.* **98** D9
Rose Belle, *Mauritius* **185** G20
Rosebery, *Tas., Austral.* **191** Z15
Rosebud, *Mont., U.S.* **100** D12
Rosebud, *Tex., U.S.* **97** P11
Rosebud Creek, *Mont., U.S.* **100** E12
Roseburg, *Oreg., U.S.* **102** J3
Rosedale, *Miss., U.S.* **94** J10
Rosedale, *Qnsld., Austral.* **191** U15
Rose Island, *Bahamas* **110** E12
Rosenberg, *Tex., U.S.* **97** R13
Rosenheim, *Ger.* **132** K6
Rose Peak, *Ariz., U.S.* **101** U9
Roses, *Bahamas* **111** G14
Rosetown, *Sask., Can.* **76** M11
Roseville, *Calif., U.S.* **103** Q5
Rosholt, *S. Dak., U.S.* **98** H8
Rosht-Kala, *Taj.* **156** K9
Rosiclare, *Ill., U.S.* **93** V6
Roşiori de Vede, *Rom.* **137** F15
Roslavl', *Russ.* **140** F5
Roslyn, *Wash., U.S.* **102** C5
Ross, *N.Z.* **193** N16
Ross, Mount, *N.Z.* **193** M19
Ross, Point, *Norfolk I., Austral.* **197** G20
Rossano, *It.* **136** K11
Ross Barnett Reservoir, *Miss., U.S.* **94** L11
Ross Dam, *Wash., U.S.* **102** A5
Rossel Island, *P.N.G.* **193** F22
Ross Ice Shelf, *Antarctica* **206** M12
Ross Lake, *Wash., U.S.* **102** A5
Ross Lake National Recreation Area, *Wash., U.S.* **102** A5
Rosso, *Mauritania* **176** G5
Rossosh', *Russ.* **140** G5
Ross River, *N. Terr., Austral.* **191** T9
Ross River, *Yukon Terr., Can.* **76** G8
Røssvatnet, lake, *Sw.* **134** F12
Rossville, *Ill., U.S.* **93** Q7
Rossville, *Qnsld., Austral.* **191** Q13
Rostaq, *Afghan.* **156** K8
Rostock, *Ger.* **132** F7
Rostov na Donu, *Russ.* **140** H4
Roswell, *Ga., U.S.* **90** K5
Roswell, *N. Mex., U.S.* **101** U14
Rota, island, *N. Mariana Is., U.S.* **196** D2
Rota *see* Songsong, *N. Mariana Is., U.S.* **196** E7
Rotan, *Tex., U.S.* **96** L7
Rothera, station, *Antarctica* **206** E4
Rothschild, *Wis., U.S.* **92** H5
Rothschild Island, *Antarctica* **206** F5
Roti, island, *Indonesia* **169** N14
Roto, *N.S.W., Austral.* **191** X12
Roto, *Pukapuka Atoll, Cook Is., N.Z.* **198** Q2
Rotorua, *N.Z.* **193** K19
Rotterdam, *Neth.* **138** H11
Rotuma, island, *Fiji* **194** J8
Roubaix, *Fr.* **138** J10
Rouen, *Fr.* **138** J9
Round Island *see* Yalewa Kalou, *Fiji* **198** G6
Round Island, *Mauritius* **185** E21
Round Island Passage, *Fiji* **198** G6
Round Mountain, *Nev., U.S.* **103** Q9
Round Rock, *Tex., U.S.* **97** P10
Roundup, *Mont., U.S.* **100** D10
Rounga, Dar, *Af.* **174** H7
Roura, *Fr. Guiana* **121** E18
Rouses Point, *N.Y., U.S.* **88** E12
Rouyn-Noranda, *Que., Can.* **77** P18
Rovaniemi, *Fin.* **135** E15
Rovereto, *It.* **136** E9
Rovieng, *Cambodia* **167** N11
Rovinj, *Croatia* **136** F10
Rowa Islands *see* Reef Islands, *Vanuatu* **198** A2
Rowena, *N.S.W., Austral.* **191** W14
Rowland, *N.C., U.S.* **90** K11
Rowley Island, *Nunavut, Can.* **77** F17
Roxas, *Philippines* **169** D14
Roxas, *Philippines* **169** E13
Roxboro, *N.C., U.S.* **90** G11
Roy, *Mont., U.S.* **100** C10
Roy, *N. Mex., U.S.* **101** R14
Royale, Isle, *Mich., U.S.* **92** D6
Royal Oak, *Mich., U.S.* **93** N11
Royal Society Range, *Antarctica* **207** N14
Royan, *Fr.* **138** M8
Roy Hill, *W. Austral., Austral.* **191** T3
Royston, *Ga., U.S.* **90** K6
Rožňava, *Slovakia* **132** K10
Rst Bank, *Arctic Oc.* **223** F19
Rua, island, *Jaluit Atoll, Marshall Is.* **196** L7
Ruahara, island, *Penrhyn, Cook Is., N.Z.* **199** A17
Ruapehu, Mount, *N.Z.* **193** L19
Ruapuke Island, *N.Z.* **193** R15
Ruatoria, *N.Z.* **193** K21
Ruawai, *N.Z.* **193** J18
Rub al Khali, desert, *Asia* **146** H4
Rubtsovsk, *Russ.* **140** L11
Ruby, river, *Mont., U.S.* **100** E7
Ruby, *Alas., U.S.* **105** G14
Ruby Dome, *U.S.* **78** F5
Ruby Mountains, *Nev., U.S.* **103** N11
Rudan, *Iran* **153** H16
Rudbar, *Afghan.* **157** R2
Rūdnyy, *Kaz.* **154** C11
Rudolf, Lake *see* Turkana, Lake, *Eth.-Kenya* **179** H14
Rudolph, Ostrov, *Russ.* **140** C12
Rudong (Juegang), *China* **162** K10
Rudyard, *Mich., U.S.* **92** F11
Rufiji, river, *Tanzania* **179** M14
Rufino, *Arg.* **124** L11
Rufisque, *Senegal* **176** H4
Rugby, *N. Dak., U.S.* **98** E5
Rügen, island, *Ger.* **132** E7
Ruhnu, island, *Estonia* **135** L16
Ru'i, *Afghan.* **156** L6
Rui'an, *China* **163** N9
Rui Barbosa, *Braz.* **123** H16
Ruiché, *Bioko, Eq. Guinea* **184** M7
Ruidosa, *Tex., U.S.* **97** Q1
Ruidosa, *Tex., U.S.* **97** X4
Ruidoso, *N. Mex., U.S.* **101** U13
Ruidoso Downs, *N. Mex., U.S.* **101** U13
Ruijin, *China* **163** P6
Ruivo, Pico, *Madeira Is., Port.* **184** M3
Rukuruku Bay, *Fiji* **198** G6
Rukwa, Lake, *Tanzania* **179** M13
Rule, *Tex., U.S.* **96** K7
Ruleville, *Miss., U.S.* **94** J10
Ruma, *Yug.* **137** F13
Rumaylah, 'Urūq ar, *Saudi Arabia* **152** M10
Rumbalara, *N. Terr., Austral.* **191** U9
Rumbek, *Sudan* **178** G12
Rum Cay, *Bahamas* **111** F14
Rumford, *Me., U.S.* **89** F15
Rumoi, *Jap.* **164** F13
Rumung, island, *Yap Is., F.S.M.* **197** C18
Runanga, *N.Z.* **193** N17
Runaway, Cape, *N.Z.* **193** K20
Runde, river, *Zimb.* **182** G12
Rundeng, *Indonesia* **168** H4
Rundu, *Angola* **182** F8
Rundu, *Namibia* **182** F8
Runge, *Tex., U.S.* **97** S10
Rungwa, river, *Tanzania* **179** M13
Rungwa, *Tanzania* **179** M13
Runit, island, *Enewetak Atoll, Marshall Is.* **196** H8
Running Water Draw, *Tex., U.S.* **96** H4
Runu, *Yap Is., F.S.M.* **197** C18
Ruo, island, *Chuuk, F.S.M.* **197** B16
Ruoqiang, *China* **160** G7
Rupat, island, *Indonesia* **168** H6
Rupert, *Idaho, U.S.* **100** H6
Rupert, Rivière de, *Que., Can.* **77** M19
Ruppert Coast, *Antarctica* **206** N9
Rupununi, river, *Guyana* **121** F14
Rurrenabaque, *Bol.* **122** J6
Rurutu, island, *Fr. Polynesia, Fr.* **199** H15
Rusanovo, *Russ.* **140** E10
Ruse, *Bulg.* **137** G16
Rushan, *Taj.* **156** J9
Rush City, *Minn., U.S.* **98** J12
Rushford, *Minn., U.S.* **98** L13
Rush Springs, *Okla., U.S.* **96** H10
Rushville, *Ill., U.S.* **93** R4
Rushville, *Ind., U.S.* **93** R10
Rushville, *Nebr., U.S.* **98** M2
Rusk, *Tex., U.S.* **96** M14
Ruskin, *Fla., U.S.* **91** U7
Russas, *Braz.* **123** E17
Russell, *Kans., U.S.* **99** S6
Russell Cave National Monument, *Ala., U.S.* **95** G16
Russell Islands, *Solomon Is.* **197** N18
Russellville, *Ala., U.S.* **95** H14
Russellville, *Ark., U.S.* **94** F7
Russellville, *Ky., U.S.* **95** D15
Russia, *Eur.-Asia* **140** H10
Russian, river, *Calif., U.S.* **103** Q2
Russian Fort Elizabeth, *Hawaii, U.S.* **106** C5
Russian Mission, *Alas., U.S.* **104** J12
Russkaya Gavan', *Russ.* **140** D12
Russkaya Polyana, *Russ.* **140** K10
Rust'avi, *Rep. of Georgia* **149** C19
Ruston, *La., U.S.* **94** L8
Rutaki Passage, *Rarotonga, Cook Is., N.Z.* **198** Q9
Ruteng, *Indonesia* **169** M13
Ruth, *Nev., U.S.* **103** P12
Rutherfordton, *N.C., U.S.* **90** J8
Rutland, *Vt., U.S.* **88** H12
Rutland Island, *Andaman Is., India* **159** Q14
Rutog, *China* **160** J4
Ruvuma, river, *Af.* **174** M10
Ruwāq, Jabal ar, *Syr.* **150** H9
Ruwenzori, peak, *Dem. Rep. of the Congo* **178** J12
Rwanda, *Af.* **178** K12
Ryan, *Okla., U.S.* **96** J10
Ryazan', *Russ.* **140** F6
Rybinsk, *Russ.* **140** F7
Rybinskoye Vodokhranilishche, *Russ.* **140** F7
Rybinsk Reservoir, *Eur.* **130** D11
Rye, *Colo., U.S.* **101** P13
Ryegate, *Mont., U.S.* **100** D9
Rye Patch Reservoir, *Nev., U.S.* **103** N8
Ryn Peski, *Kaz.* **154** E5
Ryōtsu, *Jap.* **164** M11
Ryōtsu Wan, *Jap.* **164** L11
Ryukyu Islands (Nansei Shotō), *Jap.* **165** Y1
Ryukyu Trench, *Pac. Oc.* **218** G4
Ryzhovo, *Russ.* **141** E19
Rzeszów, *Pol.* **132** J11

S

Sa, *Thai.* **166** J9
Sa'a, *Solomon Is.* **197** P20
Sa'ādatābād, *Iran* **153** G15
Saarbrücken, *Ger.* **132** H4
Saaremaa, island, *Estonia* **135** L15
Saba, island, *Leeward Is.* **113** F15
Sab'Ābār, *Syr.* **150** J9
Šabac, *Yug.* **137** F13
Sabadell, *Sp.* **139** P10
Sabae, *Jap.* **165** P9
Sabah, *Malaysia* **168** G12
Sabana, Archipiélago de, *Cuba* **110** G8
Sabana de La Mar, *Dom. Rep.* **111** L19
Sabanalarga, *Col.* **120** B5
Sabaneta, *Dom. Rep.* **111** L17
Sabaneta, Puntan, *Saipan, N. Mariana Is., U.S.* **196** A5
Sabang, *Indonesia* **169** J13
Şabanözü, *Turk.* **148** D8
Sabaya, *Bol.* **122** K6
Şāberī, Hāmūn-e, *Afghan.* **157** Q1
Sabetha, *Kans., U.S.* **99** R9
Şabḩā, *Jordan* **150** L7
Sabhā, *Lib.* **177** D14
Sabidana, Jebel, *Af.* **174** F10
Sabinal, *Tex., U.S.* **97** R8
Sabinal, Cayo, *Cuba* **110** H11
Sabinas Hidalgo, *Mex.* **108** E11
Sabine, river, *U.S.* **79** M14
Sabine, *Tex., U.S.* **97** Q16
Sabine Lake, *La.-Tex., U.S.* **94** Q6
Sabinosa, *Canary Is., Sp.* **184** R3
Sable, Cape, *Fla., U.S.* **91** Y9
Sable, Cape, *N.S., Can.* **77** Q22
Sable, Île de, *New Caledonia, Fr.* **198** A6
Sable Island, *N.S., Can.* **77** P23
Sabrina Coast, *Antarctica* **207** N20
Sabtang, island, *Philippines* **169** A14
Sabunçu, *Azerb.* **149** D23
Sabura, *Pak.* **157** Q6
Şabyā, *Saudi Arabia* **152** N8
Sabzak Pass, *Afghan.* **156** M3
Sabzevār, *Iran* **153** C15
Sacaca, *Bol.* **122** K7
Sacajawea Peak, *Oreg., U.S.* **102** F9
Sac City, *Iowa, U.S.* **99** N10
Sachigo, river, *Ont., Can.* **77** L15
Sachs Harbour, *N.W.T., Can.* **76** D11
Sackets Harbor, *N.Y., U.S.* **88** G8
Saco, *Me., U.S.* **89** H15
Saco, *Mont., U.S.* **100** B11
Sacramento, river, *Calif., U.S.* **103** N4
Sacramento, *Calif., U.S.* **103** R4
Sacramento Mountains, *N. Mex., U.S.* **101** U13
Sacramento Valley, *U.S.* **78** F3
Sacred Falls, *Hawaii, U.S.* **106** D11
Şa'dah, *Yemen* **152** P9
Sadda, *Pak.* **157** N9
Saddat ash Shuqqah, *Yemen* **152** N12
Saddle Mountain, *Idaho, U.S.* **100** G6
Saddle Mountains, *Wash., U.S.* **102** D6
Saddle Peak, *Andaman Is., India* **159** P14
Saddle Road, *Hawaii, U.S.* **107** L19
Şadḩ, *Oman* **153** N15
Sadiqabad, *Pak.* **157** T8
Sadiya, *India* **158** F15
Sado, island, *Jap.* **164** L11
Sadon, *Myanmar* **166** E7
Sae Islands, *P.N.G.* **193** B19
Şafājah, region, *Saudi Arabia* **152** H7
Safata Bay, *Samoa* **198** L3
Saffar Kalay, *Afghan.* **157** R3
Säffle, *Sw.* **134** L12
Safford, *Ariz., U.S.* **101** U9
Safi, *Mor.* **176** B7
Şāfītā, *Syr.* **150** G7
Safotu, *Samoa* **198** K2
Safranbolu, *Turk.* **148** C8
Saga, *China* **160** L6
Saga, *Jap.* **165** R4
Sagae, *Jap.* **164** L12
Sagaing, *Myanmar* **166** G6
Sagami Nada, *Jap.* **165** Q12
Sagar, *India* **158** H6
Sagar, *India* **159** P4
Sagarejo, *Rep. of Georgia* **149** C19
Sage Creek, *Mont., U.S.* **100** A8
Sag Harbor, *N.Y., U.S.* **89** N13
Saghyz, river, *Kaz.* **154** E7
Saghyz, *Kaz.* **154** E7
Saginaw, *Mich., U.S.* **92** L11
Saginaw Bay, *Mich., U.S.* **92** K12
Saglek Bay, *Nfld., Can.* **77** J20
Sagu, *Myanmar* **166** H5
Saguache, *Colo., U.S.* **101** N12
Sagua de Tánamo, *Cuba* **111** K13
Sagua la Grande, *Cuba* **110** G8
Saguaro National Park, *Ariz., U.S.* **101** V7
Sagunto-Sagunt, *Sp.* **139** R9
Saḩāb, *Jordan* **150** M7
Şaḩam, *Oman* **153** J15
Sahamalaza, Baie de, *Madagascar* **183** E17
Sahara, desert, *Af.* **174** F3
Sahara, *Jap.* **164** G13
Saharan Atlas, mountains, *Af.* **174** D4
Saharanpur, *India* **158** E6
Saharsa, *India* **158** G11
Sahel, region, *Af.* **174** G4
Sahiwal, *Pak.* **157** P10
Sahiwal, *Pak.* **157** R11
Sahl Rakbah, plain, *Saudi Arabia* **152** L7
Şaḩrā' al Ḩijārah, desert, *Iraq* **152** F9
Sahuaripa, *Mex.* **108** D7
Sai, *Jap.* **164** H13
Sai Buri, *Thai.* **167** S9
Saïda, *Alg.* **176** B10
Sa'īdābād, *Iran* **153** F15
Saidapet, *India* **159** Q7
Saidor, *P.N.G.* **193** C19
Saidu, *Pak.* **156** M10

Saigō, *Jap.* **165** N7
Saigon *see* Ho Chi Minh City, *Vietnam* **167** P13
Saihan Tal *see* Sonid Youqi, *China* **162** A5
Saijō, *Jap.* **165** R6
Saiki, *Jap.* **165** S5
Sailolof, *Indonesia* **169** J17
Saimaa, lake, *Fin.* **135** H17
Saimbeyli, *Turk.* **148** G11
Sain, Chenal, *Wallis and Futuna, Fr.* **198** E12
Saindak, *Pak.* **157** S1
Saint Albans, *Vt., U.S.* **88** F12
Saint Albans, *W. Va., U.S.* **90** D8
Saint André, Cap, *Af.* **174** M11
Saint-André, *Réunion, Fr.* **185** G16
Saint Andrew Bay, *Fla., U.S.* **91** R3
Saint Andrews, *N.Z.* **193** Q17
Saint Andrews, *Scot., U.K.* **138** E8
Saint Ann's Bay, *Jam.* **110** M11
Saint Anthony, *Idaho, U.S.* **100** G7
Saint Anthony, *Nfld., Can.* **77** L23
Saint Arnaud, *Vic., Austral.* **191** Y12
Saint-Augustin, *Que., Can.* **77** L22
Saint Augustin Bay, *Af.* **174** P11
Saint Augustine, *Fla., U.S.* **91** R9
Saint-Barthélemy, island, *Leeward Is.* **113** F15
Saint-Benoît, *Réunion, Fr.* **185** G17
Saint-Brieuc, *Fr.* **138** K8
Saint Catherines Island, *Ga., U.S.* **91** P9
Saint Charles, *Idaho, U.S.* **100** J7
Saint Charles, *Mich., U.S.* **92** L11
Saint Charles, *Minn., U.S.* **98** L13
Saint Charles, *Mo., U.S.* **99** S15
Saint Clair, river, *Mich., U.S.* **92** M13
Saint Clair, *Mich., U.S.* **92** L13
Saint Clair, *Mo., U.S.* **99** T14
Saint Clair, Lake, *Mich., U.S.* **92** M13
Saint Clair Shores, *Mich., U.S.* **92** M13
Saint Cloud, *Fla., U.S.* **91** T9
Saint Cloud, *Minn., U.S.* **98** J10
Saint Croix, island, *Virgin Is., U.S.* **113** F13
Saint Croix, river, *Me., U.S.* **89** D19
Saint Croix, river, *Minn.-Wis., U.S.* **98** H12
Saint Croix Falls, *Wis., U.S.* **92** G2
Saint Croix Island International Historic Site, *Me., U.S.* **89** E19
Saint Croix National Scenic Riverway, *Minn.-Wis., U.S.* **92** G2
Saint David, *Ariz., U.S.* **101** V8
Saint David Islands *see* Mapia, Kepulauan, *Indonesia* **169** J19
Saint David's Island, *Bermuda, U.K.* **111** F18
Saint-Denis, *Fr.* **138** K10
Saint-Denis, *Réunion, Fr.* **185** F16
Saint-Dié, *Fr.* **138** K12
Saint-Dizier, *Fr.* **138** K11
Saint Edward, *Nebr., U.S.* **99** P7
Sainte Genevieve, *Mo., U.S.* **99** T15
Saint Elias, Mount, *Alas., U.S.* **105** J19
Saint Elias Mountains, *Alas., U.S.* **105** J20
Sainte Marie, Cap, *Madagascar* **183** J16
Sainte Marie, Nosy, *Madagascar* **183** F18
Sainte-Marie, *Martinique, Fr.* **113** J17
Sainte-Rose, *Réunion, Fr.* **185** G17
Saintes, *Fr.* **138** M9
Sainte-Suzanna, *Réunion, Fr.* **185** F16
Saint-Étienne, *Fr.* **138** M11
Saint Eustatius, island, *Leeward Is.* **113** G15
Saint Francis, river, *U.S.* **79** J15
Saint Francis, *Kans., U.S.* **99** R3
Saint Francis, *Me., U.S.* **89** A17
Saint Francis, *S. Dak., U.S.* **98** M4
Saint Francis Bay, *Af.* **174** R8
Saint Gallen, *Switz.* **132** K5
Saint George, *Bermuda, U.K.* **111** F18
Saint George, *Qnsld., Austral.* **191** V14
Saint George, *S.C., U.S.* **90** M9
Saint George, *Utah, U.S.* **101** Q5
Saint George, Cape, *Fla., U.S.* **91** S4
Saint George, Cape, *P.N.G.* **193** C22
Saint George, Point, *Calif., U.S.* **102** L1
Saint George Island, *Alas., U.S.* **104** M9
Saint George Island, *Fla., U.S.* **91** R4
Saint George's, *Grenada* **113** M17
Saint George's Channel, *Nicobar Is., India* **159** T15
Saint George's Channel, *Ire.-U.K.* **138** H6
Saint George's Channel, *P.N.G.* **193** C22
Saint George's Island, *Bermuda, U.K.* **111** F18
Saint-Gilles-les-Bains, *Réunion, Fr.* **185** G15
Saint Helena, island, *Atl. Oc.* **184** G4
Saint Helena, *Calif., U.S.* **103** R3
Saint Helena Bay, *S. Af.* **182** M7
Saint Helena Sound, *S.C., U.S.* **91** N10
Saint Helens, *Oreg., U.S.* **102** E3
Saint Helens, Mount, *Wash., U.S.* **102** E4
Saint-Hyacinthe, *Que., Can.* **77** P20
Saint Ignace, *Mich., U.S.* **92** G10
Saint Ignatius, *Mont., U.S.* **100** C5
Saint James, *Minn., U.S.* **98** L10
Saint James, *Mo., U.S.* **99** T14
Saint-Jean, Lake, *Que., Can.* **77** N20
Saint Joe, river, *Idaho, U.S.* **100** C4
Saint John, island, *Virgin Is., U.S.* **113** F13
Saint John, river, *Me., U.S.* **89** B16
Saint John, *Kans., U.S.* **99** U6
Saint John, *N. Dak., U.S.* **98** D5
Saint John, *N.B., Can.* **77** P21
Saint John, *Wash., U.S.* **102** D9
Saint Johns, river, *Fla., U.S.* **91** R8
Saint Johns, *Ariz., U.S.* **101** T9
Saint Johns, *Mich., U.S.* **92** L11
Saint John's, *Antigua* **113** G16
Saint John's, *Nfld., Can.* **77** M24
Saint Johnsbury, *Vt., U.S.* **89** F13
Saint Jona Island *see* Iony, Ostrov, *Russ.* **141** H20
Saint Joseph, river, *Ind., U.S.* **93** P10
Saint Joseph, *La., U.S.* **94** M9
Saint Joseph, *Mich., U.S.* **93** N9
Saint Joseph, *Mo., U.S.* **99** R10
Saint Joseph, *Trin. & Tobago* **113** P17
Saint Joseph, Lake, *N. Amer.* **74** G7
Saint-Joseph, *New Caledonia, Fr.* **198** C8
Saint-Joseph, *Réunion, Fr.* **185** J16
Saint Joseph Bay, *Fla., U.S.* **91** R4
Saint Kilda, island, *Scot., U.K.* **138** D6
Saint Kitts, island, *St. Kitts and Nevis* **113** G15
Saint Kitts and Nevis, *N. Amer.* **113** G16
Saint-Laurent du Maroni, *Fr. Guiana* **121** E17
Saint Lawrence, river, *N. Amer.* **74** G9
Saint Lawrence, Gulf of, *Can.* **77** N22
Saint Lawrence Island, *Alas., U.S.* **104** G9
Saint Lawrence Islands National Park, *N.Y., U.S.* **88** F9
Saint-Leu, *Réunion, Fr.* **185** H15
Saint-Lô, *Fr.* **138** K8
Saint Louis, river, *Minn., U.S.* **98** G12
Saint Louis, *Mich., U.S.* **92** L11
Saint Louis, *Mo., U.S.* **99** T15
Saint-Louis, *New Caledonia, Fr.* **198** E8
Saint-Louis, *Réunion, Fr.* **185** H15
Saint-Louis, *Senegal* **176** G4
Saint-Louis du Nord, *Haiti* **111** L16
Saint Lucia, *N. Amer.* **113** K17
Saint Lucia, island, *N. Amer.* **74** N12
Saint Lucia, Cape, *S. Af.* **182** K12
Saint Lucia, Lake, *S. Af.* **182** K12
Saint Lucia Channel, *Martinique, Fr.-St. Lucia* **113** K17
Saint-Malo, *Fr.* **138** K8
Saint-Marc, *Haiti* **111** L16
Saint-Marc, Canal de, *Haiti* **111** L15
Saint Maries, *Idaho, U.S.* **100** C3
Saint Marks, *Fla., U.S.* **91** R5
Saint Martin, island, *Leeward Is.* **113** F15
Saint Martinville, *La., U.S.* **94** P9
Saint Marys, river, *Fla.-Ga., U.S.* **91** Q8
Saint Marys, *Ga., U.S.* **91** Q8
Saint Marys, *Kans., U.S.* **99** S9
Saint Marys, *Ohio, U.S.* **93** Q11
Saint Marys, *Pa., U.S.* **88** M5
Saint Marys, *Tas., Austral.* **191** Z16
Saint Marys, *W. Va., U.S.* **90** C8
Saint Mary's Bay, *Nfld., Can.* **77** M24
Saint Marys City, *Md., U.S.* **90** D14
Saint-Mathieu, Pointe de, *Fr.* **138** K7
Saint Matthew Island, *Alas., U.S.* **104** J8
Saint Matthews, *S.C., U.S.* **90** L9
Saint-Maurice, river, *Que., Can.* **77** P19
Saint Michael, *Alas., U.S.* **104** G12
Saint Michaels, *Ariz., U.S.* **101** R9
Saint Moritz, *Switz.* **132** K5
Saint-Nazaire, *Fr.* **138** L8
Saint Paul, *Minn., U.S.* **98** K11
Saint Paul, *Nebr., U.S.* **99** P6
Saint-Paul, *Réunion, Fr.* **185** G15
Saint-Paul, Île, *Ind. Oc.* **184** K10
Saint Paul I., *Alas., U.S.* **104** M9
Saint Pauls, *N.C., U.S.* **90** J11
Saint Paul's Point, *Pitcairn I., U.K.* **199** Q23
Saint Peter, *Minn., U.S.* **98** K11
Saint Peter and Saint Paul Rocks, *Atl. Oc.* **184** F2
Saint Petersburg, *Fla., U.S.* **91** U7
Saint Petersburg (Leningrad), *Russ.* **140** D6
Saint-Philippe, *Réunion, Fr.* **185** H17
Saint-Pierre, *Réunion, Fr.* **185** H16
Saint-Pierre and Miquelon, islands, *Atl. Oc.* **77** N23
Saint Pierre Island, *Seychelles* **183** C18
Saint Pölten, *Aust.* **132** K8
Saint-Quentin, *Fr.* **138** J10
Saint Rogatien Bank, *Hawaii, U.S.* **106** M6
Saint Simons Island, *Ga., U.S.* **91** P9
Saint Stanislas Bay, *Kiritimati, Kiribati* **197** B22
Saint Stephen, *S.C., U.S.* **90** L10
Saint Thomas, island, *Virgin Is., U.S.* **113** F13
Saint Thomas, *N. Dak., U.S.* **98** E7
Saint-Tropez, *Fr.* **139** N12
Saint Veit, *Aust.* **132** L7
Saint Vincent, island, *N. Amer.* **74** P12
Saint Vincent, *Minn., U.S.* **98** D8
Saint Vincent, Cape, *Af.* **174** P11
Saint Vincent, Cape, *Eur.* **130** J1
Saint Vincent, Gulf, *Austral.* **190** K10
Saint Vincent and the Grenadines, *N. Amer.* **113** L17
Saint Vincent Island, *Fla., U.S.* **91** R4
Saint Vincent Passage, *St. Lucia-St. Vincent and the Grenadines* **113** L17
Saipan, island, *N. Mariana Is., U.S.* **196** A4
Saipan, *Palau* **196** R9
Saipan Channel, *Saipan, N. Mariana Is., U.S.* **196** D4
Saipan Harbor, *Saipan, N. Mariana Is., U.S.* **196** B4
Sairang, *India* **158** H14
Saito, *Jap.* **165** S5
Saivomuotka, *Sw.* **135** D14
Sajama, Nevado, *Bol.* **122** K6
Sajyang Pass, *China* **160** N10
Sakai, *Jap.* **165** Q9
Sakaide, *Jap.* **165** Q7
Sakaiminato, *Jap.* **165** P7
Sakākah, *Saudi Arabia* **152** F7
Saka Kalat, *Pak.* **157** U4
Sakakawea, Lake, *N. Dak., U.S.* **98** F3
Sakami, river, *Que., Can.* **77** M18
Sakami, *Que., Can.* **77** M18
Sakami, Lac, *Que., Can.* **77** M18
Sakania, *Dem. Rep. of the Congo* **178** P11
Sakao (Lathi), island, *Vanuatu* **198** C2
Sakarya, river, *Turk.* **148** D6
Sakata, *Jap.* **164** L12
Sakçagöze, *Turk.* **148** H12
Sakhalin, Ostrov, *Russ.* **141** J21
Sakhar, *Afghan.* **157** N5
Şäki, *Azerb.* **149** C21
Sakishima Shotō, *Jap.* **194** C1
Sakon Nakhon, *Thai.* **166** K11
Sakrand, *Pak.* **157** V7
Saky, *Ukr.* **133** M16
Sal, island, *Cape Verde* **185** B17
Sal, Cay, *Bahamas* **110** F8
Sala, *Sw.* **135** K13
Salada, Gran Laguna, *Arg.* **125** S9
Salada, Laguna, *Mex.* **108** B5
Saladas, *Arg.* **124** H13
Saladillo, *Arg.* **124** M12
Salado, river, *Arg.* **124** H11
Salado, river, *Arg.* **124** M13
Salado, river, *Arg.* **124** M9
Salaga, *Ghana* **180** G10
Salahīyah, *Syr.* **150** G8
Sala'ilua, *Samoa* **198** K2
Salala, *Sudan* **179** C14
Salālah, *Oman* **153** P14
Salamanca, *Chile* **124** K7
Salamanca, *Mex.* **108** H11
Salamanca, *N.Y., U.S.* **88** K5
Salamanca, *Sp.* **139** Q6
Salamat, Bahr, *Chad* **177** K15
Salamis, ruins, *Cyprus* **148** L9
Salang Tunnel, *Afghan.* **156** L7
Salani, *Samoa* **198** L3
Salapaly Bay, *Af.* **174** P11
Salatiga, *Indonesia* **168** M9
Salavan, *Laos* **166** L12
Salavat, *Russ.* **140** J7
Salaverry, *Peru* **122** G2
Salawati, island, *Indonesia* **169** J17
Sala-y-Gómez, island, *Pac. Oc.* **195** L19
Sala y Gómez Ridge, *Pac. Oc.* **219** M18
Salazie, *Réunion, Fr.* **185** G16
Salda Gölü, *Turk.* **148** H5
Saldanha, *S. Af.* **182** M7
Sale, *Vic., Austral.* **191** Z13
Salebabu, island, *Indonesia* **169** G16
Saleimoa, *Samoa* **198** L3
Salekhard, *Russ.* **140** F11
Salelologa, *Samoa* **198** K2
Salem, *Ark., U.S.* **94** E9
Salem, *Ill., U.S.* **93** T6
Salem, *Ind., U.S.* **93** T9
Salem, *India* **159** Q6
Salem, *Mass., U.S.* **89** K15
Salem, *Mo., U.S.* **99** U14
Salem, *N.H., U.S.* **89** J14
Salem, *Ohio, U.S.* **93** P15
Salem, *Oreg., U.S.* **102** G3
Salem, *S. Dak., U.S.* **98** L7
Salem, *Va., U.S.* **90** F10
Salem, *W. Va., U.S.* **90** C9
Salerno, *It.* **136** J10
Salgueiro, *Braz.* **123** F16
Salida, *Colo., U.S.* **101** N12
Şalīf, *Yemen* **152** P8
Salihli, *Turk.* **148** F4
Salihorsk, *Belarus* **133** G13
Salima, *Malawi* **183** E13
Salina, *Kans., U.S.* **99** T7
Salina, *Utah, U.S.* **101** N7
Salinas, river, *Calif., U.S.* **103** U5
Salinas, *Calif., U.S.* **103** T4
Salinas, *Ecua.* **120** K1
Salinas Peak, *N. Mex., U.S.* **101** U12
Salinas Pueblo Missions National Monument (Gran Quivira), *N. Mex., U.S.* **101** T12
Saline, river, *U.S.* **79** K14
Salines, Point, *Grenada* **113** M16
Salinópolis, *Braz.* **123** C14
Salisbury, *Guam, U.S.* **196** B12
Salisbury, *Md., U.S.* **90** D15
Salisbury, *Mo., U.S.* **99** S12
Salisbury, *N.C., U.S.* **90** H9
Salisbury, *Eng., U.K.* **138** H8
Salisbury, Ostrov, *Russ.* **140** C12
Salisbury Island, *Nunavut, Can.* **77** H18
Salish Mountains, *Mont., U.S.* **100** B5
Şalkhad, *Syr.* **150** L8
Sallisaw, *Okla., U.S.* **96** G14
Salluit, *Que., Can.* **77** H18
Salmās, *Iran* **152** B10
Salmon, river, *Idaho, U.S.* **100** E4
Salmon, *Idaho, U.S.* **100** F6
Salmon Bank, *Hawaii, U.S.* **106** K2
Salmon Falls Creek Reservoir, *Idaho, U.S.* **100** J4
Salmon Gums, *W. Austral., Austral.* **191** X4
Salmon Peak, *Tex., U.S.* **97** R7
Salmon River Canyon, *Idaho, U.S.* **100** E5
Salmon River Mountains, *Idaho, U.S.* **100** F4
Salo, *Fin.* **135** J15
Salome, *Ariz., U.S.* **101** T5
Salonga, river, *Dem. Rep. of the Congo* **178** K9
Salonica *see* Thessaloníki, *Gr.* **137** J15
Salonta, *Rom.* **137** E14
Salpaus Ridge, *Eur.* **130** D8
Salpausselkä, ridge, *Fin.* **135** J16
Sal Rei, *Cape Verde* **185** C17
Sal'sk, *Russ.* **140** H4
Salt, river, *Ariz., U.S.* **101** T7
Salta, *Arg.* **124** F9
Salt Cay, *Turks and Caicos Is., U.K.* **111** J18
Saltfjorden, *Nor.* **134** E12
Salt Fork Arkansas, river, *Okla., U.S.* **96** E9
Salt Fork Brazos, river, *Tex., U.S.* **96** K6
Salt Fork Red, river, *Tex., U.S.* **96** H7
Saltillo, *Mex.* **108** F11
Salt Lake City, *Utah, U.S.* **100** L7
Salto, *Uru.* **124** J13
Salton Sea, *Calif., U.S.* **103** Y11
Salt Range, *Pak.* **157** P10
Salt River Range, *Wyo., U.S.* **100** H8
Saltville, *Va., U.S.* **90** G8
Saluafata Harbour, *Samoa* **198** L4
Saluda, river, *S.C., U.S.* **90** K8
Saluda, *S.C., U.S.* **90** K8
Salûm, *Egypt* **177** C17
Salûm, Gulf of, *Af.* **174** D8
Salvación, Bahía, *Chile* **125** W6
Salvador (Bahia), *Braz.* **123** H17
Salvador, Lake, *La., U.S.* **94** Q11
Salvador, Port, *Falk. Is., U.K.* **125** W13
Salvage Islands, *Af.* **174** D1
Salween, river, *Asia* **146** J10
Salween *see* Nu, river, *China* **160** N10
Salween *see* Thanlwin, river, *Myanmar* **166** G7
Salyan, *Azerb.* **149** E22
Salyersville, *Ky., U.S.* **95** C19
Salzbrunn, *Namibia* **182** J7
Salzburg, *Aust.* **132** K7
Salzwede, *Ger.* **132** F6
Samaipata, *Bol.* **122** K8
Samalaeulu, *Samoa* **198** K2
Samâlût, *Egypt* **177** D18
Samaná, *Dom. Rep.* **111** L20
Samaná, Bahía de, *Dom. Rep.* **111** L19
Samaná, Cabo, *Dom. Rep.* **111** L20
Samana Cay (Atwood), *Bahamas* **111** G15
Samandağ, *Turk.* **148** K11
Samangan *see* Aybak, *Afghan.* **156** L7
Samani, *Jap.* **164** G14
Samar, island, *Philippines* **169** D15
Samara, river, *Eur.* **130** E13
Samara, *Russ.* **140** H7
Samarai, *P.N.G.* **193** E21
Samarinda, *Indonesia* **168** J12
Samarqand, *Uzb.* **154** L12
Sāmarrā', *Iraq* **152** D9
Samar Sea, *Philippines* **169** D14
Samarskoye, *Kaz.* **155** D18
Samba, *India* **157** P12
Sambalpur, *India* **158** K9
Sambava, *Madagascar* **183** E18
Sambir, *Ukr.* **132** J11
Samboja, *Indonesia* **168** J12
Samborombón, Bahía, *Arg.* **124** M13
Samburg, *Russ.* **140** G12
Samch'uk, *S. Korea* **162** E14
Samdari, *India* **158** G3
Same, *Tanzania* **179** L14
Sami, *Pak.* **157** V3
Şāmiţah, *Saudi Arabia* **152** P8
Samnangjin, *S. Korea* **162** G14
Samo, *P.N.G.* **193** C21
Samoa, *Pac. Oc.* **198** K2
Samoa Islands, *Pac. Oc.* **194** J10
Sámos, island, *Gr.* **137** L17
Samothrace *see* Samothráki, island, *Gr.* **137** J16
Samothráki (Samothrace), island, *Gr.* **137** J16
Sampacho, *Arg.* **124** L10
Sampit, *Indonesia* **168** K10

Sampwe, *Dem. Rep. of the Congo* **178** N11
Sam Rayburn Reservoir, *Tex., U.S.* **97** N15
Samrong, *Cambodia* **166** M10
Sam Son, *Vietnam* **166** J12
Samson, *Ala., U.S.* **95** N16
Samsun, *Turk.* **148** C11
Samu, *Indonesia* **168** K11
Samui, Ko, *Thai.* **167** Q8
Samundri, *Pak.* **157** Q11
Samur, *Afghan.* **157** Q1
Samut Prakan, *Thai.* **166** M9
Samut Songkhram, *Thai.* **167** N8
San, river, *Cambodia* **166** M13
San, *Jap.* **165** X2
San, *Mali* **176** H8
Şan'ā' (Sanaa), *Yemen* **152** P9
Sanaa see Şan'ā', *Yemen* **152** P9
Sanae IV, station, *Antarctica* **206** A12
Şanāfīr, island, *Saudi Arabia* **152** G5
Sanaga, river, *Af.* **174** J6
San Agustín, *Col.* **120** G4
San Agustin, Cape, *Philippines* **169** F15
Sanak Islands, *Alas., U.S.* **104** P12
Sanām, *Saudi Arabia* **152** K9
San Ambrosio, Isla, *Chile* **118** K2
Sanana, island, *Indonesia* **169** K15
Sanandaj, *Iran* **152** C11
San Andreas, *Calif., U.S.* **103** R5
San Andrés, Isla de, *Col.* **109** M20
San Andres Mountains, *N. Mex., U.S.* **101** V12
San Andrés Tuxtla, *Mex.* **109** J13
San Andros, *Bahamas* **110** E11
San Angelo, *Tex., U.S.* **97** N7
San Antonio, river, *Tex., U.S.* **97** S11
San Antonio, *Chile* **124** L6
San Antonio, *N. Mex., U.S.* **101** T12
San Antonio, *Saipan, N. Mariana Is., U.S.* **196** C4
San Antonio, *Tex., U.S.* **97** R9
San Antonio, Cabo, *Arg.* **124** M14
San Antonio, Cabo de, *Cuba* **110** H3
San Antonio, Mount, *Calif., U.S.* **103** X9
San Antonio, Punta, *Mex.* **108** C5
San Antonio Bay, *Tex., U.S.* **97** T12
San Antonio de los Cobres, *Arg.* **124** E9
San Antonio de Ureca, *Bioko, Eq. Guinea* **184** N7
San Antonio Missions National Historical Park, *Tex., U.S.* **97** R9
San Antonio Mountain, *Tex., U.S.* **97** U3
San Antonio Oeste, *Arg.* **125** Q10
Sanat, island, *Chuuk, F.S.M.* **197** C16
San Augustine, *Tex., U.S.* **97** N15
Sanāw, *Yemen* **153** N13
Sanawad, *India* **158** J5
San Benedicto, Isla, *Mex.* **108** H6
San Benito, *Tex., U.S.* **97** W11
San Bernardino, *Calif., U.S.* **103** X9
San Bernardino Strait, *Philippines* **169** D15
San Bernardo, *Chile* **124** L7
San Blas, *Mex.* **108** E8
San Blas, Archipelago de, *Pan.* **109** N22
San Blas, Cape, *Fla., U.S.* **91** R4
San Blas, Punta, *Pan.* **109** N21
San Borja, *Bol.* **122** J7
San Carlos, *Arg.* **124** F9
San Carlos, *Ariz., U.S.* **101** U8
San Carlos, *Philippines* **169** E14
San Carlos, *Venez.* **120** C7
San Carlos de Bariloche, *Arg.* **125** Q7
San Carlos de Bolívar, *Arg.* **124** M12
San Carlos de Río Negro, *Venez.* **120** G9
San Carlos Reservoir, *Ariz., U.S.* **101** U8
Sánchez, *Dom. Rep.* **111** L19
Sanchor, *India* **158** H3
Sanchung, *Taiwan, China* **163** Q10
San Clemente, island, *U.S.* **78** K4
San Clemente, *Calif., U.S.* **103** Y9
San Clemente Mountains, *Calif., U.S.* **103** Z8
San Cristóbal, *Arg.* **124** J11
San Cristóbal, *Cuba* **110** G5
San Cristóbal, *Dom. Rep.* **111** M19
San Cristóbal, *Venez.* **120** D6
San Cristóbal, Isla, *Galapagos Is., Ecua.* **195** G21
San Cristobal, island, *Solomon Is.* **197** Q20
San Cristóbal de Las Casas, *Mex.* **109** K15
Sancti Spiritus, *Cuba* **110** H9
Sancy, Pico de, *Eur.* **130** H4
Sand, *Nor.* **134** L10
Sandakan, *Malaysia* **168** G12
Sandal, Baie de, *New Caledonia, Fr.* **198** C9
Sanday, island, *Scot., U.K.* **138** C8
Sand Cay, *India* **159** Q2
Sanders, *Ariz., U.S.* **101** S9
Sanderson, *Tex., U.S.* **97** Q4
Sandersville, *Ga., U.S.* **90** M7
Sand Hills, *U.S.* **78** F11
Sandia Crest, *N. Mex., U.S.* **101** S12
San Diego, *Calif., U.S.* **103** Z9
San Diego, *Tex., U.S.* **97** U10
San Diego de los Baños, *Cuba* **110** G5
Sandıklı, *Turk.* **148** F6
Sand Island, *Hawaii, U.S.* **106** K2
Sand Island, *Santa Cruz Is., Solomon Is.* **197** P22
Sand Island, *Wis., U.S.* **92** E4
Sandoa, *Dem. Rep. of the Congo* **178** N10
Sandon Iwa, *Jap.* **165** W3
Sandoy, island, *Faroe Is., Den.* **134** J6
Sand Point, *Alas., U.S.* **104** N12
Sandpoint, *Idaho, U.S.* **100** B4
Sandspit, *B.C., Can.* **76** K7
Sand Springs, *Mont., U.S.* **100** C11
Sand Springs, *Okla., U.S.* **96** F12
Sandstone, *Minn., U.S.* **98** H12
Sandstone, *W. Austral., Austral.* **191** V3
Sandur, *Faroe Is., Den.* **134** J6
Sandusky, *Mich., U.S.* **92** L13
Sandusky, *Ohio, U.S.* **93** P13
Sandviken, *Sw.* **135** K13
Sandwich, *Ill., U.S.* **93** N6
Sandwich Bay, *Nfld., Can.* **77** K22
Sandy, *Utah, U.S.* **100** L7
Sandy Cape, *Austral.* **190** G16
Sandy Creek, *Tex., U.S.* **97** R12
Sandygaçy, *Turkm.* **154** N10
Sandy Island, *Mauritius* **185** J19
Sandy Lake, *Ont., Can.* **77** M15
Sandy Point, *Andaman Is., India* **159** R14
Sandy Point, *Bahamas* **110** D11
Saneku, *Jap.* **165** W3
San Felipe, *Chile* **124** K7
San Felipe, *Col.* **120** G9
San Felipe, *Mex.* **108** B5
San Felipe, *Venez.* **120** B8
San Felipe, Cayos de, *Cuba* **110** H5
San Felipe Pueblo, *N. Mex., U.S.* **101** R12
San Félix, Isla, *Chile* **118** K2
San Fernando, *Calif., U.S.* **103** X8
San Fernando, *Chile* **124** L7
San Fernando, *Mex.* **108** F12
San Fernando, *Sp.* **139** T6
San Fernando, *Trin. & Tobago* **113** P17
San Fernando de Apure, *Venez.* **120** D9
San Fernando de Atabapo, *Venez.* **120** F9
Sanford, *Colo., U.S.* **101** P12
Sanford, *Fla., U.S.* **91** T9
Sanford, *Me., U.S.* **89** H15
Sanford, *N.C., U.S.* **90** H11
San Francique, *Trin. & Tobago* **113** P17
San Francisco, river, *N. Mex., U.S.* **101** U10
San Francisco, *Arg.* **124** J11
San Francisco, *Arg.* **124** K9
San Francisco, *Calif., U.S.* **103** S3
San Francisco Bay, *U.S.* **78** G3
San Francisco del Oro, *Mex.* **108** E9
San Francisco de Paula, Cabo, *Arg.* **125** V9
San Francisco Mountain, *Ariz., U.S.* **101** R7
San Gabriel, river, *Tex., U.S.* **97** P11
San Gabriel, *Ecua.* **120** H3
Sangamner, *India* **158** L4
Sangamon, river, *Ill., U.S.* **93** R5
Sangar, *Russ.* **141** G17
Sangareddi, *India* **158** M6
Sang Bast, *Iran* **153** C16
Sang Bor, *Afghan.* **156** M2
Sangeang, island, *Indonesia* **169** M13
Sang-e Masheh, *Afghan.* **157** N6
Sanger, *Calif., U.S.* **103** T7
Sanger, *Tex., U.S.* **96** K11
San Germán, *P.R., U.S.* **111** N22
Sanggan, river, *China* **162** D5
Sanggou Wan, *China* **162** F10
Sangha, river, *Cameroon-Congo* **181** K18
Sanghar, *Pak.* **157** V7
Sangihe, island, *Indonesia* **169** H15
Sangihe, Kepulauan, *Indonesia* **169** H15
San Gil, *Col.* **120** E6
Sangin, *Afghan.* **157** P4
Sangkulirang, *Indonesia* **168** H12
Sangli, *India* **158** M4
Sangola, *India* **158** M4
Sangolquí, *Ecua.* **120** J3
San Gorgonio Mountain, *Calif., U.S.* **103** X10
Sangowo, *Indonesia* **169** H16
Sangre de Cristo Mountains, *Colo., U.S.* **101** P13
San Gregorio, *Uru.* **124** K14
Sangre Grande, *Trin. & Tobago* **113** P17
Sang Sang, *Nicar.* **109** L18
Sangvor, *Taj.* **156** H9
Sangzhi, *China* **162** L2
Sanhe, *China* **161** B15
Sanibel Island, *Fla., U.S.* **91** W8
San Ignacio, *Arg.* **124** G15
San Ignacio, *Bol.* **122** J9
San Ignacio, *Mex.* **108** D6
Saniquellie, *Liberia* **180** G7
San Javier, *Arg.* **124** J12
Sanjiang, *China* **163** P2
San Joaquin, river, *Calif., U.S.* **103** T6
San Joaquín, *Bol.* **122** H7
San Joaquin Valley, *U.S.* **78** G3
San Jon, *N. Mex., U.S.* **101** S15
San Jorge, Golfo, *Arg.* **125** T9
San Jorge Island, *Solomon Is.* **197** M18
San José, *C.R.* **109** N19
San José, *Guatemala* **109** L15
San José, Golfo, *Arg.* **125** R10
San Jose, *Calif., U.S.* **103** S4
San Jose, *N. Mex., U.S.* **101** R13
San Jose, *Saipan, N. Mariana Is., U.S.* **196** C4
San Jose, *Tinian, N. Mariana Is., U.S.* **196** C8
San Jose, Isla, *Mex.* **108** F7
San José de Amacuro, *Venez.* **121** C13
San José de Jáchal, *Arg.* **124** J8
San José de Las Lajas, *Cuba* **110** G6
San José del Guaviare, *Col.* **120** G6
San José de Mayo, *Uru.* **124** L14
San José de Ocuné, *Col.* **120** F7
San Juan, river, *Utah, U.S.* **101** P8
San Juan, *Arg.* **124** K8
San Juan, *Dom. Rep.* **111** M18
San Juan, *P.R., U.S.* **111** M23
San Juan, *Peru* **122** J4
San Juan, Cabo, *Arg.* **125** X11
San Juan Bautista, *Calif., U.S.* **103** T4
San Juan Bautista, *Para.* **122** N10
San Juan Capistrano, *Calif., U.S.* **103** Y9
San Juan del Norte, *Nicar.* **109** M19
San Juan del Sur, *Nicar.* **109** M18
San Juan Islands, *Wash., U.S.* **102** A3
San Juan Mountains, *Colo., U.S.* **101** P11
San Juan y Martinez, *Cuba* **110** H5
San Julián, Bahía, *Arg.* **125** U9
San Justo, *Arg.* **124** J12
San Justo, *Arg.* **124** L13
Sankeshwar, *India* **159** N4
Sankuru, river, *Dem. Rep. of the Congo* **178** L9
San Lázaro, Cabo, *Mex.* **108** E6
Şanlıurfa, *Turk.* **149** H13
San Lorenzo, *Arg.* **124** K12
San Lorenzo, *Ecua.* **120** H2
San Lorenzo, Cabo, *Ecua.* **120** J1
Sanlúcar de Barrameda, *Sp.* **139** S6
San Luis, *Arg.* **124** L9
San Luis, *Colo., U.S.* **101** P13
San Luis, *Cuba* **111** K13
San Luis, *Guatemala* **109** K16
San Luis, Lago de, *Bol.* **122** H8
San Luis de Palenque, *Col.* **120** E7
San Luis Obispo, *Calif., U.S.* **103** V5
San Luis Potosí, *Mex.* **108** G11
San Luis Reservoir, *Calif., U.S.* **103** T5
San Luis Río Colorado, *Mex.* **108** B6
San Manuel, *Ariz., U.S.* **101** V8
San Marcos, *Col.* **120** C5
San Marcos, *Tex., U.S.* **97** Q10
San Marino, *Eur.* **136** G9
San Martin, station, *Antarctica* **206** E5
San Martín, river, *Bol.* **122** H8
San Martín, *Arg.* **124** K8
San Martín, *Col.* **120** F6
San Martin, Cape, *Calif., U.S.* **103** U4
San Martín, Lago, *Arg.* **125** V7
San Martín de los Andes, *Arg.* **125** Q7
San Mateo, *Calif., U.S.* **103** S3
San Mateo, *N. Mex., U.S.* **101** S11
San Matías, Golfo, *Arg.* **125** Q10
Sanmen Wan, *China* **162** M10
Sanmenxia, *China* **162** G3
San Miguel, island, *Calif., U.S.* **103** X5
San Miguel, river, *Bol.* **122** J8
San Miguel, *El Salv.* **109** L17
San Miguel Bay, *Philippines* **169** C14
San Miguel Creek, *Tex., U.S.* **97** S9
San Miguel de Huachi, *Bol.* **122** J7
San Miguel del Monte, *Arg.* **124** M13
San Miguel de Tucumán, *Arg.* **124** G9
Sanming, *China* **163** P7
San Nicolás, *Arg.* **124** L12
San Nicolas, island, *Calif., U.S.* **103** Y7
Sannikova, Proliv, *Russ.* **141** D17
Sannohe, *Jap.* **164** J13
San Pablo, *Philippines* **169** C13
San Pedro, river, *Ariz., U.S.* **101** V8
San Pedro, *Arg.* **124** E10
San Pedro, *Arg.* **124** L12
San Pedro, *Para.* **122** M10
San Pedro de las Colonias, *Mex.* **108** F10
San Pedro de Macorís, *Dom. Rep.* **111** M20
San Pedro Sula, *Hond.* **109** K17
Sanpoil, river, *Wash., U.S.* **102** B7
San Quintín, *Mex.* **108** B5
San Rafael, river, *Utah, U.S.* **101** N8
San Rafael, *Arg.* **124** L8
San Rafael, *Bol.* **122** J9
San Rafael, *Calif., U.S.* **103** R3
San Rafael, *N. Mex., U.S.* **101** S11
San Rafael, Cabo, *Dom. Rep.* **111** L20
San Rafael del Yuma, *Dom. Rep.* **111** M20
San Remo, *It.* **136** F7
San Roque, *Saipan, N. Mariana Is., U.S.* **196** B5
San Saba, river, *Tex., U.S.* **97** P8
San Saba, *Tex., U.S.* **97** N9
San Sebastián de la Gomera, *Canary Is., Sp.* **184** Q4
San Salvador, *El Salv.* **109** L16
San Salvador (Watling), island, *Bahamas* **111** F14
San Salvador de Jujuy, *Arg.* **124** E9
San Severo, *It.* **136** H11
Sansha, *China* **163** P9
Sanshui, *China* **163** R4
San Simeon, *Calif., U.S.* **103** V5
San Simon, *Ariz., U.S.* **101** V9
Sansui, *China* **163** N1
Santa Ana, island, *Solomon Is.* **197** Q21
Santa Ana, *Bol.* **122** H7
Santa Ana, *Calif., U.S.* **103** X9
Santa Ana, *El Salv.* **109** L16
Santa Ana, *Philippines* **169** B14
Santa Anna, *Tex., U.S.* **97** N8
Santa Bárbara, *Chile* **125** N6
Santa Bárbara, *Mex.* **108** E9
Santa Barbara, island, *Calif., U.S.* **103** Y7
Santa Barbara, *Calif., U.S.* **103** W6
Santa Barbara Channel, *Calif., U.S.* **103** X6
Santa Catalina, island, *Calif., U.S.* **103** Y8
Santa Catalina, island, *Solomon Is.* **197** Q21
Santa Catalina, Gulf of, *Calif., U.S.* **103** Y8
Santa Catarina, *São Tomé and Príncipe* **185** D19
Santa Clara, *Calif., U.S.* **103** S4
Santa Clara, *Cuba* **110** H9
Santa Clara, Isla, *Pac. Oc.* **195** M23
Santa Clotilde, *Peru* **122** D4
Santa Cruz, island, *Calif., U.S.* **103** X7
Santa Cruz, river, *Arg.* **125** V8
Santa Cruz, river, *Ariz., U.S.* **101** W8
Santa Cruz, *Bol.* **122** K8
Santa Cruz, *Braz.* **123** F18
Santa Cruz, *Calif., U.S.* **103** T4
Santa Cruz, *Canary Is., Sp.* **176** C5
Santa Cruz, *Madeira Is., Port.* **184** M3
Santa Cruz, *São Tomé and Príncipe* **185** D20
Santa Cruz, Isla, *Galapagos Is., Ecua.* **195** G21
Santa Cruz Cabrália, *Braz.* **123** J16
Santa Cruz de la Palma, *Canary Is., Sp.* **184** Q4
Santa Cruz del Norte, *Cuba* **110** G7
Santa Cruz del Sur, *Cuba* **110** K11
Santa Cruz de Tenerife, *Canary Is., Sp.* **184** Q5
Santa Cruz do Sul, *Braz.* **122** P11
Santa Elena, *Venez.* **121** E13
Santa Elena, Cabo, *C.R.* **109** N18
Santa Elena Peninsula, *S. Amer.* **118** D1
Santa Fe, *Arg.* **124** K12
Santa Fe, *N. Mex., U.S.* **101** R12
Santa Helena, *Braz.* **122** E10
Santa Inés, Isla, *Chile* **125** X7
Santa Inês, *Braz.* **123** E14
Santa Isabel, island, *Solomon Is.* **197** L17
Santa Isabel, *Arg.* **124** M9
Santa Isabel, Pico de, *Bioko, Eq. Guinea* **184** M7
Santa Lucía, *Arg.* **124** H13
Santa Lucía, *Arg.* **124** J8
Santa Lucía, *Cuba* **110** G5
Santa Lucía, *Uru.* **124** L14
Santa Lucia Range, *Calif., U.S.* **103** U4
Santa Luzia, island, *Cape Verde* **185** B15
Santa Margarita, Isla, *Mex.* **108** F6
Santa Maria, island, *Vanuatu* **198** B2
Santa Maria, *Braz.* **122** D9
Santa Maria, *Braz.* **122** P11
Santa Maria, *Calif., U.S.* **103** W5
Santa Maria, *Cape Verde* **185** B17
Santa María, *Arg.* **124** G9
Santa María, *Peru* **122** D4
Santa Maria, Cabo de, *Angola* **182** E5
Santa Maria, Cape, *Bahamas* **111** F13
Santa María, Cayo, *Cuba* **110** G10
Santa María, Isla, *Galapagos Is., Ecua.* **195** G21
Santa Maria da Vitória, *Braz.* **123** H14
Santa María de Nanay, *Peru* **122** E4
Santa Marta, *Col.* **120** B5
Santa Marta Grande, Cabo de, *Braz.* **123** P13
Santa Monica, *Calif., U.S.* **103** X8
Santa Monica Mountains National Recreation Area, *Calif., U.S.* **103** X7
Sant Ana, *São Tomé and Príncipe* **185** D20
Santana, *Braz.* **123** H15
Santana, *Madeira Is., Port.* **184** M3
Santana do Livramento, *Braz.* **122** P10
Santander, *Sp.* **139** N7
Santander Jiménez, *Mex.* **108** F12
Santanilla, Islas, *Hond.* **109** J19
Sant' Antioco, island, *It.* **136** K7
Santanyí, *Sp.* **139** R11
Santa Paula, *Calif., U.S.* **103** X7
Santaquin, *Utah, U.S.* **100** L7
Santarém, *Braz.* **122** D11
Santarém, *Port.* **139** R4
Santaren Channel, *Bahamas* **110** F9
Santa Rita, *Guam, U.S.* **196** D10
Santa Rita, *Venez.* **120** B7
Santa Rita do Weil, *Braz.* **122** D6
Santa Rosa, *Arg.* **124** M10

Santa Rosa, island, *Calif., U.S.* **103** X6
Santa Rosa, *Arg.* **124** K9
Santa Rosa, *Bol.* **122** G6
Santa Rosa, *Calif., U.S.* **103** R3
Santa Rosa, *Hond.* **109** L16
Santa Rosa, *N. Mex., U.S.* **101** S14
Santa Rosa, *Peru* **122** G5
Santa Rosa, *Peru* **122** J5
Santa Rosa (Gu Achi), *Ariz., U.S.* **101** V7
Santa Rosa, Mount, *Guam, U.S.* **196** B12
Santa Rosa and San Jacinto Mountains National Monument, *Calif., U.S.* **103** Y10
Santa Rosa Beach, *Fla., U.S.* **91** Q3
Santa Rosa Island, *Fla., U.S.* **91** Q2
Santa Rosalía, *Mex.* **108** D6
Santa Rosa Range, *Nev., U.S.* **102** L9
Santa Teresa, *N. Terr., Austral.* **191** T9
Santa Victoria, *Arg.* **124** D11
Santa Vitória do Palmar, *Braz.* **122** Q11
Santa Ynez, *Calif., U.S.* **103** W6
Santa Ynez Mountains, *Calif., U.S.* **103** W6
Santee, river, *S.C., U.S.* **90** L11
San Telmo Point, *N. Amer.* **74** P4
Santiago, *Chile* **124** L7
Santiago, *Dom. Rep.* **111** L18
Santiago, *Pan.* **109** P20
Santiago, Isla, *Galapagos Is., Ecua.* **195** G21
Santiago, Punta, *Bioko, Eq. Guinea* **184** N7
Santiago de Baney, *Bioko, Eq. Guinea* **184** L8
Santiago de Compostela, *Sp.* **139** N5
Santiago de Cuba, *Cuba* **111** K13
Santiago del Estero, *Arg.* **124** G10
Santiago Ixcuintla, *Mex.* **108** G9
Santiago Papasquiaro, *Mex.* **108** F9
Santiago Peak, *Tex., U.S.* **97** Q2
Santigi, *Indonesia* **169** H13
Santo André, *Braz.* **123** M13
Santo Ângelo, *Braz.* **122** P11
Santo Antão, island, *Cape Verde* **185** A15
Santo António, *Cape Verde* **185** D17
Santo António, *São Tomé and Príncipe* **185** B21
Santo Antônio do Içá, *Braz.* **122** D6
Santo Corazón, *Bol.* **122** K9
Santo Domingo, *Dom. Rep.* **111** M19
Santo Domingo, Cay, *Bahamas* **111** J13
Santo Domingo Pueblo, *N. Mex., U.S.* **101** R12
Santop, Mount, *Vanuatu* **198** G3
Santos, *Braz.* **123** M14
Santos Dumont, *Braz.* **122** F6
Santos Plateau, *Atl. Oc.* **217** R7
Santo Tomás, *Peru* **122** J5
Santo Tomé, *Arg.* **124** H14
San Valentín, Monte, *Chile* **125** T6
San Vicente, *Saipan, N. Mariana Is., U.S.* **196** C5
San Vincente del Caguán, *Col.* **120** G5
San Vito, Capo, *It.* **136** L9
Sanya, *China* **163** V1
San Ygnacio, *Tex., U.S.* **97** V8
Sanyuan, *China* **162** G2
São Bento do Norte, *Braz.* **122** E18
São Borja, *Braz.* **122** P10
São Cristóvão, *Braz.* **123** H17
São Félix do Xingu, *Braz.* **122** F12
São Filipe, *Cape Verde* **185** E15
São Francisco, river, *Braz.* **123** J14
São Francisco, Ilha de, *Braz.* **123** N13
São Gabriel, *Braz.* **122** P11
São Gabriel da Cachoeira, *Braz.* **122** C6
São João da Aliança, *Braz.* **123** J13
São João del Rei, *Braz.* **123** L14
São José, Baía de, *Braz.* **123** D15
São José de Anauá, *Braz.* **122** C8
São José dos Campos, *Braz.* **123** M14
São Leopoldo, *Braz.* **122** P12
São Lourenço, Ponta de, *Madeira Is., Port.* **184** M4
São Lourenço do Sul, *Braz.* **122** Q12
São Luís, *Braz.* **123** D15
São Luís, Ilha de, *Braz.* **123** D15
São Manuel *see* Teles Pires, river, *Braz.* **122** F10
São Marcos, Baía de, *Braz.* **123** D15
São Marcos Bay, *S. Amer.* **118** D10
São Mateus, *Braz.* **123** K16
São Miguel do Araguaia, *Braz.* **122** H12
Saona, Isla, *Dom. Rep.* **111** M20
Saône, river, *Fr.* **138** L11
Saonek, *Indonesia* **169** J17
Saoner, *India* **158** K6
São Nicolau, island, *Cape Verde* **185** B16
São Paulo, *Braz.* **123** M13
São Paulo de Olivença, *Braz.* **122** D6
São Raimundo Nonato, *Braz.* **123** G15
São Romão, *Braz.* **122** E6
São Roque, Cabo de, *Braz.* **123** F18
São Sebastião, Cape, *Af.* **174** P10
São Sebastião, Ponta, *Mozambique* **183** H13
São Tiago, island, *Cape Verde* **185** D16
São Tiago, *Cape Verde* **185** D16
São Tomé, island, *São Tomé and Príncipe* **185** D19
São Tomé, *São Tomé and Príncipe* **185** C20
São Tomé, Cabo de, *Braz.* **123** M15
São Tomé and Príncipe, *Atl. Oc.* **184** F5
Saoute, Wādī, *Syr.* **150** L9
São Vicente, island, *Cape Verde* **185** B14
São Vicente, *Madeira Is., Port.* **184** M3
São Vicente, Cabo de, *Port.* **139** S4
Sap, Tonle, *Asia* **146** K11
Sapanca, *Turk.* **148** D6
Sapanjang, island, *Indonesia* **168** M11
Sapele, *Nig.* **181** H13
Sapelo Island, *Ga., U.S.* **91** P9
Şaphane Dağı, *Turk.* **148** F5
Saposoa, *Peru* **122** F3
Sapphire Mountains, *Mont., U.S.* **100** D6
Sappho, *Wash., U.S.* **102** B2
Sapporo, *Jap.* **164** G13
Sapri, *It.* **136** J11
Sapudi, island, *Indonesia* **168** M11
Sapulpa, *Okla., U.S.* **96** F12
Saqqez, *Iran* **152** C10
Sara Adasy, island, *Azerb.* **149** F22
Sarāb, *Iran* **152** B11
Saraburi, *Thai.* **166** M9
Saraféré, *Mali* **176** H8
Saraguro, *Ecua.* **120** L3
Sarahs, *Turkm.* **154** N9
Sarajevo, *Bosn. and Herzg.* **136** G12
Sarakhs, *Iran* **153** B17
Saranac Lake, *N.Y., U.S.* **88** G11
Saranac Lakes, *N.Y., U.S.* **88** G10
Sarangani Islands, *Philippines* **169** G15
Sarangpur, *India* **158** J5
Saransk, *Russ.* **140** G6
Sarapul, *Russ.* **140** H8
Sarasota, *Fla., U.S.* **91** V7
Sarasota Bay, *Fla., U.S.* **91** V7
Saratoga, *Wyo., U.S.* **100** K11
Saratoga Springs, *N.Y., U.S.* **88** J11
Saratov, *Russ.* **140** H6
Sarāvān, *Iran* **153** G18
Sarawak, *Malaysia* **168** H10
Saray, *Turk.* **148** C4
Saray, *Turk.* **149** F18
Sarayköy, *Turk.* **148** G4
Sar Banader, *Afghan.* **157** R3
Sarbāz, *Iran* **153** H17
Sarbīsheh, *Iran* **153** E17
Sarcelle, Passe de la, *New Caledonia, Fr.* **198** E9
Sardar Chah, *Pak.* **157** T4
Sardegna (Sardinia), island, *It.* **136** J7
Sardinia *see* Sardegna, island, *It.* **136** J7
Sardis, ruins, *Turk.* **148** F4
Sardis, *Miss., U.S.* **94** H11
Sardis Lake, *Miss., U.S.* **94** H11
Sar-e Howz, *Afghan.* **156** L4
Sar-e Pol (Sari Pol), *Afghan.* **156** L5
Sargent, *Nebr., U.S.* **99** P5
Sargodha, *Pak.* **157** P10
Sargo Plateau, *Arctic Oc.* **222** H6
Sarh, *Chad* **177** K15
Sarhadd, *Afghan.* **156** K11
Sārī, *Iran* **153** C13
Sariá, island, *Gr.* **137** M17
Sarigan, island, *N. Mariana Is., U.S.* **196** B2
Sarıgöl, *Turk.* **148** G4
Sarıkamış, *Turk.* **149** D17
Sarina, *Qnsld., Austral.* **191** T14
Sarinleey, *Somalia* **179** J16
Sari Pol *see* Sar-e Pol, *Afghan.* **156** L5
Sariwŏn, *N. Korea* **162** E12
Sarıyar Baraji, *Turk.* **148** E7
Sarıyer, *Turk.* **148** C5
Sarız, *Turk.* **148** G11
Sarjektjåkko, peak, *Sw.* **135** E13
Sarkari Tala, *India* **158** F2
Şarkîkaraağaç, *Turk.* **148** G7
Şarkışla, *Turk.* **148** F11
Şarköy, *Turk.* **148** D3
Sarles, *N. Dak., U.S.* **98** D6
Sarmi, *Indonesia* **169** K20
Sarmiento, *Arg.* **125** S8
Särna, *Sw.* **134** J12
Sarny, *Ukr.* **133** H13
Saroma Ko, *Jap.* **164** E15
Saros Körfezi, *Turk.* **148** D3
Sarowbi, *Afghan.* **156** M8
Sarowbi, *Afghan.* **157** P8
Sar Passage, *Palau* **196** P11
Sarqan, *Kaz.* **155** G17
Sarria, *Sp.* **139** P5
Sartène, *Fr.* **139** P13
Sarufutsu, *Jap.* **164** D14
Saruna, *Pak.* **157** V6
Sarupsar, *India* **158** E4
Särur, *Azerb.* **149** E19
Saruu, *Kyrg.* **156** E14
Saryesik-Atyraū Qumy, *Kaz.* **155** G16
Sarygamysh Köli, *Uzb.-Turkm.* **154** J8
Saryözek, *Kaz.* **155** H17
Saryqamys, *Kaz.* **154** G7
Saryqopa Köli, *Kaz.* **154** D11
Sarysay, *Kaz.* **154** E9
Saryshagan, *Kaz.* **155** G15
Sarysu, river, *Kaz.* **154** G12
SaryTash, *Kyrg.* **156** G10
Sarzhal, *Kaz.* **155** D17
Sasalaguan, Mount, *Guam, U.S.* **196** D10
Sasamungga, *Solomon Is.* **197** L15
Sasaram, *India* **158** H9
Sasebo, *Jap.* **165** R3
Saskatchewan, *Can.* **76** L12
Saskatchewan, river, *N. Amer.* **74** G5
Saskatoon, *Sask., Can.* **76** M12
Sasolburg, *S. Af.* **182** J10
Sason, *Turk.* **149** G16
Sasora, *Indonesia* **169** K20
Sassafras Mountain, *S.C., U.S.* **90** J7
Sassandra, *Côte d'Ivoire* **180** H8
Sassari, *It.* **136** J7
Sassnitz, *Ger.* **132** E7
Sasstown, *Liberia* **180** H7
Sasykoli, *Russ.* **140** J5
Sasyqköl, lake, *Kaz.* **155** F18
Sata, *Jap.* **165** T4
Satadougou Tintiba, *Mali* **176** J6
Satala, ruins, *Turk.* **149** E14
Sata Misaki, *Jap.* **165** U4
Satanta, *Kans., U.S.* **99** U4
Satara, *India* **158** M4
Sataua, *Samoa* **198** K1
Satawal, island, *F.S.M.* **196** Q5
Satawan Atoll, *F.S.M.* **196** Q6
Sätbaev, *Kaz.* **154** F12
Satbarwa, *India* **158** H9
Satilla, river, *Ga., U.S.* **91** P6
Satipo, *Peru* **122** H4
Satkania, *Bangladesh* **158** J14
Satna, *India* **158** H7
Sato, *Jap.* **165** T3
Satpura Range, *India* **158** K4
Satu Mare, *Rom.* **137** D14
Satun, *Thai.* **167** S8
Satupa'itea, *Samoa* **198** L2
Sauce, *Arg.* **124** J13
Sauda, *Nor.* **134** L10
Saudárkrókur, *Ice.* **134** E3
Saudi Arabia, *Asia* **152** J8
Saugatuck, *Mich., U.S.* **92** M9
Saugerties, *N.Y., U.S.* **88** L11
Sauk Centre, *Minn., U.S.* **98** J10
Sauk City, *Wis., U.S.* **92** L5
Saukorem, *Indonesia* **169** J18
Sauk Rapids, *Minn., U.S.* **98** J11
Sault Sainte Marie, *Mich., U.S.* **92** F11
Sault Sainte Marie, *Ont., Can.* **77** P17
Saumlaki, *Indonesia* **169** M17
Saunders Coast, *Antarctica* **206** N10
Saupon Point, *Guam, U.S.* **196** B11
Saura, *Kaz.* **154** H5
Saurimo, *Angola* **182** C8
Sausalito, *Calif., U.S.* **103** S3
Sava, river, *Bons. and Herzg.-Yug.* **137** F13
Savage, *Mont., U.S.* **100** C13
Savai'i, island, *Samoa* **198** K2
Savalou, *Benin* **180** G12
Savanna, *Ill., U.S.* **93** N4
Savannah, river, *Ga.-S.C., U.S.* **90** M8
Savannah, *Ga., U.S.* **91** N9
Savannah, *Mo., U.S.* **99** R10
Savannah, *Tenn., U.S.* **95** G13
Savannakhét, *Laos* **166** L11
Savanna-la-Mar, *Jam.* **110** M10
Savaştepe, *Turk.* **148** E3
Save, river, *Mozambique* **182** H12
Säveh, *Iran* **152** C12
Savissivik, *Greenland, Den.* **75** C20
Savo, island, *Solomon Is.* **197** N18
Savona, *It.* **136** F7
Savonlinna, *Fin.* **135** H17
Savoonga, *Alas., U.S.* **104** G10
Savukoski, *Fin.* **135** D15
Savur, *Turk.* **149** H15
Savusavu, *Fiji* **198** G7
Savusavu Bay, *Fiji* **198** H7
Savu Sea, *Indonesia* **169** N14
Sawada, *Jap.* **164** M11
Sawah, *Indonesia* **168** H11
Sawahlunto, *Indonesia* **168** J6
Sawa-i-lau, island, *Fiji* **198** H5
Sawai Madhopur, *India* **158** G5
Sawankhalok, *Thai.* **166** K8
Sawatch Range, *Colo., U.S.* **101** N12
Sawdāḩ, Jabal as, *Lib.* **177** D14
Sawe, *Indonesia* **168** H4
Sawi, *Thai.* **167** Q8
Sawkanah, *Lib.* **177** D14
Şawqirah, *Oman* **153** N15
Şawqirah, Ghubbat, *Oman* **153** N16
Sawtooth National Recreation Area, *Idaho, U.S.* **100** G5
Sawtooth Range, *Idaho, U.S.* **100** G4
Sawu, island, *Indonesia* **169** N14
Saxby Downs, *Qnsld., Austral.* **191** S12
Say, *Niger* **176** J10
Saya de Malha Bank, *Ind. Oc.* **220** H7
Sayanogorsk, *Russ.* **141** L13
Şaydā (Sidon), *Leb.* **150** J6
Sayḩūt, *Yemen* **153** Q13
Saylac, *Somalia* **179** F16
Sayötesh, *Kaz.* **154** H6
Sayram Hu, *China* **160** E6
Sayre, *Okla., U.S.* **96** G8
Sayre, *Pa., U.S.* **88** L8
Saywūn, *Yemen* **152** P11
Sayylyk, *Russ.* **141** E18
Saza'i Kalan, *Afghan.* **156** L5
Sazin, *Pak.* **156** L11
Sbaa, *Alg.* **176** D10
Sebastián Vizcaíno, Bahía, *Mex.* **108** C5
Scammon Bay, *Alas., U.S.* **104** H11
Scandia, *Kans., U.S.* **99** R7
Scandinavia, region, *Eur.* **130** C7
Scarborough, *Trin. & Tobago* **113** N17
Scarborough, *Eng., U.K.* **138** F9
Scatterbreak Channel, *Fiji* **198** G8
Schefferville, *Que., Can.* **77** L20
Schell Creek Range, *Nev., U.S.* **103** Q12
Schenectady, *N.Y., U.S.* **88** J11
Schertz, *Tex., U.S.* **97** R10
Schofield, *Wis., U.S.* **92** H5
Schofield Barracks, *Hawaii, U.S.* **106** D10
Schouten Islands, *P.N.G.* **193** C18
Schroeder, *Minn., U.S.* **98** F13
Schuckmannsburg, *Namibia* **182** F9
Schulenburg, *Tex., U.S.* **97** R12
Schuyler, *Nebr., U.S.* **99** P8
Schwerin, *Ger.* **132** F6
Sciacca, *It.* **136** L9
Scilly, Isles of, *Eng., U.K.* **138** J6
Scioto, river, *Ohio, U.S.* **93** S13
Scipio, *Utah, U.S.* **100** M7
Scobey, *Mont., U.S.* **100** A12
Scofield Reservoir, *Utah, U.S.* **100** M8
Scooba, *Miss., U.S.* **95** K13
Scotland, *U.K.* **138** E7
Scotland, *S. Dak., U.S.* **98** M7
Scotland Neck, *N.C., U.S.* **90** G13
Scott, Mount, *Oreg., U.S.* **102** J4
Scott Base, station, *Antarctica* **207** N13
Scott City, *Kans., U.S.* **99** T4
Scott City, *Mo., U.S.* **99** U16
Scott Coast, *Antarctica* **207** N14
Scott Glacier, *Antarctica* **207** K21
Scott Islands, *B.C., Can.* **76** L7
Scott Point, *Mich., U.S.* **92** G9
Scottsbluff, *Nebr., U.S.* **99** N1
Scotts Bluff National Monument, *Nebr., U.S.* **99** P1
Scottsboro, *Ala., U.S.* **95** G16
Scottsburg, *Ind., U.S.* **93** T9
Scottsdale, *Ariz., U.S.* **101** U7
Scottsville, *Ky., U.S.* **95** D16
Scottville, *Mich., U.S.* **92** K9
Scranton, *Pa., U.S.* **88** M9
Scribner, *Nebr., U.S.* **99** P8
Scrubby Creek, *Qnsld., Austral.* **191** P12
Scyros *see* Skíros, island, *Gr.* **137** K15
Seadrift, *Tex., U.S.* **97** T12
Seaford, *Del., U.S.* **90** D14
Seagraves, *Tex., U.S.* **96** L4
Sea Island, *Ga., U.S.* **91** P9
Sea Islands, *U.S.* **79** L19
Seal, river, *Man., Can.* **77** K14
Seal, Cape, *S. Af.* **182** M9
Sea Lake, *Vic., Austral.* **191** Y11
Seal Cay, *Bahamas* **111** H13
Seal Cays, *Turks and Caicos Is., U.K.* **111** J17
Sealevel, *N.C., U.S.* **90** J14
Sealy, *Tex., U.S.* **97** R13
Searchlight, *Nev., U.S.* **103** V12
Searcy, *Ark., U.S.* **94** G9
Searles Lake, *Calif., U.S.* **103** V9
Seaside, *Oreg., U.S.* **102** E2
Seaside Park, *N.J., U.S.* **88** P11
Seaton Glacier, *Antarctica* **207** C19
Seattle, *Wash., U.S.* **102** C4
Sebago Lake, *Me., U.S.* **89** G15
Sebakor, Teluk, *Indonesia* **193** C14
Sebastian, *Fla., U.S.* **91** U10
Sebastian, Cape, *Oreg., U.S.* **102** K1
Sebastián Vizcaíno Bay, *N. Amer.* **74** L3
Sebastopol, *Calif., U.S.* **103** R3
Sebatik, island, *Indonesia* **168** G12
Sebeka, *Minn., U.S.* **98** G10
Seben, *Turk.* **148** D7
Sebeş, *Rom.* **137** E15
Sebewaing, *Mich., U.S.* **92** K12
Şebinkarahisar, *Turk.* **149** E13
Sebring, *Fla., U.S.* **91** U9
Sebuyau, *Malaysia* **168** H10
Sechura, Bahía de, *Peru* **122** F1
Sechura Desert, *S. Amer.* **118** E1
Second Cataract, *Sudan* **178** C12

Second Mesa, *Ariz., U.S.* **101** R8
Secos, Ilhéus (Ilhéus do Rombo), *Cape Verde* **185** D15
Secretary Island, *N.Z.* **193** Q15
Sécure, river, *Bol.* **122** J7
Security, *Colo., U.S.* **101** N13
Sedalia, *Mo., U.S.* **99** T12
Sedan, *Kans., U.S.* **99** V9
Seddon, *N.Z.* **193** N18
Sedeh, *Iran* **153** D16
Sedom, *Israel* **151** P6
Sedona, *Ariz., U.S.* **101** S7
Sedro Woolley, *Wash., U.S.* **102** A4
Seeheim, *Namibia* **182** K7
Seferihisar, *Turk.* **148** F2
Sefid Kers, mountains, *Afghan.* **156** J9
Sefid Kuh Mountains (Paropamisus Range), *Afghan.* **156** M3
Seg, Lake, *Eur.* **130** C10
Segamat, *Malaysia* **167** U10
Segbana, *Benin* **180** F12
Segezha, *Russ.* **140** D7
Seghe, *Solomon Is.* **197** M16
Ségou, *Mali* **176** H7
Segovia, *Sp.* **139** Q7
Seguam Island, *Alas., U.S.* **104** Q7
Séguéla, *Côte d'Ivoire* **180** G8
Seguin, *Tex., U.S.* **97** R10
Seguntur, *Indonesia* **168** H12
Sehwan, *Pak.* **157** V7
Seiling, *Okla., U.S.* **96** F9
Seinäjoki, *Fin.* **135** H15
Seine, river, *Fr.* **138** K9
Sekerangi Passage, *Penrhyn, Cook Is., N.Z.* **199** A17
Sekikawa, *Jap.* **164** M12
Sekondi-Takoradi, *Ghana* **180** H10
Sek'ot'a, *Eth.* **179** E15
Sekseüil, *Kaz.* **154** F10
Selah, *Wash., U.S.* **102** D6
Selaru, island, *Indonesia* **169** M17
Selatan, Bunguran *see* Natuna Selatan, Kepulauan, *Indonesia* **168** H9
Selawik, *Alas., U.S.* **105** E13
Selawik Lake, *Alas., U.S.* **105** E13
Selayar, island, *Indonesia* **169** L13
Selby, *S. Dak., U.S.* **98** J5
Selden, *Kans., U.S.* **99** S4
Seldovia, *Alas., U.S.* **105** K16
Selendi, *Turk.* **148** F4
Selenga, river, *Russ.* **141** L15
Selenge, river, *Mongolia* **160** C11
Selfoss, *Ice.* **134** F2
Selfridge, *N. Dak., U.S.* **98** H4
Seligman, *Ariz., U.S.* **101** S6
Selima Oasis, *Sudan* **178** C12
Selkirk Mountains, *Idaho, U.S.* **100** A3
Sellheim, *Qnsld., Austral.* **191** S13
Sells, *Ariz., U.S.* **101** V7
Selma, *Ala., U.S.* **95** L15
Selma, *Calif., U.S.* **103** T6
Selma, *N.C., U.S.* **90** H12
Selmer, *Tenn., U.S.* **95** G13
Selvas, region, *S. Amer.* **118** E3
Selway, river, *Idaho, U.S.* **100** D4
Selwyn, *Qnsld., Austral.* **191** S11
Selwyn Mountains, *Yukon Terr., Can.* **76** F9
Selwyn Strait, *Vanuatu* **198** D3
Semarang, *Indonesia* **168** M9
Sembé, *Congo* **181** K17
Şemdinli, *Turk.* **149** H19
Semeru, peak, *Indonesia* **168** M10
Semey (Semipalatinsk), *Kaz.* **155** D17
Semichi Islands, *Alas., U.S.* **104** N2
Seminoe Dam, *Wyo., U.S.* **100** J11
Seminoe Reservoir, *Wyo., U.S.* **100** J11
Seminole, *Okla., U.S.* **96** G12
Seminole, *Tex., U.S.* **96** L4
Seminole, Lake, *Fla.-Ga., U.S.* **91** Q4
Semiozernoe, *Kaz.* **154** C11
Semipalatinsk *see* Semey, *Kaz.* **155** D17
Semipalatinsk Nuclear Test Range, *Kaz.* **155** D16
Semisopochnoi Island, *Alas., U.S.* **104** P4
Semnān, *Iran* **153** C14
Semporna, *Malaysia* **168** G12
Sen, river, *Cambodia* **166** M11
Senaja, *Malaysia* **168** F12
Senaki, *Rep. of Georgia* **149** B16
Sena Madureira, *Braz.* **122** F6
Senanga, *Zambia* **182** F9
Senatobia, *Miss., U.S.* **94** H11
Sendai, *Jap.* **164** L13
Sendai, *Jap.* **165** T4
Sendhwa, *India* **158** K4
Senduruhan, *Indonesia* **168** J9
Seneca, *Kans., U.S.* **99** R9
Seneca, *Oreg., U.S.* **102** H7
Seneca, *S.C., U.S.* **90** K6
Seneca Falls, *N.Y., U.S.* **88** J7
Sénégal, river, *Mauritania-Senegal* **176** G5
Senegal, *Af.* **176** H5
Senhor do Bonfim, *Braz.* **123** G16
Senj, *Croatia* **136** F11
Senja, island, *Nor.* **134** D12
Senmonorom, *Cambodia* **167** N13
Sennar, *Sudan* **179** E13
Senneterre, *Que., Can.* **77** P18
Sens, *Fr.* **138** K10
Sensuntepeque, *El Salv.* **109** L16
Sentinel, *Okla., U.S.* **96** G8
Sentinel Range, *Antarctica* **206** H8
Senyavin Islands, *F.S.M.* **196** Q8
Seoni, *India* **158** J7
Seoul *see* Sŏul, *S. Korea* **162** E13
Sepasu, *Indonesia* **168** J12
Sepi, *Solomon Is.* **197** M18
Sepik, river, *P.N.G.* **193** C18
Sept-Îles, *Que., Can.* **77** M21
Sepupa, *Botswana* **182** G8
Sequim, *Wash., U.S.* **102** B3
Sequoia National Park, *Calif., U.S.* **103** T8
Serang, *Indonesia* **168** L8
Serasan, island, *Indonesia* **168** H9
Serbia, *Yug.* **137** F14
Serebryansk, *Kaz.* **155** D18
Şereflikoçhisar, *Turk.* **148** F9
Seremban, *Malaysia* **167** U9
Serengeti Plain, *Tanzania* **179** K13
Sergeya, Ostrova, *Russ.* **141** D13
Sergino, *Russ.* **140** G10
Sergiyev Posad, *Russ.* **140** F6
Serian, *Malaysia* **168** H9
Serik, *Turk.* **148** H6
Seringa, Serra da, *Braz.* **122** F12
Serkovo, *Russ.* **141** G13
Sermata, island, *Indonesia* **169** M16
Sermata, Kepulauan, *Indonesia* **169** M16
Sernyy Zavod, *Turkm.* **154** L8
Serov, *Russ.* **140** H9
Serowe, *Botswana* **182** H10
Serpa, *Port.* **139** S5
Serpentine Lakes, *Austral.* **190** H7
Serpent Island, *Mauritius* **185** E21
Serpent's Mouth, channel, *Trin. & Tobago* **113** Q16
Serpukhov, *Russ.* **140** F6
Serra do Navio, *Braz.* **122** C12
Serres, *Gr.* **137** J15
Serrezuela, *Arg.* **124** J9
Serrinha, *Braz.* **123** H16
Sertão, region, *S. Amer.* **118** F10
Serti, *Nig.* **181** G15
Serui, *Indonesia* **169** K19
Sesfontein, *Namibia* **182** G5
Sesheke, *Zambia* **182** F9
Setana, *Jap.* **164** G12
Sete Lagoas, *Braz.* **123** K14
Sete Quedas Falls, *S. Amer.* **118** J7
Sétif, *Alg.* **176** A11
Seto, *Jap.* **165** P10
Setouchi, *Jap.* **165** W3
Settat, *Mor.* **176** B8
Setté Cama, *Gabon* **181** M15
Settlement, *Kwajalein Atoll, Marshall Is.* **196** N5
Settlement, *Wake I., U.S.* **196** F8
Setúbal, *Port.* **139** R4
Seul, Lac, *Ont., Can.* **77** N15
Seul Choix Point, *Mich., U.S.* **92** G9
Sevan, *Arm.* **149** D19
Sevana Lich, *Arm.* **149** D19
Sevastopol', *Ukr.* **133** M16
Seven Islands Bay, *Nfld., Can.* **77** J20
Severn, river, *Ont., Can.* **77** L16
Severn, *S. Af.* **182** J9
Severnaya Dvina, river, *Russ.* **140** E8
Severnaya Zemlya (North Land), *Russ.* **141** C14
Severnyy, *Russ.* **140** F11
Severobaykal'sk, *Russ.* **141** K16
Severodvinsk, *Russ.* **140** E8
Severo Kuril'sk, *Russ.* **141** G23
Severomorsk, *Russ.* **140** D9
Severo Sibirskaya Nizmennost', *Russ.* **141** F13
Sevi, *Russ.* **141** L13
Sevier, river, *Utah, U.S.* **100** M6
Sevier Desert, *Utah, U.S.* **100** M6
Sevier Lake, *Utah, U.S.* **101** N6
Sevilla, *Col.* **120** F4
Sevilla (Seville), *Sp.* **139** S6
Seward, *Alas., U.S.* **105** K16
Seward, *Nebr., U.S.* **99** Q8
Seward Peninsula, *Alas., U.S.* **104** F12
Sewell, *Chile* **124** L7
Seychelles, *Ind. Oc.* **184** G9
Seydi, *Turkm.* **154** L10
Seydişehir, *Turk.* **148** H7
Seydisfjördur, *Ice.* **134** F4
Seyfe Gölü, *Turk.* **148** F9
Seyhan, river, *Turk.* **148** H10
Seyhan Barajı, *Turk.* **148** H10
Seyitgazi, *Turk.* **148** E6
Seylla Glacier, *Antarctica* **207** F19
Seymchan, *Russ.* **141** E20
Seymour, *Ind., U.S.* **93** S9
Seymour, *Iowa, U.S.* **99** Q12
Seymour, *Tex., U.S.* **96** K8
Seymour, *Vic., Austral.* **191** Z12
Seymour, *Wis., U.S.* **92** J6
Sfax, *Tun.* **177** B13
's Gravenhage (The Hague), *Neth.* **138** H11
Sha, river, *China* **163** P7
Shabwah, *Yemen* **152** Q11
Shache, *China* **160** G4
Shackleton Coast, *Antarctica* **207** L13
Shackleton Ice Shelf, *Antarctica* **207** K21
Shackleton Range, *Antarctica* **206** E11
Shadehill Reservoir, *S. Dak., U.S.* **98** H3
Shaduzup, *Myanmar* **166** E6
Shafter, *Nev., U.S.* **102** M12
Shafter, *Tex., U.S.* **97** Q1
Shafter, *Tex., U.S.* **97** X4
Shageluk, *Alas., U.S.* **105** H13
Shaghan, river, *Kaz.* **154** F8
Shaghan, *Kaz.* **155** D17
Shag Rocks, *S. Amer.* **118** R9
Shahbā' (Philippopolis), *Syr.* **150** K8
Shah Bandar, *Pak.* **157** X7
Shahdadkot, *Pak.* **157** T7
Shahdadpur, *Pak.* **157** V7
Shahdol, *India* **158** J8
Shahgarh, *India* **158** F2
Shaḥḥāt (Cyrene), *Lib.* **177** B16
Shahjahanpur, *India* **158** F7
Shah Juy, *Afghan.* **157** P6
Shah Malan, *Afghan.* **157** Q4
Shah Maqsud Range, *Afghan.* **157** P5
Shahpur, *India* **158** M5
Shahpur, *Pak.* **157** P10
Shahpur Chakar, *Pak.* **157** V7
Shahr-e Bābak, *Iran* **153** F14
Shahrig, *Pak.* **157** R6
Shāhrūd, *Iran* **153** C14
Shaighalu, *Pak.* **157** Q7
Shajapur, *India* **158** J5
Shakhbuz, *Azerb.* **149** E19
Shakhtakhty, *Azerb.* **149** F19
Shakhtersk, *Russ.* **141** J21
Shaktoolik, *Alas., U.S.* **104** G12
Shallowater, *Tex., U.S.* **96** K5
Shalqar, *Kaz.* **154** F9
Shalqar Köli, *Kaz.* **154** D6
Shām, Jabal ash, *Oman* **153** K16
Shamattawa, *Man., Can.* **77** L15
Shambe, *Sudan* **178** G12
Shamkhor, *Azerb.* **149** D20
Shammar, Jabal, *Saudi Arabia* **152** G7
Shamokin, *Pa., U.S.* **88** N8
Shamrock, *Tex., U.S.* **96** G7
Shamva, *Zimb.* **182** F12
Shandan, *China* **160** H11
Shandong Bandao, *China* **162** F9
Shandur Pass, *Pak.* **156** L10
Shangcai, *China* **162** J5
Shangcheng, *China* **162** K6
Shangchuan Dao, *China* **163** S4
Shangdu, *China* **162** B5
Shanghai, *China* **162** K10
Shanghang, *China* **163** Q6
Shangnan, *China* **162** H3
Shangombo, *Zambia* **182** F8
Shangqiu, *China* **162** H6
Shangrao, *China* **162** M7
Shangshui, *China* **161** K15
Shangxian, *China* **162** H2
Shangyi, *China* **162** C5
Shangyou, *China* **163** P5
Shaniko, *Oreg., U.S.* **102** G5
Shannon, river, *Ire.* **138** G5
Shantar Islands, *Asia* **146** D12
Shantarskiye Ostrova, *Russ.* **141** H20
Shantou (Swatow), *China* **163** R6
Shanxian, *China* **162** H6
Shanyang, *China* **162** H2
Shanyin, *China* **162** D5
Shanyincheng, *China* **162** D5
Shaoguan, *China* **163** Q4
Shaowu, *China* **163** N7
Shaoxing, *China* **162** L9
Shaoyang, *China* **163** N3
Shapa, *China* **163** S3
Shaqrā', *Saudi Arabia* **152** J10
Shaqrā', *Yemen* **152** R10
Shar, *Kaz.* **155** D17
Shār, Jabal, *Saudi Arabia* **152** G5
Sharan, *Afghan.* **157** N7
Sharbaqty, *Kaz.* **155** C16
Sharbatāt, *Oman* **153** N15
Sharbatāt, Ra's ash, *Oman* **153** N16
Sharhulsan, *Mongolia* **160** E12
Shari, *Jap.* **164** E16
Sharjah, *U.A.E.* **153** J15
Shark Bay, *Austral.* **190** G1
Sharlawuk, *Turkm.* **154** L7
Sharm el Sheikh, *Egypt* **151** U4
Sharon, *Pa., U.S.* **88** M3
Sharon Springs, *Kans., U.S.* **99** S3
Sharpe, Lake, *S. Dak., U.S.* **98** L5
Sharuhen, ruins, *Israel* **151** N4
Sharwayn, Ra's, *Yemen* **153** Q13
Shar'ya, *Russ.* **140** F7
Shashe, river, *Botswana-Zimb.* **182** H11
Shashi, *China* **162** L4
Shasta, Mount, *Calif., U.S.* **102** M4
Shasta Lake, *Calif., U.S.* **102** M4
Shatskiy Rise, *Pac. Oc.* **218** F7
Shatt al Arab, river, *Iran-Iraq* **152** F11
Shattuck, *Okla., U.S.* **96** F7
Shaumyan, *Azerb.* **149** D20
Shaumyani, *Rep. of Georgia* **149** C18
Shaunavon, *Sask., Can.* **76** N11
Shaw, *Miss., U.S.* **94** J10
Shawano, *Wis., U.S.* **92** J6
Shawinigan, *Que., Can.* **77** P19
Shawnee, *Kans., U.S.* **99** S10
Shawnee, *Okla., U.S.* **96** G11
Shawnee, *Wyo., U.S.* **100** H13
Shaxian, *China* **163** P7
Shaybārā, island, *Saudi Arabia* **152** J5
Shay Gap, *W. Austral., Austral.* **191** S3
Shaykh 'Uthmān, *Yemen* **152** R9
Shaymak, *Taj.* **156** J12
Shchūchīnsk, *Kaz.* **155** C13
Shebar Pass, *Afghan.* **156** M7
Shebele, river, *Af.* **174** J11
Shebelē, Wabē, *Eth.* **179** H16
Sheberghan, *Afghan.* **156** K5
Shebir, *Kaz.* **154** G6
Sheboygan, *Wis., U.S.* **92** K7
Sheboygan Falls, *Wis., U.S.* **92** K7
Sheep Mountain, *Colo., U.S.* **100** L11
Sheep Range, *Nev., U.S.* **103** T12
Shefar'am, *Israel* **150** K5
Sheffield, *Ala., U.S.* **95** G14
Sheffield, *Tex., U.S.* **97** P5
Sheffield, *Eng., U.K.* **138** G8
Shekhupura, *Pak.* **157** Q12
Shelbina, *Mo., U.S.* **99** R13
Shelburne, *N.S., Can.* **77** Q22
Shelby, *Mich., U.S.* **92** K9
Shelby, *Miss., U.S.* **94** J10
Shelby, *Mont., U.S.* **100** B7
Shelby, *N.C., U.S.* **90** J8
Shelby, *Ohio, U.S.* **93** P13
Shelbyville, *Ill., U.S.* **93** S6
Shelbyville, *Ind., U.S.* **93** S9
Shelbyville, *Ky., U.S.* **95** B17
Shelbyville, *Tenn., U.S.* **95** F15
Sheldon, *Iowa, U.S.* **98** M9
Sheldon Point, *Alas., U.S.* **104** H11
Shelek, *Kaz.* **155** H17
Shelikhova, Zaliv, *Russ.* **141** E21
Shelikof Strait, *Alas., U.S.* **105** L15
Shelikhov Gulf, *Asia* **146** C12
Shell Beach, *Guyana* **121** C14
Shelley, *Idaho, U.S.* **100** H7
Shell Lake, *Wis., U.S.* **92** G2
Shellman, *Ga., U.S.* **91** P5
Shelter Cove, *Calif., U.S.* **103** N1
Shelton, *Nebr., U.S.* **99** Q6
Shelton, *Wash., U.S.* **102** C3
Shemakha, *Azerb.* **149** D22
Shemgang, *Bhutan* **158** F13
Shemonaīkha, *Kaz.* **155** D18
Shemya Island, *Alas., U.S.* **104** N2
Shenandoah, river, *Va., U.S.* **90** D11
Shenandoah, *Iowa, U.S.* **99** Q9
Shenandoah, *Pa., U.S.* **88** N8
Shenandoah, *Va., U.S.* **90** D11
Shenandoah National Park, *Va., U.S.* **90** D11
Shenchi, *China* **162** D4
Shendam, *Nig.* **181** G15
Shengxian, *China* **162** M9
Shenmu, *China* **162** D3
Shennongjia, *China* **162** K3
Shenqiu, *China* **162** J6
Shenyang, *China* **162** B11
Shenzhen, *China* **163** S5
Sheoganj, *India* **158** H3
Sheopur, *India* **158** G5
Shepetivka, *Ukr.* **133** H13
Shepherd, *Ill., U.S.* **93** R3
Shepherd Islands, *Vanuatu* **198** E3
Shepparton, *Vic., Austral.* **191** Y12
Sherbrooke, *Que., Can.* **77** P20
Sherburn, *Minn., U.S.* **98** L10
Shereiq, *Sudan* **179** C13
Sheridan, *Ark., U.S.* **94** H8
Sheridan, *Mont., U.S.* **100** E7
Sheridan, *Wyo., U.S.* **100** F11
Sheridan, Cape, *Nunavut, Can.* **77** A16
Sherkaly, *Russ.* **140** G10
Sherlovaya, *Russ.* **141** L17
Sherman, *Tex., U.S.* **96** K12
Sherman Mills, *Me., U.S.* **89** D18
Sherman Peak, *U.S.* **78** E7

Sherobod, *Uzb.* **154** M12
Sherridon, *Man., Can.* **77** L13
Sherwood, *N. Dak., U.S.* **98** D4
Shetland Islands, *Scot., U.K.* **138** B8
Shetpe, *Kaz.* **154** H6
Shexian, *China* **162** L8
Sheyang (Hede), *China* **162** H9
Sheyenne, river, *N. Dak., U.S.* **98** F7
Sheyenne, *N. Dak., U.S.* **98** F6
Sheykh Sho'eyb *see* Lāvān, island, *Iran* **153** H13
Shḩīm, *Leb.* **150** J6
Shiashkotan, island, *Russ.* **141** H23
Shibām, *Yemen* **152** P11
Shibata, *Jap.* **164** M12
Shibecha, *Jap.* **164** F16
Shibetsu, *Jap.* **164** E14
Shibetsu, *Jap.* **164** F16
Shibushi Wan, *Jap.* **165** T5
Shicheng, *China* **163** P6
Shidao, *China* **162** F10
Shidler, *Okla., U.S.* **96** E12
Shīeli, *Kaz.* **154** H12
Shiguaigou, *China* **162** C3
Shiḩan, *Yemen* **153** N13
Shihezi, *China* **160** E7
Shijiazhuang, *China* **162** E5
Shikarpur, *India* **158** G9
Shikarpur, *Pak.* **157** T7
Shikine Shima, *Jap.* **165** Q12
Shikoku, island, *Jap.* **165** S7
Shikotan, island, *Russ.* **141** K23
Shikotsu Ko, *Jap.* **164** G13
Shili, *Kaz.* **154** D10
Shiliguri, *India* **158** G11
Shiliu *see* Changjiang, *China* **163** U1
Shilka, *Russ.* **141** L17
Shilla, peak, *India* **157** P15
Shillong, *India* **158** G13
Shiloh National Military Park, *Tenn., U.S.* **95** G13
Shilou, *China* **162** F3
Shimabara, *Jap.* **165** S4
Shimada, *Jap.* **165** Q11
Shima Hantō, *Jap.* **165** Q10
Shimanovsk, *Russ.* **141** K19
Shimen, *China* **162** L3
Shimizu, *Jap.* **164** F14
Shimizu, *Jap.* **165** Q11
Shimoda, *Jap.* **165** Q11
Shimoga, *India* **159** P4
Shimokoshiki, *Jap.* **165** T3
Shimonoseki, *Jap.* **165** R5
Shimono Shima, *Jap.* **165** Q3
Shinapaaru, *Rota I., N. Mariana Is., U.S.* **196** D8
Shināş, *Oman* **153** J15
Shindand, *Afghan.* **157** N2
Shiner, *Tex., U.S.* **97** R11
Shingbwiyang, *Myanmar* **166** D6
Shingphel, *Bhutan* **158** F13
Shingū, *Jap.* **165** R9
Shinjō, *Jap.* **164** L12
Shinkay, *Afghan.* **157** Q6
Shinkay Hills, *Afghan.* **157** P7
Shinkolobwe, *Dem. Rep. of the Congo* **178** N11
Shinnston, *W. Va., U.S.* **90** C9
Shinonoi, *Jap.* **165** N11
Shinyanga, *Tanzania* **179** L13
Shiono Misaki, *Jap.* **165** R9
Shiping, *China* **160** P11
Ship Island, *Miss., U.S.* **94** P12
Shipki La, *India* **158** D7
Shippensburg, *Pa., U.S.* **88** P6
Ship Rock, *N. Mex., U.S.* **101** Q10
Shiprock, *N. Mex., U.S.* **101** Q10
Shipu, *China* **162** M10
Shipwreck Beach, *Hawaii, U.S.* **107** G15
Shiquan, *China* **162** J1
Shiquanhe, *China* **160** J4
Shirakami Misaki, *Jap.* **164** H12
Shirase Coast, *Antarctica* **206** M10
Shirase Glacier, *Antarctica* **207** C17
Shīrāz, *Iran* **153** F13
Shire, river, *Malawi* **183** F13
Shireet, *Mongolia* **161** E13
Shiren, *China* **162** B13
Shiretoko Misaki, *Jap.* **164** E16
Shiriya Zaki, *Jap.* **164** H13
Shir Khan, *Afghan.* **156** K7
Shīr Kūh, *Iran* **153** E14
Shiroishi, *Jap.* **164** M13
Shirone, *Jap.* **164** M11
Shirshov Ridge, *Pac. Oc.* **218** C9
Shishaldin Volcano, *Alas., U.S.* **104** P11
Shishmaref, *Alas., U.S.* **104** E11
Shishou, *China* **162** L4
Shitai, *China* **162** L7
Shiv, *India* **158** G2
Shivpuri, *India* **158** H6
Shivwits Plateau, *Ariz., U.S.* **101** R5
Shixian, *China* **162** A14
Shiyan, *China* **162** J3
Shizhu, *China* **162** L1
Shizugawa, *Jap.* **164** L13
Shizuishan, *China* **160** G12
Shizuishan, *China* **162** D1
Shizunai, *Jap.* **164** G14
Shizuoka, *Jap.* **165** Q11
Shkin, *Afghan.* **157** P8
Shkodër, *Alban.* **137** H13
Shmidta, Ostrov, *Russ.* **141** C14
Shoghot, *Pak.* **156** L10
Sholapur, *India* **158** M5
Shollar, *Azerb.* **149** C22
Shonian Harbor, *Palau* **196** P11
Shonzhy, *Kaz.* **155** H17
Shorkot, *Pak.* **157** Q10
Shorobe, *Botswana* **182** G9
Shortland, island, *Solomon Is.* **197** L14
Shortland Islands, *Solomon Is.* **197** L14
Shosambetsu, *Jap.* **164** E13
Shoshone, river, *Wyo., U.S.* **100** F10
Shoshone, *Calif., U.S.* **103** U10
Shoshone, *Idaho, U.S.* **100** H5
Shoshone Falls, *U.S.* **78** E6
Shoshone Lake, *Wyo., U.S.* **100** G8
Shoshone Mountain, *Nev., U.S.* **103** T10
Shoshone Mountains, *Nev., U.S.* **103** Q9
Shoshone Range, *Nev., U.S.* **103** Q9
Shoshoni, *Wyo., U.S.* **100** H10
Shostka, *Ukr.* **133** G15
Shotor Khun Pass, *Afghan.* **156** M4
Shoval, *Israel* **151** N5
Shōwa, *Jap.* **164** K12
Show Low, *Ariz., U.S.* **101** T9
Shpola, *Ukr.* **133** J15
Shreveport, *La., U.S.* **94** L6
Shroud Cay, *Bahamas* **110** E12
Shū, river, *Kaz.* **155** H14
Shu'ab, Ra's, *Yemen* **153** R14
Shuangcheng, *China* **161** D17
Shuangchengzi, *China* **160** G10
Shuangliao, *China* **161** E16
Shuangliao, *China* **162** A11
Shuangyang, *China* **162** A12
Shuangyashan, *China* **161** C18
Shubarqudyq, *Kaz.* **154** E8
Shucheng, *China* **162** K7
Shukpa Kunzang, *India* **156** M15
Shule, river, *China* **160** G9
Shulgareh, *Afghan.* **156** K6
Shumagin Islands, *Alas., U.S.* **105** P13
Shumanay, *Uzb.* **154** J9
Shumen, *Bulg.* **137** G17
Shumshu, island, *Russ.* **141** G23
Shunchang, *China* **163** P7
Shungay, *Kaz.* **154** E4
Shungnak, *Alas., U.S.* **105** E14
Shuoxian, *China* **162** D4
Shuqualak, *Miss., U.S.* **95** K13
Shuraabad, *Azerb.* **149** C23
Shūrāb, *Iran* **153** D15
Shurakian, *Afghan.* **157** P4
Shurchi, *Uzb.* **154** M12
Shūr Gaz, *Iran* **153** G16
Shur Tappeh, *Afghan.* **156** K6
Shurugwi, *Zimb.* **182** G11
Shūsf, *Iran* **153** E17
Shūshtar, *Iran* **152** E11
Shuyak Island, *Alas., U.S.* **105** L15
Shuyang, *China* **162** H8
Shwebo, *Myanmar* **166** G6
Shwedaung, *Myanmar* **166** J5
Shwegu, *Myanmar* **166** F6
Shwegyin, *Myanmar* **166** K6
Shweli, river, *Myanmar* **166** F6
Shymkent, *Kaz.* **155** J13
Shyngghyrlau, *Kaz.* **154** D7
Shyok, river, *Pak.* **156** L13
Shyok, *India* **156** M15
Sia, *Indonesia* **169** M19
Siahan Range, *Pak.* **157** U4
Sialkot, *Pak.* **157** P12
Siantan, island, *Indonesia* **168** H8
Siapa, river, *Venez.* **120** G11
Siargao, island, *Philippines* **169** E15
Siau, island, *Indonesia* **169** H15
Šiauliai, *Lith.* **135** M16
Sibay, *Russ.* **140** J8
Šibenik, *Croatia* **136** G11
Siberia, region, *Russ.* **141** H13
Siberut, island, *Indonesia* **168** J5
Siberut, Selat, *Indonesia* **168** J5
Sibi, *Pak.* **157** S7
Sibidiro, *P.N.G.* **193** E18
Sibigo, *Indonesia* **168** H4
Sibiti, *Congo* **181** M16
Sibiu, *Rom.* **137** E15
Sibley, *Iowa, U.S.* **98** M9
Siboa, *Indonesia* **169** J13
Sibolga, *Indonesia* **168** H5
Sibsagar, *India* **158** F15
Sibu, *Malaysia* **167** U16
Sibuco, *Philippines* **169** F14
Sibut, *Cen. Af. Rep.* **178** H9
Sibutu Passage, *Philippines* **169** G13
Sibuyan, island, *Philippines* **169** D14
Sibuyan Sea, *Philippines* **169** D14
Sicasica, *Bol.* **122** K6
Sichon, *Thai.* **167** Q8
Sichuan Basin, *Asia* **146** H10
Sicily, island, *It.* **136** L10
Sicily, Strait of, *It.* **136** L8
Sicuani, *Peru* **122** J5
Sidas, *Indonesia* **168** J9
Siddhapur, *India* **158** H3
Siddipet, *India* **158** M6
Side, ruins, *Turk.* **148** J6
Sîdi Barrâni, *Egypt* **177** C17
Sidi Bel Abbès, *Alg.* **176** A10
Sidi Ifni, *Mor.* **176** C7
Sidmouth, Cape, *Austral.* **190** B12
Sidney, *Iowa, U.S.* **99** Q9
Sidney, *Mont., U.S.* **100** C13
Sidney, *N.Y., U.S.* **88** K9
Sidney, *Nebr., U.S.* **99** P2
Sidney, *Ohio, U.S.* **93** Q11
Sidney Lanier, Lake, *Ga., U.S.* **90** K6
Sidon *see* Şaydā, *Leb.* **150** J6
Sidorovsk, *Russ.* **140** G12
Sidra, Gulf of, *Af.* **174** D7
Siedlce, *Pol.* **132** G11
Siegen, *Ger.* **132** G5
Siem Pang, *Cambodia* **166** M12
Siem Reap, *Cambodia* **167** N11
Siena, *It.* **136** G9
Sierra Blanca, *Tex., U.S.* **97** V3
Sierra Blanca Peak, *N. Mex., U.S.* **101** U13
Sierra Colorada, *Arg.* **125** Q8
Sierra Leone, *Af.* **180** F6
Sierra Madre del Sur, *Mex.* **108** J10
Sierra Madre Occidental, *Mex.* **108** D10
Sierra Madre Oriental, *Mex.* **108** D8
Sierra Maestra, *Cuba* **110** K11
Sierra Mojada, *Mex.* **108** E10
Sierra Vista, *Ariz., U.S.* **101** W8
Sífnos, island, *Gr.* **137** L16
Sigatoka, *Fiji* **198** J5
Sigavé (Leava), *Wallis and Futuna, Fr.* **198** E11
Sigave, Anse de, *Wallis and Futuna, Fr.* **198** E11
Sighetul Marmatiei, *Rom.* **137** D15
Sighişoara, *Rom.* **137** E15
Sighnaghi, *Rep. of Georgia* **149** C19
Siglufjördur, *Ice.* **134** E3
Signal Peak, *Ariz., U.S.* **101** U5
Sigourney, *Iowa, U.S.* **99** P13
Siguiri, *Guinea* **180** E7
Sihora, *India* **158** J7
Sihui, *China* **163** R4
Siirt, *Turk.* **149** G16
Siis, island, *Chuuk, F.S.M.* **197** C15
Sikar, *India* **158** F5
Sikasso, *Mali* **176** J7
Sikeston, *Mo., U.S.* **99** V16
Sikhote Alin' Range, *Asia* **146** E13
Síkinos, island, *Gr.* **137** M16
Sil, river, *Sp.* **139** P5
Silat, *Indonesia* **168** J10
Silchar, *India* **158** H14
Şile, *Turk.* **148** C5
Siler City, *N.C., U.S.* **90** H11
Silet, *Alg.* **176** F11
Silgarhi, *Nepal* **158** E8
Silhouette, island, *Seychelles* **185** N19
Silifke, *Turk.* **148** J9
Siling Co, *China* **160** K7
Silisili, Mount, *Samoa* **198** K2
Silistra, *Bulg.* **137** F16
Silivri, *Turk.* **148** C4
Siljan, lake, *Sw.* **135** K13
Silkeborg, *Den.* **134** N11
Siloam Springs, *Ark., U.S.* **94** E6
Silogui, *Indonesia* **168** J5
Silopi, *Turk.* **149** H17
Silsbee, *Tex., U.S.* **97** P15
Šilutė, *Lith.* **135** N15
Silvan, *Turk.* **149** G15
Silvânia, *Braz.* **123** J13
Silvassa, *India* **158** K3
Silver Bay, *Minn., U.S.* **98** F13
Silver Bell, *Ariz., U.S.* **101** V7
Silver City, *Idaho, U.S.* **100** H3
Silver City, *Mich., U.S.* **92** E5
Silver City, *N. Mex., U.S.* **101** U10
Silver City, *Nev., U.S.* **103** Q6
Silver Creek, *Oreg., U.S.* **102** H7
Silver Lake, *Oreg., U.S.* **102** J5
Silver Peak, *Nev., U.S.* **103** S9
Silver Plains, *Qnsld., Austral.* **191** P12
Silver Spring, *Md., U.S.* **90** C13
Silverton, *Colo., U.S.* **101** P11
Silverton, *Oreg., U.S.* **102** F3
Silverton, *Tex., U.S.* **96** H6
Silves, *Braz.* **122** D10
Silvies, river, *Oreg., U.S.* **102** H7
Sima, *Comoros* **185** N16
Simansih, *Indonesia* **168** K5
Simao, *China* **160** P10
Şīmareh, river, *Iran* **152** D11
Simav, river, *Turk.* **148** E4
Simav, *Turk.* **148** F5
Simbo, island, *Solomon Is.* **197** M15
Simcoe, Lake, *Ont., Can.* **77** Q18
Simdega, *India* **158** J9
Simeulue, island, *Indonesia* **168** H4
Simferopol', *Ukr.* **133** M16
Simi, *Gr.* **137** M17
Simikot, *Nepal* **158** E8
Simi Valley, *Calif., U.S.* **103** X8
Simla, *Colo., U.S.* **100** M14
Simla, *India* **158** D6
Simpang, *Indonesia* **168** J7
Simpson Desert, *Austral.* **190** G10
Simpson Peninsula, *Nunavut, Can.* **77** F16
Simrishamn, *Sw.* **135** N13
Simushir, island, *Russ.* **141** H23
Sinai, region, *Egypt* **151** R3
Sinai, Mount *see* Mûsa, Gebel, *Egypt* **151** T3
Sinan, *China* **162** M1
Sinbang-ni, *N. Korea* **162** C13
Sinbaungwe, *Myanmar* **166** J5
Sinbokchang, *N. Korea* **162** C14
Sincelejo, *Col.* **120** C5
Sinclair, *Wyo., U.S.* **100** J11
Sinclair, Lake, *Ga., U.S.* **90** M6
Sin Cowe Island, *Spratly Is.* **168** E11
Sındırgı, *Turk.* **148** E4
Sindoa, Mount, *New Caledonia, Fr.* **198** D8
Sines, *Port.* **139** S4
Sines, Cabo de, *Port.* **139** S4
Singa, *Sudan* **179** E13
Singapore, *Asia* **167** V11
Singapore Strait, *Indonesia-Singapore* **168** H7
Singaraja, *Indonesia* **168** M11
Singavi, Mount, *Wallis and Futuna, Fr.* **198** E11
Sing Buri, *Thai.* **166** M8
Singida, *Tanzania* **179** L13
Singkaling Hkāmti, *Myanmar* **166** E6
Singkawang, *Indonesia* **168** J9
Singkep, island, *Indonesia* **168** J7
Singleton, *N.S.W., Austral.* **191** X14
Sinh Ho, *Vietnam* **166** G10
Sinj, *Croatia* **136** G11
Sinjai, *Indonesia* **169** L13
Sinjār, *Iraq* **152** C8
Sinkat, *Sudan* **179** C14
Sinkiang, region, *China* **160** F5
Sinnamary, *Fr. Guiana* **121** E18
Sinnar, *India* **158** L4
Sinó, Ponto do, *Cape Verde* **185** B17
Sinop, *Braz.* **122** H11
Sinop, *Turk.* **148** C10
Sinop Burnu, *Turk.* **148** B10
Sinp'o, *N. Korea* **162** C14
Sintang, *Indonesia* **168** J10
Sint Nicolaas, *Aruba, Neth.* **112** M8
Sinton, *Tex., U.S.* **97** T11
Sinŭiju, *N. Korea* **162** D11
Siorapaluk, *Greenland, Den.* **75** B19
Sioux Center, *Iowa, U.S.* **98** M9
Sioux City, *Iowa, U.S.* **99** N8
Sioux Falls, *S. Dak., U.S.* **98** L8
Sioux Lookout, *Ont., Can.* **77** N15
Sioux Rapids, *Iowa, U.S.* **98** M10
Sipapo, Cerro, *Venez.* **120** E9
Siping, *China* **162** A11
Sipiwesk, *Man., Can.* **77** L14
Siple, Mount, *Antarctica* **206** M7
Siple Coast, *Antarctica* **206** L11
Siple Island, *Antarctica* **206** M7
Sipura, island, *Indonesia* **168** K5
Sira, *India* **159** P5
Siracusa (Syracuse), *It.* **136** L11
Siraha, *Nepal* **158** G10
Şiran, *Turk.* **149** E14
Sirdaryo, *Uzb.* **155** K13
Sir Edward Pellew Group, islands, *Austral.* **190** C10
Siret, river, *Eur.* **130** H9
Sirḩān, Wādī as, *Jordan* **151** P8
Sirhān, Wādī as, *Saudi Arabia* **152** F6
Siri, Jabal, *Af.* **174** F9
Sīrīk, *Iran* **153** H16
Sirik, Tanjong, *Malaysia* **168** H10
Sirkka, *Fin.* **135** D14
Sirmaur, *India* **158** H8
Şırnak, *Turk.* **149** H17
Sirsa, *India* **158** E5
Sir Thomas, Mount, *Austral.* **190** G7
Sirur, *India* **158** L4
Şirvan, *Turk.* **149** G16
Sisak, *Croatia* **136** F11
Sisaket, *Thai.* **166** L11

Sisian, Arm. 149 E20
Siskiyou Mountains, Calif.-Oreg., U.S. 102 L2
Sisophon, Cambodia 166 M10
Sisseton, S. Dak., U.S. 98 J8
Sīstān, region, Iran 153 E17
Sīstān, Daryācheh-ye, Iran 153 F17
Sister Bay, Wis., U.S. 92 H8
Sisters, Oreg., U.S. 102 G4
Sistersville, W. Va., U.S. 90 C8
Sitapur, India 158 F7
Sitía, Gr. 137 N17
Sitian, China 160 F9
Sítio da Abadia, Braz. 123 J14
Sitka, Alas., U.S. 105 L22
Sitka National Historical Park, Alas., U.S. 105 L22
Sittwe (Akyab), Myanmar 166 H4
Siufaalele Point, Manua Is., Amer. Samoa, U.S. 198 P3
Siufaga, Manua Is., Amer. Samoa, U.S. 198 P3
Siulagi Point, Manua Is., Amer. Samoa, U.S. 198 N3
Siuri, India 158 H11
Siuslaw, river, Oreg., U.S. 102 H2
Sivas, Turk. 148 E12
Siverek, Turk. 149 H14
Sivrihisar, Turk. 148 E7
Siwa, Egypt 177 D17
Siwalik Range, India 158 C5
Siwan, India 158 G9
Sixaola, C.R. 109 N20
Six Feet, Pitcairn I., U.K. 199 Q23
Sixian, China 162 J7
Sixth Cataract, Sudan 179 D13
Siyäzän, Azerb. 149 C22
Siziwang Qi, China 162 B4
Sjælland, island, Den. 134 P12
Skadovs'k, Ukr. 133 L16
Skagafjördur, Ice. 134 E3
Skagen, Den. 134 M11
Skagerrak, strait, Den.-Nor. 134 M10
Skagit, river, Wash., U.S. 102 B5
Skagway, Alas., U.S. 105 J21
Skardu, Pak. 156 L13
Skeena, river, B.C., Can. 76 J8
Skeleton Coast, Namibia 182 G5
Skellefteå, Sw. 135 G14
Skellefteälven, river, Sw. 135 F13
Skiatook, Okla., U.S. 96 E12
Skibbereen, Ire. 138 H5
Skidmore, Tex., U.S. 97 T11
Skien, Nor. 134 L11
Skikda, Alg. 176 A12
Skíros (Scyros), island, Gr. 137 K15
Skive, Den. 134 N11
Skokie, Ill., U.S. 93 N7
Skomvær, island, Nor. 134 E11
Skopje, Maced. 137 H14
Skopunarfjørdur, Faroe Is., Den. 134 J6
Skövde, Sw. 134 L12
Skovorodino, Russ. 141 K18
Skowhegan, Me., U.S. 89 F16
Skudeneshavn, Nor. 134 L9
Skull Valley, Ariz., U.S. 101 S6
Skunk, river, Iowa, U.S. 99 P13
Skye, Island of, Scot., U.K. 138 D7
Skykomish, Wash., U.S. 102 C5
Slantsy, Russ. 140 D6
Slater, Mo., U.S. 99 S12
Slatina, Rom. 137 F15
Slaton, Tex., U.S. 96 K5
Slave, river, Alta., Can. 76 J11
Slave Coast, Af. 180 H11
Slavonski Brod, Croatia 136 F12
Sławno, Pol. 132 E9
Slayton, Minn., U.S. 98 L9
Sleeper Islands, Nunavut, Can. 77 K17
Sleeping Bear Dunes National Lakeshore, Mich., U.S. 92 H9
Sleepy Eye, Minn., U.S. 98 K10
Sleetmute, Alas., U.S. 105 J14
Slessor Glacier, Antarctica 206 E11
Slidell, La., U.S. 94 P11
Slide Mountain, U.S. 79 E20
Sligo, Ire. 138 F6
Slite, Sw. 135 M14
Sliven, Bulg. 137 G16
Sloan, Nev., U.S. 103 U12
Slonim, Belarus 132 F12
Slovakia, Eur. 132 J9
Slovenia, Eur. 136 E10
Slov"yans'k, Ukr. 133 J17
Sluch, river, Ukr. 133 H13
Słupsk, Pol. 132 E9
Slutsk, Belarus 133 F13
Slyudyanka, Russ. 141 L15
Smackover, Ark., U.S. 94 J8
Smallan, Pak. 157 R7
Smallwood Reservoir, Nfld., Can. 77 L21
Smara, W. Sahara, Mor. 176 D6
Smeïda see Taoudenni, Mali 176 E8
Smethport, Pa., U.S. 88 L5
Smidovich, Russ. 140 D11
Smidovich, Russ. 141 K20

Smila, Ukr. 133 J15
Smiltene, Latv. 135 L17
Smith see Sumisu, island, Jap. 194 B3
Smith, river, Mont., U.S. 100 C8
Smith Arm, N.W.T., Can. 76 F10
Smith Bay, Alas., U.S. 105 B14
Smith Bay, Nunavut, Can. 77 C16
Smith Center, Kans., U.S. 99 R6
Smithers, B.C., Can. 76 K8
Smithfield, N.C., U.S. 90 H12
Smithfield, Utah, U.S. 100 J7
Smithfield, Va., U.S. 90 F14
Smith Glacier, Antarctica 206 L7
Smith Island, Nunavut, Can. 77 J17
Smith Mountain Lake, Va., U.S. 90 F10
Smith River, B.C., Can. 76 H9
Smith River, Calif., U.S. 102 L2
Smith Sound, Nunavut, Can. 77 C16
Smithville, Tex., U.S. 97 Q11
Smoke Creek Desert, Nev., U.S. 103 N6
Smokey Hill, river, U.S. 78 H11
Smoky, river, Alta., Can. 76 L9
Smoky Bay, S. Austral., Austral. 191 X8
Smoky Hill, river, Kans., U.S. 99 T6
Smoky Hills, Kans., U.S. 99 S6
Smoky Mountains, Idaho, U.S. 100 G5
Smøla, island, Nor. 134 H10
Smolensk, Russ. 140 E10
Smolensk-Moscow Upland, Eur. 130 E10
Smyley Island, Antarctica 206 G6
Smyrna, Del., U.S. 90 C14
Smyrna, Ga., U.S. 90 L5
Smyrna, Tenn., U.S. 95 E15
Smyrna see İzmir, Turk. 148 F3
Snake, river, N. Amer. 74 H3
Snake Range, Nev., U.S. 103 Q13
Snake River Plain, Idaho, U.S. 100 H5
Snåsa, Nor. 134 G11
Sneads, Fla., U.S. 91 Q4
Sneeu Berg, Af. 174 Q8
Snezhnogorsk, Russ. 141 G13
Snøhetta, peak, Nor. 134 J11
Snohomish, Wash., U.S. 102 B4
Snoqualmie, Wash., U.S. 102 C4
Snoqualmie Pass, Wash., U.S. 102 C5
Snowdon, peak, Eur. 130 E4
Snowflake, Ariz., U.S. 101 T9
Snow Hill, Md., U.S. 90 D15
Snow Hill Island, Antarctica 206 C4
Snowville, Utah, U.S. 100 J6
Snowy, river, Austral. 190 M13
Snug Corner, Bahamas 111 H15
Snuol, Cambodia 167 N12
Snyder, Okla., U.S. 96 H9
Snyder, Tex., U.S. 96 L6
Soala see Sokolo, Mali 176 H7
Soalala, Madagascar 183 F16
Soanierana-Ivongo, Madagascar 183 F18
Soan Kundo, S. Korea 162 H13
Soap Lake, Wash., U.S. 102 C7
Sobradinho, Represa de, Braz. 123 G16
Sobral, Braz. 123 E16
Sochi, Russ. 140 H3
Society Islands, Fr. Polynesia, Fr. 199 D15
Socompa, Chile 124 E8
Socorro, Col. 120 E6
Socorro, N. Mex., U.S. 101 T12
Socorro, Isla, Mex. 108 H6
Socotra (Suquṭrá), island, Yemen 153 R15
Soc Trang, Vietnam 167 Q12
Soda Lake, Calif., U.S. 103 V11
Sodankylä, Fin. 135 E15
Soda Springs, Idaho, U.S. 100 H7
Soddy-Daisy, Tenn., U.S. 95 G17
Södertälje, Sw. 135 L14
Sodiri, Sudan 178 E12
Sodo, Eth. 179 G14
Soekmekaar, S. Af. 182 H11
Sofia see Sofiya, Bulg. 137 H15
Sofiya (Sofia), Bulg. 137 H15
Sōfu Gan (Lot's Wife), island, Jap. 194 C3
Sogamoso, Col. 120 E6
Soğanlı, river, Turk. 148 C8
Sognefjorden, Nor. 134 K9
Sogo Nur, China 160 F11
Sögüt, Turk. 148 E6
Sögüt Gölü, Turk. 148 H5
Sögwip'o, S. Korea 162 J13
Sogxian, China 160 K8
Sohâg, Egypt 177 D18
Sohano, P.N.G. 197 J13
Sohüksan Do, S. Korea 162 H12
Sojat, India 158 G4
Sokch'o, S. Korea 162 E14
Söke, Turk. 148 G3
Sokhumi, Rep. of Georgia 149 A15
Sokol, Russ. 140 F7
Sokol, Russ. 141 E16
Sokol, Russ. 141 F20

Sokółka, Pol. 132 F11
Sokolo (Soala), Mali 176 H7
Sokoto, river, Nig. 180 E12
Sokoto, Nig. 181 E13
Sol, Ponta do, Cape Verde 185 C17
Sola, Cuba 110 J11
Solander Island, N.Z. 193 R15
Solano, Punta, Col. 120 E3
Sol de Julio, Arg. 124 H10
Soldotna, Alas., U.S. 105 J16
Soledad, Calif., U.S. 103 U4
Soledad, Col. 120 B5
Solhan, Turk. 149 F15
Solikamsk, Russ. 140 G9
Solimões (Amazon), river, S. Amer. 118 D5
Solitary Islands, Austral. 190 J15
Sollefteå, Sw. 135 H13
Sóller, Sp. 139 R10
Sol'Iletsk, Russ. 140 J7
Solo, island, Fiji 198 J7
Solok, Indonesia 168 J6
Solomon, river, Kans., U.S. 99 S7
Solomon, Ariz., U.S. 101 U9
Solomon, Kans., U.S. 99 S7
Solomon Islands, Pac. Oc. 197 K17
Solomon Sea, Solomon Is. 197 M14
Solon Springs, Wis., U.S. 92 F3
Solor, island, Indonesia 169 M14
Solov'yevsk, Russ. 141 K18
Šolta, island, Croatia 136 G11
Solţānābād, Iran 153 B16
Soltan Bagh, Afghan. 157 N7
Soltan-e Bakva, Afghan. 157 P3
Solvay, N.Y., U.S. 88 J8
Solwezi, Zambia 182 D10
Solyplayas, Canary Is., Sp. 184 Q7
Soma, Turk. 148 E3
Sōma, Jap. 164 M13
Somali, region, Eth. 179 G16
Somali Basin, Ind. Oc. 220 G6
Somalia, Af. 179 J17
Somaliland, region, Somalia 179 F17
Somali Peninsula, Af. 174 H12
Somaloma, Rochers, Wallis and Futuna, Fr. 198 E11
Sombrero, island, Leeward Is. 113 E15
Sombrero Channel, Nicobar Is., India 159 S15
Somers, Mont., U.S. 100 B5
Somerset, Bermuda, U.K. 111 F16
Somerset, Colo., U.S. 101 N11
Somerset, Ky., U.S. 95 D18
Somerset, Pa., U.S. 88 P4
Somerset Island, Bermuda, U.K. 111 F16
Somerset Island, Nunavut, Can. 77 E15
Somersworth, N.H., U.S. 89 H15
Somerton, Ariz., U.S. 101 V4
Somerville, Tenn., U.S. 94 G12
Somerville, Tex., U.S. 97 Q12
Sommariva, Austral. 191 U13
Somme, river, Fr. 138 J10
Somosomo, Fiji 198 G8
Somosomo Strait, Fiji 198 H8
Somuncurá, Meseta de, Arg. 125 Q9
Son, river, India 158 H10
Sönch'ön, N. Korea 162 D12
Sonda, Pak. 157 W7
Sondar, India 157 N13
Sønderborg, Den. 134 P11
Sondrio, It. 136 E8
Song, Malaysia 167 V16
Song, Malaysia 168 H10
Song Cau, Vietnam 166 M14
Songea, Tanzania 179 N14
Songhua, river, China 161 C18
Songhua Hu, China 162 A13
Songjiang, China 162 L10
Songkhla, Thai. 167 R9
Song Ma, Vietnam 166 H10
Songnim, N. Korea 162 E12
Songsong (Rota), Rota I., N. Mariana Is., U.S. 196 E7
Songxi, China 163 N8
Songxian, China 162 H4
Songzi, China 162 L3
Son Ha, Vietnam 166 L14
Son Hoa, Vietnam 167 N14
Sonid Youqi, China 162 A5
Sonid Youqi (SaihanTal), China 162 A5
Sonid Zuoqi (Mandalt), China 162 A5
Son La, Vietnam 166 H11
Sonmiani, Pak. 157 V5
Sonmiani Bay, Pak. 157 W5
Sonoma, Calif., U.S. 103 R3
Sonora, Calif., U.S. 103 R6
Sonora, Tex., U.S. 97 P6
Sonoran Desert, U.S. 78 K6
Sonoran Desert National Monument, Ariz., U.S. 101 U6
Sonqor, Iran 152 D11
Sonsón, Col. 120 E5
Sonsonate, El Salv. 109 L16
Sonsorol Islands, Palau 194 F2
Soperton, Ga., U.S. 91 N7

Sopron, Hung. 132 K8
Sopur, India 156 M12
Sopwer, Mochun, Chuuk, F.S.M. 197 A15
Sopweru, island, Chuuk, F.S.M. 197 A15
Sorah, Pak. 157 U7
Sorang, Kaz. 155 E14
Sorezaru Point, Solomon Is. 197 L15
Sorgun, Turk. 148 E10
Soria, Sp. 139 P8
Sorkh Ab, Afghan. 157 P3
Sorkh Kowtal Temple, Afghan. 156 L7
Sørkjosen, Nor. 135 C13
Soroca, Mold. 133 K13
Sorocaba, Braz. 123 M13
Sorol Atoll, F.S.M. 196 Q3
Sorong, Indonesia 169 J17
Sørøya, island, Nor. 135 C13
Sorrento, It. 136 J10
Sør Rondane Mountains, Antarctica 207 B15
Sorsele, Sw. 135 F13
Sortavala, Russ. 140 D7
Sørvágur, Faroe Is., Den. 134 J5
Sŏsan, S. Korea 162 F13
Sösan, Sw. 135 F13
Sosanlagh Bay, Rota I., N. Mariana Is., U.S. 196 E7
Sosna, Russ. 141 J15
Sosanjaya Bay, Rota I., N. Mariana Is., U.S. 196 E7
Sosnogorsk, Russ. 140 F9
Sosnovo Ozerskoye, Russ. 141 L16
Sosnowiec, Pol. 132 H9
Soso Bay, Fiji 198 K6
Sos'va, Russ. 140 G10
Sos'va, Russ. 140 H9
Souanké, Congo 181 K17
Soubré, Côte d'Ivoire 180 H8
Soudan, N. Terr., Austral. 191 S10
Souillac, Mauritius 185 H20
Sŏul (Seoul), S. Korea 162 E13
Soure, Braz. 123 C13
Souris (Mouse), river, N. Dak., U.S. 98 E3
Sour Lake, Tex., U.S. 97 Q15
Sousa, Braz. 123 F17
Sous le Vent, Îles, Fr. Polynesia, Fr. 199 E14
Sousse, Tun. 177 A13
South Africa, Af. 182 K9
South Alligator, river, Austral. 190 B8
South Ambo Channel, Kwajalein Atoll, Marshall Is. 196 M5
Southampton, N.Y., U.S. 89 N13
Southampton, Eng., U.K. 138 H8
Southampton, Cape, Nunavut, Can. 77 J16
Southampton Island, Nunavut, Can. 77 H16
South Andaman, Andaman Is., India 159 Q14
South Aulatsivik Island, Nfld., Can. 77 K21
South Australia, Austral. 191 V9
South Australian Basin, Ind. Oc. 221 N17
Southaven, Miss., U.S. 94 G11
South Baldy, peak, N. Mex., U.S. 101 T11
South Bay, Fla., U.S. 91 V10
South Bend, Ind., U.S. 93 N9
South Bend, Wash., U.S. 102 D2
South Boston, Va., U.S. 90 G11
South Branch Potomac, river, W. Va., U.S. 90 C11
South Caicos, island, Turks and Caicos Is., U.K. 111 J17
South Cape, Fiji 198 H8
South Cape see Ka Lae, Hawaii, U.S. 107 Q19
South Carolina, U.S. 90 K9
South Cay, Jam. 110 P11
South Channel, Enewetak Atoll, Marshall Is. 196 J8
South Charleston, W. Va., U.S. 90 E8
South China Sea, Asia 146 L11
South Dakota, U.S. 98 K2
Southeast Indian Ridge, Ind. Oc. 220 P10
Southeast Pacific Basin, Pac. Oc. 219 Q19
Southeast Pass, Jaluit Atoll, Marshall Is. 196 M8
South East Point, Kiritimati, Kiribati 197 C24
Southeast Point, Tarawa, Kiribati 197 E17
Southend on Sea, Eng., U.K. 138 H9
Southern Alps, N.Z. 193 P16
Southern Bight, Bahamas 110 F11
Southern Bug, river, Eur. 130 G10
Southern Cross, W. Austral., Austral. 191 W3
Southern Indian Lake, Man., Can. 77 K14
Southern Pines, N.C., U.S. 90 J11
Southern Uplands, Eur. 130 E4
Southesk Tablelands, Austral. 190 E6
South Fiji Basin, Pac. Oc. 218 M9
South Fork, Colo., U.S. 101 P12
South Fork Owyhee, river, Nev., U.S. 102 L10
South Fork Shenandoah, river, Va., U.S. 90 D11
South Fork Solomon, river, Kans., U.S. 99 S5
South Fulton, Tenn., U.S. 94 E12
South Geomagnetic Pole, Antarctica 207 K16
South Georgia, S. Amer. 118 R9
South Grand, river, Mo., U.S. 99 T11
South Haven, Mich., U.S. 92 M9
South Henik Lake, Nunavut, Can. 77 J14
South Hill, Va., U.S. 90 G12
South Indian Basin, Southern Oc. 225 L15
South Island, N.Z. 193 Q17
South Korea, Asia 162 F15

South Lake Tahoe, *Calif., U.S.* **103** Q6
South Loup, river, *Nebr., U.S.* **99** P5
South Magnetic Pole, 2002, *Antarctica* **207** R19
South Male Atoll, *Maldives* **159** V3
South Malosmadulu Atoll, *Maldives* **159** U3
South Milwaukee, *Wis., U.S.* **92** L7
South Nahanni, river, *N.W.T., Can.* **76** G9
South Negril Point, *Jam.* **110** N10
South Orkney Islands, *Antarctica* **206** A4
South Ossetia, republic, *Rep. of Georgia* **149** B18
South Pacific Ocean, *Pac. Oc.* **194** M11
South Pass, *Kwajalein Atoll, Marshall Is.* **196** N5
South Passage, *Kiritimati, Kiribati* **197** B22
South Pittsburg, *Tenn., U.S.* **95** G16
South Platte, river, *Colo., U.S.* **100** L14
South Point, *Jaluit Atoll, Marshall Is.* **196** N8
South Ponte Vedra Beach, *Fla., U.S.* **91** R9
Southport, *N.C., U.S.* **90** K12
South Portland, *Me., U.S.* **89** H16
South Sandwich Trench, *Southern Oc.* **224** D9
South San Francisco, *Calif., U.S.* **103** S3
South Saskatchewan, river, *Alta.-Sask., Can.* **76** M11
South Shetland Islands, *Antarctica* **206** C3
South Shore, *Ky., U.S.* **95** A19
South Sioux City, *Nebr., U.S.* **99** N8
South Taranaki Bight, *N.Z.* **193** L18
South Tasman Rise, *Ind. Oc.-Pac. Oc.* **218** Q6
South Uist, island, *Scot., U.K.* **138** D6
South Valley Canal, *Egypt* **177** E18
South West Bay, *Vanuatu* **198** D2
South West Cape, *Austral.* **190** M15
Southwest Cay, *Jam.* **110** P11
Southwest Indian Ridge, *Ind. Oc.* **220** Q3
Southwest Pacific Basin, *Pac. Oc.* **218** M11
Southwest Pass, *Jaluit Atoll, Marshall Is.* **196** M7
Southwest Passage, *Enewetak Atoll, Marshall Is.* **196** H7
Southwest Point, *Bahamas* **110** D11
Southwest Rift, *Hawaii, U.S.* **107** N19
Southwest Rock, *Jam.* **110** P10
South Yolla Bolly Mountains, *Calif., U.S.* **103** N3
Souvannakhili, *Laos* **166** L12
Sovetskaya Gavan', *Russ.* **141** K21
Sovetskiy, *Russ.* **140** G10
Soweto, *S. Af.* **182** J10
Sōya, *Jap.* **164** D13
Sōya Misaki, *Jap.* **164** D13
Soyo, *Angola* **182** B5
Spaatz Island, *Antarctica* **206** G6
Spain, *Eur.* **139** Q6
Spalding, *Nebr., U.S.* **99** P6
Spanish Fork, *Utah, U.S.* **100** L7
Spanish Peak, *Oreg., U.S.* **102** G6
Spanish Town, *Jam.* **110** N12
Sparkman, *Ark., U.S.* **94** H8
Sparks, *Nev., U.S.* **103** P6
Sparta, *Ga., U.S.* **90** L7
Sparta *see* Spárti, *Gr.* **137** L14
Sparta, *Ill., U.S.* **93** U5
Sparta, *Tenn., U.S.* **95** F17
Sparta, *Wis., U.S.* **92** K4
Spartanburg, *S.C., U.S.* **90** J8
Spárti (Sparta), *Gr.* **137** L14
Spartivento, Capo, *It.* **136** K7
Spearfish, *S. Dak., U.S.* **98** K1
Spearman, *Tex., U.S.* **96** F6
Speedwell Island, *Falk. Is., U.K.* **125** W12
Speightstown, *Barbados* **113** L19
Spencer, *Idaho, U.S.* **100** G7
Spencer, *Ind., U.S.* **93** S8
Spencer, *Iowa, U.S.* **98** M10
Spencer, *N.C., U.S.* **90** H9
Spencer, *Nebr., U.S.* **98** M6
Spencer, *W. Va., U.S.* **90** D8
Spencer, Cape, *Austral.* **190** L9
Spencer Gulf, *Austral.* **190** K10
Spezand, *Pak.* **157** R6
Sphinx, ruins, *Egypt* **177** C18
Spicer Islands, *Nunavut, Can.* **77** F17
Spiess Seamount, *Southern Oc.* **224** C11
Spin Buldak, *Afghan.* **157** Q5
Spirit Lake, *Idaho, U.S.* **100** B3
Spirit Lake, *Iowa, U.S.* **98** M10
Spiro, *Okla., U.S.* **96** G14
Spitsbergen Bank, *Arctic Oc.* **223** F16
Spitsbergen Fracture Zone, *Arctic Oc.* **223** H14
Split, *Croatia* **136** G11
Split Lake, *Man., Can.* **77** L14
Spokane, river, *Wash., U.S.* **102** B8
Spokane, *Wash., U.S.* **102** C9
Spoloshino, *Russ.* **141** J16
Spoon, river, *Ill., U.S.* **93** P4
Spooner, *Wis., U.S.* **92** G3
Sporades, islands, *Eur.* **130** K9
Sprague, river, *Oreg., U.S.* **102** K5
Sprague, *Wash., U.S.* **102** C8
Sprague Lake, *Wash., U.S.* **102** C8
Sprague River, *Oreg., U.S.* **102** K4
Spratly Island, *Spratly Is.* **168** F10
Spratly Islands, *S. China Sea* **168** F10
Spray, *Oreg., U.S.* **102** G6
Spremberg, *Ger.* **132** G7
Springbok, *S. Af.* **182** L7
Spring Creek, *W. Austral., Austral.* **191** Q6
Springdale, *Ark., U.S.* **94** E6
Springdale, *Wash., U.S.* **102** B8
Springer, *N. Mex., U.S.* **101** Q14
Springerville, *Ariz., U.S.* **101** T9
Springfield, *Colo., U.S.* **101** P15
Springfield, *Fla., U.S.* **91** R3
Springfield, *Idaho, U.S.* **100** H6
Springfield, *Ill., U.S.* **93** R5
Springfield, *Ky., U.S.* **95** C17
Springfield, *Mass., U.S.* **89** L13
Springfield, *Minn., U.S.* **98** K10
Springfield, *Mo., U.S.* **99** V12
Springfield, *Ohio, U.S.* **93** R12
Springfield, *Oreg., U.S.* **102** H3
Springfield, *S. Dak., U.S.* **98** M7
Springfield, *Tenn., U.S.* **95** E15
Springfield, *Vt., U.S.* **89** H13
Spring Grove, *Minn., U.S.* **98** L13
Spring Hill, *Tenn., U.S.* **95** F15
Springhill, *La., U.S.* **94** K7
Spring Mountains, *Nev., U.S.* **103** U11
Springsure, *Qnsld., Austral.* **191** U14
Spring Valley, *Ill., U.S.* **93** P5
Spring Valley, *Minn., U.S.* **98** L12
Springview, *Nebr., U.S.* **98** M5
Springville, *N.Y., U.S.* **88** K5
Spruce Knob, *W. Va., U.S.* **90** D10
Spruce Mountain, *Nev., U.S.* **103** N12
Spruce Pine, *N.C., U.S.* **90** H7
Spur, *Tex., U.S.* **96** K6
Squaw Creek, *Idaho, U.S.* **100** G3
Sredinnyy Khrebet, *Russ.* **141** F22
Sredne Sibirskoye Ploskogor'ye, *Russ.* **141** F14
Sredniy, *Russ.* **141** F21
Sretensk, *Russ.* **141** L17
Sriharikota Island, *India* **159** P7
Srikakulam, *India* **158** M9
Sri Kalahasti, *India* **159** P7
Sri Lanka, island, *Asia* **146** L7
Sri Lanka (Ceylon), *Asia* **159** U6
Srinagar, *India* **156** M12
Srivardhan, *India* **158** M3
Städjan, peak, *Sw.* **134** J12
Stadlandet, peninsula, *Nor.* **134** J9
Stafford, *Kans., U.S.* **99** U6
Staked Plain *see* Estacado, Llano, *N. Amer.* **74** L5
Stakhanov, *Ukr.* **133** J18
Stalingrad *see* Volgograd, *Russ.* **140** H5
Stalowa Wola, *Pol.* **132** H11
Stambaugh, *Mich., U.S.* **92** G6
Stamford, *Conn., U.S.* **88** M11
Stamford, *N.Y., U.S.* **88** K10
Stamford, *Tex., U.S.* **96** L8
Stamford, Lake, *Tex., U.S.* **96** L8
Stamps, *Ark., U.S.* **94** J7
Stamsund, *Nor.* **134** E12
Stanberry, *Mo., U.S.* **99** R10
Stancomb-Wills Glacier, *Antarctica* **206** D11
Standish, *Mich., U.S.* **92** K11
Stanford, *Ky., U.S.* **95** C17
Stanford, *Mont., U.S.* **100** C9
Staniard Creek, *Bahamas* **110** E11
Stanley, *Falk. Is., U.K.* **125** W13
Stanley, *Idaho, U.S.* **100** G5
Stanley, *N. Dak., U.S.* **98** E3
Stanley, *Tas., Austral.* **191** Y15
Stanley, *Wis., U.S.* **92** H4
Stanley, Port, *Vanuatu* **198** D2
Stanovaya, *Russ.* **141** D19
Stanovoye Nagor'ye, *Russ.* **141** K16
Stanovoy Khrebet, *Russ.* **141** J18
Stanton, *N. Dak., U.S.* **98** F4
Stanton, *Nebr., U.S.* **99** P8
Stanton, *Tex., U.S.* **96** M5
Stanwood, *Wash., U.S.* **102** B4
Staples, *Minn., U.S.* **98** H10
Stapleton, *Nebr., U.S.* **99** P4
Stara Zagora, *Bulg.* **137** H16
Starbuck, *Minn., U.S.* **98** J9
Starbuck, *Wash., U.S.* **102** D8
Starbuck Island, *Kiribati* **194** H12
Star City, *Ark., U.S.* **94** J9
Stargard Szczeciński, *Pol.* **132** F8
Stargo, *Ariz., U.S.* **101** U9
Starke, *Fla., U.S.* **91** R8
Starkville, *Colo., U.S.* **101** Q14
Starkville, *Miss., U.S.* **94** J12
Starobil's'k, *Ukr.* **133** H18
Starogard Gdański, *Pol.* **132** F9
Starorybnoye, *Russ.* **141** F14
State College, *Pa., U.S.* **88** N6
Stateline, *Nev., U.S.* **103** Q6
Staten Island *see* Estados, Isla de los, *Arg.* **125** Y10
Statesboro, *Ga., U.S.* **91** N8
Statesville, *N.C., U.S.* **90** H9
Staunton, *Ill., U.S.* **93** S4
Staunton, *Va., U.S.* **90** E11
Stavanger, *Nor.* **134** L9
Stavropol', *Russ.* **140** J4
Stavropol' Plateau, *Eur.* **130** G13
Stavrós, *Gr.* **137** J15
Stavrós, *Gr.* **137** K14
Stawell, *Vic., Austral.* **191** Z11
Stayton, *Oreg., U.S.* **102** G3
Steamboat Springs, *Colo., U.S.* **100** L11
Stebbins, *Alas., U.S.* **104** G12
Steele, *N. Dak., U.S.* **98** G5
Steels Point, *Norfolk I., Austral.* **197** F20
Steelton, *Pa., U.S.* **88** P7
Steelville, *Mo., U.S.* **99** T14
Steens Mountain, *Oreg., U.S.* **102** K8
Steese Highway, *Alas., U.S.* **105** F17
Stefansson Island, *Nunavut, Can.* **77** D14
Steffen, Cerro, *Arg.* **125** S7
Steinbach, *Man., Can.* **77** N14
Steinhatchee, *Fla., U.S.* **91** R6
Steinkjer, *Nor.* **134** H11
Stella Maris, *Bahamas* **111** F13
Stepanakert *see* Xankändi, *Azerb.* **149** E20
Step'anavan, *Arm.* **149** D18
Stephen, *Minn., U.S.* **98** E8
Stephens, *Ark., U.S.* **94** J7
Stephens, Port, *Falk. Is., U.K.* **125** W12
Stephenson, *Mich., U.S.* **92** H7
Stephenson, Mount, *Antarctica* **206** F5
Stephenville, *Nfld., Can.* **77** M23
Stephenville, *Tex., U.S.* **96** M10
Stepnogorsk, *Kaz.* **155** C14
Steps Point, *Tutuila, Amer. Samoa, U.S.* **198** N7
Sterling, *Colo., U.S.* **100** L15
Sterling, *Ill., U.S.* **93** N5
Sterling, *Kans., U.S.* **99** T7
Sterling, *N. Dak., U.S.* **98** G5
Sterling City, *Tex., U.S.* **96** M6
Sterling Heights, *Mich., U.S.* **92** M13
Sterling Highway, *Alas., U.S.* **105** K16
Sterlitamak, *Russ.* **140** J7
Stettler, *Alta., Can.* **76** M10
Steubenville, *Ohio, U.S.* **93** Q16
Stevenson, *Wash., U.S.* **102** E4
Stevens Point, *Wis., U.S.* **92** J5
Stevens Village, *Alas., U.S.* **105** E16
Stevensville, *Mont., U.S.* **100** D5
Stewart, *B.C., Can.* **76** J8
Stewart, *Nev., U.S.* **103** Q6
Stewart, Isla, *Chile* **125** Y8
Stewart Island, *N.Z.* **193** R15
Steyr, *Aust.* **132** K7
Stickney, *S. Dak., U.S.* **98** L6
Stigler, *Okla., U.S.* **96** G14
Stikine, river, *B.C., Can.* **76** H8
Stillwater, *Minn., U.S.* **98** J12
Stillwater, *Okla., U.S.* **96** F11
Stillwater Range, *Nev., U.S.* **103** P8
Stilwell, *Okla., U.S.* **96** F14
Stinnett, *Tex., U.S.* **96** F5
Stirling City, *Calif., U.S.* **103** P4
Stirling Island, *Solomon Is.* **197** L14
Stjørdalshalsen, *Nor.* **134** H11
Stockdale, *Tex., U.S.* **97** R10
Stockholm, *Sw.* **135** L14
Stocks Seamount, *Atl. Oc.* **217** Q9
Stockton, *Calif., U.S.* **103** R5
Stockton, *Ill., U.S.* **92** M4
Stockton, *Kans., U.S.* **99** S6
Stockton, *Mo., U.S.* **99** U11
Stockton Lake, *Mo., U.S.* **99** U11
Stoke, *Eng., U.K.* **138** G8
Stokes, Bahía, *Chile* **125** X7
Stokes, Mount, *N.Z.* **193** M18
Stolbovoy, Ostrov, *Russ.* **141** D17
Stolin, *Belarus* **133** G13
Stonehaven, *Scot., U.K.* **138** E8
Stonehenge, *Qnsld., Austral.* **191** U12
Stones River National Battlefield, *Tenn., U.S.* **95** F15
Stonewall, *Miss., U.S.* **95** L13
Stonewall, *Okla., U.S.* **96** H12
Stony, river, *Alas., U.S.* **105** J14
Stony Rapids, *Sask., Can.* **76** K12
Stora Lulevatten, lake, *Sw.* **135** E13
Storavan, lake, *Sw.* **135** F13
Støren, *Nor.* **134** H11
Storkerson Bay, *N.W.T., Can.* **76** D11
Storlien, *Sw.* **134** H11
Storm Lake, *Iowa, U.S.* **99** N10
Stornoway, *Scot., U.K.* **138** D7
Storsjön, lake, *Sw.* **134** H12
Storuman, *Sw.* **135** G13
Story, *Wyo., U.S.* **100** F11
Story City, *Iowa, U.S.* **99** N11
Stoughton, *Wis., U.S.* **92** L5
Stoyba, *Russ.* **141** K19
Strahan, *Tas., Austral.* **191** Z15
Stralsund, *Ger.* **132** E7
Stranda, *Nor.* **134** J10
Strangways, *S. Austral., Austral.* **191** V9
Stranraer, *Scot., U.K.* **138** F7
Strasbourg, *Fr.* **138** K12
Strasburg, *N. Dak., U.S.* **98** H5
Strasburg, *Ohio, U.S.* **93** Q14
Strasburg, *Va., U.S.* **90** C11
Stratford, *Tex., U.S.* **96** F5
Strathalbyn, *S. Austral., Austral.* **191** Y10
Strathcona, Mount, *Antarctica* **207** K21
Stratobowl, site, *S. Dak., U.S.* **98** L2
Stratton, *Colo., U.S.* **100** M15
Stratton, *Me., U.S.* **89** E15
Stratton, *Nebr., U.S.* **99** R3
Strawberry Mountain, *Oreg., U.S.* **102** G7
Strawberry Reservoir, *Utah, U.S.* **100** L8
Strawn, *Tex., U.S.* **96** L9
Streaky Bay, *S. Austral., Austral.* **191** X9
Streator, *Ill., U.S.* **93** P6
Streeter, *N. Dak., U.S.* **98** G6
Strelka, *Russ.* **141** F20
Streymoy, island, *Faroe Is., Den.* **134** J6
Strezhevoy, *Russ.* **140** H11
Strickland, river, *P.N.G.* **193** D18
Stringtown, *Okla., U.S.* **96** H12
Stromsburg, *Nebr., U.S.* **99** Q7
Strömstad, *Sw.* **134** L11
Strömsund, *Sw.* **134** H12
Stroud, *Okla., U.S.* **96** F12
Stroudsburg, *Pa., U.S.* **88** N9
Stryy, *Ukr.* **132** J11
Stuart, *Fla., U.S.* **91** V10
Stuart, *Nebr., U.S.* **99** N6
Stuart, *Va., U.S.* **90** G9
Stuart Island, *U.S.* **78** P2
Stuart Lake, *B.C., Can.* **76** K8
Stuart Range, *Austral.* **190** H9
Stump Lake, *N. Dak., U.S.* **98** F7
Stumpy Point, *N.C., U.S.* **90** H15
Stung Treng, *Cambodia* **166** M12
Sturgeon Bay, *Wis., U.S.* **92** H8
Sturgis, *Ky., U.S.* **95** C14
Sturgis, *Mich., U.S.* **93** N10
Sturgis, *S. Dak., U.S.* **98** K2
Sturt Stony Desert, *Austral.* **190** G11
Stuttgart, *Ark., U.S.* **94** H9
Stuttgart, *Ger.* **132** J5
Stykkishólmur, *Ice.* **134** E2
Suai, *E. Timor* **169** N15
Suakin, *Sudan* **179** C14
Suakin Archipelago, *Af.* **174** F10
Suao, *Taiwan, China* **163** Q10
Subaşı Dağı, *Turk.* **149** G16
Subay', Urūq, *Saudi Arabia* **152** K8
Subei, *China* **160** G9
Subeita, ruins, *Israel* **151** P4
Subi, island, *Indonesia* **168** H9
Sublette, *Kans., U.S.* **99** U4
Subotica, *Yug.* **137** E13
Suceava, *Rom.* **137** D16
Sucre, *Bol.* **122** K7
Sud, Canal du, *Haiti* **111** M15
Sud, Pointe du, *Seychelles* **185** P20
Sudan, *Af.* **178** E12
Sudan, region, *Af.* **174** G3
Sudan, *Tex., U.S.* **96** J4
Sudbury, *Ont., Can.* **77** P18
Sudd, wetland, *Af.* **174** H9
Suddie, *Guyana* **121** D14
Sud-Est, Passe du, *Gambier Is., Fr. Polynesia, Fr.* **199** R21
Sudeten, region, *Eur.* **130** G7
Sud-Ouest, Passe du, *Gambier Is., Fr. Polynesia, Fr.* **199** R20
Sudr, *Egypt* **151** R1
Suðuroy, island, *Faroe Is., Den.* **134** J5
Sue, river, *Sudan* **178** H11
Suez *see* El Suweis, *Egypt* **151** Q1
Suez, Gulf of, *Egypt* **151** R1
Suez Canal, *Egypt* **151** N1
Suffolk, *Va., U.S.* **90** F14
Sugar City, *Colo., U.S.* **101** N14
Sugar City, *Idaho, U.S.* **100** G7
Sugar Land, *Tex., U.S.* **97** R13
Sugarloaf Key, *Fla., U.S.* **91** Y8
Suğla Gölü, *Turk.* **148** H7
Suhai Hu, *China* **160** G9
Şuḩār, *Oman* **153** J15
Suhbaatar, *Mongolia* **160** C12
Suheli Par, atoll, *India* **159** R2
Şuhut, *Turk.* **148** F6
Suichang, *China* **162** M8
Suichuan, *China* **163** P5
Suide, *China* **162** E3
Suining, *China* **160** L12
Suining, *China* **162** H8
Suining, *China* **163** P2
Suixi, *China* **162** H7
Suixi, *China* **163** S2
Suizhong, *China* **162** C9
Suizhou, *China* **162** K4
Sujawal, *Pak.* **157** W7
Sukabumi, *Indonesia* **168** M8
Sukadana, *Indonesia* **168** J9
Sukagawa, *Jap.* **164** M13

Sūkh, *Uzb.* **155** L14
Sukhona, river, *Eur.* **130** C11
Sukhothai, *Thai.* **166** K8
Sukkur, *Pak.* **157** T7
Sukumo, *Jap.* **165** S6
Sula, Kepulauan, *Indonesia* **169** K15
Sulaiman Range, *Pak.* **157** S8
Sulanheer, *Mongolia* **161** F13
Sula Sgeir, island, *Scot., U.K.* **138** C7
Sulawesi (Celebes), island, *Indonesia* **169** K13
Sulei, island, *Solomon Is.* **197** M18
Süleymanlı, *Turk.* **148** H11
Sulima, *Sierra Leone* **180** G6
Sulina, *Rom.* **137** F18
Sullana, *Peru* **122** E2
Sulligent, *Ala., U.S.* **95** J13
Sullivan, *Ill., U.S.* **93** R6
Sullivan, *Ind., U.S.* **93** S7
Sullivan, *Mo., U.S.* **99** T14
Sulphur, river, *Tex., U.S.* **96** K14
Sulphur, *La., U.S.* **94** P7
Sulphur, *Okla., U.S.* **96** H11
Sulphur Cone, *Hawaii, U.S.* **107** N19
Sulphur Springs, *Tex., U.S.* **96** K13
Sulphur Springs Draw, *Tex., U.S.* **96** L4
Sultan Dağları, *Turk.* **148** G7
Sultanhanı, *Turk.* **148** G8
Sultanpur, *India* **158** G8
Sulu Archipelago, *Philippines* **169** G13
Sulu Basin, *Pac. Oc.* **218** J3
Sülüklü, *Turk.* **148** F7
Sülüktü, *Kyrg.* **156** G8
Suluova, *Turk.* **148** D11
Sulu Sea, *Philippines* **169** E13
Sumampa, *Arg.* **124** H10
Sumas, *Wash., U.S.* **102** A4
Sumatra, island, *Asia* **146** L10
Sumaúma, *Braz.* **122** F9
Sumba, island, *Indonesia* **169** N13
Sumba, *Faroe Is., Den.* **134** J6
Sumbawa, island, *Indonesia* **168** M12
Sumbawanga, *Tanzania* **178** M12
Sumbe, *Angola* **182** D5
Sumburgh Head, *Scot., U.K.* **138** C9
Sumisu (Smith), island, *Jap.* **194** B3
Summer Lake, *Oreg., U.S.* **102** K5
Summerland Key, *Fla., U.S.* **91** Y9
Summersville, *W. Va., U.S.* **90** D9
Summerville, *Ga., U.S.* **90** K4
Summerville, *S.C., U.S.* **90** M10
Summit, *Miss., U.S.* **94** N10
Summit Mountain, *Nev., U.S.* **103** P10
Summit Peak, *Colo., U.S.* **101** P12
Sumner, *Iowa, U.S.* **98** M13
Sumoto, *Jap.* **165** Q8
Sumprabum, *Myanmar* **166** D7
Sumpter, *Oreg., U.S.* **102** G8
Sumqayıt, *Azerb.* **149** D23
Sumrall, *Miss., U.S.* **94** M12
Sumter, *S.C., U.S.* **90** K10
Sumy, *Ukr.* **133** H16
Sun, river, *Mont., U.S.* **100** C7
Sunagawa, *Jap.* **164** F13
Sunam-dong, *N. Korea* **162** B14
Sunbaron Roads (Tinian Harbor), *Tinian, N. Mariana Is., U.S.* **196** C7
Sunburst, *Mont., U.S.* **100** A7
Sunbury, *Pa., U.S.* **88** N7
Sunbury, *Vic., Austral.* **191** Z12
Sunchales, *Arg.* **124** J11
Sunch'ŏn, *N. Korea* **162** D12
Sunch'ŏn, *S. Korea* **162** G13
Sun City, *Ariz., U.S.* **101** T6
Sunda, Selat, *Indonesia* **168** L8
Sundance, *Wyo., U.S.* **100** F13
Sundar, *Malaysia* **168** G11
Sundarbans, delta, *Bangladesh-India* **158** J12
Sundargarh, *India* **158** J9
Sunday see Raoul Island, island, *Kermadec Is., N.Z.* **194** L9
Sunderland, *Eng., U.K.* **138** F8
Sundi, *São Tomé and Príncipe* **185** A20
Sündiken Dağ, *Turk.* **148** E7
Sundown, *Tex., U.S.* **96** K4
Sundsvall, *Sw.* **135** J13
Sunflower, Mount, *Kans., U.S.* **99** S3
Sungaianyar, *Indonesia* **168** K12
Sungaibatu, *Indonesia* **168** J9
Sungai Kolok, *Thai.* **167** S9
Sungaipenuh, *Indonesia* **168** K6
Sungai Petani, *Malaysia* **167** S9
Sung Men, *Thai.* **166** K8
Sungurlu, *Turk.* **148** E9
Sunnyside, *Utah, U.S.* **100** M8
Sunnyside, *Wash., U.S.* **102** E6
Sunnyvale, *Calif., U.S.* **103** S4
Sun Prairie, *Wis., U.S.* **92** L5
Sunray, *Tex., U.S.* **96** F5
Sunset Beach, *Hawaii, U.S.* **106** D10
Sunset Crater Volcano National Monument, *Ariz., U.S.* **101** S7
Suntar Khayata, Khrebet, *Russ.* **141** G19
Suntsar, *Pak.* **157** V2
Sun Valley, *Idaho, U.S.* **100** G5
Sunwu, *China* **161** B17
Sunyani, *Ghana* **180** G10
Suomen Ridge, *Eur.* **130** C8
Suomenselkä, ridge, *Fin.* **135** H15
Suonenjoki, *Fin.* **135** H16
Supai, *Ariz., U.S.* **101** R6
Superior, *Ariz., U.S.* **101** U7
Superior, *Mont., U.S.* **100** C5
Superior, *Nebr., U.S.* **99** R7
Superior, *Wis., U.S.* **92** E2
Superior, *Wyo., U.S.* **100** J10
Superior, Lake, *U.S.-Can.* **79** C15
Süphan Dağı, *Turk.* **149** F17
Supiori, island, *Indonesia* **193** B15
Support Force Glacier, *Antarctica* **206** G10
Supu, *Indonesia* **169** H16
Sup'ung Reservoir, *China-N. Korea* **162** C12
Suquṭrá see Socotra, island, *Yemen* **153** R15
Şūr, *Oman* **153** K17
Şūr (Tyre), *Leb.* **150** K5
Sur, Point, *Calif., U.S.* **103** U4
Sura see Makhfar al Ḩammām, *Syr.* **150** E11
Surab, *Pak.* **157** T5
Surabaya, *Indonesia* **168** M10
Sūrak, *Iran* **153** J16
Surakarta, *Indonesia* **168** M9
Suramana, *Indonesia* **169** J13
Surat, *India* **158** K3
Surat, *Qnsld., Austral.* **191** V14
Surat Thani, *Thai.* **167** Q8
Sürétiméat, Mount, *Vanuatu* **198** B2
Surf City, *N.C., U.S.* **90** K13
Surgidero de Batabanó, *Cuba* **110** G6
Surgut, *Russ.* **140** H11
Surigao, *Philippines* **169** E15
Surin, *Thai.* **166** M10
Suriname, *S. Amer.* **121** F16
Surin Nua, Ko, *Thai.* **167** Q7
Sürmene, *Turk.* **149** D14
Surprise, Île de la, *New Caledonia, Fr.* **198** A5
Surrey, *B.C., Can.* **76** M8
Surt, *Lib.* **177** C14
Surt, Gulf of, *Lib.* **177** C14
Surtanahu, *Pak.* **157** V8
Surtsey, island, *Ice.* **134** G2
Suruç, *Turk.* **149** J13
Suruga Wan, *Jap.* **165** Q11
Surulangun, *Indonesia* **168** K6
Sūsah (Apollonia), *Lib.* **177** B16
Susaki, *Jap.* **165** R6
Susamyr, *Kyrg.* **156** E11
Susanville, *Calif., U.S.* **103** N5
Suşehri, *Turk.* **149** E13
Susitna, river, *Alas., U.S.* **105** H16
Susitna, river, *U.S.* **78** P4
Susoh, *Indonesia* **168** G4
Susquehanna, river, *Pa., U.S.* **88** N7
Susquehanna, *Pa., U.S.* **88** L9
Susques, *Arg.* **124** E9
Susubona, *Solomon Is.* **197** M18
Susulatna, river, *Alas., U.S.* **105** G14
Susuman, *Russ.* **141** F20
Susunu, *Indonesia* **193** B14
Susupe, *Saipan, N. Mariana Is., U.S.* **196** C4
Susurluk, *Turk.* **148** E4
Sutak, *India* **157** N14
Sütçüler, *Turk.* **148** H6
Sutherland, *Nebr., U.S.* **99** P4
Sutherland, *S. Af.* **182** L8
Sutherlin, *Oreg., U.S.* **102** J3
Sutlej, river, *Asia* **146** H7
Sutter Creek, *Calif., U.S.* **103** R5
Sutton, river, *Ont., Can.* **77** L16
Sutton, *Nebr., U.S.* **99** Q7
Sutton, *W. Va., U.S.* **90** D9
Suttsu, *Jap.* **164** G12
Sutwik Island, *Alas., U.S.* **105** N14
Su'u, *Solomon Is.* **197** N19
Suva, *Fiji* **198** J6
Suvadiva Atoll (Huvadu), *Maldives* **159** W3
Suwa, *Jap.* **165** P11
Suwałki, *Pol.* **132** F11
Suwannaphum, *Thai.* **166** L11
Suwannee, *Fla., U.S.* **91** S6
Suwanose Jima, *Jap.* **165** V3
Suwarrow Atoll, *Cook Is., N.Z.* **194** J11
Suwŏn, *S. Korea* **162** F13
Suzhou, *China* **162** J7
Suzhou, *China* **162** K9
Suzu, *Jap.* **164** M10
Suzuka, *Jap.* **165** Q9
Suzu Misaki, *Jap.* **164** M10
Svartisen, glacier, *Nor.* **134** F12
Svatove, *Ukr.* **133** H18
Svay Rieng, *Cambodia* **167** P12
Sveg, *Sw.* **134** J12
Svendborg, *Den.* **134** P11
Sverdlovs'k, *Ukr.* **133** J18
Sverdrup Channel, *Nunavut, Can.* **77** B15
Sverdrup Islands, *Nunavut, Can.* **77** B15
Svetogorsk, *Russ.* **140** D7
Svilengrad, *Bulg.* **137** H16
Svir', river, *Eur.* **130** C10
Svobodnyy, *Russ.* **141** K19
Svolvær, *Nor.* **134** E12
Svyataya Anna Fan, *Arctic Oc.* **222** F12
Svyataya Anna Trough, *Arctic Oc.* **222** D12
Svyatoy Nos, Mys, *Russ.* **141** D17
Swain Reefs, *Austral.* **190** F15
Swainsboro, *Ga., U.S.* **90** M7
Swains Island, *Pac. Oc.* **194** J10
Swakop, river, *Namibia* **182** H6
Swakopmund, *Namibia* **182** H6
Swan, river, *Austral.* **190** K2
Swan, river, *Mont., U.S.* **100** C6
Swan Peak, *Mont., U.S.* **100** C6
Swanquarter, *N.C., U.S.* **90** H14
Swan River, *Man., Can.* **77** M13
Swansboro, *N.C., U.S.* **90** J13
Swansea, *Wales, U.K.* **138** H7
Swans Island, *Me., U.S.* **89** G18
Swanton, *Vt., U.S.* **88** E12
Swan Valley, *Idaho, U.S.* **100** H8
Swart Berg, *Af.* **174** R7
Swatow see Shantou, *China* **163** R6
Swaziland, *Af.* **182** J11
Sweden, *Eur.* **135** M16
Sweeney Mountains, *Antarctica* **206** F7
Sweetgrass, *Mont., U.S.* **100** A7
Sweet Home, *Oreg., U.S.* **102** G3
Sweetwater, river, *Wyo., U.S.* **100** J10
Sweetwater, *Tenn., U.S.* **95** F18
Sweetwater, *Tex., U.S.* **96** L7
Sweetwater Lake, *N. Dak., U.S.* **98** E6
Swellendam, *S. Af.* **182** M8
Świdwin, *Pol.* **132** F8
Swift Current, *Sask., Can.* **76** N11
Świnoujście, *Pol.* **132** F8
Switzerland, *Eur.* **132** K4
Sydney, *N.S., Can.* **77** N23
Sydney, *N.S.W., Austral.* **191** Y14
Sydney Bay, *Norfolk I., Austral.* **197** G20
Sydney Point, *Banaba, Kiribati* **197** E20
Syeri, *Indonesia* **169** K19
Syktyvkar, *Russ.* **140** F8
Sylacauga, *Ala., U.S.* **95** K16
Sylhet, *Bangladesh* **158** H13
Sylva, *N.C., U.S.* **90** J6
Sylvania, *Ga., U.S.* **90** M8
Sylvania, *Ohio, U.S.* **93** N12
Sylvester, *Ga., U.S.* **91** P5
Sylvester, *Tex., U.S.* **96** L7
Sylvester, Lake, *Austral.* **190** D9
Synya, *Russ.* **140** F10
Syowa, station, *Antarctica* **207** B17
Syracuse see Siracusa, *It.* **136** L11
Syracuse, *Kans., U.S.* **99** U3
Syracuse, *N.Y., U.S.* **88** J8
Syracuse, *Nebr., U.S.* **99** Q9
Syr Darya, river, *Asia* **146** F6
Syria, *Asia* **150** F11
Syrian Desert, *Asia* **146** F3
Syrian Gates, *Turk.* **148** J11
Sysy Basa, *Russ.* **141** H18
Syzran', *Russ.* **140** H7
Szczecin, *Pol.* **132** F8
Szczecinek, *Pol.* **132** F9
Szeged, *Hung.* **132** L10
Székesfehérvár, *Hung.* **132** K9
Szolnok, *Hung.* **132** L10
Szombathely, *Hung.* **132** K8

T

Taakoka, island, *Rarotonga, Cook Is., N.Z.* **198** Q9
Taapuna, *Tahiti, Fr. Polynesia, Fr.* **199** N15
Taapuna, Passe de, *Tahiti, Fr. Polynesia, Fr.* **199** N15
Taatioe, Mount, *Rurutu, Fr. Polynesia, Fr.* **199** K23
Tâba, *Egypt* **151** R5
Tabago, *P.N.G.* **197** K14
Ţābah, *Saudi Arabia* **152** H8
Tabalo, *P.N.G.* **193** B20
Tabar Islands, *P.N.G.* **193** B21
Ţabas, *Iran* **153** D15
Ţabas, *Iran* **153** D17
Tabelbala, *Alg.* **176** C9
Tabiang, *Banaba, Kiribati* **197** D20
Tabiang, *Tarawa, Kiribati* **197** G17
Tabik, island, *Kwajalein Atoll, Marshall Is.* **196** K1
Tabik Channel, *Kwajalein Atoll, Marshall Is.* **196** K2
Tabiteuea, island, *Kiribati* **194** G8
Tabiteuea, *Tarawa, Kiribati* **197** G18
Tablas, island, *Philippines* **169** D14
Table, Pointe de la, *Réunion, Fr.* **185** H17
Table Rock Lake, *Mo., U.S.* **99** V11
Tabontebike, *Tarawa, Kiribati* **197** E17
Tábor, *Czech Rep.* **132** J7
Tabor, *Russ.* **141** D18
Tabora, *Tanzania* **179** L13
Tabor City, *N.C., U.S.* **90** K11
Tabou, *Côte d'Ivoire* **180** H7
Tabrīz, *Iran* **152** B10
Tabu, Motu, *Ua Huka, Fr. Polynesia, Fr.* **199** M23
Tabuaeran (Fanning Island), *Kiribati* **194** F12
Tabūk, *Saudi Arabia* **152** G6
Tabunifi, *Yap Is., F.S.M.* **197** D18
Tacheng, *China* **160** D6
Tacloban, *Philippines* **169** D15
Tacna, *Ariz., U.S.* **101** U5
Tacna, *Peru* **122** K6
Tacoma, *Wash., U.S.* **102** C4
Tacuarembó, *Uru.* **124** K14
Tacutu, river, *S. Amer.* **118** C6
Tad, *Pak.* **157** V3
Tademaït, Plateau du, *Alg.* **176** D10
Tadine, *New Caledonia, Fr.* **198** D10
Tadjmout, *Alg.* **176** E11
Tadjoura, Gulf of, *Af.* **174** G11
Tadmur (Palmyra), *Syr.* **150** G10
Tadoule Lake, *Man., Can.* **77** K14
Tadoussac, *Que., Can.* **77** N20
Tadpatri, *India* **159** N6
T'aean, *S. Korea* **162** F13
Taegu, *S. Korea* **162** G14
Taejŏn, *S. Korea* **162** F13
Taenga, island, *Fr. Polynesia, Fr.* **199** E19
Tafahi, island, *Tonga* **194** J10
Tafalla, *Sp.* **139** P8
Tafassasset, Oued, *Alg.* **176** E12
Tafí Viejo, *Arg.* **124** G9
Tafonsak, *Kosrae, F.S.M.* **197** A18
Taft, *Calif., U.S.* **103** V7
Taft, *Tex., U.S.* **97** T11
Taftān, Kūh-e, *Iran* **153** G17
Taga, *Samoa* **198** L2
Taganrog, *Russ.* **140** H4
Tagant, region, *Af.* **174** F2
Tagawa, *Jap.* **165** R4
Taghaz, *Afghan.* **157** R3
Tagounit, *Mor.* **176** C8
Tagtabazar, *Turkm.* **154** N10
Taguatinga, *Braz.* **123** H14
Tagula, island, *P.N.G.* **193** F22
Tagum, *Philippines* **169** F15
Tagus, river, *Eur.* **130** J1
Tahaa, island, *Fr. Polynesia, Fr.* **199** A23
Tahan, peak, *Malaysia* **167** T10
Tahanea, island, *Fr. Polynesia, Fr.* **199** E18
Tahat, Mount, *Alg.* **176** E11
Ţāherī, *Iran* **153** H13
Tahgong, Puntan, *Tinian, N. Mariana Is., U.S.* **196** A7
Tahi, point, *Bora-Bora, Fr. Polynesia, Fr.* **199** K14
Tahiti, island, *Fr. Polynesia, Fr.* **199** P16
Tahlab, river, *Pak.* **157** T2
Tahlab, Dasht-i-, *Pak.* **157** S2
Tahlequah, *Okla., U.S.* **96** F14
Tahoe, Lake, *Calif.-Nev., U.S.* **103** Q6
Tahoe City, *Calif., U.S.* **103** Q6
Tahoka, *Tex., U.S.* **96** K5
Taholah, *Wash., U.S.* **102** C2
Tahoua, *Niger* **176** H11
Tahtalı Dağ, *Turk.* **148** F12
Tahtalidaği, peak, *Turk.* **148** J5
Tahuata, island, *Hiva Oa, Fr. Polynesia, Fr.* **199** N20
Tahueia, *Tubuai, Fr. Polynesia, Fr.* **199** K21
Tahueia, Mouillage de, *Tubuai, Fr. Polynesia, Fr.* **199** J21
Tahulandang, island, *Indonesia* **169** H15
Tahuna, *Indonesia* **169** G15
Tai'an, *China* **162** G7
Taiarapu, Presqu'île de, *Tahiti, Fr. Polynesia, Fr.* **199** P18
Taiaro, island, *Fr. Polynesia, Fr.* **199** E18
Taibei see T'aipei, *Taiwan, China* **163** Q10
Taibus Qi (Baochang), *China* **162** B6
T'aichung, *Taiwan, China* **163** R9
Taidong see T'aitung, *Taiwan, China* **163** S10
Taigu, *China* **162** F4
Taihang Shan, *China* **162** F5
Taihape, *N.Z.* **193** L19
Taihe, *China* **163** P5
Tai Hu, *China* **162** K9
Taihu, *China* **162** L6
Taiki, *Jap.* **164** G15
Tailai, *China* **161** D16
Tailem Bend, *S. Austral., Austral.* **191** Y10
Tain, *Scot., U.K.* **138** D7
T'ainan, *Taiwan, China* **163** S9
Taining, *China* **163** P7
Taiof, island, *P.N.G.* **197** J13
T'aipei (Taibei), *Taiwan, China* **163** Q10
Taiping, *Malaysia* **167** T9
Taipingot, peak, *Rota I., N. Mariana Is., U.S.* **196** E7
Tairapa, Passe, *Manihi, Fr. Polynesia, Fr.* **199** K17
Taira Shima, *Jap.* **165** V3
Taishan, *China* **163** S3
Taita, Mount, *Tubuai, Fr. Polynesia, Fr.* **199** K21
Taitao, Peninsula de, *Chile* **125** T6

T'aitung (Taidong), Taiwan, China 163 S10
Taivalkoski, Fin. 135 F16
Taiwan, Asia 163 R10
Taiwan, island, Taiwan, China 163 R10
Taiwan Strait, China 163 S8
Taiyuan, China 162 E4
Taizhou, China 162 J9
Taizhou see Linhai, China 162 M10
Ta'izz, Yemen 152 R9
Tajarhī, Lib. 177 E14
Tajikistan, Asia 156 H9
Tajima, Jap. 164 M12
Tajo, river, Sp. 139 R6
Tak, Thai. 166 K8
Taka, island, Jaluit Atoll, Marshall Is. 196 M7
Taka Atoll, Marshall Is. 196 F4
Takāb, Iran 152 C11
Takahe, Mount, Antarctica 206 L7
Takaiu, Pohnpei, F.S.M. 197 F14
Takaka, N.Z. 193 M17
Takamatsu, Jap. 165 Q7
Takamori, Jap. 165 S5
Takaoka, Jap. 165 N10
Takapau, N.Z. 193 L19
Takapoto, island, Fr. Polynesia, Fr. 199 D18
Takara Jima, Jap. 165 V3
Takaroa, island, Fr. Polynesia, Fr. 199 D18
Takasaki, Jap. 165 N11
Takatik, island, Pohnpei, F.S.M. 197 F14
Tā-kaw, Myanmar 166 H7
Takayama, Jap. 165 P10
Takefu, Jap. 165 P9
Takengon, Indonesia 168 G4
Takeo, Cambodia 167 P11
Takeo, Jap. 165 R4
Take Shima, Jap. 165 U4
Tākestān, Iran 152 C12
Taketa, Jap. 165 S5
Takfon, Taj. 156 H7
Takhtabrod, Kaz. 154 C12
Takhteh Pol, Afghan. 157 Q5
Taki, P.N.G. 197 K14
Takikawa, Jap. 164 F13
Taklimakan Desert, Asia 146 G8
Taklimakan Shamo, China 160 G5
Taksimo, Russ. 141 K17
Takuan, Mount, P.N.G. 197 K14
Takua Pa, Thai. 167 Q7
Takum, India 158 F14
Takume, island, Fr. Polynesia, Fr. 199 E19
Takuua, island, Penrhyn, Cook Is., N.Z. 199 B18
Takuua Passage, Penrhyn, Cook Is., N.Z. 199 B18
Tal, Pak. 156 L10
Talagang, Pak. 157 P10
Talaimannar, Sri Lanka 159 S7
Talamanca, Cordillera de, N. Amer. 74 Q8
Talangbatu, Indonesia 168 L6
Talara, Peru 122 E1
Talas, Kyrg. 156 E10
Talaud, Kepulauan, Indonesia 169 G16
Talavera de la Reina, Sp. 139 Q6
Talbot, Cape, Austral. 190 B6
Talbot Inlet, Nunavut, Can. 77 C16
Talbotton, Ga., U.S. 90 M5
Talca, Chile 124 M7
Talcahuano, Chile 125 N6
Taldora, Qnsld., Austral. 191 S11
Taldyqorghan, Kaz. 155 G17
Talhar, Pak. 157 W7
Talia, S. Austral., Austral. 191 X9
Taliabu, island, Indonesia 169 K15
Talihina, Okla., U.S. 96 H14
Tali Post, Sudan 178 H12
Taliwang, Indonesia 168 M12
Talkeetna, Alas., U.S. 105 H16
Talkeetna Mountains, Alas., U.S. 105 H16
Talladega, Ala., U.S. 95 J16
Tall 'Afar, Iraq 152 C9
Tallahassee, Fla., U.S. 91 Q5
Tall al Abyaḑ, Syr. 150 D11
Tall al Aḩmar (Til Barsip), Syr. 150 D10
Tallapoosa, river, Ala., U.S. 95 L16
Tallapoosa, Ga., U.S. 90 L4
Tallassee, Ala., U.S. 95 L16
Tall Birāk, Syr. 150 D14
Tall Ḩalaf, ruins, Syr. 150 C13
Tallinn (Reval), Estonia 135 K16
Tall Kalakh, Syr. 150 G7
Tall Kūjik, Syr. 150 C16
Tall Tamir, Syr. 150 D13
Tallulah, La., U.S. 94 L10
Talnakh, Russ. 141 F13
Talodi, Sudan 178 F12
Talofofo, Guam, U.S. 196 D10
Talofofo Bay, Guam, U.S. 196 D11
Taloga, Okla., U.S. 96 F9
Talok, Indonesia 169 H13
Taloqan, Afghan. 156 K8
Talorha, Mauritania 176 F6
Talos Dome, Antarctica 207 Q15
Taloyoak, Nunavut, Can. 77 F15
Talshand, Mongolia 160 E10
Talsi, Latv. 135 M16
Taltal, Chile 124 F7
Tama, Iowa, U.S. 99 N12
Tamakautonga, Niue, N.Z. 199 B20
Tamale, Ghana 180 F10
Tamana, island, Kiribati 194 G8
Tamanoura, Jap. 165 S2
Tamanrasset, Alg. 176 F11
Tamarin, Mauritius 185 G19
Tamatoa, Tubuai, Fr. Polynesia, Fr. 199 K21
Tamazunchale, Mex. 108 H12
Tambacounda, Senegal 176 H5
Tambalan, Indonesia 168 H11
Tambelan, Kepulauan, Indonesia 168 H8
Tambisan, Malaysia 169 G13
Tambo, Qnsld., Austral. 191 U13
Tambora, peak, Indonesia 168 M12
Tambov, Russ. 140 G6
Tambura, Sudan 178 H11
Tamch, Mongolia 160 D9
Tamchaket, Mauritania 176 G6
Tame, Col. 120 E7
Tamel Aike, Arg. 125 U7
Tamiahua, Mex. 108 H12
Tam Ky, Vietnam 166 L14
Tamotoe, Passe, Tahiti, Fr. Polynesia, Fr. 199 P17
Tampa, Fla., U.S. 91 U7
Tampa Bay, Fla., U.S. 91 U7
Tampere, Fin. 135 J15
Tampico, Mex. 108 G12
Tampin, Malaysia 167 U10
Tampoc, river, Fr. Guiana 121 F17
Tam Quan, Vietnam 166 M14
Tamrida see Hadīboh, Yemen 153 R14
Tamsagbulag, Mongolia 161 D15
Tamshiyacu, Peru 122 E4
Tamsweg, Aust. 132 K7
Tamu, Myanmar 166 F5
Tamuning, Guam, U.S. 196 C11
Tamworth, N.S.W., Austral. 191 X14
Tana, river, Fin.-Nor. 135 C15
Tana, river, Kenya 179 K15
Tana, Nor. 135 B15
Tana, Lake, Af. 174 G10
Tanabe, Jap. 165 R8
Tanacross, Alas., U.S. 105 G18
Tanaga Island, Alas., U.S. 104 P5
Tanagomba Harbor, Solomon Is. 197 M18
T'ana Hāyk', Eth. 179 F14
Tanahbala, island, Indonesia 168 J5
Tanahgrogot, Indonesia 168 K12
Tanahjampea, island, Indonesia 169 M13
Tanahmasa, island, Indonesia 168 J5
Tanahmerah, Indonesia 169 M21
Tanami, N. Terr., Austral. 191 S7
Tanami, Mount, Austral. 190 E7
Tanami Desert, Austral. 190 D8
Tanana, river, Alas., U.S. 105 F15
Tanana, Alas., U.S. 105 F15
Tanapag, Saipan, N. Mariana Is., U.S. 196 B5
Tanavuso Point, Fiji 198 H6
Tancheng, China 162 H8
Tanch'ŏn, N. Korea 162 C14
Tandil, Arg. 125 N12
Tandil, Sierra del, S. Amer. 118 M6
Tandlianwala, Pak. 157 Q11
Tando Adam, Pak. 157 V7
Tando Allahyar, Pak. 157 V7
Tando Bago, Pak. 157 W8
Tando Muhammad Khan, Pak. 157 W7
Tandur, India 158 L7
Tanega Shima, Jap. 165 U5
Tanen Range, Thai. 166 J7
Tanezrouft, region, Alg.-Mali 176 E9
Ţanf, Jabal aţ, Syr. 150 J11
Tanga, Tanzania 179 L15
Tangail, Bangladesh 158 H12
Tanga Islands, P.N.G. 193 C22
Tanganyika, Lake, Af. 178 L12
Tange Promontory, Antarctica 207 B19
Tanggu, China 162 D7
Tanggula Range, Asia 146 H9
Tanggula Shan, China 160 K7
Tanghe, China 162 J4
Tangi, India 158 L10
Tangier, Mor. 176 A8
Tango, Jap. 165 P8
Tangorin, Qnsld., Austral. 191 T12
Tangra Yumco, China 160 K6
Tangse, Indonesia 168 G4
Tangshan, China 162 D8
Tanguisson Point, Guam, U.S. 196 B11
Tangyuan, China 161 C18
Tanimbar, Kepulauan, Indonesia 169 N17
Tanimbili, Santa Cruz Is., Solomon Is. 197 Q23
Tanjore see Thanjavur, India 159 R6
Tanjungbalai, Indonesia 168 H5
Tanjungbatu, Indonesia 168 H12
Tanjungkarang-Telubketung, Indonesia 168 L7
Tanjungpandan, Indonesia 168 K8
Tanjungpinang, Indonesia 168 J7
Tanjungredep, Indonesia 168 H12
Tank, Pak. 157 P9
Ta-n-Kena, Alg. 176 D12
Tankovo, Russ. 141 J13
Tanna, island, Vanuatu 198 H4
Tännäs, Sw. 134 J12
Tannu Ola, Khrebet, Russ. 141 M13
Tannur, ruins, Jordan 151 P6
Tanobato, Indonesia 168 J5
Tanot, India 158 F2
Tânout, Niger 176 H12
Tanowrah, Afghan. 157 N2
Ţanţa, Egypt 177 C18
Tan-Tan, Mor. 176 C7
Tanumbirini, N. Terr., Austral. 191 Q9
Tanzania, Af. 179 M14
Tao, river, China 160 J11
Tao, Ko, Thai. 167 Q8
Tao'er, river, China 161 D16
Taojiang, China 162 M3
Taole (Mataigou), China 162 D1
Taonan, China 161 D16
Taongi Atoll, Marshall Is. 196 E4
Taos, N. Mex., U.S. 101 Q13
Taoudenni (Smeïda), Mali 176 E8
Taouz, Mor. 176 C9
Taoyuan, China 162 M3
T'aoyüan, Taiwan, China 163 Q10
Tapa, Estonia 135 K16
Tapachula, Mex. 109 L15
Tapajós, river, Braz. 122 E10
Tapak, island, Pohnpei, F.S.M. 197 F14
Tapan, Indonesia 168 K6
Tapana, island, Vava'u Group, Tonga 198 M11
Tapanahoni, river, Suriname 121 F16
Tapauá, river, Braz. 122 E7
Tapawera, N.Z. 193 M17
Tapeta, Liberia 180 H7
Taphan Hin, Thai. 166 L9
Tapi, river, India 158 K4
Tapiche, river, Peru 122 F4
Tapini, P.N.G. 193 D19
Tapiwa, Banaba, Kiribati 197 D20
Taplejung, Nepal 158 F11
Tapora, Passe, Tahiti, Fr. Polynesia, Fr. 199 P17
Tappahannock, Va., U.S. 90 E13
Tapu, Motu, Bora-Bora, Fr. Polynesia, Fr. 199 K13
Tapuaenuku, peak, N.Z. 193 N18
Tapuaetai, island, Aitutaki Atoll, Cook Is., N.Z. 198 R12
Tapuamu, Tahaa, Fr. Polynesia, Fr. 199 A23
Tapueraha, Passe de, Tahiti, Fr. Polynesia, Fr. 199 Q17
Tapul Group, Philippines 169 G13
Tapunui, island, Penrhyn, Cook Is., N.Z. 199 A17
Tapurucuará, Braz. 122 C7
Taputapu, Cap, Tutuila, Amer. Samoa, U.S. 198 M6
Taputimu, Tutuila, Amer. Samoa, U.S. 198 N7
Ţaqah, Oman 153 P14
Taquari, river, Braz. 122 K10
Tar, river, N.C., U.S. 90 H12
Tara, Qnsld., Austral. 191 V14
Tara, Russ. 140 J10
Ţarābulus (Tripoli), Leb. 150 H7
Ţarābulus (Tripoli), Lib. 177 B13
Tarakan, island, Indonesia 168 H12
Tarakan, Indonesia 168 H12
Tarakite-iti, island, Manihiki Atoll, Cook Is., N.Z. 199 C14
Taranaki, Mount, N.Z. 193 L18
Taranto, It. 136 J12
Taranto, Golfo di, It. 136 J12
Tarapacá, Col. 120 K8
Tarapaina, Solomon Is. 197 N20
Tarapoto, Peru 122 F3
Taraqu, ruins, Afghan. 157 R1
Tarara, P.N.G. 197 K14
Tarasa Dwip, Nicobar Is., India 159 S15
Tarata, Peru 122 K6
Taratai, island, Tarawa, Kiribati 197 F17
Taratai, Tarawa, Kiribati 197 F17
Tarauacá, river, Braz. 122 F5
Tarauacá, Braz. 122 F5
Taravai, island, Gambier Is., Fr. Polynesia, Fr. 199 Q20
Taravai, Gambier Is., Fr. Polynesia, Fr. 199 Q20
Taravao, Tahiti, Fr. Polynesia, Fr. 199 P17
Taravao, Baie de, Tahiti, Fr. Polynesia, Fr. 199 P17
Tarawa (Bairiki), Tarawa, Kiribati 197 G17
Tarawera, Mount, N.Z. 193 K19
Taraz, Kaz. 155 J14
Tarazit Massif, Af. 174 F5
Tarazona, Sp. 139 P8
Tarbaghatay Zhotasy, Kaz. 155 E18
Tarbert, Scot., U.K. 138 D6
Tarbes, Fr. 139 N9
Tarboro, N.C., U.S. 90 H13
Tarbrax, Qnsld., Austral. 191 S12
Tarcoola, S. Austral., Austral. 191 W9
Tardun, W. Austral., Austral. 191 W2
Taree, N.S.W., Austral. 191 X15
Ţarfā, Ra's aţ, Saudi Arabia 152 N8
Tarfaya, Mor. 176 C6
Targhee Pass, Mont., U.S. 100 F8
Tari, P.N.G. 193 D18
Ţarīf, U.A.E. 153 K14
Tarija, Bol. 122 L7
Tarikere, India 159 P5
Tariku-Taritatu Plain, Indonesia 169 K20
Tarim, river, China 160 F6
Tarim Pendi, China 160 F6
Tarin Kowt, Afghan. 157 P5
Taritatu, river, Indonesia 193 C17
Tarkastad, S. Af. 182 L10
Tarkio, Mo., U.S. 99 Q9
Tarko Sale, Russ. 140 G12
Tarkwa, Ghana 180 H10
Tarlac, Philippines 169 C13
Tarma, Peru 122 H4
Tarn, river, Fr. 139 N10
Tärnaby, Sw. 134 F12
Tarnak, river, Afghan. 157 Q5
Tarnobrzeg, Pol. 132 H11
Tarnów, Pol. 132 J10
Ţārom, Iran 153 G15
Taroom, Qnsld., Austral. 191 U14
Tarpon Springs, Fla., U.S. 91 U7
Tarpum Bay, Bahamas 110 E12
Tarrabool Lake, Austral. 190 D9
Tarrafal, Cape Verde 185 B14
Tarrafal, Cape Verde 185 B15
Tarrafal, Cape Verde 185 D16
Tarragona, Sp. 139 Q10
Tarraleah, Tas., Austral. 191 Z16
Tarras, N.Z. 193 Q16
Tarsus, Turk. 148 J10
Tarta, Turkm. 154 K6
Tartagal, Arg. 124 D10
Tartu, Estonia 135 L17
Ţarţūs (Tortosa), Syr. 150 G7
Taruia Passage, Penrhyn, Cook Is., N.Z. 199 B17
Tarutao, Ko, Thai. 167 S8
Tarutung, Indonesia 168 H5
Tarvisio, It. 136 E10
Tasāwah, Lib. 177 E13
Tasböget, Kaz. 154 H11
Tascosa, Tex., U.S. 96 G4
Taseyevo, Russ. 141 K14
Tashanta, Russ. 140 M12
Tash Gozar, Afghan. 156 K6
Tashk, Daryācheh-ye, Iran 153 F14
Tashkent see Toshkent, Uzb. 155 K13
Tashkepri, Turkm. 154 N10
Tash-Kömür, Kyrg. 156 F10
Tasiilaq, Greenland, Den. 75 C22
Tasikmalaya, Indonesia 168 M9
Tasiusaq, Greenland, Den. 75 C20
Taskan, Russ. 141 F20
Taskesken, Kaz. 155 F18
Taşköprü, Turk. 148 C9
Tasman, N.Z. 193 M18
Tasman Bay, N.Z. 193 M18
Tasman Fracture Zone, Southern Oc. 225 N13
Tasmania, island, Austral. 190 M15
Tasman Peninsula, Austral. 190 M16
Tasman Plain, Pac. Oc. 218 P7
Tasman Sea, Pac. Oc. 194 N6
Taşova, Turk. 148 D11
Tassialouc, Lake, Que., Can. 77 K18
Tassili-n-Ajjer, region, Alg. 176 E12
Tassili Oua-n-Ahaggar, region, Alg. 176 F11
Tas Tumus, Russ. 141 G17
Tasure, Solomon Is. 197 L15
Tataacho Point, Rota I., N. Mariana Is., U.S. 196 D7
Tatafa, island, Ha'apai Group, Tonga 198 Q7
Tatakoto, island, Fr. Polynesia, Fr. 199 E21
Tatamba, Solomon Is. 197 M18
Tatarsk, Russ. 140 K11
Tatarskiy Proliv, Russ. 141 J21
Tatar Strait, Asia 146 D13
Tate, Ga., U.S. 90 K5
Tateyama, Jap. 165 Q12
Tathlina Lake, N.W.T., Can. 76 H10
Tathlīth, Saudi Arabia 152 M9
Tatkon, Myanmar 166 H6
Tatnam, Cape, Man., Can. 77 K15
Tatuí, Braz. 123 M13
Tatum, N. Mex., U.S. 101 U15
Tatvan, Turk. 149 G16
Tau, island, Manua Is., Amer. Samoa, U.S. 198 P3
Tau, island, Tongatapu, Tonga 198 H12
Tau, Manua Is., Amer. Samoa, U.S. 198 P3
Tauá, Braz. 123 F16
Tauak Passage, Pohnpei, F.S.M. 197 F13
Tauanap, Mochun, Chuuk, F.S.M. 197 B14
Taubaté, Braz. 123 M14
Tauenai Channel, Pohnpei, F.S.M. 197 G13
Tauere, island, Fr. Polynesia, Fr. 199 E20
Taugarau, island, Manihi, Fr. Polynesia, Fr. 199 K18
Tauhunu, island, Manihiki Atoll, Cook Is., N.Z. 199 B13
Tauhunu, Manihiki Atoll, Cook Is., N.Z. 199 B13

Taula, island, Vava'u Group, Tonga 198 M11
Taulaga, Swains I., Amer. Samoa, U.S. 198 R3
Taumako, island, Santa Cruz Is., Solomon Is. 197 N24
Taumarunui, N.Z. 193 L19
Taumatawhakatangihangakoauauotamateapokaiwhenuaki-tanatahu 305, peak, N.Z. 193 M19
Taum Sauk Mountain, Mo., U.S. 99 U15
Taunga, island, Vava'u Group, Tonga 198 M11
Taunggok, Myanmar 166 J5
Taunggyi, Myanmar 166 H6
Taungoo, Myanmar 166 J6
Taungup Pass, Myanmar 166 J5
Taunsa, Pak. 157 R9
Taunton, Mass., U.S. 89 L15
Taunton, Eng., U.K. 138 H8
Taupo, N.Z. 193 K19
Taupo, Lake, N.Z. 193 L19
Taupo Tablemount, Pac. Oc. 218 N7
Tauragė, Lith. 135 N16
Tauranga, N.Z. 193 K19
Taurere, Pointe, Bora-Bora, Fr. Polynesia, Fr. 199 L14
Taurus see Toros Dağları, mountains, Turk. 148 H7
Taurus Mountains, Asia 146 E3
Taūshyq, Kaz. 154 G5
Tautama, island, Pitcairn I., U.K. 199 Q23
Tautau, island, Tahaa, Fr. Polynesia, Fr. 199 A23
Tautira, Tahiti, Fr. Polynesia, Fr. 199 P17
Tautu, Aitutaki Atoll, Cook Is., N.Z. 198 Q11
Tautua, island, Penrhyn, Cook Is., N.Z. 199 B18
Tauu Islands, P.N.G. 197 H16
Tavaerua, island, Aitutaki Atoll, Cook Is., N.Z. 198 Q12
Tavai, Wallis and Futuna, Fr. 198 E11
Tavas, Turk. 148 G4
Tavda, Russ. 140 H9
Taverner Bay, Nunavut, Can. 77 G17
Tavernier, Fla., U.S. 91 Y10
Taveuni, island, Fiji 198 H8
Tavşanlı, Turk. 148 E5
Tavua, Fiji 198 H6
Tavu-Na-Sici, island, Fiji 198 K9
Tawai, India 158 F16
Tawake, Fiji 198 G8
Tawakoni, Lake, Tex., U.S. 96 L13
Tawang, India 158 F13
Tawas City, Mich., U.S. 92 J12
Tawau, Malaysia 168 G12
Tawi Tawi, island, Philippines 169 G13
Tawu, Taiwan, China 163 S9
Ţāwūq, Iraq 152 C9
Taxco, Mex. 108 J11
Taxiatosh, Uzb. 154 J9
Taxkorgan, China 160 G4
Taxtako'pir, Uzb. 154 J9
Tayan, Indonesia 168 J9
Tayandu, Kepulauan, Indonesia 169 L18
Taygonos, Poluostrov, Russ. 141 E21
Taylakova, Russ. 140 J11
Taylor, Ariz., U.S. 101 T9
Taylor, Mich., U.S. 92 M12
Taylor, Tex., U.S. 97 P11
Taylor, Mount, N. Mex., U.S. 101 S11
Taylor Glacier, Antarctica 207 N14
Taylor Highway, Alas., U.S. 105 G18
Taylors, S.C., U.S. 90 J7
Taylorsville, Miss., U.S. 94 M12
Taylorville, Ill., U.S. 93 S5
Taymā', Saudi Arabia 152 G6
Taymyr, Ozero, Russ. 141 E14
Taymyr, Poluostrov, Russ. 141 F13
Tay Ninh, Vietnam 167 P12
Taypaq, Kaz. 154 E6
Tayshet, Russ. 141 K14
Taytay, Philippines 169 E13
Ţayyebāt, Iran 153 C17
Taz, river, Russ. 140 G12
Taza, Mor. 176 B9
Tazawa Ko, Jap. 164 K13
Tazawako, Jap. 164 K13
Tazewell, Va., U.S. 90 F8
Tāzirbū, Lib. 177 E16
Tazovskiy, Russ. 140 G12
Tazovskiy Poluostrov, Russ. 140 F12
Tba P'arvani, lake, Rep. of Georgia 149 C18
T'bilisi (Tiflis), Rep. of Georgia 149 C18
Tchibanga, Gabon 181 M15
Tchin-Tabaradène, Niger 176 H11
Tczew, Pol. 132 F9
Teaehoa, Pointe, Hiva Oa, Fr. Polynesia, Fr. 199 N20
Te Afualiku, island, Funafuti, Tuvalu 197 J22
Teague, Tex., U.S. 97 N12
Teahupoo, Tahiti, Fr. Polynesia, Fr. 199 Q17
Teaiti Point, Rarotonga, Cook Is., N.Z. 198 Q9
Teakava, island, Gambier Is., Fr. Polynesia, Fr. 199 Q21
Te Anau, N.Z. 193 Q15
Te Anau, Lake, N.Z. 193 Q15
Teaoraereke, Tarawa, Kiribati 197 G17
Tearinibai, Tarawa, Kiribati 197 F17
Tea Tree, N. Terr., Austral. 191 T8
Te Ava i te Lape, passage, Funafuti, Tuvalu 197 J23
Teava Moa, Passe, Raiatea, Fr. Polynesia, Fr. 199 B24
Teavanui, Passe, Bora-Bora, Fr. Polynesia, Fr. 199 K13
Teavapiti, Passe, Raiatea, Fr. Polynesia, Fr. 199 B23
Teavaraa, Passe de, Tahiti, Fr. Polynesia, Fr. 199 Q16
Teavaro, Moorea, Fr. Polynesia, Fr. 199 N14
Tébessa, Alg. 176 B12
Tebingtinggi, island, Indonesia 168 J7
Tebingtinggi, Indonesia 168 H5
Techla, W. Sahara, Mor. 176 E5
Tecka, Arg. 125 R7
Tecomán, Mex. 108 J9
Tecpan, Mex. 108 K11
Tecuala, Mex. 108 G9
Tecuci, Rom. 137 E16
Tecumseh, Mich., U.S. 92 M12
Tecumseh, Nebr., U.S. 99 R9
Tecumseh, Okla., U.S. 96 G11
Teec Nos Pos, Ariz., U.S. 101 Q9
Teel, Mongolia 160 D11
Tefala, island, Funafuti, Tuvalu 197 L22
Tefarerii, Huahine, Fr. Polynesia, Fr. 199 H14
Tefé, river, Braz. 122 E7
Tefé, Braz. 122 D7
Tefenni, Turk. 148 H5
Tegal, Indonesia 168 M9
Tégua, island, Vanuatu 198 A1
Tegucigalpa, Hond. 109 L17
Teguise, Canary Is., Sp. 184 P8
Tehachapi, Calif., U.S. 103 V8
Tehachapi Mountains, Calif., U.S. 103 W8
Tehachapi Pass, Calif., U.S. 103 V8
Te Hapua, N.Z. 193 G17
Tehek Lake, Nunavut, Can. 77 H14
Tehoohaivei, Cap, Hiva Oa, Fr. Polynesia, Fr. 199 M21
Tehrān, Iran 153 C13
Tehuacán, Mex. 108 J12
Tehuantepec, Mex. 109 K13
Tehuantepec, Golfo de, Mex. 109 L14
Tehuantepec, Istmo de, Mex. 109 K14
Tehuata (Rekareka), island, Fr. Polynesia, Fr. 199 E19
Teide, Pico de, Canary Is., Sp. 184 Q5
Teiko, Motu, Gambier Is., Fr. Polynesia, Fr. 199 R20
Tejen, Turkm. 154 M9
Tejenstroy, Turkm. 154 N9
Tejo, river, Port. 139 R5
Tekamah, Nebr., U.S. 99 P9
Tekapo, Lake, N.Z. 193 P16
Te Karaka, N.Z. 193 K20
Tekax, Mex. 109 H16
Tekeli, Kaz. 155 G17
Tekirdağ, Turk. 148 C3
Tekirova, Turk. 148 J6
Tekkali, India 158 L9
Tekman, Turk. 149 E16
Teknaf, Bangladesh 158 K14
Tekoa, Wash., U.S. 102 C9
Tekokota, island, Fr. Polynesia, Fr. 199 E19
Tekopua, island, Aitutaki Atoll, Cook Is., N.Z. 198 Q12
Te Koutu Point, Aitutaki Atoll, Cook Is., N.Z. 198 Q11
T'elavi, Rep. of Georgia 149 B19
Tel Aviv-Yafo, Israel 150 M5
Telde, Canary Is., Sp. 184 Q6
Telebekelel Ngerael, channel, Palau 196 K11
Telefomin, P.N.G. 193 C17
Telegraph Creek, B.C., Can. 76 H8
Telekitonga, island, Ha'apai Group, Tonga 198 R7
Telekivavau, island, Ha'apai Group, Tonga 198 Q7
Telele, island, Funafuti, Tuvalu 197 L23
Telén, Arg. 124 M9
Telescope Peak, Calif., U.S. 103 U9
Teles Pires, river, S. Amer. 118 E6
Teles Pires (São Manuel), river, Braz. 122 F10
Teljo, Jebel, Af. 174 G8
Tell Atlas, mountains, Af. 174 C4
Tell City, Ind., U.S. 93 U8
Teller, Alas., U.S. 104 F11
Tellicherry, India 159 Q4
Telloh see Lagash, ruins, Iraq 152 E10
Tell Tayinat, ruins, Turk. 148 J11
Telluride, Colo., U.S. 101 P11
Telsen, Arg. 125 R9
Telšiai, Lith. 135 N16
Telukbutun, Indonesia 168 G9
Telukdalem, Indonesia 168 J4
Teluk Intan, Malaysia 167 T9
Tema, Ghana 180 H11
Te Manga, peak, Rarotonga, Cook Is., N.Z. 198 Q9
Tematagi, island, Fr. Polynesia, Fr. 199 H20
Tembagapura, Indonesia 169 L20
Tembenchi, Russ. 141 H14
Temerloh, Malaysia 167 U10
Teminabuan, Indonesia 169 J18
Temirtaū, Kaz. 155 D14
Temoe (Timoe), island, Fr. Polynesia, Fr. 199 H23
Temora, N.S.W., Austral. 191 Y13
Tempe, Ariz., U.S. 101 U7
Temple, Okla., U.S. 96 J10
Temple, Tex., U.S. 97 P11
Temple Bay, Austral. 190 B12
Temuco, Chile 125 P6
Temuka, N.Z. 193 P17
Tena, Ecua. 120 J3
Tenakee Springs, Alas., U.S. 105 K22
Tenali, India 159 N7
Tenararo, island, Fr. Polynesia, Fr. 199 G22
Tenarunga, island, Fr. Polynesia, Fr. 199 G22
Tenasserim, Myanmar 166 L7
Tenasserim, river, Myanmar 167 N8
Tenasserim, Myanmar 167 N8
Ten Degree Channel, India 159 R14
Tendō, Jap. 164 L13
Tendürek Dağı, Turk. 149 F18
Ténéré, desert, Niger 176 F12
Tenerife, island, Canary Is., Sp. 184 Q5
Tengako, island, Funafuti, Tuvalu 197 J24
Tengasu, island, Funafuti, Tuvalu 197 L22
Tengchong, China 160 N10
Te Nggano, lagoon, Solomon Is. 197 R19
Tengiz, oil well, Kaz. 154 G7
Tengiz Köli, Kaz. 155 D13
Tengxian, China 162 G7
Tengxian, China 163 R2
Tenino, Wash., U.S. 102 D3
Tenjo, Mount, Guam, U.S. 196 C10
Tenkasi, India 159 S5
Tenke, Dem. Rep. of the Congo 178 N11
Tenkiller Ferry Lake, Okla., U.S. 96 F14
Tenkodogo, Burkina Faso 180 E11
Tennant Creek, N. Terr., Austral. 191 S9
Tennessee, river, Tenn., U.S. 95 E14
Tennessee, U.S. 95 F13
Tennessee Pass, Colo., U.S. 100 M12
Tennille, Ga., U.S. 90 M7
Tenoka, island, Gambier Is., Fr. Polynesia, Fr. 199 Q20
Tenosique, Mex. 109 K15
Tensaw, river, Ala., U.S. 95 N14
Ten Sleep, Wyo., U.S. 100 G11
Ten Thousand Islands, Fla., U.S. 91 X9
Teófilo Otoni, Braz. 123 K15
Teoho Ote Papa, Pointe, Ua Huka, Fr. Polynesia, Fr. 199 N23
Teohotepapa, Pointe, Hiva Oa, Fr. Polynesia, Fr. 199 M21
Tepa, Wallis and Futuna, Fr. 198 B11
Tepaeture, Pointe, Gambier Is., Fr. Polynesia, Fr. 199 Q20
Tepako, Pointe, Wallis and Futuna, Fr. 198 B12
Tepa Point, Niue, N.Z. 199 B20
Tepati, Tahiti, Fr. Polynesia, Fr. 199 Q17
Tepé, Bioko, Eq. Guinea 184 L8
Tepe Musyan, ruins, Iran 152 E11
Tepic, Mex. 108 H9
Teplice, Czech Rep. 132 H7
Tepu, Tubuai, Fr. Polynesia, Fr. 199 K20
Te Puka, island, Manihiki Atoll, Cook Is., N.Z. 199 B13
Tepuka, island, Funafuti, Tuvalu 197 J22
Tepuka, Te Ava, Funafuti, Tuvalu 197 J22
Tepuu, Pointe, Tubuai, Fr. Polynesia, Fr. 199 K20
Téra, Niger 176 H9
Terae, island, Penrhyn, Cook Is., N.Z. 199 A17
Teraina (Washington Island), Kiribati 194 F12
Teramo, It. 136 H10
Teratak, Indonesia 168 J9
Tercan, Turk. 149 E15
Tereai, island, Rangiroa, Fr. Polynesia, Fr. 199 K15
Terek, river, Eur. 130 H13
Terenos, Braz. 122 L11
Teresina, Braz. 123 E15
Terhazza, ruins, Mali 176 E8
Terihi, island, Hiva Oa, Fr. Polynesia, Fr. 199 N21
Termas de Río Hondo, Arg. 124 G10
Terme, Turk. 148 C12
Términos, Laguna de, Mex. 109 J15
Termiz, Uzb. 154 M12
Ternate, Indonesia 169 J16
Terni, It. 136 H9
Ternopil', Ukr. 132 J12
Terrace, B.C., Can. 76 K8
Terracina, It. 136 H10
Terralba, It. 136 J7
Terrassa, Sp. 139 P10
Terrebonne Bay, La., U.S. 94 R10
Terre Haute, Ind., U.S. 93 S7
Terreiro Velho, São Tomé and Príncipe 185 B21
Terrell, Tex., U.S. 96 L12
Terry, Mont., U.S. 100 D12
Tersakan Gölü, Turk. 148 G8
Teru, Pak. 156 L10
Teshekpuk Lake, Alas., U.S. 105 B14
Teshikaga, Jap. 164 F15
Teshio, river, Jap. 164 E13
Teshio, Jap. 164 E13
Teshio Sanchi, Jap. 164 E14
Tesiyn, river, Mongolia 160 C9
Teslin, Yukon Terr., Can. 76 G8
Tessalit, Mali 176 F10
Tessaoua, Niger 176 H12
Tessenei, Eritrea 179 E14
Tetas, Punta, Chile 124 E7
Te Tautua, Penrhyn, Cook Is., N.Z. 199 B18
Tete, Mozambique 182 F12
Te Teko, N.Z. 193 K20
Tetepare, island, Solomon Is. 197 M16
Tetere, Russ. 141 J15
Tetiaroa, island, Fr. Polynesia, Fr. 199 E16
Tetlin, Alas., U.S. 105 G18
Teton, river, Mont., U.S. 100 C8
Teton Range, Wyo., U.S. 100 G8
Tétouan, Mor. 176 A9
Tetovo, Maced. 137 H14
Tetufera, Mount, Tahiti, Fr. Polynesia, Fr. 199 P16
Tetutu, Pointe, Ua Huka, Fr. Polynesia, Fr. 199 N23
Teuaua (Hat), island, Ua Huka, Fr. Polynesia, Fr. 199 N23
Teuco, river, Arg. 124 F12
Teulada, Capo, It. 136 K7
Teuri Tō, Jap. 164 E13
Tevahavaha, island, Manihiki Atoll, Cook Is., N.Z. 199 C14
Tevai, island, Santa Cruz Is., Solomon Is. 197 R24
Tevaro, island, Rangiroa, Fr. Polynesia, Fr. 199 K17
Teveiroa, island, Bora-Bora, Fr. Polynesia, Fr. 199 K13
Tevere, river, It. 136 H9
Teverya (Tiberias), Israel 150 K6
Tewantin, Qnsld., Austral. 191 V15
Texarkana, Ark., U.S. 94 J6
Texarkana, Tex., U.S. 96 K15
Texas, U.S. 97 N4
Texas City, Tex., U.S. 97 R14
Texas Point, Tex., U.S. 97 Q16
Texhoma, Okla., U.S. 96 E5
Texico, N. Mex., U.S. 101 S15
Texline, Tex., U.S. 96 E3
Texoma, Lake, Okla.-Tex., U.S. 96 J12
Texon, Tex., U.S. 97 N5
Teylan, Afghan. 156 L4
Teywarah, Afghan. 157 N4
Tezpur, India 158 G14
Thabana Ntlenyana, peak, Lesotho 182 L11
Thabaung, Myanmar 166 K5
Thabazimbi, S. Af. 182 J10
Thaga Pass, India 158 D7
Thagyettaw, Myanmar 166 M7
Thai Binh, Vietnam 166 H12
Thai Hoa, Vietnam 166 J12
Thailand, Asia 166 L9
Thailand, Gulf of, Thai. 167 P9
Thai Nguyen, Vietnam 166 G12
Thal, Pak. 157 N9
Thalabarivat, Cambodia 166 M12
Thal Desert, Pak. 157 Q10
Thamarīt, Oman 153 N14
Thames, river, Eng., U.K. 138 H8
Thamūd, Yemen 152 N12
Thana, Pak. 157 S3
Thandaung, Myanmar 166 J6
Thane, India 158 L3
Thangool, Qnsld., Austral. 191 U15
Thanh Hoa, Vietnam 166 J12
Thanh Tri, Vietnam 167 Q12
Thanjavur (Tanjore), India 159 R6
Thanlwin (Salween), river, Myanmar 166 G8
Tharabwin, Myanmar 167 N8
Thar Desert see Great Indian Desert, India-Pak. 157 S9
Thargomindah, Qnsld., Austral. 191 V12
Tharthār Lake, Iraq 152 D9
Tha Sala, Thai. 167 Q8
Thássos, island, Gr. 137 J16
Thatcher, Ariz., U.S. 101 U9
Thaton, Myanmar 166 K7
Thatta, Pak. 157 W7
Thaungdut, Myanmar 166 F5
Thayawthadanngyi Kyun, Myanmar 167 N7
Thayer, Mo., U.S. 99 V14
Thayet, Myanmar 166 J5
The Brothers see Al Ikhwān, islands, Yemen 153 R14
The Alley, Jam. 110 N11
Thebes, ruins, Egypt 177 E19
Thebes see Thívai, Gr. 137 L15
The Bluff, Bahamas 110 D12
The Bottom, Saba, Neth. 113 F15
The Brothers, islands, Bahamas 111 H13
The Caves, Qnsld., Austral. 191 T15
The Dalles, Oreg., U.S. 102 F5
Thedford, Nebr., U.S. 99 P4
Theebine, Qnsld., Austral. 191 V15
The Everglades, swamp, Fla., U.S. 91 X9
The Father, peak, P.N.G. 193 C21
The Hague see 's Gravenhage, Neth. 138 H11
The Heads, point, Oreg., U.S. 102 K1
The Isles Lagoon, Kiritimati, Kiribati 197 B23
Thelon, river, N.W.T., Can. 77 H13
The Lynd, Qnsld., Austral. 191 R13
Theodore, Qnsld., Austral. 191 U14
Theodore Roosevelt, river, Braz. 122 F9
Theodore Roosevelt Lake, Ariz., U.S. 101 T8
Theodore Roosevelt National Park (North Unit), N. Dak., U.S. 98 F2
Theodore Roosevelt National Park (South Unit), N. Dak., U.S. 98 G2
The Pas, Man., Can. 77 M13
The Pennines, hills, Eur. 130 E4
The Remarkables, peak, N.Z. 193 Q15
Thermopolis, Wyo., U.S. 100 G10
The Rope, Pitcairn I., U.K. 199 Q23
The Sisters, islands, Seychelles 185 N21

The Slot see New Georgia Sound, Solomon Is. 197 MI6
The Snares, islands, N.Z. 194 Q7
Thessalon, Ont., Can. 77 QI7
Thessaloníki (Salonica), Gr. 137 JI5
Thessaly, region, Eur. I30 K8
The Steppes, Kaz. 154 E8
The Triangle, Myanmar 166 E7
The Twins, S. Austral., Austral. 191 W9
The Valley, Anguilla, U.K. 113 FI5
Thibodaux, La., U.S. 94 QIO
Thief River Falls, Minn., U.S. 98 E9
Thielsen, Mount, Oreg., U.S. 102 J4
Thiès, Senegal 176 H4
Thika, Kenya 179 KI4
Thimphu, Bhutan 158 FI2
Thingeyri, Ice. 134 E2
Thinkèo, Laos 166 JIO
Thio, New Caledonia, Fr. 198 D8
Thionville, Fr. 138 JII
Thíra, island, Gr. 137 MI6
Third Cataract, Sudan 178 CI2
Thiruvananthapuram see Trivandrum, India 159 S5
Thisted, Den. 134 NII
Thistilfjördur, Ice. 134 E4
Thitu Island, Spratly Is. 168 DII
Thívai (Thebes), Gr. 137 LI5
Thjórsá, river, Ice. 134 F2
Tho Chu, Dao, Vietnam 167 QIO
Thoen, Thai. 166 K8
Thohoyandou, S. Af. 182 HII
Thomas, Okla., U.S. 96 F9
Thomaston, Ga., U.S. 90 M5
Thomaston, Me., U.S. 89 GI7
Thomasville, Ala., U.S. 95 MI4
Thomasville, Ga., U.S. 91 Q5
Thomasville, N.C., U.S. 90 HIO
Thompson, river, Iowa, U.S. 99 QII
Thompson, Man., Can. 77 LI4
Thompson, Utah, U.S. 101 N9
Thompson Falls, Mont., U.S. 100 C5
Thomson, river, Austral. 190 FI2
Thomson, Ga., U.S. 90 L7
Thongwa, Myanmar 166 K6
Thonon, Fr. 138 LI2
Thonon, Switz. 132 K4
Thonze, Myanmar 166 K6
Thoreau, N. Mex., U.S. 101 SIO
Thórisvatn, lake, Ice. 134 G3
Thorndale, Tex., U.S. 97 PII
Thorne Bay, Alas., U.S. 105 L23
Thornton, Colo., U.S. 100 LI3
Thorntonia, Qnsld., Austral. 191 SIO
Thorp, Wash., U.S. 102 D5
Thorp, Wis., U.S. 92 H4
Thórshöfn, Ice. 134 E4
Three Forks, Mont., U.S. 100 E7
Three Kings Islands, N.Z. 193 GI7
Three Lakes, Wis., U.S. 92 G6
Three Pagodas Pass, Myanmar-Thai. 166 L7
Three Points, Cape, Ghana 180 HIO
Three Rivers, Mich., U.S. 93 NIO
Three Rivers, Tex., U.S. 97 TIO
Three Sisters, peak, Oreg., U.S. 102 H4
Three Sisters Islands, Solomon Is. 197 P2O
Throckmorton, Tex., U.S. 96 K8
Throssell, Lake, Austral. 190 H5
Thunder Bay, Mich., U.S. 92 HI2
Thunder Bay, Ont., Can. 77 PI5
Thung Song, Thai. 167 R8
Thunkar, Bhutan 158 FI3
Thurmont, Md., U.S. 90 BI2
Thurso, Scot., U.K. 138 C8
Thurston Island, Antarctica 206 K5
Thylungra, Qnsld., Austral. 191 UI2
Tiamahana, Passe, Tahaa, Fr. Polynesia, Fr. 199 B23
Tianjin (Tientsin), China 162 D7
Tianjun, China 160 HIO
Tianlin, China 160 PI2
Tianmen, China 162 L4
Tianqiaoling, China 162 AI4
Tian Shan, Asia 146 F8
Tianshan see Ar Horqin Qi, China 162 A9
Tianshifu, China 162 CII
Tianshui, China 160 JI2
Tianshuihai, China 156 LI5
Tianzhu, China 163 NI
Tiarei, Tahiti, Fr. Polynesia, Fr. 199 NI7
Tiaret, Alg. 176 AIO
Tiari, New Caledonia, Fr. 198 C6
Tiaro, Qnsld., Austral. 191 UI5
Tiaro Bay, Solomon Is. 197 NI8
Ti'avea, Samoa 198 L4
Tibagi, river, Braz. 122 MI2
Tibasti, Sarīr, Lib. 177 EI4
Tibati, Cameroon 181 HI6
Tiber, river, Eur. I30 J6
Tiberias see Teverya, Israel I50 K6
Tibesti, mountains, Chad 177 FI5
Tibet, region, China 160 K6

Tibet, Plateau of, China 160 J6
Tibiri, Niger 176 JII
Tiboku Falls, Guyana 121 EI4
Tibooburra, N.S.W., Austral. 191 WII
Tibrikot, Nepal 158 F9
Tibugá, Golfo de, Col. 120 E3
Tiburón, Isla, Mex. 108 C6
Tíchît, Mauritania 176 G7
Ticonderoga, N.Y., U.S. 88 GI2
Ticul, Mex. 109 HI6
Tiddim, Myanmar 166 F4
Tidjikdja, Mauritania 176 G6
Tidore, Indonesia 169 JI6
Tidra, Île, Mauritania 176 F4
Tiel, Senegal 176 H5
Tieling, China 162 BII
Tielong, China 160 H5
Tielongtan, China 156 LI6
Tientsin see Tianjin, China 162 D7
Tierra Amarilla, Chile 124 G7
Tierra Amarilla, N. Mex., U.S. 101 QI2
Tierra Blanca Creek, Tex., U.S. 96 H4
Tierra del Fuego, island, S. Amer. 118 R5
Tieyon, S. Austral., Austral. 191 U8
Tiffin, Ohio, U.S. 93 PI2
Tiflis see T'bilisi, Rep. of Georgia 149 CI8
Tifton, Ga., U.S. 91 P6
Tiga, Île, New Caledonia, Fr. 198 CIO
Tiger Bay, Af. 174 N6
Tigray, region, Eth. 179 EI4
Tigre, river, Peru 122 E3
Tigris, river, Asia 146 F4
Tigyaing, Myanmar 166 F6
Tīh, Gebel el, Egypt 151 R3
Tihamah, region, Asia 146 H3
Tihāmat ash Shām, region, Saudi Arabia 152 L7
Tijuana, Mex. 108 A5
Tikamgarh, India 158 H6
Tikanlik, China 160 F7
Tikapai, island, Manihiki Atoll, Cook Is., N.Z. 199 BI3
Tikchik Lakes, Alas., U.S. 105 KI3
Tikehau, island, Fr. Polynesia, Fr. 199 DI7
Tikei, island, Fr. Polynesia, Fr. 199 DI8
Tikhoretsk, Russ. 140 H4
Tikhvin, Russ. 140 E6
Tikopia, island, Solomon Is. 194 J7
Tikrīt, Iraq 152 D9
Tiksi, Russ. 141 EI6
Tiladummati Atoll, Maldives 159 T3
Til Barsip see Tall al Aḥmar, Syr. I50 DIO
Tilbooroo, Qnsld., Austral. 191 VI2
Tilburg, Neth. 138 HII
Tilden, Nebr., U.S. 99 N7
Tillabéri, Niger 176 HIO
Tillamook, Oreg., U.S. 102 F2
Tillamook Head, Oreg., U.S. 102 E2
Tillanchang Dwip, Nicobar Is., India 159 SI5
Tillia, Niger 176 HII
Tilloo Cay, Bahamas 110 CI2
Tilpa, N.S.W., Austral. 191 WI2
Timan Ridge, Eur. I30 AII
Timanskiy Kryazh, Russ. 140 E9
Timaru, N.Z. 193 PI7
Timbalier Bay, La., U.S. 94 RII
Timbalier Island, La., U.S. 94 RIO
Timbaúba, Braz. 123 FI8
Timbédra, Mauritania 176 G7
Timber Creek, N. Terr., Austral. 191 Q7
Timber Lake, S. Dak., U.S. 98 J4
Timbío, Col. 120 G4
Timbuktu see Tombouctou, Mali 176 G8
Timbun Mata, island, Philippines 169 GI3
Timimoun, Alg. 176 CIO
Timiris, Cap (Mirik), Mauritania 176 F4
Timiris, Cape, Af. 174 FI
Timiryazevskiy, Russ. 140 KI2
Timişoara, Rom. 137 EI4
Timmiarmiut, Greenland, Den. 75 D22
Timmins, Ont., Can. 77 PI7
Timmonsville, S.C., U.S. 90 KIO
Timms Hill, Wis., U.S. 92 HI4
Timoe see Temoe, island, Fr. Polynesia, Fr. 199 H23
Timor, island, E. Timor-Indonesia 169 NI5
Timor Sea, Indonesia 169 NI6
Timote, Arg. 124 MII
Timpanogos Cave National Monument, Utah, U.S. 100 L7
Timpson, Tex., U.S. 96 MI5
Timsah, Buheirat el (Lake Timsah), Egypt 151 PI
Timsah, Lake see Timsâh, Buheirat el, Egypt 151 PI
Tims Ford Lake, Tenn., U.S. 95 GI6
Timiti's Crack, Pitcairn I., U.K. 199 Q23
Tinaca Point, Philippines 169 GI5
Tinajo, Canary Is., Sp. 184 P8
Tinakula, island, Santa Cruz Is., Solomon Is. 197 P22
Ti-n-Amzi, river, Mali-Niger 176 GIO
Tindouf, Alg. 176 D7
Tindouf, Sebkha de, Alg. 176 D8
Tinggoa, Solomon Is. 197 RI9
Tingmerkpuk Mountain, U.S. 78 M2
Tingo María, Peru 122 G3

Tingri, China 160 L6
Tinharé, Ilha de, Braz. 123 HI6
Tinian, island, N. Mariana Is., U.S. 196 A7
Tinian Harbor see Sunbaron Roads, Tinian, N. Mariana Is., U.S. 196 C7
Tinnenburra, Qnsld., Austral. 191 VI3
Tinogasta, Arg. 124 H8
Tinrhert, Hamada de, Alg.-Lib. 176 DI2
Tinsukia, India 158 FI5
Tintina, Arg. 124 GII
Tintinara, S. Austral., Austral. 191 YIO
Ti-n-Zaouâtene, Alg. 176 FIO
Tioga, N. Dak., U.S. 98 E2
Tioman, island, Malaysia 167 UII
Tipp City, Ohio, U.S. 93 RII
Tipperary, N. Terr., Austral. 191 P7
Tipton, Calif., U.S. 103 U7
Tipton, Ind., U.S. 93 Q9
Tipton, Iowa, U.S. 99 PI4
Tipton, Mo., U.S. 99 TI2
Tipton, Okla., U.S. 96 H8
Tipton, Mount, Ariz., U.S. 101 R5
Tiptonville, Tenn., U.S. 94 EI2
Tiputa, Rangiroa, Fr. Polynesia, Fr. 199 KI6
Tiputa, Passe de, Rangiroa, Fr. Polynesia, Fr. 199 KI6
Tiracambu, Serra do, Braz. 123 EI4
Tīrān, island, Saudi Arabia 152 G4
Tīrān, Strait of, Egypt 151 U4
Tirana see Tiranë, Alban. 137 JI3
Tiranë (Tirana), Alban. 137 JI3
Tiraspol, Mold. 133 LI4
Tire, Turk. 148 G3
Tirebolu, Turk. 149 DI3
Tîrgovişte, Rom. 137 FI6
Tîrgu Jiu, Rom. 137 FI5
Tîrgu Mureş, Rom. 137 EI5
Tirich Mir, peak, Pak. 156 LIO
Tirnavos, Gr. 137 LI4
Tir Pol, Afghan. 156 MI
Tirso, river, It. 136 J7
Tiruchchendur, India 159 S6
Tiruchchirappalli, India 159 R6
Tirunelveli, India 159 S6
Tirupati, India 159 P7
Tiruppattur, India 159 R6
Tiruppur, India 159 R5
Tiruvannamalai, India 159 Q6
Tisaiyanvilai, India 159 S6
Tishomingo, Okla., U.S. 96 JI2
Tis Isat Falls (Blue Nile Falls), Eth. 179 FI4
Tista, river, India 158 GI2
Tisza, river, Eur. I30 H8
Titan Dome, Antarctica 206 JI2
Titicaca, Lago, Bol.-Peru 122 J6
Titikaveka, Rarotonga, Cook Is., N.Z. 198 Q9
Titule, Dem. Rep. of the Congo 178 JII
Titusville, Fla., U.S. 91 T9
Titusville, Pa., U.S. 88 L4
Tiva, Tahaa, Fr. Polynesia, Fr. 199 A23
Tivaru, island, Rangiroa, Fr. Polynesia, Fr. 199 KI5
Tizimín, Mex. 109 HI6
Tiznit, Mor. 176 C7
Tiz Ouzou, Alg. 176 AII
Tlemcen, Alg. 176 BIO
Tmassah, Lib. 177 EI4
Tmiet, island, Jaluit Atoll, Marshall Is. 196 L9
Toadlena, N. Mex., U.S. 101 RIO
Toagel Mid Passage, Palau 196 PII
Toagel Mlungui (West Passage), Palau 196 MII
Toahotu, Tahiti, Fr. Polynesia, Fr. 199 PI7
Toamaro, island, Raiatea, Fr. Polynesia, Fr. 199 B23
Toamaro, Passe, Raiatea, Fr. Polynesia, Fr. 199 B23
Toamasina, Madagascar 183 FI8
Toano, Va., U.S. 90 EI3
Toataratara, Pointe, Rurutu, Fr. Polynesia, Fr. 199 L23
Toau, island, Fr. Polynesia, Fr. 199 EI8
Toay, Arg. 124 MIO
Tobago, island, Trin. & Tobago 113 NI8
Toba Kakar Range, Pak. 157 R6
Toba Tek Singh, Pak. 157 QIO
Tobermorey, N. Terr., Austral. 191 TIO
Tobermory, Qnsld., Austral. 191 VI2
Tobi, island, Indonesia 169 HI7
Tobi, island, Palau 194 G2
Tobin, Mount, Nev., U.S. 103 N9
Tobi Shima, Jap. 164 KI2
Toboli, Indonesia 169 JI3
Tobol, river, Russ. 140 K8
Tobol'sk, Russ. 140 JIO
Tobona, island, Solomon Is. 197 MI7
Tobruk see Ţubruq, Lib. 177 CI6
Tobyl, river, Kaz. 154 BII
Tobyl, river, Kaz. 154 CIO
Tobyl, Kaz. 154 CIO
Tocal, Qnsld., Austral. 191 TI2
Tocantínia, Braz. 123 GI3
Tocantinópolis, Braz. 123 FI3
Tocantins, river, Braz. 123 FI3
Toccoa, Ga., U.S. 90 K6
Toco, Chile 124 D7

Toco, Trin. & Tobago 113 PI7
Toconao, Chile 124 E8
Tocopilla, Chile 124 D7
Todmorden, S. Austral., Austral. 191 V9
Todoga Saki, Jap. 164 KI4
Todos os Santos Bay, S. Amer. 118 GII
Todos Santos, Mex. 108 F7
Todos Santos, Bahía de, Mex. 108 B5
Tofino, B.C., Can. 76 M7
Tofte, Minn., U.S. 98 FI3
Tofua, island, Ha'apai Group, Tonga 198 P6
Toga, island, Vanuatu 198 AI
Tōgane, Jap. 165 PI3
Togiak, Alas., U.S. 104 LI2
Togian, Kepulauan, Indonesia 169 JI4
Togliatti, Russ. 140 H7
Togo, Af. 180 GII
Togtoh, China 162 C4
Togyz, Kaz. 154 F9
Tohatchi, N. Mex., U.S. 101 RIO
Tohiea, Mount, Moorea, Fr. Polynesia, Fr. 199 NI4
Tohma, river, Turk. 148 FI2
Tohopekaliga, Lake, Fla., U.S. 91 T9
Toi, Jap. 164 HI3
Toi, Niue, N.Z. 199 B2O
Toibalawe, Andaman Is., India 159 RI4
Toili, Indonesia 169 JI4
Toi Misaki, Jap. 165 T5
Toiyabe Range, U.S. 78 G5
Tojikobod, Taj. 156 H9
Tok, Alas., U.S. 105 GI8
Tokachi Dake, Jap. 164 FI4
Tōkamachi, Jap. 165 NII
Tokar, Sudan 179 DI4
Tokara Kaikyō, Jap. 165 U4
Tokara Rettō, Jap. 165 V3
Tokarevka, Kaz. 155 DI4
Toka Sand Cay, island, Pukapuka Atoll, Cook Is., N.Z. 198 RI
Tokat, Turk. 148 EII
Tŏkch'ŏn, N. Korea 162 DI2
Tokelau, islands, Kiribati 194 HIO
Tokerau, island, Penrhyn, Cook Is., N.Z. 199 AI7
Toki, Jap. 165 PIO
Toki Point, Wake I., U.S. 196 F8
Tokmak, Ukr. 133 KI7
Tokmok, Kyrg. 156 DI2
Toko, Russ. 141 JI9
Tokomaru Bay, N.Z. 193 K2O
Tokoro, river, Jap. 164 FI5
Tokoroa, N.Z. 193 KI9
Toksook Bay, Alas., U.S. 104 JII
Toksun, China 160 F7
Toktogul, Kyrg. 156 EIO
Tokung, Indonesia 168 JII
Tokuno Shima, Jap. 165 X2
Tokunoshima, Jap. 165 X2
Tokushima, Jap. 165 R8
Tokuyama, Jap. 165 R5
Tōkyō, Jap. 165 PI2
Tōkyō Wan, Jap. 165 PI2
Tokzar, Afghan. 156 L5
Tol, island, Chuuk, F.S.M. 197 CI4
Tôlañaro, Madagascar 183 JI7
Tolarno, N.S.W., Austral. 191 XII
Tolbo, Mongolia 160 C8
Tolchin, Mount, Antarctica 206 HII
Toledo, Iowa, U.S. 99 NI2
Toledo, Ohio, U.S. 93 NI2
Toledo, Oreg., U.S. 102 G2
Toledo, Sp. 139 R7
Toledo, Wash., U.S. 102 D3
Toledo Bend Reservoir, U.S. 79 LI4
Toli, China 160 D6
Toliara, Madagascar 183 HI6
Tolitoli, Indonesia 169 HI4
Tol'ka, Russ. 140 HI2
Tolleson, Ariz., U.S. 101 U6
Tollya, Zaliv, Russ. 141 DI4
Tolo, Teluk, Indonesia 169 KI4
Tolosa, Sp. 139 N8
Toltén, Chile 125 P6
Tolti, Pak. 158 B5
Tolú, Col. 120 C4
Toluca, Mex. 108 JII
Tomah, Wis., U.S. 92 K4
Tomahawk, Wis., U.S. 92 H5
Tomakomai, Jap. 164 GI3
Tomanivi, peak, Fiji 198 H6
Tomar, Braz. 122 C8
Tomari, Jap. 164 HI3
Tomaszów Mazowiecki, Pol. 132 HIO
Tombador, Serra do, Braz. 122 GIO
Tombe, Solomon Is. 197 MI6
Tombigbee, river, Ala., U.S. 95 LI3
Tombouctou (Timbuktu), Mali 176 G8
Tombstone, Ariz., U.S. 101 W9
Tombua, Angola 182 E5
Tomé, Chile 124 M6
Tomea, island, Indonesia 169 LI5
Tomil, Yap Is., F.S.M. 197 DI8

Tomil Harbor, *Yap Is., F.S.M.* **197** D18
Tomini, Teluk, *Indonesia* **169** J13
Tomman, island, *Vanuatu* **198** E2
Tommot, *Russ.* **141** H18
Tomo, river, *Col.* **120** E8
Tomo, *New Caledonia, Fr.* **198** D8
Tomotu Noi (Lord Howe Island), *Santa Cruz Is., Solomon Is.* **197** Q22
Tompa, *Russ.* **141** K16
Tompkinsville, *Ky., U.S.* **95** D16
Tom Price, *W. Austral., Austral.* **191** T2
Tomsk, *Russ.* **140** K12
Tomsyu, *Russ.* **141** E18
Tomtor, *Russ.* **141** F17
Tom White, Mount, *Alas., U.S.* **105** J18
Tonalá, *Mex.* **109** K14
Tonami, *Jap.* **165** N10
Tonantins, *Braz.* **122** D6
Tonasket, *Wash., U.S.* **102** A7
Tønder, *Den.* **134** P11
Tondou Massif, *Af.* **174** H8
Tonga, *Pac. Oc.* **194** K10
Tonga, *Sudan* **178** F12
Tonga Islands, *Pac. Oc.* **194** K10
Tong'an, *China* **163** Q7
Tongareva *see* Penrhyn Atoll, island, *Cook Is., N.Z.* **194** H12
Tongariki, island, *Vanuatu* **198** E3
Tongatapu Group, *Tonga* **194** K10
Tonga Trench, *Pac. Oc.* **218** M10
Tongcheng, *China* **162** K6
Tongchuan, *China* **162** G2
Tongdao, *China* **163** P2
Tongde, *China* **160** J11
Tongguan, *China* **161** J13
Tonghua, *China* **162** B12
Tongjiang, *China* **161** C18
Tongju-ri, *N. Korea* **162** C12
Tongliao, *China* **162** A10
Tongling, *China* **162** L7
Tonglu, *China* **162** L9
Tongo, *N.S.W., Austral.* **191** W12
Tongoa (Kuwaé), island, *Vanuatu* **198** E3
Tongoy, *Chile* **124** J6
Tongren, *China* **163** N1
Tongshi, *China* **163** U1
Tongtian (Yangtze), river, *China* **160** J9
Tongue, river, *Mont., U.S.* **100** E12
Tongue of the Ocean, bay, *Bahamas* **110** F11
Tongue River Reservoir, *Mont., U.S.* **100** F11
Tongxian, *China* **162** D7
Tongxin, *China* **160** H12
Tonj, *Sudan* **178** G12
Tonk, *India* **158** G5
Tonkawa, *Okla., U.S.* **96** E11
Tonkin, Gulf of, *Asia* **146** J11
Tonle Sap, *Cambodia* **167** N11
Tōno, *Jap.* **164** K13
Tonoas (Dublon), island, *Chuuk, F.S.M.* **197** C15
Tonopah, *Nev., U.S.* **103** R9
Tønsberg, *Nor.* **134** L11
Tonto National Monument, *Ariz., U.S.* **101** U8
Tonumea, island, *Ha'apai Group, Tonga* **198** R6
Tonya, *Turk.* **149** D14
Toodyay, *W. Austral., Austral.* **191** X2
Tooele, *Utah, U.S.* **100** L7
Toomaru, Mount, *Raiatea, Fr. Polynesia, Fr.* **199** B23
Toompine, *Qnsld., Austral.* **191** V12
Toopua, island, *Bora-Bora, Fr. Polynesia, Fr.* **199** K13
Toopua Iti, island, *Bora-Bora, Fr. Polynesia, Fr.* **199** K13
Toora Khem, *Russ.* **141** L14
Toowoomba, *Qnsld., Austral.* **191** V15
Top, Lake, *Eur.* **130** B9
Topaze Bay, *Mauritius* **185** J19
Topeka, *Kans., U.S.* **99** S9
Topock, *Ariz., U.S.* **101** S4
Topolobampo, *Mex.* **108** E7
Toppenish, *Wash., U.S.* **102** E6
Topsail Beach, *N.C., U.S.* **90** K13
Top Springs, *N. Terr., Austral.* **191** Q8
Toquima Range, *Nev., U.S.* **103** Q9
Torbalı, *Turk.* **148** G3
Torbat-e Ḩeydarīyeh, *Iran* **153** C16
Torbat-e Jām, *Iran* **153** C17
Torbay, *Eng., U.K.* **138** J7
Torbay, *W. Austral., Austral.* **191** Y3
Torbert, Mount, *Alas., U.S.* **105** J15
Torch Lake, *Mich., U.S.* **92** H10
Tordesillas, *Sp.* **139** P6
Töre, *Sw.* **135** F14
Torghay, *Kaz.* **154** E11
Torgo, *Russ.* **141** J17
Torino (Turin), *It.* **136** F7
Tori Shima, *Jap.* **165** Y1
Torixoreu, *Braz.* **122** J11
Torkestan Mountains, *Afghan.* **156** L4
To'rko'l, *Uzb.* **154** K9
Torneå *see* Tornio, *Fin.* **135** F15
Torneälven, river, *Eur.* **130** B8
Torneträsk, lake, *Sw.* **135** D13
Torngat Mountains, *Nfld., Can.* **77** J20
Tornillo, *Tex., U.S.* **97** V2
Tornio (Torneå), *Fin.* **135** F15
Torniojoki, river, *Fin.-Sw.* **135** E14
Tornquist, *Arg.* **125** N11
Tōro, *Jap.* **164** F15
Toro, *Sp.* **139** P6
Toro, Cerro del, *Arg.* **124** H7
Torokina, *P.N.G.* **193** D22
Torom, *Russ.* **141** J20
Toronto, *Kans., U.S.* **99** U9
Toronto, *Ohio, U.S.* **93** Q16
Toronto, *Ont., Can.* **77** Q18
Toropets, *Russ.* **140** E6
Toros Dağı, *Turk.* **148** H9
Toros Dağları (Taurus), *Turk.* **148** H7
Torrance, *Calif., U.S.* **103** X8
Torrens, Lake, *Austral.* **190** J10
Torreón, *Mex.* **108** F10
Torres Islands, *Vanuatu* **198** A1
Torres Strait, *Austral.* **190** A12
Torres Vedras, *Port.* **139** R4
Torrington, *Conn., U.S.* **88** L12
Torrington, *Wyo., U.S.* **100** J14
Torrutj, island, *Kwajalein Atoll, Marshall Is.* **196** M5
Torsby, *Sw.* **134** K12
Tórshavn, *Faroe Is., Den.* **134** J6
Tortola, island, *British Virgin Is., U.K.* **113** F14
Tortolì, *It.* **136** J8
Tortosa, *Sp.* **139** Q9
Tortosa *see* Ţarţūs, *Syr.* **150** G7
Tortosa, Cap, *Sp.* **139** Q9
Tortue, Île de la, *Haiti* **111** K16
Tortuga Island, *S. Amer.* **118** A5
Tortum, *Turk.* **149** E16
Ţorūd, *Iran* **153** C14
Torug-Art, *Kyrg.* **156** G12
Torul, *Turk.* **149** D14
Toruń, *Pol.* **132** F9
Tõrva, *Estonia* **135** L17
Tosashimizu, *Jap.* **165** S6
Tosa Wan, *Jap.* **165** R7
Tosca, *S. Af.* **182** J9
To Shima, *Jap.* **165** Q12
Toshka Lakes, *Egypt* **177** E18
Toshkent (Tashkent), *Uzb.* **155** K13
Tostado, *Arg.* **124** H11
Tosu, *Jap.* **165** R4
Tosya, *Turk.* **148** D9
Totegegie, island, *Gambier Is., Fr. Polynesia, Fr.* **199** Q21
Toteng, *Botswana* **182** G9
Totia, island, *Manihiki Atoll, Cook Is., N.Z.* **199** C15
Totiw, island, *Chuuk, F.S.M.* **197** C15
Totness, *Suriname* **121** E16
Tôto, *Angola* **182** B6
Totokafonua, island, *Vava'u Group, Tonga* **198** M11
Totolom, peak, *Pohnpei, F.S.M.* **197** F14
Totora, *Bol.* **122** K7
Totoya, island, *Fiji* **198** K8
Tottan Hills, *Antarctica* **206** C11
Tottori, *Jap.* **165** P7
Totu Tofari, island, *Bora-Bora, Fr. Polynesia, Fr.* **199** K14
Toubkal, Jebel, *Mor.* **176** C8
Tougan, *Burkina Faso* **180** E9
Touggourt, *Alg.* **176** B12
Touho, *New Caledonia, Fr.* **198** C7
Toul, *Fr.* **138** K11
Touliu, *Taiwan, China* **163** R9
Toulon, *Fr.* **139** N12
Toulouse, *Fr.* **139** N9
Toummo, *Niger* **177** F14
Toungo, *Nig.* **181** G16
Tournavista, *Peru* **122** G4
Touros, *Braz.* **123** E18
Tours, *Fr.* **138** L9
Touside, Pic, *Af.* **174** F6
Touwsrivier, *S. Af.* **182** M8
Tovuz, *Azerb.* **149** D19
Towada, *Jap.* **164** J13
Towada, *Jap.* **164** J13
Towada Ko, *Jap.* **164** J13
Towanda, *Pa., U.S.* **88** L8
Tower, *Minn., U.S.* **98** F12
Towner, *N. Dak., U.S.* **98** E5
Townsend, *Mont., U.S.* **100** D8
Townsend, *Va., U.S.* **90** F14
Townsville, *Qnsld., Austral.* **191** S13
Towot, *Sudan* **179** H13
Towraghondi, *Afghan.* **156** L2
Towrzi, *Afghan.* **157** R5
Towson, *Md., U.S.* **90** C13
Toyah, *Tex., U.S.* **97** N2
Toyahvale, *Tex., U.S.* **97** P2
Tōya Ko, *Jap.* **164** G13
Toyama, *Jap.* **165** N10
Toyama Wan, *Jap.* **165** N10
Toyohashi, *Jap.* **165** Q10
Toyooka, *Jap.* **165** P8
Toyotomi, *Jap.* **164** D13
Tozeur, *Tun.* **176** B12
Tqvarch'eli, *Rep. of Georgia* **149** B16
Trabzon, *Turk.* **149** D14
Tracy, *Calif., U.S.* **103** S4
Tracy, *Minn., U.S.* **98** L9
Traer, *Iowa, U.S.* **99** N12
Trail, *B.C., Can.* **76** M9
Traíra, river, *Braz.* **122** C5
Traira, river, *Col.* **120** H8
Traîtres, Baie des, *Hiva Oa, Fr. Polynesia, Fr.* **199** N20
Tralee, *Ire.* **138** G5
Tranås, *Sw.* **135** M13
Trancas, *Arg.* **124** F9
Trang, *Thai.* **167** R8
Trangan, island, *Indonesia* **169** M18
Trangie, *N.S.W., Austral.* **191** X13
Tranqueras, *Uru.* **124** J14
Trans-Amazon Highway, *Braz.* **122** E10
Transantarctic Mountains, *Antarctica* **206** F11
Trans-Canada Highway, *B.C., Can.* **76** L8
Transylvania, region, *Eur.* **130** H9
Transylvanian Alps, mountains, *Rom.* **137** F15
Trapani, *It.* **136** L9
Trapper Peak, *Mont., U.S.* **100** E5
Traralgon, *Vic., Austral.* **191** Z13
Trarza, region, *Af.* **174** F1
Trat, *Thai.* **167** N10
Traverse, Lake, *Minn.-S. Dak., U.S.* **98** J8
Traverse City, *Mich., U.S.* **92** J10
Travis, Lake, *Tex., U.S.* **97** Q10
Trayning, *W. Austral., Austral.* **191** X3
Treasurers Island, *Santa Cruz Is., Solomon Is.* **197** N24
Treasury Islands, *Solomon Is.* **197** L14
Trebil, *Iraq* **152** E7
Tregrosse Islets, *Austral.* **190** D15
Treinta-y-Tres, *Uru.* **124** L15
Trelew, *Arg.* **125** R10
Trelleborg, *Sw.* **134** P12
Tremblant, Mount, *N. Amer.* **74** H8
Tremiti, Isole, *It.* **136** H11
Tremonton, *Utah, U.S.* **100** J7
Trenary, *Mich., U.S.* **92** F8
Trenque Lauquen, *Arg.* **124** M11
Trento, *It.* **136** E9
Trenton, *Mich., U.S.* **93** N12
Trenton, *Mo., U.S.* **99** R11
Trenton, *N.J., U.S.* **88** P10
Trenton, *Nebr., U.S.* **99** R4
Trenton, *Tenn., U.S.* **94** E12
Trepassey, *Nfld., Can.* **77** M24
Tres Arroyos, *Arg.* **125** N12
Tres Esquinas, *Col.* **120** H5
Três Lagoas, *Braz.* **122** L12
Tres Montes, Golfo, *Chile* **125** T6
Tres Montes, Península, *Chile* **125** T5
Tres Picos, Cerro, *Arg.* **125** R7
Tres Puntas, Cabo, *Arg.* **125** T10
Tres Zapotes, ruins, *Mex.* **109** J13
Treviso, *It.* **136** E9
Triabunna, *Tas., Austral.* **191** Z16
Triàngulos, Arrecifes, *Mex.* **109** H15
Tribulation, Cape, *Austral.* **190** C13
Tribune, *Kans., U.S.* **99** T3
Trichur, *India* **159** R5
Trieste, *It.* **136** F10
Trikora, Puncak, *Indonesia* **193** C16
Trincomalee, *Sri Lanka* **159** S8
Trinidad, island, *Trin. & Tobago* **113** P17
Trinidad, *Bol.* **122** J7
Trinidad, *Calif., U.S.* **102** M1
Trinidad, *Colo., U.S.* **101** P14
Trinidad, *Cuba* **110** H9
Trinidad, Golfo, *Chile* **125** V6
Trinidad, Isla, *Arg.* **125** P11
Trinidad and Tobago, *N. Amer.* **113** N17
Trinidad Head, *Calif., U.S.* **102** M1
Trinity, river, *Calif., U.S.* **102** M2
Trinity, river, *Tex., U.S.* **97** P14
Trinity, *Tex., U.S.* **97** P14
Trinity Bay, *Nfld., Can.* **77** M24
Trinity Beach, *Qnsld., Austral.* **191** R13
Trinity Islands, *Alas., U.S.* **105** N15
Trinity Peninsula, *Antarctica* **206** C4
Trinity Range, *Nev., U.S.* **103** N8
Trinkat Island, *Nicobar Is., India* **159** S15
Trion, *Ga., U.S.* **90** K4
Tripoli *see* Ţarābulus, *Leb.* **150** H7
Tripoli *see* Ţarābulus, *Lib.* **177** B13
Trípoli, *Gr.* **137** L14
Tripolitania, region, *Lib.* **177** C13
Tripp, *S. Dak., U.S.* **98** M7
Tristan da Cunha Group, *Atl. Oc.* **184** J4
Tristan da Cunha Island, *Atl. Oc.* **174** R2
Tristao, Îles, *Guinea* **180** E4
Trivandrum (Thiruvananthapuram), *India* **159** S5
Trnava, *Slovakia* **132** K9
Trobriand Islands, *P.N.G.* **193** D21
Trofors, *Nor.* **134** G12
Trois-Bassins, *Réunion, Fr.* **185** G15
Trois-Rivières, *Que., Can.* **77** P20
Troitsk, *Russ.* **140** J8
Trollhättan, *Sw.* **134** M12
Trombetas, river, *Braz.* **122** C10
Tromsø, *Nor.* **135** C13
Trona, *Calif., U.S.* **103** V9
Tronador, Monte, *Arg.* **125** Q7
Trondheim, *Nor.* **134** H11
Trondheimsfjorden, *Nor.* **134** H11
Tropic, *Utah, U.S.* **101** P7
Trostyanets', *Ukr.* **133** H16
Trou d'Eau Douce, *Mauritius* **185** G21
Troup, *Tex., U.S.* **96** M14
Trout Creek, *Utah, U.S.* **100** M5
Trout Lake, *N.W.T., Can.* **76** H10
Trout Lake, *Ont., Can.* **77** N14
Trout Peak, *Wyo., U.S.* **100** F9
Trout River, *Nfld., Can.* **77** M23
Troy, ruins, *Turk.* **148** D2
Troy, *Ala., U.S.* **95** M16
Troy, *Kans., U.S.* **99** R10
Troy, *Mo., U.S.* **99** S14
Troy, *Mont., U.S.* **100** B4
Troy, *N.C., U.S.* **90** H10
Troy, *N.Y., U.S.* **88** J11
Troy, *Ohio, U.S.* **93** R11
Troy, *Oreg., U.S.* **102** E9
Troyes, *Fr.* **138** K11
Troy Peak, *Nev., U.S.* **103** R11
Truckee, river, *Nev., U.S.* **103** P6
Truckee, *Calif., U.S.* **103** Q6
Trujillo, *Hond.* **109** K18
Trujillo, *Peru* **122** G2
Trujillo, *Sp.* **139** R6
Trujillo, *Venez.* **120** C7
Truk Islands *see* Chuuk, *F.S.M.* **196** Q6
Truk Lagoon *see* Chuuk Lagoon, *F.S.M.* **197** B15
Trumann, *Ark., U.S.* **94** F11
Trumbull, Mount, *Ariz., U.S.* **101** Q6
Truro, *Eng., U.K.* **138** J7
Truro, *N.S., Can.* **77** P22
Truth or Consequences, *N. Mex., U.S.* **101** U11
Tsagaan Bogd Uul, peak, *Mongolia* **160** F10
Tsagaannuur, *Mongolia* **160** C8
Tsagan Aman, *Russ.* **140** J5
Ts'ageri, *Rep. of Georgia* **149** B17
Tsagveri, *Rep. of Georgia* **149** C17
Tsahir, *Mongolia* **160** D10
Tsaka La, *India* **158** C7
Tsalka, *Rep. of Georgia* **149** C18
Tsangpo *see* Yarlung, river, *China* **160** L8
Tsao *see* Tsau, *Botswana* **182** G8
Tsarevo, *Bulg.* **137** H17
Tsau (Tsao), *Botswana* **182** G8
Tschida, Lake, *N. Dak., U.S.* **98** G3
Tsenhermandal, *Mongolia* **161** D13
Tsentral'nyy, *Russ.* **141** G20
Tses, *Namibia* **182** J7
Tsetsegnuur, *Mongolia* **160** D9
Tsetserleg, *Mongolia* **160** D11
Tshabong, *Botswana* **182** J8
Tshane, *Botswana* **182** H8
Tshela, *Dem. Rep. of the Congo* **178** L7
Tshikapa, *Dem. Rep. of the Congo* **178** M9
Tshofa, *Dem. Rep. of the Congo* **178** L10
Tshootsha, *Botswana* **182** H8
Tshuapa, river, *Dem. Rep. of the Congo* **178** K10
Tsiigehtchic, *N.W.T., Can.* **76** E9
Tsil'ma, river, *Eur.* **130** A11
Tsimlyansk Reservoir, *Eur.* **130** G12
Tsiombe, *Madagascar* **183** J16
Tsipanda, *Russ.* **141** H19
Ts'khinvali, *Rep. of Georgia* **149** B18
Tsnori, *Rep. of Georgia* **149** C20
Tsu, *Jap.* **165** Q9
Tsubame, *Jap.* **164** M11
Tsuchiura, *Jap.* **165** P13
Tsugaru Kaikyō, *Jap.* **164** H12
Tsuma, *Jap.* **165** N7
Tsumeb, *Namibia* **182** G7
Tsuruga, *Jap.* **165** P9
Tsuruga Wan, *Jap.* **165** P9
Tsuruoka, *Jap.* **164** L12
Tsushima, *Jap.* **165** Q3
Tsutsu, *Jap.* **165** Q3
Tsuyama, *Jap.* **165** Q7
Tsyurupyns'k, *Ukr.* **133** L16
Tuahora, Pointe, *Bora-Bora, Fr. Polynesia, Fr.* **199** K14
Tuakau, *N.Z.* **193** J19
Tual, *Indonesia* **169** L18
Tuamotu Archipelago, *Fr. Polynesia, Fr.* **199** D18
Tuan Giao, *Vietnam* **166** G10
Tuangku, island, *Indonesia* **168** H4
Tu'anuku, *Vava'u Group, Tonga* **198** L11
Tuapa, *Niue, N.Z.* **199** B20
Tuapse, *Russ.* **140** H3
Tuaran, *Malaysia* **168** F12
Tuasivi, *Samoa* **198** K2
Tuasivi, Cap, *Samoa* **198** K2
Tuatapere, *N.Z.* **193** R15
Tuauru, river, *Tahiti, Fr. Polynesia, Fr.* **199** N16
Tubac, *Ariz., U.S.* **101** W7
Tuba City, *Ariz., U.S.* **101** R7

Ţūbah, Qaşr aţ, Jordan 151 N7
Tubarão, Braz. 122 P13
Tubmanburg, Liberia 180 G6
Tubou, Fiji 198 J9
Ţubruq (Tobruk), Lib. 177 C16
Tubuai, island, Fr. Polynesia, Fr. 199 H16
Tubuai Islands see Austral Islands, Fr. Polynesia, Fr. 195 K13
Tucacas, Venez. 120 B9
Tucano, Braz. 123 G16
Tucavaca, river, Bol. 122 K9
Tuckerman, Ark., U.S. 94 F10
Tucker's Town, Bermuda, U.K. 111 F18
Tuckerton, N.J., U.S. 88 Q10
Tucson, Ariz., U.S. 101 V8
Tucumcari, N. Mex., U.S. 101 S15
Tucumcari Mountain, N. Mex., U.S. 101 S15
Tucupita, Venez. 120 C12
Tucuruí, Braz. 123 D13
Tucuruí, Represa de, Braz. 123 E13
Tudela, Sp. 139 P8
Tuen, Qnsld., Austral. 191 V13
Tuensang, India 158 G15
Tufi, P.N.G. 193 E20
Tufts Plain, Pac. Oc. 219 D13
Tufuone, Wallis and Futuna, Fr. 198 B11
Tufu Point, Manua Is., Amer. Samoa, U.S. 198 P4
Tufuvai, Tonga 198 K12
Tugela Falls, Af. 174 Q8
Tug Fork, river, Ky.-W. Va., U.S. 95 C20
Tūghyl, Kaz. 155 E19
Tuguegarao, Philippines 169 B14
Tugur, Russ. 141 J20
Tui, Sp. 139 P5
Tuineje, Canary Is., Sp. 184 Q7
Tukangbesi, Kepulauan, Indonesia 169 L14
Tukao, Manihiki Atoll, Cook Is., N.Z. 199 A14
Tukchi, Russ. 141 H20
Tukosméra, Mount, Vanuatu 198 H4
Tūkrah, Lib. 177 C15
Tuktoyaktuk, N.W.T., Can. 76 D10
Tukums, Latv. 135 M16
Tula, Mex. 108 G11
Tula, Russ. 140 F6
Tulaghi, island, Solomon Is. 197 N19
Tulak, Afghan. 157 N3
Tulare, Calif., U.S. 103 U7
Tulare Lake Bed, Calif., U.S. 103 U6
Tularosa, N. Mex., U.S. 101 U12
Tulcán, Ecua. 120 H3
Tulcea, Rom. 137 F17
Tulelake, Calif., U.S. 102 L4
Tuli, Zimb. 182 H11
Tulia, Tex., U.S. 96 H5
Tulit'a, N.W.T., Can. 76 F10
Ţūlkarm, West Bank 150 L5
Tullah, Tas., Austral. 191 Z15
Tullahoma, Tenn., U.S. 95 F16
Tullamore, N.S.W., Austral. 191 X13
Tulle, Fr. 138 M10
Tully, Qnsld., Austral. 191 R13
Tulsa, Okla., U.S. 96 F12
Tuluá, Col. 120 F4
Tulun, Russ. 141 L14
Tulu Welel, peak, Eth. 179 G14
Tum, Indonesia 169 K17
Tumacacori National Historical Park, Ariz., U.S. 101 W7
Tumaco, Col. 120 H3
Tumaco, Ensenada de, Col. 120 H3
Tumbes, Peru 122 E2
Tumby Bay, S. Austral., Austral. 191 X9
Tumd Youqi, China 162 C3
Tumd Zuoqi, China 162 C4
Tumen, river, China-N. Korea 162 B14
Tumen, China 162 A14
Tumeremo, Venez. 121 D13
Tumkur, India 159 P5
Tumon Bay, Guam, U.S. 196 B11
Tumu, peak, Manua Is., Amer. Samoa, U.S. 198 N1
Tumucumaque, Serra de, S. Amer. 118 C7
Tumu Point, Pohnpei, F.S.M. 197 F13
Tumwater, Wash., U.S. 102 D3
Tunas de Zaza, Cuba 110 J9
Tunceli, Turk. 149 F14
Tunchang, China 163 U1
Tundubai, Sudan 178 E10
Tunduma, Tanzania 179 N13
Tunduru, Tanzania 179 N14
Tungabhadra, river, India 159 N5
Tunga Pass, India 158 E14
Tungkang, Taiwan, China 163 S9
Tungsha Ch'üntao, China 163 T6
Tungsha Tao (Pratas Island), Taiwan, China 163 T6
Tungua, island, Ha'apai Group, Tonga 198 Q6
Tunguskhaya, Russ. 141 G17
Tunica, Miss., U.S. 94 G11
Tunis, Tun. 177 A13
Tunis, Gulf of, Af. 174 C6
Tunisia, Af. 176 B12
Tunja, Col. 120 E6
Tununak, Alas., U.S. 104 J11
Tunuyán, Arg. 124 L8
Tuo, river, China 160 L12
Tuolumne, river, Calif., U.S. 103 S5
Tupã, Braz. 122 L12
Tupai (Motu Iti), island, Fr. Polynesia, Fr. 199 E15
Tupelo, Miss., U.S. 95 H13
Tupelo National Battlefield, Miss., U.S. 95 H13
Tupi, Philippines 169 F15
Tupinier, Cape, Kosrae, F.S.M. 197 B18
Tupiza, Bol. 122 L7
Tupper Lake, N.Y., U.S. 88 G10
Tūpqaraghan Tübegi, Kaz. 154 G5
Tupungato, Cerro, S. Amer. 118 L4
Túquerres, Col. 120 H3
Tura, India 158 G12
Tura, Russ. 141 H14
Turabah, Saudi Arabia 152 L8
Turakh, Russ. 141 E16
Turan Lowland, Asia 146 F6
Tur'at Maşīrah, Oman 153 L17
Ţurayf, Saudi Arabia 152 E7
Turbaco, Col. 120 B5
Turbat, Pak. 157 V2
Turbo, Col. 120 D4
Turda, Rom. 137 E15
Tureia, island, Fr. Polynesia, Fr. 199 G21
Turfan see Turpan, China 160 F8
Turghan Pass, Afghan. 156 K9
Turgut, Turk. 148 F7
Turgutlu, Turk. 148 F3
Turhal, Turk. 148 D11
Türi, Estonia 135 K16
Turi, peak, Huahine, Fr. Polynesia, Fr. 199 G14
Turiaçu, Baía de, Braz. 123 D14
Turiaçu, Braz. 123 D14
Turin see Torino, It. 136 F7
Turkana, Lake (Lake Rudolf), Eth.-Kenya 179 H14
Türkeli, island, Turk. 148 D3
Turkey, Asia 148 F7
Turkey, river, Iowa, U.S. 98 M13
Turkey, Tex., U.S. 96 J6
Turkey Creek, W. Austral., Austral. 191 R6
Türkistan, Kaz. 155 J13
Türkmen Aylagy, Turkm. 154 L6
Türkmenbashy, Turkm. 154 K6
Türkmenbashy Aylagy, Turkm. 154 K6
Türkmen Dağı, Turk. 148 E6
Turkmenistan, Asia 154 L7
Turks and Caicos Islands, Atl. Oc. 111 J17
Turks Island Passage, Turks and Caicos Is., U.K. 111 J17
Turks Islands, Turks and Caicos Is., U.K. 111 J18
Turku (Åbo), Fin. 135 K15
Turkwel, river, Kenya 179 J14
Turlock, Calif., U.S. 103 S5
Turnagain, Cape, N.Z. 193 M19
Turner, Mont., U.S. 100 A10
Turpan (Turfan), China 160 F8
Turpan Depression, Asia 146 G9
Turpan Pendi, China 160 F8
Turquino, Pico, Cuba 110 K12
Tursunzoda, Taj. 156 J7
Turtle see Vatoa, island, Fiji 198 L10
Turtle Lake, N. Dak., U.S. 98 F4
Turtle Mountain, N. Dak., U.S. 98 D5
Tuscaloosa, Ala., U.S. 95 K14
Tuscarora, Nev., U.S. 102 M10
Tuscola, Ill., U.S. 93 R6
Tuscola, Tex., U.S. 96 M8
Tuscumbia, Ala., U.S. 95 G14
Tuskegee, Ala., U.S. 95 L16
Tutak, Turk. 149 E17
Tuticorin, India 159 S6
Tuting, India 158 E15
Tutira, N.Z. 193 L20
Tutoko, Mount, N.Z. 193 Q15
Tuttle Creek Lake, Kans., U.S. 99 S8
Tutu, island, Fiji 198 G7
Tutuala, E. Timor 169 M16
Tutuila, island, Amer. Samoa, U.S. 198 M7
Tutumu, Solomon Is. 197 N19
Tuvalu, Pac. Oc. 194 H8
Tuvuca, island, Fiji 198 H9
Ţuwayq, Jabal, Saudi Arabia 152 J10
Tuwayq Mountains, Asia 146 H3
Tuxpan, Mex. 108 G9
Tuxpan, Mex. 108 H12
Tuxtla Gutiérrez, Mex. 109 K14
Tuyen Hoa, Vietnam 166 K12
Tuyen Quang, Vietnam 166 G11
Tuy Hoa, Vietnam 167 N14
Tūysarkān, Iran 152 D11
Tuz Gölü, Turk. 148 F8
Tuzigoot National Monument, Ariz., U.S. 101 S7
Tuzla, Bosn. and Herzg. 136 F12
Tuzla Gölü, Turk. 148 F11
Tuzluca, Turk. 149 E18
Tveitsund, Nor. 134 L11
Tver', Russ. 140 F6
Tvøroyri, Faroe Is., Den. 134 J6
Tweed Heads, N.S.W., Austral. 191 W15
Twentynine Palms, Calif., U.S. 103 X11
26 Baky Komissary, Azerb. 149 E23
Twin Bridges, Mont., U.S. 100 E7
Twin Buttes Reservoir, Tex., U.S. 97 N7
Twin City, Ga., U.S. 90 M8
Twin Falls, Idaho, U.S. 100 H5
Twin Peaks, Idaho, U.S. 100 F5
Twin Peaks, U.S. 78 D6
Twin Valley, Minn., U.S. 98 G8
Twisp, Wash., U.S. 102 B6
Twizel, N.Z. 193 P16
Two Butte Creek, Colo., U.S. 101 P15
Two Buttes, Colo., U.S. 101 P16
Two Harbors, Minn., U.S. 98 G13
Two Rivers, Wis., U.S. 92 K7
Tyab, Iran 153 H15
Tybee Island, Ga., U.S. 91 N9
Tygda, Russ. 141 K19
Tyler, Minn., U.S. 98 K9
Tyler, Tex., U.S. 96 M14
Tylertown, Miss., U.S. 94 N11
Tymbáki, Gr. 137 N16
Tymvou, Cyprus 148 L8
Tynda, Russ. 141 K18
Tyndall, S. Dak., U.S. 98 M7
Tyonek, Alas., U.S. 105 J16
Tyre see Şūr, Leb. 150 K5
Tyrone, N. Mex., U.S. 101 V10
Tyrone, Okla., U.S. 96 E6
Tyrone, Pa., U.S. 88 N5
Tyrrell, Lake, Austral. 190 L11
Tyrrhenian Sea, Eur. 130 K6
Tyugyuren, Russ. 141 E18
Tyukalinsk, Russ. 140 J10
Tyumen', Russ. 140 J9
Tyup, Kyrg. 156 D14
Tzaneen, S. Af. 182 H11
Tziá see Kéa, island, Gr. 137 L15

U

Uaboe, Nauru 197 E23
Ua Huka, island, Fr. Polynesia, Fr. 195 H14
Ua Pu, island, Fr. Polynesia, Fr. 195 H14
Uaroo, W. Austral., Austral. 191 T2
Uatio, Île, New Caledonia, Fr. 198 E9
Ubá, Braz. 123 L15
Ubangi, river, Af. 174 J7
Ubauro, Pak. 157 T8
Ube, Jap. 165 R5
Ubeda, Sp. 139 S7
Uberaba, Braz. 123 K13
Uberlândia, Braz. 123 K13
Ubombo, S. Af. 182 K12
Ubon Ratchathani, Thai. 166 L11
Ubundu, Dem. Rep. of the Congo 178 K11
Ucar, Azerb. 149 D21
Ucayali, river, S. Amer. 118 E2
Uch, Pak. 157 S9
Uch Adzhi, Turkm. 154 M10
Uchiura Wan, Jap. 164 G13
Uchiza, Peru 122 G3
Uchquduq, Uzb. 154 J11
Udachnyy, Russ. 141 G16
Udaipur, India 158 H4
Udayagiri, India 158 L9
Uddevalla, Sw. 134 M12
Uddjaure, lake, Sw. 135 F13
Uderolal, Pak. 157 V7
Udgir, India 158 L5
Udhampur, India 157 N12
Udine, It. 136 E10
Udintsev Fracture Zone, Pac. Oc. 218 R11
Udipi, India 159 P4
Udon Thani, Thai. 166 K10
Udot, island, Chuuk, F.S.M. 197 C15
Udskaya Guba, Russ. 141 J20
Udu Point, Fiji 198 G8
Uebonti, Indonesia 169 J14
Ueda, Jap. 165 N11
Uele, river, Dem. Rep. of the Congo 178 J10
Uelen, Russ. 141 A21
Uelzen, Ger. 132 F6
Ufa, river, Eur. 130 C14
Ufa, Russ. 140 H8
Ufra, Turkm. 154 K6
Ugab, river, Namibia 182 G6
Ugarit see Ra's Shamrah, ruins, Syr. 150 E6
Uglovoye, Russ. 141 K19
Ugol'nyye Kopi, Russ. 141 B21
Ugum, river, Guam, U.S. 196 D10
Uhrichsville, Ohio, U.S. 93 Q15
Uige, Angola 182 C6
'Uiha, island, Ha'apai Group, Tonga 198 Q7
'Uiha, Ha'apai Group, Tonga 198 Q7
Uinta, river, Utah, U.S. 100 L9
Uinta Mountains, Utah, U.S. 100 L8
Ŭisŏng, S. Korea 162 F14
Uitenhage, S. Af. 182 M9
Ujae Atoll, Marshall Is. 196 G3
Ujajiivan, island, Kwajalein Atoll, Marshall Is. 196 L4
Ujelang Atoll, Marshall Is. 196 G1
Uji Guntō, Jap. 165 T3
Ujiie, Jap. 165 N12
Ujjain, India 158 J5
Ujungpandang (Makassar), Indonesia 169 L13
Ujung Raja, cape, Indonesia 168 G4
Uke Shima, Jap. 165 X3
Ukhiya, Bangladesh 158 K14
Ukhrul, India 158 G15
Ukhta, Russ. 140 F9
Ukiah, Calif., U.S. 103 Q2
Ukiah, Oreg., U.S. 102 F7
Uki Ni Masi Island, Solomon Is. 197 P20
Ukmergė, Lith. 135 N17
Ukraine, Eur. 133 J14
Uku, Jap. 165 R3
Ukulahu, island, Maldives 159 U3
Uku Shima, Jap. 165 R3
Ula, Turk. 148 H4
Ulaanbaatar (Ulan Bator), Mongolia 160 D12
Ulaangom, Mongolia 160 C9
Ulaanjirem, Mongolia 160 E12
Ulaga, Russ. 141 F17
Ulan Bator see Ulaanbaatar, Mongolia 160 D12
Ulanhad see Chifeng, China 162 B8
Ulanhot, China 161 D16
Ulansuhai Nur, China 162 C2
Ulan Ude, Russ. 141 L16
Ulaş, Turk. 148 F12
Ulawa, island, Solomon Is. 197 N20
Ulchin, S. Korea 162 F14
Uldz, river, Mongolia 161 C14
Uldz, Mongolia 161 C13
Uleåborg see Oulu, Fin. 135 F15
Uleguma, island, Maldives 159 T3
Ulen, Minn., U.S. 98 G8
Uliastay (Javhlant), Mongolia 160 D10
Ulingan, P.N.G. 193 C19
Ulithi Atoll, F.S.M. 196 P3
Ülken Borsyq Qumy, Kaz. 154 F9
Ullŭng Do (Dagelet), S. Korea 162 E15
Ulm, Ger. 132 J5
Ulmarra, N.S.W., Austral. 191 W15
Ulsan, S. Korea 162 G15
Ulu, Russ. 141 H18
Ulubat Gölü, Turk. 148 D4
Uluborlu, Turk. 148 G6
Ulu Dağ (Mount Olympus), Turk. 148 D5
Ulufala Point, Manua Is., Amer. Samoa, U.S. 198 P4
Uluiutu, island, Wallis and Futuna, Fr. 198 A11
Ulukışla, Turk. 148 H9
Ulul, island, F.S.M. 196 Q5
Ulundi, S. Af. 182 K11
Ulungur Hu, China 160 D7
Ulus, Turk. 148 C8
Ulvéah see Lopévi, island, Vanuatu 198 E3
Ul'yanovsk, Russ. 140 H7
Ulysses, Kans., U.S. 99 U3
Ulytaū, mountains, Kaz. 154 E12
Uman, island, Chuuk, F.S.M. 197 C15
Uman', Ukr. 133 J14
Umari, Indonesia 169 L19
Umaria, India 158 J7
Umarkot, Pak. 157 V8
Umatac, Guam, U.S. 196 D10
Umatac Bay, Guam, U.S. 196 D10
Umatilla, river, Oreg., U.S. 102 F8
Umatilla, Oreg., U.S. 102 E7
Umba, Russ. 140 D8
Umboi, island, P.N.G. 193 C20
Umbukul, P.N.G. 193 B20
Umeå, Sw. 135 G14
Umeälven, river, Sw. 135 G13
Umfors, Sw. 134 F12
Umikoa, Hawaii, U.S. 107 L20
Umm al Arānib, Lib. 177 E14
Umm al Qaywayn, U.A.E. 153 J15
Umm as Samīm, Oman-Saudi Arabia 153 L15
Umm Bugma, site, Egypt 151 S2
Umm Durmān see Omdurman, Sudan 179 D13
Umm Lajj, Saudi Arabia 152 J6
Umm Qaşr, Iraq 152 F11
Umm Urūmah, island, Saudi Arabia 152 H5
Umnak Island, Alas., U.S. 104 Q9
Umpqua, river, Oreg., U.S. 102 J2
Umred, India 158 K7
Ŭmsŏng, S. Korea 162 F13
Umtata, S. Af. 182 L11
Umuahia, Nig. 181 H14
Umuna, island, Vava'u Group, Tonga 198 L12
Unadilla, Ga., U.S. 91 N6
Unai Obyan, beach, Saipan, N. Mariana Is., U.S. 196 D5
Unai Pass, Afghan. 156 M7
Unalakleet, Alas., U.S. 105 G13
Unalaska, Alas., U.S. 104 P10
Unalaska Island, Alas., U.S. 104 P10
'Unayzah, Jordan 151 Q6

'Unayzah, *Saudi Arabia* **152** H9
'Unayzah, Jabal, *Iraq* **152** E7
Unayzah, Jabal', *Jordan* **150** L12
Uncía, *Bol.* **122** K7
Uncompahgre Peak, *Colo., U.S.* **101** P11
Uncompahgre Plateau, *Colo., U.S.* **101** N10
Underwood, *N. Dak., U.S.* **98** F4
Ungama Bay, *Af.* **174** K10
Ungava Bay, *Nunavut, Can.* **77** J19
Ungava Peninsula, *N. Amer.* **74** E8
Unggi, *N. Korea* **162** B15
União da Vitória, *Braz.* **122** N12
Unikar, Mochun, *Chuuk, F.S.M.* **197** C16
Unimak Island, *Alas., U.S.* **104** P11
Unimak Pass, *Alas., U.S.* **104** P10
Unini, river, *Braz.* **122** D8
Union, island, *St. Vincent and the Grenadines* **113** M17
Union, *Miss., U.S.* **94** L12
Union, *Mo., U.S.* **99** T14
Union, *Oreg., U.S.* **102** F8
Union, *S.C., U.S.* **90** J8
Unión, Bahía, *Arg.* **125** P11
Union City, *Ohio, U.S.* **93** R11
Union City, *Pa., U.S.* **88** L3
Union City, *Tenn., U.S.* **94** E12
Union Point, *Ga., U.S.* **90** L6
Union Springs, *Ala., U.S.* **95** L16
Uniontown, *Ala., U.S.* **95** L14
Uniontown, *Pa., U.S.* **88** P3
Unionville, *Mo., U.S.* **99** Q12
Unionville, *Nev., U.S.* **103** N8
United Arab Emirates, *Asia* **153** K14
United Kingdom, *Eur.* **138** E8
United States, *N. Amer.* **75** J16
United States, Geographic Center of the 50, *U.S.* **98** J1
United States Naval Station, *Cuba* **111** L14
United States Range, *Nunavut, Can.* **77** A16
Unity, *Oreg., U.S.* **102** G8
University Park, *N. Mex., U.S.* **101** V12
Unnao, *India* **158** G7
Unst, island, *Scot., U.K.* **138** B9
Ünye, *Turk.* **148** D12
Uoleva, island, *Ha'apai Group, Tonga* **198** P7
Upata, *Venez.* **120** C12
Upemba, Lake, *Af.* **174** L8
Upernavik Kujalleq, *Greenland, Den.* **75** C20
Upham, *N. Dak., U.S.* **98** E4
Upington, *S. Af.* **182** K8
Upolu, island, *Samoa* **198** L3
Upolu Point, *Hawaii, U.S.* **107** J19
Upper Arlington, *Ohio, U.S.* **93** R13
Upper Darby, *Pa., U.S.* **88** P9
Upper Guinea, *Af.* **174** H3
Upper Hutt, *N.Z.* **193** M19
Upper Kama Upland, *Eur.* **130** C13
Upper Klamath Lake, *Oreg., U.S.* **102** K4
Upper Lake, *Calif., U.S.* **102** L6
Upper Missouri River Breaks National Monument, *Mont., U.S.* **100** C9
Upper Peninsula, *U.S.* **79** D15
Upper Red Lake, *Minn., U.S.* **98** E10
Upper Sandusky, *Ohio, U.S.* **93** Q12
Uppsala, *Sw.* **135** K14
Upshi, *India* **158** C6
Upton, *Wyo., U.S.* **100** G13
'Uqayribāt, *Syr.* **150** F9
Ur, ruins, *Iraq* **152** F10
Urabá, Gulf of, *S. Amer.* **118** B2
Urad Houqi, *China* **162** B1
Urad Qianqi, *China* **162** C2
Urad Zhongqi, *China* **162** B2
Urakawa, *Jap.* **164** G14
Ural, river, *Eur.* **130** F14
Uralla, *N.S.W., Austral.* **191** W15
Ural Moutnains, *Russ.* **140** J8
Urana, *N.S.W., Austral.* **191** Y13
Urandangi, *Qnsld., Austral.* **191** S10
Urania, *La., U.S.* **94** M8
Uranium City, *Sask., Can.* **76** J12
Uranu, island, *Chuuk, F.S.M.* **197** B14
Uraricoera, river, *Braz.* **122** B8
Uraricoera, *Braz.* **122** B9
Uravan, *Colo., U.S.* **101** N10
Urawa, *Jap.* **165** P12
Urbana, *Ill., U.S.* **93** R6
Urbana, *Ohio, U.S.* **93** R12
Urbandale, *Iowa, U.S.* **99** P11
Urbano Noris, *Cuba* **110** K12
Urbano Santos, *Braz.* **123** D15
Urbett, island, *Jaluit Atoll, Marshall Is.* **196** K8
Urdzhar, *Kaz.* **155** F18
Uréparapara, island, *Vanuatu* **198** B2
Ures, *Mex.* **108** C7
Urganch, *Uzb.* **154** K9
Urgut, *Uzb.* **154** L12
Uriah, Mount, *N.Z.* **193** N17
Uribia, *Col.* **120** A6
Uriondo, *Bol.* **122** L7
Ūrītskīy, *Kaz.* **154** B11
Uritskoye, *Russ.* **141** H17
Urla, *Turk.* **148** F2
Urmia, Lake *see* Orūmīyeh, Daryācheh-ye, *Iran* **152** B10
Üroteppa, *Taj.* **156** G7
Urt Moron, *China* **160** H8
Uruana, *Braz.* **123** J13
Uruapan, *Mex.* **108** J10
Urubamba, river, *Peru* **122** H5
Urucará, *Braz.* **122** D10
Uruçuí, *Braz.* **123** F15
Uruçuí, Serra do, *S. Amer.* **118** F8
Urugi, *Jap.* **165** P10
Uruguai, river, *Braz.* **122** N11
Uruguaiana, *Braz.* **122** P10
Uruguay, *S. Amer.* **124** K14
Uruguay, river, *S. Amer.* **118** K7
Urukthapel (Ngeruktabel), island, *Palau* **196** P11
Ürümqi, *China* **160** E7
Uruno Point, *Guam, U.S.* **196** B11
Urup, island, *Russ.* **141** J23
Usa, river, *Eur.* **130** A12
Usa, *Jap.* **165** R7
Uşak, *Turk.* **148** F5
Usakos, *Namibia* **182** H6
Usarp Mountains, *Antarctica* **207** Q15
Ushakova, Ostrov, *Russ.* **141** C13
Ushakovskoye, *Russ.* **141** B19
Ushibuka, *Jap.* **165** S4
Ushi Point, *Tinian, N. Mariana Is., U.S.* **196** A8
Ushtobe, *Kaz.* **155** G17
Ushuaia, *Arg.* **125** Y9
Ushumun, *Russ.* **141** K19
Usinsk, *Russ.* **140** F10
Usol'ye Sibirskoye, *Russ.* **141** L15
U.S.S. Arizona Memorial, *Hawaii, U.S.* **106** E11
Ussuri, river, *Asia* **146** E12
Ussuriysk, *Russ.* **141** M21
Ustica, island, *It.* **136** K10
Ust' Ilimpeya, *Russ.* **141** H15
Ust' Ilimsk, *Russ.* **141** K15
Ust' Kamchatsk, *Russ.* **141** E22
Ust' Kamenogorsk *see* Öskemen, *Kaz.* **155** D18
Ust' Kamo, *Russ.* **141** J14
Ust' Kut, *Russ.* **141** K15
Ust' Maya, *Russ.* **141** G19
Ust' Mil', *Russ.* **141** H19
Ust' Nera, *Russ.* **141** F19
Ust' Olenek, *Russ.* **141** E16
Ust' Omchug, *Russ.* **141** F20
Ust' Ordynskiy, *Russ.* **141** L15
Ust' Usa, *Russ.* **140** F10
Ust' Yansk, *Russ.* **141** E17
Ust' Yudoma, *Russ.* **141** H19
Ustyurt Plateau, *Kaz.-Uzb.* **154** H7
Usu, *China* **160** E7
Usuki, *Jap.* **165** R5
Usumacinta, river, *N. Amer.* **74** P6
Uta, *Indonesia* **169** L19
Utabetsu, *Jap.* **164** G15
Utah, *U.S.* **100** M7
Utah Lake, *Utah, U.S.* **100** L7
Utara, Bunguran *see* Natuna Besar, Kepulauan, *Indonesia* **168** G8
Ute Creek, *N. Mex., U.S.* **101** Q14
Utete, *Tanzania* **179** M15
Uthai Thani, *Thai.* **166** L8
Uthal, *Pak.* **157** V6
Utiariti, *Braz.* **122** H10
Utica, *N.Y., U.S.* **88** J9
Utiel, *Sp.* **139** R8
Utirik Atoll, *Marshall Is.* **196** F4
Utkela, *India* **158** L9
Utnur, *India* **158** L6
Utopia, *N. Terr., Austral.* **191** T9
Utraula, *India* **158** G8
Utrecht, *Neth.* **138** H11
Utrera, *Sp.* **139** S6
Utsunomiya, *Jap.* **165** N12
Uttaradit, *Thai.* **166** K8
Utuado, *P.R., U.S.* **111** M22
Utuloa, *Wallis and Futuna, Fr.* **198** B11
Utupua, island, *Santa Cruz Is., Solomon Is.* **197** Q23
Uturoa, *Raiatea, Fr. Polynesia, Fr.* **199** B23
Utva, river, *Kaz.* **154** D7
Utwa, *Kosrae, F.S.M.* **197** B18
Uummannaq, *Greenland, Den.* **75** C21
Uusikaupunki, *Fin.* **135** J15
Uvalde, *Tex., U.S.* **97** R8
Uvéa *see* Ouvéa, Île, island, *New Caledonia, Fr.* **198** C8
Uvea, island, *Wallis and Futuna, Fr.* **198** B11
Uvinza, *Tanzania* **178** L12
Uvol, *P.N.G.* **193** D21
Uvs Nuur, *Mongolia* **160** C9
Uwajima, *Jap.* **165** R6
'Uwayriḑ, Harrat al, *Saudi Arabia* **152** G6
'Uweinat, Jebel, *Sudan* **178** B11
Uxin Qi (Dabqig), *China* **162** E2
Uxmal, ruins, *Mex.* **109** H16
Uyar, *Russ.* **141** K13
Uyuni, *Bol.* **122** L7
Uyuni, Salar de, *Bol.* **122** L7
Uzbekistan, *Asia* **154** J9
Uzbel Shankou, pass, *China-Taj.* **156** H11
Uzhhorod, *Ukr.* **132** J11
Užice, *Yug.* **137** G13
Üzümlü, *Turk.* **148** H4
Uzunköprü, *Turk.* **148** C3

V

Vaal, river, *S. Af.* **182** K10
Vaasa, *Fin.* **135** H14
Vác, *Hung.* **132** K9
Vacaville, *Calif., U.S.* **103** R4
Vache, Île à, *Haiti* **111** N15
Vadodara, *India* **158** J3
Vadsø, *Nor.* **135** B15
Værøy, island, *Nor.* **134** E11
Vaga, river, *Eur.* **130** C11
Vágar, island, *Faroe Is., Den.* **134** J5
Vaghena, island, *Solomon Is.* **197** L16
Vahanga, island, *Fr. Polynesia, Fr.* **199** G22
Vahitahi, island, *Fr. Polynesia, Fr.* **199** F21
Vahituri, island, *Rangiroa, Fr. Polynesia, Fr.* **199** L17
Vaiaau, *Raiatea, Fr. Polynesia, Fr.* **199** B23
Vaiau, Passe, *Tahiti, Fr. Polynesia, Fr.* **199** Q17
Vaiden, *Miss., U.S.* **94** K11
Vaiea, *Niue, N.Z.* **199** C20
Vaiere, island, *Penrhyn, Cook Is., N.Z.* **199** C17
Vaigalu, *Samoa* **198** L4
Vaihiria, Lac, *Tahiti, Fr. Polynesia, Fr.* **199** P16
Vail, *Colo., U.S.* **100** M12
Vailala, *Wallis and Futuna, Fr.* **198** B11
Vailoa, *Samoa* **198** K2
Vailoatai, *Tutuila, Amer. Samoa, U.S.* **198** N7
Vaimalau, *Wallis and Futuna, Fr.* **198** B11
Vaini, *Tongatapu, Tonga* **198** J11
Vaionifa, Passe, *Tahiti, Fr. Polynesia, Fr.* **199** P18
Vaipae, *Aitutaki Atoll, Cook Is., N.Z.* **198** Q11
Vaipaee, *Ua Huka, Fr. Polynesia, Fr.* **199** N23
Vaipeka, *Aitutaki Atoll, Cook Is., N.Z.* **198** P11
Vairaatea, island, *Fr. Polynesia, Fr.* **199** F21
Vairo, *Tahiti, Fr. Polynesia, Fr.* **199** Q17
Vaitahu, *Hiva Oa, Fr. Polynesia, Fr.* **199** N20
Vaītape, *Bora-Bora, Fr. Polynesia, Fr.* **199** K14
Vaitoare, *Tahaa, Fr. Polynesia, Fr.* **199** B23
Vaitogi, *Tutuila, Amer. Samoa, U.S.* **198** N7
Vaitupu, island, *Tuvalu* **194** H9
Vaitupu, *Wallis and Futuna, Fr.* **198** B11
Vai'utukakau Bay, *Vava'u Group, Tonga* **198** L11
Vaka'eitu, island, *Vava'u Group, Tonga* **198** M11
Vakfıkebir, *Turk.* **149** D14
Vakhan, region, *Afghan.* **156** K10
Vakhrushev, *Russ.* **141** J22
Vakhsh, river, *Taj.* **156** H8
Valcheta, *Arg.* **125** Q9
Valdai Hills, *Eur.* **130** E10
Valdepeñas, *Sp.* **139** R7
Valdés, Península, *Arg.* **125** R10
Valdez, *Alas., U.S.* **105** J17
Valdez, *Ecua.* **120** H2
Valdivia, *Chile* **125** P6
Valdivia, *Col.* **120** D4
Valdivia Fracture Zone, *Pac. Oc.* **219** P18
Val-d'Or, *Que., Can.* **77** P18
Valdosta, *Ga., U.S.* **91** Q6
Vale, *Oreg., U.S.* **102** H9
Valença, *Braz.* **123** H16
Valença, *Port.* **139** P5
Valence, *Fr.* **138** M11
Valencia, *Sp.* **139** R9
Valencia, *Venez.* **120** B9
Valencia, Lago, *S. Amer.* **118** A4
Valentine, *Nebr., U.S.* **98** M4
Valentine, *Tex., U.S.* **97** P1
Valentine, *Tex., U.S.* **97** W4
Valera, *Venez.* **120** C7
Valga, *Estonia* **135** L17
Valier, *Mont., U.S.* **100** B7
Valjevo, *Yug.* **137** G13
Valka, *Latv.* **135** L17
Valkeakoski, *Fin.* **135** J15
Valkyrie Dome, *Antarctica* **207** D15
Valladolid, *Mex.* **109** H16
Valladolid, *Sp.* **139** P7
Vallecito Reservoir, *Colo., U.S.* **101** P11
Valle de la Pascua, *Venez.* **120** C10
Valledupar, *Col.* **120** B6
Valle Fértil, Sierra del, *Arg.* **124** J8
Valle Formozo, *São Tomé and Príncipe* **185** D20
Vallegrande, *Bol.* **122** K8
Vallehermoso, *Canary Is., Sp.* **184** Q4
Vallejo, *Calif., U.S.* **103** R3
Vallenar, *Chile* **124** H7
Valletta, *Malta* **136** M10
Valley Center, *Kans., U.S.* **99** U7
Valley City, *N. Dak., U.S.* **98** G7
Valley Falls, *Kans., U.S.* **99** S9
Valley Falls, *Oreg., U.S.* **102** K6
Valley Mills, *Tex., U.S.* **97** N11
Valley Station, *Ky., U.S.* **95** B16
Valmeyer, *Ill., U.S.* **93** T4
Valmiera, *Latv.* **135** L17
Valona *see* Vlorë, *Alban.* **137** J13
Valozhyn, *Belarus* **132** F12
Valparaiso, *Fla., U.S.* **91** Q2
Valparaiso, *Ind., U.S.* **93** P8
Valparaíso, *Chile* **124** L6
Valparaíso, *Mex.* **108** G10
Vals, Tanjung, *Indonesia* **193** D16
Valsad, *India* **158** K3
Valverde, *Canary Is., Sp.* **184** R4
Van, *Turk.* **149** G17
Van, Lake, *Asia* **146** F4
Vana, *Santa Cruz Is., Solomon Is.* **197** R23
Vanadzor, *Arm.* **149** D18
Van Alstyne, *Tex., U.S.* **96** K12
Vanavana, island, *Fr. Polynesia, Fr.* **199** G21
Vanavara, *Russ.* **141** J15
Van Blommestein Meer, *Suriname* **121** E16
Van Buren, *Ark., U.S.* **94** F6
Van Buren, *Me., U.S.* **89** A18
Vanceboro, *Me., U.S.* **89** D19
Vanceboro, *N.C., U.S.* **90** H13
Vanceburg, *Ky., U.S.* **95** A19
Vancouver, *B.C., Can.* **76** M8
Vancouver, *Wash., U.S.* **102** F3
Vancouver Island, *B.C., Can.* **76** L7
Vandalia, *Ill., U.S.* **93** S5
Vandalia, *Mo., U.S.* **99** S14
Vandalia, *Ohio, U.S.* **93** R11
Vanderbilt, *Mich., U.S.* **92** H11
Vanderford Glacier, *Antarctica* **207** M21
Van Diemen, Cape, *Austral.* **190** A7
Van Diemen Gulf, *Austral.* **190** A8
Vänern, lake, *Sw.* **134** L12
Vangaindrano, *Madagascar* **183** H17
Van Gölü, *Turk.* **149** G17
Vangunu, island, *Solomon Is.* **197** M17
Vangunu, Mount, *Solomon Is.* **197** M16
Vangviang, *Laos* **166** J10
Van Horn, *Tex., U.S.* **97** V4
Vanikolo, island, *Santa Cruz Is., Solomon Is.* **197** R23
Vanikolo Islands, *Santa Cruz Is., Solomon Is.* **197** R23
Vanimo, *P.N.G.* **193** B17
Vanino, *Russ.* **141** K21
Vanj, *Taj.* **156** J9
Vankarem, *Russ.* **141** A20
Vännäs, *Sw.* **135** G14
Vannes, *Fr.* **138** K8
Van Ninh, *Vietnam* **167** N14
Vannøy, island, *Nor.* **135** C13
Vanrhynsdorp, *S. Af.* **182** L7
Vanrook, *Qnsld., Austral.* **191** R12
Vansbro, *Sw.* **134** K12
Vansittart Island, *Nunavut, Can.* **77** G16
Vantaa, *Fin.* **135** J16
Van Tassell, *Wyo., U.S.* **100** H14
Vanua, island, *Fiji* **198** H9
Vanuatu, *Pac. Oc.* **198** B3
Van Wert, *Ohio, U.S.* **93** Q11
Vao, *New Caledonia, Fr.* **198** E9
Vao, Nosy, *Madagascar* **183** F16
Varadero, *Cuba* **110** G7
Varanasi (Banaras), *India* **158** H9
Varangerfjorden, *Nor.* **135** C15
Varangerhalvøya, peninsula, *Nor.* **135** B15
Varas, *Afghan.* **157** N4
Varaždin, *Croatia* **136** E11
Varberg, *Sw.* **134** M12
Vardø, *Nor.* **135** B15
Varėna, *Lith.* **135** N17
Varese, *It.* **136** E8
Varkaus, *Fin.* **135** H16
Varna, *Bulg.* **137** G17
Varnville, *S.C., U.S.* **90** M9
Varto, *Turk.* **149** F16
Varungga Point, *Solomon Is.* **197** L16
Varzob, *Taj.* **156** H7
Vasafua, island, *Funafuti, Tuvalu* **197** K22
Vaskess Bay, *Kiritimati, Kiribati* **197** B22
Vaslui, *Rom.* **137** E17
Vassar, *Mich., U.S.* **92** L12
Västerås, *Sw.* **135** K13
Västervik, *Sw.* **135** M13
Vasto, *It.* **136** H10
Vasyl'kiv, *Ukr.* **133** H14
Vasyugan'ye, wetland, *Asia* **146** E8
Vaté, Île *see* Éfaté, *Vanuatu* **198** F3
Vathí, *Gr.* **137** L17
Vatia, *Tutuila, Amer. Samoa, U.S.* **198** M8
Vatia Point, *Fiji* **198** H6
Vatia Bay, *Tutuila, Amer. Samoa, U.S.* **198** L8
Vatican City, *Eur.* **136** H9
Vaticano, Capo, *It.* **136** K11
Vatnajökull, *Ice.* **134** F3
Vatneyri, *Ice.* **134** E2
Vatoa (Turtle), island, *Fiji* **198** L10
Vättern, lake, *Sw.* **135** M13

Vatu, Vanua, Fiji 198 J9
Vatuki, island, Fiji 198 G7
Vatukoula, Fiji 198 H6
Vatulele, island, Fiji 198 J6
Vatu Vara, island, Fiji 198 H8
Vaughn, Mont., U.S. 100 C7
Vaughn, N. Mex., U.S. 101 S13
Vaupés, river, Col. 120 H7
Vauvilliers, Île, New Caledonia, Fr. 198 C9
Vauvilliers, Point, Kosrae, F.S.M. 197 B17
Vav, India 158 H3
Vavara, Motu, Huahine, Fr. Polynesia, Fr. 199 G14
Vava'u, island, Tonga 198 L12
Vava'u Group, Tonga 194 K10
Vavitu see Raivavae, island, Fr. Polynesia, Fr. 199 J17
Vavuniya, Sri Lanka 159 S7
Vawkavysk, Belarus 132 F12
Växjö, Sw. 135 M13
Vayegi, Russ. 141 C21
Vaygach, Ostrov, Russ. 140 E10
Veblen, S. Dak., U.S. 98 H7
Vega, island, Nor. 134 G11
Vega, Tex., U.S. 96 G4
Vegreville, Alta., Can. 76 L11
Veharnu, island, P.N.G. 197 H14
Vekai, island, Fiji 198 H9
Velarde, N. Mex., U.S. 101 R12
Velé, Wallis and Futuna, Fr. 198 E11
Velé, Pointe, Wallis and Futuna, Fr. 198 E12
Veles, Maced. 137 H14
Vélez, Col. 120 E5
Velhas, river, Braz. 123 K14
Velikaya, river, Eur. 130 D9
Velikiye Luki, Russ. 140 E5
Velikiy Novgorod, Russ. 140 E6
Velikonda Range, India 159 N6
Veliko Tŭrnovo, Bulg. 137 G16
Vélingara, Senegal 176 H5
Vella Gulf, Solomon Is. 197 M15
Vella Lavella, island, Solomon Is. 197 L15
Velletri, It. 136 H9
Vellore, India 159 Q6
Vel'sk, Russ. 140 F7
Velva, N. Dak., U.S. 98 F4
Vema Fracture Zone, Atl. Oc. 216 M7
Vema Fracture Zone, Ind. Oc. 220 H8
Vema Seamount, Atl. Oc. 217 S14
Venable Ice Shelf, Antarctica 206 H6
Venado Tuerto, Arg. 124 L11
Venango, Nebr., U.S. 99 Q3
Venetie, Alas., U.S. 105 E17
Venezia (Venice), It. 136 F9
Venezuela, S. Amer. 120 D8
Venezuela, Golfo de, Venez. 120 B7
Vengurla, India 159 N3
Veniaminof, Mount, Alas., U.S. 105 N13
Venice, Fla., U.S. 91 V7
Venice see Venezia, It. 136 F9
Venice, La., U.S. 94 R12
Venice, Gulf of, It. 136 F10
Venkatapuram, India 158 M7
Vennesund, Nor. 134 G11
Vent, Îles du, Fr. Polynesia, Fr. 199 F16
Ventnor City, N.J., U.S. 88 Q10
Ventspils, Latv. 135 M15
Ventuari, river, Venez. 120 F10
Ventura, Calif., U.S. 103 X7
Vénus, Pointe, Tahiti, Fr. Polynesia, Fr. 199 N16
Vera, Arg. 124 H12
Vera, Sp. 139 S8
Vera, Bahía, Arg. 125 S10
Veracruz, Mex. 109 J13
Veraval, India 158 K2
Verçinin Tepesi, Turk. 149 D15
Verdalsøra, Nor. 134 H11
Verde, river, Ariz., U.S. 101 T7
Verde, Arroyo, river, Arg. 125 Q9
Verde, Cape, Af. 174 G1
Verde, Cay, Bahamas 111 H13
Verde, Península, Arg. 125 P11
Verden, Ger. 132 F6
Verdigre, Nebr., U.S. 99 N7
Verdigris, river, U.S. 79 J13
Verdun, Fr. 138 K11
Verga, Cap, Guinea 180 F4
Vergara, Chile 124 D7
Vergara, Uru. 124 K15
Vergennes, Vt., U.S. 88 G12
Véria, Gr. 137 J14
Verín, Sp. 139 P5
Verkhneimbatsk, Russ. 141 H13
Verkhneye Penzhino, Russ. 141 D20
Verkhnyaya Amga, Russ. 141 H18
Verkhoyanskiy Khrebet, Russ. 141 F17
Verkhoyansk Range, Asia 146 C11
Vermelharia, Ponta da, Cape Verde 185 B15
Vermelho, river, Braz. 122 J12
Vermilion Bay, La., U.S. 94 Q8
Vermilion Cliffs National Monument, Ariz., U.S. 101 Q7
Vermilion Lake, Minn., U.S. 98 F12
Vermillion, S. Dak., U.S. 98 M8
Vermont, U.S. 88 G12
Vernadsky, station, Antarctica 206 D4
Vernal, Utah, U.S. 100 L9
Vernon, Ala., U.S. 95 J13
Vernon, Tex., U.S. 96 J8
Vernonia, Oreg., U.S. 102 E3
Vero Beach, Fla., U.S. 91 U10
Verona, It. 136 F9
Verona, Miss., U.S. 95 H13
Versailles, Fr. 138 K10
Versailles, Ky., U.S. 95 B17
Versailles, Mo., U.S. 99 T12
Verte, Pointe, Wallis and Futuna, Fr. 198 E12
Vertientes, Cuba 110 J10
Veselyy, Russ. 141 J17
Vesoul, Fr. 138 K12
Vesterålen, islands, Nor. 134 D11
Vestfjorden, Nor. 134 E12
Vestfold Hills, Antarctica 207 G20
Vestmanna, Faroe Is., Den. 134 J6
Vestmannaeyjar, islands, Ice. 134 G2
Veststraumen Glacier, Antarctica 206 C11
Vestvågøy, island, Nor. 134 E12
Vesuvio, peak, It. 136 J10
Vétaounde, island, Vanuatu 198 A2
Vetapalem, India 159 N7
Vetavuua, island, Fiji 198 G9
Vetluga, river, Eur. 130 C12
Vevaru, island, Maldives 159 V3
Vezirköprü, Turk. 148 D10
Viacha, Bol. 122 J6
Viana do Castelo, Port. 139 P5
Viangchan (Vientiane), Laos 166 K10
Viareggio, It. 136 G8
Viborg, Den. 134 N11
Vibo Valentia, It. 136 K11
Vic, Sp. 139 P10
Vicente Guerrero, Mex. 108 B5
Vichada, river, Col. 120 F8
Vichy, Fr. 138 L10
Vici, Okla., U.S. 96 F8
Vicksburg, Mich., U.S. 93 N10
Vicksburg, Miss., U.S. 94 L10
Vicksburg National Military Park, Miss., U.S. 94 L10
Victor, Colo., U.S. 101 N13
Victor, Idaho, U.S. 100 G8
Victor, Mount, Antarctica 207 C16
Victor Harbor, S. Austral., Austral. 191 Y10
Victoria, river, Austral. 190 C7
Victoria, Austral. 191 Z12
Victoria, B.C., Can. 76 M8
Victoria, Chile 124 C7
Victoria, Chile 125 N6
Victoria, Kans., U.S. 99 S6
Victoria, Seychelles 185 P20
Victoria, Tex., U.S. 97 S12
Victoria, Va., U.S. 90 F12
Victoria, Lake, Af. 179 K13
Victoria, Mount, Myanmar 166 H5
Victoria, Mount, P.N.G. 193 E20
Victoria Falls, Zambia-Zimb. 182 F10
Victoria Island, N.W.T.-Nunavut, Can. 77 E13
Victoria Land, Antarctica 207 Q14
Victoria River Downs, N. Terr., Austral. 191 Q7
Victoria Strait, Nunavut, Can. 77 F14
Victorica, Arg. 124 K12
Victorica, Arg. 124 M9
Victorville, Calif., U.S. 103 W9
Victory Peak see Pobedy Peak, China-Kyrg. 156 E15
Vicuña, Chile 124 J7
Vidalia, Ga., U.S. 91 N7
Vidalia, La., U.S. 94 M9
Vidin, Bulg. 137 G14
Vidisha, India 158 J6
Vidor, Tex., U.S. 97 Q16
Vidzy, Belarus 132 E12
Viedma, Arg. 125 Q11
Viedma, Lago, Arg. 125 V7
Vienna see Wien, Aust. 132 K8
Vienna, Ga., U.S. 91 N6
Vienna, Ill., U.S. 93 V6
Vienna, W. Va., U.S. 90 C8
Vienne, Fr. 138 M11
Vientiane see Viangchan, Laos 166 K10
Vieques, island, P.R., U.S. 111 M24
Vierzon, Fr. 138 L10
Vieste, It. 136 H11
Vietnam, Asia 166 L14
Viet Tri, Vietnam 166 H12
Vieux Fort, St. Lucia 113 L17
Vigan, Philippines 169 B13
Vigía Chico, Mex. 109 H17
Vigo, Sp. 139 P5
Vihari, Pak. 157 R10
Vijayawada, India 159 N7
Vík, Ice. 134 G2
Vikenara Point, Solomon Is. 197 M18
Vikhorevka, Russ. 141 K14
Vikna, Nor. 134 G11
Vilaba, Sp. 139 N5
Vila Bittencourt, Braz. 122 D6
Vila da Ribeira Brava, Cape Verde 185 B15
Vila de Moura, Port. 139 S5
Vila Murtinho, Braz. 122 G7
Vilanculos, Mozambique 183 H13
Vila Nova de Gaia, Port. 139 Q5
Vila Real de Santo António, Port. 139 S5
Vila Velha, Braz. 122 B12
Vila Velha, Braz. 123 L16
Vilhelmina, Sw. 135 G13
Vilhena, Braz. 122 H9
Viljandi, Estonia 135 L16
Vil'kitskogo, Proliv, Russ. 141 D14
Villa Ahumada, Mex. 108 C9
Villa Alberdi, Arg. 124 G9
VillaÁngela, Arg. 124 G12
Villa Atuel, Arg. 124 L8
Villa Cañás, Arg. 124 L11
Villach, Aust. 132 L7
Villacidro, It. 136 K7
Villa Dolores, Arg. 124 K9
Village, Manihi, Fr. Polynesia, Fr. 199 K17
Villa Grove, Ill., U.S. 93 R7
Villaguay, Arg. 124 K13
Villa Guillermina, Arg. 124 H12
Villahermosa, Mex. 109 K14
Villalonga, Arg. 125 P11
Villa María, Arg. 124 K11
Villa Martín, Bol. 122 L6
Villamontes, Bol. 122 L8
Villanueva, Mex. 108 G10
Villanueva, N. Mex., U.S. 101 S13
Villa Ocampo, Arg. 124 H12
Villa Regina, Arg. 125 P9
Villarrica, Chile 125 P6
Villarrica, Lago, Chile 125 P7
Villa Unión, Arg. 124 H8
Villa Unión, Mex. 108 G8
Villavicencio, Col. 120 F6
Villazón, Bol. 122 L7
Villena, Sp. 139 R8
Ville Platte, La., U.S. 94 N8
Villisca, Iowa, U.S. 99 Q10
Villupuram, India 159 Q7
Vilnius, Lith. 135 N17
Vilyuy, river, Asia 146 D10
Vilyuy, river, Russ. 141 G17
Vilyuysk, Russ. 141 H17
Vilyuyskoye Vodokhranilishche, Russ. 141 H16
Vina, Calif., U.S. 103 P4
Viña del Mar, Chile 124 K6
Vinalhaven, Me., U.S. 89 G17
Vinaròs, Sp. 139 Q9
Vincennes, Ind., U.S. 93 T7
Vincennes Bay, Antarctica 207 M21
Vincent, Point, Norfolk I., Austral. 197 F20
Vindelälven, river, Sw. 135 G13
Vindeln, Sw. 135 G14
Vindhya Range, India 158 J4
Vineland, N.J., U.S. 88 Q10
Vinh, Vietnam 166 J12
Vinh Chau, Vietnam 167 Q12
Vinh Long, Vietnam 167 P12
Vinita, Okla., U.S. 96 E13
Vinnytsya, Ukr. 133 J13
Vinson Massif, Antarctica 206 H8
Vinton, Iowa, U.S. 99 N13
Vinton, La., U.S. 94 P6
Vinukonda, India 159 N7
Viqueque, E. Timor 169 M15
Vir, Taj. 156 J10
Virac, Philippines 169 C15
Virachei, Cambodia 166 M13
Viranşehir, Turk. 149 H14
Virawah, Pak. 157 W9
Virden, Ill., U.S. 93 S5
Virden, Man., Can. 77 N13
Virden, N. Mex., U.S. 101 V10
Vire, Fr. 138 K8
Virgenes, Cape, S. Amer. 118 R5
Virgin, river, Ariz., U.S. 101 Q5
Virgin, river, Nev., U.S. 103 T13
Virgin Gorda, island, British Virgin Is., U.K. 113 F14
Virginia, U.S. 90 E11
Virginia, Ill., U.S. 93 R4
Virginia, Minn., U.S. 98 F12
Virginia Beach, Va., U.S. 90 F14
Virginia City, Mont., U.S. 100 E7
Virginia City, Nev., U.S. 103 Q6
Virginia Falls, Yukon Terr., Can. 76 G9
Virgin Islands, Lesser Antilles 113 F13
Viroqua, Wis., U.S. 92 K3
Virovitica, Croatia 136 E12
Virrat, Fin. 135 H15
Virtsu, Estonia 135 L16
Virú, Peru 122 G2
Virudunagar, India 159 R6
Vis, island, Croatia 136 G11
Visalia, Calif., U.S. 103 U7
Visayan Sea, Philippines 169 D14
Visby, Sw. 135 M14
Viscount Melville Sound, N.W.T.-Nunavut, Can. 77 D13
Viseu, Braz. 123 D14
Vishakhapatnam, India 158 M9
Vishnevka, Kaz. 155 D14
Vista, Calif., U.S. 103 Y9
Vista Alegre, Braz. 122 E6
Vistula, river, Eur. 130 F8
Viterbo, It. 136 H9
Vitichi, Bol. 122 L7
Viti Levu, island, Fiji 198 J6
Viti Levu Bay, Fiji 198 H6
Vitim, river, Russ. 141 J16
Vitim, Russ. 141 J16
Vitor, Peru 122 J5
Vitória, Braz. 122 D12
Vitória, Braz. 123 L16
Vitória da Conquista, Braz. 123 J16
Vitoria-Gasteiz, Sp. 139 P8
Vitoria Seamount, Atl. Oc. 217 R8
Vitré, Fr. 138 K8
Vitsyebsk, Belarus 133 E14
Vittangi, Sw. 135 E14
Vittoria, It. 136 M10
Vityaz Trench, Pac. Oc. 218 L9
Viveiro, Sp. 139 N5
Viver, Sp. 139 Q9
Vivi, river, Russ. 141 H14
Vivi, Russ. 141 H14
Vivian, La., U.S. 94 K6
Viwa, island, Fiji 198 H5
Vizcaíno, Desierto de, Mex. 108 D6
Vize, Turk. 148 C4
Vize, Ostrov, Russ. 141 C13
Vizianagaram, India 158 M9
Vladikavkaz, Russ. 140 J4
Vladimir, Russ. 140 F6
Vladimirovskiy, Kaz. 154 B11
Vladivostok, Russ. 141 M21
Vlorë (Valona), Alban. 137 J13
Vod Ab, Afghan. 156 J9
Voh, New Caledonia, Fr. 198 C7
Vohemar see Iharaña, Madagascar 183 D18
Volborg, Mont., U.S. 100 E12
Volcano, Hawaii, U.S. 107 N21
Volcano Islands (Kazan Rettō), Jap. 194 C4
Volda, Nor. 134 J10
Volga, river, Russ. 140 H5
Volga, S. Dak., U.S. 98 K8
Volga, Source of the, Eur. 130 D10
Volga-Don Canal, Eur. 130 F12
Volga River Delta, Kaz. 154 G4
Volga Upland, Eur. 130 F12
Volgograd (Stalingrad), Russ. 140 H5
Volgograd Reservoir, Eur. 130 F13
Volkhov, river, Eur. 130 D10
Volksrust, S. Af. 182 K11
Volnovakha, Ukr. 133 K18
Volodarskoye, Kaz. 154 B12
Vologda, Russ. 140 F7
Vólos (Iolkós), Gr. 137 K15
Volta, Lake, Ghana 180 G11
Volta, Pointe de, Wallis and Futuna, Fr. 198 E12
Voltaire, Cape, Austral. 190 B5
Volyn-Podolian Upland, Eur. 130 G9
Volzhskiy, Russ. 140 H5
Vonavona, island, Solomon Is. 197 M16
Vopnafjördur, Ice. 134 F4
Vóries Sporádes, islands, Gr. 137 K15
Voring Plateau, Atl. Oc. 216 B13
Vorkuta, Russ. 140 F11
Vormsi, island, Estonia 135 K16
Voronezh, Russ. 140 G5
Voronin Trough, Arctic Oc. 222 D11
Vorontsovka, Russ. 141 J16
Võru, Estonia 135 L17
Vorukh, Taj. 156 G8
Vosges, mountains, Eur. 130 G5
Voss, Nor. 134 K10
Vostochnaya, Russ. 141 E13
Vostochnyy (Vrangel'), Russ. 141 M21
Vostochnyy Sayan, mountains, Russ. 141 K13
Vostok, station, Antarctica 207 K16
Vostok Island, Kiribati 195 H13
Volta, Lake, Af. 174 H3
Votkinsk, Russ. 140 H8
Votlo, Vanuatu 198 E3
Voyageurs National Park, Minn., U.S. 98 E11
Voyampolka, Russ. 141 E22
Voyvozh, Russ. 140 F9
Voza, Solomon Is. 197 K15
Vozhgora, Russ. 140 F9
Voznesens'k, Ukr. 133 K15
Vrang, Taj. 156 K10
Vrangel' see Vostochnyy, Russ. 141 M21
Vrangelya, Ostrov (Wrangel Island), Russ. 141 B19
Vratsa, Bulg. 137 G15
Vršac, Yug. 137 F14
Vryburg, S. Af. 182 K9

Vryheid, S. Af. 182 KII
Vuagava, island, Fiji 198 K9
Vunaniu Bay, Fiji 198 J6
Vung Tau, Vietnam 167 PI3
Vunindawa, Fiji 198 J6
Vunisea, Fiji 198 K6
Vunivutu Bay, Fiji 198 G7
Vyatka, river, Eur. 130 DI2
Vyazemskiy, Russ. 141 K2I
Vychegda, river, Eur. 130 BI2
Vychegda Lowland, Eur. 130 BI2
Vyg, Lake, Eur. 130 CIO
Vym', river, Eur. 130 BI2
Vytegra, Russ. 140 E7

W

Wa, Ghana 180 FIO
Waar, island, Indonesia 169 KI9
Wabao, Cape, New Caledonia, Fr. 198 DIO
Wabasca, river, Alta., Can. 76 KIO
Wabash, river, Ill.-Ind., U.S. 93 T7
Wabash, Ind., U.S. 93 Q9
Wabasha, Minn., U.S. 98 KI3
Wabasso, Fla., U.S. 91 UIO
Wabeno, Wis., U.S. 92 H6
Wabowden, Man., Can. 77 LI4
Wabuk Point, Ont., Can. 77 LI6
Waco, Tex., U.S. 97 NII
Waco Lake, Tex., U.S. 97 NII
Wad, Pak. 157 U5
Wadayama, Jap. 165 P8
Waddenzee, Neth. 138 GII
Waddington, Mount, B.C., Can. 76 L8
Wadena, Minn., U.S. 98 HIO
Wadena, Sask., Can. 76 MI2
Wadesboro, N.C., U.S. 90 JIO
Wadeye, N. Terr., Austral. 191 P7
Wadi Halfa, Sudan 178 BI2
Wādī Mūsá (Elchi), Jordan 151 Q6
Wadley, Ga., U.S. 90 M7
Wad Medani, Sudan 179 EI3
Wadomari, Jap. 165 X2
Wadsworth, Nev., U.S. 103 P7
Wadsworth, Ohio, U.S. 93 PI4
Wadu, island, Maldives 159 T3
Waelder, Tex., U.S. 97 RII
Waeshe, Mount, Antarctica 206 M8
Wafangdian, China 162 DIO
Wager Bay, Nunavut, Can. 77 GI5
Wagga Wagga, N.S.W., Austral. 191 YI3
Wagin, W. Austral., Austral. 191 X3
Wagner, S. Dak., U.S. 98 M7
Wagoner, Okla., U.S. 96 FI3
Wagon Mound, N. Mex., U.S. 101 RI4
Wagontire Mountain, Oreg., U.S. 102 J6
Wahai, Indonesia 169 KI7
Wahaula Heiau, Hawaii, U.S. 107 N22
Wah Cantonment, Pak. 157 NIO
Wahiawa, Hawaii, U.S. 106 DII
Wahoo, Nebr., U.S. 99 P8
Wahpeton, N. Dak., U.S. 98 H8
Wai, India 158 M4
Wai, Indonesia 169 KI6
Wai, Koh, Cambodia 167 QIO
Waiakoa (Kula), Hawaii, U.S. 107 GI7
Waialeale, peak, Hawaii, U.S. 106 B5
Waialua, Hawaii, U.S. 106 DIO
Waialua Bay, Hawaii, U.S. 106 DIO
Waianae Range, Hawaii, U.S. 106 DIO
Waiau, river, N.Z. 193 RI5
Waibeem, Indonesia 169 JI8
Waigama, Indonesia 169 KI7
Waigeo, island, Indonesia 169 JI7
Waihee, Hawaii, U.S. 107 GI6
Waiheke Island, N.Z. 193 JI9
Waikabubak, Indonesia 169 NI3
Waikahalulu Bay, Hawaii, U.S. 107 JI6
Waikapu, Hawaii, U.S. 107 GI6
Waikapuna Bay, Hawaii, U.S. 107 Q2O
Waikato, river, N.Z. 193 KI9
Waikawa, N.Z. 193 RI6
Waikiki Beach, Hawaii, U.S. 106 EII
Waikoloa Village, Hawaii, U.S. 107 LI9
Waikouaiti, N.Z. 193 QI6
Wailagi Lala, island, Fiji 198 G9
Wailea, Hawaii, U.S. 107 HI6
Wailua, Hawaii, U.S. 106 B6
Wailua, Hawaii, U.S. 107 GI7
Wailuku, river, Hawaii, U.S. 107 M2I
Wailuku, Hawaii, U.S. 107 GI6
Waimanalo Beach, Hawaii, U.S. 106 EI2
Waimarama, N.Z. 193 L2O
Waimate, N.Z. 193 QI7
Waimea, Hawaii, U.S. 106 C5
Waimea, Hawaii, U.S. 106 DIO
Waimea (Kamuela), Hawaii, U.S. 107 KI9
Waimea Canyon, Hawaii, U.S. 106 B5

Wainaworasi, Solomon Is. 197 Q2O
Waingapu, Indonesia 169 NI3
Wainunu Bay, Fiji 198 H7
Wainwright, Alas., U.S. 105 BI3
Waiohinu, Hawaii, U.S. 107 PI9
Waiohonu Pictographs, Hawaii, U.S. 107 HI8
Waioli Mission, Hawaii, U.S. 106 B5
Waipa, river, N.Z. 193 KI9
Waipahi, N.Z. 193 RI6
Waipahu, Hawaii, U.S. 106 EII
Waipio Valley, Hawaii, U.S. 107 KI9
Waipu, N.Z. 193 HI8
Waipukurau, N.Z. 193 LI9
Wairokai Harbor, Solomon Is. 197 N2O
Waïsisi, Vanuatu 198 H4
Waïsisi Bay, Vanuatu 198 H4
Waitsburg, Wash., U.S. 102 E8
Wajima, Jap. 164 MIO
Wajir, Kenya 179 JI5
Wakasa Wan, Jap. 165 P9
Wakatipu, Lake, N.Z. 193 QI5
Wakaya, island, Fiji 198 H7
WaKeeney, Kans., U.S. 99 S5
Wakefield, Kans., U.S. 99 S8
Wakefield, Mich., U.S. 92 F5
Wakefield, Nebr., U.S. 99 N8
Wake Forest, N.C., U.S. 90 HI2
Wake Island, Pac. Oc. 196 F8
Wakema, Myanmar 166 K5
Wakhan Mountains, Afghan. 156 KIO
Wakhjir Pass, Afghan.-China 156 KI2
Wakkanai, Jap. 164 DI3
Wakuach, Lac, Que., Can. 77 K2O
Wakunai, P.N.G. 193 D22
Wakuya, Jap. 164 LI3
Wala, New Caledonia, Fr. 198 B6
Wałbrzych, Pol. 132 H8
Walcott, Lake, Idaho, U.S. 100 H6
Walden, Colo., U.S. 100 LI2
Waldo, Ark., U.S. 94 J7
Waldo Lake, Oreg., U.S. 102 H4
Waldorf, Md., U.S. 90 DI3
Waldport, Oreg., U.S. 102 G2
Waldron, Ark., U.S. 94 G6
Walea, Selat, Indonesia 169 JI4
Wales, U.K. 138 G8
Wales, Alas., U.S. 104 FIO
Wales Island, Nunavut, Can. 77 GI6
Walgreen Coast, Antarctica 206 K6
Walhalla, N. Dak., U.S. 98 D7
Walhalla, S.C., U.S. 90 J6
Walikale, Dem. Rep. of the Congo 178 KII
Walkaway, W. Austral., Austral. 191 W2
Walker, Minn., U.S. 98 GIO
Walker Lake, Nev., U.S. 103 Q7
Walkerville, Mont., U.S. 100 E7
Wall, S. Dak., U.S. 98 L3
Wallabadah, Qnsld., Austral. 191 RI2
Wallaby Plateau, Ind. Oc. 221 KI4
Wallace, Idaho, U.S. 100 C4
Wallace, N.C., U.S. 90 JI2
Wallace, Nebr., U.S. 99 Q4
Wallal Downs, W. Austral., Austral. 191 S3
Wallam Creek, Austral. 190 HI3
Wallara, N. Terr., Austral. 191 U8
Wallaroo, S. Austral., Austral. 191 XIO
Walla Walla, Wash., U.S. 102 E8
Wallis, Îles, Pac. Oc. 194 J9
Wallops Island, Va., U.S. 90 EI5
Wallowa, Oreg., U.S. 102 F9
Wallowa Mountains, Oreg., U.S. 102 F9
Walls, Scot., U.K. 138 B8
Walnut Canyon National Monument, Ariz., U.S. 101 S7
Walnut Cove, N.C., U.S. 90 GIO
Walnut Ridge, Ark., U.S. 94 EIO
Walong, India 158 FI6
Walsenburg, Colo., U.S. 101 PI3
Walsh, Colo., U.S. 101 PI6
Walterboro, S.C., U.S. 90 M9
Walter F. George Reservoir, Ala., U.S. 95 MI7
Walters, Okla., U.S. 96 J9
Walters Shoal, Ind. Oc. 220 M4
Walton, N.Y., U.S. 88 K9
Walvis Bay, Namibia 182 H6
Walvis Ridge, Atl. Oc. 217 SI3
Walyahmoning Rock, Austral. 190 J3
Wama, Afghan. 156 M9
Wamba, river, Dem. Rep. of the Congo 178 M8
Wamba, Dem. Rep. of the Congo 178 JII
Wamego, Kans., U.S. 99 S9
Wamena, Indonesia 169 L2O
Wami, river, Tanzania 179 MI5
Wamsasi, Indonesia 169 KI5
Wamsisi, Indonesia 169 KI6
Wamsutter, Wyo., U.S. 100 KIO
Wana, Pak. 157 P8
Wanaaring, N.S.W., Austral. 191 WI2
Wanaka, N.Z. 193 QI6
Wanaka, Lake, N.Z. 193 QI6

Wan'an, China 163 P5
Wanchese, N.C., U.S. 90 GI5
Wanderer Bay, Solomon Is. 197 NI8
Wanding, China 160 P9
Wando, S. Korea 162 HI3
Wandoan, Qnsld., Austral. 191 VI4
Wangal, Indonesia 193 DI5
Wanganui, river, N.Z. 193 LI9
Wanganui, N.Z. 193 LI9
Wangaratta, Vic., Austral. 191 YI3
Wangary, S. Austral., Austral. 191 Y9
Wangdu, China 162 E6
Wangiwangi, island, Indonesia 169 LI4
Wang Kai, Sudan 178 GI2
Wangpen Yang, China 162 LIO
Wangqing, China 162 AI4
Wanigela, P.N.G. 193 E2O
Wanione, Solomon Is. 197 P2I
Wankaner, India 158 J2
Wanlaweyn, Somalia 179 JI7
Wanning, China 163 U2
Wanow, Afghan. 157 P5
Wanxian, China 162 KI
Wanyuan, China 162 JI
Wanzai, China 163 N5
Wapakoneta, Ohio, U.S. 93 QII
Wapato, Wash., U.S. 102 D6
Wapello, Iowa, U.S. 99 PI4
Wappapello, Lake, Mo., U.S. 99 VI5
Wapsipinicon, river, Iowa, U.S. 99 NI3
War, W. Va., U.S. 90 F8
Waranga Basin, Austral. 190 LI2
Warangal, India 158 M7
Waraseoni, India 158 K7
Waratah, Tas., Austral. 191 ZI5
Warbreccan, Qnsld., Austral. 191 UI2
Warburton, W. Austral., Austral. 191 U6
Warden, Wash., U.S. 102 D7
Ward Hunt Island, Nunavut, Can. 77 AI6
Waren, Indonesia 169 KI9
Ware Shoals, S.C., U.S. 90 K7
Warialda, N.S.W., Austral. 191 WI4
Warmbad, Namibia 182 K7
Warm Springs, Ga., U.S. 90 M4
Warm Springs, Nev., U.S. 103 RIO
Warm Springs, Va., U.S. 90 EIO
Warm Springs Reservoir, Oreg., U.S. 102 H8
Warner Mountains, Calif.-Oreg., U.S. 102 L6
Warner Robins, Ga., U.S. 90 M6
Warner Valley, Oreg., U.S. 102 K6
Waroona, W. Austral., Austral. 191 X2
Warora, India 158 K6
Warrabri, N. Terr., Austral. 191 S9
Warracknabeal, Vic., Austral. 191 YII
Warrawagine, W. Austral., Austral. 191 S4
Warrego, river, Austral. 190 HI3
Warren, Ark., U.S. 94 J8
Warren, Mich., U.S. 92 MI3
Warren, Minn., U.S. 98 E8
Warren, Ohio, U.S. 93 PI5
Warren, Pa., U.S. 88 L4
Warrender, Cape, Nunavut, Can. 77 DI6
Warrensburg, Mo., U.S. 99 TII
Warrenton, Ga., U.S. 90 L7
Warrenton, Oreg., U.S. 102 E2
Warrenton, S. Af. 182 K9
Warrenton, Va., U.S. 90 DI2
Warri, Nig. 181 HI3
Warrina, S. Austral., Austral. 191 V9
Warrington, Fla., U.S. 91 QI
Warrnambool, Vic., Austral. 191 ZII
Warroad, Minn., U.S. 98 D9
Warsa, Indonesia 169 JI9
Warsaw, Ind., U.S. 93 P9
Warsaw, N.C., U.S. 90 JI2
Warsaw see Warszawa, Pol. 132 GIO
Warsaw, Va., U.S. 90 EI3
Warszawa (Warsaw), Pol. 132 GIO
Waru, Indonesia 169 KI7
Warwick, Qnsld., Austral. 191 VI5
Warwick, R.I., U.S. 89 LI4
Wasado, peak, Indonesia 193 CI5
Wasaka, Vanuatu 198 B2
Wasam, Pak. 156 KIO
Wasatch Range, Utah, U.S. 100 K7
Wasco, Calif., U.S. 103 V7
Wasco, Oreg., U.S. 102 F5
Waseca, Minn., U.S. 98 LII
Washap, Pak. 157 U3
Washburn, Me., U.S. 89 BI8
Washburn, N. Dak., U.S. 98 F4
Washburn, Wis., U.S. 92 F4
Washburn, Mount, Wyo., U.S. 100 F8
Washington, U.S. 102 C5
Washington, D.C., U.S. 90 CI3
Washington, Ga., U.S. 90 L7
Washington, Ill., U.S. 93 Q5
Washington, Ind., U.S. 93 T8
Washington, Iowa, U.S. 99 PI3
Washington, Kans., U.S. 99 R8

Washington, Mo., U.S. 99 TI4
Washington, N.C., U.S. 90 HI3
Washington, Pa., U.S. 88 P3
Washington, Utah, U.S. 101 Q5
Washington, Wis., U.S. 92 H8
Washington, Cape, Antarctica 207 PI4
Washington, Cape, Fiji 198 K6
Washington, Mount, N.H., U.S. 89 GI4
Washington Court House, Ohio, U.S. 93 RI2
Washington Island see Teraina, Kiribati 194 FI2
Washington Island, Wis., U.S. 92 H8
Washita, river, Okla., U.S. 96 HII
Washougal, Wash., U.S. 102 F4
Washtucna, Wash., U.S. 102 D8
Washuk, Pak. 157 T4
Wasilla, Alas., U.S. 105 JI6
Wasior, Indonesia 169 KI9
Waskaganish, Que., Can. 77 MI8
Waswanipi, Lac, Que., Can. 77 NI9
Watampone, Indonesia 169 LI3
Waterbury, Conn., U.S. 88 MI2
Water Cay, Bahamas III GI3
Water Cays, Bahamas IIO FII
Wateree Lake, S.C., U.S. 90 K9
Waterford, Ire. 138 G6
Waterloo, N. Terr., Austral. 191 Q7
Waterloo, Ill., U.S. 93 T4
Waterloo, Iowa, U.S. 99 NI2
Waterman, Isla, Chile 125 Y8
Watersmeet, Mich., U.S. 92 F6
Waterton-Glacier International Peace Park, Mont., U.S. 100 A6
Watertown, N.Y., U.S. 88 G8
Watertown, S. Dak., U.S. 98 K8
Watertown, Wis., U.S. 92 L6
Water Valley, Miss., U.S. 94 HI2
Waterville, Kans., U.S. 99 R8
Waterville, Me., U.S. 89 FI6
Waterville, Minn., U.S. 98 KII
Waterville, Wash., U.S. 102 C6
Watford City, N. Dak., U.S. 98 F2
Watkins Glen, N.Y., U.S. 88 K7
Watling see San Salvador, island, Bahamas III FI4
Watonga, Okla., U.S. 96 F9
Watrous, N. Mex., U.S. 101 RI3
Watsa, Dem. Rep. of the Congo 178 JI2
Watseka, Ill., U.S. 93 Q7
Watson, S. Austral., Austral. 191 W8
Watson Lake, Yukon Terr., Can. 76 H9
Watsonville, Calif., U.S. 103 T4
Watts Bar Lake, Tenn., U.S. 95 FI7
Watubela, Kepulauan, Indonesia 169 LI8
Wau, P.N.G. 193 DI9
Wau, Sudan 178 GII
Waubay, S. Dak., U.S. 98 J7
Wauchope, N. Terr., Austral. 191 S9
Wauchula, Fla., U.S. 91 U8
Waukarlycarly, Lake, Austral. 190 E4
Waukegan, Ill., U.S. 92 M7
Waukesha, Wis., U.S. 92 L6
Waukon, Iowa, U.S. 98 MI3
Wauneta, Nebr., U.S. 99 Q3
Waupaca, Wis., U.S. 92 J6
Waupun, Wis., U.S. 92 K6
Waurika, Okla., U.S. 96 JIO
Wausa, Nebr., U.S. 99 N7
Wausau, Wis., U.S. 92 H5
Wauseon, Ohio, U.S. 93 NII
Wautoma, Wis., U.S. 92 K5
Wauwatosa, Wis., U.S. 92 L7
Wave Hill, N. Terr., Austral. 191 R7
Waverly, Iowa, U.S. 98 MI2
Waverly, N.Y., U.S. 88 L8
Waverly, Nebr., U.S. 99 Q8
Waverly, Ohio, U.S. 93 SI3
Waverly, Tenn., U.S. 95 EI4
Waverly, Va., U.S. 90 FI3
Wawa, Ont., Can. 77 PI7
Wāw al Kabīr, Lib. 177 EI4
Waxahachie, Tex., U.S. 96 MI2
Waya, island, Fiji 198 H5
Wayamli, Indonesia 169 HI6
Waycross, Ga., U.S. 91 P7
Wayne, Nebr., U.S. 99 N8
Waynesboro, Ga., U.S. 90 M8
Waynesboro, Miss., U.S. 95 MI3
Waynesboro, Pa., U.S. 88 Q6
Waynesboro, Tenn., U.S. 95 FI4
Waynesboro, Va., U.S. 90 EII
Waynesburg, Pa., U.S. 88 P3
Waynesville, Mo., U.S. 99 UI3
Waynesville, N.C., U.S. 90 H6
Waynoka, Okla., U.S. 96 E9
Wazah, Afghan. 157 N8
Wazirabad, Pak. 157 PII
Wé, New Caledonia, Fr. 198 C9
We, island, Indonesia 168 F3
Weatherford, Okla., U.S. 96 G9
Weatherford, Tex., U.S. 96 LIO
Weaverville, Calif., U.S. 102 M3

Webb City, *Mo., U.S.* **99** VII
Webster, *Mass., U.S.* **89** L14
Webster, *S. Dak., U.S.* **98** J7
Webster City, *Iowa, U.S.* **99** NII
Webster Groves, *Mo., U.S.* **99** TI5
Webster Springs, *W. Va., U.S.* **90** D9
Weda, *Indonesia* **169** J16
Weda, Teluk, *Indonesia* **169** J16
Weddell Island, *Falk. Is., U.K.* **125** WII
Weddell Plain, *Southern Oc.* **224** EIO
Weed, *Calif., U.S.* **102** M3
Weeki Wachee, *Fla., U.S.* **91** T7
Weeping Water, *Nebr., U.S.* **99** Q9
Wei, river, *China* **160** J12
Wei, river, *China* **162** G2
Weichang, *China* **162** B7
Weifang, *China* **162** F8
Weihai, *China* **162** FIO
Weilmoringle, *N.S.W., Austral.* **191** WI3
Weimar, *Tex., U.S.* **97** RI2
Weinan, *China* **162** H2
Weipa, *Qnsld., Austral.* **191** PI2
Weir, river, *Austral.* **190** HI4
Weirton, *W. Va., U.S.* **90** B9
Weiser, river, *Idaho, U.S.* **100** F3
Weiser, *Idaho, U.S.* **100** F3
Weishan, *China* **162** H7
Weishan Hu, *China* **162** H7
Weissenfels, *Ger.* **132** G6
Weiss Lake, *Ala., U.S.* **95** HI7
Weixi, *China* **160** MIO
Welbourn Hill, *S. Austral., Austral.* **191** V9
Welch, *W. Va., U.S.* **90** F8
Weldiya, *Eth.* **179** FI5
Weldon, *N.C., U.S.* **90** GI3
Welford, *Qnsld., Austral.* **191** UI2
Weligama, *Sri Lanka* **159** T7
Welker Seamount, *Pac. Oc.* **219** CI4
Welkom, *S. Af.* **182** KIO
Wellesley Islands, *Austral.* **190** CII
Wellington, *Colo., U.S.* **100** LI3
Wellington, *Kans., U.S.* **99** V7
Wellington, *N.Z.* **193** MI8
Wellington, *Nev., U.S.* **103** Q7
Wellington, *Tex., U.S.* **96** H7
Wellington, Isla, *Chile* **125** V6
Wellington, Lake, *Austral.* **190** MI3
Wellington Bay, *Nunavut, Can.* **77** FI3
Wells, *Me., U.S.* **89** HI5
Wells, *Minn., U.S.* **98** LII
Wells, *Nev., U.S.* **102** MI2
Wells, *Tex., U.S.* **97** NI4
Wells, Lake, *Austral.* **190** G5
Wellsboro, *Pa., U.S.* **88** L7
Wellston, *Ohio, U.S.* **93** SI3
Wellsville, *Mo., U.S.* **99** SI3
Wellsville, *N.Y., U.S.* **88** K6
Wellsville, *Ohio, U.S.* **93** QI6
Wellton, *Ariz., U.S.* **101** U5
Wels, *Aust.* **132** K7
Welsh, *La., U.S.* **94** P7
Welshpool, *Vic., Austral.* **191** ZI2
Wenatchee, *Wash., U.S.* **102** C6
Wenchang, *China* **163** U2
Wencheng, *China* **163** N9
Wenchi, *Ghana* **180** GIO
Wendell, *Idaho, U.S.* **100** H5
Wendeng, *China* **162** FIO
Wendesi, *Indonesia* **169** KI9
Wendover, *Nev., U.S.* **102** MI3
Wendover, *Utah, U.S.* **100** K5
Wengyuan, *China* **163** R5
Wenling, *China* **163** NIO
Weno, *Chuuk, F.S.M.* **197** BI5
Weno (Moen), island, *Chuuk, F.S.M.* **197** BI5
Wenshan, *China* **160** PII
Wensu, *China* **160** F5
Wentworth, *N.S.W., Austral.* **191** XII
Wenzhou, *China* **163** N9
Werdër, *Eth.* **179** GI7
Weri, *Indonesia* **193** CI4
Werris Creek, *N.S.W., Austral.* **191** XI4
Weser, river, *Eur.* **130** F6
Weskan, *Kans., U.S.* **99** S3
Weslaco, *Tex., U.S.* **97** WIO
Wesleyville, *Pa., U.S.* **88** K3
Wessel Islands, *Austral.* **190** A9
Wessington, *S. Dak., U.S.* **98** K6
Wessington Springs, *S. Dak., U.S.* **98** L6
Wesson, *Miss., U.S.* **94** MII
West, *Tex., U.S.* **96** MII
West Allis, *Wis., U.S.* **92** L7
West Antarctica, *Antarctica* **206** J8
West Bank, *Asia* **150** M5
West Bay, *La., U.S.* **94** RI2
West Bay, *Fla., U.S.* **91** R3
West Bend, *Wis., U.S.* **92** L7
West Branch, *Iowa, U.S.* **99** PI3
West Branch, *Mich., U.S.* **92** JII
Westbrook, *Me., U.S.* **89** HI5
Westbrook, *Tex., U.S.* **96** M6
Westby, *Wis., U.S.* **92** K4
West Caicos, island, *Turks and Caicos Is., U.K.* **III** JI6
West Cape Howe, *Austral.* **190** L3
West Caroline Basin, *Pac. Oc.* **218** J5
West Chester, *Pa., U.S.* **88** P9
Westcliffe, *Colo., U.S.* **101** NI3
West Columbia, *Tex., U.S.* **97** RI3
West Des Moines, *Iowa, U.S.* **99** PII
West End, *Bahamas* **110** CIO
West End Point, *Cayman Is., U.K.* **110** L8
Westerly, *R.I., U.S.* **89** MI4
Western, river, *Nunavut, Can.* **77** GI3
Western Australia, *Austral.* **191** U3
Western Channel, *Jap.* **165** Q3
Western Desert, *Egypt* **177** DI7
Western Dvina, river, *Eur.* **130** E9
Western Ghats, mountains, *India* **158** L3
Western Plateau, *Austral.* **190** F4
Western Sahara, *Af.* **176** E5
Western Sayan Mountains, *Asia* **146** E9
Westerville, *Ohio, U.S.* **93** RI3
West Falkland, island, *Falk. Is., U.K.* **125** WII
Westfall, *Oreg., U.S.* **102** H9
West Fayu Atoll *see* Pigailoe, *F.S.M.* **196** Q5
Westfield, *Mass., U.S.* **88** LI2
Westfield, *N.Y., U.S.* **88** K4
West Fork Poplar, river, *Mont., U.S.* **100** BI2
West Fork Trinity, river, *Tex., U.S.* **96** K9
West Frankfort, *Ill., U.S.* **93** U6
West Glacier, *Mont., U.S.* **100** B6
West Grand Lake, *Me., U.S.* **89** EI8
West Helena, *Ark., U.S.* **94** HIO
Westhope, *N. Dak., U.S.* **98** D4
West Ice Shelf, *Antarctica* **207** H21
West Indies, islands, *N. Amer.* **74** N9
West Islet, *C.S.I. Terr., Austral.* **191** TI6
West Lafayette, *Ind., U.S.* **93** Q8
West Landing, *Majuro Atoll, Marshall Is.* **196** GIO
West Liberty, *Iowa, U.S.* **99** PI4
West Liberty, *Ky., U.S.* **95** BI9
West Mariana Basin, *Pac. Oc.* **218** H5
West Memphis, *Ark., U.S.* **94** GII
Westminster, *Md., U.S.* **90** BI3
Westminster, *S.C., U.S.* **90** K6
West Monroe, *La., U.S.* **94** L8
Westmoreland, *Qnsld., Austral.* **191** RIO
Westmorland, *Calif., U.S.* **103** YII
West Nicholson, *Zimb.* **182** GII
Weston, *Mo., U.S.* **99** SIO
Weston, *W. Va., U.S.* **90** C9
Weston Point, *Tabuaeran, Kiribati* **197** B20
West Palm Beach, *Fla., U.S.* **91** VIO
West Passage *see* Toagel Mlungui, *Palau* **196** MII
West Plains, *Mo., U.S.* **99** VI3
West Point, *Austral.* **190** L9
West Point, *Jaluit Atoll, Marshall Is.* **196** M7
West Point, *Ga., U.S.* **90** M4
West Point, *Ky., U.S.* **95** BI6
West Point, *Miss., U.S.* **95** JI3
West Point, *N.Y., U.S.* **88** MII
West Point, *Nebr., U.S.* **99** P8
West Point, *Va., U.S.* **90** EI3
Westport, *Calif., U.S.* **103** P2
Westport, *Ire.* **138** F5
Westport, *N.Z.* **193** NI7
Westport, *Wash., U.S.* **102** D2
Westray, island, *Scot., U.K.* **138** C8
West Siberian Plain, *Asia* **146** D8
West Spit, *Enewetak Atoll, Marshall Is.* **196** H7
West Union, *Iowa, U.S.* **98** MI3
West Valley City, *Utah, U.S.* **100** L7
West Virginia, *U.S.* **90** C9
Westwego, *La., U.S.* **94** QII
Westwood, *Calif., U.S.* **103** N5
Westwood Downs, *N.S.W., Austral.* **191** WII
West Wyalong, *N.S.W., Austral.* **191** XI3
West Yellowstone, *Mont., U.S.* **100** F8
West York Island, *Spratly Is.* **168** EII
Wetar, island, *Indonesia* **169** MI5
Wetaskiwin, *Alta., Can.* **76** LIO
Wetumka, *Okla., U.S.* **96** GI2
Wetumpka, *Ala., U.S.* **95** LI6
Wewahitchka, *Fla., U.S.* **91** R4
Wewak, *P.N.G.* **193** CI8
Wewoka, *Okla., U.S.* **96** GI2
Wexford, *Ire.* **138** G6
Weyburn, *Sask., Can.* **76** NI2
Weymouth, Cape, *Austral.* **190** BI2
Whakapunake, peak, *N.Z.* **193** K20
Whakatane, *N.Z.* **193** K20
Whale Cay, *Bahamas* **110** DII
Whaler Anchorage, *Tabuaeran, Kiribati* **197** B20
Whalsay, island, *Scot., U.K.* **138** B9
Whangamata, *N.Z.* **193** JI9
Whangarei, *N.Z.* **193** HI8
Wharton, *Tex., U.S.* **97** RI3
Wharton Basin, *Ind. Oc.* **221** KI3
Wheatland, *Wyo., U.S.* **100** JI3
Wheatland Reservoir, *Wyo., U.S.* **100** JI3
Wheaton, *Minn., U.S.* **98** J8
Wheeler, *Tex., U.S.* **96** G7
Wheeler Lake, *Ala., U.S.* **95** HI5
Wheeler Peak, *N. Mex., U.S.* **101** QI3
Wheeler Peak, *Nev., U.S.* **78** J9
Wheeling, *W. Va., U.S.* **90** B9
Wheelwright, *Ky., U.S.* **95** C20
Whidbey, Point, *Austral.* **190** K9
Whim Creek, *W. Austral., Austral.* **191** S2
Whiskeytown Shasta-Trinity National Recreation Area, *Calif., U.S.* **102** M3
White, river, *Ark., U.S.* **94** HIO
White, river, *Colo., U.S.* **100** LIO
White, river, *Ind., U.S.* **93** T7
White, river, *Nev., U.S.* **103** QI2
White, river, *S. Dak., U.S.* **98** M2
White, river, *Tex., U.S.* **96** K6
White, *S. Dak., U.S.* **98** K8
White, Lake, *Austral.* **190** E7
White Bird, *Idaho, U.S.* **100** E4
White Butte, *N. Dak., U.S.* **98** H2
White Cliffs, *N.S.W., Austral.* **191** WI2
White Cloud, *Mich., U.S.* **92** K9
White Deer, *Tex., U.S.* **96** G6
Whitefish, *Mont., U.S.* **100** B5
Whitefish Point, *Mich., U.S.* **92** FIO
Whitefish Point, *Mich., U.S.* **92** FIO
White Hall, *Ark., U.S.* **94** H9
White Hall, *Ill., U.S.* **93** S4
Whitehall, *Mich., U.S.* **92** L9
Whitehall, *Mont., U.S.* **100** E7
Whitehall, *N.Y., U.S.* **88** HI2
Whitehall, *Ohio, U.S.* **93** RI3
Whitehall, *Wis., U.S.* **92** J3
Whitehorse, *Yukon Terr., Can.* **76** G8
White Island, *Antarctica* **207** CI9
White Island, *Nunavut, Can.* **77** GI6
White Lake, *La., U.S.* **94** Q8
White Mountain, *Alas., U.S.* **104** FI2
White Mountains, *Calif., U.S.* **103** S8
White Mountains, *N.H., U.S.* **89** FI4
White Mountains National Recreation Area, *Alas., U.S.* **105** FI6
White Nile *see* Abyad, El Bahr el, river, *Sudan* **179** FI3
White Pine, *Mich., U.S.* **92** F5
White Plains, *N.Y., U.S.* **88** MII
White River, *S. Dak., U.S.* **98** L4
Whiteriver, *Ariz., U.S.* **101** T9
White River Junction, *Vt., U.S.* **89** HI3
White Salmon, *Wash., U.S.* **102** E5
White Sands National Monument, *N. Mex., U.S.* **101** VI2
Whitesboro, *Tex., U.S.* **96** KII
Whitesburg, *Ky., U.S.* **95** D20
White Sea, *Eur.* **130** BIO
White Sea-Baltic Canal, *Eur.* **130** BIO
White Sulphur Springs, *Mont., U.S.* **100** D8
White Sulphur Springs, *W. Va., U.S.* **90** E9
Whitetail, *Mont., U.S.* **100** AI2
Whiteville, *N.C., U.S.* **90** KII
Whiteville, *Tenn., U.S.* **94** FI2
White Volta, river, *Af.* **174** G3
Whitewater, *Mont., U.S.* **100** BII
Whitewater, *Wis., U.S.* **92** M6
Whitewater Baldy, peak, *N. Mex., U.S.* **101** UIO
Whitewood, *Qnsld., Austral.* **191** SI2
Whitewright, *Tex., U.S.* **96** KI2
Whitman, *Nebr., U.S.* **99** N3
Whitman Mission National Historic Site, *Wash., U.S.* **102** E7
Whitmire, *S.C., U.S.* **90** K8
Whitmore Mountains, *Antarctica* **206** JIO
Whitney, Lake, *Tex., U.S.* **96** MII
Whitney, Mount, *U.S.* **78** H4
Whittier, *Alas., U.S.* **105** JI7
Wholdaia Lake, *N.W.T., Can.* **77** JI3
Whyalla, *S. Austral., Austral.* **191** XIO
Wialki, *W. Austral., Austral.* **191** W3
Wibaux, *Mont., U.S.* **100** CI3
Wichita, river, *Tex., U.S.* **96** J9
Wichita, *Kans., U.S.* **99** U7
Wichita Falls, *Tex., U.S.* **96** J9
Wichita Mountains, *Okla., U.S.* **96** H9
Wick, *Scot., U.K.* **138** D8
Wickenburg, *Ariz., U.S.* **101** T6
Wickepin, *W. Austral., Austral.* **191** X3
Wickett, *Tex., U.S.* **97** N3
Wickiup Reservoir, *Oreg., U.S.* **102** H4
Wickliffe, *Ky., U.S.* **94** DI2
Wicklow, *Ire.* **138** G6
Wide Bay, *P.N.G.* **193** C21
Wien (Vienna), *Aust.* **132** K8
Wiener Neustadt, *Aust.* **132** K8
Wiesbaden, *Ger.* **132** H5
Wiggins, *Miss., U.S.* **94** NI2
Wight, Isle of, *Eng., U.K.* **138** J8
Wikieup, *Ariz., U.S.* **101** S5
Wilberforce, Cape, *Austral.* **190** A9
Wilbur, *Wash., U.S.* **102** C7
Wilburton, *Okla., U.S.* **96** HI3
Wilcannia, *N.S.W., Austral.* **191** WI2
Wilczek, Zemlya, *Russ.* **140** CI2
Wildcat Peak, *Nev., U.S.* **103** QIO
Wildrose, *N. Dak., U.S.* **98** E2
Wildwood, *Fla., U.S.* **91** S8
Wildwood, *N.J., U.S.* **88** RIO
Wiley, *Colo., U.S.* **101** NI5
Wilhelm, Mount, *P.N.G.* **193** CI9
Wilhelm II Coast, *Antarctica* **207** H21
Wilhelmina Gebergte, peak, *Suriname* **121** FI5
Wilhelmina Mountains, *S. Amer.* **118** B7
Wilhelmshaven, *Ger.* **132** F5
Wilkes-Barre, *Pa., U.S.* **88** M8
Wilkes Island, *Wake I., U.S.* **196** F8
Wilkes Land, *Antarctica* **207** QI8
Wilkins Coast, *Antarctica* **206** E5
Willacoochee, *Ga., U.S.* **91** P6
Willamette, river, *Oreg., U.S.* **102** G3
Willapa Bay, *Wash., U.S.* **102** D2
Willapa Hills, *Wash., U.S.* **102** D3
Willard, *N. Mex., U.S.* **101** SI2
Willard, *Ohio, U.S.* **93** PI3
Willard, *Utah, U.S.* **100** K7
Willcox, *Ariz., U.S.* **101** V9
Willemstad, *Neth.* **112** M9
Willeroo, *N. Terr., Austral.* **191** Q8
William, Mount, *Austral.* **190** LII
William Creek, *S. Austral., Austral.* **191** V9
William Dannelly Reservoir, *Ala., U.S.* **95** LI5
Williams, *Ariz., U.S.* **101** S7
Williams, *Calif., U.S.* **103** Q4
Williams, *Minn., U.S.* **98** EIO
Williams, *W. Austral., Austral.* **191** X3
Williamsburg, *Ky., U.S.* **95** DI8
Williamsburg, *Va., U.S.* **90** FI3
Williams Island, *Bahamas* **110** EIO
Williams Lake, *B.C., Can.* **76** L8
Williamson, *W. Va., U.S.* **90** E7
Williamson Glacier, *Antarctica* **207** M20
Williamsport, *Pa., U.S.* **88** M7
Williamston, *N.C., U.S.* **90** HI3
Williamston, *S.C., U.S.* **90** K7
Williamstown, *Ky., U.S.* **95** AI8
Williamstown, *W. Va., U.S.* **90** C8
Willis, *Tex., U.S.* **97** QI4
Willis Islets, *Austral.* **194** J5
Williston, *N. Dak., U.S.* **98** E2
Williston, *S.C., U.S.* **90** L8
Williston Lake, *B.C., Can.* **76** J9
Willits, *Calif., U.S.* **103** P2
Willmar, *Minn., U.S.* **98** JIO
Willow City, *N. Dak., U.S.* **98** E5
Willowlake, river, *N.W.T., Can.* **76** HIO
Willowra, *N. Terr., Austral.* **191** S8
Willows, *Calif., U.S.* **103** P4
Willow Springs, *Mo., U.S.* **99** VI3
Wills Point, *Tex., U.S.* **96** LI3
Wilmington, *Del., U.S.* **90** BI4
Wilmington, *Ill., U.S.* **93** P7
Wilmington, *N.C., U.S.* **90** KI2
Wilmington, *Ohio, U.S.* **93** SI2
Wilmington, *S. Austral., Austral.* **191** XIO
Wilmore, *Ky., U.S.* **95** CI7
Wilmot, *Ark., U.S.* **94** K9
Wilmot, *S. Dak., U.S.* **98** J8
Wilsall, *Mont., U.S.* **100** E8
Wilson, *Ark., U.S.* **94** FII
Wilson, *Kans., U.S.* **99** T6
Wilson, *N.C., U.S.* **90** HI2
Wilson, *Okla., U.S.* **96** JII
Wilson, *Tex., U.S.* **96** K5
Wilson, Mount, *Colo., U.S.* **101** PIO
Wilson, Mount, *Oreg., U.S.* **102** F4
Wilson Creek, *Wash., U.S.* **102** C7
Wilson Hills, *Antarctica* **207** RI5
Wilson Lake, *Ala., U.S.* **95** GI4
Wilson Lake, *Kans., U.S.* **99** S6
Wilson's Creek National Battlefield, *Mo., U.S.* **99** VI2
Wilsons Promontory, *Austral.* **190** MI3
Wilson Strait, *Solomon Is.* **197** MI5
Wilton, *N. Dak., U.S.* **98** G4
Wiluna, *W. Austral., Austral.* **191** V4
Winamac, *Ind., U.S.* **93** P8
Winchester, *Idaho, U.S.* **100** D3
Winchester, *Ind., U.S.* **93** RIO
Winchester, *Ky., U.S.* **95** BI8
Winchester, *Tenn., U.S.* **95** GI6
Winchester, *Va., U.S.* **90** CI2
Winchester Bay, *Oreg., U.S.* **102** H2
Wind, river, *Wyo., U.S.* **100** H9
Wind, river, *Yukon Terr., Can.* **76** E9
Windber, *Pa., U.S.* **88** P5
Wind Cave National Park, *S. Dak., U.S.* **98** LI
Winder, *Ga., U.S.* **90** K6
Windhoek, *Namibia* **182** H7
Windom, *Minn., U.S.* **98** LIO
Windorah, *Qnsld., Austral.* **191** UI2
Window Rock, *Ariz., U.S.* **101** R9
Wind River Range, *Wyo., U.S.* **100** H9
Windsor, *Colo., U.S.* **100** LI3
Windsor, *Conn., U.S.* **89** LI3
Windsor, *Mo., U.S.* **99** TI2

Windsor, *N.C., U.S.* **90** G13
Windsor, *Ont., Can.* **77** R17
Windsor, *Vt., U.S.* **89** H13
Windsor Forest, *Ga., U.S.* **91** N9
Windward Islands, *N. Amer.* **74** P12
Windward Passage, *Cuba-Haiti* **111** L14
Winfield, *Ala., U.S.* **95** J14
Winfield, *Kans., U.S.* **99** V8
Wini, *Indonesia* **169** N15
Winifred, *Mont., U.S.* **100** C9
Wininen, island, *Chuuk, F.S.M.* **197** C16
Winion, Mochun, *Chuuk, F.S.M.* **197** C16
Winipirea, island, *Chuuk, F.S.M.* **197** B15
Winipiru, island, *Chuuk, F.S.M.* **197** C14
Winisk, river, *Ont., Can.* **77** L16
Wink, *Tex., U.S.* **97** N3
Winkelman, *Ariz., U.S.* **101** U8
Winlock, *Wash., U.S.* **102** D3
Winneba, *Ghana* **180** H10
Winnebago, *Minn., U.S.* **98** L11
Winnebago, Lake, *Wis., U.S.* **92** K6
Winnemucca, *Nev., U.S.* **102** M9
Winnemucca Lake, *Nev., U.S.* **103** N7
Winner, *S. Dak., U.S.* **98** M5
Winnett, *Mont., U.S.* **100** D10
Winnfield, *La., U.S.* **94** M8
Winnibigoshish, Lake, *Minn., U.S.* **98** F10
Winnipeg, *Man., Can.* **77** N14
Winnipeg, Lake, *Man., Can.* **77** M14
Winnipegosis, *Man., Can.* **77** M13
Winnipegosis, Lake, *N. Amer.* **74** G5
Winnipesaukee, Lake, *N.H., U.S.* **89** H14
Winnsboro, *La., U.S.* **94** L9
Winnsboro, *S.C., U.S.* **90** K9
Winnsboro, *Tex., U.S.* **96** L14
Winona, *Kans., U.S.* **99** S3
Winona, *Minn., U.S.* **98** L13
Winona, *Miss., U.S.* **94** J11
Winooski, *Vt., U.S.* **88** F12
Winslow, *Ariz., U.S.* **101** S8
Winslow, *Me., U.S.* **89** F16
Winston-Salem, *N.C., U.S.* **90** H10
Winter Garden, *Fla., U.S.* **91** T8
Winter Haven, *Fla., U.S.* **91** U8
Winter Park, *Fla., U.S.* **91** T9
Winters, *Calif., U.S.* **103** R4
Winters, *Tex., U.S.* **96** M7
Winterset, *Iowa, U.S.* **99** P11
Winthrop, *Me., U.S.* **89** F16
Winthrop, *Minn., U.S.* **98** K10
Winthrop, *Wash., U.S.* **102** B6
Wirrulla, *S. Austral., Austral.* **191** X9
Wisas, island, *Chuuk, F.S.M.* **197** D16
Wiscasset, *Me., U.S.* **89** G16
Wisconsin, river, *Wis., U.S.* **92** J5
Wisconsin, *U.S.* **92** J3
Wisconsin Dells, *Wis., U.S.* **92** K5
Wisconsin Rapids, *Wis., U.S.* **92** J5
Wiseman, *Alas., U.S.* **105** E16
Wishek, *N. Dak., U.S.* **98** H5
Wishram, *Wash., U.S.* **102** F5
Wisła, river, *Pol.* **132** G9
Wismar, *Ger.* **132** F6
Wisner, *La., U.S.* **94** M9
Wisner, *Nebr., U.S.* **99** N8
Witchcliffe, *W. Austral., Austral.* **191** Y2
Witten, *S. Dak., U.S.* **98** M5
Wittenberge, *Ger.* **132** F7
Wittenoom, *W. Austral., Austral.* **191** T3
Witu Islands, *P.N.G.* **193** C20
Włocławek, *Pol.* **132** G9
Wodonga, *Vic., Austral.* **191** Y13
Wohlthat Mountains, *Antarctica* **207** B14
Wojejairok, island, *Kwajalein Atoll, Marshall Is.* **196** L4
Wojejairok Pass, *Kwajalein Atoll, Marshall Is.* **196** L4
Wokam, island, *Indonesia* **169** L19
Wolauna, *Pohnpei, F.S.M.* **197** G13
Woleai Atoll, *F.S.M.* **196** Q4
Wolf, river, *Wis., U.S.* **92** H6
Wolf Creek, *Mont., U.S.* **100** C9
Wolf Creek, *Tex., U.S.* **96** F7
Wolf Creek, *Mont., U.S.* **100** D7
Wolf Creek, *Oreg., U.S.* **102** K2
Wolf Creek Pass, *Colo., U.S.* **101** P12
Wolfeboro, *N.H., U.S.* **89** H14
Wolfe City, *Tex., U.S.* **96** K12
Wolfforth, *Tex., U.S.* **96** K5
Wolf Point, *Mont., U.S.* **100** B12
Wollaston, Islas, *Chile* **125** Y9
Wollaston Lake, *Sask., Can.* **77** K13
Wollaston Peninsula, *N.W.T.-Nunavut, Can.* **76** E12
Wollogorang, *N. Terr., Austral.* **191** R10
Wollongong, *N.S.W., Austral.* **191** Y14
Wolo, *Indonesia* **169** K13
Wondai, *Qnsld., Austral.* **191** V15
Wongan Hills, *W. Austral., Austral.* **191** W2
Wongawal, *W. Austral., Austral.* **191** U4
Wŏnju, *S. Korea* **162** F14
Wŏnsan, *N. Korea* **162** D13
Wonthaggi, *Vic., Austral.* **191** Z12
Wonti, *Indonesia* **193** B16
Woodall Mountain, *Miss., U.S.* **95** G13
Woodbine, *Ga., U.S.* **91** Q8
Woodbridge, *Va., U.S.* **90** D13
Woodburn, *N.S.W., Austral.* **191** W15
Woodburn, *Oreg., U.S.* **102** F3
Woodbury, *N.J., U.S.* **88** Q9
Wood Lake, *Nebr., U.S.* **99** N5
Woodlake, *Calif., U.S.* **103** U7
Woodland, *Calif., U.S.* **103** Q4
Woodland, *Me., U.S.* **89** E19
Woodland, *Wash., U.S.* **102** E3
Woodland Park, *Colo., U.S.* **100** M13
Woodlark, island, *P.N.G.* **193** E22
Wood River, *Nebr., U.S.* **99** Q6
Wood River Lakes, *Alas., U.S.* **105** K13
Woodruff, *S.C., U.S.* **90** J8
Woodruff, *Utah, U.S.* **100** K8
Woods, Lake, *Austral.* **190** D8
Woods, Lake of the, *U.S.-Can.* **79** B13
Woodsboro, *Tex., U.S.* **97** T11
Woods Cross, *Utah, U.S.* **100** K7
Woodsfield, *Ohio, U.S.* **93** R15
Woods Hole, *Mass., U.S.* **89** L15
Woodstock, *Qnsld., Austral.* **191** S12
Woodstock, *Va., U.S.* **90** D11
Woodstown, *N.J., U.S.* **88** Q9
Woodsville, *N.H., U.S.* **89** G13
Woodville, *Miss., U.S.* **94** N9
Woodville, *N.Z.* **193** M19
Woodville, *Tex., U.S.* **97** P15
Woodward, *Okla., U.S.* **96** E8
Woody Head, *Austral.* **190** J15
Woomera, *S. Austral., Austral.* **191** W10
Woonsocket, *R.I., U.S.* **89** L14
Woonsocket, *S. Dak., U.S.* **98** L7
Woorabinda, *Qnsld., Austral.* **191** U14
Wooramel, *W. Austral., Austral.* **191** U1
Wooster, *Ohio, U.S.* **93** P14
Worbab, island, *Kwajalein Atoll, Marshall Is.* **196** N5
Worcester, *Mass., U.S.* **89** K14
Worcester, *S. Af.* **182** M8
Worcester, *Eng., U.K.* **138** H8
Worden, *Mont., U.S.* **100** E10
Workai, island, *Indonesia* **169** M19
Worland, *Wyo., U.S.* **100** G10
Worth, Lake, *Tex., U.S.* **96** L11
Wortham, *Tex., U.S.* **96** M12
Worthington, *Minn., U.S.* **98** L9
Wosi, *Indonesia* **169** J16
Wotho Atoll, *Marshall Is.* **196** F3
Wotje Atoll, *Marshall Is.* **196** G5
Wowoni, island, *Indonesia* **169** L14
Wrangel Island *see* Vrangelya, Ostrov, *Russ.* **141** B19
Wrangell, *Alas., U.S.* **105** L23
Wrangell Mountains, *U.S.* **78** P5
Wrangell-Saint Elias National Park and Preserve, *Alas., U.S.* **105** H18
Wrangel Plain, *Arctic Oc.* **222** G8
Wray, *Colo., U.S.* **100** L16
Wreck Point, *Af.* **174** Q6
Wrecks, Bay of, *Kiritimati, Kiribati* **197** B23
Wrens, *Ga., U.S.* **90** M7
Wright, *Wyo., U.S.* **100** G12
Wright Brothers National Memorial, *N.C., U.S.* **90** G15
Wright Patman Lake, *Tex., U.S.* **96** K15
Wrightsville, *Ga., U.S.* **90** M7
Wrightsville Beach, *N.C., U.S.* **90** K13
Wrigley Gulf, *Antarctica* **206** N7
Wrocław, *Pol.* **132** H9
Wu, river, *China* **163** N1
Wu'an, *China* **162** F5
Wubin, *W. Austral., Austral.* **191** W2
Wubu, *China* **162** E3
Wuchang, *China* **161** D17
Wuchuan, *China* **162** C4
Wuchuan, *China* **162** M1
Wuchuan, *China* **163** S2
Wuda, *China* **162** D1
Wudan *see* Ongniud Qi, *China* **162** A8
Wudaoliang, *China* **160** J9
Wudi, *China* **162** E7
Wudinna, *S. Austral., Austral.* **191** X9
Wufeng, *China* **162** L3
Wugang, *China* **163** N2
Wuhai, *China* **160** G12
Wuhai, *China* **162** C1
Wuhan, *China* **162** L5
Wuhe, *China* **162** J7
Wuhu, *China* **162** K8
Wukari, *Nig.* **181** G15
Wular Lake, *India* **156** M12
Wulian, *China* **162** G8
Wuliaru, peak, *Indonesia* **193** D14
Wum, *Cameroon* **181** H15
Wundowie, *W. Austral., Austral.* **191** X2
Wuning, *China* **162** M6
Wunlah, *Indonesia* **169** M17
Wuntho, *Myanmar* **166** F6
Wupatki National Monument, *Ariz., U.S.* **101** R7
Wuping, *China* **163** Q6
Wuqi, *China* **162** F2
Wuqia, *China* **160** F4
Wuqing, *China* **162** D7
Wurarga, *W. Austral., Austral.* **191** V2
Wurung, *Qnsld., Austral.* **191** R11
Würzburg, *Ger.* **132** H6
Wushan, *China* **162** K2
Wusi, *Vanuatu* **198** C1
Wust Seamount, *Atl. Oc.* **217** T12
Wusuli, river, *China* **161** C19
Wutai, *China* **162** E5
Wutongqiao, *China* **160** L11
Wuvi Shan, *Asia* **146** H12
Wuvulu Island, *P.N.G.* **193** B18
Wuwei, *China* **160** H11
Wuwei, *China* **162** K7
Wuxi, *China* **162** K2
Wuxi, *China* **162** K9
Wuxue, *China* **162** L5
Wuyiling, *China* **161** C17
Wuyi Shan, *China* **163** P6
Wuyuan, *China* **162** B2
Wuyuan, *China* **162** M7
Wuzhai, *China* **162** D4
Wuzhen, *China* **162** K4
Wuzhong, *China* **160** H12
Wuzhou, *China* **163** R3
Wyandot Seamount, *Atl. Oc.* **217** T14
Wyandra, *Qnsld., Austral.* **191** V13
Wylie Lake, *S.C., U.S.* **90** J9
Wyloo, *W. Austral., Austral.* **191** T2
Wymore, *Nebr., U.S.* **99** R8
Wynbring, *S. Austral., Austral.* **191** W8
Wyndham, *W. Austral., Austral.* **191** Q6
Wyndmere, *N. Dak., U.S.* **98** H8
Wynne, *Ark., U.S.* **94** G10
Wynnewood, *Okla., U.S.* **96** H11
Wynniatt Bay, *N.W.T., Can.* **77** D13
Wyoming, *U.S.* **100** H11
Wyoming, *Mich., U.S.* **92** L9
Wyoming Range, *Wyo., U.S.* **100** H8
Wytheville, *Va., U.S.* **90** F8
Wyville Thomson Ridge, *Atl. Oc.* **216** D12

X

Xaafuun, *Somalia* **179** F19
Xaçmaz, *Azerb.* **149** C22
Xaignabouri, *Laos* **166** J9
Xainza, *China* **160** K7
Xai-Xai, *Mozambique* **182** J12
Xalapa, *Mex.* **109** J13
Xalin, *Somalia* **179** G18
Xangdin Hural, *China* **162** A3
Xangongo, *Angola* **182** F6
Xankändi (Stepanakert), *Azerb.* **149** E20
Xánthi, *Gr.* **137** J16
Xanthus, ruins, *Turk.* **148** J4
Xapecó, *Braz.* **122** N11
Xapuri, *Braz.* **122** G6
Xarardheere, *Somalia* **179** H18
Xar Moron, river, *China* **162** A4
Xar Moron, river, *China* **162** A9
Xau, Lake, *Botswana* **182** H9
Xayar, *China* **160** F6
Xèng, river, *Laos* **166** H10
Xenia, *Ohio, U.S.* **93** R12
Xépôn, *Laos* **166** K12
Xi, river, *China* **163** R4
Xiachuan Dao, *China* **163** S3
Xiaguan, *China* **160** N10
Xiajiang, *China* **163** N5
Xiamen (Amoy), *China* **163** Q8
Xi'an, *China* **162** H2
Xianfeng, *China* **162** L2
Xiang, river, *China* **163** P3
Xiangfan, *China* **162** K4
Xianghuang Qi (Hobot Xar), *China* **162** B5
Xiangkhoang, *Laos* **166** J10
Xiangning, *China* **162** G3
Xiangshan (Dancheng), *China* **162** M10
Xiangtan, *China* **163** N4
Xiangyin, *China* **162** M4
Xianju, *China* **162** M9
Xiantao, *China* **162** L4
Xianyou, *China* **163** Q8
Xiaogan, *China* **162** K5
Xiao Hinggan Ling, *China* **161** B16
Xiaojiang, *China* **163** N9
Xiaoshan, *China* **162** L9
Xiaoyi, *China* **162** F4
Xiapu, *China* **163** P9
Xichang, *China* **160** M11
Xifeng, *China* **162** B11
Xifeng, *China* **162** F1
Xigazê, *China* **160** L7
Xiliao, river, *China* **162** A10
Xilinhot, *China* **162** A7
Ximiao, *China* **160** G10
Xin Barag Youqi, *China* **161** C14
Xin Barag Zuoqi, *China* **161** C15
Xinbin, *China* **162** B12
Xincai, *China* **162** J5
Xinfeng, *China* **163** Q5
Xinfeng, *China* **163** R5
Xinfengjiang Shuiki, *China* **163** R5
Xing'an, *China* **163** P2
Xingcheng, *China* **162** C9
Xinghai, *China* **160** J10
Xinghe, *China* **162** C5
Xinghua, *China* **162** J9
Xinghua Wan, *China* **163** Q8
Xingning, *China* **163** R6
Xingshan, *China* **162** K3
Xingtai, *China* **162** F5
Xingu, river, *S. Amer.* **118** E7
Xinguara, *Braz.* **123** F13
Xingxian, *China* **162** E3
Xingxingxia, *China* **160** F9
Xingyi, *China* **160** N12
Xingzi, *China* **162** M6
Xinhe, *China* **162** F6
Xinhua, *China* **163** N3
Xinhuang, *China* **163** N1
Xinhui, *China* **163** S4
Xining, *China* **160** H11
Xinji, *China* **162** E6
Xinjiang, *China* **162** G3
Xinjin, *China* **162** D10
Xinmin, *China* **162** B10
Xinning, *China* **163** P2
Xinpu *see* Lianyungang, *China* **162** H8
Xinshao, *China* **163** N3
Xinwen, *China* **162** G7
Xinxiang, *China* **162** G5
Xinxing, *China* **163** S3
Xinyang, *China* **162** K5
Xinye, *China* **162** J4
Xinyi, *China* **162** H8
Xinyi, *China* **163** S2
Xinyuan, *China* **160** E6
Xinzhou, *China* **162** E4
Xique Xique, *Braz.* **123** G15
Xishui, *China* **162** L6
Xiushan, *China* **162** M1
Xiushui, *China* **162** M5
Xiuyan, *China* **162** C11
Xiuying, *China* **163** T2
Xiva, *Uzb.* **154** K9
Xixian, *China* **162** J5
Xixiang, *China* **162** J1
Xo'jayli, *Uzb.* **154** J9
Xorkol, *China* **160** G8
Xuan'en, *China* **162** L2
Xuanhan, *China* **162** K1
Xuanhua, *China* **162** C6
Xuan Loc, *Vietnam* **167** P13
Xuanwei, *China* **160** N11
Xuanzhou, *China* **162** L8
Xuchang, *China* **162** H5
Xudat, *Azerb.* **149** C22
Xuddur, *Somalia* **179** H16
Xudun, *Somalia* **179** G17
Xuí, *Braz.* **122** R11
Xulun Hoh *see* Zhenglan Qi, *China* **162** B6
Xun, river, *China* **163** R2
Xunke, *China* **161** B17
Xunwu, *China* **163** Q6
Xunyi, *China* **162** G1
Xupu, *China* **163** N2
Xuwen, *China* **163** T2
Xuyong, *China* **160** M12
Xuzhou, *China* **162** H7

Y

Yaak, *Mont., U.S.* **100** A4
Ya'an, *China* **160** L11
Yabbenohr, island, *Kwajalein Atoll, Marshall Is.* **196** L3
Yablonovyy Khrebet, *Russ.* **141** L16
Yacata, island, *Fiji* **198** H8
Yachats, *Oreg., U.S.* **102** G2
Yacimiento Río Turbio, *Arg.* **125** W7
Yacuiba, *Bol.* **122** L8
Yadgir, *India* **158** M5
Yadkin, river, *N.C., U.S.* **90** G9
Yadong, *China* **160** M7
Yadua, island, *Fiji* **198** G6
Yafi, *Indonesia* **169** K21
Yagasa, island, *Fiji* **198** K9
Yağca, *Turk.* **148** H6
Yaguajay, *Cuba* **110** H9
Yahyalı, *Turk.* **148** G10
Yaita, *Jap.* **165** N12
Yakacık, *Turk.* **148** J11

Yakapınar, *Turk.* 148 J10
Yakeshi, *China* 161 C15
Yakima, *river, Wash.- U.S.* 102 D6
Yakima, *Wash., U.S.* 102 D6
Yakishiri Jima, *Jap.* 164 EI3
Yakmach, *Pak.* 157 S3
Yakoma, *Dem. Rep. of the Congo* 178 H10
Yakossi, *Cen. Af. Rep.* 178 H10
Yaksha, *Russ.* 140 G9
Yaku Shima, *Jap.* 165 U4
Yakutat, *Alas., U.S.* 105 J20
Yakutat Bay, *Alas., U.S.* 105 J20
Yakutsk, *Russ.* 141 G18
Yala, *Sri Lanka* 159 T8
Yala, *Thai.* 167 S9
Yale, *Mich., U.S.* 92 L13
Yale, *Okla., U.S.* 96 F12
Yalewa Kalou (Round Island), *island, Fiji* 198 G6
Yalgoo, *W. Austral., Austral.* 191 V2
Yalleroi, *Qnsld., Austral.* 191 U13
Yallock, *N.S.W., Austral.* 191 X12
Yalobusha, *river, Miss., U.S.* 94 J11
Yalong, *river, China* 160 M11
Yalova, *Turk.* 148 D5
Yalta, *Ukr.* 133 M16
Yalu, *river, China–N. Korea* 162 C11
Yalvaç, *Turk.* 148 G6
Yamada, *Jap.* 164 K14
Yamagata, *Jap.* 164 L12
Yamaguchi, *Jap.* 165 Q5
Yamal, Poluostrov, *Russ.* 140 F11
Yamas, *Indonesia* 169 K21
Yamato Glacier, *Antarctica* 207 C16
Yamato Mountains *see* Queen Fabiola Mountains, *Antarctica* 207 C16
Yamba, *N.S.W., Austral.* 191 W15
Yambio, *Sudan* 178 H11
Yambol, *Bulg.* 137 H16
Yamdena, *island, Indonesia* 169 M17
Yamethinn, *Myanmar* 166 H6
Yammaw, *Myanmar* 166 E7
Yamma Yamma, Lake, *Austral.* 190 G11
Yamoussoukro, *Côte d'Ivoire* 180 G8
Yampa, *river, Colo., U.S.* 100 L10
Yamzho Yumco, *China* 160 L7
Yana, *river, Russ.* 141 F17
Yanagawa, *Jap.* 165 R4
Yanai, *Jap.* 165 R6
Yan'an, *China* 162 F2
Yanbu' al Baḥr, *Saudi Arabia* 152 J6
Yancannia, *N.S.W., Austral.* 191 W12
Yanchang, *China* 162 F3
Yancheng, *China* 162 J9
Yanchi, *China* 162 E1
Yanchuan, *China* 162 F3
Yandé, Île, *New Caledonia, Fr.* 198 B6
Yandina, *Solomon Is.* 197 N18
Yandoon, *Myanmar* 166 K6
Yangbajain, *China* 160 L7
Yangchun, *China* 163 S3
Yangi Qal'eh, *Afghan.* 156 J8
Yangi Qal'eh, *Afghan.* 156 L4
Yangjiang, *China* 161 Q14
Yangjiang, *China* 163 S3
Yangon (Rangoon), *Myanmar* 166 K6
Yangquan, *China* 162 E5
Yangshan, *China* 163 Q4
Yangshuo, *China* 163 Q2
Yangtze, *river, Asia* 146 G12
Yangtze *see* Tongtian, *river, China* 160 J9
Yangtze *see* Jinsha, *river, China* 160 N11
Yangtze *see* Chang Jiang, *river, China* 162 L6
Yangtze, Mouth of the, *China* 162 K10
Yangtze, Source of the, *Asia* 146 H9
Yangtze Gorges, *China* 162 K2
Yangxian, *China* 162 H1
Yangxin, *China* 162 L5
Yangyang, *S. Korea* 162 EI4
Yangyuan, *China* 162 C5
Yangzhou, *China* 162 J8
Yanhe, *China* 162 M1
Yanji, *China* 161 EI8
Yanji, *China* 162 AI4
Yankeetown, *Fla., U.S.* 91 S7
Yankton, *S. Dak., U.S.* 98 M7
Yano-Indigirskaya Nizmennost', *Russ.* 141 EI7
Yano-Oymyakonskoye Nagor'ye, *Russ.* 141 F17
Yanqi, *China* 160 F7
Yanshan, *China* 162 E7
Yanshan, *China* 163 N7
Yanskiy, *Russ.* 141 F17
Yanskiy Zaliv, *Russ.* 141 E17
Yantabulla, *N.S.W., Austral.* 191 W12
Yantai, *China* 162 F10
Yanuca, *island, Fiji* 198 G8
Yao, *Jap.* 165 Q9
Yaoundé, *Cameroon* 181 J16
Yaoxian, *China* 162 G2
Yap, *island, Yap Is., F.S.M.* 197 D18
Yapen, *island, Indonesia* 169 K19

Yapen, Selat, *Indonesia* 169 K19
Yapero, *Indonesia* 169 L20
Yap Islands, *F.S.M.* 196 P2
Yap Trench, *Pac. Oc.* 218 J5
Yaqaqa, *island, Fiji* 198 G7
Yaqeta, *island, Fiji* 198 H5
Yaqui, *river, Mex.* 108 D7
Yaquina Head, *Oreg., U.S.* 102 G2
Yara, *Cuba* 110 K12
Yaraka, *Qnsld., Austral.* 191 U12
Yaralıgöz, *peak, Turk.* 148 C9
Yardımcı Burnu, *Turk.* 148 J6
Yardymly, *Azerb.* 149 F22
Yaren, *Nauru* 197 F22
Yarí, *river, Col.* 120 H6
Yarım, *Yemen* 152 Q9
Yaring, *Thai.* 167 S9
Yarkant, *river, China* 160 F5
Yarle Lakes, *Austral.* 190 J8
Yarlung (Brahmaputra) (Tsangpo), *river, China* 160 L8
Yarma, *Turk.* 148 G8
Yarmouth, *N.S., Can.* 77 Q21
Yarnell, *Ariz., U.S.* 101 T6
Yaroslavl', *Russ.* 140 F6
Yaroua, *island, Fiji* 198 J9
Yarraden, *Qnsld., Austral.* 191 Q12
Yarraloola, *W. Austral., Austral.* 191 T2
Yartsevo, *Russ.* 141 J13
Yarumal, *Col.* 120 D4
Yasawa, *island, Fiji* 198 G6
Yasawa Group, *Fiji* 198 H5
Yasin, *Pak.* 156 K11
Yasinza'i Kalay, *Afghan.* 157 Q4
Yasothon, *Thai.* 166 L11
Yasun Burnu, *Turk.* 148 D12
Yasur Volcano, *Vanuatu* 198 H4
Yata, *river, Bol.* 122 G7
Yatağan, *Turk.* 148 H4
Yatakala, *Niger* 176 H9
Yaté, *New Caledonia, Fr.* 198 E9
Yates Center, *Kans., U.S.* 99 U9
Yathkyed Lake, *Nunavut, Can.* 77 J14
Yato, *Pukapuka Atoll, Cook Is., N.Z.* 198 Q2
Yatsushiro, *Jap.* 165 S4
Yauca, *Peru* 122 J4
Yauco, *P.R., U.S.* 111 N22
Yaupi, *Ecua.* 120 J4
Yavatmal, *India* 158 K6
Yavoriv, *Ukr.* 132 J11
Yawatahama, *Jap.* 165 R6
Yawri Bay, *Sierra Leone* 180 G5
Yaylâdağı, *Turk.* 148 K11
Yaynangyoung, *Myanmar* 166 H5
Yazd, *Iran* 153 EI4
Yazdān, *Afghan.* 157 N1
Yazdān, *Iran* 153 DI7
Yazılıkaya, *Turk.* 148 F6
Yazlıca Dağı, *Turk.* 149 H17
Yazman, *Pak.* 157 S10
Yazoo, *river, Miss., U.S.* 94 K10
Yazoo City, *Miss., U.S.* 94 K11
Ye, *Myanmar* 166 L7
Yebyu, *Myanmar* 166 M7
Yecheng (Kargilik), *China* 160 G4
Yeeda, *W. Austral., Austral.* 191 R5
Yegua Creek, *Tex., U.S.* 97 Q12
Yei, *Sudan* 178 H12
Yekaterinburg, *Russ.* 140 H9
Yekateriny, Proliv, *Russ.* 141 K23
Yelets, *Russ.* 140 G5
Yélimané, *Mali* 176 H6
Yelizavety, Mys, *Russ.* 141 H21
Yell, *island, Scot., U.K.* 138 B9
Yellandu, *India* 158 M7
Yellow, *river, Asia* 146 G12
Yellow *see* Huang, *river, China* 160 K11
Yellow, *river, Fla., U.S.* 91 Q2
Yellow, Mouth of the, *China* 162 E8
Yellow, Source of the, *Asia* 146 G9
Yellowknife, *N.W.T., Can.* 76 H11
Yellow Sea, *Asia* 146 G12
Yellowstone, *river, Mont., U.S.* 100 D11
Yellowstone Lake, *Wyo., U.S.* 100 F8
Yellowstone National Park, *Wyo., U.S.* 100 F8
Yellville, *Ark., U.S.* 94 E8
Yelm, *Wash., U.S.* 102 D3
Yel'sk, *Belarus* 133 G14
Yelverton Bay, *Nunavut, Can.* 77 A15
Yelwa, *Nig.* 181 F13
Yemanzhelinsk, *Russ.* 140 J8
Yemassee, *S.C., U.S.* 90 M9
Yemen, *Asia* 152 P9
Yen Bai, *Vietnam* 166 G11
Yendi, *Ghana* 180 F11
Yeniçağa, *Turk.* 148 D7
Yenice, *river, Turk.* 148 G11
Yenice, *Turk.* 148 F8
Yeniceoba, *Turk.* 148 F8
Yeniköy, *Turk.* 148 H6

Yenişehir, *Turk.* 148 D5
Yenisey, *river, Russ.* 141 F13
Yenisey-Angara, Source of the, *Asia* 146 F9
Yenisey Gulf, *Asia* 146 C8
Yeniseysk, *Russ.* 141 K13
Yeniseyskiy Zaliv, *Russ.* 141 F13
Yen Minh, *Vietnam* 166 F11
Yenyuka, *Russ.* 141 J17
Yeola, *India* 158 K4
Yeppoon, *Qnsld., Austral.* 191 T15
Yerbogachen, *Russ.* 141 J15
Yerema, *Russ.* 141 J15
Yerevan, *Arm.* 149 E18
Yergeni Hills, *Eur.* 130 G13
Yerilla, *W. Austral., Austral.* 191 W4
Yerington, *Nev., U.S.* 103 Q7
Yerköy, *Turk.* 148 E9
Yermak Plateau, *Arctic Oc.* 223 H14
Yermo, *Calif., U.S.* 103 W10
Yeroḥam, *Israel* 151 P5
Yeşilhisar, *Turk.* 148 G10
Yeşilırmak, *river, Turk.* 148 D11
Yeşilkent, *Turk.* 148 J11
Yeşilova, *Turk.* 148 H5
Yessey, *Russ.* 141 G14
Yetman, *N.S.W., Austral.* 191 W14
Ye-u, *Myanmar* 166 G6
Yeu, Île d', *Fr.* 138 L8
Yevlax, *Azerb.* 149 D21
Yevpatoriya, *Ukr.* 133 M16
Yexian, *China* 162 F9
Yeysk, *Russ.* 140 H14
Ygatimí, *Para.* 122 M11
Yi, *river, China* 162 G8
Yi, *river, Uru.* 124 L14
Yibin, *China* 160 M11
Yichang, *China* 162 L3
Yicheng, *China* 162 K4
Yichuan, *China* 162 F3
Yichun, *China* 161 C17
Yichun, *China* 163 N5
Yigo, *Guam, U.S.* 196 B11
Yijun, *China* 162 G2
Yilan, *China* 161 C18
Yildiz Dağları, *Turk.* 148 B4
Yıldızeli, *Turk.* 148 E11
Yiliang, *China* 160 N11
Yinan, *China* 162 G8
Yinchuan, *China* 160 H12
Yinchuan, *China* 162 D1
Yindarlgooda, Lake, *Austral.* 190 J4
Yindi, *W. Austral., Austral.* 191 W5
Ying, *river, China* 161 K15
Yingcheng, *China* 162 L3
Yingde, *China* 163 R4
Yingkou, *China* 162 C10
Yingshan, *China* 162 K5
Yingshang, *China* 162 J6
Yingxian, *China* 162 D5
Yining (Gulja), *China* 160 E6
Yin Shan, *China* 162 B2
Yirga 'Alem, *Eth.* 179 G15
Yirol, *Sudan* 178 G12
Yirrkala, *N. Terr., Austral.* 191 P10
Yishan, *China* 163 Q1
Yishui, *China* 162 G8
Yitong, *China* 162 A12
Yitulihe, *China* 161 B15
Yiwu, *China* 160 F9
Yiwu, *China* 162 M9
Yixian, *China* 162 C9
Yixing, *China* 162 K9
Yiyang, *China* 162 M4
Yiyuan, *China* 162 G8
Ylig Bay, *Guam, U.S.* 196 D11
Ylivieska, *Fin.* 135 G15
Yoakum, *Tex., U.S.* 97 R11
Yobe, *river, Af.* 174 G6
Yocona, *river, Miss., U.S.* 94 H11
Yogyakarta, *Indonesia* 168 M9
Yoichi, *Jap.* 164 G19
Yokadouma, *Cameroon* 181 J17
Yokkaichi, *Jap.* 165 Q9
Yoko, *Cameroon* 181 J16
Yokoate Shima, *Jap.* 165 W3
Yokohama, *Jap.* 164 H13
Yokohama, *Jap.* 165 P12
Yokote, *Jap.* 164 K13
Yola, *Nig.* 181 F16
Yoloten, *Turkm.* 154 M10
Yom, *river, Thai.* 166 K8
Yomra, *Turk.* 149 D14
Yona, *Guam, U.S.* 196 C11
Yonago, *Jap.* 165 P7
Yonezawa, *Jap.* 164 K12
Yonezawa, *Jap.* 164 M12
Yŏngan, *N. Korea* 162 B14
Yong'an, *China* 163 P7
Yongchun, *China* 163 Q8

Yongdeng, *China* 160 H11
Yŏngdŏk, *S. Korea* 162 F14
Yŏngdŭngp'o, *S. Korea* 162 E13
Yongfu, *China* 163 Q2
Yonggyap Pass, *India* 158 E15
Yongkang, *China* 162 M9
Yongshun, *China* 162 M2
Yongtai, *China* 163 P8
Yongxin, *China* 163 N5
Yongxing, *China* 163 P4
Yongzhou, *China* 163 P3
Yonkers, *N.Y., U.S.* 88 N11
Yonne, *river, Fr.* 138 K10
York, *Ala., U.S.* 95 L13
York, *Nebr., U.S.* 99 Q7
York, *Pa., U.S.* 88 P7
York, *S.C., U.S.* 90 J8
York, *Eng., U.K.* 138 G8
York, Cape, *Austral.* 190 A12
York, Cape, *N. Amer.* 74 C7
Yorke Peninsula, *Austral.* 190 K10
Yorkton, *Sask., Can.* 77 N13
Yorktown, *Tex., U.S.* 97 S11
Yorktown, *Va., U.S.* 90 F14
Yoron Jima, *Jap.* 165 X2
Yoro Shima, *Jap.* 165 W2
Yortan Tepe, *ruins, Turk.* 148 F3
Yosemite National Park, *Calif., U.S.* 103 S6
Yoshii, *river, Jap.* 165 Q7
Yoshkar Ola, *Russ.* 140 G7
Yos Sudarso *see* Dolak, *island, Indonesia* 169 M20
Yost, *Utah, U.S.* 100 J6
Yŏsu, *S. Korea* 162 G14
Yotvata, *Israel* 151 R5
You, *river, China* 160 P12
Young, *N.S.W., Austral.* 191 Y13
Young, Mount, *Austral.* 190 C9
Young's Rock, *Pitcairn I., U.K.* 199 Q23
Youngstown, Ohio, *U.S.* 93 P16
Youth, Isle of *see* Juventud, Isla de la, *Cuba* 110 J5
Youxian, *China* 163 N4
Youyang, *China* 162 M1
Youyi Feng, *China–Mongolia* 160 C8
Yovo, *P.N.G.* 197 H14
Yozgat, *Turk.* 148 E10
Ypé Jhú, *Para.* 122 M10
Ypsilanti, *Mich., U.S.* 92 M12
Yreka, *Calif., U.S.* 102 L3
Yrghyz, *river, Kaz.* 154 F10
Yrghyz, *Kaz.* 154 E10
Ysabel Channel, *P.N.G.* 193 B20
Ysyk Köl, *Kyrg.* 156 EI3
Ysyk-Köl *see* Balykchy, *Kyrg.* 156 EI2
Ytterån, *Sw.* 134 H12
Ytyk Kyuyel', *Russ.* 141 G18
Yu, *river, China* 161 P13
Yuan, *river, China* 162 M3
Yuan (Red), *river, China* 160 P10
Yuan'an, *China* 162 K3
Yuanbaoshan, *China* 162 B8
Yüanli, *Taiwan, China* 163 Q9
Yüanlin, *Taiwan, China* 163 R9
Yuanling, *China* 162 M2
Yuanqu, *China* 162 G4
Yuba, *river, Calif., U.S.* 103 Q4
Yuba City, *Calif., U.S.* 103 Q4
Yūbari, *Jap.* 164 F14
Yuben', *Taj.* 156 K10
Yūbetsu, *Jap.* 164 E15
Yucatan Channel, *N. Amer.* 74 N7
Yucatán Peninsula, *Mex.* 109 H16
Yucca, *Ariz., U.S.* 101 S5
Yucca Flat, *Nev., U.S.* 103 T11
Yucca Valley, *Calif., U.S.* 103 X10
Yucheng, *China* 162 F7
Yuci, *China* 162 E4
Yuendumu, *N. Terr., Austral.* 191 T8
Yueqing, *China* 163 N9
Yueyang, *China* 162 M4
Yugan, *China* 162 M7
Yugorenok, *Russ.* 141 G19
Yugorskiy Poluostrov, *Russ.* 140 F11
Yugoslavia, *Eur.* 137 F13
Yuhuan Dao, *China* 163 N10
Yukagir, *Russ.* 141 E17
Yukagirskoye Ploskogor'ye, *Russ.* 141 E19
Yukon, *river, N. Amer.* 74 C1
Yukon, *Okla., U.S.* 96 G10
Yukon, Source of the, *N. Amer.* 74 E3
Yukon-Charley Rivers National Preserve, *Alas., U.S.* 105 F18
Yukon Delta, *U.S.* 78 P2
Yukon Flats, *U.S.* 78 N4
Yukon Plateau, *N. Amer.* 74 D3
Yukon Territory, *Can.* 76 F8
Yüksekova, *Turk.* 149 H18
Yulara, *N. Terr., Austral.* 191 U7
Yuleba, *Qnsld., Austral.* 191 V14
Yüli, *Taiwan, China* 163 R10
Yuli, *China* 160 F7

Yulin, *China* 162 E3
Yulin, *China* 163 R2
Yuma, *Ariz., U.S.* 101 U4
Yuma, *Colo., U.S.* 100 LI5
Yumen (Laojunguan), *China* 160 GIO
Yumenzhen, *China* 160 GIO
Yumurtalık, *Turk.* 148 JIO
Yunan, *China* 163 R3
Yunaska Island, *Alas., U.S.* 104 Q8
Yuncheng, *China* 162 G3
Yungas, region, *S. Amer.* 118 G5
Yunhe, *China* 161 MI6
Yunotsu, *Jap.* 165 P6
Yunta, *S. Austral., Austral.* 191 XIO
Yunxi, *China* 162 J3
Yunxian, *China* 162 J3
Yunxiao, *China* 163 R7
Yunyang, *China* 162 K2
Yuribey, *Russ.* 140 FI2
Yurimaguas, *Peru* 122 F3
Yushan, *China* 162 M8
Yü Shan, *Taiwan, China* 163 RIO
Yusufeli, *Turk.* 149 DI6
Yutian, *China* 160 H5
Yutian, *China* 162 D7
Yuxi, *China* 160 PII
Yuxian, *China* 162 D6
Yuxian, *China* 162 E5
Yuza, *Jap.* 164 LI2
Yuzawa, *Jap.* 164 KI3
Yuzhno Sakhalinsk, *Russ.* 141 K22
Yuzhnyy, Mys, *Russ.* 141 F2I

Z

Za (Mekong), river, *China* 160 K9
Zabaykal'sk, *Russ.* 141 LI7
Zabīd, *Yemen* 152 Q8
Zābol, *Iran* 153 EI7
Zābolī, *Iran* 153 HI8
Zabrze, *Pol.* 132 H9
Zacapa, *Guatemala* 109 LI6
Zacatecas, *Mex.* 108 GIO
Zadar, *Croatia* 136 GII
Zadoi, *China* 160 K9
Zafra, *Sp.* 139 R6
Zagora, *Mor.* 176 C8
Zagreb, *Croatia* 136 EII
Zagros Mountains see Kūhhā-ye Zāgros, *Iran* 152 DII
Zāhedān, *Iran* 153 FI7
Zahirabad, *India* 158 M6
Zaḩlah, *Leb.* 150 J7
Ẕahrān, *Saudi Arabia* 152 N9
Zaječar, *Yug.* 137 GI4
Zakamensk, *Russ.* 141 MI5
Zakataly, *Azerb.* 149 C2O
Zakhodnyaya Dvina, river, *Belarus* 133 EI4
Zākhū, *Iraq* 152 B9
Zákinthos, *Gr.* 137 LI4
Zákinthos (Zante), island, *Gr.* 137 LI4
Zakopane, *Pol.* 132 JIO
Zalaegerszeg, *Hung.* 132 L8
Zalantun, *China* 161 CI6
Zalău, *Rom.* 137 DI4
Ẕalim, *Saudi Arabia* 152 K8
Zamakh, *Yemen* 152 PII
Zambezi, river, *Af.* 174 N8
Zambezi, *Zambia* 182 E9
Zambezi, Source of the, *Af.* 174 M8
Zambezi River Delta, *Af.* 174 NIO
Zambia, *Af.* 182 EIO
Zamboanga, *Philippines* 169 FI4
Zamindavar, region, *Afghan.* 157 Q3
Zamora, *Ecua.* 120 L3
Zamora, *Sp.* 139 P6
Zanaga, *Congo* 181 MI7
Zanda, *China* 160 K4
Zanderij, *Suriname* 121 EI6
Zanesville, *Ohio, U.S.* 93 RI4
Zangla, *India* 157 NI4
Zanjān, *Iran* 152 BII
Zante see Zákinthos, island, *Gr.* 137 LI4
Zanthus, *W. Austral., Austral.* 191 W5
Zanzibar, island, *Tanzania* 179 MI5
Zanzibar, *Tanzania* 179 MI5
Zaouatallaz, *Alg.* 176 EI2
Zaoyang, *China* 162 K4
Zaozhuang, *China* 162 H7
Zapadno Sibirskaya Ravnina, *Russ.* 140 HII
Zapala, *Arg.* 125 P7
Zapata, *Tex., U.S.* 97 V8
Zapata, Peninsula de, *Cuba* 110 H7
Zapiga, *Chile* 124 C7
Zapiola Ridge, *Atl. Oc.* 217 U7
Zaporizhzhya, *Ukr.* 133 KI7
Zara, *Turk.* 148 EI2
Zarafshon, *Uzb.* 154 KII
Zaragoza, *Sp.* 139 P8

Zarand, *Iran* 153 FI5
Zaranj, *Afghan.* 157 Q2
Zárate, *Arg.* 124 LI2
Zaraza, *Venez.* 120 CIO
Zard Kūh, *Iran* 152 EI2
Zaria, *Nig.* 181 FI4
Zaruma, *Ecua.* 120 L2
Żary, *Pol.* 132 G8
Zaskar Mountains, *China-India* 157 NI4
Zatish'ye, *Russ.* 141 D2O
Zatobyl, *Kaz.* 154 BII
Zāwiyat Masūs, *Lib.* 177 CI5
Zawr, Ra's az, *Saudi Arabia* 152 HI2
Zayaki Jangal, *Pak.* 157 T5
Zaysan, *Kaz.* 155 EI9
Zaysan Köli, *Kaz.* 155 EI9
Zayü, *China* 160 M9
Zealand, island, *Eur.* 130 E6
Zednes, peak, *Mauritania* 176 E6
Zeeland, *Mich., U.S.* 92 M9
Ẕefat, *Israel* 150 K6
Zeil, Mount, *Austral.* 190 F8
Zelee, Cape, *Solomon Is.* 197 P2O
Zelenoe, *Kaz.* 154 E6
Zemio, *Cen. Af. Rep.* 178 HIO
Zemongo, *Cen. Af. Rep.* 178 GIO
Zencirli, site, *Turk.* 148 HII
Zenica, *Bosn. and Herzg.* 136 GI2
Zeni Su, *Jap.* 165 RII
Zenobia, ruins, *Syr.* 150 EI3
Zeravshan Range, *Taj.* 156 H8
Zereh Depression, *Afghan.* 157 R2
Zestap'oni, *Rep. of Georgia* 149 BI7
Zeya, *Russ.* 141 KI9
Zghartā, *Leb.* 150 H7
Zgierz, *Pol.* 132 GIO
Zhalpaqtal, *Kaz.* 154 D5
Zhaltyr, *Kaz.* 155 DI3
Zhanatal, *Kaz.* 154 GIO
Zhanatas, *Kaz.* 155 JI3
Zhanay, *Kaz.* 154 GIO
Zhangaaly, *Kaz.* 154 F5
Zhangaözen, *Kaz.* 154 H6
Zhangaqala, *Kaz.* 154 E5
Zhangaqorghan, *Kaz.* 154 HI2
Zhangbei, *China* 162 C6
Zhangguangcai Ling, *China* 161 DI8
Zhangjiakou, *China* 162 C6
Zhangping, *China* 163 Q7
Zhangpu, *China* 163 R7
Zhangwu, *China* 162 BIO
Zhangye, *China* 160 GII
Zhangzhou, *China* 163 Q7
Zhangzi, *China* 162 G4
Zhanhua, *China* 162 E8
Zhanjiang, *China* 163 T2
Zhanyi, *China* 160 NII
Zhao'an, *China* 163 R7
Zhaoqing, *China* 163 R3
Zhaosu, *China* 160 E6
Zhaotong, *China* 160 MII
Zhaoxian, *China* 162 E6
Zhapo, *China* 163 S3
Zhaqsy, *Kaz.* 154 CI2
Zharma, *Kaz.* 155 EI8
Zharmysh, *Kaz.* 154 H6
Zharqamys, *Kaz.* 154 F8
Zhashui, *China* 162 H2
Zhaslyk, *Uzb.* 154 H8
Zhayylma, *Kaz.* 154 DIO
Zhayyq (Ural), river, *Kaz.* 154 E6
Zhdanov, *Azerb.* 149 E2I
Zhecheng, *China* 162 H6
Zhelezinka, *Kaz.* 155 BI5
Zheleznodorozhnyy, *Russ.* 140 F9
Zheleznogorsk, *Russ.* 140 F5
Zhem, river, *Kaz.* 154 F8
Zhenba, *China* 162 JI
Zhenghe, *China* 163 N8
Zhenglan Qi (Xulun Hoh), *China* 162 B6
Zhengxiangbai Qi, *China* 162 B6
Zhengzhou (Chengchow), *China* 162 H5
Zhenjiang, *China* 162 K8
Zhenlai, *China* 161 DI6
Zhenping, *China* 162 J2
Zhenyuan, *China* 160 PIO
Zhenyuan, *China* 162 FI
Zhenyuan, *China* 163 NI
Zhetiqara, *Kaz.* 154 CIO
Zhexi Shuiki, *China* 163 N3
Zhezqazghan, *Kaz.* 154 FI2
Zhicheng, *China* 162 L3
Zhidan, *China* 162 F2
Zhigansk, *Russ.* 141 GI7
Zhijiang, *China* 163 N2
Zhilaya Kosa, *Kaz.* 154 F6
Zhil'gur, *Russ.* 141 HI8
Zhilinda, *Russ.* 141 FI5
Zhlobin, *Belarus* 133 FI4

Zhob, river, *Pak.* 157 Q8
Zhob, *Pak.* 157 Q8
Zhokhova, Ostrov, *Russ.* 141 CI7
Zhongba, *China* 160 L5
Zhongdian, *China* 160 MIO
Zhongning, *China* 160 HI2
Zhongshan, station, *Antarctica* 207 G2O
Zhongshan, *China* 163 Q3
Zhongwei, *China* 160 HI2
Zhongxian, *China* 162 LI
Zhongxiang, *China* 162 K4
Zhosaly, *Kaz.* 154 GII
Zhoukou, *China* 162 H5
Zhoushan, *China* 162 LIO
Zhoushan Dao, *China* 162 LIO
Zhoushan Qundao, *China* 162 LIO
Zhu (Pearl), river, *China* 163 S4
Zhuanghe, *China* 162 DII
Zhucheng, *China* 162 G8
Zhuji, *China* 162 M9
Zhuolu, *China* 162 C6
Zhuozhou, *China* 162 D6
Zhuozi, *China* 162 C4
Zhuozi Shan, *China* 162 DI
Zhupanovo, *Russ.* 141 F23
Zhuryn, *Kaz.* 154 E8
Zhushan, *China* 162 J2
Zhuxi, *China* 162 J2
Zhuzhou, *China* 163 N4
Zhympity, *Kaz.* 154 D6
Zhytomyr, *Ukr.* 133 HI3
Zi, river, *China* 162 M3
Ziarat, *Pak.* 157 R6
Zibak, *Afghan.* 156 K9
Zibo, *China* 162 F8
Zichang, *China* 162 F2
Zielona Góra, *Pol.* 132 G8
Zigana Geçidi, *Turk.* 149 DI4
Zigar, *Taj.* 156 J8
Zigey, *Chad* 177 HI4
Zigong, *China* 160 LI2
Zigui, *China* 162 K3
Ziguinchor, *Senegal* 176 H4
Zile, *Turk.* 148 EII
Žilina, *Slovakia* 132 J9
Zillah, *Lib.* 177 DI5
Zima, *Russ.* 141 LI5
Zimbabwe, *Af.* 182 GII
Zimnicea, *Rom.* 137 GI6
Zinder, *Niger* 176 JI2
Žingažir, *Taj.* 156 HII
Zinjibār, *Yemen* 152 RIO
Zion, *Ill., U.S.* 92 M7
Zion National Park, *Utah, U.S.* 101 P6
Ziway Hāyk', *Eth.* 179 GI5
Zixi, *China* 163 N7
Zixing, *China* 163 P4
Ziyang, *China* 162 JI
Ziyuan, *China* 163 P2
Zizhou, *China* 162 E3
Zlatoust, *Russ.* 140 J8
Zlatoustovsk, *Russ.* 141 J2O
Zlín, *Czech Rep.* 132 J9
Zmari Sar, *Afghan.* 157 Q5
Zmeinogorsk, *Russ.* 140 LII
Znamenka, *Kaz.* 155 DI7
Znojmo, *Czech Rep.* 132 J8
Ẕofar, *Israel* 151 Q5
Zogang, *China* 160 L9
Zolochiv, *Ukr.* 132 JI2
Zolochiv, *Ukr.* 133 HI7
Zolotaya Gora, *Russ.* 141 KI8
Zomba, *Malawi* 183 EI3
Zongo, *Dem. Rep. of the Congo* 178 H8
Zonguldak, *Turk.* 148 C7
Zor Dağ, *Turk.* 149 EI8
Zorkol Lake, *Taj.* 156 JII
Zorritos, *Peru* 122 E2
Zoushi, *China* 162 M3
Zouxian, *China* 162 G7
Zrenjanin, *Yug.* 137 FI3
Ẕufār, region, *Oman* 153 NI4
Zugdidi, *Rep. of Georgia* 149 BI6
Zululand, region, *S. Af.* 182 KI2
Zumberge Coast, *Antarctica* 206 G7
Zumbo, *Mozambique* 182 EII
Zunhua, *China* 162 D8
Zuni, river, *Ariz., U.S.* 101 S9
Zuni, *N. Mex., U.S.* 101 SIO
Zunyi, *China* 160 MI2
Zürich, *Switz.* 132 K5
Zur Kowt, *Afghan.* 157 N8
Zuru, *Nig.* 181 EI3
Zuwārah, *Lib.* 177 BI3
Zvishavane, *Zimb.* 182 GII
Zvolen, *Slovakia* 132 K9
Zwickau, *Ger.* 132 H7
Zwolle, *La., U.S.* 94 M6
Zwolle, *Neth.* 138 GII

Zyrya, *Azerb.* 149 D23
Zyryanka, *Russ.* 141 EI9
Zyryanovo, *Russ.* 141 HI3
Zyryanovsk, *Kaz.* 155 DI9

MOON INDEX

LUNAR EQUIVALENTS

Lacus ....*lake*
Mare ....*sea*
Montes ....*range*
Oceanus ....*ocean*
Palus ....*marsh*
Rupes ....*scarp*
Sinus ....*bay*
Vallis ....*valley*

All other entries are craters

A

Abel **229** MI8
Abulfeda **229** KI4
Aestuum, Sinus **228** GI2
Agrippa **229** HI3
Aitken **230** KI2
Albategnius **229** KI3
Al-Biruni **230** F6
Alden **230** L8
Aliacensis **229** LI3
Almanon **229** KI4
Alpes, Montes **228** DI2
Alpes, Vallis **229** DI3
Alphonsus **228** KI2
Altai, Rupes **229** LI4
Amundsen **229** QI3
Anaxagoras **228** BI2
Anaximenes **228** BII
Anders **231** MI5
Anderson **230** GI2
Anguis, Mare **229** FI8
Ansgarius **229** KI9
Antoniadi **231** PI3
Apenninus, Montes **228** GI2
Apianus **229** LI3
Apollo **231** MI4
Appleton **230** EII
Archimedes **228** FI2
Aristarchus **228** F9
Aristillus **228** EI2
Aristoteles **229** DI4
Arnold **229** CI4
Artamonov **230** F7
Arzachel **229** KI3
Atlas **229** DI5
Australe, Mare **230** N7
Avicenna **231** DI7
Avogadro **230** CI2
Azophi **229** KI4

B

Baade, Vallis **228** N8
Babbage **228** CIO
Babcock **230** H6
Baillaud **229** BI4
Bailly **228** QIO
Balboa **228** F6
Balmer **229** LI8
Banachiewicz **229** HI9
Barocius **229** MI4
Barringer **231** LI5
Barrow **229** CI3
Bel'kovich **229** BI6
Bell **231** FI8
Bellingshausen **231** PI4
Belyaev **231** FIO
Berosus **229** EI7
Bettinus **228** PII
Billy **228** K8
Birkhoff **231** CI4
Blancanus **228** PI2
Blanchard **231** PI6
Boguslawsky **229** QI4
Boltzmann **231** PI6
Bond, W. **229** CI3
Borman **231** MI5
Bose **231** NI3
Boussingault **229** QI4
Bragg **231** DI7
Brianchon **228** BII
Bridgman **230** D9
Brouwer **231** MI6
Buffon **231** MI6
Bullialdus **228** KIO
Büsching **229** MI4
Byrd **229** BI3
Byrgius **228** L7

C

Cabannes **231** PI3
Cabeus **228** QI2
Campbell **230** DII
Cannizzaro **231** CI6

Cantor **230** E8
Capuanus **228** MII
Carnot **231** DI4
Carpatus, Montes **228** GIO
Carpenter **228** BII
Casatus **228** QII
Cassini **229** EI3
Catharina **229** KI5
Caucasus, Montes **229** EI3
Chaffee **231** MI4
Chamberlin **230** P9
Chandler **230** EI2
Chaplygin **230** JIO
Chapman **231** CI7
Chappell **231** DI3
Charlier **231** EI6
Chebyshev **231** MI6
Chrétien **230** NII
Clairaut **229** NI3
Clavius **228** NI2
Cleomedes **229** FI7
Cockcroft **231** FI4
Cognitum, Mare **228** JIO
Colombo **229** KI6
Compton **230** C9
Comstock **231** FI7
Condorcet **229** GI8
Copernicus **228** HII
Cordillera, Montes **231** KI8
Coriolis **230** HI2
Coulomb **231** CI6
Crisium, Mare **229** GI7
Crüger **228** K7
Curie **230** L6
Curtius **229** PI3
Cyrano **230** KII
Cyrillus **229** KI5

D

Daedalus **230** JI2
D'Alembert **230** DI2
Dante **231** FI3
Darwin **228** L7
Davisson **231** MI3
Debye **231** DI3
Delambre **229** JI4
DeLaRue **229** CI5
Dellinger **230** J9
Demonax **229** QI4
Desargues **228** BIO
De Sitter **229** BI3
Deslandres **228** LI2
Dobrovol'skij **230** K9
Doppelmayer **228** LIO
Doppler **231** KI4
Drygalski **228** QII

E

Eddington **228** F7
Einstein **228** G6
Elvey **231** GI9
Emden **231** CI3
Endymion **229** DI5
Englehardt **231** HI4
Eötvös **230** M9
Epidemiarum, Palus **228** LIO
Eratosthenes **228** GII
Erro **230** H6
Esnault-Pelterie **231** DI5
Euctemon **229** BI3
Eudoxus **229** DI3
Euler **228** FIO
Evershed **231** EI4

F

Fabricius **229** NI5
Fabry **230** D8
Fecunditatis, Mare **229** JI7
Fermi **230** L8
Fersman **231** GI7
Firmicus **229** HI8
Fitzgerald **231** FI3
Fizeau **231** PI5
Flammarion **228** JI2
Fleming **230** G7
Fontenelle **228** CI2
Fowler **231** EI5
Fracastorius **229** LI5
Fra Mauro **228** JII
Franklin **229** EI6
Freundlich **231** FI2
Frigoris, Mare **228** CII
Furnerius **229** MI7

G

Gadomski **231** EI5
Gagarin **230** KIO

Galois **231** KI5
Gamow **230** CII
Gärtner **229** CI4
Gassendi **228** KIO
Gauricus **228** LI2
Gauss **229** DI7
Geminus **229** EI6
Gemma Frisius **229** LI4
Gerard **228** D8
Gerasimovich **231** LI7
Gibbs **229** KI9
Gilbert **229** JI8
Goddard **229** GI9
Goldschmidt **229** BI3
Green **230** H8
Grimaldi **228** J7
Grissom **231** NI5
Gruemberger **228** PI2
Gutenberg **229** JI6
Guyot **230** H7

H

Haemus, Montes **229** GI3
Hagecius **229** PI5
Hahn **229** EI8
Hansteen **228** K8
Hartmann **230** H9
Hase **229** MI7
Hausen **228** Q9
Hayn **229** BI5
Heaviside **230** JI2
Hecataeus **229** LI9
Helberg **231** FI9
Helmholtz **229** QI5
Henyey **231** GI5
Hercules **229** DI5
Hermite **228** AI2
Herodotus **228** F9
Herschel, J. **228** CII
Hertz **230** G7
Hertzsprung **231** HI7
Hess **230** NI2
Hevelius **228** H7
Heymans **231** BI4
Hilbert **230** K7
Hipparchus **229** JI3
Hirayama **230** J6
Houzeau **231** KI7
Hubble **229** FI9
Humboldt **229** LI8
Humboldtianum, Mare **229** CI6
Humorum, Mare **228** L9

I

Icarus **231** JI3
Imbrium, Mare **228** EII
Ingenii, Mare **230** MII
Inghirami **228** N9
Ioffe **231** KI6
Iridum, Sinus **228** DIO

J

Jackson **231** FI4
Jansky **229** HI9
Janssen **229** NI5
Jarvis **231** MI5
Joliot **230** E6
Joule **231** FI5
Jules Verne **230** MIO
Julius Caesar **229** HI4
Jura, Montes **228** DIO

K

Kane **229** CI4
Karpinskiy **230** CI2
Kästner **229** JI9
Keeler **230** JII
Kekulé **231** GI6
Kepler **228** H9
Kibal'chich **231** HI5
King **230** H7
Kircher **228** PII
Klaproth **228** QII
Kohlschütter **230** GIO
Kolhörster **231** GI7
Komarov **230** FIO
Kondratyuk **230** K8
Konstantinov **230** GII
Korolev **231** JI4
Kostinskiy **230** G8
Kovalevskaya **231** EI6
Krafft **228** G7
Krasovskiy **231** HI3
Kugler **230** P9
Kurchatov **230** EIO

L

La Caille **229** LI3
Lagrange **228** M8
Lamarck **228** L7
Lamb **230** N8
Lamé **229** KI8
Landau **231** DI6
Langemak **230** J8
Langrenus **229** JI8
La Pérouse **229** KI8
Larmor **231** FI3
Lavoisier **228** D8
Lebedev **230** N9
Lebedinskiy **231** HI4
Leeuwenhoek **231** LI3
Legendre **229** MI8
Le Gentil **228** QII
Leibnitz **230** MI2
Lemaitre **231** PI4
Letronne **228** J9
Leuschner **231** HI8
Levi-Civita **230** L9
Licetus **229** MI3
Lilius **229** NI3
Lomonosov **230** E7
Longomontanus **228** NII
Lorentz **231** EI8
Lucretius **231** JI8
Lyman **230** PII
Lyot **229** PI7

M

Mach **231** GI5
Macrobius **229** FI6
Maginus **228** NI2
Maksutov **231** MI4
Mandel'shtam **230** HII
Manzinus **229** PI3
Marconi **230** JIO
Marginis, Mare **229** GI9
Marius **228** G8
Markov **228** C9
Maunder **231** KI9
Maurolycus **229** MI4
Maxwell **230** E7
McAuliffe **231** LI5
McLaughlin **231** CI7
McMath **231** GI3
McNair **231** MI5
Medii, Sinus **228** HI2
Mee **228** NIO
Meitner **230** K7
Mendel **231** NI6
Mendeleev **230** H9
Mercurius **229** DI6
Mersenius **228** L8
Messala **229** DI7
Metius **229** MI5
Mezentsev **231** BI4
Michelson **231** HI7
Milanković **231** BI3
Millikan **230** D9
Milne **230** M8
Minkowski **231** NI4
Minnaert **230** PI2
Mitra **231** FI5
Mohorovičić **231** KI4
Moretus **228** PI2
Mortis, Lacus **229** DI4
Moscoviense, Mare **230** FIO
Murakami **231** LI5
Mutus **229** PI4

N

Nansen **230** BI2
Nassau **231** LI3
Nectaris, Mare **229** KI5
Neper **229** GI9
Nernst **231** DI8
Neujmin **230** L9
Newton **228** QI2
Niepce **231** BI4
Nöther **231** BI5
Nubium, Mare **228** KII
Numerov **231** QI3

O

Oken **229** NI7
Olbers **228** H7
Olcott **230** F7
Omar Khayyam **231** CI6
Onizuka **231** MI4
Oppenheimer **231** MI3
Oresme **230** MII
Orientale, Mare **231** LI9
Orontius **228** MI2
Ostwald **230** G8

P

Pallas **228** HI2
Palmieri **228** L9
Papaleksi **230** HII
Paracelsus **230** KII
Parenago **231** FI7
Pascal **228** BII
Paschen **231** KI5
Pasteur **230** K7
Patsaev **230** K9
Pauli **230** NIO
Pavlov **230** LIO
Perepelkin **230** J8
Petavius **229** LI7
Petermann **229** BI4
Petropavlovskiy **231** EI7
Petzval **231** PI5
Phillips **229** LI8
Philolaus **228** BI2
Phocylides **228** P9
Piccolomini **229** LI5
Pilâtre **228** P9
Pingré **228** P9
Pitatus **228** LII
Pitiscus **229** NI4
Pizzetti **230** M8
Planck **230** PIO
Planck, Vallis **230** PIO
Plaskett **231** BI3
Plato **228** DI2
Playfair **229** LI3
Plinius **229** GI5
Plutarch **229** FI8
Poincaré **230** NI2
Poinsot **231** BI3
Polzunov **230** F8
Poncelet **228** BII
Pontécoulant **229** PI6
Posidonius **229** FI4
Poynting **231** GI6
Prandtl **230** PII
Procellarum, Oceanus **228** E8
Proclus **229** GI6
Ptolemaeus **228** JI2
Purbach **228** LI2
Putredinis, Palus **229** FI3
Pyrenaeus, Montes **229** KI6
Pythagoras **228** BIO

R

Racah **230** KI2
Raimond **231** GI4
Rayleigh **229** EI8
Razumov **231** EI7
Reinhold **228** HIO
Resnik **231** MI4
Rheita **229** MI6
Rheita, Vallis **229** MI6
Riccioli **228** J6
Riemann **229** DI8
Riphaeus, Montes **228** JIO
Robertson **231** FI8
Roche **230** MIO
Röntgen **231** EI8
Rook, Montes **231** LI8
Roris, Sinus **228** D9
Rosenberger **229** PI5
Rowland **231** DI3
Rozhdestvenskiy **231** BI3
Rumford **231** LI4
Russell **228** E7

S

Sacrobosco **229** LI4
Saha **230** J6
Scaliger **230** M7
Scheiner **228** PII
Schickard **228** N9
Schiller **228** NIO
Schlesinger **231** DI5
Schliemann **230** JIO
Schlüter **228** J6
Schneller **231** EI3
Schomberger **229** QI3
Schrödinger **230** QII
Schrödinger, Vallis **230** QIO
Schuster **230** HIO
Schwarzschild **230** BII
Scobee **231** LI5
Scott **229** QI3
Seares **230** BI2
Sechenov **231** JI5
Segner **228** PIO
Serenitatis, Mare **229** FI4
Seyfert **230** F8
Sharonov **230** GI2
Shayn **230** FI2
Short **228** QI2

Sierpinski **230** LII
Sirsalis **228** K8
Sklodowska **230** L7
Smith **231** LI5
Smoluchowski **231** CI6
Smythii, Mare **229** HI9
Snellius **229** LI7
Sommerfeld **231** CI3
Somni, Palus **229** GI6
Somniorum, Lacus **229** EI5
Spencer Jones **230** GII
Spitzbergensis, Montes **228** EI2
Spumans, Mare **229** HI8
Stebbins **231** CI4
Stefan **231** DI6
Sternberg **231** GI7
Sternfeld **231** LI5
Stevinus **229** MI7
Stiborius **229** MI5
Stöfler **229** MI3
Störmer **230** CII
Strabo **229** CI5
Struve **228** F7
Subbotin **230** L9
Szilard **230** E8

T

Taurus, Montes **229** FI6
Teneriffe, Montes **228** DI2
Theaetetus **229** EI3
Theophilus **229** JI5
Thomson **230** LI2
Tikhov **230** CI2
Timocharis **228** FII
Tranquillitatis, Mare **229** HI5
Tranquillity Base **229** HI5
Trumpler **230** FI2
Tsander **231** HI5
Tsiolkovsky **230** K9
Tycho **228** MI2

U

Undarum, Mare **229** HI8

V

Valier **230** HI2
Van de Graaff **230** LI2
Van der Waals **230** N9
Van Rhijn **230** DIO
Van't Hoff **231** CI5
Vaporum, Mare **229** GI3
Vasco da Gama **228** G6
Vavilov **231** JI6
Vendelinus **229** KI7
Vening Meinesz **230** HII
Vernadskiy **230** F8
Vesalius **230** J7
Vestine **230** E7
Vieta **228** L8
Vlacq **229** NI5
Volkov **230** K8
Volta **228** C9
Von der Pahlen **231** LI6
Von Kármán **230** MI2
Von Neumann **230** EII
Von Zeipel **231** EI5

W

Walther **229** LI3
Wargentin **228** N9
Waterman **230** L9
Wegener **231** DI7
Wells **230** D9
Werner **229** LI3
Weyl **231** GI7
White **231** NI4
Wiechert **230** QI2
Wiener **230** EIO
Wilhelm **228** MII
Wilsing **231** KI5
Wilson **228** QII
Wrottesley **229** LI7
Wyld **230** J6

Y

Yablochkov **230** CIO
Yamamoto **230** CI2

Z

Zach **229** PI3
Zagut **229** LI4
Zeeman **231** QI4
Zhukovskiy **231** HI3
Zsigmondy **231** CI6
Zucchius **228** PIO

SPACECRAFT LANDING OR IMPACT SITES

Apollo II (Tranquillity Base) **229** HI5
Apollo I2 **228** JII
Apollo I4 **228** JII
Apollo I5 **229** FI3
Apollo I6 **229** JI4
Apollo I7 **229** GI5
Luna 2 **229** FI3
Luna 5 **228** JIO
Luna 7 **228** H9
Luna 8 **228** H7
Luna 9 **228** H7
Luna I3 **228** F8
Luna I5 **229** GI7
Luna I6 **229** JI7
Luna I7 **228** EIO
Luna I8 **229** HI7
Luna 2O **229** HI7
Luna 2I **229** FI5
Luna 23 **229** GI7
Luna 24 **229** GI8
Orbiter I **230** HII
Orbiter 2 **230** H6
Orbiter 3 **231** GI9
Orbiter 5 **228** J6
Ranger 4 **231** KI7
Ranger 6 **229** GI4
Ranger 7 **228** JII
Ranger 8 **229** HI5
Ranger 9 **228** KI2
Surveyor I **228** J9
Surveyor 2 **228** HI2
Surveyor 3 **228** JII
Surveyor 4 **228** HI2
Surveyor 5 **229** HI4
Surveyor 6 **228** HI2
Surveyor 7 **228** MI2

Printed in Verona, Italy

ACKNOWLEDGMENTS

CONSULTANTS

PHYSICAL AND POLITICAL MAPS

Bureau of the Census, U.S. Department of Commerce

Bureau of Land Management, U.S. Department of the Interior

Central Intelligence Agency (CIA)

National Geographic Maps

National Imagery and Mapping Agency (NIMA)

National Park Service, U.S. Department of the Interior

Office of the Geographer, U.S. Department of State

U.S. Board on Geographic Names (BGN)

U.S. Geological Survey, U.S. Department of the Interior

WORLD THEMATIC SECTION

Earth's Rocky Exterior
STEVE RAUZI, JON SPENCER
Arizona Geological Survey

BRAD SINGER
University of Wisconsin—Madison

The Internet
MARGARET MURRAY
Cooperative Association for Internet Data Analysis (CAIDA)

Structure of the Earth
LAUREL M. BYBELL
U.S. Geological Survey (USGS)

BRUCE WARDLAW
USGS

Surface of the Earth
PETER W. SLOSS
NOAA National Geophysical Data Center (NGDC)

Technology and Globalization
Center for Defense Information

Non-Proliferation Project at the Carnegie Endowment for International Peace

TIM KELLY AND ASSOCIATES
Strategic Planning Unit, International Telecommunication Union

United Nations Development Programme (UNDP)

World Biodiversity
Conservation International

TED MUNN
Institute for Environmental Studies, University of Toronto

C. HILTON-TAYLOR
International Union for Conservation of Nature and Natural Resources

World Wildlife Fund (WWF)

World Biosphere
MANUEL COLUNGA-GARCIA (ENTOMOLOGY), PATRICK J. WEBBER (PLANT BIOLOGY), DAVID T. LONG (GEOLOGICAL SCIENCES), STUART H. GAGE (ENTOMOLOGY), CRAIG K. HARRIS (SOCIOLOGY)
Earth System Science Education Program, Michigan State University

World Climate
Center for Climatic Research, University of Wisconsin—Madison

H. MICHAEL MOGIL

World Economy
DANIEL CANNISTRA
Ernst and Young LLP

SUSAN MARTIN
Institute for the Study of International Migration, Georgetown University

World Bank

World Energy
KARL GAWELL
Geothermal Energy Association

HUGH D. GUTHRIE AND VENKAT K. VENKATARAMAN
National Energy Technology Laboratory (NETL) of the U.S. Department of Energy (DOE)

DENNIS ELLIOTT, DOUGLAS GEORGE, PAMELA GRAY-HANN, DAVID RENNE
National Renewable Energy Laboratory (NREL)

CONNIE BROOKS
Sandia National Laboratories

MARSHALL REED
U.S. Department of Energy (DOE)

JOHN HAMMOND
U.S. Energy Association

CHRISTOPHER FLAVIN
Worldwatch Institute

World Environmental Stresses
MARC LEVY
Center for International Earth Science Information Network (CIESIN), Columbia University

ANNA STABRAWA, SHEILA EDWARDS, MUNYARADZI CHENJE, TESSA GOVERSE, AND MARION CHEATLE
Global Environment Outlook Section, Division of Early Warning and Assessment (DEWA), United Nations Environment Programme (UNEP)

TED MUNN
Institute for Environmental Studies, University of Toronto

UNEP World Conservation Monitoring Centre (UNEP-WCMC)

PAUL REICH
U.S. Department of Agriculture, Natural Resources Conservation Service

World Resources Institute

World Food
Food and Agriculture Organization of the United Nations (FAO)

World Health and Education
CARLOS CASTILLO-SALGADO, ENRIQUE LOYOLA-ELIZONDO, AND BYRON CRAPE
Pan American Health Organization (PAHO)/World Health Organization (WHO)

World Land Cover
MATTHEW C. HANSEN, ROB A. SOHLBERG
University of Maryland

World Landforms
SHARON G. JOHNSON
San Francisco State University

MIKE SLATTERY
Texas Christian University

L. ALLAN JAMES
University of South Carolina

World Languages
IVES GODDARD
Smithsonian Institution

World Minerals
Mineral Information Institute

W. DAVID MENZIE
USGS Minerals Information Team

World Population
GREGORY YETMAN
Center for International Earth Science Information Network (CIESIN), Columbia University

CARL HAUB
Population Reference Bureau

World Protected Lands
UNEP World Conservation Monitoring Centre (UNEP-WCMC)

UNESCO World Heritage Centre

World Religions
ARTHUR GREEN, REUVEN KIMELMAN
Brandeis University

BOB THURMAN, NEGUIN YEVARI
Columbia University

RICHARD JAFFE
Duke University

STEPHEN FIELDS, ARIEL GLUCKLICH
Georgetown University

HARRY YEIDE, JR.
George Washington University

TODD JOHNSON

International Population Center, San Diego State University

World Trade
United Nations Conference on Trade and Development (UNCTAD)

World Trade Organization (WTO)

World Weather
H. Michael Mogil

Steve Goodman
NASA Marshall Space Flight Center

REGIONAL THEMATIC MAPS
Gregory Yetman
Center for International Earth Science Information Network (CIESIN), Columbia University

Freddy Nachtergaele
Food and Agriculture Organization of the United Nations (FAO)

Carl Haub
Population Reference Bureau

W. David Menzie
USGS Minerals Information Team

FLAGS AND FACTS
Whitney Smith
Flag Research Center

Carl Haub
Population Reference Bureau

ANTARCTICA
Roland Warner
Antarctic Cooperative Research Centre and Australian Antarctic Division

David G. Vaughan
Bedmap Consortium, British Antarctic Survey

Kenneth Jezek
Byrd Polar Research Center, Ohio State University

Mark R. Drinkwater
European Space Agency

Whitney Smith
Flag Research Center

Graham Bartram
The Flag Institute

Scott Borg
National Science Foundation (NSF) Antarctic Division

Tony K. Meunier
USGS Polar Program

OCEANS

Oceanography
Eric J. Lindstrom
National Aeronautics and Space Administration (NASA)

Keelin Kuipers
National Atmospheric and Oceanic Administration (NOAA)

Bob Molinari
NOAA

Bruce Parker
NOAA/National Ocean Service (NOS)

Richard A. Schmalz, Jr.
NOAA

SPACE

General
Stephen P. Maran

Robert E. Pratt
National Geographic Maps

The Moon
Paul D. Spudis
Lunar and Planetary Institute, Houston, Texas

The Planets
Henry Kline
NASA Jet Propulsion Laboratory (JPL)

The Solar System
Lucy McFadden
University of Maryland, College Park

The Universe
Todd J. Henry
Harvard-Smithsonian Center for Astrophysics

Edmund Bertschinger
Massachusetts Institute of Technology

Donald P. Schneider
Pennsylvania State University

Marc Postman
Space Telescope Science Institute (STScI)

Christopher D. Impey
University of Arizona

R. Brent Tully
University of Hawaii

August E. Evrard
University of Michigan

APPENDIX

Geographic Comparisons
John Kammerer

National Imagery and Mapping Agency (NIMA)

George Sharman
NOAA/NESDIS/NGDC

Peter H. Gleick
Pacific Institute for Studies in Development, Environment, and Security

R.L. Fisher
Scripps Insitution of Oceanography

Philip Micklin
Western Michigan University

Glossary
Rex Honey
University of Iowa

Bernard O. Bauer
University of Southern California

Major Cities of the World
Carl Haub
Population Reference Bureau

Political Entities and Status
Leo Dillon
Department of State, Office of the Geographer

Harm J. de Blij
Michigan State University

Carl Haub
Population Reference Bureau

ART AND ILLUSTRATIONS

Pages 20–21, *Continents Adrift in Time*: Christopher R. Scotese/PALEOMAP Project; *Cutaway of the Earth*: Tibor G. Tóth; *Tectonic block diagrams*: Susan Sanford

Pages 22–23, *Rock Cycle and Reading Earth History*: ChrisOrr.com and XNR Productions

Page 26, *Fictional Landforms*: Shusei Nagaoka; *Dunes*: ChrisOrr.com

Page 27, *Rivers*: Steven Fick/Canadian Geographic; *Glacial Landforms*: Steven Fick

Pages 28–29, *Earth Surface Elevations and Depths, A Slice of Earth, and Hypsometry*: Peter Sloss, *NOAA National Geophysical Data Center*

Page 33, *Global Air Temperature Changes, 1850–2000*: Reproduced by kind permission of the Climatic Research Unit

Pages 36–37, *The Water Cycle, Air Masses, Jet Stream, Weather Fronts, Cloud Types*: ChrisOrr.com

Page 38, *Biosphere Dynamics*: Earth Science System Education Program, Michigan State University, and ChrisOrr.com; *Earth System Dynamics*: Edward Gazsi; *Size of the Biosphere*: The COMET Program and ChrisOrr.com; *Biosphere over Time*: Earth Science System Education Program, Michigan State University

Pages 40–41, *The Natural World*: NG Maps. Source data provided by World Wildlife Fund. *Threatened Ecoregions*: Source data provided by Conservation International. *Projected Biodiversity Status*: Source data provided by World Wildlife Fund.

Page 52, *Growth of World Trade*: World Trade Organization

Page 56, *Fossil Fuel Extraction*: ChrisOrr.com and XNR Productions

Pages 60–61, All graphics reproduced from Pan American Health Organization, Special Program for Health Analysis. Regional Core Health Data Initiative; Table Generator. Washington D.C., 2001. (http://www.paho.org/English/SHA/coredata/tabulator/new Tabulator.htm)

Pages 66–67, *Centers of Technological Innovation*: UNDP Human Development Report 2001 and Wired magazine, May 2000; *Milestones in Technology*: Adapted from UNDP Human Development Report 2001; *Teledensity*: NG Maps. Source data provided by TeleGeography, Inc. (www.telegeography.com) and the International Telecommunication Union. The Fuller Projection map design is a trademark of the Buckminster Fuller Institute © 1938, 1967, and 1992. All rights reserved.

Pages 68–69, All images provided by the Cooperative Association for Internet Data Analysis (CAIDA), located at the San Diego Supercomputer Center (SDSC). CAIDA is a research unit of the University of California at San Diego (UCSD). URL: www.caida.org. This work was sponsored by the National Science Foundation-funded "Internet Atlas" project ANI 9996248. Images used by permission, UC Regents.

Pages 212–213, All illustrations by ChrisOrr.com

Pages 236–237, *The Universe*: Ken Edward

Page 352, Tibor G. Tóth

ACKNOWLEDGMENTS

SATELLITE IMAGES

CONTINENTAL SATELLITE IMAGES: NASA/Jet Propulsion Laboratory (JPL)/California Institute of Technology/Advanced Very High Resolution Radiometer (AVHRR) Project/Cartographic Applications Group (CAG).

The Cartographic Applications Group manipulated more than 500 NOAA weather satellite images acquired by the AVHRR instrument to create satellite coverages at one-kilometer resolution (one pixel of data equals one kilometer on the Earth). Using hundreds of multidate NOAA AVHRR satellite scenes and imaging in the visible and near-infrared wavelengths, the mosaics were created in a rapid fashion using semiautomated software procedures based on JPL's VICAR/IBIS image processing and GIS software.

DUSTJACKET AND TITLE PAGE, WorldSat International Inc. from NOAA data; Robert Stacey.

PAGES 12–13, *WORLD*: NASA/Goddard Space Flight Center (GSFC). Images and animations by Jesse Allen, Science Systems and Applications, Inc. Data provided by the MODIS Ocean Team and the University of Miami Rosenstiel School of Marine and Atmospheric Science Remote Sensing Group.

PAGE 27, *MISSISSIPPI RIVER DELTA*: Centre National d'Etudes Spatiales (CNES).

PAGES 28–29, *SNOW DEPTH AND SEA ICE*: Data provided by NASA/GSFC, Don Cavalieri and Dorothy Hall; processed by Gene Carl Feldman. *CLOUD AMOUNT*: Data provided by NASA/GISS, William B. Rossow; processed by NASA/GSFC, Gene Carl Feldman. *DAY AND NIGHT TEMPERATURE DIFFERENCE*: Data provided by NASA/GSFC, Joel Susskind; processed by Gene Carl Feldman. *VEGETATION*: Data provided by NASA/GSFC, Compton J. Tucker; processed by Gene Carl Feldman.

PAGES 30–31, *GLOBAL LAND COVER CLASSIFICATION AT 1KM SPATIAL RESOLUTION USING A CLASSIFICATION TREE APPROACH*: Hansen, M.C., DeFries, R.S., Townshend, J.R.G., and Sohlberg, R., 2000, *International Journal of Remote Sensing*, volume 21, numbers 6 and 7, pp. 1331–1364. (Note: Data was derived from NOAA/AVHRR and NASA.)

PAGE 32, *IMAGES CREATED ORIGINALLY FOR THE GLOBE PROGRAM BY NOAA's NATIONAL GEOPHYSICAL DATA CENTER, BOULDER, COLORADO, U.S.A. CLOUD COVER*: International Satellite Cloud Climatology Project (ISCCP); National Aeronautics and Space Administration (NASA); Goddard Institute for Space Studies (GISS). *PRECIPITATION*: Global Precipitation Climatology Project (GPCP); International Satellite Land Surface Climatology Project (ISLSCP). *SOLAR ENERGY*: Earth Radiation Budget Experiment (ERBE); Greenhouse Effect Detection Experiment (GEDEX). *TEMPERATURE*: National Center for Environmental Prediction (NCEP); National Center for Atmospheric Research (NCAR); National Weather Service (NWS).

PAGE 36, *HURRICANE IMAGE*: National Oceanic and Atmospheric Administration, National Environmental Satellite, Data, and Information Service (NOAA/NESDIS).

PAGE 37, *EL NIÑO IMAGE SEQUENCE*: Courtesy Robert M. Carey, NOAA. *LIGHTNING IMAGE*: NASA Marshall Space Flight Center Lightning Imaging Sensor (LIS) Instrument Team, Huntsville, Alabama.

PAGE 58, *LIGHTS OF THE WORLD*: Composite image: NOAA, National Geophysical Data Center. Raw satellite data: U.S. Air Force Defense Meteorological Satellite Program.

PAGE 62, *OZONE DEPLETION*: David Larko, SESDA Program, NASA Goddard Space Flight Center.

PAGE 208, *SURFACE ELEVATION*: Byrd Polar Research Center, Ohio State University. *ICE SHEET THICKNESS*: Bedmap Project. *ICE FLOW VELOCITY*: Roland Warner, Antarctic Cooperative Research Centre and Australian Antarctic Division. *SEA ICE MOVEMENT AND WIND FLOW*: *SEA ICE VELOCITY DATA*: Mark R. Drinkwater and Xiang Liu, Jet Propulsion Laboratory/California Institute of Technology; *SURFACE WINDS*: Based on data from David H. Bromwich, Ohio State University, and Thomas R. Parish, University of Wyoming.

PAGES 226–227, *UGC10214 ("TADPOLE GALAXY") IMAGE*: NASA / Holland Ford, Johns Hopkins University; Mark Clampin and George Hartig, Space Telescope Science Institute; Garth Illingworth, University of California Observatories/Lick Observatory.

PAGES 228–229 AND 230–231, *CLEMENTINE TOPOGRAPHIC MAP OF THE MOON*: Courtesy of the Lunar and Planetary Institute, Houston, Texas.

PAGES 234 AND 235, *THE PLANETS*: Courtesy of NASA/JPL/Caltech.

PHOTOGRAPHY

FRONT JACKET
(up), ImageState;
(ct), Powerstock;
(lo), Adriel Heisey

BACK JACKET
George Steinmetz;

INTERIOR
PAGE 22, (UP), R.D. GRIGGS, USGS;
PAGE 22, (CT), SHARON G. JOHNSON;
PAGE 22, (LO), DAVID MUENCH;
PAGE 23, RAYMOND GEHMAN/NGS IMAGE COLLECTION;
PAGE 24, (LE), JOEL SARTORE/www.joelsartore.com;
PAGE 24, (CT), ROGER RESSMEYER/CORBIS;
PAGE 24, (UP RT), GEORGE F. MOBLEY;
PAGE 24, (LO RT), JAMES D. BALOG;
PAGE 25, (UP LE), JAMES P. BLAIR;
PAGE 25, (UP CT), LYLE ROSBOTHAM;
PAGE 25, (UP RT), ADRIEL HEISEY;
PAGE 25, (LO LE), MARC MORITSCH/NGS IMAGE COLLECTION;
PAGE 25, (LO CT), PETER ESSICK;
PAGE 25, (LO RT), SAM ABELL, NGS;
PAGE 26, (LE), PETER ESSICK;
PAGE 26, (CT), DOUGLAS R. GRANT/TERRACON GEOSCIENCE INTERNATIONAL;
PAGE 26, (RT), TOM & PAT LEESON;
PAGE 27, (UP CT), ROB BRANDER;
PAGE 27, (UP RT), GEORGE VENI & JAMES JASEK;
PAGE 27, (LO LE), SHARON G. JOHNSON;
PAGE 27, (LO RT), DOUGLAS R. GRANT/PARKS CANADA;
PAGE 30, (UP LE), TOM & PAT LEESON/PHOTO RESEARCHERS;
PAGE 30, (UP RT), MICHAEL NICHOLS/NGS IMAGE COLLECTION;
PAGE 30, (LO LE), STEPHEN J. KRASEMANN/PHOTO RESEARCHERS;
PAGE 30, (LO CT LE), ROD PLANCK/PHOTO RESEARCHERS;
PAGE 30, (CT LE), JIM STEINBERG/PHOTO RESEARCHERS;
PAGE 30, (CT RT), MATTHEW C. HANSEN, UNIVERSITY OF MARYLAND;
PAGE 30, (LO CT RT), GREGORY G. DIMIJIAN/PHOTO RESEARCHERS;
PAGE 30, (LO RT), SHARON G. JOHNSON;
PAGE 31, (LE), GEORG GERSTER/PHOTO RESEARCHERS;
PAGE 31, (LO CT LE), ROD PLANCK/PHOTO RESEARCHERS;
PAGE 31, (LE CT), JIM RICHARDSON;
PAGE 31, (RT CT), GEORGE STEINMETZ;
PAGE 31, (LO CT RT), STEVE MCCURRY;
PAGE 31, (RT), B. & C. ALEXANDER/PHOTO RESEARCHERS;
PAGE 33, SHARON G. JOHNSON;
PAGE 48, (LE), JODI COBB, NATIONAL GEOGRAPHIC PHOTOGRAPHER;
PAGE 48, (RT), JAMES L. STANFIELD;
PAGES 48–49, TONY HEIDERER;
PAGE 49, (LE), THOMAS J. ABERCROMBIE;
PAGE 49, (RT), ANNIE GRIFFITHS BELT;
PAGE 55, (LE), STEVEN L. RAYMER/NGS IMAGE COLLECTION;
PAGE 55, (CT), RICHARD OLSENIUS/NGS IMAGE COLLECTION;
PAGE 55, (RT), JIM RICHARDSON;
PAGE 57, (UP), JIM RICHARDSON;
PAGE 57, (UP CT), MARK C. BURNETT/PHOTO RESEARCHERS;
PAGE 57, (CT), COURTESY NATIONAL RENEWABLE ENERGY LABORATORY;
PAGE 57, (LO CT), JOHN MEAD/SCIENCE PHOTO LIBRARY/PHOTO RESEARCHERS;
PAGE 57, (LO), JOHN MEAD/SCIENCE PHOTO LIBRARY/PHOTO RESEARCHERS;
PAGE 58, (UP LE), CHARLES D. WINTERS/PHOTO RESEARCHERS;
PAGE 58, (CT LE), RUSS LAPPA/PHOTO RESEARCHERS;
PAGE 58, (LO LE), MINERAL INFORMATION INSTITUTE/www.mii.org
PAGE 58, (UP CT), PHILLIP HAYSON/PHOTO RESEARCHERS;
PAGE 58, (CT), MARK A. SCHNEIDER/PHOTO RESEARCHERS;
PAGE 58, (LO CT), STEVEN HOLT/STOCKPIX.com;
PAGE 58, (UP RT), MINERAL INFORMATION INSTITUTE/www.mii.org
PAGE 58, (CT RT), RUSS LAPPA/PHOTO RESEARCHERS;
PAGE 58, (LO RT), RUSS LAPPA/PHOTO RESEARCHERS;
PAGE 59, (UP LE), U.S. GEOLOGICAL SURVEY;
PAGE 59, (CT LE), E.R. DEGGINGER/PHOTO RESEARCHERS;
PAGE 59, (LO LE), U.S. GEOLOGICAL SURVEY;
PAGE 59, (UP CT), U.S. GEOLOGICAL SURVEY;
PAGE 59, (CT), MINERAL INFORMATION INSTITUTE/www.mii.org
PAGE 59, (LO CT), U.S. GEOLOGICAL SURVEY;
PAGE 59, (UP RT), KENNETH W. LARSEN, COURTESY SMITHSONIAN INSTITUTION, NMNH;
PAGE 59, (CT RT), KENNETH W. LARSEN, COURTESY SMITHSONIAN INSTITUTION, NMNH;
PAGE 59, (LO RT), U.S. GEOLOGICAL SURVEY;
PAGE 65, (LE), ART WOLFE/GETTY IMAGES;
PAGE 65, (CT), RICHARD NOWITZ/NGS IMAGE COLLECTION;
PAGE 65, (UP RT), JAMES P. BLAIR;
PAGE 65, (LO RT), SARAH LEEN;
PAGES 70–71, PETER ESSICK;
PAGE 73, LYLE ROSBOTHAM;
PAGES 114–115, MICHAEL NICHOLS/NGS IMAGE COLLECTION;
PAGE 116, L. SCOTT SHELTON;
PAGES 126–127, KENNETH GARRETT;
PAGE 129, WINFIELD I. PARKS, JR.;
PAGES 142–143, DAVID BREASHEARS;
PAGE 144, PAUL CHESLEY/NGS IMAGE COLLECTION;
PAGES 170–171, GEORGE STEINMETZ;
PAGE 173, KENNETH GARRETT;
PAGES 186–187, DAVID DOUBILET;
PAGE 189, MEDFORD TAYLOR;
PAGES 202–203, G. KOOYMAN/POLAR IMAGES;
PAGE 205, MARIA STENZEL

PRINCIPAL REFERENCE SOURCES

AAAS (American Association for the Advancement of Science) Atlas of Population and Environment. Markham, Victoria Dompka, ed. Berkeley and Los Angeles, California: University of California Press, 2000.

Columbia Gazetteer of the World. Cohen, Saul B., ed. New York: Columbia University Press, 1998.

Encyclopedia of Global Environmental Change. Munn, R. E., et. al., eds. Chichester, England: John Wiley & Sons Ltd., 2001.

Environmental Information and Assessment Technical Report: Global Assessment of Acidification and Eutrophication of Natural Ecosystems. United Nations Environment Programme/Research for Man and Environment, 1998.

Global Desertification Vulnerability. Washington, D.C.: United States Department of Agriculture, Natural Resources Conservation Service, Soil Survey Division, World Soil Resources, 1998.

Global Distribution of Original and Remaining Forests, 2000. United Nations Environment Programme/World Conservation Monitoring Centre.

Global Dominant Ecosystem Classes (map). Rome, Italy: The Food and Agriculture Organization of the United Nations and the International Institute for Applied System Analysis, 2000.

Global Environment Outlook, 2000. United Nations Environment Programme, 1999.
Gridded Population of the World (GPW), Version 2. Palisades, New York: Center for International Earth Science Information Network (CIESIN), Columbia University; Internattional Food Policy Research Institute (IFPRI); and World Resources Institute (WRI). Available at http://sedac.ciesin.columbia.edu/plue/gpw.

Hilton-Taylor, C. *2000 IUCN Red List of Threatened Species.* Gland, Switzerland, and Cambridge, UK: IUCN, 2000.

How Many Online? Nua.com, 2002.

Human Development Report, 2001. New York: United Nations Development Programme (UNDP), Oxford University Press, 2001.

International Trade Statistics, 2001. Geneva, Switzerland: World Trade Organization.

MacKenzie, Fred T. and Judith A. MacKenzie. *Our Changing Planet: An Introduction to Earth System Science and Global Environmental Change.* 2nd ed. Upper Saddle River, New Jersey: Prentice Hall, 1998.

Matras, Judah. *Populations and Societies.* Englewood Cliffs, New Jersey: Prentice Hall, 1973.

McKnight, Tom L. *Physical Geography: A Landscape Appreciation.* 5th ed. Upper Saddle River, New Jersey: Prentice Hall, 1996.

Merriam Webster's Geographical Dictionary, 3rd ed. Springfield, Ma.: Merriam-Webster, Incorporated, 1997.

Miller, G. Tyler. *Environmental Science: Working with the Earth.* 7th ed. Canada: Wadsworth Publishing Company, 1999.

Mineral Commodity Summaries, 2002. Minerals Information Team, U.S. Geological Survey (USGS). Reston, Virginia: U.S. Government Printing Office.

Monroe, James S. and Reed Wicander. *The Changing Earth: Exploring Geology and Evolution.* St. Paul, Minnesota: West Publishing Company, 1994.

National Geographic Atlas of the Ocean. Washington, D.C.: The National Geographic Society, 2001.

National Geographic Atlas of the World, 7th ed. Washington, D.C.: The National Geographic Society, 1999.

Nuclear Notebook, Natural Resources Defense Council.

Raven, Peter H., Ray F. Evert and Susan E. Eichlorn. *Biology of Plants.* 6th ed. New York, New York: W.H. Freeman and Company/Worth Publishers, 1999.

Revenga, Carmen, Siobhan Murray, Janet Abramovitz, and Allen Hammond. *Watersheds of the World: Ecological Value and Vulnerability.* Washington, D.C.: World Resources Institute, 1998.

State of the World's Fisheries and Aquaculture, 2000. Rome, Italy: Food and Agriculture Organization of the United Nations, 2000.

State of the World's Forests, 2001. Rome, Italy: Food and Agriculture Organization of the United Nations, 2001.

The Statesman's Yearbook, 137th ed. Turner, Barry, ed. Exeter, United Kingdom: MacMillan Press Ltd., 2001.

Statistical Yearbook, 1999. United Nations Educational, Scientific and Cultural Organization. Paris and Lanham: UNESCO Publishing and Bernan Press, 1999.
Strahler, Alan and Arthur Strahler. *Physical Geography: Science and Systems of the Human Environment.* 2nd ed. John Wiley & Sons, Inc, 2002.

Tarbuck, Edward J. and Frederick K. Lutgens. *Earth: An Introduction to Physical Geology.* 7th ed. Upper Saddle River, New Jersey: Prentice Hall, 2002.

The World Almanac and Book of Facts, 2002. New York, New York: World Almanac Educatoin Group, Inc., 2002.

World Christian Encyclopedia: A Comparative Survey of Churches and Religions in the Modern World. 2nd ed. Barrett, David B., et al., eds. New York: Oxford University Press, 2001.

World Development Indicators, 2001. Washington, D.C.: World Bank.

World Resources 2000–2001—People and Ecosystems: The Fraying Web of Life. Washington, D.C.: World Resources Institute, 2000.

The World Factbook 2001. Washington, D.C.: Central Intelligence Agency, 2001.

The World Health Report 2001. Annex 5. Selected National Health Accounts indicators for all Member States, estimates 1997 and 1998. Geneva: World Health Organization, 2001.

World Investment Report, 2001. New York and Geneva: United Nations Conference on Trade and Development, 2001.

World Urbanization Prospects: The 2001 Revision. Population Division of the Department of Economic and Social Affairs of the United Nations Secretariat. New York: United Nations, 2002.

PRINCIPAL ONLINE SOURCES

British Antarctic Survey
www.nerc-bas.ac.uk

Central Intelligence Agency
www.cia.gov

Conservation International
www.conservation.org

Energy Information Agency
www.eia.doe.gov

Food and Agriculture
Organization of the UN
www.fao.org

Mineral Information Institute
www.mii.org

National Aeronautics
and Space Administration
www.nasa.gov

National Atmospheric
and Oceanic Administration
www.noaa.gov

National Climatic Data Center
www.ncdc.noaa.gov

National Imagery and
Mapping Agency
www.nima.mil

National Park Service
www.nps.gov

National Renewable
Energy Laboratory
www.nrel.gov

Population Reference
Bureau
www.prb.org

United Nations
www.un.org

UN Conference on Trade
and Development
www.unctad.org

UNDP
www.undp.org

UNEP-WCMC
www.unep-wcmc.org

UNESCO
www.unesco.org

UN Population Division
www.unpopulation.org

U.S. Geological Survey
www.usgs.gov

World Bank
www.worldbank.org

World Conservation Union
www.iucn.org

World Health Organization
www.who.int

World Resources Institute
www.wri.org

World Trade Organization
www.wto.org

Worldwatch Institute
www.worldwatch.org

World Wildlife Fund
www.worldwildlife.org

KEY TO FLAGS AND FACTS

The National Geographic Society, whose cartographic policy is to recognize de facto countries, counted 192 independent nations in mid-2002. Within this atlas, fact boxes for independent nations, most dependencies, and U.S. states are placed on or next to regional maps that show the areas they represent. Each box includes the flag of a political entity, as well as important statistical data. Boxes for some dependencies show two flags—a local one and the flag of the administering country. Because Paraguay and the state of Oregon have different designs on the obverse and reverse sides of their flags, their fact boxes show both sides of their flags.

The statistical data provide highlights of geography, demography, and economy. These details offer a brief overview of each entity; they present general characteristics and are not intended to be comprehensive studies. The structured nature of the text results in some generic collective or umbrella terms. The industry category, for instance, includes services in addition to traditional manufacturing sectors. Space limitations dictate the amount of information included. For example, the only languages listed for the U.S. are English and Spanish, although many others are spoken.

Fact boxes are arranged alphabetically by the conventional short forms of the country or dependency names (except for the Oceania and Islands of Africa fact boxes, where country and dependency boxes are grouped separately). The conventional long forms of names appear within colored stripes; if there are no long forms, the short forms are repeated. This policy has two exceptions: For U.S. states, nicknames are shown inside the colored stripes, and for French overseas departments, the words "Overseas Department of France" appear inside the colored stripes.

AREA accounts for the total area of a country, U.S. state, or dependency, including all land and inland water delimited by international boundaries, intranational boundaries, or coastlines.

In the POPULATION category, the figures for U.S. state populations are from the U.S. Census Bureau's 2001 midyear estimates. Two figures are listed for the CAPITAL and LARGEST CITY of each state. The city-proper figure, from 2000 census data provided by the U.S. Census Bureau, shows the number of people who live within the incorporated city limits. The larger metro-area figure represents the number of people who live within a metropolitan area, a broader designation that includes both a city proper and the surrounding urbanized region. This figure is from the Census Bureau's *1999 Population Estimates for Metropolitan Areas (MAs)*, which includes figures for metropolitan statistical areas (MSAs), consolidated metropolitan statistical areas (CMSAs), and primary metropolitan statistical areas (PMSAs). Metropolitan areas and their geographic boundaries can cross state borders and are defined on the basis of population as well as other factors. State capitals with populations of less than 50,000 do not

have MSAs defined for them; in those cases, only city-proper population figures are shown.

POPULATION figures for independent nations and dependencies are mid-2002 figures from the Population Reference Bureau in Washington, D.C. Next to CAPITAL is the name of the seat of government, followed by the city's population. Capital city populations for both independent nations and dependencies are from 2001 United Nations estimates and represent the populations of metropolitan areas. Both POPULATION and CAPITAL figures for countries, dependencies, and U.S. states are rounded to the nearest thousand. Under RELIGION, the most widely practiced faith appears first. "Traditional" or "indigenous" connotes beliefs of important local sects, such as Maya in Middle America. Under LANGUAGE, if a country has an official language, it is listed first. Often, a country may list more than one official language. Otherwise both RELIGION and LANGUAGE are in rank ordering. LITERACY generally indicates the percentage of the population above the age of 15 who can read and write. There are no universal standards of literacy, so these estimates (from the CIA's *World Factbook*) are based on the most common definition available for a nation. LIFE EXPECTANCY represents the average number of years a group of infants born in the same year can be expected to live if the mortality rate at each age remains constant in the future.

GDP PER CAPITA is Gross Domestic Product divided by midyear population estimates. GDP estimates for independent nations and dependencies use the purchasing power parity (PPP) conversion factor designed to equalize the purchasing powers of different currencies. For U.S. states, equivalent measurements to GDP on the intranational level have been used. PCI, or PER CAPITA INCOME, figures from the U.S. Bureau of Economic Analysis are presented; PCI divides total personal income by midyear population and does not adjust for PPP.

Individual income estimates such as GDP PER CAPITA and PCI are among the many indicators used to assess a nation's well-being. As statistical averages, they hide extremes of poverty and wealth. Furthermore, they take no account of factors that affect quality of life, such as environmental degradation, educational opportunities, and health care.

ECONOMY information for the independent nations and dependencies is divided into three general categories: Industry, Agriculture, and Exports. Because of structural limitations, only the primary industries (Ind), agricultural commodities (Agr), and exports (Exp) are reported. Agriculture serves as an umbrella term for not only crops but also livestock, products, and fish. In the interest of conciseness, agriculture for the independent nations presents, when applicable but not limited to, two major crops, followed respectively by leading entries for livestock, products, and fish.

NA indicates that data are not available.

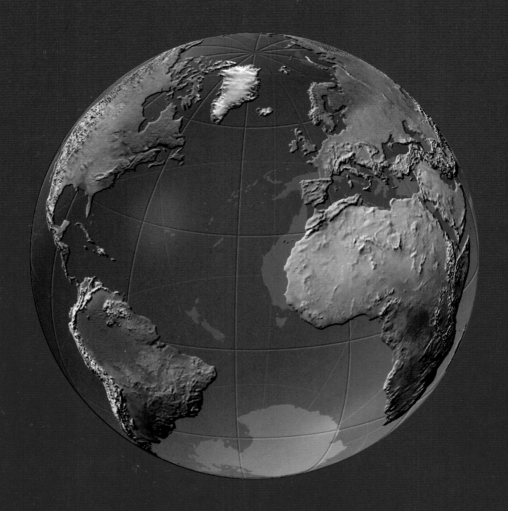

FAMILY
REFERENCE
ATLAS *of the World*

PUBLISHED BY THE NATIONAL GEOGRAPHIC SOCIETY

John M. Fahey, Jr.	President and Chief Executive Officer
Gilbert M. Grosvenor	Chairman of the Board
Nina D. Hoffman	Executive Vice President

PREPARED BY THE BOOK DIVISION

Kevin Mulroy	Vice President and Editor-in-Chief
Charles Kogod	Illustrations Director
Marianne R. Koszorus	Design Director

STAFF FOR THIS ATLAS

Carl Mehler	Project Editor and Director of Maps
Laura Exner, Thomas L. Gray, Joseph F. Ochlak, Nicholas P. Rosenbach	Map Editors
Sam Chernawsky, Kyle T. Rector, and XNR Productions	Map Research and Compilation
Matt Chwastyk, Gregory Ugiansky	Map Production Managers
James Huckenpahler, Kyle T. Rector, Martin S. Walz, and XNR Productions	Map Production
National Geographic Maps: Kevin Allen, Director of Map Services; Jan D. Morris, Project Manager; Mary Kate Cannistra, Windy A. Robertson	Geographic Information System (GIS) Support
National Geographic Maps: Michael J. Horner, David B. Miller, Scott A. Zillmer	Contributing Geographers
Carolinda E. Averitt, Lisa Lytton, Rebecca Lescaze, Alex Novak	Text Editors

Jesse Allen, Elisabeth B. Booz, Patrick Booz, Carlos Castillo-Salgado, Manuel Colunga-Garcia, Byron Crape, Laura Exner, Ellen Ficklen, Stuart H. Gage, Matthew C. Hansen, Craig K. Harris, Eric Lindstrom, David T. Long, Enrique Loyola-Elizondo, Stephen P. Maran, W. David Menzie, H. Michael Mogil, Rhea Muchow, Ted Munn, Margaret Murray, Antony Shugaar, Brad Singer, Peter W. Sloss, Paul D. Spudis, Priit J. Vesilind, Andrew J. Wahll, Patrick J. Webber, Joe Yogerst	Contributing Writers
Sam Chernawsky, Principal; Elizabeth B. Booz, Rhea Muchow, Joseph F. Ochlak, Anne E. Withers	Text Researchers
Lyle Rosbotham, Principal; Jennifer Christiansen, Megan McCarthy, Susan K. White	Book Design
Sadie Quarrier	Photo Editor
Meredith Wilcox	Photo Assistant
ChrisOrr.com, Tibor G. Tóth	Art and Illustrations
R. Gary Colbert	Production Director

MANUFACTURING AND QUALITY CONTROL

Christopher A. Liedel	Chief Financial Officer
Phillip L. Schlosser	Managing Director
John T. Dunn	Technical Director
Vincent P. Ryan	Manager

Reproduction by Quad/Graphics, Alexandria, Virginia
Printed and Bound by Mondadori S.p.A., Verona, Italy

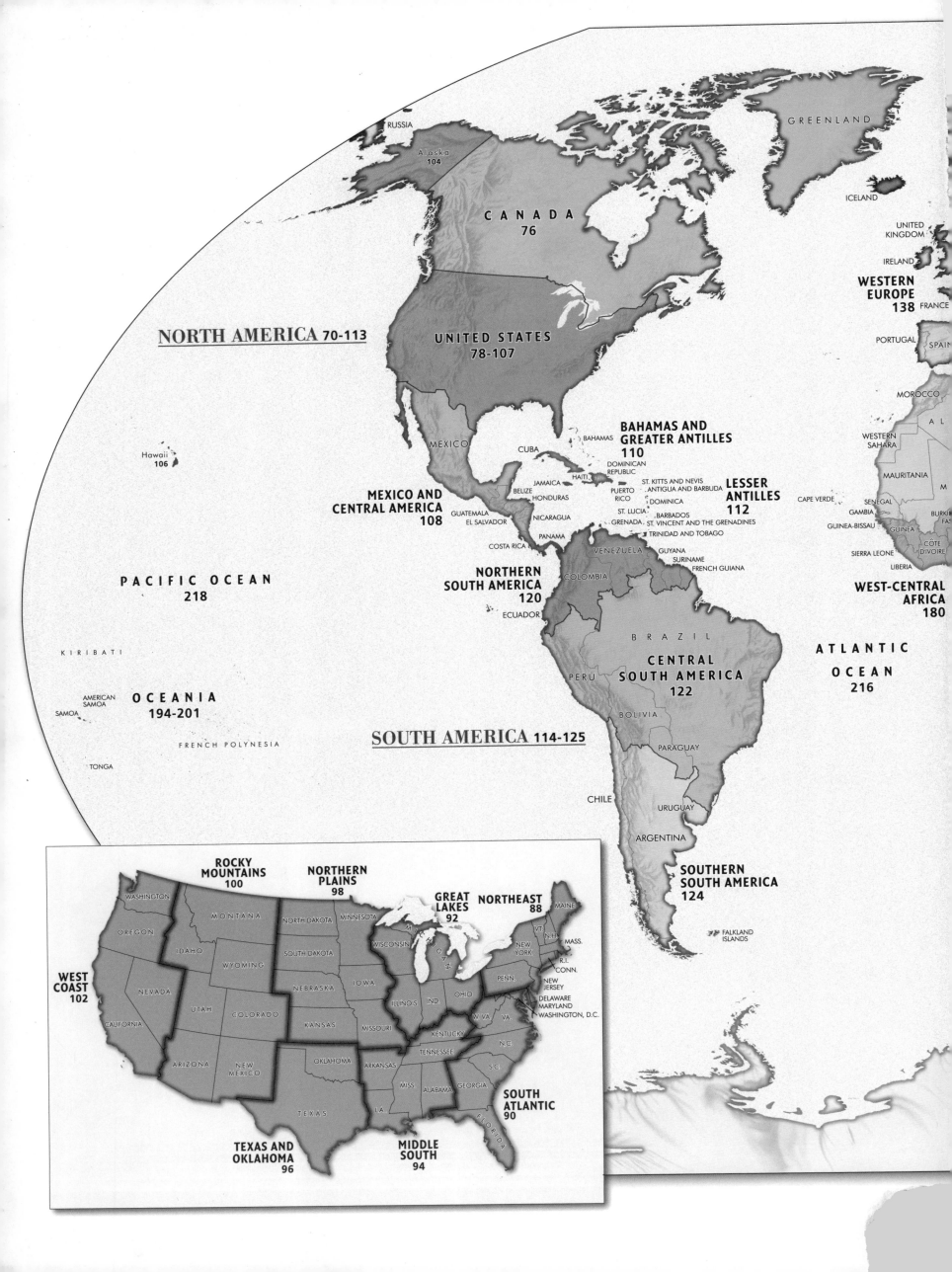

RUSSIA

GREENLAND

Alaska
104

ICELAND

CANADA
76

UNITED
KINGDOM

IRELAND

WESTERN
EUROPE
138 FRANCE

NORTH AMERICA 70-113

UNITED STATES
78-107

PORTUGAL SPAIN

MOROCCO

WESTERN
SAHARA

A L

MEXICO

BAHAMAS

BAHAMAS AND
GREATER ANTILLES
110

MAURITANIA M

Hawaii
106

CUBA

DOMINICAN
REPUBLIC

MEXICO AND
CENTRAL AMERICA
108

JAMAICA
BELIZE
HONDURAS
GUATEMALA
EL SALVADOR   NICARAGUA

HAITI

PUERTO
RICO

ST. KITTS AND NEVIS
ANTIGUA AND BARBUDA

DOMINICA

LESSER
ANTILLES
112

CAPE VERDE

SENEGAL
GAMBIA

BURKI
FA

ST. LUCIA   BARBADOS
GRENADA ST. VINCENT AND THE GRENADINES
TRINIDAD AND TOBAGO

GUINEA-BISSAU   GUINEA

SIERRA LEONE

CÔTE
D'IVOIRE

COSTA RICA
PANAMA

VENEZUELA   GUYANA
SURINAME
FRENCH GUIANA

LIBERIA

PACIFIC OCEAN
218

NORTHERN
SOUTH AMERICA
120

COLOMBIA

ECUADOR

WEST-CENTRAL
AFRICA
180

KIRIBATI

B R A Z I L

ATLANTIC

OCEAN
216

AMERICAN
SAMOA

OCEANIA
194-201

PERU

CENTRAL
SOUTH AMERICA
122

SAMOA

FRENCH POLYNESIA

SOUTH AMERICA 114-125

BOLIVIA

TONGA

PARAGUAY

CHILE

URUGUAY

ARGENTINA

SOUTHERN
SOUTH AMERICA
124

FALKLAND
ISLANDS

WASHINGTON

ROCKY
MOUNTAINS
100

NORTHERN
PLAINS
98

GREAT
LAKES
92

NORTHEAST
88

MAINE

MONTANA

NORTH DAKOTA

MINNESOTA

VT.
N.H.

OREGON

IDAHO

SOUTH DAKOTA

WISCONSIN

MICHIGAN

NEW
YORK

MASS.

R.I.
CONN.

WYOMING

NEBRASKA

IOWA

PENN.

WEST
COAST
102

NEVADA

UTAH

COLORADO

ILLINOIS

IND.

OHIO

NEW
JERSEY

DELAWARE
MARYLAND
WASHINGTON, D.C.

CALIFORNIA

KANSAS

MISSOURI

KENTUCKY

W.VA.   VA.

ARIZONA

NEW
MEXICO

OKLAHOMA

ARKANSAS

TENNESSEE

N.C.

S.C.

MISS.   ALABAMA   GEORGIA

TEXAS

LA.

SOUTH
ATLANTIC
90

TEXAS AND
OKLAHOMA
96

MIDDLE
SOUTH
94

FLORIDA